CONFLICT, LANGUAGE, AND SOCIAL PRACTICE IN MEDIEVAL SOCIETIES

THE MEDIEVAL COUNTRYSIDE

VOLUME 24

General Editor
Phillipp Schofield, Aberystwyth University

Editorial Board
Laurent Feller, Université Paris 1 Panthéon-Sorbonne
Paul Freedman, Yale University
Thomas Lindkvist, Göteborgs universitet
Sigrid Hirbodian, Universität Tübingen
Peter Hoppenbrouwers, Universiteit Leiden
Piotr S. Górecki, University of California, Riverside
Sandro Carocci, Università degli Studi di Roma Tor Vergata
Julio Escalona, Consejo Superior de Investigaciones Científicas, Madrid
Pere Benito i Monclús, Universitat de Lleida

Previously published volumes in this series
are listed at the back of the book.

Conflict, Language, and Social Practice in Medieval Societies

Selected Essays of Isabel Alfonso, with Commentaries

edited by

JULIO ESCALONA, ÁLVARO CARVAJAL CASTRO, *and* CRISTINA JULAR PÉREZ-ALFARO

with commentaries by

JEAN BIRRELL, FRANÇOIS BOUGARD, WARREN BROWN, PETER COSS, WENDY DAVIES, CHRIS DYER, ROS FAITH, FRANÇOIS FORONDA, PAUL FREEDMAN, PIOTR S. GÓRECKI, JOHN HUDSON, ANDRÉ EVANGELISTA MARQUES, JESÚS RODRÍGUEZ VELASCO, PHILLIPP SCHOFIELD, STEPHEN D. WHITE, CHRIS WICKHAM

BREPOLS

This book was produced with support from the Spanish Government's
Agencia Estatal de Investigación [MCIN/ AEI/10.13039/501100011033],
Refs: PID2020-112506GB-C44, PID2020-116104RB-I00, and RYC2020-030272-I.

British Library Cataloguing in Publication Data
A catalogue record for this book is available from the British Library.

© 2024, Brepols Publishers n.v., Turnhout, Belgium.

All rights reserved. No part of this publication may be reproduced,
stored in a retrieval system, or transmitted, in any form or by
any means, electronic, mechanical, photocopying, recording,
or otherwise without the prior permission of the publisher.

ISBN 978-2-503-60389-6
eISBN 978-2-503-60390-2
DOI 10.1484/M.TMC-EB.5.132049
ISSN 1784-8814
eISSN 2294-8430

Printed in the EU on acid-free paper.

D/2024/0095/107

Table of Contents

List of Illustrations   11

Abbreviations   13

Foreword   19

**Introduction: Dealing with the Past, Dealing with the Present.
Yet another Talk with Isabel Alfonso**
Isabel Alfonso Antón, Julio Escalona, Cristina Jular Pérez-
Alfaro, and Álvaro Carvajal Castro   21

Part I
Medieval Minds

Chapter 1
On Friendship

Amicitia: Early Writings, a Revelation, and the Identity of a Historian
François Foronda   39

On _Amicitia_ in Medieval Spain: A Document that Merits Study
Isabel Alfonso   49

Chapter 2
On the Language and Practice of Negotiation

Commentary
Wendy Davies   59

**The Language and Practice of Negotiation in Medieval Conflict
Resolution (Castile-León, Eleventh–Thirteenth Centuries)**
Isabel Alfonso   67

Chapter 3
On Judicial Rhetoric and Political Legitimation

Justice, Power, and Legitimation
John Hudson   87

Judicial Rhetoric and Political Legitimation in Medieval León-Castile
Isabel Alfonso   93

TABLE OF CONTENTS

Chapter 4
On Memory and Identity

Words, Again …
Piotr S. GÓRECKI 129

Memory and Identity in Judicial *pesquisas* in Medieval León-Castile
Isabel ALFONSO 141

Chapter 5
Two Approaches to Justice and Vengeance

Commentary
Stephen D. WHITE 169

Vengeance, Justice, and Political Struggle in Castilian Medieval Historiography
Isabel ALFONSO 171

Vengeance and Justice in the Poem of the Cid
Isabel ALFONSO 207

Part II
Community Ties and Social Differentiation

Chapter 6
On Social Differentiation in Rural Communities

Middlemen and Intermediaries in Medieval Village Society
Christopher DYER 245

Local Power and Internal Differentiation in the Rural Communities of Galicia
Isabel ALFONSO 251

Chapter 7
On Social Differentiation within Rural Communities

Commentary
Phillipp R. SCHOFIELD 271

Exploring Difference within Rural Communities in the Northern Iberian Kingdoms, 1000–1300
Isabel ALFONSO 277

Part III
Conflict and Competition

Chapter 8
On Violence

The Social Logic of Vengeance: Towards a Reading of Isabel Alfonso's Work on Conflict Resolution
André Evangelista Marques — 295

Death without Vengeance? The Regulation of Violence in Local Settings (Castile-León 13th c.)
Isabel Alfonso — 305

Chapter 9
On Peasants and the Law

The Historiography of Peasant Resistance to Seigneurial Authority 333
Paul Freedman

Peasants and the Law: Legal Avenues in their Struggle (Castile and León, 10th–13th Centuries)
Isabel Alfonso — 345

Chapter 10
On Rural Churches and Peasant Struggles

On Rural Churches and Peasant Struggles
Chris Wickham — 365

Rural Churches in the North of Castile: A Religious Dimension to Peasant Struggles during the Middle Ages
Isabel Alfonso — 371

Chapter 11
Two Anthropological Approaches to Peasants and Lords

A Commentary on 'Peasant Opposition to Labour Services' and 'The Rhetoric of Seigneurial Legitimation'
Jean Birrell — 401

Pacts, Conventions, and Contracts between Lords and Peasants in Anglo-Norman England 407
Rosamond FAITH

Peasant Opposition to Labour Services in Castile and León: Forms and Symbolic Significance 413
Isabel ALFONSO

The Rhetoric of Seigneurial Legitimation in the *Fueros* of León (11th to 13th Centuries)
Isabel ALFONSO 441

Chapter 12
On Punishment and Exemplary Violence

Commentary 465
Warren C. BROWN

***Corpus Delicti* and Exemplary Violence**
Isabel ALFONSO 475

Chapter 13
On Disputes and Wrongdoings

Written Disputes: Just the Tip of the Iceberg 505
François BOUGARD

Land Disputes and *malfetrías* among the Medieval Nobility in Castile and León
Isabel ALFONSO 509

Chapter 14
On Revolting Noblemen

Questioning the Evidence: Political History and Social Mentality
François FORONDA 551

***Desheredamiento* and *Desafuero*, or the Alleged Justification of a Revolt of the Nobility**
Isabel ALFONSO 557

Part IV
Historians' Minds

Chapter 15
On Cistercians and Feudalism

Commentary   591
Peter Coss

Cistercians and Feudalism
Isabel ALFONSO   601

Chapter 16
Three Review Articles

How to Read
Jesús RODRÍGUEZ VELASCO   627

Continuity and Documentary Revelation, or Mutation and Feudal Revolution?
Isabel ALFONSO   631

Historical Discourse as History
Isabel ALFONSO   645

Naming Violence and Controlling its Legitimation
Isabel ALFONSO   659

Full List of Publications by Isabel Alfonso   673

List of Illustrations

Tables

Table 5.1. Corpus of texts discussed in the text   175

Table 11.1. Distribution of extant *fueros* for the
provinces of León, Palencia, Burgos and Zamora   444

Figures

Figure 6.1. Pedro Romeu and his family group   259

Figure 6.2. Information about Doyane and his family group   262

Figure 8.1. Members of the Rojas family group   307

Figure 8.2. Relatives of María Gutiérrez   312

Figure 8.3. Representatives in the agreement   313

Abbreviations*

AHN   Archivo Histórico Nacional

AlfonsoV   Fernández del Pozo, José María, 'Alfonso V, rey de León. Estudio Histórico-Documental', in *León y su Historia. Vol. 5* (León: Centro de Estudios e Investigación San Isidoro, 1984), pp. 10–262.

AlfonsoVI   Gambra, Andrés, *Alfonso VI, cancillería, curia e imperio. Vol. II, Colección diplomática* (León: Centro de Estudios e Investigación San Isidoro).

AlfonsoVIII   González, Julio, *El Reino de Castilla en la época de Alfonso VIII. Vol. 3: Docuentos (1191–1217)* (Madrid: Escuela de Estudios Medievales, 1960).

AlfonsoIX   González, Julio, *Alfonso IX* (Madrid: CSIC, 1944).

BNE   Biblioteca Nacional de España

C1344   Catalán, Diego, and Soledad Andrés Castellanos, *Crónica General de España de 1344* (Madrid: Fundación Ramón Menéndez Pidal).

CAI   'Chronica Adefonsi Imperatoris', in *Chronica Hispana saecvli XII. Pars I (Corpus Christianorum, Continuatio Medievalis LXXI)*, ed. by Maya Sánchez (Turnhout: Brepols, 1990), pp. 109–248. For the English translation: Barton, Simon, and Richard A. Fletcher, *The World of El Cid: Chronicles of the Spanish Reconquest* (Manchester: Manchester University Press, 2000)

Carrizo   Casado, Concha, *Colección diplomática del Monasterio de Carrizo. Vol. I (969–1260)* (León: Centro de Estudios e Investigación San Isidoro, 1983).

CatAstorga   Cavero Domínguez, Gregoria, and Encarnación Martín López, *Colección documental de la catedral de Astorga. Vol. 1 (646–1126)* (León: Centro de Estudios e Investigación San Isidoro, 1999).

CatBurgos   Garrido Garrido, José Manuel, and Francisco Javier Pereda Llarena, *Documentación de la catedral de Burgos (804–1293). 4 vols* (Burgos: J.M. Garrido Garrido, 1983–1984

---

*   Charters are cited by the number of the edition in which they are published, followed by the year to which they are dated.

14   ABBREVIATIONS

CatLeon   Sáez, Emilio, *Colección documental del archivo de la Catedral de León (775–1230)*. *Vol. I (775–952)* (León: Centro de Estudios e Investigación San Isidoro, 1987); Sáez, Carlo and Emilio Sáez, *Colección documental del archivo de la Catedral de León (775–1230)*. *Vol. II (953–85)* (León: Centro de Estudios e Investigación San Isidoro, 1987); Ruiz Asencio, José Manuel, *Colección documental del archivo de la Catedral de León (775–1230)*. *Vol. III (986–1031)* (León: Centro de Estudios e Investigación San Isidoro, 1987); Ruiz Asencio, José Manuel, *Colección documental del archivo de la Catedral de León (775–1230)*. *Vol. IV (1032–1109)* (León: Centro de Estudios e Investigación San Isidoro, 1987); Fernández Catón, José María, *Colección documental del archivo de la Catedral de León (775–1230)*. *Vol. V (1109–1187)* (León: Centro de Estudios e Investigación San Isidoro, 1990).

CatValladolid Mañueco Villalobos, Manuel, *Documentos de la Iglesia Colegial de Santa María la Mayor (hoy metropolitana) de Valladolid (1917–1920)* (Valladolid: Sociedad de Estudios Históricos Castellanos, 1917).

CatZamora   Martín, José Luis, *Documentos Zamoranos I. Documentos del Archivo Catedralicio de Zamora. Primera parte (1128–1261)* (Salamanca: Ediciones Universidad de Salamanca, 1982).

CAX   González Jiménez, Manuel, *Crónica de Alfonso X* (Murcia: Real Academia Alfonso X el Sabio, 1999). For the English translation, see Thacker, Shelby, and José Escobar, *Chronicle of Alfonso X* (Lexington: University Press of Kentucky, 2002) (for the translation, page numbers are provided in square brackets in the references).

ColFueros   Muñoz y Romero, Tomás, *Colección de fueros municipales y cartas pueblas de los reinos de Castilla, León, Corona de Aragón y Navarra* (Madrid: Imprenta de Don José María Alonso: 1847).

CVR   Ruiz Asencio, José Manuel, and Mauricio Herrero Jiménez, eds, *Crónica de Veinte Reyes* (Burgos: Ayuntamiento de Burgos, 1991).

EE   *Estoria de España*

Espéculo   *Los códigos españoles concordados y anotados. Vol. 6* (Madrid: Imprenta de La Publicidad, 1847–1851), pp. 7–212.

FernandoI   Blanco Lozano, Pilar, 'Colección diplomática de Fernando I (1037–1065)', *Archivos Leoneses* 79–80 (1986), 7–212.

FernandoII   González, Julio, *Regesta de Fernando II* (Zaragoza: Instituto de Historia Jerónimo Zurita, 1943).

ABBREVIATIONS 15

FernandoIII González, Julio, *Reinado y diplomas de Fernando III* (Córdoba: Monte de Piedad y Caja de Ahorros de Córdoba, 1980).

FB Martínez Díez, Gonzalo, *Los fueros locales en el territorio de la provincia de Burgos* (Burgos: Caja de Ahorros Municipal, 1982).

FGN de Ilarregui, Pablo, and Segundo Lapuerta, *Fuero General de Navarra* (Pamplona: Imprenta Provincial, 1869).

FL Rodríguez Fernández, Justiniano, *Los Fueros del Reino de León. Vol. 2: Documentos* (León: Ediciones Leonesas, 1981).

FP Rodríguez Fernández, Justiniano, *Palencia: Panorámica foral de la provincia* (Palencia: Merino, 1981).

FPlasencia Ramírez Vaquero, Eloísa, *El Fuero de Plasencia. Vol. 1. Estudio Histórico y Edición crítica del texto* (Mérida: Editora Regional de Extremadura, 1987).

FSepúlvedaR Sáez, Emilio, Rafael Gilbert, and Manuel Alvar, *Los fueros de Sepúlveda. Edición crítica y apéndice documental* (Segovia: Diputación Provincial, 1953).

Fuero Real *Los códigos españoles concordados y anotados. Vol. 1* (Madrid: Imprenta de La Publicidad, 1847–1851), pp. 349–424.

Fuero Viejo *Los códigos españoles concordados y anotados. Vol. 1.* (Madrid: Imprenta de La Publicidad, 1847–1851), pp. 223–303.

FV González Díez, Emiliano, *El régimen foral vallisoletano. Una perspectiva de análisis organizativo del territorio* (Valladolid: Diputación Provincial de Valladolid, 1986).

FZ Rodríguez Fernández, Justiniano, *Los fueros locales de la provincia de Zamora* (Valladolid: Junta de Castilla y León, 1990).

Hinojosa Hinojosa, Eduardo, *Documentos para la historia de las instituciones de León y de Castilla (siglos X–XIII)* (Madrid: Centro de Estudios Históricos, 1919).

HospitalBurgos Palacín Gálvez, Mª. del Carmen, and Luis Martínez García, *Documentación del Hospital del Rey Burgos (1136–1277)* (Burgos: Ediciones J.M. Garrido Garrido, 1990).

Huelgas Lizoain Garrido, José Manuel, *Documentación del Monasterio de las Huelgas de Burgos. Vol. 1 (1116–1230)* (Burgos: Ediciones

16 ABBREVIATIONS

J.M. Garrido Garrido, 1985); Lizoain Garrido, José Manuel, *Documentación del Monasterio de las Huelgas de Burgos. Vol. 2 (1231–1262)* (Burgos: Ediciones J.M. Garrido Garrido, 1985).

MVega — Serrano, Luciano, *Cartulario del monasterio de Vega* (Madrid: Centro de Estudios Históricos, 1927).

Partidas — *Los códigos españoles concordados y anotados. Vols 2–5* (Madrid: Imprenta de La Publicidad, 1847–1851). For the English translation: Burns, Robert I., ed., and Samuel P. Scott, trans., *Las siete partidas*, 7 vols (Philadelphia: University of Pennsylvania Press, 2001).

PCG — Menéndez Pidal, Ramón, and Diego Catalán, *Primera Crónica General de España, con un estudio actualizado de Diego Catalán* (Madrid: Gredos, 1977–1979).

PMH-DC — *Portugaliae Monumenta Historica a saeculo octavo post Christum usque ad quintumdecimum, Diplomata et Chartae. Vol. 1*, ed. by Alexandre Herculano de Carvalho e Araujo and Joaquim José da Silva Mendes Leal (Lisbon: Academia das Ciências de Lisboa, 1867–1873).

PoemCid — Montaner Frutos, Alberto, *Cantar de Mío Cid* (Barcelona: Crítica, 1993). For the English translation, see Hamilton, Rita, and Janet Perry, trans., *The Poem of the Cid: A New Critical Edition of the Spanish Text* (Manchester: Manchester University Press, 1975).

SDSilos — Vivancos Gómez, Miguel C., *Documentación del monasterio de Santo Domingo de Silos (954–1254)* (Burgos: J.M. Garrido Garrido, 1988).

SIDueñas — Reglero de la Fuente, Carlos, *El monasterio de San Isidro de Dueñas. Un priorato cluniacense hispano (911–1478). Estudio y colección documental* (León: Centro de Estudios e Investigación San Isidoro, 2005).

SFPSahagun — Herrero de la Fuente, Marta, *Colección diplomática del Monasterio de Sahagún (857–1300). Vol. II (1000–1073)* (León: Centro de Estudios San Isidoro, 1988); Herrero de la Fuente, Marta, *Colección diplomática del Monasterio de Sahagún (857–1300). Vol. III (1073–1110)* (León: Centro de Estudios San Isidoro, 1988); Herrero de la Fuente, Marta, *Colección diplomática del Monasterio de Sahagún (857–1300). Vol. IV (1110–1199)* (León: Centro de Estudios San Isidoro, 1991); Fernández Flórez, José A., *Colección diplomática del monasterio de Sahagún (857–1300). Vol. V (1200–1300)* (León:

Centro de Estudios e Investigación San Isidoro, 1994).

SJBurgos
Peña Pérez, Francisco Javier, *Documentación del Monasterio de San Juan de Burgos (1091–1400)* (Burgos: Ediciones J.M. Garrido Garrido, 1983).

SMCogolla-L
Ledesma Rubio, María Luisa, *Cartulario de San Millán de la Cogolla (1076–1200)* (Zaragoza: Anubar, 1989).

SMRioseco
Cadiñanos Bardeci, Inocencio, *Monasterio cisterciense de Santa María de Rioseco, Valle de Manzanedo-Villarcayo: historia y cartulario* (Villarcayo: Asociación de Amigos de Villarcayo, 2002).

SMMoreruela
Alfonso, Isabel, *La colonización cisterciense en la Meseta del Duero. El dominio de Moreruela (siglos XII–XIV)* (Zamora: Instituto de Estudios Zamoranos Florián de Ocampo, 1986).

SMOteroDueñas
Fernández Flórez, José Antonio, and Marta Herrero de la Fuente, *Colección documental del monasterio de Santa María de Otero de las Dueñas, vol. 1 (854–1108)* (León: Centro de Estudios e Investigación San Isidoro, 1999).

SPArlanza
Serrano, Luciano, *Cartulario de San Pedro de Arlanza, antiguo monasterio benedictino* (Barcelona: Imprenta de Rafael Ibáñez de Aldecoa, 1925).

SPLaturce
García Turza, Francisco Javier, *Documentación medieval del monasterio de San Prudencio de Monte Laturce (siglos X–XV)* (Logroño: Instituto de Estudios Riojanos, 1992).

SPRamirás
Lucas Álvarez, Manuel, and Pedro Pablo Lucas Domínguez, *San Pedro de Ramirás. Un monasterio femenino en la Edad Media. Colección diplomática* (Santiago de Compostela: Convento de San Francisco, 1988).

SPRocas
Duro Peña, Emilio, *El monasterio de San Pedro de Rocas y su colección documental* (Orense: Instituto de Estudios Orensanos Padre Feijóo, 1972).

SREntrepeñas
Ruiz Asencio, José Manuel, and others, *Colección documental del monasterio de San Román de Entrepeñas (940–1068). Colección documental del Monasterio de San Miguel de Escalada (940–1605)* (León: Centro de Estudios e Investigación San Isidoro, 2000).

SSCelanova
Andrade Cernadas, José Miguel, Marta Díez Tíe, and Franciso Javier Pérez Rodríguez, *O tombo de Celanova: estudio introducto-*

rio, edición e índices (ss. IX–XII), 2 vols (Santiago de Compostela: Consello da Cultura Galega, 1995).

SSOña-A   del Álamo, Juan, *Colección diplomática de San Salvador de Oña: (822–1284). 2 vols* (Madrid: CSIC, 1950).

SSOña-O   Oceja Gonzalo, Isabel, *Documentación del Monasterio de San Salvador de Oña (1032–1350). 4 vols* (Burgos: J.M. Garrido Garrido, 1983–1986).

SToribioII   Álvarez Llopis, Elisa, Emma Blanco Campos, and José Ángel García de Cortázar, *Colección diplomática de Santo Toribio de Liébana: 1300–1515* (Santander: Fundación Marcelino Botín, 1994).

SZCarrion   Pérez Celada, Julio Antonio, *Documentación del Monasterio de San Zoilo de Carrión (1047–1300)* (Burgos: J.M. Garrido Garrido, 1986).

TBZ   Sánchez Rodríguez, Marciano, *Tumbo Blanco de Zamora* (Salamanca: Self-edited, 1985).

VC   Fernández Ordóñez, Inés, *'Versión Crítica' de la* Estoria de España: *Estudio y edición desde Pelayo hasta Ordoño II* (Madrid: Fundación Ramón Menéndez Pidal, 1993).

Foreword

As one of the contributors to this volume once stated, Isabel Alfonso is remarkable for her constant effort to bring to Spanish historians the advances of international English-language scholarship in history — not just medieval — and anthropology, and to make Spanish-speaking medieval research relevant to a wider international audience. As fair as this portrait is, it also brings to the forefront the paradox that most of Isabel's history writing is published in Spanish and is, therefore, not available to an English-speaking readership. This is certainly not the case for some outstanding contributions, such as her 1991 *Past & Present* article, or her edited volumes *Building Legitimacy* and *The Rural History of Medieval European Societies*, but it affects a large number of works that many perceive as the most representative and impactful of her production.

With all this in mind, we decided that, instead of the more common format of a collective volume of essays, we would try and offer Isabel a different kind of Festschrift. It would be a volume of assorted essays by her, translated into English, and yet it would retain the spirit of a collection of pieces by colleagues and friends. We so chose to ask a number of international scholars who have met and collaborated with Isabel through the years, and write short commentaries to introduce and discuss her pieces. A sort of scholarly version of the 'X reacts to Y' genre that is popular in the social media. The impressive line-up speaks for itself about the scope and quality of Isabel's connections.

Making a selection of her most representative articles and book chapters in Spanish proved a complicated matter. Inevitably, quite a few fine articles had to be discarded simply because there were too many of them. At the same time, we felt that some of the texts that were already available in English were too important and characteristic of her work to be left out without detriment to the volume. Gradually a consolidated selection of twenty texts took shape.

The next step was to assign them to the contributors, and this is when things began to get interesting. From the outset, it was our aim to give the commentators as much freedom as possible. Their texts had to be scholarly, of course, but the authors could decide whether to get a bit more personal or not, whether to be more or less critical, whether to stick strictly to the work or bring into the discussion some of the casuistry they themselves worked with, and so on. It was even up to them to put a title to their contribution or not! So they got creative. This is why at times the volume departs from the standard one-to-one format. François Foronda, clearly indulging on the personal side, proposed to write a commentary on Isabel's very first publication, which we had not initially considered. His choice proved much inspired, as this allowed us to present Isabel in the very first steps of her career. No good deed goes unpunished, though, and François later payed for his by kindly agreeing to write a second commentary in replacement of another commentator who was ultimately unable to participate. Likewise, Jean Birrell and Ros Faith decided to write a commentary each on both of Isabel's articles from the volumes on the *Anthropology of Seigneurial Revenue*. Same articles, two very different 'reactions'. For our part, we felt that it made sense to ask Stephen D. White to write jointly about Isabel's two pieces on Justice and Vengeance, given that they are so closely related. Likewise, Jesús Rodríguez Velasco graciously accepted our challenge to comment on three review articles that were selected because they showcase Isabel as a reader and critic of historical literature. Isabel is an astonishingly sharp yet generous reader, as all who have had the opportunity to pass their own writings through her lens are well aware. Jesús made a fine job of bringing to light this lesser-known aspect of her work.

Getting adequate English translations was by far the hardest, most time-consuming task of all. Isabel's Spanish prose is rich, nuanced and complex, and not at all easy to translate. The editors are immensely grateful to Julian Thomas, Deirdre Casey, and Nicholas Callaway for their translations from the Spanish, and to Jean Birrell, who kindly translated the French texts, but also to Isabel herself, who had the enormous patience to return again and again to her own texts until the translations were fully perfected.

A volume of this kind could have been arranged in countless ways. After several attempts, we opted for a structure that seems to us to reflect well the main aspects of Isabel's production, even if the extension varies much from one section to another. Part I comprises pieces about language, discourse and political legitimation; Part II deals with social differentiation within medieval rural communities. Part III, the lengthiest, deals with justice and dispute settlement. Part IV, finally, is devoted to Isabel's historiographical criticism.

The editorial work of several years came to a very pleasant end when Isabel invited the editors for an afternoon of food and drink at her terrace (an informal historical think-tank where more than one research project has taken shape). The conversation that we had there has become the introduction to this volume, which — at times despite Isabel's slight reticence — we feel that provides the essential biographical background to place her historical writing in context.

Behold, the deed is now done and the editors would like to express their endless gratitude to all the contributors for their enthusiastic response to our invitation and for their invaluable patience with our seemingly endless editorial process. And, of course, to Isabel for the gift of a historical work that is as rigorous as it is inspiring.

ISABEL ALFONSO ANTÓN, JULIO ESCALONA,
CRISTINA JULAR PÉREZ-ALFARO, AND ÁLVARO
CARVAJAL CASTRO

Introduction

Dealing with the Past, Dealing with the Present.
*Yet another Talk with Isabel Alfonso**

We academics usually relate to each other — get to know each other, criticize each other, admire each other — through our publications. The formality of that written record, with its peer reviews and thematic conferences, can make us forget that we are also members of a community, or rather, of a cloud of interconnected communities that are largely oral. They feed on the spoken word and dialogue through seminars, conferences, congresses and, above all, a multitude of informal conversations, where academic rigour leaves room for emotions and passion. Isabel — or Maribel, as she is known interchangeably — is one of those historians capable of producing a particularly intense impression through conversation. Over the years, casual exchanges with her have served to probe papers, discuss books, outline projects and, above all, raise doubts. Doubts of all kinds about almost anything. Fertile doubts. Constructive doubts that have enabled us to move forward.

The terrace of Maribel's apartment in Madrid, thick with plants and flowers in the spring, has been the setting for many of these conversations. Informal talks, sharing wine and ideas, that more often than not are purely for pleasure, but on occasion have even spawned entire research projects. It was also the setting of yet another conversation, the one that we will reconstruct here. Those who know Maribel will agree that it is impossible to interview her outright, as she rebels against the dynamics of the question-and-answer format. With her, only a choral chat is possible. These pages are the memories of one such chat, sharing food, drinks, and emotions. One more conversation with someone who has left her mark through conversation.

Maribel, your training differs significantly from that of other Spanish medievalists of your generation. This is surely key to understanding your history writing, and how your work relates to that of your colleagues. You studied at the Faculty of Political and Economic Sciences of the Complutense University of Madrid in the 1960s. How do you remember that time? What were your concerns when you started?

---

* Warm thanks are due to Nicholas Callaway for revising the English style of this text.

Conflict, Language, and Social Practice in Medieval Societies: Selected Essays of Isabel Alfonso, with Commentaries, ed. by Julio Escalona Monge, Álvaro Carvajal Castro, and Cristina Jular Pérez-Alfaro, TMC 24 (Turnhout: Brepols, 2024), pp. 21–34

BREPOLS ❦ PUBLISHERS   10.1484/M.TMC-EB.5.132454

IA: The 1960s? Phew! I don't remember. I'm a historian, but dates ...

Not bad for a start: 'I'm a historian, but dates ...' [laughs].

IA: Well, the first thing to consider is where I came from. I have always been a voracious reader, but originally I did not have much access to books. I come from a family with a peasant background and low social status, in which books were rare. For me, just getting my hands on a book at all was a miracle. Imagine how fascinated I was when I discovered the library at the Instituto Isabel la Católica, the secondary school I attended! I read everything, everything! But I read in a somewhat anarchic way, without much order. At university it was totally different. At first, I was surrounded by a lot of friends who, despite being rebellious youths, still came from posh families. In the first semesters, for instance, many of my female classmates still celebrated their 'debut'! It was a noticeable social distance that made me feel a bit insecure. Then I started to meet different people and gradually began to change as I absorbed other currents of thought, like what today we would call feminism. That meant a rebellion with respect to the upbringing I had received. I also associate reading with watching films. I learned so much by reading everything from film reviews to all kinds of books on cinema. It is part of an education that was also distilled through conversations with my peers.

The second issue is my choice of studies itself, Political Science. I chose it because it was very 'cross-cutting', and provided a very broad outlook, although it was not always easy for me. In fact, I dropped out in the second year because I failed History! [laughs] The kind of History we were taught in first and second year was just awful. There was this famous professor who asked us the names of Louis XIV's mistresses! So I quit and took a clerical job at a bank, where I lasted three months, at which point the director told me that I had better get back to my studies, because whenever the work was slow, I would pick up a book and read, and that, of course, was not part of my job description. When I got back to university, my outlook had changed. It was a time when university demonstrations were a daily occurrence, and that also triggered a political shift in me.

That is very interesting. The School of Political Science of the Complutense University was founded in 1943 as a symbol of Francoism, but things had changed quite a bit by the time you got there.

IA: Exactly. Supposedly open-minded professors, such as Díez del Corral or José María Maravall, had actually taught in their blue Falange shirts in the early years, but in my time those sacred cows had more politically 'progressive' assistants, such as Antonio Elorza and José Álvarez Junco. I won't bore you with my student life there, but I do want to highlight two of the subjects that were most important to me. One of them was the History of Ideas, in second year. It was an enormous discovery for me. Instead of a single textbook, we had the whole history of thought, of political ideas, at our reach. The other was the History of Institutions, taught by Luis García de Valdeavellano. His courses always focused on very monographic issues, like specific aspects of Modern History, or the transition from Late Antiquity to the Middle Ages, and so on. I was an outstanding student, and I was put in charge of the Seminar's library. It was a very good library, with lots of foreign literature.

Luis García de Valdeavellano was a very important figure in Spanish medievalism at that time. He had been a disciple and collaborator of Claudio Sánchez-Albornoz and had an international education. What was it like to work under his supervision?

IA: Perhaps one of the most interesting aspects of his teaching was the attention he paid to the analysis of documents. It was an activity that he turned into a core practice of the Seminar. The other was his exhaustive, rigorous methods ('pride in a job well done', as he called it). He deemed himself an old liberal and an 'internal exile',[1] and this impregnated many informal conversations held daily at the Seminar. The backdrop to these conversations was mostly the rupture that the Civil War had brought about with respect to the Second Republic's secular culture, which he strove to keep alive and pass along to us.

You finally chose to work on rural history by studying a monastic domain. It was an emerging research strand at the time, and you approached it in a very personal way.

IA: Yes, Valdeavellano knew of my peasant provenance and he initially suggested that I should do a PhD applying Marc Bloch's *charactères originaux* to the rural history of Spain. Surely tempting, but too broad for a thesis, right? In the end, I chose to study the monastic domain of Santa María de Moreruela (Zamora). The goal was to approach this rather local subject from a renewed perspective stemming from French historiography, which at that time was very influential both in Spain and elsewhere. At that time, Marxism was also quickly spreading in Spanish academic circles. Taking a Marxist perspective, however, was out of the question with Valdeavellano. His approach was very much socioeconomic, but never Marxist. In fact, the reception of Marxism marked a generational break between students and their professors. Mine, however, was not a militant position. For me, Marxism represented an opportunity to delve deeper in conceptual terms, but I was always careful to keep a distance from its more simplistic versions.

Being in a Social Sciences environment with a fundamentally late-modern or contemporary orientation, it's a bit surprising that you turned towards medieval history. Was that an easy move to make?

IA: Not at all. I didn't have any training in palaeography or any background as a historian. Valdeavellano's wife, Pilar Loscertales, who was the head of the *Clero* Section of the Archivo Histórico Nacional, trained me in palaeography, together with Consuelo Vázquez de Parga. I learned Latin and palaeography 'on the fly' as I went through the documents. This was before the boom in charter editions that took place in Spain starting in the 1980s, and most of the material was unpublished, as was the case with Moreruela.

---

1   The term 'internal exile' was used under Franco's regime to designate people who, without having been forced to leave the country, had suffered a more or less traumatic removal from their professional careers or public positions.

And how did your relationship with other medievalists come about?

IA: As a medievalist I really felt increasingly out of place in Political Science, and strived to connect with medievalists from other institutions. It was probably through the seminars of Abilio Barbero's group, and also those organised at Gonzalo Anes's chair of Economic History, to which they brought the latest developments in historiography. Those were very fruitful events. There I met Ángel García Sanz and Jesús Sanz, with whom I would always have a great rapport, and also Reyna Pastor, who had recently arrived in Madrid [as an exile from the Argentine dictatorship] and with whom I later made the move to the CSIC.

Before that, you spent a year in Birmingham in 1987. The choice of the United Kingdom is interesting, bearing in mind that the Spanish medievalists of your generation were usually brought up learning French, and that the influence of French historiography was enormous. The obvious destination at that time would have been France. Why then the UK, and in what way did Birmingham influence your career?

IA: That's true. Some years earlier I had actually considered going to France, and I even got a grant from the Juan March Foundation to work with Georges Duby (I still have the letters I exchanged with him), but for various reasons I didn't end up going. Birmingham, then, was a total turning point. As I said before, I felt out of place in Political Science, and I had begun to collaborate in the research project being led by Reyna Pastor at the CSIC. I really liked Reyna's work. I also loved Rodney Hilton's work, and this is why I chose Birmingham. I remember discovering the library, and the many hours I spent reading there. The highlight, though, were the Friday seminars. They were organized by the postdoctoral researchers, and met at the homes of the participants. The term's kick-off was at Rodney Hilton and Jean Birrell's home. There I met Chris Wickham, with whom I became very good friends. By then he had published *The Mountains and the City*,[2] which I think is a fundamental book and certainly had a great impact on me. The core of his approach, which brings you close to fields like anthropology, for example, was already there. I love how he connects small details from our daily life with the phenomena of the past societies he studies. I also met Peter Coss, with whom I later had a very fruitful exchange. People like Chris Dyer, with whom I shared an interest in rural and peasant history, Julia Barrow, Nicholas Brooks, John Edwards, John Haldon, Dick Holt, and Robert Swanson were also in Birmingham, and researchers like Grenville Astill, Ros Faith and Jinty Nelson also participated in these seminars. Later, I enjoyed a brief stay at King's College London, which allowed me to learn more about Jinty's work, and, thanks to other stays at the Institute of Historical Research, I was able to work in its excellent library — and the British Library too! – and attend the famous Wednesday early medieval seminars, where an enormously dynamic group of medievalists met. It was very important for me to get to know all these groups and their work. It also gave rise to great friendships that I still maintain today.

---

2   Wickham, *The Mountains and the City.*

The way you describe what your contact with Chris Wickham meant to you is very revealing for those of us who have read and learned from your work. It is your own reading of his work, of course, because for you the 'micro' approach has always been very important.

IA: Yes, indeed. I love to approach things from a 'micro' perspective. Later on, for example, I met Giovanni Levi and I was also very interested in his 'micro-history'.

Birmingham had a noticeable influence on your later publications. Your article in Past & Present *on Cistercians and Feudalism,[3] for example, although largely the result of your earlier work on Moreruela, marked a shift towards a broader approach, don't you think?*

IA: Not really. The article took up the 'Epilogue' of my book on Moreruela[4] — which hadn't aroused much interest — broadening its focus based on the available literature in English. I saw it as a necessary critique of the historiography, although it was a difficult one for me to write. I questioned the arguments of very important scholars who represented the dominant discourse (I remember that later Susan Reynolds told me that I should have gone even further). I'm really not sure to what extent Birmingham changed my way of doing history. The project I worked on there was about rural communities, and I read everything I could find on the subject. I also remember that at that time Miquel Barceló was at Birmingham too, and he — always the archaeologist — kept asking me, 'How are you going to research rural communities without digging?' Well, I didn't have a fully outlined plan. I was simply learning as I went, just as I did with my thesis, trying to better understand the kinds of questions I was asking myself. Actually, I don't think I ever really had a defined project until I came to focus on the study of disputes. When I read Wendy Davies and Paul Fouracre's book[5] — another crucial milestone — I thought that it was an approach that had to be explored for Iberia, which was a project I felt like taking on.

Your return to Madrid marked a U-turn. You left your tenured position at the Complutense and joined the CSIC, where you've stayed ever since.

IA: Indeed, it was a very important change. On the one hand, I quit the university and, with it, the frustration that teaching entailed for me. I was never allowed to delve deep into the current debates surrounding each topic, which was what I was really interested in discussing. On the other hand, the CSIC meant a full-time research job and a very different kind of teaching, mostly through research seminars. Those were years of major intellectual dynamism, when we all felt like we were generating new ways of working. The research projects led by Reyna Pastor were hugely inspiring, as were the seminars we organised, inviting Spanish and foreign historians. They always led to endless discussions livened up by a group of bright young students — now renowned historians in their own right.

---

3 See chapter 15 of this volume.
4 Alfonso, *La colonización cisterciense*.
5 Davies and Fouracre, eds, *The Settlement of Disputes*.

After joining the CSIC, you began to address a broader range of topics. Without losing sight of rural sociology, you expanded your approach to include the study of conflict and justice, which you have already mentioned, along with a new element that you hadn't studied previously: the exploration of the political sphere, which you began to develop in the late 1990s.

IA: Well, I wouldn't say that my work was rural sociology. At that time, there was a lot of work being done on rural sociology, but usually with very little historical sense. Was I a sociologist or a historian? Well, it never seemed to me that the boundaries between the two disciplines should be a rigid one.

Even so, your primary interest in peasant communities, which was already present in your study on Moreruela, really comes to the fore in your 1990s work on rural communities, especially in Galicia, which remains a point of reference.[6] How was that influenced by your joining the CSIC?

IA: It was to some extent, but not as much as it might seem. Obviously, the work on Galicia was part of a CSIC research project in which I was in charge of studying that aspect. However, I think that what weighs most heavily for me is the peasant origin of my own family, and my interest in understanding the mechanisms of domination and how people live and coexist in local rural societies. This has been part of my work from the outset. I was born in Barcelona because my father had left his village, and my mother with him, like so many others of their generation. My grandparents and all my other relatives had stayed behind, though. We visited every summer, and during that time we personally experienced the transition from a traditional society to the industrial world. No exaggeration: the village I knew in my childhood did not have electricity. I suppose that the influence of Marxism, the idea of studying domination and power, was added on to my personal link with the peasant world. For example, I think that my article on *Peasants and the Law[7]* owes a lot to the work of E. P. Thompson. But there were other influences too, of course.

It is interesting that among those references you highlight E. P. Thompson, whose work seems to have little to do with the medieval period. The dialogue with specialists in other historical periods is also a constant in your work. In fact, another very important milestone in your career was joining the Spanish Society of Agrarian History (SEHA),[8] which is largely dominated by modern historians. Was that at all problematic?

IA: It was certainly important to join the editorial board of the journal *Historia Agraria*, which was by then trying to broaden its chronological range of interests. For me, whether it was modern or contemporary history was not a barrier, because

---

6 Alfonso, 'Poder local y diferenciación interna'; Alfonso, 'La comunidad campesina'. An English version of the former may be found in chapter 6 of this volume.

7 See chapter 9 of this volume.

8 Now re-branded as Sociedad de Estudios de Historia Agraria (see http://seha.info/es). Isabel Alfonso carried out for years a very intense work in the Board of Directors of the SEHA and in the Editorial Board of the journal *Historia Agraria*.

I have always questioned those conventional boundaries and have rather favoured cross-cutting themes that can be approached in different periods, from different disciplines. Moreover, there are specific aspects of those later periods that have a very direct bearing on our own work as medievalists. In any case, participating in such forums was a major effort, since it was very difficult to get medieval research accepted; still, I do believe that favouring this integration was important work that needed to be done.

A fundamental output of your participation in the SEHA was the dossier on the historiography of medieval rural societies in Europe in Historia Agraria.[9] *It was pretty bold to bring together studies from such disparate areas.*

IA: At a certain point, I became very aware of how the different national historiographical traditions, together with our recent past, determine our way of thinking, as is the case with Francoism in Spain. I was very interested in having an international group of people reflect on how the historiography on the rural world had developed in different countries and its effects on the strands of research followed in each case. This has to do with the way in which I approach the work done on other countries. For me it is not so much a matter of knowing the history of other countries in depth as of being interested in the questions raised in their historiographies.

The effort was well appreciated, considering that shortly after it was reprinted twice, in book format by Publicacions de la Universitat de València and in English by Brepols.

IA: Yes, the English translation became the first volume in Brepols' newly created series 'The Medieval Countryside'. I was invited to join the Editorial Board, first with Paul Freedman as General Editor and later with Phillipp Schofield, when he took up the role. That was a fantastic opportunity to learn more about the historiography on other European regions, and above all to help disseminate some of the finest recent works on medieval Iberia to an international audience.

Let us go back in time for a moment. When you joined the CSIC you also began to work on disputes and judicial scenarios, probably the most recognizable and widespread aspect of your production. Perhaps the clearest starting point is the 1997 Hispania *dossier.[10] In the context of what was being written on the subject at that time in Spain, this monograph seems to have come from another planet.*

IA: For me personally it was very important, and there you can indeed see the influence of my stay in England. As I said, Davies and Fouracre's book was a real inspiration. To put that special issue together, I had to reach out to people I respected intellectually and whose work interested me a great deal — and they agreed to take

---

9 Special issues 'La historia rural de las sociedades medievales europeas: trayectorias y perspectivas, 1' in *Historia Agraria*, 31 (2003), 11–86 and 'La historia rural de las sociedades medievales europeas: trayectorias y perspectivas, 2', *Historia Agraria*, 33 (2004), 13–106. The whole collection was later reprinted in Spanish (Alfonso, ed., *La historia rural*) and in English (Alfonso, ed., *The Rural History*).

10 Special issue 'Desarrollo legal, prácticas judiciales y acción política en la Europa medieval', *Hispania*, 197 (1997), 879–1077.

part! Stephen D. White, for example, was a fundamental reference for me, although I was critical of the way in which he — and also Patrick Geary, for instance — assumed that medieval dispute-resolution processes reached a turning point in the eleventh century, after which everything was different. I did not see such a clean-cut change. I always tend to focus more on the continuities.

Paradoxically, that dossier broadened your academic network abroad and generated a discussion that was very ambitious in scope, but it was published for a Spanish-speaking audience, and it seems like Spanish medievalism at the time was not ready to assimilate it. In a certain sense, one could think that the relevance was not in the publication itself but rather in the extent to which it contributed to the internationalization of your career, which would then be further strengthened with the Acción Integrada *with St Andrews.*[11]

IA: I must admit that much of the historiography that most interested me was being written abroad. As for the dossier, I always suspected it would have a limited impact in Spain. Anyway, things have changed and maybe it will prove more significant for the younger generations. It certainly gave me the stimulus to keep going in this direction. Shortly afterwards, in 1999, I did a short stay in Los Angeles and contacted Piotr S. Górecki and Warren C. Brown. Their work has also been very useful as a reference against which to contrast my own research on conflict and dispute resolution, allowing me to connect it with a number of elements from legal anthropology. This was already present in the article I published with Cristina Jular in the year 2000.[12] At about the same time, John Hudson and I launched the *Acción Integrada* on 'Political Discourses and Forms of Legitimation', which enabled me to further develop my relationships with many colleagues working in that field. I think the resulting volume, *Building Legitimacy*, was an important landmark.[13]

Building Legitimacy, *soon followed by* Lucha Política [Political Struggle], *was a materialization of the expansion of your research interests into the political sphere, which was also marked by a profound interest in the work done on the subject in other disciplines.*[14]

IA: Yes. They were the result of a very intense research project I worked on side by side with Julio Escalona. *Building Legitimacy* is also relevant because it has been cited even outside the field of medievalism. This seems significant to me, because, although historians sometimes draw from other social sciences to theorize and build their own arguments (and I think this is well reflected in some of my own work), our publications are rarely cited in other disciplines. This book clearly had more audiences than we initially anticipated.

---

11 The *Acción Integrada* was a bilateral project between the University of St Andrews (UK) and the Centro de Estudios Históricos – CSIC, jointly directed by Isabel Alfonso and John Hudson. It ran from 1999 to 2001, and culminated in a symposium at St Andrews on *Political Discourses and Forms of Legitimation*.

12 Alfonso and Jular Pérez-Alfaro, 'Oña contra Frías'.

13 Alfonso, Kennedy, and Escalona, eds, *Building Legitimacy*.

14 Alfonso, Escalona, and Martin, eds, *Lucha política*.

You are definitely right to say that the influence of other social sciences is evident in your research. For example, some of your work from the early 2000s, such as your chapters in the volumes on the anthropology of seigneurial revenue, show how you were interweaving your own background in rural history and peasant-lord conflicts with an increasing interest in legal anthropology.[15]

Yes, my readings in anthropology in general, not just legal anthropology, were intensifying at that time. In London, I got to know Simon Roberts and Maurice Bloch, whose work broadened my own set of questions. This is reflected in my contributions to the 2000 and 2002 Valladolid and Jaca colloquia on the anthropology of seigneurial revenue, which you've just mentioned. Those were very lively meetings, with the participation of many colleagues with whom I established fruitful connections, like Monique Bourin, Laurent Feller, Paul Freedman, Julien Demade, Joseph Morsel, and Phillipp Schofield. A similar anthropological approach, but more oriented toward political matters, inspired my collaboration with Claude Gauvard, Dominique Barthélemy, and François Bougard in events like the Rome conference on Revenge.[16] Around the same time, I also connected with François Foronda, who had recently joined the Casa de Velázquez and whose views on medieval political processes I have always enjoyed so much.

Many other important things were happening during this time as well. By then you had come into contact with Georges Martin and the SIREM group in France, which critically contributed to expanding the scope of your research.[17] *More than ten years of collaboration with the SIREM have left a very recognizable impact on your work, including the study of sources that you had barely used until then, such as chronicles, epics, literature ...*

IA: Joining G. Martin's group at the SIREM was a fantastic opportunity. I was most interested in the work of G. Martin himself, and also in that of others such as Amaia Arizaleta, Francisco Bautista, Inés Fernández Ordóñez, Fernando Gómez Redondo and Jesús Rodríguez Velasco. It opened up a different world to me. It was then that I started working on the Chronicle of Alfonso X, and also on other texts such as the *Siete Partidas*, the *Poema de Mío Cid*, and the work of Infante Don Juan Manuel, and took up the challenge of exploring their underlying and explicit discourses.[18] I found it fascinating to incorporate these philological approaches into my own research on these sources. It enriched my understanding of the texts and broadened the possibilities of delving further into the societies I studied. I also think that there

---

15 Alfonso, 'La contestation paysanne'; Alfonso, 'La rhétorique de légitimation seigneuriale'. See chapter 11 of this volume.

16 Alfonso, 'Vengeance, justice et lutte politique'. See chapter 5 of this volume.

17 The SIREM (Séminaire Interdisciplinaire de Recherches sur l'Espagne Médiévale) was a French CNRS Research Group (GDP 2378) that brought together numerous historians and philologists working on medieval Iberia, directed by Georges Martin. It was later reformulated as the GDRE AILP ('Approche interdisciplinaire des logiques de pouvoir dans les sociétés ibériques médiévales'). See http://ailp.ens-lyon.fr.

18 Alfonso, 'Venganza y justicia'; Alfonso, 'Vengeance, justice et lutte politique'; Alfonso, 'El cuerpo del delito'; Alfonso, 'Desheredamiento y desafuero'. See chapters 5, 12, and 14 of this volume.

are very promising grounds for collaboration there. As I pointed out in my review of G. Martin's book,[19] the discourses of medieval literary texts need to be studied within the historical processes of political and ideological competition, of which they are an essential factor. Specialists in literature are obviously aware of this, but I feel that, when it comes to characterizing historical contexts, there is a certain disconnection with the more current debates in the historiography. Historians can contribute a great deal to these studies by bringing in ongoing historiographical developments to the reconstruction of the texts' historical contexts.

With the passage of time, this warning may seem obvious, but it was not at all so at that time. There was a very strong tendency, perhaps as a result of the postmodern critique, to place texts and narratives on a purely discursive plane, as something divorced from reality; a reality that, moreover, became ultimately unattainable. This critical article on Martin's book is part of a set of pieces of historiographical reflection — such as your commentary on D. Barthélemy's book[20] — that say a lot about your own approach to scholarship.

IA: That was also a huge task. I was not completely persuaded by the idea of the 'documentary revelation'. To me, it seemed more like a 'historiographic revelation', derived from the fact that the social changes with which this 'revelation' was associated had largely been overlooked. I think it showed how difficult it is to keep interdisciplinary practice coherent, that is, to make a critical and consistent use of both the source material and the insights from the different disciplines informing historical analysis. This is something that I regard as crucial.

Certainly, the fact that you are an excellent text critic, both of the bibliography and of the sources themselves, plays an important role in all of this.

IA: Yes, but I do not think it's because I have a special knack for linking certain texts with others. Obviously, it's built upon my background and the knowledge I have accumulated over time, but it's not something that I consciously deploy. Rather, I have come to integrate it naturally into my work practice. In the end, those skills are part of the toolbox I use to analyse texts, and this is a cumulative process. My ability to ask myself questions about a text is much greater now than it was before. As you read and reflect, your capacity to incorporate resources — in short, to gain a better understanding of things — increases. Basically, it's a learning process. This is what encourages me, what keeps me alive.

Let's now turn to your latest project, PRJ.[21] It has involved a titanic ten-year effort to build a database, which is something very different from the work you were doing before, and

---

19 Alfonso Antón, 'El discurso histórico como historia'. See chapter 16 of this volume.

20 Alfonso, 'Continuidad y revelación documental'. See chapter 16 of this volume.

21 The PRJ project ('Procesos Judiciales en las Sociedades Medievales del Norte Peninsular'), directed by Isabel, was developed in two phases between 2007 and 2013. Its main outcome was a database bringing together documentation relating to disputes and dispute resolution in the Iberian north up to 1100 (http://prj.csic.es). A volume of studies derived from the project's colloquia is currently in press.

which has allowed you to go through practically all the extant documents from the north of the peninsula from before 1100. This is striking, because at first sight such a meticulous reading of the documents that is so typical of you would seem at odds with the approach that building up a large database requires, as it privileges regularities over particularities. Has this changed your way of looking at the documents?

IA: That's a good question, but I don't really think that it has. The truth is that when I came up with the PRJ project, I had reached a point where I was a bit tired of theoretical approaches, and needed to work on something more empirical. On the one hand, I wanted to develop a mechanical tool to process the documents. The work that Julio Escalona and I undertook to design this database was exhausting, but also enormously inspiring, and all the subsequent work of compiling, disambiguating, and processing the documents allowed me to find new nuances in the texts at every step. For this I have collaborated with scholars such as José Miguel Andrade, André Marques, and Josep María Salrach, among others. On the other hand, it is true that I soon discovered the frustration of constantly seeing enormously attractive texts pass before my eyes without being able to stop and scrutinise them in detail like I normally would. Nevertheless, I am well aware that the large corpus of charters we have registered reveals some general aspects of the overall record that the particular analysis of specific documents cannot, and that in so doing it facilitates comparison — if we manage to ask the right questions, of course. I believe that the PRJ design process has laid the groundwork for a set of questions that will allow us to explore further issues in the future, both in relation to the whole charter corpus and to possible regional variations. There is still a lot of work to do.

In any case, working on a database has not entirely forced you to give up the 'micro' approach. On the contrary, one could say that you have broadened it, for example, by focusing on the materiality of documents.[22]

IA: This brings me back to what I said before: the process of inquiry must be enriched by opening up the scope, and in this case, this has meant taking materiality into account. The materiality of the documents can make you question how you interpret their textual content. Thinking more about the character of the documents and their transmission has been very important for the book we are about to publish, which brings together some important results from the PRJ project.[23]

To conclude, you can be described as a rara avis *among medievalists, in Spain of course, but also abroad. It is not common for historians to have an initial training in Social Sciences and then devote themselves to the study of the Middle Ages. Perhaps that is the origin of your interest in other disciplines, and of your eagerness to connect the past with the present.*

IA: Well, I should specify that my primary interest is in the questions asked in other disciplines, not so much in their methods as in the conceptual perspectives from

---

22 Alfonso, 'El formato de la información judicial'.
23 Alfonso, Andrade and Marques, eds, *Records and Processes*.

which they approach the problems. As I said before, the same thing happens to me regarding different national historiographies. As for the relationship between the past and the present, people always say, 'History is the science that studies change'. But why don't we study continuity more? Rituals, for example, or why certain power strategies maintain their effectiveness. I think historians should ask more often why there are things that keep having the same effectiveness (horrible things, generally, in terms of power). That is why I also think that, if I were to focus on other historical periods, even if the sources were not the same, I would be dealing with very similar concerns.

It seems only natural to close this talk with a final question about this book. It brings together, now in English, some of your most significant works, with contributions from many of the historians with whom you have had a relationship of collaboration and friendship over the years. Ultimately, it is almost a choral historiographical dialogue. What do you think an international audience can expect from this volume?

IA: This is very difficult for me to answer. I certainly believe that it boasts a first-class line-up of commentators that will be very engaging. Quite probably, too, a number of people working on these issues will appreciate having the English version of these papers now (in fact, I know there are people who would have liked to read my texts at the time they were published). It may also be useful to teachers who want to recommend readings to their students. But beyond that, I have no idea. What I do think is that the format you have chosen for this volume is very stimulating and I hope it will be well received. And I am delighted, of course, with the response of all the friends and colleagues who have participated, and with the care with which they have engaged with it. It really makes me very happy.

INTRODUCTION 33

Bibliography

Alfonso, Isabel, *La colonización cisterciense en la Meseta del Duero. El dominio de Moreruela (siglos XII–XIV)* (Zamora: Instituto de Estudios Zamoranos Florián de Ocampo, 1986)

Alfonso, Isabel, 'La comunidad campesina', in *Poder monástico y grupos domésticos en la Galicia foral (siglos XIII–XV)*, ed. by Reyna Pastor and others (Madrid: CSIC, 1990), pp. 302–72

Alfonso, Isabel, 'Poder local y diferenciación interna en las comunidades rurales gallegas', in *Relaciones de poder, de producción y de parentesco en la Edad Media y Moderna: aproximación a su estudio*, ed. by Reyna Pastor (Madrid: CSIC, 1990), pp. 203–24

Alfonso, Isabel, 'Continuidad y revelación documental o mutación y revolución feudal', *Hispania*, 189 (1995), 301–13

Alfonso, Isabel, 'El discurso histórico como historia', *Hispania*, 192 (1996), 349–63

Alfonso, Isabel, 'Desheredamiento y desafuero, o la pretendida justificación de una revuelta nobiliaria', *Cahiers de linguistique et de civilisation hispaniques médiévales*, 25 (2002), 99–129

Alfonso, Isabel, 'Venganza y justicia en el Cantar de Mío Cid', in *El Cid: de la materia épica a las crónicas caballerescas*, ed. by Carlos Alvar Ezquerra, Fernando Gómez Redondo and Georges Martin (Alcalá de Henares: Universidad de Alcalá, 2002), pp. 41–69

Alfonso, Isabel, 'La contestation paysanne face aux exigences de travail seigneuriales en Castille et Léon: Les formes et leur signification symbolique', in *Pour une anthropologie du prélèvement seigneurial dans les campagnes médiévales (XIe–XIVe siècles): réalités et représentations paysannes. Colloque tenu à Medina del Campo du 31 mai au 3 juin 2000*, ed. by Monique Bourin and Pascual Martínez Sopena (Paris: Publications de la Sorbonne, 2004), pp. 291–320

Alfonso, Isabel, 'Vengeance, justice et lutte politique dans l'historiographie castillane du Moyen Âge', in *La vengeance, 400–1200*, ed. by Dominique Barthélemy, François Bougard and Régine Le Jan (Rome: École française de Rome, 2006), pp. 383–419

Alfonso, Isabel, 'La rhétorique de légitimation seigneuriale dans les fueros de León (XIe– XIIIe siècles)', in *Pour une anthropologie du prélèvement seigneurial dans les campagnes de l'Occident médiéval (XIe–XIVe siècles). Les mots, les temps, les lieux*, ed. by Monique Bourin and Pascual Martínez Sopena (Paris: Publications de la Sorbonne, 2007), pp. 229–52

Alfonso, Isabel, ed., *The Rural History of Medieval European Societies: Trends and Perspectives* (Turnhout: Brepols, 2007)

Alfonso, Isabel, 'El cuerpo del delito y la violencia ejemplar', in *Cuerpo derrotado: cómo trataban musulmanes y cristianos a los enemigos vencidos (Península Ibérica, ss. VIII– XIII)*, ed. by Maribel Fierro and Francisco García Fitz (Madrid: CSIC, 2008), pp. 397–431

Alfonso, Isabel, ed., *La historia rural de las sociedades medievales europeas. Tendencias y perspectivas* (Valencia: Publicacions de la Universitat de València, 2008)

Alfonso, Isabel, 'El formato de la información judicial en la Alta Edad Media peninsular', in *Chartes et cartulaires comme instruments de pouvoir: Espagne et Occident chrétien (VIIIe– XIIe siècles)*, ed. by Julio Escalona and Hélène Sirantoine (Toulouse: Méridiennes-Université de Toulouse-Le Mirail, CSIC, 2013), pp. 191–218

Alfonso, Isabel, José M. Andrade Cernadas, and André Evangelista Marques, eds, *Records and Processes of Dispute Settlement in Early Medieval Societies: Iberia and Beyond* (Leiden: Brill, forthcoming)

Alfonso, Isabel, Julio Escalona, and Georges Martin, eds, *Lucha política: condena y legitimación en la España medieval*, Annexes des Cahiers de Civilisation Hispanique Médiévale, 16 (Lyon: ENS Éditions, 2004)

Alfonso, Isabel, and Cristina Jular Pérez-Alfaro, 'Oña contra Frías o el pleito de los cien testigos: una pesquisa en la Castilla del siglo XIII', *Edad Media. Revista de Historia*, 3 (2000), 61–88

Alfonso, Isabel, Hugh Kennedy, and Julio Escalona, eds, *Building Legitimacy: Political Discourses and Forms of Legitimation in Medieval Societies* (Leiden: Brill, 2004)

Davies, Wendy, and Paul Fouracre, eds, *The Settlement of Disputes in Early Medieval Europe* (Cambridge: Cambridge University Press, 1986)

Wickham, Chris, *The Mountains and the City: The Tuscan Apennines in the Early Middle Ages* (Oxford: Clarendon Press, 1988)

PART I

Medieval Minds

Language and Concepts

CHAPTER 1

On Friendship

with a commentary by François Foronda

Conflict, Language, and Social Practice in Medieval Societies: Selected Essays of Isabel Alfonso, with Commentaries, ed. by Julio Escalona Monge, Álvaro Carvajal Castro, and Cristina Jular Pérez-Alfaro, TMC 24 (Turnhout: Brepols, 2024), pp. 37–55

BREPOLS ❧ PUBLISHERS   10.1484/M.TMC-EB.5.132455

FRANÇOIS FORONDA

Amicitia

*Early Writings, a Revelation,
and the Identity of a Historian*[*]

I was not aware when I chose this piece that it was the first article of Isabel Alfonso to be published. I knew, of course, given that she defended her thesis in 1980, that it was one of her first publications, but not that it was the very first. I chose it, to the best of my recollection, at the beginning of summer 2015, when Cristina Jular told me of the festschrift she and Julio Escalona were proposing to organise. My choice was confirmed in an exchange of emails between 2 and 4 October 2015 — what would a historian seeking to retrace the stages in his academic career do, these days, without his electronic memory?

The editors will not mind, I hope, if I refer to their surprise. It was, after all, quite natural. I had not chosen one of Maribel's 'big' articles. It consists simply of an edition of a document, together with some brief introductory comments. Nevertheless I still, in 2015, retained a vivid memory of this article. I had discovered it after the Third Seminar on the Political Contract held in Madrid in 2008, as I was compiling a footnote for my introduction to the volume (eventually published in 2014) in which I argued that the contract was the essential political structure of political societies.[1] In this footnote,[2] also influenced by the contributions of the participants at one of the meetings of the Second Seminar, on the archaeology of the culture of pacts,[3] I suggested several possible avenues of research into the age of the contractual system. I also emphasised that the use of pacts by Spanish monasteries may have preserved contractual practices and formulas that were older, even ancient, if we accept the relationship proposed by Patricia Balbín Chamorro between, on the one hand, the *hospitium* and the Hispano-Roman *patrocinium*, and on the other, the *fueros*; I further suggested that the revival of these practices and formulas within monastic communities, but also spreading from them to other groups or communities then in the process of formation and stabilisation, may have been associated with the establishment of the Clunisians and Cistercians in the Iberian peninsula. It was while reading the works of Charles Julian Bishko on the pactual tradition in Hispanic monasticism, and of Antonio Linage Conde on the origins of Benedictine monasticism in the Iberian Peninsula,[4] that I discovered this 'little' article of Maribel.

---

[*] Translated from the French by Jean Birrell.
[1] Foronda, 'Du Contrat', pp. 5–13.
[2] Foronda, 'Du Contrat', pp. 10–11.
[3] Foronda and Carrasco Manchado, eds, *El contrato político*, part one, p. 121.
[4] I do not give precise references to the works just cited as they are given in the footnote in question.

I can no longer recall the precise circumstances of this discovery, but its impact remains undiminished in my mind. I spoke earlier of a vivid memory. At the time, reading this article was like a revelation. The 'it was like an apparition' of Gustave Flaubert, as he introduces his account of Frédéric Moreau's first sight of Madame Arnoux, in his *Education sentimentale*, is too present in my mind for me not to smile ironically as I write the word. Revelation. But it is how I felt. As I read, I had the feeling I had encountered a *parole-graine*. I first came across this expression when I was defending my master's degree at the beginning of June 1994. It was spoken by Patrick Boucheron, who had been invited onto the jury by Claude Gauvard. Whether he was the first to use it or simply one of several who introduced it into French university circles and to my generation in the 1990s I do not know. I may have heard it later, in the mouths of others, to mean the words of a master, the full import of which is only later appreciated by their students, when they have germinated within them, and they are capable of appreciating them. In the introduction to his thesis, which he defended at the end of June 1994, Patrick Boucheron uses this phrase to evoke the effect of the mastery of Pierre Toubert, while noting its African origin.[5] Yet the African expression, in fact *la graine de la parole*, rather than *parole-graine*, has a slightly different meaning. The Bamanan expression *kuma koloma yoro yèrè yèrè*, which Mamadou Diawara translated by the phrase *la graine de la parole*, refers to the core of something spoken, the essence, the heart of the matter, the crux, and it is what is brought out by the authoritative words of the elders before concluding a debate.[6]

However that may be, the *parole-graine* and *la graine de la parole* nicely evoke the words of a master, in a relationship of authority that is part of a culture of orality still very present in a Parisian university in the 'professorial age'. Before bibliometric criteria became the sole standard by which academic authority is measured, the impact of certain words spoken during the course of a seminar was still the real marker of academic consequence. It was probably among medievalists that I heard this expression. And it may well be, given that some of them are still inclined to view their role through the prism of the medieval world of men of scholarship, a primarily clerical milieu, that the expression *parole-graine* owed its success to the way it stirred implicit memories of the Christian model of the master-sower, associated with the parable of the sower.[7]

All this takes us a long way from the consummate authority which characterises Isabel Alfonso, always ready to engage in debate, blessed with a rare tendency to question, applied first to herself; indeed she would probably reject the very idea that she ever exercised such authority. Nevertheless, reading Maribel's article of 1973 at the very end of the first decade of the twentieth century, thus long after the event, I recognised a type of writing for which I still probably retained a certain nostalgia. I immediately regretted that I had not recognised it much earlier, so strongly did this *parole-graine* confront me afresh with the 'heart of the matter' or 'crux of the problem'

---

5 Boucheron, *Le pouvoir de bâtir*, p. 10.
6 Diawara, *La graine de la parole*.
7 Matthew 13.1–23; Mark 4.1–20; Luke 8.4–15.

of my research into the contract, at the very moment when the time had come for me to engage in a first reassessment.[8]

In the introduction to the edition and discussion of the treaty of friendship drawn up on 28 July 1156 between the monastery of Moreruela and the concejo of Castrotorafe, dealing with ownership of the localities of Moreruela and Emaces, Maribel declares her aim to frame *amicitia* within the history of mentalities, in terms of social and economic relations. Here I was suddenly presented with the rationale for a project, the pressing need to undertake a history of *amicitia* as a social institution, and an articulation of its ultimate purpose, that is, a way of approaching the construction of the social, or better, societal, and hence political, bond. These few lines published by Maribel in 1973 had for me the force of a dazzling intuition. I chose this article in 2015 because it would provide me with an opportunity to tell her what my intellectual response had been on the belated discovery of one of the articles of her youth. This I now do.

Since the nineteenth century, the university festschrift has generally taken the form of a collection of articles. This is a point I made in the introduction to one of the three volumes offered to Claude Gauvard, which consisted of contributions by former students with doctorates at the time of his retirement.[9] In the light of this tradition, the format proposed by the editors for this act of homage to Maribel is ground breaking. I find it interesting, even welcome, in that it invites the contributors to retrace in their own minds the history of their relationship with Maribel; or at least that is how I interpret it, but then I belong to a French university generation perhaps particularly prone to *ego-histoire*.[10]

I first met Maribel in Paris, at the end of 1996. I had been thinking about a medieval history thesis on an Iberian subject since the autumn of 1995, a project which led, in 1997, to a viva for a DEA entitled 'Parler au roi. Le cas des royaumes de Castille et Aragon au XVe siècle'. It was then that Claude Gauvard drew my attention to a paper which 'Madame Alfonso' was to deliver on 6 November at the seminar of Dominique Barthélémy.[11] If I attended, I might meet her. The reader may get a good idea of the content of her paper, entitled 'Cambio legal y acción política en la Europa medieval', from her article 'Campesinado y derecho: la vía legal de su lucha', the final version of

---

8 For a second review, after the conference on the constitutional question organised in 2014 in Madrid (Foronda and Genet, eds, *Des chartes aux constitutions*), see my definition: 'Contrat', in Gauvard and Sirinelli, eds, *Dictionnaire*, pp. 123–26.

9 Foronda, 'Violences souveraines', pp. 1–6.

10 The practice of *ego-histoire* is necessary in France to acquire accreditation (*habilitation*) to supervise research, the diploma required for appointment to a university professorship. It gave rise, in 2011, to the collection *Itinéraires* in the Editions de la Sorbonne, in which my own has now been published (Foronda, *Les retours*). Memories of my accreditation to supervise research, awarded 16 June 2018, inevitably turn my thoughts to Carlos Estepa, who died the following August, and who had agreed to sit on my jury. I think also of his funeral mass in León with, among others, Cristina, Julio, and Maribel.

11 I should here emphasise Maribel's contribution to the debate on the revolution of the year 1000, in particular in the publication of a critical note on Dominique Barthélémy's *La société dans le comté de Vendôme*: Alfonso, 'Continuidad y revelación documental'.

which she had sent to the journal *Noticiario de Historia Agraria* a few days earlier.[12] I was then a young researcher and frequent attender at the seminar of Claude Gauvard, where one of the recurring themes was the social production of the norm, with a strong emphasis on the mechanisms of interaction; for me, therefore, 'Madame Alfonso' was using a language with which I was familiar in order to examine the normative relationship between lords and peasants. And, though the subject of my thesis was remote from this topic and its time frame, I knew then that Maribel would become, for me, a point of reference.

I do not remember if we met again before I arrived in Madrid in September 2000 as a member of the Casa de Velázquez. I do, however, remember the close attention with which she read my first published works, on fictive cousinhood, on valour, on meeting places, and on the transformation of speaking to the king into the king speaking.[13] And the reader will have realised that the additional significance I attribute to my choice to comment on Maribel's very first article is that it evokes the pleasing memory of a dialogue begun, even an understanding established, on the basis of these youthful writings. Nor do I forget Maribel's invitation to take part in the conference 'Lucha Política' which she organised with Julio Escalona and Georges Martin in December 2001. It gave me the opportunity to present in Spain, having already done so in France,[14] the first public act of redefinition of the subject of my thesis,[15] which provoked, if only for a moment, a degree of incomprehension in my Spanish co-supervisor, José Manuel Nieto Soria.

After my period at the Casa de Velázquez, Maribel found me a post as visiting scholar at the Instituto de Historia in 2002–2003, which meant I could be attached to a research centre while I remained in Madrid to complete my thesis. Of course, Maribel was on the jury in December 2003. I could list other elements in the intellectual and personal dialogue I have maintained with her ever since. But the reasons for my choice of her first published article for this volume must by now be sufficiently clear. It remains for me (at last!) to present it.

The simplest way to do this is perhaps by means of a *synthèse d'article*. This is the exercise required of students at Paris 1 in their second year, as part of the tutorials for the introductory course to the History of the Middle Ages. It is intended to

---

12 The article was submitted on 29 October 1996. It was essentially the communication Maribel had made at the seventh Seminario de Historia Agraria (later the Sociedad Española de Historia Agraria and now the Sociedad de Estudios de Historia Agraria) organised at Baeza in June 1995, the acts of which were published by this review in three numbers in 1996–1997. Maribel's paper was published in the third: Alfonso, 'Campesinado y derecho'. [Editors' note: See the English version in chapter 9 of this volume].

13 Foronda, 'Le roi se trouve un cousin' (I no longer remember if I also addressed to Maribel this my very first article, an extract from my *mémoire de maîtrise*, which Jean-Philippe Genet decided to publish in a series of studies undertaken by students he had introduced to IT methodology: 'Les lettres de Louis XI: en quête de la formule', *Mémoire vive. Bulletin de l'association française pour l'histoire et l'informatique*, 12/13 (1994–1995), 57–65); Foronda, 'Bravoure, norme et autorité'; Foronda, 'Les lieux de rencontre'; Foronda, 'Du dit au roi au dit royal'.

14 At a meeting of the seminar of Claude Gauvard and Robert Jacob, in March of that same year.

15 Foronda, 'La *privanza*'.

train them in the methods of documentary criticism, and each session begins with a critical reading of an article written by a given historian as a way of introducing the specific theme. Maribel's article lends itself particularly well to an exercise of this type in that it is itself a commentary on and edition of a document. To perform this exercise, students not only read and summarise the article but also explore its place in the author's output, researching the context of its publication and examining its critical apparatus, all of which enables them to contextualise its production and understand its structure. Let us adopt this approach and proceed as if the article was intended to introduce a hypothetical tutorial devoted to the practices of friendship in the Middle Ages. It is also time for me to distance myself a little from the author.

The article is the work of a doctoral student who describes herself as about to submit her thesis — first announcement (n. 1). In fact it was not until 1980 that she did this, and with the title 'La colonización cisterciense en la Meseta del Duero: el ejemplo de Moreruela'. A comparison of the titles of the thesis and the article seems to show a discrepancy, as it is at first sight difficult to see what friendship is doing in the context of a doctoral research project in the field of rural history, specifically the formation of a monastic lordship, in this case Cistercian. This would be, however, to forget the extent to which, in the years from 1950 to the 1970s, rural history constituted a laboratory of methodological renewal, under the direct or indirect influence of a historical materialism which required historians to investigate jointly the relations of production and of domination, which converged in the *seigneurie*.

A striking evidence of the fruitfulness of this laboratory was the debate provoked from the late 1980s by the concept of 'feudal revolution', of which the thesis of Pierre Bonnassie on Catalonia (1976) was a paradigmatic expression. In fact something happened in rural history in the early 1970s and was still happening, with a sort of thirst to catch up on the part of Spanish historiography. It explains why talented young historians were attracted to this field, which they could legitimately see as still in the pioneering forefront of social history. Thus the discrepancy I imagined was no such thing, and a comparison of the title of the article and that of the subsequent thesis reminds us that the practice of friendship documented by this publication of 1973 had a role in the construction and implementation of landed, territorial and social domination. Friendship and domination, equality and inequality, it is here that we find the discrepancy, or the problem to be addressed.

With regard to this historiographical ferment, in which the intellectual positions adopted were not entirely uninfluenced by ideological commitment, a second discrepancy emerges. It lies in the fact that Isabel Alfonso's article was published in the *Boletín de la Real Academia de la Historia*, the first number of which appeared in 1877. In the early 1970s it offered all the guarantees of academicism, even positivism. Isabel Alfonso's article was primarily an edition of a document, appearing in the Miscellany section of this journal, and it was only one component of a subsequent documentary series whose imminent publication in her thesis (n. 10) was disclosed by its author — a second announcement.[16] We should not, however, project backwards

---

16 Her thesis includes 211 items, preserved in Madrid, Archivo Histórico Nacional and Zamora, Archivo Histórico Provincial.

onto the Academia of that time or its journal the received idea of them that might be held by a doctoral student of today. This would be a serious error. In comparison with the University or with Spanish research institutes at the end of the Franco era, the Academia of the late 1960s, while hardly a free space, was by reason of its very academicism, the site of a certain tolerance, at any rate a place where the revival of historical professionalism could re-engage with the Spanish liberal tradition.[17]

The supervisor of Isabel Alfonso's thesis, Luis García de Valdeavellano, a pupil of Claudio Sánchez Albornoz, himself a pupil of Eduardo de Hinojosa,[18] had been elected to the Academia in 1958 at the suggestion of Ramón Carande. In 1961 a colleague of García de Valdeavellano at the Faculty of Political Sciences of the Complutense University, where he held the chair of History of Institutions, José Antonio Maravall, who himself held the chair of History of Spanish Thought, was also elected. In this Madrid Faculty, these academicians, with Luis Díez del Corral, who held the chair of History of Ideas and Political Forms (and who would be elected to the Real Academia de la Historia in 1973), created a Department of History which, for a whole generation of Spanish historians, was a sort of oasis of liberty.[19] It was in this department that Isabel Alfonso defended her thesis in 1980. It now becomes possible to understand the announcements made in her article (of the imminent completion of her thesis and of a documentary collection) and to broach more generally this article's purpose. Under cover of publishing a document, it seems to me, the author is presenting herself to scholarly society, with a statement of her intellectual filiation and her affiliation to a school.

This statement was probably encouraged by her 'patron'. In the same journal, a few years earlier, Luis García de Valdeavellano had shown a particular interest in the monastic lordship of Moreruela.[20] His student's article signals a succession under way as regards a space, an archive and a problem to be addressed.[21] Nor does Isabel Alfonso appear reluctant to assume the role of student: she refers to her teacher's supervision in her first footnote and ends her article with a string of references to García de Valdeavellano's *Historia de España*, namely notes 14, 15, 16, 17, 18 and 19, the last in the article. A quick calculation reveals that nearly 37% of her critical apparatus consists of references to the master. On the same tack, we may wonder how much of the formulation of the proposition laid out at the beginning of the article ('*amicitia is essentially a way of understanding and approaching social relations in connection, of course, with the development of certain economic practices*' [my italics]) is owed to García de Valdeavellano, given his intellectual evolution from the history of law to a connected history of political institutions with a strong bias towards economic and social history. It may be that the historiographical landmarks proposed by Isabel

---

17 Peiró Martín, 'Aspectos de la historiografía', p. 26; Sarasa Sánchez, 'El medievalista', pp. 34–35.

18 In her thesis, Maribel refers to the three of them together as masters of the Spanish school of legal history: Alfonso, 'La colonización cisterciense', p. xxviii.

19 Elorza, 'Luis García de Valdeavellano'.

20 García de Valdeavellano, 'Sobre los fueros', esp. p. 195.

21 Further, the pact of friendship published by Isabel Alfonso in 1973 is flagged by García de Valdeavellano in his n. 7 ('Sobre los fueros', p. 197).

Alfonso with regard to *amicitia* were the result of work read at the suggestion of García de Valdeavellano. I think in particular of an article by Eduardo de Hinojosa and another by Ramón Prieto Bances,[22] which now seems somewhat confusing it is so dense, but which nevertheless enabled her to differentiate *amicitia* from 'artificial fraternity' and to highlight the conciliatory function performed by *amicitia* in practice.

Isabel Alfonso in 1973, the voice of her master? But hers was nevertheless a distinctive voice — this is the third announcement. We may start here with the second footnote, in which Isabel Alfonso justifies what I see as a sideways move (hence perhaps her *claro está* which tends to deny this in the sentence underlined above). If I speak here of a 'sideways move' it is because the subject of her thesis commits her a priori to discuss a seigneurial regime and her second article — which falls into the category of 'big' articles — seems significantly more focused on this subject.[23] Whereas in the article of 1973 Isabel Alfonso seeks less to engage with a seigneurial regime — although of course she does this (¡claro está!), given that the pact of friendship she edited was part of the establishment of this regime — than to present a document that could be used for a history of mentalities.

Such a history dominates the second footnote, in which she quotes Maravall's just published great work, his *Estado moderno y mentalidad social* (Madrid, 1972). But she also quotes another, even more recently published, book which, one imagines led to some hasty reading within the History Department of the Faculty of Political Sciences, namely Manuel Tuñon de Lara's *Metodología de la historia social en España* (Madrid, 1973). It is not a big book, but important given the role of intermediary assumed by the author, most notably as regards the work of French historians, and also his flair for synthesis and questioning. The generation of up and coming historians to which Isabel Alfonso belonged probably found in it numerous *parole-graines*.

In the same footnote she cites, before Tuñon de Lara, Georges Duby, but not his 1961 article on the history of mentalities,[24] to which Tuñon de Lara refers in his *Metodología*.[25] She cites, rather, his *L'an mil*, which came out in 1967 in the excellent *Collection Archives* established in 1964 by Pierre Nora and published by Julliard with the aim of providing the wider public with access to the material of historians, that is, their sources. This choice allowed Isabel Alfonso both to refer to an elementary principle of source criticism, that is, the need to investigate the social production of sources, and to clarify that the pact of friendship she was publishing was basically the expression of a certain social mentality, more specifically, a monastic milieu.

A doctoral student today, under the influence of the scholarly turn, would write at greater length. She might deal, for example, with the circumstances in which the document had been preserved, in order to establish more clearly any consequences for the source — with all that would mean for the length of the notes. And she might also make more of an important piece of information Isabel Alfonso includes at the

---

22 Prieto Bances, 'Los amigos'.

23 Alfonso, 'Las sernas'.

24 Duby, 'Histoire des mentalités'.

25 He gives 1967 as date of publication in his chapter on the history of social mentalities, but 1961 in his brief bibliography (Tuñón de Lara, *Metodología*, pp. 134, 181).

beginning of her edition, but which she does not fully exploit: 'Chirograph. Two copies are preserved'. Should this lead us to conclude that the copy intended for Castrotorafe was never handed over by the monastery? That this pact of friendship thus remained a dead letter? That the monastery might ultimately impose its domination by leaving this treaty of friendship without juridical effect? It hardly matters. As briefly formulated in 1973, the methodological caution demonstrated by Isabel Alfonso looks like the personal conviction of a rising young historian: issue-based history, whatever the subject it addresses, cannot avoid the problem of sources.

It is in the light of this personal conviction that we may now understand the third announcement in this article of 1973, which is methodological and problematic in nature. After a few historiographical milestones concerning the institution of *amicitia* and its relationship to 'artificial brotherhood', and a brief overview of the possible interests of those involved, Isabel Alfonso writes: 'I think it is important to try to understand (as far as possible, based on the documentation preserved) the processes whereby this pact was ultimately signed, in order to better analyse it'. Here, we are back with the question of the social production of the document.

I shall not recapitulate Maribel's argument — which would risk my article turning out to be longer than hers! I shall instead emphasise the extent to which this discussion of documentary production reveals a social mechanism which runs like a common thread through the later publications of its author: conflict and its resolution, domination and negotiation, social change. In *amicitia*, in its different meanings as a function of the position of the 'partners' to the agreement and the value system they each bring to it, there emerges one of the principal themes of the work of Isabel Alfonso. We may therefore see her 'sideways move' of 1973 as the founding act of a historian's identity.

Bibliography

Alfonso, Isabel, 'Campesinado y derecho: la vía legal de su lucha (Castilla y León, siglos X–XIII)', *Noticiario de Historia Agraria*, 13 (1997), 15–31

Alfonso, Isabel, 'Continuidad y revelación documental o mutación y revolución feudal', *Hispania*, 189 (1995), 301–13

Alfonso, Isabel, 'La colonización cisterciense en la Meseta del Duero: el ejemplo de Moreruela' (unpublished, Universidad Complutense, 1980)

Alfonso, Isabel, 'Las sernas en León y Castilla. Contribución al estudio de la relaciones socio-económicas en el marco del señorio medieval', *Moneda y Crédito*, 129 (1974), 153–210

Barthélemy, Dominique, *La société dans le comté de Vendôme de l'an mil au XIVe siècle* (Paris: Librairie Artheme Fayard, 1993)

Boucheron, Patrick, *Le pouvoir de bâtir. Urbanisme et politique édilitaire à Milan (XIVe–XVe siècles)* (Rome: Ecole française de Rome, 1998)

Diawara, Mamadou, *La graine de la parole. Dimension sociale et politique des traditions orales du royaume Jaara (Mali) du XVe au milieu du XIXe siècle* (Stuttgart: F. Steiner Verlag, 1990)

Duby, Georges, 'Histoire des mentalités', in *Encyclopédie de la Pléiade. L'histoire et ses méthodes*, ed. by Charles Samaran (Paris: 1961), pp. 937–66

Elorza, Antonio, 'Luis García de Valdeavellano, la humildad del investigador', *El País*, 29 May 1985

Foronda, François, 'Les lieux de rencontre. Espace et pouvoir dans les chroniques castillanes du XVe siècle', in *'Aux marches du palais'. Qu'est ce qu'un palais médiéval? Actes du VIIe Congrès international d'Archéologie Médiévale, Le Mans-Mayenne 9–11 septembre 1999*, ed. by Annie Renoux (Le Mans: Publications du LHAM, Université du Maine, 2001), pp. 123–34

Foronda, François, 'Le roi se trouve un cousin: les lettres de Louis XI à Antoines de Chabannes', *Médiévales*, 35 (1998), 141–50

Foronda, François, 'Bravoure, norme et autorité en Castille au XVe siècle', in *L'individu et la guerre, special number of the review Hypothèses 98. Travaux de l'Ecole doctorale d'Histoire de l'Université Paris I Panthéon-Sorbonne*, ed. by Sylvain Venayre (Paris: Publications de la Sorbonne, 1999), pp. 29–36

Foronda, François, 'Du dit au roi au dit royal: traces et transformations de la parole au roi dans la Castille de la fin du XVe siècle', in *Ces obscurs fondements de l'autorité, special number of the review Hypothèses 2000. Travaux de l'Ecole doctorale d'Histoire de l'Université Paris I Panthéon-Sorbonne*, ed. by François Foronda (Paris: Publications de la Sorbonne, 2001), pp. 231–39

Foronda, François, 'La *privanza* dans la Castille du bas Moyen Âge. Cadres conceptuels et stratégies de légitimation d'un lien de proximité', in *Lucha política: condena y legitimación en la España medieval*, ed. by Isabel Alfonso Antón, Julio Escalona, and Georges Martin (Lyon: ENS Éditions, 2004), pp. 153–97

Foronda, François, 'Violences souveraines. D'une tradition universitaire à un objet historique', in *Violences souveraines au Moyen Age. Travaux d'un école historique*, ed. by François Foronda, Christine Barralis, and Bénédicte Sère (Paris: Presses Universitaires de France, 2010), pp. 1–6

Foronda, François, 'Du Contrat ou de la structure proprement politique des sociétés politiques', in *Avant le contrat social. Le contrat politique dans l'Occident médiéval. XIIIe–XVe siècle*, ed. by François Foronda (Paris: Publications de la Sorbonne, 2014)

Foronda, François, *Les retours. Lieux de mémoires d'une vocation historienne* (Paris: Editions de la Sorbonne, 2019)

Foronda, François and Ana Isabel Carrasco Manchado, eds, *El contrato político en la Corona de Castilla. Cultura y sociedad política entre los siglos X al XVI* (Madrid: Dykinson, 2008)

Foronda, François and Jean-Philippe Genet, eds, *Des chartes aux constitutions. Autour de l'idée constitutionelle en Europe (XIIe–XVIIIe siècle)* (Paris – Rome: Editions de la Sorbonne – Ecole française de Rome, 2019)

García de Valdeavellano, Luis, 'Sobre los fueros de las villas de Iffanes (1220) y de Angueira (1257). Notas para el estudio del señorío del monasterio ciscercience de Moreruela', *Boletín de la Real Academia de la Historia*, 166–2 (1970), 193–226

Gauvard, Claude, and Jean-François Sirinelli, eds, *Dictionnaire de l'historien* (Paris: Presses universitaires de France, 2015)

Peiró Martín, Ignacio, 'Aspectos de la historiografía universitaria española en la primera mitad del siglo XX', *Revista de Historia Jerónimo Zurita*, 73 (1998), 7–28

Prieto Bances, Ramón, 'Los amigos en el Fuero de Oviedo', *Anuario de Historia del Derecho Español*, 23 (1953), 203–46

Sarasa Sánchez, Esteban, 'El medievalista en el franquismo', *Revista de Historia Jerónimo Zurita*, 82 (2007), 27–38

Tuñón de Lara, Manuel, *Metodología de la historia social de España* (Madrid: Siglo XXI, 1973)

ISABEL ALFONSO

On *Amicitia* in Medieval Spain

A Document that Merits Study*

Among the wealth of unpublished documents that I have gathered and studied while writing my doctoral dissertation on the Cistercian colonization of the Duero Plateau,[1] I came across the present document, which I find to be of interest for the study of the term *amicitia* in the Middle Ages. To my knowledge no one has of yet undertaken an in-depth study of this institution in Spain, taking into account the many facets that show up in medieval Spanish documents. I believe that such a study would be a worthwhile task not only as a contribution to the history of institutions, but also to the history of mentalities, as *amicitia* is essentially a way of understanding and approaching social relations in connection, of course, with the development of certain economic practices.[2]

Hinojosa was perhaps the first to refer to this institution (albeit in passing), in his important study on artificial brotherhood in Spain,[3] pointing out that *amicitia* and *fraternitas* are in some cases used interchangeably.[4] However, more important for our purposes is his paper on the Germanic element in Spanish law,[5] where he provides interesting documents for the study of *amicitia* when discussing blood feuds

---

* Original publication: Alfonso, Isabel, 'Sobre la *amicitia* en la España medieval. Un documento de interés para su estudio', *Boletín de la Real Academia de la Historia*, 170 (1973), 379–86. Translated by Julian Thomas.

1 A dissertation that I will soon be defending at the Facultad de Ciencias Políticas y Sociología, with the supervision of Professor Luis G. de Valdeavellano.

2 See the important study by Maravall, *Estado Moderno*, in particular the third part, 'Los cambios de mentalidad en relación con las nuevas formas políticas y económicas' and more specifically vol. 2, p. 134. Given that the document published here is from the collection of a monastery, I would like to highlight the need to bear in mind the type of documents used to trace the history of people's attitudes. Indeed, the mentality reflected in a document is that of the people who wrote it or had it written in the broad sense, i.e. the group of people from whom the documents in question originated. When studying the mental attitudes and representations of the collective psychology around the year 1000, G. Duby wrote, 'Leur témoignage, sans doute, demeure limité, parce qu'il émane d'un cercle tres restreint, celui "des intellectuels", parce qu'il offre seulement le point de vue des hommes d'Église, ou plus précisément des moines ...' (Duby, *L'an mil*, p. 29). Tuñón de Lara, *Metodología*, pp. 133–73.

3 I will cite from De Hinojosa y Naveros, 'La fraternidad artificial'; first published as de Hinojosa y Naveros, Eduardo, 'La fraternidad artificial en España', *Revista de Archivos, Bibliotecas y Museos*, 1 (1905), 1–18. Hinojosa studies artificial brotherhood essentially as regards the domestic community, i.e. as an institution that establishes artificial kinship ties.

4 De Hinojosa y Naveros, 'La fraternidad artificial', p. 272 and n. 38.

5 De Hinojosa y Naveros, 'El elemento germánico'; first published in German as de Hinojosa y Naveros, 'Das germanische Element'. As Galo Sánchez points out in his 1915 Spanish translation, the origin of the study was a lecture delivered by Hinojosa at the International Historical Congress in Berlin, held on 12 August 1908.

50 ISABEL ALFONSO

in Spanish law. He points out the equivalence between the terms *pax, securitas* and *assecuratio* and *amicitia*, as well as their use to signify reconciliation among the Frisians.[6]

In 1946 Emilio Sáez published a document[7] that he presented as a contribution to the study of artificial brotherhood but that, in my opinion, without denying the relationships it may have with said institution, is essentially a pact of friendship between two individuals to defend a property that they owned jointly. I believe that *amicitia* has a broader sphere of application, and does not bind the two individuals who agree to it into such a close bond as in the case of *fraternitas*. It was Prieto Bances who studied this institution in the greatest depth, from an essentially legalistic perspective, in his paper on friends in the Oviedo *fuero*, to which I will return later on.[8]

The document I am publishing here is a friendship pact between the monastery of Moreruela and the municipal council of Castrotorafe, which specifies the clauses of the agreement. The inhabitants of Castrotorafe must swear that their friendship with the monastery will be solid and permanent. Does this mean that it is implied (by those drawing up the document, in this case the monastery) that the inhabitants of Castrotorafe are the only ones who might have an interest in breaking off the pact? If so, it seems clear that the party most interested in signing the pact is the monastery, which to a certain extent is imposing the agreement upon the people of Castrotorafe. Certainly, the fact that we can find similar promises of perpetual peace being sworn to Ponce de Cabrera, majordomo to Alfonso VII the Emperor, constitutes further evidence of the authority wielded by the monastery.[9] The people of Castrotorafe must also promise to defend and aid the monastery, which in turn promises to exercise in the town's favour the considerable influence its order holds with the monarchs and princes. Moreover, in what is perhaps the key point of the pact, the council of Castrotorafe must promise not to disturb the property of the two villages that the monastery was granted through a charter issued by the Emperor: Moreruela de Suso and Emaces.

I think it is important to try to understand (as far as possible, based on the documentation preserved)[10] the processes whereby this pact was ultimately signed, in order to better analyse it. In 1146 Alfonso VII donated the village of Emazas, with

---

6 De Hinojosa y Naveros, 'El elemento germánico', p. 443 and n. 123.

7 Sáez, 'Un diploma interesante'.

8 Prieto Bances, 'Los amigos'.

9 In 1143 Ponce de Cabrera (who at that time was not yet the royal majordomo), received the village of Moreruela de Frades *diu desertam* ('long abandoned') so that a monastery could be built there (AHN. CLERO-SECULAR_REGULAR, Car.3548, N.11). Therefore, the document published here refers to Ponce de Cabrera as 'constructori Morerole', perhaps referencing his personal protection of the monastery. According to Sánchez Belza, Ponce de Cabrera 'from 1145 until his death was majordomo to the Emperor' (Sánchez Belda, *Chronica Adefonsi Imperatoris*, p. 248). However, in April 1144 he was already working for the king in Zamora, verifying, in his capacity as royal majordomo, a donation made to the monastery of Moreruela by the village of Manzanal (AHN. CLERO-SECULAR_REGULAR, Car.3548, N12).

10 I am referring to the largely unpublished collection of documents of the Monastery of Moreruela, preserved at Madrid, Archivo Histórico Nacional and at Zamora, Archivo Histórico Provincial, which I have transcribed in full, and which will be included as an appendix to my doctoral dissertation.

all its possessions and servants, *hereditario iure* to the monastery of Moreruela,[11] and in 1153 the same king donated half of the village of Moreruela de Suso 'which the men from Castrotorafe held. I donate and give you this half so that you hold it together with the other half that is yours'.[12] In 1156 the present friendship pact was signed. Everything, and especially the cited fragment, seems to indicate that the inhabitants of Castrotorafe were victims of the monastery's process of expansion. It is to be expected, then, that they would have protested and tried to regain ownership over what they saw as their rightful property.[13] This is why the monastery, the more powerful of the two parties, made them sign this friendship pact, which would have consolidated the monastery's privileged position over the municipality. We must not overlook the period in which this document was drawn up. According to Valdeavellano,[14] during the reign of Alfonso VII the profound transformations to social and economic life initiated in the eleventh century had finally reached maturity: 'the Empire of Alfonso VII adopts new economic practices, and clearly signals an increase in the development of economic activities brought on by the rebirth of commerce, the demographic and topographic growth of the urban population centres, and an increase in the circulation of currency [...]. But [...] in any case, some of the fundamental traits of the Hispano-Christian economy of the earliest middle ages still persist. Indeed, economic life maintains its predominantly agrarian character, and agricultural production and land ownership continue to remain essentially unchanged, although in León and Castile the seigneurial economy of the great estate has already prevailed over the system of smallholdings'.[15]

In other words, the eleventh and twelfth centuries witnessed not only the founding of the great manorial estates in León and Castile, but also major urban development as municipalities were formally established. The municipal councils became increasingly important, already enjoying certain jurisdictions,[16] and in some

---

11 AHN. CLERO-SECULAR_REGULAR, Car.3548, N.13.

12 'quam tenebant homines de Castru Turafe. Dono et concedo uobis eandem medietatem ut habeatis eam cum alia alia (*sic*) medietate que uestra est' (AHN. CLERO-SECULAR_REGULAR, Car.3548, N.14).

13 The village of Emazas or Emaces is mentioned in the *Fuero* whereby Alfonso VII acknowledges the inhabitants of Castrotorafe as falling within the village's limits: 'We grant a letter of surety [...] to you, the council of Castrotorafe and assign your boundaries, from Emaces, Villa Relio [...]'. ('Nobis facimus cartulam et scripturam firmitatis [...] a vobis concilio de Castrotoraf, damus a vobis terminos per Enmances villa Relio') (ColFueros, p. 480). As for the town of Moreruela de Suso, the donation document itself states that it was in the hands of the men of Castrotorafe. What he have, then, is a clear case of alienation of villages belonging to a town, with ownership being transferred over to a monastery. 'The policy of alienating villages belonging to a town' — states María del Carmen Carlé — 'in particular for the benefit of a third party, had age-old precedents. And [...] throughout the entire Middle Ages municipalities fought with true zeal in their desperate attempts to preserve their village limits [...] against the monarchs' policy of alienation, tirelessly donating villages, towns and Crown properties. This practice deserves further study' (Carlé, *Del concejo medieval castellano-leonés*, pp. 191–92; see, in particular, the section entitled 'Enajenación del término').

14 García de Valdeavellano, *Historia de España*, vol. 2, pp. 456 and ff.

15 García de Valdeavellano, *Historia de España*, vol. 2, pp. 457–58.

16 García de Valdeavellano, *Historia de España*, vol. 2, p. 480.

instances already fending off the ambitions of their powerful seigneurial neighbours, with varying degrees of success.

In the aforementioned article by Prieto Bances, friendship is defined (with a mind to Hinojosa's prior statements on the matter) in the following terms: 'Friendship, apart from affection, is peace, and those who live in peace are "friends" united by a social bond that may have legal consequences, as law is a system of peaces'.[17]

Clearly, in the document at hand, friendship is understood to mean peace, such that we also find the synonyms 'pactum amiciciarum', 'volumus etiam ut in oc pacis at caritatis uinculo', and 'Facta carta pacis et dilectionis'. 'But peace', continues Prieto Bances, 'varies in accordance with its origin. There is peace born of love and peace born of mutual interests or of violence, and to each of these types of peace corresponds a different sort of friendship. In the first case we have natural, Aristotelian friendship; in the second, negotiated friendship; and in the third, imposed friendship'.[18] Further on he states that manorial friendship can be extended through collective pacts. The small private struggles between towns or communities and the monasteries often ended in agreements making reference to love as peace and to friends as the faithful.[19]

The friendship pact between Moreruela and Castrotorafe appears to put an end to these struggles, and in it the monastery clearly emerges as the victor, imposing its 'friendship', with all that this entails, upon the town. As mentioned earlier, the mentality reflected in the document is evidently that of the monks. In order to achieve a balanced picture, we would need to learn what the men who made up the municipal council of Castrotorafe thought of this 'friendship'. It is only in light of the monastery's fears that they might break off the deal that we can infer friction between the two mentalities, friction that should be studied in relation to the socioeconomic development of both social groups.

---

17 García de Valdeavellano, *Historia de España*, vol. 2, pp. 204–05.
18 García de Valdeavellano, *Historia de España*, vol. 2, p. 205.
19 García de Valdeavellano, *Historia de España*, vol. 2, p. 224.

Appendix: The Document

28 July 1156

Friendship pact made by the monastery of Moreruela with the municipality of Castrotorafe, concerning the villages of Moreruela and Emaces.

AHN. CLERO-SECULAR_REGULAR, Car.3548, no. 17 and 16. Chirograph. Two copies are preserved.

(English translation)
In the name of God. I, Gonzalo, abbot of Moreruela, together with my brethren, make a friendship pact with the council of Castrotorafe, binding both us and our successors, and binding both them and their successors who belong to their kin and inhabit that *villa*. The pact that was vowed by us and by count Ponce [de Cabrera], builder of Moreruela, establishes that the friendship bond between they and us shall be firm and perpetual, and that they shall always defend and assist us to their ability, and that we shall love them and assist them as we can in accordance to our class before kings and princes. We also wish that in this pact and love bond which you make with us, which is being heard by all the council, you promise, namely, that *quatinus superior* Moreruela and Emaces, which the Emperor granted us with a charter. Neither you, nor your kin, nor anyone among you acting under your advice shall beg kings and princes for the abovementioned *villas* nor accept anything that they may be willing to grant them in all what belongs to the monks of Moreruela without our will and consent and of the monks there serving God. Moreover, we include you in our prayers and in all our favours so that God Almighty preserves and guards your souls and bodies and guides you to eternal life, amen. This charter of peace and love was made on the fifth day of the calends of August, Era 1194 [AD1156], governing León and Toledo Alfonso the Emperor, and being price in Zamora count Ponce [de Cabrera] and bishop Esteban, of blessed memory.

Those who were present:

(1st Col.)

Juan, witness.

Pedro, witness.

Domingo, witness.

Miguel Pérez, confirms it.

Pelayo Gustioz, confirms it.

Martín Pérez, confirms it (Signum).

(2nd Col.)

Pelayo Muñoz, confirms it.

Rodrigo Pérez, confirms it.

Diego Almadrán, confirms it.

(3rd Col.)

Juan Pérez, confirms it.

Pelayo Miguéliz, confirms it.

Fernán Cabeza, confirms it. (Signum)

(Signum): Brother Tomás, who wrote [it], confirms it.

(Original text)

In Dei nomine. Ego Gundisaluus abbas Morerole cum fratribus meis, facimus pactum amiciciarum cum / concilio de Castro Toraph, tam pro nobis quam pro successoribus nostris et ipsi tam pro se quam pro successoribus ipsorum que de / genere illorum fuerint et in uilla illa morati fuerint. Pactum tale est quod ipsi iurauerint nobis et comiti Pontio / constructori Morerole ut firma et perpetua sit amicicia inter nos et illos et ipsi semper defendant et adiuuent nos / et nostra pro posse suo et nos diligamus et adiuuemus eos pro ut potuerimus secundum ordinem nostram apud reges et / principes. Volumus etiam ut in hoc pacis et caritatis uinculo quod nobiscum facitis audiente omni concilio promittatis / quatinus superior Morerola uidelicet et Emaçes quas nobis imperator per cartam dedit. Nec uos nec parentela uestra neque / ullus hominum inter uos manens consilio uestro quo quomodo apud reges uel principus uillas illas superius iam dictas petat / uel dare uolentes accipiat in quantum Morerola monachorum fuerit sine uoluntate et consensu nostro uel mouachorum ibidem / Deo militantium. Super hec recipimus uos in orationibus et in cunctis beneficiis nostris ut De \u/[s] qui omnia potest / conseruat et cuostodiat corda et corpora uestra et ad uitam eternam per ducat amen. Facta carta pacis et dilectionis V° kalendas / augusti era MCLXXXXIIII. Imperante in Legione et Toleto Adefonso imperatore. Existente principe in Zemora / Pontio comite. Episcopo bone memorie Stephano.

Qui presentes fuerunt:

(1ª Col.)

Johannis test.

Petrus test.

Dominicus test.

Michaelis Petriz cf.

Pelagius Gusteus cf.

Martinus Petriz cf. (Signum).

(2ª Col.)

Pelai Muniz cf.

Rodericus Petriz cf.

Didacus Almadran cf.

(3ª Col.)

Johannis Petriz cf.

Pelagius Michaelis cf.

Fernan Cabeza cf. (Signum)

(Signum): Frater Thomas qui notuit cf.

Bibliography

Carlé, Mª. del Carmen, *Del concejo medieval castellano-leonés* (Buenos Aires: Instituto de Historia de España, 1968)

De Hinojosa y Naveros, Eduardo, 'Das germanische Element im Spanischen Rechte', *Zeitschrift der Savigny Stiftung für Rechtsgeschichte: Germanistische Abteilung*, 31–1 (1910), 282–359.

De Hinojosa y Naveros, Eduardo, 'La fraternidad artificial en España', in *Obras. Vol. 1*, ed. by Eduardo de Hinojosa y Naveros (Madrid: Instituto Nacional de Estudios Jurídicos, 1948 [1905]), pp. 257–78.

De Hinojosa y Naveros, Eduardo, 'El elemento germánico en el derecho español', in *Obras. Vol. 2*, ed. by Eduardo Hinojosa y Naveros (Madrid: CSIC, 1955), pp. 405–70.

Duby, Georges, *L'an mil* (Paris: Julliard, 1967).

García de Valdeavellano, Luis, *Historia de España. De los orígenes a la baja edad media*, 2 vols (Madrid: Revista de Occidente, 1963).

Maravall, José Antonio, *Estado Moderno y Mentalidad Social, siglos XV a XVII*, 2 vols (Madrid: Revista de Occidente, 1972).

Prieto Bances, Ramón, 'Los amigos en el Fuero de Oviedo', *Anuario de Historia del Derecho Español*, 23 (1953), 203–46.

Sáez, Emilio, 'Un diploma interesante para el estudio de la fraternidad artificial', *Anuario de Historia del Derecho Español*, 17 (1946), 751–52.

Sánchez Belda, Luis, *Chronica Adefonsi Imperatoris. Edición y estudio* (Madrid: CSIC, 1950).

Tuñón de Lara, Manuel, *Metodología de la historia social de España* (Madrid: Siglo XXI, 1973)

CHAPTER 2

On the Language
and Practice of Negotiation

with a commentary by Wendy Davies

Conflict, Language, and Social Practice in Medieval Societies: Selected Essays of Isabel Alfonso, with Commentaries, ed. by Julio Escalona Monge, Álvaro Carvajal Castro, and Cristina Jular Pérez-Alfaro, TMC 24 (Turnhout: Brepols, 2024), pp. 57–84

BREPOLS ✠ PUBLISHERS   10.1484/M.TMC-EB.5.132456

WENDY DAVIES

Commentary

Although her publications focus on northern Iberia in the later middle ages, Isabel Alfonso's knowledge ranges much farther. She is exceptionally well read, bringing the discipline of the social scientist, an awareness of a wider world and a grasp of social process to bear on the particularities of medieval Spain, as the paper here reprinted clearly demonstrates. It was first published in Spanish in 2005, and then in English for Stephen D. White's Festschrift as this paper's focus on negotiation reflects White's own major contribution to the historiography of dispute settlement. The key question is the relationship between rules, on the one hand, and practice on the other. Were decisions made in judicial courts on the basis of strict legal norms or was there flexibility in their application? Indeed, there were circumstances in which conflicting parties came to a formal agreement without reference to legal norms at all; negotiating thereby meant acting outside the rules.

Professor Alfonso's paper draws on many discussions of these issues — once characterized as 'normative versus processual' by Brown and Górecki[1] – including the volume on early medieval dispute settlement which colleagues and I published in 1986, itself influenced by White's early writings.[2] Our book, which ranged across Europe from the Byzantine East to the Scottish North, laid great emphasis on practice in court — what did people actually do? — as opposed to the legal historians' perspective of what people ought to have done; we concluded, amongst other points, that going to court was for most parties a strategic choice, especially because the court was the most public kind of forum in which to negotiate and consequently being in court brought support and pressure to the negotiation.[3] Our approach was subsequently criticised for not allowing that norms could constrain negotiation, which might itself depend on the threat of coercion. Since then, Stephen D. White produced further fundamental papers on strategic choice and on power.[4] A series of individual studies explored aspects of judicial practice in their socio-political contexts — notably François Bougard's *La justice dans le royaume d'Italie* of 1995, Bruno Lemesle's *Conflits et justice au moyen âge* of 2008, and Josep Salrach's *Justícia*

---

1 Brown and Górecki, 'What Conflict Means', p. 7.
2 Davies and Fouracre, eds, *The Settlement of Disputes*.
3 Davies and Fouracre, eds, *The Settlement of Disputes*, pp. 233–37.
4 Note especially White, 'Proposing the Ordeal'; White, 'From Peace to Power'; White, 'Tenth-Century Courts'.

Wendy Davies has published extensively on early medieval societies in the Celtic-speaking European areas and in the Iberian peninsula. Her work on dispute settlement is a major reference in the field.

i poder a Catalunya abans de l'any mil in 2013, a volume which acknowledges a debt to Professor Alfonso's inspiration.[5] Since the 1980s a series of collections on conflict and justice in medieval Europe has also developed an awareness of practice and of social context in different regions: *La giustizia nell'alto medioevo* at Spoleto, published in 1995; a Birmingham conference on *The Moral World of the Law*, in which Professor Alfonso participated, published in 2000; a French millennial celebration, *La justice en l'an mil*, published in 2003, the year of Brown and Górecki's American collection, *Conflict in Medieval Europe*.[6] In England in recent years some anthropologists turned back to law, but law with the different twist of the 'legalism' school, in which the articulation of rules and the use of generalizing principles are viewed as a regular aspect of social life; thereby law itself is an outcome of social process and writing law down can serve to record practice.[7] Beyond the legalism school, many historians nowadays insist that norm and process are not alternatives: as Matthew Innes put it, the 'interpenetration between local "customary" practice and universalising written norms' was such in the early middle ages that one cannot possibly maintain that they were in any kind of opposition.[8]

Throughout this generation of productive research and reinterpretation of medieval conflict, Professor Alfonso, as this volume shows, has herself contributed fundamental papers on the social and political context of judicial conflict and on the wider networks of alliance and confrontation in which judicial conflict was embedded.[9] Her paper reproduced here argues that Spanish legal codes of the central middle ages not only allowed for but positively encouraged the making of agreements, and encouraged arbitrators to work hard to achieve reconciliation. The criteria used in making settlements were not so much those of written law codes but rather those that referred to a 'moral sense of law shared by a broader social universe' — in a precise foreshadowing of the arguments of English legalism. The paper emphasizes the importance of agreement and negotiation but demonstrates unequivocally, in a later medieval Spanish context, that norms were themselves flexible and that the process of negotiation could itself affect the formulation of norms. There was a continuing dialectic between rule and process.

Most of the examples cited come from the twelfth and thirteenth centuries, although the paper ranges across the period from eleventh to fourteenth centuries. This raises the interesting question of whether or not such practices and values were a new development of the central middle ages or a continuation from an earlier period. The corpus of pre-eleventh-century charters certainly includes many examples of

---

5 Bougard, *La justice*; Lemesle, *Conflits et justice*; Salrach, *Justícia i poder*.

6 *La giustizia nell'Alto Medioevo, secoli IX–XI*; Coss, ed., *The Moral World of the Law*; Castan et al., *La justice en l'an mil*.

7 For a very clear exposition, Dresch, 'Legalism, Anthropology, and History'. See also Pirie and Scheele, 'Justice, Community, and Law'.

8 Innes, 'Charlemagne, Justice and Written Law', p. 179; cf. Wickham, *Courts and Conflict*, pp. 303–12; Humfress, 'Law and Custom under Rome', pp. 23–47.

9 Alfonso, 'Resolución de disputas'; Alfonso, 'Litigios por la tierra'; Alfonso, 'Judicial rhetoric'; Alfonso, 'Memoria e identidad'.

COMMENTARY   61

agreements, of several types, including those made both in and beyond the context of a judicial court. It also includes many citations of, and references to, legal norms. Visigothic law is frequently cited and, as Graham Barrett has demonstrated, is even more frequently reflected in the words of ninth- and tenth-century charters.[10] This is certainly a very different kind of corpus from the *fueros* and *Partidas* cited by Professor Alfonso and it might be thought that citation of a seventh-century body of law implied the very opposite of dialogue between rule and process. However, as several scholars have pointed out, this was not a fixed and unchanging body of seventh-century law: it was cited accurately and inaccurately; it was adapted; it could be ignored; and occasionally material appears to have been added to later recensions of *Forum Iudicum* that were not present in the earlier law, such as that on use of the ordeal. Nevertheless it was reflection and citation of the ancient corpus that was most characteristic rather than the formulation of new norms. Legal norm was a useful point of reference although it did not necessarily determine all judicial decisions. From the early eleventh century, however, there were changes as law became less explicitly conservative and more open to innovation. It is this new kind of practice that provides the context for Professor Alfonso's relationship between process and rule-formation in the twelfth and thirteenth centuries.

As for making agreements in the early middle ages: Otero de las Dueñas charter no. 4, for example, a record of 8 February 946 which survives on a badly damaged single sheet, details the settlement of a property dispute between lay parties.[11] Although some of the detail has been lost, it is clear that one Pedro had entered the disputed property, moved boundary markers and harvested some of Bera's crop; and it is indicated, without detail, that Pedro and his brother Vicente in turn had a case against Bera. In court in Valdoré, in the valley of the river Esla in the southern foothills of the Cantabrian Mountains, in the presence of the legal officer, the *saio*, and a judge, both parties came to an agreement (*atiba*) that Bera's boundaries should in future be respected, as well as an agreement to forgo claims for both parties' damages and to share the costs of the court case. The priest Ermegildo acted as guarantor for the deal. This must have been a negotiated outcome and the way the record is constructed, unusually for these charters, seems to reflect the process of negotiation: cast in short sentences, it reads like speech, with a series of events, recounted in the first person, at times repetitively, by Vicente; concluding with a final section in which Bera, also in the first person but now in the present tense, outlines the nature of their agreement. It is as if the two parties stood before the writer, who attempted to set down what they said, more or less as they said it.

Otero no. 4 is particularly interesting because we can see two lay parties negotiating. Agreements involving ecclesiastical parties are more common in the early middle ages and Otero charter no. 43, another charter on a single sheet, of 1 June 997, evidences a more typical kind of case. Here there had been intrusion into monastic property by two people, Velito and Calendo, who had begun to cultivate it for themselves. In

---

10 Barrett, *Text and Textuality in Early Medieval Iberia*.
11 SMOteroDueñas4 (946); the editors provide a valuable reconstruction of most of the document.

court in Valdoré, before Count Flaino Muñoz and judges, the parties agreed that the intrusion should stop and Cipriano, the spokesman for the monastery (headed by an abbess), waived the due penalty. This time, however, the negotiation was assisted by *boni homines*, mediators. The record is again cast in the first person, with patches of past-tense recounting, again concluding with first-person statements of commitment by both parties; we can again almost see the parties standing in court and making their points.[12] Here was another negotiation, this time with helpers.

Although good examples of agreements made by negotiation can be found in ninth- and tenth-century texts, it would be nonsense to suggest that all recorded agreements came about through negotiation at that time. Most records of agreements that followed intrusion into monastic property document an advantage secured by the monastery. In the monastery of Valdevimbre's action against a group of local people from San Juan en Vega over water to power their mills, the monks twice claimed that the peasants were taking so much water there was not enough left for the monastery's mill; and the king twice sent judges to measure the water levels, declaring each time that there was enough water for everyone. The case is recorded because, although the peasants were successful in maintaining their access to water, the final declaration provides for them to give assistance to the monastery when its mill needed repair; despite their success, in the course of this case the peasants acquired an obligation.[13] Persistence brought Valdevimbre an advantage, as it did to many monasteries. In the later ninth and especially in the tenth century monasteries used the courts to gain advantages like this. They took judicial action against lay aristocrats and against groups of peasants and now and then against other monasteries, priests or bishops.[14] On many occasions monasteries went to a king's court in a bid for ruler support, using the royal court as a tool to extend their property base. Some of the great monasteries, like Sahagún and San Millán, went on to forge particularly strong associations with kings (of León and Pamplona respectively) in the eleventh century.[15] The records of the agreements concluded in such cases were constructed in order to document privilege and advantage and were hardly the outcome of negotiation. Plenty of agreements there may have been in the early middle ages but agreement did not always imply negotiation.

There were, however, signs of change round about the year 1000. Where negotiation occurred with the help of mediators, references to the mediators, *boni homines*, are rare before the late tenth century, although there is a Portuguese case of 943 in which they spoke for an acknowledged killer and persuaded the *dominus* Ansur to make

---

12 This record is written on the dorse of the original charter which recorded the donation of the land in dispute (SMOteroDueñas21, 976).

13 CatLeon128 (938).

14 For many examples, see Davies, *Windows on Justice*, ch. 7.

15 Professor Alfonso delivered an exemplary study of Sahagun's use of royal connections at an international conference in London in 2011, unfortunately not included in the published proceedings of the conference. For San Millán, see García de Cortázar, *El dominio del monasterio de San Millán*, pp. 137–92 especially.

COMMENTARY 63

up the deficit in the compensation due to the dead man's family.[16] Except for this Portuguese case, all the pre-1000 examples of intercession by *boni homines* come from the *meseta* and from the 990s, and there are many more examples from the eleventh century. It looks as if this diplomatic habit — the phrase *rogare cum bonis hominibus* ('to ask with *boni homines*') is a standard formula for describing a petition[17] — in reality reflects a developing practice of mediation in the later tenth century. What the late tenth-century texts seem to show is an increasing tendency to classify those who took useful and responsible collective action as 'suitable' and 'qualified'. There was a current of feeling by the year 1000 that sought to designate group action by reputable people as legitimate and by so doing it enhanced the legitimating function of the actions. The implication is that the emphasis on negotiation was increasing.

So, negotiated agreements were certainly made in the early middle ages and although legal norms were often invoked they could be manipulated. On the other hand, many recorded agreements were concluded because of political and social pressure — with little or no element of negotiation. Shifts in the approach to the formulation of legal rules and an increasing insistence on the legitimating role of negotiators in the later tenth and eleventh centuries seems to have opened the way for more negotiation and for the exhortations to achieve reconciliation. And as documentation of conflict extends in the later middle ages we see more of relations at local levels and their continued redefinition. Understanding context, as Professor Alfonso insists, is essential and power relations cannot be ignored, triangulating between norm and action. Repeated conflict and negotiation in the later middle ages were therefore 'processes of confrontation in which the values that articulate a shared political culture operate and are constructed'.

---

16 PMH-DC53 (943).
17 See Martínez Díez, 'Terminología jurídica', pp. 260, 261–3, and Martínez Sopena, 'La justicia en la época asturleonesa', pp. 241, 245, 248.

Bibliography

La giustizia nell'Alto Medioevo, secoli IX–XI. Atti della 44ª Settimana di studio (Spoleto, 11–17 aprile 1996) (Spoleto: Centro Italiano di Studi sull'Alto Medioevo, 1997)

Alfonso, Isabel, 'Resolución de disputas y prácticas judiciales en el Burgos medieval', in *Burgos en la Plena Edad Media. III Jornadas Burgalesas de Historia* (Burgos: Asociacion Provincial de Libreros de Burgos, 1994), pp. 211–43

Alfonso, Isabel, 'Litigios por la tierra y "malfetrías" entre la nobleza medieval', *Hispania*, 57–197 (1997), 917–55

Alfonso, Isabel, 'Judicial Rhetoric and Political Legitimation in Medieval León-Castile', in *Building Legitimacy. Political Discourses and Forms of Legitimacy in Medieval Societies*, ed. by Julio Escalona, Isabel Alfonso and Hugh Kennedy (Leiden: Brill, 2004), pp. 51–88

Alfonso, Isabel, 'Memoria e identidad en las pesquisas judiciales en el área castellano-leonesa medieval', in *Construir la identidad en la Edad Media. Poder y memoria en la Castilla de los siglos VII a XV*, ed. by José Antonio Jara Fuentes, Georges Martín and Isabel Alfonso (Cuenca: Universidad de Castilla-La Mancha, 2011), pp. 249-79

Barrett, Graham, *Text and Textuality in Early Medieval Iberia* (Oxford: Oxford University Press, 2023)

Bougard, François, *La justice dans le royaume d'Italie: de la fin du VIIIᵉ siècle au début du XIᵉ siècle* (Paris: École française de Rome, 1995)

Brown, Warren C., and Piotr Górecki, 'What Conflict Means: The Making of Medieval Conflict Studies in the United States, 1970–2000', in *Conflict in Medieval Europe: Changing Perspectives on Society and Culture*, ed. by Warren C. Brown and Piotr Górecki (Aldershot: Ashgate, 2003), pp. 1–35

Castan, Nicole et al., *La justice en l'an mil. Actes du colloque du 12 mai 2000*, Histoire de la justice, 15 (Paris: Association Française pour l'Histoire de la Justice, 2003)

Coss, Peter, ed., *The Moral World of the Law* (Cambridge: Cambridge University Press, 2000)

Davies, Wendy, *Windows on Justice in Northern Iberia, 800–1000* (Abingdon: Routledge, 2016)

Davies, Wendy, and Paul Fouracre, eds, *The Settlement of Disputes in Early Medieval Europe* (Cambridge: Cambridge University Press, 1986)

Dresch, Paul, 'Legalism, Anthropology, and History: A View from Part of Anthropology', in *Anthropology and History* ed. by Paul Dresch and Hannah Skoda (Oxford: Oxford Scholarship, 2012), pp. 1–37

Humfress, Caroline, 'Law and Custom under Rome', in *Law, Custom, and Justice in Late Antiquity and the Early Middle Ages*, ed. by Alice Rio (London: King's College London, 2011), pp. 23–47

Innes, Matthew, 'Charlemagne, Justice and Written Law', in *Law, Custom, and Justice in Late Antiquity and the Early Middle Ages*, ed. by Alice Rio (London: King's College London, 2011), pp. 155–203

Lemesle, Bruno, *Conflits et justice au Moyen Âge. Normes, loi et résolution des conflits en Anjou aux XIᵉ et XIIᵉ siècles* (Paris: Presses Universitaires de France, 2008)

Martínez Díez, Gonzalo, 'Terminología jurídica en la documentación del reino de León. Siglos IX–XI', in *Orígenes de las lenguas romances en el Reino de León, siglos IX–XII* (León: Centro de Estudios e Investigación San Isidoro, 2004), vol. 1, pp. 229–72

Martínez Sopena, Pascual, 'La justicia en la época asturleonesa: entre el *Liber* y los mediadores sociales', in *El lugar del campesino. En torno a la obra de Reyna Pastor*, ed. by Ana Rodríguez (Valencia: Publicacions de la Universitat de València, 2007), pp. 239–60

Pirie, Fernanda, and Judith Scheele, 'Justice, Community, and Law', in *Legalism: Community and Justice*, ed. by Fernanda Pirie and Judith Scheele (Oxford: Oxford University Press, 2014), pp. 1–24

Salrach, Josep M., *Justícia i poder a Catalunya abans de l'any mil* (Vic: Eumo, 2013)

White, Stephen D., 'Proposing the Ordeal and Avoiding It: Strategy and Power in Western French Litigation, 1050–1110', in *Cultures of Power: Lordship, Status, and Process in Twelfth-Century Europe*, ed. by Thomas N. Bisson (Philadelphia: University of Pennsylvania Press, 1995), pp. 89–123

White, Stephen D., 'From Peace to Power: the Study of Disputes in Medieval France', in *Medieval Transformations. Texts, Power, and Gifts in Context*, ed. by Esther Cohen and Mayke De Jong (Leiden: Brill, 2001), pp. 203–18

White, Stephen D., 'Tenth-Century Courts at Mâcon and the Perils of Structuralist History: Re-reading Burgundian Judicial Institutions', in *Conflict in Medieval Europe*, ed. by Warren C. Brown and Piotr Górecki (Aldershot: Ashgate, 2003), pp. 37–68

Wickham, Chris, *Courts and Conflict in Twelfth-Century Tuscany* (Oxford: Oxford University Press, 2003)

ISABEL ALFONSO

The Language and Practice of Negotiation in Medieval Conflict Resolution (Castile-León, Eleventh–Thirteenth Centuries)*

A recent cartoon by one of our most scathing graphic journalists shows a contemporary character dressed as a modern Moses holding the Tablets of the Law, which appear crossed out, proclaiming, 'There are no commandments, everything is negotiable'.[1] I do not remember the political context in which the cartoon was published, but it evidently seemed to point to a widespread social principle which accepts that negotiation is preferable to dispute and that peaceful solutions are better than hostile and violent ones; an ethical assumption surely rooted in another, more pragmatic, cultural principle which can be summed up in a well-known proverb: 'an ill agreement is better than a good judgement'.[2]

However, on reconsidering this cartoon in the context of this essay, it seemed to me that, despite its apparent obviousness — which is only the result of our own assumptions — the cartoon can be interpreted in different ways which will allow me to allude to some of the issues which are worth bearing in mind when thinking about negotiation. It is tempting to believe that the arguments about the predominance of negotiation in conflict resolution in the societies of the past that are currently being postulated correspond to a need and a desire to advocate negotiation as the most appropriate and peaceful resource for settling the multiple differences and tensions, with their diverse dimensions and scales, that emerge in present-day societies between individuals or groups. It is nevertheless essential to reflect on the roots of this current historiographical discourse to understand why negotiation has gone from a factor that was practically ignored to one which has become predominant. These reasons for this are undoubtedly to be found in the present, and it is useful to identify them, among other reasons because, as we know, they condition — more or less consciously and explicitly — our perception of the past.

---

* Original publication: Alfonso, Isabel, 'Lenguaje y prácticas de negociar en la resolución de conflictos en la sociedad castellano-leonesa medieval', in *Negociar en la Edad Media/Négocier au Moyen Âge*, ed. by María Teresa Ferrer, Jean-Marie Moeglin, Stéphane Péquignot and Manuel Sánchez. Anejos del Anuario de Estudios Medievales 61 (Barcelona: CSIC, 2005), pp. 45–65. It was thereafter published in English translation as 'The Language and Practice of Negotiation in Medieval Conflict Resolution (Castile-León, Eleventh-Thirteenth Centuries)', in *Feud, Violence and Practice: Essays in Medieval Studies in Honor of Stephen D. White*, ed. by Belle. S. Tuten and Tracey. L. Billado (Farnham: Asghate, 2010).

1 'No hay mandamientos todo es negociable', cartoon by El Roto, *El País*, 19 September 1999.

2 For the literal version in Spanish ('Más vale mala avenencia que buena sentencia') see Correas, *Vocabulario de refranes*. The adage also has an equivalent in French: 'Un mauvais arrangement vaut mieux qu'un bon procès'.

Two ideas are seemingly opposed to negotiation: on one hand, a normative system which the process of negotiation would seem to exclude; and on the other hand, war and violence in general, since negotiation is associated with peace and to achieve this, any method is valid. The cartoon by El Roto expresses a critique of the mystification that is often present when referring to these ideas. Can we therefore maintain that to negotiate is to act outside the rules? That it is the non-violent way to resolve conflicts? That its fundamental aim is peace? That it is the most effective and the fairest of the different conflict resolution tools? That it is a widespread resource, to which all groups and social strata have similar access?

These and other questions form part of some of the, until very recently, undiscussed premises in the historiography of conflict resolution in the Medieval period, owing to the fact that the study of negotiation in the field of law, traditionally the field of reference for any kind of dispute resolution, is relatively new. This is linked to a shift in orientation — common to the social sciences — toward the study of processes and social practices instead of institutions and structures. This new perspective in law has been fundamental, shifting from a focus on courts and the substantive law supposedly applied in their sentences to an analysis of the — not always formal, not always judicial — processes used by litigants to search for solutions to their conflicts. It is therefore an approach that takes as its starting point the interests, values and strategies of those participating in a dispute and the way in which they perceive, appeal to and use the law, as well as the means and forums they look for to resolve their differences. And it is with this perspective in mind that negotiation has acquired new significance.[3]

Toward the end of the 1980s, when I began to work on this subject matter, I thought it symptomatic of the delay in Spain's reception of these new processual approaches, that a book on arbitration published in 1981,[4] despite being a legal study of this institution, was not included in the bibliographies of any of the manuals on history of law or of constitutional history in Spanish universities. Nor did these monographs include terms such as settlement, agreement, friendship, or love in their indexes as part of law and of the routine methods used to resolve disputes, as the studies of M. Clanchy or S. White were doing at the time elsewhere in Europe.[5] Rather, they reflected the widely accepted dichotomy, both inside and outside legal historiography, that opposed adjudication and formal justice to compromises and arbitration, viewing the latter as extrinsic to judicial mechanisms in the limited terms in which these were conceived. In this way, they ignored that our medieval legal culture also shared the principle that agreements triumph over law and love over trials; in other words that sentences divide litigants and agreements unite them; that agreements go beyond law and amicable resolution goes beyond legal sentences, as

---

3   White, '*Pactum legem vincit*'; White, 'Feuding and Peace-Making'; Geary, 'Vivre en conflit'; Geary, 'Extra-judicial means of conflict resolution'; Davies and Fouracre, eds, *The Settlement of Disputes*; Roberts and Comaroff, *Rules and Processes*.

4   Merchán Álvarez, *El arbitraje*.

5   White, '*Pactum legem vincit*'; Clanchy, 'Law and Love'. My observations in Alfonso, 'Resolución de disputas', p. 233.

THE LANGUAGE AND PRACTICE OF NEGOTIATION   69

indicated by the Anglo-Norman author of the *Leges Henrici Primi* with the expression
'Pactum ... legem vincit et amor judicium', the idea being that a sentence may be able
to end a dispute between two parties, but it cannot restore peace between them.[6]

Nor was it taken into account that our most Romanistic legal codes such as the
Espéculo or the *Partidas*,[7] those that are considered to have abolished — at least in
theory — the most archaic forms of justice and imposed fairer and more rational
forms, also made room for agreements as a way of resolving differences. Moreover,
settlements were postulated as,

> something that men must greatly covet among themselves, and especially those
> in litigation or dispute on some matter to which they claim right. And hence we
> say, that when some put their disputes in the hands of arbitrators, those who
> receive them must work hard to reconcile them, passing judgement and resolving
> so they may remain in peace.[8]

Peace was highlighted as the main objective of the resolution, underlining the role
of the arbitrators in the process and the legal nature of these as justices of free will,
whose appointment was also a matter of agreement: 'However the other arbitration
judges cannot be appointed, rather by the agreement of both parties, as mentioned
above'.[9] This same article 4 of the third *Partida* contains an extensive regulation
of the conciliation process, with provisions about the types of *jueces de auenencia*
('settlement judges') there could be, how they should be appointed, what issues
can, or cannot, be put to them, who can act as arbitrators, how these cases must be
dealt with, and so on.[10]

Likewise in the *Fuero Viejo* arbiters are *amigos* ('friends'), and the term *avenencia*
('settlement') is used to refer to the agreement by both sides on their appointment.[11] In
general, as in local law which also regulates these modes of resolution, arbitrators are
referred to in terms which highlight their legal nature and their pacifying, reconciliatory

---

6   An expression used by White as a title for the article cited in n. 5, which has become a classic on the
    subject.
7   I quote from *Los codigos españoles*.
8   'cosa que los omes deben mucho cobdiciar entre sí, e mayormente aquellos que han pleyto, o
    contienda sobre alguna razón en que cuidan aver derecho. E por ende decimos, que quando algunos
    meten sus pleytos en mano de auenidores, que aquellos que lo reciben, mucho se deuen trabajar de
    los auenir, juzgandolos, e librandolos, de manera que finquen en paz' (Partidas III.4.26).
9   'Mas los otros jueces de alvedrio non pueden ser puestos, si non por avenencia de ambas las partes,
    asi como suso es dicho' (Partidas III.4.1.2). Similar to the *Espéculo*: 'Aun y a otros alcalles a que llaman
    de avenencia. E estos pueden ser puestos con placer de amas las partes' ('There are even another type
    of magistrates, those called arbitration magistrates. And these can be appointed with the consent of
    both parties') (Espéculo IV.2); and to the *Fuero Real*: 'Alcalde [...] a placer de amas las partes, que
    lo tomen por avenencia, para juzgar algun pleito' ('magistrate [...] with the consent of both parties,
    which can appoint him by agreement to pass judgement on some case' (Fuero Real I.7.2); 'alcaldes de
    avenencia en que las partes avinieren de estar a su juicio' ('arbitration magistrates, whose judgements
    both parties agree to accept') (Fuero Real II.13.4).
10 Partidas III. 4.23 to 35.
11 Fuero Viejo, III.1.1.

and consentaneous role: *alcaldes e abenidores* ('magistrates and arbitrators'); *alcaldes de conveniença* ('magistrates of consensus').[12]

There are several concepts that articulate this legal vocabulary and that, in my view, are worth retaining: reconciliation — sometimes the word settlement is used — conciliation in friendship, pacification, as objectives of this *juyzio de avenidores* ('judgement of arbitrators'),[13] which 'means both arbitrators and friends of the community'[14] that pass judgement according to their *aluedrio* ('free will'). The concept of free will, which leaves the resolution to the judgement and ideas of the arbitrator-judges themselves, those that are said to be common friends of both parties and are chosen by them to intervene in the resolution of their differences, seems to include the Romano-Canonical distinction between these 'arbitrators' and the 'arbiters'; those that resolve disputes according to the law, and although in the doctrine and casuistry of the Alphonsine code, these two forms of arbitration become confused,[15] the difference can be appreciated between the qualities attributed to each. However, it is important not to forget the purely formal character of this dichotomy between a normative resolution and one that is a product of the personal decision of the judges, inasmuch as the criteria used in an amicable settlement were in no way outside of the law. Indeed, although they do not appeal to substantive law, they do refer to common conceptions of fairness, to a moral sense of law shared by a social universe which is broader than the more restrictive and formalised one present in institutionalised courts.[16] The dialectic, in any case, between norms and practices of resolution is highly complex and belongs to one of the most interesting current lines of research, as I will mention later on.

My intention here is not so much to analyse the legal culture of negotiation mentioned in these legal texts, despite its undeniable interest, but to emphasise some aspects of the most common negotiation practices used in the resolution of disputes which I believe are still central to the important debate that is to be had in this area. This involves looking at the way in which solutions were negotiated judicially and extrajudicially, as well as the relationship between these two ways of resolving conflicts and the role of legal norms in both areas. This also necessitates an analysis of how both practices were affected by the formalisation of power structures, including the judicial authorities. To achieve this, I will use the research I have carried out on the subject in Castile and León.[17]

---

12 FSepúlvedaR, § 195; and FPlasencia, § 720, on which see Merchán Álvarez, *El arbitraje*, p. 68, where more information is given.

13 Partidas III.4.35.

14 'quiere tanto dezir como aluedriadores e comunales amigos' (Partidas III.4.23).

15 As stated by Merchán Álvarez, *El arbitraje*, pp. 69–77.

16 This social interdependence is the central theme in the works collected in Coss, ed., *The Moral World of the Law*.

17 Alfonso, 'Resolución de disputas'; Alfonso and Jular Pérez-Alfaro, 'Oña contra Frías'; Alfonso, 'Conflictos en las behetrías'; Alfonso, 'Litigios por la tierra', and Alfonso, 'Campesinado y derecho' [Editors' note: For an English translation of the latter two, see chapters 13 and 9 of this volume]. Reference is also made to the more extensive bibliography quoted in the abovementioned text.

THE LANGUAGE AND PRACTICE OF NEGOTIATION   71

Perhaps the main conclusion of these studies — in which I adopted a processual approach —, at least in relation to the issue that concerns us here, was to confirm the negotiated nature — even in the case of the more formalised royal courts — of many of the settlements of disputes that the preserved documentation allows us to minimally contextualise. This confirmation would seem to question specific deep-seated conceptions in our historiography which will appear throughout the analysis of some of the disputes I will use to illustrate specific aspects of these trials and their semantics.[18]

The majority of the cases analysed refer to land disputes between ecclesiastical institutions and local nobility, as this is the kind of conflict about which most information has been preserved, in Castilian areas of La Bureba, centred on the monastery of Oña, or in parts of León that came under the sphere of influence of the cathedral of León or the important monastery of Sahagún. The study of these disputes allows us to see that antagonism between secular groups and ecclesiastical institutions was part of a more complex process of social interaction from which alliances were not excluded, with the fragmented nature of landownership and the power it entails as a principal factor in both groups. The negotiation of relationships within these local frameworks constituted one of the undeclared aims of litigation, in other words, disputes could be seen as a negotiation strategy. I will briefly mention one of these conflicts.

In 1229, after intermittent disputes between the monastery of Oña and some minor noblemen from Tamayo, a town near the monastery, over contradictory rights over estates in the town, having been brought before various courts, the conflict passed to the royal court. In the document which records this,[19] it is possible to perceive the vocabulary of agreements in a court traditionally considered as the site of adjudication par excellence, in which the explicit rules of law are supposedly applied, and out of which one of the parties comes victorious and the other is declared guilty. However, King Fernando III confirmed the settlement which don Lope Díaz de Haro, a Castilian baron who at the time held office as *adelantado*, had undertaken by way of an inquiry. The inquiry had been carried out to verify the *behetría* estates that the knights claimed from the monastery, alleging that the monastery had bought them from their vassals after the Cortes de Nájera had forbidden such transactions. The result of this process was that only two plots were given to the nobles, who, from then on agreed not to claim any more land from Oña, nor to acquire them from their vassals:

> and for these claims that existed between them, don Lope Diaz, with the consent of both parties, made the following settlement, that those two *solares* in the aforementioned *benfetria* should belong to the nobles, and that these should waive the *solares* belonging to the monastery and be banned from buying the *heredamientos* in the monastery's *solares*. And both parties requested from me, King Fernando, to have this settlement that don Lope Diaz had made between

---

18 The cited cases are further developed and contextualised in the works mentioned in the corresponding footnotes.
19 SSOña-A452 (1229).

them confirmed and granted in a charter. And I, King Fernando, by the grace of God King of Castile and of Toledo, by request of the abbot, and Garçi Lopez, and don Tello, and Lope Garcia, who came in agreement unto me that I may execute and confirm this settlement, execute and confirm it with my charter, which I have had sealed with my seal.[20]

In this case, it can be seen that the norm invoked to justify the nobles' claim is not questioned, nor are the reported sales of the properties; the issues at stake are the facts, in this case the dates when the transfers took place. The agreement, a negotiation, is arbitrated by a territorial authority and ratified by the king.

In other situations, also under the dominion of the same Burgos monastery, more direct forms of resolution, without intermediaries, or at least formal ones, were documented. This is the case for the agreement seemingly sought by Oña, after unsuccessful claims by relatives of the nobles of Tamayo mentioned earlier. The terms of this agreement are clearly those of a 'direct' negotiation. In 1287, the prior and convent of Oña claims to undertake 'litigation and agreement with you',[21] doña Toda Ortiz, daughter of don Sancho Martínez de Briviesca; and goes on to describe the contents of the agreement:

- The monks give her the house they possess in Piérnigas, with its vassals and all the rights associated with it, which must be returned upon her death with all the improvements made, respecting in addition the situation of the vassals.

- In exchange, they will receive everything claimed by them in previous disputes and that was possessed by the woman at the time.

- In addition, the woman promises to manage the division of the inheritance with her cousins, so that the monastery may receive its part.

- Other conditions are also stipulated as guarantees, which do not concern us here.

- The two parties jointly consent to and finalise everything mentioned in the letter, and ask the public clerk of Oña to draw up a charter-party, each side sealed with the other party's seal.

- The negotiation was undertaken in the presence of witnesses, which are repeatedly mentioned as seeing, hearing and attending the negotiation, and

---

20 'et por estas demandas que eran entr'ellos, don Lop Diaz, a placer damas las partes fizo tal avenencia, que aquellos dos solares de la benfetria sobredichos, que fuesen de los caualleros, et de los solares que eran del monesterio que se partiesen dellos et que non pudiesen comprar los heredamientos destos solares del monesterio. Et desta abenençia que don Lope Diaz fizo entr'ellos, pidieron merçed amas las partes a mi rey don Ferrando, que gela confirme et que gela otorgue con mi carta. Et yo don Ferrando, por la gracia de Dios rey de Castiella et de Toledo, por ruego del abbad, et de Garçi Lopez et de don Tello, et de Lope Garcia, que avenidos uinieron ante mi, que yo que esta avenencia otorgase et confirmarse, et you otorgola et confirola et con mi carta robrola, et fiz sellar con mio siello pendien't' (SSOña-A452, 1229).

21 'pleyto e postura connusco' (SSOña-O313, 1287).

THE LANGUAGE AND PRACTICE OF NEGOTIATION 73

whose testimony will serve to guarantee compliance with the agreement.

It would seem that it was not always possible for Oña to reach this kind of direct and bilateral agreement with these same families, as can be inferred from the difficulties arising over the exchange of two houses or exploitation centres in different villages. The nature of these difficulties is not specified, but a manuscript from 1294 mentions that, 'because they could not settle on the exchange, they put it to friends',[22] and later on, the non-acceptance of the exchange would necessitate another arbitration, although the mediator-friends seem to come from the two groups in dispute, and a special role is accorded to the intervening third parties, making it more similar to a bilateral process.[23] What follows is a description of the events:

In 1294, making use of a very common formula in this type of agreements, each party appoints one of the *amigos* ('friends') and another is jointly appointed, and confers on them the power to resolve the issue as they see fit, promising to accept their decision — 'and they gave them full power for whatsoever these friends may settle, or set to rights, or judge, so that both parties shall consent to it and accept it for evermore'.[24] Any party in violation of the agreement would owe the other 9,000 *morabetinos*, maintaining the arbitrators' decision — 'and endorsing that said by the aforementioned friends'.[25] The first compromise is therefore to designate third parties and to promise to accept their decision.

Once the friends receive this dispute over the exchange, at the request of both parties, as repeated in the letter, 'having the counsel of *boni homines*'[26] and by the power given to them by the two parties through their consent, they will decide, *iudgando* ('by judgement'), and order the distribution of the assets that is the object of the exchange. The actual occurrence of this exchange seems to be extremely slow, because the document includes the guarantors given almost a year later by the nobleman to the monastery to guarantee the said exchange under the agreement stipulated. It is therefore possible to infer that the negotiation process performed a series of unrelated functions that were at least as important as the final settlement. Each stage of this negotiation had witnesses who endorsed it.

However, the settlement reached did not last. In 1295[27] the abbot brought repeated actions, complaining that the other party was occupying, without his consent, the house handed over during the exchange, and five years later, the parties called for more arbitration which, this time, is couched in more technical terminology.[28] So in 1300, in a public session in the cemetery of the church of San Román in Burgos, before several magistrates and clerks of the city, the two parties commit themselves

---

22 'por razon que non se podien abenir en el camio, pusieronlo en amigos' (SSOña-O402, 1294).

23 Rouland, *L'anthropologie juridique*.

24 'et dieronles conplido poder que, quanto estos amigos mandasen abiniesen o conpusieresen o iudgasen, amas las partes que esten por ello e que lo ayan por firme para siempre' (SSOña-O402, 1294).

25 'e que uala lo que dixieren los amigos sobredichos'.

26 'auido conseio con bonos omnes'.

27 SSOña-O417 (1295).

28 SSOña-O467 (1300); SSOña-O468 (1300); SSOña-O469 (1301).

once more to the decision of 'magistrates, arbitrators and amicable compositeurs of the claims and disputes'[29] between them. Time has elapsed, and the nobleman from Tamayo is now accompanied by his son. During this new session, the parties say they are 'resolved to put all these aforementioned claims and disputes and contests and suits […] in the hands and in the power of friends, and we shall put them and place them in their hands and in their power'.[30] Three friends are appointed: two royal magistrates and one prior from the monastery, who are also described as *omnes buenos* (*boni homines*) that will hear each party's claims and anything else they wished to argue before them:

> and those friends shall discover the whole truth through as many parties as may be necessary and in any such manner they see fit, *in keeping with the order of the fuero and the law or otherwise*. And anything that they, all three as one or two of them without the other, *order or judge or set to rights or settle or will whether by charter or by judgement or by free will, judging, arbitrating or setting to rights or settling* in any way they may see fit, both parties consent and accept, accepting the outcome for evermore [And should they not, they shall pay to the other party 1000 *maravedíes* by agreement and pact]. And the agreement paid or not paid, should be worth what they, all three of them as one or two of them without the other, order, or judge, or set to rights, or settle, or will, in any such way as said by them or seen fit by them.[31]

There is undoubtedly much that is formulaic in this document, but the fact that in this formula different ways to reach an agreement and what constitutes negotiation begin to merge, with the emphasis on the decision taken by elected third parties, on the final agreement reached, rather than on the legality of the means of verifying what happened, or the way in which this is decided, is worth bearing in mind and attention should be paid to the terms underlined, which state that the procedures be limited — or not — to the *fuero* or to the law. It is this explicitly recognised flexibility in relation to the norms — not of the norms themselves, as it is usually sustained –, that should be remembered.

The parties made a mutual commitment to appear, in any time or place, in person or by proxy, in answer to any summons issued by the good men arbitrating, with a

---

29 'alcaldes, arbitros e amigables componedores en los pleytos e en las demandas'.

30 'abenidas en poner todas estas demandas e querellas e contiendas e pleytos sobredichos […] en manos e en poder de amigos, e ponemoslo e metemoslo en so poder e en so mano'.

31 'e los dichos amigos que sepan toda la verdat por quantas partes la pudieren saber en qualquier manera que ellos por bien touieren, *guardando la orden del fuero e del derecho o non la guardando*. E todo quanto ellos, todos tres en vno o los dos dellos sin ell otro, *mandaren o iudgaren o compusieren o avinieren o aluedriaren, quier por fuero, quier por iuyzio, quier por aluedrio, iudgando, arbitrando, componiendo o aviniendo* en qualquier manera que ellos por bien touieren, amas las partes lo otorgamos e lo auemos e lo auremos por firme agora e en todo tiempo. [Y si no lo hacen pechen a la otra parte 1000 maravedíes por postura e paramiento]. E la postura pagada o non pagada, que vala lo que ellos, todos tres en vno o los dos dellos sin ell otro, mandaren o iugaren o compusieren o avinieren o aluedriaren, en qualquier manera que lo ellos dixieren o por bien touieren'.

fine of 20 *maravedíes* if they did not attend. These *boni homines* were given the right to follow the case and to be counted as present if they did not attend after three summons. The abbot and the convent also make explicit their commitment to be present and to comply with 'everything that may be judged by the aforementioned friends'.[32] They also request that the king and his *Adelantado mayor* in Castile enforce that which these friends 'judge or set to rights or settle',[33] and promise, on pain of a fine of 1000 *maradevíes*, not to act against them as a result of their findings:

> we promise that to these *boni homines*, in whose hands we have put these aforementioned suits and disputes and contests and claims, that we shall not bring suit against them nor dispute with them nor whatsoever they may say or do or judge or will in these aforementioned suits.[34]

They end by naming guarantors to ensure that the compromise is kept and complied with, and request that it be written up by the public clerk of Burgos in three public charters.

Another document that has come down to us is that which mentions the decision taken a month later by the *amigos* ('friends') appointed in the church of Santa María in Burgos inside the new cloister, 'setting to rights, settling, willing, ordering we sentence',[35] the distribution between the parties of that which was deemed to belong to them, and is detailed in the charter. The transactional nature of this resolution and of the possibly hotly contested negotiation, can be clearly seen in the last clause, in which the judges manage, as they expressly state, to award a certain sum of *maravedíes* and a certain amount of *fanegas* of wheat and barley to the secular litigants to encourage them to compromise, so that 'they may always have great willingness to serve the monastery of Onna and be indebted to the abbot and the convent',[36] and to ensure their acceptance of the decision taken, which doubtless did not favour them. The nature of this type of arbiters and the complexity of their work, which makes clear their links to the parties as well as their knowledge of the issue in which they are to mediate and the context in which it occurs, and therefore, of the power relations existing between those in dispute and the social network in which they are immersed, including the mediators themselves, whose own interests are not entirely external to these processes.[37]

---

32 'todo quanto fuere iudgado por los amigos sobredichos'.
33 'iugaren o compusieren o abinieren'.
34 'prometemos que a estos ommes buenos, en cuyo mano e en cuyo poder metemos estos pleytos e querellas e contiendas e demandas sobredichas, que les nunca mouamos pleyto nin querellemos dellos nin contra ellos por cosa que digan o fagan o iudguen o aluedrien o fablen en estos pleytos sobredichos'.
35 'componiendo, abiniendo, aluedriando, mandando iudgamos'.
36 'ayan siempre mayor talento de seruir al monasterio de Onna e de guardar los bonos debdos que an con el abbat e con el conuento'.
37 The position of power held by third parties mediating in disputes has been emphasised in Roberts and Comaroff, *Rules and Processes*. The mediators' own interests have been highlighted by in one particular case by Péquignot, '*Interponere partes suas*'.

Another case, that of the bishop and chapter of León, allows us to observe the social dynamic in which disputes and negotiations are both a sign and result of the competition between secular social groups from the low nobility and church institutions vying for power and control of local relationships.[38] In 1117 the bishop of León and a group of low-ranking nobles concluded an agreement to resolve a dispute over the estates of a monastery to which both parties claimed rights.[39] Indeed, after verifying that each side possessed the said rights, they agreed in council to make a pact registered — 'the assembled a meeting and by agreement they reached a pact and covenant'.[40] In the first part, they specified that the nobles renounced their claim to the monastic estates held — 'so that this *hereditarii* shall relinquish the *hereditates* of the monastery that they are withholding';[41] that the bishop would build and populate the monastery, and that he would require their counsel to appoint and remove the abbot from office — 'and the bishop shall build and populate the monastery and appoint and remove the abbot according to their advice'.[42]

The *hereditarii*, as these knights were also termed, committed, in the second part, to use their power to protect and increase the assets and estates of the disputed monastery — 'and this *hereditarii* shall always assist the abbot of the monastery in his affairs, and use their power to defend it and enlarge the monastery with their *hereditates*';[43] while the abbot in turn promised to receive them at the monastery whenever necessary, even to take them in in case of extreme poverty, to dwell and serve God there as heirs:

> and if any of them passed through the monastery and wished to be lodged there, he should be granted this as an *hereditarius* by the power of the abbot and without been charged for it, and if any of them became needy and wished to live in the monastery and serve God, he should be allowed to do so and honourably enjoy it by the power of the abbot who is at the monastery at that time.[44]

Therefore, in this pact, which was backed up by a fine of 500 *solidi* for the offender, each party recognises their socially ascribed role: the nobles as defenders of the abbot's assets; and the monks and the monastic institution as protectors of various needs of their, hereafter, allies in relation to any unexpected circumstances that may occur during their lives.

---

38 Alfonso, 'Litigios por la tierra', pp. 929–42.

39 CatLeon1358 (1117).

40 'conuenerunt concilium et fecerunt inter se pactum simul et placitum tali uidelicet pactione'.

41 'quod ipsi hereditarii dimittant hereditates ipsius monasterii quas retinent'.

42 'et episcopus construat et populetur illud monasterium, et per consilium eorum preponat et deponat abbatem'.

43 'et quod ipsi hereditarii semper auxilientur sui rebus abbati ipsius monasterii, et defendant pro posse suo, et amplificent illud monasterium suis hereditatibus'.

44 'et quicumque illorum pertransiens in monasterio hospitari uoluerit, recipiatur sicut hereditarius, non agrauantur, sed pro posse abbatis, et si forte aliquis illorum ad inopiam deuenerit, atque in monasterio morari et ibidem Deo deseruire uoluerit, recipiatur et honeste teneatur pro posse abbatis qui eo tempore monasterio prefuerit'.

One last case, this time in the documentation of Sahagún, allows us to see the way in which the renewal of the relationships resulting from this type of agreements is inherited and negotiated by descendants; the case documents two generational stages of this dynamic, something which can only be inferred in other cases.

In 1199,[45] Fernando Pérez, belonging undoubtedly to the same social stratum of low-ranking nobility, reached an agreement with the prior don Pedro, in the presence of the good men of Villárdiga and Cañizo, relating to an estate in the first of the two towns, which, together with his relatives, he had attempted to appropriate violently:

> Before the *boni homini* of Villardiga and Cañizo I make this agreement and charter regarding the *hereditas* of Villargida, which I forcefully seized and wished to extort claiming that I had it from my parents, and that by no means should San Salvador have it.[46]

The account, which publicly corroborates old alliances and agreements between the monastery and the person speaking, articulated through the exchange and possession of estates, points to a kind of negotiation that seems to have been very widespread and which is quite well documented: the donation of land to a religious institution, in exchange for another belonging to the monastery, ceded with a lifelong tenancy and which could be handed down to sons. The difficulties involved in this transmission led to disputes similar to the one mentioned here, in which the heir claims to be obliged to act, even by using force, in order that his rights, denied by the monastery, might be recognised:

> My part on that that *hereditas* was as follows: the *hereditas* in Población, which is nearby Cañiza, belonged to my father; and my father granted this *hereditas* to the monastery of San Salvador, as per the following agreement: that he should remain as a friend and relative of the house of San Salvador forever, and that he should be buried there, as he has been buried, and that he should hold this *hereditas* and Villárdiga for his lifetime, and that after his death it should remain in the hands of his son, I, Fernando Pérez; and if it was not given to me, I should then receive an *hereditas* in Población. The prior denied all this and said that this was by no means true, but false.[47]

---

45 SFPSahagun1530 (1199).
46 'facio talem conuenienciam et talem kartulam, coram bonis hominibus de Uillardiga et de Cannizo, super hereditate de Uillardiga, quam ego per forciam et per meos parentes uolebam extorquere, ut nequaquam eam haberet domus Sancti Saluatoris'.
47 'Super quam hereditatem talis era mea racio, uidelicet: quod hereditas de Populatura, que est circa Cannizo, fuerat patris mei; et ipsam hereditatem obtulerat pater meus, monasterio Sancti Saluatoris, tali conueniencia: ut esset amicus et familiaris domus Sancti Saluatoris semper, et ut sepeliret se, sicut est sepultus, et ut ipsam hereditatem et Uillardiga teneret eam in uita sua, et post mortem remaneret michi, filio suo, Fernando Petri; quod si michi non daretur, habebam ego recipere hereditatem de Populatura. Quod totum dominus prior dextruebat et nequaquam dicebat esse uerum, set falsum'.

ISABEL ALFONSO

In this way, a new *conveniencia* ('agreement') was reached that renewed on a similar basis, although in this case dropping the claims, the bonds of friendship and familiarity previously initiated by the father:

> Finally, once falseness was removed and peace between each party was restored, I, Fernando Pérez, who inquired into all this, for the salvation of my soul and the remission of my sinful deeds, by spontaneous will waive my claim to it, so that these monks may have me in their prayers and spiritual goods, in life and death.[48]

Disputes involving claims to various hereditary rights, as in these cases, seem to be an important element in a wider strategy aimed at the continued redefinition of power relations at local level through these kinds of negotiations. The channels and methods used, and the courts in which these claims were aired differed, but even in the agreements that seem more direct, it is the presence of a partly institutionalised public audience, like the one present in the local assemblies or councils mentioned previously, which gave strength and effectiveness to these kinds of negotiations.

One of the most interesting aspects to come out of the study of these cases is the interdependence, in some cases, of royal justice, arbitral justice and negotiated resolutions. This connection between the judicial and other more informal conflict resolution mechanisms prevents us from maintaining the much generalised definitions about the nature of each. Litigants strategically use the different possibilities available to them, in order to resolve their differences or achieve their objectives. This was the case in the suit between the knights of Tamayo and the monks of Oña which ended, at least as far as we can see from the documentation, in the appeal to the authority of the king to confirm a previous settlement. These available channels are superbly illustrated, due to the rich documentation preserved, in a case which for a long time opposed the same monastery of Oña and the council of Frías because of the effects that the population and facilities of this royal *villa* on the monastic assets and estate. I will now briefly describe the stages documented in this long conflict.[49]

- In 1270 in the royal court of Burgos, the attorneys of the parties agree to an inquiry to verify the status of the assets and rights in dispute, using their influence to appoint the inquirers: two royal magistrates, and a third designated by the king. The arbitral nature of the process stems from this initial settlement about the way in which it should be carried out and the appointment of the key figures, with the inclusion of royal authority in the process.[50]

---

48 'Tandem, remota perfidia et pace ex utraque parte reformata, ego Fernandus Petri, qui hoc totum inquirebam, pro remedio anime mee et pro abluendis peccatorum meorum facinoribus, dimisi spontanea uoluntate ut amplius talia non inquirirem, et ut ipsi monachi reciperent me in orationibus suis et in spiritualibus bonis, in uita et in morte'.

49 There is a detailed analysis of this conflict in Alfonso and Jular Pérez-Alfaro, 'Oña contra Frías'; to which I refer the reader for more information.

50 The role of the inquirers as mediators is clear in the provisions of the Fuero de Puebla de Sanabria of

- Ten years later, in 1280, the resolution of the dispute is put in the hands of three arbitrator magistrates, also appointed by the parties involved and by order of king Alfonso in the form of his son the infante Sancho — 'appointed with the consent of both parties and by order of the infante Sancho'.[51] Royal authority and arbitration remain linked.

- In 1281 the first arbitral sentence finds in favour of the monastery. There is no information on the negotiation processes that undoubtedly took place; what is established and publicised is a 'judicial truth' to legitimise the resolution arrived at.

- This arbitration sentence would need three attachments: two in 1281, when one by one, in front of many witnesses and with great ritual, the assets recognised in the trial were handed over to Oña; and another in 1282.

- However, in 1283, the case is reopened due to a claim made by the abbot of Oña, alleging that the people of Frías had nullified the previous resolution by obtaining a *desaforada* ('illegal') charter from king Sancho. The local council's strategy and its, at least momentary, effectiveness reveals the short-circuiting that central power was subject to in practice.

- Nothing more is mentioned until, ten years later, in 1292,[52] there appears a resolution reached directly between the litigants with the aim, rhetorical but realistic, of 'living together in harmony and more peacefully'[53] than previously and respecting their obligations to one another, through a *good settlement and love* that would be contracted in writing:

> Shall it be known to those who read this charter how we don Domingo, by the grace of God abbot of Oña, and the convent of the same place and we, the council and magistrate and jurors of Frias, of the town and villages, seeking to maintain between us a *good understanding and love so that we may live together in peace and enjoy a more harmonious coexistence* than we have had up to the present, now and forever, and so that the good relations between us be always kept, come resolved to make an agreement in the manner described herein.[54]

1220: 'E si algunos omes ovieren entre sí contienda e metieren en el pleito en mano de pesquisidores, aquelos pesquisidores avénganlos a buena fe sin mal enganno daquesta guissa: que si los contendedores fueran de la villa, los pesquisidores avéngalos fasta tercer día, e si fueren del alfoz, fasta nueve días; más si fueren de fuera del alfoz o de su término, avéngalos luego que tornaren a la villa; e si el pesquisidor parare el pleito por revuelta, peche la demanda e de allí delante non faga ninguna pesquisa' ('And if some men should have disputes between them and put the suit in the hands of inquirers, those inquirers must settle the dispute in good faith and without deception in the following way: if the opponents are from the town, the inquirers must reconcile them before three days, if they are from the surrounding area, before nine days; and if they are from outside the municipality, they must reconcile them as soon as they arrive in the town; and if the inquirer stops the suit, he shall pay the fine and must not continue inquiring any more' (FZ42, 1220, § 25).

51 'dados a voluntad de amas las partes e por mandamiento del infant Sancho'.
52 SSOña-O381 (1292).
53 'beuir los unos con los otros en paz e mas sosegadamente'.
54 'Sepan quantos esta carta uieren como nos don Domingo, por la gracia de Dios abbad de Onna, et

The practical motives for this change are described in the settlement: in short, that each party would receive the assets located nearest to it, recognising the goodness to come out of the dispute: 'And for this reason, we will be able to live always in peace with each other and there be no reason henceforth to dispute or bring any more suits against each other'.[55]

This transaction, named 'agreement and firmness' ('postura e firmedumbre'), is a judicial manoeuvre which demonstrates well the relationship between justice and negotiation, because the agreement between the litigants results in evermore pragmatic foundations in this last stage of the long process, using interesting legal subterfuges, such as complying with the previous sentence of the arbitrator magistrates, despite the change implied by excepting the assets now exchanged and, of course, complying with, in spite of the directness of the negotiation, the king's will, as the agreement could not be maintained in any other way — 'pleasing our lord the king and signing his charters, as in no other way could this be made stable by either of the parties'.[56] Indeed, one year later, Sancho IV confirms this change in the name of the council 'that both parties resolved to keep love between them and leave behind disputes and arguments'.[57] There is therefore a clear acceptance by the royal authority of the effectiveness of these extrajudicial negotiations, direct and informal, in reaching effective resolutions of differences between parties, and which is fully coherent with the law included in the code of *Partidas* mentioned above.

But there is another side to this royal confirmation that is of special relevance in the context of the debate on the role of norms in negotiation processes for the resolution of conflicts. In order to ensure that the new situation reached by the council and the monastery could never be broken, the king reversed a legal provision, that which forbade assets belonging to the *realengo* from becoming part of the *abadengo* and vice versa, a norm already invoked by the nobles of Tamayo to justify their claims against Oña in the case mentioned above. The royal revocation means that this norm, contrary to that practiced in the Cortes de Nájera where it was established a century before, could never be invoked to break the agreement made. This case clearly shows how substantive norms can be affected in processes of resolution, including those that, like this one, used less institutional channels: 'It is agreed that this exchange shall not be impeded nor undone at any time owing to the fact that the *reganlengo* should not pass to the *abbadengo* nor the *abbadengo* to the *reganlengo*, nor for any

---

el conuiento des mismo logar et nos, el conceio e el alcalle e los iurados de Frias, de uilla e de aldeas, queriendo catar Carrera en commo siempre aya entre nos *buena abenençia e amor e podamos beuir los unos con los otros en paz e mas sosegadamente* que fasta aquí uiquiemos, agora e en todo tiempo, e sean siempre guardados los buenos debdos que auemos los unos con los otros, venimos avenidos de fazer abenençia e camio en la manera que aquí sera escripto'.

55 'E por esta razon, podremos beuir siempre en paz los unos con los otros e non fincara y razon ninguna porque deuamos daqui adelante contender nin auer pleyto en uno'.

56 'plaziendo al rey nuestro sennor e firmandolo por sus cartas, ca en otra manera non se podria fazer que estable fuesse pora ninguna de las partes'.

57 'que amas las partes abenieronse de aver entre si amor e se partir de contienda e de porfía' (SSOña-O399, 1293).

THE LANGUAGE AND PRACTICE OF NEGOTIATION   81

other reason there may be, but rather remain always firm and valid'.[58] This is another of aspect worth highlighting.[59]

Negotiation practices, which in the cases mentioned up to now were mostly led by low-ranking nobles, or urban elites, are also documented between other social groups, both at the highest political level, and among the peasantry. These relate to internal relationships within these groups and relationships with other groups or institutions.

In the case of the peasants, research into the contexts in which the statutes regulating local life, the *fueros*, were written — the short *fueros* in which we have traditionally seen conditions imposed by a lord on an oppressed peasantry — has shown the transactional nature of many of these charters, by revealing peasant action and movements aimed at achieving more favourable tenancy or rent conditions, greater mobility and use of their land, and so on: in short, more autonomy. These actions clearly indicate the competence of peasants organised into small councils to take part in the legal formulation of their demands and to strategically use legal procedures. It has been shown that the normative definition of the lord/peasant relationship, embodied in these documents, took place in processes of continual conflict and negotiation, in which the law functioned as an emblem, but also as a parameter, of the legitimation of power, as a means of defining real practices and processes, activities and behaviour. Testimonies, for example, of the pressure for the compliance with the rhetoric of the good lord reflect this capability well.[60]

I will outline one last case to show the multiple forms that the rural population's capacity for negotiation could take. In 1315[61] several heads of households, some of them women, that were vassals of the king, of the abbey of Santillana and the monastery of Oña, made a pact, for them and their children, to become vassals of Garcilaso de la Vega because he had favoured them in taxation and protected them since then — 'he did us good and favoured us [...] he exempted fifteen of us from the king's tax register and protected us until now'.[62] The people promise to serve him as *vasallos a señor* 'vassals to their lord', on the condition that he and his sons or those of the manor, continue to protect and help them — 'that they support us and protect us, and do not do us injustice or suchlike'.[63] Two points should be highlighted in this agreement. On one hand, the internal negotiation process that must have taken place in these communities in order to take the decision to abandon their traditional lords and decide on another; and on the other, no less relevant, the capability to set in writing the resources they would have right to

---

58 'Et tenemos por bien que se non enbargue nin se desate este camio en ningun tiempo del mundo por razon que es defendido que el reganlengo non pase al abbadengo nin el abbadengo al reganlengo, nin por otra razon ninguna que pueda seer, mas que finque siempre firme e ualedero'.

59 On the invocation of this same norm in other cases, see Alfonso, 'Conflictos en las behetrías'.

60 Alfonso, 'Campesinado y derecho'.

61 SSOña-O550 (1315).

62 'nos fizo bien y merced [...] nos fizo rraer quince pecheros de la cabeza de los padrones del rey e nos amparastes fata aquí'.

63 'que nos guarden y nos amparen, que ningunos non nos fagan tuerto nin demas'.

should the new lord or his officials not comply with the agreement, in other words, if he did them *tuerto* ('injustice') instead of protecting them. They would therefore be able to file a complaint, first with the lords' stewards and then with the lords themselves, whom they could abandon and choose another if they breached the agreement — 'that we take a lord that does right unto us'.[64] In compensation, the lord was reciprocally insured against an unjustified abandonment by the vassals, as these had to accept to pay 'by litigation and by agreement with you we pay 50 *maravedíes* each person'[65] if, while protected, they decided to transfer to another lord. The clauses recognising, although only in theory, the ability of the peasants to appeal against their lords' breaches of contract require further detailed study, because they reflect a set of power relations that are less one-sided than usually accepted.[66] Nor must we underestimate the importance of the patronage offered to vassals, as a symbol and result of the accumulation of the political capital that this protection implies, in the construction of hegemony in the face of other noble powers. In addition, it is in this type of agreement, where the moral, but also the normative and political images, with all of their practical meaning, of the good and bad lord, and the converse image of the good and bad vassal, gradually take shape; in other words, it is in these processes of confrontation in which the values that articulate a shared political culture operate and are constructed.

There are several conclusions that have been drawn from the analysis of the modes of conflict resolution in the areas studied, using the proposed processual perspective, that are worth highlighting in this context:

- The practice of resolving disputes through extrajudicial compromises — through direct negotiation, mediation of third parties or arbitrators — was, as in all medieval Europe, commonplace. Furthermore, the predominance of resolutions agreed upon by the litigants, of compromises in the royal courts, sometimes reached through apparently strict adjudication methods, show an interest in renegotiating pre-existing relationships using clearly political processes. The continuity of these forms of struggle and judicial and extrajudicial negotiation that are documented throughout the period calls into question the impact attributed to the legal and institutional developments of the twelfth and thirteenth centuries. The existence of the latter was undoubtedly important, but within a dialectical, not exclusive, relationship which must be the subject of more research in the future.[67] In fact, the 'infrajudicial' has become a specific field of study in the modern era.

- Violence is not absent, rather it plays and active role in processes of resolution through settlement or compromise, and forms part of the strategies used to

---

64 'nos que tomemos señor que nos faga derecho'.
65 'por pleito y por postura que conbusco ponemos 50 maravedis cada persona'.
66 Some of these clauses are commented on in Alfonso, 'Campesinado y derecho'.
67 This was the central thesis in the monograph Alfonso, Isabel, *Desarrollo legal, prácticas judiciales y acción política en la Europa medieval*, Hispania, 197 (1997), 879–1077. On this complex relationship, one of the most interesting recent contributions has been Wickham, *Legge, patriche e conflitti*.

achieve an improved position in the negotiations. The strategic use of violence observed here does not serve to justify it, but it does serve to distance it from an essentialist discourse which links it to more primitive social phases of consubstantial disorder and anarchy.[68]

- Negotiated forms of conflict resolution seem to be better guarantors of social order in medieval societies than coercion by the political apparatus. However, this does not mean that the aim of every negotiation is to achieve peace, as the rhetoric claims, rather it serves to reproduce the power relations generated by conflicts, to change them, or simply to limit them. The questions raised at the outset cannot be answered using abstract concepts, but must be explained in relation to the contexts in which the practices took place, because not only are the semantics of negotiation a cultural construction — and as such it should be understood — but also the power relations, the disparities in power, of the parties negotiating differs greatly, and is therefore a variable that cannot be excluded from any explanatory model.[69]

- The formation of sets of values and norms, which are the reference points in a negotiation processes, and which are also constructed during these processes, is a field of research requiring further attention.[70]

---

68 Alfonso, 'Los nombres de la violencia' [Editors' note: For an English translation, see chapter 16 of this volume]; Brown and Górecki, eds, *Conflict in Medieval Europe*.
69 Alfonso and Jular Pérez-Alfaro, 'Oña contra Frías'.
70 Central theme in the Research Project, 'Cultura, lenguaje y prácticas políticas en las sociedades medievales. Un estudio comparado sobre la construcción de valores compartidos y las formas de su contestación', funded by the Ministry of Science and Technology [BHA2002–03076].

Bibliography

Alfonso, Isabel, 'Resolución de disputas y prácticas judiciales en el Burgos medieval', in *Burgos en la Plena Edad Media. III Jornadas Burgalesas de Historia* (Burgos: Asociacion Provincial de Libreros de Burgos, 1994), pp. 211–43

Alfonso, Isabel, 'Campesinado y derecho: la vía legal de su lucha (Castilla y León, siglos X–XIII)', *Noticiario de Historia Agraria*, 13 (1997), 15–31

Alfonso, Isabel, 'Litigios por la tierra y "malfetrías" entre la nobleza medieval', *Hispania*, 57–197 (1997), 917–55

Alfonso, Isabel, 'Conflictos en las behetrías', in *Los señoríos de behetría*, ed. by Carlos Estepa Díez and Cristina Jular Pérez-Alfaro (Madrid: CSIC, 2001), pp. 227–60

Alfonso, Isabel, 'Los nombres de la violencia y el control de su legitimación', *Hispania*, 61/2 (2001), 691–706

Alfonso, Isabel, and Cristina Jular Pérez-Alfaro, 'Oña contra Frías o el pleito de los cien testigos: una pesquisa en la Castilla del siglo XIII', *Edad Media: Revista de Historia*, 3 (2000), 61–88

Brown, Warren C., and Piotr Górecki, eds, *Conflict in Medieval Europe: Changing Perspectives on Society and Culture* (Hampshire: Ashgate, 2003)

Clanchy, Michael, 'Law and Love in the Middle Ages', in *Disputes and Settlements: Law and Human Relations in the West*, ed. by John Bossy (Cambridge: Cambridge University Press, 1983), pp. 47–67

Correas, Gonzalo, *Vocabulario de refranes y frases proverbiales y otras fórmulas comunes de la lengua castellana* (Madrid: Tip. de la Rev. de Archivos, Bibliotecas y Museos, 1924 [1627])

Coss, Peter, ed., *The Moral World of the Law* (Cambridge: Cambridge University Press, 2000)

Davies, Wendy, and Paul Fouracre, eds, *The Settlement of Disputes in Early Medieval Europe* (Cambridge: Cambridge University Press, 1986)

Geary, Patrick, 'Vivre en conflit dans une France sans État: typologie des mécanismes de règlement des conflits (1050–1200)', *Annales ESC*, 41–5 (1986), 1107–33

Geary, Patrick, 'Extra-Judicial Means of Conflict Resolution', in *La giustizia nell'Alto Medioevo, secoli V–VIII. Atti della 42ª Settimana di studio (Spoleto, 7–13 aprile 1994)* (Spoleto: Centro Italiano di Studi sull'Alto Medioevo, 1995), pp. 569–605

Merchán Álvarez, Antonio, *El arbitraje: estudio histórico-jurídico* (Sevilla: Universidad de Sevilla, 1981)

Péquignot, Stéphane, '*Interponere partes suas*: les bons offices de Jacques II d'Aragon entre les cours de Naples et de Majorque, 1301–1304', in *L'intercession au Moyen Âge et au début de l'époque moderne*, ed. by Jean-Marie Moeglin (Genève: Droz, 2004), pp. 215–61

Roberts, Simon, and John Comaroff, L., *Rules and Processes: The Cultural Logic of Dispute in an African Context* (Chicago: The University of Chicago Press, 1981)

Rouland, Norbert, *L'anthropologie juridique* (Paris: Presses Universitaires de France, 1988)

White, Stephen D., '*Pactum legem vincit et amor judicium*: The Settlement of Disputes by Compromise in Eleventh-Century Western France', *The American Journal of Legal History*, 22–4 (1978), 281–308

White, Stephen D., 'Feuding and Peace-Making in Touraine around the Year 1100', *Traditio*, 42 (1986), 196–263

Wickham, Chris, *Legge, patriche e conflitti. Tribunali e risoluzione delle dispute nella Toscana del XII secolo* (Roma: Viella, 2000)

CHAPTER 3

On Judicial Rhetoric
and Political Legitimation

with a commentary by John Hudson

Conflict, Language, and Social Practice in Medieval Societies: Selected Essays of Isabel Alfonso, with Commentaries, ed. by Julio Escalona Monge, Álvaro Carvajal Castro, and Cristina Jular Pérez-Alfaro, TMC 24 (Turnhout: Brepols, 2024), pp. 85–125

BREPOLS ❦ PUBLISHERS

10.1484/M.TMC-EB.5.132457

JOHN HUDSON _____

Justice, Power, and Legitimation

In 'Judicial Rhetoric and Political Legitimation in medieval León-Castile' Isabel Alfonso makes a major contribution to various historiographical trends of the late twentieth and early twenty-first centuries. Most obviously she focuses on the discourse of texts, to reveal both the authors' aims and the underlying assumptions and ideologies. In addition, she examines materials that had once been of interest primarily to historians of law, to give them a wider relevance. And thirdly she explores processes of legitimation of power, a move away from earlier twentieth-century concentration on forms of exercise of power.

Central to the article's argument is that 'in the judicial sphere, royal legitimation was promoted through the employment of diverse rhetorical devices. These deserve careful analysis, as they served not only to define the dynamics of power, but also to establish moral portraits of those who wielded it'.[1] The article is of particular interest in that it examines co-existing legitimatory discourses: one framed in terms of the restoration of order, another in terms of truth.[2] Most of the information comes from ecclesiastical documents concerning 'legal suits brought before the king by ecclesiastical institutions intent on reclaiming property that had been seized from them or jurisdiction that had been usurped'.[3] That documents from different diplomatic categories use the same discourse indicates that 'employment of justificatory discourses that described royal policies that were favourable to the Church can be attributed to motives that went far beyond mere compliance with diplomatic convention'.[4]

How did legitimation work? Documents could exclude matters that might be 'unsavoury', and instead focus on restoration, royal justice, and royal genealogy. Take a confirmation by Alfonso VII for the monastery of Sahagún: according to the article, 'the king used this document to establish a connection between his protection of the monastery and the continuity and legitimacy of his family line'.[5] This discourse

---

1   See below, p. 96. Note also p. 95: 'The term "legal rhetoric" is employed here in reference to the existence and significance of discourses developed to represent the royal activities of judging and settling disputes, or even simply presiding over judicial purposes. This specific term is used because the discourses in question clearly had an audience.' The thoughts in this piece owe much to the years of collaboration I have enjoyed with mediaevalists at the CSIC, collaborations that started with an invitation from Maribel Alfonso. I am also grateful to Kimberley Knight and Steve White for their comments on an earlier draft of the piece.

2   See below, p. 96.

3   See below, p. 95.

4   See below, p. 107.

5   See below, p. 108. See also p. 102 'The ecclesiastical discourse […] employs the rhetoric of restoration

John Hudson, University of St Andrews

of restoration was supplemented by a related one, broader than protection of the Church; the latter extended to 'the guardianship of the peace, health, and stability of the kingdom. This effectively legitimized the king's authority by distancing it from his power as an individual and presenting it as both public and superior in nature'; hence 'a good king was supposed to be the source of all good things and offer protection against all evils'.[6] The basis of this depiction of good kingship went back to Isidore of Seville and thence to the Bible.[7] Thus 'the political activities of the kings [...] were legitimated through the development of a discourse that contrasted order with disorder, and good deeds with bad. A firm association was also thus developed between divine and secular power through the repeated affirmation that the latter was entrusted to kings through the will and grace of the former'.[8]

Meanwhile, a second form of discourse was at work, wherein ownership of land was raised to become synonymous with 'the truth'. The ideas were linked semantically, and 'the pursuit of a legal claim became the conceptual equal of the pursuit of both truth and justice'.[9] Royal justice thus became linked to truth through a process whereby the truth was effectively objectified in the judicial arenas whose business they record. This process was a circular one: 'legal decisions acquired the status of truth as a result of the authority invested in the methods through which that truth had been ascertained'; that authority 'in turn derived from the power that ordered the implementation of those methods'; and that power 'was itself legitimized in the process, along with the forum in which the whole process unfolded'.[10]

The power was royal, the forum was the royal assemblies exercising judicial functions. The use of accounts of judicial hearings to suggest legitimatory discourses is very fruitful. However, Maribel also reveals the necessary awareness of the problems involved. How ideas were generated, the ways in which they reached texts, is necessarily obscure: 'a model of good kingship was developed through a process of which we are still largely ignorant'.[11] Given the nature of the surviving sources, it is unlikely that even reading a much wider range of sources will much diminish that ignorance.

There is a further problem, of which Maribel again demonstrates her awareness: are the sources being examined as texts *with* legitimatory functions? Or are they being examined as texts *that reveal* legitimatory processes? Or both? Maribel's answer is 'both'. She writes that 'the documents themselves [...] as records of royal justice not only contained important expressions of power, but also served as a fundamental tool in its creation'.[12] This raises the question of the audience for these documents, an issue the article discusses only to a limited degree because of its specific interests.[13] Was

---

to legitimize royal justice and presents royal genealogies in such a way as to emphasize their positive aspects while totally suppressing other less savoury ones'.

6 See below, p. 112.
7 See below, p. 112.
8 See below, p. 117.
9 See below, p. 117.
10 See below, p. 123.
11 See below, p. 112.
12 See below, p. 93.
13 See below, pp. 116–17.

JUSTICE, POWER, AND LEGITIMATION 89

there an initial, public reading, suited to the employment of legitimatory rhetoric? And how far were the documents read thereafter?[14] As with historical writing — also much studied by those interested in practices of legitimation — the means by which an audience was reached are far from clear, and therefore the degree to which the texts might serve propagandistic purposes uncertain.[15] It is not so much a question of whether the assertions of the sources 'were understood (and possibly even shared despite being disputed) by the political community to which they were directed and within which the disputes with which they were associated took place'; rather it is a question of how far the assertions in the sources were directed at the political community.[16] Not just the generation but also the dissemination of legitimatory ideas 'is necessarily obscure'.

However, Maribel is not only arguing that the texts served legitimatory purposes but more importantly that they reveal legitimatory processes: 'it was the dialectic interaction between king and aristocratic groupings that provided the yardstick whereby individual monarchs' authority and the effectiveness of its imposition were measured: through which, in other words, their power was legitimized'.[17] Assemblies such as that where Alfonso V received liturgical acclamation and was raised to the throne of his forefathers in the royal seat of León clearly promoted his position as legitimate and authoritative ruler.[18] The ecclesiastical sources give us some sense of the ways in which legitimation worked in this context, but there is a considerable danger that other discourses be overlooked. How do developing secular chivalric discourses fit into the legitimation of royal authority, discourses of the sort that might have raised to high standing a king such as William Rufus of England, to whom monastic historians were profoundly hostile?[19] And the focus on discourse may lead to a neglect of other methods of establishing authority, of deterring challenge. Punishment by royal justice may fit into a rhetoric of royal judicial authority, but it was much besides rhetoric:

> The king invoked the biblical mandate *ne patieris maleficos* and ruled that 'evildoers' be condemned to exemplary execution. Then, to show that he was in earnest, he hung a few wrongdoers in the presence of the assembled company.[20]

---

14 On audience, see also below, pp. 93–94.

15 See below, p. 94 'The predominantly ecclesiastical nature of these sources obviously conditions the information they contain to such an extent that their origin must be kept constantly in mind by anyone attempting their interpretation. It is therefore very important that we take into account their function with respect to the institutions that issued them, and the context that lent credibility to their contents, though this, of course, is not necessarily described by the texts themselves. [...] Although they describe judicial processes that took place within the context of royal assemblies, they are not necessarily the work of legal scribes who recorded the business transacted there for strictly administrative purposes'.

16 See below, p. 95.

17 See below, p. 94.

18 See below, p. 100.

19 See e.g. Gillingham, 'Kingship, Chivalry and Love'.

20 See below, p. 115.

Furthermore, if one is to understand the ways in which mediaeval regimes were legitimised, it may be necessary to pay as much attention to processes of unintentional legitimation as to the strategies of legitimation and authority building. For example, each time a legal arrangement or dispute was conducted in terms of fiefs or inheritances, those bases of royal — and also aristocratic — authority were reaffirmed, even when the possession of a particular fief or particular inheritance was contested.[21] In these ways existing discourses, practices, and institutions were reproduced and reinforced.

A further issue to ponder, then, is the notion that there is a 'dialectical relationship between the exercise of power and its legitimation' — a notion perhaps implying that the exercise of power and the legitimation of power are necessarily independent processes.[22] The legitimation of power may be better seen as a part of the exercise of power, legitimation and exercise both working through the same actions and the same discourses. To classify an act as one of violence may have been a means to bring it into the remit of the royal courts as well as to justify its hearing there, at a time when jurisdictional rights over property cases were less clear.[23] Similarly, the hearing of complaints is a vital function of any figure in power, and the language of complaint runs through the documents analysed in the article.[24] The aim of the ruler was to be the most effective answerer of complaints, to instil the assumption that he was the proper source of remedy: the distinction between exercise of power and its legitimation breaks down. Practice and legitimation of practice may be inseparable.

All such analyses of the legitimation of royal authority may be furthered by a comparative approach. To a historian of England, much in Maribel's article is familiar. For example, there is justification through both the good old law or custom and an emphasis on the legitimacy of new royal law.[25] There are royal investigations into the truth. But interestingly it is in the rhetoric of truth that a significant difference can be found between the Leonese-Castilian rhetoric and the English. In the Spanish documentation the word 'ueritas' seems occasionally to be used to mean 'good title' to property in a way in which — so far as I am aware — it is not in England; thus there is reference to men 'who used to hold those inheritances *sine ueritate*'.[26] Such a difference of usage re-emphasises the significance of the way in which these Leonese-Castilian texts sometimes objectify 'the truth'.

As I have said, one of the great virtues of Maribel's article is that it examines more than one legitimatory discourse. This leads on to a final thought. When I first visited the CSIC, at Maribel's invitation in 1998, I was impressed by the continuation of work — including hers of course — in the *Annales* tradition, integrating the social, the economic, the political. The shift to a focus on discourse, and indeed on legitimation

---

21 My thinking here is influenced by the writings within 'Critical Legal Studies'; a good starting point is Kelman, *A Guide to Critical Legal Studies*.

22 See below, p. 90; also pp. 93–94.

23 See McHaffie, 'Law and Violence'. See below, p. 100.

24 See below, p. 105 ('querimonia'), p. 109 ('querela').

25 See below, p. 113. Note also p. 108 for justification through the activity of grandparent.

26 See below, p. 100; note also pp. 106, 117, 118. cf. p. 103 'ueritatem ignorantes', and also pp. 118, 119. Note also p. 122 for developments taking place without the influence of Roman Law.

of power, can endanger such a commitment to *histoire totale*. Yet really it should just be an additional step towards completeness of analysis. Maribel's project on 'Procesos Judiciales en los del norte peninsular (ss. IX–XI)' allows such a development. The material assembled is analysable from a multiplicity of perspectives. The welcome renewed focus on the more discretely judicial and legal aspects given, for example, by Wendy Davies' work on the workings of courts in northern Iberia can be continued alongside assessment of legitimatory and other discourses.[27] And crucially, the mass of material will allow the analysis of disputes within their socio-economic circumstances. Such analysis will be invaluable both for its own sake and for the better understanding of the legitimatory discourses of the documents that Maribel analyses so well in the present piece.

---

27 See e.g. Davies, 'Summary justice'. However, note also Reynolds, 'Assembly government'.

Bibliography

Davies, Wendy, 'Summary Justice and Seigneurial Justice in Northern Iberia on the Eve of the Millennium', *Haskins Society Journal*, 22 (2012), 43–58

Gillingham, John, 'Kingship, Chivalry and Love: Political and Cultural Values in the Earliest History Written in French: Geoffrey Gaimar's *Estoire des Engleis*', in *Anglo-Norman Political Culture and the Twelfth-Century Renaissance: Proceedings of the Borchard Conference on Anglo-Norman History, 1995*, ed. by Charles Warren Hollister (Woodbridge: Boydell, 1997), pp. 33–58

Kelman, Mark, *A Guide to Critical Legal Studies* (Cambridge MA: Harvard University Press, 1987)

McHaffie, Matthew, 'Law and Violence in Eleventh-Century France', *Past and Present*, 238 (2018), 3–41

Reynolds, Susan, 'Assembly Government and Assembly Law', in *Gender and Historiography: Studies in the Earlier Middle Ages in Honour of Pauline Stafford*, ed. by Janet L. Nelson, Susan Reynolds, and Susan Johns (London: University of London Press, 2012), pp. 191–99

ISABEL ALFONSO

Judicial Rhetoric and Political Legitimation in Medieval León-Castile[*]

Royal assemblies — variously referred to as *concilia, curiae,* or *cortes* in contemporary documents — have often been studied in their guise as the forerunners of their better developed institutional descendants, be they parliaments, royal tribunals, or royal consultative assemblies.[1] Those who have studied them have therefore for the most part concentrated on evaluating the king's capabilities or limitations with respect to the judicial, legislative, and governmental tasks that the development of those institutions demanded.[2]

This area of investigation, which has usually been approached from decidedly traditional analytical angles, proves richly rewarding when seen from a novel perspective, from which royal assemblies are perceived as public spaces in which the distribution of political power was debated and legitimized; in which certain behavioural models concerning the transmission and maintenance of power and the functions of those who wielded it were enacted and consolidated while others were — either explicitly or by implication — rejected; in which reputation, prestige, honour, and dignity, as well as their opposite qualities, received public expression; in which political relations were competitively negotiated and defined; and in which participants were educated in the practices upon which that political competition was based.[3]

I shall adopt this perspective in order to examine the processes of legitimation that developed in the context of royal judicial assemblies and the discourses that these generated. I shall pay particular attention to those royal gatherings presented by the sources as courts at which a king heard and resolved disputes. An important aspect of this investigation concerns the ways by which the king's own image and authority, as well as the nature of his power are constructed before the community of lay and ecclesiastical aristocrats attending royal judicial assemblies. Indeed, it

---

[*] Original publication: Alfonso, Isabel, 'Judicial Rhetoric and Political Legitimation in Medieval León-Castile', in *Building Legitimacy: Political Discourses and Forms of Legitimacy in Medieval Societies*, ed. by Julio Escalona, Isabel Alfonso and Hugh Kennedy (Leiden: Brill, 2004), pp. 51–88.

[1] This paper was originally presented at the University of St Andrews in March 2001 at one of the sessions of the symposium entitled *Political Discourses and Processes of Legitimation*, held jointly by the Consejo Superior de Investigaciones Científicas, Madrid, and the Department of Medieval History of the University of St Andrews. I am very grateful to the members of that department for their criticism and suggestions for improvements, and to Julio Escalona, Stephen D. White, Susan Reynolds and Paul Fouracre for their useful comments on its most recent draft.

[2] See, for example, the collection of studies published in *Cortes, Concilios y Fueros; Las Cortes de Castilla y León en la Edad Media; Las Cortes de Castilla y León, 1188–1988,* and the bibliography that is cited there.

[3] For a discussion of the political sphere as an area in which rivals competed over resources, see Alfonso, 'Venganza y justicia' [Editors' note: For an English translation, see chapter 5 of this volume].

was the dialectic interaction between king and aristocratic groupings that provided the yardstick whereby individual monarchs' authority and the effectiveness of its imposition were measured: through which, in other words, their power was legitimized.

It is not the purpose of this article to comment on the means whereby royal courts were convoked or the nature of those who attended. Neither is it to describe the disputes that were heard there. Suffice it to say that these assemblies are presented in our sources as royal gatherings whose most exalted members often enjoyed close ties to the king. They are generally depicted as solemn and magnificent affairs which we might classify as public spectacles of a ritual type, ideally suited to the ideological representation of royal authority.

Careful analysis of these gatherings reveals much, not only about the official discourses of legitimation that were developed there, but also about the mechanisms whereby royal judicial assemblies were transformed into spaces of legitimation in their own right. The analysis of those mechanisms is another of the principal aims of this investigation.

The records of certain court cases brought before the kings of León and Castile in the eleventh and twelfth centuries by some of the most important religious institutions of those kingdoms provide the documentary basis upon which this investigation is constructed.[4] These texts touch upon three different issues. The first concerns the documents themselves, which as records of royal justice not only contained important expressions of power, but also served as a fundamental tool in its creation. The second concerns the idea that royal courts were important environments of socialization where cultural values were transmitted and learned. The third concerns the concept of legitimation as a social, political and cultural process.

Bearing in mind the comparative framework within which this study has been conceived, it is worth reflecting briefly on the nature of the documents on which it is based to interpret them, and the ways in which their analysis has been approached. It is also worth emphasizing the need to deepen our knowledge regarding their production, conservation, and functions. The predominantly ecclesiastical nature of these sources obviously conditions the information they contain to such an extent that their origin must be kept constantly in mind by anyone attempting their interpretation. It is therefore very important that we take into account their function with respect to the institutions that issued them, and the context that lent credibility to their contents, though this, of course, is not necessarily described by the texts themselves. It is also essential to note that most of our sources concerning this period are not in fact originals, but later copies that were preserved in twelfth-century cartularies. The implications of this fact are in urgent need of further investigation.[5] Finally, we must examine closely those aspects of our sources that might be identified as topoi of the

---

4 The documentary collections used are those of the Cathedrals of León and Astorga and the monasteries of Celanova and Sahagún, together with some editions of the royal charters of Alfonso V, Alfonso VI, Fernando II, Alfonso IX.

5 See Lucas Álvarez, *Las cancillerías reales (1109–1230)*; Lucas Álvarez, *Cancillerías reales astur-leonesas (718–1072)*, for a study of the diplomatics of royal documents, and Fernández Flórez, *La elaboración de los documentos*, on the production of documents in the Christian kingdoms of Western Iberia.

formulation of legal narrative. Rather than simply representing procedural formalities or conventional formulae, I will argue that these constituted communicative and representative strategies designed to dress the claims and resolutions made at royal judicial assemblies in a cloak, of justice and, in the final analysis, legitimacy.[6]

Most of the documents examined here concern legal suits brought before the king by ecclesiastical institutions intent on reclaiming property that had been seized from them or jurisdiction that had been usurped. Although they describe judicial processes that took place within the context of royal assemblies, they are not necessarily the work of legal scribes who recorded the business transacted there for strictly administrative purposes. Instead, they are for the most part narratives formulated by ecclesiastical litigants who, despite recording the arguments put forward by their adversaries, presented a version of events that was invariably conditioned by a desire to enhance the legitimacy of a ruling that found in their own favour. However, our sources' obvious partiality should not blind us to the fact that their assertions with respect to the functions of the Crown, justice and criminality, rights and obligations and the proper means whereby these should be transmitted were understood (and possibly even shared despite being disputed) by the political community to which they were directed and within which the disputes with which they were associated took place. Just as Martin has said of heroic narratives, one might say that the language of these sources establishes models of both 'good' and 'bad' behaviour.[7]

We know very little about the process whereby these documents were written and made public. However, some of them contain evidence suggesting that they were issued after the passing of judicial decisions in order that they might then be read out and publicly ratified before the assemblies that had contributed to and witnessed the debates and resolutions they recorded. The documents themselves therefore did not, as is commonly assumed, simply represent an official record of judgements that could be presented in the event of future legal challenges. At a more fundamental level, they also served as vehicles for the communication of the means whereby those decisions had been made, and the social networks that had been activated in the process. In this sense, these documents were themselves the fruit of a process of political legitimation, and should be considered as social constructs in which language and practice were inextricably linked. It is for this reason that we must pay especially close attention to the processes whereby our sources were created. Although they certainly do not conform to any single diplomatic model and their contents vary widely, they nevertheless display certain common elements that deserve comment.

The term 'legal rhetoric' is employed here in reference to the existence and significance of discourses developed to represent the royal activities of judging and setting disputes, or even simply presiding over judicial processes. This specific term is used because the discourses in question clearly had an audience. By examining

---

6 On the nature, and classification of procedural documents see Prieto Morera, 'El proceso en el Reino de León', pp. 386–89. For an interesting discussion of the character of judicial narratives in the context of Italian communal justice, see Wickham, *Legge, patriche e conflitti*.

7 Martin, 'Le récit héroïque', p. 150.

96   ISABEL ALFONSO

the 'judicial rhetoric' used in our sources, it is possible to identify those elements within them that contribute most significantly to the fulfilment of their function as self-reinforcing social and political instruments. As proposed by Miller, such rhetoric, far from merely representing discursive convention, is in fact intricately bound up with both power and violence.[8] It is worth noting that the very production of the documents on which this study is based presupposed the recognition of royal power and represented a declaration of its validity and a glorification of royal justice. In this respect, I shall argue that the nature of royal authority was to a great extent defined and consolidated within the context of royal justice, which constituted what Maurice Bloch would term 'practical political ideology'.[9]

In the judicial sphere, royal legitimation was promoted through the employment of diverse rhetorical devices. These deserve careful analysis, as they served not only to define the dynamics of power, but also to establish moral portraits of those who wielded it. In examining them, I will focus first of all on those discourses that emphasized the restoration of social order, and then on the rhetoric of truth that is to be found within them.

Judicial Rhetoric and the Politics of Restoration

In 1018, the Abbot of Sahagún, one of the most powerful monasteries in the Kingdom of León, requested Alfonso V's help in rectifying the damage it had suffered during the king's minority due to the unlawful entry of royal officials (*scurrones*) into monastic settlements and the unjust and unprecedented demands they had made of them. This request was framed by an appeal to common knowledge of how Sahagún had been founded and endowed by the king's ancestors:

> It is known by many and not to a few has it been declared that King Don Alfonso and his wife, Doña Jimena, built a monastery called Santos Facundo y Primitivo on the shore of river Cea, and that to this monastery they granted full-ownership of *villae*, together with their inhabitants, as is written in their charter. They remained in possession of this places since the time of this king, and then of his brother King Ramiro, and of those who succeeded them in the kingdom, until the days of Alfonso, son of Prince Vermudo, during whose infancy the royal officers entered those *villae* and behaved unsuitably. In the face of this the brethren, together with their abbot, the beloved Egilanus, felt defiled, for they were undergoing actions that were not contemplated in the old customs.[10]

---

8   Miller, *Bloodtaking*, p. 3.
9   Bloch, *Political Language*.
10 'A multis quidem est notum et non a paucis manet declaratum eo quod edificauit rex domnus Adefonsus et coniux eius domna Xemena arcisterium, uocabulo Sancti Facundi et Primitiui; super crepidinis aluei Ceia; et ad ipsum monasterium concederunt uillas et omnes habitants in eas ab integro, secundum quod in eius testamentum resonat. Tenentes fratres de hunc locum iam taxatum tempore ipsius regis, postea frater eius Raimrus rex uel qui post eos suceeserunt in regno usque ad

This complaint was heard in the Monastery of Sahagún itself by the king who, we are informed, had been guided there along with his wife the Queen Elvira, by the will of God once Alfonso had attained his majority. The document recording the event employs direct speech to report the plea made by the abbot and monks as they lay prostrate at the king's feet: 'Our lord and great prince! Lend your ears to hear and your heart to understand this document that was issued by your grandparents':

> and this prince, with full understanding and truthful discernment, together with his wife, the glorious Queen Elvira, was led by God to the house and to those holy bodies, and they received them with gladness and full of joy and happiness. Seating in this monastery, the abbot who ruled it, together with his brethren, fell to the prince's feet and said: 'Our lord and great prince! Prepare your ears to hear and your heart to understand and listen to the charter that your forefathers issued'.[11]

Moved to mercy by this outburst, Alfonso V had the testament that the monks had presented to him read out in the presence of all of the magnates of his court, after which he recognized its validity and confirmed it before the assembled company, with the words: 'Let this pact, which was custom in ancient times, be confirmed and strengthened':

> He, truly moved by mercy, ordered that this charter be read before all the magnates of his palace and then, recognizing that the fact was true, said before the whole assembly: 'This agreement shall remain valid and firm as it was customary in the ancient times'.[12]

The narrative is then continued in the first person by the king who, appealing to divine mercy and to the memory of his grandparents, issued a charter of restoration exempting the monastery's settlements from the dues that had allegedly been wrongfully demanded of them (these were taxes that were habitually mentioned in royal concessions of fiscal immunity like fines for homicide, theft, and kidnapping) and confirming the integrity of the monks' jurisdiction:

---

dies Adefonsi, prolis Ueremudi principis, adhuc permanente in puericia, ingressi fuerunt scurrones in eius uillulis et fecerunt in eis quod illis non decebat. Dum uiderunt se ipsi fratres, una cum abbate carum Egilani, in angustia positi et que faciebant super eos quod ab antiquis temporibus usualem non abuerant' (SFPSahagun404, 1018). A twelfth-century copy in the cartulary known as *Becerro Gótico de Sahagún*, Madrid, AHN, Códices, L.989, fol. 8ᵛ.

11 'et ipse principe, plenum intellectum et uera intelligendum, duxit eum Deus, una pariter cum coniuge eius gloriosa regina Geluira, ad ipsum domum et corpos sanctos; et collegerunt eos, cum susceptione et omni gaudio et letitia plene. Sedentes intus monasterii, ipse abbas qui regebat hunc monasterium cecidit, una pariter cum collegas suos, ad pedes ipsius principis et dixerunt: "Domnus noster et princeps magne! Pone aurem ad audiendum et cor ad intelligendum et audi hunc scriptum que fecerunt aui tui"' (SFPSahagun404, 1018).

12 'Ille, uero, motus misericordia, ordinauit coram omnes magnates palacii legere ipsum testamentum et dum agnouit ueraciter factum dixit coram omni concilio: Abeat roborem et firmitatem pactum istum quod ab antiquis temporibus fuit usum'. (SFPSahagun404, 1018).

And thenceforth, I, Alfonso, supported in the throne of my grandparents by God's mercy, grant to you, Abbot Don Egilanus, and all [the community of] Santos Facundo y Primitivo, a charter of restoration so that from now onwards none shall disturb those *villas* that are under your rule, neither for homicides, nor for thefts, abductions, nor for any other reason. They shall remain rightly and fully under your control.[13]

It is remarkable how this text establishes an association between royal greatness and policies aimed at the restoration of monastic dominions in three distinct ways. In the first instance, it does so by describing in great detail the *ad hoc* transformation of the cloister into a forum of royal justice: the monastery, which is the scene of the action, is presented as a sacred space to which kings are guided by divine providence, and a fundamental point of contact between secular and spiritual powers.[14] Secondly, it contrasts periods of political order and political disorder, and links them to both the weakness or strength of individual monarchs and the fortunes of the monastery itself. In connection with this, it also describes a specific type of royal legitimacy which it links explicitly to the protection of monastic property. It thus relates the history of the foundation and endowment of the monastery by Alfonso V's royal ancestors in such a way as to emphasize his descent from the illustrious kings Alfonso III, who reigned during the second half of the ninth century, and Ramiro, who is not further identified. It goes on to state that the monastery had enjoyed its endowments in peace from the time of those kings until Alfonso V's own minority, omitting any mention of other reigns and events that were detrimental to the monastery, of which we are informed by other sources. In this case such an omission seems to have been made in order to contrast more clearly the two distinct phases into which the royal career of the king before whom they were airing their grievances was divided.[15]

---

13 'Ob inde, sub misericordia Domini, ego Adefonsus, in solio auorum meorum fultus, uobis domno Egila abba uel omnium Santorum Facundi et Primitiui facio uobis scriptum restaurationis ut amplius et deinceps non faciant uobis unam, in omnes uestras uillas, inquietationem, que uestra ordinacione discurrunt: non pro omicidio, nee pro furto, nee pro roixo, nee pro aliqua causa, sed sana et integrata maneat sub dicioni uestre' (SFPSahagun404, 1018).

14 On the construction of spaces of power, see De Jong and Theuws, eds, *Topographies of Power*.

15 The references to kings made in this document are vague enough to lend themselves readily to erroneous interpretations. Indeed, its identification of Ramiro as the king's brother supports Isla's theory that the Alfonso mentioned in the document was in fact Alfonso IV the Monk (Isla Frez, 'La monarquía leonesa', p. 47). However, the document's own identification of Alfonso and his wife as the monastery's founders leads me to believe that it in fact refers to Alfonso III. This is also the opinion of Herrero, who has edited the document (Herrero de la Fuente, *Colección Diplomática del Monasterio de Sahagún, Vol. II*, pp. 49–51). It is of course possible that the original version of the charter, written by the famous Sampiro (monk, priest, bishop and royal notary), referred to and distinguished additional kings, and that the twelfth-century scribe who copied it, acting in accordance with different interests from those of the original author, edited them out, retaining only the idea of Alfonso V's restorative efforts and his ties to Sahagún's great royal founder. Indeed, Herrero's study indicates that the preambles of many earlier documents were suppressed when they were copied for inclusion in the cartulary (Herrero de la Fuente, *Colección Diplomática del Monasterio de Sahagún, Vol. II*, pp. xxx–xxxvii). It is possible that the King Ramiro who is mentioned in the document was in fact Ramiro II, given the favourable attitude displayed

JUDICIAL RHETORIC AND POLITICAL LEGITIMATION IN MEDIEVAL LEÓN-CASTILE   99

The documents recording the numerous disputes brought before Alfonso V, even before he attained his majority, by the powerful Galician monastery of Celanova contain discourses of legitimacy that were rather more complex and multi-faceted than those found in the Sahagún documents. The sheer abundance of legal battles waged by Celanova can perhaps be attributed to its being under the patronage of the most powerful member of the Galician nobility, Count Gutierre Menéndez and the proximity that that nobleman's position as regent granted him to the king's own person. His status and political position may also have lain behind the fact that some of the monastery's judicial records can be seen as both monastic and familiar chronicles, as it were. By establishing genealogical connections between the house of the Galician count and the royal family, these narratives effectively emphasized the legitimacy of both, since explicit statements of kin connections, far from being neutral, are heavily loaded with meaning.[16]

The surviving documentary record of a Celanovan case of 1007 is typical in this respect.[17] The arguments put forward to justify the claims of Celanova's abbot are developed in the context of a long and complex narrative relating the history of the territories under dispute in connection with the authority of the families of both king and count, whose genealogies and continuity are shown to be closely interlinked. We are informed that the property was confiscated by Alfonso III from its original owner, a rebellious dux called Vitiza, and given instead to Count Hermenegildo Gutiérrez, who had loyally quashed the duke's uprising. The count and his descendants, among whom the document cites Bishop Rosendo, the founder of Celanova, were confirmed in their possession of the confiscated property by all of the kings who followed Alfonso. These confirmations are mentioned in the course of the narrative, as are the uncertainties that threatened the property's integrity due to hereditary divisions made by Count Hermenegildo himself. The document also identifies a section of the property that was donated to Celanova by Bishop Rosendo and the dux Froila, who were the children of Count Gutierre Menéndez and therefore also direct descendants of Count Hermenegildo, but also the text states that the monastery had no problem in holding onto the territory until after the brothers had died. Thereafter, we are told, outsiders with no local connections usurped this monastic property, thereby incurring 'not a few but many ills' ('disturbationes […] non paruae sed multe') and provoking the first of many disputes about it to be brought before a royal court — this time that of Vermudo II (982–99), who ruled that the property should be returned to the monastery and the order of his royal ancestor respected. Together with the bishops and magnates of his court, Vermudo also confirmed the bequests made to Celanova by Bishop Rosendo. However, we are told that after his death, 'thiefs and foreign men' ('raptores et extranei homines') once again seized the disputed territories.

---

by Sampiro in his chronicle towards that monarch, which is discussed by Isla in the work cited above (Isla Frez, 'La monarquía leonesa', p. 45).

16 Bourdieu, *El sentido práctico*, ch. 2, pp. 267 ff.

17 AlfonsoV-4 (1007). A copy in the cartulary known as *Tumbo de Celanova*, Madrid, AHN, Códices, L. 986, fols 4ᵛ–5ʳ. [Editors' note: this charter has also been edited as SSCelanova3 (1007). The full text of this latter edition is available at the PRJ's website: http://prj.csic.es/descargarPDF.php?id=215 [Date accessed: 22 February 2022].

The narrative continues by introducing Alfonso V, who had been called upon to arrange the latest resolution of the dispute, of whom it paints the most magnificent of pictures. Born by God's will, he was said to have been raised to the throne of his forefathers in the royal seat of León with the unanimous approval of a great council that had gathered there and also with divine approval:

> And when the abovementioned king, Don Vermudo, died, God raised his offspring, Don Alfonso, and being gathered in one assembly, those from Castile, *Terra de Foris* [León], Galicia and Asturias, elevated the king to the chair of his grandparents and parents in the royal seat in León, all together in one accord, praising and thanking God.[18]

The document then proceeds to list the king's many qualities — 'and the abovementioned king, the emperor, who knows all, and distributes all, and judges everything rightfully' ('et rex supra dictus imperator iam sciens omnia, et diuidens cuncta et prout opus erat recte diiudicans universa') —[19] by way of introduction to the subject of the old dispute that had been brought before him and Count Menendo Gonzalez by the abbot and monks of Celanova.[20] The count is described as divinely appointed regent and tutor of the king and also as governing the region of Galicia by divine will and royal command:

> And then the abovementioned Abbot Manilla, together with the brethren of the abovementioned monastery, complained to the aforesaid and most serene prince in many places, and before the great Count Menendo González, appointed tutor and regent, who governed in peace all the lands of Galicia under God's and the king's authority.[21]

The description of the hearing, which took place in a Galician village, contains a detailed account of the count's genealogy, through which he is linked to the original aristocratic owner of the disputed territories. His family history is then used to justify the court's decision that the disputed bequests should be returned to the monastery without delay and thenceforth enjoyed by the monks in peace, as they had been held 'without truth' by its adversaries:

> Once the king was seating in *Villa Gomarici*, and together with him was the said duke Menendo González, who was a descendant of the offspring of Count

---

18 'Et defuncto autem supradicto rege domno Uerremudo (*sic*), suscitauit Deus semen illius regem domnum Adefonsum et collecto concilio Castelle, terre Forinseze, Galleciense uel Asturiense, leuauerunt cum regem super cathedram auorum et parentum suorum in sede regia Legionense, omnes una uoluntate Deo laudes reddentes et gratias agentes' (AlfonsoV-4, 1007).

19 Andrade reads *dividiens* (AlfonsoV-4, 1007).

20 The association made here between Alfonso V and David has been identified in Isla Frez, *Realezas hispánicas*, p. 96.

21 'Iterum facit ipse supradictus Manilla abbas, et fratres supradicti monasterii, querimoniam ante prefatum et serenissimun principem in multis locis, et ante cum sedentem comes magnus Menindus Gundisaluit, qui ex sub divino nutu creator et nutritor erat et omnem terram Gallecie, sub Dei et ipsius imperio regis, iuri quieta obtineba' (AlfonsoV-4, 1007).

Hermenegildo, of blessed memory, and a grandson of the abovementioned bishop, and having been purified and blessed, the king and this count appointed a judge of the palace, Pelayo, son of Aroalvus, who had been designated as a royal judge, to go to the lands of the abovementioned districts and to call before him all the *infanzones* and all the men who held those estates unlawfully, or had acquired them through purchase, or by any request, from the death of the abovementioned bishop until now, so that they relinquished them to the monastery without delay and without any further attack or disruption.[22]

In the event, however, this decision was never imposed as the king, moved to mercy together with the count and the abbot of Celanova, renegotiated the conditions under which these men, who had originally been described as thieves and foreigners but were now identified as members of the lower nobility (*infanzones*), were either to return the property in question or continue to possess it as monastic tenants.[23]

And moved by mercy, that most serene prince, and that count and that abbot, Manilla, ordered that those who held or possessed those estates be given half of their price by the monastery if there were men living [in them], and if the men were dead they should be deprived of them and everything should be returned to the monastery.[24]

The questions raised by this document are too numerous and wide-ranging for us to attempt to answer them all within the context of the present study. There are, however, a few whose relevance to our topic deserves special emphasis. It is clear, for example, that a narrative such as this, in which the continuity of a royal line of descent is stressed while interruptions in its genealogical history are quietly swept under the carpet, was not constructed merely to record the result of a monastic land dispute.[25] Through their account of the history of these disputed lands, the monks of Celanova presented their claim as having a certain status that was linked to both the

---

22 'Et rex in uilla Gomarici sedens et ipse iam dictus dux Menendus Gundisaluit, qui ex semine supra memorati Hermegildi comitis descendit et neptus supra dicti pontificis et ab eo sanctificatus et benedictus abebatur, elegit rex et ipse comes iudicem de palatio Pelagium, Aroalui filiium, qui iudex erat constitutus a rege, ut ueniret in medio terre supradicte mandationes et uenirent ante eum omnes infanzones et homines qui ipsas hereditates sine ueritate tenebant, siue de comparatione, uel de quacumque petitione uel de obitum supradicti pontificiis usque nunc tempus, relinquerunt eas post partem monasterii absque alia dilatione et sine aliqua postea irruptione uel disturbatione' (AlfonsoV-4, 1007).

23 It is interesting to note that it was in fact *infanzones* as representatives of local power groups, who were the principal claimants and occupants of monastic property. I have examined the tensions that existed between these groups and monastic institutions in various different areas and periods in Alfonso, 'Resolución de disputas'; Alfonso, 'Litigios por la tierra' [Editors' note: For an English translation, see chapter 13 of this volume]; Alfonso, 'Conflictos en las behetrías', with further bibliography.

24 'Et misericordia motus, ipse serenissimus princeps, et ipse comes et ipse Manillani abbas, ordinauerunt ad ipsos qui ipsas hereditates tenebant uel possidebant, ut ornarent eis medium pretium, de parte ipsorum monasteriorum unde fuerint homines uiui, unde fuerint autem mortui careant omnia ab integro et tornet se totum post partem monasterii' (AlfonsoV-4, 1007).

25 One might, for example, examine the very object of the dispute, as the terminology used to describe

fortunes of the monarchy and the relationship of their own patrons with the king. The process whereby the monks thus consolidated their status also served clearly to reinforce the foundations on which Alfonso V's own power rested as this, just like the possession of land, as legitimized through proof of inheritance. What is more, the passage of rime is marked in this narrative by successive royal confirmations of an original donation to the monastery in such a way as to present royal policy as one of continuous protection of ecclesiastical patrimony. Finally, the document's depiction of this public legal ritual in such a way as to emphasize the historical continuity of the monastery's patronage by the king's royal forefathers must also be interpreted as an affirmation of a kind of inherited symbolic capital, which was the collective fruit of all of the individual alliances through which its subjects' blood, prestige, and superiority were exalted before the political community in the assembly. Both trials described in the document, the one heard by Vermudo II and the other brought before Alfonso V, are presented in such a way as to negate the possibility that the monastery's adversaries might have had any worthwhile arguments with which to defend their claims against Celanova. Instead, they are depicted as acts of restitution of property over which the Church held unchallengeable rights.[26] Although this is clearly a biased account, it nevertheless hints at the difficulties faced by this Galician abbey when it came to imposing their exclusive dominance on areas in which they had to compete with other power groups.

This ecclesiastical discourse thus employs the rhetoric of restoration to legitimize royal justice and presents royal genealogies in such a way as to emphasize their positive aspects while totally suppressing other less savoury ones. This is most evident in the case of Fernando I (1037–1065), whose assumption of the throne of León as a result of his marriage is presented as following smoothly and directly on from the reign of his father-in-law, Alfonso V. What this version of events fails to reveal is that his path to the throne was in fact rather bloody and led to the death of his brother-in-law and rival Vermudo III on the battlefield on which the two clashed. In this case, it is particularly interesting to note that the position of a king who was, according to general opinion, the founder of a new dynasty was legitimized through his representation as the continuator of the ideals and spirit attributed to the reigns of his wife's most illustrious royal ancestors.[27] This is illustrated in the lengthy preamble to one of Fernando I's judgments.[28] The stated aim of this introductory narrative, in which

---

it varies greatly through the document (*omnen terram, mandationes de […] et homines habitants, hereditates mandationem*).

26 The phrase *cunctis uiuentibus inreuocabiliter hereditas est* is especially interesting in this respect, as it is reminiscent of the terms used to express the concept of absolute ownership 'against the world' identified by Milson as a constituent part of the property law that was imposed in England by Common Law (Milsom, *The Legal Framework of English Feudalism*; Milsom, *Historical Foundations of the Common Law*). A critique of the rigidity of his interpretation of these terms, which in my view is justified, can be found in White, 'Inheritances and Legal Arguments'. However, the appearance of this phrase may be the result of interpolations made in the twelfth century copy of the document in which it appears.

27 A more generalized overview of these reigns can he found in Isla Frez, *Realezas hispánicas*.

28 CatAstorga306 (1046). It is a seventeenth-century cartulary copy preserved in Madrid, BNE, MS 1195b, fols 14–15.

JUDICIAL RHETORIC AND POLITICAL LEGITIMATION IN MEDIEVAL LEÓN-CASTILE   103

Fernando I addresses the assembled court in the first person, is to render a faithful account of the events that led up to the ruling in question. In his speech, the king makes an explicit link between his own political agenda concerning the restoration and protection of Church property and that of his father-in-law, Alfonso V — who is also described as 'Great' in the document — which had been cut short by the celebrated king's death. This document, which was drawn up in 1046, is among those most often cited as evidence of Fernando I's reconstructive policies. It is therefore also extremely relevant with respect to the 'rhetoric of legitimacy' that we have been discussing. Its preamble begins with an account of how Femando, king by the grace of God, gathered his faithful subjects together at a royal council. There he, together with his wife Queen Sancha, celebrated the good deeds of his predecessor Alfonso V, who, after defeating the Muslims, had summoned a council at which he had ordered the restitution of ecclesiastical property and enlarged the holdings of the Church in general:

> Under the authority [of Christ] and of his mother, Saint Mary always Virgin. I, Fernando, king by the will of God, together with my wife, Queen Sancha, have seen for it to be known and understood by the council of the faithful our kingdom, and by those present and by those who shall be born in the future, so that all of them shall comprehend and acknowledge, and recognize as truthful, all the good deeds that were made in the days of Prince Don Alfonso [V], our father-in-law, who defeated the Muslims, and enlarged the churches and increased their properties, and summoned all his faithful men to a council, and ordered that each should have their estates, both the church as well as those of the highest and the lowest orders in the provinces of his kingdom.[29]

The narrative continues with an account of the anarchy that followed Alfonso V's death, with special reference to the damage done at that time to ecclesiastical property and the kingdom's faithful as a result of the armed conflicts that broke out among its subjects:

> After the death of this most glorious and serene king, of blessed memory, some wicked men, ignorant of the truth, arose in his kingdom and seized and damaged the estates of the Church, and the faithful of the kingdom were reduced to nothing. And this was because they all slaughtered each other with their swords.[30]

---

29 'Sub ipsius imperio et illius genitricis Sanctae Mariae semper virginis. Fredinandus, gratia Dei rex, una cum uxore mea Sanctia, Regina, scire atque nosse facere curauimus fideli concilio regni nostri ut presents et quia postea ad synodum posteritatis nostrae nascendo venture sun tut vere sciant et intellegant, atque certe agnoscant eo quod in diebus domini Adefonsi principis, soceri nostri, quanta et qualia bona fecerint regioni suae qui omni tempore vitae suae gentem muzleimitarum detruncauit, et ecclesias ampliavit et val de omnibus bonis suis ditavit et omnes homines fideliter ad synodum congregauit, atque unus quisque hereditatem suam habere precepit tam ecclesiis su cunctis magnis, vel minimis regni sui provinciis' (CatAstorga306, 1046).

30 'Post mortem uero ipsius divae memoriae gloriossissimi et serenissimi regis, surrexerunt in regnum suum viri peruersi, veritatem ignorantes et extraneaverunt atque vitiauerunt hereditates ecclesiae et

104   ISABEL ALFONSO

It is onto this bleak background that the subject of the new king's project of ecclesiastical restoration is introduced once, as is also the case in the previous narratives we have examined, the divine approval in which his ascent to the throne was shrouded has been emphasized, combined in this case with the acceptance of 'the faithful', who are also identified here as victims of the political turmoil described:

> And after a long time, with the care of divine clemency and the protection of His mercy, we were granted the apex of the Kingdom, and received the throne of glory from the Lord's hand and from all the faithful.[31]

We are then informed that the king had inherited his reconstructive policies from his royal ancestors, and that these consisted in ordering royal enquiries into ecclesiastical holdings, appointing bishops in every see, for them to restore churches and make the Christian faith recover, so that, by his authority, they maintain both 'within the framework of the Church':

> we ordered that the estates of the church be investigated, as we know it was done by our ancestors and earlier kings. We ordered that bishops be appointed to the sees for the churches to be restored and for the restoration of the Christian faith, so that under our authority they could honestly obtain their dioceses and estates and control them firmly under the power of the church.[32]

It was in precisely this restorative context that Fernando I sent out one of his faithful royal officials (*sayon*) to investigate the rights claimed by the bishopric of Astorga over certain properties. The mission must have been a rather difficult one, as the unfortunate royal official to whom it was entrusted met his death at the hands of the inhabitants of the disputed settlement while on the job. The king subsequently summoned a legal assembly at which he, 'choosing the truth of heaven' ('caelum veritatis eligentes'), invoked both Canon Law and Gothic legal codes before establishing exemplary punishments for the rebellious peasants and ordering the restitution of their village to the see of Astorga. The document recording these events is extremely well known due to its relevance to the history of peasant uprisings and their suppression, and deserves much more detailed analysis than I can undertake here.[33]

---

fideles regni ipsius ad nihilum redacti sunt. Proter quod unusquisque ipsorum unus inter alio gladio se tracidauerint' (CatAstorga306, 1046).

[31] 'Post plurimis namque temporibus, diuina procurante clementia et eius misericordia protegente, dum nos apicem Regni concedimus, et tronum gloriae de manu Domini et ab universis fidelibus accepimus' (CatAstorga306, 1046).

[32] 'iussimus perquirere haereditates ecclesiae, sicut ab antecessoribus nostris et prioribus regibus facta cognovimus fecimus ordinare per illas sedes episcopos ad restaurandum ecclesias et recreandum fidei christianae, per nostrum nanque auctoritatem illius diocessis et haereditatibus fideliter acquississent et sub potestate eclesiae firmiter subiugassent' (CatAstorga306, 1046).

[33] This document has been studied in both Pastor, *Resistencias y luchas campesinas* and Cabero Domínguez, *Astorga y su territorio*. In a recent article, J. J. Larrea questions both of their theses and disputes the existence of the political transformations that have been associated with the repression of this peasant community (Larrea, 'Villa Matanza'). This disagreement, however, forms part of a broad and longstanding debate over the transition of medieval Christian Iberia to feudalism into which we cannot enter here.

JUDICIAL RHETORIC AND POLITICAL LEGITIMATION IN MEDIEVAL LEÓN-CASTILE 105

Astorga's cathedral archives also contain another, later document in which a similar narrative is employed to highlight Fernando I's efforts at ecclesiastical restoration.[34] Just like its forerunners, this charter also makes much of the general disorder that followed the death of Alfonso V, whom it describes as 'great prince' ('princeps magnus'). Unlike the documents we have just been looking at, however, it also mentions his successor, Vermudo III, under whom, it blandly states, that no property was restored to the church. It then goes on to contrast what is identified as a general decline under Vermudo III with the improvements made by the current king, Fernando I, who is also described as 'great' (*magnus*), through the restitution of bishops to their sees and the granting of legal protection to Church property:

> For many years that remained as it is stated in the charter. The abbots, monks, and nuns hold it undisturbedly under the power of the bishop of the diocese of Astorga, to which they rendered service and paid obedience in a peaceful manner, as it was commanded by all the bishops of Astorga, until death took the great prince, King Don Alfonso, and then the enemies of the church throughout the land ruled by this aforementioned king became restless. In those very days, before his descendant, King Don Vermudo, had received the kingdom, Ero Salidiz, together with his sons, rose violently and seized that monastery from those monks and abbots of Santa María who persisted there, and turned that monastery into a fortress. After some time, the great prince, King Fernando, ruler of the the principality of León, together with his wife, Queen Doña Sancha, by God's command and his own, promised out of his ready mind to appoint Don Diego, even if undeserving, as bishop of that see, and so it was done, and they granted him permission to investigate all the debts and the truth of the see of Astorga, that is, whatever was due to its service.[35]

The family of usurpers described here were members of the local nobility who gave up their claims to ownership of the disputed monastery and acknowledged its belonging to the bishopric:

> That great prince ordered that Ero Salitiz and his sons appear before him. And then Bishop Don Diego denounced them and readily wished them to be judged together with others, as he had commanded, and as did the king and his judges.

---

34 CatAstorga353 (1057). A seventeenth-century copy in Madrid, BNE, MS 1195b, fol. 633.

35 'Permansit ibi plures annos secundum in testamento resonat, tenuerunt illum iuri quieto abbates, monachos vel sorores, sub potestate episcopi sedis astoricensis, et fecerunt ex eo servitum et obedientiam, secundum illos ordinaverint omnes episcopus astoricensis more pacifico usque dum rapuit mors ad principe magno rex domino Adefonso, et tunc soliciti fuerunt omnis adversariis ecclesiae in omnem terram que regebat ille princeps iam de super nominato. In illis vero diebus, antequam regnum accepisset prolem eius, rex domino Bermudo, subrexit Ero Salidiz et filios eijus, per violentia, ut presumpserit ipso monasterio de ipsos monachos et abbates de Sancta Maria, qui ibidem erant permanentes fecerunt illos esse ex torres de ipso monasterio. Ad aliquanto tempore, princeps magno rex Fredinando, in Legione principato regente, cum uxore sua regina domina Sanctia, iussio Dei et illius, annuit mens spontanea ordinare episcopo in sedis astoricensi domino Didaco quamvis indigno, sicuti et fecerunt, et dederunt illi licentia ut exquireret omnem debitum et veritatis huius sedis astoncense qui proprium est debitum ibidem servire' (CatAstorga353, 1057).

But those said people refused to face the bishop in court over that monastery and recognized that it belonged to the estates of Santa María and the lords of that see.[36]

The bishop and canons of Astorga were not alone in lamenting the loss of ecclesiastical property which they reclaimed through royal courts. The archives of the aforementioned Leonese monastery of Sahagún, to cite one more example, contain a document which records a longstanding dispute concerning such property. Once again, churchmen can be seen to have added weight to their claims by associating the stability of their own holdings in particular, and that of the Church in general, with the strength and glory of royal authority:

> a dispute arose [...] before the most serene king, Don Fernando, may his kingdom and his empire be blessed. Abbot Don Ecta, together with Sahagún's college of monks, claimed *Villa Antoniano* and its estates by its ancient boundaries, as it was written in his ancient charter, and as the brethren had governed them from the days of the most serene king, Don Ramiro, until the land had become kingless and the Holy Church had lost its truth.[37]

On visiting Sahagún, Fernando I also issued another charter at the monks' request in which he restored to them the jurisdiction they had exercised over some settlements in a nearby region, after recognizing the written evidence that they had read out before him as truthful and legitimate:

> And I recognize that the charters were truthful and legitimate, and under God's mercy I, the said King Fernando, together with my wife, Queen Sancha, grant you this charter of restoration.[38]

It has been suggested by the editor of Sahagún's cartulary that this document may in fact have been modelled on another, earlier, diploma dating from the reign of Alfonso V which we have already discussed. She also suggests that the issues of restoration and confirmation that are highlighted in these and other documents represent repetitions of borrowed diplomatic formulae.[39] Although diplomatic

---

36 'Ipse autem princeps magnus iussit venire in eius presentia Ero Salitiz et suos filios. Tunc calumniavit eos episcopus dominus Didacus et voluntarie desideravit super ilium facere iudicium et cum plures secundum ille ordinaverit, et ipse rex et eorum judices, seu et illos iam suprataxatos reunxerunt facere judicium cum illo episcopo super ipsa monasteria et cognovenmt quod erat proprium debitum de Sancta Maria et domos de ipsa sede' (CatAstorga353, 1057).

37 'orta fuit intemtio [...] ante serenissimo rege domno Fredenando, cuius regnum et imperium sit in benedictione. Dicebat ipse Abbas domno Ecta, cum collegio fratrum de Santo Facundo, pro Uilla Antoniano et suas hereditates de suis terminis antiquis, sicut in suo testamento antiquo resonat; et quomodo eam iurificarunt fratres in diebus serenissimi regis domni Ranemiri, usque dum peruenit terra sine rege et ecclesia sancta non habebat ueritatem' (SFPSahagun514, 1048). A twelfth-century copy in *Becerro Gótico de Sahagún*, fols 190ᵛ–191ʳ. We shall comment further on the contents and eloquence of this document at a later point.

38 'Vt cognaui quia ueridica essent testamenta et legitima, sub misericordia Domini, ego, iam dictum Fernandus rex, una cum coniuge mea Sancia regina, facimus uobis scriptum restauracionis' (SFPSahagun534, 1049). A twelfth-century copy in *Becerro Gótico de Sahagún*, fol. 11ᵛ.

39 Herrero de la Fuente, *Colección Diplomática del Monasterio de Sahagún, Vol. II*, pp. xl–xli.

JUDICIAL RHETORIC AND POLITICAL LEGITIMATION IN MEDIEVAL LEÓN-CASTILE   107

similarities certainly do exist between these documents, they do not contradict my proposition that the language represents more than the mere repetition of conventional topoi. Indeed, not only do the documents in question display significant variations — like for example the uncharacteristic absence of any allusion to the judicial assembly which reached the decision recorded in the last of them — but the rhetoric of restoration also appears in other contemporary documents that fall into different diplomatic categories. This provides a clear indication that our sources' employment of justificatory discourses that described royal policies that were favourable to the Church can be attributed to motives that went far beyond mere compliance with diplomatic convention. This is further indicated by the presence of such discourses in the documentation of other religious institutions of the period.

The points of reference employed in the development of these discourses changed over time. For example, a document issued by Alfonso VI in 1068 attributes his restorative activity with respect to Sahagún to the same motives as had purportedly inspired Alfonso III before him. However, on this occasion Alfonso III was not identified as the monastery's founder but rather as its restorer; the monastery's adversaries were more vaguely described, as was the chronology of their aggression; and in the final analysis all damage done over the years to the monastery's property was attributed to the devil himself:[40]

> A long time ago God inspired the heart of Prince Alfonso, together with her wife, Queen Doña Jimena, so that venerable place be restored, and he returned all the goods that God had granted it, as it was contained in its charters and was preserved in the parchments that were written by ancient scribes, by royal edicts conforming with God's will, and ordered that all its estates and *villas*, unharmed and intact, be confirmed to this holy and venerable place. Then eventually, injustice arose everywhere and the charity of many faded, and this deed was undone and did not stay as the said charters contain. But then Alfonso, son of the Emperor Fernando, to whom God granted wisdom, knowledge, and intelligence, due to the suggestion of the congregation of the brethren of that place, together with the abbot, called Gonzalo, the provision of divine mercy and his own honour, approved that the possessions of this place should be restored. This great king, pious and merciful, together with all the magnates of his palace, declared that all its villas, together with the men that inhabited those *villas* or who should come to inhabit them, should remain unharmed and that no one should disturb them, as it used to be, under royal authority.[41]

---

40 It is worth noting that weight is added to the monastery's claims in this case when the document in which they are recorded specifies that on this occasion the king restored to the monastery all the possessions listed in its charters and protected by documents drawn up by ancient scribes (*pictoribus*).

41 'A multis namque temporibus transmisit Deus in corde principis Adefonsi, una cum coniuge sua domna Xemena, regina, ut restauraretur hoc uenerabile locum et ut redderet illi, de omnibus bonis quod illi Dominus dederat, quod habebatur in suis scriptionibus et tuebatur in membranis que fuerant scripta ab antiquis pictoribus, per precepta regum priorum permitente Dei uoluntate, et iussit ut omnes suas hereditates et suas uillas illesas et intactas stabilirent ad ipsum sanctum et uenerabile

In this case the restorative activity of a king who is presented as great, pious, merciful, and divinely endowed with wisdom, knowledge, and intelligence, takes the form of a royal confirmation of the monastery's fiscal and jurisdictional immunity.

We can take this argument further. Some later Castilian-Leonese reigns also provide documents concerning some of the same religious institutions mentioned above, in which discourses of legitimation similar to those we have already encountered are employed. Although this is not always explicitly linked to royal assemblies, its connection to environments where royal justice was administered can usually be inferred. These diplomas date from the twelfth century and, although penned by ecclesiastical clerks, were undoubtedly issued by royal chanceries,[42] yet the rhetoric they deploy is very much the same.

One such document, issued in 1126 by Alfonso VII, 'inflamed by divine inspiration' ('diuina inspiratione inflamatus'), contains a confirmation of the monastery of Sahagún's holdings and its immunity from royal taxation.[43] Just as his predecessors had done before him, the king used this document to establish a connection between his protection of the monastery and the continuity and legitimacy of his royal family line. In it, he emphasizes the activity of his grandparents — 'supported in the throne of my grandparents by God's mercy' ('misericordia Dei fultus in solio auorum meorum') —, who had been great benefactors of Sahagún, and whose generosity he wanted to both emulate and surpass:

> I, King Alfonso, son of Count Raimundo and Queen Urraca, in honour of that groom, namely Christ, son of God, and His Holy bride, namely the Church, mindful of my own weakness, supported in the throne of my grandparents by God's mercy, in the hope of eternal life, for the remission of my sins and for the souls of my parents, determined to uphold and enhance royal largesse towards, as well as royal authority over, the monastery of the holy martyrs Facundus and Primitivus. For this reason, inflamed by divine inspiration, the request of Bernardo, abbot of the said monastery, and moved by all the convent of monks, uphold under royal authority that dependency of the said monastery that is called Cofiñal.[44]

---

locum. Tunc demum, surgente in omnibus iniquitate et refrigerente multorum caritate, detractum est hoc opus et non permansit sicut in superioribus scripcionibus habebatur. Modo uero, annuit serenitas nostris principis Adefonsi, filii Fredinandi imperatoris, permisit in eum Donunus sapienciam et sciencientiam (*sic*) atque intelligenciam et currentes omnes congregationis fratres ipsius loci, una cum abate Gundisaluo nomine suggerentes regi et procurante diuina pietate et honorificentia ipsius regis iterum ut aliquid de rebus suis restauraret hunc locum. Rex magnus, pius et miserieors, una cum omnes magnati palatii, ut omnes suas uillas, elegit cum toth hominess qui ibi habitant uel posmodum ad habitandum uenerint, permaneant illesas ut nullus eas inquietet, sicut prius solebant, in iuri regio' (SFPSahagun680, 1068). A twelfth-century copy in *Becerro Gótico de Sahagún*, fols 4ᵛ–5ʳ.

42 This period is generally believed to have witnessed the birth of the Royal Chancery in León-Castile (Fernández Flórez, *La elaboración de los documentos*, pp. 123 ff.).

43 SFPSahagun1227 (1126).

44 'Ego rex Adefonsus, comitis Raymundi et regine Urrace filius, ad honorem ipsius sponsi, uidelicet, Christi filii Dei eiusdemque sponse sante, uidelieet, Ecclesie, mee fragilitatis memor, misericordia Dei fultus in solio auorum meorum, spe uite eterne et pro remisione peccatorum meorum et pro

The document makes no mention of the conflict-ridden reign of the king's mother, Queen Urraca. This is, however, alluded to in another royal diploma issued only months before, which describes the disasters that were visited on the *regnum Hyspanum* during the seventeen years that followed the death of his grandfather, Alfonso VI, when he himself was young and ignorant and bereft of illustrious parents and the land suffered due to the internecine fighting of its magnates:

> In the eternal salvation of the Lord, God, I, Alfonso, by God's grace king and lord of all Spain, son of Count Raimundo and Queen Urraca, salute you, Abbot Don Bernardo, and all the monks, both present and future, that live in the monastery of Sahagún according to its rules. After my grandfather, don Alfonso, who had benefited the monastery of Sahagún with great and magnificent gifts, followed the way of all flesh, I was left young and ignorant, bereft of illustrious parents, and for seventeen years the Kingdom of Spain suffered innumerable misfortunes inflicted by its own magnates, who were fighting against each other.[45]

This charter continues with a first-person narrative in which the king relates that he had been entrusted to the guardianship of the abbot and townsmen of Sahagún during those tempestuous years in order that he might be spared the wicked influence of the faction that had supported his mother — 'In that tempestuous time of so many calamities, I was entrusted to the guardianship of the abbot and the townsmen of the *villa*, so that I be spared the wicked influence of my mother and his faction' ('Qua temptestate, ab abate et a burgensibus in uilla ad tutelam tantarum calamitatum sum receptus, ubi a matre eiusque partes defensatibus acriter sum sepe infestatus').[46] He thus establishes a framework to justify the detailed confession that follows, in which he describes his contributions to the damage suffered by the monastery during the disturbances. These included seizing gold, silver, and other monastic possessions for himself and his knights, without respect to the monastery's jurisdiction and grants, both royal and papal, imposing a royal official on the town of Sahagún, replacing its old customs with new laws, and sharing out monastic settlements and other possessions among his knights:

---

animabus parentum meorum, decreui munire et sublimare regia munificentia, simul et auctoritate, monasterium sanctorum martirum Facundi et Primitiui. Idcirco, diuina inspiratione inflamatus atque precibus Bernardi, abbatis supradicti monasterii, totiusque monachorum conuentus permotus, munio, regia auctoritate, quandam decaniam predicti monasterii que uocatur Cofinniale' (SFPSahagun1227, 1126).

45 'Ego Adefonsus, Dei gratia tocius Hyspanie rex et dominus, comitis Reymundi et Urracee regine filius, domno Bernardo, abbati, et omnibus monachis, tam presentibus quam futuris, in cenobio quo est Dompnis Sanctis regulariter uiuentibus, in Domino Deo aeternam salutem. Postquam auus meus dompnus, uidelicet, Adefonsus uiam tocius carnis est ingressus, qui monasterium Santi Facundi largis et magnificis ditauit muneribus remansi ego puerulus et inscius, duobus clarissimis orbatus parentibus, et regnum Hypanum decem et septem annorum temporibus innumeros sustinuit casus, a propriis conculcatum proceribus, inter se, pro se, dimicantibus' (SPFSahagun1226, 1126).

46 It is clear that the author of this document, king's chaplain, who was standing in for the chancellor on this occasion ('regie damus capellani, cacellarii uice facentis'), employed the term *infestatus* in a negative sense to mean 'politically manipulated').

110   ISABEL ALFONSO

Then, pressed by many needs and driven by the irresponsibility of youth, I inflicted many wrongdoings on the said abbot and the monks, as I now, with better judgement, I acknowledge. I took gold, silver and properties from the abbey for me and my knights; I breached its monastic preserve, the royal grants and the Roman privileges; I seized its *villae* against right and divine law; I violated the old and new customs; and distributed the *villae* and some other possessions, both kept at the monastery and elsewhere, among my knights.[47]

By the time this document was issued, we are reassured, the kingdom had been pacified and the king had repented of his actions and decided, in the interests of his own salvation and the stability of the kingdom, to repair the damage that had been done. He therefore confirmed the monastery's independent lordship and immunity from royal jurisdiction:

Then God's grace appeased that tempest, and rightfully reunited the kingdom, which had been divided wrongfully, and bestowed understanding and honour again on me in my better age, and I determined to amend the said wrongdoings. Seized, then, by the fear and love of God and the veneration of the Holy Martyrs Facundus and Primitivus, and by due reverence to my grandfather of blessed memory, King Alfonso, who is buried there, I return to the abbot and the monks all the estates and possessions that I and others laid waste. I confirm the monastic preserve, the privileges, both royal and Roman, and whatever charters had been duly made for the fear of God, without impairment. Also, I restore whatever *villae* in all my kingdom were and must be yours, with churches and parishes, inside and outside the monastic preserve, whether populated recently or for long or deserted, according to the ancient customs. And I reaffirm that nothing of what my grandfather, Alfonso, king of blessed memory, conferred upon you, shall be demanded from you and from this place. And for the salvation of my soul and the stability of my kingdom, I shall shut the officers out of this *villa*, and hereafter in no occasion shall any other lord, except for the abbot and the monks, control this or any of the other *villae*, and I shall not grant on loan any other of Sahagún's lands in the future. I promise, and confirm this promise, that the abbot of this monastery shall not be substituted by any other lord unless this is decided with the consent of the congregation of the said monastery; and that no one from the royal offspring shall be entitled to requisition the monastery or any part of its estates, or to possess any of the inheritances [it may receive according to] secular law, nor any of the lands subjected to its lordship.[48]

---

47 'Vnde, multis neccessitatibus coangustatus et leui adolescentie sensu agitatus, supradicto abbati et monachis multa iniuste, ut modo iam meliori sensu recognosco, intuli; aurum et argentum et substantiam monasterii, ad meum et meorum militum sumptum, accepi; cautum et regalia, necnon Romana priuilegia, infregi; uille prefecturn, contra ius et fas, imposui; consuetudines antiguas, nouas inducens, immutaui; uillas ceterasque possessiones, intus et extra, mihi militantibus, distribui' (SPFSahagun1226, 1126).

48 'Nunc, uero, quia tantam procellam, Dei gratia aliquatinus sedauit, regnumque in parte male diuisum bene coadunauit michique meliorem aetatem, intellectum, honorem prestitit, ad me reuersus,

Although there is no space here to embark on the detailed analysis such rich source material clearly deserves, a brief consideration of its language and contents serves to illustrate the typical readiness with which a discourse concerning the royal defence of ecclesiastical property was adopted in this and other diplomas of Alfonso VII. This king, who at his most explicit declared himself 'concerned for the peace and advantage of God's church' ('de quiete et utilitate ecclesie Dei sollicitus'),[49] seems to have taken to heart the saying of the Church Fathers that kings should endow and patronize the Church because 'He who builds the house of God builds for himself', with which he introduced one of his donations to the Cathedral of León:

> The ancient Holy Fathers advised the kings of the secular institutions to benefit and enlarge God's churches. Learning the disposition of the doctrine, as it is indeed written that 'he who builds the house of God builds for himself', I, Alfonso, King of Spain by the grace of God, grant.[50]

It is clear that the defence and protection of the patrimony and privileges of the Church were both attributed to and demanded of the king, Furthermore, his greatness and majesty were defined in relation to his ability to fulfil these tasks. This is well illustrated in the preamble to one of Alfonso VII's most generous concessions to Sahagún:

> It is in the interest of royal majesty, as it is evident even for the less cultivated, that churches and holy places and land do not undergo any wrongdoing, and to defend the truth and the alms and the benefits granted in deference to God [...] to visit, assist and honour [them].[51]

---

mala supradicta emendare disposui. Correptus, ergo, timore et amore Dei ueneratione sanctorum martyrurn Facundi et Primitiui, necnon et reuerentia aui mei bone memoriae Regis Adefonsi, ibidem sepulti, omnes hereditates et possessiones, a me et ab aliis ui direptas, monasterio, abbati et monachis restituo; cautum, consuetudines, priuilegia, tam regalia quam Romana, et kartas a quibuslibet Deum timentibus, rite factas, absque ulla diminutione, confirmo; uillas, etiam, cunctas que in toto regno meo uestri iuris fuerunt uel esse debent, cum aecclessis et parrochiis, intra uel extra cautum, longe uel prope populatas uel desertas, secundum priscos usus, uobis redintegro. Et ut nichil aliud uel aliter quam auo meo, regi bone memoriae Adefonso, antecessores uestri caritatiue exhibuerunt, a uobis uel a loco isto exigam, itidem, confirmo. Pro remedia, quoque, anime mee et mei regni stabilitate, prefectum a uilla tali tenore excludam ut deinceps ulla occasione in illa nec in aliis omnibus nullum alium dominum, nisi abbatem et monachos preferam, nec alicui terram Sancti Facundi ulterius in prestamine concedam. Promitto, etiam, et promittendo confirmo, ut nulla alterius monasterii persona, nisi quam concors congregatio predicti cenobii elegerit, in ibi abbas substituatur; nec alicui, unquam, ex proieniae regum, sit licitum monasterium Sancti Facundi uel aliquam partem ex suis hereditatibus, pro seculari hereditate, requirere, uel in eis aliquod ius secularis hereditationis seu terrene subiectionis dominium possidere' (SPFSahagun1226, 1126).

49 SFPSahagun 1269 (1140). Original.

50 'Antiqua sanctorum patrum institutio terrenis regibus precipit ut ecclesias Dei hereditent et amplificent. Scriptum quippe est "qui domum Dei hedificat semetipsum hedificat", quam institutionem doctrine conperiens, ego Adefonsus gratia Dei Yspanie rex dono' (CatLeon1404, 1132). Original.

51 'Regie maiestatis interesse, et iam minus eruditis certum est, ecclesias et sacra loca non solum ab iniuria fueri et defendere verum eciam elemosinarum et beneficiorum in Dei obsequium [...] uisitare, fouere et honorare' (SFPSahagun1248, 1131). Copy dated to 1411.

This discourse of legitimation was not, moreover, simply limited to the use of the rhetoric of social restoration with which each successive monarch affirmed his hold on the crown, and was in turn affirmed in his position by those powers on whom his own authority depended. It also employed a different rhetoric of good government through which royal protection of the Church was linked to the guardianship of the peace, health, and stability of the kingdom.[52] This effectively legitimized the king's authority by distancing it from his power as an individual and presenting it as both public and superior in nature. In this way, a model of good kingship was developed through a process of which we are still largely ignorant. It demanded love for, and defence of, justice, respect for old laws and new legislation, and the resolution of conflicts. According to this model, a good king was supposed to be the source of all good things and offer protection against all evils. It is a model whose development is worth charting as it eventually came to represent the foundation of a political culture whose effects were extremely far-reaching and whose constituent parts represented means of legitimation that could he employed in a wide range of different contexts and situations.

The preambles of a number of diplomas issued by Fernando I, by emphasizing that those kings who enjoy divine assistance from the Holy Trinity promote all that is good and reprove all that is bad — 'With the divine and heavenly assistance from the Holy Trinity […] promoting all that is good and reproving all that is bad' ('Sub diuino et caelesti auxilio sancta et indiuidua Trinitas. […] eligens quod bonum est et quod malum est reprobans') —, precede and justify the king's decisions. Thus, the restoration of bishops to their sees and their subsequent maintenance, chief among the good deeds attributed to good Christian kings, opens Fernando I's aforementioned diploma of 1046 to the see of Astorga.[53] Likewise, the exemplary generosity of the Christian king heads a document drawn up one year later recorded the donation of an estate to the Bishop of León.[54] This invocation had already been formulated already in the late tenth century in the preamble of a charter issued by Vermudo II on behalf of his royal notary and chronicler, Bishop Sampiro.[55] On that earlier occasion, a king's subjection of his rebellious subjects was also celebrated as model royal behaviour inasmuch as the donated goods provened from confiscation of the rebels' property. This model was clearly of Isidorian inspiration, and a reflection of a biblical ideal of kingship which Sampiro himself celebrated in the chronicle he penned at the beginning of the eleventh century.[56]

---

52 The formula 'For the salvation of my soul and the stability of my kingdom' ('Pro remedio, quoque, anime mee et mei regni stabilitate') certainly predates the period under discussion. Although I have not been able to find it among the diplomatic formulae that Amancio Isla has identified in connection with early medieval Iberian kingships, it occurs in Merovingian legislation (I thank Paul Fouracre for this information). However, what interests us here is the moment in which it is revived and once again assimilated into the royal documents that we are commenting.

53 CatAstorga306 (1046). A seventeenth-century copy in Madrid, BNE. MS 1195b, fols 14–15.

54 SFPSahagun505 (1047). A twelfth-century copy in *Becerro Gótico de Sahagún*, fols 80ᵛ–81ʳ.

55 CatLeon581 (998?). Preserved in a copy of 1020.

56 The Isidoran inspiration of these documents is noted by Isla in his comparison of the virtues attributed to these kings (Isla Frez, *Realezas hispánicas*, pp. 81–88).

JUDICIAL RHETORIC AND POLITICAL LEGITIMATION IN MEDIEVAL LEÓN-CASTILE   113

By representing their royal subjects in the context of judicial assemblies through which they imposed order and harmony on the litigants, these documents also established a clear association between their royal person and the establishment of peace. The year both 1089 witnessed a rather peculiar hearing which is particularly interesting in this respect and because it concerns the formulation of norms in the context of a judicial assembly.[57] On that occasion, the bishop of León, trusting in the justice of his lord the king, brought a case against the king's own sister, Urraca. In the document recording this event the king, Alfonso VI, confesses that it was his desire to put an end to the confusion and disorder that afflicted his kingdom that moved him to judge the case. The king is thus presented as a peacemaker taking charge of law and order in his kingdom with the consent and advice of the members of his curia:

> A dispute arose between the Infanta, Doña Urraca, daughter of King Fernando, and the Bishop of León, Don Pedro, over the estates and the villeins of Saint Mary of León. The Infanta, the said Doña Urraca, seized those villeins and their estates, which belonged to Saint Mary, and for this reason the Bishop, Don Pedro, suffered a great harm, and claimed that if the Infanta took away the villeins, she should not seized the estates as well, for they had been granted to the church of León by kings and others for it to have them forever without any opposition. Then the bishop, trusting the justice of his lord, King Don Alfonso, brought a lawsuit over this before the king. After that, King Don Alfonso, who was in Villalpando, wishing to put an end to the great disorder and conflicts in his reign, called for her sisters, Infanta Doña Urraka and Infanta Doña Elvira, and with the latters' consent and corroboration, at a hearing and assembly of his counts and barons, of the greatest of his school, and of the best of his land, and of all of those who had been called to his court, issued this pact and confirm this charter [...] King Don Alfonso had this charter written and confirmed [to be valid] in all his kingdom, and ordered that if he or any of his kin, or of the kin of counts and nobles, should try to breach his charter, he should be cursed and excommunicated in this world and the next, together with Judas, the Lord's traitor, and suffer infernal punishment in hell, and for his temerity he shall render twice what he disturbed and pay one thousand marks of silver to the king, and this charter shall remain firm.[58]

---

57   CatLeon1244 (1089). Preserved in a twelfth-century copy.
58   'Orta fuit intencio inter infantam domnam Urracam, filiam Fredinandi regis, et Legionensem episcopum domnum Petrum super hereditates et uillanos Sancte Marie de Legione. Infantissa enim domna Urraca leuauat illos uillanos cum sua hereditate que pertinebat ad Sanctam Mariam, et pro ista causa episcopus domnus Petrus tenebat grandem calumniam, et dicebat quod, si ipsa infantissa leuabat illos uillanos, non debebat leuare illas hereditates, quas reges et alii per hereditatem Legionensi ecclesie dederant, ut eas in perpetuum sine contradictione haberet. Tunc episcopus, confidens de iusticia domini suis regis domni Adefonsi, fecit grandem querelam de hoc coram ipso rege. Postea uero domnus Adefonsus rex, cum esset in Uilla Alpando, uolens tollere grandem confusionem et grandem baraliam de regno suo, uocauit ad se germanas suas, infantem domnam Urrakam et infantem domnam Geloiram, et illis autorizantibus et affirmantibus per iudicium et

114 ISABEL ALFONSO

It is also interesting that this document refers to a legal battle of a distinctly aristocratic nature, in which the bishop of a powerful see confronted a member of the kingdom's highest nobility over the possession of territory and dependent peasants. In this case the king's credentials as peacemaker are promoted through a description of a regulation that he attempted to impose universally — 'to impose in all his kingdom' ('affirmauit in toto regno suo') on the transfer of property, through which he prohibited property transfers between different modes of lordship (royal, ecclesiastical or the two kinds of lay noble lordships).[59]

Rhetoric such as this, which emphasizes the re-establishment of social order through the proper exercise of royal justice — which in this case is specified as the formulation of regulations dedicated to the maintenance of a peaceful society — is to be found in various guises throughout the documentation of twelfth century León and Castile. It is, however, in the description of the great royal assembly that was summoned to attend Alfonso VII's coronation in León to be found in the *Chronica Adefonsi Imperatoris*, that it receives its most ritualized expression.[60] On that occasion, we are told, archbishops, bishops, and abbots, counts and princes, dukes, and judges all gathered in the royal to await the day of the king's crowning — 'a council held in León, the royal city, with the presence of archbishops, bishops, and abbots, counts and princes, dukes, and judges that there were in the kingdom' ('concilium apud Legionem civitatem regiam cum archiepiscopis, episcopis, et abbatibus, comitibus et principibus, ducibus et iudicibus, qui in illius regno erant') —, on which they were joined by the queen and the king's sister as well as the king of Pamplona, and a great multitude of monks, priests, and common people — 'There came a great multitude of monks, priests, and innumerable common people to see and to hear and to speak the divine word' ('Venit autem et maxima turba monachorum et clericorum, necnon et plebs innumerabilis ad videndum sive ad audiendum vel ad loquendum verbum divinum'). The proceedings lasted three days. On the first, the spiritual wellbeing of the kingdom was dealt with at a meeting that took place in the Cathedral of León. On the second, with great ceremony Alfonso VII was crowned and received the title of Emperor, also in the city's cathedral. Then, on the third and last day, the focus shifted to the 'royal palaces' ('palatiis regalibus'), where all 'gathered together' ('iuncti sunt') in order to legislate on those issues 'that touched on the health of all Spain' ('quae pertinent ad salutem regni totius Hispanie'). Interestingly enough, the series of legal

---

consilium comitum, baronum suorum et maiorum de sua escola et meliorum de sua terra, cunctis uocalis ad suam curiam, fecit istum plazum [o placitum] et affirmauit hoc scriptum [...] Hoc scriptum fecit fieri rex domnus Adefonsus et affirmauit in toto suo regno, et statuit ut si ille aut allquis de genere suo aut de genere comitum aut nobilium hoc suum scriptum infringere temptaret; maledictus et anathemizatus esset in hoc seculo et in futuro cum Iuda Domini traditore in inferno lueret penas inferni et pro temeritatis ausu duplet quantum inquietauerit et ad partem regis mille marchas argenti persoluat et hoc scriptum firmum permaneat' (CatLeon1244, 1089).

59 I have pointed out elsewhere the lack of attention to the general character of these legal dispositions despite the fact that they clearly set a precedent for those that were formulated at the Court of Nájera one century later (Alfonso, 'Litigios por la tierra', p. 951).

60 CAI, I.69–71.

acts passed on this occasion faithfully reflected those made by many previous rulers on their accession to the throne.

Through the first day, the king 'issued legal codes for the whole of his kingdom in accordance with those that had been in use in his royal grandfather's time [Alfonso VI]' ('deditque imperator mores et leges in universe regno suo, sicut fuerunt in diebus avi sui Regis domni Adefonsi'). This served to legitimize his authority not only by presenting him in the role of lawmaker, but also by reminding his subjects of the continuity of his royal inheritance and his continuation of the good government of his royal ancestors.

The second consisted of an 'order that the churches of his kingdom be given back all the dependents that had been taken from them unlawfully and without a trial' ('iussitque restituere universis ecclesiis omnes habitatores et familias, quas perdiderant sine iuditio et iustitia'). In this case, this particular aspect of Alfonso VII's general policy of restoration, which was explicitly and exclusively concerned with the defence of the patrimony and jurisdiction of the Church, was presented not as a purely ecclesiastical matter, but as an issue that affected the health of the entire kingdom.

In the third day, the king ordered the restoration of all the lands and settlements that had been destroyed by war — 'he also ordered that all the villages and territories that had been destroyed during war time be populated and vineyards and trees be planted' ('praecepitque villas et terms, quae fuerant destructae in tempore bellorum, populare, et plantare vineas et omnia arbusta'). Thereafter, he ruled that his judges should judge righteously in order to put an end to the crimes of those men, both rich and poor, who had been discovered acting unjustly and who had contravened rules made by kings, princes, magnates, judges, and other authorities:

> he also ordered that all judges should act severely to eradicate the crimes of those men who had been found acting unjustly and against the decrees of the kings, princes, authorities and judges, and some be hanged from trees, some have their hands and feet cut, without sparing the rich and generous or the paupers, but rather rightfully judge them according to their guilt.[61]

In addition to this, the king invoked the biblical mandate *ne patieris maleficos* and ruled that 'evildoers' be condemned to exemplary execution. Then, to show that he was in earnest, he hung a few wrongdoers in the presence of the assembled company: 'Thereafter he ordered that the evildoers should by no means be endured, as the Lord said to Moses, "Do not allow the wicked to live", and in the presence of all, he captured som of those evildoers and hanged them on a gibbet' ('Praeterea iussit nullomodo suferri maleficos, sicut Dominus dixit Moysi "Ne patieris maleficos", et in conspectus omnium, capti sunt aliqui operarii inquitatis et suspense sunt in patibulis'). The last of this series of royal decrees was addressed to the municipal authorities of the

---

61 'iussitque omnibus iudicibus stricte vitia eradicare in illis hominibus qui contra iustitiam et decreta regnum et principum et potestatum e iudicum invenirentur, et illi alios in lignis suspendentes, alios truncatis manibus aut pedibus relinquentes: non divitibus vel generosis plusquam pauperibus parcentes, sed totum secundum modum culpae discernentes, iuste iudicaerunt' (CAI, I.71).

regions of Toledo and Extremadura, who were directed to make war on the infidel each year in order to avenge God and protect Christian laws.

This detailed description of the great assembly that gathered for Alfonso VII's coronation, written by an anonymous twelfth-century chronicler, is undoubtedly unique as far as our sources are concerned. Despite its singularity, however, it is infused with the same rhetoric that we have discovered in all of the other documents examined so far, which elaborates on the image of the king as the guardian of the kingdom's health, the restorer of ecclesiastical patrimony, the rectifier of the ravages of war, and the administrator of exemplary justice.

Alfonso VII's diplomas offer many more examples through which this image of royal greatness is promoted. One of them describes the kings Lenten meditation in the Leonese monastery of Sahagún — in whose scriptorium a large proportion of his documentary output originated — and relates the king's desire to encourage good deeds and stamp out evils in his kingdom — 'it is our concern that in our kingdom the honest deeds grow and the dishonest and wicked are duly eradicated' ('curandum summopere nobis est ut queque honesta in regno nostros succrescant et inhonesta atque iniqua consulte extirpetur').[62] Another describes how he replaced the bad old laws of the town of Sahagún with a new, improved, charter after mediating in the resolution of a conflict.[63]

If we pause to consider just one more document, we will have proved beyond doubt the continuity in our twelfth-century sources of the association of restorative royal power with the image of model kings who combined the functions of judge, legislator, and peacemaker. It was issued by Alfonso VII's Leonese successor, Fernando II, in order to record the ruling he made in favour of the Bishopric of Lugo against the *cives* of that cathedral city in 1161.[64] Its preamble contains a royal exaltation of the judicial process in which kings are attributed 'the tasks of maintaining justice, banishing evils, protecting the rights of churches and upholding Canon Law, and confirming and extending royal donations to religious institutions' ('Regum est officium iustitiam colere, mala extirpare, bona bonis tribuere, et iura ecclesiastica lege canonum et regum donatione instituta conservare, conseruataque in melius propagare'). When legislating in favour of the see of Lugo and against that town's municipal authorities, Fernando II claimed to do so by divine inspiration — 'advised by divine inspiration [and] the grace of God' ('Dei gratia [...] diuina inspiratione monitus') — in order to put an end to the many wrongs — 'many crimes and many wrongdoings' ('multa facinora et quamplures iniurias') — that had been done to that church, and because he desired all concerned to live together in peace — 'I wish that everyone lives in peace' ('omnes enim uolo uiuant in pace').[65]

---

62 SFPSahagun1256 (1136). Original.
63 SFPSahagun1314 (1152). Original.
64 FernandoII-6 (1161). Twelfth-century copy in Madrid, BNE, MS 1195b, fols 14–15.
65 A 'discourse of peace' is also employed by Fernando II's successor, Alfonso IX, who, having heard that his 'kingdom was greatly disturbed by wrongdoers' ('regnum ualde turbatum erat per malefactores') in the first year of his reign, acted to banish that 'violence and those evils' (uiolentias et iuniurias') from his kingdom, by issuing extremely interesting decrees, although their dating and content are strongly debated (AlfonsoIX-12 (1188)). See Pérez-Prendes, 'La potestad legislativa'.

Our brief foray into the archives of the religious institutions of eleventh and twelfth-century León and Castile has demonstrated that the political activities of the kings of those kingdoms were legitimated through the development of a discourse that contrasted order with disorder, and good deeds with bad. A firm association was also thus developed between divine and secular power through the repeated affirmation that the latter was entrusted to kings by the will and grace of the former. It was a discourse that represented a fundamental component of the political ideology transmitted by kings through the legal arena that provided the physical setting for the administration of royal justice. Any discussion of the rhetoric employed in the development of this discourse would be incomplete if it avoided the controversial issue of the way in which texts reflect reality, since the use of the term 'rhetoric' itself implies that the texts are not to be taken at face value. We must therefore be aware of the dangers of accepting without question our sources' accounts of the reconstructive efforts they attribute to their various royal subjects. In other words, we should be wary of interpreting the discourse of restoration that they promote as anything other than a resource of legitimation.[66] Above all, we must accept that tool of legitimation as an important element of medieval social reality and strive to learn more about its construction and employment, and development over time.

Judicial Rhetoric and the Politics of Truth

We must now turn our attention to another fundamentally important aspect of the development of the legitimacy attached to judicial places. This concerns the relationship that is established between justice and truth, terms whose synonymy is established through the presentation of the judicial process as a process of truth. This connection between the two concepts endowed the courts with which they were associated with unimpeachable credentials as forums of legitimation. They were thus promoted as environments in which a certain 'truth' was identified and presented in the form of 'justice', and where rights were both defined and legitimized. In the process, the ownership of land was elevated to a level where it also became synonymous with the 'truth', Semantically speaking, therefore, 'justice' (*iustitia*), came to encompass both 'truth' (*veritas*) and 'right' (*directum*) in our sources. In this context, the pursuit of a legal claim became the conceptual equal of the pursuit of both truth and justice.

In 1043, Fernando I and his wife Queen Sancha responded to a claim made by the Bishop of León to an estate that had been lost to his see since the 'time of persecution' ('tempore persecutionis') by commissioning a legal investigation into the 'truths' of their kingdom's churches in order that they might confirm their rights accordingly — 'we ordered that the truth of the churches be investigated and ordered that should

---

66 The long persistence of discourses based upon restorative power, the improvement of justice and order, as well as the recreation of historical memory and legitimacy by those who hold such a power has often led historians to take those narratives at face value, as descriptions of real events. Centuries later, the old rhetoric still writes its effects on its readers.

hold their rights as they had persisted since the times of their ancestors' ('iussimus perquirere ueritates ecclesiis et precepimus eas stare per directum sicut ab antecessoribus permanserant').[67] In keeping with the restorative rhetoric of such proceedings, the royal couple went on to state that, 'while they heard the "truth", they also understood that he who restores is more worthy than he who builds' ('dum audiuimus ueritatem [...] intelleximus quia melius est qui restaurant quam qui hedificat').

As we have already seen, this discourse promoted the mutual support of church and monarchy to such an extent as to make the two institutions inseparable. The dependence of religious institutions on a favourable monarchy is most eloquently expressed in the aforementioned document recording the claims made by the Abbot of Sahagún on the lordship of an estate.[68] In that document, the abbot is reported to have claimed that the property in question had belonged to his monastery from the time of Ramiro III until that time when 'the land was without king and the Holy Church without truth' ('peruenit terram sine rege et ecclesia santa non habebat ueritatem'). This was a reference to the disorder associated with the reign of Vermudo II which, according to this document, lasted until Alfonso V took up the rule and 'the Church was able to recover the truth' ('ecclesia Dei habere cepit ueritatem'). In a similar vein, a document issued by the Cathedral of Lean praises Fernando I 'for ordering an investigation into all the rights and "truths" of the bishopric' ('ut exquireret omnem debitum et veritatis hujus sedis').[69]

This association between justice and truth established through legal proceedings is apparent before the reign of Fernando I. One document of 1012, for example, tells of a dispute between the monastery of Celanova and a layman who was the nephew of one of its monks.[70] The case was brought before Alfonso V, who ordered one of his royal officials to take control of the disputed property 'until both parties to the quarrel had attended his council and each had arrived at the truth of the matter' ('usque quando devenissent ad concilium et abuissent unus cum alios veritatem'). The king also ordered one of his counts 'to give them the truth [...] until the cause of the truth had been defined in his presence' ('que dedisset veritatem [...] usque definissent inde ante eum causam veritatis'). The count in turn delegated the job to another, whom he ordered to be a truthful judge of the case and to deliver to its litigants both judgment and the truth in such a way as to decide with which side the truth lay, and then to grant that side the undivided possession of the disputed property:

> and he ordered that Pelagio Strofediz be his deputy and truthful judge of this case, to deliver [to the litigants] both judgment and the truth, so that the party on whose side the truth lay was granted the undivided possession of the estate without any disturbance and free of any other claimant, and so he did.[71]

---

67 CatLeon1007 (1043). Preserved in a twelfth-century copy in the cartulary known as *Tumbo Legionense*, León, Archivo de la Catedral, MS 11, fol. 22$^{r-v.m.}$

68 See p. 106.

69 CatAstorga353 (1057). A seventeenth-century copy in Madrid, BNE. MS 1195b, fol. 633.

70 SSCelanova548 (1012). A copy in the *Tumbo de Celanova*, fols 188^r–188^v.

71 'et ordinavit ad Pelagio Strofediz ut fuisset suo vicario et iudice verifico de ista actione, et dedisset inter eos iudicium et veritatem, et cui dedisset veritas ipsa hereidtas possidisset omnia iuri quieto absque alio herede ita et fecit' (SSCelanova548, 1012).

JUDICIAL RHETORIC AND POLITICAL LEGITIMATION IN MEDIEVAL LEÓN-CASTILE 119

In the event, the property was granted to the monastery because the defendant recognized 'in truth' the 'truth' of the document presented by the monks to support their case — 'he recognized […] in truth that the document presented by the monks was truthful and they should be confirmed the possession of that estate forever without disturbance' ('agnovit […] in veritate quia erat ipsa scriptura verifica et debent semper robore abere pro quo ipsam hereditatem obtineant iuri quieto'). In other cases, compromise agreements (*convenientiae*) were implemented to settle disputes when their judges found that both litigants 'were in possession of the truth' ('ueritatem tenebant').[72]

Such inquiries into the 'truth' referred primarily to ecclesiastical patrimony and were justified through their representation as obedient responses to expressions of divine will. Thus at the 1017 Council of León, Alfonso V supported his legislation by claiming that the law stated that whoever 'made truth' did so in compliance with God's will, and that he who denied the truth defrauded God — 'we shall investigate the truth as prescribed by the law, for the law says that whoever makes truth complies with God wills, and whoever denies the truth defrauds God' ('inquiramos ueritatem sicut lex docet, quia legem dicit ut qui ueritatem facit Dei uoluntatem adimplet. Deo enim fraude facit qui ueritatem resindet').[73] In this way, the taking of royal decisions is presented by our sources in such a way as to emphasize the desire of kings to deliver decisions that were just, legal, and accordance with truth and right. Thus in the aforementioned 1046 diploma Fernando I is said to have been moved by the 'zeal of truth' ('caelum veritatis') when judging the case of the rebellious peasants of the village of Matanza, whom he defeated and imprisoned before deciding that according to both Canon Law and the Visigothic Law they should be re-incorporated into the jurisdiction of the bishopric that they had rejected.[74]

---

72 SFPSahagun514 (1048). A twelfth-century copy in the *Becerro Gótico de Sahagún*, fols 190ᵛ–191ʳ.

73 AlfonsoV-19a (1017). A thirteenth-century copy is in the cartulary of Braga Cathedral, the so-called *Liber Fidei*, Braga, Arquivo Distrital de Braga, C-GCartulários, fol. 1ʳ–1ᵛ. Another clause of the same code applies the same method of inquiry to seigneurial contexts: 'whoever is in debt shall go to his lord to accept his truth, and if the latter refused to grant it, he shall gather two or three [persons] from that village who shall testify on the truth of the matter and they shall appear before the judges chosen by the council, who shall give him the truth' ('qui habuerit debitum uadat ad domino suo pro accipere sua ueritate et si noluerit eam dare in uoce det duas uel IIIes de ipsa uilla que uideant ueritas et postea pergant ante ipsos iudices qui in concilio electi sunt et dent illi sua ueritate'). Compare with the version of these same laws recorded in the twelfth-century cartulary of Oviedo Cathedral known as *Liber Testamentorum*, (Oviedo, Catedral de Oviedo, Códices, 1, fols 54ᵛ–57ʳ (AlfonsoV-19b, 1017).

74 'We, moved by the zeal of truth and overthrown by such arrogance, ordered to capture these men and put them in jail, so that they were punished in this present life for the deeds they have committed and others, seeing this, could take example. We then decided that this should be judged according to the most holy Canon Law, and to what is found in Visigothic law, in Book II, on rebellions and opposition to the king and regarding the latter's attributes, and to what is prescribed and inscribed in the writings of the ancient Holy Fathers' ('Nos vero caelum veritatis eligentes et horum taliam superbiam prosternentes iussimus comprehendere ipsi homines et in ergastuli mittere, ut aliquid ex facto suo presenti in vita recipient et ceteris in hac opinione exemplo fiat. Elegimus etiam ex eis quidquid in santissimum canonem et goticam legem invenitur de rebelionibus et contradictoribus regis, siue de facultatibus eorum sicut in libro secondo et in eius titulo constitutum vel exaratum a prioribus santis patribus scriptum esse decernitur') (CatAstorga306, 1046). A seventeenth-century copy in Madrid, BNE, MS 1195b, fols 14–15.

120   ISABEL ALFONSO

How was this 'truth' ascertained? On which foundations did its authority rest? The search for the 'truth' which is described in that León code as both legal mandate and divine will was in practice pursued through inquisitive mechanisms such as judicial inquiries. The evidence presented at such inquiries was often of a written nature, and the documents in which it was recorded were authenticated by the testimony of the litigants themselves. The case brought before Alfonso V in 1014 by the Portuguese monastery of Guimarães illustrates not only this process, but also the way in which the practice it represents predated the legal norms from which it was commonly assumed to have proceeded.[75] The document recording this case relates that the monks of Guimarães, who had had all of their documents authenticated at the court of every new king since the foundation of their monastery, had been challenged by 'wicked slanderers' who claimed those documents to be false — 'wicked and iniquitous men arose against this monastery of Guimaraes, claiming that those documents were not truthful' ('surrexerunt omnes inique et maliciantes contra ipso monasterio Vimaranes, narrauerunt ei quomodo non errant ipsos testamentos uerificos').[76] It also tells that the monks testified to the veracity of their documents after they had been read out before the assembled council and the truth of their contents had been investigated. This process resulted in a new royal ratification of the disputed monastic documentation, which could be produced as a guarantee of the monastery's possessions in the face of future attacks on its patrimony. One needs look no further than the preamble of the charter that contained this ratification to discover the function that was attributed to the documents to which it refers, as it most explicitly states that it was written in order that all might be informed that the narrative it relates was a 'true account' — 'It should not be doubted but rather should remained known by may widely recognised by many as truth' ('Ambiguum quidem non est sed multis plerisque manet connitum atque notissimum in ueritate').

In this context, it is fitting to consider cases in which false documents were burned in order that the 'truth' might be established, as the identification of falsifications and their destruction were among the functions attributed to judicial assemblies.[77] Indeed, it is impossible to overstress the importance of written documents in the legal contexts we have been discussing. The written word was such an important legitimizing weapon in the battle to impose and gain recognition for any single version of past events, that protecting the documents that recorded them was of the utmost importance. What they most needed protecting from were fires, both those that started accidentally and those that resulted from more sinister causes. It is not surprising,

---

75 AlfonsoV-15 (1014).

76 It would be worth investigating this claim with respect to the types of documents to which it refers (*testamenta, agnitiones, notitiae* ...) in order to discover more both about the nature of monastic archives and how these supported their owners' claims to credibility.

77 This occurred in a case in which the charters produced by one of the sides to a dispute were found to be falsifications and were ordered to be burned — '[this documents were] late and false and abhorrent [and so] they ordered they be burnt and invalidated' ('posteriores et falsas et aborrendas mandarunt eas cremare et fuissent inualidas'); PMH-DC225 (1014). Cited by Prieto Morera in his commentary on the dispute (Prieto Morera, 'El proceso en el Reino de León', p. 479).

JUDICIAL RHETORIC AND POLITICAL LEGITIMATION IN MEDIEVAL LEÓN-CASTILE   121

then, to find that some royal confirmations were clearly drafted in response to the needs of those who had lost documents through fire.[78] Although the causes of those fires, which were generally perceived as divine punishment, were rarely specified, the destruction of the charters of one's adversaries clearly represented a recognized strategy of political aggression. This is well illustrated by a document, issued in 1058, recording a case brought before Fernando I by the bishop of Astorga in an attempt to reclaim some villages that had been usurped by men who, like preying wolves, had attacked his see by seizing all of its documents, which they had then burned at the devil's own prompting — 'Ecta Rapinatiz and his sons arose like wolves against the bishopric and seized all its documents and led by the devil they burned them' ('surrexit Eeta Rapinatiz et filiis suis sicut lupis super hanc sedem et aprehenderunt omnes scripturas et cremaverunt eas zelo diaboli ductus').[79] The case was resolved when the accused men personally recognized the truth of the allegations levelled against them before a council at which many *boni homini* who lived in the disputed area were present — 'they recognized the truth [...] with their own tongue in the council, and many sons of good men who lived there were present' ('agnoverunt se in veritate [...] cum propria sua lingua in hoc concilio, necnon et multorum filii bonorumque hominum ibidem stantium atque residentium').[80] This public recognition was to be maintained in the memory of all those present, but was also committed to the written record and preserved in the cathedral's archives to serve as a more permanent guarantee of the see's property.

In 1063, Fernando I dealt with another dispute, this time between two monasteries. In this case, he ordered his 'most faithful deputy' ('fidelissimum vicarium') Fernando Osoriz 'to summon all the nobles and wise men who were familiar with the truth to make justice between both monasteries' ('convocassent omnes nobiles et sapientes qui bene nouerant veritatem ut discemerent iustitiam inter utrosque monasterios'). The 'judges and noble magistrates' ('iudices et nobiles magistratus') who had been summoned to the task duly ordered one of the disputing parties to provide witnesses to testify as to the 'truth' regarding their monastery during the reign of Alfonso V — 'suitable witnesses to testify as to what the truth is' ('testes ydoneos que iurassent quia est ueritas'). The document recording this case details the sworn testimony of the witnesses presented — 'we truthfully testified as to what was true' ('ita verifice iuramus quia est veritas') — and then describes the division of the disputed goods, made and confirmed in the king's presence, which it states was made publicly — 'Once all that was determined and the division agreed upon we put it down in writing publicly, and in the king's presence we read it aloud in order to confirm it and ensure its stability' ('Omnia taxata vel division fermata publice

---

78 AlfonsoV-6 (1007), is a request for a royal confirmation of privileges that had been destroyed by fire. AlfonsoV-33 (1027) is a confirmation of the diplomas belonging to the cathedral of Lugo that had been kept in its *scriniis et tesauris* and had been lost through fire.

79 CatAstorga361 (1058). An eighteenth-century copy in the *Tumbo Negro*, fol. 42.

80 Later, when returning the disputed property, these men confessed that they did so 'according to the laws and the judges determined in the council, and we recognised the truth and thus acted' (secundum leges et judices elegerunt in hoc concilio et nos in veritate fuimus conscious sic facimus').

exaravimus, et coram Regis presentia adstabiliendum vel confirmandum protulimus').[81] The 'truth' about the property of the Church was thus gradually incorporated into the documentary registers of religious institutions.

The preamble to a charter we have already discussed provides an emphatic example of the ecclesiastical imposition of the value of written evidence as a guarantee of rights gained through disputes brought before judicial assemblies. It contains a commandment that the resolutions of those assemblies, which it describes using the term 'agreement' (*agnitio*), should be committed to writing in order that they might always be remembered by the people and therefore never lose their force:

> The ancient fathers and doctors taught that past, present and future agreements should be written, so that they are always remembered and known in the present and their knowledge transmitted to those coming after so that they are firmly confirmed and irrevocably held.[82]

In the same vein, the preamble to yet another legal narrative relates its committal to the written record to the maintenance of the 'truth' as it had been defined and recognized in the context of royal justice: 'We made this document and issued this charter so that it is acknowledged to be true by whoever reads it or hears and the truth receives full and firm recognition'.[83] According to these documents, this method of ascertaining and defining past events was well established in León and Castile well before the influence of Roman Law made its way into those kingdoms. A hundred years later, at the end of the twelfth century, we see it again being employed by Fernando II, another Leonese monarch, who stated unequivocally in the preamble to a judicial settlement that when judgments were not committed to writing, they were consigned to oblivion instead — 'It is most frequently the case that if that which is settled by judgement is not committed to script, it is consigned to oblivion instead' ('Plerumque contingere solet ut ea que per iuditum diffiniuntur nisi in scripto redigantur posteris obliuini tradantur').[84] This document of 1186 records a dispute in which the authorities of a powerful royal town confronted the oft-cited monastery of Sahagun 'before the king and his court' ('coram rege et eius curia'). It employs very refined language and presents its subject in a notably formal and institutionalized light. It states that the sentence handed down by the king in this case was based, not on consideration of the law, but on the truth as it had been ascertained by a royal inquiry — 'In this case the

---

81 SSCelanova260 (1063). A twelfth-century copy in the *Tumbo de Celanova*, fol. 95ᵛ. This monastery also brought another dispute before Fernando I during which the king ordered that 'whatever was their truth' ('quantum erat sua veritate') should be ascertained through the testimony of witnesses in a council 'where not a few people of fine descent attended' ('ubi fuerunt non modica multorum filii multorum benenatorum'); SSCelanova300 (1063).

82 'Antiqui enim patres atque doctores de preterita presentia atque future agnitionem scribere docuerunt, ut agnita in memoria semper esse ut et presentes scirent, et scienda cuncta posteris relinquerent et confirmata firmiter et inreuocabiliter tenerent' (AlfonsoV-4, 1007). A twelfth-century copy in the *Tumbo de Celanova*, fols 4ᵛ–5ʳ.

83 'Hoc autem scriptum facimus et cartula decernimus ut quisquis legeret vel audierit vera esse fateatur agnitionem veritatis plenam habeat firmitatem' (CatAstorga353, 1057).

84 SFPSahagun1423 (1186). Original.

JUDICIAL RHETORIC AND POLITICAL LEGITIMATION IN MEDIEVAL LEÓN-CASTILE   123

judicial settlement was so reached: once the investigators had been appointed, they sought for the truth, and whoever held the estate during the days of the Emperor until his death shall freely possess it' ('In quia causa iuditiali sententia deffinitum est: ut, datis exquisitoribus, ueritas inquireretur et qui in diebus imperatoris et ad mortem eius hereditatem illam tenebat ipse eam libere possideret'). This sentence was in fact a compromise solution reached in the interests of peace — 'to make peace' ('pro pace conformanda') — that, temporarily at least, resolved the quarrel. As we have already seen, such negotiated resolutions were sometimes reached because the judges ruled that both parties to a dispute were 'in possession of the truth'.

The documents we have been discussing demonstrate the process whereby the truth was effectively objectified in the judicial arenas whose business they record.[85] This process was a circular one through which legal decisions acquired the status of truth as a result of the authority invested in the methods with which that truth had been ascertained, which in turn derived from the power that ordered the implementation of those methods, which was itself legitimized in the process, along with the forum in which the whole process unfolded. This process and its circularity were described by Foucault when he examined the relationship between power, law, and truth in an attempt to identify the source of the authority that can bestow the status of truth on a given version of events.[86] The relevance and interest of his aim to apply historical analysis to what he termed 'the politics of truth' through the examination of historical judicial practices cannot be doubted. Indeed, leaving aside his contradictory and widely questioned assertions concerning the model of political development that should have accompanied the establishment of the truth through inquiries and the innovation that would have implied in terms of judicial convention, we can agree with Foucault that this type of judicial inquiry in effect represented a 'means of exercising power'.[87]

The evidence of the judicial narratives we have been discussing allows us to extend this argument one step further, as the way in which they represent royal power has more to do with its legitimation than its exercise. Their function was not only to record actions based on established truth, but also to use that truth, and the methods by which it was ascertained, to justify the power that imposed it. It is between the lines of this dialectical relationship between the exercise of power and its legitimation that

---

85 We are in fact far from the 'zealous search for an objective truth' or the 'material rather than formal truth' which Prieto Morera associates with these documents (Prieto Morera, 'El proceso en el Reino de León', pp. 432, 480).

86 Foucault presents a consideration of this problem, which underlies his work in its entirety, in Foucault, Microfísica del poder, and in Foucault, La verdad y las formas jurídicas.

87 Foucault proposed that the revival of this method of judicial investigation accompanied the recovery of Roman Law in the twelfth century, signified the demise of previous magical or irrational judicial practices in which the function of a trial was not so much to establish the truth, but to decide which party to a dispute was the strongest. It was his opinion that the re-introduction of the judicial inquiry transformed those previous legal practices and led to the development of new forms of justice (Foucault, La verdad y las formas jurídicas, pp. 60–85). For the challenges that have been made to others who have shared Foucault's opinion see: Reynolds, Kingdoms and Communities; Davies and Fouracre, eds, The Settlement of Disputes; Bougard, 'La justice dans le royaume d'Italie'; Wickham, 'Justice in the Kingdom of Italy'; Nelson, 'Kings with Justice'; Alfonso, 'Litigios por la tierra' White, 'La traición'.

I believe one can discern the process whereby the superiority of royal power and jurisdiction were established. It is a process in urgent need of further investigation.

Bibliography

El Reino de León en la Alta Edad Media. Vol. 1: Cortes, Concilios y Fueros (León: Centro de Estudios e Investigación San Isidoro, 1988)

Las Cortes de Castilla y León en la Edad Media. Actas de la primera etapa del Congreso Científico sobre la Historia de las Cortes de Castilla y León (Burgos, 30 de septiembre a 3 de octubre de 1986), 2 vols (Valladolid: Cortes de Castilla y León, 1988)

Las Cortes de Castilla y León, 1188–1988. Actas de la tercera etapa del Congreso Científico sobre la historia de las Cortes de Castilla y León (León, del 26 a 30 de septiembre de 1988), 2 vols (Valladolid: Cortes de Castilla y León, 1990)

Alfonso, Isabel, 'Resolución de disputas y prácticas judiciales en el Burgos medieval', in *Burgos en la Plena Edad Media. III Jornadas Burgalesas de Historia* (Burgos: Asociación Provincial de Libreros de Burgos, 1994), pp. 211–43

Alfonso, Isabel, 'Litigios por la tierra y "malfetrías" entre la nobleza medieval', *Hispania*, 57–197 (1997), 917–55

Alfonso, Isabel, 'Conflictos en las behetrías', in *Los señoríos de behetría*, ed. by Carlos Estepa Díez and Cristina Jular Pérez-Alfaro (Madrid: CSIC, 2001), pp. 227–60

Alfonso, Isabel, 'Venganza y justicia en el Cantar de Mío Cid', in *El Cid: de la materia épica a las crónicas caballerescas*, ed. by Carlos Alvar Ezquerra, Fernando Gómez Redondo, and Georges Martin (Alcalá de Henares: Universidad de Alcalá, 2002), pp. 41–70

Bloch, Maurice, *Political Language and Oratory in Traditional Society* (London: Academic Press, 1975)

Bougard, François, 'La justice dans le royaume d'Italie aux IXe–XIe siècles', in *La giustizia nell'Alto Meioevo (secoli IX–XI). XLIV Settimana di Studio del Centro Italiano de Studio sull'Alto Medioevo* (Spoleto: Centro Italiano di Studi sull'Alto Medioevo, 1997), pp. 133–78

Bourdieu, Pierre, *El sentido práctico* (Madrid: Taurus, 1991)

Cabero Domínguez, María Consolación, *Astorga y su territorio en la edad media (s. IX–XIV). Evolución demográfica, económica, social, político-administrativa y cultural de la sociedad astorgana medieval* (León: Universidad de León, 1995)

Davies, Wendy, and Paul Fouracre, eds, *The Settlement of Disputes in Early Medieval Europe* (Cambridge: Cambridge University Press, 1986)

De Jong, Mayke, and Frank Theuws, eds, *Topographies of Power in the Early Middle Ages* (Leiden: Brill, 2001)

Fernández Flórez, José A., *La elaboración de los documentos en los reinos hispánicos occidentales (ss. VI–XIII)* (Burgos: Institución Fernán González, 2002)

Foucault, Michel, *Microfísica del poder* (Madrid: Ediciones de la Piqueta, 1979)

Foucault, Michel, *La verdad y las formas jurídicas* (Barcelona: Gedisa, 1995)

Isla Frez, Amancio, 'La monarquía leonesa según Sampiro', in *Historia social, pensamiento historiográfico y Edad Media. Homenaje al Prof. Abilio Barbero de Aguilera*, ed. by María Isabel Loring García (Madrid: Ediciones del Orto, 1997), pp. 33–57

Isla Frez, Amancio, *Realezas hispánicas del año mil* (A Coruña: Edicios do Castro, 1999)

Larrea, Juan José, 'Villa Matanza', in *Les sociétés méridionales à l'âge féodal: Espagne, Italie et su de la France X^e–XIIIe s. Hommage à Pierre Bonnassie*, ed. by Hélène Débax (Tolouse: Université de Toulouse-Le Mirail, 1999), pp. 223–28

Lucas Álvarez, Manuel, *El reino de León en la Alta Edad Media. Vol. 5: Las cancillerías reales (1109–1230)* (León: Centro de Estudios e Investigación San Isidoro, 1993)

Lucas Álvarez, Manuel, *El Reino de León en la Alta Edad Media. Vol. 8: Cancillerías reales astur-leonesas (718–1072)* (León: Centro de Estudios e Investigación San Isidoro, 1995)

Martin, Georges, 'Le récit héroïque castillan (Formes, enjeux sémantiques et fonctions socio-culturelles)', *Cahiers d'Études Hispaniques Médiévales*, 11 (1997), 139–52

Miller, William I., *Bloodtaking and Peacemaking: Feud, Law, and Society in Saga Iceland* (Chicago: The University of Chicago Press, 1990)

Milsom, S. F. C., *The Legal Framework of English Feudalism* (Cambridge: Cambridge University Press, 1976)

Milsom, S. F. C., *Historical Foundations of the Common Law* (London: Butterworths, 1981 [1969])

Nelson, Janet L., 'Kings with Justice, Kings without Justice: An Early Medieval Paradox', in *La giustizia nell'Alto Meioevo (secoli IX–XI). XLIV Settimana di Studio del Centro Italiano de Studio sull'Alto Medioevo* (Spoleto: Centro Italiano di Studi sull'Alto Medioevo, 1997), pp. 797–823

Pastor, Reyna, *Resistencias y luchas campesinas en la época del crecimiento y consolidación de la formación feudal: Castilla y León, siglos X–XIII* (Madrid: Siglo XXI, 1980)

Pérez-Prendes, José Manuel, 'La potestad legislativa en el reino de León (Notas sobre el Fuero de León, el concilio de Coyanza y las Cortes de León de 1188', in *El Reino de León en la alta Edad Media. Vol. 1: Cortes, concilios y fueros* (León: Centro de Estudios e Investigación San Isidoro, 1988), pp. 495–545

Prieto Morera, Agustín, 'El proceso en el Reino de León a la luz de los diplomas', in *El Reino de León en la Alta Edad Media. Vol. 2: El ordenamiento jurídico del reino* (León: Centro de Estudios e Investigación San Isidoro, 1992), pp. 381–520

Reynolds, Susan, *Kingdoms and Communities in Western Europe, 900–1300* (Oxford: Clarendon Press, 1984)

White, Stephen D., 'Inheritances and Legal Arguments in Western France, 1050–1150', *Traditio*, 3 (1987), 55–103

White, Stephen D., 'La traición en la ficción literaria. Derecho, hecho y ordalías en la narrativa y la épica en francés antiguo', *Hispania*, 57–197 (1997), 957–80

Wickham, Chris, 'Justice in the Kingdom of Italy in the Eleventh Century', in *La giustizia nell'Alto Meioevo (secoli IX–XI). XLIV Settimana di Studio del Centro Italiano de Studio sull'Alto Medioevo* (Spoleto: Centro Italiano di Studi sull'Alto Medioevo, 1997), pp. 179–250

Wickham, Chris, *Legge, patriche e conflitti. Tribunali e risoluzione delle dispute nella Toscana del XII secolo* (Roma: Viella, 2000)

CHAPTER 4

On Memory and Identity

with a commentary by Piotr S. Górecki

Conflict, Language, and Social Practice in Medieval Societies:Selected Essays of Isabel Alfonso, with Commentaries, ed. by Julio Escalona Monge, Álvaro Carvajal Castro, and Cristina Jular Pérez-Alfaro, TMC 24 (Turnhout: Brepols, 2024), pp. 127–165

BREPOLS ❧ PUBLISHERS   10.1484/M.TMC-EB.5.132458

PIOTR S. GÓRECKI

Words, Again ...

'Truth is not truth'
Rudy Giuliani

'A heavy crash shook the forest from end to end'
Lewis Carroll

Words

One lesson of our troubled times is the importance of words: their meaning, role in forming concepts, and capacity to specify (or obscure) phenomena.[1] These attributes are affected by what might be called their societal life over time: their circulation, use, adaptation, and fluidity of reference. Beginning about three decades back into the past century, we have experienced thoroughgoing critical reassessments of key words designating big areas of order in medieval Europe: *feudalism*, the *state*, *violence*, the *fief*, *ritual*, and most recently *kinship*.[2] Words like these possess two quite different capacities. They can designate semantic fields — open-ended areas of interest, that, once named, may blossom into new fields of inquiry. Or, they can directly identify specific phenomena. The two capacities can converge, so that in the course of the inquiry a semantic field refracts into a range of precise phenomena.[3] Or, a word can continue along its variegated societal life.

In our profession, few words have enjoyed a societal life as rich and influential as *memory* and *identity*. Each now works in both capacities, but with unusually complicated results. Their meanings have expanded so widely that each now covers — refers to, or specifies — an exceedingly broad range of phenomena, themselves as open-ended as the principal two words. In their core, now still current, dictionary meanings, *identity* refers either to some basis, or criterion, for identifying an item, or to a designation of two or more items as identical (essentially or exactly similar); while *memory* refers to the many cognitive states related to remembering and forgetting.[4]

---

1 On words and this distinction, I remain indebted to Reynolds, *Fiefs and Vassals*, pp. 12–16; Reynolds, 'Fiefs and Vassals after Twelve Years', pp. 17–20.
2 In addition to the classical works by Brown, 'The Tyranny of a Construct'; Bisson, 'The "Feudal Revolution"'; White, 'The "Feudal Revolution": II'; Barthélémy, *The Serf, the Knight, and the Historian*, Reynolds, *Fiefs and Vassals*, and Buc, *The Dangers of Ritual*, see most recently Hummer, *Visions of Kinship*.
3 Examples: Brown, *Violence in Medieval Europe*; Reynolds, 'The Historiography of the Medieval State'; Reynolds, 'Fiefs and Vassals after Twelve Years'.
4 Ligon Bjork and Bjork, eds, *Memory*.

Piotr S. Górecki, University of California Riverside

Among us, historians, the great expansion of meanings attached to these two words has been in a complex, cognitive direction.

Identity has evolved toward a personal trait. As such, it entails a social and a cognitive aspect: membership in a collectivity; and a shared understanding of that collectivity's existence, criteria of membership, and importance. The current breadth of *identity* is a result of two variables. On the one hand, there is viewpoint. Who exactly experienced the membership and its understandings? It can be us, historians, as we discern past identities by classifying people into groups: 'women', 'rustics', 'peasants', 'knights', 'Poles', and so forth. Or, it can be the past people themselves, as they classified their contemporaries, ancestors, or their own selves along similar lines. The latter gives us, historians, a sense of who the people we study thought they were.[5] On the other hand, there is degree of implication. A past text may present no discernible viewpoint at all, yet logically, necessarily imply, in the past world upon which it reflects, that same recognition of identity by someone, or some group — not directly specified, but hovering somewhere between the author, the people upon whom the author was reflecting, and specific actors. Or, we may infer identity even less directly and more implicitly, from attributes of texts produced in quantities sufficient to create meaningful patterns and contexts. This happens when a document, or a cluster of documents, appear to concern a collectivity, and to reflect on the part of its authors or of its actors an aim, or at least an inner logic, related to the collectivity's existence and significance, even if no one actually asserts it.[6]

The result has been a major proliferation of meanings of *identity*.[7] Insofar as a classification uses a proper name for a collectivity, it points us toward an identity rooted in ethnicity, in a people, in a specific city, in other kinds of bounded territory, in family, in type of religious observance, in knighthood, or in lordship. When experienced over long spans of time, or imagined as extending into a primeval past, identity assumes the form of collective myth, including ethnogenesis. When linked to deliberate activity by (or, directed toward) a collectivity, meant to sustain its membership, identity rests on performance and re-enactment — commemoration.[8] Hence one of many areas of connection between identity and memory. When sustained or experienced over time, identity *becomes* memory — in, in its own turn, one meaning of that word.

On its side, *memory* has evolved toward a synonym-at-large for a wide spectrum of modes of cognition. One is knowledge. Another is a text. A third is a record. A fourth is evidence, especially its use as proof. A fifth is the range of human activities entailing, and surrounding, the creation, use, interpretation, and retention of the above four. I do not mean to overstate! Clearly, these modes are closely, indeed seamlessly related. For example, the type of knowledge discussed by Isabel Alfonso in this article simply *is* memory, in one meaning of that word: knowledge as experienced over time, cognitively processed, subject to recall, interpretation, distortion, or oblivion,

---

5   This is my most specific definition of identity; Górecki, 'Words, Concepts, and Phenomena', pp. 144–53.

6   This type of analysis is one of the many contributions of Koziol, *The Politics of Memory and Identity*.

7   An interesting example: Pleszczyński and others, eds, *Imagined Communities*.

8   Connerton, *How Societies Remember*, pp. 41–104.

made permanent in the written record, and accessed and potentially further modified through that record. In my own work, I myself have treated knowledge as memory outright, or as linked to memory seamlessly and without additional specification.[9]

Nevertheless, these words do have different meanings, so as a result much of the literature plainly blurs rather than distinguishes memory itself. As a result, it is difficult today to think of any cognitive activity affecting or referring to groups and extending over time, that is *not*, in some sense or another, identity, or memory, or both. This history of two words calls for attention and conceptual refinement. For both purposes, Isabel's splendid article is both an example and a resource.

The Article

Isabel sets up her subject ingeniously. As her source of material, she selects an event that, in its very essence, entails remembering (and forgetting): the inquest. For me, specialized in a very different part of Europe, this is a most happy choice, as the inquest entails elements that are highly comparable across time and space.[10] Intrinsically, by definition, the inquest means a placement of a group of people under oath, and elicitation from them of some desired knowledge. That basic framework presupposes other elements, which varied widely across time, place, and type of inquest: an agent with the power to place others under oath, and persuade (or compel) them to disclose knowledge; a protocol for that disclosure and its recording; and the elicited knowledge itself, that is, the cognitive experience by the participants in the inquest of the subject matter elicited, recorded, and sometimes generated, in its course.

The type of inquest Isabel has selected here, the *pesquisa*, was forensic. It was judicial, and took place at the phase of a trial that yielded knowledge comprising proof. Isabel brilliantly situates the *pesquisa* in the bigger story of the twelfth- and thirteenth-century medieval courts.[11] The importance of inquiry as an act of power puts it at the conjunction of the adversarial and the inquisitorial acquisition of knowledge. Its availability as an option to judges as well as to the parties places it between adversarial and *ex officio* proceedings. Its quest for knowledge possessed by people recruited from larger populations resonates with the roles of socially-based reputation (*fama*), as initial evidence and as proof. No less importantly, the *pesquisa* was an alternative to adjudication, actively sought by the parties in extra-judicial dispute settlement.

As told here, the *pesquisa* emerges as a great, and (for us) thoroughly enjoyable story. We learn a great deal about it as an event: its composition, location, protocol (for example, the assembling of the witnesses and their testimony either in sequence, person by person, or simultaneously as a group), and all kinds of variations in practice and circumstance. I cannot recall reading prose that is quite this good in telling

---

9 Górecki, *The Text and the World 1160–1310*, pp. 55–106.
10 Górecki, 'Piast Poland and the Legal Systems', p. 10.
11 Brundage, *Medieval Canon Law*, pp. 143–51.

us — simply put — *what happened* at a forensic event of any kind. This treatment of the *pesquisa* is excellent legal history in its currently updated conceptual profile, to which Isabel has made major contributions throughout her scholarly career.[12]

The inquest, and *this* inquest, lead Isabel, and us as readers, seamlessly to the article's two principal subjects. The link of the inquest with memory is knowledge, as experienced over time. The link with identity is the social composition of the witnesses. Both links hinge on two schematically simple (though in their particulars doubtless complicated) human acts: speech, consisting of a question and an answer; and its reconfiguration in writing. The smallest unit, or bit, of the resulting record is a short written report, narrating the question and the answer. A sub-theme of the article is Isabel's treatment of those resulting units as texts — short pieces of narrative, each spanning one question and one utterance. In that treatment, two topics are to me especially notable.

The first is the close attention to the epistemological significance of the testimony: the meaning, and the quality, of the knowledge elicited in the *pesquisa*. That attention arises at two moments: back then, at the *pesquisa* itself; and today, in Isabel's close treatment of this subject. At both moments, the issue is framed with reference to one word: *truth*. The record applies this word to the testimonies jointly with enhancing adjectives: 'good truth', 'fair truth', and the like. To us, such enhancements of *truth* seem like redundant amplifications. But to them, they problematize truth. The adjectives imply a recognition of veracity as a sliding scale, culminating with a distinct — the best possible — level. Glimpsed here is a brief but fascinating moment in the medieval articulation of (what was once called) objective knowledge. In our postmodern professional folklore, neither *knowledge* nor *truth* now enjoy a comfortable, let alone a happy, societal life. So today I could not be more grateful to Isabel for bringing to the centre of our attention this vivid concern by our medieval predecessors with this exact subject: the meaning, and the multiple levels, of empirical certainty.

The textual direction leads Isabel inexorably to (in her own word) the 'rhetoric' of the recorded testimony. This aspect of testimonies preserved as texts has been another important area of Isabel's work,[13] reflecting a major historiographical current spanning the past several decades: a broad interest in the 'rhetoric', or 'rhetorical' dimension, of texts. In its turn, this word has long enjoyed an exuberant yet slightly unusual societal life. Its precise meaning always was, and is, the skill of effective expression and the learned discipline of its acquisition. The medieval phase of rhetoric thus understood drew a surge of attention between the 1970s and the 1990s.[14] In the course of that inquiry and ever since, the word in addition appears to refer to all the literary or compositional aspects of a text, typically sought in order to infer the apparent purpose of the text itself, and, lurking behind it, of its author or authors. Once discerned, 'rhetoric' enhances the effectiveness of the text, first, as a literary

---

12 In addition to articles in this book, see the fine tribute in Davies, *Windows on Justice*, pp. 19–20, nn. 54–55.

13 Alfonso, 'Judicial Rhetoric'.

14 Conley, *Rhetoric*; other literature, Górecki, 'Rhetoric, Memory and Use of the Past', pp. 267–20 (nn. 34, 42–43, 49, 51).

mode whereby the text 'represents' its subject, and, second, as in itself the source — the creation, or the conjuring up — of the subject 'represented', by the text itself.

Curiously, *rhetoric* has not, it seems to me, emerged as a semantic field. Uses of this word by historians are not meant principally to specify *rhetoric* beyond its conventional, well-understood meaning. Rather, the word is employed axiomatically — with an apparent certainty as to what it means — in order to characterize an attribute of a text: in assertions that a text, or its fragment, are 'rhetorical'; or, that its form, expression, or purpose add up, in some sense, to 'rhetoric'; or, that the text's 'rhetoric' relates to its quality or force as an assertion, as a truthful or verisimilar expression, and the like. In this article, Isabel appears to use this word in this axiomatic sense, producing, for me, one moment of unclarity. I am uncertain about what is meant by that attribute, and the value added of its discernment.

One possibility can be ruled out. Isabel does not enter the conundrum, already a bit weathered when the original article was published ten years ago, concerning the status of 'rhetoric', or the 'rhetorical', as the essential 'reality' inherent in a text. Epistemological scepticism flashes once, in a disclaimer that testimony was not 'merely' or 'simply' rhetorical, but is otherwise absent. Elsewhere, there is a highly tangible point of departure, as Isabel discerns rhetoric in speech: that smallest unit of the written record which reports one question and one answer. But, regarding speech, possibilities abound. Does this attention convey insight into speech? Its transition to writing? The possible routinization of the *pesquisa* as a text, at its oral or written phases? Then there is power. Did the interrogation tend to elicit responses under duress? Something else? All of the above appears to be meant, so that, on the subject of rhetoric, the article raises important possibilities but does not quite clinch them.

That same textual material traces, in this article, *memory* and *identity*. The conceptual overgrowth around each word presents a good moment for a distinction: between them, and the other, related but different types or levels of cognition — above all, knowledge.[15] My interest in that difference was piqued by my recent work with two remarkable Polish documents: records of papal trials of the Teutonic Order held in Poland in 1320–1321 and 1339, over allegations by the Polish king regarding grievous damage inflicted on the Kingdom and its people.[16] The centrepiece of each document is a dossier recording numerous testimonies, uttered in response to interrogatories. The dossiers resemble the *pesquisa* insofar as their smallest unit — constituent bit — is one question and one answer. Each unit, and all of them together, elicit and permanently fix in writing three cognitive states: knowledge, memory, and identity.[17]

This source provides a good, crisp empirical basis for my distinction — especially between the main two subjects and knowledge generally. As in that other work, in this comment I focus on knowledge, because its attainment — the quest for a

---

15 A recent treatment of records related to such cognitive states is Head, *Making Archives 1400–1700*, pp. 43–66.

16 *Lites ac res gestae inter Polonos Ordinemque Cruciferorum*, ed. by Zakrzewski; *Lites ac res gestae inter Polonos Ordinemque Cruciferorum*, ed. by Chłopocka; Górecki, 'Memory'.

17 Milliman, 'The Slippery Memory of Men'; Bieniak, 'Litterati'; Bieniak, '"Milites"'; Bieniak, 'Środowisko świadków'.

PIOTR S. GÓRECKI

'truth' that was 'good', or 'fair' — was the most explicit aim of the *pesquisa*, and, more generally, because knowledge is the independent variable affected by memory meant in its most exact sense, remembering and forgetting. Knowledge also relates to identity, both in the general sense of classification — insofar as that knowledge is acquired, processed, and retained differently by different social groups — and in its exact sense: an awareness, by someone in the overall population, of that group difference and its significance. As presented in the two Polish trials, the testimony bearing memory and identity is differentiated along a continuum of cognitive states, ranging from their most specific meanings, through related kinds of cognition, all the way to knowledge in a general sense.[18] In the rest of this comment, I attempt to reconfigure Isabel's examples of memory and identity along that continuum.

Memory

Isabel opens the entire article with an explicit reference to the act, or fact, of remembering. The actors in the *pesquisa* designated the elicited knowledge, and its expression in writing, as in and of themselves 'memory', or 'remembrance' — remembered matter — while a subset of the witnesses asserted, with that word, that they 'remember[ed]' the knowledge they reported. To Isabel, this double reportage of 'memory' defines the *pesquisa* as a process and a genre. The explicit references prompt her to present the *pesquisa*, right from the get-go, as, in and of itself, 'memory'. All the elicited knowledge is — as a cognitive state, is experienced and processed as — memory. Thus, my proposed distinction seems to disappear. However, this identification depends crucially on the frequency of such references. If they were universal, then the study of this inquest *becomes* the study of memory, and I am done. However, in several places Isabel implies that the witness references to memory were occasional, and cites a handful of utterances reporting actual remembering by the witnesses. I assume that the citations are not all such utterances — but are they typical, and if so, how? A fuller placement of this detail in the written record would have been helpful in discerning memory lodged, right from the get-go, at the most exact end of my continuum.

Also near that end is knowledge experienced across big units of time — replicated, reiterated, and potentially altered, processes that surely involved remembering and forgetting. In contrast to actual assertions of remembering, that kind of testimony seems absolutely ubiquitous in the *pesquisa*. Witnesses reported having acquired knowledge from ancestors across generations, or in the course of their lives, with (in this body of evidence, and excellent analysis) especially fascinating references to early youth and old age; and, they identified other chronological markers placing their knowledge at specific times in their past.[19] A long legacy of personal experience in a specialized activity or skill served a similar purpose, as a basis for chronological orientation over its evolution or transition.

---

18 Górecki, 'Memory', pp. 178–81.
19 Myśliwski, *Człowiek średniowiecza*, pp. 205–300.

Equally close to memory in the specific sense, is commemoration: practices purposefully designed to impart and preserve knowledge over time, thereby sustaining or creating memory. One such practice is an inscription made upon the human body, sufficiently intense to be memorable. A lovely instance, cited by Isabel, is Chris Wickham's celebrated report of whipping young people at legal transactions, toward the victims' later recollection of their occurrence and (perhaps) meaning. This mnemonic use of violence was part of boundary perambulation — an activity nicely linking Isabel's article with my work. For her, perambulation is perhaps *the* most prominent example of commemoration. For me, it is by far the best documented collective practice in medieval Poland related to a legal transaction of any kind.[20] As documented in Spain and in Poland, perambulation is linked to several phenomena that together comprise memory in the most specific sense: knowledge; its evolution over time; and performative acts involving the human body — motion, sensory perception, and the marking of objects with cuts, signs, or letters.

Thanks to reading Isabel's article, I now think that, much like memory, perambulation sits along a continuum. Most closely related to remembering, mis-remembering, or forgetting, are: (1) perambulations elicited by someone's doubt about the location of a previously existing boundary — so that the core issue was loss or absence of memory; (2) moments in their course when the participants paused along the way and performed demonstrative acts — bodily gestures such as kneeling or oath-taking; (3) explicit descriptions of those or other acts as mnemonic; and (4) attribution to the participants of traits closely related to memory, above all seniority of age, reputation, or experience (including in the act of remembering). Where such evidence is absent, I would describe the role of a perambulating group as confirming or altering knowledge in the general sense, further away from memory along the continuum.

Most distant from memory is one specific use of knowledge elicited by the *pesquisa*: proof. Proof is presented in this article as an instance of the medieval hierarchy of proofs, from the most desirable downward, in a sequence of default options.[21] In this case, the best proof was knowledge acquired by a witness directly — by seeing, hearing, or taking part in the contested circumstances — in strong preference to knowledge mediated by all the factors noted throughout the article: human agency, passage of time, or cognitive transition — that is, memory. Specifically regarding proof, memory recedes — is put in its place, so to speak — in favour of knowledge understood in its most direct meaning. I note this disjunction of the best proof from memory with interest because of a similar preference for directly acquired knowledge reflected in the witness testimonies regarding the Teutonic Order.[22]

---

20 Górecki, 'Communities of Legal Memory', p. 129 (n. 8), p. 133 (n. 25), pp. 140, 146–51; Górecki, *The Text and the World*, pp. 99–106, 163, 249; with much debt to Myśliwski, 'Zjawiska cudowne'; Myśliwski, 'Powstanie i rozwój granicy liniowej'; Myśliwski, 'Boundary Delimitation'.
21 Analogously to the placement of the ordeal in a hierarchy of proofs; Bartlett, *Trial by Fire and Water*, pp. 24–33.
22 Górecki, 'Memory', pp. 177–78, 181.

Identity

On the subject of identity, the article poses the ambiguity of viewpoint. Identity is here discerned above all from the perspective of the historian, Isabel, as she classifies the witnesses into social groups, such as 'knights', clerics, women, and others. In addition, she presents us with many examples of identity lodged at the clearest end of the continuum — as witnesses described themselves, in the first person singular, as 'knights', townspeople, 'clergymen', 'cobblers', and the rest, sometimes amplified relationally, as someone else's 'vassals' or 'subjects'; and, as scribes reported such utterances by witnesses in the third person singular: that they 'said', 'asserted', or 'claimed' their place in their worlds this way.

Equally reflective of identity is a recurrent description of the witnesses, also by scribes in the third person singular, in terms of an attribute, not group classification. That attribute is what Isabel calls 'honorability': a high moral and cognitive standing within some surrounding social world — seniority meant polyvalently — articulated with the adjectives 'worthy', 'good', 'old', and their superlative enhancements, contrasting the people thus designated favourably with that surrounding social world. This is an excellent, meaningful discernment of identity, because this attribute bridges several viewpoints. Even though in the record it describes witnesses, and is not articulated *by* them, its use in the *pesquisa* logically, necessarily implies a broad social recognition of its reality — including on the part of the people thus classified, as well as their contemporaries.

On the other hand, I am slightly puzzled by Isabel's treatment of the genesis of this attribute. In the opening sentence of the second section, she appears to assert that 'honorability' was generated — actually created — by the *pesquisa* itself, in its process, in order to enhance, right up front, the quality of the testimony gathered from the people thus designated. While this observation is intriguing, it raises, as developed here, a question for me. In the evidence I know best, of the various kinds of inquest in medieval Poland, that same attribute, reported in language (apparently) identical to the *pesquisa*, always appears as a preexisting qualification: a fully independent variable, possessed by the attesting population prior to an inquest, and the reason for their selection and for the high value of their knowledge and testimony. To be sure, in medieval Poland that qualification was, in its turn, further enhanced by participation in the inquest, which is presumably what Isabel means here. While therefore on this subject we are, I think, not in disagreement, here is another place I would have welcomed a slightly fuller explanation.

In some other parts of the article where social classifications are presented as identity, I am less certain whose viewpoint Isabel is reporting. One classification seems sharply removed from identity — lodged at the other end of my continuum. It is women. To be sure, women are of utmost importance in this article, but for a different reason, to which I will turn momentarily. As a marker of identity, womanhood poses the viewpoint problem with a special acuity. Isabel identifies a subset of witnesses as women, so this is certainly an act of classification by a historian. But did those witnesses identify themselves as women, or otherwise with reference to gender, sex, or sex difference? Unless I missed something, the answer is negative. Isabel does not describe either the testifying women, or the scribes, or any other voice from the *pesquisa*, as broaching this subject — in any of its variants: womanhood, sex difference, gender. The apparent absence of gender awareness is perplexing. This whole subject was so important as a source of identity, in its core sense — as subjectively felt, articulated experience — in so many medieval contexts that I wonder whether the *pesquisa* was one of them. At the moment, that is not clear.

Where women matter crucially in this article is on the subject of their knowledge, as disclosed in the *pesquisa*. Isabel splendidly revises one part of the historiographical representation of knowledge possessed by women: the emphasis on (supposedly) female-gendered subjects such as domesticity, the familial sphere, spatial interiority, and the like. While, like all good revision, Isabel does not diametrically reject the presence of such subjects in women's *pesquisa* testimonies, her reassessment emphasizes instead the prominence in their testimonies of subjects that are common in their range and frequency throughout the witness testimonies in their totality — meaning, logically, in testimonies offered by men. Here, as presented in this article, is Isabel's great contribution to gender. The social meaning of sex difference is simultaneously complicated and enriched.

In addition, like so many other aspects of what is meant here by identity, this revision loops us, the readers, back to memory. Insofar as knowledge — now including knowledge possessed by women — overlaps specifically with memory, Isabel has here provided an important revision of 'women's memory', as a cognitive state specific to that group or population.[23] However, this is an implication — yet another welcome perspective opened for us by Isabel — rather than an explicit conclusion, or link. It is but one example of the two big, subjects underlying of this article — visible, yet not quite clinched, perhaps yet to be written in one more dedicated section: the multiple connections between 'memory' and 'identity', each across its wide range of meanings; and, the 'debate' about each and both.

---

23 Fentress and Wickham, *Social Memory*, pp. 137–43; van Houts, ed., *Medieval Memories*.

Bibliography

Lites ac res gestae inter Polonos Ordinemque Cruciferorum, ed. by Ignacy Zakrzewski (Poznań: Nakładem Biblioteki Kórnickiej, 1890–1892)

Lites ac res gestae inter Polonos Ordinemque Cruciferorum, ed. by Helena Chłopocka, (Wrocław: Wydawnictwo Polskiej Akademii Nauk, 1970)

Alfonso, Isabel, 'Judicial Rhetoric and Political Legitimation in Medieval León-Castile', in Building Legitimacy: Political Discourses and Forms of Legitimacy in Medieval Societies, ed. by Julio Escalona, Isabel Alfonso, and Hugh Kennedy (Leiden: Brill, 2004), pp. 263–89

Barthélémy, Dominique, The Serf, the Knight, and the Historian (Ithaca: Cornell University Press, 2009)

Bartlett, Robert J., Trial by Fire and Water: The Medieval Judicial Ordeal (Oxford: Clarendon Press, 1986)

Bieniak, Janusz, '"Litterati" świeccy w procesie warszawskim z 1339 roku', in Cultus et cognitio. Studia z dziejów kultury średniowiecznej, ed. by Stefan Kuczyński (Warsaw: Państwowe Wydawnictwo Naukowe, 1976), pp. 97–106

Bieniak, Janusz, '"Milites" w procesie polsko-krzyżackim z 1339 roku', Przegląd Historyczny, 75 (1984), 503–14

Bieniak, Janusz, 'Środowisko świadków procesu polsko-krzyżackiego z 1339 r.', in Genealogia. Kręgi zawodowe i grupy interesu w Polsce średniowiecznej na tle porównawczym, ed. by Jan Wroniszewski (Toruń: Uniwersytet Mikołaja Kopernika, 1989), pp. 5–35

Bisson, Thomas N., 'The "Feudal Revolution"', Past & Present, 142 (1994), 6–42

Brown, Elizabeth A. R., 'The Tyranny of a Construct: Feudalism and Historians of Medieval Europe', American Historical Review, 79 (1974), 1063–88

Brown, Warren C., Violence in Medieval Europe (London: Longman, 2011)

Brundage, James, A., Medieval Canon Law (London: Routledge, 1995)

Buc, Philippe, The Dangers of Ritual: Between Early Medieval Texts and Social Scientific Theory (Princeton: Princeton University Press, 2001)

Conley, Thomas, Rhetoric in the European Tradition (Chicago: University of Chicago Press, 1990)

Connerton, Paul, How Societies Remember (Cambridge: Cambridge University Press, 1989)

Davies, Wendy, Windows on Justice in Northern Iberia, 800–1000 (Abingdon: Blackwell, 2016)

Fentress, James, and Chris Wickham, Social Memory (Oxford: Blackwell, 1992)

Górecki, Piotr, 'Rhetoric, Memory and Use of the Past: Abbot Peter of Henryków as Historian and Advocate', Cîteaux: Commentarii Cistercienses, 48 (1997), 261–94

Górecki, Piotr, 'Communities of Legal Memory in Medieval Poland, c. 1200–1240', Journal of Medieval History, 24 (1998), 127–54

Górecki, Piotr, 'Words, Concepts, and Phenomena: Knighthood, Lordship, and the Early Polish Nobility, c. 1100–c. 1350', in Nobles and Nobility in Medieval Europe: Concepts, Origins, Transformations, ed. by Anne Duggan (Woodbridge: Boydell, 2000), pp. 115–55

Górecki, Piotr, 'Piast Poland and the Legal Systems of Medieval Europe: A Case Study', Quaestiones Medii Aevi Novae, 20 (2015), 5–34

Górecki, Piotr, The Text and the World: The Henryków Book, its Authors, and Their Region, 1160–1310 (Oxford: Oxford University Press, 2015)

Górecki, Piotr, 'Memory: An Unlikely Case Study of Genocide', in *A Cultural History of Genocide, vol. 2: The Middle Ages*, ed. by Melodie H. Eichbauer (London: Bloomsbury, 2021), pp. 165–87 and 197–201

Head, Randolph C., *Making Archives in Early Modern Europe: Proof, Information, and Political Record-Keeping, 1400–1700* (Cambridge: Cambridge University Press, 2019)

Hummer, Hans, *Visions of Kinship in Medieval Europe* (Oxford: Oxford University Press, 2018)

Koziol, Geoffrey, *The Politics of Memory and Identity in Carolingian Royal Diplomas: The West Frankish Kingdom (840–987)* (Turnhout: Brepols, 2012)

Ligon Bjork, Elizabeth, and Robert A. Bjork, eds, *Memory* (San Diego: Academic Press, 1996)

Milliman, Paul, *'The Slippery Memory of Men': The Place of Pomerania in the Medieval Kingdom of Poland* (Leiden: Brill, 2013)

Myśliwski, Grzegorz, 'Zjawiska cudowne w pisarstwie średniowiecznym (XII–początek XIII w.)', *Przegląd Historyczny*, 81 (1990), 405–22

Myśliwski, Grzegorz, 'Powstanie i rozwój granicy liniowej na Mazowszu (XII–poł. XVI wieku)', *Kwartalnik Historyczny*, 101 (1994), 3–24

Myśliwski, Grzegorz, 'Boundary Delimitation in Medieval Poland', in *Historical Reflections on Central Europe: Selected Papers from the Fifth World Congress of Central and East European Studies, Warsaw 1995*, ed. by Stanislav Kirschbaum (Houndmills: Palgrave, 1999), pp. 27–36

Myśliwski, Grzegorz, *Człowiek średniowiecza wobec czasu i przestrzeni. Mazowsze od XII do poł. XVI wieku* (Warsaw: Wydawnictwo Krupski i S-ka, 1999)

Pleszczyński, Andrzej, and others, eds, *Imagined Communities: Constructing Collective Identities in Medieval Europe* (Leiden: Brill, 2018)

Reynolds, Susan, *Fiefs and Vassals: The Medieval Evidence Reinterpreted* (Oxford: Oxford University Press, 1994)

Reynolds, Susan, 'The Historiography of the Medieval State', in *Companion to Historiography*, ed. by Michael Bentley (London: Routledge, 1997), pp. 117–38

Reynolds, Susan, 'Fiefs and Vassals after Twelve Years', in *Feudalism: New Landscapes of Debate*, ed. by Sverre Bagge, Michael H. Gelting, and Thomas Lindkvist (Turnhout: Brepols, 2011), pp. 15–26

Van Houts, Elisabeth, ed., *Medieval Memories: Men, Women and the Past, 700–1300* (Harlow: Routledge, 2001)

White, Stephen D., 'The "Feudal Revolution": II', *Past & Present*, 152 (Aug., 1996), 205–23

ISABEL ALFONSO

Memory and Identity in Judicial *pesquisas* in Medieval León-Castile*

Pesquisas as Judicial Proceedings and Witness Records

In a debate on *Identity and Memory*, the process of judicial inquiry through the interrogation of witnesses (*pesquisa*) deserves special attention. This process, which became customary in medieval societies very early on in that period, explicitly sought to mobilise the memories of those summoned regarding the issues under investigation. Hence, the records of the testimonies in these *pesquisas* were sometimes expressively qualified as a 'remembrance' (*remembranza*), since this is how memory was understood, as remembrance or as a memory of times long past (*acuerdo de luengo tiempo*).[1]

Pesquisas became the evidentiary instrument deemed to have the greatest legitimacy for the resolution of a wide range of disputes and conflicts throughout the Middle Ages. Legal and political historians, assuming the objectivity claimed by this method for investigating and finding the truth, have regarded them as a step forward in the rationalisation of law and justice. This development has been linked to the institutional strengthening of the public powers, which used *pesquisas* in the *ex officio* prosecution of crimes against the community.[2] Without delving further into the sophisticated legal debates raised around this issue, recent studies have revealed the existence of a long-term legal culture in which the oral testimony of witnesses (the basis of all *pesquisas*) prevailed over written statements.[3] This method has been

---

* Original publication: Alfonso, Isabel, 'Memoria e identidad en las pesquisas judiciales en el área castellano-leonesa medieval', in *Construir la identidad en la Edad Media. Poder y memoria en la Castilla de los siglos VII a XV*, ed. by José Antonio Jara Fuentes, Georges Martin and Isabel Alfonso (Cuenca: Universidad de Castilla-La Mancha, 2010), pp. 248–79. Translated by Julian Thomas.

1 In the archives of the Cathedral of Burgos there is a 'Charter of the memories pertaining to the dispute' between the monastery of Ibeas and various councils 'over their boundaries and over pasture lands' ('Carta de remembranza de la contienda [...] sobre los terminos e sobre los pastos'). This contains the *pesquisa* that had been ordered by King Fernando III to resolve the dispute, and records the joint testimonies of seventeen witnesses (CatBurgos505, 1217). The testimony of four old men in front of the knights and the council of Tamayo was also qualified as a *remembrança* in the claim made by the Abbott of Oña to clarify some of his monastery's estates, which had been concealed (SSOña-A501, 1245). The witnesses in the *pesquisa* between the monastery of Oña and the council of Frías were questioned on the notion of memory (SSOña-O213, 1280).

2 This issue is dealt with in Cerdá Ruiz-Funes, 'En torno a la pesquisa'. For a general overview see Berman, *Law and revolution*.

3 The study of memory in the judicial field, and of the legal value of oral testimonies, has become an important issue in the last two decades at least. See Delumeau, 'La memoire'; Wickham, 'Gossip and Resistance'; Fentress and Wickham, *Social Memory*; Alfonso, 'Resolución de disputas'; Smail, 'Archivos de conocimiento'; and more recently his Smail, *The Consumption of Justice*; Górecki,

shown to have been used long before the twelfth and thirteenth centuries, when the legal changes related to the reception and development of Roman law supposedly occurred.[4] As far as the practice was concerned, this instrument of judicial inquiry varied over time in ways that cannot yet be fully ascertained due to the lack of systematic studies. However, it may be more appropriate to see the changes that historians have perceived as a result of the growing abundance and accuracy of written records of inquests, as well as of the increasing regulation of their use by courts.[5] This is suggested by the increase in the number of more or less complete *pesquisas* that have been preserved from the twelfth century, and especially from the thirteenth century onwards. For many others we only have the summaries presented during court proceedings or mere references indicating that they were requested and even carried out, but nothing else.

In general terms, the procedure seems to have followed a similar pattern: after the initial lawsuit about a disputed fact or right had been filed, the judges or the third parties who were summoned to participate would order or propose an investigation (*inquisitio*) in order to clarify the disputed issues. The *pesquisidores*, who were elected by the authority in question or sometimes appointed by the parties concerned, would conduct the questioning. It was they who generally selected and summoned the witnesses, though very often these were put forward by the litigants. The written records of their depositions by public notaries, which formed the basis on which the case was to be resolved, would be sent in the form of a closed letter to the authority that had requested the investigation. In other cases, they were developed as 'proof' (*probanza*) for the parties, aimed at substantiating their claims and demonstrating the validity of their arguments. This was the general litigation process, but its practical results were highly diverse. The diversity of records may be largely due to the degree

---

'Communities of legal memory'; Bedell, 'Memory and proof'; Alfonso and Jular Pérez-Alfaro, 'Oña contra Frías'; Wickham, *Legge, patriche e conflitti*; Branco, 'Memory and Truth'; Oliva Herrer, *Justicia contra señores*. These studies are at the crossroads of several discussions and debates on the relationship between oral culture and written culture, and about social memory and collective identity, to which I will refer throughout the following pages.

4 On *pesquisas* as a well-established judicial practice throughout the eleventh century, which was even used to restore the content of lost or destroyed documentation, see Alfonso, 'Judicial rhetoric', esp. pp. 78–85. This study dealt with the construction of truth in the judicial sphere in the early Middle Ages. It contains a critique of the arguments made by Foucault — perhaps the most influential author in the historiography in general—, who, accepting the theses of those who regarded them as a product of the increasing influence of Roman law, emphasised the radical change that *pesquisas* made to the concept of truth. For more on the importance of this method in restoring written documents lost during the early Middle Ages, see Brown, 'When documents are destroyed or lost'; this practice has been attested for Catalonia by Bowman, *Shifting Landmarks*.

5 The purpose of this regulation can be seen in some documents issued by Alfonso X (CatBurgos149, 1278) and Sancho IV (SFPSahagun1874, 1294). Delumeau, 'La memoire', pp. 45–46; and Bedell, 'Memory and proof', p. 25; provide arguments along the same lines. Branco, 'Memory and Truth', p. 2, more explicitly links the changes to the growing strength of the written form, and alongside with it, the development of notarial attestation. Of great interest to our understanding of the complex changes in the *pesquisa* method is the chapter by Lemesle, 'L'enquête contre les épreuves'. This volume collects the papers delivered at a symposium held in 2004 at the Ecole française in Rome, to which I have only had access once this study had been completed.

and forms of preservation, but could also be linked to a number of factors, including: the drafting of the record; the field or fields in which the *pesquisa* was carried out; the identity of the parties in dispute; and also the type of disputes, given that the content of the questionnaire, the identity of the informants, and the recollections required varied accordingly. Re-establishing the context in which each of the *pesquisas* occurred is therefore essential for a proper understanding of the information they provide. Here, however, only the more general aspects will be addressed.

While the documents in Leon-Castile are in varying degrees of preservation, even a cursory review reveals that *pesquisas* were used as fully standardised instruments of inquiry in connection with different types of issues, both fiscal and judicial.[6] Notwithstanding the controversial nature of the former, *pesquisas* seem to have been used not only in adversarial processes but also in *ex officio* ones. They were launched by various kinds of authorities in all types of litigation involving litigants of all sorts (individuals or groups, secular or ecclesiastical) and resulted in a broad range of resolutions. Their use was not limited to formal courts or mere adjudication processes. Rather, negotiation and agreement could be at the very root of the investigations when pursued by arbitrators or requested by the parties in dispute.[7] As we will later see, there are numerous cases in which litigants agreed to initiate a *pesquisa* regarding the claims made, and/or on the appointment of the investigators, who were therefore somehow deemed to be mediators or arbitrators.[8] However, there were also other

---

6 A good example of a simple inquiry to distribute and collect payments or royal orders can be a letter from Alfonso X which gave assurances that *pesquisas* would be used lawfully and accurately illustrates the damages — inherent to the practices of fiscal collection — that could be caused by their misuse (CatBurgos149, 1278).

7 The dispute over pasture boundaries and estates between the Cathedral of Burgos and its vassals of La Aguilera of the one part, and Juan Pérez and his vassals of Gumiel de Mercado, of the other part, was placed by King Alfonso X into the hands of mediators (*avenidores*) to find out the truth from the *hombres buenos* of the nearby towns (CatBurgos192, 1285). In the conflict between the chapter of the Cathedral of León and the heirs of Villavicencio about the obligations demanded by the former, Queen Violante explained that it was agreed that testimonies would be given by *hombres buenos* who knew the truth about the use of the disputed obligations; the statements made by eleven informants have been preserved (CatLeon2559, 1291; CatLeon2560, 1291). Other cases of *pesquisidores* / arbitrators: SSOña-O631 (1280); CatBurgos192 (1285). See also the following note.

8 A good example of the arbitral nature of *pesquisas* from the moment when the person who would carry out the interrogation was appointed, can be found in the complaint raised by the abbot of Oña against Alfonso Pérez de Terminón with regards to the estates that the latter held on behalf of the monastery; the two parties 'agreed to have the dispute settled by worthy men', who are named, and also that these men 'shall found the fair truth and make a fair inquiry into these complaints and these claims, and that the parties shall hear [that truth], and that once both parties have heard it, they shall decide what is right [...] and the judgement they issue shall be valid' ('touieron por bien de poner este pleyto en bonos omnes [para que] supiesen buena verdad e buena pesquisa de todas estas querelas e estas demandas en ommes bonos, e que oyan las partes, e oyendo amas las partes, que iudgasen aquello que fuese derecho [...] e que uala el iuyzio que ellos dieren'). The appointees, who called themselves mayors, once they found out the truth, sentenced the defendant and imposed penalties on him (SSOña-O235, 1281). In the dispute that the abbot of Silos and the council of San Pedro de la Villa brought before Fernando III, the litigants 'agreed to have it settled by means of a pesquisa' and the king 'ordered a pesquisa to be made' ('abinieronse de meterlo por pesquisa [...] mandelo pesquirir') (SDSilos121, 1233). It was also the disputing parties who chose the arbitrators

pesquisas which appear to have been made by the interested parties themselves, following similar procedures.[9]

As written records of oral inquests, judicial *pesquisas* gave rise to an informative body of material with a particular narrative. This is evident both in their initiation and in the questions of the *pesquisidores*, as well as in the 'accounts' (*dichos*) or statements of those summoned to testify as witnesses. This narrative character operates on several levels: on the statement of the objective; on the findings, which, particularly when provided as summaries, were formalised as a coherent story aimed at justifying one's own claims against those of the opponent's; and even when accounts fragmented among many voices are presented as 'proof' (*probanza*) by a party in order to support the validity of its arguments.[10] Despite not being homogeneous in either their preservation or in how they were carried out, these must be accepted as a very special source, one whose 'intrinsic logic' may be useful to restore.[11] In my opinion, this logic derives from the rhetorical formulation of the objectives generally used in all *pesquisas*, which is one of their characteristic features. Namely, they are said to be initiated to find out the truth about the disputed facts or rights. This explicit purpose is repeatedly stated in different ways, which included the reports that men of either party were selected to 'seek out the truth',[12] those that contained a royal order commanding 'an inquiry into the truth regarding some churches',[13] and those that urged the *pesquisidores* to 'find out the fair truth from as many parties as you can learn it' about the claim at stake.[14]

This rhetoric was enhanced by the oaths sworn by the witnesses to tell the whole truth about what they knew or had seen or heard about the matter under investigation

---

who would hear the claim between the council and the heirs of Clavijo, and the monastery of San Prudencio de Laturce concerning the pasture areas (SPLaturce65, 1291).

9 In 1270 the legal representatives of the Monastery of Oña and the council of Frías submitted their demands to Alfonso X. They requested and agreed to a *pesquisa*, intervened in the appointment of the *pesquisidores*, and possibly also in the selection of witnesses and in the recording and rendering of their answers. The arbitral nature of this long lawsuit, notwithstanding the royal nature of the judicial framework in which it took place, is highlighted in the study on the exceptional material preserved. In addition to the *pesquisa*, in which over a hundred witnesses appeared, we have daily records of the trial where this *pesquisa* was used (Alfonso and Jular Pérez-Alfaro, 'Oña contra Frías'). The study by Oliva Herrer, *Justicia contra señores*, is largely based on the 'proofs' (*probanzas*) or testimonies presented by the litigant parties.

10 Although guided by the questions, the responses often constitute real stories that are narrated as being credible; as an example, see that of don Samuel de Bilforado, reproduced later in n. 53, and that of Per Yuannez of Arroyuelo in n. 54. This narrative nature of the depositions was pointed out, among others, by Delumeau, 'La memoire'. p. 47; Bedell, 'Memory and proof', pp. 23–24; Oliva Herrer, *Justicia contra señores*, pp. 96–105. On the theoretical aspects on memory, see Fentress and Wickham, *Social Memory*, pp. 47–59.

11 Oexle convincingly proposed the usefulness of restoring the logic of the sources in Schmitt and Oexle, eds, *Les tendances actuelles*.

12 'and they chose men to inquire into the truth from both sides' ('Et elegerunt de una parte et de alia homines qui exquisissent inde ueritatem') (CatLeon695, 1011).

13 'perquirire ueritates de ecclesiis' (CatLeon1007, 1043).

14 'sepades buena verdat, por quantas partes pudierdes saber' (SFPSahagun1876, 1294; SFPSahagun1878, 1294). See also *supra*, the document cited in n. 8.

and on which they were being examined. It seems that each witness was sworn in individually, and it became routine to include, after his name and other personal data and before transcribing his answers with more or less detail, the phrase 'sworn in and questioned' to indicate that the witnesses had taken the oath and that the questions had been put to them. However, only very rarely did the public notaries record their oaths. More frequently, reference is made to the fact that witnesses were sworn in by the laying of hands on the holy Gospels or on these and the cross: 'Before all of them, those four men who had been sworn in on the Holy Gospels narrated everything that is written in this charter'.[15] Sometimes it is specified that it was the mayor who was holding the gospels while oath was taken.[16] The oath ritual was a most solemn act and a practice that was widespread and deeply rooted in all realms of society. It was taken as an assurance of truth and commitment in many different situations for it somehow externalised and made social values explicit.[17]

Since all answers given under oath were considered to be truthful, they also reinforced the rhetoric mentioned above, and thus became the most common form of legal evidence. Therefore, judging on the basis of truthful *pesquisas* was a fundamental feature of medieval justice: 'that man [the *merino*] shall judge in accordance to the inquiries on the truth'.[18] Evidence of resolutions made after the completion of the relevant inquest is therefore abundant, showing how judges issued their rulings based on the fair truth that they found in all the places where they were able to investigate: 'and once the truth was investigated all throughout the region and in all those places where we could learn it [...] we deemed that truth to be good'.[19] The findings in *pesquisas* were taken as the basis for the final decision and made official. They thus became a truth that was not only asserted in the specific case in question, but could also be strategically invoked later as and when appropriate. This occurred, for instance,

---

15 'Delante de estos todos, aquelos cuatro hombres jurados sobre Santos Evangelios dijeron lo que está en esta carta escrito'.

16 SSOña-A501 (1245); SDSilos140 (1251); SPLaturce116 (1378). It is striking that, in contrast with the widespread taking of oaths on the Gospels, in the *pesquisa* into the alleged exemption by the monastery of Oña from payment of the *fonsadera*, the *pesiquisidor*, on behalf of the king and queen were to ask the *hombres buenos* 'to tell what they knew by the truth they owed to their natural lords' ('quel dixiesen lo que ende sabien, por la verdad que auian a decir a sus sennores naturales') (SSOña-O410, 1294). I do not know if this formula is an exception or an indication of a different political and ideological position.

17 In the text that records the dispute between the monastery of Sahagún and the people of Grajal, oaths were taken in a broad range of situations, including those establishing extrajudicial settlements (SFPSahagun126, 1152). See Le Roy Ladurie, *Montaillou*, pp. 548–51; and also Verdier, ed., *Le serment* for more on the importance of oaths as legal evidence and the way in which they externalised the values and the bonhomie involved in local practices. The author also discusses the formal diversity of oaths depending on where they were made (in the fields they were made on a body part or on any food intended for the body, while in more educated settings people were sworn in on the calendar or on the Gospels).

18 'iudicet illo homine per exquisicione de ueritate' (SFPSahagun949, 1095).

19 'e havida la verdad por toda la comarca o por todos los logares que la podemos saber [...] fallamos por buena verdat' (SPLaturce65, 1219); 'in all nearby areas and places to find out the truth' ('por vicinas partes et loca et reperta veritat') (SFPSahagun1266, 1139).

when the litigants referred to previous *pesquisas* in which rights had been defined and awarded and which were questioned again later, or when witnesses used them to substantiate their knowledge. This was the case for several witnesses questioned about the grounds of the rights claimed by the council of Frías over those alleged by the monastery of Oña. Some of them claimed to know something because they had seen the *pesquisa* once it had been done: 'and don Lope had ordered it to be investigated and I saw the inquiry once it was done';[20] others argued that they had heard that 'Frías had won [the dispute] thanks to an inquiry that King Don Alfonso had ordered'.[21] The *pesquisa* was therefore accepted as a means of defining rights and of legitimising an acquisition; it made ownership public and legally accepted. Memory, which was recreated in, and fed by, these acts, clearly constituted an essential element of the construction and dissemination of social knowledge, both as a recollection of actual inquiry practices and of the documents where it was contained. *Pesquisas*, as archives of memory, became memorable objects in themselves.[22]

This chapter will focus on the social aspect of oral memory as mobilised in lawsuits and laid down in writing during the *pesquisa* process. The purpose is to seek further insight into the meaning and effect that the practice of inquiring (*perquirir*) may have had on the agents whose memories were collected and on the social environments in which they lived. By examining the elements that defined the identity of witnesses, the nature of their memories, and the credibility accorded to them, relevant issues can be discussed in connection with the core subject of this debate. This review will be limited to some of the *pesquisas* preserved in the documents from some of the ecclesiastical institutions in the area of Castile and Leon during the middle centuries of the medieval period.

---

20 The context of the answer is worth reproducing here. The *pesquisidor* '[said]in his question that those from Frías said that their neighbours from Cebolleros used to cut [wood] and graze [their cattle] with those from Mijangos in the hills in the times of King Don Alfonso and ever since, and that these [rights] are now been seized from them and that for this they will lose them, unlawfully and with no justification, and that this is what he knows' ('en la pregunta que dizien los de Frías que los sos vecinos de Cebolleros que usaron encortar e en pacer con los de Mijangos en los montes, en tiempo del rey don Alfonso e dent aca, e que ge lo embargan agora e que los pendran por ello, sin razon e sin derecho, que es lo que ent sabe'). The witness 'said that he had seen and he knows that they had already had another dispute over that hill, in the times of don Lope; and that don Lope had ordered and inquiry on it to be done, and that I saw that inquiry once it had been made, and that don Lope had decreed that those from Cebolleros should cut [wood] with those from Mijangos in the communal land but not in the rest' ('dijo que vio e que sabe que ya otra uegada ouieron contienda sobre este monte, en tiempo de don Lope; e don Lope mandolo pesquirir e que ui la pesquisa fecha e don Lope que mando que los de Cebolleros cortasen con los de Mijangos en el monte defuso e en lo al non') (SSOña-O231, 1280).

21 'por pesquisa que mando fazer el rey don Alfonso lo gano Frias' (SSOña-O231, 1280).

22 In another pesquisa from the monastery of Oña caused by a dispute with the Monastery of Rodilla about plots of land, boundaries and *pechos* (rents), many of the fourteen witnesses admitted that their memories of those issues came from having heard their parents or other old *hombres buenos* say repeatedly that they had seen a *pesquisa* take place on the same issues: 'that they have heard their father, who was and old good man who lived over a hundred years, say many times that he had seen a *pesquisa* being made between the people of the Monastery and the Abbot of Oña' ('que oyera a su padre, que era omme bueno antigo, que visquiera bien çien annos, dezir muchas uezes que el viera fazer pesquisa entre los de Monesterio e el abat de Onna') (SSOña-O568, 1317).

The Identity of Witnesses and the Criteria that Gave Credence to their Memories

Given the rhetoric involved in any *pesquisa*, being summoned as a witness to answer questions from the *pesquisidores* publicly qualified any such individual as truthful and legally trustworthy, and thus bestowed upon him the status of an *hombre bueno* (lit. a 'worthy man'). All of the informants were required to meet such requirements, and compliance was then confirmed when they were sworn in to tell the truth about the matters on which they were questioned. There are very substantial examples of how this requirement was sometimes made explicit. That occurs in a case involving the Cathedral of Oviedo in the late eleventh century, when King Alfonso VI 'ordered that an inquiry should be made by truthful and knowledgeable men'.[23] A *pesquisa* carried out in 1152 at the request of the monks of Sahagún against the violent acts regularly perpetrated by the inhabitants of Grajal against the dam that fed one of their mills also serves to illustrate this requirement. This *pesquisa* was convened and the complaint was heard by Princess Sancha, sister of King Alfonso VII, who presided over the process. Two of her 'elderly knights, of good life and fame and fearful of God' selected fourteen men to be questioned from seven nearby localities, to be identified from among 'the oldest and most respected and prestigious men they could possibly find'.[24] Their testimonies would be also ratified by two other inhabitants of the accused village whose honourability was also emphasised: 'the elders of the valley and the honourable of the community'.[25] In an area to the east of the above, don Oriol, as royal *merino* in the whole of Bureba, also gathered the council and twelve of the best reputed men to question them in order to settle a dispute over a meadow between San Millán and the men of Santa Maria de Ribarredonda.[26] Good reputation thus became a sign of distinction that identified the actors in the *pesquisas*, both those who were summoned to be questioned, and those who were appointed to ask those questions. Although the economic and social status of each of these groups was very different, there was a circular logic that fed back into the whole process. There seemed to be a widespread awareness of the consequences (both symbolic and material) of having a good or bad personal reputation; hence care was taken in maintaining the former and avoiding the latter.[27]

---

23 'iussit inde exquisitionem facere per omnes ueridicos et sapitores' (AlfonsoVI-112, 1090). It is perhaps interesting to take into account that in various sales between private individuals of goods located in the territory of Sahagún the term *sapitores* (wise men) identifies some of those who appear on the list of witnesses after *merinos* and *sayones*, and before other confirming witnesses. See SFPSahagun1265 (1138); SFPSahagun1267 (1139); SFPSahagun1270 (1140) — in the last one in the vernacular *sabidores*.

24 'milites antiguos, bone uite et fame et timentes Deum [...] de antiquioribus et melioris uite et fame qui possent inuenire' (SFPSahagun1266, 1139–1152).

25 'antiquos ualle et honorabiles omni plebi' (SFPSahagun1266, 1139–1152).

26 'duodecim ergo de melioribus concilii' (SMCogolla-L294, 1178).

27 Some recent studies fittingly posing theoretical questions about the social dimension of personal reputation are collected in Fenster and Smail, eds, *Fama*. See, in particular, Wickham, 'Fama and the Law', pp. 15–26, on legal aspects of reputation in Italian courts; and Bowman, 'Infamy and Proof', on infamy in Visigothic law and in *Las Partidas* of Alfonso X.

As shown in the cases mentioned above and in many others too numerous to mention here, in general terms those called to testify had to conform to certain identity criteria regarding two aspects that were often concurrent: older age, valued in terms of having earlier and more direct knowledge of the facts under investigation; and a good personal and social reputation, which gave assurance of the truthfulness of the testimonies. This is illustrated in a particular dispute between the monks of Sahagún and the council of Belver, caused by the monks' alleged exemption from the payment of *yantares*. The fact that one of the witnesses was identified as 'a good and elderly man that had been mayor of the locality in many occasions' fitted the mandate given to the *pesquidores* 'so that they should learn the truth from the *omnes bonos* and the eldest of the place as to whether the prior and the monks gave the *yantar* to Kind Don Alfonso and to the current King Don Sancho'.[28]

The recollections or memories of the eldest members of the community did not seem to be a mere rhetorical statement; rather, the general question about the witness's age and the time that their memories dated back to — both of which were included in the majority of interrogations — indicated the importance attached to the age of the witnesses. Their degree of knowledge seemed to be linked to the years they had lived, an association between knowledge and old age that is clearly made in the royal charter by Alfonso VI cited above when the knowledgeable (*sapitores*) are identified as 'those of a very old age'.[29] The frequency with which some people claimed to be 'septuagenarians', 'octogenarians' or even 'centenaries' suggests that life expectancy in these medieval societies was greater than has been assumed. It is difficult, however, to decide how reliable the age claimed by the witnesses was. Scholars who have studied this matter have come to different, and even opposite, conclusions. For example, Delumeau (regarding people of Arezzo and Siena), and Bedell (regarding people in England) considered the claims to be reliable, and on that basis attempted to deduce the temporal perception of the witnesses' memories, and the importance of their testimonies for the construction of local past events.[30] However, Branco, for the Portuguese area of Braga, has questioned the plausibility of these claims. For her, they are a mere indication of elderly status, rather than a record of actual age. She believes that this seems inconsistent with their obligation to confirm both how they knew their age, and the evidence they provided to the *pesquisidores* to that effect. In her opinion, the only explanation for this contradiction was that they deliberately, albeit piously, lied.[31]

It should be noted that all three works cited focused on specific *pesquisas* about a given dispute between particular litigants. The considerations of these authors are only applicable to specific cases. By adopting a more general view, as proposed

---

28 'omme bono e ançiano que fuera alcalde del lugar muchas veguadas [...] que sopiessen verdad enos omnes bonos e mays ançianos del lugar sse dieran yantar el prior o los monges, al rey don Alfonso y a este rey don Sancho' (SFPSahagun1861, 1291; SFPSahagun1862, 1291).

29 'iam in decrepita etate positos'. See n. 23, AlfonsoVI-112, 1090.

30 Delumeau, 'La memoire', pp. 49–53; Bedell, 'Memory and proof', pp. 11–15. Both include charts of the reported ages and the nature of the recollections that formed the basis of their testimonies.

31 Branco, 'Memory and Truth', pp. 14–17.

here, the data from the *pesquisas* used tends to confirm that the self-reported age of witnesses was aimed at supporting allegations closely pertaining to the prescription of disputes over property or jurisdiction, or simply sought to emphasise long-term memories. In some specific instances, however, it may be worth engaging in an analysis such as that conducted by the authors mentioned above, where the facts mentioned by the witnesses could allow their claimed age to be verified. In the absence of this type of analysis, when witnesses answered the question about their age (which did not happen in all cases), they seem to have been under the generally accepted assumption that old age itself was sufficient to validate their memories. When they were asked about the time period that their recollections dated back to and replied accordingly, their answers appear to have been directly linked to the specific issue being investigated. Rarely did they allude to political events, and their recollections were more often related to their own life cycles, which is more indicative of the ways in which memory is reproduced than of the actual age of the witnesses.[32] These impressions can be illustrated by some examples. In the *pesquisa* filed by the monastery of Sahagún in the early thirteenth century to defend its rights in many churches against the claims of the Cathedral of León, more than one hundred and forty witnesses questioned provided vague answers about their age and could not say with any degree of certainty how old they were. One of them, however, a layman called Domingo Martín from Villardefrades, argued that he remembered that when Count Nuño carried King Alfonso as a child, he was older than the king.[33] Another witness, Pedro Nicolas, a *miles* from Bundregales, said 'he had heard from his mother and tutors that he had been born in the same week that the emperor died'.[34] Rodrigo Nicolás, his brother, also a *miles* from the same place, admitted that he only knew

---

32 For example, the recollections of Tellum Gutierrez de Villada, the third witness in the Grajal case, referred to his childhood, puberty and adulthood up to the present. When he was asked 'he said that he was over eighty six years old since he had been a child and recalled [living] in his father's house, and later as a young man he very often went to grind the wheat of his father to the mill of *Villasalit*, and also for himself; and later he took a wife' ('dixit quod erant plusquam octoginta et sex anni ex quo ipse erat puer ut recordabatur in domo patris sui; et postquam iuuenis multociens iuit ad molendum triticum patris sui ad molendina de Uillasalit, etiam pro se, postquam recepit uxorem'), and he went on to describe that he had actually witnessed the collapse of the dam under investigation (SFPSahagun1313, 1152).

33 'he did not know how old he was, but he remembered that when Count Nuño carried Alfonso as a child he was older than the king' ('de se non sit quot annorum sit, et bene recordatur quando comes Nunio portabat puerum regem Aldefonsus, et erat iste maioris etatis quam rex' (SFPSahagun1849, 1215: witness 30). The witness seems to allude to some of the events that took place between 1159 and 1162, when the Lara family fought for the guardianship of King Alfonso VIII, then a child, against the rival Castro family, who were allies of his uncle, the King of León, Fernando II. Therefore, this witness must have been about 80 years old; witness 32, another layperson from the same place, also referred to this fact to situate his age.

34 'natus est ea septimana quo mortuus fui imperator, secundum quod audiuit a matre sua et a tutoribus suis' (SFPSahagun1849, 1215: witness 14). This means that he must have been fifty-eight years old, since Emperor Alfonso VII died in 1157. The recollection of witness 33 also referred to the emperor's death, but he claimed that 'he had already been born and remembered well that men mourned the emperor's death' ('iam natus erat quando mortuus est imperator, et bene recordatur quod uidit homines flere propter mortem illius') (SFPSahagun1849, 1215).

that he was eighteen years younger than him.[35] Sometimes the answers belie a certain irony and even sarcasm, such as that produced by Fernando Guastonis, another monastery *solariego* from Villavicencio who, when asked what his age was, or what he thought his age was, remarked that he was old enough to know the facts that he was being asked about.[36] Another example is that concerning Juan Cuzelon from Grajal, who simply responded 'the one I know', but claimed to have memories from seventy years before.[37]

The witnesses who testified in the *pesquisa* conducted by a procurator from San Zoilo of Carrión to endorse the rights of his monastery in numerous churches against the Bishop of Palencia also provided vague estimates of their age. These, however, used different time references to place their memories.[38] One of them, Martín Peláez, a layman from Frómista, recalled the time when 'there was an interdict in the kingdom due to the marriage of the King of Leon [and] no religious services were held in the church of San Martín'.[39] Another, don Fernando de Arconada, said 'he did not know his age, but he had memories from fifteen years before Alarcos'.[40] Juan Boardo of Villaomet claimed he was a quinquagenarian 'and remembered the *curia* held in Carrión when the King of Castile gave his daughter in marriage to the King of León'.[41] Having said that, the memories of the more than one hundred and fifty witnesses who were questioned for this *pesquisa* were primarily concerned with personal issues related to attending the celebrations of monastic vigils, or the period in which they lived and were brought up (*nutritus*) in the monastery — or they simply mentioned that they had seen or heard it under various circumstances.[42]

---

35 'When asked about his age, he answered that he did not know, but that his brother [...] was eighteen years younger than him' ('Interrogatus quo annorum sit, respondit quod nescit; set frater suus, proxime supradictus, exedit eum in XVIII annos') (SFPSahagun1849, 1215).

36 'I am old enought to know about this' ('bene habeo tantum quod bene scio istud') (SFPSahagun1849, 1215).

37 'quid scit ego' (SFPSahagun1849, 1215: witnesses 48 and 109).

38 SZCarrión84 (1220): witness 13. For more information on knowledge and assessment of time by the witnesses in this inquest, I refer to the study by Gautier-Dalché, which I only found after writing this paper, and which supplements my own findings in greater detail Gautier-Dalché, 'Connaissance de l'age'.

39 'cum regnum inderticto suppositum occasione matrimonii regis legionensis, ecclesia Santi Martini nihilominus diuina officia celebrabat' (SZCarrión84, 1220). This witness refers to the bull of excommunication issued by Innocent III in 1204 because of the marriage of King Alfonso IX of Leon to Berengaria, daughter of Alfonso VIII, given their kinship.

40 'De etate, nescit, set recordatur a XV annis ante Alarcus' (SZCarrión84, 1220). This is witness 8 from those who were questioned about the Church of San Facundo Arconada; since Alarcos had been conquered by the Almohad in 1195, the recollection of this witness, according to his account, dated back to the 1180s; other witnesses linked their memories to the time when *Opte* was taken.

41 'et recordari a tempore curie que fuit Carrionis, quando rex Castella tradidit filiam suam nuptii regi legionensi' (SZCarrión84, 1220). This is witness 12 of those who were questioned about the pontifical *tercia* in Villaomed. He alluded to the *curia* of Carrión held in 1188 and the arrangements for the wedding of Alfonso IX, which sealed the peace between the two kingdoms. On the splendour and importance of this *curia* held in the monastery church of San Zoilo, see González, *El Reino de Castilla en la época de Alfonso VIII*, t. 1, pp. 705–07.

42 SZCarrión84 (1220): witness 28, Juan Dominguez de Marcella, was asked how he knew the Church of Frómista if he was not from there and 'he said that every year during his childhood he used to come to the vigils to Martin Beatus of Frómista and always found monks of San Zoilo in charge' ('dixit quo

The issue of credibility being based on older age takes on a whole different meaning here. Being older was no longer directly equated with having more knowledge, or at least this was somewhat questioned. It was superseded by having direct experience. This could come from a variety of situations, either due to profession and/or status, or to having lived in the places which were covered in the *pesquisa*, or even because they had been told about it were simply aware of it as it was part of shared knowledge.

Other elements related to identity need to be discussed before exploring the various criteria for knowledge to be deemed to be authoritative and attributed greater credibility. The personal identity of the witnesses in these *pesquisas* was also often defined by their place of origin, as well as by their place of residence. Sometimes, if origin and residence are different, this provides data about a significant level of mobility.[43] Identity could also be defined by kinship;[44] by profession (butchers, shepherds, shoemakers, farmers, gardeners); as well as by social status, often confused with profession: distinctions were made between laymen (knights and squires) and churchmen (priests, priors, monks or mere clergymen). An important identifying factor was also the nature of the witnesses' ties to others, as well as being vassals or *solariegos*. In the *pesquisa* filed by Sahagún to defend its jurisdiction over numerous churches against the claims of the Cathedral of León, one hundred and forty-two witnesses appeared before the bishops of Orense and Segovia, who were acting as papal delegates. Most of them were laymen who claimed to be subjects (*solariegos*) of the abbot. Five of the witnesses said they were knights (*miles*); and nineteen claimed to be clergymen, including several monks from the same monastery. For others no ties of dependency are stated. This is also the case in the *pesquisa* related to some churches disputed by the Monastery of Oña and the Cathedral of Burgos, in which witnesses included both laymen and clergymen. It must be noted that, in general, the number of laymen involved in formal ecclesiastical disputes was higher than that of clergymen. This indicates that the 'churches' concerned and affected everyone, not only in terms of worship, but also as material suppliers of most of their income and, to a certain extent, of the personnel in charge of them. The sociability generated around all of these aspects provided much of the knowledge that fed the memories of these people. In any case, within the same *pesquisa*, both laymen — noblemen and *milites* —, and churchmen — priors and monks — were usually questioned. One of

---

quolibet anno a pueritia sua uenire consueuerat ad uigilias beati Martini de Fromesta et inuenieat semper monachos Sancti Zoyli dominantes'). Witness 29 answered in the same way; another said they had been fostered there.

43 See, for example, the responses of more than seventy witnesses in the *pesquisa* held to settle the dispute between the monastery of Oña and the clergymen from Liencres on the church of Santa Olalla. The latter claimed that it was a communal church, namely, that it belonged to clergymen who were the sons and heirs of some village dwellers (SSOña-O601, 1323–1329).

44 The high number of sons of clergymen who appear in the case of Liencres (cited in note 39) is noteworthy. This is partly explained by the nature of the dispute, as it was a claim made by the village dwellers for the church to remain in the hands of their sons. On the social fabric that provided the context for this dispute, see a study to be published shortly, which was presented at the colloquium entitled *Medieval Peasants revisited*, held at the University of California, Huntington Library, in May, 2008. [Editors' note: Later published as Alfonso, 'Iglesias rurales'. For an English translation, see chapter 10 of this volume].

152   ISABEL ALFONSO

the most interesting aspects of the *pesquisa* related to the conflict between Oña and Frías is precisely the complexity and diverse nature of the social fabric affected by it. Of the one hundred and twenty witnesses from more than fifty localities, ninety-four identified themselves as vassals of more than forty-five different lords.[45]

Despite the scarcity of the information available, it is important to consider the gender identity of the witnesses. Generally speaking, for the cases here studied the statements made by Robert Durand about the Portuguese area of Seia and by Chris Wickham about Italian Tuscany regarding the male-dominated nature of the memories invoked and recorded in *pesquisas*[46] could well be accepted, since most of the witnesses were men. However, it should be noted that in the areas of León-Castile covered by these inquiries, the testimonies of some women are also documented, albeit only sporadically and in very small numbers. In the inquiry launched by the monastery of San Pedro de Arlanza concerning the rents owed by their vassals in Contreras, together with five *hombres buenos*, two — good and old — women were also questioned, and their testimony was summarised alongside the men's.[47] A higher proportion of women, although still in the minority, can be seen in the *pesquisa* conducted by the attorney (*procurador*) monk from San Zoilo of Carrión on the rights of his monastery over several churches in the Bishopric of Palencia. More than one hundred witnesses were called to testify in each of the places where the disputed churches were located, nine of which were women. Several of them were identified as widows, some claimed to be centenarians, others did not know their age, but they all acknowledged that they remembered similar information to that provided by their neighbours, and had obtained that information in different ways. They either had heard it from their parents, or had seen statements — such as the assignation of mandates — that the monastery owned the churches, and none of them had witnessed (in whole or in part) that they belonged to the Bishop of Palencia. Direct knowledge and personal experience is also claimed, as in the case of a woman who together with her husband had held one of the disputed churches. Finally, they all certainly shared common knowledge, one which seemed to combine all sources of information. What was seen, heard, or participated in was then spread and communicated in the various spheres of local society, thus becoming part of the public domain. This was very clearly stated by *Maria Iohannes, relicta Gomecii*, when she claimed: 'I know what everyone in the village knows', that the church of San Facundo had always belonged to the sacristan of San Zoylo and that the bishop had his share in it.[48] This woman seemed to be aware that it was precisely this collective character that granted her knowledge authority, and it is likely that she received it as such.[49]

---

45   Alfonso and Jular Pérez-Alfaro, 'Oña contra Frías', pp. 79–81, and end tables: I, specifying the place of origin of each witness; and II, specifying the lords whose vassals they claimed to be.

46   Durand, 'La mémoire des campagnes portugaises', pp. 366; Wickham, 'Fama and the Law', pp. 23–24.

47   SPArlanza160 (1289).

48   'ego scio omnes sciumus quis sumus in uilla' (SZCarrión84, 1220).

49   On the paradigm of shared knowledge and the universality of its formulation in medieval European legal culture, see Smail, 'Archivos de conocimiento', p. 1051. He has developed his arguments in later works, especially in Smail, *The Consumption of Justice*.

More evidence can be added to the fact that the testimony and memories of women were sometimes taken into account in judicial *pesquisas* in this area, but the recollections provided above suffice to nuance some of the findings that have been made in other areas. Most significantly, women's knowledge has been regarded as partial, that is, as limited to certain issues and restricted to some spheres. Where there are testimonies from women, such as in the rich urban record of late medieval Marseille studied by Daniel Smail, these are considered to pertain to the domestic sphere and to family matters, such as births and deaths.[50] When testimonies are non-existent, as in the Portuguese or Italian areas mentioned before, this is explained in the same terms, on the basis that men and women occupied different social spaces, and therefore, that since the statements collected would have depended on the type of matters being investigated, some of them would have been supposedly known only to men's memories.[51] The evidence related to the Castile and León areas, even if scarce, partially questions this differentiation (at least in terms of time and space), since the regulations at the time sought to govern and perhaps even construct this difference.[52]. Knowledge was more socially diffuse in the local areas, in the small rural communities that were periodically mobilised by *pesquisidores*. While it seems certain that, as in other areas, the testimonies of women were not granted the same legal status as those of men, women's participation in the construction of both family and community memories was more significant than can be inferred from their small presence in inquests — as the authors mentioned above recognize. This does not deny the existence of differentiated memories; they were different, but that differentiation was not only gender based. Clergymen, for example, included among their memories many incidents of their church 'careers', just as monks recalled events occurred within their monastic enclosure. The knowledge held by these latter groups was also coloured to a greater extent by written memories, though this are not necessarily absent in other groups. The recollections recorded in the *pesquisas* appear to be very dense and fluid because they deal with issues that in one way or another affected and mattered to all.

To return to the question of the authoritativeness conferred on statements, it is neither possible nor desirable to separate the identity of the witnesses from

---

50 Smail, *The Consumption of Justice*. pp. 233–40.
51 In this regard, Chris Wickham presumed that the lack of female testimonies in the Tuscan area covered by his *pesquisas* could be due to the fact that they were disputes about land and the church, which means that they privileged a male-specific public space. However, he added, rightly in my opinion, that the private *fama*, the legal concept of 'rumour' (which could include women) may have been constructed in a less formal and hierarchical, and more interesting way. Still, it did not give rise to the kind of legally acceptable common knowledge, at least in those kinds of disputes and during this period (Wickham, 'Fama and the Law', p. 24). The same lack of female witnesses is noted by Oliva with regards to the *probanzas* from León-Castile in the early modern period, which he also attributed to its lack of legal value even if some *concejo* ordinances recognised the legal capacity of women to testify (Oliva Herrer, *Justicia contra señores*, pp. 109–10). In a similar vein, although emphasising shared responsibility and collaboration in the task of preserving the past, see Van Houts, *Memory and Gender*.
52 For more in-depth discussion on this subject, see Madero Eguía, 'Savoirs féminins'.

their sources of information, because the more direct those sources were, the more credibility they were granted. In many *pesquisas* the experience of the witnesses was more highly valued than their age, and it was thus on this basis that they were selected in order to support the information gathered. This is clearly evident in the *pesquisa* initiated by the lawsuit brought by the monastery of Sahagún against the governor (*tenente*) of the village of Melgar and his vassals, who did not respect the jurisdiction of the monastery and the use of pastures in some places. Those responsible for the investigation said they had asked:

> in as many places as they could to men of worthy ascendancy who said that they had grazed [their cattle] many times, and to other men who had been shepherds and had been grazing their cattle in the preserve of Sahagún for a long time, and to other men in the boundaries.[53]

Among the twenty-three witnesses summoned, many were identified as shepherds who claimed that their knowledge about the area reserved to the monastery was based on their experience in watching the monastery's cattle over a number of years, 'for they were around and had seen it'.[54] This was the case even if, besides shepherds, there were shoemakers or gardeners, or even squires who had been involved in the control of cattle.[55] They all provided information because they had witnessed improper conduct by the governors from Melgar against whom Sahagún had brought the lawsuit, due to the work that they had performed. Another *pesquisa* was carried out to determine the pasture rights of Uranave and Puentedura, two small localities in Burgos under the control of the monastery of Silos, which were denied to them by the people of another village. The first witness 'swore and said that he had been a shepherd for ten years in that hill' and that he had seen how dwellers of the two villages within the boundaries indicated 'grazing [their cattle] and cutting [wood] and lying and defending'.[56] This answer was confirmed by other witnesses, although none were identified as shepherds. Direct knowledge derived from experience was also adduced in cases involving either income or a title that resulted in the right to receive such income. It was common for witnesses in these cases to support their statements by identifying themselves as having been collectors of such income at some point, which undoubtedly made their testimony more convincing. These include

---

53 'por quantas partes pudiemos en omnes fiiosdalgo, que dizien que fueran en correr las yeruas muchas vezes, et en otros omnes que fueron pastores que anduvieron paciendo con sus ganados en el coto de Sant Fagunt muy grant tiempo, et en otros omnes de las fronteras' (SFPSahagun1878, 1294).

54 'porque andaba allí y lo viera' (SFPSahagun1878, 1294).

55 SFPSahagun1878 (1294). Witness 3 identified himself as a shoemaker from Sahagún. When questioned, he stated that he had been a shepherd and had looked after the cattle in the areas reserved to the monastery and elsewhere for more than fifteen or twenty years. Witness 4, a gardener from the village of Sahagún, said that he was an apprentice and had kept cattle on the monastery's pastures, which is why he was in a position to testify. Witness 5 was a shepherd from Perales. Witness 6 was also an apprentice from Perales and had watched his cattle on the pastures of Sahagún and in the monastery's enclosure.

56 'juro e dixo que fue diez annos en aquel monte pastor [...] uio paçeer e cortar e iazer e deffender' (SDSilos121, 1233).

individuals who claimed to have collected *procuraciones*[57] or *infurciones*[58] that were due. There were also those who said that they had collected royal revenues, such as some of the witnesses questioned on their collection of the *fonsadera* from the vassals of Oña, who recounted why and how they had collected it.[59] This was also common in cases of disputes over ecclesiastical rights. Some witnesses were individuals who claimed that they had been *terceros*, a name given to those responsible for collecting the *tercias* or third parts into which the tithing was divided. One of such witnesses was Martinus Grandini, a layman from Villaomez, in the *pesquisa* carried out into the *tercia pontifical* of that town. He said that because 'he had been *terciarius* and made the division' he knew that a *tercia* was divided between the steward and the bishop of Palencia, another *tercia* was for the *concejo*, and the other one for the chaplain.[60] This procedure was ratified by many of his neighbours, as they had also participated in its collection at some point in the past. Another aspect that could also be discussed is the knowledge that came from another type of involvement, such as that claimed by witnesses testifying on their own obligations. However, this issue deserves more attention than can be afforded in these pages.[61]

---

57 SSOña-O107 (1209).
58 CatLeon2560 (1291). Witness 4, for example, stated that he collected *infurciones* on orders from the person in charge of Villavivencio by the chapter of the church of León.
59 SSOña-O410 (1294). Witness 8, don Samuel Bilforado, when asked, 'said that he had sometimes collected the payments that those in the land gave as payment of the *fonsaderas* that were due to the king and to the bishopric of Burgos on behalf of Count don Loppe, but he said that he had never demanded any payment for the *fonsadera* to the vassals of the abbot of Oña, with the exception of a *fonsadera* that Juan Mateo, a royal cup-bearer, had collected by force, which had been collected on his behalf by Pedro Fernández of Oña; and that for this reason the abbot of Oña was greatly upset, for it went against the privileges and exemptions and liberties that had been granted to them by the kings, as their vassals were exempted from the payment of the *fonsadera*; and he said that Juan Mateo had promised that he would pay back everything that they had collected from their vassals for that reason, and that he would never demand it again' ('dixo que el que cogiera algunas uezes dineros en la tierra de las fonsaderas que dauan al rey en el obispado de Burgos paral conde don Loppe, mas dixo que el nunqua demandara ninguna cosa por razon de fonsadera a los vasallos del abbat de Onna, saluo de vna fonsadera que ouo cogido Iohan Mathe, camarero mayor del rey, por fuerça, e ouola cogido por el Pero Ferrandez de Onna; et que por esta razon el abbat de Onna que se agrauiara mucho, porque les pasaua contra los privilegios e las franquezas e las libertades que ellos tenien de los reyes, porque non auien a dar fonsadera ninguna los sus vasallo; et dixo que Iohan Mathe quel prometiera quel que ge lo pecharie quanto les auien tomado a sus uasallos por esta razon, e que nunqua ge lo demandarie mas').
60 'fuerat terciarius et diuiserat' (SDSilos84, 1220).
61 That was the case of the witnesses in the dispute between Oña / Frías who came from some of the disputed places. For example, when Per Yuannez of Arroyuelo, identified as a vassal of the abbot of Oña and resident in Frías, said 'that he did not know anything about those things, but only about one property that was in Arroyuelo, a village that is under the control of Oña, and that he lives in this property and that he always gives to the abbot of Oña for that property two *almudes* of bread and two *obras* every year for the *serna* and the *yantar* of the abbot of Oña, just as all his other neighbours; and he did that like those from Frías, as [payment for the] *fonsadera* and for the *moneda*, and met every rent in the same manner as the neighbours of Frías; and that should a fine be due from that property, it was those from Frías who collected it' ('que no sabie nada de todas estas cosas, saluo de I solar que es en Arroyuelo, una aldea que es de Oña, e el que mora en este solar e que da sienpre por este solar al abbat de Oña dos almudes de pan e dos obras en el año pora serna e yantar al abad de Oña, como los

The mere fact of living in the same place or region, which was certainly another form of experience, also provided an important level of knowledge. This is why many witnesses alluded to the degree of closeness as proof. Any knowledge acquired visually, as well as orally, or as a result of having been told, provided many specific details that affected the degree of credibility of each individual's claim to knowledge. So likely was it that someone living in a particular place would have witnessed or heard about the issue at stake that facts claimed not to have been seen nor heard were deemed not to have occurred.[62] This was certainly the perception of the priest of San Nicolás de Espinosa, who, when asked about the money that the clergy were required to give to the abbot of Oña for their churches, replied that they had only given money for twenty years; and that if payments had occurred earlier, he would have known about it, as he had always dwelt in the area.[63] He made the same argument regarding attendance to the episcopal council: he had seen no priest or monk go; if they had attended, he would have seen them. This also happened with interdicts, one of the acts with the greatest capacity to prove who held ecclesiastical power. It was one of the most frequently asked questions in *pesquisas* related to jurisdictional disputes between bishops and abbots. The practice of excommunication seemed to have been resorted to all too often and was the subject of widespread comment in terms of who had been excommunicated and why. Juan, a priest from Pino and a witness in the above *pesquisa*, stated that he had never seen any bishop, archdeacon or archpriest of Burgos lay interdicts in churches close to Oña; 'and that if he had not heard about it happening in more remote areas either', it was because they had not been laid, 'as if they had he would have heard comments about it as he was in the area'.[64] The term *clamour* (public fame) clearly refers to widespread discussions about some events, especially those that contributed to constructing personal 'fame', shared knowledge about individual and collective affairs. The combination of statements regarding an active and direct participation in the events to be elucidated, and the knowledge resulting from 'public fame' produced the most conclusive results, that is, the most conclusive and broadly legitimised truths. In my opinion, however, it is the dynamic relationship between both types of knowledge that needs to be highlighted.[65]

---

otros sus vecinos; e todo lo al fazielo commo los de Frias en fonsadera e en moneda e en todo pecho asi commo los otros vecinos de Frias, et, si calonna acaecie en este solar que la leuauan los de Frias'); and when asked 'for how long he remembered that to be the custom in that property', he answered 'that ever since he had been aware until now and that it was at least 40 years and that he had heard his father say that they used to do it like that in the time of King Don Alfonso and ever since' ('por cuanto tiempo aca se acuerda que vso asi este solar [...] que de que el alcanzo a aca que a bien 40 años e que oyo decir a so padre que usara asi en tiempo del rey don Alfonso e despues aca' (SSOña-O231, 1280: witness 10).

62 Though it was also possible to claim lack of knowledge because 'it was in the mountains and very far away' ('de montanis est et remotus'), as did a *solariego* from Sahagún with respect to a dispute between his abbot and the Bishop of León (CatLeon1849, 1215: witness 2).

63 'and if anyone would have been given to the abbot over the last twenty years, I would know about it, for I have lived continuously in that land for that long' ('et si aliquid daretur abbati a XX annis supra, sciret iste, cum tanto tempore fecerit moram continuam in terra illa').

64 'et dicit se non audiuisse quod posuerit interdictum in aliis que remotiores erant quod, si fieret, audiuisset clamorem, cum esset in terra'.

65 The problems posed by the existence of different versions of this common knowledge and the

Pesquisas (practice) and Social Memory

In order to gain a better understanding of the nature of the memories in question, it is important to discuss the means and methods used in judicial investigations, and the way in which they were recorded in writing. These include knowing whether *pesquisidores* followed a questionnaire and who designed it; if they visited the place where the witnesses lived, or whether the witnesses were required to go to a specific place when summoned; whether their appearance was voluntary or compulsory; how the summons were made and how the witnesses were questioned; and how their testimonies were recorded. These are all aspects of a widespread practice that regularly affected many people over extensive geographic areas, who were questioned about their knowledge regarding a wide range of matters. Despite the information on these issues being very scattered and fragmentary, systematic research would undoubtedly yield interesting data. The discussion here will deal with some of the methods and scope of witness examinations.

It is no simple matter to ascertain how witness testimonies were collected; whether witnesses were questioned in public, or kept apart from the others and questioned individually. These details were not usually included in the records, but they are relevant for clarifying whether or not these type of memories were social in nature. In many cases the hearing was clearly public. This was the case when the four old men of the small community of Tamayo in Burgos were required to detail their recollections about the assets to which the abbot of Oña claimed ownership rights in front of the knights who ruled there, which took place in the presence of a significant number of men who were explicitly listed as witnesses to be examined. Their statements, which went beyond matters concerning monastic interests, would have served to disclose the profound and detailed knowledge they had about the very active dynamic of family and community transactions that lay behind the changing status of the *solares* and their various elements and dependencies. Hearing these recollections would have fed the memories of those who were listening to them.[66] Seven informants from Contreras (including two elderly women) also testified publicly under oath about their knowledge concerning income due from the vassals of Arlanza. They were questioned in the local church in front of an audience composed of knights and *hombres buenos* from the council. Their answers were recorded jointly and became, at least for a while, the truth about local monastic rights.[67] In both cases the image conveyed was that of the oldest members of the community testifying and sharing their memories with small local councils. The majority of the *pesquisas*, however, included statements from various communities from a wider area, indicating a larger pool of knowledge.[68]

---

competition between them have been intentionally left out in this chapter. These can be seen, for example, in the *pesquisa* related to the properties of the Cathedral of León in Villavicencio (CatLeon2559, 1291; CatLeon2560, 1291).

66 SSOña-A501 (1245). For more on the context in which the *pesquisa* took place, see Alfonso, 'Resolución de disputas'.

67 SPArlanza160 (1289).

68 These communities seem to be in line with the concept devised in Górecki, 'Communities of legal

In 1214 Sancho IV launched a *pesquisa* after the protest made by the monastery of Oña that its exemption from payment of the *fonsadera* was not being respected by royal collectors. It was held before an audience that had come from throughout the Burgos area to hear the testimony of the eighteen *hombres buenos* who had been summoned. The royal notary who recorded the proceedings noted that many of the witnesses came from the city of Burgos, while others came from the area around the city.[69] Public examination of the witnesses seems to have been the norm in royal *pesquisas* about rights. The envoys sent by Alfonso III of Portugal to perform the *Inquiriçoes* on the rights of the King in the various districts of his administration must have proceeded in that way, as remarked by Robert Durand in his study on the *pesquisas* in one of these districts. As Durand did, one needs to wonder the extent to which the first testimonies served as a guide to the responses given by later witnesses. However, this cannot be easily verified. The greater detail generally contained in the testimonies of those who were first questioned could be attributed more to the method followed by the scribes who recorded the proceedings than to the public who listened to the testimonies. In fact, the detailed recording of the first testimonies may have served more as a reference for the scribe than for the witnesses that were questioned later. There are frequent references to the fact that the witnesses had sworn to and endorsed what the first witness had said, as well as statements that the answers were the same but for certain aspects they did not know or for extra pieces of information they had added. However, on the basis of these references it is not easy to ascertain whether the witnesses had been questioned privately or in public. The witnesses might have heard previous testimonies, or the scribe heard them and established parallels of his own accord between the various answers in order to avoid repetitions. This is evident when the records are only a summary of the various depositions, having found agreement between them, regardless of how the witness examination took place.[70] In any case, when recollections were verbalised in public, *pesquisas* can be taken as an exercise in social memory, as an example of shared memories that did not exclude discrepancies, and of the very process of sharing and/or disputing those memories.

Even if we do not always know how it was performed, it is clear that the ritual of *commemoration* (in its most literal meaning of 'remembering together') which

---

memory', a local study on how the legal memories of communities operated as a source of legal knowledge and records. He reconstructed the collective activities by which the groups involved in the legal transactions recognised and remembered them, as well as the physical, personal and environmental anchors at play in their collective memory.

69 'the ommes buenos that are here recorded are witnesses to this and saw and heard about those testimonies [followed by their names] as well as many other ommes buenos from Burgos and from outside Burgos' ('Desto son testigos que uieron e oyeron dezir estos dichos destos ommes buenos que aquí son escriptos [followed by their names] et otros muchos ommes buenos de Burgos e de fuera de Burgos') (SSOña-O410, 1294). The documentary dossier on this lawsuit is fairly informative about the procedure carried out in the *pesquisa*.

70 This seems to have been how the monk Silos, who had claimed to have done the *pesquisa* on behalf of his lord the abbot, proceeded. The *pesquisa* had been ordered by the *merino mayor* in Castile. In his records the answers of twelve informants from three different villages coincided with what had been said by the first witnesses (SDSilos140, 1251).

accompanied these public interrogations mainly occurred in inquiries into boundaries. In many cases these were accompanied together with the *apeo*, a *perambulation* and the setting of markers on recognised borders. These are *pesquisas* that generally, but not exclusively, originated from conflicts over pasture boundaries. Sometimes, as in the conflict between the monastery of Silos and the men from San Pedro de la Villa, it was the witnesses themselves who showed the *pesquisidores* (jointly appointed as arbitrators by the litigants) where the boundaries were, took them to the location in question and walked through with them.[71] The setting of markers on the boundaries — as remembered by the nine witnesses in this case — was carried out by the royal *merino* after King Fernando III, before whom the lawsuit had been brought, approved the *pesquisa*.[72] In the light of the abundant evidence found, this approach must have been commonplace. On the occasion of the dispute about grazing rights between the sacristan of Sahagún and the small Valdavida community in Leon, the latter demanded that a *pesquisa* be conducted, as

> the worthy and elderly men that lived in the land and knew about it should come and swear on the Holy Gospels and go to those places, and walk around them, and that which they said that belonged to the council of Valdavida should remain in its possession, and that which they said that belonged to the *sacristania* should remain in its possession.[73]

All of the gestures involved in the practice of remembering and identifying marks on the ground also served to fix them in memory. The awareness that these memories had to be regularly updated, and the need for them to be learned and internalised from childhood could lead to educational practices that were not without violence in some cases. As documented by Wickham, there were some places in Tuscany where the children were whipped in front of the boundary markers so that they would remember them.[74] In the *pesquisas* I have studied I have not seen references to any similar mnemonic rituals, but *apeos* and demarcations were possibly accompanied by acts that served similar purposes. Further research on this material would surely provide interesting information on practices and rituals that would have been subsequently incorporated into so-called popular folklore. Testimonies collected in recent studies about the *pesquisas* discussed here provide further insight into

---

71 'And these men who testified in this *pesquisa*, walked and perambulated it together with the inquirers and the royal *merino*' ('Et estos omes que dixieron esta pesquisa, andidieronlo e apearonlo a estos pesquisidores e al merino del rey') (SDSilos140, 1251).

72 SDSilos121 (1233).

73 'omnes buenos e ançianos auie en la tierra que lo sabien, et que veniessen y e iurassen sobre santos Euangelios e que fuessen a los logares e que los andudiessen e por o dixiessen que era del conçeio de Valdauida, que ffincasse por suyo; e lo que dissiesen que era de la sacritania, que ffincasse por suyo' (SFPSahagun1868, 1292).

74 'in memoria forum faciebat verberare pueros super terminos' ('the assembly made the children speak about their memories of the limits'). The author considers that this violent defence of the boundaries was part of the public *fama* of the place (Wickham, *Legge, patriche e conflitti*, p. 140). For similar forms of mobilisation of local knowledge in perambulations in some Polish areas, see Górecki, 'Communities of Legal Memory', pp. 146–51.

the mechanisms used to fix the memories in place, and their gestural nature. The criteria whereby witnesses claimed to know the facts show the importance of public performance, of the gestures and conversations employed for the dissemination of a wide range of information that created common knowledge to be known and discussed by all. The *pesquisas* worked not only in terms of mobilising memory, but also as a means of fixing recollections, of verifying them, of securing a certain *fama*. I have already mentioned the circular nature of this construction.

Witness examination did not always take place in open and public spaces. There is evidence of *pesquisas* where some witnesses were questioned separately from the rest. This was perhaps either to prevent the first statement from conditioning the responses of subsequent witnesses, or for other reasons unknown to us. This is how two *hombres buenos* who were entrusted with performing a major inquest into the depopulated area of Fuenteungrillo were said to have proceeded in the fifteenth century. The subject matter was a dispute on the boundaries of Fuenteungrillo between the monastery of Matallana and other lords: 'they interrogated separately in secret' numerous witnesses.[75] It is tempting to attribute this individual questioning to the late date of the inquest, but this method of questioning had been documented in earlier periods. In the inquiry undertaken by Queen Sancha to settle the lawsuit brought before her by the monastery of Sahagún against the people from Grajal, once the best and eldest had been selected, she asked for them to be separated and called individually to testify in her presence.[76] However, despite the explicit decision to question the witnesses separately from each other, the last two witnesses who were questioned acknowledged that 'everything that had been said by the previous witnesses was true'.[77] How did these men know the testimony given by earlier witnesses, if they had testified separately? In this case a potential self-reference made by the narrator can be ruled out, as the text states that the responses had been communicated to them before they were interrogated. Why was this done, why were they specifically told about this? Everything indicates that pragmatic reasons led the queen, who was the judge, investigator and narrator of the case in the first person, to inform the last two witnesses of the content of had been said previously before asking them about the content of the previous statements. This might have been due to the fact that their confessions proved the violent and improper actions that the people from Grajal had been accused of, in which both of them had also been involved. These last two witnesses, therefore, testified knowing the testimonies that had accused them, and having obtained assurances against potential reprisals for their confessions for themselves and for their neighbours.

This is a very interesting document, not only due to the wealth of descriptions it provides of how the people from León acted during the investigation but also due to

---

75 'apartadamente en secreto preguntaron' (AHN Clero, Carpeta 3417/10, 1405–1407). I am grateful to Carlos Reglero for the copy of this *pesquisa* that he gave me years ago. In order to contextualise it, I refer to his work Reglero de la Fuente, 'Señores y vasallos'.

76 'And they were separated. And once separated, I called them one by one to come alone in my presence' ('Et statim separaui eos. Quibus separatis, vocaui unumquemque per se solum, coram me') (AHN Clero, Carpeta 3417/10, 1405–1407).

77 'uera sunt omnia que testes dixerunt' (AHN Clero, Carpeta 3417/10, 1405–1407).

its narrative nature, which can be analysed from different perspectives.[78] My comments here, however, are only intended to draw attention to the close connection between statements given in private and confessed in public, between oral statements, their written rendering, and the collective hearing of their public reading, all of which somewhat seemed to occur as part of a continuum. This widespread practice of reading publicly to convey and transmit the content of texts deserves further investigation. In the Grajal document, once the queen, through the confession of the two elders, discovered the collective plot — of men and women, young and old — that was behind the annual breakdown of the mills dam,[79] she summoned everyone from the area 'men as well as women' to read to them the statements made by the *hombre buenos* who had been questioned.[80] So great was the dread and fear felt by those who listened to these that they could not speak.[81] The text discusses how these emotions caused the community to halt their action, and their subsequent formal submission to the monastic dictates. It is precisely this knowledge of the testimonies that incriminated them that initiated the description of a generally well-known ritual, which led to the guilty parties to be forgiven. The queen requested that, to escape punishment, they should acknowledge, and seek the abbot and monks' forgiveness for the harm that they had unjustly caused; that they should collectively agree that the charges that had been read to them were true; and that they should abide by any compensatory measures that might be established.[82] Not surprisingly, the narrative logic of the queen's text hailed the general feeling of joy resulting from having restored peace and charity among the parties in the dispute.[83]

The emotional account of the settlement of this lawsuit by reading aloud the records of confessions comes to show that it is not appropriate to use dichotomies that deny or deprecate the existing overlap between the public and private, on one hand, and between oral and written communication, on the other. This provides

---

78 A sharp reconstruction of the peasant plot and the context in which it took place is made in Martínez Sopena, *Tierra de Campos occidental*, pp. 352–56.

79 There was a sworn collective agreement so that if they were questioned, they would all answer 'as if they had a single mouth' ('omnes uno ore') with one same argument, that the breaking of the dam was 'an old, long-standing custom' ('ex antiquitate et consuetudine longa') (SFPSahagun1266, 1139–1152).

80 being all in my presence, I read to them the statements that the witnesses had made' ('tam uiros quam feminas [...] omnibus coram me stantibus, legi eis omnia predictorum testium dicta') (SFPSahagun1266, 1139–1152).

81 'Hearing this, the men and women from Grajal felt an inmense fear, and because of this fear they could not speak' ('Quibus auditis, homines et femine de Graliare ingenti pauore timuerunt et per timore loqui non potuerunt') (SFPSahagun1266, 1139–1152).

82 'And all the men and women said that everything that had been read to them was true, and begged me to dispose the way in which they should compensate for it and they would freely fulfil it' ('Tunc dixerunt omnes uiri et femine quod uera erat omnia que coram eis legeram, et deprecabantur me quod mandarem eis quam emendam fecerent et ipsi libenter adimplerent') (SFPSahagun1266, 1139–1152).

83 'and once peace and charity between them were restored, they receded with joy' ('et refformata pace et karitate inter eos, recesserunt omnes cum gaudio') (SFPSahagun1266, 1139–1152). The work of Barbara Rosenwein, especially her book Rosenwein, *Emotional communities*, which reviews the old and new accounts on the subject, is essential reading on emotions as fundamental elements in expressing certain social relationships.

new data to the current historiographic debate on the relationship between those two spheres and between those two modes of communication and qualifies this traditional dichotomy.[84] The authority conferred to the written text was clearly reinforced by the performative character that was given to the public reading of its contents. Sometimes the mere knowledge of the existence of written documents, either because they had been seen or even read, served to support the arguments of many testimonies in favour of those who held them, as was the case of papal bulls and royal privileges. There was therefore an interconnection, more than an opposition, between these written or oral forms of transmitting memory, and also among the spheres where it was transmitted. The memory contained in the *pesquisas* that have been discussed here was part of a long process that in many cases began much earlier, during childhood and adolescence, within the family, as well as being the result of personal memories being reactivated by having been summoned to testify. External settings were also involved, such as for those people whose upbringing or work occurred outside the home and started early. Memory formation thus extended to broader and more diverse aspects of life. Hence the attention that must be paid to the data on processes of coexistence and sociability prior to the completion of *pesquisas*, for they constituted the social fabric in which news was created and disseminated. They shaped and articulated quotidian exchanges which resulted in common knowledge, what everyone knew, the public *fama* about which they were sometimes asked.[85] The allusions to this *fama* in their answers, in their factual, interpretative or personal aspects, were commonplace. Even when witnesses made their depositions on an individual basis, their perceptions were shared and ratified as extended memory, which was not merely individual. Data on preliminary conversations to prepare the answers in advance is contained in one of the *pesquisas* in the conflict between the monastery of Oña and the Cathedral in Burgos about their churches. When asked whether he had been given instructions regarding his deposition, Juan, a priest from Pino, replied that 'before leaving his home land' to make his statement as a witness, 'he had agreed on', or had discussed 'his recollections with the elders who lived there'.[86] Another one, a layman called Domingo Iohannis de Terminón, denied having been instructed, but acknowledged that before going to Valladolid he had talked to his neighbours in the council, noting that he had nevertheless not said anything against his conscience.[87] The authority granted to the information by the *foro* in the council is evidenced by

---

84 Regarding reading, visibility, oral transmission, and writing as inseparably connected forms rather than contradictory dimensions of knowledge and memory retention, I refer only to some of the many existing studies containing additional literature: Innes, 'Memory, Orality and Literacy'; Geary, 'Land, Language and Memory', p. 172; Bedell, 'Memory and proof', p. 24; Oliva Herrer, *Justicia contra señores*, pp. 122–31; Keller, 'Oralité et écriture': y Kuchenbuch, 'Oralité et écriture'.

85 'if it was or is publicly said and known in the regions' ('si era o es publica boz e fama por las comarcas').

86 'antequam recederet de terra sua acordauit se cum aliqui senibus de terra sua' [Editors' note: The verb 'acordar' in the original medieval Castilian means both 'to remember' and 'to agree to something'].

87 'sitting at the council, he had agreed with his neighbours [on what he would tell], but he said that he had not said anything against his conscience' ('acordauit se cum uicinis suis sedendo in concilio, nec dixit aliquid contra conscienciam suam, ut dicit') (SSOña-O107, 1209).

how often witnesses in many *pesquisas* said that they knew something because they 'had heard it from the elders of the council'.[88] This practice of remembering and discussing together issues on which they would be asked about with other elders or their neighbours during meetings of the council is a clear exercise of social memory. Several of the aspects here addressed advise against a radical distinction between public and private statements, between social and individual memory. The process of constructing personal memories undoubtedly has social dimensions, and takes place through various avenues and methods of communication in multiple areas of sociability that are worthy of further study.

---

88 'oyeron a los viejos en concejo' (SSOña-A458, 1229).

Bibiography

Alfonso, Isabel, 'Resolución de disputas y prácticas judiciales en el Burgos medieval', in *Burgos en la Plena Edad Media. III Jornadas Burgalesas de Historia* (Burgos: Asociación Provincial de Libreros de Burgos, 1994), pp. 211–43

Alfonso, Isabel, 'Judicial Rhetoric and Political Legitimation in Medieval León-Castile', in *Building Legitimacy. Political Discourses and Forms of Legitimacy in Medieval Societies*, ed. by Julio Escalona, Isabel Alfonso and Hugh Kennedy (Leiden: Brill, 2004), pp. 51–88

Alfonso, Isabel, 'Iglesias rurales en el norte de Castilla: una dimensión religiosa de las luchas campesinas en la Edad Media', in *Sombras del Progreso. Las huellas de la historia agraria*, ed. by Ricardo Robledo (Barcelona: Crítica, 2010), pp. 27–65

Alfonso, Isabel, and Cristina Jular Pérez-Alfaro, 'Oña contra Frías o el pleito de los cien testigos: una pesquisa en la Castilla del siglo XIII', *Edad Media: Revista de Historia*, 3 (2000), 61–88

Bedell, John, 'Memory and Proof of Age in England 1272–1327', *Past & Present*, 162 (1999), 3–27

Berman, Harold J., *Law and Revolution: The Formation of the Western Legal Tradition* (Cambridge, MA: Harvard University Press, 1983)

Bowman, Jeffrey A., 'Infamy and Proof in Medieval Spain', in *Fama: The Politics of Talk and Reputation in Medieval Europe*, ed. by Thelma S. Fenster and Daniel L. Smail (Ithaca: Cornell University Press, 2003), pp. 95–117

Bowman, Jeffrey A., *Shifting Landmarks. Property, Proof, and Dispute in Catalonia around the Year 1000* (Ithaca: Cornell University Press, 2004)

Branco, María J., 'Memory and Truth: The Strange Case of the Witness Enquiries of 1216 in the Braga-Toledo Dispute', *Historical Research*, 203 (2006), 1–20

Brown, Warren C., 'When Documents are Destroyed or Lost: Lay People and Archives in the Early Middle Ages', *Early Medieval Europe*, 11–4 (2002), 337–66

Cerdá Ruiz-Funes, Joaquín, 'En torno a la pesquisa y procedimiento inquisitivo en el derecho castellano-leonés de la Edad Media', *Anuario de Historia del Derecho Español*, 32 (1962), 483–518

Delumeau, Jean-Pierre, 'La memoire des gens d'Arezzo et de Sienne a travers des depositions de temoins (VIIIᵉ–XIIᵉ s.)', in *Temps, Memoire, Tradition au Moyen Âge. Actes des congrès de la Société des historiens médiévistes de l'enseignement supérieur public* (Aix-en-provence: Université de Provence, 1983), pp. 43–66

Durand, Robert, 'La mémoire des campagnes portugaises', in *Campagnes médiévales: l'homme et son espace. Études offertes à Robert Fossier*, ed. by Elisabeth Mornet (Paris: Publications de la Sorbonne, 1995), pp. 363–73

Fenster, Thelma S., and Daniel L. Smail, eds, *Fama: The Politics of Talk and Reputation in Medieval Europe* (Ithaca: Cornell University Press, 2003)

Fentress, James, and Chris Wickham, *Social Memory* (Oxford: Blackwell, 1992)

Gautier-Dalché, Jean, 'Connaissance de l'age et évaluation de la durée chez les habitants de quelques agglomérations du diocèse de Palencia selon une enquête de 1220', *Anuario de estudios medievales*, 19 (1989), 191–204

Geary, Patrick, 'Land, Language and Memory in Europe, 700–1100', *Transactions of the Royal Historical Society (Sixth Series)*, 9 (1999), 169–84

González, Julio, *El Reino de Castilla en la época de Alfonso VIII*, 3 vols (Madrid: Escuela de Estudios Medievales, 1960)

Górecki, Piotr, 'Communities of Legal Memory in Medieval Poland, c. 1200–1240', *Journal of Medieval History*, 24–2 (1998), 127–54

Innes, Matthew, 'Memory, Orality and Literacy in an Early Medieval Society', *Past & Present*, 158 (1998), 3–36

Keller, Hagen, 'Oralité et écriture', in *Les tendances actuelles de l'histoire du Moyen Âge en France et en Allemagne: actes des colloques de Sèvres (1997) et Göttingen (1998) organisées par le Centre National de la Recherche Scientifique et le Max-Planck-Institut für Geschichte*, ed. by Jean-Claude Schmitt and Gerhard Oexle (Paris: Éditions de la Sorbonne, 2002), pp. 127–42

Kuchenbuch, Ludolf, 'Ecriture et oralité. Quelques compléments et approfondissements', in *Les tendances actuelles de l'histoire du Moyen Âge en France et en Allemagne: actes des colloques de Sèvres (1997) et Göttingen (1998) organisées par le Centre National de la Recherche Scientifique et le Max-Planck-Institut für Geschichte*, ed. by Jean-Claude Schmitt and Gerhard Oexle (Paris: Éditions de la Sorbonne, 2002), pp. 127–42

Le Roy Ladurie, Emmanuel *Montaillou, village occitan, de 1294 à 1324* (Paris: Gallimard, 1975)

Lemesle, Bruno, 'L'enquête contre les épreuves. Les enquêtes dans la région angevine (XIIᵉ-début XIIIᵉ siècle)', in *L'enquête au Moyen Âge*, ed. by Claude Gauvard (Rome: École française de Rome, 2008), pp. 41–74

Madero Eguía, Marta, 'Savoirs féminins et construction de la vérité. Les femmes dans la preuve testimoniale en Castille au XIIIᵉ siècle', *Crime, Histoire & Sociétés*, 3–2 (1999), 5–21

Martínez Sopena, Pascual, *La Tierra de Campos occidental: poblamiento, poder y comunidad del siglo X al XIII* (Valladolid: Institución Cultural Simancas, 1985)

Oliva Herrer, Rafael, *Justicia contra señores. El mundo rural y la política en tiempos de los Reyes Católicos* (Valladolid: Universidad de Valladolid, 2004)

Reglero de la Fuente, Carlos, 'Señores y vasallos en una aldea castellana medieval: Fuenteungrillo (siglos XIII–XIV)', *Edad Media: revista de historia*, 4 (2001), 113–39

Rosenwein, Barbara, *Emotional Communities of the Early Middle Ages* (Ithaca: Cornell University Press, 2006)

Schmitt, Jean-Claude, and Gerhard Oexle, eds, *Les tendances actuelles de l'histoire du Moyen Âge en France et en Allemagne: actes des colloques de Sèvres (1997) et Göttingen (1998) organisées par le Centre National de la Recherche Scientifique et le Max-Planck-Institut für Geschichte* (Paris: Éditions de la Sorbonne, 2002)

Smail, Daniel L., 'Archivos de conocimiento y la cultura legal de la publicidad en la Marsella medieval', *Hispania*, 197 (1997), 1049–77

Smail, Daniel L., *The Consumption of Justice: Emotions, Publicity, and Legal Culture in Marseille, 1264–1423* (Ithaca: Cornell University Press, 2003)

Van Houts, Elisabeth, *Memory and Gender in Medieval Europe, 900–1200* (London: Palgrave, 1999)

Verdier, Raymond, ed., *Le serment*, 2 vols (Paris: C.N.R.S. Éditions, 1992)

Wickham, Chris, 'Gossip and Resistance among the Medieval Peasantry', *Past & Present*, 160 (1998), 3–24

Wickham, Chris, *Legge, pratiche e conflitti. Tribunali e risoluzione delle dispute nella Toscana del XII secolo* (Roma: Viella, 2000)

Wickham, Chris, 'Fama and the Law in Twelfth-Century Tuscany', in *Fama: The Politics of Talk and Reputation in Medieval Europe*, ed. by Thelma S. Fenster and Daniel L. Smail (Ithaca: Cornell University Press, 2003), pp. 15–26

CHAPTER 5

Two Approaches to Justice and Vengeance

with a commentary by Stephen D. White

Conflict, Language, and Social Practice in Medieval Societies: Selected Essays of Isabel Alfonso, with Commentaries, ed. by Julio Escalona Monge, Álvaro Carvajal Castro, and Cristina Jular Pérez-Alfaro, TMC 24 (Turnhout: Brepols, 2024), pp. 167–240

BREPOLS ❧ PUBLISHERS   10.1484/M.TMC-EB.5.132459

STEPHEN D. WHITE

Commentary

As Isabel Alfonso points out in 'Vengeance, Justice, and Political Struggle in Castilian Medieval Historiography', prejudices, anachronisms, and ideological presuppositions have been deeply imbedded in scholarship on feuding and violent revenge in medieval Castile. The same, one might add, can also be said of studies on these subjects in medieval European societies generally. Not only is vengeance commonly represented, in William Ian Miller's words, as 'crazed, uncontrolled, subjective [...], admitting no reason, no rule of limitation, [...] unruled and ruleless';[1] it has also been viewed as an automatic response to the killing or injury of a relative and as the cause of 'an endless cycle of violence' — a phrase favoured by those who see feuding and anarchy as two sides of the same coin.[2] As Alfonso points out, moreover, because previous scholars have regarded 'private' or 'family' revenge as totally incompatible with 'public' justice and other judicial practices organized under royal authority, including 'public' sanctions on criminal acts, they have tried to use both legal and literary sources to show that the development of the latter necessarily entailed the suppression of the former, the formulation and enforcement of new regulatory norms on violence generally, and the end of an anarchic era of lawlessness, blood revenge, and cruelty. In these ways, she rightly maintains, previous scholars have provided us with a deeply flawed narrative of the middle ages that satisfies modern ideological prejudices without illuminating medieval political practice or culture.

However, in the article already mentioned on vengeance, justice, and political struggle in the *Legend of the Seven Infantes of Lara*, the *Romanz del infante García*, and *The Cid* and in 'Vengeance and Justice in the *Poem of the Cid*', Isabel Alfonso does more than undermine the assumptions already mentioned about the stark oppositions between public and private, between vengeance and justice, and between conflict between families and conflict between political rivals. At the same time, without bypassing the necessary work of meticulously analysing and dating the manuscripts of different versions of the literary works that her papers consider, she uses an innovative approach to the study of the texts themselves to construct an important argument about how honour and shame were negotiated, both in court and out of court, in an aristocratic society where honour by birth was recognized, but still had to be maintained and competed for in practice, if it was not to be lost.

---

1 Miller, 'In Defense of Revenge', p. 73.
2 For example, according to Pinker, *The Better Angels of Our Nature*, p. 538, 'Feuding and anarchy go together'.

Stephen D. White is the Candler Professor of Medieval History (emeritus) at Emory University, Atlanta, GA, USA.

In both articles, Alfonso also contests the conventional view that vengeance is necessarily lawless and bloody and leads inevitably to endless feuding by showing: first, that the authors of all four of the literary texts under consideration invoked well-established norms in order to distinguish 'good' vengeance from 'bad'; and, second, that these stories depicted multiple forms of vengeance, including ones that have been erroneously classified as being unique to 'public' justice under royal authority. Her papers also demonstrate that medieval courts could serve not simply as forums for the adjudication of lawsuits, but as political and juridical arenas for taking vengeance on wrong-doers and shaming them and for re-negotiating honour among all participants in a court hearing.

For these reasons, although the main targets of Alfonso's two articles are the contestable assumptions of previous scholarship on vengeance, violence, and conflict, her papers can now help us to frame critical responses to two new, interrelated trends in the study of medieval vengeance and feuding: first, the virtual abandonment of 'feud' as a subject of scholarly inquiry in favour of the study of vengeance, with a particular focus on violent revenge; and, second, the adoption of assumptions drawn from the work of a particular school of psychologists that vengeance, in all its forms, is the expression of an irrational emotional urge that is universal among humans, because it is supposedly hard-wired into the human brain.[3] However, as one can see from her work, whether or not medievalists continue to find heuristic value in the concept of feuding, they cannot make sense of the ongoing conflicts among nobles to which this term has been applied by reducing them to a series of emotionally driven acts of revenge; instead, they must conceptualize them as socio-political processes that were significantly shaped by cultural norms, including a sense of aristocratic honour, and did not suddenly disappear with the advent of royally sponsored justice.

Bibliography

Miller, William I., 'In Defense of Revenge', in *Medieval Crime and Social Control*, ed. by Barbara A. Hanawalt and David Wallace (Minneapolis: University of Minnesota Press, 1999), pp. 70–89

Pinker, Steven, *The Better Angels of Our Nature: Why Violence has Declined* (New York: Viking Books, 2011)

White, Stephen D., 'The Feelings in the Feud: The Emotional Turn in the Study of Medieval Vengeance', in *Disputing Strategies in Medieval Scandinavia*, ed. by Kim Esmark and others (Leiden: Brill, 2013), pp. 281–311

White, Stephen D., 'The Peace in the Feud Revisited: Feuds in the Peace in Medieval European Feuds', in *Making Early Medieval Societies: Conflict and Belonging in the Latin West, 300–1200*, ed. by Kate Cooper and Conrad Leyser (Cambridge: Cambridge University Press, 2016), pp. 281–311

---

3 On these two trends, see White, 'The Feelings in the Feud'; and White, 'The Peace in the Feud Revisited', p. 238.

ISABEL ALFONSO

Vengeance, Justice, and Political Struggle in Castilian Medieval Historiography*

The topic of vengeance as a violent practice typically arouses a vast amount of prejudices and anachronisms. Our very perceptions of what is just and unjust violence — and it would be interesting to list expressions of one and the other — are embedded in the analysis of medieval vendettas. The initial assumption is that in a certain period, blood feuds were the required response in situations when a relative had been killed, or had been the victim of a serious injury or attack. These actions in turn triggered similar or more severe reactions, in an endless cycle of violence which was difficult to appease. This notion of societies with bloody and unregulated practices of self-defence is widespread in historiography, and Spanish scholarship is not an exception. Advocates of this view describe a process whereby family and private blood feuds were gradually replaced with forms of public justice (greater involvement of authorities, limits placed, etc.). The 'primitive sense of revenge' was ultimately undermined by regulatory norms, which prevented people from 'taking justice into their own hands'.[1]

This evolutionary approach has been applied to both legal documentation and literary narratives, with the result that legal or literary historians and philologists are often mutually reinforcing. It is true that these assumptions are not always explicit, but they surface in numerous arguments, as it happens when certain traits — allegedly derived from the 'Germanic' origins of the Castilian epics, such as for example, the 'bloodthirstiness' and the cruelty of the vengeful actions in epic narratives, are said to illustrate 'one of the most persistent and anachronistic criminal justice systems in Europe'.[2] In fact, the 'Germanic' epithet seems to feed the semantics of cruelty and bloody violence, whether without any further explanation, or through circular arguments, to the extent that, in the absence of other chronological data, violence is even used to date these narratives.[3] These assumptions are so widespread and

---

* Original publication: Alfonso, Isabel, 'Vengeance, justice et lutte politique dans l'historiographie castillane du Moyen Âge', in *La vengeance, 400–1200*, ed. by Dominique Barthélemy, François Bougard and Régine Le Jan (Rome: École française de Rome, 2006), pp. 383–419. Translated from the original French version by Jean Birrell.

1 This was, for example, J. L. Martín's argument. He understood that local codes abolished ancient private law practices (Martín, 'Relectura del fuero de Salamanca', p. 536).

2 Pérez-Prendes, *Curso de Historia del Derecho Español 1*. This author saw the issue as 'a certain struggle between private initiative, which tended to perpetuate long-running enmity (*saña vieja*), as in the cycle of the *infantes* of Lara, and public initiative, which had some modest success stories, as that of closing the cycle of vengeance by way of a declaration included in local codes that any killing caused by asserting that right would not trigger a further deadly feud' (Pérez-Prendes, *Curso de Historia del Derecho Español 1*, p. 1222).

3 An example of the circular nature of these arguments is Alvar and Alvar, eds, *Épica medieval española*,

entrenched that they condition the understanding not only of vindictive practices, but also of the existing continuities between the various ways in which conflicts were resolved in the past.

Two of the most obvious assumptions that emerge from these arguments are: 1) that vengeance and justice are antithetical and consecutive forms of settling cases of blood or injurious actions; and 2) that a distinction was established between family and political fights. An investigation of some well-known cases from a perspective I have already tested elsewhere,[4] questioning such dichotomies and discontinuities, would contribute to a better understanding of vengeance and the social processes in which it was represented, as well as to clarify the role it played in the political culture of the societies under study. These cases correspond to three epic narratives in which revenge appears as a central element of the plot, at least in certain passages: the *Legend of the Seven Infantes of Lara*, the *Romanz del infante García*, and the *Poem of the Cid*.

The *Legend of the Seven Infantes of Lara* notably describes the death of these noble youths and their father's captivity in Córdoba due to the treason of their maternal uncle and his wife, followed by the subsequent vengeance that Mudarra, the bastard son born in captivity (and, in some versions, the infants' mother), inflicted on the traitors.

The *Romanz del infante García* tells of the death of this *infante*, son of the Count of Castile. He was the victim of an old enmity that was stoked when he went to León to meet his fiancée the *infanta* Sancha, sister of the King of León. The *infanta*, in turn, avenged his iniquitous death by directly executing one of the killers. The others, in some versions, were put to death by King Sancho of Navarre, brother-in-law of the dead infant.

The third part of the *Poem of the Cid* narrates how the Cid took revenge for the bloody attack inflicted on his daughters by their husbands, the *infantes* of Carrión. This revenge took place in a parliament (*cortes*) convened by the king in Toledo. There the Cid recovered his honour and the reputation of his lineage through a judicial combat waged by his vassals, in which the *infantes* were humiliated, beaten and dishonoured for the injurious act they had committed.

The Sources

The transmission of these stories is of great interest, as the available narratives differ in three essential aspects. The events narrated in the *Legend of the infantes of Lara* are the earliest of the three narratives, as they date back to the second half of the tenth century. However, the only version that has come down to us is a romance prose text inserted in thirteenth-century chronicles. It was not contained in the earlier Latin chronicles, nor was it preserved in any narrative poem.[5] On the death

---

pp. 50 ff. See also Accutis, *La leggenda degli Infanti di Lara*, which has been aptly criticised for his systematic efforts to link the most archaic elements of the plot to an alleged 'Germanic' society and code of values. Cf. Escalona, 'Épica, crónicas y genealogías', p. 132.

4 Alfonso, 'Venganza y justicia'. [Editors' note: For the English version of this article, see Chapter 5 in this volume].

5 This legend has been the object of particularly thorough study thanks to the efforts of Menéndez Pidal and the subsequent studies that they generated. It is not my intention to review them

of the *infante García*, which occurred in the first quarter of the eleventh century, no texts have been preserved in verse form. The event was, however, echoed in Latin chronicles. In vernacular chronicles it was inserted in prose form as a *romanz*.[6] The *Poem of the Cid* is set in the late eleventh century. Both the poem — the only *chanson de geste* that has been preserved, recognised as the masterpiece of Spanish medieval literature — and the prose versions of the Latin and vernacular chronicles have come down to us. However, the story of revenge that is of interest here is narrated only in the latter and in the *Poem*.[7]

A common denominator of these narratives is that all three have been preserved in a romance prose version incorporated into the *Estoria de España* (EE), which began to be compiled in the court of Alfonso X the Wise during the last third of the thirteenth century. That is why my analysis will focus primarily on this corpus of texts, to which one still has to refer as *Primera Crónica General de España* (PCG), as it was called by Menéndez Pidal nearly one century ago.[8] This is partly due to the fact that it remains the only existing complete edition, and partly due to the insufficient familiarity of historians with the great textual complexity revealed by recent philological studies about the different families of manuscripts and codices in which these texts have been preserved.[9] In brief, the EE should no longer be accepted as a homogeneous whole that emerged from King Alfonso X's workshop. Instead, only the part of the EE up to the first quarter of the eleventh century in Pidal's edition can be said to have been inspired by King Alfonso X. This corresponds to a first draft called *Versión primitiva* (VP) (*c.* 1270–1274), and contains the stories *of* the *infantes of Lara* and of the *infante*

---

extensively. Suffice to say, from the perspective being used here, that Menéndez Pidal, as was customary among scholars in that period — the first edition was published in 1896 –, intended to show that the epic genre not only existed in Spain, but was as important as that of other countries. He argued that if epic narratives had been preserved in their true and original wording 'our poems would be worthy of being included alongside the *Nibelungen* and the *Garin le Loherain*, masterpieces of bloody epic revenge' (Menéndez Pidal, *La Leyenda de los Infantes de Lara*, p. 11).

6 The story of the death of the last Castilian count has also been the subject of numerous studies, precisely because it is the one of the narratives most directly related to a historically documented fact. In several works, Menéndez Pidal focused on separating the imaginary from the real in the information transmitted in connection with the attempt to find traces of this lost *romanz*. See Menéndez Pidal, 'El elemento histórico', amended and enhanced in Menéndez Pidal, 'El "romanz del Infant García"'. See also chapter XI in Catalán and de Bustos, eds, *La épica medieval española*.

7 The first and most complete study of the narrative epic was also conducted by R. Menéndez Pidal. See Menéndez Pidal, *Cantar de Mio Cid*. For a recent critical edition of the *Poem*, regarded as one the best, see Montaner Frutos, *Cantar de Mio Cid*. In French, see the excellent translation in Martin, *Chanson de Mon Cid*. For an English translation, see Hamilton and Perry (trans.), *The poem of the Cid*.

8 Menéndez Pidal and Catalán, *Primera Crónica General*.

9 These studies form a very large and important group, of which two collective studies can serve as a reference. I consider both of these essential for the dissemination of their achievements among historians, and were the result of two seminars on Alfonso X's the Wise EE and the chronicles deriving from it. They are Martin, ed., *La historia alfonsí*; and Fernández Ordóñez, ed., *Alfonso X el Sabio*. An indispensable reference for the history of Castilian prose are Gómez Redondo, *Historia de la prosa medieval 1*; and Gómez Redondo, *Historia de la prosa medieval 2*, both with extensive bibliography on these issues.

174 ISABEL ALFONSO

García.[10] From that moment onwards, the EE in PCG is an extended revision dated to the reign of Sancho IV, which has been therefore called *Versión amplificada de 1289* (VA1289). The story of the *Cid* was inserted in the latter. Nevertheless, as we shall later see, the date of this section also needs to be amended.[11]

The significance of these remarks becomes clearer when taking into account the ideology underlying the variations of each of the EE versions, even those made during a single reign. It was recently discovered that the second redaction of the EE (*c.* 1282–1284) was definitely inspired by King Alfonso X himself. It has become known as the *Versión crítica* (VC),[12] as it meant a radical revision of the first draft. Since the content of this version covers up to the twelfth century, the three epic narratives under discussion here were included in it, making this the principal point of comparison with the other two versions mentioned.[13]

The ways in which these epic stories are inserted into the main narrative of EE has long been a major issue for specialists seeking to unearth the traces of and reconstruct the lost epic narratives.[14] More recently, the focus has shifted to exploring the purpose of, and reasons for, the different versions of the 'same' story, aiming to better understand the various political contexts in which they were made and received; and the various audiences to which they were addressed.[15] The debate

---

10 The first two stories are in a section dedicated to the history of the Astur-Leonese kings from Ramiro I to Vermudo III (PCG, chs. 628–801), preserved in the *primitive* version, also known as *vulgar* or *concise*. Today we know that this version 'is simply the most genuine representative of the first draft', as noted by I. Fernández Ordoñez in an enlightening and complex study which explained that the testimonies in this *concise* version and the text recast in 1289 were the same, because its compilation had already been completed. See Fernández Ordóñez, 'La transmisión textual', pp. 228–35. See also, in that same book, de la Campa, 'Las versiones alfonsíes'. D. Catalán had already noted that Menéndez Pidal, contrary to his 1896 study, had used the text of the *concise* version for the edition of the *Legend of the Infantes of Lara* included in Menéndez Pidal and Catalán, *Reliquias de la poesía épica*, p. xxviii.

11 The first draft of King Alfonso's story was partially rewritten in 1289. Given its ideological distance from the King's thought, it should be cautiously considered to be a 'chronicle' and not a 'version', as noted by Crespo, 'Las Estorias de España', pp. 119–21. But it must also be remembered that the codex drafted in the fourteenth century in which it was preserved contains significant interpolations, one of which is precisely the story of the Cid's revenge, as previously indicated. On the ideological differences between the 1289 chronicle of Sancho IV's reign and Alfonso X's *Estorias*, and together with Crespo's chapter, see Fernández Ordóñez, 'La transmisión textual', p. 234; as well as Fernández Ordóñez, 'Variación en el modelo historiográfico', pp. 61–65.

12 On the political reasons for the different versions, see Fernández Ordóñez, *Versión Crítica*. The author summarizes her conclusions about the ideological radicalization of this version in Fernández Ordóñez, 'Variación en el modelo historiográfico', pp. 49–61. See also de la Campa, 'Las versiones alfonsíes', pp. 88–106.

13 According to Fernández Ordóñez, 'La transmisión textual', p. 232, the section of the *Versión Crítica* where our three stories are contained is literally copied in the textual tradition of the *Crónica de veinte reyes* (Ruiz Asencio and Herrero Jiménez, eds, *Crónica de Veinte Reyes*), which is the one I will use here to refer to this version.

14 As J. B. Crespo noted, we must remember here that when in the late nineteenth century Menéndez Pidal began the textual study of the *Estoria de España*, he did so with the aim of reconstructing the Spanish epic tradition in an almost archaeological manner, seeking what was left of it in the songs. See Crespo, 'Las Estorias de España', p. 125.

15 This is the approach taken by the most recent studies, as those cited in n. 9. For an overview of

VENGEANCE, JUSTICE, AND POLITICAL STRUGGLE

about the incorporation of epic poems into historiographical discourse remains very active and interesting, and in my opinion has not been convincingly resolved. This is largely due to the fact that the discussion ultimately revolves around the problem of the convergence or confrontation between two models of thought which included the culture, discourse, ideas and values of the two dominant powers, the royal and the aristocratic. These were two ways of looking at the past, of building a memory of it, of understanding the relationships between the two powers, and even of using a certain literary genre.[16] I hope that the comparative analysis of these three stories of vengeance, however indirectly, can also contribute to this debate. I will also use the so-called *Crónica de 1344* (C1344), because it provides a longer version of the story of the *infantes* of Lara, although the reasons for this being so are still disputed.[17] The following table summarises the corpus of texts under discussion:

Table 5.1. Corpus of texts discussed in the text. (1) These chapters were incorporated in the d-14th century, as indicated in n. 81.

Infantes of Lara	*Infante* García	Mío Cid
EE (VP, h.1270) (ed. in PCG, h. 736–43 and 751)	EE (VP, h.1270) (ed. in PCG, ch. 787, 788, 789)	PoemCid, vv. 2278–3730
EE (VC, h. 1283) CVR, Book V, ch. VII–XIII and XX	EE (VC, h. 1283) CVR, Book VII, ch. V–VII	EE (VC, h. 1283) CVR, ch. LXXV–LXXXIII
C1344, ch. I–XII		EE (VA1289) (ed. in PCG, ch. 929–47 (1)

Good and Bad Vengeances

A key feature in this analysis is that vengeance as a process for the reparation of a dishonourable offense — not always resulting in death — was constructed both positively and negatively in these texts. The stories were articulated around bad and good vengeful actions. There was no condemnation of vengeance in the abstract,

---

the debate, see Gómez Redondo, *Historia de la prosa medieval 1*, p. 652, n. 403. See also Genet, ed., *L'histoire et les nouveaux publics*.

16 This, for example is one of the main focuses of the interpretation by F. Gómez Redondo in his continued attempt to reconstruct the reception settings of the texts studied. See Gómez Redondo, 'La materia cidiana', p. 99. On epic memory as a feature of the nobility, see Gómez Redondo, *Historia de la prosa medieval 2*, p. 667. Similar questions, but with different answers have been discussed by G. Spiegel for French prose literature in Spiegel, *Romancing the past*.

17 This is a noble chronicle written by the Count of Barcelos in the mid-fourteenth century. He built upon very diverse historiographical material but did not use any of the different redactions of Alfonso X's EE. Rather, his main sources are the Galician-Portuguese translations of later versions of Alfonso X's works, namely the *Crónica de 1289* and the *Crónica de Castilla*. On these texts and for relevant references see Fernández Ordóñez, 'La transmisión textual', pp. 258–59. In C1344 the most significant variations are precisely those in the *chanson de geste*, particularly in the legend of the infants of Lara, on which see Gómez Redondo, *Historia de la prosa medieval 2*, pp. 1227–28. For a recent contribution questioning the origin of these chronicle as an offshoot of PGC and advancing a new dating for the story of the *infantes* of Lara, see Escalona, 'Épica, crónicas y genealogías', p. 168.

176 ISABEL ALFONSO

or a presentation of the recourse to justice as being the most suitable course. Some revenges were presented as unjust and unjustified and others as proper and legitimate. The right to take revenge, to do justice, seemed to be part of the latter. These three narratives will be examined from this perspective below (see the Annex for an identification of the differences between them).

As in the other two narratives, in the *Legend of the Infantes of Lara*[18] the opposition between 'bad' and 'good' types of vengeance is illustrated by the contrast between the scheme of the *infantes'* aunt and uncle, doña Lambra and Ruy Vázquez, who plotted to kill them and hold their father captive in Muslim Córdoba; and the vengeance inflicted on the conspirators as a just response for their actions. These events are set in the second half of the tenth century, in the reigns of kings Ramiro III and Vermudo II in León and Count Garci Fernández in Castile.[19]

Evil forms of revenge were condemned, as in other narratives, by presenting the perpetrators in a negative light. The events took place during the wedding of Ruy Vázquez, the maternal uncle of the *infantes*, and doña Lambra, cousin of the Castilian count. The first part of the drama revolves around this 'mala mujer' (bad woman),[20] who instigated the injurious competition that would lead to the bloody clashes in which the *infantes* were involved. In the last, and fifth, week of the wedding celebrations, doña Lambra encouraged them to prove their courage on the field with their first cousin, who was shown to be bragging about being the best in front of the ladies. This caused the first bloody incident, as the younger *infante* hit him so hard that he fell down dead. Ruy Vázquez's angry response to what looked like an accidental death occurred after the well-known female mourning ritual, intended to cause the aggressor to be punished by invoking the dishonourable attack perpetrated.[21] But the chronicler discredited the exaggeration of this first revenge, as Ruy Vázquez, 'with great anger' ('con gran yra') injured his nephew badly and triggered a broader fight. This would only be prevented by the restraint shown by the *infantes* and the joint mediation by their father and the count, who managed to persuade Ruy Vázquez to forgive them.[22] The fight was thus 'appeased and settled' ('apaziguada y avenida') when Ruy Vázquez agreed to take them into his service and promised to do good to them 'so that through him they would be worthier', as expressly requested by their father.[23]

---

18 My comments are based on the version in PCG, ch. 736–43 and 751, with references to variants relevant for my argument in VC; CVR, book V, ch. XIII and XXL; and C1344, ch. I–XII in Menéndez Pidal's edition in Menéndez Pidal, *La Leyenda de los Infantes de Lara*, pp. 249–314.

19 PCG, ch. 736–43 (death of King Ramiro), followed in 751 (reign of King Vermudo II). In VC, the events only take place during the reign of the latter.

20 While presented as 'a very distinguished woman' ('una dueña de muy gran guisa') at the start of the narrative, she would later become the instigator of the vengeful acts planned by her husband, Ruy Vázquez.

21 The mourning in this case was for the personal dishonour incurred, rather than for the victim. Doña Lambra 'began to yell, weeping soundly, and claiming that no woman had ever been dishonoured in her wedding as she had there been' ('començo a dar grandes uozes, llorando muy fuerte, et diziendo que nunqua dueña assi fuera desondrada en sus bodas como ella fuera alli') (PCG, ch. 736, p. 432). On this ritual, see Miller, 'Choosing the Avenger'.

22 'se amigaron vnos con otros' ('they restored the friendship between them') (VC, p. 121).

23 'en maner que ellos valiesen más' (PCG, ch. 736, p. 432). VC is even more explicitly with regards to the nature of the obligation assumed by the uncle 'that he would honour them in all he could as his

It must be noted that this concept of value, of the ways of acquiring it or losing it, and of having it recognised, refused, defended and increased, was very important, as the social identity of the actors, their honour and their reputation were built around it, which was a common feature in these accounts.[24]

Another similar episode that took place after the wedding illustrates firstly how resolutions, even those as formally friendly as the one described above, did not necessarily override the feelings of hostility; and secondly, that any excuse could be used to bring those feelings to the fore once again. There was a second incident in which doña Lambra expressed her discomfort when she saw that same *infante* swimming half-naked, and decided to take revenge for the earlier death: 'I shall thus take revenge for the thump and the death of my cousin'.[25] She sent one of her men to throw at him a cucumber full of blood, promising to shelter him from the *infante's* foreseeable aggressive response. Everything happened as planned, and when the seven brothers became aware that doña Lambra was behind the apparent game, they killed her vassal, whom she was protecting under her coat. Several aspects, also emphasised by the chronicler, are worthy of note:

1. The existing trust was breached. This aggravated the insult instigated by doña Lambra and revealed her true feelings towards the *infants*, 'for they thought that they were in good terms with her, and that she loved her without malice, but in this they were fouled'.[26]

2. Another ritual was included to encourage revenge for the last offense received, or to seek support to take it. On this occasion, the *infante* who had been insulted — in light of the laughing attitude of his brothers — urged them to engage in vengeance. He claimed that if the same had happened to them 'I would not want to live one day more until I had taken revenge, and since you took that deed for a game, may God make you repent'.[27]

3. Doña Lambra offered her vassal her protection, hiding him under her coat, and therefore prevented the infants from pursuing a less bloody reaction than had been originally intended.

---

nephews and as his own flesh' ('que les faría toda la onrra quel pudiesse commo a sus sobrinos e su carne') (VC, p. 122).

24 On the dispute on personal value in the *Poem of the Cid*, see Alfonso, 'Venganza y justicia', p. 65. A. Dacosta places the notion of 'valer mas' (being of greater worthiness) at the centre of the ethics of medieval Biscayan hidalgos, on which see Dacosta, *Los linajes de Bizcaia*.

25 'assí tomare yo uengança de la punnada et de la muerte de mio primo'.

26 'ca tenien ellos que bien estauan con ella, et que ella los amaua sin toda arte; mas eran ellos engannados en esto'. VC explains that doña Lambra's attitude was due to the hatred she felt ('le desamaua de coraçon'), while C1344 notes that 'she could not have felt for them a more intense mortal hatred' ('ca ella los desamaua mortalmiente que mas non podía'). This expression displays a profound aversion and is also a manner of making public a mortal enmity. See n. 34.

27 'Yo no querría uiuir un día mas fasta quel non uengasse; et pues que vos leuades en iuego tal fecho como este et tal desondra, mande Dios que uos aun repintades ende'. Miller noted the effectiveness of this type of incitement, which consisted in the virtual exchange of roles or situations. See Miller, 'Choosing the Avenger', pp. 175–94.

4. The woman engaged in mourning, thus instigating vengeance for the death of her vassal and for the dishonour that this act had brought upon her. This time the ritual involved placing the body on a bench in the middle of her palace and crying, together with all of her women, for three days in a prodigious way ('que por marauilla fue'), tearing her clothes apart and calling herself a widow and claiming 'that she had no husband' ('que non auie marido').[28] This provocation was exacerbated when her husband appeared:

She came to him, scratched all over,[29] and fell to his feet asking for mercy, claiming that she was stricken by grief for the dishonour that her cousins had brought upon her, and asking him to repair her in the name of God as he deemed proper.[30]

She obtained from him the promise that he would satisfy her request in a manner that would make everyone talk about it.

5. The resolution of this dispute was also highlighted. Despite the hostility of one of the parties, an amicable settlement to the dispute was negotiated, as had been done previously, this time without the mediation of the count. Ruy Vázquez called a meeting with the father of the *infantes* in a neutral area between within his domains[31] to discuss the dishonouring of his wife, and there 'they came to terms with each other'.[32] The *infantes* were left again in the care of their uncle so that, after finding out who had caused the dispute, he would do 'whatever he deemed righteous and was just'.[33] Ruiz Vázquez appeared to accept this using flattery, deceit and false words so that they would not mistrust him, and in order to better plan his revenge.

At various times, therefore, the chronicler presented an opposition between the behaviour of the infants, who only responded to undeserved insults and proposed and accepted legal and peaceful solutions, and the deceptive and treacherous behaviour of their aunt and uncle, who felt for them a 'mortal hatred'[34] and broke

---

28 VC notes that she 'called herself repeatedly a widow, forsaken by both husband and lord)' ('llamandose muchas vegadas bibda e desanparada de marido e de señor'), thus enhancing the circle of people who could take responsibility for avenging the dishonour she was proclaiming (VC, p. 122).

29 VC also notes 'e descabeñada' (and dishevelled).

30 'Fuese pora ell toda rascada et llorando mucho de los oios, et echose a sus pies pidiendol merced quel pesasse mucho de la desondra que auie recebida de sus sobrinos, et que por Dios et por su mesura quel diesse ende derecho'. Ruy Vázquez's response is a premonition of a great vengeance: 'Do not let this trouble you and refrain yourself, for I promise you that you shall obtain justice in a manner that everyone will talk about'. ('Non uos pese et sofrituos [in the sense of refraining oneself], ca yo uos prometo que tal derecho uos de ende que tod el mundo aura que dezir dello') (PCG, ch. 738, p. 434). The use of the term *derecho* ('justice') has no ironic connotations. It expresses the right to act in order to pursue justice and to deliver the vengeance planned.

31 On the 'medianedo', the name of that judicial space, see García de Valdeavellano, *Curso de historia de las instituciones españolas*, p. 558.

32 'pusieron su amor unos con otros'.

33 'aquello que touiesse por bien et fuesse derecho'.

34 The expression 'desamor mortal' (mortal aversion) clearly alluded to an 'enemistad mortal' (mortal enminity), and only appears in C1344 to emphasise the contrast between the *infantes'* trust in the love

the vassal pacts of friendship established during each of these confrontations. This culminated in the great treacherous revenge that led their father into captivity and to the death of the infants. This kind of bloody, treacherous and unjustified revenge as the one perpetrated by Ruy Vázquez against his brother-in-law and nephews, which undermined the legal procedures in place,[35] was therefore condemned in the narrative. In order to carry it out, he had to deceive everybody: he deceived his own sister regarding the reasons for sending her husband to Córdoba;[36] deceived her husband about his mission;[37] and finally the *infantes* by taking them to the host where they would die.[38] It is the construction of these actions as treason that justified and legitimised the later revenge. The victims were portrayed as innocents who invoked divine punishment. When the *infantes* discovered their uncle's betrayal, they appealed to God's vengeance: 'may God never forgive you for what you have done to us'.[39] At the same time, their foster father thus addressed Ruy Vázquez: 'You treacherous and evil man, look at what you have done to all your nephews! May God punish you for this, for people all over the world shall talk about this betrayal'.[40]

In addition, the revenge would also cause the death of all involved, including the enemy Moor forces with which the traitor allied himself. That is why the behaviour of Ruy Vázquez was also reviled. The context in which these acts originated was no longer festive, private, and familial. This was intended to show that the deep political antagonisms and the struggles for power involved in these local settings had much wider effects and implications, as Julio Escalona recently very convincingly stated.[41] To some extent, it also involved corrupting the legitimised objectives of the fight against the Moors, which was now fed by revenge and personal ambitions. And in the long

---

of their aunt and her deceptive behaviour, although 'desamor' ('aversion') was also mentioned in the two other versions. On the juridical dimension of the expression see Bartlett, '"Mortal Enmities"'.

35 The festive context in which these fights take place legally exempts the infants from the first death. The legal reparation for the violence perpetrated that they seek discredits the exaggerated responses that Ruy Vázquez schemes to take revenge for the dishonour, as her women demands. This is regulated, for example, in the *Fuero Real*: 'If a man dishonours the groom or the bridge in the day of their wedding, he shall pay five hundred *sueldos*, and if he does not have them he shall pay what he has' (Fuero Real IV.5.12 and also IV.17.7).

36 Ruy Vázquez lied to him and said that he would return from Córdoba a rich man.

37 The mission proposed by Ruy Vázquez to his brother-in-law before Almanzor in order to ask him for the financial help that he had been promised for his weddings, hid the intended treachery, as he sent letters in Arabic in which he asked Almanzor to have him killed, alleging that he had dishonoured him and his wife 'et porque non me puedo dellos uengar aca en la tierra de los cristianos, [assí como yo querria]' ('and because I cannot take revenge on them in Christian lands [as I wished]'). The words in square brackets are omitted in VC. Can we see in this argument the assumption that the vengeance he was seeking was not legitimized in Castile?

38 'mas todo esto que les el mandaua fazer todo era engaño et nemiga' ('but all he ordered them to do was deceitful and a hoax'). These episodes, which are described in great detail, made up the betrayal on which Ruy Vázquez based his vindictive plan.

39 'nunca te perdone Dios por lo que aquí nos hiciste'.

40 '¡Traydor e ome malo, como as traydo todos tus sobrinos! Dios te de por ende mal galardon, ca en todo el mundo fablaran los omes desta trayçion'.

41 The recent contribution by J. Escalona explains the confrontation between Lara and Salas to achieve territorial hegemony. See Escalona, 'Épica, crónicas y genealogías'.

version of C1344 the count's personal authority was affected, as Ruy Vázquez, buoyed by his victory in the battle in which the *infantes* died, rebelled against the count and conquered all his fortresses. The count's personal authority and power would only be recovered when Mudarra's revenge was fulfilled. In this version it was ultimately the count's political weakness that prevented the *infantes'* father from taking revenge on his return from Córdoba. This was explicitly stated by the count himself in the mourning episode to which he had been summoned along with all the relatives and friends of the victims, to which I shall refer later.

As in the case of the Cid or that of the *infante* García discussed below, the 'good' type of vengeance was legitimised in opposition to the 'bad' type of vengeance, presented as treason. Hence they were depicted as required acts of reparation that were not only moral, but also social and political in nature. The perpetrators of the former were also the 'goodies'. While the complexity of this process cannot be discussed here in detail, for the sake of my argument I will outline the main guidelines of the way in which the texts we are analysing portray the avenging of the deaths of the infants and consider the variations between them The two versions of the EE narrate only the revenge of Mudarra, the child conceived during the father's captivity in Córdoba. The narrator pre-empts his audience/readers of this revenge in the passage where he describes the compassion that Almanzor felt for Gonzalo Gustioz when, reading the letter in which he was asked to order his be-heading and organise a battle to kill his sons, he discovered the hatred that Ruy Vázquez felt against him. He decided to give him a Moorish woman to conceive his child, who would later become the avenging subject: 'he was the one who avenged his father and his brothers, the seven infants, for the betrayal schemed by Ruy Vázquez, for which he killed him'.[42]

The theme of the son that was begotten to avenge the others included in this legend is one of those mythical subjects that have attracted great attention and, indeed, much has been written about the role and significance of this character.[43] I will not discuss these aspects, but will only note that his revenge was also in line with legal procedures, although these were less accurate or formalised than those to be seen the *Poem of the Cid*. In the two versions of EE, Mudarra began his revenge as a judicial court procedure: by daring the traitor before the count, listening to the denial of his dare, trying to attack him for it, granting truces and then directly executing him afterwards for his cunning, lies and betrayals when he tried to flee.[44] Thus ends the

---

42 'Fue el que uengo a su padre et a sus hermanos los vii infantes por la traycion que les boluiera Ruy Vazquez, ca le mato ell por ende'.

43 For a commentary and further references see Escalona, 'Épica, crónicas y genealogías', p. 139.

44 Once Mudarra has confessed to his father that the reason why he has come to Salas is 'to avenge your dishonour and the death of the seven *infantes*' ('uengar la uuestra desonrra et la muerte de los vii infants'), they depart towards the count's palace, together with a great number of knights. Once there he challenges Ruy Vázquez, who denies the charges. Mudarra is thus moved to unsheathe his sword and tries to hurt him, but he is prevented from doing so by the count, who grants the culprit a three day truce. The chronicler does not explain what the aim of the truce was, maybe because he assumed that the audience would know. Was it to give them time to prepare a judicial duel, as in the *Poem of the Cid*? Was it to enable the person challenged to seek refuge in the face of the declaration of public enmity that the challenge entailed, as envisaged in the *fueros*? He only notes that at night, when

story in the two Alfonso X's versions. In the much longer version included in C1344, the revenge for the death of the seven *infantes* would have two episodes over the body of the guilty party: one, which also featured Mudarra, the *infantes'* stepbrother, who was victorious that time, but did not kill the traitor in judicial combat; and the other, in which doña Sancha, the mother, ritually and symbolically humiliated and dishonoured Ruy Vazquez's body, after having him executed.

The ground for the first of these episodes was prepared by the narrator using the same tone and context of the EE version. It follows a similar outline, notwithstanding some substantial differences on which I cannot dwell here. An appeal to the authority of the count is also made. After the process of incorporating Mudarra into Christian society (through baptism), into the family (by maternal adoption), and into the knightly order (through the investiture)[45] had been completed, the count appointed Mudarra *alcalde mayor* and entrusted him with the mission of recovering all of the fortresses usurped by the rebel, while at the same time avenging the death of the *infantes*. In this version the traitor was not challenged in the count's court, but on the battlefield. Mudarra, after a long chase, proposed that they should fight each other in judicial combat.[46] Ruy Vázquez was then defeated but not killed.[47] His death, in the C1344 version, served as justification for a second vindictive episode.

As in the story of the *infante* García, in this chronicle there was a final episode in the revenge process that featured a woman. In this case too, this is the episode that has been most deprecated for being the most archaic and barbaric, as the *infantes'* mother expresses her wish to drink the blood of the traitor as she had previously dreamt of. She was eventually dissuaded by Mudarra, who said that such treacherous blood should not be part of such a loyal body. This episode, however, did not stray far from legal parameters, both human and divine, as doña Sancha became both

---

he was trying to escape, he was caught by Mudarra, who fell on him shouting 'Die, you treacherous, cunning and renegade man!' ('Morras, aleuoso, falsso et traydor'). The blow was such that his body was split and he fell dead on the ground. The thirty knights that were with him were also killed.

45 The first version of EE does not mention any of these rituals, while VC ends the narration with a flashback to relate his baptism and, indirectly, his investiture as a knight: 'Agora sabet aquí los que esta estoria oydes que quando este Mudarra González llegó de Córdoua a Salas, que lo fizo batear su patre e tornólo christiano, ca antes moro era, e fue muy buen cabavallero e mucho esfforçado en quanto buivio' ('Those of you who listen to this story must now know that when Mudarra González came from Córdoba to Salas, his father had him baptized and turned him into a Christian, for before that he had been a Moor, and he was a very noble knight and very vigorous in all he lived through') (VC, p. 128). The reference to Mudarra's baptism is the most striking and significant aspect of VC, which is rather known for suppressing elements from the first version. Was Alfonso X trying to make Mudarra stand out, as he was the one destined to re-establish comital authority? Was this a way of reinforcing his legitimacy as a good avenger? A list of the elements suppressed in VC can be found in de la Campa, 'Las versiones alfonsíes', p. 104.

46 'mientes traydor, mas tu daras oy derecho de quantas trayciones e aleves pensaste; e para se acabar ello [...] lidiemos nos uno por otro' ('you are lying, traitor, but you shall pay today for all the betrayals and treasons you schemed; and to put an end to it [...] let us fight each other').

47 A topic of interest that arises in line with this confrontation is the responsibility of vassals for their assistance to their lords and ladies engaging in unlawful practices. Once again this comes to show how these stories dealt with issues that affected, and were discussed in, the political community that they targeted.

182   ISABEL ALFONSO

an active subject and a judge in the revenge process. Of the various punishments suggested to her, she arrogated to herself the right to choose the type of justice to be done: 'but I want to do justice as I please, and with the consent of God and don Mudarra, I now want to be the *alcalle* of this deed'.[48]

The expressions 'doing justice' and 'to be the *alcalle* of this deed' are worth bearing in mind, as these explicit statements are the most suitable to illustrate my arguments about the relationship, and even conceptual identity, between revenge and justice; and about the public nature of the avenging subject. In this case, it was ordered that the scene where it had all begun, the rostrum of the wedding,[49] be reproduced and the traitor be hanged there, so that each of those affected by his betrayal would be able to do justice on his body. It literally meant the opening of a process of collective revenge, although this was not the term used:

> And I decree that the relatives of the people who died in battle with his sons, and whoever may have been wronged by him, shall come to throw darts or assegais or lances or whatever other weapons at his body, so that the traitor's flesh shall be cut into pieces, and that once he has fallen to the ground, everyone should throw stones at him'.[50]

And that is what they did. They displayed the body for public view so that everyone passing would curse him instead of praying for him. As in the *Poem of the Cid*,[51] the story in this version also ended with a moral: And whoever commits a betrayal shall be cursed in this manner.[52] In this way the revenge became a public and ritual punishment, which sought to denigrate a bloody betrayal.

The end of doña Lambra, the traitor's wife, whom the count referred to as a 'most treacherous woman' (*grande alevosa*) or as a 'known traitor and bad woman', depending on the version, when she begged him for mercy by appealing to the family relationship between them, followed similar lines After all she had a joint responsibility for the reproached acts:

> You lie as a most treacherous woman, for you supported all the betrayals and harms that he did, and you were the lady and queen of my fortresses. From now on I shall not protect you anymore, and I shall order don Mudarra to burn you

---

48   'mas pero esta justiçia yo quiero faser a toda mi voluntad, e queriendo Dios e don Mudarra, yo quiero agora ser alcalle deste fecho'.

49   An allusion to 'damned' weddings, a common epithet used to censure the type of alliance that they sealed.

50   'todos los que eran parientes de aquellos que murieran en la batalla con sus fijos, e otros quales quier a que el mal mereciese, que vinieren lanzar con dardos o con asconas o con varas de lanzar, o con otras armas quales quier, en tal manera que las carnes del traydor fueseen todas partidas en pedazos, e desque cayere en tierra, que entonces le apedreasen todos'.

51   With this moral, which is not included in prose versions, the author expressed a juridical and moral ideal of vengeance: 'If someone dishonours a woman and leaves her, he shall suffer the same or a worse fate'. ('¡Qui buena duena escarneçe, e la dexa después, | Atal le contesca o siquier peor' [PoemCid, vv. 3706–3707]). See Alfonso, 'Venganza y venganza' [Editors' note: For an English translation, see chapter 5 of this volume).

52   'E por esta guisa es maldito aquel que traycion fase'.

alive, and to have your flesh broken apart by dogs, and thus shall your soul be lost forever.[53]

The final curse of this chronicler ('Mal sieglo aya! Amen') certainly shows his bias, but also how he was able to use the narrative resources to emotionally involve his listeners or readers. The purpose was to play the same didactic and moralising role that both the chronicle and historiography also assumed.

Before moving on to discuss the next narrative, I want to emphasise here the great importance of mourning rituals, the emotions and gestures in which they were manifested, as they acted as driving forces for good and bad acts of revenge. I have pointed out such episodes, which occurred in parallel to each insult or aggression, but the mourning of the death of the *infantes*, which would provoke the great revenge that triggered this legend, was even more dramatic than normal. Their father, when he recognised the heads of his children and the foster father who raised them, fell as dead to the ground. Then he cried so abundantly that it was a miracle that nobody could see this and not cry. It was in tears that he praised each of them for their good deeds. These laments were reproduced in a direct and detailed style in C1344, where the mourning process took on an unusual dimension. It was in this context that the father decided to conceive a son who would take revenge.[54] This version also narrated the great mourning of the mother, who summoned those who were 'of his kin and lineage, including Count Garci Fernández himself, and then very large groups came and mourned deeply for the *infantes*.'[55] But her mourning, as the father's before, did not lead to immediate revenge due to the political weakness caused by the treacherous rebel, who had left the would-be avengers powerless to retaliate:

> When he was leaving the wake, count don Garci Fernández said: my friends, this wrong will never be repaired, and you have no reason to make it again; the traitor, Ruy Vázquez, has raised against me, holding a land that I cannot regain from him in response to the deaths of these infants; everyone must go back to his house and beware of the traitor, as given the fortresses that he controls he could do you a great harm.[56]

---

53 'Mentides, como grande aleuosa, ca vos basteçíestes todas estas trayciones e males que el fiso, e vos erades señora e rreyna de las mis fortalesas. De aquí adelante non uos atreguo el cuerpo, e mandare a don Mudarra que vos faga quemar uiua, e que espedaçen canes las vuestras carnes et vuestra alma sera perdida para siempre'. In the two EE versions Mudarra, taken into consideration the kinship between doña Lambra and the count, waits until the death of the latter to effect the deed.

54 The contradictions between the different versions with regards to the status of the Moorish woman and the nature of her relationship with the *infantes*' father are well known. C1344 presented her as the sister of Almanzor himself, while the relationship, rather than a long-standing love affair initiated since the beginning of his captivity, is portrayed as an occasional encounter, even as a forced one aimed exclusively at bringing forth the avenger son.

55 'del su debdo e linaje y el propio conde Garci Fernandez luego vinieron muy grandes conpañas e fisieron muy grant duelo por los infantes'.

56 'E en partiendose del duelo, dixo el conde don Garçi Ferrandes: amigos, este dapno nunca se puede cobrar, e non auedes por que lo faser mas; el traydor de Ruiz Vazquez alçoseme con la terra, e non la puedo del cobrar por la muerte destos infantes; daqui cada uno se vaya para su casa, e guardese del traydor, ca podriades del rreçebir grant dapno por las fortalesas que tiene' (C1344, pp. 288–89).

Therefore, in this version the subsequent vengeance and the return to the social and political order it entailed attained greater significance.

In the story about the death of the *infante* García included in the EE[57] we also find an evaluation of, and an opposition between the two types of vengeance. This is constructed by means of rhetorical resources that are similar to the ones used in the previous story. Treacherous vengeance corresponds to the one which, invoking and ancient enmity, the sons of Count Vela carried out against the *infante* García, son and successor of the count of Castile, when he was to marry the sister of the king of León. The response in retribution for that act is presented as legitimate vengeance.

The death of the young Castilian *infante*, which was also accounted for in the Latin chronicles, was always judged as being treacherous. According to the *Chronica naiarensis* the perpetrators of the killing 'ducti enuidia [...] innocuum occiderunt' ('were driven by envy and killed an innocent man').[58] In his *Chronicon Mundi*, Bishop Lucas de Tuy stated that it was 'memores malorum' ('the memory of the evils') that caused the 'enormi sacrilegio perpetrato' ('immense sacrilege that was committed').[59] The archbishop of Toledo Rodrigo Jiménez de Rada thought that 'odium prodictionis' ('the hatred of treason') was behind the murderous action that led to the treacherous killing of the *infante*.[60] We know that for composing this episode the redactors of the EE explicitly used the last two chronicles, as well as a *romanz* now lost that complemented the information of those texts. Thus it was written that the sons of Count Don Vela 'recalling the harm and the dishonour that their father, Count Don Sancho, had brought to them, and how he had expelled them from Castile, reckoned that they could take revenge if they so wanted'.[61]

As Lucas de Tuy, Alfonso X's redactor described them as being moved by the memory of the ills suffered, which were considered to be sufficient to justify revenge, as they were categorised as dishonourable. So rather than claiming that the revenge was unjustified, in line with Jiménez de Rada, the judgement in EE focused on the deceptive and treacherous way in which it was schemed and performed. Initially, the Vela brothers welcomed the *infante* and paid tribute to him, kissing his hand 'as is customary in Spain' ('assi como es costumbre de Espanna'),[62] and thus became his vassals. Then they received tenures from him, as they had requested, and promised 'that they would serve him with them as his natural vassals', and repeating the kissing of hands.[63] The narrator emphasised that they had gained his confidence through the pact of friendship inherent in homage, to draw attention to the treacherous revenge that would be committed later:

---

57 My commentaries are also based on the PCG version, ch. 787, 788, 789, though noting the significant variations in VC, CVR, Book VII, ch. V–VII.

58 Estévez Sola, ed., *Chronica Naierensis*, Liber II, 41 and Liber III, 2.

59 Tuy, *Chronicon mundi*, Liber IV, 44.

60 Jiménez de Rada, *Historia de rebus Hispanie*, Liber V, XXV.

61 'acordaronse del mal e de la desonrra que su padre, el conde don Sancho, les fiziera e de commo les echara de Castilla, touieron que tenien tiempo de uengarse si quisiessen'.

62 This is specified by Archbishop Jiménez de Rada, but is omitted in VC.

63 'seruirte con ellas como a sennor cuyos naturales somos'.

VENGEANCE, JUSTICE, AND POLITICAL STRUGGLE   185

and being then under the protection of the sons of Count Vela thanks to the homage that they paid to him, he sought his wife doña Sancha, and saw her, and talk to her as much as we wanted and as he pleased.[64]

The young count's trust was also highlighted when he responded to Sancha's call to caution about him being unarmed. She knew that 'there were men in the land that wished him harm' ('omnes auie en la tierra quel querien mal'), and that he had never damaged anyone. And yet, the Vela brothers were ill-advised in 'evilness, falseness and treason' ('malo, falso y de trayción') and planned how to kill him while searching for a justification for their intended murder.[65] As one of them said:

> I know how we can find a reason to justify his killing. We shall place a wooden panel in the middle of the street. The Castilian knights are men who enjoy these things, so they will want to come and take solace. We will then initiate a fight with them over the throwing of the lances, and we will kill them all in this manner.[66]

As in the legend of the *infantes of Lara*, the setting for this first revenge was festive, and the pretext was also causing a fight, which indicates the impunity that this environment provided for violence. The narrator described how everything happened, as well as the enormity of the massacre, in which not only the infant, but also the knights who accompanied him were killed, with some aggravating circumstances. The murderer Vela was the godfather the *infante*, who was barely thirteen years old, and killed him in front of the church of San Juan. The count himself boasted about what he had done before doña Sancha and the magnates assembled in the palace. Those assembled could not believe that he had dared commit 'such a great betrayal' ('tan gran traycion'), which escalated the violence between the various parties involved. The Vela brothers killed many other friends and vassals of the *infante*. According to EE, following Lucas de Tuy and Jiménez de Rada, the mourning of *infanta* Sancha was so sorrowful that she seemed to be dead rather than alive and wanted to be buried in the same grave as the *infante*.[67] The chronicler acknowledged that up to this point he had followed the information in Latin given by Lucas de Tuy and the Archbishop

---

64 'et seyendo ya el seguro de los fijos del conde don Vela por ell omenage quel fizieran, fuesse por su esposa donna Sancha, et uiola, et fablo con ella quanto quiso a su sabor'.

65 The word *traycion* (betrayal) is omitted in VC.

66 'Yo se en que guisa podremos mouer razon dond ayamos achaque por quel matemos. Alcemos un tablado en medio de la rua, et los caualleros castellanos, como son omnes que se precian desto, querran y uenir a assolazarse, et nos bolueremos estonces pelea con ellos sobrell alançar, et matarlos emos a todos desta guisa' (PCG, ch. 788). Variants in VC, ch. VI, affect the use of direct style but entail no change in the sense of the passage.

67 Lucas de Tuy says that Sancha 'made a great mourning over Count García and buried him honourably next to her father, King Alfonso [the V], in the church of San Juan' ('fecit planctum magnum super ducem Garsiam et sepeliuit eum honorifice iusta regem Adefonsum patrem suum in ecclesia sancti Iohannis'); Jiménez de Rada: 'The bride, who had barely relished the bliss of her fiancé, who was a widow before being married, cried and her tears merged with the blood of the murdered, and she repeated incessantly that she had died together with him. When he was taken to the church of San Juan to be buried next to the father of her fiancé, she wanted to be buried with him'. ('Sponsa uero sponsi dulcedine uix gustata ante uidua quam traducta fletu lugubri semiuiua lacrimas cum occisi

of Toledo, which in Alfonso X's VC was considered to be totally truthful. He then introduced a *chanson* in Spanish that told a different version of the story.[68] The epic narrative does indeed contain some variations regarding the setting in which the *infante* was killed and the mourning of doña Sancha which above all affect the later episode of the good revenge, the *digna ultione* referred to by the *Naiaerense* (the only Latin chronicle that mentions it). In the other two, the Vela brothers escaped to the mountains. In Lucas de Tuy's chronicle they explicitly escape from the 'multitudo' that 'conflueret ad vindicandam mortem Garcie ducis' (the crowd that got together to demand the death of Dux García),[69] which implies that to some extent this was what must have been done. But the *chanson* inserted into the two Alfonso X's versions of the EE, despite considering them to be a legend, recounts two revenges — or two episodes of the same process, as in the case of the infants of Lara —, both good and justified: 1) that of King Sancho III the Older against the Vela brothers, and 2) that of the *infanta* Sancha on another count who also participated in the death of the *infante* and who personally dishonoured her.

In the first episode, 'the treacherous counts', as they were called by the narrator, did not flee to the mountains but to the castle de Monzón, on the Castillian border, where after having been warned by the *tenente*, king Sancho appeared with his sons and seized all the guilty parties, except the person who offended the *infante*, who escaped in disguise. When the Velas saw them arrive, they rightly guessed their fate: 'these [people] come only to take revenge for the death of the *infante* García'.[70] They were in fact burnt after having been harshly punished as traitors who had killed their master.[71] The chronicler thus invoked an explicit rule against treason similar in nature to that written in the same Alfonso X's *scriptorium* where the EE was written, whereby betrayal was considered 'one of the most serious and odious crimes which a person can commit'.[72]

---

sanguine anmiscebat, se occisam ingeminants cum occiso. Qui cum in ecclesia santi Iohannis cum patre sponse sepeliretur, er ipsa cum sepulto uoluit sepeliri').

68 PCG, ch. 788: 'assi fue como el arçobispo et don Lucas de Tuy lo cuentan en su latin, dize aquí en el castellano la estoria del Romanz dell inffant Garcia dotra manera, et cuentalo en esta guisa' ('and this is how Archbishop don Lucas de Tuy narrates it in his Latin, the story of the *Romanz of the infante Garcia* is here recorded in Castilian in a different fashion, and it is told in this manner'). VC, ch. VI, omits any reference to the Latin chroniclers and simply notes: 'Mas commo quier que esta sea la verdat, la estoria del rromançe desde infante diz desta otra guissa' ('And since this is the truth, the story of the *chanson* of this infant is told in this other manner').

69 The romance edition of this work adds 'los cuerpos de los queles fuelgan en el lugar que se dize Gordon en la villa que se dize Çeruera' ('whose bodies lounged in that place that is called Gordon, in the village called Cervera') (Tuy, *Crónica de España*, p. 338).

70 'que estos non uienen por al sinon por uengar la muerte dell inffant Garcia'.

71 'Quemaronlos y luego, faziendoles antes muy grandes penas como a traydores que mataran a su señor' ('They burnt them after inflicting a very harsh punishment upon them, as traitors who had killed their lord'). VC only mentions King Sancho, noting that they were burnt alive in the fire ('viuos en fuego') but omitting the justification for this.

72 'vno de los mayores yerros, e denuestos, en que los omes pueden caer' (Partidas VII.2.Preamble). The consideration of betrayal as a contagious disease in this text deserves to be taken into account, as it alluded to a perception of evil — and by implication, of good — as attitudes that took root and

The identity of the avenging subjects is one of the most significant elements in the plot of any revenge story, and it is therefore the most open to manipulation. In particular, major discrepancies can be found in the various versions of the chronicles regarding the role played by king Sancho de Navarra throughout the story. Discrepancies occur with regards to his role in the episode when he accompanied the *infante* to the court in León, to whether or not he was the driving force behind the request that he be granted the title of Castilian king, and in his speech at the funeral and, especially, in the revenge process. These events were told differently according to the intended logic to be derived from the narrative, which would deserve further study. Although the involvement of the king of Navarra in the vengeance was not made explicit, the political benefit seems clear. It is true that he was the victim's brother-in-law and also a relative of the *infante*, but these links were not invoked to explain his revenge. For example, the absence of the Leonese king, Vermudo III, who was Sancha's brother and had participated the arrangement of the wedding, is surprising, for he was brother-in-law of both the murdered *infante* and of the king. His stay in Oviedo does not seem to be sufficient to completely leave him out of the retaliation for the murder committed by his vassals, which also caused the planned political alliance with the Castilians to fail. The major role played by King Sancho, who killed the 'killers', as stated in the *Chronica Naierensis* and emphasized in the prose version of the *Romanz* in EE, was related to the king's function in the political landscape of the period. In the narrative of the *Romanz*, the second episode of revenge was linked to the hegemonic ambitions of the King of Navarra. After executing the traitors and being received as lord of the strongholds and territories that were under the control of the *infante* Garcia in the Castilian border, he went to León for the marriage of his son Fernando with the very *infanta* Sancha, whose condition for accepting the wedding was that he should take revenge on the traitor, who was still alive, on her behalf:

> that if he did not get back at Fernant Laynez, who took part in the death of the *infante* García and slapped her and took her by the hair, her body would never reach that of Fernando, his son.[73]

The second episode of this vindictive process started at this point. It referred back to the mourning of this Leonese infant, which was again the device that explained the logic and assessment of vengeance that arose from that pain. To the mourning described in nearly all of the chronicles, the epic narrative adds two scenes. In one of them Sancha offered her life in exchange for that of the infant, and in the other, she stood over his body and asked to be buried with him. In both she was reviled by the traitor Fernán Laínez, who first slapped her in the face and then took her by the hair and knocked her down. She now called for these grievances, together with his

---

were transmitted almost physiologically, which were also acquired and learnt by example. The need to jointly analyse the legal and historiographic work of Alfonso X has been rightly raised, in my opinion, in Fernández Ordóñez, 'Variación en el modelo historiográfico', p. 74.

73 'que si la non uengasse del traydor Fernant Laynez que fuera en la muerte del inffant Garcia et diera a ella una palmada en la cara et la messara de los cabellos, que nunqua el su cuerpo antes llegarie al de don Fernando su fijo'.

involvement in the death of her fiancé, to be avenged, but not by her. The fulfilment of this wish then became a condition for the new political alliance. The narrator tells how once the fleeing count was captured by order of King Sancho, he was delivered to the *infante* for her to administer justice 'doing what she pleased with him and to make justice as she willed',[74] with details of how this took place:

> Then doña Sancha took him and made him pay as she saw fit, and she proceeded in this manner: she herself took a knife in her hand and cut his hands, with which he had injured the *infante* and herself, and then she cut his feet, with which he walked during that deed, and then she cut his tongue, with which he had talked about his betrayal, and once she had done all this she took his eyes out, with which he had seen everything. And once this was done to him, she called for a mule to make him ride it and take it to as many villages and markets as there existed in Castile and in the land of León, where he committed his betrayal, saying and announcing everywhere that it was due to the death of the *infante* García, which Fernando Laínez had caused, that the latter was so suffering.[75]

The exemplary nature of the narrative-act was evident and explicit, and the meaning of this literal and metaphorical reproduction of the attack (which echoed the one performed by the other Sancha, mother of the *infantes* of Lara), was along the same lines. The critical recasting of EE ordered by Alfonso X *c.* 1238 did not include this avenging ritual on the body of the traitor, but the fact that the details were missing did not change the purpose of the vengeance: 'and she administered justice as she saw fit, as he had killed with his own hands'. It is important to bear in mind that vengeance and justice were regarded as being synonyms in both versions, and the direct nature of this female vengeance.[76]

---

74 'fiziesse dell lo que quisiesse et la justicia que touiesse por bien'.

75 'Estonces donna Sancha tomol et fizo justicia en el qual ella quiso, et fizola en esta guisa: tomo un cuchiello en su mano ella misma, et taiole luego las manos con que el firiera all inffant et a ella misma, desi taiol los pies con que andidiera en aquel fecho, despues sacole la lengua con que fablara la traycion; et desque esto ouo fecho, sacole los oios con que lo uiera todo. Et desquel ouo parado tal, mando adozir una azemila et ponerle en ella et leuarle por quantas uillas et mercados auie en Castiella et en tierra de Leon do el fiziera aquella traycion, dexiendo et pregonando sobrel cada logar que por la muerte que aquel Fernant Laynez basteçiera al inffant Garcia et fuera ell en ella, padecie ell aquello'.

76 'Et ella fizo en él su justiçia, qual touo por bien, asi quel mató con sus manos mesmas'. It may be noted that a similar story is found in the *Libro del Cavallero Zifar* (*Book of the Knight Zifar*), when King Zifar orders that the traitor Nasón must be killed: 'I order that your tongue is brought out through your neck for the words that you said against me, and that your head is cut off for you resorted to others to savage my land, and that you are burnt and made dust for the fire that you set to it, so that you shall not be eaten by dogs or by birds, for they would be infected by your treachery. Rather, they shall collect that dust and throw it to the lake that lies in the confine of my kingdom, which they called Lake Solfareo, where no fish nor any other living being has ever been found'. ('Mando que vos saquen la lengua por el pescueço por las palabras que dixistes contra mi, e que vos corten la cabeça que vos fezistes cabo de otro[s] para correr la mi tierra, e que vos quemen e vos fagan polvos por la quema que en ella fezistes, porque nin vos coman canes nin aves, ca fincarian enconadas de la vuestra traycion; mas que cojan los polvos e los echen en aquel lago que es en cabo del mi regno, a que dizen lago Solfareo, do nunca ovo pes nin cosa biva del mundo'). The parallel is noted in Cacho Blecua, 'La

The last part of the *Poem of the Cid* — the version of the poem — narrates how the Cid's daughters were scorned and bloodily dishonoured by their own husbands, the infants of Carrión, who claimed that it was their vengeance for having been reviled and shamed in their father-in-law's court in Valencia. In connection with this vengeance, the poet or chronicler stressed that the *infantes* were cowardly, treacherous and deceitful, and that their aggression was a mere reflection of their vile character. In contrast with this portrayal, the characters of the Cid and his vassals are presented in a positive light. They called upon the king to fulfil their rights, and to take revenge for the ills and dishonour they had suffered. The king, who was regarded as having some responsibility in terms of the reparation, convened an assembly in Toledo and initiated a procedure that ended in a judicial combat between the *infantes* and the Cid's vassals. In this fully regulated judicial duel, the former were humiliated, vanquished and dishonoured for the injuries they had inflicted upon their wives, and the Cid recovered the honour (*honra*) and value of his lineage. The Cid's vengeance before the king's assembly was a political process that reflected one of the means used for rights to be demanded, granted, taken, and obtained.

This account, in which none of the vengeful acts resulted in killings, brought closure to the epic poem of the Cid. I analysed it in detail in a previous study which discussed the relationship between vengeance and justice that I develop in this paper.[77] Here it serves as a reference point to assess whether this relationship between vengeance and justice changed or was maintained in the prose version of this narrative in the EE. It must also be noted that from Alfonso X's workshop only the text of VC, dated to *c.* 1283, remains for this part. It is the one considered to be closest to the Poem,[78] since the text contained in PCG did not even belong to the extension made in Sancho IV's court in 1289. The draft of the initial EE version used for the episode discussed here had a 'gap' in the compilation that was filled 'by a copyist who worked in the fourteenth century'.[79] Moreover, it has been discussed whether the epic narrative used to write the EE was the poem that survived to present times, at least in the case of one of the two extant versions of the EE.[80] Fernando Gómez Redondo, for example, after analysing the formulae used to insert the themes related to the Cid in PCG, considered this section to be based on a different version of the *Poem*, aimed at a different target audience. He noted that the epic themes in the narration became chivalric, and this is why, despite the similarities in the plot between the verses from the *Poem* and those from PCG, the greater thematic development of the latter seems to be due to different

---

crueldad del castigo', p. 68, n. 10, from where I have taken the quote. According to Cacho, in the text 'vengeance is replaced with the implementation of the law, although the outcome is the same'.

77 Alfonso, 'Venganza y justicia'.

78 Pattison, 'El Mio Cid del Poema'.

79 This was explained by Inés Fernández Ordóñez, when she very clearly systematised the hand-written transmission of the EE and all derived chronicles, indicating that this is why there is no direct source for the first draft. See Fernández Ordóñez, 'La transmisión textual', pp. 233–35. For a systematic comparison between the two versions, see Dyer, *El Mio Cid del taller alfonsí*.

80 Catalán, 'Las crónicas generales', pp. 104–14.

190   ISABEL ALFONSO

expectations on the part of the audience, whereby chivalric values were proposed to support courtesan identity.[81]

In the context of this debate, and without any attempt at comprehensiveness, it would be of interest to make some remarks on the nature of the variations or refinements in the description of the conflict that can be identified between the version in PCG, on the one hand, and the *Poem* and VC, on the other. PCG maintained the central plot of the *Poem*: the censuring of vengeance and its perpetrators, the *infantes* of Carrión; and the justification of another vengeance in which the key players, the Cid and his vasalls, were praised. Various aspects could be discussed here, but the focus will only be on two of them: the tension between the different options to take vengeance by lawful means and the more formalised chivalric ethic as a reference point for this conduct. As was the case with the previous narratives of the *infantes of Lara* and of the *infante García*, in that of the Cid law and vengeance were also part of the same semantic field, as they were presented as being interchangeable. For example, when the *infantes* were planning their attack on their wives, they claimed that they would seek *derecho* (right) in retaliation for the scorn and shame they had suffered from the Cid's circle when their cowardice had been brought to light.[82] Once they had obtained their right, that is, after they had assaulted their wives when they were taking them to Carrión, they proclaimed that vengeance had been wreaked.[83] The same argument was heard from the Cid and his vassals, when they complained about the aggression suffered by the Cid's daughters. It is within this group that different ways of *tomar derecho* (obtaining right) were suggested in order to punish the *infantes* for their action and take revenge. These will be discussed in detail below.

The vassals that accompanied the Cid's daughters when they left Valencia were the first ones who, in view of the gravity of the situation, argued that it was better to engage in combat with the *infantes* than to return to the Cid and face his inquiries.[84] Alternatively, they also contemplated resorting to the king to claim that

---

81   Fernando Gómez Redondo held that it is appropriate to talk about *cantares*, and reviewed the various explanations that have been provided about the variations between the *Poem* and the different versions of the EE. He suggested that attention ought to be paid to the recipients of those poetic and chronicled works and the mechanisms involved in the relation between the text and the audiences in order to understand the four Cid figures he identified in PCG. See Gómez Redondo, 'La materia cidiana'.

82   'mal dia yo naçi et vos, si dello derecho non auemos' ('cursed was the day in which you and I were born, if we do not obtain redress for this'); or 'mal dia nos nasciemos, si non auemos derecho del' ('cursed was the day in which we were born, if we do not obtain redress for this') (PCG, pp. 603–04).

83   'And now you will see how your father and your lineage avenge you, for we have been avenged for the dishonour he brought upon us in Valencia with the lion' ('Et agora ueredes commo uos uengara vuestro padre et uuestro linaje, ca nos ya uengados somos de la deshonra que nos el fizo en Valencia con el leon') (PCG, p. 609).

84   'My friends, these *infantes* committed evil against their wives, the daughters of our lord the Cid, and they are our ladies, for we paid homage to them before their father and we acknowledged them as our ladies, and the Cid granted us knighthood so that we would honour the obligations we have towards them and their father […] we would better […] kill the *infantes* for the evil they committed rather than going back to the Cid, for we should not come before him if we failed to avenge him in any manner' ('Amigos, estos infantes fizieron mal fecho en sus mugeres, fijas del Çid nuestro sennor, et

justice be done if they could not find the *infantes*.[85] Their dialogue was articulated on the basis of the vassals' duty to defend and help their lord to seek his right and redress for having been dishonoured, and taking revenge for a wrong-doing before appearing before their lord with dignity. Accordingly, they all agreed that none of them would change their lord 'fasta que el Çid aya alcançado el derecho que deue auer sobresto' ('until the Cid had obtained the right to which he was entitled for the events occurred'), and committed to remain in the court of king Alfonso until the Cid was avenged. This tension between taking direct, immediate revenge and pursuing vengeance through a judicial claim was maintained throughout the entire procedure before the king's assembly in Toledo. It did not take the form of a constant threat of outbreaks of violence, as these were attributed to the side (*bando*) of Carrión both in the *Poem* and in the chronicle. This violence, which would escalate the conflict, was not regarded as a legitimate alternative, but as a manifestation of the 'locura de algunos de la corte que se mueuen contra mi' ('the madness of some in the court who plot against me'), as the Cid argued in the face of provocation. Therefore, the vassals were advised not to use aggressive language that could be used as a justification by the *infantes*. These are the different alternatives to take revenge by lawful means that the actors envisage in PCG version and which I deem noteworthy.

The Cid himself, when he voiced his challenge before the king and asked him to take responsibility for the events, requested that he be granted redress from the men of Carrión for the wrongdoings and dishonour they had caused him. He claimed that, if the king's assembly failed to repair the ills suffered, he would take justice into his own hands with the help of God and the truth he demanded.[86] Furthermore, if the king refused,[87] he would go

> to the prized estate of Carrión and grab them by the throat, hold them prisoners and carry them off to Valencia, where my daughters — their wives — are, and I will force penance upon them for what they have done and feed them the delicacies they deserve.[88]

---

ellas son nuestras sennoras, ca omenaie les fiziemos ante su padre o las rescebiemos por sennoras, et el Çid nos fizo caualleros por guardar todos estos debdos que auemos con ellas et con su padre [...] mas nos ualdrie [...] matar con los infantes por el mal fecho que fizieron, que non que nos tornassemos por el Çid; ca si nos dotra manera non punnamos del vengar, non somos pora paresçer antel') (PCG, p. 610).

85 'To tell him "all the truth so that he can make justice as it should be made for such an evil deed"' ('Toda la uerdat por que faga y aquella justicia que se deue fazer sobre atan mal fecho') (PCG, p. 610).

86 'My lord, give me redress for the evil and the dishonour that they have brought upon me [...] and if you do not make amends for it at your court, please be merciful and let me deal with them, for I will seek my right with the help of God and with the truth I am claiming for' ('Señor, datme derecho dellos, del mal et de la deshonrra que me fizieron [...] et si vos por uuestra corte non fazedes emendar, sea la uestra merced, et dexat a mi con ellos, ca yo tomare mio derecho con Dios et con la uerdat que demando'), (PCG, pp. 619–20).

87 'for if you did not feel sorrow, my lord' ('porque si a vos non pesare, sennor'), seemingly referring to the joint responsibility that he is demanding from the king.

88 'a la su heredat de Carrion de que se ellos preçiian, et y los prendere por las gargantas, et leuarlos he comigo presos pora Valencia o son mis fijas et sus mugeres, et y los fare yo tomar penitencia de lo que fizieron, et darles he a comer de aquellos maniares que meresçeen' (PCG, p. 620).

Therefore, the threat to implement the law of retaliation and vengeance on the same terms as the damaged sustained was part of the dispute resolution process, even metaphorically, as in this case. The king's response, once he had accepted his part in the dishonour caused to the Cid, came to show that the alternatives mentioned above were perfectly legitimate. However, the king stated that, as they were already gathered before the assembly, it was no longer possible to demand justice in any other way but by resorting to the judicial process:

> But given that you are already at my court, it is no longer time to request it from me in any other manner, but you shall accuse them of the deed they committed, and they shall abide the sentence that the judges that I have appointed pass.[89]

This option was invoked again to stop the violence that broke out between them several times during the procedure: 'Neither you nor they shall behave like that before me, for your right shall not be diminished in any manner'.[90] In this climate the judicial procedure followed its course, including the verbal duel between the parties, which was used by the Cid and his vassals to proclaim that they had been dishonoured, denounce the premeditation of the *infantes*, and dare them to prove it wrong in a judicial combat. This procedure was explicitly perceived and regarded as vengeance for the dishonour caused to the Cid. One of the instances of this was when the Cid advised the vassals who were to engage in duel that they should ensure that 'he should be relieved of his shame and they should stand as good knights, providing redress and honour for his daughters and for his lord King Alfonso'.[91] The vassals' final gratitude to God for their victory was an even more expressive way of showing how they understood and perceived the actions undertaken. The Cid kneeled down, blessed and praised the name of God for the revenge they had taken on the *infantes* of Carrión, and said to his wife and daughters: 'you and your daughters are now avenged, may the name of God be praised, now we can marry them without shame'.[92] His daughters also knelt down and thanked God for the revenge that He granted them for the great dishonour that the *infantes* had brought upon them.[93] The chronicler persistently attributed the ultimate responsibility for this 'vengeance that God inflicted upon the *infantes* of Carrión'[94] to God, which prompted the Cid to order eight days of festivities to be held in Valencia.

This representation of the judicial procedure as the framework within which the vengeance had taken place is no different from the one found in the *Poem* and in

---

89 'Mas pues que en la mia corte estades, non es ya tiempo de demandargelo en otra manera sinon que los metades vos en culpa del fecho que fizieron, et ellos que se saluen segunt la sentencia que dieren los alcalles que yo he dado' (PCG, p. 620).

90 'Non auedes vos nin ellos por que venir a tanto ante mi, ca de uestro derecho non vos menguara nada' (PCG, p. 621).

91 'tirassen a el de vergüenza et ellos fincasen por buenos caballeros et diessen bengança et onrra a sus hijas et al rey don Alfonso su señor' (PCG, p. 624).

92 'agora sodes vengada y vuestras fijas, et loado sea el nombre de Dios, agora las podremos casar sin vergüenza' (PCG, p. 624).

93 'agradecieron a Dios la venganza que les diera de la gran deshonra que les hicieran los infantes' (PCG, p. 624).

94 'venganza que Dios le diera de los infantes de Carrión'.

VC.[95] What seems to differ in the PCG version is the greater level of specification of the ethical code with respect to which chivalric behaviour was judged. The acts of cowardice of the *infantes* during their stay in Valencia — namely to their fear of the lion and their fleeing from battle — which were disclosed before the assembly in the first challenge, merited the reproach of the Cid's young vassal. They had failed to show their bravery on these occasions, and later attacked the women as if they were men who could defend themselves. This reproach was condensed in the *Poem* in a single verse: 'They are women and you are men' [v. 3347],[96] whereas in PCG it was made by invoking a form of ethics that justified that they had been challenged to a duel for their maliciousness:

> and they proved their force against them, as if they were also men who could defend themselves. And for this they acted as if they were cowards and vile men who are not worthy of chivalry, for they displayed their power against women, who are such a weak thing. And for this I challenge them for their maliciousness.[97]

This type of ethics was the yardstick by which a knight could deserve to be regarded as 'good' or 'evil', as a 'good' or a 'bad' knight errant. Failing to fulfil the duty of vengeance, or failing to fulfil such duty in accordance with the established code, led to being deemed as a 'bad' knight errant. This was how Pero Bermúdez said he felt when he arrived in Valencia to tell the Cid what had happened to his daughters, uttering a sentence that encompassed the full meaning of the *tempus* that marked the decisions to be made on the possible resolution strategies for revenge:

> My uncle and lord, for the love of God I beg you to feel in your heart the evil that those treacherous men from Carrión have inflicted upon you, and upon us altogether with you. I do not know what to say, but I regard myself as a bad knight errant, because I have failed to avenge you before coming back to you, and I truly say to you that if I failed to do so, or die, or venture, or finish it [...]. And for the love of God I beg your favour so that you shall not refrain, that we shall ride and present charges and make a claim, for this is something we should not forego.[98]

The values that characterised a good knight extended to his swords: when he recovered his two famous swords, called Colada and Tizón, which he had given to

---

95 'Señor Dios, a ti gracias e mercedes porque mis fijas son oy asy vengandas' (VC, p. 243).
96 'Ellas son mugieres e vós sodes varones'.
97 'et mostraron contra ellas su esfuerço, assy commo si fuessen otros omnes que se les pudiesen amparar. Et por esto paresce que fizieron a guisa de couardes et de viles omnes en que non a prez ninguno de caualleria: en mostrar su poder contra mugeres, que son tan feble cosa. Et por esto rieptolos por aleuosos' (PCG, p. 621).
98 'Mio tío y sennor, por amor de Dios vos ruego que vos sintades en uuestro coraçon del mal daquellos falsos de Carrión que rescebistes vos, et nos todos conuusco. Et no se que vos diga, más tengome por mal andante porque vos non uengue ante que a vos tornasse; et bien vos digo uerdat, que si fallara en que, o yo muriera o me auenturara o lo acabara [...]. Et por amor de Dios vos demando en merçed que non vos detengades, et caualguemos et vayamoslo acalonnar y demandar, ca non es cosa que deuamos echar en vagar' (PCG, p. 614).

his sons-in-law, the Cid resorted to irony to oppose his own bravery to theirs. He contrasted how he had earned them with little they had used them:

> With the aim of honouring my daughters I granted you to be cared by the *infantes* of Carrión, but they were not good for you, and they kept you hungry, as during the time you stayed with them they did not feed you in the manner I used to do. Now God has had mercy on you and has released you, and you have come back to my hands. And I was fortunate to receive you, and you were fortunate to receive me.[99]

Also, in order to counteract the contempt that the *infants* exhibited for his status and position to justify their aggression, the Cid boasted before the assembly about his high value as an ally: 'there is no Christian king who would not regard as proper of a good knight errant to marry my daughters, other than this betrayers. Lord, redress me for the evil and the dishonour they have brought upon me'.[100] The expression 'bien andantes' (referring to the good knight errant) epitomises the chivalric virtues that made up one's reputation and prestige: valour in battle, the defence of women, loyalty as vassals, observance of the rules of friendship, etc. These qualities were featured by the Cid's group and were used to contrast their revenge, guided by God, with that effected by the *infantes*, inspired by the devil).[101]

Discussion

Several aspects merit further attention in connection with the content of these stories. These include their narrative articulation around the assessment of the actors' behaviour; and the logic of reparation governing this social process, which condemned treason and legitimised punishment in response (a process where the deep antagonisms generated by competition and political fights were often identified). To conclude, I will only focus on the two aspects that I believe are the most controversial: the role of women in vengeance processes and the relationship between vengeance and justice.

---

99 'Et por onrrar a mis fijas, diuos con ellas en guarda a los infantes de Carrion, mas non eran ellos por a vos, et trayenuos fanbrientas, et en el tiempo con que con ellos andudiestes non uso ceuauan como yo vos solia ceuar, et fizouos Dios merçed que saliestes de catiuo et venistes a las mis manos; et yo fuy bienandante en cobrar a vos, et vos fuestes bien andantes en cobrar a mi' (PCG, p. 618).

100 'non ay rey cristiano que se non touiese por bien andante de casar con las mis fijas, demas estos alevosos. Señor, datme derecho dellos, del mal et de la deshonrra que me fizieron' (PCG, p. 619).

101 The Cid pre-empted what was going to happen (which his wife's intuition had warned him about) and said that if 'the devil moved them to do such wrong, they would pay for it dearly' (el diablo les fiziesse tan mal fecho fazer, caro les costarie' (PCG, p. 608).

Women and Vengeance

Except for the story of the Cid, in the other two narrations one of the revenge episodes that was represented in a positive light (the one described in the bloodiest way) featured a woman. As mentioned earlier, the key role of female characters and the cruelty of their vengeance have been seen to link Spanish stories with the great 'Germanic' epic, thus also showing the archaic nature of society in Castilla-León.[102] However, the cruelty of this violence did not specifically seem to be a female feature, nor was it always assessed negatively. The way in which king Zifar ordered the traitor Nasón to be executed did not differ much from the two cases of revenge taken by women in the narratives here.[103] In all cases the traitors' bodies suffered mutilations associated with the transgressions committed by them, and this appeared to be quite frequent in the penal system then current in the various legal codes.[104] In addition, the vengeance wreaked by King Sancho of Navarre on the *infante* García's murderers, as well as the revenge taken by Count García Fernández on doña Lambra, involved grave physical punishment that was not very different from that attributed to women.[105] Cruelty was not characterised as being absolute but relative, and therefore it was postulated as a ruler's positive feature in various legal and doctrine treatises of the period when the seriousness of the offence committed required it: 'The king, the prince or the governor of the kingdom must be cruel against cruel, evil and treacherous men and those who commit any sort of evil'.[106] This idea of truly cruel chastisement, and of the exemplary nature of a particular form of punishment, was central to the legal works of Alfonso the Wise.[107] In my view, the fact that the major female characters

---

102 Interestingly, Menéndez Pidal used a circular argument to support his idea that these episodes of vengeance must have taken place in the later periods. He said: 'It is generally believed that great barbaric customs in a narrative are a sign that it was older, but the study of the evolution of medieval epic narratives contradicts this common belief […] until the thirteenth century women who had been scorned did not take revenge personally. It was only in later developments of the legend in the fourteenth century that the features of *female ferocity* were introduced, which show a decadence in epic taste' [my emphasis], without explaining what he means by decadence (Menéndez Pidal, 'El "romanz del Infant García"', p. 78).

103 See n. 76.

104 See a more detailed commentary in Alfonso Antón, 'El cuerpo del delito' [Editors' note: For an English translation, see chapter 12 of this volume].

105 Of the Velas, PCG (p. 789) says that 'they burnt them, but only after inflicting very heavy punishments upon them as traitors who had killed their lord' ('quemaronlos y luego, faziendoles antes muy grandes penas como a traydores que mataran a su señor'); the VC version only notes that 'they were arrested and burnt alive' ('prisolos e quemólos vivos en fuego') (VC, p. 152). For doña Lambra, C1344 envisages the following: 'I shall send Mudarra to burn you alive and to have dogs to break apart your flesh, and your soul shall be lost forever' ('mandare a Mudarra que vos faga quemar uiua, e que espedaçen canes las vuestras carnes, e la vuestra alma sera perdida para siempre' (C1344, p. 313).

106 'Cruel debe ser el rey o prínçipe o regidor de reyno contra los crueles e malos e traydores e tratadores de todo mal'. See Walsh, 'El libro de los doze sabios', p. 92. The logic that compelled and legitimised cruelty towards someone who behaved cruelly must be noted here.

107 It is so argued in the Partidas VII.Preamble. The *Fuero Real* prescribes the following: 'Any man who kills another one treacherously […] shall be arrested and hanged' ('Todo home que matare a otro a traycion […] arrastrenle por ello, e después enforquenlo' (Fuero Real IV.17.2).

executed crude avenging justice should be understood in the context of a fair exercise of power, without assuming any outdated atavism to support the thesis of a remote origin for these narratives.

The analysis of the forms of female revenge certainly requires further research. Not only to document the cases of an increasing number of vengeful women characters, which will surely appear if the necessary effort is made to find them, but rather to explore the reasons why they were represented in such a way from other perspectives. In other words, to renew the theoretical frameworks to interpret them. Important progress has been made in seeking to understand how the gender system worked in past societies; that is, how relationships between men and women were perceived according to the factors and functions that were not strictly biological which differentiated them. It is precisely the historical dimension of this construction of different codes that needs further study, as shown by the works of J. Nelson, C. Clover, or N. Pancer on the medieval period, which are the basis for my own reflections.[108] The issue of female violence among the power elite (of which revenge is one form), hinges on a debate focused primarily on ascertaining whether the violent actions carried out by women characters were intended to substitute or virilise some activities related to certain situations or times of the life cycle of women; or whether these actions could be explained by a code of shared values, in which honour was not solely a male virtue. It would be interesting to explore to what extent the sources of power were common or differentiated; in other words, the degree to which birth, wealth, and social networks were shared resources, as were the mechanisms simultaneously put in place to maintain them.[109] These issues, albeit schematically explained, would allow for new readings to be made of the Spanish narratives of vengeance by women.

The application of gender and kinship codes different from the reading of the legend of the *infantes* of Lara has allowed Julio Escalona to explain the various versions of the legend existing in the two chronicles discussed here; and the fact that one of them, translating the story into an agnatic system, excluded the revenge of the mother of the *infantes*, as it was not in accordance with the social usage and prevailing mentality in the kingdom in the late thirteenth century. He has also been able to explain why C1344, even if composed at a later date, maintained that revenge episode, which according to Escalona, could only be due to the fact that there were hardly any changes in the sources of this chronicle. The consistency of a cognatic system or the strong presence of the female line, within which retaliation made sense, remained intact.[110] Escalona's

---

108 Nelson, 'Queens as Jezebels'. For a state-of-the-art, see Nelson, 'Family, Gender and Sexuality in the Middle Ages'; Clover, 'Regardless of Sex'. It was part of Partner, ed., *Studying Medieval Women*; Pancer, *Sans peur et sans vergogne*.

109 The debate is very well summarized and assessed in N. Pancer's book, which provides the key references.

110 Escalona, following Clover, argues that both doña Lambra and the infants' mother act as 'virtual widows', the first inducing her husband, the second taking action in view of his disability — read as equivalent to feminity (Escalona, 'Épica, crónicas y genealogías', pp. 134–73). It must be noted, though, that two episodes question the father's disability: his blindness is miraculously cured with the ring carried by Mudarra, and then he volunteers to personally fight against the traitor due to his being more able in combat tan Mudarra himself (C1344, pp. 299 and 309).

arguments were very detailed and well-reasoned, and convincingly clarified how a local legend, whose meaning was perfectly explained in this context, and which was a key element in the genealogy of the most powerful Castilian aristocratic family, the Laras, could be incorporated into the royal chronicle. That the material on this family arrived at the workshop alfonsino after having been manipulated by the monks of Arlanza, as Escalona suggests, perhaps explains the omission of the mother's revenge. Nonetheless, what is more problematic is understanding why two chronicles that were close in time, PCG and C1344, adapted their sources to different gender and kinship systems; why one was focused on a world of male relationships, whereas the other recreated a different one that was predominantly female, considered to be more archaic. Furthermore, if we accept that the redactors of PCG[111] assumed codes of behaviour that were sexually differentiated, what would have to be explained is why they failed to also exclude the revenge of *infanta* Sancha for the death of her fiancé, the *infante* García, which was included only a few chapters later.

The difficulties raised by the interpretation of the active presence of female violence increase when considering that in other episodes both chronicles seemed to have assigned a different role to men and women. Thus, in the episode in which the father of the *infantes* married the Moorish woman in order to conceive the avenging son, it was stated that only if a son was born would vengeance be carried out. For as the C1344 version explicitly notes, if a daughter was conceived, Almanzor would marry her off.[112] This different behaviour was also described in the mourning scene before the heads of her children, when the Moorish woman reproached him that he cried like a woman and failed to act like a man. However, in this case, the reproaches were used to instigate revenge, or at least to act vengefully. To analyse the two versions: in *PCG*, when witnessing the intense pain of the father, which brought him even to want to die (as his own wife had said upon learning of the death of her children, and the *infanta* Sancha before the body of her beloved), the Moorish women (p. 442) said to him:

> recover your strength, lord Don Gonzalo, and stop crying and being sorry, for I had twelve sons who were all very good knights, and fate had the twelve of them killed on the same day in a battle, but for that I did not fail to comfort myself and maintain my endurance. And if *I, a woman, endured as I did* and I did not seek

---

111 That is, for these two stories, it was the redactors of the two Alfonso X's versions of EE.

112 'And he said [in response to question of the Moorish woman]: "If he were a man, I would provide him two nurses to raise him well, and once he was old enough to distinguish good from evil I would tell that he is my son and ask them to send him to me to Castile, to Salas"' ('Et el dixo [como respuesta a la pregunta de la mora] "si fuere uaron, darledes dos amas quel crien muy bien, et pues que fuere de edat que sepa entender bien et mal dezirledes como es mio fijo, et enuiarmeledes a Castilla, a Salas"') (PCG, p. 442); 'And he said [in response to the question of the Moorish woman]: "I will tell you this: take the half of this ring, and if he is a male, give it to him once he has come of age, and tell him to seek me in Salas de Barbadillo [...] and if she is a women, give her to your brother Almanzor, who may well arrange marriage for her"' ('E el le dixo [como respuesta a la pregunta de la mora]: "esto yo vos dire; tomad esta media sortija, e si fuere ome dar gela, desque fuere de hedat, e dezit le que me vaya buscar a Salas de Baruadiello [...]; e si fuere muger dat la a Almançor, vuestro hermano, que la podra muy bien casar"') (C1344, p. 215).

198   ISABEL ALFONSO

to be killed nor let myself die for it, *why should you, a man, do so?* For you shall never recover your sons no matter how much you cry for them. And what good will it bring you to kill yourself like that?[113]

The Moorish woman, portrayed as Almanzor's sister in the C1344 version, also consoled him by telling him how much she had suffered when her husband and seven children had been killed, and despite her pain, she had not wanted to die:

comfort yourself, Christian, for you seem to me to be a coward, for they tell me that when the Moors and the Christians have an field battle, the living go over the dead craving for fighting; and since this is not something you can wage, I think you would greatly suffered what I, a women, endured.[114]

In these texts, the fact that the female character set herself as a reference for more courageous behaviour in similar situations should perhaps be interpreted in the sense that what was assessed was non-gendered weakness and impotence, rather than the specific gender of the actor.[115] But it is in the PCG version of the story of the Cid, added to the EE prepared in Alfonso X's workshops, where an ideology involving a more marked sexual differentiation can be found. This is consistent with explicit chivalrous ethics, such as when the vassals of the Cid reproached the *infantes* of Carrion for their cowardice and wickedness, as they had proved their value against women, 'that are such a weak thing' ('que son tan feble cosa'), as if they were men who could defend themselves.[116] Weakness was constructed here as a specifically female attribute, and the female victims of aggression in this story were avenged by the men of their family.

This information requires reflection on the nature of the contradictions perceived within the same chronicle. On the one hand, women were portrayed as avengers, while on the other, children had a different fate depending on their sex. And also, as in the last case mentioned above, weakness (as a female trait) was set in opposition to strength (as a male trait). Claiming that these texts collected together materials

---

113   'Esforçad, sennor don Gonçalo, et dexad de llorar et de auer pesar en uos, ca yo otrossi oue XII fijos et muy buenos caualleros, et assi fue por uentura que todos XII me los mataron en un dia en batalla; mas pero non dexe por ende de conortarme et de esforçarme. Et pues *yo que so mugier me esforce* et non di por ende tanto que me yo matasse nin me dexe morir, *quanto mas lo deues fazer tu que eres uaron?* ca por llorar tu mucho por tus fijos non los podras nunqua cobrar por ende; ¿et que pro te tiene de te matar assi?'(PCG, p. 442). Emphasis is mine.

114   'conortat uos, christiano, que mucho vos veo cobarde, ca me dizen que quando los moros e los christianos auedes alguna lid campal, que pasades los biuos sobre los muertos con grant coyta de lidiar; e pues vos esto non podedes librar, bien cuedo que mal sofreriades lo que yo sofri, que so mujer' (C1344, pp. 213–14).

115   This is Clover's main argument in Clover, 'Regardless of Sex'.

116   'and they showed their force against them, as if they were also men who could defend themselves. And for this they acted as if they were cowards and vile men who are not worthy of chivalry, for they displayed their power against women, who are such a weak thing' ('et mostraron contra ellas su esfuerço, assy commo si fuessen otros omnes que se les pudiesen amparar. Et por esto paresce que fizieron a guisa de couardes et de viles omnes en que non a prez ninguno de caualleria: en mostrar su poder contra mugeres, que son tan feble cosa') (PCG, p. 621).

from many different sources does not seem to be consistent with attributing specific global objectives to these chronicles. If it is deemed to have been proven that these objectives required the partial manipulation of sources and some omissions, it should be accepted that this also affected the information provided, and how it was maintained. It seems to be more appropriate to take a non-essentialist perspective regarding the differentiation in the relationships between men and women, and to accept the historical character of the notions that constructed and represented such differentiation in terms and along lines that are not yet understood sufficiently well. What should be noted as a basis for future research is that, in the Castilian society of the thirteenth and fourteenth centuries within which these stories were written, revenge episodes carried out by women characters were not exceptions, nor did female characters act in place of any of the men in their family; nor were they presented as uncontrolled emotional reactions, but as social processes designed and planned with a specific purpose, in which personal, family and political aspects appeared to be closely interwoven. This indicates that it is necessary, first, to question principles of behavioural differentiation between the men and women other than those strictly defined by sex; and secondly, to investigate to what extent, from when and until when, honour and family reputation was a shared issue.[117]

The process of the formation of a chivalric code disseminated through epic narratives, to which the construction of aggression, force and violence as being exclusively male was predominantly attributed, should be seen as a longer, more complex, possibly less linear process than has been previously considered. The study of this process needs further research to explain the coexistence of representations of female violence that did not conform to this rigid code of behaviour.

Vengeance or Justice?

It also seems doubtful that the dichotomies mentioned in my initial comments can be maintained. The discourse about revenge contained in the texts discussed did not place in opposition the two consecutive and exclusive models of revenge with opposing logics. Bad behaviour in conflict resolution was censured and legitimised a vengeance which was seen as justice. This was intended as reparation for offenses and injuries, and as punishment of evil in general. These objectives were assumed by royal power in such a royal contemporary text as the *Fuero Real*, where it is stated that 'a people cannot thrive without its king, who is its head appointed by God to bring good and to avenge and prohibit evil'.[118]

---

[117] Lucy Pick notes that in the stories of the early medieval Christian chronicles from the ninth century men and women at the royal court first played different roles in relation to power, while later gender relationships between them are confined to the family group, a public sphere in which they share and distribute power among themselves (Pick, 'Gender in the early Spanish chronicles', esp. 245–46). N. Pancer reaches a very similar conclusion with regards to Merovingian queens in Pancer, *Sans peur et sans vergogne*.

[118] 'el pueblo non puede auer bien sin su rey que es su cabeza et puesto por Dios por adelantar el bien e pora uengar e uedar el mal' (Fuero Real, I.2.2). Alfonso VI is praised as an 'avenger of evil' ('vengador del mal') en Ubieto Arteta, *Crónicas Anónimas de Sahagún*, p. 24. A similar image is also found in a

This Code explicitly recognised the right of revenge in its title regarding homicides, by exempting from death he who killed in aid of another man who must take revenge 'for his lineage' (*se deua uengar por linage*) (including his father, son, grandfather or brother), or who killed in any other manner as long as he could prove that he had the right to do so;[119] and regulating other unpunished homicides in cases of maliciousness and betrayal. The terms of justice and revenge were interchangeable and assumed in judicial language. In the *Partidas*, accusation was defined as a way of claiming revenge, where notions of punishment, revenge and exemplariness were closely connected.

> A charge brought by one man against another before a judge, declaring him to be guilty of some offense which he alleges that he has committed, and asking the judge to take vengeance upon him, is properly called an accusation. Such an accusation is of great benefit to all the men of the entire country, for by means of it, when it is proved, the malefactor is justly punished, and the party who sustained the wrong is avenged.[120]

And it explicitly recognised that those who felt dishonoured had the right to claim severe punishment and revenge as reparation for their grievance, indicating how the judge should act in such a case.[121] However, it is this same *Partida* which defined and condemned evil vengeance, indissolubly linking it to deception and betrayal — a malice that uproots loyalty from the heart — as one of its fourteen possibilities: 'for so great is the turpitude and wickedness of evil-disposed men who commit a crime of this kind, that they do not venture to take vengeance upon those whom they hate in any other way, except secretly and by treachery'.[122] But in fact it was embedded in the deeper and broader core of relationships of human hostility, where the malevolence of men against others was made apparent: 'Men influenced by hatred are induced to treat one another badly [...] we hold that those who exert themselves in this manner commit a very serious offense, and take wicked vengeance without reason'.[123] These

---

letter of Yvo of Chartres to Luis VI, in a passage in which there is a clear notion of retributive justice: 'Faciat itaque gladius regalis officium suum ad vindictam malorum, ut sicut pios colligit mansetudine, sic impios coerceat justa severitate' ('May the royal sword do its work to punish the wicked, so that, just as he welcomes the pious with mildness, so he will the wicked be bent with just severity') (Yvo of Chartres, Letter 253, PL, 162, col. 259B).

119 Fuero Real, IV.17.1.

120 'Propiamente es dicha acusacion profaçamiento que vn ome faze a otro ante del juzgador afrontandolo de algun yerro que dize que fizo el acusado e pidiendo que le faga venganza. E tiene grand pro tal acusación a todos los omes de la tierra comunalmente. Ca por ella quando es prouada se escarmienta derechamente el mal fechor, e recibe venganza aquel que recibio el tuerto' (Partidas VII.1.1). When identifying those who could make an accusation, women (among others) were expressly excluded, except for the accusations related to the king or the kingdom, or for damage personally received by them, or by their relatives to the fourth degree (Partidas VII.1.2).

121 Partidas VII.9.21.

122 'tan grande es la vileza, e la maldad de los omes de mala ventura que tal yerro fazen, que non se atreven a tomar vengança de otra guisa de los que mal uieren, si non encubiertamente, e con engaño' (Partidas VII.2.1).

123 'Muevense los omes a buscar mal vnos a los otros por malquerencia que han entre si [...] e tenemos que fazen muy gran yerro, e toman mala vengança sin razon' (Partidas VII.29.11).

assessments could be easily applied to any of the evil vengeances narrated in the three narratives discussed, where 'malevolence' and 'mortal disaffection', which triggered action, also revealed the character of the enmity between the actors. It would exceed the limits of this paper to review the numerous other data that would enable us to discuss the culture of revenge further, as Andrea Zorzi has for the Italy of the Comuni. Zorzi found a conceptual equivalence between justice and revenge in the doctrinal, literary and legal texts he analysed. Revenge appeared in those texts as a virtuous form of justice, since the mayors of the Comuni considered public justice to be an act of fast, hard, diligent and honourable revenge.[124] Spanish urban statutes also carefully regulated and limited judicial redress of homicides, clearly distinguishing between on the one hand, just and legitimate reparations and punishments, and on the other hand, reparations and punishments that were to be censured and condemned. In this context, I do not believe that it is justified to oppose the logic of justice to that of revenge, since both are part of the same semantic field, as I have attempted to show. It would be necessary to expand the scope of analysis to include within it all friendship-enmity and political struggle processes in which these vengeful events were originated and enacted, as well as the discourses that accompanied them.[125]

---

124 Zorzi, 'La cultura della vendetta'.
125 White, 'Un imaginaire faidal', convincingly argues that there is an interweaving of practice and discourse on medieval violence.

ISABEL ALFONSO

Annex

Comparison between Narratives

	Infantes de Lara	Infante García	Poem of the Cid
Wrongful vengeance	**Actors:** they are kin to the victims. They are portrayed in a negative light as cowards, felons, and traitors. The wicked traits of their character persist and increase throughout the story. The same applies to those in their entourage.	**Actors:** they are not related to the victim. They are portrayed in a negative light as traitors. They create bonds of vassalage as a deception. Their bad qualities persist and increase throughout the story. The same applies to their support group.	**Actors:** they are kin to the victims. They are consistently portrayed in a negative light as cowardly, petty, and treacherous. Their behaviour and bad qualities persist and increase throughout the story. The same applies to their support group.
	Justification: offences on a festive occasion that clearly show ill will, latent rivalries, provocation, defamation, refusal to repair insults peacefully.	**Justification:** old enmity.	**Justification:** offenses on a festive occasion that evidence their bad faith.
	Execution: firstly, provocation by insults; secondly, by means of cheating, treacherously. It occurs in secret and is very bloody and cruel.	**Execution:** provoking a fight on a festive occasion (which highlights their bad faith). It entails the breaking a prior alliance and betrayal.	**Execution:** it occurs in secret and is presented as deceptive, treacherous, sanguinary, and dishonest.
	Outcome: there are many victims and they all die. The nephews of the perpetrators and a brother-in-law are captured (the intention was to kill the latter). Family and political alliances are broken; ostensible enmity is displayed and a treacherous homicide is committed; in addition, many other people are victims because vengeance is treacherously organised as a fight.	**Outcome:** a fatal victim results from a treacherous homicide, the matrimonial alliance between León and Castile breaks up, a woman is dishonoured in the context of vengeance.	**Outcome:** the wives of the culprits are seriously injured and dishonoured; there is a ritual process of repudiation, and family and political alliances are broken; ostensible enmity.

	Infantes de Lara	Infante García	Poem of the Cid
Mourning for the victims	It is the beginning of a process of 'restorative vengeance'. There are several sequences of mourning: 1) that of the father in Córdoba before the heads of his sons; 2) the one that occurs when he returns to his wife and his lineage (including the political authority).	It is the beginning of a process of 'restorative vengeance': the bride.	It is the beginning of a process of 'restorative vengeance'.

	Infantes de Lara	Infante García	Poem of the Cid
Just vengeance	**Actors:** they are portrayed in a positive light as brave and loyal. Their qualities and behaviour are gradually enhanced. They suffer the consequences of the other vengeance.	**Actors:** they are portrayed in a positive light as brave (courageous) and loyal. Their personal qualities are enhanced. They suffer the consequences of the other vengeance. While collective participation is on the foreground, two characters appear as the executioners: the male hero, engendered in order to avenge the death of his half-brothers; and the mother, who performs the humiliating and exemplary ritual. Both present themselves as real and metaphorical judges: as (1) royal officer, and (2) local judge.	**Actors:** they are portrayed in a positive light as loyal. Their qualities are progressively enhanced. They suffer the consequences of the other vengeance. Two characters appear as executors: the male heroes, led by King Sancho of Navarre, who execute the traitors after subjecting them to punishment (there is no description of the judicial process, but there is an explicit application of the legal penalty); and the 'wife' or fiancée, who performs the degrading and exemplary ritual. Both of them become the real and metaphorical judges, as they explicitly present themselves.
	Justification: previous evils and dishonours.	**Justification:** previous deaths and betrayals.	**Justification:** a death inflicted treacherously.
	Execution: openly and publicly in various settings: before the king (requesting his involvement in the process because of his responsibility); in the judicial forum convened for this purpose; in a judicial duel that exposes the deceit and treachery perpetrated by the offenders before all.	**Execution:** vengeance is accomplished openly and publicly in various settings, in two stages: before the count (who is involved in the trial as an authority); and in the courtroom: challenge to the perpetrator, truces, prosecution, judicial duel (deemed more appropriate than a general battle); death of the perpetrator and physical punishment.	**Execution:** openly and publicly in various settings: royal prosecution and execution of the perpetrators (though there is no narrative of the trial); involvement of the king (who is also a relative of the victim) in a judicial setting (at least metaphorically); death and corporal punishment of the perpetrator, public display. Similarly, the two sequences of vengeance are represented here as acts of justice.
	Outcome: the culprits are defeated (wounded, but not dead) and humiliated, defamed and degraded politically. Vengeance and justice are accomplished. Enmity remains unresolved. From a political perspective the balance of power changes (through political proximity to the king, through alliances with the royal heirs of Navarre, through the enhanced reputation of the Cid).	**Outcome:** the culprits die and are dishonoured. Vengeance and justice are accomplished. Enmity remains unresolved. From a political perspective the balance of power changes: at a higher level, the authority of the count is strengthened; at a local level, the evil lord of Lara disappears, and the foundations of an honourable lineage for this important aristocratic house are laid.	**Outcome:** the culprits die and are dishonoured and publicly displayed. Vengeance and justice are accomplished; enmity remains unresolved. From a political perspective the balance of power changes: at a higher level, the authority of the king of Navarre is strengthened; also, as we know, in Castile and León the death would lead to a change in power.

	Infantes de Lara	Infante García	Poem of the Cid
Exemplarity	It emerges from the two sequences.	It emerges from the two sequences. Throughout the story, other issues and the ways of solving them are introduced, for example, the discussion on the responsibility that can be attributed to vassals in relation to the betrayal of their lord, or the defence of the duel between two fighters instead of group confrontation.	It emerges from the two sequences.

Bibliography

Accutis, Cesare, *La leggenda degli Infanti di Lara* (Turin: Einaudi, 1978)

Alfonso Antón, Isabel, 'El cuerpo del delito y la violencia ejemplar', in *El cuerpo derrotado: cómo trataban musulmanes y cristianos a los enemigos vencidos (Península Ibérica, ss. VIII–XIII)*, ed. by Maribel Fierro and Francisco García Fitz (Madrid: CSIC, 2008), pp. 397–431

Alfonso, Isabel, 'Venganza y justicia en el Cantar de Mío Cid', in *El Cid: de la materia épica a las crónicas caballerescas*, ed. by Carlos Alvar Ezquerra, Fernando Gómez Redondo, and Georges Martin (Alcalá de Henares: Universidad de Alcalá, 2002), pp. 41–70

Alvar, Carlos and Manuel Alvar, eds, *Épica medieval española* (Madrid: Cátedra, 1991)

Bartlett, Robert J., '"Mortal Enmities": The Legal Aspect of Hostility in the Middle Ages', in *Feud, Violence and Practice: Essays in Medieval Studies in Honor of Stephen D. White*, ed. by Belle Stoddard Tuten and Tracey Lynn Billado (Farnham: Ashgate, 2010), pp. 197–212

Cacho Blecua, José Manuel, 'La crueldad del castigo: el ajusticiamiento del traidor y la "pértiga" educadora en el Libro del Cavallero Zifar', in *Aragón en la Edad Media: sesiones de trabajo. IV Seminario de Historia Medieval* (Zaragoza: Universidad de Zaragoza, 1995), pp. 59–89

Catalán, Diego, 'Las crónicas generales y el Poema de Mio Cid', in *El Cid, poema e historia: actas del Congreso Internacional (Burgos, 12–16 de julio, 1999)*, ed. by César Fernández Alonso (Burgos: Ayuntamiento de Burgos, 2000), pp. 105–14

Catalán, Diego and María del Mar de Bustos, eds, *La épica medieval española. Desde sus orígenes hasta su disolución en el romancero*, Obras Completas de R. Menéndez Pidal. Vol. XIII. (Madrid: Espasa-Calpe, 1992)

Clover, Carol J., 'Regardless of Sex: Men, Women, and Power in Early Northern Europe', *Representations*, 44 (1993), 1–28

Crespo, Juan Bautista, 'Las Estorias de España y las crónicas generales', in *Alfonso X el Sabio y las crónicas de España* ed. by Inés Fernández Ordóñez (Valladolid: Servicio de Publicaciones de la Universidad de Valladolid, 2001), pp. 107–32

Dacosta, Arsenio, *Los linajes de Bizcaia en la Baja Edad media: Poder, parentesco y conflicto* (Bilbao: Universidad del País Vasco, 2003)

de la Campa, Mariano, 'Las versiones alfonsíes de la Estoria de España', in *Alfonso X el Sabio y las crónicas de España*, ed. by Inés Fernández Ordóñez (Valladolid: Servicio de Publicaciones de la Universidad de Valladolid, 2000), pp. 83–106

Dyer, Nancy Joe, *El Mio Cid del taller alfonsí: versión en prosa en la Primera Cronica General y en la Crónica de veinte reyes* (Newark, DE: Juan de la Cuesta, 1995)

Escalona, Julio, 'Épica, crónicas y genealogías. En torno a la historicidad de la Leyenda de los Infantes de Lara', *Cahiers de Linguistique Hispanique Médiévale*, 23 (2000), 113–73

Estévez Sola, Juan Antonio, ed., *Chronica Hispana saeculi XII. Pars II. Chronica Naierensis* (Turnhout: Brepols, 1995)

Fernández Ordóñez, Inés, 'Variación en el modelo historiográfico alfonsí en el siglo XIII: las versiones de la "Estoria de España"', in *La historia alfonsí: el modelo y sus destinos (siglos XIII–XV)*, ed. by Georges Martin (Madrid: Casa de Velázquez, 2000), pp. 41–74

Fernández Ordóñez, Inés, 'La transmisión textual de la "Estoria de España" y de las principales "Crónicas" de ella derivadas', in *Alfonso X el Sabio y las crónicas de España*, ed. by Inés Fernández Ordóñez (Valladolid: Servicio de Publicaciones de la Universidad de Valladolid, 2001), pp. 219–64

Fernández Ordóñez, Inés, ed., *Alfonso X el Sabio y las crónicas de España* (Valladolid: Servicio de Publicaciones de la Universidad de Valladolid, 2001)

García de Valdeavellano, Luis, *Curso de historia de las instituciones españolas: de los orígenes al final de la Edad Media*, 3ª edn (Madrid: Alianza, 1984 [1968])

Genet, Jean-Philippe, ed., *L'histoire et les nouveaux publics dans l'Europe médiévale (XIIIe– XVe siècle). Actes du colloque international organisé par la Fondation europeéenne de la science (Casa de Velázquez, Madrid, 23–24 avril 1993)* (Paris: Éditions de la Sorbonne, 1993)

Gómez Redondo, Fernando, *Historia de la prosa medieval castellana. Vol. 1. La creación del discurso prosístico: el entramado cortesano* (Madrid: Cátedra, 1998)

Gómez Redondo, Fernando, *Historia de la prosa medieval castellana. Vol. 2. El desarrollo de los géneros. La ficción caballeresca y el orden religioso* (Madrid: Cátedra, 1999)

Gómez Redondo, Fernando, 'La materia cidiana en la crónica general alfonsí: tramas y fórmulas', in *Teoría y práctica de la historiografía hispánica medieval*, ed. by Aengus Ward (Birmingham: The University of Birmingham Press, 2000), pp. 99–123

Jiménez de Rada, Rodrigo, *Opera omnia I. Historia de rebus Hispanie sive historia gothica*, ed. by Juan Fernández Valverde (Turnhout: Brepols, 1987)

Martin, Georges, *Chanson de Mon Cid. Cantar de Mio Cid* (Paris: Aubier, 1996)

Martin, Georges, ed., *La historia alfonsí: el modelo y sus destinos (siglos XIII–XV)* (Madrid: Casa de Velázquez, 2000)

Martín, José Luis, 'Relectura del fuero de Salamanca. La venganza de la sangre', *Príncipe de Viana. Anejo. Homenaje a José María Lacarra*, 3 (1986), 531–38

Menéndez Pidal, Ramón, *La Leyenda de los Infantes de Lara* (Madrid: Espasa-Calpe, 1971 [1896])

Menéndez Pidal, Ramón, *Cantar de Mio Cid. Texto, gramática y vocabulario. 3 vols* (Madrid: Imprenta de Bailly-Baillière é Hijos, 1908–1911)

Menéndez Pidal, Ramón, 'El elemento histórico en el "Romanz dell Infant Garcia"', in *Studi letterari e linguistici dedicati a Pio Rajna nel quarantesimo anno del suo insegnaimento* (Firenze: Tip. E. Ariani, 1911), pp. 41–85

Menéndez Pidal, Ramón, 'El "Romanz del Infant García" y Sancho de Navarra antiemperador', in *Historia y epopeya* (Madrid: Centro de Estudios Históricos, 1934), pp. 29–98

Menéndez Pidal, Ramón, and Diego Catalán (eds), *Primera Crónica General de España, con un estudio actualizado de Diego Catalán* (Madrid: Gredos, 1977–1979)

Menéndez Pidal, Ramón, and Diego Catalán, *Reliquias de la poesía épica española: acompañadas de Epopeya y Romancero I. Reproducción de la edición príncipe de dos obras de Ramón Menéndez Pidal, adicionadas con una introducción crítica de Diego Catalán* (Madrid: Gredos, 1980)

Miller, William I., 'Choosing the Avenger: Some Aspects of the Bloodfeud in Medieval Iceland and England', *Law and History Review*, 1–2 (1983), 159–204

Nelson, Janet L., 'Queens as Jezebels: The Careers of Brunhild and Balthild in Merovingian History', *Studies in Church History Subsidia*, 1 (1978), 31–77

Nelson, Janet L., 'Family, Gender and Sexuality in the Middle Ages', in *Companion to Historiography*, ed. by Michael Bentley (London: Routledge, 1997), pp. 153–76

Pancer, Nira, *Sans peur et sans vergogne. De l'honneur et des femmes aux premiers temps mérovingiens* (Paris: Albin Michel, 2001)

Partner, Nancy, F., ed., *Studying Medieval Women: Sex, Gender, Feminism* (Cambridge, MA: Medieval Academy of America, 1993)

Pattison, David G., 'El Mio Cid del Poema y el de las crónicas: evolución de un héroe', in *El Cid: de la materia épica a las crónicas caballerescas*, ed. by Carlos Alvar Ezquerra, Fernando Gómez Redondo, and Georges Martin (Alcalá de Henares: Universidad de Alcalá, 2002), pp. 23–27

Pérez-Prendes, José Manuel, *Curso de Historia del Derecho Español. Volumen I. Introducción, fuentes y materiales institucionales* (Madrid: Universidad Complutense de Madrid, 1989)

Pick, Lucy, K., 'Gender in the early Spanish chronicles from John of Biclar to Pelayo of Oviedo', *La corónica: A Journal of Medieval Hispanic Languages, Literatures & Cultures*, 32–3 (2004), 227–48

Spiegel, Gabrielle, *Romancing the past. The rise of Vernacular Prose Historiography in Thirteenth-Century France* (London: University of California Press, 1993)

Tuy, Lucas de, *Crónica de España*, ed. by Julio Puyol y Alonso, *Crónica de España. Primera edición del texto romanceado*, (Madrid: Real Academia de la Historia, 1926)

Tuy, Lucas de, *Chronicon mundi*, ed. by Emma Falque Rey, *Chronicon mundi (Corpus Christianorum Continuatio Mediaevalis, 74)*, (Turnhout: Brepols, 2003)

Ubieto Arteta, Antonio, *Crónicas Anónimas de Sahagún* (Zaragoza: Anubar, 1987)

Walsh, John K., 'El libro de los doze sabios o, Tractado de la nobleza y lealtad (ca. 1237)', *Anejos del Boletín de la Real Academia Española*, 29 (1975), 71–118

White, Stephen D., 'Un imaginaire faidal. La représentation de la guerre dans quelques chansons de geste', in *La vengeance, 400-1200*, ed. by Dominique Barthélemy, François Bougard, and Régine Le Jan (Rome: École française de Rome, 2006), pp. 175–98

Zorzi, Andrea, 'La cultura della vendetta nel conflitto politico in età comunale', in *Le storie e la memoria. In onore di Arnold Esch*, ed. by Roberto delle Donne and Andrea Zorzi (Firenze: Firenze University Press, 2002), pp. 135–70

ISABEL ALFONSO

Vengeance and Justice
in the Poem of the Cid*

Justice or Vengeance?

One of the best known and most studied fictional trials in the medieval period is the one heard by the royal court of Alfonso VI where the parties involved were the Cid and his sons-in-law, the *infantes* of Carrión. The trial constitutes the third and last part of the *Poem*. For the purposes of the reading proposed in this chapter, a widely quoted description of the third *cantar* made by Fletcher is reproduced below:

> At the opening of the third *cantar* the *infantes* are shown up as cowards and ridiculed by the Cid's followers in an incident when a captive lion escapes from its cage in the Cid's palace in Valencia. Further mockery is provoked by their failure to distinguish themselves in a battle against the Moroccan ruler Búcar. *The* infantes *plan to avenge these slights.* They depart for Castile with their brides. On their way they stop for the night in the forest of Corpes. On the following morning, having sent away all their servants, they strip their wives of their clothes, beat them senseless with their belts and spurs, and leave them for dead. The women are discovered and rescued by the Cid's nephew. *Rodrigo decides to avenge his family's honour* by seeking legal redress. He appeals to the king, who responds by summoning a solemn meeting of the royal court at Toledo. In court the Cid successfully claims restitutions of his daughters' dowries. The *infantes* are subsequently defeated in judicial duels by the Cid's champions. *The honour of the Cid has thus been vindicated* and he is rendered even more illustrious by the subsequent remarriage of his daughters into the royal houses of Aragon and Navarre.[1]

According to Fletcher, vengeance (in its various forms), is evidently the central theme of this story, as shown by the three highlighted passages above. However, he believed that the Cid was 'seeking legal redress rather than personal revenge by violence',[2] following a well-rooted tradition in which the Cid, unlike other epic heroes, 'rules out vengeance in favour of a legal compensation judicially adjudicated at the King's court', as Menéndez Pidal suggested.[3] A widespread image of el Cid was thus

---

* Original publication: Alfonso, Isabel, 'Venganza y justicia en el Cantar de Mío Cid', in *El Cid: de la materia épica a las crónicas caballerescas*, ed. by Carlos Alvar Ezquerra, Fernando Gómez Redondo and Georges Martin (Alcalá de Henares: Universidad de Alcalá, 2002), pp. 41–69. Translated by Julian Thomas.

1 Fletcher, *The Quest for El Cid*, pp. 191–92.
2 Fletcher, *The Quest for El Cid*, p. 194.
3 Menéndez Pidal, *La España del Cid*, p. 618.

constructed whereby he was not guided by 'his thirst of vengeance for the affront he had suffered', but 'is always portrayed as humane and a defender of justice'.[4]

This clear dichotomy between vengeance and justice has been maintained — albeit not without contradictions — in recent studies which oppose private forms of vengeance to public forms of justice; private law to public law; and feudal practices to royal justice. They claim that the *Poem* 'attacks the then current right to private vengeance, that old aristocratic recourse'[5] used by the *infantes*, as a criminal act and according to the applicable legislation in the late twelfth century, admits only *riepto* (challenge). These oppositions invoke a very rigid notion of vengeance as a literally bloody action, which continued to be associated with the impulse of taking immediate personal reprisals.[6]

It could be argued that such legal-oriented studies attempt to establish differences between lawful and unlawful forms of reparation. However, the problem is not that simple, because our perceptions of lawful vs unlawful and public vs private involve certain assumptions that are not necessarily consistent with those prevailing in the society under study. These assumptions seem to arise from an ideal model of the workings of justice and the law constructed by modern jurists, who connect it with the linear development of a state power capable of prevailing over private interests. I have discussed elsewhere the numerous and significant implications of adopting this approach.[7] Here I only wish to note how this model has been the basis for an image of early medieval society in which the recurrent conflicts among the nobility are described as uncontrolled violent endeavours bolstered by feelings of vengeance. These are depicted as being aimed only at destroying adversaries, by engaging in interminable cycles of private confrontations only limited and controlled by the influence of the Church and the growth of the monarchies, armed with a new public law influenced by the Roman tradition. The earlier period is characterized by 'bloody vengeance', whilst the later one is defined by 'challenge' (*riepto*), a regulated combat used to resolve honour issues. Separating challenge (as a lawful procedure) from vengeance (as an unlawful form of violence) can be misleading. It obscures and distorts the antagonistic relationships that involved open competition between groups or individuals in an aristocratic society such as that described in the *Poem*.[8] Interpreting the *Poem*'s challenge and the judicial duel that brought the procedure to a close as a new means for the king to administer justice, is moreover in stark contrast with other studies of the literary and legal aspects of European epics that see it as an ordeal-like type of proof of feudal nature, which has been criticised by the authors of these literary works in connection with the renovation of the judicial proceedings that

---

4 García de Valdeavellano, *Historia de España*, p. 496.

5 Lacarra, El 'Poema de Mio Cid', p. 98.

6 Montaner Frutos, *Cantar de Mio Cid*, comments to vv. 2763–2984 and v. 2309. The debate is broad and somewhat homogeneous. It is very well summarised by Montaner in the notes to his edition. This is the edition that will be used in my references to the *Cantar*.

7 Alfonso, 'Introducción: desarrollo legal', pp. 879–83.

8 Spanish legal historians traditionally differentiate *riepto* from 'judicial duel'. See a criticism, and an approach that connects *riepto*, insult, vengeance and ordeal in legal texts, in Madero Eguía, 'El riepto'; Madero Eguía, *Manos violentas*.

they claimed was taking place.[9] Both interpretations show that this type of analysis can be problematic. They operate as if the model constructed to explain the practice was, in fact, the cause of the practice. According to Bourdieu, doing this would fail to account for the constituent elements of that practice, including its development, timeline and purpose.[10]

Some anthropology-based studies have questioned these approaches and theoretical foundations, at least over the last decade, by focusing on other issues and providing new frameworks to understand the old problems related to social order and control. These studies have suggested that these processes, either violent or judicial, should be analysed within the dynamics of political competition. They have advocated that it is difficult to identify the beginning and the end of these conflicts, as old enmities and partnerships were taken up again as and when it was convenient. Resolutions were not final but contingent upon the correlation of forces at play, in which honour and reputation were crucial in terms of attained status.[11]

My proposal is to make a reading of the third *Cantar* of the *Poem* along these lines, in order to understand the overall political culture of that period, which is still understudied in Spain. The main issues are the loss and recovery of honour, loyalty and friendship. The story provides research material to deal with some of the key themes to recognise the forms of competition and political action in medieval aristocratic society; of a highly regulated moral and cultural universe shared by its members; and of the political community that was intended to be the audience for these heroic narratives, as aptly remarked by G. Martin.[12]

Vengeance as a Political Process: Taking Revenge before the Royal Court

Much of the knowledge about vengeance as a socio-political and cultural practice (as proposed by Verdier) can be applied to the process described here, as a relationship in which violence and compensation may be exchanged between rival groups through judicial rituals.[13] As highlighted by Miller, vengeance is more than a constructed series of open actions, and it is not reduced to an avenging death. It is the relationship between groups, the state of mind of the participants, the challenging, antagonistic, cold positions held by them, all of which fill the intervals

---

9   For a critique of this European historiography on the epic genre in the terms described here, see White, 'La traición'.

10 Bourdieu, *El sentido práctico*, p. 138.

11 There are numerous studies along these lines. Only the most relevant for this discussion are mentioned here: White, '*Pactum ... legem vincit*'; White, 'Feuding and Peacemaking'; Geary, 'Vivre en conflit'; Miller, *Bloodtaking*; Alfonso, 'Resolución de disputas'; Alfonso, 'Litigios por la tierra'; Hyam, 'Feud and the State'; Bartlett, 'Mortal Enmities'.

12 Martin, 'Le récit héroïque'.

13 Verdier, 'Le système vindicatoire'. The three volumes that make up this work are undoubtedly interesting, particularly to understand the construction of a strict concept of vengeance as opposed to a concept of state justice.

210 ISABEL ALFONSO

between one hostile confrontation and the next.[14] The third part of the *Cantar*, which hinges on a debt of honour and the recovery of that honour through the final ritual of the judicial duel, also narrates and accounts for that web of relationships and attitudes of the confronted groups, their latent hostility and the pretext to make it explode.

In the *Cantar* there is a contrast between two types of vengeance that is assessed through the rhetorical construction of the confronted groups as good and bad.[15] It is clear that the *infantes* were the evildoers. They were constructed as such from the very beginning of the third part of the Cantar, when they were described as being scared when a lion escaped from the Cid's palace in Valencia. Their fear was used to present two opposed attitudes: that held by the Cid's vassals, who surrounded and protected him; and that held by his sons-in-law who ran away instead of facing the lion and protecting the Cid when he was asleep:

> Salió s' de la red e desató s' el león | En gran *miedo* se vieron por medio de la cort | Enbraçan los mantos los del Campeador | E cercan el escaño e fincan sobre so señor | Ferrán Gonçález [...] | Non vio allí do s'alçasse, nin cámara abierta nin torre. | Metió s' so'l escaño, tanto ovo el pavor | Diego Gonçález por la puerta salió | diziendo de la boca: '¡Non veré Carrión!' | Tras una viga lagar metió s' con grant pavor, | el manto y el brial todo suzio lo sacó [vv. 2282–91]

(The lion struggled loose and escaped from his net. Great fear seized them in the middle of the hall, and the Cid's men wrapped their cloaks about their arms and surrounded the couch to protect their lord. Fernando González [...] found no open door nor towers; so in his panic he crawled under the couch. Diego González made off through the door, crying: 'I shall never see Carrión again!' In his terror he got behind the wine press and made his cloak and tunic all filthy).[16]

The following verses are also used to place the Cid's bravery, who, upon waking, contained the lion and placed it back in its net, in opposition to the *infantes'* fear, who remained in their hiding place, and the embarrassment they felt later:

> Mio Çid por sos yernos demandó e no los falló | maguer los están llamando ninguno non responde. | Cuando los fallaron, ellos vinieron assi sin color | ¡non viestes tal juego commo iva por la cort! | mandólo vedar mio Çid el Campeador. | Muchos' tovieron por embaídos los ifantes de Carrión: | fiera cosa les pesa d'esto que les cuntió [vv. 2304–2310]

(When the Cid asked for his sons-in-law they were nowhere to be found. Everyone was calling to them, but they made no answer. When they were discovered they were pale with fear. You never saw such mockery as then went

---

14 Miller, *Bloodtaking*, pp. 179–220.

15 The terms used to describe groups depend on the situation and functions sought by the individual who devises the classification (Bourdieu, *El sentido práctico*, p. 144).

16 PoemCid, § 112. The emphasis is mine.

round the palace. The Cid forbade it to continue, but the *infantes* felt that they had been put to shame and deeply resented all that had happened).[17]

The colour of fear is its absence, the facial expression of that feeling, their faces becoming pale. These obvious signs were the object of people's irony and teasing, which the Cid stopped, although he could not prevent the *infantes* from feeling offended and ashamed. This twofold concept of *embaídos* is an accurate illustration of how shame operated as a mechanism of social control.[18] This episode, which portrayed the shame of cowardice, was the building block on which the avenging process of the *infantes* was constructed.

The negative representation of the *infantes* continued with the description of their cowardice upon the siege of Valencia by the Moors, since unlike el Cid and his men, the *infantes* were frightened of engaging in combat [vv. 2315–2337]. All the elements employed in the narration serve to contrast the behaviour, valour and feelings of the infantes with those of the Cid's vassals.[19] This is not a simplistic or linear contrast; rather, it is complex and sophisticated, since at times the Cid was seen in his court admiring his sons-in-laws' decision to fight, and how they were appreciated for it. This involves a recovery of their 'honour' (*honra*), and the intention to publicise this:

> Grant fue el día en la cort del Campeador | Después que esta batalla vencieron e al rey Bucar mató. | Alçó la mano, a la barba se tomó: | '¡Grado a Chistus, que del mundo es señor, | cuando veo lo que avía sabor: | que lidiaran comigo en campo mios yernos amos a dos! | Mandados buenos irán d'ellos a Carrión, | commo son ondrados e avervos han grant pro' [vv. 2474–2481]

> (There was a great rejoicing in the Campeador's palace after this victory and the death of King Búcar. The Cid raised his hand and grasped his beard. 'Thanks be to Christ, Lord of this world', he said, 'I have seen my desire fulfilled! My sons-in-law have both fought in battle by my side; good news of them will go to Carrión, for they have won honour for themselves and will hereafter be a great help to us').[20]

It is also worth mentioning that the honour attributed to the *infantes* of Carrión was not due to their birth, but linked to their presumed valour in battle. Their cowardice was also recognised regardless of their blood. This information and some other details to be discussed later seem useful to question another dichotomy that has been attributed to the author of the *Poem* between blood-based nobility and merit-based nobility, which is claimed to have antagonised two social groups.[21] This opposition, which has been widely assumed to be the ideological backbone of the *Poem*, needs

---

17 PoemCid, § 112.
18 On the concept of shame, see Miller, *Humiliation*, pp. 117–24; 131–36 and 157–95. For a very interesting analysis of this notion in lay low medieval discourse, see Cacho Blecua, 'La vergüenza'.
19 See a discussion of the accumulation of ignominious data, both in the moral and the legal realm in Montaner Frutos, *Cantar de Mio Cid*, p. 616.
20 PoemCid, § 120.
21 Georges Martin, in the introduction to this remarkable bilingual verse edition of the *Poem*

to be reconsidered. In my view, there is no such opposition, since both honour and reputation operate as elements of a symbolic capital that, despite having been inherited, must be earned and increased. This capital had to be reaffirmed before others in different ways. Thus some messages were sent to Carrión to report on the valour shown by the *infantes*, which would be unnecessary if such dichotomy were accepted, and their status and honour were merely inherited. The great riches won by los *infantes* were a reason for joy in the Cid's court, but only added to their positive behaviour, as this integrated them into the family. Honour was linked to success in battle, but also to family membership and relationships.

> Algo veyé mio Cid de lo que era pagado, | alçó los ojos, estava adelant catando| e vio venir a Diego e a Fernando, | amos son fijos del conde don Gonçalo. | Alegrós' mio Cid, fermoso sonrisando: | '¡Venides, mios yernos, mios fijos sodes amos! | Sé que de lidiar bien sodes pagados| a Carrión de vós irán buenos mandados, | commo al rey Bucar avemos arrancado. | Commo yo fio por Dios e en todos los sos santos, | D'esta arrancada nós iremos pagados' [vv. 2438–2448]

> (There was one thing that the Cid saw that gave him great satisfaction. As he raised his eyes and looked ahead, there coming towards him were Diego and Fernando, the sons of Don Gonzalo. The Cid smiled a happy smile and said: 'Here you come, my sons-in-law, nay, rather my sons, both of you. I know you have borne yourselves well in the fighting. Good reports of you will reach Carrión telling how we have defeated King Búcar. As I trust in God and all His saints we shall have reason to be proud of this victory').[22]

However, the poet continued to portray los *infantes* as having failed to integrate. They were also shown to be secretly scheming to leave for Carrión, to scorn and abandon their wives, and to be planning their noble status and a better marriage:

> 'Vayamos por Carrión, aquí mucho detardamos | averes levaremos grandes que valen grant valor, | Escarniremos las fijas del Canpeador. | D'aquestos aueres siempre seremos ricos omnes. | Podremos casar con fijas de reyes o de enperadores| ¡Ca de natura somos de condes de Carrión!' [vv. 2550–2554]

> ('Let us go to Carrión, for we have delayed too long here. We shall carry off our great wealth and we shall show our contempt for the daughters of the Cid! With these great possessions we shall be rich for life, we shall be able to marry daughters of kings or emperors, for we are descended from the counts of Carrión').[23]

This idea that they would become 'noble men' (*ricos hombres*, lit. 'wealthy men') given the bounty obtained and the potential to marry the daughters of kings or emperors supports my argument further. Blood nobility, even if based on a title, could disappear; a noble birth and great deeds were better together than in isolation. The

---

summarises his works on these issues. See Martin, *Chanson de Mon Cid*, pp. 29–46; PoemCid, vv. 1375–76.

22   PoemCid, § 119.

23   PoemCid, § 123–24.

VENGEANCE AND JUSTICE IN THE POEM OF THE CID   213

hegemony that noble men had attained in that social context, and the fact that this had become a sort of title or a sign of a dignified status clearly indicates that success in war and the spoils obtained were very important for that blood nobility in terms of the relationship they sought to develop with royalty through marriages, and also by obtaining positions in the court, benefits, etc. Some scholars have claimed that these were separate aspects, but in fact they were part of one and the same political dynamic.

The idea of *vengeance* was not expressed by the *infantes* until later, when they announced to their wives the humiliation they would inflict on them. Nonetheless, the farewell scene in Valencia, when the Cid showed great deference towards his sons-in-law granting them a dowry in coins, mules, and horses, as well as the two famous swords, already serves to signal what the narrator immediately presented as treason and falsehood, due to the actions that would be perpetrated by the *infantes* of Carrión. This was obviously a narrative strategy to create dramatic tension, a foreshadowing of events to come. It is worth noting that the poet becomes explicitly involved in the narration by judging the behaviour of the characters. The attitude of the *infantes* towards their wives in Corpes was a stepping stone in them being constructed as evil characters, since they concealed their intended treachery with signs of affection:

> Todos eran idos, ellos cuatro solos son; | Tanto mal comidieron los ifantes de Carrión: | 'Bien lo creades, don Eluira e doña Sol: | 'aquí seredes escarnidas, en estos fieros montes, | oy nos partiremos e dexadas seredes de nós, | non abredes part en tierras de Carrión. | Irán aquestos mandados al Cid Campeador; | nos vengaremos por aquésta la del león' [vv. 2712–2719]
>
> (When all the rest had gone on and only those four were left alone, the Infantes set about carrying out their wicked plan. [To their wives they said] 'Do you hear, Doña Elvira and Doña Sol? We are going to show our contempt and scorn for you here in this wild forest. Today we shall separate and you will be abandoned by us. You will then have no claim to any of our lands in Carrión. This is the news that will go to the Cid Campeador; this is the vengeance for the dishonour with the lion').[24]

At this stage in the narration, the reason alleged by the *infantes* for taking revenge hardly seems convincing, compared with the appalling humiliating act they were about to engage in. In the construction of their personalities, their treacherous, disloyal and false ambition outweighed the reason provided for vengeance. Given the level of sophistication of the story and the careful treatment of the characters, I believe this is deliberate. It seems to be a narrative device to condemn this type of vengeance and place it in opposition to the other type of vengeance to be wreaked by the Cid. Due to the way in which the *infantes* are presented, their vengeance was not only dishonourable, but was also used to show their meanness. This is a combination of their intention to gain more status (vengeance for our marriages) and the humiliation suffered by them when their cowardice was exposed (what they

---

24 PoemCid, § 128.

called the lion's dishonour), and it would serve to dishonour them even further.[25] In addition, the way in which they inflicted humiliation on their wives made them appear viler. It involved causing them serious physical injuries (which left them virtually dead). The poet used this humiliating display of scorn to give pace and tension to the narration, by suggesting what might happen if the Cid appeared at that precise moment.[26] It seems as if the poet had aligned the plot with the *Partidas*, in which the following claim is made:

> ca tan grande es la vileza, e la maldad de los omes de mala ventura, que tal yerro fazen, que non se atreven a tomar vengança de otra guisa de los que mal quieren, si non encubiertamente e con engaño.

> (for so great is the turpitude and wickedness of evil-disposed men who commit a crime of this kind, that they do not venture to take vengeance upon those whom they hate in any other way, except secretly and by treachery).[27]

The repeated references made by the *infantes* to their prestigious genealogical credentials need to be understood in the narrative context of their disproportionate claims to power and valour:

> Por los montes do ivan, ellos ívanse alabando. | 'De nuestros casamientos agora somos vengados; | non las deviemos tomar por barraganas | si non fuéssemos rogados, | pues nuestras parejas non eran pora en braços; | ¡La desondra del león assí s'irá vengando!' [vv. 2757–2763]

> (They went off through the woods highly pleased with themselves. As they went they said boastfully: 'Now we are avenged for our marriages. We should not have taken them even as concubines, unless we had been formally asked; they were not equals in rank or fit to be our lawful wives. By acting as we have done we have our revenge for the dishonour we suffered in the episode of the lion').[28]

The negative representation of the *infantes* as being cowardly and evil in the first part of the third *Cantar* was plausibly expanded to cover their support group. It was accentuated by their fear in the face of the *cortes* being convened [vv. 2985–2987], and the ulterior motives attributed to them by the poet [vv. 3007–3011]. The name of *bando* given to them also needs to be understood in this sense, as in my view it was used as a narrative device to delegitimise any acts committed by this group. The nature of their association, however, does not seem to be different to that of the Cid's *mesnada*. In the same *Cantar* other data were provided that suggested that they were not two different forms of political group, but two opposing ways of assessing the same one.[29] This will be discussed further at a later stage in this chapter.

---

25 vv. 2720–2756. According to Miller, this humiliation is defined by reference to pretence; in this case, by cowards pretending to be brave (Miller, *Humiliation*, pp. 131–74).

26 On forms of humiliation, see Madero Eguía, *Manos violentas*, ch. 2.

27 Partidas VII.2.1.

28 PoemCid, § 130.

29 At the assembly that was convened in the banks of the Tagus, to which the *infantes* of Carrión attended, the king's men were characterized as *mesnadas*:

The construction of the 'good ones' is part of the same logic, which is not only narrative, but is also in line with a certain social rationale. In the third *Cantar* this is most noticeable precisely in how the Cid's group made arrangements for the *corte* [vv. 3000–3106], which is contrasted with the representation made of the men that accompanied the *infantes*: 'Bien aguisado viene el Çid con todos los sos; | buennas conpannas, que assi an tal sennor [vv. 3022–3023] [...] con éstos cúmplanse ciento de los buenos que ý son' [v. 3072] (The Campeador came well prepared, with a great following of vassals worthy of such a lord [...] One hundred good men here present will make up your numbers).[30]

It is interesting to note how the description of their apparel and hidden weapons, which could make them a *bando*, was presented in positive terms, as it was attributed to their mistrust of the *infantes*. It was intended to assert their position and demand their rights, to impress their adversaries and to ensure that they would not be dishonoured if the *infantes* of Carrión attempted such an action. Fear (*pavor*), attributed to cowardice in the case of the *infantes*, was presented as a sign of caution in the case of the Cid. His valour was shown to rely on the qualities and bravery of his group of armed men,

'velmezes vestidos por sufrir las guarnizones, | de suso las lorigas, tan blancas commo el sol, | sobre las lorigas, armiños e pelliçones, | e que no parescan las armas, bien presos los cordones; | so los mantos las espadas, dulces e tajadores: | d'aquesta guisa quiero ir a la cort, | por demandar myos derechos e dezir mi razón. | Si desondra buscaren ifantes de Carrión, | do tales ciento touier, bien seré sin pauor'. | Respondieron todos: 'Nos esso queremos, señor'. | Assí commo lo á dicho todos adobados son [vv. 3073–3083]

('I wish you all to put on your padded tunics which help you to bear the armour, over them your coats of mail shining like the sun and, over these, ermine or other fur tunics with strings pulled tight to hide the coats of mail; under your cloaks carry your sharp, well-tempered swords. That is how I wish to go to the court to demand justice and plead my case. If the *infantes* of Carrión should commit any breach of the peace, I shall fear nothing with a hundred like you behind me'.

Con el rey atantas buenas conpannas, | los yffantes de Carrión mucho alegres andan | [...] | El rey don Alfonsso apriessa caualga, | cuendes e podestades e muy grandes mesnadas; | los yfantes de Carrión lieuan grandes conpannas. | Con el rey van leoneses e mesnadas galizianas [vv. 1974–1982] ([The king] was himself bringing a large train of nobles. The Infantes of Carrión were in high feather [...]. Without delay King Alfonso rode off with his retinue of counts and barons and a vast company of vassals. The Infantes of Carrión had their own fine escort; in the King's suite there were Leonese and Galicians') (PoemCid, § 103). This is also how the Cid, once forgiven, refers to his men: 'Gradéscolo a Dios del çielo e después a vós | e as estas mesnadas que están aderredor' [vv. 2037–2038] ('For it I thank God, then you and these my vassals who stand here with me') (PoemCid, § 104). Earlier on in the text the term *compaña* is used to refer to both the king's and the Cid: 'La conpanna del Çid creçe e la del rey mengó' [v. 2165] ([The Cid's] party increased in number while the King's grew smaller) (PoemCid, § 107). For a note on the opposing meaning of the terms *mesnada* and *band*, see Martin, *Chanson de Mon Cid*, p. 40.

30 PoemCid, § 135 and 137.

216   ISABEL ALFONSO

They answered with one accord: 'We agree to do what you wish'. As they said this they all made ready).[31]

The representation of this group, their weapons and the way the Cid was dressed [vv. 3085–3103] was intended to dazzle the court, and also ultimately the listeners and readers so that they could feel and understand the admiration that was going to be caused by the Cid's greatness, chivalry and pain. This way of bending the audience and the assembly in their favour was a tremendous deployment of power, a very efficient display of symbolic capital: 'cuerdamientre entra mio Cid con todos los sos, | El va en medio e los ciento aderredor [vv. 3105–3106] ([The Cid] entered with sober mien, surrounded by his hundred followers).[32] This was illustrated by the impact caused by his group's entry, and the signs of deference he received from the members of the *cortes*, including the king himself [vv. 3107–3122]. The opposition between good and evil persisted for as long as the entire *cortes* were convened and in the ritual held before them. This opposition was shown in the description of the attitudes held by the parties and their groups in view of the judicial session taking place in the city. This will be elaborated further in the specific section dealing with this session. Nevertheless, it is worth bearing in mind this normative dimension that involved emotions and gestures attributed to the characters in the positive or negative presentation of their actions. This indicated that the author used social conventions to assess the appropriateness or otherwise of such expressions.[33] By employing these rhetorical devices, the vengeance wreaked by the Cid was shown to be justified, whereas that inflicted by the *infantes* was reproved. The Cid's feelings of vengeance were already implicit in his words when he heard about the tremendous scorn suffered by his daughters [vv. 2826–2834]. Several aspects are to be highlighted in this regard:

- The Cid pondered his actions, he did not act on impulsive rage: 'cuando ge lo dizen a mio Çid el Campeador, | una grand ora pensó e comidió' [vv. 2827–2828] (and when they told the Cid he meditated for a long time).[34]

- He talked ironically about the 'honour' (ondra) given to him by the *infantes* in a negative exchange that referred to the 'dishonour' caused: '¡Grado a Christus, que del mundo es señor, | cuando tal ondra me an dada los ifantes de Carrión!' [vv. 2830–2831] ('Thanks be to our Lord Jesus Christ' (he said) 'for this honour the Infantes of Carrión have done me').[35]

---

31 PoemCid, § 137.

32 PoemCid, § 137.

33 As noted by James A. Averill, emotions can be understood as socially constituted syndromes or transitory social roles, which are part of the rhetoric through which the actions taken by the various actors are constructed favourably or unfavourably. This is cited in the most valuable White, 'The Politics of Anger'.

34 PoemCid, § 131.

35 PoemCid, § 131.

- He swore by his beard, which was honourable because it had not been denigrated, not by God, that *the infantes* would not succeed in causing him the dishonour they sought to inflict: '¡Par aquesta barba que nadi non messó, | non la lograrán los ifantes de Carrión' [vv. 2832–2833] ('By this beard which no one has ever plucked, they [the Infantes of Carrión] will not succeed in dishonouring me').[36]

- He did not mention that his daughters had been abandoned and their marriage had been broken; instead, he used positive terms to talk about how he would find a better match for them. This seemed to be the most appropriate way to abort the dishonour resulting from the unilateral, scornful destruction of the marriage, in the context of exchange and reciprocity discussed above: 'que a mis fijas bien las casaré yo!' [v. 2834] ('for I shall make better marriages for my daughters').[37]

- At that point he did not refer to the pain suffered by his daughters. It was only when his daughters returned to Valencia after having been injured and humiliated that the Cid proclaimed what can be regarded as an invocation for ordeal, since he mentioned God in connection with his vengeance:

'Venides, mis fijas, Dios vos curie de mal | Yo tomé el casamiento, mas non osé dezir ál. | ¡Plega al Criador, que en cielo está | que vos vea mejor casadas d'aquí en adelant! | De mios yernos de Carrión Dios me faga vengar!' [vv. 2890–2894]

('Here you are, my daughters! May God protect you from all harm! I accepted this marriage, for I did not dare do otherwise. May it please Heaven to let me see you better married in the future! May God grant me vengeance on my sons-in-law of Carrión!').[38]

However, it can be considered that the political process involved in the vengeance had already started with the expressions of pain of his closest vassals, when they collected his daughters in San Esteban de Gormaz:

'en los días de vagar | toda nuestra rencura sabremos contar'. | Lloravan de los oios las dueñas e Álbar Fáñez, | e Pero Vermúez conortado las ha: | 'Don Eluira e doña Sol, cuidado non ayades, | cuando vós sodes sanas e bivas e sin otro mal; | buen casamiento perdiestes, mejor podredes ganar. | ¡Aun veamos el día que vos podamos vengar!' [vv. 2862–2868]

('when we have more leisure, we shall be able to tell you all we have suffered'. The ladies and Álvar Fáñez wept, and Pedro Bermúdez spoke these comforting words: 'Doña Elvira and Doña Sol, do not distress yourselves, seeing that you are safe and alive and have nothing more to trouble you. One good marriage has

---

36 PoemCid, § 131.

37 PoemCid, § 131.

38 PoemCid, § 132. The relationship with the divinity in the *Poem* was explored by M. Lacomba in an excellent Memoria de DEA (Lacomba, 'Honneur'). I am grateful to the author for allowing me to read this work.

been dissolved but you will be able to make a better one. We hope a time will come when we may avenge you!').[39]

It is striking that emphasis was placed on the broken marriage and the reparation of the humiliation through a better match, rather than on the physical and moral damage suffered. It shows how the *honra* and honour that could result from marriage alliances and the disloyalty and damage caused when they were broken was so important in that society that reparation was not only aimed at punishing those responsible, but at recovering *honra* through more honourable alliances. It seemed to have been generally accepted that a married woman who had been abandoned by her husband needed to clear her family's *honra* and her own through a better marriage.

The next event described was the Cid's daughters being welcomed by their mother and the plan immediately put in place by the Cid (the *tempo* of vengeance).[40] He sent an envoy to the king to inform him of the dishonour suffered, that is, to involve him in the reparation through gestures and expressions that mobilised his participation:

> El que en buen ora naxo non quiso tardar, | Fablós' con los sos en su poridad, | Al rey Alfonso de Castiella pensó de enviar: | '¿Ó eres, Muño Gustioz, mio vasallo de pro? | En buen ora te crié a ti en la mi cort. | Lieves el mandado a Castiella al rey Alfonso, | por mi bésale la mano d'alma e de coraçón, | cuemo yo so su vassallo e él es mio señor, | d'esta desondra que me an fecha los ifantes de Carrión| que.l' pese al buen rey d'alma e de coraçón. | Èl casó mis fijas, ca non ge las dí yo; | cuando las han dexadas a grant deshonor, | si desondra ý cabe alguna contra nós, | la poca e la grant toda es de mio señor. | Mios averes se me han levado que sobejanos son, | Esso me puede pesar con la otra desonor. | Adúgamelos a vistas o a juntas o a cortes, | Como aya derecho de ifantes de Carrión, | Ca tan grant es la rencura dentro de mi coraçón' [vv. 2898–2916]

(The Cid wasted no time but took counsel immediately with his vassals in private and decided to send a message to King Alfonso of Castile [...] 'Muño Gustioz, my brave vassal, I am fortunate in having you among those of my household. You shall carry this message to King Alfonso in Castile. Kiss his hand with cordial respect from me — for I am his vassal and he is my lord. Entreat him to consider as a deep and serious grievance the dishonour done to me by the *Infantes* of Carrión. The King was responsible for this marriage of my daughters, for I myself did not give them away. The dishonourable desertion they have suffered is not merely an insult to me, it is a far greater one to my lord the King, who is responsible for both. They have taken great sums of money from me, which I also consider as an injury. Let the King summon the *infantes* to judicial

---

39 PoemCid, § 132.
40 For some highly informative considerations on the importance of timing in exchange social practices (both positive and negative), see Bourdieu, *El sentido práctico*, pp. 126–29 y 138–40.

meetings, assemblies or solemn courts to render me justice for the wrong they have done to me, which rankles in my heart').[41]

This is in anticipation of the claim that the Cid's vassals were to bring before the king, which would take place again in his presence before the *cortes* convened in the monastery of Sahagún in León, after the hand-kissing and humiliation ritual [vv. 2934–2952]. This scene, usually interpreted as the Cid discharging responsibility for the dishonour suffered, should be seen instead as a strategy to involve the king. It was a way of gathering his support and certainly invoked the responsibility of the king as the lord who had arranged the marriage and proposed the now broken alliance. These circumstances caused great resentment in his heart, and hence he asked the king to convene the *infantes* before the appropriate forum to seek reparation (*derecho*). These expressions of indignation were a well-known means of recovering honour and initiating the avenging process, which was positively presented by the explicit invocation made by el Cid. It is true that there is and was a more or less regulated legal framework that governed relationships and social practices in that political community of lords and vassals. These were invoked by el Cid to legitimise his demands.[42]

The king's involvement, presented by the narrator as being self-evident, made vengeance and justice inseparable in this process. As perceived by many scholars, the king, acting as a judge, became a defender of a type of public justice versus private justice, and took on the role of an avenger. He accepted his responsibility and expressed his regret and sorrow that the marriage had taken place. In addition, he showed his wish to help el Cid to assert his right by convening the *cortes*:

> El rey vna gran ora calló e comidió:[43]| 'Verdad te digo yo que me pesa de coraçón, | E verdad dizes en esto tú, Muño Gustioz, | ca yo casé sus fijas con ifantes de Carrión. | fizlo por bien, que fuesse a su pro; | ¡siquier el casamiento fecho non fuesse oy! | Entre yo e mio Cid pésanos de coraçón, | ayudarl'é a derecho, sí.n' salue el Criador, | lo que non cuidava fer de toda esta sazón, | Andarán mios porteros por todo mio reino, | pregonarán mi cort pora dentro en Toledo. | Que allá me vayan cuendes e ifançones; | mandaré cómmo ý vayan ifantes de Carrión| e cómmo den derecho a mio Cid el Campeador' [vv. 2953–2966]

> (The King remained silet for a long time, reflecting on the matter. 'I am gravely concerned about this, Muño Gustioz [...] What you say is true, for I did give the Cid's daughters in marriage to the *infantes* of Carrión. I did it for the best, thinking that it would be to their advantage. Now I wish the marriage had never taken place. I am as much grieved about it as the Cid, and I promise to do him justice, as I hope for salvation. I shall do something I have not considered doing for a long time. My royal couriers will travel throughout the kingdom, announcing

---

41 PoemCid, § 132–33.
42 On the different strategies of formalisation, see also Bourdieu, *El sentido práctico*, pp. 183–84; Roberts and Comaroff, *Rules and Processes*.
43 The parallel with el Cid's reaction when he heard about the humiliation is worth noting [v. 2828].

the assembly of a solemn court of justice at Toledo and requiring all counts and baronets to attend. To it I shall summon the *infantes* and demand that they give satisfaction to the Cid').[44]

Here again the expression *dar derecho* means giving reparation,[45] rather than the widespread idea that a trial involved applying substantive rules to clearly defined and sanctioned criminal offences. These expressions (giving, obtaining, helping [el Cid] to assert his rights) were related to a resolution process that involved the very political community to which the affected groups belonged. The damages inflicted and the dishonour caused by it affected the very essence of their relationships, and also the groups that supported them.

The King also informed the Cid that the *cortes* would be convened and reassured him (*aseguramiento*) so that he would go a Toledo in person. He declared that he had convened the *cortes* out of affection for him,[46] and that he and his group would be treated honourably. These expressions showed that the king was part of the vindictive process of reparation, as he took sides and prejudged the outcome. He did not wait until he had listened to the accused, and did not presume their innocence. He was not an impartial judge, not even ideally, as some scholars have argued,

'e que non aya rencura podiendo yo vedallo. | Dezidle al Campeador, que en buen ora nasco, | que d'estas siete semanas adóbes' con sus vasallos, | véngam a Toledo, esto.l' dó de plazo. | Por amor de mio Cid esta cort yo fago, | saludádmelos a todos, entr' ellos aya espaçio, | d'esto que les avino aun bien serán ondrados!' [vv. 2967–2973]

('No wrong shall be done to him if I can prevent it. Tell the Campeador to prepare to come to Toledo with his vassals within seven which — which is the term I allow him. I am calling this court for the Cid's sake. Greet them all in Valencia on my behalf and tell them to be of good cheer, for from this disgrace which has befallen them honour will accrue').[47]

Full, specific details cannot be provided here about the session held by the *cortes*. However, it is worth stressing that the process of mobilisation of support by the groups started there [vv. 2975–3014]. From that time onwards, the dispute continued in the extraordinary assembly convened by the king in Toledo. The narration described the whole procedure that took place in this courtly and judicial venue, including the places and spaces within it, and the importance of other peoples' perceptions. All outward signs of *honra* were depicted accordingly, and this resulted in some parties being ennobled and others being shamed, with group distinction and identity established by apparel, gestures and the unequal deference given to each of them. The *corte* was clearly

---

44 PoemCid, § 133.

45 The relationship between vengeance and rights was already identified in Madero Eguía, 'El riepto', p. 855.

46 On the political content of this concept, the paper Martin, 'Amour' is particularly interesting, even if it disagrees with the opinion noted in n. 21. See also Jaeger, 'L'amour des rois'.

47 PoemCid, § 134.

VENGEANCE AND JUSTICE IN THE POEM OF THE CID   221

a space to socialise and learn all the practices that made up the game of honour.[48] It was the arena where all the issues related to honour were resolved; where all scorns and damages suffered were penalised, and *honra* was recovered. It was the ultimate socio-political context *par excellence* in this hierarchical community of equals. Two specific events seem to be particularly important in understanding the relationships underlying the assembly, constituted by royal vassals and their *mesnadas*. One took place prior to the formal meeting, namely the response given by the Cid when he was welcomed, which was an affirmation of the political friendship they shared:

> besóle la mano e después le saludó: | '¡Grado a Dios cuando vos veo, señor! | Omíllom' a vós e al conde don Remond, | E al conde don Anrich e a cuantos que ý son. | ¡Dios salue a nuestros amigos e a vós más, señor!' [vv. 3034–3038]

> (He kissed the King's hand and then his mouth. 'I am thankful to see you here. I give you my humble greetings, Count Raymond, Count Henry and all here present. God save our friends and above all you, our lord and King!').[49]

This was a way of gathering support for his cause, to turn those responsible for hearing the case to his favour, but also to state that he belonged to a political community from which he had been expelled. The *Poem* was clearly the narration of the recovery of honour by the Cid, but also a full ritual of re-entry into the social group to which he belonged.

The second outstanding event is related to the lines of antagonisms existing in the assembly. On the one hand, the king made a rhetorical statement noting that the counts appointed as *alcaldes* (judges, in this context) in the case did not belong to the *bando* of Carrión;[50] and, on the other, pronounced himself as the pacifier of any potential revolts in this regard. He then threatened to unleash his wrath and expel from his kingdom any parties who revolted:

> 'alcaldes sean d'esto [...] | el conde don Anrich e el conde don Remond| e estos otros condes que del vando non sodes. | Todos meted ý mientes, ca sodes connoscedores, | Por escoger el derecho, ca tuerto non mando yo. | D'ella e d'ella part en paz seamos oy; | juro por Sant Esidro, el que bolviere mi cort| quitarme á el reino, perderá mi amor. | Con el que toviere derecho, yo d'essa parte me só' [vv. 3135–3142]

> ('Let Counts Henry and Raymond act as judges in this case and with them other counts who do not belong to the Carrión faction. All of you give it your closes attention as experts to choose the right, for I will authorise no wrong. Let peace reign between the two parties. I swear by St Isidore that anyone who disturbs the court shall lose my favour and leave my kingdom. I side with the party which is proved to be in the right').[51]

---

48 Bourdieu, *El sentido práctico*, pp. 124–28.
49 PoemCid, § 135.
50 The term *bando*, included here in that of *mesnadas*, provides stronger evidence for my argument on this point.
51 PoemCid, § 137.

The *corte* was therefore the venue where the political community of the kingdom was represented. This community was made up of friendship and antagonism, of both implicit and explicit competition. Power within it was reinforced by being recognised, and the drive for action was to obtain more *honra*, more prestige, to maintain one's current status, to gather more allies or to gain the king's or the other major figures' favour. The ritual of the spaces each person occupied, of the protocol and ceremony described in the *Poem*, acquired its full value in this symbolic competition. In this context the king became legitimised as a higher power, as he was the arbitrator and a pacifier in these disputes and acted in support of the law. This rhetoric aimed at legitimising power clearly served to affirm it, but this did not indicate that the king was defending any type of new law or a different kind of justice. These forms of resolution, these judicial practices, as shown by recent studies, were old and would continue to be in force for a long time.[52]

The detailed development of the procedure in the *cortes* in Toledo is well known. It included the return of swords and the dowry, as well as the challenge and final combat. But at this stage it is worth highlighting the meaning of certain events:

The Cid began his address by thanking the king for having agreed to hold the assembly. This was a way of informing the audience that he had the king's support, which at that point was assumed by all present: 'Mio Cid la mano besó al rey e en pie se leuantó: | "Mucho vos lo gradesco commo a rey e a señor, | por cuanto esta cort fiziestes por mi amor"' [vv. 3145–3147] ('The Cid stood up and did obeisance to the King. "I am truly grateful", he said, "to you as my king and my lord for summoning this court for my sake"').[53]

The fact that the Cid presented the spurning of his daughters as an attack on the king's honour was tantamount to publicly transferring responsibility to, and involving him in the recovery of such honour: 'Esto les demando a ifantes de Carrión: | por mis fijas que.m' dexaron yo non he deshonor | ca vós casastes, rey, sabredes qué fer oy' [vv. 3148–3150] ('With regard to the Infantes of Carrión, my complaint is this. In deserting my daughters they did not dishonour to me, for you gave them in marriage and you will know what to do on that score today').[54]

Moreover, the Cid's claim is structured in three parts, which makes for a greater interest and narrative effect. Firstly, his claim to have his swords returned, as they were symbols of his gains, his feats and his value as a man. They were also a symbol of the rupture of the family and of his friendship with the *infantes*, a way to declare them his enemies and making the scorn suffered publicly known. The nature of relationships between lords, not only with the king, was also articulated around political 'love', the loss of which seemed to result from the same type of disloyalty. The judges (*alcaldes*) were aware of these rules and conventional practices that were legal, political and moral at the same time, and thus granted that 'todo esto es razon',

---

52 Alfonso, 'Litigios por la tierra'; White, 'La traición'; Hyam, 'Feud and the State'; Bartlett, '"Mortal Enmities"'. Studies on the low Middle Ages show that there was no single process of legal change, but rather an amalgamation of different practices of conflict resolution. Some interesting works on this are Vallerani, *Il sistema giudiziario*; Smail, 'Common Violence'; Dean, 'Marriage and Mutilation'.

53 PoemCid, § 137.

54 PoemCid, § 137.

'mas cuando sacaron mis fijas de Valençia la mayor, | yo bien las quería d'alma
e de coraçón, | diles dos espadas, a Colada e a Tizón| (éstas yo las gané a guisa
de varón), | que.s' ondrasen con ellas e sirviessen a vós. | Cuando dexaron mis
fijas en el robredo de Corpes, | comigo non quisieron aver nada e perdieron mi |
amor; | ¡denme mis espadas cuando mios yernos non son!' | Otorgan los alcaldes:
'Tod esto es razón'. [vv. 3151–3159]

('When they took my dearly beloved daughters away from Valencia I gave
them two swords, Colada and Tizón — which I won by my own skill — that
they might gain honour with them in your service. When they abandoned my
daughters in the oak forest of Corpes they showed that they wished to have no
more connexion with me and broke all bonds of friendship and affection. Let
them give me back the swords, as they are no longer my sons-in-law'. The judges
confirmed the justice of this plea).[55]

The symbolic nature of weapons was again seen in the joy felt by the Cid when he
recovered them (described by the poet as the joy of vengeance), and handed them
to the two vassals who would take part in the duel. It must be remembered that
these swords were to be used to materially execute vengeance in the final combat:

Sacaron las espadas Colada e Tizón, | pusiéronlas en mano del rey so señor. |
Saca las espadas e relumbra toda la cort, | las maçanas e los arriazes todos d'oro
son, | maravíllanse d'ellas todos los ommes buenos de la cort [vv. 3175–3179] [...]
alegrós'le todo el cuerpo, sonrrisós de coraçón; | alçava la mano, a la barba se
tomó: | 'Par aquesta barba que nadi non messó, | assí s' irán vengando don Eluira
e doña Sol' [vv. 3180–3187]

(They brought out the swords, Colada and Tizón, and placed them in the
hand of the King, their liege lord. When the swords were drawn they dazzled the
whole court with their golden pommels and cross-guards, to the amazement of
all beholders [...] The joy that filled his heart was seen in his smile and every
movement of his body. He raised his hand and grasped his beard saying: 'By this
beard that none has ever plucked, they will help me to take vengeance for Doña
Elvira and Doña Sol').[56]

The strategy of claiming the weapons in the first place was successful, as it led the
infantes to believe that there would be no claim against them for the dishonour they
had caused, and that they would be able to have an amicable relationship with the king,

Dixo el conde don García: 'A esto fablemos nós'. | Essora salién aparte ifantes de
Carrión| con todos sus parientes e el vando que ý son; | apriessa lo ivan trayendo e
acuerdan la razón: | 'Aún grand amor nos faze el Cid Campeador| cuando desondra
de sus fijas no nos demanda oy, | bien nos avendremos con el rey don Alfonso. |
Démosle sus espadas, quando assí finca la boz, | e cuando las toviere partirse á
la cort; | ya más non avrá derecho de nós el Cid Campeador' [vv. 3160–3169]

---

55 PoemCid, § 137.
56 PoemCid, § 137.

(Count García (Ordóñez) said: 'We should like to consult about this matter'. Then the *Infantes* of Carrión went aside to discuss the question with all their relations and their party there. They decided at once to accede to the request saying: 'The Cid Campeador does us a great favour by not demanding satisfaction today for the insult to his daughters. We shall easily come to an understanding with King Alfonso. Let us give the Cid his swords, as he has ended his pleading, so that when he has received them he will leave the court and make no more demands on us').[57]

This speech is very important. Not only, as has been argued, because it was adapted to the statutory legal procedures, but because it showed that the *infantes* realised that the king had chosen to take sides, and their fear of losing his affection as a result. Their objectives were maintaining their links with him and the position this involved. When they agreed to return the swords as required, they publicly declared that they were the king's vassals:

Con aquesta fabla tornaron a la cort: | 'Merçed, ya, rey don Alfonsso, sodes nuestro señor! |No lo podemos negar, ca dos espadas nos dio; | cuando las demanda e d'ellas ha sabor, | dárgelas queremos delant estando vós' [vv. 3170–3174]

(They returned to the court to announce this decision: 'We beg permission to speak, King Alfonso, our liege lord. We cannot deny that the Cid gave us two swords. As he demands them and wishes to have them returned we shall give them to him here in your presence').[58]

These are signs that the honour dispute was ultimately about belonging to the king's circle, the most influential political circle. It should not be forgotten that the original reason for the old enmity mentioned in the poem from the start was the fight for power in the court, in which the Cid had been defeated. Therefore, it was the king's friendship and love that was at stake, rather than any formal aspects of upward mobility within the noble strata, which have been excessively emphasised, in my view.

Secondly, the Cid's claim for the return of the dowry (three thousand silver marks) involved an additional material and symbolic break of the marriage alliance. All the arguments used were part of that logic of exchange discussed above; it entailed the repayment of the amount previously delivered in order to cease the connection embodied by those objects,

'Otra rencura he de ifantes de Carrión. | Cuando sacaron de Valencia mis fijas amas a dos, | en oro e en plata tres mill marcos les di yo. | Yo faziendo esto, ellos acabaron lo so: | ¡denme mis averes, cuando mios yernos non son!' [vv. 3202–3206]

('I have a further complaint to make against the *Infantes* of Carrión. When they took my daughters away from Valencia, I gave them three thousand marks in gold and silver. In spite of this generosity on my part, they carried out what they had planned to do. Let them give me back my money as they have ceased to be my sons-in-law').[59]

---

57 PoemCid, § 137.
58 PoemCid, § 137.
59 PoemCid, § 137.

The difficulties that the *infantes* had to return those goods in coins and their offer to pay them back in lands raised a number of issues that I cannot elaborate on at this point.[60] Briefly, their offer was interpreted as another rhetorical opposition between two social levels and their different economic bases. This kind of request has often been documented as a final stage of judicial proceedings, such as in the well-known ritual whereby the convicted party begged to be forgiven and to be allowed to pay the monetary amount demanded as a fine or compensation in lands.

Much has also been discussed about the reasons why the king received part of that money.[61] It may have been intended to acknowledge his involvement in bringing the marriage into being, as aptly argued by Hinojosa.[62] This would highlight the importance of the broken marriage, as all the assets that somehow symbolised the alliance were claimed back. The rupture affected the king, who refused to receive a payment as gratitude, since it had dishonoured him. His refusal, albeit in retrospect, indicated that he had taken a stance and considered the action performed by the *infantes* to be illegitimate:

> 'Nós bien la sabemos aquesta razón, | que derecho demanda el Cid Campeador.| D' estos tres mill marcos los dozientos tengo yo, | Entr'amos me los dieron los ifantes de Carrión. | Tornárgelos quiero, ca tan desfechos son, | Enterguen a mio Cid, el que en buen ora nació. | Cuando ellos los an a pechar, non ge los quiero yo' [vv. 3229–3234]

> (We realise that the Cid has right on his side in this matter. Of these three thousand marks I hold two hundred which the *infantes* gave to me on the conclusion of the match. As they are so impoverished, I shall return this sum to them. Let them pass it on to the Cid, for, if they have to pay back these marks, I have no wish to keep them).[63]

But what should be highlighted, as in the case of the swords, is that this act carried some symbolic overtones, in terms of the legitimacy of the money they had received, and the rejection of that money by the king. It was a way for material objects to be endowed with a certain moral quality; swords and money should be deserved, and their exchange could cause dishonour for the receiver, or otherwise. Objects carried honour or dishonour, as they were attached to the subjects of the exchange and to their actions.[64] The second section of this passage is more complicated than it seems and has sometimes been misunderstood.[65] When the king assumed that they had to

---

60 For further elaboration on this interpretation, see Montaner Frutos, *Cantar de Mio Cid*, n. 3223.

61 Alberto Montaner reviewed and discussed the various interpretations given to this. See Montaner Frutos, *Cantar de Mio Cid*, n. 3231.

62 De Hinojosa y Naveros, 'El Derecho en el Poema del Cid', pp. 213–14.

63 PoemCid, § 137.

64 Cf. here the reflections on this issue made by don Juan Manuel to his son in his *El libro enfenido*, ch. XVIII, where he notes that of moneys 'that are not rightfully won [lords] should make no treasure' (Blecua, ed., *Don Juan Manuel. Obras completas*, p. 175). Perceptions with regards to coin possession and exchange would be worth investigating, in line with works such as those collected in Parry and Bloch, eds, *Money*.

65 See Montaner Frutos, *Cantar de Mio Cid*, n. 3231.

pay them ('los han de pechar'), he seemed to make a clear reference to the judicial compensation owed by the *infantes* for having abandoned their wives. They were certainly being judged on those grounds, but there was in fact a renegotiation of the relationship that had been formalised through the exchange of assets (swords, money ...) and then broken by the return of those assets. The fact that the Cid later refused to retain those moneys payable to him [vv. 3502–3503] as compensation for the damage suffered (to the benefit of the king) seems to be part of the same game.

Thirdly, the exchange was more complex: the *infantes* responded to the honour granted to them with dishonour. And it was this dishonour that they needed to reimburse the Cid for. Therefore, when the money had been returned, the el Cid made a third demand, which he claimed was the major one and he could not forget. That was when, 'in God's name' ('por amor de caridad'), he requested the king's mercy,

> Estas apreciaduras mio Cid presas las ha, | sos omnes las tienen e d' ellas pensarán; | mas cuando esto ovo acabado, penssaron luego d' al: | '¡Merced, ya rey e señor, por amor de caridad! | La rencura mayor non se me puede olbidar' [vv. 3250–3254]
>
> (The Cid accepted the payment in kind and handed over the various items to the care of his followers. When this business was finished, another point was brought forward (by the Cid): 'I beg a favour of my lord the King in God's name. I cannot forget my greatest cause of complaint').[66]

The conflict gradually and subtly became a dispute about relationships, about political affection and disaffection which, to a certain extent, affected the entire aristocratic community represented in the *Poem*. The Cid addressed the court as a whole, appealed to their solidarity in the face of the dishonour suffered and invoked the moral obligation of challenging,

> 'Oídme toda la cort e pésevos de mio mal; | los ifantes de Carrión, que.m' desondraron tan mal, | a menos de riebtos no los puedo dexar' [vv. 3255–57]
>
> ('Let the court hear me and sympathise with me in the wrong I have suffered. I cannot allow the Infantes of Carrión, who have done me such dishonour, to escape without a challenge').[67]

It was at that point that the verbal duel began, the public exchange of insults and reproaches that the challenge (*riepto*) constituted. The Cid challenged them to fight as a result of their actions, and stated that he would submit himself to the *corte* if they were found to be right. This challenge was used to publicise the actions carried out by the *infantes* and define the offence they had committed, which included betraying his trust, breaking their marriage covenants, causing el Cid's daughters physical injuries and abandoning them. The lack of a known reason meant that such infamous and vile actions seemed worse, and therefore that the worth of the *infantes* decreased. This behaviour diminished the perpetrators' value and reputation and also their honour in legal terms, which was submitted to the judgement of the court:

---

66 PoemCid, § 138.
67 PoemCid, § 138.

VENGEANCE AND JUSTICE IN THE POEM OF THE CID   227

'Dezid, ¿qué vos merecí, ifantes de Carrión, | en juego o en vero o en alguna razón? | Aquí lo mejoraré en juvizio de la cort. | ¿A qué m' descubriestes las telas del coraçón? | A la salida de Valencia mis fijas vos di yo | con muy grand ondra e averes a nombre. | Cuando las non queriedes, ya canes traidores, | ¿por qué las sacávades de Valencia, sus honores? | ¿A que las firiestes a cinchas e a espolones? | Solas las dexastes en el robredo de Corpes | a las bestias fieras e a las aves del mont. | ¡Por cuanto les fiziestes menos valedes vós! | Si non recudedes, véalo esta cort'. [vv. 3258–3269]

('Tell me, *infantes* of Carrión, what injury, real or imaginary, have I ever done to you? I am willing here and now to make it good as the court may decide. Why did you wound my deepest feelings? When you left Valencia I entrusted my daughters to you with all due honour and abundant wealth. If you had no love for them, you treacherous dogs, why did you take them from their estates in Valencia? Why did you strike them with belts and spurs? You abandoned them in the oak forest of Corpes, at the mercy of wild beasts and birds of prey. In doing this you have incurred infamy. If you do not give satisfaction for this crime, let the court pass judgement').[68]

The later responses of each party in the verbal duel, despite following well-known legal formulae, included specific strategies that turned the dispute into an assessment of the value of the alliance; in other words, of the capital it involved for the parties, which is described in detail below.

Count *don* García, previously presented as an enemy of the Cid, asked mercy of the king, 'greatest in all Spain' ('el meior de toda Espanna') and adduced the higher social hierarchy of the *infantes* de Carrión as a reason for them having abandoned their wives. His strategy not only attempted to ridicule the Cid's long beard as a sign of honour, but it also involved a negative assessment of the honour and types of alliances established between them. The *infantes* of Carrión proclaimed themselves to be of 'such a nature' ('natura tal') that they should never had accepted their wives even as concubines; he wondered who had dared to give them to the *infantes* as wives, making an implicit allusion to the king's decision. The count stated that they were right to have left their wives and despised the Cid's challenge, that is, his demand,

El conde don Garçia en pie se levantava: | '¡Merced, ya rey, el mejor de toda España! | Vezós' mio Cid a llas cortes pregonadas; | Dexóla crecer e luenga trae la barba, | los unos le han miedo e los otros espanta. | Los de Carrión son de natura tal, | non ge las devién querer sus fijas por varraganaso | ¿quién ge las diera por parejas o por veladas? | Derecho fizieron porque las han dexadas, | cuanto él dize non ge lo preciamos nada' [vv. 3270–3280]

(Count García (Ordóñez) rose to his feet and said: 'Give me leave to speak, O King, greatest in all Spain. The Cid is used to attending meetings of this solemn court of justice; he allowed his beard to grow long to strike terror in the hearts of

---

68 PoemCid, § 139.

all. The lords of Carrión are of such noble lineage that they should not consider his daughters fit to be their concubines. Who gave them to them as lawful wedded wives? They did right in deserting them. We care nothing for his accusation').[69]

This response to the Cid's challenge can be considered to be a bluff to disparage the opposing party, as if he were trying to score some points in their verbal duel by suggesting that the Cid was not worthy of the claims he made. Appealing to a presumed superior *natura* was part of this logic, although interestingly it was used to negate the scornful and aggressive character of the actions committed by the *infantes*. Reference was made to a community of 'equals' among whom the game of honour was played; and to the fact that outsiders were not supposed to play that game, at least not at that level. However, the very fact that he responded to the challenge showed to what extent they tacitly acknowledged what they were trying to negate with their words.

The Cid replied by praising his own beard, which had been ridiculed before, and arguing what constituted honour. He made prior resentments explicit and mentioned the old animosity between them resulting from an episode in which he had dishonoured count *don* García by plucking his beard. This strategy allowed the Cid to discredit the counter-arguments made by his opponent:

Essora el Campeador prísos' a la barba | '¡Grado a Dios, que cielo e tierra manda! | Por esso es luenga, que a delicio fue criada. | ¿Qué avedes vós, conde, por retraer la mi barba? | Ca de cuando nasco a delicio fue criada, | ca non me priso a ella fijo de mugier nada | nimbla messó fijo de moro nin de cristiana, |commo yo a vós, conde, en el castiello de Cabra, | cuando pris a Cabra e a vós por la barba. | Non ý ovo rapaz que non messó su pulgada, | la que yo messé aún non es eguada'. [vv. 3280–3290]

(At this the campeador grasped his beard and answered: 'Thanks be to almighty God, it is long because it has had much loving care lavished on it. What reproach can you cast on my beard? All my life it has been my chief delight. No woman's son has ever plucked it an no one, Moor or Christian, ever tore it — as happened to yours, Count, in the castle of Cabra. When I took Cabra and plucked your beard, there was not a lad but tore out his bit. The piece that I pulled out has still not grown even again').[70]

The next intervention was that by Fernán González, one of the *infantes*. He asked the Cid to abandon his claim, as he had already been duly paid. This time the tactic used was to harm the reputation of his adversary by depicting him as a quarrelsome troublemaker. He attempted to show that the Cid was trying to intensify the conflict (*varaja*) between them. He also insisted on their high social status, which meant that they deserved to marry the daughters of kings and emperors, and not the 'daughters of petty nobles' ('fijas de ifançones'). Fernán González at that stage repeated that leaving their wives was the right thing to do, and that their worth had increased — rather than decreased — as a result:

---

69 PoemCid, § 140.
70 PoemCid, § 140.

VENGEANCE AND JUSTICE IN THE POEM OF THE CID   229

Ferrán Gonçalez en pie se levantó, | a altas vozes odredes equé fablo: | '¡Dexássedes vós, Cid, de aquesta razón! |De mvuestros averes de todos pagado sodes; | non creciés *varaja* entre nós e vós. | De natura somos de condes de Carrión, | Deviemos casar con fijas de reyes o de enperadores, | ca non pertencién fijas de ifançones; | porque las dexamos derecho fiziemos nós, | más nos preciamos, sabet, que menos no' [vv. 3291–3300]

(Fernando González stood up and shouted: 'Forbear to press this claim, Cid; now that you have your money's worth returned, you may be content. We have no wish to continue this mutual strife. We are of the family of the counts of Carrión and have a right to marry the daughters of kings and emperors, and the daughters of pety nobles are not our equals. We did right in deserting them, and in doing so we are raised, not lowered, in the esteem of the world').[71]

At that point the Cid urged those in his group to take action and engage in duel, by calling dumb (*mudo*) to Pedro Vermúdez,

Mio Cid Ruy Díaz a Pero Vermúez cata: | '¡Fabla, Pero mudo, varón que tanto callas! | Yo las he fijas e tu primas cormanas, | a mí lo dizen, a ti dan las orejadas, | Si yo respondier, tú non entrarás en armas!' [vv. 3301–3305]

(The Cid Ruy Díaz looked at Pedro Bermúdez and said: 'Speak, Pedro Mudo, you silent man! They are my daughters but they are also your cousins. They insult me but they aim to strike you cheek. If I take up the challenge, you will have no chance of defending their cause').[72]

His vassal then issued a personal challenge and accused the previous speaker of having lied. This was an insult that questioned his reputation, as it made public their cowardly actions and lies, such as their having run away from a battle, which had been concealed until then. By doing so he showed that Fernán was fatuous and pretentious, and that he was a liar with low worth. 'Lengua sin manos, cómo osas fablar?' ('You handless tongue, how dare you talk?'), he said, in opposition to the criticism he had received.

Pero Vermúez conpeçó de fablar; | detiénes' le la lengua, non puede delibrar, | mas cuando enpieça, sabed, nol' da vagar: | '¡Dirévos, Cid, costunbres auedes tales, | siempre en las cortes Pero Mudo me llamades; | bien lo sabedes, que yo non puedo más; | por lo que yo ovier a fer por mí non mancará. | ¡Mientes, Ferrando, de quanto dicho has: | por el Campeador mucho valiestes más! | Las tus mañas yo te las sabré contar. | Miémbrat' cuando lidiamos cerca Valençia la grand: | pedist las feridas primeras al Campeador leal, | vist un moro, fústel' ensayar, | antes fuxiste que a él te allegasses. | Si yo non uviás, el moro te jugara mal; | passé por ti, con el moro me of de ayuntar, | de los primeros colpes, ofle de arrancar. | Did' el cauallo, tóveldo en poridad, | fasta este día no lo descubrí a nadi. | Delant

---

71 PoemCid, § 141. My emphasis.
72 PoemCid, § 142.

mio Cid e delante todos ovístete de alabar | que mataras el moro e que fizieras barnax; | croviérontelo todos, mas non saben la verdad, | e eres fermoso mas mal varragán! | ¡Lengua sin manos, cuémo osas fablar?' [vv. 3305–3328]

(Pedro Bermúdez spoke in his turn, a little tongue-tied at first, but once he started there was no stopping him. 'I declare, Cid, you have got into the habit in every assembly of calling me Pedro Mudo! You know very well that I cannot help my defect of speech, but I shall not fail where deeds are concerned [...] You lie, Fernando, in all you have said. It was an honour for you to be connected with the Campeador. I could tell a few tales about you! Remember what happened when we were fighting near Valencia. You asked the Cid's permission to deal the first blows. You caught sight of a Moor and went forward to pit yourself against him, but you ran away instead, before you came up to him. If I had not gone to your aid, that Moor would have got the better of you. I outstripped you, engaged the Moor and defeated him at once. I gave you his horse and kept quiet about it, and have not told it to a soul until now. You were able to boast to the Cid and everyone else that you had killed the Moor and won your spurs. They all believed you but they do not know the truth. You are a handsome fellow, but a coward. You handless tongue, how dare you talk?').[73]

This shows how information circulated, how reputation was created and destroyed, and how it depended on other people's opinion. Along these lines, Pedro Vermúdez exclaimed:

'¡Riébtot' el cuerpo por malo e por traidor, | esto t'lidiaré aquí ant'el rey don Alfonso ¡ | Por fijas del Cid don Eluira e doña Sol, | por cuanto las dexastes menos valedes vós. | Ellas son mugieres e vós sodes varones, | en todas guisas más valen que vós. | Cuando fuere la lid, si ploguiere al Criador, | tú lo otorgarás a guisa de traidor; | de cuanto he dicho verdadero seré yo' [vv. 3343–3351]

('I therefore challenge you in person as an evildoer and traitor. I shall maintain this in combat with you here in the presence of King Alfonso. On behalf of the Cid's daughters, Doña Elvira and Doña Sol. By deserting them you incurred infamy. They are women and you are a man, but they are your superiors in every way. When — God willing — it comes to fighting you will confess yourself a traitor, and I shall prove myself right in all I have said').[74]

The vile action of attacking women was used to justify the challenge and the objective of the intended fight. This was to show the value they attributed to themselves and denied to others, hence the challenge was to prove 'myself right in all I have said' ('¡De quanto he dicho verdadero seré yo!'). The role of the duel was to construct a judicial truth, the one on which actual reputation was based; this was the true value, which depended on what other people knew or believed, and on the authority of the venue in question to give certainty to those beliefs. This was the context in which

---

73 PoemCid, § 143 (with modifications in the last verse to keep the literal sense).
74 PoemCid, § 144.

truth was established. The truth/falsehood dialectic to a large extent articulated the discourse of the parties.

The next intervention featured the other *infante*. He emphasised their higher level in the hierarchy, the disparity between the parties to the alliance and the fact that they did not regret having abandoned the Cid's daughters. He said that he would fight to show that their honour was increased by having left them,

> Diego Gonçalez odredes lo que dixo: | 'De natura somos de los condes más limpios. | ¡Estos casamientos non fuessen aparecidos, | por consagrar con mio Cid don Rodrigo. | Porque dexamos sus fijas aún no nos repentimos; | mientra que bivan pueden aver sospiros, | lo que les fiziemos serles ha retraído. | ¡Esto lidiaré a tod el más ardido: | que por que las dexamos ondrados somos nós!' [vv. 3353–3360]

> (Then Diego González spoke: 'We are high-born nobles and we should not have made these marriages or entered into any kind of relationship with the Cid, Don Rodrigo. We do not repent of deserting his daughters, but they will regret it, for as long as they live what we did will be cast upt to them. I shall defend this against the best champion: that by deserting them we gained honour').[75]

The challenge made by Martín Antolinez, another one of the Cid's vassals, included similar insults to those previously uttered: 'traitor, and liar that you are' (*aleuoso, boca sin verdad!*), and added further details to the account of the cowardly actions perpetrated by the *infantes*, providing information about the incident with the lion. He challenged his opponent in the duel by saying that he would make him confess his treason and lies,

> Martín Antolínez en pie se leuantaua: | '¡Cala, aleuoso, *boca sin verdad*! | Lo del león non se te debe olvidar' | […] | 'Yo lo lidiaré, non passará por ál: | fijas del Cid, porque las vós dexastes, | en todas guisas, sabed que más que vós valen. | ¡Al partir de la lid, por tu boca lo dirás | que eres traydor e mintist de cuanto dicho has!' [vv. 3361–3371]

> (Martín Antolínez rose to his feet and said: 'Hold your tongue, traitor and liar that you are. Do not forget what happened with the lion. I am bound to fight you on this point — that, because you deserted them, the Cid's daughters are superior to you in every respect. When the fight is over you will confess yourself a traitor and that everything you have said is a lie').[76]

Another narrative device used by the poet to antagonise the public and readers was the unfavourable description of the *infante* who replied. He was presented as being red in the face because he had overeaten and his words were unwise:

> Asur Gonçález entrava por el palaçio | manto armiño e un brial rastrando, | vermejo viene, ca era almorzado, | en lo que fabló avié poco recabdo [vv. 3373–3376]

---

75 PoemCid, § 145.
76 PoemCid, § 146. My emphasis.

(Ansur González entered the hall, dragging his ermine cloak and his tunic. Red-faced, he came straight from the table, and there was little sense in what he said).[77]

This description was further emphasised by Munio Gustioz, the third of the Cid's vassals who intervened:

'¡Calla, alevoso, malo e traidor! | Antes almuerzas que vayas a oración; | a los que das paz fártaslos aderredor. | Non dizes *verdad* a amigo ni ha sennor, | falso a todos e más al Criador, | en tu amistad non quiero aver ración. | ¡Fazertélo he dezir, que tal eres cual digo yo!' [vv. 3382–3389]

('Hold your tongue, you wicked and deceitful traitor! You always breakfast before going to say your prayers, and when you give the kiss of peace you belch in people's faces. You lie to friend and lord — false to them all and still more to God. I want no part in your friendship. I shall make you confess that you are such a man as I say').[78]

These vassals undermined the ironic reproaches made by the *infante* about the low status of the Cid and his ambitious intentions when he became related with the Carrión family. It is another example of the truth/falsehood dialectic, in which the *infantes* were urged to confirm that what was being said was true.

'¡Ya varones! ¿Quién vio nunca tal mal? | ¿Quién nos darié nuevas de mio Cid el de Bivar? | Fuesse a río d'Ovirna los molinos picar | e prender maquilas, commo lo suele far, | ¿Quí.l' darié con los de Carrión a casar?' [vv. 3376–3381]

('Gentlemen, who ever saw such a thing? Who ever heard of the Cid, that fellow from Vivar? Let him be off to the river Ubierna to dress his millstones and collect his miller's tolls as usual. Who gave him the right to marry into the Carrión family?').[79]

The dispute about the each of the parties' worth throughout the verbal confrontation turned into a dispute based on worth resulting from one's personal conduct, rather than family status, as intended by the *infantes* of Carrión. But, as has been held by some scholars, was there an opposition between personal honour and lineage honour, which reflected a separation between different groups? In this assessment of the honour and *honra* of the members of each of the groups, emphasis was certainly placed on appropriate conduct, but with respect to shared values, without it being necessarily linked to a particular group. Blood and merit complemented each other, and inherited honour was to be maintained and increased through honourable behaviour and relationships. I do not believe that there was a proposal to advocate the existence of two distinct political groups (indicating a different relationship with the king), as argued by Martin.

---

77 PoemCid, § 147.

78 PoemCid, § 149. My emphasis.

79 PoemCid, § 148. For other interpretations of these verses, which have been used to substantiate a supposed opposition in the *Cantar* between two levels of nobility, see Montaner Frutos, *Cantar de Mio Cid*, nn. 3379–80.

VENGEANCE AND JUSTICE IN THE POEM OF THE CID   233

These public verbal exchanges in which the honour and prestige of the litigants were disputed should be understood as being part of a political culture and certain practices of the struggle for power. These practices continue to be embedded in present-day Spanish electoral culture, where resources such as slander, making charges against the other side and disclosure of private information are used to disparage the leader of the opposing party. While these practices have been officially questioned, they are effective in political processes. The dialectical elements in this fight are different in form only.

The following verses of the *Cantar* [vv. 3392–3426] show how the *corte* fulfilled more than one role. During the process two knights acted on behalf of the *infantes* de Navarra y de Aragón to ask his daughters in marriage, and he demanded a decision from the king. The king silenced the *corte* ('fizo callar la cort') and granted his approval of the marriages, as they would bring the Cid honour, consideration and wealth ('ca crécevos ý ondra e tierra e onor'). This was followed by a ritual of consents and a public assessment of the political capital involved in this alliance, including the repercussions for the various groups present in the court.[80] The narration, which included solemn oaths and homage ('fes e los omenajes') exchanged by them, led to the conclusion that these acts must have been fairly similar to those previously performed with respect to the *infantes*.

The challenge of Minaya, cousin of the victims, also needs to be discussed. He was impatient to be allowed to proclaim his own resentment (*rencura*) against the *infantes*:

Minaya Álbar Fáñez en pie se levanto: | '¡Merced vos pido, commo a rey e a señor, e que non pese esto al Cid Campeador! | Bien vos di vagar en toda esta cort, | dezir querría yacuanto de lo mio.' | Dixo el rey: 'Plazme de coraçón, | dezid, Minaya, lo que oviéredes sabor'. | 'Yo vos ruego que me oyades toda la cort, | ca grand rencura he de ifantes de Carrión. | Yo les di mis primas por mandado del rey Alfonso, | ellos las prisieron a ondra e a bendición; | grandes averes les dio mio Cid el Campeador. | Ellos las han dexadas a pesar de nós: | ¡riébtoles los cuerpos por malos e por traidores! | De natura sodes de los de Vanigómez, | onde salién condes de prez e de valor; | mas bien sabemos las mañas que ellos han oy' [vv. 3429–3445]

(Minaya Álvar Fernández rose to his feet and said: 'I beg you leave to speak, my king and lord, with all due respect to the Cid Campeador. I have kept silent through all these proceedings but now I wish to have my say in the matter'. The King replied: 'You have my permission to speak. Say what you wish, Minaya'. Minaya continued: 'I ask all here in this court to listen to me, for I have a great complaint to make against the Infantes of Carrión. I gave them my cousins in marriage on behalf of King Alfonso, and the marriage was celebrated. The Cid gave them great wealth but they, in defiance of us, abandoned their wives. I challenge them as wicked traitors. You belong to the family of the Beni-Gómez, which has

---

80 'A muchos plaze de tod esta cort, | mas non plaze a los ifantes de Carrión' [3427–3428] ('Many were pleased at this event, but not the Infantes of Carrión') (PoemCid, § 149).

produced counts of valour and worth. But well we know the evil manners of these young men today').[81]

In this case, while the reproach revolved around the nature/manners (*natura/mañas*) dichotomy, the first element, honour resulting from lineage appreciation (*prez*) and worth (*valor*), was not undermined; rather, it was their behaviour (their manners) that was disparaged. This clearly supports the argument I proposed earlier: in the *Poem* there was no opposition between birth nobility and merit nobility, since they could be complementary. In fact, the logic of the narration can be understood better now. The account of the duel was interrupted to include the new wedding of the Cid's daughters, because the last challenge was related to the greater honour that would ensue. They would kiss the hands of their cousins and call them ladies, given their marriage to the sons of kings. This is a good illustration of the desirable, rather than opposing, bond between blood and merit. It showed that honour and value, as well as prestige and reputation, had a contingent nature in the society described by the poet. The content of the last challenge, made by a relative and vassal of the king, was that the honour of the Cid had increased. And should anyone deny it, he put himself forward claiming that we would uphold his statement ('pora tod el mejor'),

> 'Antes las aviedes parejas pora en braços | agora besaredes sus manos e lamarlas hedes señoras, | averlas hedes a servir mal que vos pese a vós. | Grado a Dios del cielo e a aquel rey don Alfonso, | así l' crece la ondra a mio Cid el Campeador. |En todas guisas tales sodes cuales digo yo; | si ay qui responda o dize de no, | yo só Álbar Fáñez, pora tod el mejor!' [vv. 3450–5456]

> ('Once you had them as wives and equals, but now you will kiss their hands and acknowledge them as your superiors. You will have to do them service, however, unwillingly. I thank God and good King Alfonso, for thus is the honour of the Cid enhanced. In every respect you are such men as I say. If anyone should answer or contradict me, I am Álvar Fáñez and will uphold my statement').[82]

This was a strong challenge. It is worth noting this personal way of challenging, which involved showing one's own worth versus that of the opponents. It was a personal battle in the most and the least physical sense, as it was a challenge based on each person's social identity. This ritual of self-representation was perhaps the most daring and sophisticated. It provided a definition of one's identity with respect to conventional, shared values, and it was at the same time a ritual of affiliation to political society. Therefore, it was a ritual that served to legitimise the values of the group, certain models of behaviour and political actions.[83] The challenge was accepted by the second *infante* and the court was the venue used for this demonstration, in the different senses of the word.

---

81 PoemCid, § 149.

82 PoemCid, § 148.

83 On the ritual acts of acknowledgement that all groups need to construct themselves and maintain themselves as such, a key contribution to understand these processes is that made Bourdieu, *El sentido práctico*, pp. 232–37.

Gómez Peláyet en pie se levantó: | '¿Qué val, Minaya, toda essa razón? | Ca en esta cort afartos ha pora vós, | e qui ál quisiesse, serié su ocasión. | Si Dios quisiere que d'ésta bien salgamos nós, | después veredes qué dixiestes o qué no'. [vv. 3457–3462]

(Gómez Peláez rose and said: 'What is the use of all this talk, Minaya? For in this court there are more than enough to take you on, and he who said otherwise would do so at his peril. If God wills that we should come off best in this affair, we shall then see what there was in your claim').[84]

The king intervened to put an end to this exchange of insults, of the verbal injury that is the stuff of challenges. He established that the fight between the first six men who had challenged each other would take place at sunrise,

Dixo el rey Alfonsso: '¡Fine esta razón! | Non diga ninguno d'ella más una entención | Cras sea la lid, cuando saliere el sol, | D' estos tres por tres que rebtaron en la cort' [3463–3466]

(The King said: 'Enough of this. Let no one make any further allegations. The combat shall take place tomorrow at sunrise between the three on each side who took part in the challenge before the court').[85]

However, the *infantes* wanted to postpone the confrontation, and gave the excuse that they did not have any weapons or horses. They asked to be granted a longer period of time to travel to their land and bring what they needed. The king agreed and gave them three weeks before the fight would take place in the banks of Carrión. He declared that anyone who failed to appear would be considered to have been vanquished and to be a traitor. The Cid returned to Valencia and left his knights and troops under the king's protection, which every good vassal deserved from his lord. It is interesting how the poet once again ensured that the positive value given to the protagonist also had repercussions for the king himself. The good king/good vassal dialectic was reciprocal and to a large extent served as the basis for the public morality of domination in this social class [vv. 3467–3485].

The first session at the *corte* in Toledo therefore ended with the king taking the Cid's vassals under his protection while the Cid returned to Valencia. This included a full farewell ritual in deference to them and also to the rest of the assembly. It also showed signs of generosity from Rodrigo towards the king and the major lords of the *corte*, a full demonstration of power and wealth intended to deploy his worth and *honra* at the same time [vv. 3486–3532]. These were again political rituals of deferential exchange, in which their vassal friendship was affirmed. The Cid advised his men and repeated what he expected of them, which was condensed succinctly into the expression 'better dead than defeated', because they had vowed to assume a debt of honour that had to be repaid:

El Campeador a los que han de lidiar tan bien los castigó: | [...] | 'Buenos mandados me vayan a Valencia de vós'. | Dixo Martín Antolínez: '¿Por qué lo

---

84 PoemCid, § 148.
85 PoemCid, § 148.

dezides, señor?' Preso avemos el debdo e a passar es por nós; | podedes oír de muertos, ca de vencidos no [vv. 3523–3529]

(The Cid gave wise advice to those who were to take part in the combat [...] 'in Valencia I may hear good reports of your conduct'. Martín Antolínez answered: 'Why do you say this? We have undertaken this duty and it is for us to see it through. You may hear of us as dead but not as defeated').[86]

The Duel as a Resolution

The ritual of the duel began with the description of the groups that would engage in combat. The opposition between good and evil was made apparent in this section: whereas the *infantes* were presented as being unpunctual, having bad intentions, and being frightened and liable for the actions committed, the Cid's vassals were portrayed as being punctual, courageous, and confident in the judicial trial they were about to face and in the king's support of the outcome [vv. 3533–3603]. Above all, however, the judicial trial they were going to face was conferred full value — its authority being legitimised and its power formalised — by the way in which the assembly, and the king within it, are presented as guarantors of the law. The king stood as the arbitrator of the fight, its procedures and its outcome,

Troçida es la noche, ya quiebran los albores; | Muchos se juntaron de buenos ricos omnes | por ver esta lid ca avien de ende sabor | por querer el derecho e non consentir el tuerto | Demas sobre todos y es el rey don Alfonsso [vv. 3545–3548]

(The night had passed and dawn was about to break, when a great crowd of nobles assembled to witness the combat, which they were eager to behold. Above all, King Alfonso was there to see that justice was done and no wrong).[87]

The fight began with an independent description of each of the combats. This seemed to be intended to hide the fact that they took place at the same time. The narration is full of force and tension for the outcome to be known, with the public surrounding the field of combat. One by one, with everyone's expectant eyes on them, the men of Carrión were defeated and the king ordered that the field be vacated [vv. 3608–3692].

The *Cantar* finishes abruptly, with the king putting an end to the duel and briefly speaking about the *honra* of one party and the humiliation (*biltança*) of the other; about joy in Valencia and sadness in Carrión:

Mando librar el campo el buen rey don Alfonso, | las armas que ý restaron él se las tomó. | Por ondrados se parten los del buen Campeador, | Vencieron esta lid grado al Criador; | grandes son los pesares por tierras de Carrión [vv. 3693–3697] [...] Por malos los dexaron a los ifantes de Carrión, | complido han el debdo que

---

86 PoemCid, § 150.
87 PoemCid, § 150.

les mandó so señor; | alegre fue d'aquesto mio Cid el Campeador. | Grant es la biltança de ifantes de Carrión [vv. 3702–3705]

(King Alfonso ordered the field to be cleared. The arms of the vanquished which were left there became his property. The Campeador's champions departed with honour for they had, by God's grace, won the fight. There was great sorrow throughout the lands of Carrión […] They had proved the Infantes of Carrión traitors and so fulfilled the obligation laid on them by their lord, who was greatly rejoiced to hear it. The Infantes of Carrión had suffered a deep disgrace').[88]

But there is also a moral to the story, to which insufficient importance has been given.[89] The author expressed it as a legal/moral/avenging ideal: anyone who scorns a woman and abandons her should have the same (or worse) happen to him:

¡Qui buena duena escarneçe, e la dexa después, | Atal le contesca o siquier peor [vv. 3706–3707]

(May such a fate or worse befall anyone who treats a noble lady shamefully and then abandons her).[90]

Therefore, in terms of *honra*, there were no agreements or pacts; only victorious and defeated parties. This moral, normative lesson reduced the conflict to a dispute caused by slander and injuries where the law of talion prevailed. Vengeance had been achieved:

'¡Grado al rey del çielo, mis fijas vengadas son! […] | Sin vergüenza las casaré o a qui pese o a qui non!' [vv. 3714–3715]

('I thank God in His Heaven that my daughters are avenged! Let them now be considered quit of the estates of Carrión. I can give them in marriage without let or hindrance').[91]

These narrative strategies, taken literally, served to substantiate debates on the private or public nature of offences, and therefore, of reparation. In this way the fight for power, which has been shown in these pages, was concealed.[92]

The vengeance effectively served for the key characters to recover their *vergüenza* (*honra*, honour). This capital also seemed to have come from the new alliances with the kings of Navarra y Aragón, which made the Cid a relative of the Spanish monarchs, as explained by the poet when describing the second marriage of his daughters and

---

88 PoemCid, § 152.
89 This is how I interpret that Alberto Montaner reduced this vengeful aphorism to an individual wish of the narrator (Montaner Frutos, *Cantar de Mio Cid*, p. 676).
90 PoemCid, § 152.
91 PoemCid, § 152.
92 The study of the different forms of political struggle, of competition for power among the dominant groups, in connection with their own shaping as such, is the objective of the research project I am currently leading on *Political Struggles and Legitimisation in León-Castile (10th–15th centuries)* (PB98–0655).

the increase in honra involved. This again ratifies my interpretation that there was no opposition between the various ways of acquiring and increasing honour:

> A mayor ondra las casa que lo que primero fue. | ¡Ved quál ondra creçe al que en buen ora nació | Quando sennoras son sus fijas de Navarra e de Aragón! | Oy los reyes d'Espanna sos parientes son; | A todos alcança ondra por el que en buen ora naçió [vv. 3717–25]

> (The first marriages brought them honour, but these were better still. See what honour accrued to the Cid when his daughters became Queens of Navarre and Aragon. Today the Kings of Spain are related to him and all gain lustre from the fame of the fortunate Campeador).[93]

But what seems to be most interesting, and should be highlighted, is to ascertain the circulation of *honra*, the socio-political dynamic whereby it was acquired and lost, transmitted and regained. The Cid had lost his *honra* because his daughters had been scorned, recovered it through vengeance and increased it by obtaining a better marriage for his daughters. And later he publicised the process. The *infantes*, honourable men, lost their *honra* because of their cowardice, and failed to regain it. The vile nature of the injury and scorn they inflicted on their wives as vengeance increased their dishonour. The outcome of the duel came to corroborate and expose this situation, and demonstrated their legal incompetence, for which they had been vilified.

---

93   PoemCid, § 152.

Bibliography

Alfonso, Isabel, 'Resolución de disputas y prácticas judiciales en el Burgos medieval', in *Burgos en la Plena Edad Media. III Jornadas Burgalesas de Historia* (Burgos: Asociación Provincial de Libreros de Burgos, 1994), pp. 211–43

Alfonso, Isabel, 'Introducción: desarrollo legal, prácticas judiciales y acción política en la Europa medieval', *Hispania*, 47197 (1997), 879–83

Alfonso, Isabel, 'Litigios por la tierra y "malfetrías" entre la nobleza medieval', *Hispania*, 57–197 (1997), 917–55

Bartlett, Robert J., '"Mortal Enmities": The Legal Aspect of Hostility in the Middle Ages', in *Feud, Violence and Practice: Essays in Medieval Studies in Honor of Stephen D. White*, ed. by Belle Stoddard Tuten and Tracey Lynn Billado (Farnham: Ashgate, 2010), pp. 197–212

Blecua, José Manuel, ed., *Don Juan Manuel. Obras completas* (Madrid: Gredos, 1983)

Bourdieu, Pierre, *El sentido práctico* (Madrid: Taurus, 1991)

Cacho Blecua, José Manuel, 'La vergüenza en el discurso del poder laico desde Alfonso X a Don Juan Manuel', in *Actas del VI Congreso Internacional de la Asociación Hispánica de Literatura Medieval (Alcalá de Henares, 12–16 de septiembre de 1995)*, ed. by José Manuel Lucía Megías (Alcalá de Henares: Universidad de Alcalá, 1997), pp. 343–412

de Hinojosa y Naveros, Eduardo, 'El Derecho en el Poema del Cid', in *Obras, I*, ed. by Eduardo de Hinojosa (Madrid: 1948)

Dean, Trevor, 'Marriage and Mutilation: Vendetta in Late Medieval Italy', *Past & Present*, 157 (1997), 3–36

Fletcher, Richard A., *The Quest for El Cid* (Oxford: Oxford University Press, 1991)

García de Valdeavellano, Luis, *Historia de España*, 2 vols (Madrid: Revista de Occidente, 1968)

Geary, Patrick, 'Vivre en conflit dans une France sans État: typologie des mécanismes de règlement des conflits (1050–1200)', *Annales ESC*, 41–5 (1986), 1107–33

Hyam, Paul, 'Feud and the State in Late Anglo-Saxon England', *Haskins Society Journal*, 40–1 (1991), 1–21

Jaeger, C. Stephen, 'L'amour des rois: structure sociale d'une forme de sensibilité aristocratique', *Annales E.S.C.*, 46–3 (1991), 547–71.

Lacarra, María Eugenia, *El 'Poema de Mio Cid': Realidad histórica e ideología* (Madrid: Porrúa, 1980)

Lacomba, Marta, 'Honneur et Perception de Dieu dans le Poema de Mio Cid' (unpublished, Université París 13, 1997)

Madero Eguía, Marta, 'El riepto y su relación con la injuria, la venganza y la ordalía (Castilla y León, siglos XIII y XIV)', *Hispania*, 47–167 (1987), 805–61

Madero Eguía, Marta, *Manos violentas, palabras vedadas. La injuria en Castilla y León (siglos XIII–XV)* (Madrid: Taurus, 1992)

Martin, Georges, *Chanson de Mon Cid. Cantar de Mio Cid* (Paris: Aubier, 1996)

Martin, Georges, 'Amour (Une notion politique)', *Cahiers d'Études Hispaniques Médiévales*, 11 (1997), 169–206

Martin, Georges, 'Le récit héroïque castillan (Formes, enjeux sémantiques et fonctions socio-culturelles)', *Cahiers d'Études Hispaniques Médiévales*, 11 (1997), 139–52

Menéndez Pidal, Ramón, *La España del Cid* (Madrid: Espasa-Calpe, 1969 [1934])

Miller, William I., *Bloodtaking and Peacemaking: Feud, Law, and Society in Saga Iceland* (Chicago: The University of Chicago Press, 1990)

Miller, William I., *Humilation, and other Essays on Honor, Social Discomfort, and Violence* (New York: Cornell University Press, 1993)

Parry, Jonathan Parry, and Maurice Bloch, eds, *Money and the Morality of Exchange* (Cambridge: Cambridge University Press, 1989)

Roberts, Simon and John Comaroff, L., *Rules and Processes: The Cultural Logic of Dispute in an African Context* (Chicago: The University of Chicago Press, 1981)

Smail, Daniel, 'Common Violence and Inquisition in Fourteenth-Century Marseille', *Past & Present*, 151 (1996), 28–59

Vallerani, Massimo, *Il sistema giudiziario del comune di Perugia. Conflitti, reati e processi nella seconda metà del XIII secolo* (Perugia: Deputazione di storia patria per l'Umbria, 1991)

Verdier, Raymond, 'Le système vindicatoire. Esquisse théorique', in *La Vengeance: Études d'ethnologie, d'histoire et de philosophie. Volume I: Vengeance et pouvoir dans quelques sociétés extra-occidentales*, ed. by Raymond Vedier (Paris: Éditions Cujas, 1980), pp. 12–42

White, Stephen D., '*Pactum ... legem vincit et amor judicium*: The Settlement of Disputes by Compromise in Eleventh-Century Western France', *The American Journal of Legal History*, 22-4 (1978), 281–308

White, Stephen D., 'Feuding and Peacemaking in Touraine around the Year 1100', *Traditio*, 42 (1986), 196–263

White, Stephen D., 'La traición en la ficción literaria. Derecho, hecho y ordalías en la narrativa y la épica en francés antiguo', *Hispania*, 57–197 (1997), 957–80

White, Stephen D., 'The Politics of Anger', in *Anger's Past: The Social Uses of an Emotion in the Middle Ages*, ed. by Barbara Rosenwein (Ithaca: Cornell University Press, 1998), pp. 127–52

PART II

Community Ties and Social Differentiation

CHAPTER 6

On Social Differentiation in Rural Communities

with a commentary by Christopher Dyer

Conflict, Language, and Social Practice in Medieval Societies: Selected Essays of Isabel Alfonso, with Commentaries, ed. by Julio Escalona Monge, Álvaro Carvajal Castro, and Cristina Jular Pérez-Alfaro, TMC 24 (Turnhout: Brepols, 2024), pp. 243–267

BREPOLS ✠ PUBLISHERS   10.1484/M.TMC-EB.5.132460

CHRISTOPHER DYER

Middlemen and Intermediaries
in Medieval Village Society

Isabel Alfonso wrote a typically acute and original analysis of the social history of a sample of Galician villages, based on a close reading of the archives of monastic landholders. She was aware of records showing that lessees took over the administration of lords' rents in the sixteenth century. Historians had argued that this introduced a new complexity into the social hierarchy, and signalled the end of the direct relationship between lords and peasants, as the lessees were collecting rents on the lords' behalf. Isabel argued that this was not new, and that such middlemen were already part of the social hierarchy in the thirteenth and fourteenth centuries. She focussed on elite landed families, who included wealthy peasants, some of them on the fringes of the nobility, and some of whom became parish clergy. They had close relationships with the local monasteries, becoming their clients, and acting as their agents. They in turn built up a following of local allies, including their relatives and neighbours. These categories of wealthy, well-connected and influential clerics and laymen formed an intermediate rank between lords and peasants. Relationships in these complex rural societies were not based entirely on the exercise of lordship from above, and deference and resistance from below, but on ties of kinship, friendship, patronage, clientage and neighbourhood. These subtle and indirectly documented connections can only be detected by very careful and subtle techniques of historical analysis.

For historians of medieval English society some of the details of the Galician villages studied by Isabel are unexpected and very different from the villages that we study. The role of the parish clergy as landholders and active participants in the secular world would not be easily parallelled in England. The institutions were clearly working in different ways, so that in England parish clergy could be recruited from among the sons of the local gentry, but they would not become active in land holding and forming alliances in the way that Galician clergy did. Many English parish clergy were outsiders, and might come from another region.

Social historians of medieval England recognize the potential importance of clientage, kinship and other informal relationships in rural society, but find it difficult to detect them in the sources available. Perhaps we could explore these themes if we devoted more time and energy to the deeds (charters), leases and similar documents that were exploited so successfully by Isabel. Deeds survive in their hundreds for some English villages, but they are not as abundant as those in Spain, and not so informative. They are sources neglected by medieval historians, who are seduced by the great quantities of detailed data in manorial court records.

Christopher Dyer, University of Leicester

246   CHRISTOPHER DYER

There are parallels for the Galician elites. From a thorough study of the village of Sherington in Buckinghamshire, based on deeds and royal court records, John de Cave was found to be a royal justice and rector of a parish church in the mid thirteenth century when it was possible to pursue the two occupations simultaneously. He lent money in some quantity, and spent the profits on acquiring property. He leased the moated manor house in Sherrington (but not the manor itself) and bought a great deal of land there. He also held land in various midland villages, including some leased from Ramsey Abbey. His brother Simon de Cave was the vicar of Carnaby in Yorkshire, but he was in minor orders and incurred the disapproval of church reformers. Like his brother, he was a money lender, as was revealed by legal proceedings in 1260. He inherited John's land, and for a time lived in Sherington, but lost some land in a nearby village when he was caught up in the troubles that followed the civil war of 1258–1265.[1]

In the same village, the career of John de Chebenhale can be traced between 1339 and 1364, when he was operating as a merchant in the towns of Newport Pagnell and Stony Stratford, but he also served for three years as bailiff for the absentee rector of Sherington. He prospered sufficiently to be able to buy 100 acres of land in the village in 1364.[2] One sees people bearing some resemblance to Isabel's elites taking on many roles, as we would say multi-tasking, combining clerical and legal professions with commercial interest and land holding. John de Cave had a connection with a monastery, but the monastic affiliations of English villagers in general were not as strong as those in Galicia. The de Caves and de Chebenhale were certainly superior to peasants, but fell short of achieving conventional aristocratic, noble or gentry status. They cannot be fitted into a single pigeon hole. As well as demonstrating the complexities of their society to modern historians, they show that medieval people, for all of their repetition of the three orders idea, in their own lives did not conform to that model social structure.

Although it is possible to recognize these similarities between Galician and English rural society, the general point needs to be pursued about the inadequacy or rather the incompleteness of the 'lord and peasant' characterisation of medieval society in England. The following social categories will be considered: large landholders with various ways of acquiring and managing their lands; agents and intermediaries; patronage and clientage among peasants, and commercial middlemen.

Any list of manorial tenants will show us that the majority held yardlands, half-yardlands and smaller holdings, so that the top tier held 30–40 acres, but there was a handful, or even just one or two located above them with large holdings and often light services. Their details were recorded in the twelfth and thirteenth centuries, but they were the successors of tenants dating back to before 1066. The Old English term radmen (riding men) was used in 1170 to describe Jordan and Randolph who each held a half-hide (two yardlands or about 60 acres) at Ripple in Worcestershire.[3] They had the duty to attend the courts of the hundred and the shire (that is the

---

1 Chibnall, *Sherington*, pp. 54–58.
2 Chibnall, *Sherington*, pp. 135–36.
3 Hollings, ed., *The Red Book of Worcester*, p. 167.

county court of Worcestershire and of the hundred of Oswaldslow, a subdivision of the shire) to represent the lord's tenants at Ripple. Although the term radman was not used in a survey of 1266–7 of the Gloucester Abbey manor of Aldsworth, three tenants clearly belonged (or their predecessors had belonged) to that category. Almaric de Collesburne, William Barebast and William de Hyda each held a half hide amounting to 96 acres. Their rents — one owed 4s., another 12s. and a third 16s. — were quite light, at 2d. per acre or less. They were also expected to do 'foreign service' which would mean riding to deliver letters or attend courts, an honourable and rather prestigious duty. Their wealth and status can be judged by the heriot that would be levied when each tenant died, which was a horse with its harness and the tenant's arms, perhaps a sword and lance.[4]

This type of tenant had deep roots, and persisted into the later middle ages, when elite landholders were called franklins. A scatter of franklins paid their poll tax at a higher rate in 1379 and they were awkwardly positioned between the upper peasantry and lesser gentry. In the thirteenth century we find tenants with unusually large holdings who seem to have accumulated their land piecemeal by a combination of purchase, marriage and rewards for service. An example might be Richard le Bedel who stands out in a survey of the Coventry Priory manor of Priors Marston in 1279. He held from the monastic lord a yardland, with extra holdings of 5 acres and 20 acres, making 55 acres, but in addition he sublet from other tenants four smaller parcels of land amounting to 17 ½ acres, and his combined accumulation of more than 70 acres make him the wealthiest man (in terms of land) in the village.[5] His rise was partly through his own enterprise in negotiating sub tenancies, which he presumably purchased, but his surname, 'beadle' being a manorial official, hints that he benefitted from association with his monastic lord. The late thirteenth century was a good time to be tenant of many acres in a village producing wheat and other grain, some of which would have been consumed by the growing population of the city of Coventry.

These tenants of larger holdings would often have been large-scale agricultural producers for the market, but an alternative would be to sublet in order to draw a cash income, and leave their tenants to work the land. Subletting is often undocumented, and in the case of customary tenants was restricted by the lord and therefore concealed by the tenants. It is sometimes revealed in the type of document studied by Isabel Alfonso, a deed from a monastic archive. In the early thirteenth century Arbury Priory, a rural monastery in north Warwickshire, received a grant from John Vitor of Coleshill of rents with a total value of 16s. per annum, which had been paid to him by six subtenants. As is often the case, we know little of the background.[6] Did the subtenants belong to Vitor's clientage, as would have been the case in Galicia? Presumably his grant would make them tenants of the Priory, so that a middle tier between lord and peasant was being removed by Vitor's grant. There are also deeds of the same period showing Vitor receiving grants of land. He may have been

---

4 Hart, *Historia*, p. 184.
5 John, ed., *Warwickshire Hundred Rolls*, pp. 210–12.
6 Watkins, *The Early Records of Coleshill*, pp. 69–70.

buying land and rents for his own profit, or he may have been acting on behalf of the monastery. A complicating factor arises from credit relations, again a feature of landed society often hidden from view. John Vitor may have been lending money and gathering parcels of land from those who could not pay him back in cash. Or he could have borrowed money from the monastery, and his grant of his assets was to satisfy their demands for repayment.

John Vitor's position as a gatherer of rent from his subordinates which ultimately benefited a monastery connects him to the Galician lessees who collected a portfolio of peasant rents and paid a leasehold rent to the monks. A more direct parallel comes from English lessees of manors, who acquired the rents and services of tenants as well as the demesne. Such manorial leases were reduced in numbers in the thirteenth century as most lords took on the direct management of their manors so they would gain the full profits. Manors were more often farmed out in the twelfth century, and then we encounter figures like Henry Bucvinte who leased the manor of Kensworth in Hertfordshire from the canons of St Paul's Cathedral in 1152. He was to pay the lords £5 per annum in the first year, increasing by the seventh year to £10. A danger was foreseen that the lessee would oppress the peasant tenants (of whom there were eleven in 1086) to the long-term disadvantage of the canons, so the lease included the condition that he would treat the men of the manor 'reasonably'. A glimpse of Bucvinte's supporters and possible clients is given in the lease, as five pledges are named, including Gervase Pevrel and his brother Jordan.[7] Whenever we see a lease, especially a lease of a major asset like Kensworth manor, the possibility of subletting must be envisaged. When leasing of demesnes and occasionally whole manors became the normal way of managing an estate in the late fourteenth and fifteenth centuries 'under farmers' were commonplace, again reinforcing the impression of a multi-layered rural society.

In the transfer and acquisition of land agents and brokers could play an important role. These middlemen were of particular concern to monasteries because mortmain legislation of 1279 prevented them from buying land except when they had a licence from the crown. The most efficient way of proceeding, while remaining within the law, was for an individual outside the monastery to buy land as it became available, and then to grant the accumulated properties in a single transaction under the terms of a 'general' licence. The individuals are quite easily identified from their distinctive multiple grants of land — people like Peter de Blokley and William de Passenham who aided Coventry Priory's acquisition of property in the city of Coventry in the fourteenth century.[8] Their names derive from villages on the outer edge of Coventry's sphere of influence, about whom we know nothing, but they must have been well-informed men of affairs, with practical knowledge of the property market. John de Standish was active in the countryside, helping to transmit land sold by Walter de Bret of Pitchcombe into the hands of Gloucester Abbey around 1300.[9] These well informed and responsible agents might be compared with the feoffees who

---

7 Hale, ed., *The Domesday of St Paul's*, pp. 128–29.
8 Goddard, *Lordship and Medieval Urbanisation*, pp. 121–25.
9 Melland Hall, 'Pynchenecumbe'.

helped in the management of the property of the lay aristocracy, and were trusted to receive grants of estates in order to keep them until they passed them on to an heir.

For English social historians the main route of access to the workings of medieval village society comes from the manor court and its records. A pioneering study of interactions between peasants which can be compared with Isabel's work came from Richard Smith, when he examined the links of kinship and neighbourhood among peasants in a Suffolk village in the late thirteenth century. He detected evidence of better-off peasants, for example with holdings of 14 acres, exercising patronage over smallholders with only an acre or two. The elite peasants employed these poor neighbours, lent them money, and acted as pledges in the court, which meant guaranteeing that the requirements of the court were obeyed.[10] Other researchers have explored relationships among peasants and put more emphasis on connections between social equals based on family and kinship.[11] Causes of friction and peace-making among quarrelling villagers have been explored, but again these allies and enemies tended to be middling and better off peasants rather than rich and poor.[12] There is room for more research because many historians have noted that peasants employed one another and acted as pledges, without pursuing the likely exercise of patronage associated with inequality of wealth, power and influence among villagers.

Trade could have been conducted without middlemen, as in an ideal world grain, livestock, dairy produce and wool were sold by the producer directly to the consumer without handling fees and extra charges. The real commercial world was more complicated and involved intermediaries who profitably performed a service in identifying purchasers and delivering goods. Dealers are often not identified, so in the grain trade there are only a few references to traders identified by the occupational descriptions of badgers, bladers and cornmongers. Specialists in the trade were scarce because dealing in grain was a side line for many other traders. The poultry trade can sometimes be revealed by the activities of poulterers who bought the birds from the many (often female) small-scale producers, assembled the numbers required in aristocratic households and in towns, and delivered them to the consumers.[13] Dealers in wool and cloth are more visible, and can often be found in rural settings, especially in the fifteenth and early sixteenth centuries. Pottery manufacture is a rural industry lacking much written documentation, but abundantly represented by its material remains. Pottery made at Hanley Castle in Worcestershire is found in large quantities around the kilns themselves at Hanley, but also in the towns and villages where it was used over much of the west midland region and extending into south Wales. But how were the pots transferred from the kilns to the kitchens where they were used? The answer must be that a network of traders developed, not called potmongers because they dealt in other goods with woodland origins, who efficiently distributed thousands of modest, cheap, but essential assets to everyone cooking, serving and storing food and drink.

---

10 Smith, 'Kin and Neighbours'.
11 Razi, 'Family, Land and Village Community'.
12 Schofield, 'Peasants and the Manor Court'.
13 Dyer, 'Peasants and Poultry', esp. p. 116.

Isabel's example of Galician village society has stimulated these thoughts, and suggests the gaps in our knowledge which ought to be remedied by further research. The strength of Isabel's article is that it provides an interpretation of Galician society, but she develops ideas that can be applied to medieval society in general. Every region has its different characteristics, but in our research we benefit from the stimulation of general insights and hypotheses.

Bibliography

Chibnall, A. C., *Sherington. Fiefs and Fields of a Buckinghamshire Village* (Cambridge: Cambridge University Press, 1965)

Dyer, Christopher, 'Peasants and Poultry in England, 1250–1540', *Quaternary International*, 543 (2020), 113–18

Goddard, Richard, *Lordship and Medieval Urbanisation. Coventry 1043–1355* (Woodbridge: Boydell, 2004)

Hale, William, ed., *The Domesday of St Paul's* (London: Camden Society, 1858)

Hart, William H., *Historia et Cartularium Monasterii Sancti Petri Gloucestriae*, Vol. 3, Rolls Series (London: Longman, 1867)

Hollings, Marjory, ed., *The Red Book of Worcester* (London: Worcestershire Historical Society, 1934–1950)

John, Trevor, ed., *Warwickshire Hundred Rolls of 1279–1280* (Oxford: Oxford University Press, 1992)

Melland Hall, John, 'Pynchenecumbe – Abstracts of Original Documents in the Register of St Peter's Gloucester', *Transactions of the Bristol and Gloucestershire Archaeological Society*, 14 (1889–1890), 141–62

Razi, Zvi, 'Family, Land and Village Community in Late Medieval England', *Past & Present*, 93 (1981), 3–36

Schofield, Phillipp, R., 'Peasants and the Manor Court: Gossip and Litigation in a Suffolk Village at the Close of the Thirteenth Century', *Past & Present*, 159 (1998), 3–42

Smith, R. M., 'Kin and Neighbours in a Thirteenth-Century Suffolk Community', *Journal of Family History*, 4 (1979), 219–56

Watkins, Andrew, *The Early Records of Coleshill c. 1120–1549* (Stratford-upon-Avon: The Dugdale Society, 2018)

ISABEL ALFONSO

Local Power and Internal Differentiation in the Rural Communities of Galicia*

Of the major assumptions about the social past of Galicia, one key element used to explain its history, and even its immediate present, is the formation of a social group of *frades* and *fidalgos*, upon which recent research has been able to shed new light.[1] This group was made up of non-productive rentiers, in the most literal sense. Their emergence and consolidation in the societal structure of rural Galicia has been dated to the sixteenth century, when they took advantage of favourable circumstances to settle as *foreros* (lease-holders) on monastic lands. They therefore took part in collecting the rent that the peasants who farmed the land had to pay to the monasteries. In this view, it was the nature of the leasing system known as the *foro* — the most widespread form of land management in Galicia — that allowed this group of intermediaries to develop and gain strength, as they integrated with full force into the structure of rural society, managing to take control of half of all surplus production. Thus, this process is interpreted as calling into question the binary opposition between large-scale landowners and those who worked the land, since — we are told — starting in the sixteenth century peasants and lords ceased to constitute the two poles of rural society.[2]

Such arguments, largely made by historians of the modern era, implicitly or explicitly assume that, by contrast, in the medieval period there did exist such a direct relationship between peasants and lords, one which was broken at the dawn of the modern era.[3] The medieval historiography upon which these authors base their ideas allows, to a certain extent, for such clear-cut assertions, despite medievalists'

---

* Original publication: Alfonso, Isabel, 'Poder local y diferenciación interna en las comunidades rurales gallegas', in *Relaciones de poder, de producción y de parentesco en la Edad Media y Moderna: aproximación a su estudio*, ed. by Reyna Pastor. Biblioteca de Historia 1 (Madrid: Consejo Superior de Investigaciones Científicas, 1990), pp. 203–23. Translated by Nicholas Callaway.

1 Essential references are Villares, *La propiedad de la tierra en Galicia*; Villares, *Foros, Frades y Fidalgos*, with an extensive, indispensable bibliography. For the subject matter explored here, see esp. c. III 'A Fidalguía' and c. IV 'Evolución histórica do foro'.

2 Villares, *La propiedad de la tierra en Galicia*, p. 123, and more generally, pp. 68–105.

3 I believe this applies, for example, to the reception of this argument in valuable geographic studies such as J. García Fernández: 'In the Middle Ages the *foro* established a direct relationship between the owner, i.e. the lord, and the peasant. [Later on], the relationship becomes an indirect one, losing its feudal character [...] The *forero* of the modern period is not, therefore, the peasant of the medieval period, but rather a rentier of the land. The *foro* had by then lost its original meaning, which is why the *subforo* has been seen as a corrupted form of the *foro* that pushed the peasantry into abject poverty, rendering futile its efforts to increase the yields of the land' (García Fernández, *Organización del espacio*, pp. 101–02, as per the original). Likewise, Villares, *La propiedad de la tierra en Galicia* states explicitly, in studying the formation of the house or domain of Lagariños, that 'generally speaking, the sixteenth century is when notaries and squires insert themselves between the peasants and the monasteries'.

252   ISABEL ALFONSO

unflagging insistence in pointing out not only the complexity of rural social structures, but also the existence of stratification both in the heart of the peasantry as well as among the dominant groups.[4] These studies show that throughout the medieval period, not just peasants, but also 'people of the most varied social backgrounds' received leases of monastic properties.[5] However, in part because these contracts lacked the formal legal status they would attain in subsequent periods, and in part due to their low statistical representation in the overall documentary corpus, it is only from the late fifteenth century onwards that historians have traced the importance of this one upwardly mobile social group, ignoring the fact that *foro* contracts already existed in earlier periods.[6]

In a recent synthesis of medieval rural society, Cortázar has shown just how difficult it is to analyse social differentiation and hierarchization during this period. In his view, these difficulties come down to 'the lack of social stratification models' — the telling title he has given to the final section of his chapter on this topic. Indeed, he judges as insufficient the range of social categories used to define the stratification of rural society on the eve of the fourteenth century.[7] Within this hierarchy, on the

---

4   See e.g. Portela, *La región del Obispado de Tuy*; Rodríguez Galdo, *Señores y campesinos*; Mariño Veiras, *Señorío del monasterio de Meira*.

5   Mariño Veiras, *Señorío del monasterio de Meira*, p. 191. M. X. Rodríguez Galdo has likewise pointed out how over her study's three centuries the properties of the Church end up 'in the hands of the *foreros*, who are usually peasants, but on occasion are also lay and ecclesiastic lords, *hidalgos*, scribes, notaries, artisans, etc.' (Rodríguez Galdo, *Señores y campesinos*, p. 153). E. Portela explains how the economic hardships of the second-tier rural nobility during the thirteenth century pushed them to seek assistance from the ecclesiastic nobility, such that, by becoming beneficiaries of the latter's lands, they in turn became dependent on them' (Portela, *La región del Obispado de Tuy*, p. 234).

6   I am referring to *subforo* contracts, a form of subtenancy, which in the works cited in note 4 are studied separately from *foro* contracts proper. *Subforo* is closely tied to this class of intermediaries, whose first signs of emergence E. Portela, for example, situates in the fourteenth century 'the interest of certain second-tier nobles and, most of all, certain members of the bourgeoisie, in exploiting the benefits for intermediaries that the very administrative structure of the cathedral domain facilitated, is what explains the emergence of the *subforo* in the fourteenth century' (Portela, *La región del Obispado de Tuy*). For D. Mariño and M. X. Rodríguez Galdo, the adverse circumstances of the late fifteenth and early sixteenth centuries, along with the social conflicts among the peasantry, is what forced the clergy to put in place intermediaries in order to ensure rent was collected and properties kept under control (Mariño Veiras, *Señorío del monasterio de Meira*. p. 192 and Rodríguez Galdo, *Señores y campesinos*, p. 220, respectively), a process that was closely linked to the rise of the *subforo*. D. Mariño points out that prior to the fourteenth century, the lack of legal standardization makes it impossible to quantify the phenomenon (Mariño Veiras, *Señorío del monasterio de Meira*, p. 123), and in the fifteenth century the *foros* no longer satisfied the initial aim of keeping the populace in place, expanding farmland, and making general improvements. Rather, from this point on a new series of intermediaries arise, advocating for the creation of the *subforo*, which would eventually be legally enshrined (Mariño Veiras, *Señorío del monasterio de Meira*, pp. 123–24). I wish to point out how an overly formalist interpretation of property transfer documents has kept medievalists from enriching their arguments with the wealth of information that they themselves have brought to light and analysed, instead by and large taking up the inherited wisdom relegating the *subforo* and the intermediary social group to the modern period (Portela, *La región del Obispado de Tuy*, p. 309; Mariño Veiras, *Señorío del monasterio de Meira*, p. 193; Rodríguez Galdo, *Señores y campesinos*, p. 210).

7   García de Cortázar, *La sociedad rural*, pp. 149–78.

second tier, beneath the king and the high lay and ecclesiastic nobility, he places 'the community's intermediaries, *hidalgos* and *hombres buenos*, a true village aristocracy, occasionally in contact, too, with the bourgeoning townsmen. These are, by definition,' he says, 'the rentiers managing the rents of the nobility', while recognizing the need to study the issue in greater depth.

My goal is not to add to the information we already have about the *foros* granted to non-farmers prior to the sixteenth century. Rather, I believe that what is needed in any study on the social structures of the medieval countryside are different perspectives and new hypotheses so that we can craft a more nuanced approach to the testimonies with which we are already familiar. Over the last several years, microanalytical research has proven very effective in European historiography, enabling us to reach a more concrete understanding of the societies of the past.[8] As G. Bois has defended,[9] it is this small-scale approach that will allow us not only to understand the essential changes in the system, but also to become familiar with the men, families and farms in each individual village. As argued by G. Levi, one of the foremost representatives of microhistory, this is the approach that will enable us to arrive at a less anonymous, typological reading of social realities.[10]

It is from this perspective of local analysis that I hope to shed light — in a research project that extends far beyond the scope of this paper — on the social relations that structured the rural communities in one area of the Galician province of Ourense during the medieval period. Tracing ties of kinship and neighbourhood, uncovering patterns of antagonism and solidarity, determining how networks of patronage and clientship were built, and even naming some of the key players, is work that will necessarily yield elements to help us understand how social differentiation worked in practice, and how power took shape and became stratified at the local level.

The source materials for this work in progress are from monastic institutions in the Diocese of Ourense: Ramiranes, Rocas, Santa Cristina y San Esteban de Ribas de Sil, Montederramo, Melón, Sobrado de Trives, Celanova, San Clodio, and more. These collections are irregular, both in absolute figures and in terms of the centuries that they cover. Here, although I will also make use of prior and subsequent information, I will work with documents from the thirteenth and fourteenth centuries, which exhibit a greater degree of regularity and homogeneity. The documentation is mostly made up of leases (*cartas forales*). These legal documents, despite their apparent uniformity, express the various social hierarchies, as is also true of the less frequent donations, purchases and exchanges.[11] This documentation sheds light on highly localized areas that revolve around the monasteries' sphere of influence, but with

---

8 Some of the most recent publications that have inspired my research are: Davies, *Small Worlds*; Wickham, *The Mountains and the City*. I share many of the theoretical and conceptual approaches in Sabean, *Power in the Blood*, on villages in the Duchy of Württemberg in the modern period. Some results of G. Levi's work on a seventeenth-century Piedmont village can be found in his book Levi, *L'eredità immateriale*.

9 Bois, 'Poder y parentesco'.

10 Levi, 'Terra e strutture familiari', p. 1095.

11 The expression *carta foral* encompasses a wide array — in both form and content — of agrarian

highly diverse relationships to the real political centres — the region's towns (*villas*) and castles — as well as to the bishop of Ourense.

With the help of the abundant documentation from the nunnery of Ramiranes, we will focus on the valley of the same name, along with the surrounding mountains to the southeast. The cartulary of this convent is the corpus I have been able to study the most exhaustively so far, as it provides easy access to almost 600 documents, of which over 350 date from the thirteenth to fourteenth centuries and concentrate on a relatively small area.[12]

The valley is irrigated by the Tuño River (called Eires in the documents), a tributary of the Arnoya, which goes on to join the Miño from its left bank. It is an area with a relatively dense settlement pattern of modestly sized village territories (*villas*) that appear to contain a diffuse network of tiny settlements, as can be inferred from the frequent mention of *locos* ('places') associated to dwellings. The territory (*termino*) of these *villas* is first documented during the thirteenth century, just before or at the same time as the parish becomes the dominant spatial frame of reference. Although there were many of them, churches are not documented in every village. It is, therefore, a settlement pattern in the process of defining itself territorially, as certain local centres begin to acquire predominance. This is expressed from the early thirteenth century by the fact that people — not just the land — start to be named as inhabitants of a given place or parish. Determining the logic behind this process of self-definition, along with the elements that make up the identity of these communities, is part of the task that lies ahead.[13]

Generally speaking, the *villas* and *locos* seem to contain the living quarters (house and enclosures) of the *casales*, which were the basic units of production. For the area and period under study, however, the *casal* (roughly, 'household') seems to be more of an organizational concept than a coherent and stably structured unit, although in some cases a single *casal* may constitute the settlement itself. In the texts from Ramiranes, throughout the century most of the land grants consist of plots, or groups of isolated plots, belonging to a larger farming unit, e.g. *leira de casal de Monte en villa de Eires* ('a strip of land belonging to *casal de Monte* in the *villa* of Eires'), or *un terreno de casal de X* ('a piece of land of *casal X*'). The plots associated with a *casal* had clearly

---

land grants. I use the term in the general sense, making specifications as necessary, in order to avoid unnecessary labels or schematic typologies.

12   The documentation has been published in SPRamirás. Documents from the mid-fourteenth century onwards have not been transmitted in full, but only in summaries, which rules out the same sort of in-depth analysis carried out up to this point.

13   The common Spanish word *aldea*, which is used for example in the 1199 *Fuero* of nearby Milmanda (AlfonsoIX-19, 1199) to refer to its outlying villages, is not used in Ramiranes until the fifteenth century — assuming that the summary of SPRamirás473 (1450) is literal, since the term *aldea* is not used in any prior record. Therefore, here I will not use *aldea* as a synonym of *villa*, as one normally would in Spanish. The hierarchical sense that the term retains even today, with a *villa* being larger than an *aldea*, may lead to confusion for periods in which these processes are still underway. I will therefore use the terms 'local community' or 'local society' as a concept that expresses the social interrelations mediated by diverse factors of ownership, tenancy, kinship, clientship, neighbourhood, etc. Understood in this way, community exists even without institutional formalization, and in sparsely populated areas.

defined boundaries, but were generally mixed in with other plots belonging to different *casales*. As such, these are terms that cover heavily fragmented groups of lands, which are granted, alienated or transmitted separately, and thus not forming cohesive units. While this topic and its subsequent evolution merit a more careful examination, it is beyond the scope of this paper, although it will come up throughout.[14]

The economic reorganization apparently reflected in these massive land leases (*foro*) starting in the thirteenth century, overseen by the monastic land managers — and not just in Ramiranes — is especially aimed, at least at the outset, at clearing uncultivated woodland (*monte*). As such, it is difficult to interpret them as having resulted from the disintegration of a theoretical 'reserve' that had previously been farmed directly.[15] But what about leases of already cultivated land? Were they part of estates that had previously been farmed directly? Classic bipartite domains were not at all widespread in these regions — certainly not in Ramiranes, in any case. While this issue must of course be developed in greater depth, I am inclined to believe that what mainly takes place in the thirteenth century, in parallel to the expansion of farmland, is that many earlier customary-law 'contracts' between the monasteries and people who were in fact already their dependents, were finally put into writing.[16]

Given how spread out the settlements and plots of farmland are, the frame of reference I will use is the parish (*feligresía*), which is the unit that, throughout the period under study, most clearly comes to predominate, and which will help us to organize the data and track the overall process. On either side of the aforementioned Eires river are many of the *villas* and *locos* about which we have the most information, nestled in the Ramiranes valley, an area of fertile soil stretching between two low mountains, Silvaoscura to the west and Paizás to the east. They belong to, or are gradually incorporated into, on the left bank, the parishes of Santa María de Villameá, San Salvador de Penosiños, Santiago de Rubias, and the monastery of San Pedro de Ramiranes itself; and, on the right, Santa María de Freás, San Jorge de Acevedo, and San Salvador de Paizás. Santa Eufemia and Santa María de Milmanda are located between the two branches of the Eires, and, in the mountains, to the southeast, are Santa María and San Pedro de Leirado. They are parishes that have survived into the present with little variation, but which, in the period under study, were just being consolidated.[17]

---

14 The bibliography on peasant households as the feudal system's basic units of production is as extensive as it is irregular. On Galicia, see, in addition to the works cited in n. 4, Pallares and Portela, 'Aproximación al estudio'; Jiménez Gómez, 'Análisis de la terminología'.

15 On the characteristics of Galicia's woodlands, its highly fragmentary farmlands, and the ecological conditions contributing to the porous distribution and small size of the region's settlements, see García Fernández, *Organización del espacio*, esp. pp. 80 ff., and in general the entire second part of the book.

16 I do believe that it would be of great interest to consider some of the issues that historians of other regions of Europe have raised regarding whether there was differentiation between tenants based on those who had a written contract and those who did not. In England this is the difference between copy and customary tenants, and in Italy, between *libellarii* and *massaricii*. See a good summary of the relevant approaches and bibliography in Wickham, *The Mountains and the City*, pp. 224–37.

17 Risco, *Geografía general*.

We do not know when the parish churches were founded, but isolated data that match up with known processes from other areas indicate that they 'belonged' to certain families or even communities of *hereditarii* before gradually being passed on to the monastery. These churches possess assets indicative of prior devotion and alliances, and which form the material basis of the power of their clergymen. In this area the latter are closely connected to Ramiranes, so much so that they form part, alongside the nuns, of the conventual chapter. The rural clergy's ties to the monasteries is a relatively widespread phenomenon throughout medieval Europe, either because the churches had become the property of a nearby monastery, or because the monastery had become the churches' patron, thereby gaining the right to represent them. However, in Ramiranes, as with other convents, the fact that it was a female monastery explains the multiple functions that the clergymen there had to fulfil. Duro Peña, who is well-versed in the monastic life of Ourense, has suggested that this association of clerics and monks, as in other monasteries in the region, could derive from its origins as the double monastery of a kin group.[18] Some of these clergymen are particularly well documented, and, by examining their family ties and local connections, we can begin to analyse the network of relationships and models of social organization of these rural communities of parishioners, in which they seem to have played a major role. *Fernandus Martini*,[19] prelate of Villamediana (today Villameá), is a good example of a landowner who forged ties with the monastery in order to consolidate his power at the local level. This can be inferred from the fact that he founded an anniversary service for the monastery's deceased nuns and clerics with the donation of a *casal* in the *villa* of Eires, in the parish in which he would eventually become rector. We do not know if the church was already a family possession, but he did manage to pass it on to his son *Martino Fernandi*, who, in turn, would go on to earn the rank of priest, as well as becoming administrator of the assets of the *opera* of Sancti Petri.[20] Both were key players in the community, but the son's activities and power perhaps illustrates better what it meant to be a parish priest. He participates as a witness as well as a scribe in many of the monastery's affairs, but comes to occupy a preeminent position in those that directly affect what we can assume to be his own family assets (whether enjoyed through ownership or tenancy). Thus, when another cleric, *Fernandus Petri*, was granted in *foro* a strip of

---

18 Duro Peña, 'El monasterio de San Pedro de Ramiranes', pp. 36–39. This opinion is taken up in Lucas Álvarez and Lucas Domínguez, *San Pedro de Ramirás*, pp. 34–37. According to E. Portela, the two characteristics that clearly stand out in eleventh-century Galician monasteries (similarly to those in nearby Portugal studied by Mattoso), are the fact that they were double monasteries, and that they were founded through family estates. Their eventual incorporation into Cluny did not keep their patrons, who were members of the various dominant social groups, from making political and economic use of the monasteries and priories. Portela, *La colonización cisterciense*, p. 30 ff.

19 Data on Fernandus Martini: SPRamirás11, 12, 14, 19, 27, 29.

20 While this is impossible to prove, it is by no means improbable. The fact that Martino Fernandi appears in certain transactions involving assets that belonged to Fernandus Martini, along with the former's patronymic, appears to indicate ties that go beyond the mere administrative duties of a rector, or even the administration of the rest of his church's assets. The information appears in documents SPRamirás10, 14, 19, 23, 27, 28, 29, 30, 41, 51, 78, 92.

land in the *casal* that *Fernandus Martini* had donated, among the usual authorities cited as legitimizing the documents (the king, the bishop of Ourense, the abbot of Celanova, or the royal delegates in Santa Cruz and Milmanda) we also find the *prelatus ecclesie de Villamediana Martinus Fernandi*. Similarly, he appears separately at the head of the list of witnesses in a document granting the cleric *Petro Iohannis* a portion of woodland near the monastery, bordering on vineyards said to belong to *Martinus Fernandi* and to *don Fernandus Martini*.

The documents do not mention the size or condition of his estate, but do indicate that he held the *casal* in Eires, and that he gained rent and vassals by leasing out portions of it. Both the aforementioned cleric and one *Rodericus Fernandi* were *foreros* of strips of land (*leiras*) of this *casal*, and had to pay Fernandus Martini part of the land's yields as rent, in addition to their heirs becoming his vassals. His position as prelate of the local church would enable him to form his own clientship network, such that in 1250 we find him at the head of a group of relatives and neighbours, transferring to *Pedro Velasco* and his wife lands belonging to *casales* in his parish. These people are smallholders — their plots are cited as boundary references — and are also *foreros* of certain lands belonging to the *casales* of the monastery. Some appear as witnesses, but not all of them, and not often. They may have continued to farm these lands now under the control and management of *Pedro Velasco*,[21] who in turn paid rent and might himself have worked the land, while perhaps still belonging to the group of notables, or *bonos homines*, of the society of the valley. To his actions in other periods we will return further along.[22] Born in Villamediana — where he had connections to the previous parish priest, from whom in 1225 he received a *leira* of inherited land in *foro* — he was a landowner who sold several lands to the monastery, and appears to have risen through the ranks of society, as demonstrated by the multiple grant mentioned above. Late in life he shows up as judge in a case pitting Ramiranes against Celanova.

San Salvador de Penosiños may be another example of a church controlled by a landowning and *forero* family in the same area. The church was led by the *Lupi* family, members of which can be found among the nuns and clerics who head the church throughout the thirteenth century. Even in the fourteenth century, a member of the clan shows up as the monastery's cellarer: *Alfonso Petri*, son of *Petrus Lupi*. We will return to them later on.[23]

We will now turn to other members of the chapter of Ramiranes who, despite appearing not to have a permanent pastoral mission there, cannot be regarded as mere

---

21 Data on Pedro Velasco: SPRamirás 12, 33, 75, 78, 153, 197.

22 This somewhat vague term seems to refer to a broad category of people vested with a certain degree of local public authority in resolving conflicts, reaching agreements, establishing rents, and acting as judges or *inquisitores*; in other words, having the authority to enforce the law. Of interest for observing how this term spread to other regions of Europe is the definition given in the glossary section of Davies and Fouracre, eds, *The Settlement of Disputes*.

23 A group of people who share the last name Lupi and have ties to the parish of San Salvador de Penosiños. Exactly how they are related is not always clear, but there is enough sound data to infer some type of kinship. However, it is beyond the scope this paper to examine the details of each individual case.

administrators of the conventual estate either. They certainly do not form a homogeneous group by any measure, whether social, economic, or, least of all, ecclesiastic. Indeed, the ecclesiastic ranks they are able to attain throughout their lives are surely linked to their family status and their alliances inside and outside the monastery. They benefit from monastic grants of various sorts and under diverse conditions. Some of them hold monastic farmlands, from which they in turn lease out plots for rent. We have already seen the rectors of Villamediana, but their situation is also shared by men like *Petrus Menendi*,[24] *Fernandus Roderici*,[25] *Martinus Petri*[26] and several others, who collect and store in their granaries the rents produced by the lands they have given in *foro*. In other cases it is not clear whether they are actually detached from working the land directly, as they are still obliged to cultivate and pay rent for plots received directly from the monastery or through other clerics who held them from it. This is likely the situation of the aforementioned clerics *Fernando Petri* and *Pedro Iohannis*, who received *leiras* from the prelate of Villamediana. It is also the case of the priest *Pedro Villanova*,[27] who, alongside his brother *Michael Petri*, obtained lands in similar conditions, in terms of farming and rents, as those of many *foreros*. This is also similar to the circumstances of clerics tenanting vineyards bordering on other lands being farmed.[28] Thus, as payers or recipients of rent, or in both roles at different points in time, the clergymen of Ramiranes seem to be at the centre of a clientship network that defines relationships with the outside world through the monastery, its nuns and its patrons, as well as locally, both with the various ranks of the peasantry (which are not always fully defined), as well as with the region's *milites* and squires.

Of the latter, we know quite a bit about *Petrus Petri, dictus Romeus*,[29] *de Penosiños*, although it is unclear whether this geographical reference is based on his family origins or on properties he acquired in the area. Penosiños is a parish dedicated to the Holy Saviour, located to the north of the parish of Villameá, in the foothills of mount Silvaoscura, which, as we have seen, delimits the valley of Ramiranes from the west. *Pedro Romeu* appears to have entered the monastic clientship network through cleric *Fernando Petri* — with whom, based on the last name, we can imagine there may have been family ties. In 1238 the latter gave Romeu a *leira* from the *casal de Monte* that the cleric had in the *villa* of Eires. The grant was for Romeu's lifetime, without the ability to pass it on, and with the obligation to pay a quarter of the land's annual yields into Petri's granary. In subsequent years *Pedro Romeu* shows up among the monastic witnesses, and in 1251 is recorded as one of a group of *milites* linked to the monastery, who took part in a relatively important ceremony that merits examination, given its similarity to another event held that same year that centreed directly on Romeu.[30]

---

24 Data on *Pedro Menendi*: SPRamirás27, 29, 31, 32, 35, 47, 52 bis.
25 Data on *Fernando Roderici*: SPRamirás52, 66, 82, 117, 132, 133.
26 Data on *Martinus Petri*: SPRamirás14, 27, 28, 30, 45, 47, 49, 55, 57, 67, 132, 137, 235.
27 Data on *Pedro Villanova*: SPRamirás19, 20, 21, 22, 35. He also appears as a witness in many others.
28 Documents regarding Montecillo: SPRamirás3, 10, 13, 19, 25, 29, 36.
29 Data on *Pedro Romeu*: documents SPRamirás26, 80, 83, 89, 111, 121, 122(?), 132, 144, 155, 158, 199, 200, 221. See Fig. 6.1.
30 SPRamirás83 (1251): 'do et concedo tibi Petro Gomez sextam partem hereditatis que est in uilla aut in termino de Leirado, de ipso nostro casali et dicitur Cidilubu. Do tibi ipsam tali pacto quod tenas

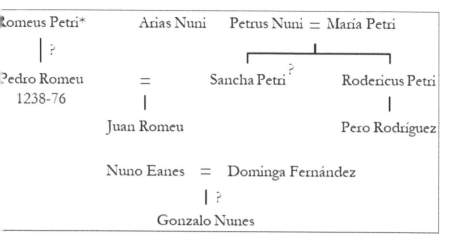

Figure 6.1. Pedro Romeu and his family group.[31]

In both cases, they are lifetime grants aimed at recovering the monastery's properties and incorporating them into the farming operation (*casal, heredad*) to which they belong. However, it is not so much a matter of territorial integration, but rather one

---

eam in uita tua et ad mortem tuam permaneat libera in pace ipso iam dicto casali. Statuo etiam tecum quod quantum potueris pro ueritate inuenire per te at per alios bonos homines quod abet ipsum casal in Retortoiru et in quantis eciam locis in ipsa uilla aut in suo termino scias inde ueritatem et extrae illam per custam tuam et per custam monasterii Ramiranis, scilicet de rousuas, et tene ipsam in uita tua' (I give and grant you, Pedro Gómez, one sixth of the estate that is in the village and territory of Leirado, belonging to our casal, which is called Cidilubu. I give it to you with the understanding that you have said casal during your lifetime and after your death it shall be released peacefully. I also order that you shall inquire truthfully, whether by yourself or through homines bonos, what newly claimed land belongs to this casal in Retortoiro and in whatever other places inside that village and its territory, that you find out the truth on your own behalf and that of the monastery of Ramiranes).

SPRamirás89 (1251): 'damus atque concedimus tibi Petro Romeu et uxori tue Sancie Petri unam nostram hereditatem quam abemus in termino de Penosiños in loco qui dicitur Abrigeiras, et fuit de domna Sancia Petri. Damus uobis ipsam hereditatem quomodo illam melius potueritis inuenire cum bonis omnibus sibi pertinentibus, tali pacto quod in uita uestrorum anborum detis inde clericis et monialibus Ramiranis XII solidos pro quadragesima mediante quando canitur "Letare Iherusalem"; et abeatis ipsam in uita uestra per hoc pactum. Post mortem uestram permaneat libera in pace supradictis clericis et monialibus Ramiranis' (We give and grant you Pedro Romeu and your wife Sancia Petri an estate of ours that we have in the territory of Penosiños, in the place called Abrigeiras, which used to belong to doña Sancia Petri. We give our estate as good as you find it, with all its appurtenances, on the condition that during your lives both of you give to the clerics and nuns of Ramiranes twelve solidi by mid-Easter, when they usually sing 'Letare Iherusalem', and that you have it for your life under this agreement, and after your death, let it return peacefully to the aforesaid clerics and nuns of Ramiranes').

31 We do not know the names of Pedro Romeu's ancestors. He may have been the son of Romeus Petri, a public notary and scribe who served Bishop Juan of Orense (SPRocas28, 1256).

of verifying and asserting their rights over them. In both cases, the assets granted (including the ones they will recover) reveal certain family ties that are traceable in the case of *Fernando Petri*, and explicit in that of *Pedro Romeu*, describing assets in the place called *Abrigeiros* that had belonged to his wife, *doña Sancha Petri*. In contrast, neither of the two grants includes rent, since, in my opinion, the twelve *solidi* that *Pedro Romeu* and his wife are to pay to the clerics and nuns of Ramiranes each year 'in the middle of Easter, when they usually sing *Letare Iherusalem*' should not be understood as rent.

Perhaps there is nothing more to say about the parallels between the two transactions. *Pedro Romeus* is a *miles* accompanied by *milites*; *Pedro Gómez*, the subject of the other document, is a *bonus homo* aided in his pursuit of the truth by 'other good men'. In any case, rather than comparing the circumstances of two individuals, it is more interesting to compare their family and social contexts, which I have begun to examine in the case of *Pedro Romeus de Penosiños*, and which we will see further on in the case of *Pedro Gómez de Leirado*. However, before moving on, there are a few more considerations about the texts at hand that will be important to bear in mind during our analysis. These documents are about Ramiranes's seigneurial power; about how it is exercised locally by the *milites* and *bonos homines*, who are part of the monastery's clientship network; about how it is contested by peasants who collaboratively conceal plots provisionally cleared out of the woodland (*rousas*); about the profits it yields and the rents they will receive upon verification. In short, the relationships of domination and dependence that this situation engenders at multiple levels. We will have the opportunity to return to this subject when discussing the local political milieu of each of the various communities.

For now we will continue with *Pedro Romeu*, who by the mid-thirteenth century was established in Penosiños, with *casales* bordering the woodland called Monte del Mayordomo, also bordered by the cleric *Iohannes Lupit* on one side, and by Lupit's father, *Lupo Ordiniii*, on the other. This situates him among the relatively important landowners and tenants. Years later, it is in this parish, San Salvador, that Romeu and his wife received 'for your lifetime all the rights and appurtenances that we (Ramiranes) have in Vincis and in the land that Ihoannes Petri (a servant of the aforementioned cleric *Iohannes Lupit*) held in *foro* from us'. According to this pact, *Pedro Romeu* was obliged, at wine-pressing time, to furnish either one modius of wine or one maravedí, two capons, one sack of wheat, and *unan quartam de vino*. Although not specified in the document, based on other similar contracts we can infer that *Pedro Romeu* would in turn receive rent for the part that had already been leased to him via *foro*, situating this contract among one of the various forms of *subforo*, although this is not made explicit.

He continues to appear as a witness in documents that, while probably drawn up in the monastery, refer to lands outside the valley of Ramiranes, in Deva and Valongo, parishes along the banks of the river Miño on the other side of mount Silvaoscura. It is logical to imagine that this type of ceremonies, which at times brought together people from an array of places linked in one way or another to Ramiranes, must have served to showcase the links and ties formalized in the document being drawn up, while also serving as an occasion to establish or renew alliances with those in

LOCAL POWER AND INTERNAL DIFFERENTIATION   261

attendance. It is therefore worthwhile to examine who attended such gatherings and with whom, and on which occasions certain individuals came together to act as witnesses to these signing ceremonies.

Before turning to *Petro Nuni*, another *miles* present at many of the same signings as *Pedro Romeu*, we might first have a look at the fate of *Romeu's* assets and status. He last appears as a witness in 1276, when he must have been over sixty, alongside his son *Juan Romeu*,[32] also a squire, meaning that the younger Romeu inherited his father's clientship relations, although he never appears as a *miles*. Recall, however, that we do not know how many of the older Romeu's properties and tenancies were granted just for his own lifetime. In fact, in 1311 the monastery seems to have absorbed the portion purchased by *Pedro Romeu*, in Abrigeiros, joining them to the two *quartas* that they already possessed. In exchange, *Juan Romeu* receives, for his lifetime 'and no more', the *casal* of Monte, of which his father had received a tract in his youth. The notable insistence on the tenancy's temporary nature, and on the fact that upon his death it must be returned to the monastery empty, 'without any contents', seems to indicate that perhaps Juan Romeu's designs in fact were just the opposite. His son, *Nuno Eanes*, the grandson of *Pedro Romeu*, seems only to inherit the family ties to Ramiranes and the benefits that such a relationship entails.[33] This same year, one month later, we see him alongside his wife, Dominga Fernández, receiving two *casales* in the parish of Penosiños, which they can indeed pass on for one generation after them to a person of similar condition. However, they will have to pay rent in proportion to the harvest, along with other customary rights, thus becoming monastic vassals.

Petro Nuni is another *miles* with significant assets in the parish of Penosiños:[34] two *casales* in the hamlet of Calvos form part of the properties that he gives his wife *María Petri*, 'as a donation and for the purchase of your body, and as a bridal payment'. However, it appears that *Petro Nuni* actually possessed many more assets, including one *casal* in Orvan, to the south of the area at hand, and another in Ramiranes, both part of the properties paid to the bride *en arras*. This last property, in Ramiranes, is where Petro Nuni's daughter *Sancha Petri* lived. While it is tempting to infer that this is the wife of *Pedro Romeu*, this cannot be verified in the documentation, beyond learning that she possessed family assets in the area, and that we can only follow her lineage through this line. It is equally unclear whether the *almunario* who was present when Jacebanes was granted in *foro* to a group of eight families is the same *Petrus Nuni* or someone else by the same name, nor is it clear how he might be related to the nuns and other relevant figures who share his last name. What is clear is that he intervenes in socially important events, such as a ceremony held in the presence of the bishop, the archdeacon and a canon of the Cathedral of Ourense, where he acts as witness to a grant benefiting Pedro Abad in Valongo, a parish where the grantee will later become parish priest, and where Petro Nuni himself has several possessions. We know some of his men — *Matinus Silvester homo de don Petrus Nuni* — and we also know

---

32   Data on Juan Romeu: SPRamirás211, 234, 265, 266.
33   Data on Nuno Eanes: SPRamirás265, 266.
34   Data on Petro Nuni-Munit: SPRamirás23, 28, 32, 35, 54, 81(?), 83, 109(?), 121, 187, 227.

Don Johannis Fernandi	=	Doña Sancia Gundisalui
	Don Gundisaluus Iohannis	

Figure 6.2. Information about Doyane and his family group.

that he was majordomo to *Doyane*,[35] a clearly important character who is beyond the scope of this paper. In both spatial and social terms, then, his circle of relations appears to be broader than that of Pedro Romeu, but nevertheless remains within the local society we are examining, although he likely had alliances with and even belonged to the regional lay nobility.

So far, we have focused mainly on the clerics and notables of the valley parishes, but it will be useful to return to our examination, begun several pages ago, of the similarities and differences with other groups of *villas* in the mountains. Leirado is a *villa* in the Penagache mountains, to the southwest of the valley of Ramiranes, which had two associated churches, San Pedro and Santa María. Abbess Ona of Ramiranes disputed the patronage of these two churches with the clerics *Petrus Ermigii and Martinus Ermigii*, in a 1259 suit before the bishop of Ourense, alleging that the *ius patronatus* belonged to the monastery, as it had been bequeathed by Rodrigo Fernández and Pedro Gómez from her grandparents' line, who were memorialized in that church. Advised by experts, the bishop's verdict awarded this right in its entirety to the abbess, and ordered the cited rectors to receive Ona as patron on behalf of the monastery.[36]

This document is of great interest, because it reveals frictions between two family groups within the same *villa*. The fact that such a tiny settlement had two churches might also be a reflection of this situation. Other documents offer grounds for further inquiry. We have seen how in 1251 *Pedro Gómez* received from the monastery one sixth of an estate in the *casal* of Cidilibu, with the obligation to determine which other plots belonged to this *casal* within the *villa* and outlying areas of Leirado.[37] His ties to Ramiranes are underscored in 1256, when he declares himself their humble vassal and stipulates that he should be buried there ('mandum ibi corpus meum'), donating all his properties in Leirado, including his corresponding share of the churches of Santa María and San Pedro — the subject of the future suit involving the abbess.

This is not, however, a will written up late in life, but rather a business deal that will affect his personal circumstances for at least twenty more years, when, as an old man, he finally ratifies this donation and requests a ration of food and clothing from the monastery. Following this act, we see that his status on the majority of his properties changes to that of tenant, which is in fact rather common among other landowners. His circumstances, however, appear not to worsen; on the contrary, everything indicates that they actually improve. He continues to collect rent from those supposedly working these lands, between early September and St Martin's day

---

35 Data on *Doyane*: SPRamirás52, 218, 227. I am inclined to believe that it is the same man who appears as tenant of Santa Cruz and Milmanda during the same period. See Fig. 6.2.

36 SPRamirás137 (1259).

37 Data on Pedro Gómez: SPRamirás83, 133, 137, 213.

(11 November), and stipulates that should he die between these dates, the rent should be passed on to the monastery chapter. But during his own lifetime he will not have to give anything to the monastery; rather, in light of his material and personal ties, it is the monastery that will each year give him 'three modii of rye, one of millet and four modii of wine, the cereal at threshing and the wine at the pressing [...] and also one pig, or eight solidi in its place, by St Martin and also thirty solidi at Christmas for clothing'.

There are reasons to believe that this act was a way of becoming a lay participant (*porcionero*) without having a pastoral mission or living in the monastery, since it envisages the possibility of staying there as a guest, thereby receiving the same rations as a clergyman. Moreover, Pedro Gómez takes this donation of his assets and his person to the extreme of promising to defend it 'from that woman that claims to be my daughter and from the one I now live with'. There is no indication as to why he disinherits these two women. Pedro Gómez's close alliance with Ramiranes could have been an attempt to become the parish priest of the two churches, or at least to reinforce his local standing against the *Hermigii*, a more powerful family with ties to Milmanda, the most politically important centre in the surrounding area.

The *Hermigii* family had assets in Leirado; for example, farmlands of *Maiore Hermigii* and *María Hermigii*, probably the sisters of the two aforementioned clerics, are cited there as bordering on the *casal* in Lama that the monastery leases out by *foro* in 1253. Given the dispute mentioned earlier, it is to be assumed that up until this point the *Hermigii* had operated outside the monastic sphere.[38] We are told nothing about the clerics' allegations in the suit, nor about who filed them, but the very fact of acting as rectors, along with other isolated bits of evidence, shows that they must indeed have had such rights. The ruling in favour of the monastery does not do away with them, but merely integrates them into the monastery's clientship, forcing them to recognize the abbess as their patron. Information from the last third of the thirteenth century through the fourteenth century sheds light on the *casales* in this parish that were held by members of this family, whose tenancy was passed down throughout the period. They refer to *Don Hermigio* as owning one of the *casales* in Leirado. I believe that this common ancestor is *Hermigio Munionis*, who in a 1219 document from Ramiranes shows up as a judge in Milmanda, and in 1223 and 1225 as tenant of the Castle of Santa Cruz. *Don Hermigio* is among those present at a private act of sale held in Milmanda (1232). Sometime after the suit, in 1271, the monastery granted, alongside another *casal*, most of the *casal* of Fondoes, 'which used to belong to Don Hermigio', to the knight *Martino Hermigii*, which is the same name as one of the rectors of the churches of Leirado, and possibly the same man who in 1254 appeared as a witness alongside *Didacus Hermigii* and *Laurencius Hermigii*, mayor of Milmanda, in an important monastic ceremony. In exchange for the goods received, *Martin Hermigii*, leaves upon his death another *casal* in Leirado and orders that his body be buried at the monastery of Ramiranes. We know that through the wife of this

---

38 Here again I have used this patronymic, which is quite unusual in this corpus, to encompass a group whose ties are confirmed directly or indirectly by other information. I have left out all cases giving rise to doubt. Data on them: SPRamirás9, 11, 14, 17, 78, 83, 86, 101, 111, 137, 157, 176, 187, 227, 231, 280, 322.

knight — *Mayor Stephani* — the foregoing *casal*, along with three others, as well as hereditary estates, leases, rights and renders in the parish of Santa María de Leirado, were all passed on to *Rodrigo Hermiges*, clearly a descendant of this line, who lived in Milmanda. The monastery allowed him to keep these assets until the mid-fourteenth century. This family, connected to the tenancy of the fortress of Milmanda and to its council, clearly formed part of the nobility, even though not all of its members enjoyed the same status. A study of this kin group would fall outside the scope of both our documentation and our aims with this paper, merely aimed at determining their impact at the local level.

The relatively scant documentation on Leirado offers little more information, but there is still a bit more that can be said. The confrontation between the *Hermigii* clerics and Ramiranes for control over the churches of Leirado — along with the clerics' alleged affront against the abbess — ultimately indicates that neither of these groups had total control over the *villa* or, by extension, its inhabitants. It is this tension that perhaps enabled independent landowners to emerge, the *hereditarii de Leirado* or *hereditarii de Quintela*, who show up in boundary descriptions throughout this area.[39] Historians are far from having determined the nature of this group of people, generally assuming that they are free smallholders whose ties with the monasteries, via *foro* contracts, grow progressively stronger as more and more woodland is cleared. This also appears to be the case in our area of study, but there are still unresolved questions that I will merely raise. For example, how are we to understand the fact that Ramiranes promises to protect its *foreros* in Jacebanes, except from *hereditarii* demanding services of them?[40] I wonder if the term in question, *hereditatores* or *heredes*, might actually involve multiple realities, as in the case of *boni homines* or even *vasallos*. Moreover, the fact that they are named in the plural indicates that they form a group acting as such. Likewise, when *hereditarii* are mentioned among the boundaries of adjacent lands, or when they grant an asset, the term seems to indicate a common possession. To cite just one case, in Vegas de Deva, in the lower part of Leirado, one document describes a plot that borders on *hereditatoribus de Leirado*, as well as a plot that Vivian Munit held from *hereditatoribus*.[41] Could it be that there is some sort of consortium or *germanitas* in which the assets — even if they are divided up — remain within the family group? Some documents mention *socios* or *heredes*; the fact that monasteries allow and even plan for siblings or relatives to be admitted as *socios*, *participes* or *consortes* entitled to take part in an inherited *foro*, may indicate

---

39 SPRamirás11, 86, 168.

40 SPRamirás28 (1240): 'et semper setis fideles vasalli de monasterio supradicto, et monasterium defendat uos pro posse suo contra omnes. Quod si non potuerit det uos amparatorem; tantum non amparet uos contra hereditarios quo uos faciatis eis servicium' (That you forever be loyal vassals of said monastery and that the monastery shall protect you as best as it can from everyone. And if it cannot, that it shall provide you with a defender to fend for you except from the hereditarii to whom you pay service'). The clause is repeated in SPRamirás146 (1262) and SPRamirás169 (1268), with the only difference that in them tantum is replaced by tamen. The text's meaning, therefore, is not completely clear.

41 SPRamirás86 (1251).

that it is a widespread practice. Thus, we ought not to imagine it as being restricted to smallholders or the humblest of the *foreros*.[42]

Despite the limited information available on Leirado, we know from a 1218 *inquisitio* ordered by Alfonso IX at the request of Celanova that it fell within the jurisdictional space of this monastery, which adds another level of authority to the ones we have already discussed.[43] However, based on the documents we have already examined, as well as the *inquisitio* itself (which shows how difficult it was for this jurisdictional authority to define itself territorially), we can question the practical effectiveness of exercising such power without defining it at the local level on a personal basis.[44] Let us recall the agreement between Ramiranes and *Pedro Gómez* (in which Celanova does not participate at all, despite the fact that the place in question falls under its jurisdiction), alongside other *boni homines*, to seek out the truth regarding estates that had been lost, and along with them rents and other unpaid benefits. In the document, he agrees to share the costs with the monastery, indicating both a difficult and costly situation (suits? complaints? paid alliances?) and reveals how individuals could find themselves caught up in the actual intricacies of power struggles. But it also points to the means used for its legitimation; a truth investigated by *boni homines* and ratified as such can ultimately reach greater consensus.

The jurisdictions overlap, intersect and mix because the settlement pattern is so diffuse, limiting the ability to effectively control the peasant population. This is what makes it interesting to investigate the real workings of these communities beneath their formally recognized authorities, whose effectiveness depends on their ability to work from within the very social structure of these communities. In the case of *Leirado*, a *villa* outside the jurisdiction of Ramiranes, we have seen the two most prominent family clans face off; in fact, the monastery allied itself with the weaker side, a *bonus homo*, against members of the lesser aristocracy, which controlled the church. Another example of a *bonus homo* could be *Vivian Munit*, a tenant who pays rent to the monastery, in addition to being a *forero* of the local *hereditatores*. On these and other peasants who worked the land, there is such little information in the documents that we can hardly examine them here.

---

42 There is a very interesting suit from SPRamirás3 (1137) between Ramiranes and Álvaro Rubio with his associates, who in the rest of the document are referred to simply as *hereditatores*, of whom Álvaro Rubio acts as representative (*vocifero*) in the trial held before the emperor. On *participes* and *consortes* see SPRamirás56 (1248), where the monastery, after leasing a tract of woodland (*monte*) in *foro* to Munio Gundisalui and his wife María Fernandi, agrees 'that in said woodland Juan González and Pedro González and Rodrigo González shall participate and hold their share of four fifths, according to the above partition agreement' ('quod in predicto monte sint uobiscum Iohannes Gundisalui et P. Gundisalui et Rodericus Gundisalui, participes et consortes per quatuor quiniones ad pactum quod est diuisum superius').

43 Published by Rodríguez, 'El Coto de Celanova'.

44 The inquiry arose out of a conflict between the abbot of Celanova and don Pedro Fernández, 'knight of Caparin, tenant of the castles of Santa Cruz and Sande [...] over their jurisdiction, boundaries and legal statutes', in which the abbot declares he has been wronged by the knight. The king orders that *boni homines* be elected in order to verify which rights over these places correspond to Celanova and which to the *dominus terre*.

266 ISABEL ALFONSO

For *Villameá* and *Penosiños*, parishes in the sphere of Ramiranes,[45] we have examined the leading role of their clergymen — whether church rectors or not — in building relationships with the various layers of village society. In these societies, the lay notables — some of them militarized, like Pedro Romeu — show up in the documents as having ties to the monastery, actively taking part in the downward expansion of the latter's clientship network. We will likewise not take up the lowest echelons of peasant society in this area either, although in this case we do have the data. Suffice it to say that we do find ties of kinship, neighbourhood, friendship and clientship between this group and the other strata. The significant hierarchization of these communities is even more pronounced in Leirado.

My aim in this paper has been to demonstrate the complex differentiation of this social fabric, and the elements that mediated in the relations between people — their different options to access land and the diverse conditions of tenancy in terms of time, size, rent and obligations, but also the different clientship networks to which the land was linked. What we see, in short, is that this society, albeit stratified, cannot be reduced to a binary opposition between lords and peasants. As crucial as these strata were for social differentiation, they were conditioned by various forms of mediation and reciprocity that connected and divided rural society — from independent *foreros* to *hidalgos* who had gained entry into the nobility — in a wide variety of ways. It is by paying attention to this complex social framework that we can understand how deeply rooted and vast certain clientship networks were at the time of the monastic reform of the sixteenth century, with the imposition of the external authority of the Castilian abbots.[46] But it is also in such a context as this that we can explain the wide-reaching alliances and antagonisms that faced rural society in the late Middle Ages, whose apparent contradictions are merely superficial.

---

45 Although in Penosiños, according to the aforementioned *inquisitio* (SPRamirás41), Celanova was entitled to collect payments for certain rights.

46 See for example the clientship network centred around Abbot *Don Ares* of the monastery of Meira, which is perfectly reflected in the capitulations resulting from his negotiations with the reformist monks (Mariño Veiras, *Señorío del monasterio de Meira*, pp. 124–28).

Bibliography

Bois, Guy, 'Poder y parentesco en el siglo X en el Maçonnais', in *Relaciones de poder, de producción y de parentesco en la Edad Media y Moderna: aproximación a su estudio*, ed. by Reyna Pastor (Madrid: CSIC, 1990), pp. 1–12

Davies, Wendy, *Small Worlds: The Village Community in Early Medieval Brittany* (London: Duckworth, 1988)

Davies, Wendy, and Paul Fouracre, eds, *The Settlement of Disputes in Early Medieval Europe* (Cambridge: Cambridge University Press, 1986)

Duro Peña, Emilio, 'El monasterio de San Pedro de Ramiranes', *Archivos Leoneses*, 49 (1971), 9–74

García de Cortázar, José Ángel, *La sociedad rural en la España Medieval* (Madrid: Siglo XXI, 1988)

García Fernández, Jesús, *Organización del espacio y economía rural en la España Atlántica* (Madrid: Siglo XXI, 1975)

Jiménez Gómez, Santiago, 'Análisis de la terminología agraria en la documentación lucense del siglo XIII', in *Actas de las I Jornadas de Metodología Aplicada de las Ciencias Históricas, Vol. 2* (Santiago de Compostela: Universidade de Santiago de Compostela, 1975), pp. 115–34

Levi, Giovanni, 'Terra e strutture familiari in una comunità piemontese del '700', *Quaderni Storici*, 33–3 (1976), 1095–121

Levi, Giovanni, *L'eredità immateriale: carriera di un esorcista nel Piemonte del Seicento* (Turin: Einaudi, 1985)

Mariño Veiras, Dolores, *Señorío del monasterio de Meira (de 1150 a 1525). Espacio rural, régimen de propiedad y régimen de explotación en la Galicia Medieval* (La Coruña: Nos, 1983)

Pallares, Carmen, and Ermelindo Portela, 'Aproximación al estudio de las explotaciones agrarias en Galicia durante los siglos IX y XII', in *Actas de las I Jornadas de Metodología Aplicada de las Ciencias Históricas, Vol. 2* (Santiago de Compostela: Universidade de Santiago de Compostela, 1975), pp. 93–115

Portela, Ermelindo, *La región del Obispado de Tuy en los siglos XII al XIV. Una sociedad en la expansión y en la crisis* (Santiago de Compostela: El Eco franciscano, 1976)

Portela, Ermelindo, *La colonización cisterciense en Galicia (1142–1250)* (Santiago de Compostela: Universidad de Santiago de Compostela, 1981)

Risco, Vicente, *Geografía general reino Galicia. Provincia Orense* (Barcelona: Alberto Martín, n.d.)

Rodríguez Galdo, María Xosé, *Señores y campesinos en Galicia. Siglos XIV–XVI* (Santiago de Compostela: Pico Sacro, 1976)

Rodríguez, Justiniano, 'El Coto de Celanova (Orense) y su fuero', *Archivos Leoneses*, 73 (1983), 83–96

Sabean, David Warren, *Power in the Blood: Popular Culture and Village Discourse in Early Modern Germany* (Cambridge: Cambridge University Press, 1984)

Villares, Ramón, *Foros, frades y fidalgos. Estudios de Historia Social de Galicia* (Vigo: Edicións Xerais de Galicia, 1982)

Villares, Ramón, *La propiedad de la tierra en Galicia 1500–1936* (Madrid: Siglo XXI, 1982)

Wickham, Chris, *The Mountains and the City: The Tuscan Apennines in the Early Middle Ages* (Oxford: Clarendon Press, 1988)

CHAPTER 7

On Social Differentiation within Rural Communities

with a commentary by Phillipp R. Schofield

PHILLIPP R. SCHOFIELD

Commentary

Isabel Alfonso's valuable contribution to the memorial volume for Rodney Hilton illustrates the ways in which a Spanish medieval historiography has engaged closely with the economic history of the rural lower orders in the middle ages and also, through use of the rich sources available for parts of Spain, offered particular and unique insights into the structure of rural society and economy in this period. Alfonso's chapter, which is a published version of a paper presented to the conference just over a year after Hilton's death, examines differentiation within the medieval village, with particular reference to labour services extracted from those holding village franchises (*fueros*) in the regions of Castile and Léon. This examination allows Alfonso to offer reflection upon stratification in the medieval village, to consider the impact of labour services on different social sub-groups within high medieval village society, and to assess the ways in which labour services were assigned within these communities.

Alfonso distinguishes, amongst the peasantry, between three broad economic categories of peasant of large, medium and small-holders, with, as she describes it, 'varying capacity for subsistence' (p. 279). This she relates as much to household size as to landholding per se and the physical capacity of peasant households to provide the labour required of them. Holders of village franchises were expected to perform a variety of labour services, sometimes referred to under the broad term *sernas*, and these were distributed to an extent defined by the size of a peasant household's landholding, its working animals, or the dependence of any particular household upon its own labour (pp. 279–80). Capacity alongside other measures such as legal and social standing also served to condition the actual degree to which any tenant of a *fuero* was expected to perform their labour services.

Of great interest in this respect is Alfonso's observation that those who performed such labour services were not those who, as vassals of the lord, were necessarily required to deliver the services. At the village of Mojados, near Valladolid, seigneurial documents from the twelfth and thirteenth centuries permit a view of labour services and the negotiations of local lords with their tenants. Even wealthier peasants, including those with others 'under their protection', were expected to deliver labour services but, as Alfonso suggests, the assumption is that the wealthier tenants operating within any particular *fuero* relied upon others to perform a range of bi-annual services and, on occasion, this reliance was acknowledged within local regulations and conditioned in certain ways. So, for instance, in the 1133 Fuero de Fuentesauco, those tenants required to perform five days of labour *per annum* were allowed to use 'as vassals only the ploughmen and gardeners "living in their houses"' (p. 283). This does not necessarily imply that these individuals lived under the same roof, as part of a household, but

Phillipp R. Schofield, Aberystwyth University

may indicate, as was the case at Villavicencio as revealed in an inquest from the thirteenth century, that such ploughmen were sub-tenants of wealthier peasants; they occupied tenements and performed some or all of the services formally owed by the wealthier peasants, their landlords. Quite who these sub-vassals were or in what conditions they lived it is difficult to judge from the documents but there was clear room for main tenants to negotiate the role of such sub-vassals, these *vassalli vassallorum* ('vassals of vassals'), and to use them as substitutes for their own labour. As Alfonso, makes clear, there was evident variety in the ways these sub-vassals were employed and upon what terms. In so far as can be judged, the lords of these *fueros* accepted such an arrangement as it facilitated performance of labour rents and maintained the function and obligation of the existing tenancies.

While a good deal of the surviving evidence points to the use, by vassals, of sub-vassals who did not live under the same roof, it is also evident that members of the same household, either family members of live-in servants, might be used to perform labour rents. Seigneurial pronouncements against the use of children in such work or that any replacement should be as strong as the person replaced, point to common practices and also speak to the potential role of household members, including adolescents, women and the elderly, in agricultural work. As Alfonso also notes there is some indication here of the non-tenanted, landless labour force, often relatively hidden from view and unable to access communal rights but, as Harold Fox's study of *garciones* at Glastonbury has also shown, of likely great importance in supporting the function of the seigneurial economy in this period (p. 287).

There are a number of observations, including comparative points, that can flow from Alfonso's exciting discussion of labour service organisation according to the *fueros*. The first of these relates to source type and period. From a British and, more particularly, an English perspective, a striking feature of Alfonso's analysis is the study period. An end date of 1300 is, typically, closer to the start date for discussion of social stratification in medieval England. While there are some notable studies directed at social and economic difference amongst the peasantry of pre- and post-Conquest England, these have tended to rely on documents that have offered historians snapshots of tenure and obligation as well as occasional glimpses into the fragmentation and reallocation of units of landholding. They suggest social inequality in the medieval village without offering so much in the way of insight into the mechanisms and explanations of stratification.[1] By contrast, later sources, especially seigneurial court records in England originating in the mid-thirteenth century, begin to show interaction between peasants and uneven relations of social and economic power comparable with the kinds of materials used by Alfonso in her paper. While Alfonso's study is founded upon the more static statement of the eleventh-century *fueros* which, again to use an English source comparison, have some proximity to the extents and custumals of the twelfth and early thirteenth centuries, the later *fueros*,

---

1 See, for instance, the excellent study Douglas, *Social Structure*. For recent discussions of stratification in medieval Europe, see Aparisi Romero and Royo, eds, *Beyond Lords and Peasants*; Menant and Jessenne, eds, *Les élites rurales*.

from the thirteenth century, include insights into disputes and some sense of the negotiation around the particular terms for use of substitute labour.

While the evidence of the *fueros* speaks unequivocally to stratification, it is the glimpses offered by Alfonso's study into the process of stratification that are especially important. They offer us a view of not only the distinctions within peasant society in this period but an understanding of how that stratification worked. This, as Alfonso notes, is especially important in terms of the landless, and especially perhaps those who existed outside of their own households but found opportunity and employment working in and/or for the households of others. Unlike investigation of sub-tenants, that is those who occupied the land and houses of wealthier peasants, any opportunity to examine the lives of those without land provides a view of medieval social and economic life that, given so much of the historical record relates to land, its tenure and its associated obligations, is rare and, therefore, especially important. Such groups within medieval rural society remain, by the nature of their existence, largely hidden from us and it is often only in the incidental reference to and explanation of structures of landholding and organisation of rent that their lives are revealed at all. Harold Fox's important study of similar groups on the Glastonbury Abbey estates in the thirteenth and early fourteenth centuries addressed in detail the ways in which those without land, living and working in the households of non-kin, might be employed in the service of the seigneurial economy.[2] Of importance also here is Alfonso's reflection upon the role of other household members in the completion of seigneurial tasks. There are a number of relevant observations that may be drawn from such issues, not least the importance of the household and the houseful in the performance of labour. Recent work by a number of historians has stressed the significance of female labour and child labour in sustaining the domestic economy.[3] The evidence of the *fueros* shows both the expectation that family and household labour could be an important element in the performance of labour services as well as revealing seigneurial anxieties regarding the use of labourers of limited strength and suitability for the defined tasks.

Reflecting an historiographical tradition which has played a major role in the interpretation of seigneurial sources and the nature of rent and labour in the middle ages, Alfonso's essay recognizes that a significant part of the explanation for social and economic differentiation within the medieval rural community resides in the actions and controls of lordship. This position, which was, of course, axiomatic for historians working in a Marxist tradition, does not wholly negate, again as Alfonso's thoughtful contribution makes clear, the distinctions and tensions which existed in peasant communities and neither does it dismiss the possibility that peasants enjoyed a degree of agency and control in the organisation of their working lives. Alfonso's discussion of the *sernas* associated with these high-medieval *fueros* reminds us that a top-down allocation of obligations was conditioned by an array of factors. Some of

---

2 Fox, 'Exploitation of the Landless'.
3 See, for one recent contribution to this discussion, Whittle, 'A Critique of Approaches to "Domestic Work"'.

these factors were created by the expectations of lords, such as a direct association of labour rent with particular landholdings or, as the later work J. A. Raftis was intended to show,[4] the lord's need to preserve the capacity of their tenantry. Others were established by the expectations and pre-existing inequalities within peasant society. One instance of this relates to the ways in which peasant tenants might seek to ameliorate their own condition by negotiating with their lords over obligations as well as associated benefits.[5] The 1294 issue of a *fuero* by the Bishop of Segovia speaks to previous disputes over allocation of services and includes statements distinguishing a range of obligations according to the resources of the tenant as well as the sorts of benefits-in-kind that rent-payers might expect to receive, dependent on their status. Such details are not dissimilar to the kinds of arrangements that Jean Birrell has identified in English custumals where food rights during service are often set out in detail and with a clear sense of the expectations on the part of the tenantry.[6]

As Alfonso's discussion makes clear, earlier allocation of landholding and, no doubt, the kinds of *inter-vivos* or *post-mortem* mechanisms that facilitated both a morcellation and engrossment of peasant tenures, as well as changes in size of family and household, were important factors in both explaining stratification and, as importantly, sustaining it. In his discussion of the *garciones* at Glastonbury, Fox makes the important point that the presence of landless males reveals some stark choices made by peasant tenants, including the ejection by fathers of their own offspring into the landless labour force in order to preserve their own income and standard of living. Such a process required 'collusion among heads of households', who took in the offspring of their neighbours as servants while sending out their own children for the same reason, and was an effective exploitation of the young by their parents.[7] This adds additional nuance and dimension to the conclusions drawn from the work of Zvi Razi work on medieval Halesowen, which showed that non-inheriting offspring in wealthier peasant households and most if not all offspring in poorer peasant households might experience this centrifugal force and find themselves ejected from the family hearth.[8] Even within these cohorts the distinctions mattered greatly so that, as Judith Bennett has recently argued, young girls and young women, drawn or expelled from their homes for social, economic or simply familial reasons, may have been especially vulnerable.[9]

Rereading Isabel Alfonso's essay as part of the *Rodney Hilton's Middle Ages* volume gathered in memory of Rodney Hilton, and reflecting again on the relationship between the Anglophone and Spanish historiography of the medieval rural economy, has also served to remind me that a number of the subsequent contributors and editors of the collection, including Isabel Alfonso and the present author, were

---

4 Raftis, *Peasant Economic Development*.

5 For a brief but insightful reflection on the processes of stratification in the pre-modern community and its related historiography, see Aparisi Romero and Royo, 'Fractures in the Community'.

6 Birrell, 'Peasants Eating and Drinking'.

7 Fox, 'Exploitation of the Landless', pp. 559–60.

8 Razi, *Life, Marriage and Death*.

9 Bennett, 'Women and Poverty'.

attending a conference in Spain, at Jaca, in early June 2002 when news of Hilton's death was received. The conference, on peasant land markets and lordship, drew together European scholars working on such themes and responded to the kinds of agendas established by Hilton and others and to which Isabel Alfonso so usefully responds in this contribution. As is well known, a central tenet of Hilton's work on the medieval English peasantry was examination of the relationship between lords and their tenants. As both Marxist and non-Marxist historians of the medieval agrarian economy have identified, simple distinctions between lords on the one hand and peasants or tenants on the other mask other distinctions and economic and social inequalities which applied within peasant society. Hilton, while tending to stress that the claim of peasant class solidarity in opposition to lordship trumped divisions within peasant society, was also clear that such distinctions did exist.[10] Alfonso's contribution also makes clear the subtleties and distinctions that can be employed in close examination of seigneurial sources relating to rent and labour service; explorations into the performance of such obligations admit, increasingly, a variety of approaches to the labouring past of the middle ages and allow historians not only to examine lord-tenant relations, as exhibited through rent, but also the complexities and structures in rural society conditioned by an array of factors, of which rent was but one.

---

10 Hilton, *The English Peasantry*, pp. 54–58.

Bibliography

Aparisi Romero, Frederic, and Vicent Royo, 'Fractures in the Community: A Historiographical Review', in *Beyond Lords and Peasants. Rural Elites and Economic Differentiation in Pre-modern Europe*, ed. by Frederic Aparisi Romero and Vicent Royo (València: Publicacions de la Universitat de València, 2014), pp. 21–36

Aparisi Romero, Frederic, and Vicent Royo, eds, *Beyond Lords and Peasants: Rural Elites and Economic Differentiation in Pre-modern Europe* (València: Publicacions de la Universitat de València, 2014)

Bennett, Judith M., 'Women and Poverty: Girls on their Own in England before 1348', in *Peasants and Lords in the Medieval English Economy: Essays in Honour of Professor Bruce Campbell*, ed. by Maryanne Kowaleski, John Langdon, and Phillipp R. Schofield (Turnhout: Brepols, 2015), pp. 299–318

Birrell, Jean, 'Peasants Eating and Drinking', *Agricultural History Review*, 63 (2015), 1–18

Douglas, David C., *Social Structure of Medieval East Anglia* (Oxford: Oxford University Press, 1927)

Fox, Harold S. A., 'Exploitation of the Landless by Lords and Tenants in Early Medieval England', in *Medieval Society and the Manor Court* ed. by Zvi Razi and Richard Smith (Oxford: Oxford University Press, 1996), pp. 518–68

Hilton, Rodney, *The English Peasantry in the Later Middle Ages* (Oxford: Oxford University Press, 1975)

Menant, François, and Jean-Pierre Jessenne, eds, *Les élites rurales dans l'Europe médiévale et modern* (Toulouse: Presses universitaires de Mirail, 2007)

Raftis, James A., *Peasant Economic Development within the English Manorial System* (Montreal: Mcgill-Queens, 1996)

Razi, Zvi, *Life, Marriage and Death in a Medieval Parish: Economy, Society and Demography in Halesowen, 1270–1400* (Cambridge: Cambridge University Press, 1980)

Whittle, Jane, 'A Critique of Approaches to "Domestic Work": Women, Work and the Preindustrial Economy', *Past & Present*, 243 (2019), 35–70

ISABEL ALFONSO

Exploring Difference within Rural Communities in the Northern Iberian Kingdoms, 1000–1300*

Historical studies in Spain have been dramatically revitalized since the 1970s and 1980s, not just for the medieval period but in general. This has meant the gradual integration of Spanish work into debates and developments in other countries. The myth of Spanish difference, for long so carefully fostered by official ideology in almost every sphere, was thus questioned in its medieval dimensions as well. It is not my intention here, however, to address these historiographical developments, which are well known.[1] Rather, I will examine some issues relating to peasant communities in the north of the peninsula, in particular in regard to internal forms of inequality, a theme on which Rodney Hilton wrote many illuminating pages.[2] His influence, indeed, played a pivotal role in the shift from legal and institutional history to more social approaches among Spanish medievalists.[3]

The changing approach by historians to rural communities in medieval Castile has unquestionably been closely related to new ideas concerning the development of feudal society in the peninsula, and has benefited greatly from new critical editions of documentary sources. These allow a better appraisal of both the information these sources contain and the contexts in which they were compiled. Sadly, with a few notable exceptions, historians have been slow to integrate into their field the great potential contribution of archaeology, which in Spain is underdeveloped and usually underfunded.[4]

---

* Original publication: Alfonso, Isabel, 'Exploring Difference within Rural Communities in the Northern Iberian Kingdoms, 1000–1300', in *Rodney Hilton's Middle Ages: An Exploration of Historical Themes*, ed. by Christopher Dyer, Peter Coss, and Chris Wickham. *Past and Present*, Supplement 2 (Oxford: Oxford University Press, 2007), pp. 87–100. I am most grateful to Julio Escalona for his comments on a draft of this paper, and to Simon Doubleday (Hofstra University, New York), for the English translation.

1 One of the most recent historiographical studies in the field of medieval rural history is García de Cortázar and Martínez Sopena, 'Los estudios sobre la historia rural', originally published as part of two special issues on the rural history of medieval European societies that appeared in *Historia Agraria*, 31 (2003), and *Historia Agraria*, 33 (2004) and which included articles on England (C. Dyer and P. Schofield), France (G. Brunel and B. Cursente), Italy (L. Provero), Poland (P. Gorécki), and Germany (J. Demade), now in English in Alfonso, ed., *The Rural History*.

2 Hilton, 'Reasons for Inequality'; Hilton, *The English Peasantry*.

3 Two of his most influential books (Hilton, *Bond Men Made Free*; Hilton, ed., *The Transition from Feudalism to Capitalism*), were almost immediately translated into Spanish and the second of these two books, which introduced one of the main debates about the origins of capitalism, appeared in three Spanish editions within a very short period of time. [Editors' note: For the Spanish translations, see Hilton, *Siervos liberados* and Hilton, ed., *La transición del feudalismo al capitalismo*].

4 On this problem, Julio Escalona has been particularly eloquent. See Escalona, 'Paisaje, asentamiento y Edad Media'. See also Barceló, *Arqueología medieval*.

Scholars agree to some extent that local society offers a variegated picture in the period between the eleventh and thirteenth centuries. Diverse forms of lordship and internally divided communities are recognized, although the formalization of such differences also varied. In many cases, there were two clearly defined groups among charter witnesses, representing the free population of a community: a group of knights, and the rest of the population. The names given to these two respective groups varied according to the context. The first group were generally known as *milites* or *caballeros* ('knights'), and they enjoyed certain privileges with respect to their neighbours, from whom they were distinguished by ownership of a horse and their corresponding (at least nominal) military duties. Those belonging to the remaining population were known as *pedites* or *peones, homines, pecheros, labradores, rusticos, collazos*, to cite the most common terms. Together both groups formed the body of seigneurial dependants (sometimes called 'vassals'[5]), although villages rarely depended on a single lord and most communities were divided in their attachments to social superiors.

But there were other differences, too, both between the two groups and within their ranks, partly corresponding to material wealth but also dictated by networks of social relationship. There were some knights, for instance, who were recognized as nobles or *infanzones*, along with others such as 'village knights' ('caballeros villanos') who only in part avoided the obligations that were normally rendered by the commoners. Our understanding of the processes of social mobility which led to this type of differentiation within the most elevated ranks of peasant society has improved considerably in recent decades, as the result of attempts to identify mechanisms of seigneurial domination which influenced and/or made possible such differentiation.[6] Nevertheless, more research is still needed on a number of matters, such as the position of local knights in regard to rural communities — were they essentially outsiders, or privileged members of a cohesive social body? —, or the extent to which they were involved in agricultural production and direct management of their holdings. We also need to know more about the chronology of social differentiation and its regional variations.[7]

In villages where we witness this kind of internal stratification, we can also see that the remaining peasant population was not homogeneous, either. The sources we have in Spain for the study of inequality among peasant holdings, although far sparser than those available, for example, to English historians, allow us to trace a

---

5 'Vassals', a word confined to socially elevated feudal tenants in England, is applied in Castile to all the tenants of a lord.

6 The bibliography, already abundant, can be reviewed in the articles in two important collective volumes arising from an explicitly comparative approach to similar problems in other societies of the medieval European west: Álvarez Borge, ed., *Comunidades locales y poderes feudales; Señores, siervos, vasallos*. See also n. 14 above.

7 For my immediate area of concern, see Monsalvo Antón, 'Transformaciones sociales'; Alfonso, 'Poder local y diferenciación interna' [Editors' note: For an English translation, see chapter 6 of this volume]. See also Pastor and others, *Poder monástico y grupos domésticos*; Pastor and others, *Transacciones sin mercado* [Editors' note: For an English translation, see Pastor and others, *Beyond the Market*]; Estepa Díez, *Las behetrías castellanas*, vol. 2, pp. 275–76.

widespread, tripartite, social structure of peasants with large, medium and small holdings: that is to say, with a varying capacity for subsistence. Taking cyclical patterns into consideration, these differences mean that some households had insufficient manpower in the nuclear household, and others enjoyed a surplus. Certainly, it is not easy to go beyond generalized descriptions, or to know the relative proportions of the different sizes of peasant holding or their precise distribution in different lordships and regions, but a growing interest in family structures and community interaction has opened new avenues of scholarly inquiry.[8]

My aim here is to explore this differentiation within villages, paying special attention to the most dependent seigneurial peasants, those least visible in the sources. I believe this will allow us to identify some of the problems which underlay social antagonisms, at the same time generating less easily apparent forms of solidarity. I will concentrate on information relating to labour services exacted from the recipients of *fueros*, village franchises, in the villages of Castile and León by lay or ecclesiastical lords, in the expectation that this will throw light on stratification among the peasantry.[9] I will address three questions: 1) how these labour services affected different segments of the population, 2) who performed these services in practice, and 3) how the work was assigned within peasant households.

Seigneurial *fueros* and Social Differentiation among Dependent Peasants

Local laws (*fueros*), which varied widely in length and content, multiplied across Christian Iberia between the eleventh and thirteenth centuries, in small hamlets and villages as well as in major urban centres. The normative character that was attributed to these documents until recently has obscured the fact they are valuable sources of information for issues other than the regulation of peasant life by the lords, traditionally seen as the only social agents in the elaboration of these local statutes. Less juridical approaches have allowed us, among other things, to recognize the influence of the broader population in the design of such laws. A majority of the *fueros* were the result of resistance and struggle, the result of sustained conflicts — many of them conducted in legal terms — and prolonged negotiations.[10]

Labour services, known as *sernas* in Castile and León, or sometimes simply described by reference to the required tasks, were generally quite light, since week-work was exceptional. Most common were one or two days of labour service each month, or even three or four days per year. Nonetheless, the peasant perception of these obligations appears to have been very negative, and, as elsewhere in Europe, they performed them

---

8 See notes 17 and 18.

9 I will use the following compilations of *fueros*: FL, FZ, FP, FV.

10 Alfonso, 'Campesinado y derecho' [Editors' note: For an English translation, see chapter 9 of this volume]. For more details on the nature and content of these sources in a comparative context, see Martínez Sopena, 'Autour des *fueros*'; Alfonso, 'La contestation paysanne' [Editors' note: For an English translation, see chapter 11 of this volume]; Reglero de la Fuente, 'Le prelèvement seigneurial'.

without the 'goodwill' that their lords demanded.[11] The differences we observe in the *fueros* regarding the labour services that were required from a community or a group of vassals under the lord's jurisdiction or holding land from him (*vassallos, homines, collazos, populatores, moradores*) seem to have corresponded to a desire to exploit the particular resources of peasant families. These differences — which also existed in relation to other forms of payment — corresponded to the size of the peasants' landholdings; the number of working animals (one or two oxen or donkeys were most common); or whether they depended only on their own labour. Although there is no evidence that peasants in the same community were required to work more days than others, each was required to perform labour services related to his resources.

But these differences also had a social, juridical and political dimension, which tended to give privileges — in a wide range of conditions and contexts — to free men over bondmen, clerics over laymen, those with a horse over *peones*, the lord's officials (*alcaldes, jueces, merinos*) over others, those with a supervisory role over their neighbours, and the recently-married and widows over the rest. These privileges meant total or partial exemption from services owed by others, and, given the limited number of days of service demanded, appear to have entailed not only an economic advantage, but also a symbolic distinction and a certain prestige within the community.

Sub-Dependants as Substitutes

The perception of labour services as quintessentially servile work — a picture largely drawn from the charters themselves — has obscured the fact that those who really performed these services were not necessarily direct seigneurial vassals. In reality, the latter could oblige, request, or pay others to fulfil the services in their place. There are frequent references to peasants who had not managed to gain exemption like their more privileged neighbours, but who sent substitutes to perform them. It is worth investigating the character of these substitutions, and the relationship between dependants and substitutes, by examining a few cases.

Mojados is a village to the south of the Duero river, 14 km from Valladolid, from which we have a number of extant documents. It is an ecclesiastical lordship between two large towns, and was linked successively to the bishops of Palencia and Segovia. The bishop of Palencia had received it in a donation by Alfonso VIII in 1175, along with all its *collazos*, a term which we might translate as 'villeins' or simply 'tenants'; they were ostensibly free but actually dependent peasants. One year later, in 1176, the bishop agreed on a *fuero* with these local inhabitants.[12] This document takes the form of a charter addressed to all the vassals, without exception, so that by 'living honestly' according to the *fuero* and good customs they might merit eternal life and

---

11 For further detail, see Alfonso, 'Las sernas'. I have studied the way in which peasants view their condition in Alfonso, 'La contestation paysanne'. The classic study of resistance is Pastor, *Resistencias y luchas campesinas*.

12 FV11 (1176).

happiness.[13] Of its twenty-three clauses, we are especially interested in three here. One allows tenants to possess more than one *solar* where they can accommodate their *yugueros* ('ploughmen') or other workers, male or female.[14] Another establishes that all residents, male and female — except salaried workers — with more than 10 *maravedíes* of money, shall pay and serve the bishop.[15] The third clause obliges them to perform labour services (*sernas*) twice a year, once to plough the land and once to sow the seed, besides other duties.[16] The *fuero* does not, then, appear to be directed to the poorest members of society, even though the term *collazos*, applied to the population in the royal donation of the previous year, might seem to suggest this. In these clauses of the text, one can observe that references to the local population make a number of fine distinctions.[17] They distinguish vassals with more than one *solar*; those who implicitly have only one; men and women who live in someone else's *solar*; vassals with more than 10 *maravedíes*; those who implicitly have less than this, and the 'salaried labourers' (*soldariegos*). The latter two categories are explicitly excluded from paying tribute or performing service to the bishop. These distinctions, although they reveal a differentiated social fabric, should not be taken as clearly defined

---

13 FV11 (1176): 'I grant you these charter [...], my men and faithful vassals from Mojados, to all of you without any exception, both present and yet to come, with your *fueros* and good customs so that you shall live rightfully and honestly in this world, and that, by holding lawfully and firmly to them, after this temporal life of which Christ is far you shall happily reach the eternal life' ('facio cartam [...] uobis hominibus meis et fidelibus vasallis de Moiados generaliter omnibus sine exceptione aliqua tam presentibus quam futuris de uestris foris et bonis consuetudines quibus in hoc seculo recte et honeste uiuatis, et hec iuste et fimiter semper tenendo ab hac temporali uita ad eternam que Christus est procul feliciter perueniatis').

14 FV11 (1176), § 2: 'And I approve that you have other *solares* beyond your own should this be necessary, and that you lodge your *yugueros* and any other men and women' ('Et placet mihi quod habeatis aliut solare tantum preter uestrum ubi si neccesarie fuerit et teneatis iugueros uestros uel quoslibet homines uel mulieres'). The word *solar* is the common term for the peasant holding, the place where the house is constructed, the central nucleus of seigneurial exactions, to which cultivated lands (sometimes described as the *heredad*) are conjoined. The growing complexity of peasant tenancies, and the process of separation between *solar* and *heredad*, seems quite well developed by the thirteenth century, although we do not yet understand all their implications. For these questions, see Estepa Díez, 'Proprietà'; Álvarez Borge, 'Sobre las relaciones de dependencia'; Martínez García, 'Los campesinos solariegos' [Editors' note: For an English translation, see Martínez García, 'Solariego Peasants'].

15 FV11 (1176), § 3: 'I also establish that all men and women, whatever their kin, and except the salaried workers, who inhabit the village of Mojados and have estates and movable property worth 10 *maravedíes* or more, shall all pay and serve their lord, the bishop, under his authority, and pay him his dues' ('Pretera constituo quod omnes homines uel mulieres, cuiuscumque generit [sic] sint, quicumque in uilla de Moiados commorauerint, nisi fuerint soldariegos, habentes ualiam X morabetinorum et ultra in hereditate uel in quolibet mobili, omnes pro arbitrio et mercede episcopi pectent et seruiant domino episcopo suo').

16 FV11 (1176), § 5: 'I also order that every year you perform two *sernas* on my behalf, one on fallow land and the other at the time of sowing' ('Mando eciam quod faciatis mihi duas sernas in anno, unam in barbechar et alteram in seminar').

17 A separate clause regulates the obligations of the Jewish inhabitants. The term 'neighbour' (*vecino*) is used to regulate horizontal relationships in general, and as a global term of reference the word *qui* is used.

social strata; indeed, what needs to be investigated is the overlapping, fluidity and contingency which might be involved in these situations. The term social 'stratum' therefore needs to be understood here in a loose sense.

We know that the village of Mojados subsequently passed to the crown, which then re-granted it to the bishop of Segovia, in whose hands it remained until it was sold in the sixteenth century.[18] It was one of the bishops of Segovia who issued another *fuero* in 1294,[19] and who tells of the disputes over their duties that his predecessors had experienced in the course of the thirteenth century. These disputes, the new *fuero* stated, had damaged the bishops and given the peasants a *mala fama* ('poor reputation') as vassals. The new *fuero* consolidates some improvements in regard to taxation, and, although it does not modify the frequency of labour services, it lays down some changes in how they are to be performed and allows us to observe more clearly the different social strata living in this peasant community. Labour services are to be performed by all peasants who work using oxen or mules, but those with more than one pair of oxen are to perform the services with just one of these pairs, while those with only one ox or mule should bring it to be yoked to another. Those with only donkeys, meanwhile, no longer have an obligation to perform labour services.[20] All tenants with this obligation are to receive bread, wine and cheese twice a day. But the *alcaldes* ('local officials') and other *boni homini* ('good men') supervising the labour services are to receive meat instead of cheese[21] and do not have to perform these boon works.[22] Therefore, these arrangements do not seem to have affected the *caballeros* ('knights') as they did in other communities,[23] but rather those who formed the apparatus of the local council (*alcaldes, juez* and *escribano*)

---

18 Martínez Díez, 'Los fueros inéditos de Mojados'.

19 FV30 (1294).

20 FV30 (1294), § 1: 'These *sernas* must be performed in this manner by all of those who plough with their oxen and mules: whoever ploughs with one team shall perform the *serna* with one team, and whoever has more [than one team] shall not be forced to render more than one team; and whoever has one ox or one mule shall render it so that it is put in a team with another; and whoever ploughs with donkeys shall not be forced to perform the *serna*' ('Estas sernas deuen fazer todos los que labraren con bueys o con bestias mulares en esta guysa: el que labrare con vna yunta que faga serna con vna yunta, el que mas oyuere non sea tenudo de dar mas de vna yunta; et el que ouyere vn buey o vna bestia mular que la de para yuntar con otra; et los que labraren con bestias asnares que non sean tenudos de fazer serna').

21 FV30 (1294), § 1: 'and we order that on the day that they perform the *serna*, the *alcaldes* and all the other worthy men who supervise them shall give them bread and wine and meat to eat twice during the day, and they shall give those who plough with their oxen bread and wine and cheese twice during the day on the field, and at night, when they finish their tasks, they shall give them two breads and two half-quarters of wine' ('et el dia que fizieren la serna mandamos que a los alcalles et a los otros omes buenos que lo endereçaren que les den pan et vino et carne dos vezes al dia a comer, et a los otros que labraren con los bueys que les den pan et vino et queso dos vezes al dia con el ero, et a la noche quando dexaren de la lauor denles sendos panes et sendos medios quartos de vino').

22 FV30 (1294), § 6: 'and we deem it rightful that the *alcaldes* and the judge and the notary are excused from performing the *serna* on our behalf and of paying us the *infurcion*' ('et tenemos por bien que los alcalles et el iuez et el escriuano que sean escusados de nos fazer serna et de nos dar enfurcion').

23 The fact that *caballeros* ('knights') are not exempted does not mean that they were obliged to perform labour services, since there is no evidence that there were any in the village.

EXPLORING DIFFERENCE WITHIN RURAL COMMUNITIES 283

and the generic 'good men'. It is likely, although not certain, that most of the latter belonged to the privileged sector of the village. However, we can see that not all the wealthier peasants were formally exempt from work services, with all their servile connotations, since these services were due also from those who had more than one pair of oxen and had other people under *su bien fazer* ('their protection') and *gouernio* ('authority'),[24] even though, as in 1176, they did not have to pay for the *solar* where these people were lodged. The evidence allows us to deduce that in practice it was often the sub-dependants — when the tenant possessed them — who performed the labour service.

We know little about this last-mentioned sector of peasant society, especially those who lived in villages and hamlets, except that they were excluded from the rights afforded to their more privileged neighbours. In some cases, their domestic character is clear: in Mojados, they appear to have formed a part of the peasant household, living in an adjoining building. It is true, nonetheless, that the ambiguous expression 'morar en sus casas' ('to live in their houses'), which we find in other references to express the link between these workers and the seigneurial tenants, may signify either possession or cohabitation in these houses, so we have to assess carefully the nature of these residential arrangements.[25] Another group of references poses similar problems:

1. *Fuero* de Fuentesaúco (1133): the men of the bishop of Zamora, in this village, obliged to perform five days of labour each year, are authorized to have as vassals only the ploughmen and gardeners 'living in their houses'.[26]

2. *Fuero* de Villarmildo (1129): Countess Estefanía grants similar authorization to her *collazos* in this village, among the few who are subject to week work, for having the same type of workers under their dependency.[27]

---

24 FV30 (1294), § 2: 'and we deem it rightful that in the house in which a person lives there may be another *solar* that is not subject to the *enfurcion* in which he may keep his oxen or the men under his protection and authority, but not otherwise' ('tenemos por bien que sin la casa en que morare cada vno pueda aver otro solar sin enfurcion en que tenga sus bueys o omes que esten a su bien fazer de gouernio et en otra manera non'). The term *gouernio*, besides authority, implies a sense of responsibility for providing what was necessary for carrying out the tasks at hand.

25 The dimensions of the *solar* are unknown, but the well-entrenched equation between *solar*, house and family needs to be re-evaluated, given the many indications of complexity. What are we to think, for instance, of the ten 'hearths' (*fuegos*) within a single *solar*, used as a criterion for the *servicium temporale* ('temporal service') owed by clerics and laymen to the abbot of Oña *rationi soli*? (SSOña-O107, c. 1209). On these questions see Alfonso, 'Resolución de disputas', p. 226.

26 FZ7 (1133), § 1: 'So that no man has his vassals, nor his *yugueros*, nor his gardener living in his own house' ('Ut nullus homo habeat ibi vassalum nisi suum iugarium vel suum ortolanum qui moratus fuerit in sua propia kasa').

27 FV5 (1129), § 15: 'And to you, my dependants, I grant you this *fuero*, that you shall enjoy full authority over your gardeners and *yugueros* without any higher lord over them in their houses' ('Et uos meos populatores dono uobis foro, que abetis super uos uestros ortolanos et uestros iukeros sine alio seniore super se in domos suas').

3. *Fuero* de Villalonso and Benefarces (*c.* 1147), also a lay lordship: its men, obliged to perform only four days of *serna* each year, may have their ploughmen as vassals.[28]

In these cases, what the references reveal — at least as much as the domestic character of this population — is a subordinate level of vassalage, permitted and recognized by the lord. This is a form of dependency which, without doubt, must have encompassed a variety of situations, from servants in husbandry on yearly contracts, or labourers hired by the day, to some type of sub-tenancy, but we lack sufficient information to be precise about the nature of their accommodation. Take the case of the *yugueros*. These are better known from urban *fueros*, in which they are mentioned receiving lands and animals for working these lands separately with their families in exchange for one fifth of the product. However it is not clear that the situation of rural ploughmen can be equated to that of their urban counterparts.[29]

These forms of dependency were the object of specific negotiation in some cases. For instance, let us observe the choice the bishop of Zamora gave to one of his vassals in 1224 as the result of a dispute. He might choose either to reside personally in the hamlet of Almaraz as a direct vassal of the bishop, performing all the corresponding labour services and owing all the relevant taxes, and to keep all the *cortes*[30] populated with his own vassals. Or he might choose to leave, and to cede these sub-vassals to the direct lordship of the bishop.[31] We do not know what decision the bishop's vassal took; his options were, however, no different from those in many other cases. More generally, the possibility provided by some *fueros* of keeping a house legally inhabited, even if one did not live in the place implied the option of substituting another worker to do his services. Nonetheless, in this kind of situation, the lord's preference appears to have been that the substitute be his direct vassal, even if this vassal were to have other workers in his service.

Why this seigneurial preference? Why allow in the lordship this extra social stratum of dependants of his peasant vassals, these *vassalli vassallorum* ('vassals of vassals') which one document mentions alongside the landless — *proprios labores non habentes* ('those who did not have their own holdings')?[32] Before trying to answer these questions, it is important to stress that although the explicit legal recognition that others might take one's place in performing tenant obligations seems to be a later phenomenon, in practice this kind of substitution had been occurring for a

---

28 FZ10 (*c.* 1147), § 2: 'And those men [...] shall have their ploughmen exempted and as their vassals, so that they shall not perform any labour services' ('Et illos homines [...] habeant suos iugeros perdonatos et pro suos vasallos, ut non faciant facienda nulla').

29 Martín Cea, 'Una pequeña contribución'. See also n. 49.

30 The terminology here is rather unclear, with a dynamic rather than a fixed meaning, indicating processes that we can only partially understand at present (see n. 14, 25). This further complicates research into the nature of these sub-dependants, and the nature of their relationship with the peasants for whom they work. The problem is not unique to our sources, as has been shown in regard to the *garciones* listed in the court rolls by Fox, 'Exploitation of the Landless'.

31 We have various documents on this *aldea* ('hamlet'), which was first under lay lordship and then under episcopal lordship: FZ20 (1175); FZ38 (1194–1217); FZ46 (1224).

32 *Fuero* de Pozuelos (FP29, 1197).

long time. In order to show this, I will use a different kind of source — an inquest — which provides rich information on the practice of work on the demesne, and which reinforces and complements what we know from the *fueros*. The inquest was conducted by the cathedral of León in the late thirteenth century to ascertain the obligations their *fuero* vassals owed in Villavicencio, a village some way from the centre of their estates. One witness, asked whether he knew whether Domingo López or his wife, Sol García, performed labour services, answered that he did not, but that he had seen their *yuguero* doing so, and that this ploughman, who lived in their houses in Villavicencio, was using their oxen.[33] The context of this information makes one doubt, again, whether these ploughmen were servants in husbandry, living with the direct vassals of the cathedral in the houses they possessed in this village. Alternatively, the witness's response may equally be read to mean that the houses were inhabited by the tenants' dependent *yugueros* who went to work the demesne while the direct vassals lived in the nearby settlement of Villalpando. Another witness in the same inquest states that he is not sure whether those he has seen performing *sernas* for the bishop were doing so 'for money or for some other reason'.[34] Again, we have evidence here of the various methods which tenants on church estates might use in order to fulfil the demands associated with tenancy and/or seigneurial dependency. Another, later source indicates the same. In 1417, on their own behalf or for another, the inhabitants of Oteruelo, vassals of the abbot of San Marcelo de León, had to perform the service of threshing; moreover, those with oxen had to perform the service of ploughing with their animals and with their own personal labour, or else 'provide someone else to plough with the said oxen'.[35] They had also to gather the vintage for one day, or 'provide workers, male or female, every year'.[36]

The very terminology used to designate these workers, which seems rather imprecise to us, indicates the diversity of situations about which we have, in fact, very little information.[37] Again, the contrast is striking with the more extensive *fueros* of the cities and major towns which regulate very precisely the forms of work and payment for the segment of the population employed to cultivate the land by the (internally differentiated) group of landowners and taxpayers.[38] But in the brief *fueros* of the small seigneurial villages under consideration here, one hardly catches a glimpse of

---

33 'that he had seen their *yuguero* doing so, and that this *yuguero* lived in the houses that Domingo López and Sol Pelaz had in Villavicencio, and that he was using Domingo López and Sol Pelaz's oxen' ('que la vio fazer al su jugero que tenie los sus bues e que moraua en las suas casas de Domingo Lopez e de Sol Pelaz que auien en Vilauicens e que la fazia con los sus bues de Domingo López e de Sol Pelaz') (CatLeon2560, 1291).

34 'se por dineros si por otra cosa' (*Fuero de Oteruelo*, FL132, 1417).

35 'o dar a otro por sy que hare con los dichos buees' (*Fuero de Oteruelo*, FL132, 1417).

36 'o dar obreros o obreras cada año' (*Fuero de Oteruelo*, FL132, 1417).

37 See Reglero de la Fuente, 'Le prelèvement seigneurial'.

38 The classic study is that of R. Gibert, who from a juridical perspective analyses source material that still remains insufficiently used. See Gibert, 'El contrato de servicios'. More recently, Martín Cea, 'El trabajo en el mundo rural'. Nonetheless it is the late medieval studies that bring a more complex vision of these questions: Martín Cea, *El mundo rural castellano*; and Oliva Herrer, *La Tierra de Campos*, a study which shows the influence of Rodney Hilton and Chris Dyer in the analysis of standards of living in medieval communities.

the *no heredes, soldariegos, mancipios, yugueros,* and *obreros,* who we find — albeit not exclusively — in the employ of the most substantial tenants of the manor. All the same, in these villages there were similar groups of landless peasants, who directly fed seigneurial demands for manpower.[39] They also, as I have tried to show, met those needs of peasant tenants which were associated with the greater size of their holdings, cyclical necessities, and/or seigneurial pressure. The paucity of data make it difficult to make comparisons with the interesting interpretation of H. S. A. Fox regarding landless peasants on the manors of Glastonbury Abbey *c.* 1300.[40] Suffice it to say that given the lightness of labour services in the lordships of Castile and León, it is not possible to attribute the tenants' need for their manpower to satisfy heavy seigneurial demands, or to a seigneurial desire to profit from a tax on their labour, as in the manors Fox has studied, since they were generally exempt from any payment as dependants and tenants. In Castile-Leon, the seigneurial strategy of indirectly accepting their labour perhaps should be better understood as a more effective means of controlling both tenancies and rents.

Within the Peasant Household

Despite the scarcity of detailed evidence, it seems clear that one sector of the recipients of the *fueros* were peasants who had at their disposal another source of manpower that could be used for fulfilling labour services on seigneurial lands. But there are also signs that children or old people might be used as substitutes for the male head of the household, presumably to reserve the effective labour of men in their prime for the cultivation of the peasant holding. This was the case, above all, in less privileged peasant households which did not have dependants, or which were at that stage in the tenant's lifecycle when no sons were available for work. It is quite true that one of the issues in which knowledge needs to be extended is the internal organization of the domestic household. The difficulties of penetrating this sphere are practically insuperable, particularly when it comes to the issue of exactly who, among its members, including servants, had to perform labour services. One does not have to know who made this kind of decision within the household to guess that sending those members of the family who for physical reasons were least productive must have been one of the ways households avoided losing the labour of adult males. This decision simultaneously represented a form of resistance. Hence the seigneurial demand that children should not be sent,[41] that the replacement be as strong as the person with the obligation, and that frail and elderly villeins work separately.[42] Lords did not reject

---

39 For instance, the dependent *criazon* ('household') of 25 individuals of the monastery of San Zoilo de Carrión in the area of San Zoles in 1240 (SZCarrión101, 1240). See also Martínez Sopena, 'Las solidaridades campesinas'.

40 Fox, 'Exploitation of the Landless'.

41 *Fuero de Cañizo* (FZ53, 1234, § 12); *Fuero de Belver* (FZ33, 1208, § 50).

42 'And if any villein wants to send another man in his place, if the lord does not wish to, he shall not accept any young man unless he is as strong as the man he is replacing. If any villeins are frail or old, they shall work separetly' ('Et si algun villano quisiere imbiar en su lugar ombre logado, si el seynior

the work of women on the demesne, however. Although exemptions for widows are very generalized, in some *fueros* it is stipulated that a widow who cannot provide a male for the haymaking shall do so herself, receiving the same food in compensation as the rest of her neighbours.[43] Some other evidence further suggests that women might be obliged directly to perform these services: in a well-known case of 1040 from the famous monastery of San Millán de Cogolla, a peasant woman refused to go with her neighbours to do so, considering it *opus servile* ('servile work').[44] We have seen that women are also mentioned among dependent workers of the tenants.

It is also in this context that one must address the question of those peasants' sons who were used as servants in the houses of other peasants. This question is closely related to the character of the sub-dependent workers, whom Fox not only associates with the temporary periods characterizing the so-called servant cycle but also shows were sometimes more permanent.[45] In the case of Galicia, Reyna Pastor has shown the influence of the seigneurial policy of land concessions upon strategies of family reproduction among peasant households, which diminished or grew in size — through a kind of self-regulation well-known in later periods — to adjust to offers of seigneurial land. Pastor, nonetheless, unlike Fox, considers that the practice of young peasants serving for a period of time in the houses of their neighbours did not develop.[46] The dichotomy between periodic and permanent circulation perhaps responds more to the type of sources available than to historical reality, since the consideration of a population of rural servants or domestic workers is coming to be seen as a fundamental component in the re-evaluation of rural work. Studies of family structures need to be re-assessed along these lines, and we need a more systematic exploration of other documentary sources.

Underlying these brief remarks on social differentiation within the village, there have been two main objectives: firstly, to emphasize the existence, even in small rural communities, of a sector of the population dependent on other peasants, a sector which the documents reveal more in negative terms — as those that do not have lands, houses, or animals — than in terms of the work these dependants perform; secondly, to underline the character of this dependency, which appears to have excluded them from a direct seigneurial relationship, and also to have deprived them of communal rights. The study of the internal dynamic of the community, which has advanced so much in the last decade, must explore more deeply both the reasons for such inequality, and the role of labourers and servants in peasant communities, as Rodney Hilton indicated in works that continue to represent a valuable guide.

---

non quisiere non recibrá, nin mancebo soldado, si non fuere tal que saque ombre al mudado. Si oviere algunos villanos flacos ó vieios, labren apart'); (FGN, L. III, t. V, cp. XVII, 51).

43 *Fuero* de Abelgas (FL67, 1217, § 12): 'Widows who cannot provide males for the haymaking shall themselves collect it both in the field and in the house, and the lord shall give them food' ('Sed uidue que non dant uiros ad secandam herbam, ipsemet debent uenire ad colligendum eam tam in prato quam in domo et dominus dabis eis ad comendendum').

44 This text is edited in Alfonso, 'La contestation paysanne', Annexes [2]. [Editors' note: see chapter 11 in this volume].

45 Fox, 'Exploitation of the Landless', pp. 554–60.

46 Pastor, 'Poder monástico'.

Bibliography

Señores, siervos, vasallos en la Alta Edad Media. XXVIII Semana de Estudios Medievales. Estella, 16 al 20 de julio de 2001 (Pamplona: Gobierno de Navarra, 2002)

Alfonso, Isabel, 'Las sernas en León y Castilla. Contribución al estudio de la relaciones socio-económicas en el marco del señorio medieval', *Moneda y Crédito*, 129 (1974), 153–210

Alfonso, Isabel, 'Poder local y diferenciación interna en las comunidades rurales gallegas', in *Relaciones de poder, de producción y de parentesco en la Edad Media y Moderna: aproximación a su estudio*, ed. by Reyna Pastor (Madrid: CSIC, 1990), pp. 203–24

Alfonso, Isabel, 'Resolución de disputas y prácticas judiciales en el Burgos medieval', in *Burgos en la Plena Edad Media. III Jornadas Burgalesas de Historia* (Burgos: Asociación Provincial de Libreros de Burgos, 1994), pp. 211–43

Alfonso, Isabel, 'Campesinado y derecho: la vía legal de su lucha (Castilla y León, siglos X–XIII)', *Noticiario de Historia Agraria*, 13 (1997), 15–31

Alfonso, Isabel, 'La contestation paysanne face aux exigences de travail seigneuriales en Castille et Léon: Les formes et leur signification symbolique', in *Pour une anthropologie du prélèvement seigneurial dans les campagnes médiévales (XIᵉ–XIVᵉ siècles): réalités et représentations paysannes. Colloque tenu à Medina del Campo du 31 mai au 3 juin 2000*, ed. by Monique Bourin and Pascual Martínez Sopena (Paris: Publications de la Sorbonne, 2004), pp. 291–320

Alfonso, Isabel, ed., *The Rural History of Medieval European Societies: Trends and Perspectives* (Turnhout: Brepols, 2007)

Álvarez Borge, Ignacio, 'Sobre las relaciones de dependencia en las behetrías castellanas en el siglo XIII: hipótesis a partir del caso de las Quintanillas', in *Señorío y feudalismo en la Península Ibérica (ss. XII–XIX). Vol. 3*, ed. by Eliseo Serrano Martín and Esteban Sarasa Sánchez (Zaragoza: Institución Fernando el Católico, 1993), pp. 225–40

Álvarez Borge, Ignacio, ed., *Comunidades locales y poderes feudales en la Edad Media* (Logroño: Universidad de la Rioja, 2001)

Barceló, Miquel, *Arqueología medieval. En las afueras del 'medievalismo'* (Barcelona: Crítica, 1988)

Escalona, Julio, 'Paisaje, asentamiento y Edad Media: reflexiones sobre dos estudios recientes', *Historia Agraria*, 20 (2000), 227–44

Estepa Díez, Carlos, 'Proprietà, evoluzione delle strutture agrarie e trasformazioni sociali in Castiglia (secoli XI–XII)', in *Strutture e trasformazioni della signoria rurale nei secoli X–XIII*, ed. by Gerhard Dilcher and Cinzio Violante (Bologna: Il Mulino, 1996), pp. 411–43

Estepa Díez, Carlos, *Las behetrías castellanas*, 2 vols (Valladolid: Junta de Castilla y León, 2003)

Fox, Harold S. A., 'Exploitation of the Landless by Lords and Tenants in Early Medieval England', in *Medieval Society and the Manor Court* ed. by Zvi Razi and Richard Smith (Oxford: Oxford University Press, 1996), pp. 518–68

García de Cortázar, José Ángel and Pascual Martínez Sopena, 'Los estudios sobre la historia rural de la sociedad hispanocristiana', *Historia Agraria*, 31 (2003), 57–83

Gibert, Rafael, 'El *contrato de servicios* en el Derecho medieval español', 15 (1951), 5–129

Hilton, Rodney, *Bond Men Made Free: Medieval Peasant Movements and the English Rising of 1381* (London: Temple Smith, 1973)

Hilton, Rodney, *The English Peasantry in the Later Middle Ages* (Oxford: Oxford University Press, 1975)

Hilton, Rodney, *Siervos liberados. Los movimientos campesinos medievales y el levantamiento inglés de 1381* (Madrid: Siglo XXI, 1978)

Hilton, Rodney, 'Reasons for Inequality among Medieval Peasants', in *Class Conflict and the Crisis of Feudalism*, ed. by Rodney Hilton (London: Verso, 1990), pp. 66–78

Hilton, Rodney, ed., *The Transition from Feudalism to Capitalism* (London: New Left Books, 1976)

Hilton, Rodney, ed., *La transición del feudalismo al capitalismo* (Barcelona: Crítica, 1977)

Martín Cea, Juan Carlos, 'Una pequeña contribución al conocimiento del campesinado castellano: el yuguero', in *El pasado histórico de Castilla y León. Actas del I Congreso de Historia de Castilla y León celebrado en Valladolid, del 1 al 4 de diciembre de 1982. Vol. 1* (Burgos: Junta de Castilla y León, 1983), pp. 101–12

Martín Cea, Juan Carlos, *El mundo rural castellano a fines de la Edad Media. El ejemplo de Paredes de Nava en el siglo XV* (Valladolid: Junta de Castilla y León, 1991)

Martín Cea, Juan Carlos, 'El trabajo en el mundo rural bajomedieval castellano', in *El trabajo en la historia. Séptimas Jornadas de Estudios Históricos*, ed. by Ángel Vaca Lorenzo (Salamanca: Ediciones Universidad de Salamanca, 1996), pp. 91–128

Martínez Díez, Gonzalo, 'Los fueros inéditos de Mojados', in *Estudios en homenaje a Don Claudio Sánchez Albornoz en sus 90 años. Vol. 2* (Buenos Aires: Instituto de Historia de España, 1983), pp. 453–67

Martínez García, Luis, 'Los campesinos solariegos en las behetrías castellanas durante la Baja Edad Media', in *Los señoríos de Behetría*, ed. by Carlos Estepa Díez and Cristina Jular Pérez-Alfaro (Madrid: CSIC, 2001), pp. 187–226

Martínez García, Luis, '*Solariego* Peasants in Castile's Late Medieval *Behetrías*', in *Land, Power, and Society in Medieval Castile: A Study of Behetría Lordship*, ed. by Cristina Jular Pérez-Alfaro and Carlos Estepa Díez (Turnhout: Brepols, 2009), pp. 229–74

Martínez Sopena, Pascual, 'Las solidaridades campesinas en la Tierra de Campos durante la Edad. Media', in *Solidaritats pageses, sindicalisme i cooperativisme. Segones Jornades sobre Sistemas agraris, organització social i poder local als Països Catalans*, ed. by Jaume Barrull, Joan Josep Busqueta, and Enric Vicedo (Lleida: Institut d'Estudis Ilerdencs, 1998), pp. 93–113

Martínez Sopena, Pascual, 'Autour des *fueros* et des chartes de franchises dans l'Espagne médiévale', in *Pour une anthropologie du prélèvement seigneurial dans les campagnes médiévales (XIe–XIVe siècles): réalités et représentations paysannes. Colloque tenu à Medina del Campo du 31 mai au 3 juin 2000*, ed. by Monique Bourin and Pascual Martínez Sopena (Paris: Publications de la Sorbonne, 2004), pp. 211–37

Monsalvo Antón, José María, 'Transformaciones sociales y relaciones de poder en los concejos de frontera, siglos XI–XIII: aldeanos, vecinos y caballeros ante las instituciones municipales', in *Relaciones de poder, de producción y de parentesco en la Edad Media y Moderna: aproximación a su estudio*, ed. by Reyna Pastor (Madrid: CSIC, 1990), pp. 107–70

Oliva Herrer, Rafael, *La Tierra de Campos a fines de la Edad Media. Economía, sociedad y acción política campesina* (Valladolid: Universidad de Valladolid, 2002)

Pastor, Reyna, *Resistencias y luchas campesinas en la época del crecimiento y consolidación de la formación feudal: Castilla y León, siglos X–XIII* (Madrid: Siglo XXI, 1980)

Pastor, Reyna, 'Poder monástico y grupos domésticos foreros', in *Poder monástico y grupos domésticos en la Galicia foral (siglos XIII–XV)*, ed. by Reyna Pastor and others (Madrid: CSIC, 1990), pp. 49–234

Pastor, Reyna, and others, *Poder monástico y grupos domésticos en la Galicia foral, siglos XIII–XV* (Madrid: CSIC, 1990)

Pastor, Reyna, and others, *Transacciones sin mercado: instituciones, propiedad y redes sociales en la Galicia monástica, 1200–1300* (Madrid: CSIC, 1999)

Pastor, Reyna, and others, *Beyond the Market: Transactions, Property and Social Networks in Monastic Galicia, 1200–1300* (Leiden: Brill, 2002)

Reglero de la Fuente, Carlos, 'Le prelèvement seigneurial dans le royaume de Leon: Les évêchés de Leon, Palencia et Zamora', in *Pour une anthropologie du prélèvement seigneurial dans les campagnes médiévales (XIᵉ–XIVᵉ siècles): réalités et représentations paysannes. Colloque tenu à Medina del Campo du 31 mai au 3 juin 2000*, ed. by Monique Bourin and Pascual Martínez Sopena (Paris: Publications de la Sorbonne, 2004), pp. 411–42

PART III

Conflict and Competition
From Local Disputes to Political Struggles

CHAPTER 8

On Violence

with a commentary by André Evangelista Marques

Conflict, Language, and Social Practice in Medieval Societies: Selected Essays of Isabel Alfonso, with Commentaries, ed. by Julio Escalona Monge, Álvaro Carvajal Castro, and Cristina Jular Pérez-Alfaro, TMC 24 (Turnhout: Brepols, 2024), pp. 293–330

BREPOLS ❧ PUBLISHERS   10.1484/M.TMC-EB.5.132462

ANDRÉ EVANGELISTA MARQUES ⸻⸻⸻⸻⸻

The Social Logic of Vengeance

Towards a Reading of Isabel Alfonso's Work on Conflict Resolution

Back in 2010, while entering the final stage of my doctoral thesis, I was invited by Isabel Alfonso to join the PRJ project's research team, who had been working for some years on a survey of the entire corpus of Iberian dispute records up to 1100, now available online.[1] This brought me to work under the close supervision of an exceptionally learned and original scholar, who has played a pivotal role among historians of medieval Iberia in laying the foundations of a truly interdisciplinary and comparative history. Isabel's typically sceptical and always thought-provoking approach to the received historiography, along with an eye for detail and the ability to capture the various shades of meaning that can be derived from the sources, have allowed her to build a highly relevant and original body of work which has paved the way for much innovative research on different aspects of medieval Iberian society and politics. The present volume rightly celebrates this achievement in an original manner. My task here is not so much to gloss an article that speaks for itself in its utmost revealing micro-historical analysis of two documents from which the author draws very interesting conclusions about the social logic of vengeance, but rather to show how this piece fits into the much larger polyptych that Isabel has been painting over the last decades on the broader topic of dispute settlement and conflict resolution in medieval Iberia.

Isabel's research interests span two different areas not entirely apart from each other. On the one hand, she has paid much attention to rural history, with a special focus, first, on the monastery of Moreruela and the Cistercian 'colonization' of the Duero Valley (the topic of her doctoral thesis), and later, on the political agency of rural communities, their internal stratification and their involvement in power conflicts with external players. On the other hand, and this is hardly surprising from a student of Luis García de Valdeavellano's who started her career in academia teaching institutional history at the Universidad Complutense, Isabel devoted much

---

[1] *Judicial Processes in Early Medieval Societies in Northern Iberia (9th–11th centuries)*, at http://prj.csic. es/ [Date accessed: 22 February 2022]. The PRJ database offers access to the text of every single dispute record and full-text search capacities on the whole corpus. Complex queries are also available, allowing for cross comparison between different time frames, regions, the institutions where the records were originally produced/transmitted, forms of transmission (originals/copies), and ratios of dispute records to the overall number of extant records.

André Evangelista Marques, Universidade Nova de Lisboa

of her research effort over the last decades to the rise of conflicts and their resolution through legal disputes, violence and other forms of social and political action. The article I was asked to comment on clearly fits into this second research area, but it also examines two documents concerned with disputes between rural communities and aristocratic kinship groups, which makes the connection to the first topic all the more evident. This piece is thus particularly illustrative of Isabel's research, as indeed are others collected in the present volume.

By adopting an anthropologically inspired approach to conflicts, Isabel became one of the first, and still few, Iberian medievalists to look into the full range of norms and sociopolitical strategies that could potentially be deployed in a dispute.[2] She thus took aim at the legal paradigm that held sway in Iberian historiography until very recently and, in a long string of papers that explore different types of sources,[3] has made a decisive contribution to a whole new way of thinking about dispute settlement and conflict resolution. Two main points deserve special mention here. First, justice is no longer seen as a 'simple attribute of power',[4] consisting in the enforcement of abstract laws, but rather as part and parcel of power politics with their inherent conflicts and symbioses cutting across social strata and institutional as well as territorial scales.[5] Justice is thus reconceptualized as a political and social arena, with the focus on the social uses of law, rather than on the norm itself. Second, and perhaps more importantly for the purposes of the present commentary, judicial process is presented as one amongst several possible modes of conflict resolution. Legal disputes are often the most visible aspect — both due to the sources' nature and to historians' preconceptions — of much more complex disputing processes in the settlement of which the law, custom, compromise, violence, and other forms of public legitimation all could play a part.

Isabel's work on violence and its actual and symbolic uses is a particularly good example of the key role she has played in introducing legal and political anthropology to an Iberian audience.[6] Against traditional views of medieval (and especially 'feudal') violence as a feature of a 'primitive' society, and a means for social domination and oppression, Isabel espoused a more processual approach that has been gaining acceptance in the field of medieval studies, and especially among students of the

---

2 Despite the evident delay of Portuguese historians vis-à-vis their Spanish colleagues in the use of anthropological models, it is fair to cite here José Mattoso's innovative analysis of the inner workings of a rural community based on the late twelfth- and early thirteenth-century local codes from Riba-Côa: Mattoso, 'Da comunidade primitiva ao município'.

3 These include dispute records, by-laws and charters of privilege (which Isabel has convincingly shown are often the negotiated outcome of disputes that the texts' rhetoric tends to conceal), and narrative texts, either in prose or verse.

4 Alfonso, 'Campesinado y derecho' [Editors' note: For an English translation, see chapter 9 of this volume].

5 Alfonso and Escalona, 'Introduction'.

6 Four papers deserve special note. Two draw on documentary sources: the article commented on here, and Alfonso, 'Litigios por la tierra' [Editors' note: For an English translation, see chapter 13 of this volume]; the other two draw on narrative sources: Alfonso, 'Venganza y justicia'; Alfonso, 'Vengeance, justice et lutte politique' [Editors' note: For an English translation, see chapter 5 of this volume].

THE SOCIAL LOGIC OF VENGEANCE   297

early Middle Ages, since the 1980s.[7] According to this view, much influenced by anthropological thinking, violence was used not only as an aggressive, punitive, or dissuasive strategy to which the contending parties could resort to in a conflict, but also as a symbolic resource at the disposal of those in charge of producing some kind of oral or written account that could legitimize the whole settlement process and its outcome. Given that violence could be portrayed as either 'negative' or 'positive', according to context, it should by no means be seen as necessarily opposed to justice. In other words, the ways in which violence was socially construed become as relevant to the historian as its material realization.[8]

Isabel puts this theoretical framework to very good use in this article on vengeance and the 'regulation of violence in local settings', in which she embarks on a detailed analysis of 'the only [two Iberian] documentary pieces of this period that refer to the practice of blood feuds as it has been traditionally understood' (p. 305). The first, preserved in the monastery of Oña's cartulary, dates 1217, and records a dispute between seventeen men related to the aristocratic Rojas family and the council of Hontomín over the murder of Diego Rodríguez, a member of that family.[9] The second dates 1291, was preserved in the cartulary of Zamora cathedral, and records a dispute between the kin of Alfonso Pérez and the council of Manganeses and Junciel, following Alfonso's murder.[10] By presenting several common features regarding the disputing process and the status of the contending parties, these two texts can shed light on one another. Above all, they provide the author with illuminative case-studies of the nature and uses of vengeful violence, including the right to renounce it; and they allow for 'a more accurate, less simplistic, understanding and analysis of the very different types of violence and their various forms of resolution in these societies' (p. 306).[11] To that effect, Isabel examines two major sets of questions, while exploring both texts in parallel.

Context and Players

The first set revolves around the contexts for the disputes: the identity of the parties and other players involved, the different roles each group is seen to be playing, and the imbricated ties between them, which make for a complex local game that was brought to bear on the dispute. The author sets out to investigate the parties in both cases, starting with an attempt at a genealogical reconstruction of the individuals named as members of the aristocratic groups presented in the documents as plaintiffs.

---

7   For a good overview, see Brown, *Violence in Medieval Europe*. For an illuminating example of such a processual approach, see, among his many papers, White, 'Re-penser la violence'.

8   Alfonso, 'Los nombres de la violencia' [Editors' note: For an English translation, see chapter 16 of this volume].

9   SSOña-A409 (1217).

10   TBZ280 (1291).

11   On medieval vengeance, see Smail and Gibson, eds, *Vengeance in Medieval Europe*, and, for one example among a vast literature, Barthélemy, Bougard, and Le Jan, eds, *La vengeance*.

Special attention is paid to the distinction between natural and 'artificial' kinship bonds and to the complex mesh of alliances and dependencies that structured each group, which Isabel has tried to unravel by looking into a vast array of other records extant for each region. The issue of gender is also addressed with reference to disputes in which women, acting as plaintiffs, claim for vengeance for the death of their sons, brothers, or nephews, as is the case with the mother of Alfonso Pérez. The author concludes that age, social status and wealth seem to have played a much more important role than gender identity in women's ability to engage in a violent course of action seeking retribution. The question remains whether they could do it on their own, which does not seem to be the case in the disputes studied here. Isabel then progresses to characterize the rural communities acting as defendants. In both cases they seem to act together and take a 'collective responsibility', although litigation actually falls in the hands of 'men' from Hontomín and 'representatives' (*personeros*) from Manganeses, which allows Isabel to suggest different levels of institutional organization between the two councils.[12] The extent to which these men/representatives act as community members or rather as their leaders remains to be assessed, and one should not exclude the possibility that they were fighting for interests somehow more limited than those of the entire community. Finally, attention is paid to the 'mediators' that helped reach a final settlement in either case. They were members of ecclesiastical bodies that happened to be the lords of the rural communities, the monastery of Oña in the case of Hontomín, and the bishop and chapter of Zamora in the case of Manganeses. In the dispute opposing the Rojas to Hontomín, some of the mediators from Oña were also related by kinship and other ties to the Rojas, a family whose patronage relationship with Oña is clearly documented in a variety of records. All of this suggests a complex social and institutional fabric, forcing us to beware simplistic explanations for Oña's intervention, as Isabel perceptively notes (p. 320). I shall return to this point below.

The author's dissection of all these aspects yields a nuanced picture of the two local societies. In both disputes the dividing line not only cuts across social strata but also blends the lay and ecclesiastical spheres: the powerful Oña monastery and the Zamora bishop and cathedral side with their dependent peasant communities against the two aristocratic groups and, one could speculate, these groups' own dependents from within such communities. This unveils the intricacies of social and political action, with individuals often having to walk a thin line between their own personal interests and those — at times conflicting — of their kindred, or of any other group they might be part of. As remarked by Isabel about the 1217 dispute, the members of a 'practical kinship group' (Bourdieu) called upon to avenge the killing of a relative 'acted according to both individual strategies and group solidarity, which were more contingent than is generally accepted. Their solidarity was triggered by blood ties as well as by obligations and alliances of other kinds' (p. 311). It is also important to bear in mind that these groups were not fixed entities acting cohesively through the

---

12 I wonder, though, whether the difference should not be put down more to scribal practice, and a different choice of words by different redactors, than to actual institutional asymmetries.

whole dispute process, but rather took on different configurations at different stages, as the author shows about the 1291 case (pp. 311–13). This was probably the result of changing circumstances throughout the process. Different social and procedural scenarios might demand the intervention of different actors, and the better the contending groups could cater for such different scenarios, the better they would succeed in advancing their claim.

Disputing Processes and their Recording

This brings us to the second set of questions addressed in this article, which revolves around the processes of dispute settlement and their recording, and prompts consideration of key topics in recent conflict scholarship such as ritual, narrative, rhetoric, and the use of legal concepts. Isabel's latest work is pretty much concerned with the records themselves and the ways in which they determine our perception of the disputing processes.[13] But this sort of preoccupation can be traced back to previous papers like this one, in which the silences in the two documents are interpreted as serving the rhetorical construction of both disputes. Neither the plaintiffs nor the redactors felt the need to detail the reasons behind the murders, which clearly shows that the focus of both texts was on the settlement of the disputes, not their causes. These processes aimed not so much at deciding on right and wrong, abstractly defined, as at reaching a palatable solution that could address the interests and expectations of the parties, obviously taking into account the differences between them in terms of social status and political power. While avoiding the causes for the two conflicts, the scribes were more generous in describing the disputing processes, with both cases being framed as (a) an accusation on the part of the kinship groups, leading to (b) acts of violent redress against the rural communities portrayed as the guilty party,[14] followed by (c) the 'indulgence' and 'forgiveness' extended by the kinship groups to the communities, which works as a trigger for (d) the final settlement. This leads Isabel to perceptively note how vengeance is used by the victors as a strategy to formalize the whole narrative of the dispute and to legitimize the plaintiff role they claim for themselves and their actions in the conflict — Bourdieu's concepts of 'officialisation' and 'symbolic capital' are invoked at this point (pp. 317–19, 326).[15] On the contrary, the documents are nearly silent about the intervention of the two local councils in the process, probably because such an information would sit uncomfortably with the texts' overarching narrative.

Having considered the narrative economy of both texts, the author embarks on a detailed analysis of the 'peace-making rituals' that 'publicly sealed the settlement of a

---

13 Alfonso, 'El formato de la información judicial'. See also the 'Database' section on the PRJ website, cited above, n. 1.

14 In the case of Hontomín, only the possibility of violence seems to be contemplated.

15 Perhaps this strategy can be attributed not only to the winning parties, but also to the two ecclesiastical institutions that might have controlled the recording of the conflict, if not the process of dispute settlement itself, as I suggest below.

dispute' and of the language used by the scribes in such accounts, drawing interesting parallels with legal concepts and procedures mentioned in royal legislation (namely Alfonso X's *Partidas*) and in local by-laws. By doing so, Isabel skilfully shows how the disputing process and its textual rendering can be used as a means to understand the social and political underpinnings of a conflict. There are common elements in the sequence of events recorded by each document: forgiveness is extended by the kinship groups to the rural communities, the former commit to not engage in reprisal against the latter and to treat as traitor any individual of their kin who defies such commitment, and the ecclesiastical institutions pledge to commemorate the anniversaries of the deceased men. However, the overall structure of the two records is quite different: the 1217 text presents a straightforward description of a process that can arguably be broken down into five consecutive steps,[16] while the 1291 text is a rather more elaborate account in which four different elements are presented with more detail.[17]

Through close analysis of the two documents, Isabel was able to dissect both processes of conflict resolution and to show how they differ from one another with regard to the purposes of the settlements reached,[18] to how the players and audiences in each case determined the choice of different rituals,[19] and, more broadly, to the whole 'dynamics of the conflict'.[20] She then takes a step further from her two case-studies to discuss the interpretative models used to make sense of this kind of disputing processes. After recalling the laconic nature of her material vis-à-vis the sort of narrative sources that have moulded mainstream views of medieval vengeance, she asks a key question: 'is it just a matter of a different narrative style? Or should one think of other forms that may have been used to suppress and regulate conflicts?' (p. 328). In other

---

16 These are: the forgiveness and commitment of no retaliation by the Rojas group, the pledge by Oña to commemorate the anniversary of Diego Rodríguez's death, the 'kiss of peace' ritual, the council's pledge to a yearly payment to Oña for the deceased's anniversary, and, finally, the commitment by the Rojas to rise against any of their kin that would inflict any damage (*iniuria*) against the men of Hontomín.

17 These are: an initial peace agreement (*avenencia*) that conflates the forgiveness extended by the kinship group to the council with the conditions imposed on the latter by the former, a series of formal commitments to uphold the agreement by members of the kinship group (made in their own name and as surrogates for relatives and other men), the acceptance of the agreement by the council's representatives, who also relinquish all claims against the other party, and the subscription of some of the deceased's closest relatives, of several witnesses, and of two royal notaries public.

18 'Unilateral forgiveness' in the first case, cessation of 'the hostilities and the subsequent escalation of violence' in the second (pp. 324, 327).

19 '[In the 1291 case] the gathering of witnesses seems to include more knights, squires, and urban clerics than that in Oña. To a certain extent, written rituals arise from repetition, and perhaps this entailed special oaths specifically used for this type of audience, as the representatives of the councils of the rural communities did not make their promises under this rite of "pact and homage" ("pleyto y homenaje"), and the victim's mother was also excluded from the act. Could it have meant compromising a kind of chivalrous honour?' (p. 326).

20 'The difference between these two narratives indicates that, although the logic of revenge was the same in both areas, in its cultural and legal aspects, the dynamics of the conflict diverged depending on various factors'. (p. 327).

words, can dispute records actually shed a new light on modes of conflict resolution traditionally seen as 'violent' and 'primitive', and therefore associated with the period before the alleged establishment of a 'rational' Romano-canonical procedure in the twelfth and thirteenth centuries? Isabel answers this question by summing up a series of features that her deep and nuanced analysis of the two cases has convincingly shown to sit uncomfortably with such views on medieval violence and conflict. And she concludes that dispute records claim for a 'conceptual background' that can help us 'further our knowledge of a revenge culture perceived in relation to, rather than in opposition to, justice, and other forms of conflict resolution which have been much more long lived' (p. 328). This brings us to one of the cornerstones of Isabel's work: the rejection of a binary opposition between what she calls the 'anthropological' and the 'traditional legal' models of dispute studies.[21] Such a dichotomy, Isabel has reminded us time and again, must give way to close scrutiny of the complex blend of conflict resolution strategies used throughout the medieval period, which must be assessed on the grounds of their 'efficacy' and social embeddedness rather than their 'rationality' (p. 328).

Another more hidden, but by no means less important, strength of this article is that it lays bare the challenges that dispute records pose to the historian of medieval conflicts, and thus exposes the tricky relationship between text and reality. One of the main accomplishments of Isabel's work is to have shown how patchy and yet complex dispute records are. Not only they rely upon a highly codified (when not technical) language and ritual that were meant to produce a rhetorical effect and strike the right chord with their contemporary audiences, but they can also be ambiguous, when not intentionally misleading. Legitimation strategies largely outstrip accurate description in these texts. This makes them all the more puzzling to modern historians, who can seldom claim a full grasp of any such text. A slight departure from Isabel's interpretation on the actual role of the ecclesiastical institutions presented as mediators in the two documents examined in this article allows me to illustrate this point.

Mediators or Interested Parties?

In fact, one can use some features pointed out by the author to suggest that the two councils portrayed as the guilty parties might have played a more discrete role in both conflicts than the texts would have us believe; and that the final settlements were the result of a negotiation between aristocratic kinship groups and ecclesiastical lords over matters that might have transcended the two murders — let us not forget that the monastery of Oña and the Zamora cathedral were the lords of Hontomín and Manganeses, respectively.[22] First, the dénouement of both conflicts seems to have

---

21 Alfonso, 'Introducción: desarrollo legal'.

22 Normative sources such as by-laws and royal legislation remind us of different forms of lordly abuses and violence against rural communities. But it is important to bear in mind, as Isabel quite rightly notes, a much broader scenario where violence was the direct consequence of competition over local

been brought about by a 'spiritual' resolution: it is the commitment on the part of the two ecclesiastical bodies to say masses for the soul of the victims that leads the kinship groups to relinquish their claims and pardon the rural communities (p. 321). Second, the councils' representatives seem to play a minor role in the peace-making rituals, or at least in the accounts of such rituals (pp. 323–24); and in the 1217 case, it is even a monk from Oña that performs the peace ritual on behalf of the council — notably *receiving* the kiss of peace from the deceased's relatives (p. 322). Also in this case, and this is my third point, 'It is striking that the narrative structure of the text implied that only the noblemen — self-declared victims and therefore entitled to exert repression — might breach the agreement, and that they were the only ones who swore not to engage in such a breach' (p. 324). Given that a pledge to abide by the agreement is more often than not made by the losing party, one can surmise that the whole process, or at least its recording, was controlled by the Oña monastery, who had the capacity to impose such a commitment on the Rojas. Finally, the peace settlements 'rely more often on the memory of the people than on their written form. The fact that in these cases they were recorded in writing is probably attributable to the fact that the mediators were clergymen, as well as to other factors unknown to us.' (p. 328). One could argue, though, that the very existence of the records should be put down to the ecclesiastical bodies' intervention as a sort of co-parties in the disputes, rather than as simple mediators.

The key question is thus whether they were acting as lords and protectors of the rural communities, on account of their greater leverage to force on the aristocratic groups an agreement more favourable to the communities, or as interested parties who were directly involved in the conflicts, despite their role being intentionally downplayed by the texts' redactors.[23] Although the responsibility for the murders seems to lie with the two communities (probably with some individuals within them more than others), one could fall back on Isabel's suggestion that these murders and the ensuing disputes were but steps in broader and longer conflicts opposing lay and ecclesiastical lords to hypothesise that the rural communities were used by their ecclesiastical lords as a sort of legal proxies in disputing processes actually fought by the latter. Possible catalysts for conflict between the kinship groups and the ecclesiastical institutions include competition over lordly control of the two communities and their territories,[24] and the shared holding of property and resources

---

economic resources and of power struggles 'between various groups and institutions at different levels and degrees, within a context of fragmentation among competing lords' (pp. 318–19).

23 Isabel had previously shown in an article where she looks into conflicts between Oña and the lesser aristocrats living in the monastery's environs that the different causes for such disputes 'reflect a mesh of social bonds in which alliance and antagonism are entwined in one and the same process', Alfonso, 'Resolución de disputas' (my translation). She later explored the 'complex relationships between lay and ecclesiastical aristocracies' based on Leonese charter material, Alfonso, 'Litigios por la tierra' [Editors' note: For an English translation, see chapter 13 of this volume].

24 The detail with which the redactor of the 1291 text tries to preclude this agreement being used by the council of Manganeses to protect the 'enemies' of the kinship group that lived in the surrounding areas hints at competition, if not conflict, over territorial lordship.

as a consequence of patronal relationships.[25] If confirmed, these hypotheses would help us bring the ecclesiastical 'mediators' to the centre stage of the disputes.[26]

This is the sort of question that may well never find an answer, given the paucity of information. It begs, in any case, for a close examination of the local contexts in which conflicts originate, evolve, and eventually fade away or mutate into other conflicts, as Isabel has very convincingly shown in numerous papers in which she resorts to all kinds of extant sources in order to patiently reconstruct the social and political milieux of specific disputes. At the same time, her work forces us to look into the texts themselves and to consider the multiple ways in which they conflate social agency and symbolic systems such as norms, rituals, and indeed violence. In a nutshell, it forces us to think about the social logic of conflict.[27] By using her vast historiographical culture to ask relevant questions and her perceptive eye for the sources to find innovative answers, Isabel has built a remarkable body of work that no student of law, conflict, and politics in medieval Iberia and beyond should dispense with.

---

25 Close ties could be pinpointed at least between some members of the Rojas kinship group and Oña (pp. 320).
26 Cf. two suggestive analyses of how large monasteries such as San Millán de la Cogolla and Sahagún used homicide cases associated with conflicts over communal areas (and thence liable to collective responsibility) to assert their lordly authority over dependent communities and their communal resources: Larrea Conde, 'Obispos efímeros', at pp. 194–96; and Escalona, 'One Monk, one Donkey, one Dead Man'.
27 I paraphrase here, rather freely, the term and concept of 'social logic of the text' coined by Spiegel, 'History, Historicism, and the Social Logic of the Text'; see also Spiegel, *The Past as Text*.

Bibliography

Alfonso, Isabel, 'Resolución de disputas y prácticas judiciales en el Burgos medieval', in *Burgos en la Plena Edad Media. III Jornadas Burgalesas de Historia* (Burgos: Asociación Provincial de Libreros de Burgos, 1994), pp. 211–43

Alfonso, Isabel, 'Campesinado y derecho: la vía legal de su lucha (Castilla y León, siglos X–XIII)', *Noticiario de Historia Agraria*, 13 (1997), 15–31

Alfonso, Isabel, 'Introducción: desarrollo legal, prácticas judiciales y acción política en la Europa medieval', *Hispania*, 57–197 (1997), 879–83

Alfonso, Isabel, 'Litigios por la tierra y "malfetrías" entre la nobleza medieval', *Hispania*, 57–197 (1997), 917–55

Alfonso, Isabel, 'Los nombres de la violencia y el control de su legitimación', *Hispania*, 61–208 (2001), 691–706

Alfonso, Isabel, 'Venganza y justicia en el Cantar de Mío Cid', in *El Cid: de la materia épica a las crónicas caballerescas*, ed. by Carlos Alvar Ezquerra, Fernando Gómez Redondo, and Georges Martin (Alcalá de Henares: Universidad de Alcalá, 2002), pp. 41–69

Alfonso, Isabel, 'Vengeance, justice et lutte politique dans l'historiographie castillane du Moyen Âge', in *La vengeance, 400–1200*, ed. by Dominique Barthélemy, François Bougard, and Régine Le Jan (Rome: École française de Rome, 2006), pp. 383–419

Alfonso, Isabel, 'El formato de la información judicial en la Alta Edad Media peninsular', in *Chartes et cartulaires comme instruments de pouvoir: Espagne et Occident chrétien (VIIIe–XIIe siècles)*, ed. by Julio Escalona and Hélène Sirantoine (Toulouse: Méridiennes-Université de Toulouse-Le Mirail, CSIC, 2013), pp. 191–218

Alfonso, Isabel, and Julio Escalona, 'Introduction', in *Building Legitimacy: Political Discourses and Forms of Legitimacy in Medieval Societies*, ed. by Isabel Alfonso, Hugh Kennedy, and Julio Escalona (Leiden: Brill, 2004), pp. ix–xxiii

Barthélemy, Dominique, François Bougard, and Régine Le Jan, eds, *La vengeance, 400–1200: actes du Colloque 'La Vengeance, 400–1200' réuni à Rome les 18, 19 et 20 septembre 2003*, Collection de l'Ecole française de Rome, 357 (Rome: École française de Rome, 2006)

Brown, Warren C., *Violence in Medieval Europe* (London: Longman, 2011)

Escalona, Julio, 'One Monk, one Donkey, one Dead Man: Contexts for a Homicide in a Tenth-Century Sahagún Charter', in *Records and Processes of Dispute Settlement in Early Medieval Societies: Iberia and Beyond*, ed. by Isabel Alfonso, José Miguel Andrade, and André Evangelista Marques (Leiden: Brill, forthcoming)

Larrea Conde, Juan José, 'Obispos efímeros, comunidades y homicidio en La Rioja Alta en los siglos X y XI', *Brocar*, 31 (2007), 177–200

Mattoso, José, 'Da comunidade primitiva ao município. O exemplo de Alfaiates', in idem, *Fragmentos de uma composição medieval* (Rio de Mouro: Círculo de Leitores, 2001 [1987]), pp. 28–40

Smail, Daniel Lord, and Kelly Gibson, eds, *Vengeance in Medieval Europe: A Reader*, Readings in Medieval Civilizations and Cultures, 13 (Toronto: University of Toronto Press, 2009)

Spiegel, Gabrielle M., 'History, Historicism, and the Social Logic of the Text in the Middle Ages', *Speculum*, 65 (1990), 59–86

Spiegel, Gabrielle M., *The Past as Text: The Theory and Practice of Medieval Historiography*, Parallax – Re-visions of Culture and Society (Baltimore: Johns Hopkins University Press, 1997)

White, Stephen D., 'Re-penser la violence: de 2000 à 1000', *Médiévales (L'an mil en 2000, eds Monique Bourin and Barbara H. Rosenwein)*, 37 (1999), 99–114

ISABEL ALFONSO

Death without Vengeance?

*The Regulation of Violence in Local Settings (Castile-León 13th c.)**

Among the documents from the monastery of Oña there is a letter dated to 1217 which states that the sons, brothers and other relatives of Rodrigo Díaz de Rojas gathered in the monastery with the prior, the whole monastic community, and the Abbott of Rioseco in May of that year.[1] The purpose of their encounter was to grant formal pardon and a promise of non-aggression to the council of Hontomín for the death of Diego Rodríguez, son of Rodrigo Díaz de Rojas. The reconciliation was sealed with a kiss as a sign of perpetual peace. The people of Hontomín, who were vassals of Oña, by means of five representatives, committed to pay ten *maravedís* to the convent in order to celebrate a yearly mass for the soul of the deadman.

The cartulary of the cathedral of Zamora known as *Tumbo Blanco* preserves a copy of the agreement made in 1291 between Alfonso Pérez's relatives and the council of Manganeses and Junciel, who were vassals of the bishop.[2] Under the agreement, Alfonso Pérez's relatives forgave his death, withdrew the accusation of murder they had made, and granted a lasting truce to the council. The bishop and the chapter promised to have masses sung for the soul of the deceased. In turn, the council's representatives undertook to withdraw the complaints that they had made against the relatives and to abide with the terms of the agreement.

The similarity between these two documents, coming from institutions as far apart as Burgos and Zamora, is remarkable, as is their uniqueness. To the best of my knowledge, they are the only documentary pieces of this period[3] that refer to the practice of blood feuds as it has been traditionally understood, i.e.: acts of violence that were necessary after the killing of a relative, normally triggering a cycle of violence that was difficult to appease. The violence that is usually said to characterise medieval societies has been attributed to the proliferation of these feuds, a phenomenon that has been more often assumed than studied. This violence is portrayed as private, anarchic, unregulated, instinctive, cruel and primitive, and it is posited that it only

---

* Original publication: Alfonso, Isabel, '¿Muertes sin venganza? La regulación de la violencia en ámbitos locales (Castilla y León, siglo XIII)', in *El lugar del campesino. En torno a la obra de Reyna Pastor*, ed. by Ana Rodríguez (Valencia: Universidad de Valencia, 2007), pp. 261–87. Translated by Julian Thomas. I am grateful to Julio Escalona and Cristina Jular, who read and commented on this article.

1 SSOña-A 409 (1217). It is a copy preserved in fol. 64 of the fourteenth-century cartulary of Oña.

2 TBZ280 (1291). The editor commented upon this charter in Sánchez, 'La venganza de sangre'.

3 I refer here to those published in the collections of ecclesiastical institutions that, as is well known, may have been preserved because they were written and/or archived there.

306   ISABEL ALFONSO

became gradually controlled by the development of public bodies. These and other commonplaces such as honour codes and chivalrous ethics, which I will discuss later, are also used to explain vengeance.

Such widespread assumptions have largely prevented a more accurate, less simplistic, understanding and analysis of the very different types of violence and their various forms of resolution in these societies. This field has undergone substantial review, something to which Reyna Pastor's studies on peasant/nobility conflicts have contributed greatly.[4] These pages are intended as a recognition of that work. The first part of this chapter contains a detailed analysis of the two aforesaid documents, and some concluding remarks about the regulation of this specific type of violence will be added later.

Groups in Conflict: Kinship Groups and Peasant Communities

In both texts there was a conflict between a kinship group and a small community organised as a council. In both, the council was held responsible, and then forgiven, for the murder or death of a member of a kinship group — in one case, a brother; in the other, a son — according to the person who stood as spokesman for the group. It is worth paying attention to how these groups were structured in these situations.

Fratres et consanguinei atque parentes

In the first case, the victim belonged to a group of seventeen people who identified themselves as 'brothers', 'blood relatives' and 'relatives' ('nos omnes fratres et consanguinei atque parentes'). For the first two categories, 'brothers' and 'blood relatives', the names and kin relationships were listed in the following order: first, the two brothers, then the sister, followed by the paternal uncle with his two sons, and finally, the paternal aunt. The eleven 'relatives' were only mentioned by name, although they were all linked to the Rojas, a noble family group that is relatively well known in the region in the late Middle Ages — the dead person was referred to as the son of Rodrigo Díaz de Rojas. Speaking of 'the Rojas', though, is purely conventional in this case, as contrary to the group from Zamora, they did not purport to be either a lineage or a *bando*. In this charter they refer to themselves twice as 'of our kin and that of Diego Rodríguez' ('genere nostro uel Didaci Ruderici') or include themselves among 'all the relatives of Diego Rodríguez' ('omnes parentes Didaci Ruderici') without specifically identifying the degree of kinship between them.[5] Even a non-exhaustive review of this period's records shows eloquently the

---

4   Mainly in Pastor, *Resistencias y luchas campesinas*.

5   According to Ignacio Álvarez Borge, not even in the mid fourteenth century can they be considered to be a lineage, and they can be better described as a family group of the 'regional nobility'. He traced

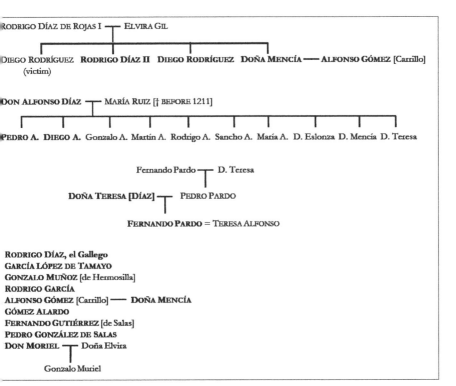

Figure 8.1. Members of the Rojas family group.

complex web of relationships that existed between them and with other families of the 'regional' and 'local' nobility.[6]

In the 1217 pardon the surname Rojas was only applied to the father of the victim. We know of his marriage to Elvira Gil and his high rank because years before they had received an estate in Los Tremellos from Alfonso VIII.[7] By this date, however, both

---

the bases of their estates and lordships, as registered in the *Libro Becerro de las Behetrías*, in Álvarez Borge, 'Los señoríos de los Rojas' [Editor's note: See an English version in Álvarez Borge, 'The Lordships of the Rojas']. The author is preparing a more extensive study on the estates of the Rojas, which will provide a better understanding of the family group and its different branches as outlined here [Editors' note: Published as Álvarez Borge, 'Poder local y poder central']. I am grateful to Ignacio for the information he has provided about the persons mentioned in the 1217 charter.

6 Carlos Estepa explained and accounted for this categories in an essential study on the subject, Estepa Díez, *Las behetrías castellanas*. This book provides the general framework that makes the microanalysis in these pages intelligible. I am grateful to Carlos for the opportunity to compare my data with his.

7 AlfonsoVIII-869 (1210). See also HospitalBurgos37 (1210). The question is whether (as I think) he is

must have been dead, as neither he nor his wife were mentioned among the injured party while his brother and sister feature at the top of the list. The information about them is uncertain due to homonymy cases, although the victim's brother whose name is the same as his father's may be related to a member of the Laras.[8]

More interesting is the fact that doña Mencía, the victim's sister, was married to Alfonso Gómez, who was listed among the unqualified relatives. Alfonso Gómez was a Carrillo, and the couple is recorded making donations to Oña together in 1243 and to San Juan de Burgos in 1245.[9] The Carrillos were another major branch of the 'regional nobility' whose origins are also very difficult to trace. A Rojas-Carrillo marriage shows that by the early thirteenth century the different branches of the nobility were already closely intertwined, even before they were clearly defined as such noble groups.[10]

After the victim's siblings, the paternal uncles were listed: don Alfonso Díaz first, and then doña Teresa. Alfonso Díaz and his prolific marriage to María Ruiz (which produced six sons and four daughters) is known from a donation they jointly made in 1211 for the soul of Alfonso's mother. They donated part of the inheritance they had received from her in Castrillo and San Lorenzo del Pisuerga to the Cathedral of Burgos. This donation was increased by the father in 1216 so that the chapter would have a clergyman sing daily masses for the dead and also pray regularly over the tomb of his wife — who presumably must have been buried in the same cathedral. At this time Alfonso Díaz claimed to be a member of the Rojas lineage, and his son Gonzalo Alfonso[11] was among the *infanzones* who acted as witnesses to the donation. In the 1217 act only the father — now a widower — was named together with his two older sons. We have more information about his second son, Diego Alfonso. Some evidence suggests that he may have been related to the Laras, as he had received at least one concession from Sancha Fernández de Lara somewhere in the Bureba. In 1245, he and his brother Sancho used the locative surname 'de Rojas' when they

---

the father or (as I. Álvarez thinks) he is the son.

8 It is hard to tell if it was the father or the son (see previous note), or even their namesake nicknamed 'el Gallego' ('the Galician'), the one that appeared with don Gonzalo Núñez de Lara in 1232 in a donation to the Monastery of San Andrés del Arroyo (Estepa Díez, *Las behetrías castellanas*, vol. 1, p. 371 and n. 15 below).

9 SSOña-A496 (1243); the witnesses included the sons of Alfonso Gómez: Rodrigo Alfonso and García Gómez. SJBurgos80 (1245); both husband and wife were listed in this donation, as well as among the *hidalgo* witnesses from the place where the land was sold.

10 C. Estepa alluded to the difficulty in identifying the Carrillos for periods before the composition of the *Libro Becerro* in the mid fourteenth century, on which see Estepa Díez, *Las behetrías castellanas*, vol. 2, pp. 378–80. The family name Carrillo was used by Alfonso Gómez in unpublished documents from the cathedral of Burgos dated to 1241–1245 (see CatBurgos628, 1241–1245; cited in Estepa Díez, *Las behetrías castellanas*, vol. 1, p. 378, n. 86).

11 CatBurgos437 (1211); CatBurgos496 (1216). On their estates and the mother's membership of the local nobility see, Estepa Díez, *Las behetrías castellanas*, vol. 1, p. 389 and vol. 2, pp. 43 and 224. Nevertheless, her burial in the Cathedral may indicate the woman's rise in status due to marriage, rather than the reverse.

DEATH WITHOUT VENGEANCE   309

testified in the inquest into the estates that Oña claimed from the knights of Tamayo, one of whom is also listed among the Rojas, as we shall see.[12]

The study of the victim's paternal aunt, doña Teresa, leads to the group that founded and had the usufruct of the hospital of Valdefuentes, the Pardos. Teresa Díaz was married to Pedro Pardo. After the death of her father-in-law Fernando Pardo, they jointly inherited the lifetime holding of Valdefuentes, granted by Alfonso VIII in 1196. Fernando Pardo was undoubtedly an important figure in the twelfth century. He appears in both the Rioseco and Las Huelgas records, and also subscribing charters issued by people in the royal entourage.[13] In the pardon charter of 1217 next to the name of Teresa Díaz — conceivably by then a widow — appears Fernando Pardo. Although the document does not precise their relationship, this is evidenced when Teresa — now the single holder of Valdefuentes — is documented with her son, named after his grandfather, who was to receive the same royal concession when she died.[14]

So siblings and brothers-in-law, uncles and cousins were the plaintiffs against the council of Hontomín for the death of one of their own. The relatives also included others whose kinship ties are undocumented, although they are often recorded acting together. Therefore, one might justifiably think of artificial kinship bonds, that is, patronage and clientship. While Rodrigo Díaz 'el Gallego',[15] Rodrigo García, and Pedro González de Salas remain undocumented, others can be identified. Thus, Gonzalo Muñoz and Gómez Alardo were jointly appointed by Alfonso VIII as inquirers in a dispute over pastures between the neighbours of Arce, Cellorigo and Miranda.[16] This strongly suggests that Gonzalo Muñoz is the same Gonzalo Muñoz de Hermosilla that also acted as inquirer in the dispute between Oña and the knights of Tamayo.[17]

One of the latter, García López de Tamayo, features too among the Rojas, although we do not know exactly his connection to the group. He is nevertheless one of its

---

12 Huelgas336 (1242); SSOña-A501 (1245). For later evidence on this individual see Estepa Díez, *Las behetrías castellanas*, vol. 1, pp. 189 and 389.

13 AlfonsoVIII-71 (1165); AlfonsoVIII-87 (1166); AlfonsoVIII-172 (1172); AlfonsoVIII-181 (1173); AlfonsoVIII-271 (1176); AlfonsoVIII-342 (1180); AlfonsoVIII-474 (1187); AlfonsoVIII-650 (1196). See also González, *El Reino de Castilla en la época de Alfonso VIII*, pp. 609–10. SMRioseco049 (1188); SMRioseco051 (1188); SMRioseco060 (1193); Huelgas42 (1196).

14 HospitalBurgos69 (1218). However, years later the hospital was repossessed by Fernando III, when Fernando Pardo, together with his wife Teresa Alfonso (perhaps his cousin?) waived their rights to it in his favour in exchange for the lifelong lease of all the hospital's possessions in Moncalvillo and Río Francos (HospitalBurgos183, 1237).

15 C. Estepa suggests that the nickname may be due to his relationship with the Lara based in Galicia, who in 1232, together with his wife Teresa Sánchez, sold an estate in Cozuelos de Ojeda to S. Andrés del Arroyo that had been received precisely by count Gonzalo Núñez de Lara. Doubt remains as to whether it is this one or the Rodrigo Diaz II of 1217, on which see Estepa Díez, *Las behetrías castellanas*, vol. 1, pp. 175, 388.

16 AlfonsoIX-905 (1213). Gómez Alardo also witnessed a donation to the monastery of Vileña — a daughter house of Las Huelgas's — by Queen Urraca López, wife of Fernando II. Don Munio, already by then abbot of Oña, appeared as first witness, and the *infanzones* included Gonzalo Gómez, son of Gómez Alardo, and the latter's brother, Gonzalo Gómez. See Huelgas173 (1222).

17 SSOña-A421 (1218). A hypothesis also put forward in Estepa Díez, *Las behetrías castellanas*, vol. 2, p. 22, who also classifies him as 'local nobility'.

best evidenced figures because of the — basically contemporary — dispute that he and his brothers had with Oña over the control of the village which gave its name to the family.[18] The same block of evidence justifies identifying Fernando Gutiérrez, another member of the group, as Fernando Gutiérrez de Salas. Not only did he appear as a witness together with the Tamayos and negotiating with Oña, but also with don Moriel, the last and most enigmatic character in the list.[19] Don Moriel was known only by his name, perhaps because of a higher social position, or simply because of his unusual name. His being mentioned in last place does not necessarily indicate a lower place in the hierarchy. Instead, he could actually be casting a protective influence over the whole group. Don Moriel appears in charters from the monastery of Rioseco and Hospital del Rey, but most significantly he was a benefactor of Las Huelgas de Burgos, where his widow, doña Elvira, was secluded, and where both the couple and their son, Gonzalo Moriel, were buried. He is most visible in his role as *merino mayor* of Castile between 1235–1239, which reflects the high position he had reached. This, however, does not clarify his relationship to the Rojas.[20] In his role as *merino* he judged a dispute of the monastery of Rioseco, which he and his wife had favoured in 1229 with a grant of the estates received from his grandmother, Elvira Muñoz de Quintanajuar. Acting as surety in this donation was Martín Alfonso, one of the many sons of Alfonso Díaz de Rojas. Don Moriel himself was also a surety in a donation that another relative, Fernando Gutiérrez de Salas, made to Las Huelgas in 1219. This confirms the identity of the latter, and shows that he accompanied Don Moriel in court as *merino*, where he appeared among the subscribers in royal diplomas.[21]

Since we do not know the naming criteria and the context and roles in which the actors sought to be identified, these 'objectivist' assertions do not support many more deductions.[22] It should be noted, though, that this prosopographic reconstruction, albeit cursory, reveals that not all of the victim's kin were summoned, or if they

---

18 A year after the act of conciliation in 1217, Garci López and his brother don Tello returned the estates that they had usurped from Oña on the grounds that they were of *behetría* status, and acknowledged the violent acts committed. They gave the abbot a 'generous horse' ('caballo generoso') as compensation. Fernando Pardo appeared as one of the witnesses to this act. On the disputes between the Tamayo knights and Oña, and their forms of resolution, see Alfonso, 'Resolución de disputas', pp. 224 and ff.

19 Huelgas134 (1219); SSOña-A422 (1219); SSOña-A450 (1229); SSOña-A466 (1231); SSOña-A475 (1236), SSOña-A480 (1236).

20 I have been unable to find evidence of don Moriel being named Rodríguez de Rojas, as stated by Pérez-Bustamante, *El gobier no*, p. 308. This seems to have been subsequently used by other historians without prior confirmation.

21 For this information see Huelgas125 (1216); Huelgas134 (1229); Huelgas136 (1229); Huelgas289 (1237); Huelgas292 (1237); Huelgas316 (1240); Huelgas317 (1240); Huelgas320 (1240); Huelgas321 (1240); Huelgas354 (1245); Huelgas355 (undated); HospitalBurgos117 (1227); HospitalBurgos155 (1231); SMRioseco140 (1229); SMRioseco155 (1237); FernandoIII-556 (1235) to FernandoIII-663 (1239).

22 This is the case of the locative surname 'Rojas', which in the 1217 Oña charter was only used by one person, but apparently entailed no exclusivity, as it was also used by other members to identify themselves in different contexts during the same time period. However, this may have occurred non simultaneously, and its use may indicate actual or intended hierarchical positions within the family group. On this topic, see Martínez Sopena, 'La evolución de la antroponimia'.

DEATH WITHOUT VENGEANCE   311

were, they were not all present (see Fig. 1, with listed members in boldface). Some could be no longer alive, some could have been too young, some could be absent, but some may have actually avoided attending. Reacting in the event of the killing of a relative was not an automatic obligation, but a whole social process involving different members of what — following Bourdieu's apt characterisation — we can call a 'practical kinship group', as different to the notional kinship group.[23] These members acted according to both individual strategies and group solidarity, which were more contingent than is generally accepted. Their solidarity was triggered by blood ties as well as by obligations and alliances of other kinds, as suggested by the complex relationships between members discussed above. However scarce the surviving information, the group in dispute with the council of Hontomín was a good example of the interweaving of both regional and local nobility. However, further research is needed as to how these relationships were maintained and reproduced, and the specific circumstances in which they were deployed. With no information about the means and the arguments through which relatives were summoned, we cannot precise how the gathering was justified, even though thanks to other studies we know that this was a very complex process.[24] Nevertheless, these considerations must be kept in mind in order to compare how the other group was presented.

Relatives, Lineage and *bando*

In our second example, a broader kinship group gathered around the victim's mother, the widow María Gutiérrez. While in the first we only know the family relationship of seven people, ranging from siblings to paternal uncles and perhaps cousins, in the latter the group is referred to as 'other relatives of ours' ('otros nostros parientes') and 'all of our *bando* and of our lineage' ('todos los de nostro bando et de nostro linage'). Specifically, they were named at four different times:

a) In the opening, in this order: the mother — who was said to be the wife of Pedro González, son of Gonzalo Domínguez de Villapando — with her surviving son and another son of her husband, the victim's step-brother; two of his paternal uncles: Ruy and Gil González; and another two individuals with the surname of González. One, the son of Arias Gonzalo, and the other, the son of Juan González, the relationship between them not being indicated.[25] In total, thus, seven people (Fig. 2).

---

23 The concept was developed in Bourdieu, *Le sens pratique*.
24 An example of this is the analysis that can be found in Miller, *Bloodtaking*, ch. 6. Here the author shows how mobilising support was an ongoing process of creating obligations. Therefore, it was related to activities which maintained kinship and affinity, clientele and vicinity ties. The formation of these groups, therefore, depended on a large number of variables. On the legal regulation of this support obligation, which penalised those who failed to appear, some evidence from the Castilian-Leon by-laws was collected in Orlandis Rovira, 'Las consecuencias del delito'.
25 M. Sánchez assumed that the victim had some paternal cousins, since he considered — without documenting it — that their fathers were brothers. But he was clearly mistaken regarding other links,

Figure 8.2. Relatives of María Gutiérrez.

b) Upon the agreement: the mother, on her own behalf and on behalf of her son, whom she *manlieva*,[26] and the two paternal uncles named above, each endorsing one brother, Gómez González (not mentioned earlier), and others whose relationship is not indicated. The group is thus reduced to five names acting and representing themselves and those of their *bando* and their lineage (a total of thirteen people) in the agreement. It should be noted the leading representative role of the two paternal uncles, while the woman only represented her son (who was anyway also represented by the second of his uncles).

c) When the truce and pardon came into effect through 'pact and homage' ('pleyto et hommage'), and a promise was made to keep this pardon forever, the leading group changes. The mother's name disappears and the two paternal uncles swear for all those whom they *manlievan*, except Alvar López, who swore for himself. The consent of the other paternal uncle, Gómez González, to be represented in the oath by his two brothers is also explicit. The group is now reduced to four.

---

such as the step-brother of the victim, whom he considered to be a son from the mother's previous marriage, even though the document explicitly stats that he was a son of the father from a previous marriage. See Sánchez, 'La venganza de sangre', pp. 99–100.

26 The meaning of this term, like so many others, is not univocal. It is interesting that the gesture of 'raising the hand to swear' ('manum levare') was still associated with the economic burden of providing security in the event of an infringement. I believe this is the meaning used here, of representation through endorsement. Cf. RAE, *Diccionario*, s.v. 'manlevar'; Alonso, *Diccionario Medieval Español*, s.v. 'manlevar'; Niermeyer, *Mediae Latinitatis Lexicon Minus*, s.v. 'manulevare'. Later on I will refer to the social significance of this type of guarantee.

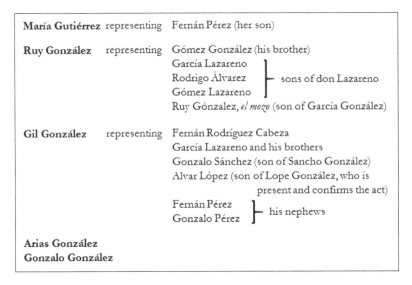

Figure 8.3. Representatives in the agreement.

d) And finally, when the commitments were secured by affixing their wax seals to the letter to be given to the council. This was done by the two paternal uncles referred in every instance above, together with Arias González, who appeared in the first, as well as the uncle who was always present.

Unlike the Rojas, I believe that the status of this group, whose oldest member claimed to be from Villalpando, is indicated indirectly by the fact that they had their own seal, as well as, perhaps, by the nature of the witnesses,[27] and most certainly by the fact that they referred to themselves with terms such as 'lineage' and *bando*, even if in this period the practical meaning of those terms is barely known.[28] In the absence of enough evidence to define the social category of the members of this group, some caution is advisable. Nothing indicates that they lived in any of the three places related to the dispute — Manganeses, Junciel and Pajares. They might have dwelt in Villalpando, the paternal grandfather's locative identification, and may have belonged to the group of local knights so well categorised by Martínez Sopena in this area.[29] If this is the case, then the *bando* does not seem to constitute an internal division of the

---

27 It must be remembered that only the seals of the two paternal uncles of the victim and another surnamed González, whose connection was not made explicit, appeared in the document. This does not mean that other members did not have seals, but may simply be an indication of the secondary role played by them in this act.

28 It is not possible here to deal with the extensive literature devoted to *bandos* and their fights, especially in the late medieval period and in urban areas. Some of the key issues can be found in Monsalvo, 'Parentesco y sistema concejil'; Díaz de Durana, ed., *La Lucha de Bandos* [Editors' note: For the English translation, see Díaz de Durana, *Anonymous Noblemen*].

29 Martínez Sopena, *La Tierra de Campos Occidental*.

community to which they belonged, as Villalpando seems to be merely a reference for the family, and there are no other territorial indications to locate their members. We must not rule out, however, that they may have formed part of the urban knights of Zamora. In any event, neither group belonged to the community that they were in conflict with, as was the case for the other group.[30] Regarding their internal hierarchy, the leading role of the paternal uncles is consistent throughout, with the inclusion of the victim's mother only in two occasions, during the accusation and upon the agreement. Conceivably, these would be the only occasions in which she would have played an active role, but she appeared too in the narration of the killings and wrongs inflicted on the people from Manganeses in the course of the conflict which they now sought to end. Unfortunately, there is not enough information to more accurately understand the extent of her involvement.

The explicit presence of women in these conflicts deserves some attention. In the case of Oña the victim's sister and aunt — of which only the latter was a widow — were present at the ritual of forgiveness where they renounced their revenge. In the Zamora case, the mother — also a widow — played a leading role in the vengeance process by making a claim and blaming the peasant council for the death of her son. An assumption that gender differentiation was critical in shaping behaviour and social representations can lead to interpretations such as that made by Marciano Sánchez, who believes that the interventions of women in revenge actions were exceptions that he attributed 'to the character of such women, somewhat hysteroid, and with a desire for prominence, which led them to break the rules'.[31] However, by considering the factors other than gender — such as age, status, wealth, etc. – that could influence men and women's roles, it is possible to offer alternative, more sophisticated explanations about the representations contained in the texts. Recent studies have proven that both age and socio-economic status were more important than sex identity in explaining the capacity to participate in these violent exchanges.[32] The fact that two of the avenging women in our texts were widows may explain their intervention in these conflicts, rather than it being the transgression of a specific social norm on inherently female behaviour. However, the presence of a sister of the victim along with her husband means that female participation cannot be explained out only thus. Of note here is that women's capacity to take violent action, as recognised in these and many other texts, precludes the holding of an essentialist view of sexual differentiation. An historical analysis is therefore advised on how such distinctions were constructed in different periods and contexts.[33]

---

30 M. Sánchez, on the contrary, noted the split or secession within the community that this conflict produced. Cf. Sánchez, 'La venganza de sangre', p. 100.

31 This author compared María Gutiérrez to María la Brava, from Salamanca, who famously avenged the death of her sons. See Sánchez, 'La venganza de sangre', p. 100.

32 N. Pancer convincingly showed the hierarchy of social relationships in the Merovingian world, and how sex was not the only significant factor involved, on which see Pancer, *Sans peur et sans vergogne*. This author very clearly analysed the status of the debate on sexual differentiation, by questioning the indiscriminate application of the modern English term 'gender' to all past societies.

33 Regarding vengeful women in our chronicles, see Alfonso, 'La vengeance' [Editors' note: For an

The Councils

Almost all that is known about the two small rural councils accused of these deaths, is that both were vassals of two ecclesiastical institutions: the powerful monastery of Oña in Burgos,[34] and the no less powerful cathedral of Zamora, although their status as vassals is only explicit for the latter: 'vassals of the bishop and of the church of Zamora' ('uassalos del obispo et de la eglisia de çamora').[35] As was the case for kinship groups, the internal organisation of the two peasant communities also differed. The spokesmen for Hontomín — 'with the voice and in the name of all the council' ('in uice atque nomine tocius concilii') — were simply called 'men' ('homines'), while those from Manganeses were presented as 'representatives' (*personeros*) of the council. This impression should be ratified with further evidence from both areas. In any case, the degree of institutional development apparently had no impact on the issues at stake, as both communities were able to send representatives to negotiate on a collective matter.[36] Five people from Hontomín were named,[37] and only four from Manganeses, a mayor (*alcalde*) among them.[38] They all remain unidentified, since they are not documented anywhere else.

What certainly deserves to be highlighted here is the sense of collective responsibility in these communities. What might have been the reasons that led these two small villages to confront such powerful kinship groups? Why did they collectively assume such responsibility? We know there were attempts to limit such extended accountability. As Reyna Pastor stated, these amendments were introduced in the so-called 'good by-laws' ('fueros buenos') because this kind of responsibility must

---

English translation, see chapter 5 of this volume].

34 The village of Hontomín lay on the road from Burgos to Villarcayo, 27 km away from the former. Hontomín, together with Pineda, had been given to Oña in 1190 by Alfonso VIII in exchange for other *villas* (SSOña-A286, 1190). This exchange was confirmed in 1231 by Fernando III (SSOña-A466, 1231; SSOña-A467, 1231). Later, Alfonso X granted Hontomín the right to hold a weekly market every Tuesday (SSOña-A603, 1272).

35 Manganeses was located south of Benavente, in the Zamora sector of Tierra de Campos, in the area of La Lampreana, and neighbouring the Villafáfila salt pans. It was donated by the king and by the Ponce de Cabrera family, to the Cathedral of Zamora in 1200 (CatZamora56, 1200). Junciel, a nearby hamlet, had also been transferred to the Cathedral following a dispute with the monastery of Moreruela (SMMoreruela80, 1226). Junciel appeared here as a subordinate annex of the council of Manganeses. Its name is not always mentioned when Manganeses is referred to. This may have been similar to the case of the Riojan suburb of Cojas with respect to Tobías, which, as shown in an inquest, were jointly responsible in cases of murder (SMCogolla-L189, 1089).

36 On these actions, see Jular Pérez-Alfaro, 'The King's Face'.

37 'We, the men of Hontomín, namely Martín Gascón, Pedro Sobrín, Martín Martín, and Juan, son of doña Helo and Gonzalo de la Vega, with the voice and in the name of all the council of Hontomín' ('Nos homines de Fomin, uidelicet Martines Gascon et Petrus Sobrin et Martines Martin et Iones filius de domna Helo et Gundisaluus de la Uega, uice atque nomine tocius concilii de Fonteomin').

38 'we made an agreement with Juan Rodríguez, the mayor, and with Pedro Juanes, and with Miguel Pérez, and with Pelayo Feibez, representatives of the council of Manganeses' ('feziemos auenencia con Johan Rodríguez el alcalde et con pedro yuanes et con miguel perez et con pelay feybez, personeros del conceyo de manganeses').

have been one of the most cumbersome and most strongly resisted.[39] Two tendencies can be observed in numerous dispositions in the by-laws. One of them pointed towards releasing the council from responsibility for killings occurred within the township boundaries if the perpetrator was unknown; the other was to prosecute only the perpetrator — individual responsibility — rather than the council as a group — collective responsibility. The well-meaning intention of these provisions was already postulated in the privilege of Alfonso VII to the council of Burgos made in 1152 to reward its good and faithful service:

> on that bad norm (*malo foro*) on homicide that you have had in Burgos so far, I declare you exempt from it, and I grant you a good and rightful statute so that if any man commits murder in Burgos or its township, he shall pay the *homicidium*, and the council shall not be held responsible and shall not have to pay the *homicidium*, and the officials of the Emperor shall demand his *homicidium* from he who killed the man.[40]

The same limitation is explicit in the by-law of Lara of 1135, which releases the council from liability for murders occurred within their boundaries and from the associated payment of *homicidium*.[41] In 1214, that is, a few years before the reconciliation event discussed, the by-law that the abbot of Oña granted the people of Cornudilla, Aldenas and Quintanilla stipulated that only the murderer had to pay (*pechar*) for his act: 'Whoever commits murder shall himself pay the *homicidium*, he and nobody else' ('Quicumque homicidium fecerit, ipsemet qui occiderit pectet illud et non alii').[42] Similar provisions were also established by Alfonso VIII in 1187 for the dwellers of the council of Valdefuentes, following the pleas made by Fernando Pardo (grandfather to the homonymous person listed among the relatives of the Rojas). The council would be exempt from liability for any dead body that was found hidden within their boundaries through oaths taken by five of its members:

> Moreover, if a man is killed or a dead man is hidden in your township, according to your by-law the council shall be released after five men have taken an oath, and then the dead shall be buried if the council so pleases, and it shall not pay for it and nobody shall demand any payment from it.[43]

---

39 See further examples in Pastor, *Resistencias y luchas campesinas*, pp. 241–43.

40 'de illo malo foro de illo homicidio, quod usque habuistis in Burgis, et modo aufero vobis eum, et dono vobis pro bono et directo foro ut omnis homo qui in Burgis uel in suo termino aliquem hominem interfecerit ipsemet pectet homicidium et non respondeat Concilium pro eo nec pectet ipsum homicidium, et maiorinus imperatoris querat suum homicidium super ipsum qui hominem interfecerit' (FB7e, 1152).

41 FB13 (1135): 'And if a man is killed in Lara or its township, the council shall not be held responsible for it nor pay the *homicidium*' ('Et si fuerit hominem occisum in Lara uel in suo terminos, non respondeat concilio per eum nec pectet homicidium').

42 SSOña-A402 (1214).

43 'Preterea, si aliqui homine mortum aliquem oculte in termino vestro proiecerint, secundum uestrum forum liberet se concilium et sacramenno saluet se cum quinque hominibus, et tunc

DEATH WITHOUT VENGEANCE 317

Some exemptions from collective responsibility can also be found in by-laws from more western villages, such as Melgar: 'And if anyone demands the *homicidium* from the council of these villages, the latter shall not be held responsible on behalf of any neighbour or any neighbour's son and shall demand it from he whoever had committed [the murder]'.[44] Interestingly, Zamora was the setting of the famous epic poem that narrates the Castilians' siege of the city and the dramatic accusation that the urban council had to face after the treacherous killing of King Sancho of Castile. As far as rhetoric goes, the famous challenge thrown by the Castilians was the broadest example of collective responsibility possible, as it addressed not only the living but also the dead, the born and unborn, the waters they drank, the clothes that they wore and the stones in the city walls.[45] The people of Zamora proposed to settle this matter through a trial by combat in which, according to the regulations, only five members of the council were to fight.[46] The fictional tone does not detract from the likelihood that such procedures were used to settle collective responsibilities, and seem to characterise the rest of the by-laws in the area.[47]

---

sepeliatur mortuus, si concilio placuerit, et nihil pro eo pectent nec ab aliquo exigatur eis pectum' (AlfonsoVIII-474, 1187).

44 'Et si algun demandar a concejo de estas villas omecillo, non responda por vecino et fijo de vecino e demanda aquel ficiere por nombre' (FP2, 970). It is difficult to be precise about the date of this by-law, as noticed by the editor in FP, pp. 45–49.

45 This story is told in PCG, § 834–44. The accusation is told as follows: 'The Castilians have lost their lord. He was killed by the traitor Vellido Dolfos, who was his vassal. After this betrayal, you protected him in Zamora. And for this I say that he is a traitor, and that whoever protects him is also a traitor if he knew of his betrayal, or consented to it, or could have stopped him. And I challenge the people of Zamora, both the highest and the lowest, both the dead and the living, both those who are to be born and those who have been born, and the waters the drink, and the clothes they wear, and even the stones of the wall' ('Los castellanos ha perdudo su sennor; et matol el traydor Vellid Adolffo seyendo su uasallo, et despues que fizo esta traycion, uos acogiestele en Çamora. Et digo por ende que es traydor el, et traydor el que lo tiene consigo, si sabie dantes de la traycion o si gela consintio o si uederagela pudo. Et riepto a los çambranos tanbien al gand como al pequenno, et al muerto tambien como al biuo, et al que es por nascer como al que es naçudo, et a las aguas que beuieren, et a los pannos que uistieren, et aun a las piedras del muro' (PCG, § 839).

46 After denying the accusation, the nobleman added: 'And you must know something: that whoever challenges the council must fight five men, first one and then another one, and that if he defeats those five, he shall stand as trustworthy, and if he is defeated by any of those five men, he shall stand as a liar' ('Et sepas una cosa; que tod aquel que riepta a conceio, que deue lidiar con cinco uno en pos otro; et si el uenciere a aquellos cinco, deue salir por uerdadero; et si alguno de aquellos cinco le uenciere, deue fincar por mintroso') (PCG, § 839).

47 José Luis Martín proposed a different reading of the provisions of the by-law of Salamanca which, in his opinion, limited blood vengeance in the same way, See Martín, 'Relectura del fuero de Salamanca', pp. 531–38.

318 ISABEL ALFONSO

Reasons for the Conflicts

What gave rise to such a strong sense of solidarity that prevented the perpetrators from being identified, both in Manganeses and in Hontomín? Was this liability voluntarily accepted or was it imposed? In order to explore possible answers to these questions, it is necessary to understand what caused this violence, and the possible reasons for the conflicts.

In both cases the reason adduced by those seeking vengeance was the direct or indirect responsibility of each council in the murder of a member of their kinship group, with no indication of place, circumstances, perpetrators, or reasons. Thus in Hontomín 'for the death of Diego Rodríguez' ('pro illa muerte Didaci Ruderici'), and in Manganeses 'for the death of Alfonso Pérez [...] which as we asserted was killed by the abovementioned council [...] or which participated in his killing' ('en razon de la muerte de Alfonso Pérez [...] que nos deziamos que lo mataran el conceyo sobredicho [...] o que fueran en lo matar'). Despite the lack of context, by merely invoking the killings, the relatives considered themselves entitled to blame and attack the party they deemed guilty, even if they only justified this implicitly by waiving their right to do so. The relatives of Diego Rodríguez termed 'indulgence' (*indulgentiam*) their promise not to retaliate against the neighbours of Hontomín for his death. The relatives of Alfonso Pérez, more eloquently, announced that they waived any claims or complaints derived from his death, by forgiving those from Manganeses.

Some evidence contained in the latter text allows for reconstructing a longer-standing conflict. According to the date of its anniversary, the killing of the Rojas member must have occurred only a few days before the pardon letter was issued.[48] In contrast, the Manganeses agreement was only reached after a longer phase of retaliation, apparently triggered by the killing, during which the lineage and *bando* of Alfonso Pérez committed 'many murders and evil deeds against the people of Manganeses as a result of this enmity' ('feycho muertes et otros males a los de Manganeses segundo esta ena enemizar'). It was this ongoing fight that the agreement intended to stop. The conditions laid out in the agreement suggest that the alleged killing did not trigger the conflict, but rather that the hostility was the context in which the killing occurred. However, it was the public declaration of enmity that gave it a lawful character and legitimised the reprisals that constituted the vengeance process, as contained in the by-laws and other rules applicable in homicide cases.[49] Framing a conflict in terms of revenge, even tacitly, was advantageous for those who were in a position to do it. It justified the hostilities and placed their cause on the shoulders of the other party.

---

48 In actual fact, the document only mentions the anniversary date, 'V idus maii' (11 May). It remains unclear how the editor concluded that that was also the date of the text.

49 Abundant evidence was collected by De Hinojosa y Naveros, 'El elemento germánico'; and from a more 'romanist' perspective in Orlandis Rovira, 'Sobre el concepto de delito'; Orlandis Rovira, 'Las consecuencias del delito'.

It moreover defined who the victims were and who the guilty party was, allowing the resolution process to be managed or controlled to their benefit.[50]

The reasons the communities had, if they ever had the chance to express them, were not recorded in writing. However, the surviving local by-laws frequently mention situations that demanded a collective response, such as force or harm to the neighbours, forced lodgements in their homes, threats to the village, or attacks from evil-doers. All these events called for community support that was recruited by invoking an *apellido*,[51] with penalties imposed on those who failed to comply and exemption if a homicide occurred in the course of action. With these considerations in mind we might speculate on the type of violence that the groups of relatives may have inflicted on the accused communities. Although it would be wiser to remember the existence of other conflict factors more directly related to the use and distribution of production resources, as well as the local struggles for power between various groups and institutions at different levels and degrees, within a context of fragmentation among competing lords. Despite the full loyalty that each lord could demand of their vassals, the most common practice was that of crossed alliances.[52] This is a terrain which is much less studied than it deserves; hence for the moment I will confine myself to an exegesis of the documents, and leave other considerations to the end.

Mediators and their Reasons for Mediating

In the two cases under discussion here, there was an intervention by third parties who mediated to achieve a resolution that would prevent or stop an escalation of violence. In both conflicts it was mainly — but not exclusively — the lords of the vassal communities that fulfilled this role. In the first case, they assembled in Oña, before its chapter, its prior, its steward and a monk, along with abbot don Rodrigo de Rioseco, who offered to say masses for the soul of the deceased and inscribe his name in the book of the monastic 'family'.[53] In the second case, it was specified that the relatives put down their claims and signed a compromise at the request of the

---

50 They are aspects of the 'officialisation process', involving the legitimation of demands, which has been well theorised by Bourdieu and has been incorporated into some innovative studies on conflict resolution that have shown its great explanatory potential (Miller, White, Wickham, Alfonso, Brown-Gorecki ...).

51 A term defined as follows in the *Partidas*: '[*Apellido*] means an appeal made by men to assist one another or to defend their property, when they are receiving injury, or suffering violence' ('Apellido quiere tanto decir como boz de llamamiento que fazen los omes para ayuntarse e defender lo suyo, quando reciben daño o fuerça') (Partidas II.26.24). The references for these cases can be found in Orlandis Rovira, 'Las consecuencias del delito', pp. 79–81 and 101.

52 For these types of alliances and enmities, see Alfonso, 'Campesinado y derecho'; Alfonso, 'Litigios por la tierra'. [Editors' note: For English translation, see chapters 9 and 13 of this volume].

53 This undoubtedly refers to the obituaries that monasteries used to keep. The symbolism of this inscription — a mechanism of integration into a spiritual community — should not be considered only as a sign of membership, but also as a mark of distinction from those who were not part of it.

320   ISABEL ALFONSO

bishop and the chapter of Zamora, who also offered to sing masses for the soul of the departed in his diocese and in those of León and Salamanca.

The role of mediators played by religious figures has been traditionally highlighted in the historiography as an aspect of their clerical status. However, even if this image is more than a reflection of official discourse and is rooted in objective facts, the reasons for this are not those generally adduced. In 1986, Stephen D. White wrote what I regard as one of the most enlightening papers about why the monks were able to mediate in local conflicts among the lay population. His analysis of the documentation in some French monasteries showed that it was their central position and their power within a dense social network that allowed churchmen to exercise that peacekeeping role, and explained why this mediation was useful and even crucial, given its effectiveness.[54]

In the first case analysed here, it seems safe to attribute the presence of the abbot of Rioseco and the major role played by the monk don Munio at the ceremony held in Oña to their links to the Rojas, which are better documented for don Munio.[55] This monk — who later became abbot of Oña — was a brother of the knights from Tamayo, one of whom, García López, was listed as a member of the Rojas family group and another, Gonzalo González, among the witnesses to the act. All characters in this group appeared repeatedly in monastic documents in a variety of situations that show the networks they were part of. Fernando Pardo, for example, witnessed the settlement of the dispute between the knights of Tamayo and Oña; years later, García López de Tamayo acted as a surety for donations to Oña, and was witness among a group of *fijosdalgo* that also included some of the Rojas. Besides Oña, other ecclesiastical institutions were included in this dense social network. The monastery of Rioseco, that of Las Huelgas, the King's Hospital, the cathedral of Burgos are arguably the most relevant, to judge from the information provided by their cartularies about the members of this kinship group. Therefore, the reasons for Oña to mediate in a conflict that directly affected one of its vassal councils cannot be attributed only to its role as lord, or to the peace-making role monks bestowed upon themselves. They need to be understood within the complex relational framework in which the actors were involved, which ultimately would also explain the conflict itself. The extant records provide only minimal information on this, perhaps because the reasons were too well-known to all those involved. However, this interpretation does not rule out that the Hontomín representatives might have actually appealed to their lords seeking protection from the noblemen's reprisals and the negotiated settlement contained in the document being discussed here.

María Gutiérrez's lineage attributed her decision to reach an agreement with the peasants of Manganeses and Junciel and halt the bloody violence, to the entreaties of the bishop and the chapter of the cathedral of Zamora, together with the masses promised for the salvation of her son:

---

54 White, 'Feuding and Peacemaking'.
55 On don Munio's identity, see Alfonso, 'Resolución de disputas', p. 225. I have no evidence supporting kinship links for Rodrigo, abbot of Rioseco between 1214 and 1230, but there are documents confirming the close ties the monastery had with many of the Rojas.

And now, understanding that this is in the service of God and for the soul of the abovementioned Alfonso Pérez, and in response to the supplication of the bishop and the chapter of Zamora, and since this bishop shall have masses sung for the soul of this Alfonso Pérez in his bishopric and in the bishoprics of León and Salamanca, and in order to halt the fighting between us, we come to an agreement.[56]

The relationships between actors are unknown here, and the ecclesiastical and lordly roles of the bishop seem to overlap when protecting his vassals. However, the time, the 'now' (*agora*) which is put into the mouths of the relatives, indicates that mediation took place at an advanced stage of the conflict. What remains to be ascertained is why a similar result was not sought from the beginning; what prevented a cessation of hostilities; and what were the reasons that led to the escalation of reprisals, although these facts can be certainly attributed to the inner logic of revenge processes.

The mediators in these conflicts not only acted to reconcile the parties and put an end to the enmity between them. They also offered the only compensation that was contemplated, which was inherent to them: praying for the soul of the victims. It must be noted that the victims were only considered as such to the extent that they were acknowledged by their avengers. The spiritual nature of this compensatory mechanism meant that the ecclesiastical mediating role was twofold: on the one hand, it related to the divinity and the afterlife, and on the other, it affected the earthly community and the peace process in the local area. It may be of interest to see how both spaces were constructed and presented.

The Peace-Making Ritual. Forgiveness and Agreement

These two texts record and describe, or merely refer to, what can be called 'peace-making rituals'. They have common elements and gestures that were recognised by all, and which publicly sealed the settlement of a dispute. Both seem to have taken place in a sacred place: in the chapter assembly in Oña and possibly also in the chapter of Zamora, in the presence not only of direct mediators but a number of witnesses who attested to the act and helped to formalise it.

In Oña, the ritual, as described, began with a solemn declaration of forgiveness by the group of the Rojas whereby they vowed not to cause the men of Hontomín, both in the present and future, any insult, defiance or hindrance, terms that contain the full semantic load of vindictive retaliation:

for the love of the Holy Saviour and for the soul of Diego Rodríguez, we, all the aforementioned, on our behalf and of behalf of all our relatives and of all the men

---

56 'Et agora entendiendo que es seruicio de dios et prol de la alma del sobredicho alfonso perez et por Ruego del obispo et del cabildo de çamora; et porque este obispo ha de fazer cantar missas por alma deste alfonso perez en el so obispado et en los obispados de leon et salamanca; et por partir contienda de entre nos feziemos auenencia'.

who are relatives of Diego Rodríguez, dismiss the council of Hontomín, and all the men who now and in the future forever [belong to it], from the death of Diego Rodríguez, and neither we, nor our relatives, shall insult, defy or hinder in any manner the men of Hontomín.[57]

This commitment was secured by what they called a 'decree' (*decretum*), which involved the submission of any of them to both divine and royal anger if they violated it: 'And we, all the above mentioned, decree that if any among our kin or among Diego Rodríguez's kin dare to breach our dismissal, they shall incur the wrath of God Almighty and the king of the land'.[58] The monks of Oña then intervened to declare that, moved by piety, they undertook to hold a plenary anniversary every year for the soul of the dead and inscribe his name in the book where all the names of the brethren were displayed. This is a term that, even when referred to the monastic family, also alluded to a spiritual brotherhood to which a chosen few belonged:

> We, the community of San Salvador, moved by piety for the soul of Diego Rodríguez [...] oblige ourselves to hold a plenary anniversary every year for the soul of Diego Rodríguez, which we shall celebrate on the fifth of the ides of May, and we shall inscribe his name in the book were the men of all our brethren are written to be seen.[59]

The parties present then witnessed how the monk, don Munio, acting on behalf of all the members of the council, was greeted by those who identified themselves as relatives of the deceased, who kissed him as a sign of eternal peace: 'And we, the relatives of Diego Rodríguez, on behalf of all [the men] of Hontomín, salute you, the monk of San Salvador, don Munio, and kiss you as a sign of eternal peace'.[60] The greeting and the kiss were, perhaps, the most widespread gestures of moral and legal reconciliation. They constituted agreements and if they were broken, they resulted in moral, social and legal sanctions that were closely intertwined.[61]

---

57 'pro amore Sancti Saluatoris atque pro anima Didaci Ruderici, nom omnes predicti [...] indulgendo dimittimus pro nobis et pro omnibus parentibus nostris et pro omnibus illis qui sunt parentes Didaci Ruderiçi omni concilio et omnibus hominibus qui nunc et futuri sunt usque inperpetuum in Fonte Omino, ut pro illa morte Didaci Ruderici nullam iniuriam neque aliquam contrariam aut aliquod impedimentum nos uel parentes nostri faciamus hominibus de Fonteomin'.

58 'Et nos omnes predicti facimus decretum, quod si aliquis ex genere nostro uel Didaci Ruderici contra indulgentiam nostram uenire presumpserit, iram Dei Omnipotentis habeat et regis terre'.

59 'Nos siquidem conuentus Sancti Saluatoris intuitu pietatis pro anima Didaci Ruderici [...] compromittimus quod per singulos annos plenum anniuersarium pro anima Didaci Ruderici, Vᵒ idus maii celebremus, et nomen illius subscribimus in libro ubi nomina omnium fratrum nostrorum subscrita esse uidentur'.

60 'Et nos omnes parentes Didaci Ruderici pro omnibus de Fonteomin, salutamus domnum Munionem monachum Santi Saluatoris et damus ei osculum in signum perpetue pacis'.

61 For more on gestures, see the evidence from the by-laws compiled in De Hinojosa y Naveros, 'El elemento germánico'; and Orlandis Rovira, 'Las consecuencias del delito'. This tradition is contained in the seventh *Partida*, which refers to the ways of establishing peace and penalties to be imposed on those who broke it: 'we decree that where any persons bear a grudge against one another by reason of

DEATH WITHOUT VENGEANCE 323

They constituted, therefore, the strongest symbol to support promises of peace, at least theoretically. It is noteworthy that the physical nature of the act of kissing, as a gestural mechanism of memory, did not occur directly between the parties, but was enacted with the mediation of the monk in the ritual held in Oña. Was it intended as a sign of distance and differentiation, rather than an attempt by the reconciling parties to becoming closer?

Only after this ritual had taken place was the council allowed to speak. Through its representatives, the council was ordered to pay the convent ten *maravedís* for the soul of the dead on the day of the anniversary of his death, that is, to defray the cost on a permanent basis. Thus a spiritual link became material income, a perennial sign of their collective guilt:

> Moreover, we, the men of Hontomín, namely Martín Gascón, Pedro Sobrín, Martín Martín, and Juan, son of doña Helo and Gonzalo de la Vega, with the voice and in the name of all the council of Hontomín, oblige ourselves and our descendants forever to pay the community of San Salvador ten *maravedís* for the soul of Diego Rodríguez on the day of his anniversary, that is, the fifth of the ides of May.[62]

After the date and list of witnesses, the document includes a solemn agreement whereby all the relatives of Diego Rodríguez agreed under oath that, were one of their own to break the agreement, they would rise against this individual and treat him as a traitor. In addition, anyone who failed to do so would be equally considered to be a traitor and a *calumniator*:[63]

> We, the abovementioned blood brothers and relatives of Diego Rodríguez, establish and take an oath, in the chapter of San Salvador, before the abovementioned witnesses, that if any of our kin commits any damage (*iniuria*) against the men of Hontomín, we all shall rise up against him as a traitor, and whoever takes part on it shall be equally considered a traitor and a wrongdoer (*calumniator*).[64]

---

homicide, dishonour, or injury, and they agree to be reconciled, for said reconciliation to be genuine two things must be done, namely, they must pardon and kiss one another' ('dezimos que quando algunos se quisieren mal por razon de omezillo, o deshonrra, o de daño, se acaeciere que se acuerden para auer su amor de consuno, e fer el amor verdadero conuiene que aya y dos cosas que se perdonen e se besen') (Partidas VII.12.4). For a monograph advancing new perspectives for the entire medieval West see Petrov, *The Kiss of Peace*. Also worth considering are the contributions collected in Gauvard and Jacob, eds, *Les rites de la justice*.

62 'Preterea nos homines de Fomin, uidelicet Martinus Gascon et Petrus Sobrin et Martinus Martin et Iohannes filius de domna Helo et Gundissaluus de la Uega, uice atque nomine tocius concilii de Fonteomin, obligamus nos atque omnes successores nostros in perpetuum ut persoluamus decem morabetinos conuentui Sancti Saluatoris pro anima Didaci Ruderici in die sui anniuersarii, scilicet V° idus maii'.

63 This term is to be understood as anyone deserving a fine, punishment, or penalty.

64 'Nos siquidem omnes predicti fratres consanguinei atque parentes Didaci Ruderici, statuimus et confirmamus et hominum facimus in capitulo Santi Saluatoris coram suprascriptis testibus, ut si aliquis ex nobis ex genere nostro pro morte Ruderici aliquam iniuriam hominibus de Fonteomin

The terms of the agreement formalised in Oña through this public ceremony of verbal promises and body gestures, were less explicit and broader than those contained in the written agreement of 1291 in Zamora. In the 1217 agreement signed in Oña there was no specific intent to define its terms; instead, this was implicitly assumed through non-aggression wording, also formalised here by means of a special 'oath' (*homino*)[65] made by the Rojas group to guarantee that their promises would be kept. The council, for its part, used the verb 'to oblige' (*obligare*) to show their perpetual commitment to pay on the anniversary of the death for the soul of the victim. It is striking that the narrative structure of the text implied that only the noblemen — self-declared victims and therefore entitled to exert repression — might breach the agreement, and that they were the only ones who swore not to engage in such a breach.

In the chapter of Zamora there was a more detailed declaration of forgiveness that contains all the terms of a truce, as well as guaranteeing perpetual peace, and establishing the conditions for its maintenance. For this, as the representatives of María Gutiérrez's lineage and *bando* gave their forgiveness and set aside any claims and complaints they may have had due to the killing and to the later events in a solemn act. The council was thus granted a truce, for the present and the future, in word or deed or counsel — a formulaic statement that refers to the multiple forms that the grievance could take:

> we forgive you and promise to do so forever [...] we dismissed them of any claim and complaint that we have or may come to have against them or against any of them due to the killing of the aforementioned Alfonso Pérez, and so we do regarding those that we held at the time this death occurred, as well as those we currently have, and of those who may arise, and we grant them a safe and secure truce, in word and deed, forever and ever, on our own behalf and on that of our *bando*.[66]

The agreement between María Gutiérrez's lineage and the representatives of the council of Manganeses and Junciel ended a feud which, according to the story, had been caused by the killing of María Gutiérrez's son. She confessed that her lineage and *bando* had inflicted deaths and other ills on those in the council, in the context of enmity that triggered the conflict. The intention was not to waive revenge, but to cease the hostilities and the subsequent escalation of violence.

---

fecerit, omnes alii insurgamus contra eum quasi contra proditorem et qui uoluerit sit pariter cum factore proditor et calumpniator'.

65 The term to indicate homage is similar to the 'pact and homage' ('pleyto e homenaje') used by the other group. See Alonso, *Diccionario Medieval Español*, under 'homenaje'; Niermeyer, *Mediae Latinitatis Lexicon Minus*, under 'hominaticus', 'hominatio', 'hominatus', 'hominium' 'hommagium'.

66 'perdonamos et seguramos pora siempre jamays [...] toda quanta demanda et querela auemos o podriamos auuer contra ellos o contra cada uno dellos por razon de la muerte del dicho Alfonso Perez et partimos dellos querella, assí de las que eran al tiempo que esta muerte acaesçio como dellas que agora son, et dellas que seran daqui adelantre et damosles bona triegua salua et segura, de dicho et de fecho et de conseyo, por en todo tiempo et por siempre jamays por nos et por todo nostro bando'.

DEATH WITHOUT VENGEANCE **325**

Despite the poor condition in which this agreement is preserved, it can be clearly recognised that it contains the legal language of the by-laws (*fueros*) on the procedures to regulate and settle various forms of 'enmity' and guarantee compliance with the agreements reached under such settlements. Although no mention was made of a challenge — a public accusation that gave entitlement to revenge –, the expression referring to the killings and damages committed — 'as a result of this enmity' ('segundo esta ena henemizar') — it can be concluded that the subsequent confrontation followed the procedures that were permitted in such acts, and that the inhabitants of this council would have been declared enemies. The scale and scope of the conflict in which several communities had been involved were also shown in other points of the agreement. These included the references to the exile of some people from Manganeses who, in order to qualify for forgiveness and the truce, were required to return to the village within two years to live there again:

> And [regarding] all of those who are now out of Manganeses, who dwelt there at the time of the death of Alfonso Pérez, if, from the day in which this charter is produced and for a period of two years, they did not wish to return to live there, from then onwards, even if they are harmed or damaged by us or by any of the abovementioned or by any of us or of our relatives or anybody among us, nor the truce neither our dismissal shall be broken, and we shall not be taken to be any less worthy for it, and for this two years they shall remain safe from us.[67]

It also included references to the involvement of the men of Pajares, another nearby location, who could not be accepted or given shelter in the village unless they engaged in a similar agreement: 'And also, the council of Manganeses shall not receive nor protect in its village against our will any man from Pajares until the latter have reached an agreement with us'.[68] Allusions were also made to laxer solidarities and therefore enmities were not confined to the boundaries of a place. The men of Manganeses had to commit not to receive any enemy of the *bando* as a neighbour, or dweller, and not to accept any such enemy but to expel him, unless he took shelter in the church or the bishop's palace. The men of the *bando* undertook that, once the enemy had been expelled, they would refrain from killing him on the same day they took him out ('el día que lo sacaren') whether in the village, the suburbs or the township:

> And also, that they shall not receive any of our enemies as a neighbour or to dwell in the village, neither protect him, nor any man that has done wrong to us, or to one of our *bando* or to anyone of us, so that, once we inform the council about it, that man shall be expelled from the village, unless he seeks shelter in

---

67 'Et que todos aquellos que son fuera de manganeses, que eran moradores hy al tiempo de la muerte de alfonso perez que, se del dia que esta carta es feycha fasta dos annos hy non quesieren uenir morar, que dende adelantre, se algun dano o mal reçibieren de nos o destos sobredichos o de alguno de nos o de nostros parientes o de cada uno de nos, que por ende non sea quebrantamento de tregua nen de perdon, et que non ualgamos menos por ende, et entre tanto, fasta estos dos annos que anden seguros de nos'.

68 'Et, otrossi, que el conceyo de manganeses non reciban nen amparen en sua uilla a nengun ome de payares contra nostra uoluntade fasta que ayan auenençia connosco'.

the church or the palace of the bishop, and once he is expelled we shall not kill him the day they take him out in the village or in the suburb or in the township of Manganeses.[69]

In this reconciliation no mention was made of a 'kiss of peace', although it was in widespread use in the western part of the kingdom.[70] There were repeated statements of 'pact and tribute' ('pleyto et tributo') made by some of the lineage members, acting for themselves and for those they represented, to fulfil the promises contained in 'this truce, and this security and this forgiveness' ('esta triega et esta segurançia et este perdon'). There were widely known sanctions to be applied to those who broke them, those imposed on a traitor:

> And we make a pact and a homage to keep this forever and ever, and if any of us goes against it in any manner, he shall be considered as a traitor, and so shall any who breaches this truce and security.[71]

What were the gestures used in this ritual, which were undoubtedly well-known to everyone? In this case, the gathering of witnesses seems to include more knights, squires, and urban clerics than that in Oña.[72] To a certain extent, written rituals arise from repetition, and perhaps this entailed special oaths specifically used for this type of audience, as the representatives of the councils of the rural communities did not make their promises under this rite of 'pact and homage' ('pleyto y homenaje'), and the victim's mother was also excluded from the act. Could it have meant compromising a kind of chivalrous honour? Certainly, the avenging group never made its status explicit, as this did not seem to be required. But a certain aggressive, rather than generous tone can be perceived in their granting of forgiveness. All that was left to do for the representatives of the council — only four men, as opposed to a numerous group of relatives — was to accept the truce and sign the agreement on behalf of their community:

> We, the abovementioned Juan Rodríguez, and Pedro Juanes, and Miguel Pérez, and Pelayo Feibez, in the name of the abovementioned council of Manganeses, for which we stand as representatives, acknowledge this and make this agreement with you in its name [...] And in the name of that same council we dismiss all our claims and complaints that the council has or may come to have against you or against the abovementioned or against any among you due to their deaths or

---

69 'et, otrossi, que non reçiban nengun nostro enemigo a uezindade nen more enlla uilla nenllo anparen nen a nengun home atas que nos o de nostro bando ou qualquier de nos vienga que nos aya feycho tuerto o mal, mays que luego quello feziermos saber al conceyo que lo eychen de la uilla, saluo se acoger a eglisia o al palaçio del obispo, et despues que lo sacaren que nos non seamos tenudos de lo matar esse dia que lo sacaren enlla uilla nen en el arraualde nen en el termino de manganeses'.

70 Orlandis Rovira, 'Las consecuencias del delito', pp. 118–20.

71 'Et fazemos pleyto et homenage de lo agardar pora siempre iamais, et qualquier de nos que contra ello uenier en alguna guyssa, que sea traydor por ello, assi como aquel quebranta triegua et segurançia'.

72 Among the witnesses present there was a knight, his squire and a clergyman from Valderas, his son, a nephew of the bishop, other clergymen, another squire and other inhabitants of Valderas.

to any other harm they received. And we promise in its name to uphold all that is contained in this charter forever and never to go against it.[73]

The asymmetry of the quarrelling groups was not resolved through the rituals and rhetoric of gestures and words, but it rather served to accentuate, or at least ratify, social distinctions. Through these acts, groups of nobles were able to appear pious and generous, indulgent in their forgiveness of serious offenses and attacks, even without the usual acts of submission. In this way they increased their prestige and reputation, which were the constituent elements of their symbolic capital. But this did not seem to undermine or enhance the effectiveness of the objectives intended through these mutual declarations. Both parties appealed to principles that strengthened their promises, and to the guarantee of non-aggression practices. The breach of those agreements, with or without homage, entailed not only legal, but also moral sanctions which affected the reputation of the defaulting party. This explains the emphasis that both texts placed on the wording of penalties for those who failed to abide by the agreements. Details were also given about what would be considered to be breaches of the truce and forgiveness, in order to prevent this type of 'legal handicap' which was a major concern for the heroes of epic poems, among others.[74]

The agreement with the council of Manganeses, which was formalised by the seals of the notaries public of Queen Violante in Valderas and of the king in Zamora, as well as the witnesses mentioned and the seals that the urban knights themselves affixed on the letter delivered to the council, also differed from the Oña document in other respects, partly due to the conflictive period and process within which it was made. So while the Rojas operated as grantors of a unilateral forgiveness granted to a guilty group, the lineage and *bando* from Zamora forgave but also received, if not forgiveness, the commitment of the council not to sue for the damages and killings inflicted. And although the truce and forgiveness always originated from the group and were never attributed to the representatives of the council, there was a recognition of the council's right and capacity to issue a legal response in the face of the attacks by the kinship group.

---

73 'Nos los sobredichos Johan rodríguez et pedro yuanes et miguel perez et pelay feybez, en nomble del conseyo sobredicho de manganeses, cuyos personeros somos, assi lo reçebimos et en so nomble fazemos auenencia conuosco [...] Et por nomble desse mismo conceyo partimos nos de todas las demandas et querelas que el conceyo han o podrien auer contra uos o contra los sobredichos o contra cada uno de uos por razon dellas muertes et dellos otros males que resçibieron. Et prometemos en so nomble de agardar todo esto que esta carta dize en todo tiempo et de non uenir contra ello'.

74 The definition of this concept in the *Partidas* is very eloquent: 'Men in Spain are accustomed to make use of the expression "to be less worthy" ("valer menos"), and this is something that when a man becomes liable to it he is no longer the peer of anyone in the court of his lord, or in a court of justice, and it causes great injury to those who commit an offense of this kind; for they cannot, from that time forward, be considered the peers of others in battle, or bring an accusation; or give testimony, or share in any honours for which good men should be selected' ('Vsan los omes decir en España vna palabra, que es, valer menos. E menos valer es cosa, que el ome que cae en ella, non es par de otro en Corte de Señor, nin en juicio: e tiene grand daño a los que caen en tal yerro. Ca non pueden dende en adelante ser pares de otros en lid, nin fazer acusamiento, nin en testimonio, nin en las otras honrras, en que buenos omes deuen ser escogidos') (Partidas VII.5.1).

328   ISABEL ALFONSO

The difference between these two narratives indicates that, although the logic of revenge was the same in both areas, in its cultural and legal aspects, the dynamics of the conflict diverged depending on various factors. It is not known whether the ease in the reconciliation between the Rojas and the men of Hontomín was encouraged by the greater power or the mediating ability of the monks; whether the conflict was less acrimonious; whether the interests at stake were not so important; or whether there were other reasons. This contrasts with the dynamics of violence that characterised the process in the township of Manganeses.[75]

Final Remarks

The documents reviewed here are tremendously terse and lack all those elements that bring colour and vibrancy to epic stories or chronicles about vendettas. These elements have become part of the conceptual background resorted to when similar conflicts are often uncritically analysed. Arguably the records of the resolution in Oña and Zamora are not even vaguely reminiscent of great narratives. They point indeed to a very different genre, with clearly different goals. But is it just a matter of a different narrative style? Or should one think of other forms that may have been used to suppress and regulate conflicts? The texts discussed here describe peace settlements that rely more often on the memory of the people than on their written form. The fact that in these cases they were recorded in writing is probably attributable to the fact that the mediators were clergymen, as well as to other factors unknown to us.

If the material here is compared with any of the known features of the traditional model, it can be found: that the right and obligation that the relatives implicitly invoked was not articulated either in terms of honour or revenge, but of retaliation for murder; that no parity existed between the parties in dispute, but there was a clear asymmetry in status and organisation; that prevailing kinship bonds and alliances were not simple matters of blood; that women were not excluded as active subjects, but were involved and even played a major role in the responses provided; that far from giving rise to endless cycles of violence, mechanisms were put in place to cease hostilities; that although many scholars would not hesitate to qualify these forms of settlement as private on the grounds that they did not involve any recognised judicial institution, there were some elements that prevent these settlements from being deemed to be private. Can a conflict in which such large groups — and the local, lordly and/or religious authorities — were involved be characterised as a private dispute? Can the category of 'private' be applied to regulated processes of reconciliation, where legal and moral guarantees were resorted to, even though no specific laws were invoked?[76]

Given the findings regarding these discrepancies from the traditional model, should we continue to think, as is often suggested, that these practices are reminiscent

---

75 Historians are increasingly paying attention to the material capabilities to maintain fights as a variable in considering resolutions, as opposed to the existence of stricter rules restraining them.

76 Only the use of the current concepts of public and private allows such a dichotomy to be maintained.

of a primitive culture that was becoming extinct? Or that the new Romanised law intended to abolish revenge? Or is it necessary to consider the latest proposals to further our knowledge of a revenge culture perceived in relation to, rather than in opposition to, justice, and other forms of conflict resolution which have been much more long lived?[77]

Bibliography

Alfonso, Isabel, 'Resolución de disputas y prácticas judiciales en el Burgos medieval', in *Burgos en la Plena Edad Media. III Jornadas Burgalesas de Historia* (Burgos: Asociación Provincial de Libreros de Burgos, 1994), pp. 211–43

Alfonso, Isabel, 'Campesinado y derecho: la vía legal de su lucha (Castilla y León, siglos X–XIII)', *Noticiario de Historia Agraria*, 13 (1997), 15–31

Alfonso, Isabel, 'Litigios por la tierra y "malfetrías" entre la nobleza medieval', *Hispania*, 57–197 (1997), 917–55

Alfonso, Isabel, 'Venganza y justicia en el Cantar de Mío Cid', in *El Cid: de la materia épica a las crónicas caballerescas*, ed. by Carlos Alvar Ezquerra, Fernando Gómez Redondo, and Georges Martin (Alcalá de Henares: Universidad de Alcalá, 2002), pp. 41–69

Alfonso, Isabel, 'Vengeance, justice et lutte politique dans l'historiographie castillane du Moyen Âge', in *La vengeance, 400–1200*, ed. by Dominique Barthélemy, François Bougard, and Régine Le Jan (Rome: École française de Rome, 2006), pp. 383–419

Alonso, Martín, *Diccionario Medieval Español desde las Glosas Emilianenses y Silenses (s. X) hasta el siglo XV* (Salamanca: Universidad Pontificia de Salamanca 1986)

Álvarez Borge, Ignacio, 'Los señoríos de los Rojas en 1352', in *Los señoríos de Behetría*, ed. by Carlos Estepa Díez and Cristina Jular Pérez-Alfaro (Madrid: CSIC, 2001), pp. 73–144

Álvarez Borge, Ignacio, 'The Lordships of the Rojas Family Group in 1352', in *Land, Power, and Society in Medieval Castile: A Study of Behetría Lordship*, ed. by Cristina Jular Pérez-Alfaro and Carlos Estepa Díez (Turnhout: Brepols, 2009), pp. 89–175

Álvarez Borge, Ignacio, 'Poder local y poder central. Servicio al rey y desarrollo patrimonial en Castilla en el siglo XIII. El merino Fernán González de Rojas y sus descendientes', *Edad Media: revista de historia*, 8 (2017), 146–76.

Barthélemy, Dominique, Bougard, François, and Le Jan, Régine, eds, *La vengeance, 400–1200* (Rome: École française de Rome, 2006)

Bourdieu, Pierre, *Le sens pratique* (Paris: Éditions de Minuit, 1980)

Díaz de Durana, José Ramón, *Anonymous Noblemen : The Generalization of Hidalgo Status in the Basque Country (1250–1525)* (Turnhout: Brepols, 2012)

Díaz de Durana, José Ramón, ed., *La Lucha de Bandos en el País Vasco: de los Parientes Mayores a la Hidalguía Universal. Guipúzcoa, de los bandos a la Provincia (siglos XIV a XVI)* (Bilbao: Universidad del País Vasco, 1998)

---

77 I refer to the contributions gathered in Barthélemy, Bougard, and Le Jan, eds, *La vengeance*, which confirm an earlier line of interpretation advanced in Zorzi, 'La cultura della vendetta' and Alfonso, 'Venganza y justicia' [Editors' note: For an English translation, see chapter 5 of this volume]. See also the bibliography cited in these works.

Estepa Díez, Carlos, *Las behetrías castellanas*, 2 vols (Valladolid: Junta de Castilla y León, 2003)

Gauvard, Claude and Jacob, Robert, eds, *Les rites de la justice. Gestes et rituales judiciaires au Moyen Âge* (Paris: Le Léopard d'Or, 1999)

González, Julio, *El Reino de Castilla en la época de Alfonso VIII*, 3 vols (Madrid: Escuela de Estudios Medievales, 1960)

Hinojosa y Naveros, Eduardo, 'El elemento germánico en el derecho español', in *Obras*, ed. by Eduardo Hinojosa y Naveros (Madrid: CSIC, 1955), pp. 405–70

Jular Pérez-Alfaro, Cristina, 'The King's Face on the Territory: Royal Officers, Discourse and Legitimating Practices in Thirteenth- and Fourteenth-Century Castile', in *Building Legitimacy: Political Discourses and Forms of Legitimation in Medieval Societies*, ed. by Isabel Alfonso, Hugh Kennedy, and Julio Escalona (Leiden: Brill, 2004), pp. 107–38

Martín, José Luis, 'Relectura del fuero de Salamanca. La venganza de la sangre', *Príncipe de Viana. Anejo. Homenaje a José María Lacarra*, 3 (1986), 531–38

Martínez Sopena, Pascual, *La Tierra de Campos Occidental: poblamiento, poder y comunidad del siglo X al XIII* (Valladolid: Universidad de Valladolid, Institución Cultural Simancas, 1985)

Martínez Sopena, Pascual, 'La evolución de la antroponimia de la nobleza castellana entre los siglos XII y XIV', in *Poder y Sociedad en la Baja Edad Media Hispánica. Estudios en homenaje al profesor Luis Vicente Díaz Martín. Vol. 1*, ed. by Carlos Reglero de la Fuente (Valladolid: Universidad de Valladolid, 2002), pp. 461–79

Miller, William I., *Bloodtaking and Peacemaking: Feud, Law, and Society in Saga Iceland* (Chicago: The University of Chicago Press, 1990)

Monsalvo, José María, 'Parentesco y sistema concejil. Observaciones sobre la funcionalidad política de los linajes urbanos en Castilla y León (siglos XIII–XV)', *Hispania*, 185 (1993), 937–69

Niermeyer, Jan Frederik, *Mediae Latinitatis Lexicon Minus* (Leiden: Brill, 1984)

Orlandis Rovira, José, 'Sobre el concepto de delito en el derecho de la alta Edad Media', *Anuario de Historia del Derecho Español*, 16 (1945), 112–92

Orlandis Rovira, José, 'Las consecuencias del delito en el derecho de la alta Edad Media', *Anuario de Historia del Derecho Español*, 18 (1947), 61–165

Pancer, Nira, *Sans peur et sans vergogne. De l'honneur et des femmes aux premiers temps mérovingiens* (Paris: Albin Michel, 2001)

Pastor, Reyna, *Resistencias y luchas campesinas en la época del crecimiento y consolidación de la formación feudal: Castilla y León, siglos X–XIII* (Madrid: Siglo XXI, 1980)

Pérez-Bustamante, Rogelio, *El gobierno y la administración territorial de la corona de Castilla*, 2 vols (Madrid: Universidad Autónoma, 1976)

Petrov, Kiril, *The Kiss of Peace: Ritual, Self, and Society in the High and Late Medieval West* (Leiden: Brill, 2003)

RAE, *Diccionario de la Lengua Española* (Madrid: RAE, 1970)

Sánchez, Marciano, 'La venganza de sangre en Zamora', *Stvdia Zamorensia*, 8 (1987), 93–104

White, Stephen D., 'Feuding and Peacemaking in Touraine around the Year 1100', *Traditio*, 42 (1986), 196–263

Zorzi, Andrea, 'La cultura della vendetta nel conflitto politico in età comunale', in *Le storie e la memoria. In onore di Arnold Esch*, ed. by Roberto delle Donne and Andrea Zorzi (Firenze: Firenze University Press, 2002), pp. 135–70

CHAPTER 9

On Peasants and the Law

with a commentary by Paul Freedman

PAUL FREEDMAN

The Historiography of Peasant Resistance to Seigneurial Authority

This 1997 study of peasants' remonstrances and litigation protesting against seigneurial oppression is of key importance not only in the evolution of Isabel Alfonso's work but in the Spanish historiography concerning resistance to oppression and resourcefulness. Not long after the publication of this article, José Ángel García de Cortázar and Pascual Martínez Sopena surveyed the previous thirty years of Iberian rural history of the Middle Ages, identifying three periods and approaches.[1] According to their scheme, the first phase (roughly 1969 to 1980) produced basic studies of seigneurial, primarily monastic, administration along with discussions of peasant insurrections. In the 1980s, under the influence of the French studies of feudalism, more attention was given to land and the workings of the seigneurial economy. This approach connected with the earlier focus on contradictions and confrontations between lords and peasants, but with a greater appreciation of the workings of a feudal system. It also emphasized the importance of small-holdings that made up monastic or aristocratic estates, a reorientation away from estate management to the constituent parts of lordship marking a turn towards the peasants themselves as producers for their own subsistence and for the benefit of their secular and ecclesiastical lords. While the extractive oppression of this system and the extra-economic power of lords was made evident, this historiographic tendency also afforded an evaluation of peasant autonomy, of what in England and America is referred to as 'peasant agency': the ability of peasants to influence their social and economic environment in more everyday forms of evasion, subversion and means other than open revolts.

From the late 1980s until the end of the century, an expansion of printed sources and archaeological research as well as an intense study of power relations based on land gave further impetus to studies of the medieval peasantry. For the 1990s in particular, Martínez Sopena has elsewhere emphasized the interest in the study of power and in particular the system of seigneurial levies outlined in the works of Carlos Estepa, Carlos Reglero, Ignacio Álvarez and Esther Peña.[2] This decade also saw an extension of research into the formerly neglected later Middle Ages, including a close evaluation of the mid-fourteenth century Libro Becerro de las

---

1   García de Cortázar and Martínez Sopena, 'The Historiography of Rural Society'. This volume updates and translates into English a series of articles that appeared under the direction of Isabel Alfonso in *Historia Agraria*, 31 (2003), pp. 9–86 and 33 (2004), pp. 11–106.
2   Freedman and Martínez Sopena, 'The Historiography of Seigneurial Income', pp. 83–97 (this part written by Martínez Sopena).

Paul Freedman, Yale University

334   PAUL FREEDMAN

Behetrías, commissioned by Pedro I, an unusually detailed, village-by-village survey of aristocratic seigneurial rights in Castile.[3]

In all these phases the work of scholars outside Spain was selectively influential, beginning with the French school of Marc Bloch, Georges Duby and Guy Bois in the 1970s and including non-medievalists' descriptions of overall periodization (Perry Anderson; Robert Brenner), indirect forms of resistance (James Scott), or peasant standards of living (Christopher Dyer).

Isabel Alfonso's article represents both a broadening of comparative focus pointed out by García de Cortázar and Martínez Sopena (citing foreign studies of routine rather than open, violent peasant struggles) and a revaluation of rural conflict. The essays in the present volume in honour of our beloved colleague, show collectively Isabel's unique role within Spanish studies of medieval society generally over the course of more than twenty-five years. Her attention to the cohesion as well as complexity of peasant village society had led to reconsideration of the resources available to and utilized by peasants in responding to the lords' demands.

What was, if not unorthodox, at least novel in 1997 was the assertion implicit in the title that the lucha of the peasantry included a vía legal; that appeals by peasant communities for legal recourse were frequent and sometimes effective. Equally radical was the assertion that judicial struggle should be seen in terms of overall everyday forms of peasant resistance: 'how the law was embedded in the daily life of the rural society' (p. 346). The implication that the word *lucha* (struggle) can be applied not only to uprisings such as the well-known late-medieval Irmandiño revolt, the Fuenteovejuna uprising or the Catalan remença war, but also to less visible, violent or unified subversion of the seigneurial regime goes against what used to be the conventional estimations of the character of the peasantry across historical boundaries, estimations shared by Marxist and neo-liberal historians. The 'normal' functioning of the seigneurial regime, the ordinary, quotidian forms of peasant opposition, the recourse to collective legal action and finally the defence of rights by violence are now seen as a continuum and a set of tactics that coexisted rather than positing a breakdown of a previously stable mode of production. In all of this, the estimation of peasants' ability to manoeuvre within an oppressive system (peasant agency) is emphasized, not simply out of sentiment in favour of the victims of injustice but from the reading of sources. These sources are extensive and, as Hipólito Rafael Oliva Herrer, writing in 2004 showed in his study of the struggles of villages in Old Castile, articulate a detailed, coherent and politically sophisticated opposition to the usurpation and extortion of the seigneurial regime.[4] For the tenth to thirteenth centuries covered here in Isabel's study, there is not the same series of territorial rebellions as in the late-fifteenth and early-sixteenth centuries, but a similar recourse to law, less visible resistance and defiance if not insurrection.

In this aforementioned spectrum of peasant forms of resistance, litigation and appeals to royal courts and authority, emphasized in this article of Isabel's, are the

---

3   Martínez Díez, ed., *Libro Becerro de las Behetrías*. On the *behetrías* as a form of secular lordship Estepa Díez, *Las behetrías castellanas*.

4   Oliva Herrer, *Justicia contra señores*.

THE HISTORIOGRAPHY OF PEASANT RESISTANCE TO SEIGNEURIAL AUTHORITY   335

most difficult to appreciate within the paradigms of rural sociology and historical theories that tended to dominate the twentieth century. This is partly because the earliest studies of medieval agrarian society throughout Europe were based on medieval legal treatises and over-estimated their normative value. Scholars such as Eduardo de Hinojosa for Catalonia, Paul Vinogradoff or H. S. Bennett for England, or Henri Sée for France assumed on the basis of legal compilations and procedures that almost all peasant tenants were of servile condition.[5] Part of the significance of the social historical approach of the Annales School, beginning before the Second World War with the pioneering insights of Marc Bloch, was to propose archival, documentary evidence in preference to reliance on generalized and theoretical statements of the jurists. Bloch himself was intrigued, even obsessed by the problem of serfdom, a prime example of social condition in relation to legislation, but his influence tended to diminish attention to questions of personal status in favour of the everyday realties of tenancy: not what peasants were called, but rather what they paid.[6] The result of this emphasis on the specific obligations and the depth of its documentation ('histoire totale', encompassing geography, soil, agriculture) was to reveal how the seigneurial regime functioned, how rent, levies and economic conditions were assessed and collected.

Such investigations offered a diversified view of the peasantry. Regardless of official social status, there were well-off and impoverished members of the same rural community. Agrarian historians presented a more socio-economic and less legalistic analysis of a seigneurial regime that functioned regardless of whether or not agriculturalists were categorized as legally unfree (villeins, or servi and the like), enforcing its extractive structure by means of organized force more than abstract and prescriptive law.

The waning historiographic authority of legal records and the triumph of social history played out in different ways in different countries. In France, Marc Bloch's legacy was the elaboration of a structure of feudal society that included the maintenance of seigneurial and ecclesiastical income and power through exploitation of the peasantry. This extraction of peasant surplus could be seen as a mode of production in conformity with Marxist theories of historical change, but whatever the theoretical assumptions, little account was made of law except by its absence. The domination of the aristocracy, posited as the result of a feudal crisis or mutation féodale around the year 1000, was achieved by defiance of legal tribunals and central administration, the imposition of new and onerous customs on a formerly free and judicially recognized class.[7] Subsequent oppression did not depend on peasants being formally defined

---

5   De Hinojosa y Naveros, *El régimen señorial*; Vinogradoff, *Villeinage in England*, pp. 43–220; Bennett, *Life on the English Manor*, pp. 3–26; 99–150; Sée, *Les classes rurales*, pp. 156–211.
6   Boutruche, *Seigneurie et féodalité* 2, p. 74, observed that Bloch had been 'tormented' by his attempts to define servile condition and its strength, weakness or absence in different parts of medieval Europe. On Marc Bloch and the problem of serfdom, Bonnassie, 'Marc Bloch'.
7   I have discussed the postwar French school of social history in Freedman, 'Georges Duby'.

as servile, but rather on a machinery of feudal extraction applied independently of a now irrelevant legal status.[8]

As applied to the study of medieval England, the same depreciation of legal definitions had the effect of raising historians' estimation of the autonomy of medieval peasants and the scope of their enterprises. English Common Law created an unusually elaborate set of rules about who was unfree, and this determined access to royal justice. Unfree tenants could not appear before the public courts and were subject to their lords' jurisdiction exclusively. In theory, the subordinate condition of villein applied to a majority of the agricultural tenants of the realm, but Anglo-American historiography of the twentieth century tended to regard unfree status as largely irrelevant, that in reality and on an everyday basis, peasants were their own masters. Their absentee manorial lords, according to the view identified with the so-called Toronto School established by Ambrose Raftis, were less important in determining what went on in the village than the peasant elites who effectively managed the local government. The economic and social divisions within the village community were of more significance than the demands of its lord.[9]

For Catalonia, reliance on legal sources also gave way to an archival, social historical research methodology. The codified Usatges de Barcelona and subsequent legislation affecting the peasantry such as the clause 'En les terres o locs' of the Corts of Barcelona in 1283, along with the 'bad customs' allowing lords to exact manifestly unjust levies, defined a servile class constituting the remences of the late Middle Ages. Beginning with the celebrated thesis of Pierre Bonnassie in the 1970s, the degradation of the Catalan peasantry was regarded as the result of aristocratic rebellion, the overthrow of comital government and the imposition of feudalism (a part of the mutation féodale of the eleventh century). Here again, as for France, the assertiveness of the milites and castellans took place in defiance of laws and procedures, rendering judicial forms irrelevant.[10]

Castile forms yet another set of teachings and approaches to the question of law and the condition of the peasantry. To the degree that mid-twentieth century historiography was influenced, if not dominated, by the teachings of Claudio Sánchez-Albornoz that Spain's crucial historical distinction was that it never experienced feudalism, the issues of seigneurial extraction or of peasant resourcefulness despite subordinate juridical status did not arise. According to the classic presentation, the Castilian agriculturalist was a free farmer who could choose his lord. This image with regard to Castile in particular was reinforced by an emphasis on the Reconquista and

---

8 Describing feudalism as a kind of machine or balance of forces operating in different directions is a hallmark of the work of Guy Bois, especially Bois, *Crise du féodalisme*.

9 Among the important and influential studies by Ambrose Raftis: Raftis, *Tenure and Mobility*; Raftis, *Warboys*. On the Toronto School, a classic if somewhat unfavourable estimation is by Razi, 'The Toronto School'.

10 Bonnassie, *La Catalogne*, pp. 735–829. On law, defiance of law and the *mutation féodale*, Salrach, 'Justicia y violencia'.

THE HISTORIOGRAPHY OF PEASANT RESISTANCE TO SEIGNEURIAL AUTHORITY   337

its opportunities, a point of view particularly popular in North America in an era when a comparison of 'frontier liberties' in Spain and the New World was put forward.[11]

The 1970s saw the rediscovery of Iberian feudalism resulting in a less favourable evaluation of Spanish exemption from seigneurial oppression. The idea of exceptionalism — that the free Castilian farmer was not oppressed by baronial overlords — was no longer maintained, part of an effort to break with the Franco regime's exaltation of Spanish distinction — as encapsulated in the tourist slogan 'España es diferente' — and to embrace Europe.[12] The Castilian behetría, regarded by Sánchez Albornoz as a model of Castilian rural liberty, was now seen as extractive and, moreover, as closely related to other European forms of feudal organization rather than constituting a peculiar or exemplary Iberian social relationship.[13]

The emphasis on feudalism in the new historiography was directed to systematic seigneurial lordship and the social conflicts it created — the struggles of Castilian tenants and villagers for their liberties across the entire period of the central and late Middle Ages.[14] As was the case elsewhere in Europe, the later Middle Ages saw a series of social conflicts, including peasant rebellions.[15] The important studies of Carlos Barros for the Galician Irmandiños and Hipólito Rafael Oliva Herrer for Castilian movements emphasize the peasants' coherent agenda of social theory justifying their actions.[16] The emphasis on mentality in these studies and its corresponding attention to everyday life and attitudes, leads to a reconsideration of the means of redress of grievances short of open rebellion, the legal aspects of the *lucha* of the peasants discussed in Isabel's article.

As Isabel points out, the prevailing tendency with regard to peasant movements had been to consider law a tool of seigneurial imposition, a means of enforcing obedience to oppression.[17] For the historiography of medieval Spain, peasant insurrections and anti-seigneurial violence have been thought of as more important than recourse to litigation. In response to Isabel Alfonso and Cristina Jular's original oral presentation on rural conflicts, offered at the VII Congreso de Historia Agraria, Reyna Pastor acknowledged that legal disputes over *fueros* and everyday forms of resistance were

---

11 Sánchez-Albornoz, *España*. For American attitudes, Lewis and McGinn, eds, *The New World Looks at its History*, which includes an article by Don Claudio (Sánchez-Albornoz, 'The Frontier'), and Charles J. Bishko, 'The Castilian as Plainsman'. For the notion of the frontier as a free and distinct space for social progress and experimentation, Powers, 'Frontier Competition'.

12 Readers of a certain age will recall the impact of Barbero and Vigil, *La formación del feudalismo* (reprinted with a new introduction by Eduardo Manzano, Barcelona, 2015). See also *La formació i expansió del feudalisme català*. Significantly, the latter volume was based on a conference in Girona on the 1200 anniversary of its conquest from the Muslims by the Franks. The subtitle of the conference was 'Girona: 1200 anys de vocació europea'.

13 Sánchez-Albornoz, 'Las behetrías'; Sánchez-Albornoz, 'Muchas más páginas sobre las behetrías'. Modern treatment of the behetrías is given in Jular Pérez-Alfaro and Estepa Díez, eds, *Land, Power, and Society*.

14 Moreta, *Malhechores-feudales*; Pastor, *Resistencias y luchas campesinas*. Compare, for Catalonia, Salrach, 'Agressions senyorials'.

15 Valdeón Baruque, *Los conflictos sociales*; Valdeón Baruque, 'Resistencia antiseñorial'.

16 Barros, *Mentalidad justiciera*; Oliva Herrer, *Justicia contra señores*.

17 Alfonso, 'Campesinado y derecho', see below, pp. 15–16.

already sufficiently taken into account, but doubted their efficacy or relevance to the history of real and active peasant resistance.[18]

At the same time, however, laws establish a basis for rights that even if suppressed in practice, can be appealed to in the course of creating movements of resistance. The *fueros* discussed by Isabel become points of reference for justifying the cases of peasant communities appealing for justice, and these appeals against new labour services (sernas), arbitrary seizures and other forms of seigneurial violence, were not futile appeals to a deaf or indifferent tribunals. In Isabel's work the search for legal redress is linked on the one hand to the strategies of everyday forms of resistance ('uso social del derecho') and, on the other, to open defiance of lordship. This later connection would later be emphasized in Oliva Herrer's study of late-fifteenth century Castile which emphasizes the ability of peasants to frame their demands politically, their use of loyalty to the ruler as a counterweight to seigneurial claims and their right to defend their autonomy by a continuum of acts including both litigation and violence.[19]

In my own work on Catalonia, I tried to show the role of jurists and legal taxonomy in both defining and enforcing servitude, a mentality of subordination.[20] Pere Benito i Monclús has noted specific examples of both legal and extra-legal resistance to demands to work on repairing castles imposed by lords on their peasant tenants in Catalonia during the period 1373–1396.[21]

The coexistence of judicial processes and active revolt can be observed in other parts of medieval Europe. It is not so much that violence results from frustration at the denial of legal remedies as that both were risky but at least sometimes effective means of responding to seigneurial violence and extortion. From about 1270 until the late fifteenth century, over 17,500 petitions of grievances were made to the English crown and parliament, many of them by villeins (unfree peasants) who were, in theory, prevented from appearing in public courts. The petitions against arbitrary and uncustomary seigneurial mistreatment precede and follow the great English Peasant Rising of 1381 and were simultaneous with numerous local rebellions.[22] There are many individual examples of English villages where litigation in the manor court, run by seigneurial authority, was punctuated or accompanied by more active resistance such as refusal to perform labour service, turning away from the manor court and boycotting it, or raising money to engage in legal procedures (including the aforementioned grievance petitions). The village and manor of Alrewas (Staffordshire) is one such case, described recently by Jean Birrell who also cites other instances and localities.[23]

Law emerges from the study of peasant-lord relations not so much as an option (as opposed to direct action) as a negotiating strategy. Recourse to judicial tribunals

---

18 Pastor, 'La conflictividad rural', especially p. 18.
19 Oliva Herrer, *Justicia contra señores*, p. 31.
20 Freedman, 'Catalan Lawyers'.
21 Benito i Monclús, 'Pleitar contra el señor'.
22 Kew (UK), The National Archives, Special Collections, Ancient Petitions, SC 8/205/10202. See Ormond, Dodd, and Musson, *Medieval Petitions*. There is an ongoing project to digitize these documents, https://www.york.ac.uk/history/research/majorprojects/medieval-petitions/ [Date accessed: 22 February 2022].
23 Birrell, 'Confrontation and Negotiation'.

THE HISTORIOGRAPHY OF PEASANT RESISTANCE TO SEIGNEURIAL AUTHORITY   339

did not mean an expectation of a definitive decision. For the decisions involving the *fueros*, Isabel shows that what are presented as royal judgments are in fact the result of compromises. The king is both adjudicator of a decision and mediator of an effective or disguised compromise.[24] Such comparisons, in turn, are not presented as the result of negotiation but as the free exchange of gifts. This is not gift-giving in the sense of reinforcing ties or demonstrating status, but rather putting a certain colouration on payments so that the lord receives tributes not out of merit or law but as a 'free gift' from the peasant tenants. Monasteries obtained in theory the *sernas* they claimed without the peasants actually performing the services, merely acknowledging they owed the service as a legal requirement.

Historians can sometimes over-emphasize how much power peasants have in negotiations. The fact that such negotiations take place behind the screen of definitive or customary statements does not mean that power is equally distributed. This has been a problem in the study of German local regulations, *Weistümer*. There are hundreds of these lists of village customs that appear to reflect the life of the people. They were collected in the nineteenth century as an act of national cultural recovery by the same brothers Grimm whose codification of fairy stories and folk-tales created an enduring impression of medieval Germany. German observers often exaggerated the authenticity of these documents as a reflection of autonomous village life and self-government. Gadi Algazi showed that in these documents the peasants were not dictating to the lords what heir immemorial customs were. Rather the lords were demanding recognition of their rights and exactions, at times dressing up new demands as ancient practice.[25] Written in regional dialects of German, the Weistümer purport to be spontaneous village testimony about local bylaws and their authenticity is enhanced by colourful practices such as the rule from the Swiss village of Fällenden that chickens could wander from their yard only a distance equivalent to how far their owner could throw a sickle from his rooftop using his left arm while clutching his left armpit with his right hand.[26] Such picturesque detail notwithstanding, Weistümer like fueros, are artful, contingent and negotiated, not declarations of long-standing custom nor recognition of long-standing rights.

When village 'customs' were adjudicated, the social relationship might be reset, but only temporarily: the conflict continued in one or another form. It is notable that among the communities discussed by Isabel in this essay is Dueñas (Palencia) which struggled for its liberties against Santa Maria de las Dueñas in the twelfth century and against secular lords during the fifteenth- and sixteenth-century.[27] If there is indeed a continuous process of struggle and negotiation, there is also, however, a difference between the different eras of medieval conflict. Oliva Herrer points to a more radical assault on the legitimacy of the seigneurie as characteristic of the late Middle Ages, visible not only in the litigation, remonstrances and rebellions that

---

24 Alfonso, 'Campesinado y derecho', p. 21.
25 Algazi, 'Lords Ask, Peasants Answer'.
26 Teuscher, *Lords' Rights and Peasant Stories*, p. 132.
27 Alfonso, 'Campesinado y derecho', pp. 23–24, based on Martínez Sopena, *Tierra de Campos occidental*, pp. 235–40; Oliva Herrer, *Justicia contra señores*, pp. 39–133.

took place under the Catholic Kings but also extensively in the *Libro de Pensamientos Variables* which puts in the mouth of the labourer, in a dialogue with the king, a series of anti-seigneurial denunciations that amount to the statement that all lordship is essentially tyranny and robbery. Rather than the compromises and discourse of gift and counter-gift characteristic of the earlier fueros and royal decisions, we have here a starker declaration of the illegitimacy of seigneurial domination and the inability of any such system to function according to a putative but discredited logic of mutuality.[28]

In the *Libro de Pensamientos Variables* the labourer protests his loyalty to the monarch and argues that only royal government has the sanction of God and can administer justice. The earlier conflicts, without displaying quite as complete a political theory of just order, also involve recourse to the king as the fount of justice and an implicit exaltation of royal impartiality against arbitrary seigneurial power. This should not be interpreted literally, as if the peasants had a naïve faith in a distant ruler, a sacred fount of justice. Comparative studies of peasant rebellions show that their protestations of loyalty to a leader above and beyond their immediate overlords are ways of defending against accusations of rebellion, asserting peasants' loyalty to a just order rather than overturning the legitimate traditions of society. In imperial Russia peasant revolts against nobles were characterized by extravagant and not completely sincere praise of the tsar.[29] In the contemporary world social scientists have in some measure heard the voice of the peasants and rediscovered their ability to figure out their situation and to justify their assertion of rights.[30] This is done through intellectual analysis, collective and individual forms of everyday resistance, subversion, and open rebellion. Isabel Alfonso has created a model for how to understand medieval peasant discontent, not as part of a stable system of confident seigneurial domination, but neither as amounting only to a series of manifest rebellions. Without exaggerating the spaces and opportunities available to ordinary rural labourers, Isabel has provided us a view of their circumstances and autonomy.

---

28 Oliva Herrer, *Justicia contra señores*, pp. 19–35.
29 Field, *Rebels*.
30 The work of James Scott, cited in Isabel Alfonso's article. See also Feierman, *Peasant Intellectuals*.

Bibliography

La formació i expansió del feudalisme català: Actes del col.loqui organitzat pel Col.legi Universitari de Girona (8–11 de gener de 1985): Homenatge a Santiago Sobrequés i Vidal, vol. 5–6 of *Estudi General (1985–1986)* (Girona and Barcelona: Col·legi Universitari de Girona and Universitat Autònoma de Barcelona, 1985–1986)

Alfonso, Isabel, 'Campesinado y derecho: la vía legal de su lucha (Castilla y León, siglos X–XIII)', *Noticiario de Historia Agraria*, 13 (1997), 15–31

Algazi, Gadi, 'Lords Ask, Peasants Answer: Making Traditions in Late Medieval Village Assemblies', in *Between History and Histories: The Making of Silences and Commemorations*, ed. by Gerald Sider and Gavin Smith (Toronto: University of Toronto Press, 1997), pp. 199–229

Barbero, Abilio and Marcelo Vigil, *La formación del feudalismo en la Península Ibérica* (Barcelona: Crítica, 1978)

Barros, Carlos, *Mentalidad justiciera de los irmandiños, siglo XV* (Madrid: Siglo XXI, 1990)

Benito i Monclús, Pere, 'Pleitar contra el señor del castillo y bajo su jurisdicción. Resistencias de los campesinos catalanes frente a la servidumbre de las obras de castell termenat', *Studia Historica. Historia Medieval*, 30 (2012), 213–35

Bennett, H.S., *Life on the English Manor (A Study of Peasant Conditions 1150-1400)* (Cambridge: Cambridge University Press, 1938)

Birrell, Jean, 'Confrontation and Negotiation in a Medieval Village: Alrewas before the Black Death', in *Survival and Discord in Medieval Society: Essays in Honour of Christopher Dyer*, ed. by Richard Goddard, John Langdon, and Miriam Muller (Turnhout: Brepols, 2010), pp. 197–211

Bishko, Charles J., 'The Castilian as Plainsman: The Medieval Ranching Frontier in La Mancha and Extremadura', in *The New World Looks at its History: Proceedings of the Second International Congress of Historians of the United States and Mexico*, ed. by Archibald R. Lewis and Thomas F. McGinn (Austin, TX: University of Texas Press, 1963), pp. 457–69

Bois, Guy, *Crise du féodalisme* (Paris: Presses de la Fondation Nationale des Sciences Politiques, 1976)

Bonnassie, Pierre, *La Catalogne du milieu du Xe à la fin du XIe siècle: croissance et mutations d'une société*, 2 vols (Toulouse: Association des Publications de l'Université de Toulouse-Le Marail, 1976)

Bonnassie, Pierre, 'Marc Bloch, historien de la servitude: réflexions sur le concept de "classe servile"', in *Marc Bloch aujourd'hui. Histoire comparée et sciences sociales*, ed. by Hartmut Atsma and André Burguière (Paris: Éditions de École des Hautes Études en Sciences Sociales, 1990), pp. 363–87

Boutruche, Robert, *Seigneurie et féodalité. Vol. 2: L'apogée (XIe–XIIIe siècles)* (Paris: Aubier-Montaigne, 1970)

Estepa Díez, Carlos, *Las behetrías castellanas*, 2 vols (Valladolid: Junta de Castilla y León, 2003)

Feierman, Steven, *Peasant Intellectuals: Anthropology and History in Tanzania* (Madison: University of Wisconsin Press, 1990)

Field, Daniel, *Rebels in the Name of the Tsar* (Boston: Houghton Mifflin, 1976)

Freedman, Paul, 'Catalan Lawyers and the Origins of Serfdom', *Mediaeval Studies*, 48 (1986), 288–314

Freedman, Paul, 'Georges Duby and the Medieval Peasantry', *Medieval History Journal*, 4–2 (2001), 259–71

Freedman, Paul, and Pascual Martínez Sopena, 'The Historiography of Seigneurial Income in Spain: A Double Approximation', in *Pour une anthropologie du prélèvement seigneurial dans les compagnes médiévales. Réalités et représentations paysannes*, ed. by Monique Bourin and Pascual Martínez Sopena (Paris: Publications de la Sorbonne, 2004), pp. 83–111

García de Cortázar, José Ángel and Pascual Martínez Sopena, 'The Historiography of Rural Society in Medieval Spain', in *The Rural History of Medieval European Societies: Trends and Perspectives*, ed. by Isabel Alfonso (Turnhout: Brepols, 2007), pp. 93–107

Hinojosa y Naveros, Eduardo de, *El régimen señorial y la cuestión agraria en Cataluña durante la Edad Media*, 2 vols (Madrid: Imp. de Fortanet, 1905)

Jular Pérez-Alfaro, Cristina and Carlos Estepa Díez, eds, *Land, Power, and Society in Medieval Castile. A Study of Behetría Lordship* (Turnhout: Brepols, 2009)

Lewis, Archibald R. and Thomas F. McGinn, eds, *The New World Looks at its History: Proceedings of the Second International Congress of Historians of the United States and Mexico* (Austin, TX: University of Texas Press, 1963)

Martínez Díez, Gonzalo, ed., *Libro Becerro de las Behetrías: estudio y texto crítico*, 3 vols (León: Centro de Estudios y Investigación San Isidoro, 1981)

Martínez Sopena, Pascual, *La Tierra de Campos occidental: poblamiento, poder y comunidad del siglo X al XIII* (Valladolid: Institución Cultural Simancas, 1985)

Moreta, Salustiano, *Malhechores-feudales: violencia, antagonismos y alianzas de clases en Castilla, siglos XIII–XIV* (Madrid: Cátedra, 1978)

Oliva Herrer, Rafael Hipólito, *Justicia contra señores. El mundo rural y la política en tiempos de los Reyes Católicos* (Valladolid: Universidad de Valladolid, 2004)

Ormond, W. H., Gwilym Dodd, and Anthony Musson, *Medieval Petitions: Grace and Grievance* (York: York Medieval Press, 2009)

Pastor, Reyna, *Resistencias y luchas campesinas en la época del crecimiento y consolidación de la formación feudal: Castilla y León, siglos X–XIII* (Madrid: Siglo XXI, 1980)

Pastor, Reyna, 'La conflictividad rural en la España medieval', *Noticiario de Historia Agraria*, 12 (1996), 13–20

Powers, James F., 'Frontier Competition and Legal Creativity: A Castilian-Aragonese Case Study Based on Twelfth-Century Municipal Military Law', *Speculum*, 52 (1977), 465–87

Raftis, Ambrose, *Tenure and Mobility: Studies in the Social History of the Mediaeval English Village* (Toronto: Pontifical Institute of Mediaeval Studies, 1964)

Raftis, Ambrose, *Warboys: Two Hundred Years in the Life of an English Mediaeval Village* (Toronto: Pontifical Institute of Mediaeval Studies, 1974)

Razi, Zvi, 'The Toronto School's Reconstitution of Medieval Peasant Society: A Critical View', *Past & Present*, 85 (1979), 141–57

Salrach, Josep M., 'Agressions senyorials i resistècies pageses en el procés de feudalització (segles IX–XII)', in *Revoltes populars contra el poder de l'estat* (Barcelona: Generalitat, 1992), pp. 11–29

Salrach, Josep M., 'Justicia y violencia: el porqué de una problemática', *Historiar*, 4 (2000), 99–113

Sánchez-Albornoz, Claudio, *España, un enigma histórico*, 2 vols (Buenos Aires: Editorial Sudamericana, 1962)

Sánchez-Albornoz, Claudio, 'The Frontier and Castilian Liberties', in *The New World Looks at its History: Proceedings of the Second International Congress of Historians of the United States and Mexico*, ed. by Archibald R. Lewis and Thomas F. McGinn (Austin, TX: University of Texas Press, 1963), pp. 27–46

Sánchez-Albornoz, Claudio, 'Las behetrías', in *Viejos y nuevos estudios sobre las institutciones medievales españolas*. Vol. 1, ed. by Claudio Sánchez-Albornoz (Madrid: Espasa Calpe, 1976), pp. 17–191

Sánchez-Albornoz, Claudio, 'Muchas más páginas sobre las behetrías', in *Viejos y nuevos estudios sobre las institutciones medievales españolas*. Vol. 1, ed. by Claudio Sánchez-Albornoz (Madrid: Espasa Calpe, 1976), pp. 195–326

Sée, Henri, *Les classes rurales et le régime domanial en France au moyen âge* (Paris: Giard et Brière, 1901)

Teuscher, Simon, *Lords' Rights and Peasant Stories: Writing and the Formation of Tradition in the Later Middle Ages* (Philadelphia: University of Pennsylvania Press, 2012)

Valdeón Baruque, Julio, *Los conflictos sociales en el reino de Castilla en los siglos XIV y XV* (Madrid: Siglo XXI, 1975)

Valdeón Baruque, Julio, 'Resistencia antiseñorial en la Castilla medieval', in *El chivo expiatorio. Judíos, revueltas y vida cotidiana en la Edad Media* (Valladolid: Ámbito, 2000), pp. 135–53

Vinogradoff, Paul, *Villeinage in England: Essays in Medieval English History* (Oxford: Clarendon Press, 1892)

ISABEL ALFONSO

Peasants and the Law

Legal Avenues in their Struggle
(Castile and León, 10th–13th Centuries)*

This study is part of a broader research on the forms of conflict resolution in medieval society, focused on judicial practice in relation to power and social structures.[1] Among other aspects, it seeks to explore the tensions and disputes in the peasant world and the means employed for their resolution. Generally speaking, it was a world largely ruled by lords, in which the powerful imposed their jurisdiction (their courts and laws, and the enforcing officers who penalised non-compliance) and regulated the rural world to their advantage. It is usually taken as a fact that peasants submitted themselves to regulatory systems that were alien to them, since they had been imposed from above. This seems to be supported by the documented predominance of defeats over victories in the judicial field, and the widespread belief that the function of the law, as a mere attribute of power, was to secure and consolidate the privileged position enjoyed by the nobility as a social group.[2] The classic studies on peasant revolts conducted by R. Hilton on England and R. Pastor on northern Spain made innovative contributions to the research on this subject by emphasising the structural nature of those revolts. Hilton also argued that 'the legal system [...] gives all of the power to the ruling class',[3] while Pastor similarly noted that 'the law was, therefore, in most cases, a fiction crafted to favour feudal power [...] since it was built by, and for, that class'.[4] Both authors seem to agree that 'the limits of that power did not arise from peasant rights being recognised, but from the strength of their resistance'.[5] It is not my aim to deny that aspects such as greater legal knowledge, access to written records, support, or ceremonial apparatus, favoured the powerful and acted as deterrents to litigate against them. However, the large number of preserved lawsuits between peasant communities and lords shows the insistence of the former in using legal channels, despite the defeats, and deserves some attention. The hypothesis argued here is that the judicial struggle of peasants was closely linked those everyday conflicts that are qualified as as resistance. Resistance had also an expression in the legal field, through the peasants' struggle to have their rights defined and recognised. This two-fold interplay reveals the specific features of their political action. In this

---

*   Original publication: Alfonso, Isabel, 'Campesinado y derecho: la vía legal de su lucha (Castilla y León, siglos X–XIII)', *Noticiario de Historia Agraria*, 13 (1997), 15–31. Translated by Julian Thomas.
1   For theoretical approaches to these matters, see Alfonso, 'Resolución de disputas'.
2   Martín Cea, El campesinado castellano, p. 39.
3   Hilton, 'Las societé paysanne et le droit', p. 15.
4   Pastor, Resistencias y luchas campesinas, p. 249.
5   Hilton, 'Las societé paysanne et le droit', p. 15.

paper I will discuss a set of local legal codes that were issued as the result of lawsuits, which clearly show that there were disputes about their content.

Additional evidence can shed further light on how the law was embedded in the daily life of the rural society under study; that is, how it related to other values that governed social life, and to what extent the defence of these values was connected to the different forms of individual and community life throughout society. The formation of a peasant class consciousness will therefore be observed from a broader, yet at the same time, more quotidian perspective than is customary when crucial collective violence phenomena are solely or primarily addressed. These issues will be developed in the second part of this paper.

The significant increase of medieval sources edited over the past decade has provided scholars with an abundant number of *fueros* from the eleventh to the thirteenth centuries. The value of these documents as social history sources has been highlighted by various historians. This is despite the fact that such documents were considered to be 'ordinances granted by the lord to his dependents', and that some studies based solely on the information contained in them have been criticised for being excessively legalistic. I propose here to draw attention to a type of *fueros* that clearly resulted from court litigation. In my view, the importance of such records lies in that, rather than being gracious concessions or imposed legal regulations that excluded the population, they can be seen as legal practice documents which inform on the conflicts and empirical facts that they regulated. Thus the value that may be attributed to them is qualitatively different. Together with these records, which resulted from legal disputes, other tensions must be considered that seem to have been settled in more informal ways. These occurred either through the mediation of third parties or by means of multiple negotiations and settlements, which were likely to have included other types of pressure and threats. The main purpose here is to highlight the negotiated nature of rules and the peasants' vested interest in having an impact on their contents, as well as their ability to do so.

The analysis that I propose is not intended to be exhaustive or even systematic in any way, although such an analysis would not be lacking in interest. I do not intend to discuss the normative content of these *fueros*. Rather, based on a selection of cases, I intend to propose, and sometimes to confirm, some hypotheses regarding the 'social use of law'[6] by peasant communities in the northern plateau of the Duero river, the main area to which the sources used refer.

The judicial formalisation of peasants' demands against their lord must be understood as one stage of a broader and longer-lasting contentious process; as one means, among others, of resolving tensions; and as a strategy to achieve often unclearly formulated objectives. It is unknown how a community made the decision to resort to the 'courts' to make a claim against their lord. Nor is it known how the costs and risks that this undoubtedly involved were assessed; how the will for collective action was summoned; how their representatives were elected; and how they discussed the form their claims would take so that they would appear to be more reasonable.

---

6 P. Martínez Sopena used this expression to refer to the use made of the *Fuero* of Logroño by the social groups vying for control of that town (Martínez Sopena, 'Las villas de la Rioja Alta').

The importance of legal discourse and the very ritual used when formulating their demands cannot be ignored either.[7] The discussions held at meetings of the local council and in other social spheres must have been decisive.

The documents are extremely varied in terms of the information they contain. Some provide data on how the conflict had developed; on the different parts of the procedure; on the authority judging it and those involved; on the arguments of the parties; on any evidence adduced or required; on the investigation undertaken on the facts or rights in dispute; on the answers of informants and their social category; on the resolution issued and its nature (including the *fuero* itself); on the sureties that the resolution would be enforced; on the means for its execution; and even on the witnesses who were present. Often only one of these pieces of information is available. However, it is enough to show the negotiated nature of many of the records that survive.

From an early date there is abundant evidence that the *fueros* and customs of peasant communities were defended before the king. In 1219, at the request of the parties involved, Fernando III confirmed and reinforced the agreement 'super foris et consuetudines' ('on rules and customs') between the local council of Villaverde and the monastery of Arlanza, which had been made earlier in the presence of Alfonso VIII.[8] This indicates that only a few years after the *fuero* had been granted to them (between 1190 and 1193), it was already being discussed and that differences remained, as shown by this new royal confirmation of the previous agreement.[9] In 1220 that same monastery reached another agreement with the local council of San Leonardo laying down the rules of the *fuero*, although apparently without any external intervention this time.[10]

Discussions on the regulations contained in *fueros* are widely documented. A dispute started between the prior of Santa Maria de Nájera and the vassals of the local council of two villages in Burgos, Cuevacardiel and Villamundar:

> because of discrepancies over the *fueros* and the rights due by these vassals to their lords, for they [the vassals] claimed that the Prior and the Convent demanded more from them [...] than they should, and also they suspect that their rights are not recognised as it is written in the grant issued by [King] don Alfonso, the Emperor, a grant that they call a privilege.[11]

Court proceedings were thus initiated, and in 1270 Alfonso X appointed an arbitrator judge to clarify the issues that had been raised. The arbitration award, which survives, further specified and seemed to maintain the original provisions from 1152, supporting the allegations of the local council about the growing pressure from their lord.

---

7 Roberts and Comaroff, *Rules and Processes*; Bloch, *Political Language*.
8 FernandoIII-83 (1219).
9 FB34 (1190–1193).
10 FB212 (1220).
11 'contienda en razón de las dubdas de los fueros et de los derechos que debian dar e fazer tales vasallos, porque ellos lo tenien que les demandava mas el Prior et el Convento [...] que non devien, et otrossi ellos temen que no les davan so derecho segunt se contiene en la carta de donación de don Alfonso el Emperador, la cual carta llaman ellos privilegio'.

348   ISABEL ALFONSO

Therefore, in this case the vassals asserted their claim and succeeded in maintaining the old regulations.[12]

It seems symptomatic of the great significance conferred on the preservation of these privileges that in 1234 the local council of Castrogeriz requested that Fernando III confirmed their *magna carta* (as they referred to it), for fear of its destruction given its age.[13] However, this should not be understood as a sign of stagnation or immutability. The appeal to an earlier *fuero* must be understood as a strategic resource in view of the real or feared deterioration of the conditions established in these documents. Some examples of these included the vassal communities of the Church of Nájera, which qualified their *fuero* as a privilege, and the local council of Castrogeriz, which referred to it as their *magna carta*. The local councils of Silos and Caleruega certainly deemed their appeal to their former *fueros* to be a strategic resource, as each of them forged theirs to confront the growing claims of the abbots, their respective lords, albeit with different outcomes.[14] In contrast, in other cases the intention could be to press for the improvement of, or exemption from, bad *fueros*, and for more beneficial *fueros* to be granted.[15] It can be argued that these expressions were part of the rhetoric of power, which so qualified the *fueros* to the advantage of the powerful; still, they cannot be considered to have been unimportant for the peasants. The fact that their view of the bad *fuero* prevailed is another example of their struggle to change it.

The case of Mojados (a village in the Castilian Extremadura), first under the bishop of Palencia, and later under the bishop of Segovia, is possibly one of the best examples of the persistent and repeated disputes between lords and communities over the content of the *fuero*.[16] These are recorded throughout the thirteenth century, and even reached the royal court. Due to their persistence in the confrontations, the people of Mojados 'gained themselves a reputation of not abiding by their lords as they should',[17] according to the bishop who, in 1293, drafted a new *fuero* to solve all discrepancies about rents and services due and denied to previous bishops. The local council requested that they determined 'in the *fuero* those things they should abide by and comply with [...] so that they [the vassals] kept their will to serve us faithfully and we kept the reason to do them good and mercy'.[18] This clarification of

---

12 Hergueta, 'Fuero de Cuevacardiel y Villamundar'.
13 FernandoIII-513 (1234).
14 Regarding the context in which such forgeries occurred, see the paper by I. Álvarez Borge on the conflicts between the local councils of the villages of Silos, Covarrubias and Caleruega and their respective monasteries, where a connection is made between the existing conflicts and both the growing pressure from the lords and the parallel strengthening of the institutional organisation of the peasant communities (Álvarez Borge, 'Los concejos contra sus señores').
15 An essential study on the socio-economic conditions in which these concessions took place and the 'tensions, pressures and negotiations' that preceded them, is Pastor, *Resistencias y luchas campesinas*, pp. 230–36. See also Martínez Sopena, *Tierra de Campos occidental*, pp. 256–64.
16 Martínez Díez, 'Los fueros inéditos de Mojados'.
17 'ouieron a ganar fama que non eran mandados a sus sennores como deuian' (Martínez Díez, 'Los fueros inéditos de Mojados').
18 'cosas çiertas por fuero que deuiesen guardar et cumplir [...] de manera que ellos ouiessen voluntad de nos seruir lealmiente et nos ouiesemos rrazon de les fazer bien merçed' (Martínez Díez, 'Los fueros inéditos de Mojados').

PEASANTS AND THE LAW   349

the normative content is the most interesting aspect of the new *fuero*, as it informs on the tensions about the original obligations: what they were, and what the improvements consisted in.

The powerful monastery of Sahagún was very often embroiled in litigations related to *fueros* with their bourgeois and peasant vassals. The repeated conflicts with the town of Sahagún and the king's intervention to appease them are well known and have been thoroughly studied.[19] In 1152 Alfonso VII was compelled to go to the town due to the great discord that had broken out between them 'over their *fueros*',[20] as the abbot and monks had demanded to define which *fueros* effectively regulated the relationship between them. It is not known who took the initiative to appeal to royal authority to resolve this conflict, but the context in which it was granted is clear. A century later, in 1255, Alfonso X admitted the 'gran desavenencia' ('great discord') that he found when he arrived at Sahagún between the monastery and the local council of the town, and how he saw fit to 'ammend the existing *fueros*',[21] thus referring to all the previous ones. No judicial process was documented, but it was clear that the king acted as a mediator in the conflict on the normative content, and he was affirmed as a judge, leaving the *Fuero Real* as a complementary law.

In 1294, his son Sancho IV had to resolve a new dispute in the same town about the aggravations that the members of the local council claimed had been caused to them by the abbot and monks, 'enforcing upon them many things that exceeded the Emperor's *fuero*, which they used to have'.[22] The monks, in turn, complained that they were not given their rights, nor was their lordship respected as thoroughly as it should. In order to settle this dispute, the king called for an *ad hoc* 'audience' with the abbot, some monks and the *boni homines* of the local council. He listened to the complaints made against the monastery, which referred mainly to the government of the town, 'to deeds of jurors and notaries',[23] according to the inquest ordered to establish the facts. While the responses of the informants, which have been preserved, are of great interest, it is not possible to deal with them here for reasons of space. Nonetheless, these comments on the conflicts about the content of the *fuero* of Sahagún can serve as a suitable introduction to the analysis of other legal complaints the same lord had to deal with in several nearby local councils that had a larger peasant population.

In the Villacete-Belver community, violence alternated with agreements, both judicial and extrajudicial, concerning the conditions set forth in *fueros* during the first half of the thirteenth century. As a result of some serious assaults committed by these 'furori repleti' ('greatly furious') men on the monastery's estate, in 1208 a 'composicio siue conuenientia' ('settlement and agreement') was established between the monastery of Sahagún and the men who inhabited the monastery's land in San

---

19   On these and previous disputes in the first third of the twelfth century, see Pastor, 'Las primeras rebeliones burguesas'; Pastor, *Resistencias y luchas campesinas*; Estepa Díez, 'Sobre las revueltas burguesas'; Martínez Sopena, *Tierra de Campos occidental*; Portela and Pallares, 'Revueltas feudales'.

20   'pro carta de foros' (FL19, 1152).

21   'emendar los fueros que habían' (FL80, 1255).

22   'pasandoles en muchas cosas a mas de como debian usar con ellos según el fuero del Emperador que solien auer' (SFPSahagún1874, 1294).

23   'a fechos de jurdos y escribanos' (SFPSahagún1874, 1294).

Salvador de Villacete after the mediation of the king and some noblemen.[24] After what seemed to be the customary ritual of forgiveness followed by the abbot granting his mercy, the town's local council settled for an agreement and appointed sureties to avoid that kind of *malefacto* ('wrongdoing') in the future. The lord's power seemingly prevailed, but in subsequent years the local council also appears to have become stronger. They obtained a royal *fuero* in 1211, and Sahagún was denied right to tithes and other ecclesiastical revenues from the other church existing in the town. Shortly afterwards, in 1214, this resulted in another *convenientia* ('agreement') with direct royal intervention, by which the local council granted the referred church to Sahagún and promised to meet its obligations.[25] The local council also promised to be loyal and defend the monastery's interests should anyone wish to harm them. However, they left the rights owed to their lord the king intact and defended the *fuero* given by him as a standard for their rights and obligations. This document, issued by the local council and confirmed by the king, was completely different from the previous one. Unsurprisingly, the monastery, declaring its good will 'for the sake of peace and all the love that I have for you',[26] could do no less than make concessions in favour of the autonomy and defence of the town, in releasing them from one third of the tithe for a period of seventeen years to fund the construction of a walled enclosure.

Nevertheless, as with many other local councils, the problems and tensions did not disappear. These are attested by two extant documents of great interest from 1231, granted by Fernando III. They were issued on the same day but made no internal reference to each other. According to one of them, after complaints made by Sahagún for the wrongs and damages committed by the local council of Belver, and in the presence of representatives of the latter, the king responded to the pleas for mercy made by all parties involved and 'took the lawsuit into [his] own hands.[27] This is a typical judicial procedure, in which the king ruled for the monastery and against the local council. The judgment ordered it to redress the wrongs committed against the monastery's assets and houses, to recover the destroyed crops and to pay damages as assessed by the three arbitrators appointed by the king. The other document, on the contrary, rather shows the King acting as a mediator between the same abbot and local council in the dispute about the abbot's demands.[28] These included payments in money, renders to build a hospice, the right of the monastery's *merino* to partake in the fines collected by the local council's mayors and a toll for all goods sold in the village, as well as ownership of the church of Santa María. After a 'longuam altercacionem' ('long confrontation'), which must be understood as an exchange of arguments and reasoning on the mutual claims submitted to the court, the king decided to mediate and as a result an amicable settlement was reached.[29] The victory of the monastery

---

24 SFPSahagún1572 (1208).
25 SFPSahagún1594 (1214).
26 'pro bono pacis et multo amore que habeo erga uso' (SFPSahagún1594, 1214).
27 'recebi el pleito en mi mano' (FernandoIII-309, 1231).
28 FernandoIII-310 (1231).
29 'with me as a mediator, a friendly agreement between them was reached in this manner' ('me mediante, amicabiliter inter eos compositum fuit isto modo') (FernandoIII-310, 1231).

did not seem to be so clear at that point. The local council succeeded in not bowing to the earlier demands of the monastery, maintained its earlier judicial 'autonomy' and control over trade, and became exempt from the toll payable to the monastery (an exemption desired by many other nearby villages).[30] However, it had to cede its rights over the two churches of the town and promise not to make any further claims to them. They reaffirmed their support of, and reverence for, the abbot, and vowed to defend him against anyone who might seek to harm him, reaffirming also, nonetheless, their 'salua regia reuerencia' ('reverence for the king').

These two documents are two sides of the same coin. They confirm that adjudication and mediation may have been present as a form of conflict resolution both in the procedures themselves and in the royal courts, despite the common assumption. The image of the king being at the same time adjudicator and mediator questions the sharp separation that has been said to exist between these two types of dispute resolution.[31] It was the socio-political context in which these disputes took place that explains the way they were resolved and the — even if provisional — outcomes achieved. I do not intend to dwell on these issues, which need to be placed in connection with the conflicts with traditional powers that emerged from the establishment of royal towns.[32]

I want to draw attention to other disputes that arose in very small communities in defence of their rights, not so much against the institutionalised lordship of a monastery or cathedral, but against certain characters who became lords under what could be considered to be a feudal contract.[33] A well-known case is that of the *fuero* of Toldanos, a village under the dominion of the Cathedral of León, which recounts how the people of this community left because it had been ceded in *prestimonio* by the Bishop to the *milite* ('knight') Rodrigo Pérez. Later on, and with protection from Count Pedro Alfonso they claimed ownership of their lands, except for the plots and other property owned by the bishop. But the bishop argued that everything belonged to the church, so the dispute lasted a long time until the bishop came to a *conuenintia*, following mediation by King Fernando II and Count Pedro. The charter then sets the terms for the inhabitants to return to the place and live under old *fueros*, with additional exemptions from certain burdens and the stipulation of the conditions for them to retain control of their land, whether they lived there or migrated. The bishop, for his part, promised never to cede the village in holding again. This event took place in 1165, a date on which these kinds of transfers (*prestimoniales*) and the issues arising from them had not yet become widespread.[34]

---

30 I refer to the rigorous analysis conducted by Martínez Sopena on the conspiracy of Grajal in Martínez Sopena, *Tierra de Campos occidental*, pp. 552–56.

31 Further development on these issues and the historical-anthropological debate surrounding them can be found in Alfonso, 'Resolución de disputas'.

32 Martínez Sopena, *Tierra de Campos occidental*, pp. 196 ff.

33 Other similar cases, due to the attempts by the lower nobility to create their own manors within existing jurisdictions, resulted in what was known as *querimonie* or quires of complaints by Catalan peasant communities demanding fulfilment of their rights under the Count's justice Salrach, 'Agressions senyorials', pp. 25 ff.

34 FL29 (1165).

A similar situation, but one narrated with more dramatic effect, was that experienced by the inhabitants of Arroyal. Having peacefully been vassals of the king, they obtained a *fuero* in the times of Alfonso VII.[35] Upon his death one Álvaro Rodríguez de Mansilla, who is not mentioned as acting under any lord, appropriated the domain, oppressed them and unlawfully deprived them of their 'foro iniuste' ('unjust *fuero*'). In this context, a tragic event unleashed the contained anger derived from such unfair behaviour. Upon the death of one of the village dwellers, Álvaro sent his relatives and his 'villico maior' ('major bailiff') to seize the dead person's house and possessions, and also wanted to plunder his heirs of all their chattels. The charter goes on to narrate how their neighbours, the entire local council of Arroyal, being aware of the strength of their union, rose up and uttered insults against Don Álvaro.[36] In their outrage, they lodged a complaint with King Alfonso in Palencia. The King — through his bailiff — returned the house to the victims of the abuse. But the complaint made by the local council was directed against the unjust exercise of power by a person who had arrogated lordship status to himself. King Alfonso instructed his 'villico maior', the one who 'oversaw all those villages',[37] to lead an enquiry in Arroyal's neighbouring villages to find which *fuero* they had had from the days of King Sancho. The text mentions the villages surveyed and the enquirers, as well as the names and responses of the peasants from one of them after they had sworn that they would tell the truth about their knowledge of the *fuero* of Arroyal.[38] The investigation continued in the same way in the other villages. Once it had been completed according to the usual procedure, the outcome was submitted to the king, who reaffirmed it and delivered it to the beneficiaries. The informants said that the dwellers from Arroyal had never done labour services (*sernas*); that they used to give a rent of two solidi from each household in March; and that they could excuse themselves from fines or injuries assessed at less than twenty solidi by their own oath, or with twelve oath-helpers, 'sicut mos est' ('as customary'), for injuries assessed over that amount. It must be assumed that these conditions were very different from those that they had been subjected to by the maligned Don Álvaro.

Given the tone in which this *fuero* was written, it may have been used to fuel the rhetoric of the righteous king and his legal protection of the weak, so widespread among medieval and later peasants. However, it is interesting to note the collective ability shown to employ legal parameters that set limits to the illegitimate or unjust use of power.

The tensions and contradictions generated as a result of the transfer of a village by its legitimate lord is clearly illustrated by the so-called *fuero* of Pinos de Babia. The *fuero* was the product of, or is contained in, an agreement, sealed by a judge from León and made in 1250 between the Abbot of the canon church of San Isidoro de Léon and

---

35 FB36 (1183).

36 'declaring collectively that what had happened to one of them could occur to all of them' ('in commune dicentes quod uni inertur nobis omnibus uenturum putemus') (FB36, 1183).

37 'preerat omnibus uilicis' (FB36, 1183).

38 'they would say the truth about what they had heard and knew about the *fuero* of Arroyal' ('dicerent quiquid uerum sentirent et scirent de foro the Arroyal') (FB36, 1183).

'all their vassals from Pinos, that is, the whole local council'.[39] The abbot recounted that the lease or agreement[40] that the monastery had entered into with Juan Pérez de Majua ought to be maintained until the end of its term, provided that it did not give the local council a treatment that was contrary to their *fuero*. Once the term of the lease had expired, if the local council agreed 'to rent it, or to pay the Abbot all the rents and rights' (I am not sure if they are indeed two alternatives), the latter 'would not be permitted to give the village in holding to any knight'.[41] It was, therefore, the transfer of the village that was being negotiated, since the Abbot went on to say that if they did not reach an agreement he 'should be entitled to lease it to whoever he pleased and to obtain with it as much benefit as he could'.[42] The monastery's obvious strategy was to secure the undisturbed collection of revenue while reversing protests against the current tenant by offering to lease the village to the local council itself. The latter fought to limit feudal power and actions that were *desaforadas* ('contrary to the law'), and to take control of the village. What these conflicts show is that the ability of lords to dispose of the villages under their lordship had some limits which were partly imposed by the people under their rule.

It seems to have been sufficiently demonstrated that the regulations defining the rights and obligations between lords and peasants occurred within a process of continuous negotiation and conflict. The context of the debate was not always or entirely, judicial, and *fueros* often only mentioned the consensus reached. There are *fueros* that reveal the gift and counter-gift process of negotiation, with reciprocity being shown by the concessions made by both parties. The *fuero* granted by the Monastery of Vega to the village local council in 1217 was formalised as a gracious concession by the Abbess 'a charter of concession, acquittal and stability'.[43] This deals with exemptions from rents owed for arable land and vineyards ceded in *prestimonio*, which they would be able to sell among themselves without paying entry fines, as well as other exemptions. The idea of a *pactum* ('pact') emerges not only from the text's vocabulary, but also from the fact that these exemptions were granted in exchange for the vassals' performing fifteen days of labour services per year at the Abbess's request 'with ready will and with good disposition'.[44] Such work renderings were extensively regulated by the nuns of this monastery.[45]

Similar negotiations took place between the nuns of San Pedro de Dueñas and the local council of the village of the same name. In 1124 the village inhabitants had gained the right to transfer their holdings to their closest kin if they died childless, without the burden of *mañería*, according to the 'consuetudo terre' ('region's custom').[46]

---

39 'todos los vasallos de Pinus, conuien a saber con todol conçeyo dessa uilla' (FL79, 1250).

40 I think that the translation by J. Rodriguez of *pleytu* as lawsuit totally distorts the meaning of this article of the *fuero* (FL79, 1250).

41 'por yeal arrendar o de le parar bien todos sos foros e todos sos derechos [...] non deue arrendar ela uilla a caualero nenguno' (FL79, 1250).

42 'sea poderoso de la arrendar a quien quesier, ye de la meter a sua prod e lo maos que podier' (FL79, 1250).

43 'cartam concessionis, absolutionis et stabilitatis' (MVega81, 1217).

44 'libenti animo et voluntate bona' (MVega81, 1217).

45 Alfonso, 'Las sernas', pp. 194–95.

46 FL11 (1124).

In 1162 the villagers were donated an extensive piece of bounded land within the village territory and some *fuero* regulations were established.[47] The wording of the *fuero*[48] clearly shows that the process was based on compromise. This is first made evident from the requirement to render work as a counter-gift.[49] It is even clearer in a paragraph placed after the date and references of authority of the document, a likely indicator that there was pressure to append it, or at least an urge to commit to script concessions that might have been offered verbally and informally. This is a clause that clarified an earlier one in the same *fuero*, and consolidated the right of free movement of peasants and the free transfer of their land, something quite extraordinary in the area, as aptly demonstrated by Martínez Sopena.[50]

In 1191 the nuns were forced to make additions to that old *fuero* which in fact annulled the last clause.[51] This, and the arguments used to achieve the concejo's 'assensu et beneplacito' ('acquiescence and consent') suggest that another issue needs to be considered, namely the nature of the conflicts over the peasants' ability to dispose of their land, and how this was recorded in the *fueros*. In what follows I want to draw attention to this important, yet insufficiently studied issue.

The text in question begins by narrating the reasons claimed for these new regulations to be developed. These were the ills, violence and theft that resulted from the relationships that the village dwellers had with knights and squires, whose children they raised, and to whom they gave their daughters as wives (while they took others as concubines), and to whom they also sold land that they had received from the monastery. The peasants were thus involved in, and were the victims of, the disputes, alliances and enmities that existed among the local powerful. The monastery, besides losing its *prestimonios*, became engaged in 'lites et causis in juidicio' ('arguments and disputes in court') with them to defend their property, and were also victims of damage and destruction, all of which resulted in a reduction of justice and the ability of the village to defend itself. In order to prevent these events, 'omnis in simul' ('all of them together') and again with the consent of the local council added the provisions contained in this document to the old *fuero*. These were intended to ban, or make the village's men to commit not to have, any ties with knights and squires, as this had been identified as the cause of all ills; or that they would at least not do so without the control and authorisation of the monastery, since it was anticipated that some alliances with the powerful may be of interest.[52] Heavy fines were contemplated,

---

47 SFPSahagún1341 (1162).

48 That 'consensual' character of 'reciprocity' and 'exchange' is also evident in the ritual of an *alboroque* worth 1 mr. as dues paid to the monastery.

49 'sernas por estos foros' ('labour services on the basis of this norms') (SFPSahagún1341, 1162).

50 Martínez Sopena, *Tierra de Campos occidental*, pp. 235 ff.

51 FL49 (1191).

52 This very close, 'nurturing' relationship that existed in practice between some peasants and local powerful families, was considered as a breach of the regulations in this context, maybe because this relationship was a sign of freedom. Still in the mid-thirteenth century, in order to circumvent the demands of the bishop of Lugo that they were 'villanos de fazendaria' ('bonded peasants'), the community of San Vicente de Muros and Santiago de Procul, in Galicia claimed, among other things, to be a *behetría* and could nurture the children of the region's knights. See Hinojosa78 (1226).

including the appropriation of all their land (not only that on loan) for those who violated such a 'salubre statum' ('benefitial statute'). The local council was said to have been summoned by a crier at the door of San Benito. Seeing that all this had been granted by means of a *fuero* for their order and peace, they received the *fuero* under that peace and were bound to comply with it. Their property was used as security, as it would protect them from the ills previously suffered. The process ended with a mutual commitment to respect it.

The monastery of San Isidoro de León seems to have had similar problems at their village of Pinos de Babia.[53] The *fuero* discussed above began with the apparently joint promise never to receive a knight or a squire, or their families, as residents or heirs in the village from that date onwards. This was followed by a commitment by both parties, jointly with the king, the *merino* and the *comendero*, to expel the knight Suero Alfonso and his relatives due to the damage that they had always caused both to the local council ('a great wrong with a great arrogance, a great loss of property') and to the monastery ('a great impairment, a great loss'), and to the fact that they did not have the right to live in the village, or to have any properties or vassals there.[54] This type of arrangement, whether formalised as a ban or as an obligation, was aimed at ensuring that the lord's property would remain subject to seigneurial rights. This was one of the most frequent and widespread *fuero* regulations, and probably also one of the least respected, as shown — among many others — by the *fueros* discussed above.[55]

These documents certainly contain a wealth of information about how the conflicts were being played out at different levels. Beyond the efforts made to reach a consensus about complying with *fuero* regulations, a wider conflict can be detected between the monasteries and the local lower nobility, who challenged their capacity to control alliances. The peasants, however, were not just a bit player in this plot, and they used their leverage to take advantage of the clashes between the other groups.

The multiple questions arising from this information need further study. I believe that the tensions and conflicts regarding whether, to what extent, and under which conditions the peasants could freely dispose of the properties in their hands (both leased and owned), reflected the practical intricacies and the significance of property transfers in and out of the community. These were not just aimed to control revenues and property, but also to monitor the peasants' networks of alliances. The social use of land to create links though transfers also operated among the peasants. Donations were made to the church and to powerful laymen so as to seek not only strong material protection, but also to create other kinds of relationships. Donations were not only conditioned by need, or by a purely economic necessity. Nor were sales.[56] Having the right to freely dispose of land in donations, sales or exchanges entailed having the ability to develop and strengthen partnerships, to find the most suitable benefactor, and to consolidate friendly relationships within the community or in a

---

53 FL79 (1250).
54 'mucho mal, mucha soberuia, gran desheredamiento [...] gran menoscabo, gran perdida' (FL79, 1250).
55 Martinez Sopena linked the breach of this clause to the crisis of large estates in the thirteenth century Martínez Sopena, *Tierra de Campos occidental*, p. 246.
56 White, *Custom, Kinship, and Gifts to Saints*; Wickham, *The Mountains and the City*; Miller, *Bloodtaking*.

wider circle. It would be interesting to investigate how the dynamics of alliances at local level worked between more or less formally distinct social groups; and how these networks of relationships that made up the fabric of local society were inherited and reproduced in local contexts, where conflicts between communities and others in higher hierarchical positions seemed to be resolved. It is essential to look at this social fabric, not only to have a comprehensive understanding of peasant/lord relationships, but also to appreciate the development of peasant class consciousness and political action on a daily basis.[57]

It was in their everyday environment that the peasants' capacity to formulate their demands in legal terms was shaped. Legal notions about access to, use of, and disposability of land, as well as accompanying obligations, were part of a wider normative context comprising the cultural values which defined social relationships, and resulted from both struggle and negotiation.[58] This was the setting for the ideological conflicts that affected the very language of class relationships, as opposing groups attempted to impose their own interpretation of activities and behaviours.

Documentary evidence shows how these medieval peasants — just as those from Sedaka many centuries later, as studied by Scott (1985) — tried to impose their own meaning on the language related to the work to be rendered to their lord. To accept that the *sernas* were done on a voluntary basis, as claimed in 1206 by the men of San Pedro de Dueñas and 'no de debito or per foro' ('not by legal obligation' or 'on the basis of the *fuero*'), as held by the Abbot of Sahagún, did not only concern peasant dignity. It also affected the very nature of the relationships between the two groups. Failure to perform compulsory tasks was penalised, but this was not the case if help was voluntary. In this litigation the powerful Abbot of Sahagún filed a claim against the community of the village of Dueñas before King Alfonso VIII.[59] The community lost, as the investigation ordered by the king proved that they were obliged to perform that work and had done so for a long time in the past, and that their property had been seized when they failed to do it.

Many years earlier, however, in 1126, in a nearby area, the inhabitants of the local council of Venialbo had succeeded in obtaining 'foros bonos' ('good *fueros*') from the Abbot of Santo Tomé, which exempted them from labour services and from giving their animals for transport unless they did that out of piety and free will.[60] This came

---

57 I have researched the complexity and tensions of this social fabric in connection with communities in Galicia and more recently in some areas of Burgos Alfonso, 'Poder local y diferenciación interna'; Alfonso, 'La comunidad campesina'; Alfonso, 'Resolución de disputas'.

58 Here I draw on the concepts of 'repertoire' and 'normative context' developed by anthropologists in works such as Roberts and Comaroff, *Rules and Processes*; Scott, *Weapons of the Weak*. Thinking in terms of a normative context involves taking into account a broad set of rules, principles and values of various types, which are partly the result of the material conditions of production and rooted in ordinary material practices. These are not external to the social actors, but result from a clash of divergent interpretations of the social order. It is in this context that one can speak of the 'social use' of law, to the extent that it constitutes the material for the construction of a 'normative discourse' under which opposing demands and interests are presented.

59 SFPSahagún1569 (1206).

60 'except whoever wanted for the sake of his soul and by his own will [...] except whoever wanted by

PEASANTS AND THE LAW   357

to formalise the voluntary nature of these work services and was a departure from the servile nature that they had always had.

In another area of Castile, approximately in the same period as the peasants in Dueñas, the powerful monastery of Oña also accepted not only that their vassals in Nuez and Montenegro would work fewer days (two instead of fifteen per year), but also that such work would be carried out as help, not as an obligation.[61] Therefore, the 'war of words' involved in the struggle to impose a certain interpretation on the activities of the social group was not without practical consequences.[62]

Another symbolic weapon used by both parties in this ideological struggle was the pressure for the fulfilment of reciprocal relationships to ensure that they were not merely rhetorical. The mutual obligations that they recognised came to reinforce a normative repertoire that each of the two groups could strategically use to serve their own interests. These principles of reciprocity, while frequently violated, should not only be understood as a legitimising ideology of domination, but also as a weapon in the hands of the weak to set limits to that domination.[63] The aforecited agreement between the Abbot of San Isidoro de León and the local council of Pinos de Babia ended with what can certainly be considered as one of the longest documents specifically dealing with reciprocity in lord/peasant relationships.[64] The local council pledged in good will to be the Abbot's faithful vassals, to pay him rents and rights and to have no other lord. The monastery promised in good will to be good lords and not to rule them unlawfully. Later they penalised any failure to comply with these agreements by referring to the value/counter-value of loyalty/disloyalty, which was defined according to the 'norm' of reciprocity: if the local council did not respect these agreements they would be worthless, as he who is disloyal to his lord, and would forfeit their whole property. And similarly worthless must be the lord who is disloyal to his vassals.[65]

---

his own will and for the sake of God' ('nisi qui voluerit pro anima sua et pro suo gradu [...] nisi qui voluerit per suo gradu et pro amore Dei') (FZ5, 1126).

61 'exonerate and acquiet you [...] from the *sernas* that you have until now performed on our behalf for fifteen days, so that we shall not demand them again from this day onwards' ('absoluemos e lessamos [...] las sernas ke fata aqui nos faziedes en quiza dias, ke nunqua uos las demandemos deste dia en adelant') (SSOña-A481, 1238); 'and so that you shall never do any *serna*. And you shall help us two days every year' ('ni fagades nunqua serna premia. E uos ke non aiudedes siempre dos días kada un anno') (SSOña-A576, 1268).

62 According to Scott, 'just who is helping whom and how much — who is the social creditor and who the debtor — in relations described as [help] is always a contested social fact [...] Struggles of precisely this kind, I believe, are common whenever classes are in direct, personal contact' (Scott, *Weapons of the Weak*, pp. 193–94). Scott considers the 'war of words' as one of the key forms of everyday resistance: 'The refusal to accept the definition of the situation as seen from above [...] while not sufficient, are surely necessary for any further or greater resistance' (Scott, *Weapons of the Weak*, p. 240). In a later book, Scott furthered the study of the relationship between what he calls elementary forms of politics, nurtured in a 'hidden transcript' that goes on unseen by, and directed against, power holders, and more organised forms of political action (Scott, *Domination*, ch. 7).

63 Scott deals extensively with the strategic use of social ideology as a symbolic weapon by patron and client and provides an interesting bibliography in Scott, *Weapons of the Weak*, pp. 198 ff.

64 FL79 (1250).

65 About clauses in leases that express aspects of reciprocity as legitimation of power, see my study on

The preceding pages show how an ideological discourse of class relations was established and how it informed everyday vocabulary. This is the context to be taken into account when considering the qualifications of good or bad applied both to *fueros* and to vassals and lords, and the synonyms that expressed their content (forceful or not, loyal/disloyal). They constituted normative values that sought to influence the behaviour of the other party through social sanctions when they were not observed.[66]

The lords' obligations to their vassals were part of the 'dominant ideology' of the three orders, and rarely went beyond the scope of vague statements about protection and help in exchange for service: 'we shall love you and you shall serve us'.[67] The preserved texts seldom show the kind of strategic manipulation of reciprocal obligations that is seen in the previous document; and even rarer still is to find them formally regulated, as was the case with the *fuero* granted by the Abbess of San Pedro de Dueñas in 1198 to the 'men who are our vassals in Mahudes'.[68] Only some isolated provisions reveal the existing tension and negotiation involved, and the demands for the lord's protection made by the vassals. It was stated that if the lord did not do right by them, they could leave their wives and children in their land and seek whomever they pleased as lord. The importance of such statements should not be underestimated if we think that the *ius maletractandi* ('right to abuse') is a privilege recognised in other places as a lordly right. The law certainly set limits — even if theoretical — on the power of the monastery. The violation of those limits undermined their authority, caused conflicts that might be harmful to it, and to some extent established the rules of the legitimate exercise of these rights. I believe that this regulatory recognition of the lords' obligations with respect to their vassals was an achievement of this peasant community.[69]

The data reviewed in these pages highlight some aspects of peasant conflicts which, in my opinion, deserve to be borne in mind:

- The normative definition of peasant/lord relationships occurred within constant processes of negotiation and conflict. The use of judicial avenues, while not always chosen by peasants, was another strategy within broader conflict

---

Galician communities Alfonso, 'La comunidad campesina', pp. 313–14.

66 See the above cited case of Mojados (*vid. supra*, pp. 348–49), where the Bishop of Segovia warned his vassals that they had gained a reputation for not abiding by their lords' rules as they should, due to their repeated refusal to meet certain lordly demands. The Cistercian monks from Moreruela, in the same spirit, asked their vassals of the village of Ifanes (modern Portugal) to be good, loyal and serviceable, as all vassals must be to their lord in all that is law and custom in our land (Alfonso, *La colonización cisterciense*). Of great interest on this subject is the chapter devoted by Scott to studying what he called the 'vocabulary of exploitation' (Scott, *Weapons of the Weak*, pp. 186 ff.).

67 'nos vobis amando, et vobis nobis serviendo' (Hinojosa41, 1157).

68 'homines qui sunt uasalli en Mahudes' (FL56, 1198).

69 The 1148 *fuero* of Covarrubias contains a similar clause, although in this case it seems to be intended to channel violent peasant reactions through the courts rather than to the lords, either directly or indirectly: 'If the lord or the *merino* should want to force them, let them defend themselves in court without suffering any fines' (FB21, 1148). It is worth referring to the paper presented by Chris Wickham in Valencia in 1993, largely inspired by Thompson, *Whigs and Hunters*, about the law as a defining element of the parameters of legitimate power. I am grateful to him for allowing me to read it as an unpublished copy. Thompson's argument on the law was also applied to custom in a chapter in Thompson, *Customs in Common*.

processes that cannot be isolated from other forms of struggle or resistance, whether peaceful or violent. It is necessary to ascertain the contexts in which the former or the latter prevailed.[70]

- The diversity of outcomes must be attributed more to specific socio-political and economic situations than to general principles of the law as a coercive instrument.

- The legalisation of forms of domination entailed by regulatory institutionalisation — the law — also involved a legal framework within which the exercise of a power purporting to be legitimate was to take place. This exercise of power involved trade-offs and rules of conduct, whose breach and violation caused de-legitimisation, violence and losses.

---

70 For the sake of clarity, this paper deliberately avoids dealing with the ways in which the struggles were presented and the factors that conditioned or determined them (degree of dependence, development of local councils, intensification of internal differentiation, greater lordly pressure, inter-nobility conflicts, economic expansion or crisis, among others).

Bibliography

Alfonso, Isabel, 'Las sernas en León y Castilla. Contribución al estudio de la relaciones socio-económicas en el marco del señorio medieval', *Moneda y Crédito*, 129 (1974), 153–210

Alfonso, Isabel, *La colonización cisterciense en la Meseta del Duero. El dominio de Moreruela (siglos XII–XIV)* (Zamora: Instituto de Estudios Zamoranos Florián de Ocampo, 1986)

Alfonso, Isabel, 'La comunidad campesina', in *Poder monástico y grupos domésticos en la Galicia foral (siglos XIII–XV)*, ed. by Reyna Pastor and others (Madrid: CSIC, 1990), pp. 302–72

Alfonso, Isabel, 'Poder local y diferenciación interna en las comunidades rurales gallegas', in *Relaciones de poder, de producción y de parentesco en la Edad Media y Moderna: aproximación a su estudio*, ed. by Reyna Pastor (Madrid: CSIC, 1990), pp. 203–24

Alfonso, Isabel, 'Resolución de disputas y prácticas judiciales en el Burgos medieval', in *Burgos en la Plena Edad Media: III Jornadas Burgalesas de Historia* (Burgos: Asociacion Provincial de Libreros de Burgos, 1993), pp. 211–43

Álvarez Borge, Ignacio, 'Los concejos contra sus señores: luchas antiseñoriales en villas de abadengo en Castilla en el siglo XIV', *Historia social*, 15 (1993), 3–28

Bloch, Maurice, *Political Language and Oratory in Traditional Society* (London: Academic Press, 1975)

Estepa Díez, Carlos, 'Sobre las revueltas burguesas en el siglo XII en el Reino de León', *Archivos Leoneses*, 55–56 (1974), 291–307

Hergueta, Narciso, 'Fuero de Cuevacardiel y Villamundar', *Revista de Archivos, Bibliotecas y Museos*, 10–1 (1907), 417–22

Hilton, Rodney, 'Las societé paysanne et le droit dans l'Anglaterre médievale', *Études rurales*, 103–04 (1986), 13–18

Martín Cea, Juan Carlos, *El campesinado castellano de la cuenca del Duero: aproximaciones a su estudio durante los siglos XIII al XV* (Valladolid: Consejo General de Castilla y León. Servicio de Publicaciones, 1983)

Martínez Díez, Gonzalo, 'Los fueros inéditos de Mojados', in *Estudios en homenaje a Don Claudio Sánchez Albornoz en sus 90 años. Vol. 2* (Buenos Aires: Instituto de Historia de España, 1983), pp. 453–67

Martínez Sopena, Pascual, *La Tierra de Campos occidental: poblamiento, poder y comunidad del siglo X al XIII* (Valladolid: Institución Cultural Simancas, 1985)

Martínez Sopena, Pascual, 'Las villas de la Rioja Alta entre los siglos XII y XIV', in *Historia de la ciudad de Logroño 2. Edad Media*, ed. by José Ángel Sesma Muñoz (Zaragoza: Ayuntamiento de Logroño, 1995), pp. 279–322

Miller, William I., *Bloodtaking and Peacemaking: Feud, Law, and Society in Saga Iceland* (Chicago: The University of Chicago Press, 1990)

Pastor, Reyna, 'Las primeras rebeliones burguesas en Castilla y León (siglo XII). Análisis histórico-social de una coyuntura', *Estudios de Historia Social*, 1 (1965), 13–101

Pastor, Reyna, *Resistencias y luchas campesinas en la época del crecimiento y consolidación de la formación feudal: Castilla y León, siglos X–XIII* (Madrid: Siglo XXI, 1980)

Portela, Ermelindo and María del Carmen Pallares, 'Revueltas feudales en el camino de Santiago. Compostela y Sahagún', in *Las peregrinaciones a Santiago de Compostela y San Salvador de Oviedo en la Edad Media. Actas del Congreso Internacional celebrado en Oviedo del 3 al 7 de diciembre de 1990*, ed. by Juan Ignacio Ruiz de la Peña (Oviedo: Gobierno del Principado de Asturias, 1993), pp. 313–34

Roberts, Simon, and John Comaroff, L., *Rules and Processes: The Cultural Logic of Dispute in an African Context* (Chicago: The University of Chicago Press, 1981)

Salrach, Josep María, 'Agressions senyorials i resistències pageses en el procés de feudalització', in *Revoltes populars contra el poder de l'Estat. Actes de les primeres Jornades de Debat (Reus, 18–20 octubre 1990)* (Barcelona: Centre de Lectura de Reus, 1992), pp. 11–29

Scott, James C., *Weapons of the Weak: Everyday Forms of Peasant Resistance* (New Haven: Yale University Press, 1985)

Scott, James C., *Domination and the Arts of Resistance: Hidden Transcripts* (New Haven: Yale University Press, 1990)

Thompson, Edward P., *Whigs and Hunters: The Origin of the Black Act* (London: Allen Lane, 1975)

Thompson, Edward P., *Customs in Common* (London: Penguin, 1991)

White, Stephen D., *Custom, Kinship, and Gifts to Saints: The Laudatio Parentum in Western France, 1050–1150* (Chapel Hill: University of North Carolina Press, 1988)

Wickham, Chris, *The Mountains and the City: The Tuscan Apennines in the Early Middle Ages* (Oxford: Clarendon Press, 1988)

CHAPTER 10

On Rural Churches and Peasant Struggles

with a commentary by Chris Wickham

Conflict, Language, and Social Practice in Medieval Societies: Selected Essays of Isabel Alfonso, with Commentaries, ed. by Julio Escalona Monge, Álvaro Carvajal Castro, and Cristina Jular Pérez-Alfaro, TMC 24 (Turnhout: Brepols, 2024), pp. 363–397

BREPOLS ❦ PUBLISHERS   10.1484/M.TMC-EB.5.132464

CHRIS WICKHAM

On Rural Churches and Peasant Struggles

This important article has a double aim. First, and for most of the text, it tracks the various ways in which rural communities contested the paying of tithe to the church in northern Castile-León, particularly in a long thirteenth century. Second, it seeks to explore the fact that such resistance had an ideological/religious element, not just an economic one: not a heretical element, or not for the most part, but at least one based on a set of religious values which were not always those of the ecclesiastical powers which tried to keep communities under control. Few people in the central middle ages denied the legitimacy of paying tithe at all (I will come back to the point), but what it should be for — whether or not it should benefit the local community first, and outside powers only second — could be an issue in any society. Maribel Alfonso here shows, very effectively, how to recognise the coherence of peasant religious values, and she also points up the fact, unavoidable for any medieval historian, that the material and the religious were inextricable in people's minds, and that it is a mistake for any of us to focus on either to the exclusion of the other (I will come back to this point too). I would add that the way that she weaves resistance into the identity of the parish as a whole, as an alternative to the institutional analyses of parish structures which abound in the literature, is in itself a path which we all need to follow. Her other work on courts and conflicts gives further resonance to this social, rather than institutional, approach. But my commentary on this article will otherwise focus on the first of Maribel's aims, for that is the one which she has the clearest evidence for, and this is why she devotes most of her text to it: on the ways and means of peasant anti-tithe resistance itself.

This article focusses on the good documentation from the monastic lordship of Oña between 1150 and 1325, although it adds enough briefer examples from other places in northern Spain to show us that Oña was by no means atypical. Oña had to deal with anti-tithe resistance from villages inside its lordship which made different sorts of claim: sometimes they said that the village church was their collective property (*difusa*, in their terminology), and that the clerics of the church were *filii vicinorum* ('sons of the inhabitants') of the village; sometimes the villagers (with their local priests) moved their religious observance to a second church, generally a chapel which they had founded themselves, which they claimed parish rights for. Either way, they claimed that they did not have to pay ecclesiastical dues (the standard European set of tithes, first-fruits, and oblations) as a result, and they defended this in lengthy court cases — they lost some, but in others they cut complex deals through arbitration over how much tithe they had to pay. Interestingly, some of these deals show that one of the things the villagers wanted most was the maintenance of the right to choose local clerics from the *filii vicinorum*; clearly, this was seen as

---

Chris Wickham, Emeritus Chichele Professor of Medieval History, Oxford University

sufficient to establish local control over the church, and presumably over the use to which tithes were put too. Villages were not, of course, homogeneous; rural élites tended, as elsewhere, to dominate, and it was these élites which provided most of the *filii vicinorum* to the local church, not necessarily with as collective a commitment as villages tended to claim. All the same, the force of these collectivities remains striking, and they were quite often relatively successful in their claims. In particular, Maribel shows that churches were the property of their local communities, large and small, very widely in northern Spain, well outside the lordship of Oña, and indeed perhaps even more so elsewhere.

Maribel remarks that she would need far too many pages to compare this local society to others in Europe, and that is indeed true: particularly if one did this with the subtlety which she shows in her own analyses. Since I know Italy best, however, I cannot avoid such comparisons; for what is striking to me is how unlike Italian disputes these Castilian ones are. Italian disputes between communities of *vicini* and lords — usually ecclesiastical patrons — were about the election of the local priest, not tithe; and it was the election itself which was at issue, not the right of the community to have priests only of local origin.[1] (Indeed, it is usually rather difficult to tell where, or which family, any documented priest was actually from, until surnames begin in the countryside). Disputes about tithe were between bishops and the lords who took over percentages of tithe in the tenth century or so and who were unwilling, in the twelfth century, to give it back except for money; or else between the local *pieve* (super-parish) and a monastery which was the patron of a chapel inside the territory of the *pieve*. The later disputes between the *pieve* and its chapels, which were breaking off into independent parishes of their own with a closer link to local communities, tended rather to be over burial dues and (often immaterial) 'reverences', not tithe.[2] The role of tithe was anyway variable inside Italy; Simone Collavini has recently argued that in Tuscany the control over tithe was marginal to lords, unlike in the Po plain.[3] The two collective volumes which have recently appeared on tithe across western Europe (particularly, but not only, France) similarly imply a relative absence of community-based conflict over tithe; in Provence, for example, disputes between local communities and ecclesiastical lords in the late middle ages hardly involved tithe at all, even if around 1300 they had been more numerous.[4]

---

1 Nanni, *La parrocchia*, pp. 159–71; Wickham, *Courts and Conflict*, e.g. pp. 93–97, 260–64.
2 Wickham, *Courts and Conflict*, pp. 238–52; Wickham, *Community and Clientele*, pp. 75–81; Violante, 'Pievi e parrocchie', pp. 737–50; Provero, 'Les dîmes'. For lords, see (among others) Violante, 'Pievi e parrocchie'; Menant, *Campagnes lombardes*, pp. 732–35, 760–64; Menant, 'Dîme et féodalité'.
3 Collavini, 'La dîme'.
4 Viader, ed., *La dîme*; Lauwers, ed., *La dîme*, in which see Butaud, 'Définition, prélèvement et gestion de la dîme', pp. 480–84, for Provence. Note, as Maribel Alfonso also does, the article on Castile and Aragón in Viader's volume, Díaz de Durana and Guinot, 'La dîme', a useful descriptive article, which at pp. 77–78 refers briefly to peasant resistance over tithe, not citing the texts which Maribel analyses. It is striking how rare the contestation of tithe-paying was in the well-documented diocese of Girona: Mallorquí, *Parròquia i societat rural*, pp. 253, 344–45, 402–03. Wood, *The Proprietary Church*, pp. 459–518, gives a very good general account of the history of tithe.

When one thinks about this relative absence, it is even odd. Tithe was a big payment, even if generally less than rent. Even late medieval state taxation, when it came back in, was rarely for larger percentages than the 10 per cent or more which genuinely does seem to have often been exacted in the parishes of Europe.[5] But communities resisted taxation, very often, and sometimes rents and seigneurial dues too (as with the collective movements which led to village *franchises, franchigie* and *fueros* across western Europe). Why they found tithe less troublesome must have something to do with the religious context for it which Maribel explores so interestingly in the final pages of her article. It also may be significant that the well-known example of Montaillou in the 1320s, where tithe was certainly resented and contested (including through the extremely religious strategy of adopting Catharism), was not only one of a strong local community, but also one in which most peasants owned their own land, so tithe was actually the main due they paid to anybody.[6] But anyway, tithe, of all the dues which peasants paid, seems to have been among the most accepted in the central and late medieval centuries. What peasants did if they wished to avoid paying it was less in the arena of claiming the right not to pay it, but rather in that of evasion. Maribel indeed begins her article with an evocation of Alfonso X banning a variety of forms of day-to-day evasion in Castile, Jim Scott's classic 'weapons of the weak'. I do not doubt that these forms of evasion were standard throughout Europe — they are little documented, precisely because they did not amount to claims of right. This again emphasises the fact that, in various villages of Castile, the ones she studies in the core of her article, tithe was indeed contested as a claim of right. And that brings us back to the particularity of Castile.

What made Castilian villages special? To me, it was the unusual strength of their communities. No village communities in Europe in the tenth century are as visible and as active as those of Castile and its neighbours; they fought over village boundaries, and they had, at least sometimes, some form of explicit community organisation, the *concilium*, as few other parts of Europe did. Importantly here, they are sometimes also documented as founding their own churches, which is very rare in the rest of Europe apart from in Catalonia, whose social patterns were in this respect (even though not others) closely parallel.[7] The interesting thing about Castile, in particular, is that when local lordship developed in the century after (say) 1050, removing — among other things — control over pastures from local communities, this did not lead to the weakening of local solidarities; and when villages established formal rights with *fueros* and similar agreements, in the late twelfth century and into the thirteenth, they called themselves by the same collective name as in the tenth, 'council', now more often Castilianised as *concejo* — indeed, larger settlements had sometimes managed to hold off seigneurial power throughout the intervening period too, in a way which was, again, very rare in the rest of Europe. In this context, it was also more likely that thirteenth-century village collectivities could be conceived as owning their own church,

---

5 Lauwers, 'Pour une histoire de la dîme', esp. pp. 18–20, 52–53, is interesting on this: is tithe a 'tax'?
6 Le Roy Ladurie, *Montaillou*, pp. 37–50.
7 For a brief comparative survey, Wickham, *Community and Clientele*, pp. 192 ff. For collective church foundation and ownership across western Europe, see Wood, *The Proprietary Church*, pp. 651–58.

something which had actually been true in many cases at the beginning, and could be used as an image — whether truly or falsely — three centuries later. (Moving to another church which was more fully under local control could be thought off as a spin-off of this too; again, the practice was unusual, although it was conceivable to Italian and French writers of canon law).[8] The emphasis on the *filii vicinorum* in Castile must have been linked to this too: for, where the church was so imbricated (a word Maribel likes) with such a tight secular society, clerics were very likely to be local leaders, and needed — more than elsewhere? — to be local themselves.

More could easily be said about these differences, and should as well, for they need to be confronted more. But we must not be romantic about them. What collective, village, autonomy also means is that the people who command locally are not outsiders but insiders. Villages were always unequal; local élites always commanded. Perhaps they did not do so with the detachment and disregard for local norms that lords did, but they did so all the same. One witness-document from 1323–4 for Liencres (prov. Cantabria), cited by Maribel, recounts how one family controlled the church until it ceded half of it to another family in payment for a killing; the image of a local family giving part of a church to end a feud is an arresting one in this context. And it is also one which makes us think further. The practical imbrication between the religious and the material meant not just that payments to outsiders could have a religious charge, but that the control of cult was inseparable from other material imperatives too. Hierarchy, and the need to make peace: how secular were they? The question is a false one, for the lay and the religious were always inextricable, here as everywhere else, despite all the attempts by western European clerical activists after 1100 to separate them out. In Montaillou, villagers were not just interested in Catharism because they opposed tithe, but also interested in Catholicism because the local priest and village leader, who was himself a Cathar, abused his powers. We know this inextricability, but we too easily forget it. This article encourages us, forces us, to do our best not to forget it.

---

8 Lauwers, 'Pour une histoire de la dîme', pp. 56–61.

Bibliography

Butaud, Germain, 'Définition, prélèvement et gestion de la dîme en Provence orientale à la fin du Moyen Âge', in *La dîme, l'Église et la société féodale*, ed. by Michael Lauwers (Turnhout: Brepols, 2012), pp. 473–506

Collavini, Simone M., 'La dîme dans le système de prélèvement seigneurial en Italie: réflexions à partir du cas toscan', in *La dîme, l'Église et la société féodale*, ed. by Michael Lauwers (Turnhout: Brepols, 2012), pp. 281–308

Díaz de Durana, José Ramón, and Enric Guinot, 'La dîme dans l'Espagne médiévale', in *La dîme dans l'Europe médiévale et moderne: actes des XXXes Journées Internationales d'Histoire de l'Abbaye de Flaran, 3 et 4 octobre 2008*, ed. by Roland Viader (Toulouse: Presses universitaires du Mirail, 2010), pp. 63–88

Lauwers, Michael, 'Pour une histoire de la dîme et du dominium ecclésial', in *La dîme, l'Église et la société féodale*, ed. by Michael Lauwers (Turnhout: Brepols, 2012), pp. 11–64

Lauwers, Michael, ed., *La dîme, l'Église et la société féodale* (Turnhout: Brepols, 2012)

Le Roy Ladurie, Emmanuel, *Montaillou, village occitan, de 1294 à 1324* (Paris: Gallimard, 1975)

Mallorquí, Elvis, *Parròquia i societat rural al bisbat de Girona, segles XIII–XIV* (Barcelona: Pagès editors, 2011)

Menant, François, *Campagnes lombardes au moyen âge. L'économie et la société rurales dans la région de Bergame, de Crémone et de Brescia du Xe au XIIIe* (Rome: Ecoles françaises d'Athènes et de Rome, 1993)

Menant, François, 'Dîme et féodalité en Lombardie, XIe–XIIIe siècles', in *La dîme dans l'Europe médiévale et moderne: actes des XXXes Journées Internationales d'Histoire de l'Abbaye de Flaran, 3 et 4 octobre 2008*, ed. by Roland Viader (Toulouse: Presses Universitaires du Midi, 2010), pp. 101–26

Nanni, Luigi, *La parrocchia studiata nei documenti lucchesi dei secoli VIII–XIII* (Rome: Universitatis Gregorianae, 1948)

Provero, Luigi, 'Les dîmes dans la territorialité incertaine des campagnes du XIIIe siècle', in *La dîme, l'Église et la société féodale*, ed. by Michael Lauwers (Turnhout: Brepols, 2012), pp. 309–34

Viader, Roland, ed., *La dîme dans l'Europe médiévale et moderne: actes des XXXes Journées Internationales d'Histoire de l'Abbaye de Flaran, 3 et 4 octobre 2008* (Toulouse: Presses universitaires du Mirail, 2010)

Violante, Cinzio, 'Pievi e parrocchie nell'Italia centrosettentrionale durante i secoli XI e XII', in *Le istituzioni ecclesiastiche della 'societas christiana' dei secoli XI–XII — Diocesi, pievi e parrocchie. Atti della sesta Settimana internazionale di studio: Milano, 1–7 settembre 1974* (Roma: Vita e pensiero, 1977), pp. 643–799

Wickham, Chris, *Community and Clientele in Twelfth-Century Tuscany: The Origins of the Rural Commune in the Plain of Lucca* (Oxford: Oxford University Press, 1998)

Wickham, Chris, *Courts and Conflict in Twelfth-Century Tuscany* (Oxford: Oxford University Press, 2003)

Wood, Susan, *The Proprietary Church in the Medieval West* (Oxford: Oxford University Press, 2006)

ISABEL ALFONSO

Rural Churches in the North of Castile

*A Religious Dimension to Peasant Struggles
during the Middle Ages**

Struggles against Tithing: Anti-Seigneurial Struggles?

In the middle of the thirteenth century, Alfonso X addressed the local councils of the towns and villages of the diocese of Zamora to remind them of their obligation to pay the tithes of all fruits to the Church *derechamente* ('rightfully'), that is, to deliver them in full view of the public, rather than secretly at night, as he knew people were doing.[1] To avoid this, he gave precise orders that in each of these places the church bells were to be rung three times at the time of tithing. The collectors, who were called *terceros* in reference to the thirds of tithes, would thus be summoned so that they could come to control the division and collection of the fruits of labour on the threshing floor without being threatened or harmed in their endeavour. In this way, the Wise King expressly denounced the apparently customary practices of the peasantry, namely, measuring the harvested crops in secret in order to reduce the tithe portion to be exacted, and threatening and exerting violence against those in charge of collecting it.

Support for the monarch's penal measures was essential to ensure that 'these things against the faith' would not occur and the obligations to the church were effectively met. In another charter, the king not only delineated the extent of fraudulent actions such as those described, but also stated that the excommunication sentences issued by bishops and prelates were scorned. In order to avoid paying the tithe, people remained excommunicated, and many died in that state. The king therefore lamented that, along with the souls, the holy church was also losing its rights.[2] In order to

---

* Original publication: Alfonso, Isabel, 'Iglesias rurales en el norte de Castilla: una dimensión religiosa de las luchas campesinas en la Edad Media', in *Sombras del Progreso. Las huellas de la historia agraria. Estudios en homenaje a Ramón Garrabou*, ed. by Ricardo Robledo (Barcelona: Crítica, 2010), pp. 27–65. Translated by Julian Thomas. An initial version of this paper was presented at the Medieval Peasants Revisited conference, held at The Huntington Library, Los Angeles, on May 16–17, 2008. I wish to thank Piotr S. Górecki for his invitation to be part of the organising committee, along with John Langdon. I am also grateful to the participants for their suggestions and, in particular, to Julio Escalona, who read and discussed the written text. This research is part of a Project included in the National R&D Plan, ref. BHA2002–03076.

1 This information is contained in two royal letters from 1255, one sent from Valladolid, dated 28 July, and another sent from Burgos dated 23 October. The former was addressed to the council of Toro and its villages and the other 'to all the local councils of the towns and villages of the diocese of Zamora'. They have been published as CatZamora150 and CatZamora153.

2 This was a complaint also brought before Alfonso X by the prior of Santa María de Valladolid in 1277

avoid the weakening of justice that this would lead to, and with the explicit objective of bringing temporal and spiritual power together (since everything comes from God), whenever necessary Alfonso X sent his *merinos* to punish those who failed to fulfil their tithing obligations. Royal orders such as the one mentioned above, which reproduced almost verbatim Title XX of the *Primera Partida*, where the tithe was justified and regulated, seem to have been addressed to all the dioceses of the kingdom in an attempt to stop the conflicts generated by the collection, and ensure that the royal portion of the tax would be levied.[3]

Can these fraudulent practices regarding tithing obligations and the disdain for remaining excommunicated be understood as forms of peasant struggle, as indicated in the title of this paper? Were there forms of peasant opposition that were recognised as purely religious, and not accompanied by some kind of doctrinal heterodoxy? Given the close relationship between these two aspects, there may be some doubt as to whether the spiritual impact attributed to these acts was related to peasants remaining excommunicated or to not paying tithes. The truth is that in the canon law already in force, those who insisted on remaining excommunicated for one year were regarded as suspected heretics; but it was also a sin not to pay tithes (as the editor of the letter to the *merinos* of Valladolid indicates).[4] The extensive preamble that preceded Alfonso X's orders in that letter also emphasised the spiritual character of the tithing obligations. It contained some of the essential points of the legitimating discourse that was intended to be assumed to ensure that everyone fulfilled their tithing duties. It is also clear that the peasants in towns and villages were the intended audience for the rhetoric that lay and ecclesiastical leaders used to justify and legitimise their demands and deductions.[5]

Attributing a spiritual character to tithe fraud, as intended by official rhetoric, may seem debatable, especially when taking into account that the forms of concealment described in the royal text were not very different from those generally used by peasants in their daily resistance to the payment of the various demands to which they were subjected by their lords, as historians have rightly pointed out.[6] Hence the anti-lord interpretation of these actions has predominated. It is possible to look into other more poorly-understood aspects that highlight the important religious dimension of these peasant movements, as proposed here; or rather, into how religion and its institutional elements were intertwined with their lives. The struggle to oppose tithes, which persisted until they were abolished in the twentieth century, was on occasion less sporadic and seemingly less radical than individual fraud, but had a broader or different meaning. That is the case when collective action was used to appropriate local centres of worship, thus appealing to more formalised and accepted resources

---

because of the same type of non-compliance with the tithing obligations denounced by the bishop of Zamora. See CatValladolid70 (1277).

3 Partidas I.20; Nieto Soria, *Iglesia y poder real*.

4 See the comments to CatValladolid70 (1277).

5 Alfonso, 'La rhétorique de légitimation seigneuriale'. For an update on the vast, but scattered, bibliography on tithing, see the review in Díaz de Durana and Guinot, 'La dîme'.

6 Hilton, *Siervos liberados*; Pastor, *Resistencias y luchas campesinas*.

RURAL CHURCHES IN THE NORTH OF CASTILE　373

for their own benefit. This was performed by following more open, formalised and, paradoxically, less-known avenues than those indicated in the king's text. These avenues showed the extent of the active opposition to parish structures from within. My intention here is to emphasise the need to conduct a more profound study of the peasants' capacity to act collectively within accepted frameworks, with the purpose of limiting, counteracting, and also opposing the impositions of ecclesiastical rule; and, it could also be said, of using alternatives to official worship. The way in which the ecclesiastical authorities rejected the claims made by peasants reveals the most crudely material interests of the religious and ecclesiastical organisation that the authorities wanted to impose on them. One of the most outstanding contributions made by Ramón Garrabou to the studies of agrarian history has been precisely recognising and emphasising the capacity for action that rural populations had as social agents. These pages are intended to be a modest tribute to his work.

It is well known and widely accepted that churches, with their changing roles, were key institutional resources for the wealth of both lay and ecclesiastical aristocracies at different social levels. These resources were strategically used by their members to negotiate power relations among themselves and were exploited for purposes of economic and social control.[7] The community struggles discussed below are intended to show how peasants used the ecclesiastical resources that they themselves ultimately produced in their own favour. In order to develop my arguments, I will focus on a series of cases from the documentary sources of the monastery of San Salvador de Oña in the province and diocese of Burgos, in which these collective struggles to appropriate and/or control the revenues from local churches are better recorded than in any others. In the second section, I will compare them with similar disputes recorded in other areas of the Iberian Peninsula. I will conclude by addressing the religious aspects of these actions. While at first glance they seem to be related to the nature of the disputed property itself (as a centre of worship and its associated rights and property), they were also related to the pious conceptions and practices of parishioners, and fed and formed the basis for key elements of their political culture.

Priests and Neighbours against the *tithe*

San Salvador de Oña was a Benedictine monastery founded at the beginning of the eleventh century by Count Sancho García of Castile to the north of Burgos, to whose diocese it belongs. It became one of the most powerful Castilian monasteries, with a vast, very fragmented and dispersed patrimony. This extended from the areas south of Burgos to the Cantabrian Sea, and included a multitude of settlements that were partially or entirely under its jurisdiction, as well as numerous churches and small

---

7　Alfonso, 'Litigios por la tierra', pp. 928–36 [Editors' note: For an English translation, see chapter 13 of this volume]. On the process of the formation and development of the great ecclesiastical property, I refer to the pages of Álvarez Borge, *Poder y relaciones sociales*, pp. 109–25; 173–238, which serve to contextualise my analysis and provide the relevant references.

monasteries. These were features that it shared with other medieval monasteries in the Iberian Peninsula and beyond.[8]

A significant number of dispute records dating from the middle of the twelfth and throughout the thirteenth centuries show small communities of clerics and lay people, mostly organised in local councils that, even though they were under the jurisdiction of the monastery of Oña, had gained control over the local church.[9] Sometimes this was the only church in the village, which they claimed to have removed from the abbey's control. In other cases, they chose a chapel as their local centre of worship and abandoned the parish church under the control of the abbey, whose rights and roles were thus diminished as it was left without its congregation or parishioners. The preserved documents show that peasants were very active participants in the negotiation of what they had to give and how it was distributed; of the part that they could retain; and of the arguments that legitimised these renders and their distribution. The local councils, with their clerics, claimed to be the managers and beneficiaries of everything concerning the local church, recognising, seemingly without problems, episcopal authority and the share of the income obtained. Their actions were closely entwined with the same arguments: the affirmation that the church had a common or collective character (*difuso*) from ancient times, (which implied that they received the ecclesiastical revenues in full), and the rights arising from the fact that the clerics were children of local inhabitants. The practical ways in which they formulated these arguments varied, as was their emphasis, but the terms or categories that were managed and opposed, although not always radically, were common: chapel as opposed to a parish church; private church as opposed to community church. Ecclesiastical rights and obligations differed, or were claimed to differ, according to such definitions. Most of the arguments made by the opposing parties revolved around these concepts. Their struggle was thus also made up of words, that is, it was discursive and conceptual in nature.[10]

These cases are well known because of the conflicts that surrounded them, and because they gave rise to litigation. Some disputes were of great duration and complexity, though the documentation that exists about them is scarce, and is also very diverse and fragmented. However, these records alone indicate the importance given to these issues, the complexity they entailed, and the mobilisation they generated within the differentiated fabric of local societies. In these the social and religious, economic, spiritual, family and communal affairs were deeply interwoven, as were the people who lived and worked in these communities, despite their differing statuses. I will now examine some of these cases.

---

8 Luciano Serrano had already noted that Oña was the most important institution in the diocese of Burgos, from the perspective of both lords and ecclesiastical authorities. Its patrimony surpassed that of the bishopric and cathedral canonry and 'the number of churches owned by it could be equated to a true diocese' (Serrano, *El obispado de Burgos*, pp. 264–73). For recent studies on the formation of the monastic domain of Oña see: Bonaudo, 'El monasterio de San Salvador de Oña'; Olmedo Bernal, *Una abadía castellana*; Ruiz Gómez, 'Las formas de poblamiento'.

9 The monastery's documentation was edited in SSOña-A, an edition subsequently completed in SSOña-O.

10 Alfonso, 'La rhétorique de légitimation seigneuriale'.

In 1293 the abbot of Oña filed a complaint before the bishop of Burgos in which he accused the inhabitants of two small communities of having left the churches of Santa María and San Nicolás.[11] According to the abbot, they had been his parishioners for more than forty years, but now attended the divine offices in the chapel of Santa Cecilia, where mass had been celebrated in the manner of a community church. The abbot asked the bishop to rectify this situation, as it was contrary to the rights inherent to the abovenamed parish churches, which belonged to his monastery. The litigation, as recorded in the proceedings, took place in various sessions during the months of July and August of that year, including allegations and replies from the representatives of each party. The final judgment was issued by an ecclesiastical judge, who was a canon of Burgos cathedral. He declared that the abandoned churches were parish churches. For that reason, the inhabitants of those communities were obliged to pay them tithes, first-fruits and oblations, and to receive the sacraments in them, that is to say, to behave as parishioners of the churches, as requested by the monks of Oña.

This situation clearly showed peasant opposition to the institutional parish church and the terms of its community space, in which context they chose another centre of worship to celebrate religious services. The inhabitants of these two Castilian villages, the councils of Berrueza and Quintanilla, both 'clérigos e legos' ('clerics and laypeople'), as they were specifically described, had come together against the power of Oña. They swore a covenant that took some time to be acknowledged before the judicial authority. It was a promise not to attend masses or make payments to parish churches. They made the decision and vowed to fulfil it by closing themselves off and establishing a chapel in between the two communities. They not only conspired to act in this way, but also defended their rights judicially through their representatives appointed to that effect. In the face of Oña's accusations that the church-chapel of Santa Cecilia, where they celebrated mass in the manner of a community church, 'was a chapel without a font, without parishioners and without sacraments',[12] they claimed that it had parishioners, tithes and appurtenances, and therefore that it met all the canonical requirements to function as a parish. The language of the text shows how the different categories that defined and distinguished the various centres of worship and the nuclei of ecclesiastical organisation had different meanings in social processes that were not without tension. These peasants, and their clergy, had decided that the chosen chapel fulfilled sufficient requirements to be considered a parish church. These groups remained within recognised criteria, but were able to add new, alternative content to those criteria.

The representatives of these communities in the trial against Oña were two clerics from each. This may induce us to concentrate our attention on the increasingly well-known peasant élites that led these community movements. However, it should not be overemphasized; as even though that was the case, it may also conceal the family relations that tied them to their communities, as well as their converging interests, expressed in the fact that they decided to regard the chapel as a community church.

---

11 SSOña-O389 (1293); SSOña-O390 (1293); SSOña-O392 (1293).
12 'era una ermita sin pila, sin parroquianos y sin sacramentos'.

One of the most interesting aspects of this lawsuit, and of many other similar ones, is precisely the overlap between laypeople and clergy. It was the community, through its clerics, that controlled the local church and the revenues collected on its behalf, and used these revenues to oppose, or at least limit, the interference of and demands from other external religious institutions.

A good illustration of this situation can be seen in the disputes occurred in the first quarter of the thirteenth century in Montenegro and in Sotoavellanos, two villages of Oña's monastic domain in the area of Herrera de Pisuerga.[13] Unlike the settlement that had resulted from the litigation discussed above, these disputes were resolved by means of amicable settlements reached in the Bishop's palaces, in Burgos and in Quintanadueñas respectively, with only a few months' difference. The records of these agreements are very different from the trial documents from the previous litigation. While both take the form of a chirograph, whereby each party retained a part, three instruments were made in Sotoavellanos. One of them was kept in the sacrarium of the cathedral of Burgos, which indicates the mediating involvement of the bishop, whether sought or imposed.

In both cases, the 'laicos et clericos' ('laypeople and clerics') in Montenegro and the 'clericos et concilio' ('clerics and local council') in Sotoavellanos, defended the community-based character of the local churches, claiming that 'they were communal since ancient times',[14] and reached a 'compositio amicabilis' ('amicable agreement') with the monks on the economic distribution of the profits. They argued that 'they had been in the possession of many sons of local members of the community, who had administered them for a long time and had received full ecclesiastical rights in them'.[15] Among other things, the distribution shows the interest of Oña in not losing the offerings from the festivity of the patron saint, which were more abundant than the standard ones. The abbot renounced the latter in order to claim half of those offered during the patron saint's festivities. This happened in Montenegro, whose church and patron saint's festivity was dedicated to St John the Baptist. It seemed that the clerics obtained a more favourable distribution than the traditional one in three parts, since they agreed that the tithes and first-fruits were to be divided into halves, without the usual third of the tithe going to the bishop. Nothing was discussed about the roles or appointment of the clergy, or about whether the church, which was the only one in the village, would remain in the hands of the locals.

In Sotoavellanos the conflict appears to have been longer. It was said that the hearing before the ordinary judges of the bishop had lasted a long time. The 1225 agreement seems to have been reached during the conduct of an inquest, and was presented as an amicable agreement (less direct than the previous one) reached through the representatives of the parties, one acting for the monastery (the abbot), and two acting for the clerics and the local council, of which one was member of the clergy and the other a layman. The dispute was not, as in Montenegro, about the

---

13 SSOña-A438 (1225); and SSOña-A439 (1225).

14 'illam fuisse diffusam ab antiquo'.

15 'in ista quasi possessione fuerant multi filii vicinorum qui in ipsa ecclesia longo tempore ministrauerant, et omnes prouentus ecclesie ex integro perceperant'.

only local church in the locality, but about one of them, that of San Pantaleón. The council's spokesmen stated that, given its community status as *difusa*, it belonged to them entirely, while Oña only recognised it as 'capilla propia' ('proprietary chapel') belonging to its church of Santa María.[16] Formally, this conflict resembles the one related to the councils of Quintanilla and Berrueza. As in those places, the church-chapel was relegated to being a centre of worship but without any entitlement to offerings. In Sotoavellanos, as in Montenegro, the distribution of the tithes also favoured the community, though to a lesser extent here, since it was only after discounting the third of the tithe for the bishop that the tithes and first-fruits would be divided into three parts. Of them only one would go to Oña, while the other two would go for the local council and the clerics. The monks from Oña had to explicitly accept that from then on, according to the custom of the land, the priests would be chosen by the local council from among the children of the locality, although they were obliged to celebrate the divine office daily in the monastic church of Santa María and to carry out the burials in their cemetery, if they chose to inter themselves there.

The choice of the priest from among the children of the local inhabitants was invoked as customary for the area. It was one of the basic formulations they used to claim a common or collective character for their churches. The objective and instrument of many of these struggles used by the community was not only to maintain the control of the centres of worship and cemeteries through their children, but, what seemed to be so much more important, the collection and enjoyment of tithes and other ecclesiastical revenues. Numerous examples have been identified which indicate the frequency and the different contexts in which these practices took place.

It is worth noting that one of the charters where these questions appear most clearly is in the *fuero* that the abbot of Oña granted in 1190 to all his vassals who lived in the town of Oña, both clerics and lay people. The numerous aspects regulated here included some particularly interesting ones, which established that the only chapel of the place was that of San Juan and San Martín; that this church would be common to all clerics and laymen who at that time owned houses and properties in Oña;[17] that half of all the tithes, first-fruits and oblations of both the living and the dead of the town would go to them; that the children of any local inhabitants who had lived in the town for fifteen years and abided by the *fuero* and were worthy of receiving

---

16 The ecclesiastical structure of Sotoavellanos seems more complicated than that of Montenegro, as there are data that show that initially the church of Santa María had been a monastery that was integrated into Oña, together with the town, as a result of a donation by Alfonso VIII (SSOña-A291, 1191). But in Sotoavellanos there was also the district of San Pantaleón, which in this process Oña also tried to submit to its jurisdiction (SSOña-A399, 1201).

17 'We grant you another *fuero*, so that neither in Santa Cruz, where there used to be one, nor in all Oña, there shall be any chapel other than chapel of San Juan and San Martín. And this chapel of San Juan and San Martín shall always be *difusa* for all the clergymen and laymen that now have houses and properties in Oña' ('Damus vobis aliud forum, ut nec in Sancta Cruce ubi solebat esse neque in tota Honia sit alia capella nisi capella Sancti Iohannis et Sancti Martini, et illa capella Sancti Iohannis et Sancti Martini sit semper diffusa omnibus tam clericis quam laicis, qui nunc habent domos et hereditates in Honia') (FB39, 1190, § 16). I think translating the term *difusa* as 'open', as Ruiz did, is contrary to a reading such as the one proposed here. Cf. Ruiz Gómez, 'Las formas de poblamiento', p. 749.

sacred orders, could be the heirs of that chapel; that the town should also receive half of the tithes of the land that other town-dwellers had in Oña, and also from half of all the land that they cultivated anywhere else.[18] This provision solved one of the most disputed aspects in terms of the territorial definition of the parishes, since the territories of neither settlements nor parishes included all the possessions of the domestic or family units, who frequently owned lands in other settlements or parishes. We do not know the tensions and struggles that happened, as in other places, in order to obtain that *fuero*, whose negotiated nature was nonetheless expressly recognised in the text.[19] What is certain is the sense of achievement of the peasants involved in these claims and clauses, who in this case obtained very favourable provisions.

It is true that clerics sometimes seemed to have acted as if they were more separated from their communities than in the cases just described. Such was the case of the priests from Matarrepudio and Villasana. These priests were faced with a claim brought by the abbot of Oña, which alleged that they wanted to celebrate mass in a parish church other than the monastic one, and that the monastery was harmed by the diversion of the revenues due. They were urged to acknowledge their guilt and stop doing so. In both cases the letter of resolution took the form of a personal renunciation; in Matarrepudio, the cleric, called Domingo *abad*, son of Don Juan de Matarrepudio, declared, echoing Oña's accusation, that the church of San Sebastián was a chapel, and that he wanted to celebrate mass there as in a parish church, to the detriment of the monastery's one: 'in this chapel I celebrated mass as if it was a parish church, to the detriment of your church, that of Santa María [...] which is our parish church'.[20] Aware as he was of the great wrong and damage this had caused to the monastery of Oña and of the great sin committed by his soul, he allowed himself to be counselled by good men, and to atone for his sin he acknowledged that when he celebrated in the chapel he did so 'maliciously and unduly',[21] as he had no right to do it. He also admitted that the church of Santa María of the same place belonged to the monastery with all its rights, and that all the things that Christians owe to the church where they are parishioners, including paying tithes and first-fruits and receiving the sacraments, were to be carried out there. He finally admitted that he had no right to either of the two churches and promised that he would never again celebrate mass in the chapel as a parish priest. The letter established sanctions if he failed to fulfil this promise, of which his own father was guarantor. The result was the same at Villasana: here, the clergyman, Don García, faced by a similar claim from Oña, had to recognise that he had attempted to do the same as the priest of Matarrepudio, celebrating mass in the village's church, San Cebrián, which is not referred to as a chapel, to the detriment of the monastery's, San Julián, which was the parish church. Oña was to have all the rights detailed in the previous letter regarding tithes and first-fruits.[22]

---

18 FB39 (1190), §18, §17 and §20, respectively.
19 With regards to the conflict-solving nature of most of the known *fueros*, see Alfonso, 'Campesinado y derecho'.
20 'la qual hermita yo cantava e quería cantar por parochial, en preiuyzio de la nuestra eglesia que dizen Sancta Maria [...] que es nuestra parrochial'.
21 'maliciosamente, como non deuía'.
22 SSOña-O350 (1291); SSOña-O378 (1292); SSOña-A563 (1263).

The arguments given by other clergymen in similar situations provide information on how widespread these practices were, and the broad range of situations in which they occurred. The priest of the church of Hornillalatorre, also in the domain of Oña, acknowledged that during the same years he also had maliciously wanted to celebrate mass there. The text, which seems to have copied the wording of the renunciations of the two previous cases but was written in Romance instead of in Latin, explicitly included the reasons adduced by the priest to justify his actions, which in his confession he had to assume as being erroneous. He had incorrectly claimed to be a son and grandson of a local inhabitant without in fact being so, and agreed that he had asked for the tithes 'sinfully and unduly'.[23]

These cases show that responsibility was attributed to, and accepted by, a priest individually. The laity in these communities only appeared as witnesses, and also as 'good men' who mediated the resolution. However, it is difficult to imagine that the clergy could act as they claimed to have done without the complicity of their neighbours. They were the actors who had to support that decision, and even agree to it, as seen in the cases discussed above. In general, to argue, as I do, that this link existed between priests and laymen in these rural communities may be regarded as a simple — albeit well-founded — hypothesis, which can only occasionally be confirmed through documentary evidence. This is true of Matarrepudio, where a separate document, parallel to and contemporary of the cleric's concession, clearly illustrates this link, as it records the promise made by the local council to pay its tithes and first fruits to Santa María, the church owned by Oña. The expression 'volver a pagar' ('to pay again') is, in my opinion, an implicit but clear recognition that at some point, together with the actions of their clerics, the people of that locality had stopped fulfilling their tithe obligations, thus making evident the local council-based organisation that must previously have supported such a movement.[24] Undoubtedly, the local council was not excluded from the *pro bono pacis* pact established by Oña directly with the clerics of the church of San Juan de Villanueva de Alfania, since the text explicitly settled and recognised that they would receive part of the income from the tithes, oblations and alms for the needs of the church.[25]

The Troublesome Distribution of Revenues

As expressed by the monks and according to the evidence, these practices had an immediate economic result that they did not try to disguise with any of the usual rhetoric. Despite presenting them as a 'fecho spiritual' ('spiritual deed') and warning that engaging in such acts could be dangerous for the soul, what they complained about was the loss of the tithes, first-fruits, oblations and other payments from the

---

23 'con pecado y como no debía' (SSOña-O416, 1294). Other charters preserve further information on the church of Santa Marina de Hornilla and the circumstances experienced there.
24 SSOña-O359 (1291).
25 SSOña-A442 (1227).

parishioners who were required to provide them.[26] But what were the implications for the peasantry of avoiding those payments? Was it simply a matter of diverting them to a different centre and other priests, or could they somehow retain them? Was it a question of piety, related to the zeal for greater control of the management of the centres of worship, or was it a question of circumventing a wider monastic domination? All these different aspects may have been more closely intertwined in their own minds, interests and emotions, than historians usually accept. The information available about who the recipients of the tithes, and other duties not paid by communities, were is very indirect. It seems likely that at least in part it went to clerics, as well as to refurbishment funds and to cover the needs of the church, as is often documented. But it is equally possible that it might have in part returned to the community itself,[27] or simply that the amount paid by the community would be decreased, resulting in a reduction of the proportion that each family individually owed, as was intended to be the case with other taxes paid to the king or to lords. In the town of Oña itself, it is very clear that half of the tithes went to the community and the other half went to the chapel. In Montenegro there also seems no doubt that the clergymen and laity received the full revenues from their church. What is clear is that a local council could save (or divert or reserve) a large amount if it decided to abandon the established church and choose a chapel as their parish church, thus ceasing to pay tithes, first-fruits and oblations, or taking them for themselves (as we have seen in one of the previous cases). This can be concluded from the assessment made in the rulings from those disputes where the claimants estimated their losses and the rebellious local council was ordered to cover the amount in full.

An example of this process is the one documented for the monastery of San Martín de Torme, which was in the diocese of Burgos but outside the scope of Oña's power. The monastery argued that the local council should return 3000 *maravedis*, which was the value of the tithes and first-fruits, along with the offerings, for the two years when they had not paid them. Similar estimates have been found in many other cases. These need not be detailed here, as the constant discussions about the multiple fractions into which tithes could be divided and the permanent tensions that their distribution entailed in practice, clearly indicate that there was a clear economic valuation of them, and a very subtle accounting of their repercussions, both when the usual recipients lost their income and when it was deducted from the peasants' production.[28] The diversity in the local practice of tithe distribution, and

---

26 In fact, this is a recurrent theme in the disputes between monastic institutions and bishoprics, or of the different dioceses among themselves, where problems of territorial demarcation of the parishes appeared more clearly. See Díaz de Durana and Guinot, 'La dîme'.

27 The explicit participation of the community was also documented in the *fuero* of Covarrubias, Mecerreyes and Barbadillo del Pez. See FB21 (1148).

28 Díaz de Durana recalled a petition submitted to the Cortes de Madrigal in 1438, according to which the deduction accounted for between 50 per cent and 70 per cent of peasant production; of the rest (between 50 per cent and 30 per cent) the seeds for the following year would also have to be subtracted. Certainly, one must agree with him that 'the analysis of the real beneficiaries of tithe collection is one of the most important issues to study in the near future' (Díaz de Durana and Guinot, 'La dîme').

the multiple collective and individual actors that competed for a portion of it, are the best indicators of its importance in the economies of all those involved. It seems to me that it is necessary to begin to use a notion of tithing that does not identify it only as income, but which is capable equally of containing its intrinsic and original meaning of a levy on production, in any of the aspects that it came to cover.[29]

The documentary material from Oña also contains other information that not only reveals more about the inter-dependence between the rural clergy and their local communities, but also about the organisational capacity that these communities had developed in aspects that were as much civil as religious, economic and social.[30] In the mid-twelfth century, the clergymen and laymen from nearly twenty settlements who lived under the monastery's control made a curious donation to the monastery — 'we, all the clergymen and laymen that inhabit these settlements under the domain of Oña'.[31] This took place exactly a year after the bishop of Burgos and the abbot of Oña had come to an agreement that the monks should be given all one third of the tithes and the 'ius parrochiale' ('parish right') that canonically belonged to all of the churches that the monastery possessed at that time, as well as to others that the cathedral had received.[32] In each of these localities an agreement had been reached to allow for a 'vecino excusado' ('exempted neighbour') who would support the monastery in refurbishing and building their respective churches under the following covenant for the salvation of their souls: that the *excusados* would be exempt from any *pecho* ('common tax') of the local council and the palace's land, that is to say, of the work they were required to perform for the lords. The neighbours thus exempt would then be obliged to deliver to the Abbot of Oña the complete tithe of all the fruits every year, without any reductions, for the repair of altars and buildings. They would not, however, be excluded from the collective property, but would share common water, pastures, meadows, hillsides and parishes with the rest of the community. They would not be excluded from any matters of common interest, except for the payment to the abbot of Oña. It was, therefore, a negotiation about the total amount of the tithes, which by this act was limited to being paid by only one of the parishioners. But the negotiation also affected the dues payable to the lord, imposed on the transfer of their holdings when they died (called *mañería* in this area and *luctuosa* in others), which they managed to reduce to a small amount

---

29 This diversity that the distribution of tithes adopted in practice is generally indicated in nearly all the studies on the subject. It has not been used to emphasise so much the latent conflict and constant negotiation that it indicated, but how it was far removed from the applicable regulations.

30 The articulation of the communities around the church is a classic theme in both the studies on the institutionalisation of the communes and the establishment of the parish network. These aspects have been substantially revised in recent years: not to question the importance of the church, but rather with the intention of highlighting the complexity and diversity of the processes that underlie its configuration. Cf. Reynolds, *Kingdoms and Communities*, Wickham, 'Gossip and Resistance'; Álvarez Borge, ed., *Comunidades locales y poderes feudales*.

31 'nos omnes clerici et laici qui sub domini de Oña sumus populati in istis uillis' (SSOña-A212, 1152). The text only names the settlements that had thitherto paid tithe to the bishop of Burgos, but not those belonging to Oña.

32 SSOña-A213 (1153).

(five *solidi*).[33] It was a commitment that all the population of these settlements, clergy and laity alike, vowed to fulfil, under threat of a penalty payable to the king. The importance of this collective action, bringing together the rural population of such a large number of villages, is undeniable, as the subsequent conflicts over the interpretation of these agreements clearly show; they were external conflicts with Oña, but also had an internal impact on the communities, when they came to decide who would be the *excusado* from payment in each of them, and who would receive the amount of their tithes.

In 1218, for example, it was specified that the clerics and laity from some of these villages (those from which Oña received tithes as a result of their agreements with the bishop of Burgos mentioned above) would choose not one but two *excusados*, following this procedure: the richest settler of each village would deliver all the tithes to the parish church with the rest of the inhabitants, and the next one below in wealth would dutifully pay tithes to the monastery of Oña: 'in those villages, the *colonus* whose goods are the wealthiest and most abundant [...] moreover, the *colonus* who lives in those villages that is second in wealth after him'.[34] In the wording of this agreement the key factor they negotiated for their clerics was seemingly the reduction of the tax burden on their inherited estates and the exemption from performing compulsory work. Therefore, the *excusado* paying the tithe appears as a concession of the local council; this is the reason why pact and commitment wording appears together with the language of donation, which both clerics and laymen were explicitly committed to fulfil.

It should be noted that these were peasant communities whose population, including clerics, not only lived under the lordship of their abbots, but also worked the monastic lands. They were the monastery's dependents, repeatedly called *collazos* or *vasallos solariegos* in the sources.[35] It is true that in this period clerics were gradually released from the duties to perform the tasks that continued to be a heavy burden on their neighbours, but it is also true that they jointly obtained favourable responses to some of the demands mentioned earlier, which were sometimes recorded in the local *fueros*. Barely a month after the pact of 1218 took place, Cereceda received a *fuero* that reproduced this negotiation, because in exchange for the same concessions, all dwellers agreed to give Oña the two *excusados* on similar terms: that the wealthiest member of the community should pay tithes to the local church and the second wealthiest should pay tithes to the convent.[36] It is likely that the other towns involved in the

---

33 The *mañería* seems to have become a tax imposed on the inherited estates of all the dependent population in general and not only, as originally, of those that died without children, called *mañeros*.

34 'ille colonus qui magis locuplex in illis villis atque copiosus [...] alius siquidem colonus qui secundus in diuittis post illum in illis villis commorauerit' (SSOña-A417, 1218). These solutions seem to have been more widespread, as can be seen from Díaz de Durana's claim that sometimes, in the cases he studied, the struggles over the share of the tithes resulted in the distribution of the village's tithed houses that would pay tribute to the clerics or the lord in the future (Díaz de Durana, 'Patronatos', p. 495).

35 In 1190, the Abbott of Oña granted the *fuero* to 'all the men of the local council of Oña, both clergymen and laymen' ('vobis omnibus collaciis Honie tam clericis quam laicis') (FB39, 1190).

36 SSOñaÁlamo418 (1218).

RURAL CHURCHES IN THE NORTH OF CASTILE   383

agreement may have also obtained a specific *fuero* that has not been preserved, but what clearly should be noted is the internal differentiation within these communities, explicitly assumed in these cases, when recognising that some parishioners were richer than others.[37] It is equally important to ascertain how the laity supported or helped the exemptions for their clergy, among other things because they were more or less directly considered to be, and possibly were, their potential beneficiaries.

The Chapel as a Place of Dissent

To complete the review of the documents from Burgos, a brief commentary will be provided on a legal dispute which provides information, on the one hand, on how there was a widespread knowledge of the implications for a church to be accepted as *difusa*, and, on the other, on the dynamics of these struggles. This was a long process focused on a coastal area of the Cantabrian Sea, very close to Santander and quite far from the monastic centre, with small and dispersed population centres. The relatively well-documented dispute appears to have begun with the complaint of the Abbot de Oña before the bishop of Burgos against several clergymen from Liencres, whom he accused of having forcefully appropriated the church of Santa Olalla de Liencres and the tithes and first fruits paid by the parishioners.[38] The abbot argued in his defence that this particular church had always belonged to the monastery of Oña, which had control over because it had been donated by King Sancho; that it used to lease it; and that it was the tenants who were in charge of appointing a chaplain for it and paying his wages.[39] The clerics who had taken it a few years earlier claimed for their part that it was a community church, that is to say, it belonged, and had always belonged, to clerics who were children of the town dwellers with inheritance rights, and therefore that the income belonged to them, which was to be distributed equally.

Testimonies survive from seventy-six witnesses from both parties (with very different places of origin and statuses) who, for slightly more than two months, from November 1323 to January 1324, were summoned to testify before the judges in connection with this case. The inquest involved a large number of people from the local community, and their answers, transcribed by the notary public of Santander,

---

37 In fact, both the amount and economic capacity of the parishioners was a constant concern for the recipients of tithes. This is illustrated by the complaints of many ecclesiastical institutions because their parishioners were the poorest. So did the Order of Calatrava in Bolaños in the face of the Cathedral of León in 1259. That is also the case of the 120 'immortal parishioners' from Aguilar de Campos (so named because when one died, he was replaced by another of 'equal value'). As a result of an agreement with the bishop of León, the local council granted those parishioners to the church of San Juan, a dependency of the monks of San Zoilo the Carrión which lacked parishioners because it was located outside the village: Martínez Sopena, *Tierra de Campos occidental*, pp. 302–03.

38 Records of the judgement, the inquiry, the sentence and its enforcement have been preserved: SSOña-O539 (1313); SSOña-O540 (1313–1319); SSOña-O601 (1323–1324); SSOña-O603 (1324); SSOña-O617 (1327); SSOña-O619 (1328); SSOña-O622 (1329).

39 Actually, the witnesses also referred to two lifetime leases that exist for this church, SSOña-A548 (1258); and SSOña-A559 (1262).

with a cleric also present, constituted a very extensive dossier. This is very rich material that deserves extensive commentary, because it provides unusual information on the social fabric in which the conflict occurred, and is not included in other official documents. I will only raise a number of issues that are relevant to the thematic thread developed here, as they help to understand the real importance of a dispute involving a single local church that lasted such a long time and was so socially wide-ranging. These questions lead one to ask about what was in fact being disputed; to rethink the value of these churches for each and every one of the groups involved; and to inquire into how this type of conflict was perceived by the witnesses, some of whom had an interest in the outcome, as explicitly stated in the inquiry.

The testimonies of the witnesses in this inquiry, which are by no means intended to be impartial and are certainly not homogeneous, show how the situation of the church had evolved during the lifetime of the witnesses, who had either direct memory of it or whose recollections had been handed down from others, and even ratified some of the points of the argumentation provided by the monastery abbot. Thus they claimed to have seen, or to have heard, that Oña had leased the church in exchange for a fixed rent; that they knew and had appointed the tenant, were aware that he designated the chaplains to celebrate masses and paid them a wage, and that when he died his son had received the church. But they also knew that for some time the tenant had ceded half the church and its income to another local family, made up of several brothers whom they also knew and named, in order to have the murder of one of them forgiven — 'para matar la enemistad' ('to appease the enmity' —; and that the murderer had had to leave (some of the witnesses even attested to having seen the pardon ritual that had taken place in the church of San Francisco, in Santander).[40] They likewise declared that they were aware that the clerics against whom Oña was engaged in the dispute had found 'letters indicating that it was a community church',[41] and how they had shown them to the bishop to have them recognised, for they claimed that at some point the church had community status, and that they had lost it due to 'mala verdad' ('bad truth'). Certainly, this interpretation, which underlies numerous statements, was intended to deny the violent appropriation which the monks were claiming. Their testimony showed that many of the witnesses were also aware that they would benefit if the local clerics prevailed in the litigation. If they came from Liencres, had got married there, or simply had their dependant in that location (as an external cleric stated), their children would be entitled to inherit the church if it was recognised as being a community church, and for this reason they openly attested that they were favourable to the clerics. However, in the information in this long inquest, there was some indication of the internal tensions that the leasing of the church entailed (in which the involvement of the accused clerics can be glimpsed), since fragmentary data suggest that before claiming it as a community church they had been its chaplains and had tried to negotiate with Oña that they should be the tenants.

---

40 On this type of violence and its resolutions, see Alfonso, '¿Muerte sin venganza?' [Editors' note: For an English translation, see chapter 8 of this volume].

41 'cartas de como era difusa'.

The information scattered across the statements of the witnesses shows the detailed knowledge they had of the different possibilities and ways of taking advantage of the institutional resource that the local worship centres were. Access to them was more differentiated than egalitarian, even when presented under the community banner. They knew that they could be tenants or *tenentes* ('holders') of these churches, or officiating clergy, or salaried chaplains; they could also be the collectors of the revenues for the varied recipients, or could have the churches sublet, and all this not always for the entire church.[42] This litigation provides two additional interesting details: on the one hand, the temporary nature of the mobilisation, which implies the choice of a political context understood as favourable, in order to raise their claims; and on the other hand, the updating of old arguments to justify that a church could have community status for the inhabitants of the locality and their children.

Further research is needed to identify the factors that made these struggles possible. Undoubtedly, one factor that must be analysed is the role played by the bishop of Burgos as both an authority and as an interested party. From the middle of the twelfth century and throughout the thirteenth century, a long and costly dispute between the bishop and the monastery of Oña for the control of the tithes of all its churches seems to have been a backdrop for these other partial and more localised struggles. The conflict, which amply exemplifies the complicated criteria that allowed and justified the tithes and their multiple fractions, had a great impact and it even reached Rome, as several bishops of other Spanish dioceses were commissioned by the pope to intervene. This again indicates that there was a strenuous and constant struggle for tithes.[43] Was it perhaps this context of monastic weakness that precipitated or made possible the invocation by the Oña-dependent rural clergy of the communal traditions referred to, in order to control their churches by arousing the support and involvement of their neighbours and parishioners, to achieve goals that were presented as beneficial to all? Undoubtedly, conflicts between large institutions and the extent and timeline in which they occurred are a variable that must be taken into account, in order to understand the smaller-scale movements analysed here. Disputes between cathedrals or between monasteries, or between a cathedral and a monastery to define their territories and resources on a diocesan scale, are (as is known) one of the general characteristics of these central centuries of the Middle Ages.[44]

---

42 It would be of interest to extend this study by looking at the leasing of those monastic houses (*casas*) that directly controlled the properties owned by monasteries in a locality, which usually included the church. In some cases, such leases were made after mobilisations such as those mentioned had taken place. The example of Sotoavellanos would illustrate the case of a local council that obtained the lease of the monastic house in the locality after having engaged in a dispute about the church (SSOña-A626, 1275).

43 On the conflicts between Oña and the Cathedral of Burgos, see Serrano, *El obispado de Burgos*, pp. 359–63. The documents on these litigations have been preserved in both the archive of Oña and the cathedral archive.

44 'The conflicts between Benedictine monasteries and bishops for parish rights, the collection of tithes and the service to the congregation are a constant in all of Roman Christianity since the twelfth century' (Reglero de la Fuente, *El monasterio de San Isidro de Dueñas*, p. 165). For specific aspects on this issue in Spain and the relevant literature, see Díaz de Durana and Guinot, 'La dîme'. Cf.,

But it is the local scale that is of interest here, and the question now is what happened in other contexts and other areas. Despite what has sometimes been held, the phenomena recorded were not unique to the diocese of Burgos, nor were they based on a particular custom that would have allowed priests and parishioners to seek greater control of local churches.[45] For the diocese of Leon it has been possible to use the data of a source as important as the so-called *Becerro de Presentaciones*, a survey from the second half of the thirteenth century that covers the situation of the centres of worship across more than a thousand villages, distributed in archdeaconries and thirty four deaneries. Fernández Flórez, who edited and studied this precious codex, was able to verify the high proportion of churches in which the local councils (to which they seem to have belonged, even if not always) presented their clerics (in 23 of the 289 churches of the archdeaconry of Valderas), as well as the important participation that many of them had in the distribution of the tithes.[46] Using the information from the *Becerro* for the ten deaneries of the western Tierra de Campos, Martínez Sopena also found that a large number of churches were owned by the local councils (out of 227 churches, they fully owned 29) and also that they played a prominent role in receiving the tithes.[47] The phenomenon of community churches and their consequent rights is also recorded in the documentary collections of cathedrals and large monasteries of other dioceses of the region, such as Zamora, Astorga or Palencia. Royal towns (Mayorga, Castroverde, Villafrechós, Aguilar de Campos, Villalpando, Villafáfila or Frómista) had several churches each and are the best known, since throughout the twelfth and thirteenth centuries, and thanks to royal support, their booming local councils absorbed church property which previously had been largely in secular hands.[48]

In the most western dioceses of the kingdom, therefore, not only the existence of important local councils has been documented, but also of small rural communities that owned their churches, elected their clerics and participated in the distribution of tithes. It is then worth investigating whether such a situation was the result of processes of collective action taken to defend the control of local churches of the same type as those discussed in connection with Oña; and whether a common

---

for comparative purposes, Wickham, *Legge, patriche e conflitti*, ch. 6, where he analyses the various patterns of ecclesiastical disputes in the Tuscan dioceses.

45 On the uniqueness of the Burgos case, see Alonso de Porres Fernández, *Las parroquias*. He argued that until the mid-nineteenth century, there had been a special regime of personal parishes in Burgos, despite repeated provisions to the contrary. Orlandis extended the idea of this situation to the dioceses of Calahorra and Pamplona (Orlandis Rovira, 'Los laicos y las iglesias rurales', pp. 289–90).

46 Fernández Flórez, 'El *Becerro de Presentaciones*', pp. 302–12.

47 Martínez Sopena interpreted this as the possible archaic remnants of the old communal property of the churches in some small places, though in the large royal towns he saw it as being a clear consequence of the great development experienced by the local councils of the area at the end of the twelfth century. Three of these towns — Castroverde, Villafrechos y Aguilar de Campos — together with their villages, had 17 churches (Martínez Sopena, *Tierra de Campos occidental*, pp. 279 and 289, Figure 6).

48 Martínez Sopena, *Tierra de Campos occidental*; Pérez Celada, *El monasterio de San Zoilo de Carrión*; Reglero de la Fuente, *El monasterio de San Isidro de Dueñas*; Reglero de la Fuente, 'Los obispos y sus sedes'.

identity was argued for, using a similar language and resorting to similar concepts. For comparative purposes, despite the undoubted interest of the conflicts that took place in the larger towns, attention will only be paid here to the information provided by studies on the smaller communities, because they bear a great resemblance to the cases studied.[49] As in the previous ones, these were local councils with a population that was dependent on the monastery that they had a dispute with. They wanted to control the appointment of the priest, to ensure that it was a son of local villagers, and to retain the greatest portion possible in the distribution of tithes and other payments. Again, as in Oña, agreements were used to try to settle these conflicts. The main differences between the two may lie in the absence of arguments to allege the communal character of the church in the case of those in the Tierra de Campos, and that there is no evidence of the collective abandonment of the parish to move to a chapel or the consequent claim to make it a parish church and benefit from the relevant rights. These differences, rather than suggesting that they might have involved different processes, may be due to the type of sources preserved, although this needs to be investigated.

However, with this caveat, and without intending to simplistically extrapolate the data from one context to another, I believe that the detailed study of the material of Oña in these pages can be useful as a benchmark to trace the possible existence of similar processes elsewhere. It is true that the term *difusa*, strongly present in the documentation from Burgos, does not appear in the sources from León,[50] but the existence of a custom shared by a group seems to remain implicit in the argument, used in this area as well, that access to the service of the local church was reserved for the children of the local inhabitants, and in the fact that the revenues would be reserved to them. In this sense, as noted by Martínez Sopena, the claims made by the rural councils were no different from those made by other church owners. For those for which data are only available regarding the tithes for the local council, some deductions can be made about the process of their acquisition, and other aspects that place these specific communities in situations similar to those that we have seen in the local councils of the domains of Oña. This, for example, may serve to confirm the hypothesis put forward by Fernández Flórez that, in the references to clergy who 'entran a racion' ('shared in a church') in the thirteenth-century Parish Register of León, the expression indicated that those clerics were the sons of villagers and that the church belonged to the local council.[51] Fernández Flórez based his hypothesis on a seventh-century council canon. However, in the light of Oña's charters, such

---

49 Reglero analyses a series of disputes faced by the small local councils in places where the lords were San Zoilo de Carrión, San Isidro de Dueñas y San Román de Entrepeñas or where these monasteries had churches. See Reglero de la Fuente, 'Los obispos y sus sedes', pp. 421–49. Some of these are also analysed in Pérez Celada, *El monasterio de San Zoilo de Carrión*; and Martínez Sopena, 'Las solidaridades campesinas'.

50 It only appears in a charter from the Cathedral of León (CatLeon1313, 1102), on which see Martínez Sopena, 'Las solidaridades campesinas', pp. 104–05. It seems to be unique, as it is not included in the *Index verborum* of the medieval Leonese documentation, which could provide possible parallels: Fernández Catón, *Index verborum*.

51 Fernández Flórez, 'El *Becerro de Presentaciones*', p. 337.

388   ISABEL ALFONSO

an early normative basis is not needed to explain, for example, why in the Leonese village of Villahiera the three *racioneros* that the local council appointed to its church were allocated two thirds of the tithes instead of one. These may have resulted from continual negotiation to retain and control the largest portion of tithes, as documented in some cases for Oña.

These deductions could be extended further to the cases of Quintanilla, Villamuera, Santa Eulalia de las Eras, and Santovenia. In 1177, the local council of Quintanilla succeeded in having at least part of its claims over the local church there included in the fuero they negotiated with the monks of San Zoilo de Carrión. The text recognises the right of the council to appoint the clerics, although they were required to abide to the monastic lordship. They could enjoy the first fruits and one third of the bread and wine destined to the church for themselves. They were also to give a third to the bishop, and they would share in half of the other, theoretically destined to the lord, who in this case was the treasurer of San Zoilo.[52] This is one of the many cases that illustrates how often the *fueros*, rather than being laws dictated from above, resulted from bottom-up mobilisations.[53] The concord of 1215 between the local council of Villamuera and the sacristan of San Zoilo was the result of prolonged tensions, and only became visible in the priority given to the local inhabitants to appoint chaplains to the church, who would receive the full wages of the chaplaincy, as well as half of a third of the bread and wine and *minucia*, along with all the oblations and gifts from the dead to the church.[54] In 1240, the local council of Santa Eulalia de las Eras, despite being placed under strong pressure from the prior of San Roman de Entrepeñas, obtained an agreement that recognised the shared right both to choose and to remove the cleric. It also established that he would be chosen from among the inhabitants of the village, although maintaining their vassalage to the monastery. This participation in appointing a clergyman jointly with the prior could be seen as an achievement by the local council, that countered the argument of the prior that 'wherever he had a cemetery, a baptismal font and a third of the tithing'[55] he was entitled to appointing the priest (a physical symbol of rights which is worth noting). On the contrary, however, it could also be interpreted as a partial loss of control since, as he had argued, they had held it for more than sixty years. It was also provided that burials and baptisms should be performed only in the monastery, and that the monastery should always receive its rights, specifying the amounts to be paid.[56] In the litigation that occurred in 1206 between the local council and the clergy of Santovenia and San Isidoro de León, there is some indication that a major fight took place, during which the people of Santovenia stopped paying tithes (although apparently no claims to communal ownership were made in this case). The prior of San Isidoro condemned such a breach as a sin and imposed that it was his *terciario prioral* who would take charge of its collection and distribution, which can be interpreted as a sign of fraud

---

52   SZCarrion49 (1177).

53   Alfonso, 'Campesinado y derecho'.

54   SZCarrión82 (1215).

55   'donde él tenía cementerio, fuente y tercia'.

56   SREntrepeñas63 (1240). Reglero de la Fuente, 'Los obispos y sus sedes', p. 426.

RURAL CHURCHES IN THE NORTH OF CASTILE   389

and mistrust.[57] The exploration of information preserved in other lists of parishes and documentary collections of later centuries would make it possible to investigate to what extent and under what conditions and forms peasants continued to struggle collectively to maintain the ownership of the local centres of worship and the control of their resources in this and in other areas.

In view of the preceding examples, perhaps the fact that in 1333 Santo Toribio de Liébana, another major monastery in the diocese of Leon in an Asturian valley, had to prohibit and penalise the installation of a baptismal font in the chapels of San Pedro and Santa María de Potes, should not be taken as isolated. The local council had engaged in a long conflict over the right to appoint a priest and the right to a portion of the tithe, and had abandoned the parish church of San Vicente, which belonged to the monastery. The information contained in the provisions of the arbitration clearly shows that the clergy and laity from Potes had not only ceased to attend daily religious services but had also ceased to pay 'all the tithes, first-fruits, oblations, renders and rights in due manner as faithful Christians should grant and pay as tithes, and not render to any other church'.[58] In this case the monastic lord sought to completely impose himself at the local council making few concessions, but litigation would be repeatedly resorted to here during subsequent centuries.[59]

Nor should we consider the late medieval conflicts surrounding the patronage of local churches carried out by the neighbours of the villages and places of Guipúzcoa, studied by Díaz de Durana, to be unique to the País Vasco.[60] The most common ones there were also concerned with the appointment and number of clergy, plus the income from tithes and associated goods and, globally, with recognition of that patronage. In this area, whose land belonged to the dioceses of Bayonne, Pamplona and Calahorra, everything seems to suggest that before the end of the fourteenth century many churches remained in the hands of the local councils, and that it was only with during the reigns of the Trastámara kings of Castile that the royal patrimony was transferred to the *Parientes Mayores* ('Elder Relatives'), as the lords of that area were called. Certainly, it is this secular, rather than ecclesiastical, identity of the new church owners that provides the greatest contrast in these cases with respect to those discussed for other areas. However, the litigations between Elder Relatives and parishioners which were brought before both the ecclesiastical authorities and the *Chancillería* in Valladolid have many similarities to the conflicts waged by the local councils in other areas. Thus in Cestona, Hernani, Cegama, and Zumea, the villagers came together and conspired to leave the old parish and tried to build another one parallel to it; appointed a cleric different from the one imposed by the lord to whom they paid their tithes; increased the *congrua* ('curacy') they were to receive from the revenues of the church; and distributed the 'casas diezmeras' ('tithe-paying households') of the village so that they would pay to the clerics or the patron, as seen

---

57 SIDueñas76 (1206).
58 'todos los diezmos, primicias, ofrendas, frutos, y derechos bien y cumplidamente como lo debían dar e diezmar fieles cristianos e no a otra iglesia ninguna'.
59 SToribioII-22 (1331); SToribioII-24 (1333).
60 Díaz de Durana, 'Patronatos'.

in the local councils of many places under the control of Oña. The local councils had certain material achievements, although whether the resolutions were more or less favourable to either side depended on the correlation of existing forces and the results were therefore contingent on this.

Research Avenues

It is not the purpose of this study to compile yet more data of similar movements,[61] but to raise some questions about their religious dimension. This, I believe, seems to have been overly subordinated to the study of the institutional development of the parish, closely linked to a focus on the Gregorian Reform that is excessively attached to the rhetoric of its proposals.[62] The anti-lord character attributed to these conflicts to some extent has also limited the inquiry into the specific religious elements that such actions entailed. And yet, without denying this anti-lord nature (it is impossible to ignore the lordly nature of both the ecclesiastical authority and lay patrons), it seems to me that the formalisation of collective actions within a religious-ecclesiastical framework has implications that deserve to be examined.

In her study of peasant resistance, Reyna Pastor already referred to the disputes in different areas of León and Castile between, on the one hand, the priests of villages and hamlets, allied with their parishioners in defence of their interests and their churches, and on the other, abbots and bishops. Pastor argued that what she called the 'clerical proletariat' (adopting Duby's concept) struggled together with the peasants against the high clergy for the distribution of tithes, in a resistance movement against the feudal advancement of the church.[63] The aspiration for autonomy of the local councils in the royal towns (in opposition to feudal powers) has also been regarded as the objective of the movements they carried out.[64] The same anti-lord character of these movements for the control of local churches and of tithe revenues was identified by Díaz de Durana regarding the struggles in the communities of Guipúzcoa and Vizcaya with their Elder Relatives, which took place from the middle of the fourteenth century until the sixteenth century.[65] The greater wealth of information provided by the judicial lawsuits of this period allowed Díaz

---

61 Some parallels in other European areas can be found in Reynolds, *Kingdoms and Communities*; Wickham, 'Gossip and Resistance'; Wickham, *Legge, patriche e conflitti*; Wood, *The Proprietary Church*. A comparative study on a wide scale would require a different approach and many more pages.

62 The exemplary study of the diocese of Oviedo made by Calleja Puerta seems to be a good example of this approach. Calleja Puerta, *La formación de la red parroquial*. The reference made to a generalised opposition from the middle of the thirteenth century by the local councils, both from the town of Oviedo itself and from the rural communities, undoubtedly has similar connotations to the conflicts discussed here, but Calleja merely indicates that the old practice of private ownership of rural churches, especially through the choice of the priest, would remain in effect in this diocese throughout the middle ages (Calleja Puerta, *La formación de la red parroquial*, pp. 120–44).

63 Pastor, *Resistencias y luchas campesinas*, pp. 157–62.

64 Martínez Sopena, *Tierra de Campos occidental*; Pérez Celada, *El monasterio de San Zoilo de Carrión*; Reglero de la Fuente, 'Los obispos y sus sedes'.

65 Díaz de Durana, 'Patronatos'.

de Durana to draw attention to the symbolic aspects that he also observed in these movements, and highlighted that the material side of the exercise of patronage rights should be analysed inseparably from the political/ideological side. I think that this line of research should be pursued and developed.[66]

The protests against tithes have generally been of the most concern in the literature associated with religious dissent and anti-clerical attitudes, and in many cases without distinction between the two. Due to the success of Le Roy Ladurie's book on Montaillou, peasant struggles against tithing have been almost inextricably associated with heretical currents.[67] The abundant information that has been preserved about the inquisitorial process to which the Montaillou peasants were subjected at the beginning of the fourteenth century allowed Le Roy Ladurie to identify the close connection that existed between the refusal to pay tithes and the ideas of the Cathar heresy which was widespread among the Occitan population. He perceived this link as the foundation of a long-standing anticlericalism, in which the resentful alienation was both spiritual and temporal.[68]

Rebellion and heterodoxy have also gone hand in hand in most interpretations of the much-studied English peasant movement of 1381, considering that the influence of Wyclif's ideas can be argued to have been at the basis of the rebels' thinking. One of the most influential works in this vein is that of Justice, as it provides an original approach to the ability of illiterate peasants to adopt and rework contesting ideas that circulated in writing in rural areas.[69] This type of association between religious dissidence movements and peasant uprisings has continued to have a strong impact on historiography, as it has a type of intrinsic force that cannot be ignored, although there is no evidence of any language coming from heterodox sources. The seductive power of this connection has partly obscured the interpretations that suggest the influence of the teachings of the Gospel on such social movements, showing that the message of egalitarianism, the main Christian idea, could feed both submission and rebellion. Le Roy Ladurie, for example, was not unaware that hostility to the rich was nourished in the Gospel, as if a New Testament orthodoxy had anticipated heretical propaganda, especially in the questions concerning the problem of poverty.[70]

It is symptomatic that in an article of great interest, Justice retracted his assumption that the English revolt had more affinity with heresy than with orthodoxy; he stated that he had failed to perceive that examples that could be taken as evidence of heterodox or dissident attitudes could contain, on the contrary, the richness of the language, thought, habits and imaginary of the pious prayer to which the peasants

---

66 One of the latest colloquia held in Flaran focused on the historiographical revision of anti-lord struggles in medieval and modern Europe, a subject that in the editors' eyes is currently under review. Oliva carried out a critical review on the studies for the Kingdom of Castile and raised new research perspectives that shifted the analysis towards cultural and communicative elements, as part of a line of research that he has developed in his later works (Oliva Herrer, 'Les luttes anti-seigneuriales').

67 Le Roy Ladurie, *Montaillou*, pp. 560–66.

68 However, it is worth noting that in Montaillou, the main tithe-takers were the dependants of the parish churches.

69 Justice, *Writing and Rebellion*, pp. 73–101.

70 Le Roy Ladurie, *Montaillou*, pp. 564–70.

were accustomed (which constituted, therefore, the moral and theological basis for their actions).[71] By doing so he aligned himself with a research approach to medieval Christianity that shows that the doctrines, rites, practices and languages of devotion, far from being frozen into a blind dogmatism, displayed an almost alarming plasticity. Even in their more normative forms, religious beliefs and sentiments were diverse, conflicting and multi-vocal, and peasants were ultimately able to use the religious resources that best articulated their worldview.[72]

The traces of heterodoxy in peasant conflicts and resistance have also been sought without success in Spanish historiography.[73] Although the heretical threat is visible above all in Lucas de Tuy's work to combat heresy, the content of the doctrines which the supposed heretics were able to disseminate, or indeed their practical impact, is scarcely known. Moreover, the simple assimilation to Catharism that has been attempted is considered by Patrick Henriet to be completely reductionist.[74] Important for the arguments I am presenting here is his observation that the religiosity of laymen was not totally different from that of the clergy. Also of interest is his distinction between legal and illegal pious practices and those that were clearly heretical. The latter were the only ones that proposed a system of salvation different from that proposed by the church (although the thread that led to it was finer than has been assumed). Certainly, it must be accepted that the religious dimension of the actions discussed in these pages seems to be more related to the nature of the actual asset under dispute, a centre of worship and its resources, rather than to any doctrinal dissent. In the light of the preserved testimonies, the argument, that movements in which the laity gave such a prominent place to their clerical neighbours should be considered to be anticlerical in nature, cannot be easily justified. Nor does it seem likely that they might have been inspired by heretical deviations, since it has been noted that the results obtained (however partial, scarce and contingent) were accepted by the ecclesiastical authority itself and, therefore, their legitimacy was recognised. And yet these agreements between local councils and lords were contrary to all the canonical legislation disseminated in councils, synods, pastoral visits, etc. Is this fact to be understood as yet another manifestation of the resistance that the application of the Gregorian Reform encountered, as an example of the difficulties in its implementation vis-à-vis the laity? It seems to me that we are now in a position to abandon this facile and teleological interpretation, and to raise questions that might allow for a more plausible explanation of the reality transmitted to us through these texts. I confess that I do not have such an explanation, and these considerations are only tentative. They result from a dissatisfaction with an explanatory model of linear evolution that was full of exceptions and diversity, attributed to the failure of the

---

71 Justice, 'Religious Dissent'.

72 Justice, 'Religious Dissent', pp. 214–15.

73 Pastor, *Resistencias y luchas campesinas*, p. 160.

74 For further references in this respect see Henriet, 'La religiosité des laïques entre IXe et XIIe siècle', p. 265. Not surprisingly, the only testimony of heretical doctrines in León conveyed by Lucas de Tuy in the thirteenth century became well known thanks to Menéndez Pelayo, *Historia de los heterodoxos españoles*.

RURAL CHURCHES IN THE NORTH OF CASTILE   393

implementation of abstract normative objectives, both concerning the establishment of the so-called classic parish church, and the complete separation of ecclesiastical property from the laity.[75]

Let us review the evidence that has been discussed so far. What were the repercussions for the people involved, when they pursued (and in many cases achieved) control of their churches and villages to varying degrees? What would have been the implications, in religious terms, of the collective refusal to attend religious services in the parish church, and to choose a separate chapel instead, and to place itself under the protection of a different saint? And of the pious gifts and offerings of a whole community being given to this centre, from the first fruits to the gifts for its dead?[76] What was the force that enabled them to act as they did?[77] I have tried to assess the economic repercussions of this control, and I have proposed that this should not be reduced to a merely defensive attitude in the face of the highly oppressive payment of tithes. But it seems to me that mobilising to achieve certain material objectives and formalising them within the religious-ecclesiastical framework must have had implications that went beyond the pious and caregiving character that has been attributed to the growing community involvement in the management of local churches.[78] We must reflect on the ways and areas in which the actors in these movements assessed the spiritual and material risks involved in not fulfilling the obligations of the church, how they accepted the dangers of sinning by

---

75 Studies on these issues have been largely conditioned by the historiography of both proprietary churches and the 'Gregorian Reform'. The latter is usually taken as a key reference for the study of actions like the ones considered here. It provides a teleological narrative for the devolution of proprietary churches to major ecclesiastical institutions in which such actions are interpreted as resistances and limitations to the 'reform'. Although it now seems to be accepted that the establishment of a parish organisation was a slow process that moved forward at irregular pace (Fernández Conde, *La religiosidad medieval 1*), the role of a yet unattained 'reform' is invoked to explain the process, rather than seeking the specific factors behind it. Perhaps the most extreme version of this model, bearing some resemblance to Spanish nationalism, was that presented in Orlandis Rovira, 'Los laicos y las iglesias rurales'. The literature on ecclesiastical reform is very abundant. See the references provided in the works collected in *La reforma gregoriana*, especially López Alsina, 'La reforma eclesiástica'. Outside of Spain, traditional approaches have been reviewed in Wood, *The Proprietary Church*; and Ramseyer, *The Transformation of a Religious Landscape*. For the territorial aspects of ecclesiastical reorganisation, it would be very useful to assume conceptually that, following Zadora-Río, the parish network did not emerge when the countryside was being populated and cultivated, but through a slow process of territorialisation in which the administrative, fiscal and religious development seemed to operate together (Zadora-Rio, 'Territoires paroissiaux', p. 21).

76 It is not certain that the choice of burial entailed that peasants would necessarily be interred in a cemetery located in a place other than that linked to the parish church, although some data point in that direction. As with parishes, with cemeteries: hardly anything was as simple, as early, or as concrete as it seemed until recently (Zadora-Rio, 'Territoires paroissiaux', p. 21). For the origin of the cemeteries in the medieval West, and their relationship to the sacred places and inhabited spaces, see also Lauwers, *La naissance du cimetière*.

77 On the power of the oath for the construction of community identity, see Sánchez León, 'El poder de la comunidad', pp. 345–49. The influence of sworn practices on the crystallisation of communities was already noted in Wickham, *Comunità e clientele*.

78 Martínez Sopena, 'Las solidaridades campesinas'; Dyer, 'The English medieval Village Community'; Schofield, *Peasant and Community*.

not paying the tithe, how they dealt with their fears that their crops might diminish or worsen because of these acts, or of being punished with excommunication and eternal condemnation if they did not immediately rectify their behaviour. Ultimately these were the risks they were explicitly advised about in many contexts through various means, using threats that sought to determine their behaviour.[79] Trying to understand the thoughts and intentions of the peasants who used a religious route for their mobilisation involves assuming that their actions were intelligible, and can therefore be investigated within the specific terms of that intelligibility. Even if one accepts that it is not possible to completely reconstruct the meaning they gave to these circumstances, it can be seen that they were consistent and well informed.[80]

The intention of this study has been to open a line of research based on the political culture of the peasantry which incorporates the religious imaginary that was part of their worldview. In addition, it is to be expected that the increasing contribution of archaeology to the historiography of parish churches and places of worship in general, masterfully identified by Zadora-Río, along with the renewed enthusiasm of García de Cortázar in his recognition of *socioeclesiología*, should raise awareness about more complex ways of studying the territories of the churches and the links of the people with them.[81] The cases discussed here seek to contribute to this complexity, both to unravelling and to understanding the processes involved.

---

79 On the sin of not meeting the tithe obligation, see Martín and Linage Conde, eds, *Religión y sociedad medieval*, p. 254. On the consequences of eternal condemnation for those who defrauded or failed to pay their tithes see Martín Cea, *El mundo rural castellano*, pp. 378–443. The section dedicated to the study of religiosity can be explored in relation to these issues, especially with regard to the involvement of the local council in the maintenance of the socio-religious order. The texts of some synodal constitutions warned of the catastrophic evils that would affect the souls, bodies and estates of those who did not pay tithes, and even to their land, which would cease to bear fruit or be invaded by plagues of caterpillars and locusts: as with those from Orense, cited in Ríos Rodríguez, 'Por su pobreza', p. 256.

80 Justice, 'Religious Dissent', pp. 209 y 311.

81 Zadora-Rio, 'L'historiographie des paroisses rurales'; García de Cortázar, 'La organización socioeclesiológica'.

Bibliography

Alfonso, Isabel, 'Campesinado y derecho: la vía legal de su lucha (Castilla y León, siglos X–XIII)', *Noticiario de Historia Agraria*, 13 (1997), 15–31

Alfonso, Isabel, 'Litigios por la tierra y "malfetrías" entre la nobleza medieval', *Hispania*, 57–197 (1997), 917–55

Alfonso, Isabel, 'La rhétorique de légitimation seigneuriale dans les fueros de León (XIe–XIIIe siècles)', in *Pour une anthropologie du prélèvement seigneurial dans les campagnes de l'Occident médiéval (XIe–XIVe siècles). Les mots, les temps, les lieux*, ed. by Monique Bourin and Pascual Martínez Sopena (Paris: Publications de la Sorbonne, 2007), pp. 229–52

Alfonso, Isabel, '¿Muerte sin venganza? La regulación de la violencia en ámbitos locales (Castilla y León, siglo XIII)', in *El lugar del campesino. En torno a la obra de Reyna Pastor*, ed. by Ana Rodríguez (Valencia: Publicaciones de la Universidad de Valencia, 2007), pp. 239–60

Alonso de Porres Fernández, César, *Las parroquias en la ciudad de Burgos: estudio histórico-jurídico de un régimen peculiar* (Burgos: Caja de Burgos, 1981)

Álvarez Borge, Ignacio, *Poder y relaciones sociales en Castilla en la Edad Media. Los territorios entre el Arlanzón y el Duero en los siglos X al XIV* (Salamanca: Junta de Castilla y León, 1996)

Álvarez Borge, Ignacio, ed., *Comunidades locales y poderes feudales en la Edad Media* (Logroño: Universidad de la Rioja, 2001)

Bonaudo, Marta, 'El monasterio de San Salvador de Oña. Economía agraria y sociedad rural', *Cuadernos de Historia de España*, 51–52 (1970), 42–122

Calleja Puerta, Miguel, *La formación de la red parroquial de la diócesis de Oviedo en la Edad Media* (Oviedo: Real Instituto de Estudios Asturianos, 2000)

Díaz de Durana, José Ramón, 'Patronatos, patronos, clérigos y parroquianos: los derechos de patronazgo sobre monasterios e iglesias como fuente de renta e instrumento de control y dominación de los parientes mayores guipuzcoanos (siglos XIV a XVI)', *Hispania sacra*, 50–102 (1998), 467–508

Díaz de Durana, José Ramón, and Enric Guinot, 'La dîme dans l'Espagne médiévale', in *La dîme dans l'Europe médiévale et moderne: actes des XXXes Journées Internationales d'Histoire de l'Abbaye de Flaran, 3 et 4 octobre 2008*, ed. by Roland Viader (Toulouse: Presses universitaires du Mirail, 2010), pp. 63–88

Dyer, Chris, 'The English Medieval Village Community and its Decline', *Journal of British Studies*, 33–4 (1994), 407–29

Fernández Conde, Francisco Javier, *La religiosidad medieval en España. Vol. 1: La Alta Edad Media (siglos VII–X)* (Oviedo: Universidad de Oviedo, 2000)

Fernández Flórez, José A., 'El *Becerro de Presentaciones*. Códice 13 del Archivo de la Catedral de León', in *León y su Historia. Miscelánea histórica. Vol. V* (León: Centro de Estudios e Investigación San Isidoro, 1984), pp. 265–565

García de Cortázar, José Ángel, 'La organización socioeclesiológica del espacio en el norte de la Península Ibérica en los siglos VIII a XIII', in *La pervivencia del concepto. Nuevas reflexiones sobre la ordenación social del espacio en la Edad Media*, ed. by José Ángel Sesma Muñoz and Carlos Laliena Corbera (Zaragoza: Gobierno de Aragón – Grupo CEMA, 2008), pp. 13–56

Henriet, Patrick, 'La religiosité des laïques entre IXe et XIIe siècle', in *Monarquía y sociedad en el reino de León. De Alfonso III a Alfonso VII. Vol. 2* (León: Centro de Estudios e Investigación San Isidoro, 2007), pp. 235–67

Hilton, Rodney, *Siervos liberados. Los movimientos campesinos medievales y el levantamiento inglés de 1381* (Siglo XXI: Madrid, 1978)

Justice, Steven, *Writing and Rebellion. England in 1381* (Berkeley: University of California Press, 1994)

Justice, Steven, 'Religious Dissent, Social Revolt and "Ideology"', in *Rodney Hilton's Middle Ages: An Exploration of Historical Themes*, ed. by Chris Dyer and Chris Wickham (2007), pp. 205–16

Lauwers, Michael, *La naissance du cimetière: lieux sacrés et terre des morts dans l'Occident médiéval* (Paris: Aubier, 2005)

Le Roy Ladurie, Emmanuel *Montaillou, village occitan, de 1294 à 1324* (Paris: Gallimard, 1975)

López Alsina, Fernando, 'La reforma eclesiástica: la generalización de un modelo parroquial renovado', in *La reforma gregoriana y su proyección en la cristiandad occidental: siglos XI–XII. XXXII Semana de Estudios Medievales, Estella, 18 a 22 de julio de 2005* (Pamplona: Institución Príncipe de Viana, 2006), pp. 421–50

Martín Cea, Juan Carlos, *El mundo rural castellano a fines de la Edad Media. El ejemplo de Paredes de Nava en el siglo XV* (Valladolid: Junta de Castilla y León, 1991)

Martín, José Luis, and Antonio Linage Conde, eds, *Religión y sociedad medieval: el catecismo de Pedro de Cuéllar (1325)* (Valladolid: Junta de Castilla y León, 1987)

Martínez Sopena, Pascual, *La Tierra de Campos occidental: poblamiento, poder y comunidad del siglo X al XIII* (Valladolid: Institución Cultural Simancas, 1985)

Martínez Sopena, Pascual, 'Las solidaridades campesinas en la Tierra de Campos durante la Edad. Media', in *Solidaritats pageses, sindicalisme i cooperativisme. Segones Jornades sobre Sistemes agraris, organització social i poder local als Països Catalans*, ed. by Jaume Barrull, Joan Josep Busqueta, and Enric Vicedo (Lleida: Institut d'Estudis Ilerdencs, 1998), pp. 93–113

Menéndez Pelayo, Marcelino, *Historia de los heterodoxos españoles*, 3 vols (Madrid: Imprenta de F. Maroto e hijos, 1880–1882)

Nieto Soria, José Manuel, *Iglesia y poder real en Castilla: el episcopado, 1250–1350* (Madrid: Universidad Complutense de Madrid, 1988)

Olmedo Bernal, Santiago, *Una abadía castellana en el siglo XI: San Salvador de Oña (1011–1109)* (Antiqua et Medievalia: Madrid, 1987)

Orlandis Rovira, José, 'Los laicos y las iglesias rurales en la España de los siglos XI y XII', in *Le istituzioni ecclesiastiche della 'societas christiana' dei secoli XI–XII. Diocesi, pievi e parrocchie. Atti della sesta Settimana internazionale di studio, Milano, 1–7 settembre 1974* (Milan: Vita e Pensiero, 1977), pp. 261–90

Pastor, Reyna, *Resistencias y luchas campesinas en la época del crecimiento y consolidación de la formación feudal: Castilla y León, siglos X–XIII* (Madrid: Siglo XXI, 1980)

Pérez Celada, Julio Antonio, *El monasterio de San Zoilo de Carrión. Formación, estructura y decurso de un señorío castellano-leonés (siglos XI al XVI)* (Burgos: Universidad de Burgos, 1997)

Ramseyer, Valerie, *The Transformation of a Religious Landscape: Medieval Southern Italy, 850–1150* (Ithaca: Cornell University Press, 2006)

Reglero de la Fuente, Carlos, *El monasterio de San Isidro de Dueñas. Un priorato cluniacense hispano (911–1478). Estudio y colección documental* (León: Centro de Estudios e Investigación San Isidoro, 2005)

Reglero de la Fuente, Carlos, 'Los obispos y sus sedes en los reinos hispánicos occidentales', in *La reforma gregoriana y su proyección en la cristiandad occidental: siglos XI–XII. XXXII Semana de Estudios Medievales, Estella, 18 a 22 de julio de 2005* (Pamplona: Institución Príncipe de Viana, 2006), pp. 195–288

Reynolds, Susan, *Kingdoms and Communities in Western Europe, 900–1300* (Oxford: Clarendon Press, 1984)

Ríos Rodríguez, María Luz, 'Por su pobreza recibirían gran fatiga. El clero parroquial auriense a fines de la Edad Media', *Medievalismo*, 17 (2007), 247–70

Ruiz Gómez, Francisco, 'Las formas de poblamiento rural en La Bureba en la Baja Edad Media. La villa de Oña' (Unpublished PhD Dissertation, Universidad Complutense de Madrid, 1988)

Sánchez León, Pablo, 'El poder de la comunidad', in *El lugar del campesino. En torno a la obra de Reyna Pastor*, ed. by Ana Rodríguez (Valencia: Publicaciones de la Universidad de Valencia, 2007), pp. 331–58

Schofield, Philip R., *Peasant and Community in Medieval England, 1200–1500* (New York: Palgrave MacMillan, 2003)

Serrano, Luciano, *El obispado de Burgos y Castilla primitiva desde el siglo V al XIII*, 3 vols (Madrid: Instituto de Valencia de Don Juan, 1935–1936)

Wickham, Chris, *Comunità e clientele nella Toscana del XII secolo. Le origini del comune rurale nella Piana di Lucca* (Roma: Viella, 1995)

Wickham, Chris, 'Gossip and Resistance among the Medieval Peasantry', *Past & Present*, 160 (1998), 3–24

Wickham, Chris, *Legge, pratiche e conflitti. Tribunali e risoluzione delle dispute nella Toscana del XII secolo* (Roma: Viella, 2000)

Wood, Susan, *The Proprietary Church in the Medieval West* (Oxford: Oxford University Press, 2006)

Zadora-Rio, Élizabeth, 'L'historiographie des paroisses rurales à l'épreuve de l'archéologies', in *Aux origines de la paroisse rurale en Gaule méridionale, IVe–IXe siècles*, ed. by Christine Delaplace (Toulouse: Errance, 2005), pp. 15–23

Zadora-Rio, Élizabeth, 'Territoires paroissiaux et construction de l'espace vernaculaire', *Médiévales*, 49 (2005), 105–20

CHAPTER 11

Two Anthropological Approaches to Peasants and Lords

with a commentary by Jean Birrell and Rosamond Faith

Conflict, Language, and Social Practice in Medieval Societies: Selected Essays of Isabel Alfonso, with Commentaries, ed. by Julio Escalona Monge, Álvaro Carvajal Castro, and Cristina Jular Pérez-Alfaro, TMC 24 (Turnhout: Brepols, 2024), pp. 399–462

BREPOLS ✠ PUBLISHERS   10.1484/M.TMC-EB.5.132465

JEAN BIRRELL

A Commentary on 'Peasant Opposition to Labour Services' and 'The Rhetoric of Seigneurial Legitimation'

The two articles by Isabel Alfonso I shall discuss here are of great interest to English medieval social and economic historians, as well as models of their kind. They were written for a conference held in 2002 with the general title *Towards an anthropology of seigneurial rent in the medieval countryside (eleventh–fourteenth centuries)*, whose proceedings were published in two volumes in French in 2007 (volume 1: *Words, times and places*, volume 2: *Peasant realities and representations*). Both articles are largely based on the evidence of *fueros*, what might loosely be called Spanish charters of franchises, and one of the virtues of this collection for English historians is to show how study of these continental records (*chartes de franchises, Weistümer* and *carte di franchigia*) can suggest fresh approaches to English manorial history. Of these charters, the Spanish *fueros* are perhaps the least well known to English historiography, which gives special value to Isabel's contributions. I will concentrate here on the way her articles can suggest fresh ways of looking, in particular, at English manorial custumals. These, it can be argued, are the nearest equivalent to charters of franchises in medieval England, sharing many parallels with them; however different the circumstances in which these records were produced, and however different the position of English peasant tenants, the similarities between these records can be fruitfully explored, as I hope to show.

The first of these two articles addresses the question of peasant opposition to labour services. Now labour services themselves, and peasant hostility to them, are both amply documented for medieval England and have frequently been discussed by English historians, if usually within the confines of an estate or manorial history. Nevertheless, these articles, based on a meticulous analysis of a large number of *fueros* from a number of different estates across Leon, cast new light on an 'old' subject. The masterly and systematic survey of the nature of these services as recorded in a large number of *fueros*, a survey of a type not familiar in English historiography, is in itself of interest. It includes, for example, the careful distinction between six separate tasks involved in cultivating corn; she also pays attention to what can too easily be treated as subsidiary aspects of these services, such as the explicit articulation of the obligation on the *corvéables* to turn up punctually when summoned, to perform whatever task was indicated by the appropriate official, and to work as long as was laid down; obligations that are balanced by those on the lord himself, on what he could demand, such as that to give adequate and public notice, that not to impose

---

Jean Birrell, Honorary Fellow, School of History and Cultures, University of Birmingham

402 JEAN BIRRELL

simultaneous or unachievable demands, and that, more frequently discussed in England, to make the customary provision of food and drink for the workers.

These checks, such as they are, on the will of the lord are attributed to the opposition of the peasants, which she identifies as an alternative strategy to more overt collective action. Of course, peasant resistance to labour services, from failure to turn up to poor performance in the field, has been amply discussed by English historians, but this has largely been on the basis of manorial court rolls, where such offences were presented and punished. This article draws our attention to the evidence of peasant resistance at, as it were, an earlier stage, through negotiation with lords, the results of which were committed to writing in *fueros*. English manorial custumals would certainly repay reading with these points in mind. What can appear at first sight as simply a list of obligations imposed on peasant tenants, often incorporated into a manorial survey and treated simply as an aspect of rent payable for a holding, can, if read carefully, reveal intense prior negotiation over a variety of issues. I refer for example not only to the detailed specifications which set limits on what could be demanded (the length, breadth and depth of ditching to be dug, for example, or the quantity of each type of corn to be threshed), but to clarifications that are effectively limitations, such as that the lord himself was responsible for specific tasks, for example carting the harvested crop from the field to the barn, even if the peasants were required to perform all the other earlier stages.

This article shows how meticulous analysis of these clauses can be fruitful not only for the light they throw on this dynamic, constantly changing, element in the relationship between lords and peasants, but for the light they can throw on peasant attitudes, generally so elusive. Again, this is helpful for English historians faced with the difficulty of accessing these attitudes, given that the sources are so heavily manorial, in the sense of being produced by manorial officials and intended to serve their purposes. But English historians have access to a very large number of manorial custumals, which, if read carefully, can be revealing. The clauses which reveal evidence of prior negotiation or dispute, indeed the very appearance of certain clauses in custumals, can be an indication of which aspects mattered to the peasant tenants.

Equally, and more generally, hostility to labour services can be deduced, she points out, from the need to specify methods of control and penalties for non-performance or poor performance. Now, reluctance to perform labour services has long been noted by English historians, as already stated, and the greater inefficiency of forced labour as opposed to wage labour has recently been impressively demonstrated, but largely on the basis of, respectively, manorial court rolls and manorial accounts. The evidence of manorial custumals enables a slightly different approach to both these aspects, and to the problems manorial lords faced in enforcing these services. For example, she discusses 'control and penalties', the need to specify both in itself evidence of a 'resistance' they were designed to counteract, which have generally been less remarked on by English historians. Control was exercised, in part, and at least in theory, by making it an obligation of some of the peasant tenants themselves, what she calls 'l'implication des victimes elle-mêmes'. She makes us ask how willingly and how effectively the supervision by these individuals that is so carefully written into many manorial custumals was exercised, and how this supervision, assuming it was

COMMENTARY 403

carried out, was viewed by those immediately affected, on both 'sides', that is, by the supervisors and the supervised, and by the community at large. Did some tenants welcome the authority and power this supervision gave? Were these clauses ever effectively implemented, or was supervision in practice left to manorial officials, acting on behalf of the lord or the community? How enthusiastically did these officials, or tenants temporarily invested with special powers, enforce these obligations? And what were the consequences for relations within the manorial community? (A fascinating aside here concerns the significance attached to ownership of a horse (p. 298), the latter, too, visible in English custumals in the obligation of certain supervising tenants to be mounted). Assuming the answers are not generally clear cut, reflecting a less than clear situation on the ground, what make the difference? All this could usefully be followed up in custumals.

It will at this point be helpful to turn to the second of Isabel's articles, in which, under the title 'The Rhetoric of Seigneurial Legitimation in *fueros*', she deals with the preambles to these documents, discussing the way they reveal, more or less explicitly, the motives of those involved and the circumstances which dictated the issue of the records. This in an area where continental historians are better served than their English fellows, as English manorial custumals typically lack explanatory preambles. This must be in part because of the form in which they mostly survive, whatever their origins (which would itself surely repay further study), that is, incorporated into manorial surveys. Within these surveys the customs and services may be recorded separately, as a discrete set of 'customs', or as part of the rent obligation of each tenant or each category of tenant — any reader of manorial surveys is familiar with the lengthy, often extremely lengthy, description of the services of a 'standard' tenant, followed by a list of those tenants whose services were identical or differed in some aspect — or in a mixture of the two; in any case, the survey/custumal often only survives in a later copy, for example as enrolled in a register or cartulary. However that may be, these are not records primarily intended, like *fueros*, to record an agreement between issuing lord and receiving peasants.

Nevertheless, some English manorial custumals do have preambles, which have been little noticed, and which the discussion in this article may help us to interpret. Isabel's article draws attention, for example, to the evidence of disputes that the *fueros* were an attempt to settle. We may wonder to what extent this was a factor in the issue of some English custumals. At Alrewas, for example, there is clear evidence in the lengthy 'preamble' which precedes the statement of the customs of the customary tenants that this was an attempt to settle tensions and disputes on the manor (the 'various disagreements and disputes' that 'have often arisen'); the preamble to an inquisition 'concerning the customs of Stoke under Hamdan' (Stoke Beauchamp) in 1251 reveals that it was made on the accession of a new lord, and includes a restatement of a declaration (probably originally made by an ancestor) that he will 'inviolably preserve' the customs recorded. These preambles suggest that a shift of attitude towards manorial custumals on the part of medieval historians would show dividends; in particular, they emerge not simply as by-products of a drive for manorial efficiency, which is not to deny that this may often have been a factor, but as the product of a particular conjuncture between the issuing lord and the affected peasants.

However, the main theme of the article under discussion here is the 'legitimising rhetoric' found in many preambles. Put briefly, it notes the desire of manorial lords to be seen as wise, benevolent and acting of their own free will, even when the document itself explicitly or implicitly suggests that they had been coerced into making the concessions recorded or into issuing the document — what she calls 'un privilege arraché par ses beneficiaries'. Such rhetoric may be rare in English manorial documents, in general so business-like and practical, but it may often be there, if one is alert for it. I will quote just one example. At Alrewas, where, as we have seen, the custumal was at least in part issued in an attempt to settle persistent local disputes, the preamble emphasises the benevolence and wisdom of the issuing lord and the respect felt for him by his tenants: the former, given his full title, 'Lord Philip de Somerville, knight, lord of the manor of Alrewas', had, according to the preamble, been appealed to by the latter, 'trusting in his faith as a good lord', and because, not only had he 'governed the manner amicably and graciously these last forty years and more' but he has more knowledge than anyone else living of the certainty of the customs of the tenants, to solve their problems by setting their customs down in writing.

The Alrewas preamble may reveal more about the mind set of the lord than that of the tenants, unless it be the latter's cunning, but Isabel points to another way in which custumals may reflect peasant attitudes, in this case, specifically, their desire to write their own history. She notes the preamble to a *fueros* of Toldanos in which the peasants have succeeded in getting their struggle mentioned — in this case, as the principal reason for the issue of the *fueros* — in a way that preserves a memory of their action and gives their own version of events. This is immensely helpful for our understanding of what may at first seem extraneous interpolations in many custumals, in which old disputes are rehearsed.

Throughout both these articles there is an emphasis on the importance of studying the vocabulary employed, the importance of which, she is sure, was appreciated by peasants as well as by lords — what she calls a 'guerre des mots'. Close attention to this can provide another way of access to the peasants' own attitude to their obligations, generally so elusive. This, too, suggests a fruitful approach to English manorial records and in particular custumals (language is the subject of another section in this same collection, which includes a pioneering article on England by Chris Dyer). Even in the form in which it reaches us, written down in Latin by a scribe who was usually employed by the manorial lord, the language use can reveal peasant attitudes in ways that are not revealed by any recorded actions. We can see, for example, in many custumals, through the vocabulary, a peasant desire to emphasise or cling onto the voluntary or honourable status of certain obligations, and even the honourable status of certain tenants. The customary tenants of one of the manors of the Benedictine Burton Abbey, for example, can be shown clinging to the description of a certain customary payment to the lord as a gift, even though in practice it was — or had become — obligatory. This it is an aspect that would surely repay further study.

While singling out certain clauses as particularly significant for her themes, Isabel insists in both of these articles on the need for an analysis of all the clauses in *fueros*, together with the preambles. Strangely, no systematic analysis of the clauses found in English manorial custumals has been attempted. This is not to ignore or downplay the many excellent studies of various aspects of surviving custumals, usually in estate — less often regional — studies. What is lacking, however, is a comparison of the clauses in a large number of surveys; ideally, of course, these would come from different estates and regions, and cover the whole period. So many questions about custumals remain unanswered: why there are such variations in what is included in different custumals; why certain types of clause, for example those dealing with liability to heriot and the form it should take, or with the duties and perquisites of manorial officials, begin to appear in custumals across estates and across the country at certain points in time; why certain custumals deal with a range of judicial or administrative matters, others hardly or not at all; and so on. English historians might well also pay attention to the origins of a range of clauses quite alien to continental charters of franchise, such as exoneration from or alleviation of certain obligations for peasants who were sick, unmarried, in childbirth and so on.

The enduring dynamism of English language historiography and its ability to revitalise itself was admiringly commented on by a contributor to a volume edited by Isabel herself.[1] The work of Isabel Alfonso, only briefly outlined here on the basis of two articles (and of course to be seen in conjunction with the other contributions to these two volumes), so valuable in itself, could also be valuable in the stimulus it gives to new research by medieval English agrarian historians interested in social relations.

Bibliography

Demade, Julien, 'The medieval countryside in German-language historiography since the 1930s', in *The rural history of medieval European societies*, ed. by Isabel Alfonso (Turnhout: Brepols, 2007), pp. 173-252

---

1 Demade, 'The Medieval Countryside', p. 237.

ROSAMOND FAITH

Pacts, Conventions, and Contracts between Lords and Peasants in Anglo-Norman England

The article by Isabel Alfonso 'The rhetoric of seigneurial legitimation in the *fueros*' of Leon (11th to 13th centuries) raises the question, relevant to all studies of social relationships in the medieval countryside, of how lords were able to appropriate from peasants significant amounts of labour, both their own and that of their draught stock, goods and money.[1] Sheer violence, while it can never be ruled out as a partial explanation, cannot stand as one by itself and Isabel Alfonso, like Marc Bloch before her, regards feudal social relations as having partly been successfully maintained by the legitimisation of landlord power in the minds of both those exploited and those exploiting them. In this penetrating article she rehearses the various forms this legitimisation took, finding in the *fueros* a wealth of peasant voices which will strike envy into the hearts of English medieval historians. She also draws attention to the importance to reinforcing such relations of the fact that lords and peasants had an 'ensemble of shared references'. Isabel Alfonso's work has, in this regard, much in common with the idea of the 'moral economy', which has had a vigorous historiographical afterlife since first introduced by Edward Thompson in 1977.[2] It has not been taken up so eagerly by medievalists but could well have a more creative and interpretative force than the 'extra-economic compulsion', propounded but never fully elucidated by Marxist historians, by means of which medieval lords secured the exploitation of the peasants on their estates.

My contribution is intended to complement that made by Jean Birrell (and we hope that Isabel will read both as a continuation of conversations the three of us have had in the past). Birrell's work, and her contribution to this volume, demonstrate that the *fueros* can very productively be related to English manorial custumals, 'the nearest equivalents of charters of franchises in medieval England'.[3] Two themes which figure particularly strongly in Isabel Alfonso's article will be considered here. One is the value that both lords and peasants placed on narratives which claim to describe, or refer to, the origins of the relationship between them. The second is the importance in these narratives of references to negotiations and settlements. Isabel

---

1 Alfonso, 'La rhétorique de légitimation seigneuriale'. I have used Birrell's translations for this volume throughout.
2 Thompson, 'The Moral Economy'.
3 Birrell, 'Manorial Custumals Reconsidered'.

Rosamund Faith is a renowned scholar who has published ground-breaking contributions to the social history of the middle ages and the conditions of medieval peasantry.

Alfonso points to the way in which the documents themselves expressly refer in their names, *'fueros buenos* or the *cartas de Libertad* [...]to an amelioration of the exchanges they purport to regulate, hence their name.' *Pactum* and similar words, she explains, reveal not only the conflicts that had occurred, but the 'involvement of the recipients in the definition of the content.' Birrell too has drawn attention to the stress in some of the preambles to English custumals on 'mutual bargaining and adjustment' between lords and their tenants.

From the period that I address, that from the mid-eleventh to the late twelfth centuries, there is no such wealth of evidence. While custumals of the type examined by Birrell survive from the 1180's, comparable earlier records are much scantier. Two pre-Conquest documents list peasants' obligations on estates owned by the church. Both include heavy labour rent and renders in kind. However, these were owed by the tied and semi-servile tenants called *geburas* on the 'inland' of each estate, the core area devoted to production for the lord's household, not from the often large numbers of other peasants on the rest of the estate, whose obligations are not listed.[4] About peasant obligations on lay estates, small estates, or outwith private landholdings altogether, we have virtually no information. A reference in the early eleventh century text known as the *Rectitudines singularum personarum* to the 'feasts' that the 'custom of the district' ruled should be provided at key points in the farming year, principally haymaking and harvest, suggest that 'boon works' were already in place.[5] At these the people of the locality, not just the estate, were accustomed to being 'requested' to work on the lord's fields: the 'feasts' are their reward.[6] Other than these, we have no reliable means of knowing from sources internal to any estate when, and by what means, the labour regimes recorded by the manorial custumals of the twelfth and thirteenth centuries had been instituted. In the eyes of near contemporaries, however, it was clear enough: labour services became fixed in the aftermath of the conquest of England by Duke William of Normandy in 1066.

We have the views of three members of the legal and administrative establishment on this topic: one wrote in the late twelfth century, one in the mid-thirteenth, one in the late thirteenth century. All considered that the imposition of labour rent on the peasantry was a direct result of the aftermath of the Conquest of 1066, and more particularly of the land settlement which distributed the estates of the English landowners to new Norman owners. In this narrative, which appears to have had currency outside establishment circles, the indigenous English at all levels of society, having been ousted in favour of incoming Normans, had had to strike hard bargains with their new lords. Richard Fitzneal, writing in the 1170's took considerable trouble to find out what he could about law and administration in Anglo-Saxon England, much of which had been absorbed into the law and administration of the new Norman regime. In 'the Dialogue of the Exchequer' he recounts what he had learned from

---

4 Survey of the manor of Tidenham, Gloucestershire: Robertson, ed., *Anglo-Saxon Charters*, CIX, 204–07; Deveson, 'The *ceorls* of Hurstbourne'.

5 Liebermann, ed., *Die Gesetze der Angelsachsen. Vol. 1*, pp. 444–53.

6 The etymology of 'boon' works, Latin *precaria*, parallels that of corvee, *co-rogata*, 'co-requested', services 'prayed for' from a group.

the 'natives', the English, about what happened shortly after the Conquest in the countryside. This is what he had been told:

all those who had fought the invaders and survived, and the heirs of those who had fallen, were deprived of all hope of recovering their former lands, farms and rents, for they counted it real gain to be allowed to live in subjection to their enemies. But over time those who had not fought [...] acquired the goodwill of their lords by devoted service and began to hold tenancies at the will of their lords, for themselves alone, however, without hope of succession [...]. But as time went on, when they were everywhere thrown out of their holdings because *odiosi* to their lords, and there was no-one to restore nor was there anyone who would restore what had been taken away [...] at last it was decreed that whatever they had been able to obtain from their lords by due renders and by a lawful agreement having taken place, should be granted to them in inviolable right. They might claim nothing in the name of succession to other property from the time of the conquered people [...] from then on they were obliged to purchase the goodwill of their lords by devoted service. Thus whoever of the conquered people possesses landed property [...] not what he considered due to him by right of succession but only what he has earned by due demands or by some agreement having taken place.[7]

Fitzneal's account could have been simply describing what he learned about the fate of landholders well above the level of the peasantry, were it not for the fact that negotiated settlements also figure in two thirteenth century accounts which specifically refer to them. The most esteemed legal text of the thirteenth century, the *de legibus* attributed to judge Bracton, described the post-Conquest settlement like this:

free men who held their holdings by free services or free customs [...]when they were thrown out by more powerful people, on returning afterwards took the same services up again to hold in villeinage, doing work for them which was servile but set and specified.[8]

The author of *Mirror of Justices*, an eccentric legal tract of the late thirteenth century may well have been drawing on Fitzneal when he wrote, using the language of feudal law, perhaps to emphasise the authority of such transactions:

contracts were made by our first conquerors when the counts were enfeoffed of counties, [...] the knights of knights of knights' fees, the villeins of villeinages [...] some received fees [...] to hold by villein custom to plough, lead loads, drive droves, weed, reap, mow stack and thresh [...] and sometimes without receiving food for this.[9]

---

7 *Dialogus de Scaccario*, ed. and trans. by Johnson, pp. 53–54.
8 Bracton, *Henry de Bracton de legibus*, vol. 2, f. 7 at 37.
9 Horne, *Mirror of Justices*.

Evidence that individual peasants contested the terms of settlements appears in a legal text broadly contemporary with Fitzneal's, the collection of laws known as the *Leis Willeme*. This purports to be 'the Laws of William (I, king of England) [...] the same which his cousin Edward held before him'.[10] It has recently been dated to the 1120's to 1130's. *Leis Willeme* is part of a wider claim in Anglo-Norman culture to derived legitimacy for the new regime from a supposed continuity from the pre-Conquest past. However, while reproducing, more or less accurately, much of the pre-Conquest law codes, the author uses several terms which were then current in Normandy to describe English conditions. One clause refers to fugitive tenants as *nativi*, 'born on' an estate, a term which would become legally equivalent to 'serf': 'Les naifs ki departe(n)t de la terre ne deivent cartre faire n'avurie quere que il ne facent leur dreit service que append a lour terre' ('Native-born who leave their land must not make a charter nor seek avowry that they do not owe the due service which belongs to their land'). Two distinct and opposed ways of thinking about law are at work here. To seek avowry was to appeal to the Old English method of personal commendation, by which an individual 'commended' himself to a powerful person who would be expected to vouch for him in court. Anglo-Norman lords, and Anglo-Norman law, preferred a once-and-for all settlement accepted by tenants as a group and without recourse to appeals to outsiders: 'Si hom volt derehdner covenant de terre ver sun seineur par ses pers de la tenure meismes qu'il apelerad a testimonie lui estuverad derehdner kar par estrange nel purrad pas derehdner' ('If a man wishes to deraign — i.e. vindicate in court — a *covenant*, agreement, about land against his lord, it is incumbent on him to deraign by his his peers of the same tenure, which are the proper deraignment for him, because by a foreigner he cannot deraign'). Nor was it acceptable that a *nativus* should 'have a charter made' in order to claim his exemption from service: the Latin translation of *Leis Willelme* gives the translation, perhaps deliberately tendentious, *ingenium*, 'device', for *carta*. The conditions established as a result of these 'negotiations' were not necessarily altogether new: what made them distinctive was that they were now fixed. These agreements were meant to bind lords and men just as surely as the Oath of Salisbury was meant to bind William's 'chief men' to him.

Whether these views accurately represented what had really happened after the Conquest is of course unknowable: English medieval historians have on the whole dismissed or ignored them. However, there is evidence that some agreements had indeed been made about peasant services and that these remained remarkably stable. The rule in *Leis Willelme* that a lord was unable to revoke a tenant holding which had been granted 'by agreement' as long as the services due from it were performed is not far from what we know from the evidence of manorial records. The commentators stress that these were private bargains made between tenants and their lords. A term used for a settlement or established arrangement in Anglo-Norman England was the French word *assise*. It was widely used for many kinds of legal rulings or agreed procedures but had a place in the vocabulary of the manor as well: it seems likely that

---

10 Liebermann, ed., *Die Gesetze der Angelsachsen. Vol. 1*, pp. 492–520.

rents that were agreed came to be called in manorial records *redditus assise*, 'rents of the assize', the rents of the 'settling' or 'establishment'. Two modern commentators have emphasised the particular nature of tenancies thought to have been established 'by agreement'. Nellie Neilson distinguished tenancies held 'by contract or special arrangement between the lord and the individual' from tenancies held 'by custom of the manor'. John Hatcher emphasised the stability of these tenures: as long as their services were performed and rents paid it was very rare for lords to revoke them. Birrell also notes that 'the fixing of labour services proved generally disadvantageous to the lords' in the thirteenth century.[11] Moreover, if the economic conditions of the time were right, tenancies settled by 'agreement' might convey economic advantage to peasants. Cash 'rents of the assize' remained stable even in periods of inflation when it would have benefited lords to have raised them, and it was possible, but extremely rare, for lords to evict a customary tenant. This illustrates an important insight of Isabel Alfonso: agreements, in setting what a lord could demand, at the same time prescribed limits to those demands.

It almost goes without saying that if it was indeed by agreement that English peasants had accepted the burden of labour rent, then their negotiation had delivered more to lords than to peasants, who now 'held' their land on less favourable terms. In England, as in Spain, it was to the profit of lords that narratives of the negotiation of 'pacts' and 'agreements' played an important part in the 'rhetoric of legitimation'. But that peasant tenants also set a great deal of store by the language of negotiation and agreement can tell us something about the moral economy of the period. In expressing a principle of reciprocity, even in this profoundly unequal society, it allowed some dignity to the oppressed.

---

11 Hatcher, 'English serfdom and villeinage'; Neilson, 'Customary rents'.

Bibliography

Dialogus de Scaccario. trans. and ed. by Charles Johnson, *Dialogus de Scaccario by Richard, son of Nigel*, (London: Nelson, 1950)

Alfonso, Isabel, 'La rhétorique de légitimation seigneuriale dans les fueros de León (XIe–XIIIe siècles)', in *Pour une anthropologie du prélèvement seigneurial dans les campagnes de l'Occident médiéval (XIe–XIVe siècles). Les mots, les temps, les lieux*, ed. by Monique Bourin and Pascual Martínez Sopena (Paris: Publications de la Sorbonne, 2007), pp. 229–52

Birrell, Jean, 'Manorial Custumals Reconsidered', *Past & Present*, 224 (2014), 3–37

Bracton, Henry de, *De Legibus et Consuetudinibus Angliae*, ed. by George E. Woodbine, trans. by Samuel E. Thorne, Vol. 4 (Cambridge, MA: Belknap Press of Harvard University Press, 1968–1977)

Deveson, Alison M., 'The *ceorls* of Hurstbourne revisited', *Proceedings of the Hampshire Field Club Archaeological Society*, 64 (2009), 105–15

Hatcher, John, 'English Serfdom and Villeinage: Towards a Reassessment', *Past & Present*, 90 (1981), 3–39

Horne, Andrew, *Mirror of Justices*, ed. by William J. Whittaker, Selden Society. 7 (London: Bernard Quaritch, 1895)

Liebermann, Felix, ed., *Die Gesetze der Angelsachsen*. Vol. 1 (Halle: Max Niemeyer, 1898)

Neilson, Nellie, 'Customary rents', in *Oxford Studies in Social and Legal History. Vol. 2*, ed. by Paul Vinogradoff (Oxford: Clarendon Press, 1910), pp. 6–219

Robertson, Agnes J., ed., *Anglo-Saxon Charters* (Cambridge: Cambridge University Press, 1956)

Thompson, Edward P., 'The Moral Economy of the English Crowd in the Eighteenth Century', *Past & Present*, 50 (1971), 76–136

ISABEL ALFONSO

Peasant Opposition to Labour Services in Castile and León

*Forms and Symbolic Significance**

The Historiographical Context

The invitation to contribute to a conference on the anthropology of seigneurial rent, in the section devoted to labour services and their symbolic value and economic importance, has given me an opportunity to revisit an article written nearly thirty years ago, and for this I am grateful to the organisers.[1] I shall begin with some observations on the historiographical and personal context in which I undertook this earlier work, as they nicely illustrate the historiographical changes that have taken place in the intervening years.

The article I wrote in the early 1970s was on the *sernas* in León and Castile, and it discussed socio-economic relations in the context of the medieval seigneurie. Amongst other things, to which I shall return, it followed the approach of those Marxist historians who hoped that their work, by revealing the conditions of subjection of the medieval peasantry, would influence practice. I remember my feeling of apprehension as I wrote of the appropriation of peasant surplus labour as surplus value, and at the same time my pride at having had the courage to overcome my fears, echoing the arguments of Marx as conveyed by Charles Parain, that is, basing myself on his authority.[2]

The fact that I am today concerned with the more symbolic aspects of these demands could be interpreted as a rejection of the materialist assumptions influencing me at the time of that earlier study. I see it, rather, as reflecting the well-known evolution of this mode of analysis, integrating into the social processes certain elements of reality which the structural approaches then in vogue had systematically excluded. This is what I shall try to show in the following pages.

I should first point out, however, that the Spanish historiographical context was also one of reaction against the 'myth' of peasant liberties as a characteristic element of our past, and that the study of the processes of the transition to feudalism was

---

* Original publication: Alfonso, Isabel, 'La contestation paysanne face aux exigences de travail seigneuriales en Castile et Léon: Les formes et leur signification symbolique', in *Pour une anthropologie du prélèvement seigneurial dans les campagnes médiévales (XIe–XIVe siècles): réalités et représentations paysannes. Colloque tenu à Medina del Campo du 31 mai au 3 juin 2000*, ed. by Monique Bourin and Pascual Martínez Sopena (Paris: Publications de la Sorbonne, 2004), pp. 291–320. Translated from the original French publication by Jean Birrell.

1 Alfonso, 'Las sernas'.

2 Alfonso, 'Las sernas', p. 154.

strongly influenced by the French model, in the desire to align our own history more closely with that of the rest of Europe.[3] In this context, the study of labour services encountered a first obstacle: the difficulty of describing as organic the relationship between the demesne and the peasant holdings in the lordships of the north of the peninsula, in accord with the so-called classic model. This difficulty was due in large part to the divergence between our documentation and that on which the model was based, as the north of the Iberian Peninsula lacks evidence of burdens of similar weight or significance; nor is their chronological evolution analogous.[4] We were still a long way from the Rome conference of 1978 and the break with this 'classic' model which then occurred, legitimising other approaches on which research could increasingly focus.[5] I believe, nevertheless, that what I said in that earlier article about the need for further research on the relationship between the various forms of peasant labour and the evolution of rents in general, though not articulated strongly enough or in a systematic manner, anticipated the soundness of this proposition, as this conference proves.

The first part of this article will consist of a brief synthesis of what is known about the most characteristic forms of labour in the lordships of the *meseta* of the north of the peninsula, beginning with the names of the works, the sources, the types of activity most frequently demanded, the grounds or criteria justifying their existence ... and ultimately the business of implementing these demands; I shall indicate in passing some aspects that deserve further comment in the light of the questionnaire so carefully compiled by Ghislain Brunel. In the second and longer part, I will discuss the forms and symbolic content of peasant resistance to these obligations.

---

3 One of the most explicit examples of this orientation, which was also the most influential for research on monastic estates in Spain, is García de Cortázar, *El dominio del monasterio de San Millán*, pp. 221, 230.

4 J. J. García Gonzalez, in his study of these charges on the estate of the monastery of Oña, likens the system of exploitation used to the Carolingian system. See García González, 'Rentas en trabajo'. See also the argument on p. 164, discussed by J. A. García de Cortázar, who believed that onerous though these levies may have been for the peasants from a psychological point of view, 'it does not seem that, from an economic perspective, and given their numbers, they could be significant enough to make them comparable to those of a classic domanial system' (García de Cortázar, *La sociedad rural*, p. 102). He was thus to some extent correcting the close similarity he had noted between this model and the mode of operation of the demesne of San Millán (García de Cortázar, *El dominio del monasterio de San Millán*, p. 223).

5 *Structures féodales et féodalisme*. The Spanish edition (Bonnassie and others, *Estructuras feudales*) has an introduction by Reyna Pastor which includes a useful summary of the proceedings of this conference.

Practical Aspects

The Vocabulary and the Sources. Questions Regarding the overall Burden and its Evolution

The vocabulary shows that compulsory labour is neither a simple historiographical object nor an artificial construction, but that it was presented and felt as such in the documentation of the period. Two factors in particular support this claim: on the one hand, the variety of terms used:[6] *sernas, operas, labores, obrerizas, ieras* (a word used only in the westernmost part of North Iberia), *servitium, serventia, facendera, ayuda*, and often the agricultural tasks demanded themselves; on the other, the uncertainty and ambiguity, the conflict between forced labour and voluntary aid, attested by the use of some words rather than others. I shall return to this aspect.

The available information is essentially ecclesiastical in origin and dates back no further than the tenth century, after which it becomes more abundant. It corresponds, therefore, to the period of the formation and expansion of the great lordships and of domination over huge sectors of the rural population.

For the early period, our main source consists of a large number of grants of immunity, which, if analysed systematically, would enable us to revisit the problem of the significance, weight and nature of labour services, and then of the individuals compelled to perform these works before they passed into the hands of lords. Were they servile works or communitarian collective levies? Was there a homogenisation of dependency, as some historians have claimed? Here, research bringing together archaeology, micro-toponymy, topography and landscape studies might provide valuable information.[7]

For the period between the eleventh and thirteenth centuries, during which these demands appear to become more widespread, though not necessarily heavier, the sources which are most informative — if this adjective can properly be used of medieval sources — are, as is well known, the *fueros*. The fact that these texts are not wholly normative allows us to get a clearer picture of these charges in practice, of their repercussions for peasant families and of the nature of resistance to them. However, a number of troubling questions remain: where and in which parts of a lordship did these obligations predominate? What are the reasons for the differences we observe? How did the weight of these demands change? I noted in my earlier article some of the problems arising from the discontinuity of the evidence for the same lordship.[8]

---

6 For a fully documented discussion of the meaning of these words, see Alfonso, 'Las sernas', pp. 159–68. On the use of *serna* in the charters from Rioja Alta as a term identifying a space, prior to its usage as an agricultural levy, and on its relevance for the organisation of space, see García de Cortázar, 'La serna', pp. 115–28. This discussion was expanded in Botella Pombo, *La serna*.

7 Botella's argument on the existence of communal spaces, cultivated severally by the whole collectivity, is unconvincing. She fails to show that the *serna* was uniquely or essentially a communal space. She takes for granted that there existed cohesive homogeneous communities with shared customs serving the interests of the group as a whole — something which has been strongly contested — and that it was upon these groups that the lords would impose their control (Botella Pombo, *La serna*, pp. 61–62).

8 Alfonso, 'Las sernas', pp. 197–98.

We have only qualitative information to indicate the focus of the protests, and how commutation came about.

The information in the *fueros* can be supplemented by a closer examination of other sources from the late Middle Ages to aid our understanding of what appears to be a general retreat from these charges during this period, a process that is little understood. The reasons for this phenomenon deserve to be re-examined. There is certainly ample evidence of reductions, commutations and even abolition, but there is considerable evidence of continuity, too, on the same or even harsher terms. Here, it seems essential to study sources dating from the late Middle Ages, as I indicated in my earlier study, and as has subsequently been emphasised by J. J. García González for the estate of Oña.[9] The information in that great enquiry, the *Libro Becerro de las Behetrías*, shows that in more than 150 out of a total of just over 2000 localities the inhabitants were required, in the mid fourteenth century, to perform labour services two or three days a year and also frequently once or twice a month. Other studies reveal that not all obligations were recorded.[10] Furthermore, the documentation for the large grants at farm, which are supposed to have ended these forms of work, more often refers to transfers or changes in beneficiary of labour services than to their abolition. The case of the *cillero* of Santa Maria del Valle granted by the bishop of Zamora in 1275 is a case in point.[11] Nor should we forget the disputes and lawsuits between the great landowners (which often but not always took the form of ecclesiastical protests against the *encomenderos*, or lay advocates), which show very clearly the advantages, even practicality, of maintaining access to peasant labour in this form, and the ferocity with which they opposed each other.[12]

It is clearly necessary to re-examine the question by comparing the different ways in which peasant labour was used in the different contexts and circumstances, not only economic; as Francesco Panero has shown, the direct link between the increase in money in circulation and the decline of labour services is by no means clear.[13]

---

9 García González, 'Rentas en trabajo', p. 176.

10 Alfonso, 'Las sernas', p. 203; Álvarez Borge, 'Dependencia campesina', esp. pp. 22–24; Martínez Díez, ed., *Libro Becerro de las Behetrías*. There is a further piece of information that is usually neglected but which needs to be considered as well (I thank J. Escalona for bringing this to my attention). L. Serrano included it in the introduction to Cardeña's *Becerro Gótico*. It consists of a few additional pages, in a fourteenth-century hand, which he partly reproduces in n. 3, pp. xii–xiv. It is a list of the rights that Cardeña enjoyed over a series of towns, probably composed as a result of an enquiry. The answers are of great interest for the subject of this study. They indicate the labour obligations that the inhabitants of these towns owed to the monastery. These obligations do not appear among the ones listed in the *Libro Becerro* for these towns. See Serrano, *Becerro Gótico de Cardeña*. I discuss this in the article cited in n. 18.

11 'And also, that in your time you should not lift the *sernas* nor make any concessions to men from outside that place, so that whatever they consist of they are lent to you' ('Otrosi, que non quitedes elas siernas nin fagades gracia dellas en uestro tiempo a los omnes de fuera del lugar, quales quier que sean que vollas hayan de fazer') (Martín, 'El cillero de Santa María del Valle', p. 77).

12 Alfonso, 'Las sernas', p. 205.

13 Panero, 'Le corvées'.

Timing, Tasks Demanded, and Regulation[14]

Among the most common demands, the obligation to work one or two days a month was one of those that persisted longest; also very common was three or four days' work a year, and other variants ranging from two to eight days a month. Weekly work is much less frequently documented, and the evidence for it seems to be limited to an early period and to concern only a clearly servile population. The principal activities for which works were demanded were as follows:

- cereal cultivation: a fairly standard obligation to perform all the tasks associated with growing this crop. In the region concerned by the *fueros* of Zamora, there were six: ploughing, hoeing, sowing, reaping, threshing and garnering. When only four works a year were demanded, it was specified that they must be performed during the months when most labour was needed, that is, between June and September

- viticulture: a less common but fairly widespread obligation. More research is needed to establish if these works were demanded additionally, if they were specific, more or less numerous, etc.

- woods: works relating to picking fruit or gathering firewood rather than specific tasks. Such works are rarely mentioned, but may have been more widespread than is suggested by the available sources

- other activities more dependent on local circumstances, such as the mowing and bringing in of hay mentioned in certain *fueros*

- carriage often appears as a *serna* associated with agricultural tasks, cereal cultivation in particular, though also viticulture, whether to the threshing floor or the lord's barn. It might also involve the transport of wood or salt. Other carrying services called *mandaderia* or *carreris* are documented due to the short distances to be covered, hence the small amount of time devoted to them by the lord's tenants

- building works and the maintenance of castles and fortresses are less well documented but survived for a long time. The word *castellaria* was not always used to indicate these charges

- other types of levy of a military, judicial or administrative nature. I believe these, like the previous category, deserve special treatment, in association with the others. I cannot, however, expand on this here.

There is evidence to show that there were sometimes limits to the arbitrary power of the lord, probably due to the strong opposition of the peasants. Among obligations by which the lord himself was bound, we may quote that to issue the summons or public announcement in advance, with adequate notice and on the customary dates,

---

14 For detailed evidence in support of this last point, see Alfonso, 'Las sernas', pp. 177–95.

under pain of loss of performance of the service; the impossibility of demanding all the works simultaneously if this had not been agreed; the obligation to feed the peasants as promised.

The obligations of those liable to labour services are regulated in great detail in some *fueros*. They include responding punctually to the summons, under pain of punishment; waiting as a group to be told what tasks to perform, that is, making themselves available to the *sayón*, the officer of justice, or to the administrator of the monastery; coming with the necessary animals and tools; working the full period specified — in this context, the works from sunrise to sunset recorded in some *fueros* were not necessarily disadvantageous, because they limited the duration of the service, as compared with other *fueros* which appear to leave this to the discretion of the lord. The works had to be done properly, for if not the peasants would be punished — especially if they did not turn up to do the work demanded.

Justifications for the Imposition.
The Unevenness of the Demands and the
Question of Exemptions and Substitutions[15]

It was fairly common for these works to be demanded collectively from persons called *vasallos, homines, rústicos, collazos*, etc., depending on the lord who had granted the *fueros*. But the obligation was often also linked to the land of the lord, the tenure granted (*prestamo*), even though the unit of assessment was the family holding. This brings us to the much debated question of whether these charges were *banal* or *foncier* in nature,[16] that is, whether the work was owed to the lord by reason of the dependence of the persons themselves or of the land they held, or both. Posed in these terms, that is, from the point of view of the nature of the link, hence of subjection and domination, the problem is difficult to resolve, because it is not always possible to establish such a clear distinction. In practice, very different degrees of dependency with regard to a single lord or several lords existed among the inhabitants of one same community, and each individual might experience differing degrees of subjection.

The various work obligations burdening a community or group of tenants, as they are documented in the *fueros*, seem essentially to respond to the desire to profit from the economic resources of the peasant families. They varied according to the existence or not of a *prestamo*, to the number of draught animals — principally oxen and donkeys — owned,[17] or to their physical strength if they had nothing else — like the *braceros* ('labourers') or workers —; in any case, they were obliged to make their

---

15 For further evidence on this issue see Alfonso, 'Las sernas', pp. 195–97.

16 The lack of a Spanish word to describe this type of agrarian rent is a major problem for Spanish historiography, particularly given that *dominical* has seigneurial connotations. The debate, often muddled, testifies to the huge number of attempts made by historians to understand the criteria justifying the different modes of appropriation of the peasant surplus (P. Martínez Sopena, I. Alfonso, J. L. Martín, C. Estepa, I. Álvarez Borge ...).

17 A horse enabled its owner to perform services that were not necessarily agricultural in nature.

PEASANT OPPOSITION TO LABOUR SERVICES IN CASTILE AND LEÓN 419

agricultural equipment (ploughs, hoes, etc.) available. By contrast, it was very rare for the number of full or part days' work to differ from one to the other.

The differences, whether in the case of obligations or exemptions, had a social, legal and political dimension, too: in different circumstances and on different estates, the free men were privileged compared with the serfs, the men of *behetría* compared with the *solariegos*, the clergy compared with the laity, and those owning a horse compared with the *peones*, as also were those who agreed to supervise and control the work of the others and the newly married and widowed, whose obligations were reduced.

If, in parallel with these aspects, to which I shall return, we analyse the information about the type of substitutions envisaged and the nature of the seigneurial reward for these works, essentially in the form of food and drink, we will be better able to understand both who actually performed these labour services and the evolution, which was far from linear, of these forms of forced labour towards other forms of labour called free. We may also, crucially, see how the recourse to the different types of labour, and their diversity and variability over time, were fundamental to the forms of seigneurial exploitation.[18]

Control and Penalties

The question of control, as we have noted, was a major preoccupation of the lords. It occasionally surfaces in the *fueros*, usually in the form of clauses stipulating sanctions in case of non- or poor performance. I dealt with this subject at some length in the article already referred to.[19] Here I shall only summarise the most notable aspects from the point of view of the peasants, so as to establish not only how they accepted or resisted the supervisory practices that were imposed upon them, but also how they became involved in them.

I have no evidence regarding the circumstances or frequency with which the peasants were required to hand over a sheep or a lamb, or its cash equivalent, for failure to perform the tasks demanded; nor do I know if they were held answerable for the negligence or ill will with which they had performed them. But the fact that the charters frequently specify penalties, and demand that these tasks be performed 'bonam laborem et sine fraude' ('with good work and without fraud'), or *libenter* ('with goodwill'), gives a clear indication of the attitude of the peasants to these demands and of their readiness to make maximum use of the 'weapons of the weak'.[20]

As is well known, among the weapons employed by the powerful to impose their authority, one of the most effective was to involve the victims themselves in policing

---

18 For further discussion on this issue, as well as on the unequal distribution of work within the peasant household, see 'Renta en trabajo y diferenciación campesina', to be published in *Historia Agraria* [Editors' note, based on I. Alfonso, pers. comm.: The article was never published as such, though the material collected and the analysis developed in its preparation would inform 'Exploring difference within rural communities in the northern Iberian Peninsula', in chapter 7 of this volume].

19 Alfonso, 'Las sernas', pp. 194–95.

20 I take the expression from Scott, *Weapons of the Weak*. Ill will is regarded as a form of negative reciprocity in Scott, *Domination*.

420   ISABEL ALFONSO

the performance of labour services. The most common way of doing this, it seems, in addition to the control exercised by the seigneurial officers, was to exempt from labour services those who took on supervision, making them appear privileged in the eyes of their peers.

I should like here to refer to a text that is exceptionally informative in this regard in order to develop the points I made in my earlier discussion of the *sernas* [1].[21] It is a 'carta absolutionis, concessionis et stabilitatis' granted by the prior and priory of the monastery of Vega to a community in which some sixty families lived exempt from the *redittu* ('rent') charged on transfers of land and vines granted in *prestamo*, plus some further dispensations. They were, however, obliged to pay tithes and dues at Martinmas, the Feast of St John and Christmas, and to perform *sernas* every fortnight 'libenti animo et voluntate bona' ('with good spirit and good will'). To ensure that this was the case, the lords were to choose two *boni homines* from the community who would swear an oath of loyalty and supervise those liable to labour services as they worked on the priory's lands. It is clear that this was not a commitment lightly entered into, as the charter envisages the possibility of refusal, with a fine of one *maravedí* in such cases; two other men were then to be appointed, and they would be excused from these works. The priors even envisaged the possibility of refusal to supervise by the men who had sworn an oath, of rebellion on their part (*rebelles*) or refusal to be *suprasernarios*. In this case, the punishment laid down was a sheep, without exemption from performance of the *sernas*.

It is true that these clauses can be interpreted, as I did myself, as evidence of a certain rebellious spirit on the part of the peasants, and of relative group solidarity, as it was only under pressure from above that they agreed to supervise the others. But this last clause reveals that their refusal was due also to the pressure applied by their peers, a pressure demonstrated within the community by the dishonour falling on anyone who agreed to collaborate with the lord — another weapon of the weak. The fact that this action was punished much more severely than the others, and that the punishment contained both material and symbolic elements shows the importance and the efficacy of practices of this type within the community.[22] It was here that the most effective measures to challenge and condemn seigneurial domination were found,[23] though also the circumstances conducive to its acceptance.

The Forms and Nature of Resistance. Symbolic Aspects

I shall now comment in some detail on several texts which document the various formulas employed by the peasantry to challenge demands for labour services and escape them entirely or at least get them reduced. I hope in this way to throw light on what this forced labour signified for the peasants themselves, on their perception

---

21   The numbers in square brackets refer to the documents in the appendix.

22   'And if anyone contradicts or slanders the aforementioned oath, he should render us a ram, however unwillingly, and abandon the work in our service' ('Et si aliquis contradixerit vel maledixerit istis supradictis iuratis, pectet unum carnerium nobis sine amore et exeat de nostro labore').

23   For the importance of these practices in peasant resistance, see Wickham, 'Gossip'.

of the hierarchies and inequalities, on the parameters of justice and the criteria used in argument and on the material consequences of a struggle which often seems more concerned with the symbolic than the purely economic aspects; lastly, I shall discuss how this situation came about. I shall in this way stay true to my aim to study labour services from the standpoint of the peasants, services which cannot in any case be dissociated from the context in which they appeared.

Both in the demand for these works and in the refusal to perform them, there was a strong symbolic content, both being closely linked to the subjection and the power which the peasants sought to reject and the lords to impose. Subjection made domination easier. This was said as late as 1315 by the abbot of the monastery of San Pedro de Montes (León) to justify the demand for these charges, referring to a particular reading of a privilege of Alfonso XI:

> the neighbours live in the estate of the monastery and are actually its dependants, even though they have a *fuero*, and thus, and in order to evidence their subjection at all times, it was decreed ever since they entered this wasteland that because they were dependants, they should serve five days each.[24]

Awareness of this fact and of its symbolic significance was clearly shared. This is revealed by struggles to assert and win public recognition of a legal status exempt from charges and a superior position associated with certain distinctions, or by actions aimed at obtaining privileged conditions. Let us look at a few examples.

The Defence of Status: *ingenuidad* and *behetría*

A well-known document from the monastery of San Millán de la Cogolla (La Rioja), dating from the beginning of the eleventh century [2], tells how a peasant woman from the village of Terrero, believing herself superior to her peers, refused to work in the fields and vines of the monastery or perform the customary servile labour along with the others:

> a peasant woman called Maior, from *villa Terrero*, regarded herself as superior to her neighbours, and did not want to go with them to work in the fields and vines of San Millán, and failed to perform the customary servile work with her neighbours.[25]

The bishop, in his pastoral capacity, met the count, Iñigo López, lord of Biscay, and other nobles to consider the abbot's complaint and rule as to the status of this peasant woman. On learning of such an *error* ('error'), the bishop told the count:

---

24 'los vecinos viven de la hacienda del propio monasterio y en realidad son criados de ese convento, aunque forenses, y así, para que constase su sujeción en todo tiempo de estos moradores, dispúsose desde los principios que entraron en este yermo que, como tales criados, sirviesen cada uno cinco días' (quoted by Puyol y Alonso, 'La Abadía de San Pedro de Montes', p. 143–44).

25 'mulier rustica nomine Maior, in villa Terrero videns se sublimiorem suis vicinis, nolevat ire cum illis in officio operis agrorum et vinearum S. Emiliani, imo comtemnebat opus servile et usuale facere cum suis vicinis'.

I gave orders to ascertain who this person was and have her brought before me. And despite her wish, this woman was unable to have herself exempted from these servitudes because it was proved that she was indeed of servile condition.[26]

At a further meeting with the count and the other nobles the bishop ordered the woman to perform the work with her fellows or be released from it on the same conditions. Thus, at the end of a legal process, this woman and her descendants were subjected to monastic domination *per secula* ('forever').

This document has been interpreted as evidence of a general slide into servitude on the part of a previously free population, as a consequence of seigneurial expansion and pressure.[27] However, the content and nature of this 'servitude', like that of the *ingenuidad* ('freedom'), are subjects that are open to debate, and on which further research is needed, as already noted. We do not have enough information and it is dangerous to generalise.

Let us remember for now the way in which the distinction between serf and *ingenuo* ('free') is in this case reduced to the obligation to labour on the lands and vines of the monastery, or exemption — total or partial — from it, and that the reason cited for demanding the works was servile ancestry.

It seems to me useful here to refer to another case from the same San Millán archive [3], which shows how the monastery, a few years later, submitted a similar complaint to King Alfonso VI. This concerned two men of the monastic town of Cihuri who, in exchange for their houses and land, had refused to perform any service or obey the abbot, claiming that they had been born *ingenuos* and exempt from all service.[28]

The king instructed his bailiffs to conduct an investigation, and the rebels, as they were described, were unable to prove the validity of their claims with the aid of witnesses or charters.[29] The king decided, therefore, for the safety of his soul, that they could keep what they had only if they agreed to perform services like the others; if not, they must return to the monastery the houses and lands they occupied, together with the movable assets, and leave.

We see in this case, in contrast to the one discussed previously, how personal legal status mattered less than possession of the land, that is, ownership of it by the monastery. This affair has given rise to a long and rather sterile debate about the nature of the demands for labour I discuss here: were the rights in question jurisdictional or linked to ownership of land? Or, what amounts to the same thing, were they obligations of a personal or a 'landed' nature? We may suppose that the same lord, in this case the abbot of San Millán de la Cogolla, enjoyed powers of a different type over the population of his estates, or that it was the status of the subject population that was different. In neither case do we know how much work they were required

---

26 'se escusare de servitute [...] quia probamus illam de tribu servili fuise [*sic*] genitam'.

27 García de Cortázar, *El dominio del monasterio de San Millán*, pp. 191, 229; Alfonso, 'Las sernas', p. 176. For a more recent assessment of this issue see Loring García, 'La expansión de la servidumbre'.

28 'for they say: we should be free and exempt from service' ('quia dicunt illi genuos vel absolutos ab servitio debemus esse').

29 'these rebels could not even present witnesses, nor charters to prove that they should be enfranchised' ('Illi quoque rebellanti nec testes, nec cartula potuerunt donare ut essent solutos').

to perform, hence the difference between the demands made on a serf and those on the tenant of a monastic land. In both cases, however, *ingenuidad* ('freedom') was linked to the non-performance of services, or at least of certain services. The *opera* ('works') owed by the peasant woman of Terrero involved the cultivation of arable land and vines, while the *servitium* ('services') demanded from the two brothers of Cihuri was not specified and limited to a vague obligation to obey (*obedire*).

We might add other considerations, which cannot be pursued here, regarding the limitations of a seigneurial justice forced to resort to royal justice to clarify the status and obligations of its subjects, although it was on the basis of local evidence that these were decided. Admittedly, the abbot had got his jurisdiction over the town and its inhabitants recognised, but it does not appear that his domination was accepted. Let us remember, however, the vocabulary both of the challenge — refusing to obey and to serve, claiming to be *ingenuos* and *solutos* ('enfranchised') — and of the repression — transforming disobedience into rebellion, asserting servitude.

It is rare to find information about the arguments used by peasants to challenge the demand for forced labour, which is what makes these documents so valuable, because, even though we may question the accuracy of the transcription of the arguments, the way in which they are presented in the seigneurial registers remains significant.

In the most westerly part of the kingdom of León, at the beginning of the twelfth century [4], the abbess of the monastery of San Dictino of Astorga crossed swords with another proud peasant: he had behaved, we are told, almost like a man of *behetría*, rejecting the domination and the obligations associated with his condition and claiming the land he possessed, it seems, from the fact of his marriage to a woman of the village (the text is unclear on this point):

> he raised his head like a serpent and claimed that his status was almost that of a man of *behetría*, and refused to be recognised [as of servile status] and to serve for it or with it, when alone or with others, service had always been rendered with that holding on behalf of the aforementioned monastery.[30]

The dispute was taken before the count don Martin, a royal judge, so he could deliver an oral judgement:

> they came in the presence of Count Don Martín, who was the judge appointed and chosen by King Alfonso with all the authority of his royalty, so that they should receive from him an oral judgement.[31]

The 'rectum et verum' ('right and truthful') judgement rendered by the count defined the circumstances in which the peasant must serve the monastery — 'so that he may dwell in that *hereditas* and serve with it on behalf of St Dictino'[32] – and the abbess,

---

30 'levavat caput velut serpens et faciebat se quasi benefactoria de foris et noleuat se cognoscere nec servire pro ea nec cum ea quando quidem cum unis quando eusdem cum aliis semper contenta se agebat cum ipsa hereditate ad partem huius monasterii iam supradicti'.

31 'venerunt inde in presentia ante comes dominus Martinus vt acciperent ab eius ore iudicium, qui erat iudez constitutus et electus a domno rege Adefonsso in toto imperio regni sui'.

32 'vt residet se in ipsa hereditate et servisse cum ea Sancto Dictino'.

424   ISABEL ALFONSO

and indicated that, if he could not fulfil his obligations, he must abandon the land in the condition in which he had received it, naming securities, and go wherever he thought fit with the grace of God. The account continues with the admission of the peasant that he had lied and a pledge to do as he was told, in words which left no doubt about the terms of his subjection:

> so that I shall hold that *hereditas* as a grant from you, work it and inhabit it and occupy it and serve with it on your behalf and acknowledge myself as one of your men, and to be under your command for all the days of my life. And if it should so occur that I no longer wish to dwell there I shall go wherever I want and leave your *hereditas* and your house as you will find it and wherever I go, if no substitute for me.[33]

Once again, therefore, we have loss of land in case of refusal of services, and even with sureties who would be held accountable. The language of the *placitum* ('plea') legitimised the sentence: the judgement is presented as fair and incontrovertible, the judge as benevolent; the peasant, by contrast, is made to appear pretentious, vain and untruthful. The final ritual of humiliation, one of the most powerful symbolic signs of subjection, took place in the presence of the bishop of Astorga and all the powerful men of the palace. We see here a royal public order that supported and sustained seigneurial domination.

This peasant who presumptuously claimed to be 'almost' of *behetría* must have shared a common sense of distinction with the peasants of the neighbouring lordships such as those of Valcabado who, two centuries later, would also claim to be men of *bienfetría* by comparison with their *solariegos* neighbours obliged to work on the lands of the bishop of Astorga with their animals and their bodies.[34] The *fuero* granted by the bishop in 1279 reveals the different treatment of each of these groups, and the way in which forced labour was here too the sign of a greater dependence with regard to episcopal authority and domination.[35] Evidence also survives of the action taken by the men of certain towns of Galicia to defend their status of *behetría* against the demands of the bishop of Lugo, and to distinguish themselves from the *villanos de fazendaria*, claiming their ties of upbringing with the local *caballeros* ('knights') as proof of their condition as free men, vassals of the master who had chosen them.[36]

These documents raise many questions: which aspects supported the peasants' demands? On what did they base their claims? *Ingenuidad* as opposed to servitude? *Behetría* as opposed to other forms of dependence? Was this a process of seigneuri-

---

33 'vt teneam ipsam hereditatem ex vestro dato, laborem eam et habitem et populem eam et seruia vobis cum ea et cognoscam vestrum hominum esse vel vestrum clamorem tenere omnibus diebus vitae meae et si mihi ocasio venerit quod animus meus non det mihi locum ibi ad auitandum vbi voluero ire vadam et relinquam vestram hereditatem et domum qualis eam inveneritis et vbi fuero si nullam supotitam per me'.

34 FL88 (1279).

35 For this *fuero* and the conflicts that flared up in the lordships of *behetría*, see Alfonso, 'Conflictos en las behetrías'.

36 Hinojosa78 (1226). For the ties created by the practices of *crianza* ('fostering'), see Alfonso, 'Conflictos en las behetrías'.

PEASANT OPPOSITION TO LABOUR SERVICES IN CASTILE AND LEÓN

alisation that turned *ingenuos* into serfs and the men of *behetría* into *solariegos*? Was it general? Were the *sernas* the essential sign of this submission?

From Forced Labour to Voluntary Aid. The War of Words

Many communities endeavoured to obtain a reduction in their labour services, or at least their conversion into voluntary levies, in default of total exemption, with very variable success. Let us look at a few examples and the context in which they took place.

Two texts from the archives of San Pedro de Arlanza, both from the second half of the eleventh century, illustrate this phenomenon. The first is an agreement between the abbots of the monasteries of Arlanza and San Quirce, in the valley of Canales, the interpretation of which is problematic.[37] It regulated the use of the common pastures by the two monasteries and all the villages in the valley and it explicitly distinguished payment of tithes, which would be obligatory, from labour services, which were to be performed voluntarily: 'they shall not perform any service unwillingly'.[38]

The second text is a *carta libertatis* of the ancient *fueros* granted by the abbot of Arlanza to the communities of Villaespasa y Rucepos.[39] Here, the ambiguity between the voluntary and obligatory nature is highly significant: in parallel with a first broad exemption — 'that you shall never have [...] to perform those *sernas*'[40] — which seems to discharge the inhabitants of the communities from the *mañería* and the *sernas* while maintaining the *anubda* or customary weekly surveillance, it later requires them to perform the customary six days' labour on the *sernas* of the monastery wherever they were needed, in addition to the voluntary contributions:

> And every year you shall all have as a custom to render six days of work in our *sernas* or wherever we shall require it, besides those that you may willingly do for us. And all of you, from the lower to the highest, shall not be exempt from this labour, but rather you shall all come together to perform it.[41]

It goes on to record the obligation to carry bread and wine to the monastery once a year, and salt of Añana: 'that you shall bring us bread and wine yearly whence we have it, and bring us half of the salt of Añana yearly forever'.[42] Many texts present voluntary consent as a privilege, a sign of free status — hence the highly symbolic value of this term. In the immunity granted by Alfonso VI, in 1103, to the inhabitants

---

37 SPArlanza61 (1062). I thank Julio Escalona for his comments on this document.
38 'sine voluntas nullum servicium me fecisent'.
39 FB4 (1089).
40 'ut non habeatis [...] ne omni tempore illas sernas laborare'.
41 'Et ut omnes in omni anno abeatis per usum VI. dies laborandi in nostras sernas vel ubi necessitas nobis fuerit, preter illum quod facietis nobis libenter. Et a minimo usque ad maximum nullus excusetur ab isto labore, set omnes in unum ad illum venite'.
42 'ut afferatis nobis unam vicem in anno panem aut uinum unde abuerimus, et in omni tempore abducatis nobis illud sal de Annana ad medietatem unam vicem in anno'.

of Foncebadón and those who lived on these territories, we read: 'no service due to any earthly authority shall be enforced [in that place, which] shall always remain *ingenuus* and free in perpetuity'.[43] In the *fuero* granted by Alfonso VIII, a century later, to the community of Pampliega we find, among other significant concessions, exemption from demands for service against their will, except for three days a year *ad laborandum* ('of work') — two days ploughing and one day pruning — on which the lord must provide them with bread, wine and meat: 'you shall not make any service against your will'.[44] It seems to me that we observe here the same dialectic between volition and imposition as in the grant by the abbot of Arlanza discussed above.

This notion of 'voluntary performance' is very explicitly articulated in the 'carta de vestros foros bonos' ('charter of your good *fueros*') granted to the 'concejo de maiores et minores' ('council of the higher and the lower') of Venialbo who had populated the monastic domain of Santo Tome of Zamora.[45] The first clause, which is separate from the rest, concerns the voluntary nature of the performance of the *sernas*: 'First of all, that no one shall perform a *serna* except whoever wills to do so for the wellbeing of his soul and on the basis of his rank' (an exemption which extended to the *fonsadera, mañería* and *nuncio*).[46] Carrying services, too, had the same voluntary character: 'And by this *fuero* they shall not lend their animals for any carrying service except whoever wills to do so on the basis of his rank and for the love of God'.[47]

These peasants, without even claiming to be of *behetría*, obtained conditions which put them on the same level as them, because they won recognition of the legal capacity to serve as they deemed fit and retain the land they had paid for, as long, of course, as they respected the *fuero*: 'And any man who lives in Venialvo shall serve outside whomever he wills and pay for his *hereditas* in Venialvo'.[48]

The goodness of the *fueros* lay essentially in the voluntary nature of the charges and the dependence, which in some sense expunged their servile nature, as well as the ability, in this case, to dispose of their property in order to be free to seek the protector they wished to serve. There is considerable evidence to show that the peasant resistance and struggles[49] which gave rise to the most favourable *fueros*[50] crystallised round these conceptions of the power of decision and free disposal of one's own labour and lands.

The inhabitants of the village of San Pedro, in the same region of León, rejected the right of the abbot of Sahagún to demand, in the *fuero*, five *sernas*, that is, impose

---

43 'nullo terreni imperii seruitio praematur sed ingenuus semper et liber permaneat euo perenni' (CatAstorga507, 1103).

44 'nec faciatis illi ullum servicium absque uoluntate uestra' (AlfonsoVIII-836, 1209).

45 FZ5 (1126).

46 'In primis, quod non faciat serna nisi qui voluerit pro anima sua et pro suo gradu'.

47 'Et non dent suas bestias in nulla carrera per foro nisi qui voluerit per suo gradu et pro amore Dei'.

48 'Et homo qui havitaverit in Venialvo serviat foras cui voluerit et habeat in Venialvo sua hereditate pagata'.

49 I discuss this question in more detail in Alfonso, 'Conflictos en las behetrías', p. 24.

50 For the *fueros buenos* ('good *fueros*') and peasant resistance, see Pastor, *Resistencias y luchas campesinas*; Martínez Sopena, *Tierra de Campos occidental*. I discuss the peasant struggle for the application of legal parameters in Alfonso, 'Campesinado y derecho' [Editors' note: For an English translation, see chapter 9 of this volume].

PEASANT OPPOSITION TO LABOUR SERVICES IN CASTILE AND LEÓN   427

them; the inhabitants claimed to do them voluntarily, meaning they could not be punished if they did not perform them. We learn this from the lawsuit concerning the basis of this obligation, which was taken before the royal courts: whether they were obliged to perform them *de debito* ('as an obligation'), *per forum*, as claimed by the abbot, or *spontanei* ('voluntarily'), as claimed by the peasants themselves [5]:

> They said that they were not obliged to perform them, and that whenever they had performed them, they had done so spontaneously, not on the basis of the *fuero*. [The abbot] said that they had performed the *sernas* as an obligation, and that whenever they did not want to perform them they were distrained until they did.[51]

The enquiry ordered by the king agreed with the abbot and the decision went in his favour: it was proved that the *sernas* had been owed since time immemorial.

There is no reference in this case to the status of the persons, or to that of the lands, but solely to the regulatory *fuero* and to custom, which demonstrates clearly their domination and dependence on the lord. I have discussed elsewhere the process of subjecting these people, and their sustained rebellion, drawing attention to the battle that was also waged at the level of language, given the practical repercussions that this or that representation of reality could have.[52] To win public recognition that the *sernas* were voluntary, not obligatory, was not simply a question of dignity, it also affected the nature of the obligation, because failure to perform what was owed might be punished, whereas failure to perform a voluntary service would not. In this case, as in many others, the peasants lost when faced with an all-powerful lord. But it is a clear illustration of the battle they waged to impose their own conception of these works and of how they perceived and claimed to perform them and also, lastly, of the nature of the relationship they wished to sustain with their masters and their lords.

Other texts from the monastery of Oña, in the eastern region of Castile, which are highly informative with regard to the circumstances and levels at which this symbolic 'war of words' was waged,[53] reveal some very favourable practical results. In several places for which the thirteenth-century *fueros* survive, the abbey of Oña had to accept not only a reduction in the number of days' work owed by the tenants each year, but also that these works were performed as an aid, not as an obligation. For example, in the *fuero* granted in 1266 to their men of Villela, Gornaz and Rebolledillo [6], the monastic lords declared:

> we lift and cancel [...] the *sernas* that you have performed until now on our behalf every fortnight, and during August every eight days, so that from this day neither we nor those who may come after us shall ever demand them from you, nor shall you ever perform any *serna* by request. If this is not breached, then you shall help us two days every year, one to sow and one to thresh. Whoever has a

---

51 'Dicebant quod non debebant eas facere, et quotiens eas fecerant, spontanei fecerant, non per forum [the abbot] dicebat quod fecerant sernas illas ex debito, et quotiens sernas illas sibi nollebant facere, pignorabantur quousque facerent'.

52 Alfonso, 'Campesinado y derecho', pp. 26–27.

53 For this crucial element in the most everyday peasant resistance, see Scott, *Weapons of the Weak*, p. 240.

yoke of oxen shall help us with it and with his body, and whoever has an ox shall help with it and with his body [...] and that you shall harvest our vines in Villilla every year, and carry the grapes to the seigneurial centre of St Olalla.[54]

The lords naturally saw the lifting of the *sernas* as a favour, and demanded significant payments in cash and kind in exchange. This favour was also extended to the obligation to carry sods to rebuild the dike, which was no longer imposed: 'and the sods that you used to carry to the dike, that you shall never carry them as an obligation'.[55] The other carrying services, of cereals to the lord's palace, were not included in the two voluntary days and were very precisely defined and regulated in this negotiated charter.

A few years earlier, in 1238, the abbot of Oña had also negotiated with his dependents of La Nuez de Río do Urbel the reduction of the obligatory annual twenty-four *sernas* in exchange for their aid two days a year and payments similar to those owed by the tenants of the other places.[56] A convention of the same type between the abbot and his men of Montenegro also survives, in which the abbot exchanged the twenty-four *sernas* for four days' aid, on the same terms.[57] We may reasonably assume, therefore, that the two days a year which the men of the monastery of Cornudilla must provide under the name of *adiutorium* ('aid'), as indicated in the charter granted in 1187 in order to improve their condition, were similar in nature and the result of similar pressure to that exercised by the tenants of the three villages previously discussed.[58]

This all shows the many attempts made by the peasants to substitute the term aid for that of service owed. The documents clearly reflect the sharp distinction between the labour provided as an obligation and the service rendered as a favour, even though this last word seems only to apply to the conduct of powerful men when demonstrating generosity and mercy, virtues which made them good lords and so justified the services and rents demanded.[59] The peasants were not taken in by this way of presenting things, this rhetoric of lordly knowledge and generosity, this reciprocity serving to justify the demand for services. These texts show, rather, how they were able to turn it to their own advantage in order to limit the arbitrary power of the lord and improve their conditions of dependency, and how they actively intervened in the formulation of the representations of reality which favoured them.

It would also be possible to analyse from the same perspective the vocabulary of the *buenos fueros* and the associated rhetoric of the *bene facere* ('doing good'), and

---

54 'absoluemus e dessamos [...] las sernas ke fata aquí nos fiziestes en quinze quinze dias, et en al agosto en ocho en ocho dias, que nunqua uos las demandemos deste dia en adelante, ni nos ni los uernan despues de nos, ni nos fagades nunqua serna por premia. Si non fuera sacado esto, que nos ayudades dos dias en cada anno, uno a sembrar et otro a trallar. El que ouiere yugo de bues que ayude con el et con so cuerpo, et el quie ouiere un bue que ayude con el e con so cuerpo [...] et que nos uendimiendes cad'anno las nuestras uinnas de Villilla, et que nos las acarredes las uvas al palacio de Sant Olalla'.

55 'et los çespedes que soliedes leuar a la presa, que non leuedes nunqua por premia'.

56 SSOña-A481 (1238).

57 SSOña-A576 (1268).

58 FB38 (1187).

59 The *Fuero General de Navarra* (FNG, Ch. xvii) draws a distinction between the food that the lords 'were obliged to give' (*son tenidos de dar*) to their *villanos* when they worked for them and that which they 'gave out of their own will' (*les dá por gracia*).

PEASANT OPPOSITION TO LABOUR SERVICES IN CASTILE AND LEÓN   429

extend such research to later sources. We might encounter situations like that of the agreement made in the mid fifteenth century between the inhabitants of Villavicencio and the admiral of Castile, don Fadrique, whose subjects they were, according to a ritual which shows very clearly the value for them of forcing their lord to recognise the reciprocity of the relationship between them. They managed in this way to procure a pledge, amongst other things:

> that the neighbours should be exempted from bringing wood from the mountain, or from any other place, and from taking it from the houses for him or for any other; and from sending a neighbour as a messenger, and from demanding *maravedís*, and from lending oxen, animals or carts to bring or carry wood, wine, grapes, rams, sheep, chickens, piglets, sacks, blankets, *novenos* or any other things, as well as from forcing any men or woman to build walls, dig or make any other labours at home or outside; unless anyone wants to do so of his own accord or for money.[60]

Individual Forms of Negotiation

As we have seen, not all the resistance and action against the *sernas* was collective. The opposite method was also found, and we cannot ignore the evidence of other forms and particular strategies (familial or group) aimed at gaining exemption from these obligations or getting them reduced, rather than contesting them, resisting them or refusing to perform them.

Some cases from the archive of the great monastery of Sahagún in León are here very revealing. They throw further light on the way in which these burdens were perceived by those who bore them, and on the value and significance they possessed in their eyes, both outside the community and within the internal system of distinctions and hierarchies whose foundations were never strictly economic, but also social, political and even symbolic.

A well-known document from this monastic archive [7] records the donation to the monastery by Diego Patrez, at the end of the eleventh century, of a piece of land in Villa Paradiso, with the whole of the adjacent holding, as the donor had received it himself from someone he calls 'domno meo' ('my lord'). What is striking about this donation is that the donor claims that he is in this way not only saving his soul but also freeing himself from all human service[61] and also that his children, to whom he reserves use of this holding, will enjoy certain additional advantages as compared with

---

60 'que fuesen escusados los vecinos de traer leña del monte, ni de otra parte, ni de lo tomar por las casas para él ni para otro; ni embiar vecino en mensagería, ni demandar maravedís, nin tomar buey, ni bestias, ni carros para traer o llevar leña, ni vino, ni vbas, ni carneros, ni ovejas, ni pollos, ni lechones, ni costales, ni mantas, ni noveno, ni otras cosas, ni tomar hombre ni muger para tapiar, cavar, ni hacer otras lauores en el lugar, ni fuera del; salvo si alguno lo quisiere por su voluntad o por dinero' (FV, pp. 72–73). For the context in which this agreement was reached, see the brief but useful article Martínez Sopena, 'El señorío de Villavicencio'.

61 'so that I shall be free of any human service for all my life' ('ut ego sim liber in omni uita mea ab omni servicio humano').

430 ISABEL ALFONSO

the other subjects of the monastery; these consisted of a lesser degree of servitude, only twelve days' service a year, together with the possibility of serving as *kauallarii* ('mounted men') if they owned a horse.

The terminology expressing these motivations, which constitute the conditions of the donation, is of considerable interest. Here, no distinction is made between serfs and *ingenuos* or between *solariegos* and men of *behetría*, as in the cases discussed above. The distinction consisted of a lesser degree of subjection, a less strict form of dependence for the descendants — 'my sons shall not be subjugated into service as strictly as others are'[62] — or a different form of service if they owned a horse — 'that if they have horses they shall serve as *kauallarii*'.[63]

These were significant material distinctions with strong symbolic connotations, which would probably serve to accentuate the internal differences within the community, marking prerogatives relating to honour and particular services, as was the case at Villarmildo, a community to which the Countess Estefanía granted a *fuero* in 1129:

> And any man who has a horse shall stand as knight and be honoured, and shall not perform any *serna* nor have a lodger on my behalf, but shall go on command as far as *Uilla Alua* and on the other side as far as the bank of the Duero.[64]

To serve like a mounted man, and to enjoy such a prerogative, is clearly associated in these documents with exemption from obligatory agricultural works. And this is clearly the significance of the — more laconic — exemptions granted to those who owned a horse in many other *fueros*, which were probably the result of a similar process.

The information provided by the texts just quoted helps us to interpret other, less explicit documents, in which the parties seem to be following a similar course of action. I will quote another, later, case from the same Sahagún archive. In 1100,[65] two brothers, Rodrigo and Pedro Vellitiz, returned their part of the land of Mathmutes to the monastery; they retained use of it as long as they lived, and their son and grandson after them, without any labour services of any sort, a privilege their descendants would also enjoy: 'we shall serve San Facundo without *serna* and *facendera* ("labour work")'. If our sons do not want to serve they shall leave that *solar* if they do not want to have *serna* and *facendera* imposed upon them'.[66] The last paragraph, however, is rather confused and it is difficult to interpret. As transcribed, it poses several problems: were the grantors reserving for their children the possibility of abandoning the land if someone claimed to impose on them the *serna* and the *facendera*, or must they only do this if they refused to perform them? The logic of the text makes the former more likely, because it may be observed that he who donates his own means of production

---

62 'filii mei non subiugati tam stricti sint in servicio sicut sunt ceteri'.

63 'quod sic habuerint kauallos serviant sicut kauallarii'.

64 'Et homo qui abuerit kauallo stet pro cauallero et sedat honorato, et non faciat mihi serna ne abeat posadero, set uadat in mandato usque ad Uilla Alua et in alia parte usque ad Riba de Dorio' (Fernández Catón, *Catálogo del archivo histórico diocesano*, pp. 18–19). See the document in the dossier presented by Carlos Reglero.

65 SFPSahagun1059 (1100).

66 'serviamus a S. Facundo sine serna et facendera. Si uero filii nostri noluerint servire exeant de ipso solare si serna et facendera noluerint imponere eis'.

PEASANT OPPOSITION TO LABOUR SERVICES IN CASTILE AND LEÓN   431

can negotiate certain conditions for use of the property, whereas he who receives probably could not. The clauses anathematising whoever might claim to deprive them of their *foro* show that they aimed to protect the conditions agreed at this point.

The negotiation conducted by another person, probably belonging to the same stratum of notables still not clearly differentiated from the peasant *serneros*,[67] is of a similar type and date.[68] This seems to be indicated by the simple fact of it being necessary to spell out that the service to be rendered in return for use of the property given to the monastery should be 'sine serna et facendera'. This condition of service was also inherited by their children, as well as the freedom to go elsewhere, that is, to decide if they wished to continue to depend on the monastery or not.

We may observe the same strategies and a similar desire to transmit comparable or even better conditions of use to their descendants in another donation of a land. Here, the donor expresses her desire to remain on the land for the rest of her days without being forced to perform labour services, because, she says, she had built her *hereditas* there, and the desire that her children should be able to live there, too, on the same conditions. The formulation here is different from that in the previous case, as she explains that they will perform the *sernas* as an aid and on request, not as an obligation.

> by this act I shall have it during my life and I shall remain exempt [from the obligations towards] the abbot of St Facundo in that *solar*, which was built in my *hereditas*; and those of my sons who may inhabit that *solar* shall always be exempt [from the obligations towards] St Facundo and shall render labour services to the abbot as an aid and on request; and if my sons or my grandsons do not remain tied to San Facundo they shall leave that *solar* to San Facundo; but if my sons or my grandsons want to remain tied to San Facundo, no abbot shall deprive them of that *solar*.[69]

There are differences between these texts, admittedly, but they seem to demonstrate the aspects I wish to emphasise: the diversity of the ties that were formed between the lords and the rural population, and the diversity also of the possibilities of renegotiating these ties; and the symbolic value of these charges in this period, as a sign of dependence associated with a servile connotation or even worse.[70]

---

67 I use the word *serneros* because this is how those who performed the sernas are designated in some documents, and because it is clear that, in the period under discussion, it was an important element in social distinction.

68 SFPSahagun1062 (1100).

69 'per tale actio ut teneam eum in uita mea et sedeam excusata de abbate Santi Facundi in illo solare, quia fuit in mea hereditate factum; et filios meos qui in illo solare morauerint sint semper excusati de Santo Facundo et dent in opera abbatis adiutorium ad rogo; et si filios meos non fuerint de Santo Facundo, uel neptos meos, dimmittant illo solare a Santo Facundo; que si ipsi mei filii uel nepti uoluerint esse de Santo Facundo, nullus abbas eis solare illo tollat' (SFPSahagun1169, 1109). Of the same type is a grant dated to 1245 (SFPSahagun1698).

70 The servile nature of forced labour, also perceived by the lords, is very clear in the *fuero* granted to the clergy of several towns of the monastery of Oña, who were exempted from 'serna, that is, from

Some Further Questions

Further questions are raised regarding the different ways of resisting or negotiating in order to obtain more favourable conditions of tenure or subjection, which should be related to those which led to substitutions and commutations; and regarding, also, the meanings attached to all of these. In which periods, circumstances and contexts did collective or more individual forms predominate — or coexist? How did those involved differ from one to the other? The answers to these questions would help to establish if, for example, there was a link between collective resistance and the power of the group of notables who were its leaders, or if, on the contrary, it was because these groups were weaker that they were forced to act jointly and transform their particular interests into common interests; or if the variants were so numerous and so complex that it is in reality impossible to establish any correlation at all, however slight. At all events, the answers to these questions would help us to a clearer understanding of the motives and the reasons for peasant actions and what impelled them to act collectively in pursuit of their ends.

---

performing servile labour as the rest of our *collazos*' ('serna id est ad laborem seruilem faciendum, sicut ceteri collaci nostri vadunt') (SSOña-A412, 1221).

Appendix

1. December 1217.

Fuero *granted by the monastery of Vega to this community, exempting it from certain rents and regulating others [fragment].*

Published: González Díez, Emiliano, *El régimen foral vallisoletano. Una perspectiva de análisis organizativo del territorio* (Valladolid: Diputación Provincial de Valladolid, 1986), doc. 17.

Per presents scriptum sit notum omnibus tam presentibus quam futuris, quod ego Armanda priorissa monaster[ii de Vega, et Petrus prior, de assensu totius nostri capituli et de mandato abba]tisse Fontisbraue facimus cartam absolutionis, concessionis et stabilitatis concilio Monasterii de [Vega et uniuersi generi eorum ibidem commoranti, pereniter valituram.

[1] Ab]soluimus itaque eos de cetero a redditu illo, quam debebant nobis annuatim de terris, et de uineis, quas tenebant [in prestimonium: et ad petitionem et volumptatem supradicti] concilii damus et concedimus ipsas terras et uineas LX hominibus tenendum absque redditu, ut habeant eas et [dividant et pignorent inter se absque ulla uenditione.

[4] Hoc] totum facimus, ut omnes de pacto tam LX quam alii exeant ad forum et libenti animo et uoluntate bon[a faciant nobis sernam ad decem et quinque dies ad uoluntatem nostram infra hebdoma]dam, sicuti in sua propia hereditate.

[5] Et unusquisque persoluat unum solidum in festo Sancti Martini de unoquoque fu[mo [...] quod a festo Sancti Iohannis usque ad Natiuitatem.

[6] Et quando] leuauerint suum panem de sua area, uocitent nostrum decimarium; et si noluerit uenire, faciant testes, et dimit[tant nostram decimam in area, et similiter de lino et uino: et hoc sit fir]mum, et aliter non fiat.

[7] Nos uero per prouidentiam et consilium duorum bonorum hominum, quos elegerimus annua[tim de suo concilio, qui sub iuramento sue fidei debent esse fideles,] in labore nostro estare super sernarios supradictos. Debemus illi dare conductum, uidelicet panem [de plena pessa et uinum et conductum sicuti nostro conventui; et ad] unum rogum, unam carnem, scilicet, inter quatuor quarta partem unius arietis, uel inter duos unam pesam ac u[accine carnis.

[8] Et qui non fuerit ad sernam pectet unum carnerium].

[9] Et sit duo homines, quos nos helegerimus in concilio noluerint iurare, unusquisque pectet unum morabetinum et nos ponamus [alios; et isti duo sint excusati de serna. Si forte sint rebelles et no]luerint stare supra sernarios, unusquisque pectet unum carnerium, et de illo die non sint excosati.

[10] Et si nos uo[luerimus departire nostram sernam, unus uadat ad unum diem et alius ua]dat ad alium diem.

[11] Et si aliquis contradixerit uel maledixerit istis supradictis iuratis, pectet unum carnerium [nobis sine amore et exeat de nostro labore.

[17] Preterea statui[mus et concedimus ut uidue que non habent in apreciamento usque ad V morabetinos, non faciant] neque aliam fazenderam, preter tres rogos in anno.

2. 1040

The bishop of Pamplona, in assembly with the count Iñigo López and other nobles, examines the case of a peasant woman who refused to perform servile works in the fields and vines of San Millán with her neighbours. Her servile origin having been proved by an enquiry, the woman and her descendants were doomed to perform these works in future.

Published: Muñoz y Romero, Tomás, *Colección de fueros municipales y cartas pueblas de los Reinos de Castilla, León, Corona de Aragón y Navarra*, Vol. 1 (Madrid: Imp. de José María Alonso, 1847), pp. 157–58.

Copy: *Tumbo de San Millán*, cap. 45, fol. 34.[71]

Tempore Garcia Regis, filii Sancio, me Sancio episcopo, pastorali cura monasterium S. Emiliani regente, contigit quod quedam mulier rustica nomine Maior, in villa Terrero videns se sublimiorem suis vicinis, nolevat ire cum illis in officio operis agrorum et vinearum S. Emiliani, imo comtemnebat opus servile et usuale facere cum suis vicinis. Ego autem cum talem audirem errorem cepi inquirire quenam esset que tale quod fecere auderet, statimque cum ante conspectum meum presentari feci. Cum autem voluit se escusare de servitute non potuit, quia probavimus illam ex tribu servili fuise genitam. Et habito concilio com comite Eneco Lupiz et aliis nobilibus, mantum equalem talem unusquisque vicinorum suorum prestare debet. Itaque illa cum omni genere suo est subposita sut hoc pecto per secula cuncta, amen.

Facta carta sub era M. LXXVIII.II Nonas Februarii, feria VI. Reinante Reye Garcia in Pampilona. Sancius Eps. conf. Eneco Lupiz Vizcayensis Comes conf. Toto concilio de Terrero testis.

3. 1077

The Abbot of San Millán submits to King Alfonso VI a complaint against two men of the town of Cihurí which belonged to him, who proclaimed themselves ingenuos and quit of all service. As they were unable to prove this, the king ordered them to submit to the same obligations as their neighbours if they wished to retain their houses, their land and their belongings, in default of which they would lose everything and be obliged to leave [fragment].

---

71 For the problems of dating and the different versions of this text, see Loring García, 'La expansión de la servidumbre', pp. 45–46.

PEASANT OPPOSITION TO LABOUR SERVICES IN CASTILE AND LEÓN

Published: Serrano, Luciano, *Cartulario de San Millán de la Cogolla* (Madrid: Centro de Estudios Históricos, 1930), doc. 232.

Copy: Becerro, fol. 67ᵛ.

Sub Christi nomine redemptoris nostri. Ego quidem Alfonsus, gratia Dei rex, facio cartam ab honorem et atrio S. Emiliani, et tibi presenti Blasio cum sociis tuis monachis. Audivi ex vobis querimoniam de Gonsalbo Sarraciniz et Bellito Sarraciniz, qui sunt in villa vestra Zufior, et vos dicitis quia volunt se exaltare et nolent ullum servitium nec per casas nec per hereditatem ad S. Emiliani obedire, et quia dicunt illi genuos vel absolutos ab omni servitio debemus esse. Unde iussi merinos meos probare hec predicto. Illi quoque rebellanti nec testes nec cartula potuerunt donare ut essent solutos, solummodo equaliter cum vicinis. Unde iubeo pro mee anime remedium ut si volunt cum vicinis equaliter servire, habeant suum, et si nolunt, tam kasas quam hereditatem et totum mobile dimittant in S. Emiliani, et illi vadant ubique volunt. Si quis autem ex regibus [...]

4. 1108

Dispute between the abbess of the monastery of San Dictino in León and a peasant of the town of Morales, who, claiming to be of behetría, *refused to serve in exchange for the land of the monastery he cultivated. The trial having been held before the count don Martin, the peasant had to recognise his vanity and his dishonesty in order to be able to remain on the lands and serve as man of San Dictino.*

Published: Cavero Domínguez, Gregoria, and Encarnación Martín López, *Colección documental de la catedral de Astorga. Vol. 1 (646–1126)* (León: Centro de Estudios e Investigación San Isidoro, 1999), doc. 544.

Copy: BN, MS 9194, fol. 103.

In era centessima quator decima sexta prius peracta millessima. Horta fuit intentio inter donna Gontina abbatissa de Santi Dictini cum uno rustico quodam pernominato Ioanne Alvariz super hereditate vna de Sancti Dictini quae erat in Valle Sancti Laurentii super Petra Alua de Susana in loco praedicto villa quos nuncupant Morales ipse iam supra prefactus rusticus Ioanne duxerat inde vxorem de supra vocitata villa et levavat caput velut serpens et faciebat se quasi benefactoria de foris et noleuat se cognoscere nec seruire pro ea nec cum ea quando quidem cum vnis quando eusdem cum aliis semper contenta se agebat cum ipsa hereditate ad partem huius monasterii iam supradicti Paulo post tempore contingit pro ista note misserunt eum sub fideiussore et venerunt inde in presentia ante comes dominus Martinus vt acciperent ab eius ore iudicium qui erat iudez constitutus et electus a domno rege Adefonsso in toto imperio regni sui ita fecerunt et iudicauit eos iam supra factus comes rectum iuditium et verum et remeauit unsquisque ad propria cum iudicio. Post ham definicionem non potuit iam sepe dicto rustico complere facere iudicium quam eu benignus comes imperauerat et cognouit se mentiossus esse et vanitatem et falsitatem contra Deum et eius monasterii conmemorato et seniori suae theneri obiurgium et rogare caepit et spopondere seruicium et humilitatem et fidelitatem teneri omnibus hominibus huius ecclesiae habitantibus non solum abbatissae sed minimo seruo seruorum eius et in presentia dominus et catholicus Pelagius astoricens episcopus et omnes magnati palatii sui vt residet se in ipsa hereditate et servisse cum ea Santo Dictino et abbatisse eius et si pre impediente diabolo occassio eius euenisset quod ibi hauitare non potuisset dimitere domum et haereditatem post partem ecclesiae qualis eam inuenerint et pergere vbi voluerit cum Domini gratia et hoc cum fide iussoribus, ob inde ego supra dictus Ioannes Alvariz vobis abbatisse Gontina et ecclesiae vestrae sancti Dictini seu abbatissis qui post vos fuerit commorantibus, facio factum side placidum legabile firmissimum super me de ipsa intentio quod vobis cum Deo valenti commissi vt teneam ipsam hereditatem ex vestro dato laborem eam et habitem et populem eam et seruia vobis cum ea et cognoscam vestrum hominum esse vel vestrum clamorem tenere omnibus diebus vitae meae et si mihi ocasio venerit quod animus meus non det mihi locum ibi ad auitandum vbi voluero ire vadam et reliquam vestram hereditatem et domum qualis eam inveneritis et vbi fuero si nullam supotitam per me vel per aliquos homine sede ipsa hereditate vel de fratribus eius fecero quomodo pariam vobis ego vel isti mei fideiussores praenominati Petro Petriz et Pelagio Dominguiz ducentos solidos de argento et insuper duplem ipsam hereditatem vobis qui voci ecclesiae vestrae pulsavit et haveatis cum euo perenni et saecula cuncta amen. Regnante rege Adefonso in Toleto et Legione cum Beatrice regina. Pelagius astoricens episcopus.

Nos fideiussores Petro Petriz et Pelagio Dominguiz hunc placidum nostrae manus roboramus.

Ego Iohannes Albaroz hunc placidum quo fieri elegi manu mea roboroui. Petro testis. Martino testis. Iohannes testis.

Pelagius diaconus notarius.

5. 1206, November 25, Palencia

Complaint submitted to King Alfonso VIII by the Abbot of Sahagún against the men of San Pedro de Dueñas who had refused to perform the five sernas which the abbot claimed were owed him according to the fuero, and claimed they had only ever performed them voluntarily. The enquiry conducted by the king proved that the abbot's complaint was justified.

Published: Fernández Flórez, José A., *Colección diplomática del monasterio de Sahagún (857–1300). Vol. V (1200–1300)* (León: Centro de Estudios e Investigación San Isidoro, 1994), doc. 1569.

Copy: Escalona, *Historia de Sahagún*, App. 3, 575, escr. CCXVI.

Notum sit omnibus, tam presentibus quam futuris, quod conuencio fuit inter domnum Pelagium, abbatem Sancti Facundi, et homines Santi Petri de las Donnas super illis quinque sernas quas idem abbas Santi Facundi demandabat eis quod debebant eas facere. Homines, uero, Sancti Petri dicebant quod non debebant eas facere, et quotiens eas fecerant, spontanei fecerant, non per forum. Abbas, quidem, dicebat quod fecerant sernas illas ex debito, et quotiens sernas illas sibi nollebant facere, pignorabantur quousque facerent. Super hoc, autem, ego A[defonsus], Dei

PEASANT OPPOSITION TO LABOUR SERVICES IN CASTILE AND LEÓN

gratia rex Castelle et Toleti, feci fieri inquisitionem a domno Guterrio Ermeildi, priore Hospitalis, et inueni per ueram inquisitionem quod abbas Santi Facundi super hoc iustitiam exigebat, et homines Santi Petri de las Donnas annuatim sernas illas sibi facere tenebantur, et faciebant eas tempore imperatoris et regis Sancii et diebus meis; etc. cum nollebant eas facere, pignorabantur pro illis.

Facta carta apud Palentium, rege exprimente, era M CC XLIIII^a, VII^a kalendas decembris.

6. 1266, April

The abbot of the monastery of Oña in Burgos regulates the payment of the sernas *by his tenants of the villages of Villella, Gornaz and Rebolledillo.*

Published: del Álamo, Juan, *Colección diplomática de San Salvador de Oña: (822–1284)*. 2 vols (Madrid: CSIC, 1950), doc. 573.

Original: AHN, Clero Regular, car. 288, n. 10.

Manifiesta cosa sea a todos los ommes que esta carta uiren et oyeren, que nos don Pero Perez por la gracia de Dios abbad de Onna et nos conuiento des mismo logar, absoluemos e dexamos a uos los nuestros vasallos de Villella et de Gornaz et de Rebollediello, a los que sodes hi agora et a los que seran hy siempre moradores, las sernas que fasta aquí nos fiziestes en quinze quinze dias, et en al agosto en ocho en ocho dias, que nunqua uos las demandemos deste dia en adelante, ni nos ni los uernan despues de nos, ni nos fagades nunqua serna por premia. Si non fuera sacado esto, que nos ayudades dos dias en cada anno, uno a sembrar et otro a trallar. El que ouiere yugo de bues que ayude con el et con so cuerpo, et el qui ouiere un bue que ayude con el et con so cuerpo et el uaron que no ouiere bue que nos ayude con so cuerpo a segar o a trillar, et el qui ouiere yugo de bestias o bestia et con ello labrare en su lauor, que nos ayude a uos con ello, et que nos fagades la lauor bien et lealmientre. Et el qui touiere la nuestra casa, de uos cada un dia destos, a cad'uno de uos de los que alli labraren, dues libras de pan de las del cuende don Sancho, la una de trigo et la otra de communa, et entre tres una quarta de vino segunt lo soledes auer, et un conducho, et que nos uendimiendes cad'anno las nuestras uinnas de Villilla, et que nos las acarredes las vuas al palacio de Sant Olalla. Et el qui touiere la nuestra casa de Villilla, que uos del una libra de pan, la media de trigo et la media de communa, a cada uno de uos, que hy labrare, et uino si lo hy ouiere, et si non ouiere hy uino, que uos den çebollas o queso. Por tal pleyt uos fazemos esta mercet et este quitamiento de las sernas que nos dedes cad'anno, el qui ouiere yugo de bues una tercia de dineros, et el qui ouiere un bue dos sueldos, et el uaron qui no ouiere bue ninguno, que uos de XV dineros, la meatat destos dineros que los paguedes por Paschua de Resurrectio, et la otra meatat por Sant Miguell, et quitamos uos el sayon que soliedes dar del sayongado, que nunqual dedes, et quitamos uos la paia, et el feno et los façes del ordio que nos soliedes dar, que numqua los dedes et los çespedes que soliedes leuar a la presa, que los non leuedes nunqua por premia. Et los de Villilla que seades tenidos de acarrear el pan del era al nuestro palacio de Sant Olalla, et los de Gornaz, que seades tenidos de acarrear el pan de Val de Call, et lo del tercio de

Sant Julian de Gornaz al palacio de Sant Olalla de Villilla, et los de Rebollediello que seades tenidos de acarrear el pan de Sant Maria de Canaleia et de Sant Andres et de San Yuannes de Rebollediello al palacio de Sant Olalla de Villilla. Et el dia que acarrearen el pan qui touiere la nuestra casa de Villilla, que de a diez bestias una fanega de ceuada, et a los ommes que las traxieren, sennas libras de pan, assi como a los de la uendimia. Et el anno que uos mandarnos acarreare el pan del era et de los otras logares que son de suso nombrados a Sant Olalla de Villilla, aquel anno que non seades tenidos de aduzir la requa del pan a Onna, el otro anno que uos seades tenidos de aduzir uuestra requa a Onna. Et porque est pleyt sea firme, nos don Pero Perez por la gracia de Dios abbat de Onna et nos conuiento des mismo logar, esta carta que mandamosla fazer, confirmamosla mandamus sellar con nuestros sellos. Fecha la carta, en el mes de abril, en el era de mill et trrezientos et quatro annos. El rey don Alffonso, con su mugier donna Yolant, regnando en Castiella, en León, en Toledo, en Gallizia, en Seuilia, en Cordoua, en Murcia, en Jahen, et en el Algarue. Don P[edro] Guzman merino mayor del regno.

7. 1093, July 25

Donation of land at Villa Paradiso made by Diego Patrez to the monastery of Sahagún. He makes this gift not only to assure the safety of his soul, but also to free himself from all human service, and so that his children should not be subject to this obligation like the other tenants and might serve as mounted men if they owned a horse.

Published: Herrero de la Fuente, Marta, *Colección diplomática del monasterio de Sahagún (857-1300). Vol. III (1073-1109)* (León: Centro de Estudios e Investigación San Isidoro, 1988), doc. 909.

Copy: Beccerro Gótico de Sahagún, fol. 38ᵛ, escr. XXIIII.

In Dei nomine. Ego Diaco Patrez facio uobis sanctis martiribus Facundo atque Primitiuo et tibi domno Diaco abbati, una cum congregacione monachorum Domnis Santis, de uno solare quod habeo in uilla qui dicitur Paradiso, cum omnia sua hereditate que continet: in terris, in uineis, in pratis et in omnibus suis prestacionibus. Facio cartulam donacionis, spontanea mea uoluntate, pro remedio anime mee, quemadmodum et michi facta est cartula donacionis de ipso solare a domno meo Tello Gutterriz. Et non solum pro remedio anime mee, uerum etiam et ut ego sim liber in omni uita mea ab omni servicio humano; et teneam eum in uita mea, tam ego quam et filii mei et filii filiorum meorum, sub iure et dominio Sancti Facundi. Et si filii mei uel nepti noluerint sub iure esse Sant Facundi, careant ipsum solarem et ipsam hereditatem que ad eum pertinet; et filii mei non subiugati tam stricti sint in servicio sicut sunt ceteri, sed ut tantummodo ponant XII dies in anno ad servicium domni abbatis; quod si habuerint kauallos seruiant sicut kauallarii.

Facta cartula donationis VIIIº kalendas augustas, era I CXXXIᵃ. Ego Diacus Petrez in hanc cartulam quam fieri iussi manu mea (*signum*) roboraui. Regnante Adefonso rege in Legione et in Toleto. Monio Godesteiz conf. Petro Uellitiz conf. Iohanne Citiz confirmat. Pro testes: Dominico, Citi, Belliti, testes. Martinus notuit (*signum*).

Bibliography

Structures féodales et féodalisme dans l'Occident méditerranéen, X^e–XIIIe siècles: bilan et perspectives de recherches. Colloque international organisé par le Centre National de la Recherche Scientifique et l'École française de Rome (Rome, 10–13 octobre 1978) (Rome: École française de Rome, 1980)

Alfonso, Isabel, 'Las sernas en León y Castilla. Contribución al estudio de la relaciones socio-económicas en el marco del señorío medieval', *Moneda y Crédito*, 129 (1974), 153–210

Alfonso, Isabel, 'Campesinado y derecho: la vía legal de su lucha (Castilla y León, siglos X–XIII)', *Noticiario de Historia Agraria*, 13 (1997), 15–31

Alfonso, Isabel, 'Conflictos en las behetrías', in *Los señoríos de behetría*, ed. by Carlos Estepa Díez and Cristina Jular Pérez-Alfaro (Madrid: CSIC, 2001), pp. 227–60

Álvarez Borge, Ignacio, 'Dependencia campesina, propiedad de los señores y señoríos en Castilla la Vieja en la Plena Edad Media', *Historia Agraria*, 19 (1999), 9–41

Bonnassie, Pierre, and others, *Estructuras feudales y feudalismo en el mundo mediterráneo* (Barcelona: Crítica, 1984)

Botella Pombo, Esperanza, *La serna: ocupación, organización y explotación del espacio en la Edad Media (800–1250)* (Santander: Tantin, 1988)

Fernández Catón, José María, *Catálogo del archivo histórico diocesano de León*, Vol. 1 (León: Centro de Estudios e Investigación San Isidoro, 1978)

García de Cortázar, José Ángel, *El dominio del monasterio de San Millán de la Cogolla (siglos X al XIII). Introducción a la historia rural de la Castilla altomedieval* (Salamanca: Universidad de Salamanca, 1969)

García de Cortázar, José Ángel, 'La serna, una etapa del proceso de ocupación y explotación del espacio', *En la España Medieval*, 1 (1980), 115–28

García de Cortázar, José Ángel, *La sociedad rural en la España Medieval* (Madrid: Siglo XXI, 1988)

García González, Juan José, 'Rentas en trabajo en San Salvador de Oña. Las sernas (1011–1550)', *Cuadernos burgaleses de Historia Medieval*, 1 (1984), 123–94

González Díez, Emiliano, *El régimen foral vallisoletano. Una perspectiva de análisis organizativo del territorio* (Valladolid: Diputación Provincial de Valladolid, 1986)

Loring García, María Isabel, 'La expansión de la servidumbre en el reino de Navarra a mediados del siglo XI: el ejemplo de Terrero', *En la España Medieval*, 12 (1989), 45–61

Martín, José Luis, 'El cillero de Santa María del Valle: una empresa señorial zamorana del siglo XIII', *Studia Zamorensia, Segunda etapa*, 2 (1981), 67–83

Martínez Díez, Gonzalo, ed., *Libro Becerro de las Behetrías: estudio y texto crítico*, 3 vols (León: Centro de Estudios y Investigación San Isidoro, 1981)

Martínez Sopena, Pascual, *La Tierra de Campos occidental: poblamiento, poder y comunidad del siglo X al XIII* (Valladolid: Institución Cultural Simancas, 1985)

Martínez Sopena, Pascual, 'El señorío de Villavicencio: una perspectiva sobra las relaciones entre abadengo y behetría', in *Homenaje a la profesora Cármen Orcástegui Gros* (Zaragoza: Universidad de Zaragoza, 1999), pp. 1015–25

Panero, Francesco, 'Le corvées nelle campagne dell'Italia settentrionale: prestazioni d'opera "personali", "reali" e "pubbliche" (secoli X–XIV)', in *Pour une anthropologie du prélèvement seigneurial dans les campagnes médiévales (XIe–XIVe siècles). Vol. 1: Réalitiés et représentations paysannes*, ed. by Monique Bourin and Pascual Martínez Sopena (Paris: Publications de la Sorbonne, 2004), pp. 365–80

Pastor, Reyna, *Resistencias y luchas campesinas en la época del crecimiento y consolidación de la formación feudal: Castilla y León, siglos X–XIII* (Madrid: Siglo XXI, 1980)

Puyol y Alonso, Julio, 'La Abadía de San Pedro de Montes', *Boletín de la Real Academia de la Historia*, 86 (1925), 116–76

Scott, James C., *Weapons of the Weak : Everyday Forms of Peasant Resistance* (New Haven: Yale University Press, 1985)

Scott, James C., *Domination and the Arts of Resistance: Hidden Transcripts* (New Haven: Yale University Press, 1990)

Serrano, Luciano, *Fuentes para la historia de Castilla. T. III: Becerro Gótico de Cardeña* (Valladolid: Cuesta, 1910)

Utrilla, Juan F., ed., *El Fuero General de Navarra: Estudio y edición de las redacciones protosistemáticas (series a y b)* (Pamplona: Gobierno de Navarra, 1987)

Wickham, Chris, 'Gossip and Resistance among the Medieval Peasantry', *Past & Present*, 160 (1998), 3–24

ISABEL ALFONSO

The Rhetoric of Seigneurial Legitimation in the *Fueros* of León (11th to 13th Centuries)*

According to the hypothesis advanced by the organisers of this conference, lords, in the preambles to charters of franchises, articulated an idealised vision of social relations, and consequently these documents allow 'an exceptional approach to representations of rent and of relations between lords and subjects'. I therefore propose here to analyse systematically the preambles of the *fueros* of León and reflect on the meaning and function of their rhetoric. I shall begin by discussing the principal characteristics of these *fueros* and the way I have organised them so as to make comparisons possible, and then look in greater detail at the preambles themselves and at the principal themes of the discourse that is expressed in them.

The *fueros* of León

The relatively recent editions of the *fueros* of four of the modern provinces of the ancient kingdom of León (Palencia, Valladolid, León and Zamora) have enabled the systematic study of a body of documents which is substantial from both a territorial and a chronological point of view and of a uniform juridical nature.[1] However, two general observations need to be made. The first concerns the territorial context: the frontiers of the kingdom of León were shifting during the period in question and seigneurial estates sometimes extended across them. The second concerns the content of this documentation, and also the chronology. Some specialists might deny the status of *fuero* to some of the documents collected in these editions. I have decided to include them, nevertheless, because I do not believe that an excessively restrictive definition of the *fueros* would significantly affect my conclusions. Although they themselves do not attempt this, in their desire to provide as full a catalogue as possible of the provincial *fueros*, the editors would accept that a modernised textual critique is needed; and it is impossible to consider these *fueros* as a homogeneous corpus.[2] They vary as a result of the differences both between the lords who granted

---

* Original publication: Alfonso, Isabel, 'La rhétorique de légitimation seigneuriale dans les fueros de León (XIe–XIIIe siècles)', in Pour une anthropologie du prélèvement seigneurial dans les campagnes de l'Occident médiéval (XIe–XIVe siècles). Les mots, les temps, les lieux, ed. by Monique Bourin and Pascual Martínez Sopena (Paris: Publications de la Sorbonne, 2007), pp. 229–52. Translated from the original French publication by Jean Birrell. Warm thanks to Cristina Jular and Julio Escalona for reading this article, and to François Foronda for his French translation.

1 FP, FV; FL; FZ. We may add to those in these editions four documents: SFPSahagun1569 (1206); SFPSahagun1612 (1218); SFPSahagun2044 (1318); SFPSahagun2576 (1398).

2 See, for example, J. Rodríguez's observations on the *fuero* of Belver (FZ, p. 150, n. 8). For the problems of studying the *fueros*, see the useful remarks of Barrero García, 'El proceso de formación'.

them and between the surviving texts, which are of variable length, leading to their being generally distinguished by this criterion. Essentially, however, their diversity is a product of the demographic and social disparities between the populations obtaining the *fueros*, and of the often very different matters they regulated. Which is to say that, although all the *fueros* served the same purpose, that is, to regulate the relationship to the seigneurial power, each *fuero* nevertheless reflected a specific set of relations.

The Preambles

What precisely should we understand by preamble? Of course, the word indicates the beginning, the introduction or prologue of the charter.[3] However, despite the best efforts of the editors to number the parts of the charter, ambiguity is still possible, because knowing where the preamble actually ends is not a simple matter.[4] For this article, and although they do not always appear at the beginning, I have chosen to treat as preamble all the declarations of intent, often of variable length, which appear within the documents. For, as already stated, my purpose here is to examine the rhetoric employed by the lords to justify their domination, their power and their position within a social order on which their consolidation and reproduction depended. With this in mind, it might perhaps be better to talk of justifications or motivations than of preambles, even though it is within the latter, in the initial section of the act, that they are usually expressed.[5]

From this perspective, which assumes joint study of the preamble and the rest of the charter, even where the two parts are autonomous, two points should be emphasised. The first concerns the description given to the act: it, too, is far from uniform and in many cases takes the form of a declaration of intent.[6] This is obvious in the case of the *fueros buenos* ('good fueros') or the *cartas de libertad* ('letters of franchise') which expressly refer to an amelioration of the arrangements they aim to regulate, hence their name. In other cases, the use of the term *pactum* ('agreement') or words with a similar meaning draws attention both to the conflicts underlying the compilation of these documents and the involvement of their recipients in the definition of the content. We must be careful, therefore, not to ignore these descriptions, as their wording is often revealing.

Second, the sanctions that are stipulated for potential offenders, which are usually recorded at the end of the charter, have received insufficient attention.[7] For it seems to me highly instructive to know who are the potential offenders they specify. In

---

3 For a first approach to the preambles and study of them, see Parisse, 'Préambules de chartes'.
4 For an example of the rather artificial nature of this separation, see n. 24 below.
5 In fact, students of diplomatics point out that the exposition of the motives may be dispersed throughout an act.
6 The most frequent expressions are: *cartam de foro; carta donationis; damus foros; cartam et stabilimentum; cartam absolutionis, concessionis, donationis et stabilitatis; cartam de liberationis; franquezas* is rare and appears only at a later date.
7 For pioneering remarks on the scarcely considered usefulness of studying these clauses, see Martín, 'Utilidad de las fórmulas "inútiles"'.

THE RHETORIC OF SEIGNEURIAL LEGITIMATION IN THE *FUEROS* OF LEÓN

many cases these are indicated only in a general manner, that is, whoever might violate the provisions, whether this was the act of the recipients or of the grantors or only the latter. As far as I can tell in these cases, the charter is a privilege extracted by its beneficiaries, they alone having an interest in its protection. So, through the sanctions, we may establish the identity of, on the one hand, those who wished the *fueros* to be maintained and respected and, on the other, those who represented a threat to them. These sanctions have other features, of course, to which I shall only allude here, such as the content of the sanction itself, spiritual, or perhaps better symbolic, and/or material.[8]

It seems to me, therefore, that the preambles cannot be separated from the body of the charter, and some of my interpretations are, in fact, based on an analysis of the relationship between the two. In any case, those present when these texts were read almost certainly did not separate their introduction from their clauses. We need also to ask, and this is another problem raised by the preambles, to what extent their content was limited to the repetition of predetermined model formularies. One way of establishing this is to pay attention not only to the intertextuality between the various preambles, but also to where they are inserted into the charter they introduce, with the intentions they proclaim being interpreted in this specific context, and not generally. We may also consider that a preamble, even when it re-uses a model formulary, assumes the ideological function of the representations it expresses.

The Organisation of the Material

Given the comparative approach adopted here, I need also to explain how I have organised my evidence to this end. As regards the purely statistical aspects, I have dealt only with material from the eleventh to the thirteenth centuries,[9] that is, a total of 243 *fueros*. Before counting the number of *fueros* with and without a preamble, I separated out the charters for which all we have is a single notice or reference, given the impossibility in such cases of establishing if a preamble existed. This reduces the number of *fueros* to 207, of which slightly more have a preamble than are without. I have also noted the identity of the persons, grantors and beneficiaries, though the latter do not appear in Table 1, as well as the description of the act. So, before embarking on the main body of my discussion, we may observe on the basis of Table 1 the number of grants by century, according to several criteria such as type of lord (king, ecclesiastic, lay) and type of act.

---

8 In some cases, while offenders against the *fuero* were punished, its defenders enjoyed a blessing: 'And may whoever sustains these *fueros* be blessed by God and Saint Mary and All the Saints' ('E todos aquellos que estos fueros mantovieren sean benditos de Dios e de Santa María e de todos los Santos') (FP2, 970).

9 For the area studied, only three *fueros* have survived from the tenth century, one of which is apocryphal. For the fourteenth and fifteenth centuries it is the *memoriales* or extracts of texts which are most plentiful; they are of limited value for this study of preambles, but I have nevertheless drawn on them when they throw light on certain aspects.

ISABEL ALFONSO

Table 11.1. Distribution of extant *fueros* for the provinces of León, Palencia, Burgos and Zamora. Figures in brackets indicate the number of *fueros* with a preamble.

Century	No of fueros	With preamble	Without preamble	Grantor	Grantor	Grantor	Type of preamble	Type of preamble	Type of preamble	Type of preamble
				King	Clergy	Laity	Good service	Dispute resolution	Pact	Fuero bueno
11th	15	11	4	9(8)	2(1)	4(2)	1	3	1	6
12th	89	50	39	23(19)	51(21)	15(10)	11	10	17	20
13th	103	47	56	39(26)	58(17)	6(3)	9	26	16	18

Table 1 shows, for example, that *fueros* granted by the kings predominated in the eleventh century, but that the main grantors in the twelfth and thirteenth centuries were ecclesiastical lords, bishops, abbots or masters of military orders. This is only logical, given that the surviving documentation comes principally from religious institutions. It was also the period when the majority of *fueros* were issued. The use of preambles seems more common in the case of those granted in the eleventh century, and more frequent in those granted by the king. These proportions prompt two observations. First, the acts may only be copies of *fueros* granted at an earlier date,[10] and second, usages, or customs, may have regulated relations between lords and peasants before the original documents were drawn up. In fact, there are sometimes explicit references to these uses and customs in the *fueros* announced as intended to regulate them, a sign, no doubt, of their lack of precision and the absence of a previous written version. In other cases, it is clear that the *fueros* are amending earlier texts. Almost all the *fueros buenos* fall into this category, as also do those which, without being so described, refer to the improvements brought by the new charter. Nevertheless, I admit to some scepticism as to the real value of these figures, which should be treated with caution, even though they enable us to compare various regional groupings and give some coherence to the interpretation. Be that as it may, it seems more helpful at this point to move to a discussion of the types of justifications put forward when the charter was granted, and indicate some of the questions their study poses.

The Thematic of the Preambles

As far as I can tell, the thematic of the preambles is very diverse.[11] They range from charters in which the grantors claim to be acting from the love of God and for the safety of their souls (reasons found, as is well known, in every act of donation) to charters in which they proclaim to be acting by reason of the good service rendered them by the beneficiaries, or of the benefit and favour they do them (improving

---

10 On the subject of the small number of originals preserved, see the remarks of the editors of the collections of *fueros* noted above.

11 I have not counted as preamble the simple declaration 'we grant it for it to be populated' ('damus ad populandum'), whatever its precise form.

THE RHETORIC OF SEIGNEURIAL LEGITIMATION IN THE *FUEROS* OF LEÓN   445

tenurial and living conditions, exemption from charges, confirmation of ancient usages, resolution of differences regarding obligations, rents, etc.). It is something of a challenge, consequently, to try to order this immense body of specious reasoning thematically, without loss of specificity.[12] The attempt must be made, nevertheless, if we wish to establish the main themes of the discourse of the *fueros*, and on this basis consider their relationship to other documentation of seigneurial origin. We then find that the preambles generally emphasise the quality and the objectives of the grant (the 'good *fuero*' and the amelioration in question), with some putting the emphasis on the reasons motivating it (good service rendered, a dispute or a conflict). However, the motives tend to turn into objectives, and their autonomy is often in reality slight, so firmly are they integrated into a single logic. For example, the 'good *fueros*' are said to be granted in return for services rendered or as a way resolving a conflict. But two main themes can nevertheless be detected. They correspond to different contexts and a differentiated image of the grantors and of the beneficiaries emerges, as also of the relationship between them, which the *fuero* claims to settle.

The Discourse of Reciprocity, or *fueros* Earned: The Rhetoric of Doing Good

In the preambles, which usually seek to justify the grant of the charter, there is frequent reference to the principal of the reward and/or the promotion of good and loyal service. This idea of the prize and the reward made the grant of the *fuero* a good in itself, so it is common to find simultaneously expressed the kindness of the concession granted and that of the service rendered. Thus when, in 1062, Fernando I granted a 'charter of benefits or of good things, *fueros*' to the local council of Santa Cristina (Zamora), he claimed to be acting for the safety of his own soul and that of his father, but also 'for the good service they had rendered [him]'.[13] The phrase is not without echoes of a feudal language, appropriate to the grant of a benefice, and the *fueros* have something of this nature about them.[14]

The perception of the *fuero* as a favour, whether maintained or augmented, to be earned as if it was a reward, is particularly clear in the *fueros* of the region under discussion, even if it is expressed in different forms, which vary with the circumstances. Without going into detail, let us say that the underlying logic of this idea, often explicitly articulated, is widely shared, and also instrumentalised according to the strategies employed by the parties concerned. From this perspective, the case of the *fuero* granted by the bishop of Palencia to his vassals of Villamuriel in 1162 is particularly telling, as it expresses the idea of a reciprocity designed to legitimise an episcopal domination which the charter seeks to define.

---

12   For discussion of this vast question from a European perspective, but for a later period, see the important article of Guyotjeannin, 'Vivre libre dans une seigneurie juste'.
13   'cartula benefactis, sive causa bonitas, foros [...] pro bono servitio quem mihi fecistis' (FZ2, 1062).
14   In fact, certain grants are presented as purely seigneurial matters: a lord, king or count, grants to another the right to grant *fueros*, in return for services rendered.

> It is right and just, and always advised by mercy, that the faithful and lawful vassals are fittingly rewarded by their lord for their good services. For that reason, I [...], albeit unworthy, do not forget the good services that you have always rendered me, and grant you, the men of Villamurial, both to those present and to those who shall come to live in this *villa*, a new charter of good *fueros*, as good and loyal vassals.[15]

Rewarding the good services rendered by the vassals is presented here as a worthy and proper act, consequence of the lord's clemency, this being materialised in the charter of 'good *fuero*' he granted them. Clearly expressed, the reward that followed the good and loyal conduct of the vassals highlights the way in which the idea of reciprocity should be understood. And the bishop returns to this point in the last paragraph of the act: 'I grant and bequeath' both to the men now present and to those to come 'so that you shall always be most faithful in everything and for everything and devoted to all good services'.[16]

In other cases, as in the *fuero* granted by the abbot of Moreruela to the Portuguese local council of Nuez in 1238, the idea of reciprocity is included in a declaration of love on the part of the lord, in response to the good services which have been rendered him: 'With a good heart and good will, for the love that I have for you, and for the services that you have rendered and will render us, we grant you and confirm this *fuero*'.[17] The idea was not new, as is shown by its use at a much earlier date by lay lords, as in this example of 'good *fuero*' granted to the vassals of Pozuelo de Campos:

> I, Martín Pérez, and Elvira Pérez, and Maior Martínez, grant you, the inhabitants of Pozuelo de Campo, this charter, which shall always be valid, so that you enjoy good *fueros*, namely the ones that they have in Villamayor, so that we shall love you and you shall serve us.[18]

This same discourse had already been invoked by Alfonso VI, in particular in the grant of *consuetudines et foros* ('customs and *fueros*') to the town of Sahagún in 1085, so his men would serve the monastery of that name:

> I, Alfonso the Emperor, moved by the will of the abbot and the community of brethren, grant the men of Sahagún these customs and *fueros*, so that they shall

---

15 'Dignum et iustum est et misericordia semper suadet ut fidelibus et legitimis uassallis digna pro bonis seruiciis fiat a domnis retributio. Propterea ego [...] licet indignus non inmemor bonorum seruiciorum quos mihi semper fecistis, facio nouiter cartam de bonis foris uobis hominibus de Uilla Morel tam presentis quam futuris in eadem uilla commorantibus sicuti bonis et cabosis uasallis' (FP20, 1162).

16 'Omnia bona dono et concede [...] ut uos semper sitis magis fideles in omnibus et per omnia et deuotiores ad omne bonum seruicium'.

17 'De buen coraçon ye de bona voluntad, ye por el amor que vos avemos, ye por el servicio que nos feziestes ye faredes, otorgamos vos ye confirmamos vos este foro' (FZ56, 1238).

18 'Ego Martinus Petriz et Elvira Petriz et Maior Martinez facimus cartam in perpetuum valituram vobis populatoribus de Pozolo de Campo, ut habeatis foros bonos, scilicet quos habent in Villamaiore, nos vobis amando et vos nobis serviendo' (FV10, 1139–1149). For the date of and revisions to this text, see the comments of its editor (FV, pp. 35–37).

THE RHETORIC OF SEIGNEURIAL LEGITIMATION IN THE *FUEROS* OF LEÓN   447

serve [this monastery] as [they serve the Lord], with full submission and humility. And [the monastery] shall defend them and they shall love it.[19]

Another source of the benefits conceded was political love, as expressed by Alfonso X in the preamble of his famous *Fuero Real*, in which, it is said, he aimed to standardise the kingdom juridically. When he granted this *fuero* to the town of Aguilar de Campoo (Palencia), he put particular emphasis, among the reasons that had led him to wish to reorganise the royal domain, on the love which the kings, his predecessors, had always felt for the said town and their desire to 'do them good in plenty and grant them favour'.[20]

Still within this logic of reciprocal gift, of mutual and necessary exchanges, other elements tended to accentuate not only the moral but also the legal nature of this reciprocity, now perceived as a divine and human imperative. This is the case with the *fuero* granted by the bishop of Palencia to his men and faithful vassals of Mojados in 1176, in which we read in the preamble: 'For both the divine and the human laws advise this: that those vassals who are always good and faithful shall receive goods for their good deeds and be rewarded in accordance to their merits'.[21]

It was on the basis of this rhetoric of reciprocal benefit that the ideal images of the good lord and good vassals were constructed,[22] and they, in their turn, gave legitimacy to a consensual domination. It is probably in the royal *fueros* that this formulation is most clearly articulated. Thus, to justify the grants, these royal *fueros* propose a positive royal model based on the concept of merciful and grateful kings, obliged to reward appropriately whoever merited it, to abolish bad customs and to encourage their men to be loyal; ultimately, this model refers to the idea of a Rewarder God, that is, a God who rewards the good and punishes the wicked.[23] Let us look at some examples. In 1180 the grant of 'good *fueros*' to two localities in the province of Palencia by Alfonso VIII is presented as one of the fundamental elements of royal majesty:

> In the name of our Lord Jesus Christ, amen. It is appropriate for the royal majesty to show mercy for the humble people, and visit those tired of the miserable oppression bringing relief, abolishing the wicked customs and granting good *fueros*. For this reason [...][24]

---

19 'Istas consuetudines et foros per voluntatem Abbatis et collegio fratrum dedi ego Adefonsus Imperatur hominibus Sancti Facundi per quos serviant ei sicut Dominus in submissione et humilitate plena. Et illi defendant eos et ament ut suos homines' (FL6, 1085).

20 'fazerles mucho bien et mercet' (FP38, 1255). For the political nature of love, see in particular Martin, 'Amour'.

21 'Diuine enim leges et humane hoc precipiunt ut semper omnes fideles et boni vassalli pro bonis bona reçipiant et una eadem mensura illis merito remeçiatur' (FV11, 1176).

22 On the way in which this rhetoric is expressed in other contexts, see my Alfonso, 'Conflictos en las behetrías'.

23 The contribution of this discourse to the qualitatively different and hierarchically superior construction of royal power deserves fuller discussion. For some aspects, see Escalona, 'Misericordia regia'.

24 'In nomine Domini nostri Ihesu Christi, amen. Regie conuenit maiestati humilibus personis mesericordiam clementer exhibere, miserabili oppressione fatigatos ope releuationis uisitare, prauas

Similarly, in 1222, Fernando III wished the 'fueros honestos y útiles' ('honest and useful *fueros*') he granted to the men of Peñafiel [5] to be regarded as the reward for their good service by his royal majesty, in a preamble in which the exchange of benefits promoted a hereditary gratitude.[25]

Other royal *fueros*, especially from the reigns of Fernando II and Alfonso IX, but also those granted by Alfonso VIII and Fernando III, emphasise the idea of a good and Catholic king.[26] Previously autonomous elements tend to merge in their lengthy preambles. These *fueros* raise important questions of diplomatic, as noted above, given that they have often only come down to us through the intermediary of copies or in a later confirmation. With this problem in mind, which cannot unfortunately be tackled here, the *fuero* of Puebla de Sanabria, granted by Alfonso IX in 1220 and known only through a copy of Alfonso X (1263) in the vernacular, is a good example of the use of the image of the Christian king:

> In the name of our Lord Jesus Christ. Amen. It is worthy and fitting for a Christian king to grant his new settlements the appropriate *fueros*, rights and judicial customs, and to confirm them in perpetuity, so that the new settlement shall benefit from the growth in goodness and worthiness of its council among the older settlements of the kingdom, and to reprimand the wicked men for their pride and to confound the arrogant for their evil, so that they shall observe the honour and value of their king in all things, and render him, and those who may come after him, good and loyal service [...] And for this reason, I, Don Alfonso, King of León, grant you, the inhabitants of Sanabria, both those now present and those to come, and all your descendants, this charter with your *fueros*; and it shall always be valid so that you, and your children, and your grandchildren, and anyone who may come after you shall live in peace and quiet, and so that the wicked and the arrogant be punished in any necessary manner in accordance to these good *fueros* that you are receiving from me for the mercy of God and for your good merits.[27]

---

aufferendo consuetudines et bonos foros inpendendo. Ea propter [...]' (FP24, 1180). *Fuero* of Villasila y Villamelendro. J. Rodríguez explains the importance for the king of these localities because they were on the frontier of the kingdom of León. Situated in the *alfoz* of Saldaña, on the high plateau of Valdavia, they later passed to the Order of Santiago (FP, pp. 126–27). See also how the bishop benefited from the preamble of the *fuero* of Palencia to locate himself on the level of the king who gave his assent (FP25, 1181). See Appendix 3.

25 FV19 (1222). See Appendix 5.

26 The expression comes from the preamble of the *fuero* conceded to Villafranca del Bierzo by Alfonso IX: 'Good and catholic King' ('Bono rey y cathólico') (FL50, 1192).

27 'En el nombre de nuestro Sennor Iesu Christo. Amén. Guisada cosa es e perteneçe a todo rey christiano de dar su puebla nueva tales fueros e tales derechos, e tales costumbres de justicia, e confirmarlos por siempre jamás, que la puebla nueva reciba acrecimiento en bondat e en valor de su conceyo entre las otras pueblas antiguas de su regno, e de apremiar a los malos en su soberbia e confonder a los soberviosos en su maldat, de manera que guarden la onrra e el prez de su rey en todas las cosas, e quel fagan buen servicio e leal a él a todos aquéllos que vernán dél [...] E por aquesto, yo, don Alffonso, rey de León, fago carta a vos, los pobladores de Senabria, tan bien a aquéllos que agora son, como a los otros que vernán después, e a toda la vuestra generación, de vuestros fueros; que sea valedera por siempre, e porque vos e vuestros fijos e vuestro nietos, e a todos aquellos que de vos

THE RHETORIC OF SEIGNEURIAL LEGITIMATION IN THE *FUEROS* OF LEÓN   449

This long preamble also makes it possible to understand the political culture on which the wise king based his vast enterprise. In this sense, the preamble of the second *fuero* granted to Peñafiel is also highly revealing, as it shows how the model of a king who was a good lord was inseparable from, while at the same time helping to construct, the model of the good vassal:

> For among all the things that kings must do, there are two that are particularly important for them: one is to favour those who have served them well and loyally, and the other to ensure that the people obliged to serve them by nature and lordship are further obliged, granting them good and favour so that in the future they are more willing to serve them and love them.[28]

This last model is characteristic of many of the texts already discussed, such as the *fueros* granted by the bishop of Palencia to his people of Villamuriel and Mojados, in which the preambles indicated who deserved to be rewarded by a 'cartam de bonis foris' ('charter of good *fueros*'), that is, faithful and loyal, good and accomplished vassals. And this was precisely how the abbot of Moreruela wished the seventy persons charged with populating his town of *Ifanes* to behave:

> we grant you our *villa* called *Iffanes* so that you populate it [...] and we grant it to you under the following terms and *fuero*: that you remain our good and loyal and accomplished vassals, as vassals shall be to their lord in all manner as is rightful and is the custom in the land where we live.[29]

In fact, all the preambles so far discussed present an ideal world. Everyone, the good king and the good lord, the good and faithful vassal, performs the role that has been assigned him. Yet we need to qualify this image, especially as in other preambles the tensions and conflicts underlying the charters, involving lords and vassals, and from

---

vernán, vivades siempre en paz y en mansedumbre, e porque los malos e los sobervios sean castigados en todas maneras segund aquestos fueros buenos que vos recibides de mí por la gracia de Dios e por los vuestros buenos merecimientos' (FZ42, 1220). I use here the original version of the privilege of Alfonso X, edited by Anta Lorenzo, 'El fuero de Sanabria'. The preamble reproduces almost literally that of the *fueros* of Mayorga, granted Fernando II in 1181 (FV13), of Villafranca in 1192 (FL50) and of Laguna de Negrillos in 1205 (FL58). The links between these *fueros* and those of the family of Benavente are studied by J. Rodríguez (FZ, pp. 170–76). He believes that the preamble repeats the ideology expressed in other items produced by the Chancellery of Alfonso X (FZ, p. 171), even if the formulation is known for earlier reigns.

28 'Porque entre todas las cosas que los reyes deven a fazer, sennaladamente estas dos les conviene mucho: la una de dar gualardon a los que bien e lealmente los sirvieron, la otra que magar los omnes sean adebdados con ellos por naturaleza e por sennorío de les fazer serviçio adebdarlos aún más fazeiéndoles bien e merçet porque cabodelante ayan mayor voluntad de los servir e de los amar' (FV26, 1264). *Fuero* of Peñafiel. In reality it is a privilege accorded to the knights of the town which completed and improved the *Fuero Real* granted a decade earlier.

29 'damos a pobrar la nostra villa de Iffanes [...] e damosvola so tal condiçion e a tal fuero: que seades nostros vasalos buenos e lealles e bien mandados, assi commo vasalos deven ser a sennor en todas las cosas que es de derecho e de costumbre en la tierra do vivimos' (FZ82, 1310). It should be noted that the editor's division of the contents in the form of articles, in order to facilitate its study, separates this information from the preamble. For a transcription more respectful of the formal structure of the document, see SMMoreruela199.

both the rural and the urban worlds, are clearly visible. Nevertheless, the models just discussed are still present, their role being that of parameters of legitimation, both to formalise certain ways of behaving and to demand, in practice, appropriate behaviour. It is particularly important, therefore, to examine the interaction between the two discourses.

The Discourse of Pact, or Disputed Charters: The Rhetoric of Order

> 'This is the pact that was reached between'; 'this pact and agreement'; 'this firmest pact and agreement'; 'we have reached and established this pact and this *fuero*'; 'regarding the dispute between [...] I imposed this agreement upon them [...] and this said agreement [...] they shall have it as *fuero*'.[30]

Formulas of this type are found in many charters. But the most significant, and generally the longest, characterise the *fueros* granted, amended or added to in the aftermath of a conflict regarding their implementation. When this happened, the grantor — who might be a lord opposed by his vassals or his dependents, or the king or a third party called on to help resolve the situation — justified his intervention, favourable or not, in a sometimes lengthy narrative which was his version of the conflict, in order to present his decision in the best light. These settlements were achieved after very different procedures and in very different circumstances. In many cases, these conflicts, described in detail, end in *pactos forales*; in others, the terms *pactum, postura* or *convenientiam* simply describe the charter, without reference to any tension.[31] It seems to me that these notions proclaiming an agreement reached must relate to an earlier negotiating process, and that it is therefore necessary to consider all these *fueros*, with or without preamble, together. The same applies in the case of the charters described as 'good *fueros*', sometimes without any further information or matching rhetoric.[32] This positive qualifier can clearly only be understood, at least implicitly, in relation to another, this time negative, in a world of shared significances, in which the norm regulating relations between lord and peasant acquires its character, good or bad. This link is explicitly affirmed when the grantors say, for example, 'we abolish the bad *fueros* [...] we grant and establish [...] all these good *fueros* in perpetuity';[33] or when we read that a lord makes a 'charter to alleviate all the bad *fueros* that you

---

30 'Hoc est pactum quod fit inter'; 'tali pacto et conuenientia; pactum firmissimum vel convenientia'; 'facimus et statuimus tale pactum et tale forum eis'; 'sobre contienda que era entre [...] pus tal auenencia entre ellas [...] y esta misma auenencia [...] dengela por fuero'.

31 A useful survey of the terms relating to the controversies in the documentation for the cathedral of León is provided in an appendix to the work of Jular Pérez-Alfaro, 'Conflictos ante tenentes y merinos'.

32 For the socio-economic context in which the good *fueros* proliferated, see Pastor, *Resistencias y luchas campesinas*; Martínez Sopena, *Tierra de Campos occidental*.

33 'Saccamus foros malos [...] damus et affirmamus [...] totos istos bonos foros usque in perpetuum' (FV14, 1181). *Fuero* of Villavarud de Rioseco, granted by lay lords.

THE RHETORIC OF SEIGNEURIAL LEGITIMATION IN THE *FUEROS* OF LEÓN   451

previously had'.[34] In the latter case, the declaration is the real reason for the act.[35] It seems important, therefore, to take account of these acts, too, admittedly without a preamble, but where the tension preceding compilation is clearly visible.[36] Similarly, the need to put the concessions granted into writing so that they do not get forgotten, a need frequently recalled in the preambles, should be seen not as the repetition of a stereotyped formula but as a way of preserving a record of the results achieved, by the lord as much as by his vassals. From this perspective, the pact granted by the prior of Nogal and the abbot of Sahagún to their settlers of Vallegera eloquently expresses the role of the *fueros* in fixing memory:

> In the name [...] Before oblivion renders the good deeds useless, it is necessary to commend them to future memories through the written record. And this is what I [...] grant and concede you, the people of Vallegera, this pact and agreement.[37]

An examination of the prescribed sanctions would certainly help to clarify the conflictual context behind the concessions which, as noted above, were extracted from the lord by his dependents when he was the only one to be suspected of a potential violation.[38]

I have discussed elsewhere how the peasants perceived the *fuero* as a weapon to be used against seigneurial arbitrariness, and how this right, achieved by negotiation, reveals not only their resistance but also the consistency of their action to this end.[39] The systematic study of the *fueros* of the kingdom of León confirms this thesis. A large number of these acts signal the conflicts arising in connection with the fixing or improvement of these local rights, so making it possible to understand more clearly the dynamic between these struggles and charters. Discussion of the preambles also makes it possible to supplement two points I made in my earlier work. First, faced with a conflictual situation, it was in the interests of the lords to demonstrate

---

34 'kartam de alleuiatione de los malos foros quod prius habebatis' (FP27, 1187). *Fuero* of Lomas, granted by the abbot of Sahagún.

35 The grant of a 'good *fuero*' might simply be presented as an act enhancing the generosity of the grantor, as in the case of the *fuero* granted by Alfonso VI to Santa María de Dueñas (FP5, 1078). Similarly, when the motives or reasons for the grant were not spelt out, the moral quality and the generosity of the grantor was indirectly enhanced by that very fact (FP5, 1078; FP24, 1180).

36 The text by which Alfonso VII amended the conditions of the old *fuero* of the town of Sahagún, to settle the discord which had arisen between its inhabitants and the monastery, clearly illustrates the problems that can arise when separated justifications are put into categories (FL19, 1152). In the table proposed here, however, these categories, sometimes presented together in a text, are adhered to (settlement of conflicts, pact, good *fuero*).

37 'In nomine [...] Ne bonorum facta prior obliuionem ducantur in irritum, necesse est per litterarum appices posterorum memorie commendare. Inde est quod ego [...] do et concedo uobis populatoribus de Ualligera tali pacto et conuenientia' (FP28, 1194). Many more examples could be quoted.

38 The charter which the heirs of Vadello granted their *collazos* ('dependents') stipulated that: 'If any *hereditarius* imbued by any malignity should break or disturb our deed, may God's wrath fall upon him and may he grieve in hell with Judas, Our Lord's traitor' ('Si quis aliquis hereditarius aliqua malignitate imbutus hoc factum nostrum frangere vel irrumpere voluerit ira Dei veniat super eum et lugeat in inferno inferior cum Iuda Domini traditore') (FP31, s. XII). This clause probably reveals the concern of the heirs regarding conflicts that might in future divide them.

39 Alfonso, 'Campesinado y derecho'.

generosity, which enabled them to emphasise the gracious nature of their concessions and/or invoke order and social peace to justify the changes to the *fuero*. Second, when the peasants — or the whole population dependent to varying degrees on the lord — were able to intervene in the narrative reconstruction of the conflict, they tried to have the memory of their battles recorded to their own advantage. And the uneven nature of the surviving documentation should be related to these processes of negotiation. I will quote just a few examples to demonstrate this.

In the second half of the thirteenth century, the abbot of Palazuelos (Valladolid) claimed mercifully to accede to the pleas of the men of this locality, who were seeking to improve the rights obtained from his predecessors:

> We, the aforementioned Abbot and the congregation, regarding those articles included in the aforementioned charter by which the aforementioned men of Palazuelos claimed that they had been burdened, and wishing to be merciful to them, lessen and temper these articles in the following manner, that is [...][40]

It is impossible to tell whether the complaints of the vassals were as peaceable as indicated in the act. However, the presentation of the *fuero* as a merciful concession from the abbot, and not as extracted, significantly changes both the representation of the relationship between the lord and his people and the image of the parties concerned. Thus the abbot is a benefactor, whereas the peasants are his obedient subjects, who entreat him to improve their condition, this improvement being granted not as a result of their resolute action but out of the kindness of their lord. Yet not long after, the descendants of these same peasants, in a text which this time transmits their collective voice, affirm their abandonment of the *fuero* of which they were the beneficiaries in order to take another they judged to be more favourable.[41] In his conflict with the council of Fuentesaúco, the bishop of Zamora, too, insists on his image as a good lord — to the point where, faced with the refusal of the council to meet his fiscal demands, the bishop declared he would be merciful, accordingly reducing the sums demanded or granting exemption. The measures subsequent to this charter, which 'Bishop don Suero established for Fuentesaúco in accordance to the will of the council',[42] even though drawn up in the same manner, struggle to conceal the underlying tension.

Nevertheless, it is the invocation of good order and social peace that constitutes the main plank in the discourse designed to legitimise the measures adopted in the *fueros*, or the meaning the lords sought to give to their law, even though it was sometimes violently challenged. From this perspective, the additions made by the sisters of the monastery of San Pedro de las Dueñas (León) to the ancient *fuero* of the city [4] are of exceptional interest.[43] These additions changed some fundamental

---

40 'Nos vero supradicti abbas et conventus super quibusdam articulis in supradicta carta contentis per quos supradicti homines de Palaçiolos se gravatos esse dicebant misericorditer cum eis agere volentes eosdem articulos temperavimus sive contraximus in hunc modum, videlicet' (FV22, 1224).

41 FV31 (1313).

42 'el obispo don Suero puso ena Fuente del Sabugo a plazer del conceyo' (FZ60, 1251).

43 FL49 (1191). See Appendix, 4. J. Rodríguez describes it as a 'neat justification' in his discussion (FL,

THE RHETORIC OF SEIGNEURIAL LEGITIMATION IN THE *FUEROS* OF LEÓN   453

points concerning the organisation of the holdings and of the peasant families, as they affected their ability to dispose of their belongings at their convenience and to establish links with more privileged groups. These possibilities were firmly denied them for the moment. But what really matters here were the reasons put forward by the seigneurial authorities to explain these measures, their 'beneficiaries' finding themselves additionally constrained, or only persuaded, to view them positively. For, on the pretext of protecting the vassals, the new prohibitions aimed to prevent the violence, damage and insults caused by ties of kinship, blood or alliance, by marriage or by fosterage (*crianza*), established between them and the group of knights and squires of the township, or caused by land transfers made to their benefit. And this aim also encouraged the people of the council to accept the 'salubre estatuto' ('beneficial charter') which the lords had decided to grant them 'of our own accord and for the sake of peace'.[44] A voluntary or forced acceptance? At all events, this collective assent was part of a seigneurial rhetoric in which consensus concealed the imposition of measures intended to contain and control what seem to have been habitual dynamics of social interaction.[45]

The need to restore order in the community featured in many *fueros* intended to resolve confrontations, but it was in the charters produced by royal intervention that it was most clearly expressed. The recurring conflicts between the convent of Sahagún and the people of that town on the route to Santiago de Compostela are well known. As early as 1152 Alfonso VII declared that it had been necessary for him to go to the monastery to settle a dispute by means of a *carta de foros* ('charter of' *fueros*) [1] granting the townspeople the measures they demanded, in order to restore peace and harmony between the parties.[46] A century later, Alfonso X declared in similar terms:

> In the name of God. Let it be known to those who may see this charter how We, Don Alfonso, King of Castile by the grace of God […] came to Sahagún and learnt about a great dispute between, on the one hand, Don Nicolas, the Abbot of Sahagún, and the congregation of this monastery and, on the other, the council of Sahagún, and we also learnt about the great disagreement and enmities among the men of the township, and wishing to settle these disagreements that existed between the Abbot and the congregation, on the one side, and the council, on the other, and the enmities that the men of the township had between them, and leave them all in a good situation, We, together with the Abbot and the convent of the monastery, decided to amend the *fueros* that had been granted to them by King Alfonso, the Emperor's grandfather, as well as those which the Emperor had later granted them together with the Abbot and the convent, and to grant

---

p. 297).

44   'per nostra observacione et bono paci'.

45   I have discussed this dynamic within rural communities in several works; see in particular Alfonso, 'Campesinado y derecho', pp. 24–26; Alfonso, 'Litigios por la tierra', pp. 939–40; Alfonso, 'Conflictos en las behetrías', pp. 246–58.

46   FL19 (1152). See Appendix 1.

them a *fuero* to regulate life from now onwards not only for those who live there but also for those who will come to live in the future.[47]

The *fuero*, instrument of order and regulator of social relations at the local level, was part of an ensemble of shared references about which it was nevertheless still possible to argue and negotiate. In many cases, this was expressed in simple formulas, such as those which frequently accompany the grants of *fuero* 'for you to live in accordance with'; or the more rhetorical formulas (like 'of your *fueros* and good customs according to which you shall live rightly and honestly in this world') which, in the seigneurial discourse, implied that norms of service and obligations should respected ('the *fuero* according to which they shall live and serve'), but which in the preambles of royal grants tended to shape a more elaborate discourse — this would primarily be used by Alfonso X in the introduction of the *Fuero Real*.[48] For the area studied, the grants of the *Fuero Real* to Peñafiel in 1256 and to Valladolid in 1265 are good examples:

> Let it be known to those who may see this charter how I [...] Since I learnt that the township of Peñafiel had not been granted a *fuero* to conduct themselves as they should, and that for this reason they had many disagreements and disputes and many enmities and that justice was not rendered as it should, I, the aforementioned King Don Alfonso, wishing to amend this harm, and together with Queen Doña Violante and with my son, the *infante* Don Fernando, grant and award them that *fuero* that I composed with the advice of my court, written in a book and sealed with my lead seal, so that they have it for the council of Peñafiel as well as for its villages and hamlets, so that all things are forever conducted in accordance with it, for them and for those who may come [...] And also to do them good and grant them favour and to reward them for all the services that they rendered the most noble and honest King Don Alfonso, my great-grandfather, and the most noble and honest King Don Fernando my father, and me before and after I started to reign, I grant and award them these liberties that are written in this privilege.[49]

---

47 'In Dei nomine. Connoscida cosa sea a quantos esta carta vieren, cuemo Nos D. Alfonso por la gracia de Dios rey de Castiella [...] viniemos a Sant Fagunt et fallamos hy grand desavenencia entre D. Nicolas abad de San Fagund et el convento desse monasterio de la una parte et el conceio de Sant Fagunt de la otra, et otrosi fallamos grandes desavenencias et enemizades entre los omes de la villa, et por toller estas desavenencias que eran entrel abad et el convento de la una parte, et el conceio de la otra, et las enemizades que los ommes dessa villa avien entre si, et ponerlos todos en buen estado, toviemos por bien de Nos con el abad et con el convento de este monasterio de emendar los fueros que avien tambien del rey D. Alfonso abuelo del emperador, cuemo los otros que les diera despues el emperador en uno con el abad et con el convento, et de les dar fuero porque vivan da aquí adelantre tambien los que son agora cuemo los que vernan despues' (FL80, 1255).

48 'fuero por que uiuades'; 'de uestris foris et bonis consuetudines quibus in hoc seculo recte et honeste viuatis'; 'foro cum quo vivant et cum quo serviant'.

49 'Conoscida cosa sea a todos los omes que esta carta vieren, como yo [...] Porque falle que la billa de Peñafiel non avie fuero conplido porque se judgaren asi como devien, et por esta razón venian muchas dubdas et contiendas et muchas enemistades et la justicia non se cunplie asi como devie, yo el sobredicho rey D. Alfonso, queriendo sacar todos estos daños, en uno con la reina Doña Violant et con mio fijo el infante D. Fernando: Doles et otorgoles aquel fuero, que yo fiz con consejo de mi corte, escripto en libro et sellado con mio seello de plomo, que lo ayan el consejo de Peñafiel, tanbien de villas

THE RHETORIC OF SEIGNEURIAL LEGITIMATION IN THE *FUEROS* OF LEÓN   455

This preamble is of particular interest. On the one hand, it seems to mark a significant change, in that the clauses of the *fuero* are no longer seen as regulating the service expected by the lord but as a norm of reference for judging and exercising justice; on the other, we find brought together in a single text everything that has characterised the earlier concessions, such as the idea of the favour, of the reward to be given in payment for services rendered, and of the grant of liberties. On this basis, the royal discourse opened the way for ideas already present in the political culture of the day ('for the benefit and advantage of this township'),[50] ideas which are increasingly related to the well-being of the kingdom, the common good, the 'benefit of all the inhabitants.'[51] The communal discourse of the towns of the royal domain also drew on this conceptual store, as appears in the agreements established by the council of Toro, legitimised in the name of the 'enhancement of the lordship of our lord the King, and for the benefit of us all.'[52]

So, seigneurial generosity and the restoration of order and social peace predominate in the thematics of the *fueros* granted to resolve conflicts. And, to an extent, the image of the good lord, bringer of peace and justice, which they transmit coincides with the imagery of the discourse discussed about. However, as also noted, in some texts the lords have a less flattering image, in a sense inverted, because they rehearse their mistakes, wrongs, excesses and possible disloyalty with regard to their vassals and the harm they do them. In other words, we have a portrait of the bad lord. But the chief characteristic of these texts is that they involve all the parties in the construction of the sought-after communitarian order, thus attributing a positive role to peasant action.

The preamble of the *fuero* of Toldanos is a particularly clear example of this. The peasants managed to get their struggle mentioned as the main reason for an act to their advantage, which therefore preserved the memory of their action and their version of events. Here, the rhetoric of doing good has disappeared, and the bishop of León was obliged to recognise the wrong he had done by granting the town, as *prestimonio*, to a *miles* ('knight'), and to accede to the petitions of inhabitants who had deserted it as a result. Admittedly, they had been able to rely on the support of a count and of King Fernando II himself to obtain the *convenientia* (agreement) which brought their conflict to an end, but this in no way diminishes the importance of

---

como de aldeas, por que se judguen por el en todas cosas para siempre jamas, ellos y los que dellos vinieren [...] Et demas por facerles bien et merced et por darles galardon por los muchos servicios que ficieron al muy noble et mucho honrrado Rey D. Alfonso mio bisabuelo et al muy noble et mucho honrrado rey D. Fernando mio padre et a mi antes que regnare et despues que regne, doles et otorgoles estas franquezas que son escriptas en este previllejo' (FV24, 1256). *Fuero* of Peñafiel. The preamble of the *Fuero Real* is however longer and a little different. Ultimately, the reason put forward for the grant was not legal deficiencies, but the reasons which made the laws necessary: discord and conflicts provoked by the diversity of human feelings and the difficulty of reconciling them (Fuero Real, p. 349).

50 'propter utilitatem et commodum ipsius ville', as declared by the bishop of Astorga and the abbess of Carrizo with the consent and acquiescence of all the council ('de consensu et beneplacito tocius concilii'), in what appears to be a pact of public order they established in agreement with their local vassals. *Fuero* of the township of Molinaseca (FL51, 1196).

51 'pro de todos los pobladores' (*Fuero* of Medina: FV35, 1258).

52 'acrecentamiento del señorio de nuestro señor el Rey, e a provecho de nos todos' (FZ72, 1280). On this discourse, see Alfonso and Jular Pérez-Alfaro, 'Oña contra Frías', pp. 73–75.

456   ISABEL ALFONSO

their mobilisation. They had forced the bishop to promise never again to grant out the town, and to settle the conditions in which they might in future dispose of their property and emigrate without losing it as a result [2].[53]

Another example is provided by the case brought by the people of the locality of Villaudela (Palencia) before royal justice to defend their rights. It resulted in public recognition of the seigneurial abuses endured by this community, in the preamble to an agreement which King Fernando III himself ordered should be given to them as *fuero*; these 'good charters, which shall remain firm forever', restored the old charter, violated by the abbot and chapter of Husillos ('for the abbot and the chapter of Husillos violated their *fueros*').[54]

Similarly, the vassals of the bishop of Segovia, well before those of the bishop of Palencia, managed to pin responsibility for disrespect of the charter on their lords. They also complained about the bad reputation they had been given by these lords, who had said of them that they had hardly behaved like loyal vassals: 'They gained fame for not obeying their lords as they should, thus causing them great harm, and complaining about this and wishing to live as vassals should live with their lord'.[55] And the language used by the people of Mojados to demand that their new bishop should enquire into the charter they enjoyed and wished to be observed, is part of a rhetoric in which the good vassal appeals to the good lord:

> They asked for our mercy so that we learnt about the life and the *fuero* that they had with those who were bishops before [...] and that we should firmly establish by *fuero* the things that they should observe and fulfil on our behalf and on that of all the bishops that may come after us, so that they would have the will to serve us loyally and we would act justly to do good to them and grant them favour.[56]

The seigneurial rhetoric of doing good is not absent from this text, but here it is the peasants who make use of the ethic of reciprocity. What seems to me a similar case is that of the agreement obtained by the men of Pinos from the abbot of San Isidoro of León. This act records not only mutual promises to observe the *fuero* between 'vassals good and loyal to the abbot and lords good and loyal to the council', but also explicitly refers to the possibility of disloyalty and violations on the part of the lord, and consequently the possibility of its devaluation.[57] That these commitments

---

53 FL29 (1165). See Appendix 2.

54 'buenas cartas, firmes para siempre [...] que los desaforava el Abbad y el cabildo de Husillos' (FP37, 1243).

55 'Ouieron a ganar fama que non eran mandados a sus sennores como deuyen con grant danno de si, doliendose ellos dende et queriendo beuir segunt deuen vasallos beuir con su sennor'. Good *fama* was not purely rhetorical but an important element in the social capital possessed or desired by every social group. This was made very plain when Alfonso X in the *Fuero Real* appealed to Holy Scriptures to declare that 'the greatest of all enemies is that who gives someone bad fame' ('que no es mayor enemigo ninguno, que aquel que dà mala fama a otro') (Fuero Real, p. 350).

56 'Pidieronnos merçed que sopiesmos la vida et el fuero que ellos ouieron con los obispos que fueron ante [...] et que le diesemos cosas çiertas por fuero que deuiesen guardar et conplir a nos et a los otros obispos que viniesen despues de nos, de manera que ellos ouieson voluntat de nos seruir lealmiente et nos ouiesemos rrazon de les fazer bien et merçed' (FV30, 1294). I discuss this *fuero* in Alfonso, 'Campesinado y derecho', p. 19.

57 'bonos uasallos e leales al abbat y bonos señores e leales al conçeyo' (FL79, 1250). For more detail

slip from the simple declaration of intent customarily included in the preamble into the charter's penal clauses seems to me a clear sign of a different balance of power.

Conclusion

The reconstruction of the processes by which the sources discussed here were drawn up and revised poses a number of problems, and not only from the diplomatic perspective. In attempting to overcome them, the results obtained by work on the legitimising function of these texts, that is, this construction of a favourable historical memory which underpins them, are particularly persuasive. And it is this perspective, in general rather neglected, that analysis of the preambles of the charters allows to be developed, because they reveal the tensions which presided over their compilation. Given the primacy of the references to these tensions, one conclusion is clear: it was negotiation of the terms of the exchanges between lords and vassals, forced by the opposition of the latter, which led to the production of these charters. These references also reveal the major — and conflictual — contribution to their compilation made by their beneficiaries; that is, by the very persons the lords wished to be good, loyal, faithful, humble and obedient subjects, called on simply passively to enjoy their generosity and protection, or receive the reward merited by their good and loyal service.[58]

That said, how far can we trust these conclusions? What should we make of the charters without a preamble? Should the absence of justification be interpreted as a sign of a seamless domination, wholly accepted? More research is needed and I hope that it will focus on, for example, relating the preambles, or their absence, more closely to the clauses, and on linking the nature of the seigneurial regime more closely to the size and organisation of the communities concerned. For only an analysis of the clauses as a whole, it seems to me, can in reality give us access to the nature of the tensions characterising the local societies, and reveal the nature of the exchanges between the various groups and the meaning they themselves wished to give them. Nevertheless, whatever its limitations, the analysis of the preambles and of their rhetoric reveals a seigneurial ideology designed to legitimise the domination exercised or only desired. But this ideology was so meaningful only because the parameters constituting it derived from a more complex ensemble of norms and social, moral and cultural values shared by the dependent groups, which explains why they contested them and appropriated them.

---

about this agreement, see my Alfonso, 'Campesinado y derecho', pp. 23–28.

58 'These customs and *fueros* [...] by which they shall serve him as a lord in complete subjection and humility' ('Istas consuetudines et foros [...] per quos serviant ei sicut dominus in submissione et humilitate plena') (FL6, 1085); 'and that you shall remain loyal and faithful' ('et ut seduatis fideles et uertadeiros') (FZ25, 1182); 'First, that they remain always as our faithful, humble and subject vassals' ('In primis, ut sint semper nostri vasalli fideles, humiles et subjecti') (FZ53, 1234); 'they shall always be good and faithful vassals of the bishop' ('sean siempre bonos uasallos e leales del obispo') (FL87–8, 1270–1279).

Appendix

1. 1152, December 18

Fuero *given to the citizens of Sahagún by King Alfonso VII and Abbot Domingo*

Published: Rodríguez Fernández, Justiniano, *Los Fueros del Reino de León. Vol. 2: Documentos* (León: Ediciones Leonesas, 1981), doc. 19.

In nomine domini Jhesuchristi. Sicut in omni contratu conditiones valere imperialis testatur authoritas, sic etiam iustitiae ratio exigit ut quae a Regibus, sive ab Imperatoribus fiunt scripto firmentur, ne temporum diuturnitate oblibioni tradantur.

Idcirco ego Adefonsus totius Hispanie Imperator videns inter Dominum Dominicum monasterii Sancti Facundi Abbatem, et eiusdem villae Burgenses discordiam exagitari pro carta de foros quam eidem Abbati suisque monachis requirebant; ut pacem inter eos facerent, ad Sanctum Facundum veni et tunc presentibus filiis meis Sancio et Fernando regibus, communicato consilio cum uxore mea Imperatrice Domna Rica, et sorore mea Domna Sancia Regina, et Raimundo Palentino et Martino Ovetensi Episcopis, et Fernando Galleciae Comiti, Gutierrio Fernandiz, et Poncio de Minerva, et aliis mei imperii melioribus, simul cum Domno Dominico monasterii Sancti Facundi Abbate, et cum omni ipsius monasterii monachorum religioso Conventu, hominibus villae Sancti Facundi tam presentibus quam futuris, et filiis suis omnique genrationi suae foros quibus vivant damus, et per testamentum istud in omnium supradictorum presentia eis roboramus et confirmamus.

[...]

Ego Adefonsus Imperator una cum supranominatis personis confringimus illos malos foros qui erant in veteri carta contra Burgenses Sancti Facundi, quia ipsi a Monachis expetebant. Et ut pacem et concordiam inter eos reformaremus cum Monachis dismissimus habendam propter libertatem romanam qui in ea resonabat.

2. 1165, August 21

Agreement between don Juan, bishop of León, and the inhabitants of Toldanos concerning the fueros they had to make with the promise of the Bishop not to give the villa in prestimonio.

Published: Rodríguez Fernández, Justiniano, *Los Fueros del Reino de León. Vol. 2: Documentos* (León: Ediciones Leonesas, 1981), doc. 29.

(Christus) Sub era MᵃCCᵃIIIᵃ et quot XIIº kalendas septembris. Cognitum est pluribus episcopum domnum Johannem sedis legionensis dedisse Toldanos cuidam militi Roderico Petri nomine in prestimonium; et propter hoc ipsi homines del Toldanos depopulauerunt eam et cum comite domno Petro Alfonsi requirebant hereditatem

THE RHETORIC OF SEIGNEURIAL LEGITIMATION IN THE *FUEROS* OF LEÓN 459

dicentes: quod debebant eam secum leuare, exceptis solaribus et ortis et palumaribus et senris et uineis et terris que erant de manifesto Sancte Marie. Episcopas autem e contra dicebat quod non debebant eam leuare, quia erat hereditas Sancte Marie; et diu super hoc contendentes deuenerunt ad talem finem. Concedente rege domno Fernando et comite domno Petro Alfonsi, episcopus domnus Johannes simul cum toto capitulo fecit eis talem conuenientiam, uidelicet […]

3. 1181, August 23

Fuero *given to the local council of Palencia by its bishop Raymond II, with the consent of his chapter and of King Alfonso VIII.*

Published: Rodríguez Fernández, Justiniano, *Palencia: Panorámica foral de la provincia* (Palencia: Merino, 1981), doc. 25.

In nomine sancte et individue Trinitatis, que a fidelibus in unitate colitur et adoratur. Opus est pietatis et ad salutem animarum prestantisimun argumentum, dominisque sive rectoribus populorum Spanie conveniens, populos sibi submissos certis et scriptis legibus gubernare, bonos instituendo foros, pravasque consuetudines abolendo, ne inter dominum et populum sibi subiectum frequens oriatur discordia et ne dominetur cum inclemencia, ut populus de infidelitate redarguatur, sed in hoc equitas, in illo fidelitas, in utroque stabilitas, mereatur approbari. Eapropter ego Raimundus secundus, Dei gratia Palentine ecclesie episcopus, bono animo et spontanea voluntate, intuitu pietatis ac misericordia et pro salute anime mee, cum consensu pariter et voluntate omnium sociorum meorum eiusdem Palentine ecclesie sancti Antonini canonicorum, necnon cum consensu et voluntate et concesione domini nostri Aldefonsi regis Castelle, ut Deus remunerator omnium bonorum ipsi regi vite conferat utriusque felicitatem, fancio cartam de foris tibi toti concilio de Palencia presenti et futuro in perpetuum valituram.

4. 1191, April 26

Additions to the old fuero *of San Pedro de las Dueñas, granted by the abbess Mayor Díaz and the prior Pedro León, with the consent and mandate of don Gutierre, abbot of Sahagún.*

Published: Rodríguez Fernández, Justiniano, *Los Fueros del Reino de León. Vol. 2: Documentos* (León: Ediciones Leonesas, 1981), doc. 49.

In Dei nomine, amen. Notum sit omnibus hominibus hanc carrtam uidentibus, quos ego domna Maior Didaci abbatissa Sancti Petri et ego Petrus Leónis prior et ego domna Hema priorissa totusque conuentus eiusdem monasterii Sancti Petri de Dominabus, una cum consensu uoluntate et mandato domini Guterri, Dei gratia abbas Sancti Facundi actotus conuentu eiusdem monasterii, necnon etiam cum assensu et beneplacito concilii Sancti Petris, facimus, ordinamus et statuimus et addicimus foro antiquo uille Sancti Petri istud que in presenti scripto sequitur. Quia plures cades uiolentie, rapine dampna et oprobria inferebantur nostris uasallis nostre uille Sancti Petri, per eo uidelicet que multi eorum erant nutricii et alumpni militum et scutifferorum et nutriebant filios et filias eorum. Pretestu quorum nos credebamus nostri uasalli deberent tueri et deffendi et nobis maior honor impendi. Et ex hoc tam nostris uasallis quam nobis secuebant contrarium quia quocienscumque ipsi generosi inter se homicidium perpetrabant, minabantur nostros uasallos et aliquociens interf-ficiebant eos pro eo que nutriebant filios inimicorum suorum et ita disipabantur tam bona nutriendum quam aliorum, et ob hoc non solum modo nos amitebamus nostros uasallos, uerum etiam foros et iura illorum. Item quod aliqui nostrorum uasallorum tradebant filias suas generosis in matrimonium et filias eorum filiis suis copulabant et alique uidae et solute fugebant se illis in coniugium uel in concubinatum. Item quod aliqui ipsorum uasallorum uendebant possessiones et hereditates quos a nobis acceperant militibus et armigeris, et propter hoc amitebamus nostras hereditates quas nostris uasallis in quibus uiuerent dederamus. Quo propter mouebamus contra eos lites et causis in judicio pro deffenssione nostrarum hereditatum et exceptis minis et obprobiis que impendebant nostris uasallis et hominibus nobis seruientibus; incurrebamus dampna grauia et expensarum, magnam destruciones, defectio justicie et deffenssionis in nostra uilla Sancti Petri. Et dicto quod, supradicti domna abbatissa et prior et priorissa totusque conuentus monasterii supradicti, considerando omnia mala qua nobis eueniunt his racionibus supradictas ad custodiendum nos et nostros uassallos et nostre uille Sancti Petri in perpetuum ut non eueniant nobis et ipsis dampna et mala quo actenus nuscunta euenisse, omnis in simul cum assensu et uoluntate et beneplacito supradicti domini Gutterrii abbas Sancti Facundi et conuentu eiusdem loci et etiam concilii Sancti Petri, in perpetuum inuiolabilis obseruandum.

[...]

[8] Et nos concilium uille Sancti Petri omnes insimul iunti iuxta portam Beati Benedicti et uocati sub uoce preconis, prout est usus et consuetudinis, uidendo que omnia ista supradicta que uos dicti domini nostri nobis datis in foro et ordinatis totum facitis, per nostra obseruacione et bono paci, ut possimus custodiri a malis et dampnis quoactenus paciebamus prout pacis per supradicta totum recipimus et concedemus quidquid resonat in presenti pagina. Et obligamus nos et omnia bona nostra et successorum nostrorum ad hoc tenendum, complendum et obseruandum in perpetuum sub pena supradicta.

5. 1222, July 23

Fuero of Peñafiel, granted by King Fernando III following the model provided by those of Ávila, Uceda and Madrid.

Published: González Díez, Emiliano, *El régimen foral vallisoletano. Una perspectiva de análisis organizativo del territorio* (Valladolid: Diputación Provincial de Valladolid, 1986).

Ut regalia gesta fidelium permaneant necesse est ut obliuionis ignauia scripture subsidio succurrantur. Cum itaque Pennefidelis concilium quod auo nostro, scilicet, domno regi Alfonso inclite recordationes, et famossissimo imperatori, necnon et auunculo nostro regi Enrico et mihi circa principium regni nostro et circa progressum in nobis quecumque uolui sempre deuote et fideliter adheserit, et uariis seruiciis sine intermissione nostre sibi obligauit tot et tam bona seruitia non decuit magestatem regiam sine remunerationis gratia pertransire. Eapropter, ego Ferdinandus, Dei gratia rex Toleti et Castelle, una cum uxore nostra Beatrice regina et cum filio nostro ynfante Alfonso, ex assensu ac beneplacito domne Berengarie, genitricis mee, et de consilio magnatum nostrorum, ut uestra inconcussa fidelitas perennis remunerationis testimonio glorietur uobis duxi foros honestos et utiles concedendos, quibus motu proprio, non ad instanciam neque ad petitionem uestram, sed supradictis et multis aliis priuatis sepe et sepius incitatus, que indecens erat magestatem regiam remuneratoria relinquerre foris duxi dignum sequentibus insignire.

Bibliography

Alfonso, Isabel, 'Campesinado y derecho: la vía legal de su lucha (Castilla y León, siglos X–XIII)', *Noticiario de Historia Agraria*, 13 (1997), 15–31

Alfonso, Isabel, 'Litigios por la tierra y "malfetrías" entre la nobleza medieval', *Hispania*, 57–197 (1997), 917–55

Alfonso, Isabel, 'Conflictos sociales en villas de behetrías', in *Los señoríos de behetría*, ed. by Carlos Estepa Díez and Cristina Jular Pérez-Alfaro (Madrid: CSIC, 2001), pp. 227–60

Alfonso, Isabel and Cristina Jular Pérez-Alfaro, 'Oña contra Frías o el pleito de los cien testigos: una pesquisa en la Castilla del siglo XIII', *Edad Media: Revista de Historia*, 3 (2000), 61–88

Anta Lorenzo, Lauro, 'El fuero de Sanabria', *Studia historica. Historia medieval*, 5 (1987), 161–72

Barrero García, Ana María, 'El proceso de formación de los Fueros Municipales (cuestiones metodológicas)', in *Espacios y fueros en Castilla-La Mancha (siglos XI–XV): una perspectiva metodológica*, ed. by Javier Alvarado Planas (Madrid: Polifemo, 1995), pp. 59–88

Escalona, Julio, 'Misericordia regia, es decir, negociemos. Alfonso VII y los Lara en la *Chronica Adefonsi imperatoris*', in *Lucha política: condena y legitimación en la España medieval*, ed. by Julio Escalona, Isabel Alfonso, and Georges Martin (Lyon: ENS Editions, 2004), pp. 101–52

Guyotjeannin, Olivier, 'Vivre libre dans une seigneurie juste. Note sur les préambules des chartes de franchises', in *Campagnes médiévales. L'homme et son espace. Etudes offertes à Robert Fossier*, ed. by Elisabeth Mornet (Paris: Publications de la Sorbonne, 1995), pp. 375–85

Jular Pérez-Alfaro, Cristina, 'Conflictos ante tenentes y merinos en los siglos XII–XIII, ¿contestación al poder señorial o al poder regio?', *Noticiario de Historia Agraria*, 13 (1997), 33–64

Martin, Georges, 'Amour (Une notion politique)', *Cahiers d'Études Hispaniques Médiévales*, 11 (1997), 169–206

Martín, José Luis, 'Utilidad de las fórmulas "inútiles" de los documentos medievales', in *Semana de historia del monacato cántabro-astur-leonés* (Oviedo: Monasterio de San Pelayo – La Industria, 1982), pp. 81–86

Martínez Sopena, Pascual, *La Tierra de Campos occidental: poblamiento, poder y comunidad del siglo X al XIII* (Valladolid: Institución Cultural Simancas, 1985)

Parisse, Michel, 'Préambules de chartes', in *Les prologues médiévaux: Actes du Colloque international organisé par l'Academia Belgica et l'École française de Rome avec le concours de la F.I.D.E.M. (Rome, 26–28 mars 1998)*, ed. by Jacqueline Hamesse (Turnhout: Brepols, 2000), pp. 141–69

Pastor, Reyna, *Resistencias y luchas campesinas en la época del crecimiento y consolidación de la formación feudal: Castilla y León, siglos X–XIII* (Madrid: Siglo XXI, 1980)

CHAPTER 12

On Punishment and Exemplary Violence

with a commentary by Warren C. Brown

Conflict, Language, and Social Practice in Medieval Societies: Selected Essays of Isabel Alfonso, with Commentaries, ed. by Julio Escalona Monge, Álvaro Carvajal Castro, and Cristina Jular Pérez-Alfaro, TMC 24 (Turnhout: Brepols, 2024), pp. 463–502

BREPOLS ❧ PUBLISHERS   10.1484/M.TMC-EB.5.132466

WARREN C. BROWN

Commentary

At the beginning of this essay, Isabel alludes to — and at the same time distances herself from — a tradition of work on medieval disputing that developed, in dialogue with social and legal anthropology, on both sides of the Atlantic in the 1970s. This tradition has, as she points out, tended to highlight negotiation, compromise, and extra-judicial ways of resolving disputes over the strict application of laws.[1] It emerged in reaction to an overly mechanical view of medieval justice produced by the positivist legal historians of the late nineteenth and first half of the twentieth centuries, represented in medieval studies by such towering figures as Heinrich Brunner.[2] These scholars treated medieval texts both narrative and archival as objective witnesses and sources of facts. Conflict resolution was a matter for laws that people followed in a rule-centred manner,[3] and for judicial institutions that followed defined and identifiable procedures and that generally produced clear results. The anthropologically-driven school of medieval dispute studies, in contrast, focused on social and political relationships and processes. Its leading lights, including in the Anglophone world Stephen D. White, Patrick J. Geary, Barbara H. Rosenwein, Geoffrey Koziol, and the Bucknell group led by Wendy Davies and Paul Fouracre, and in Germany Gerd Althoff, pointed out that the processes by which medieval people declared, managed, and resolved their disputes with each other often transcended what was recorded in a single document; we have sometimes to look at several documents, or at an array of texts from different genres, to get a complete (or at least more complete) picture of what was going on. They argued moreover that it is not only the ties of authority and obedience projected by laws that matter to how disputes were handled, but also relationships of kinship, friendship, allegiance, and raw power, and the frequently unwritten norms that structured them. They turned the tools of literary criticism loose on our sources, to show how much even archival records could be influenced by personal or political bias, or by narrative conventions; record-keeping itself emerged as a weapon in medieval conflict. It is not at all surprising, then, that these scholars and their successors have tended to cast conflict in terms of negotiation and settlement, and as one way that people constituted and reconstituted their relationships with each other, rather than as a breach of order that needed to be restored by laws and judicial institutions.

Isabel reminds us that there is another side to medieval conflict: sometimes the sources do talk about winners and losers, objective right and wrong, and

---

1 For the discussion below see Brown and Górecki, 'What Conflict Means'.
2 See e.g. Brunner, *Deutsche Rechtsgeschichte*.
3 On the 'rule-centred' approach to norms see Roberts, *Order and Dispute*.

Warren C. Brown, California Institute of Technology

disrupted order that needed to be restored. Nevertheless, her work in this essay is very different from that of the old positivists. Isabel approaches legal history as it has come to be understood at the end of the twentieth century and the beginning of the twenty-first: as the study of normative behaviour writ large; as the study of not only the institutions but also the social practices through which past societies channelled power and regulated their members' behaviour. Law strictly defined (as a set of binding norms promulgated by an authority)[4] is part of this, but not the only part, and in some situations not even the dominant part. Accordingly, as she explores how power was wielded and its exercise justified in high medieval Castile (which I think is fundamentally what this essay is all about), Isabel looks at law, as projected by Alfonso X's *Siete Partidas*, but she also reaches well beyond it. As she herself says, she is expanding legal history beyond 'the history of penal or criminal law' to look at broader criteria by which particular kinds of punishments were legitimated (p. 476). I would argue, therefore, that she is still, with her expansive understanding of 'law' and the variety of sources with which she has engaged, very much working within the recent tradition of medieval conflict studies that she takes as her point of departure.

Where Isabel comes to rest is on the human body, as a site where power, and the norms that governed it, were not only enforced but also displayed and communicated. To help us understand the norms that regulated corporal punishment in high-medieval Castile, and what prompted (or compelled) people to pay attention to them, she focuses on emotions — specifically, fear. In my opinion, this is a very important contribution. In my own work on conflict, violence, and power in medieval societies north of the Pyrenees, I have tended to think that people paid attention to norms primarily out of self-interest. While acknowledging that medieval rulers frequently resorted to violence and fear as tools of power, I have the sense that in the decentralized, low-technology societies that characterized much of Europe during the Middle Ages, they had only a limited ability to coerce obedience from their subjects on a large scale and over a long period. I have been led, therefore, to look more at the ways and at the reasons why people *chose* to acknowledge power and its normative claims, or *decided* how they were going to react to them, in line with their own needs and interests rather than at the fears that could compel them to do so.[5] Isabel, in contrast, presents social control as something that rulers sought to achieve or promote by consciously manipulating and broadcasting emotions, and especially fear, not in the context of what we might call 'state terror', but rather in the context of justice itself. The fear provoked in the malefactor by the threat of mutilation or a painful death — attacks on the body that were off-limits in non-judicial or non-military contexts — was a good and healthy fear, in the context both of justice and of warfare against non-Christians. It was positive, and its use reflected well on the ruler, because it promoted and helped maintain a common (and in the case of violence against non-Christians a universal?) good. Channelling Michel Foucault's

---

4   See e.g. the Oxford English Dictionary online, s.v. 'law, n. 1', def. I.1.a; MacCormick, *Institutions of Law*, p. 11.

5   See *inter alia* Brown, *Unjust Seizure* and Brown, *Violence in Medieval Europe*.

Discipline and Punish (which she cites),[6] Isabel illustrates how violence against the human body served as a means of communication. It did not simply communicate to its immediate victim, however. Through the display of its effects (that is, the scars or missing limbs of the living, or the bodies — or pieces of the bodies — of the dead), it kept on communicating, in ways that could transcend the immediate time and place of its application. The initial act of violence against the body of someone who had violated the accepted order served to punish; public punishment warned witnesses and anyone they communicated with against engaging in similarly disruptive behaviour; the victim's mutilation communicated this deterrent for his or her lifetime — wherever he or she went — or even beyond the grave in the case of heads and body parts distributed to various places.

By focusing, in the way that she does and with the sources that she does, on the human body as the parchment (as it were) on which this warning was inscribed and from which it was read, Isabel looks from legal history towards both literary and art history — specifically, work by literary scholars and art historians on the meaning of human skin. For example, a recent volume of essays by a group of Anglo-American scholars on flaying — that is, the deliberate removal of people's skin — in pre-modern Europe compares the actual historical practice of flaying people with representations of flaying in literature and art. The volume's contributors echo Isabel by suggesting (among other things) that flaying (which in the rare cases when it was actually carried out was above all a punishment for treason) publicly wiped out an old identity and inscribed a new one onto the body of the victim; in the case of treason, flaying indelibly marked a crime against the body politic onto the body of the traitor. The skin's preservation could communicate the meaning of its removal for generations.[7]

As Foucault does in a different context, Isabel stresses repeatedly that this kind of punishment served ultimately to reinforce the authority of the ruler.[8] We might say, then, that the kings of Castile sought to create what Barbara Rosenwein would call an 'emotional community', that is, a community in which a particular set of stimuli (in this case certain kinds of damage purposefully inflicted on people's bodies), applied according to commonly understood rules, provoke (or are supposed to provoke) emotional responses that the members of the community understand and value in the same way.[9] Isabel's sources paint a consistent picture of this emotional community: the king is entitled, either personally or through his judicial representatives, to wield violence against his subjects' bodies in order to create and spread a fear that will prompt his subjects to obey his rules; his use of fear assumes that his subjects will in fact feel fear, and respond to it, as he expects them to. This raises a question, namely, whether there may have been (as Rosenwein suggests for other times and

---

6 Foucault, *Discipline and Punish*, first published in French as Foucault, *Surveiller et punir*.
7 Tracy, ed., *Flaying in the Pre-Modern World*, p. 201. For a similar observation within the realm of more traditional legal history see Oliver, *The Body Legal*, p. 176 on scalping as punishment in Anglo-Saxon England; because hair cannot grow back on the scalped part of the head, 'not only is the transgressor publicly humiliated and physically tortured, but he is branded for life'.
8 Cf. Foucault, *Discipline and Punish*, p. 55.
9 Rosenwein, *Emotional Communities*, p. 2.

places) different emotional communities in high medieval Castile that understood fear and its use differently, and did not accept — and therefore threatened — the king's use of the emotion (cf. Foucault's argument that in early modern Europe the use of public ceremonies of violence to assert royal power required public acceptance to be effective).[10]

Isabel does something else that distances her from the positivist legal historians: rather than treating the meaning of her key terms as transhistorical absolutes, she incorporates into her argument the fact that they did not always mean what they do today; her observations raise the possibility that the meanings of some of them could differ even in various parts of the past itself. The words 'crime' and 'criminal' are a case in point. 'Crime' in English today refers to an offense against the state that the state assumes the right to punish. It derives from the Latin *crimen*, which was in the earlier Middle Ages, however, but one of several general terms for transgression in societies dominated by an undifferentiated, and highly subjective, sense of wrong. It began to develop in the direction of the modern English 'crime' in the twelfth and thirteenth centuries, when kings emerged who were powerful enough to define a wide range of offenses as wrongs against themselves that they alone had the right to police.[11] Nevertheless, in both periods of the Middle Ages *crimen* (as well as its French and Anglo-Norman cognates) referred to an offense of some kind. I was quite surprised, therefore, to learn from Isabel that 'criminal' (*criminal*) offenses, as a subset of offenses in general (*yerros*), could be defined on a completely different basis: not by the nature of an offense but by the nature of the punishment that it brought (see pp. 476–77 and n. 7). What was or was not done to the body in response to an offense in her world determined whether or not that offense was a crime, not the interests of the state; a 'crime' was a wrong 'for which [the malefactor] may suffer loss of life or limb, or some other corporal punishment, or expulsion from the country'.[12] I was similarly struck by her discussion of the two words 'prisoner' and 'captive'. I am used to thinking of these two words as synonymous, and have seen nothing in the sources with which I am familiar that might cause me to think otherwise (yet). Here, Isabel tells us that in high medieval Castile the words were related, but that their meaning depended on whether or not the person being held was 'inside' or 'outside' of Christian society. Whether one were a 'prisoner' — that is, a Christian captured by other Christians — or a 'captive' seized in a war against someone of a different religion determined how one's body could and could not be treated (see p. 485).

The distinction between 'inside' and 'outside' is central to Isabel's project. In high-medieval Castile, she argues, similar norms applied to non-Christian 'captives' as to Christian 'criminals'; their bodies were not just fair but also necessary targets (see pp. 486–87). Since a particular kind of violence against the bodies of non-Christians marked the boundary between 'inside' and 'outside', then by implication, as non-Christians were 'outside', so too were Christian 'criminals'. Isabel's observations

---

10 Rosenwein, *Emotional Communities*, as above; Foucault, *Discipline and Punish*, pp. 59–63.

11 See Hyams, *Rancor and Reconciliation*, pp. 220–21; Hudson, *The Formation of the English Common Law*, p. 44.

12 Partidas III.4.9.

are particularly apropos at the time this volume is slated to appear. In all parts of the modern world, the question of who gets to wield violence against whom turns on boundaries not only of religion but also of nationality or ethnicity, race, immigration status, etc. Violence is not acceptable against members of the 'in' group, but its use against outsiders helps define who is 'in'. It becomes vitally important, then, to figure out exactly where the 'out' group is. In Isabel's world, the boundary markers are inscribed on people, or advertised by their physical treatment.

Here again we can make an interesting comparison to medieval societies north of the Pyrenees, or at least to those with which I am most familiar, namely the ones that developed within the territory of the Carolingian Empire. Here the primary boundaries between 'inside' and 'outside', at least as far as the use of violence against human beings goes, followed the lines not of religion but of status. In Isabel's Castile, status distinctions mattered in the judicial arena; the punishments that judicial authorities might inflict on the bodies of transgressors depended on their social rank. The continuum of possible punishments appears to assume, however, that inflicting corporal punishment on any criminal was *per se* legitimate, regardless of rank. In Frankish and post-Frankish Europe, the assumptions underlying judicial punishment were different, as were those governing the treatment of enemies in war. In a world where, except on the frontiers (and later, in Crusader Palestine), all warfare pitted Christian against Christian, it was status that determined 'inside' and 'outside', and therefore the legitimacy (or not) of certain kinds of physical violence. Among the early medieval Franks, for example, only unfree people could be punished corporally, or judicially tortured. Freemen and women paid compensation for wrongs up to and including homicide. Only if a free wrongdoer refused to pay or could not pay compensation (or find enough kinspeople to help him pay it) was he left open to physical retribution (with the consequences often communicated by the public display, at a crossroads or on a fencepost, of the malefactor's mutilated body).[13] Jumping forward a few centuries, the way that status separated 'inside' from 'outside' in the context of warfare is clearly visible in Jean Froissart's *Chronicles* of the Hundred Years War. In vignette after vignette, Froissart tells us that for members of the warrior nobility of fourteenth-century western Europe, no matter which king they followed, killing, injuring, or even humiliating other nobles was generally unacceptable, even in battle. If one was defeated, one could expect to be captured and held for ransom, and to be treated decently. The rules changed when it came to members of the lower orders; they could be tortured and killed with impunity. Nowhere is this expressed more plainly than in Froissart's description of the northern French revolt of 1356 now known as the Jacquerie. In recounting a battle at Meaux, between a group of rebels and a band of nobles that had come to the rescue of some noble ladies trapped in the town, Froissart pits the well-organized and heavily armed and armoured nobles, with their banners flying, against what he describes as a disorganized mob of peasants whose members were 'small and dark and very poorly armed'.[14] The knights mowed down the Jacques like the cattle Froissart seems to have thought they were; in the

---

13 For examples see *Pactus Legis Salicae*, 11b, 158; Tours, *Historiarum libri decem*, IX.19, 256–57.
14 Froissart, *Chronicles*, p. 154.

days that followed, nobles roamed the countryside killing rustics without mercy. Froissart's descriptions of events are of course idealized and heavily stereotyped; they were clearly intended to appeal to the members of the warrior nobility who were Froissart's chief patrons and audience. Yet they are useful precisely because they make it easier for us to see how the nobles drew the lines of 'inside' and 'outside' on the bodies of the nob-noble, to their own advantage.

Part of what made the Jacques 'other' to Froissart, that is, subject to and deserving of unrestrained physical violence, was their (alleged) resort to unacceptable violence against their betters. He has the rebels raping and killing a knight's wife and daughter in front of him before killing them all, roasting a knight on a spit and forcing his wife and children to eat his flesh before killing them, etc. Evoking the kind of religious 'inside' v. 'outside' that Isabel identifies, Froissart makes the Jacques worse even than Muslims by declaring: 'Their barbarous acts were worse than anything that ever took place between Christians and Saracens'.[15] Here we see a rhetorical use of the body different from that observed by Isabel: not violence against the bodies of 'others', but rather accusations that 'others' had used violence against bodies unjustly, or sometimes that they had done so at all. Larissa Tracy has recently traced the use of such accusations by other medieval authors to draw images of 'inside' and 'outside' on a different basis, namely that of emerging national identities. As early as the twelfth century, and throughout the thirteenth and fourteenth, she argues, some Europeans sought to define themselves as members of nations (e.g., 'English' or 'French'). Literary descriptions of judicial brutality and torture formed part of this effort; like Froissart's Jacques, barbarian 'others' resorted to judicial brutality and judicial torture, while 'we' did not (in much the same way that we often today 'other' the Middle Ages themselves by telling stories or visiting museums about medieval torture).[16] In a wide-ranging study of flogging, Guy Geltner, like Isabel, notes that societies both present and past have used corporal punishment to mark and separate out internal deviants. He also points out, however, that these same societies have promoted their own collective identity at the expense of other groups by accusing them of using corporal punishment, or of using it wrongly, in an effort to cast the 'other' as 'profoundly different, brutal, and uncivilized'. Neither tactic, he argues, has disappeared in the modern world, even in the allegedly civilized West.[17] It appears that in many contexts, the lines between inside and outside have been based on different criteria. The human body, however, as a site on which to mark it, or on which to accuse others of marking it, is the common coin.

These comparisons suggest an arena in which to push Isabel's observations further: warfare among Christian principalities in high medieval Spain. Above the level of crime, Isabel alludes to political conflict among Christians, in the form of riot, or the 'seditious tumults' called *asonada* (pp. 489, 491). But it would be interesting to explore further how the Christian inhabitants of Castile conceptualized and understood full-scale warfare against Christians beyond their borders. What were

---

15 Froissart, *Chronicles*, p. 151.
16 Tracy, *Torture and Brutality*.
17 Geltner, *Flogging Others*.

COMMENTARY   471

the norms governing corporal punishment of captives in this kind of conflict? Were they treated as 'others', whether criminal others or 'outside' others? Or were they, like noble opponents in warfare north of the Pyrenees, treated as 'us'? A way in to this subject might be offered by Isabel's discussion of enmity. She notes that the law recognized 'open enmity', as a state of conflict that allowed one to treat captives in ways normally reserved only for criminals or non-Christians: 'And, where it happens that one man arrests another of noble descent, he should not put him in irons, in prison, or in stocks, or restrain him of his liberty in any other harmful or dishonourable way, unless he is his open enemy and has been so declared by judgment of court' (pp. 489–90, citing Partida II.26.17). Perhaps it was enmity that provided the norms governing how prisoners were treated when one Christian prince on the Iberian Peninsula fought another.

What Isabel says about enmity points up both how tempting and how dangerous it is to try to distinguish between 'state' norms and 'personal' norms, or 'public' and 'private' actions and motivations, in her (or any other medieval) world; a distinction that we take for granted in the twenty-first century western present did not necessarily make sense in the deep past. Here enmity, something that at first glance might seem to be intensely personal, was woven into the fabric of the law. It justified behaviour that would otherwise be illegitimate, namely physically mistreating noble captives. Legally recognized enmity thus seems to have created new lines of 'inside' and 'outside'. The lines between 'public' and 'private' also blur when Isabel notes that Castilian justice incorporated not only the king's need to keep order but the immediate victim's need for reparation (p. 486 and n. 62). Isabel's fundamental point, that Castilian justice was based on a 'pedagogical and therapeutic' conception of violence as a means by which the king promoted proper behaviour, likewise pulls together what we think of as very different social fields, namely the state and the family. It provides more fodder for an argument that Foucault made about the transition to modernity: pre-modern penal systems were so bound to the personal power of the king that in order to reform them, early modern reformers had in a sense to 'depersonalize' them by making them 'public'.[18]

In the chronicles that Isabel explores we see heads displayed and paraded while the bodies of beheaded kings were treated with respect; we see public and scripted displays of grief in which women played a central part. All of this bespeaks a rich symbolic language of gesture and counter-gesture that enabled communication across the lines of religion. But Isabel's observations about these rituals raise an interesting question about the possible distance between image and reality in narrative sources: how 'other' were the Muslims, really, if this kind of communication worked? The *Chronica Adefonsi imperatoris*, for example, describes the body parts of the defeated Munio Alfonso being treated by the Muslims — that is, being paraded, displayed, and returned — using the same symbolic language as that employed by Christians. If the Muslims and their Christian opponents 'spoke' a mutually comprehensible symbolic language, that by implication reflected shared ideals about order and about

---

18 Foucault, *Discipline and Punish*, pp. 73–82.

how the body should be treated, how different were they? Or are we witnessing here a literary rendering of the 'other' as comprehensible, in the same way as the late eleventh century epic poem *The Song of Roland* presents its Muslims as in some ways mirror images of, but in their social order and worldview exactly like its Franks?[19]

Finally: Isabel has engaged in this essay in one of the fundamental tasks of the historian: explaining how what appears incomprehensible or unacceptable in our world could be rational and acceptable in someone else's. She shows us how in some circumstances, for example, perfectly rational human beings could view cruelty as having a positive value, or think that imprisonment was not necessarily punitive (see e.g. p. 12). She thus helps us get past tropes about the irrationally or anarchically violent Middle Ages.

---

19 The editions and translations of this work are too numerous to cite; see e.g. Brault, ed., *The Song of Roland*.

Bibliography

Pactus Legis Salicae, ed. by Karl August Eckhardt, *Monumenta Germaniae Historica. Legum sectio I. Legum nationum Germanicarum, t. 4, 1*, (Hanover: Hahn, 1962)

Brault, Gerard, ed., *The Song of Roland: An Analytical Edition* (University Park, PA: Pennsylvania State University Press, 1978)

Brown, Warren C., *Unjust Seizure: Conflict, Interest and Authority in an Early Medieval Society* (Ithaca: Cornell University Press, 2001)

Brown, Warren C., *Violence in Medieval Europe* (London: Longman, 2011)

Brown, Warren C. and Piotr Górecki, 'What Conflict Means: The Making of Medieval Conflict Studies in the United States, 1970–2000', in *Conflict in Medieval Europe: Changing Perspectives on Society and Culture*, ed. by Warren C. Brown and Piotr Górecki (Aldershot: Ashgate, 2003), pp. 1–35

Brunner, Heinrich, *Deutsche Rechtsgeschichte*, 2 vols (Berlin: Duncker & Humblot, 1906)

Foucault, Michel, *Surveiller et punir. Naissance de la prison* (Paris: Gallimard, 1975)

Foucault, Michel, *Discipline and Punish: The Birth of the Prison* (New York: Vintage Books, 1979)

Froissart, Jean, *Chronicles*. trans. and ed. by Geoffrey Brereton (New York: Penguin, 1968)

Geltner, Guy, *Flogging Others: Corporal Punishment and Cultural Identity from Antiquity to the Present* (Amsterdam: Amsterdam University Press, 2014)

Hudson, John, *The Formation of the English Common Law: Law and Society from King Alfred to Magna Carta*, 2nd ed., (London: Routledge, 2018)

Hyams, Paul R., *Rancor and Reconciliation in Medieval England* (Ithaca: Cornell University Press, 2003)

MacCormick, Neil, *Institutions of Law: An Essay in Legal Theory* (Oxford: Oxford University Press, 2007)

Oliver, Lisi, *The Body Legal in Barbarian Law* (Toronto: University of Toronto Press, 2011)

Roberts, Simon, *Order and Dispute: An Introduction to Legal Anthropology* (Harmondsworth: Penguin, 1979)

Rosenwein, Barbara H., *Emotional Communities in the Early Middle Ages* (Ithaca: Cornell University Press, 2006)

Tours, Gregory of, *Historiarum libri decem*, ed. by Rudolf Buchner (Darmstadt: Wissenschaftliche Buchgesellschaft, 1967–1970)

Tracy, Larissa, *Torture and Brutality in Medieval Literature: Negotiations of National Identity* (Cambridge: D. S. Brewer, 2012)

Tracy, Larissa, ed., *Flaying in the Pre-Modern World: Practice and Representation* (Cambridge: D. S. Brewer, 2017)

ISABEL ALFONSO

Corpus Delicti and Exemplary Violence*

According to Black's Law Dictionary, the expression *corpus delicti* means:

> The body of a crime. The body (material substance) upon which a crime has been committed, e.g., the corpse of a murdered man, the charred remains of a house burned down. In a derivative sense, the substance or foundation of a crime; the substantial fact that a crime has been committed.[1]

This notion of the body as both object and evidence is important for understanding the nature of the widespread corporal punishments provided by medieval law for certain crimes. The body of the culprits is perceived to be an instrument of these acts and therefore a punishable receptacle for legally sanctioned violence. This violence that sought to roughly reproduce the damages suffered by the victim, or to punish, wound or maim, the body parts involved in the alleged crime.[2] Taking into account that in medieval Castile justice could be understood as 'another form of very great war that men use at all times', and judges as 'warriors and adversaries of those who seize control of Justice',[3] it seems relevant to look at the practical and semantic connections that were established — more often than is commonly thought — between the bodies defeated in the two main areas of confrontation and conflict resolution: trial and battle. The recent emphasis on the conciliatory character of medieval conflict resolution tends to overshadow the fact that the terms 'winners' and 'losers' are ubiquitous in the legal lexicon of this period.[4]

This paper explores how various medieval texts portrayed the physical violence inflicted on 'defeated bodies' in the judicial field and in war and the relationship between the two. It also considers the similarities and differences between the

---

* Original publication: Alfonso, Isabel, 'El cuerpo del delito y la violencia ejemplar', in *El cuerpo derrotado: Cómo trataban musulmanes y cristianos a los enemigos vencidos (Península Ibérica, ss. VIII–XIII)*, ed. by Maribel Fierro and Francisco García Fitz (Madrid: Consejo Superior de Investigaciones Científicas, 2008), pp. 397–431. Translated by Julian Thomas.

1 Black's Law Dictionary, 2nd Ed. s.v. 'Corpus Delicti'. [online]: http://thelawdictionary.org/corpus-delicti/ [Date accessed: 22 February 2022)].

2 Orlandis Rovira, 'Las consecuencias del delito'; López-Amo y Marín, 'El Derecho penal español'; Tomás y Valiente, *El derecho penal de la monarquía absoluta*; Madero Eguía, *Manos violentas*; Gauvard, *De grace especial*; Gonthier, *Le châtiment*.

3 As per Alfonso X of Castile's famous legal compilation: [judges are] 'como guerreros, e contralladores a los que embargan la Justicia', [for justice is] 'otra manera de muy gran guerra que usan los hombres en todo tiempo' (Partidas III.2.2).

4 As in the *fuero* of Soria: 'If someone who is convicted [lit. 'defeated'] for the death of a man has nothing to pay the fines with, he shall be held by the neck in the stocks' ('Si aquel que fuere vencido por muerte de omne non ouier de que pechar las calonnas, ssea metido de garganta en el çepo') (Sánchez, *Fueros castellanos de Soria*, p. 517). For recent literature on conflict resolution, see Alfonso, 'Lenguaje y prácticas de negociar' [Editors' note: For an English translation, see chapter 2 of this volume].

476 ISABEL ALFONSO

treatment of the vanquished in each sphere, in a broad, not strictly legal, sense. This approach is not that of the history of penal or criminal law. What ultimately matters here is identifying the criteria used to construct the differences and similarities in these two areas, the various types of enemies that appear in each of them and, thus, comparing how the violence with which they were treated was legitimised in each sphere. The central corpus used for this analysis consists of Alfonso the Wise's *Siete Partidas*. More than just a legal code, this work is now widely considered as a political and doctrinal treatise of great significance for understanding how the punishing of convicts was perceived and justified in mid-thirteenth century Christian Spain. It also provides an opportunity to compare legally imposed violence both in peace and war, the two contexts of justice identified by the legislator. Additionally, it gives insights into how behaviour towards prisoners in each field was regulated, and into the procedures for redeeming Christian captives. Only incidentally and indirectly does this source inform us about the treatment accorded in the Christian kingdoms to captives or people of another religion. The first part of this essay, therefore, will be devoted to the analysis of this legal code. With this conceptual and normative background, I will then examine some chronicle passages in which the treatment of the enemies defeated in judicial trials or in war is described in particular detail.

The *Siete Partidas*

Although there is a widespread tendency to reduce the judicial content of the *Siete Partidas* to the more explicit Partidas III and VII, their conceptual principles and references pervade the whole corpus. This is true despite the intricacies of the successive redactions undergone by each of the Partidas, as is now widely recognised.[5] In Alfonso X's code the passing allusions and associations are at least as interesting as the explicit rules. For example, from the mere rhetoric of Partida III, it could be thought that peacetime conflicts were resolved non-violently, by recourse to 'law and justice', in contrast with the 'might and arms' necessary in wartime.[6] However, when comparing the titles on Justice in peacetime in Partida VII, with the titles on Justice in wartime in Partida II, the principles underlying each of the two areas seem closer than the discourse of Partida III would suggest. In fact, it is Partida III that articulates a central idea of medieval justice: the necessary existence of a corporal

---

5 For the contents and writing of the Siete Partidas, see Gómez Redondo, *Historia de la prosa medieval 1*.
6 'great lords must be specially attentive to the two particular occasions on each of which they should be careful to act in a proper manner; first, the time of war, of arms, and soldiers, in opposition to strong and powerful foreign enemies; second, the time of peace, law and legal rights in opposition to internal wrong-doers and insolent persons, acting in such a way that they may be always victorious, on the one hand, by means of strength and arms, on the other, through equity and justice' ('dos tiempos han de catar los grandes en que han de estar guisados para obrar en cada vno dellos segund conuiene. El vno, en tiempo de guerra, e de armas, e de gente, contra los enemigos de fuera fuertes e poderosos. E el otro, en tiempo de paz, e de Leyes, e Fueros derechos, contra los de dentro tortizeros e soberuiosos; de manera que siempre ellos sean vencedores. Lo vno con esfuerço, e con armas; e lo al con derecho, e con justicia') (Partidas III.Preamble).

CORPUS DELICTI AND EXEMPLARY VIOLENCE   477

penalty, that is, a justice that penalises the bodies. Thus, cases are termed 'criminal' precisely whenever the defendant accused of committing certain acts 'may suffer death, maiming or another corporal chastisement' if they were proven.[7] Tellingly, the word 'criminal' does not refer to the crime, but to the penalty that the culprit may deserve. A criminal penalty, moreover, does not always relate to a crime, in the modern sense of the term. An awareness of the arguments supporting this legally imposed violence is important for understanding the perceptions that underlie or justify other types of violence.

Judicial Punishments Carried Out on Bodies

Partida VII details seven forms of punishment that judges could use to chastise those who committed *yerros* ('wrongdoings'),[8] whether by deed, in speech, in writing or by criminal association.[9] Among these punishments, only the first (death or loss of limb) and last (being publicly lashed or injured, dishonoured by being displayed in the pillory, or laid bare in the sun slathered in honey to be eaten by flies) involve direct physical damage. This does not mean that the rest of the established punishments, ranging from forced labour, life imprisonment for servants, exile with or without expropriation, to being banned from carrying out any kind of trade, did not involve physical pain and suffering, that is, violence.[10] In the code, the penalties are seemingly graded by the seriousness of the offence committed, but here come into play perceptions — both ours and theirs — of what actually constituted violence, revealing its relative nature — both then and now.[11] This was obvious in the ways judges were

---

7   Partidas III.4.9 defines criminal cases when discussing the kind of lawsuit the judge should not hear if it is against his parents or children: 'A criminal prosecution means an accusation or complaint made in court by one man against another, concerning some offence which he alleges the latter has committed, for which he may suffer loss of life or limb, or some other corporal punishment, or expulsion from the country' ('Criminal pleyto tanto quiere decir, como acusamiento, o querella que faze en juicio vn ome contra otro, sobre yerro que dize que ha hecho, de que le puede venir muerte, o perdimiento de miembro, u otro escarmiento en su cuerpo, o echamiento de tierra'). Since Partida III deals with disputes over property and lordship, it only covers situations where so-defined criminal accusations are excluded. Likewise, Partidas II.31.7 singles out *pleyto de sangre* ('a matter involving the shedding of blood') as a kind of lawsuit that could not be judged by teachers about their pupils.

8   *Yerros* generally refers to wrong, illegal, or violent acts. Its semantic content deserves a profound analysis, for the word 'crime' used here may present problems if this is not borne in mind. On penal vocabulary, see Gonthier, *Le châtiment*, pp. 9–19.

9   Partidas VII.31.3 discusses the following types of *yerros*: by deed (killing, stealing, robbing ...); in speech (reviling, insulting, or bearing false witness ...); in writing (false letters, wicked songs, malicious statements ...); by advice: where certain persons 'join together', or take an oath, or enter into an agreement or an association 'to do harm to others; or to receive enemies into the country; or to cause insurrections therein; or to encourage thieves or malefactors' ('[se] ayuntan en uno [y hacen jura, postura o cofradía] para fazer mal a otros, o para rescebir los enemigos en la tierra, o para fazer leuantamiento en ella, o para acoger los ladrones o los malhechores').

10   Partidas VII.31.4.

11   Miller has produced one of the most important insights I know about the concept of violence. He uses the term 'perspective' to refer to both its perception and its representation, as well as to the

478   ISABEL ALFONSO

allowed, or not, to have the death penalty carried out: beheading with a sword or knife, but not with a sickle;[12] burning, hanging or throwing to wild beasts, but not stoning, crucifying, or throwing anyone from a cliff, tower, bridge or the like.[13] Accordingly, there are 'some forms of penalty that no man should be given, whichever the *yerro* he might have committed'. Among these are certain actions against the face, such as marking it with hot coals, cutting the nose, gouging out the eyes or any other way that may leave a mark, because the face was made in the likeness of God. The rest of the body was deemed sufficient to fulfil the main objective of frightening people and providing public example.[14] The fact that banishment could only be imposed by the highest political authorities while death was in the hands of ordinary judges also suggests that the severity of issues deserving the former punishment had more to do with political concerns than with any objective measure of violence.[15]

The criteria defining the severity of crimes depend on the context in which they occur and are modulated by social status, age, and gender, among other factors. Social status was particularly relevant and produced complex distinctions that eloquently

------

complex process of assigning a meaning to it (Miller, *Humiliation*, ch. 2). For a discussion of the different meanings that other historians give to this notion see, Alfonso, 'Los nombres de la violencia' [Editors' note: For an English translation, see chapter 16 of this volume].

12 'the capital punishment of death [...] shall be inflicted on the party who deserved it by cutting off his head with a sword or a knife, and not with an ax, or a sickle used for reaping' ('la pena de la muerte principal [...] puede ser dada al que la mereciere, cortandole la cabeza con espada, o con cuchillo e non con segur nin con foz de segar') (Partida VII.31.6).

13 'or he may be burned, hung, or thrown to wild beasts to be killed by them; but judges shall not order any man to be stoned to death, or crucified, or cast down from a rock, tower, bridge, or any other high place' ('otrosi pueden lo quemar o en forcar, o echar a las bestias brauas, que lo maten pero los judgadores non deuen mandar apedrear ningun ome, nin crucificarlo, nin despennarlo de penna: nin de torre, nin de puente, nin de otro logar') (Partida VII.31.6).

14 'there are, however, certain kinds of punishment which should be inflicted on any man on account of an offense which he may have committed; as, for instance, branding him in the face with a hot iron; cutting off his nose, plucking out his eyes; or inflicting any other kind of punishment on him by which his face may be disfigured. This is the case because God made man in his own image, and therefore no judges should punish anyone in this way, and we forbid them to do so; for, since God wished to honor and ennoble man to such an extent as to create him in his own image, it is not fitting that because of some offense or wickedness of evil-disposed people the face of the Lord should be disfigured, or injured. Wherefore We order that judges, whose duty it is to punish men for crimes of which they are guilty order such punishment to be given on other parts of the body, and not in the face; for there are enough other places on which this can be done, so that those who see and hear of it may fear and take warning' ('algunas maneras son de penas, que las non deuen dar a ningun ome, por yerro que aya fecho: assi como señalar a alguno enla cara, quemando le con fuego caliente, o cortandole las narices, nin sacandole los ojos, nin dandole otra manera de pena en ella de que finque señalado. Esto es porque la cara del ome fizo dios a su semejanza: e porende ningund juez, non deue penar en la cara: ante defendemos que non lo haga. Ca pues Dios tanto lo quiso honrrar e ennoblecer faziendo lo a su semejanza non es guisado que por yerro, e por maldad de los malos sea desfeada, nin destorpada la figura del Señor. E porende mandamos que los judgadores que ouieren a dar pena a los omes, por los yerros que ouiessen fechos, que gela manden dar en las otras partes del cuerpo e non en la cara: ca asaz ay lugares en que los pueden penar, de manera que quien los viere, e los oyere, pueda ende rescebir miedo, e escarmiento') (Partida VII.31.6).

15 Partidas VII.31.5.

illustrate the nature of the differentiation.[16] But it is in the context of war against external enemies when wrongdoings appear to be more dangerous than those committed in other cases: 'those who engage in it have enough to do to protect themselves from damage inflicted by the enemy, without taking into account what they may suffer through their own fault'.[17] In times of war the punishment or chastisement that military leaders ordered by way of judgement against perpetrators became stricter than in ordinary situations. In the eleven laws of Partida II.28, which deals with the chastisement of crimes committed in wartime, the emphasis placed on socio-political differentiation is even greater than in the cases regulated in Partida VII. In virtually all these laws, the punishments for lower or middling people (*menores, medianos*, as they were literally called), seemed to be harsher, at least physically, than those received by the greater (*mayores*) in similar cases. In cases of insubordination, knights could be threatened or verbally reprimanded by their leader, and only if they persisted, they could have their horses killed or undergo bodily harm without the leader suffering any liability or enmity from their kindred, even if they were maimed or died in the execution of the penalty. They could also suffer penalties of debasement, which was deemed worse than death itself. In contrast, insubordinate *menores* were to be killed. Debasement, a clear factor of social distinction, was not contemplated as a punishment for *menores*.[18]

In certain cases, however, the seriousness of the 'grievance' or 'crime' (the fault committed or the damage caused, is more often fully described than designated by a specific term), was greater the higher the status of the perpetrator. As a result, the highest men of the kingdom were matched with the lowest.[19] So in cases of disloyalty or treason, *hidalgos* ('gentlemen') would be beheaded and *ricoshombres* ('higher noblemen') could be treated with the same cruelty as *hombres viles* ('commoners'): they could be thrown to the beasts for dismemberment, starved to death, or thrown into deep waters so that the fish would eat them until no trace of them was left. Moreover, if such a punishment could not be effected and *ricoshombres* died in another land, they, in addition to having their goods confiscated,

> should not be brought for burial into the country against which they arrayed themselves; for the Holy Church did not approve that they be interred in ground that

---

16 The criteria that the judges were required to take into account before establishing the penalty can serve as an example of this (Partidas VII.31.8), as well as the special consideration given to prisoners who were *caballeros* ('knights'). This suggests a separate kind of justice reserved for certain social strata (Partidas VII.29.2 and 3). The severity of criminal conduct was also defined by whether it was directed against the King or against the common good (Partidas VII.2.1). For a discussion of the political significance of this distinction, see Gómez Redondo, *Historia de la prosa medieval 1*, p. 581.

17 'ca assaz abonda a los que en ella andan de auerse de guardar, quanto mas del que les viene por culpa de los suyos mesmos' (Partidas II.28, Preamble).

18 Partidas II.28.1, 2 and 3. On the functions of humiliating and shaming rituals, see Miller, *Humiliation*, p. 161.

19 The underlying principle is that 'the better the family and the nobler the blood of men the greater should be their self-control, and solicitude to protect themselves from sin' ('Los omnes, quanto son de mayor linaje, e mas de noble sangre, tanto deuen ser mas mesurados, e mas apercibidos para guardarse, de yerro') (Partidas VII.28.2, on the penalties for a blasphemous nobleman).

is sacred, but on the other hand, it was ordered that if they should be found buried there, their bones should be removed and scattered over the fields, or burned.[20]

Apart from the symbolism embedded in the punishments described, which will be discussed later, these provisions notably portray cruelty as excessive violence.[21]

In the same wartime context regulated in Partida II, punishments that sought to reproduce in the body of the offender the evil or harm done were contemplated for those who fomented dissent or instigated fights or revolts among members of their own side. As disagreement divides and destroys, and in war men should be even 'more united in order to avoid damage and inflict it upon their enemies',[22] it was established that *medianos* and *menores* 'should be punished in proportion to the injury which [they] desired to cause [...] and must be placed in custody and [their] eyes put out on account of the treason which [they] committed, so that they might never be able to see by their means what they desired to witness'.[23] For *mayores*, however, Partida II merely established severe prison sentences without recourse to royal mercy, the same as if they had caused fights or riots; the penalty of mutilation of the bodily part that had caused the injury was reserved for *medianos* and *menores* if they injured anyone; if they caused someone's death, they 'should be buried under [the victim's] corpse, except where the deed was done in self-defence, or while in command, or when disciplining his soldiers'.[24]

Along the same lines of the literal — albeit sometimes only metaphorical — reproduction of the damages caused, punishments were set for the thefts from other companions in the host: *menores*, besides paying double the property stolen, had to be marked by having their ears or hand cut off, not only to serve as a warning to others, but as testimony in case of re-offending; *mayores* were instead exempt from corporal punishments, although not from paying compensations, and if they reoffended they would be banished as well. The code at this point describes a curious punishment ritual — allegedly established by 'the ancients' — for those who stole food.[25] As an alternative to the mutilation of ears or hands, this kind of ordeal consisted of burying the offender to the waist, and having the victim of the theft throw a spear at him from an established distance. If the accused was hit or killed, this was not

---

20 'non los deuen traer a soterrar a aquella [tierra] contra quien fueron ca non lo touo por bien Santa Eglesia que fuessen soterrados en lugares sagrados. Ante mandaron que si los fallaren y metidos que sacassen ende sus huesos e los derramassen por los campos o los quemassen' (Partidas II.28.2).

21 The most common medieval definition of cruelty, according to Baraz, was the excessive application of judicial violence (Baraz, *Medieval Cruelty*). In other texts, instead, cruelty is equated to impiety, while a negative value is not always attributed to it: Cacho Blecua, 'La crueldad del castigo'; Alfonso, 'Vengeance, justice et lutte politique' [Editors' note: For an English translation, see chapter 5 of this volume].

22 'mas acordados por guardar a si de daño et facerlo a los enemigos' (Partidas II.28.6).

23 'hayan de pena el mal que quisiesen hacer [...] ca estonce deben seer presos por el aleve que facen et sacarles los ojos porque nunca vean con ellos lo que cobdiciaban veer' (Partidas II.28.4).

24 'fueras ende si ficiese algunos destos fechos en defendiendo su cuerpo o acabdellando o castigando su compaña' (Partidas II.28.4 and 5).

25 On the political significance of invoking (or contradicting, as on this occasion) the authority of the ancients, see Gómez Redondo, *Historia de la prosa medieval 1*, pp. 512–20.

CORPUS DELICTI AND EXEMPLARY VIOLENCE   481

considered to be murder, nor was any compensation due, and if he was not hit, he was declared innocent of the charges. The Partidas saw this ritual as excessive, for it crippled the offender, and — against the aforementioned prohibition — they recommended marking his face with a hot iron, so that his crime would be apparent. If he reoffended, he could be put to death.[26] This was deemed preferable because otherwise the victim would not get his goods back and the death of the accused would be to the detriment of the host.[27]

The criminal cases contemplated in the Partidas are more numerous, but my purpose here is not to describe in detail the legitimate physical violence that allowed judges and other officials to order executions, including beheading, burning and hanging; nor is it to list the various types of mutilation and humiliation. My aim is rather to understand how the Partidas represented the function that such violence had for the political authority. It was these functions that, in my opinion, largely justified such practices.

Policy of Chastisement and Fear of Punishment

'Men should be punished for the offenses which they commit'.[28] The penal discourse of the Partidas, is based on the idea of chastisement and the fear that this generates. This is especially true of Partida VII, which purports to harshly punish those who acted arrogantly, to mete out the punishment they deserved, so that those who heard about it would be frightened and dissuaded. The severe punishments imposed on the bodies of the culprits, vanquished or defeated, served precisely to counter the naturalisation of evil that results from forgetting:

> Forgetfulness and boldness are two things which cause men to err greatly, for forgetfulness induces them not to remember the evil which can come upon them on account of the offenses which they commit, and boldness gives them daring to do those things which they should not. In this way, they practice evil so that it becomes natural to them and they received pleasure from it.[29]

Thus, a physical reminder for the punished and a reminder of fear for those who witnessed it. Such a pedagogy of punishment was not new, but it received a new impetus and was expressed with great emphasis: cruelty becomes a positive value that renders

---

26 'semeyonos mas derecha razón de los mandar señalar en las caras con un fierro caliente [porque] fuesen conoszudos por ello, et el segundo furto et la señal fuesen testimonios para escarmentarlos dándoles muerte' (Partidas II.28.6).

27 Partidas II.28.6–7. On punishments applied to the face, and the correspondence between damages committed and punishments applied, see, among others, Madero Eguía, *Manos violentas*; Cacho Blecua, 'La crueldad del castigo'. For the specific role of mutilations, see Miller, 'Choosing the Avenger', pp. 159–204.

28 'Escarmentados deuen ser los omes por los yerros que fazen' (Partidas VII.31.Preamble).

29 'Olvidança e atreuimiento, son dos cosas que fazen a los omes errar mucho. Ca el oluido los aduze, que non se acuerden del mal que les puede venir por el yerro que fizieren. E el atreuimiento les da osadía, para acometer lo que non deuen: e desta guisa, vsan el mal de manera, que se les torna como en natura recibiendo en ello plazer' (Partidas VII.Preamble).

punishments efficient. This advocates for a type of justice which 'removes by severe punishment the disputes and tumults which arise from the evil deeds committed for the pleasure of one party to the injury and dishonour of the other',[30] insisting that 'judges should endeavour to punish crime in the territory over which they have jurisdiction, after the guilty parties have been convicted or confessed'.[31] Exemplarity and chastisement became closely associated in the very notion of punishment:

> Punishment is a reparation for sin, or chastisement which is imposed by the law upon persons on account of the offences which they commit. Judges inflict this punishment upon men for two reasons; first, that they may be chastised for the crime of which they are guilty; second, in order that all those who hear or see this make take notice and warning to avoid doing wrong through fear of punishment.[32]

But *escarmiento* ('chastisement') was also defined in Partida II as the 'penalty ordered by a commander to be inflicted upon those who are guilty of offences, and resembles a judicial sentence'.[33] Hence it is not surprising that both in Partida II and VII the term *juicio de escarmiento* ('judgement of chastisement') was used to describe this type of exemplary punishments.[34] Its didactic nature resided both in 'receiving chastisement' and in 'making an example': the former referred to oneself, whereas the latter referred to the others. This is why executions were statutorily publicised: 'the execution of those who have committed acts for which they deserve death shall be public, in order that others who see and hear of it, may, for this reason, be afraid and take warning; and the *alcalde* or the crier shall state in the presence of the people the crimes for which the culprits are put to death';[35] moreover, this is why damage to the face was prohibited, since there were enough places in the body to inflict punishment, 'so that those who see and hear of it may fear and take warning'.[36]

Therefore, it was the emotion of fear and its complex nuances, ranging from suspicion and dread to terror, that was behind this rationale of *escarmentar*, which was more political and moral than legal. Fear is one of the virtuous manifestations

---

30 'tuelle por crudos escarmientos las contiendas, e los bullicios, que se levantan de los malos fechos, que se fazen a plazer de la vna parte, e a daño, e a deshonra de la otra' (Partidas VII.Preamble).

31 'punar deuen los judgadores de escarmentar los yerros, que se fazen en las tierras, sobre que han poder de judgar, despues que fueren judgados, o conocidos' (Partidas VII.31.6).

32 'Pena es enmienda de pecho, o escarmiento, que es dado según ley a algunos, por los yerros que fizieron. E dan esta pena los Judgadores a los omes, por dos razones. La vna es, porque resciban escarmiento de los yerros que fizieron. La otra es, porque todos los que lo oyeren, e vieren, tomen ejemplo e apercibimiento, para guardarse que non yerren, por miedo de las penas' (Partidas VII.31.1).

33 'pena que manda dar el cabdiello contra los que errasen como en manera de juicio' (Partidas II.28.1).

34 Partidas VII.31.8.

35 'Paladinamente deue ser fecha la justicia a los que han de morir, para escarmiento de los que lo vieren, diciendo el pregonero los yerros porque lo matan' (Partidas VII.31.11).

36 'en que los puedan penar, de manera que quien los viere, e los oyere, pueda ender rescebir miedo, e escarmiento' (Partidas VII.31.6). On the strength of these representations, in addition to the works cited in n. 2, see Jacob, *Images de la justice*. It is part of the available stock of interpretations to emphasise the political character of these rituals as part of the ceremonies of ostentation and visible power, as noted by Foucault, *Surveiller et punir*. Nevertheless, see the criticism of his arguments on 'criminal change', among others by Harding and Ireland, *Punishment*, ch. 10.

of human nature that leads someone to act as he should 'for fear of what may injure him'.[37] While in the Partidas promoting fear against the people was considered a tyrannical exercise of power to keep them submissive,[38] and although the agreements and deals made under the pressure of fear were explicitly rendered invalid,[39] inducing fear and even terror of punishment was the unequivocal goal of this criminal policy, whose philosophy pervaded the entire legal body under analysis.[40]

---

37 'The wise men thought that nature is a virtue which all things possess and which causes each to act as is proper, according to the regulations which God laid down for each. That of man is of two kinds; first, the means by which he sees and perceives what is beyond him, as, for instance, where he is troubled, and has fear of something which he thinks may injure him, and is pleased with what he believes may be to his advantage' ('Departieron los Sabios, que la natura es virtud que esta encerrada dentro de las cosas, e faze a cada vna obrar assi como conuiene, segund el ordenamiento que Dios puso en ellas. E esta es en el ome, en dos maneras. La vna de lo que vee, e siente de fuera; assi como pesarle, e auer miedo de aquello que entiende quel podrie venir daño, e plazerle de lo quel piensa que le verna bien') (Partidas II.27.2).

38 'They [the tyrants] always employed their power against the people, by means of three kinds of artifice. The first is, that persons of this kind always exert themselves to keep those under their dominion ignorant and timid, because, when they are such, they will not dare to rise up against them, or oppose their wishes' ('usaron ellos [los tiranos] de su poder siempre contra los del pueblo, en tres maneras de arteria. La primera es, que estos atales punan siempre que los de su señorio sean necios, e medrosos, porque quando tales fuesen, non osarían levantarse contra ellos, ni contrastar sus voluntades') (Partidas II.1.10).

39 Fear is defined as an emotion that determines human action, identifying the fears that render agreements and positions invalid: 'Metus means fear of death or of bodily torture, or a loss of limb or forfeiture of liberty, or of documents by which it may be defended; or of the dishonour by which a party becomes infamous; and the laws of this our book refer to fear of this kind and other similar to it when they state that a contract or agreement which a man makes through fear shall not be valid. For through such fear not only weak men, but also those who are strong, are induced to promise or perform certain things' ('Metus, miedo de muerte o de tormento de cuerpo, o de perdimiento de miembro, o de perder libertad, o las cartas, por las que podria amparar o de recibir deshonra por que fincaria enfamado; y es de este miedo del que hablan las leyes de este nuestro libro cuando dicen que pleyto e postura que hombre hace por miedo no debe valer. Pues por tal miedo se mueven a prometer o hacer cosas no solo los hombres flacos sino también los fuertes') (Partidas VII.33.7).

40 'The advantages derived from justice are very great [...] for if they are good men, they become still better by reason of it, and are rewarded for the good they accomplish. Moreover, the wicked are compelled to be good through the influence of justice, from dread of the punishment which it orders to be inflicted upon them for their evil deeds' ('Pro muy grande es el que nasce de la justicia [...] ca si son buenos, por ella se fazen mejores, recibiendo gualardones por los bienes que fizieron. E otrosi, los malos por ella han de ser buenos, recelándose de la pena, que les manda dar por sus maldades') (Partidas III.1.2); 'It happens at times, that men are accused of offenses for which, if they were convicted, they would receive corporal punishment of death or loss of limb; and, for this reason, through the fear which they have of punishment they endeavour to make terms with their adversaries, by paying them something not to proceed further with the cases' ('Acaesçe algunas vegadas, que algunos omnes son acusados de tales yerros, que si les fuesen prouados, que recebirian pena por ellos en los cuerpos, de muerte, o de perdimiento de miembro; e porende, por miedo que an de la pena, trabajanse de fazer auenencias con sus aduersarios, pechandoles algo, porque non anden adelante en el pleito') (Partidas VII.1.22). The same idea occurs in Alfonso X's earlier legal code, the Fuero Real: 'Esta es la razon que nos movio para fazer leyes, que la maldad de los omes sea refrenada por ellas, e la vida de los buenos sea segura, e los malos dejen de mal fazer por miedo de la pena' ('This is the reason that moved us to pass laws, that the wickedness of men be restrained by them, and that the life of the

But justice, we are told, is not just about punishing evil, but rather about rewarding good conduct.[41] There would not be proper justice if wrongdoers were not punished and those engaging in upright conduct were not rewarded for the good they have done.[42] It is precisely this kind of reciprocity and balance which accomplished justice:

> For each to receive good for good, and evil for evil, according to his desert, is perfect justice, which causes affairs to be maintained in good condition.[43]

Those engaging in upright conduct were encouraged to be better and the wrongdoers were inspired to make amends.[44] Fear appeared as the underside of pleasure, an emotion that led men to act in the direction 'of what they expect to produce good'.[45] The essentialism of this argument needs to be noted, as in this discourse acting right or wrong imprints a character of such a nature that it marks the moral standing of subjects. Being good or bad thus becomes a dichotomy that constitutes an ethical benchmark for actual behaviour. This can be seen in the way in which narratives constructed their characters.[46]

The proposed comparison between Partidas II and VII therefore gives a rather clear image of the meaning underlying this conception of justice focused on reward and punishment, with the aim of encouraging good behaviour and inhibiting bad conduct by promoting fear of punishment. Both were intended to set an example, although Partida II developed those ideas further, as it dealt with war-time matters, when the exercise of a justice of the type described was more urgent and necessary.

Prisoners and Captives: The Various Forms of Enmity

So far I have referred to so-called 'judicial prisoners', both in times of peace and war, that is, those accused of such actions that, if proven, 'they must die for it, or

---

good men be safe, and that through the fear of the penalty the wicked refrain from doing evil') (Fuero Real I.6.3).

41   'For justice does not only consist in punishing wicked actions but in requiting good ones' ('Ca la justicia non es tan solamente en escarmentar los males, mas aun en dar gualardon por los bienes') (Partidas II.27.2).

42   'For, as stated above, strict justice would not be done if the wicked were not chastised for the evil which they do, just as the good are rewarded for the good which they accomplish' ('Ca de otra guise non seria justicia derecha, como de suso diximos, si los malos non ouiessen escarmiento del mal que fiziessen, assi como los buenos gualardon por el bien') (Partidas II.28, Preamble).

43   'Bien por bien, e mal por mal recibiendo los omes según su merescimiento, es justicia cumplida, e que faze mantener las cosas en buen estado' (Partidas II.27. Preamble).

44   The rewards to be given for good deeds performed by men in times of war are mentioned in Partidas II.27.

45   'de lo que piensa que le venra bien'. See above, n. 38.

46   According to Gómez Redondo, Historia de la prosa medieval 1, pp. 591–97, this normative sphere provided a textual background for the literary works that channelled the type of values forged in the code. The process of constructing a moral universe of shared references has been the focus of the research project I directed on Cultura, lenguaje y prácticas políticas en las sociedades medievales: Un estudio comparado sobre la construcción de valores compartidos y las formas de su contestación, with support from the Spanish Ministerio de Ciencia y Tecnología [BHA2002–03076].

be damaged in some of their limbs'.[47] This is why they had to be held in prison and sureties could not be accepted for them, for if they were found guilty they would flee or hide for fear that those punishments would be imposed on them. Fear appears again as the driver and justification for these behaviours.

The treatment of judicial prisoners held for trial was regulated by Partida VII.29. It established how and by whom they could be legally captured; how they should be treated according to their status, fame or gender,[48] as well as the penalties for any jailors who harmed or dishonoured them. Here, the Partida followed literally the well-known but controversial sentence from Ulpian's *Digest* that 'prison should be for the purpose of keeping prisoners, and not for displaying malevolence toward them, or doing them any injury or punishing them while there'.[49] A maximum period of two

---

47 'deuen morir por ende, o ser dañados en algunos de sus miembros' (Partidas VII.29 Preamble).

48 'At night they should guard them as follows, namely; by putting them in chains or in stocks, and carefully closing the doors of the prison; and the chief jailer should every night lock the chains, the stocks, and the doors with his own hands, and take good care of the keys, leaving men inside with the prisoners to watch them all night with a light, so that they may not file their way out of the prison in which they are confined, or liberate themselves in any other way; and after dawn appears and the sun has risen, the doors of the prison should be opened so that they can see the light; and when any person desires to speak with them, they must then be brought out, one by one, those whose duty it is to guard them being present all the time' ('echandolos en cadenas, o con cepos, e cerrando las puertas de la carcel muy bien: e el carcelero mayor deue cerrar cada noche las cadenas, e los cepos, e las puertas de la carcel, con su mano mesma, e guardar bien las llaues, dexando omes dentro con los presos, que los velen con candela toda la noche, de manera que non puedan limar las prisiones en que yoguieren, nin se puedan soltar en ninguna manera: e luego que sea de dia, e el sol salido, deuenles abrir las puertas de la carcel, porque vean la lumbre. E si algunos quisiesen fablar con ellos, deuelos estonces sacar fuera vno a vno, todavía, estando delante aquellos que los han de guardar') (Partidas VII.29.6).

49 'What Penalty Keepers of Prisoners Deserve if They Do Them Any Harm, or Cause Them Any Dishonour, on Account of Hatred Which They Have for Them, or in Consideration of Something Promised to Them. Men induced by hatred, are induced to treat one another badly and some of them, at times, act thus towards prisoners by secretly giving something to those in charge of them to induce the latter to provide them with bad food or to confine them in uncomfortable prisons, or to do them harm in many other ways; and we hold that those who exert themselves in this manner commit a very serious offense, and take wicked vengeance without reason; for a prison should be for the purpose of keeping prisoners, and not for displaying malevolence towards them, or doing them any injury or punishing them while there. For this reason we order that no jailer nor any other man who has charge of prisoner, shall dare to commit any cruelty of this kind, for the sake of a reward which may be given him; or on account of any request made to him; or because of hatred which he may entertain toward said prisoners; or for any affection he may have for those who caused them to be arrested; or for any other reasons whatever; for it is sufficient for them to be prisoners and restrained of their liberty and after they are sentenced to suffer the penalty which they deserve as the laws direct. And if any knight, or keeper of prisoners should be induced by malice to do anything contrary to what is contained in this law, the judge of the district shall cause him to be put to death for doing so; and if he should be negligent in punishing a party of this kind he shall be deprived of his office as a man who is infamous, and shall receive such a penalty for his conduct as the king may think proper. The other parties who cause jailers to act in this manner shall also be punished according to the judgement of the king' ('Que pena merecen los guardadores de los presos si les fizieren mal, o deshonra, por malquerencia que les ayan, o por algo que les prometan. Muevense los omes a buscar mal los vnos a los otros por malquerencia que han entre si. E esto fazen algunos a las vegadas contra aquellos que son

486   ISABEL ALFONSO

years was stipulated for prisoners to be either tried or released. The judicial prisoners that Partida VII.29 protected were different from captives precisely because — at least in theory — 'they do not suffer any damage to their bodies'.[50] This protection, however, was primarily aimed at strengthening royal authority. It was the king that controlled the judicial process, stipulated the death penalty for non-abiding officers and held the monopoly of prisons. Without a royal mandate, nobody was allowed to set up prisons in their homes, as it was considered bold and daring, and a detriment to royal power.[51] An exception to this prohibition was the case of 'captive Moors', which I shall refer to later.

This all suggests that imprisonment did not have the punitive nature which was to be a fundamental feature of later penal systems, because it was not understood or applied as penalty. However, this idea of a purely preventive detention is at odds with some of the forms of punishment referred to in the title discussed above (which deals with criminal typology). These include life imprisonment 'en fierros' ('in chains') and forced labour of unmistakably punitive nature. This contradiction was already present in the Roman Law texts that inspired the Partidas, challenging,

----

presos, dando algo encubiertamente a aquellos que los han en guarda, porque les den mal a comer, o a beber, e que les den malas prisiones, e que les fagan mal en otras maneras muchas; e los que desto se trabajan, tenemos, que fazen muy gran yerro, e toman mala vengança sin razón. Ca la carcel deue ser para guardar los presos e non para fazerles enemiga, nin otro mal, nin darles pena en ella. E porende mandamos, e defendemos que ningún carcelero, nin otro ome que tenga presos en guarda, que non sea osado de fazer tal crueldad como esta por precio que le den, nin por ruego que le fagan, nin por malquerencia que haya contra los presos, nin por amor que aya alos que los fizieron prender, nin por otra manera que pueda ser. Ca assaz abonda de ser presos, e encarcelados, e recebir, quando sean judgados la pena que merecieren, según mandan las leyes. E si algun carcelero, o guardador de presos maliciosamente se mouiere a fazer contra lo que enesta ley es escrito, el Judgador del lugar lo deue fazer matar por ello: e si fuere negligente en non querer escarmentar atal ome como este, deue ser tollido del officio, como ome mal enfamado, e recebir pena perende, según el Rey tuuiere por bien. E los otros que fazen fazer estas cosas a los carceleros, deuenles dar pena según su aluedrio') (Partidas VII.29.11).

50   'no reciben otro mal en sus cuerpos' (Partidas VII.29.1).

51   'For no man has a right to build a prison, or to confine men therein, except the king alone, or those to whom he grants power to do so; as, for instance, his officers whom he permits, and to whom he delegates his authority to arrest and punish malefactors and the judges of cities and towns; and powerful and distinguished men who are the lords of certain lands to whom the king has given permission to do this. And if henceforth any other person should build a prison, stocks, or any place of detention by his own authority, without an order of the king, and should confine men therein, we command that he shall be put to death for his offence; and we order that our officials, where an insolent act of this kind is committed, and they are aware of it and do not punish or forbid it, or give information of it to the king, shall suffer the same penalty.' ('Ca non pertenece a otro ome ninguno, nin ha poder de mandar fazer carcel, nin meter omes a prision en ella, si non tan solamente el Rey, o aquellos a quien el otorga que lo puedan fazer, assi como sus Officiales a quien otorga, e da su poder, de prender los omes malfechores, e de los justiciar; e a los Juezes de las Cibdades, o de las Villas, e a los omes poderosos, e honrrados aque son Sennore de algunas tierras, a quien lo otorgase el Rey que lo pudiessen fazer. E si otro de aqui adelante fiziere carcel por su autoridad, o cepo, o cadena sin mandado del Rey, e metiesse omes en prision en ella, mandamos que muera por ello; e los nuestros oficiales, do fiziessen tal atrevimiento como este, si lo supieren, o lo non escarmentaren, o lo non vedasen, o lo non fizieren saber al Rey, mandamos otrosi que ayan aquella mesma pena') (Partidas VII.29.15).

CORPUS DELICTI AND EXEMPLARY VIOLENCE   487

according to historians of Antiquity, the traditional view of a linear development of imprisonment.[52] In any case, the grievous, if not punitive, nature of prison was widely recognised in legal texts and made explicit in Partida II.28, which, as we saw before, is dedicated to how those who incur in any wrongdoing at war must be punished, and which provides information about the provisions for imprisonment in such cases. Thus, for example, imprisonment and humiliating penalties are contemplated for those who disobey their commanders:

> for the sole reason that he disobeyed orders, he should be kept in custody by the king or the commander, until the enterprise is concluded, and restrained of his liberty in any way they designate, and in a dishonourable manner if they desire; as, for instance, put in heavy irons, or fetters, and be compelled to either ride on an ass, or walk carrying a chain fastened to his neck, or be attached with a rope to the tail or crupper of an animal. All these degrading punishments were imposed upon men of rank on account of the great baseness that they displayed, which caused them through cowardice to leave the ranks without the order of their superiors.[53]

This is also contemplated for those who stir discord in the companies in which they go to war, and it was decreed that if that was proved they should be inflected the wrong they intended to commit:

> he must be placed in custody, and his eyes put out on account of the treason which he committed, so that he might never be able to see by their means what he desired to witness [...] This is understood to refer to persons of middle or inferior rank, but those who are of noble descent should be kept in very strong prisons, as long as the war lasts; and even if the king id desirous of showing them mercy, they should be banished from the kingdom for as long a time as he deems proper.[54]

The explicitly punitive character of imprisonment 'on bread and water' is evident in the provision regarding those who eat their rations before due time:

> It was considered proper that this punishment should be protracted for a sufficient length of time; first, because by means of it they underwent corporal punishment by lying in prison and enduring hunger and thirst; and second, on account of the

---

52 See Torallas Tovar and Pérez Martín, eds, *Castigo y reclusión*. On imprisonment in the Middle Ages, see Serna, 'Los límites de la reclusión carcelaria'. On the nature and evolution of incarceration, despite an excessive focus on the state, see Dunbabin, *Captivity and Imprisonment*.

53 'solamente porque se desmandó debe seer preso del rey o del cabdiello; et mientre aquel fecho durare traello a quamaña prisión quisiere et a quanta deshonra, asi como en grandes fierros o en cormas, yendo caballero en asno o de pie, levandolo con cadena a la garganta, o atandolo con una soga a la cola de alguna bestia o al ataharre. Et todas estas penas de aviltamiento pusieron a los honrados homes por la grant viltanza que tovieron que facien en derramar sin mandado de sus mayorales por saber sofrir miedo' (Partidas II.28.3).

54 'ca estonce [los medianos y menores] deben seer presos por el aleve que facen et sacarles los ojos porque nunca vean con ellos lo que cobdiciaban ver [...] mas si fueren de los mayores deben seer metidos en muy fuertes prisiones mientra aquel fecho furare, asi que aun quando el rey les quisiere facer merced, que los eche del regno por quanto tiempo el toviere por bien' (Partidas II.28.4).

488   ISABEL ALFONSO

disgrace incurred, and that men might know it was imposed on account of their great imprudence or gluttony.[55]

In addition to these judicial prisoners, resulting from judicial proceedings against them for various offences, in both peacetime and wartime, Partida II identified two other types of prisoners: those who became prisoners when there was 'war among Christians', that is, among people of 'one Law'; and 'those who fall in the captivity of men of a different creed'.[56] The former were deemed to be unlawful, and their existence was prohibited; the latter, either Moors or Christians, were beyond the scope of justice.

Albeit apparently cognate, the terms 'law' and 'belief' were in fact covered by different regulatory codes, namely legal and religious, respectively. Law and belief distinguished internal from external enmity. This distinction derives mainly from the different consideration that the different types of war deserve. The first, which correspond to internal strives fought between the people of the land, are said to cause harm and dishonour. The others, which are waived 'in opposition to the enemies of the Faith, the king or the kingdom, are for the advantage and honour of the latter'.[57] The second 'is called *justa*, in Latin, which means, in Castilian, founded upon right. This happens where a man engages in it to recover his own property from the enemy, or to protect himself and it from them'.[58]

The distinction between these two types of wars and between 'prisoners' and 'captives', however, is not systematically laid out to encompass all situations. The Partidas focus on prohibiting the ill-treatment of Christian 'prisoners', but only make passing allusions to Christian captives captured by Muslims, when regulating procedures for their redemption and the compensation to be received for damages suffered in enemy territory.[59] There is no specific provision about the treatment of the Moors captured by Christians. Therefore, the information on the very different consideration that each other's captives deserved, while very explicit, is rather indirect. This will be discussed below.

The regulation of internal strife and the treatment of the prisoners resulting from it provides some indication as to how captives may have been treated. The disapproval of such conflicts underlies the prohibition of mistreating the bodies of those defeated in them. In seditious tumults ('*asonada* is the term used to refer to gatherings of people to fight each other, or to do each other harm'), no man was permitted to capture another in order to take him to prison, or kill him after he had been defeated,

---

55   'ca este escarmiento tovieron por bien que complie asaz, lo uno porque les yacie hi pena de los cuerpos yaciendo presos et sufriendo fambre et sed, et lo avergüenza porque saben los homes que les aviene por su nesciedat et por su glotonia' (Partidas II.28.9).

56   'aquellos que caen en prisión de homes de otra creencia' (Partidas II.29.1).

57   'que son fechas contra los enemigos de la Fe, o del Rey, o del Reyno, son a su pro, o a su honra' (Partidas II.26.16).

58   'llaman en latin *justa*, que quiere tanto decir en romance, como derechurera. E esta es, quando ome la faze por cobrar lo suyo de los enemigos, o por amparar a si mismos, e a sus cosas dellos' (Partidas II.23.1).

59   Partidas II.25.29 and 30.

CORPUS DELICTI AND EXEMPLARY VIOLENCE   489

or damage him. The law that established this prohibition provides a very detailed description that is worth reproducing, because it refers to the permitted treatment of the captive Moors, that is, those defeated in wars that were deemed to be just:

> No man taking part in a riot should dare to arrest another in order to make a prisoner of him — even though he may have him in his power in the field — or decapitate him, or cut his throat, or deprive him of any of his limbs, unless he wounded him while defending himself; nor has he the right to mutilate him after he has been killed, for it was not deemed proper to injure him or cut off any of his limbs. It was also considered just that those who violated this rule, where both parties were equals in rank, should themselves receive the same bodily injury which they had inflicted, and where they are persons of inferior rank, that they should be put to death on this account, and if the cannot be found, that they should lose all their property. They imposed these penalties upon those who fought; first, because they violated the prohibition of the king; and second, because they ventured to cut off a limb, which no one should do, except he who occupies the position of judge.[60]

Several aspects need to be noted: the unlawfulness of taking these prisoners; of harming their defeated bodies outside of the fight itself; of beheading or mutilating their dead bodies. All those who violated these prohibitions would suffer the same treatment if they were of equal or superior status to the defeated, or killed if their status was inferior; if they escaped all their assets would be confiscated. But this law understood that despite the ban prisoners were actually taken and, in fact, it made special provisions regarding the varying treatment of nobles depending on the degree of enmity — declared or not — between the captive and his captor:

> And, where it happens that one man arrests another of noble descent, he should not put him in irons, in prison, or in stocks, or restrain him of his liberty in any other harmful or dishonourable way, unless he is his open enemy and has been so declared by judgment of court. Nor should he confine him in such a way that he may lose his life by reason of it, or make use of him by compelling him to perform labour, or do anything else which is not suitable for him to do; but where the captive is not an enemy he should release him, after he has been sworn and has agreed that he will do not do him any harm because he took him prisoner. When the other party is unwilling to do this, he may keep him locked up for

---

60 'Atreuer non se deue ningund ome, a prender a otro en assonada, para lleuarlo a su prision, maguer lo tuuiesse en su poder en el campo, nin le ha de cortar la cabeza, nin degollar, nin desfazer miembro ninguno, si no firiendole mientra se defendiesse, nin aun después que lo ouiesse muerto, nin tuuieron por bien que lo lastimasen, nin le tajasen, miembro ninguno. E que los que contra esto fiziessen, tuuieron por derecho, que si mayores con mayores, o eguales con equales fuessen los fazedores deste lastimamiento, que recibiesen otro tal en su cuerpo, como ellos ouiessen fecho. E si fuesen los menores, que muriesen por ello. E si non los pudiessen auer, que perdiesen quanto que ouiessen. E estas pesnas pusieron a los que lidiasen; lo vno, porque se atruian contra defendimiento del Rey; e lo al, porque se atreuian a cortar miembro, lo que ninguno deue fazer, si non el que ouiesse lugar de Justicia' (Partidas II.26.17).

nine days, without inflicting any other punishment upon him, but, during this time, he should not remove him to the dominions of another king, or cause him to be ransomed, or resort to any compulsion in order to force him to do what he wishes; or wound, or kill him in any way either through rage or the enmity which he entertains towards him, which was contracted either before or after he took him prisoner.[61]

Again, Partida II.29 offers a negative depiction of those prisoners who were the result of 'war among Christians' as being illegally apprehended, by saying that such a term was applied to those

> who suffer no other bodily harm, except such as they may experience from confinement in jail, or where something is collected from them on account of the expense incurred while they were kept in custody, or where reparation is demanded for some injury caused by them. Nevertheless, they should not be put to death as soon as they have fallen into the hands of their captors, nor should any punishment be inflicted upon them, or anything else be done to them to cause their death, except where they have been arrested for some violation of law. For, under any other circumstances, the ancients did not consider it just that, after a man had been taken prisoner, he should be killed, or subjected to such severe torture that he might die in consequence of it, or be sold, or compelled to serve as a slave, or that his wife might be outraged in his presence, or he be separated from her or his children, in order to sell them apart from one another. This, however, is understood to refer to prisoners who confess the same religion, as, for instance, when a war exists between Christians.[62]

---

61 'E si acaeciesse, que alguno prendiesse a otro que sea hidalgo, non le deue meter en fierros, nin en carcel, nin en cepo, nin darle otras malas prisiones, nin deshonrradas; fueras ende si fuesse su enemigo conocido, dado por juicio. E aun a este non le deue dar prision de que muera por achaque della, nin deue seruirse del, metiendole a fazer labor, nin otra cosa que le non conuenga; mas si el preso no fuesse enemigo, deuele dexar yr sobre su omenaje, tomandole pleyto, que non le venga mal del, por razon que lo prendio. E si esto non quisiere fazer, puedele tener cerrado fasta nueve dias, non dandole otra pena: mas en este plazo, non le deue sacar a Señorio de otro Rey, nin fazerle redemir, nin darle otra pena ninguna, porque lo faga; nin ferirlo, nin matarlo a ninguna manera, por saña, nin por enemistad que le tuuiesse, nin ante, nin estonce desquel ouiesse preso. E non le deue apremiar que le faga pleyto' (Partidas II.26.17).

62 'aquellos que non reciben otro mal en sus cuerpos sinon es quanto en manera daquella prision en que los tienen, o si llevan alguna cosa dellos por razon de costa que hayan fecha teniendolos presos, o por daños que dellos hayan rescebido queriendo ende haber enmienda. Pero con todo esto non los deben luego matar a sohora después que los tovieren en su prision, nin darles pena nin facer otra cosa por que mueran, fueras ende si fuesen presos por razon de justicia: ca de otra guisa non tovieron por bien et por derecho los antiguos que después que el home toviesen preso quel matasen nin diesen grant tormento por que hobiese de morir, nil puediesen vender nin servirse del como de siervo, nin le deshonrasen la muger delante, nin apartasen a ella del nin a sus fijos para venderlos partiendolos unos dotros; pero esto se entiende de los presos de una ley, asi como quando fuese guerra entre cristianos' (Partidas II.29.1).

These prohibitions concerning 'internal' prisoners,[63] (Christians captured by Christians), which prevented them from being killed or tortured to death, from being enslaved, from having their wives dishonoured in their presence, and from separating them from their children to sell them, indirectly depict the a wide range of penalties inflicted on those captured in lawful wars, that is, the captives. It is beyond the remit of this paper to engage in further analysis of the legislation on the form of political struggle called *asonada*,[64] but it is worth emphasising, first, that royal authority is reinforced by the very act of declaring all those forms of violence to be illegitimate; and second, that the mistreatment that was prohibited for the vanquished in internal conflicts was implicitly legitimate if applied to those defeated in wars against external enemies.

The description of the cruelty attributed to men of a different religion towards Christian captives — the only ones considered by the legislator — broadens the spectrum of hardships that Moors could receive if taken captive by Christians.

> Those are properly called captives who come under the control of men embracing another belief, for those have the power to put them to death after they have taken them prisoners, on account of the contempt which they have for their religion, or they can subject them to cruel punishments, or make use of them as slaves, compelling them to perform such arduous tasks that they will prefer death to life. And, in addition to this, they are not allowed to possess their own property, but must surrender it to those who inflict all those evils upon them, or have a right to sell them whenever they desire to do so. They have also the power to commit a still greater act of cruelty, for they can separate what God united as, for instance, a husband from his wife, who become so according to law by marriage. They have, moreover, a right to violate the ties of nature, as for instance to separate children from fathers and mothers, or brothers from one another, or persons from other relatives of the same blood. They can also separate friends, which is a very serious matter, for as the union of love surpasses and is superior to that of descent and everything else, so is the affliction and sorrow greater when they are torn asunder; hence for all these reasons and on account of the many hardships which they endure, they are very properly called captives, because this is the worst misfortune that men can endure in this world.[65]

---

63 The term 'internal' should be used with caution, as it refers to groups of unknown size and boundaries. This causes difficulties in deciphering the meaning of the terms used to refer to the conflicts or the criteria used to do so. See theoretical considerations on these issues in Alfonso, 'Los nombres de la violencia'. [Editors' note: For an English translation, see chapter 16 of this volume].

64 A systematic study of this type of conflict is still lacking, particularly on its lexicon, its logic and operation. The theoretical framework for understanding these wars which have been traditionally called 'private' was outlined in my introduction to Alfonso, Escalona, and Martin, eds, *Lucha política*, pp. 9–18. I have shown its relationship with 'enmity' and 'revenge' in other studies: Alfonso, 'Venganza y justicia'; and Alfonso, 'Vengeance, justice et lutte politique' [Editors' note: For an English translation, see chapter 5 of this volume].

65 'cativos son ellos llamados por derecho aquellos que caen en prision de homes de otra creencia ca estos los matan después que los tienen presos por despreciamiento que han a la su ley, o los tormentan de crueles penas, o se sirven dellos, como de siervos, metiendolos a tales servicios, que

It does not seem too much of a risk to read this text reciprocally as a projection of the treatment that Christians would give to their captives, prisoners who, instead of being killed could be kept as servants. It is telling that the only exception to the general prohibition to have private prisons was for 'captive Moors', under the justification that they had to be prevented from fleeing to their land.[66] The text also indicates that the sufferings which would now be called moral, such as the separation from family and friends, were linked to the perception that they were more painful and cruel than others, although the rhetoric of captivity particularly stresses the loss of freedom in addition to physical suffering.[67]

In short: the exercise of criminal justice was largely projected on the bodies guilty of a crime. Social status determined different treatments, and its punitive methods consisted of various forms of capital punishment (beheading, burning, hanging, throwing to beasts, ...) and mutilation, which seem to have been designed to mark out and sever the parts of the body responsible for the acts committed. This punishment was legitimised not only by its claim to prevent disorder resulting from bad conduct by instilling fear of exemplary chastisement, but also because it involved the execution of fair well-deserved decisions,[68] with the culprits being supposedly protected in prison until their guilt was decided upon. A sense of vengeful reparation

---

querrian ante la muerte que la vida. E sin todo esto, non son señores de lo que han, pechandolo a aquellos que les facen todos estos males, o los venden, quando quieren. E aun fazen mayor crueldad, que departen lo que Dios ayunto, assi como marido de muger, que se face por ley, et por casamiento. E otrosi estreman el ayuntamiento natural assi como fijos de padres, o de madres, o hermanos de hermanos, o de los otros parientes, que son como vna sangre. Otrosi los amigos, que es muy fuerte cosa departir a vnos de otros: ca bien como el ayuntamiento del amor passa, et vence al linaje, e a todas las otras cosas; assi es mayor la cuyta, e el pesar quando se departen. Onde por todas estas razones, e otras muchas que sufren, son llamados con derecho captiuos, porque esta es la mayor malandança que los omes pueden auer en este mundo' (Partidas II.29.1).

66 'but where persons desire to build stocks in their houses to secure their Moorish captives, they can do so without a royal order, and they shall not be liable to punishment therefor, since they do so to secure the captives over whom they exercise ownership in order that they may not escape to the country of the Moors' ('Pero si algunos quisieren fazer cepos en sus casas para guarder sus Moros catiuos, bien lo pueden fazer sin mandado del Rey, e non caen porende en pena; pues que lo fazen para guardar sus catiuos en que han señorio, e lo fazen porque non se fuyan a tierra de Moros') (Partidas VII.29.15). For more on captivity and servitude, in addition to the aforementioned title, the power of the lords over them was regulated in Partidas IV.21.

67 'Men ought naturally to feel sorrow for members of their own religion when, as captives, they fall into the power of enemy, for the reason that they are deprived of liberty, which is the most precious thing which men can enjoy in this world' ('Naturalmente se deben los homes doler de los de su ley quando caen en cativo en poder de los enemigos, porque ellos son desapoderados de la libertad que es la mas cara cosa que home puede haber en este mundo') (Partidas II.29 Preamble). The high regard in which freedom is held in this text questions the place of freedom as the value *par excellence* in the contemporary world, as opposed to 'salvation', which was the other 'ultimate value' in the medieval world. As a result, the desire to make these two 'ultimate values' the axes of their different social rationales, is also called into question. A recent example of this type of dichotomous approach was proposed in Guerreau, *L'avenir d'un passé incertain*.

68 Deserving punishment for an offence or crime is different from receiving it for simply disobeying some rules. It must be remembered that any justice has more to do with the repression of behaviour than with obliging people to abide by the rules.

was also present in the nature of the justice meted out.[69] It was a justice that seemed to explicitly exclude the captives or prisoners of just wars who, unlike the others, fell under the authority and power of their lords and masters who were allowed to exercise any kind of (mis)treatment. Nevertheless, in my opinion, it included some elements that indicate the use of a penal logic — or at least a penal discourse — regarding captives. In other words, their treatment, or violence against their 'defeated bodies', was regulated and subject to procedures of legitimisation that could be understood in the same context as that of the criminal policy described above. To illustrate this, it is necessary to look to other texts.

Chronicles

The Chronicles belong to a very different narrative genre, which partly explains the different nature of the information that they provide. But just as important as the kind of writing were their objectives and the public to whom they were addressed, since these elements determined how their contents were presented and their characters treated. It is necessary, therefore, to provide the broadest context possible for the testimonies contained in them.

However, the exploration below is experimental. It is intended, on the one hand, to assess the scope, character and relationship between forms of physical punishment in judicial contexts and in times of war. On the other hand, it is meant to investigate the way in which corporal punishment was perceived, in an attempt to understand the kind of values that were invoked to justify its imposition, the emotions that it sought to mobilise in the different actors involved, and the functions explicitly attributed to rituals which currently tend to be seen as macabre.

The Justice of Kings

This section will look first at the *Chronica Adefonsi Imperatoris*,[70] an anonymous mid-twelfth century Latin chronicle that narrates the reign of Alfonso VII in two parts. The first details the kingdom's internal restoration and the second presents the fight against the Muslims. In order to exalt the figure of the King and his restoration policies, the first part highlights how authoritatively he undertook the exercise of justice as soon as he was crowned emperor. On the third day of the coronation assembly gathered in León in 1135 he ordered the judges to severely judge and eradicate the

---

69 For example, the chastisement of the wrongdoer and the vengeance of the victim are the two functions of the process following an accusation that a *yerro* had been committed (Partidas I.1.1; Partidas VII.9.21).

70 CAI. Regarding the chronicle's author, M. Pérez González attributes this 'true medieval biblical epic' to a literate cleric who might have been an unofficial chronicler of the monarch, a contemporary of the story being narrated and eyewitness to some facts, who belonged to the high clergy and was very fond of everything from León (Pérez González, ed., *Crónica del Emperador Alfonso VII*, pp. 18–25). On the problems involved in the interpretation of this chronicle, the objectives of its author, and the context in which it was written, also see Baloup, 'Reconquête et croisade'.

vices of those who had acted against justice and the decrees of kings, princes, lords and judges; they met this mandate by hanging some from timber, and hewing the hands or feet of others, not sparing the rich or influential more than the poor, but deciding according to the degree of guilt of each.[71] The story goes on to describe how some miscreant were publicly captured and hanged on the gallows.[72] The narration highlights the exemplary function of a justice that emphasised the severity of the physical punishment and the egalitarian way in which it was inflicted, backed by the authority and power of the emperor.[73]

The *Estoria de España* (*History of Spain*) is another chronicle that, like the *Partidas*, was started under the aegis of Alfonso X.[74] A version of this work preserved in a composite codex formed between 1340–1345, includes a section covering all the reigns from Alfonso VII to Fernando III, although the materials used could date from further back. A rather peculiar chapter of this manuscript is dedicated to the 'emperor's justice'. This chapter gathers together in a vignette, which includes a moral, the elements of exemplarity and social equality that characterised imperial justice in the previous chronicle.[75] The narrative tells of the legal defence made by the emperor of the rights of a commoner against the violence of an *infanzón* who was ordered to be arrested and hanged. Thus, the story goes, the emperor pacified the land:

> and the fear that arose among all the men of the land because of this deed was so great that no one in the land ever dared to harm another. And this deed of justice, and others like this, were done by the Emperor, who was thus feared by the people, and everyone conducted his own affairs in peace[76]

---

71 'and he commanded all the judges to eradicate severely vice in those men who were discovered to be acting contrary to justice and to the decrees of kings, nobles, authorities and judges. They, for their part, judged justly, hanging some from the gallows, leaving others to have their hands or feet cut off, not sparing the wealthy nor the highborn any more than the poor, but distinguishing everything according to the level of guilt' ('iussique omnibus stricte iudicibus uitia eradicare in illis hominibus qui contra iustitiam et decreta regum et principum et potestatum et iudicum inueniretur. At illi alios in lignis suspendentes, alios truncatis manibus aut pedibus relinquentes, non diuitibus uel generosis plus quam pauperibus parcentes, sed totum secundum modum culpe discernentes, iuste iudicauerunt') (CAI, I.71).

72 'in the sight of all, some of these workers of iniquity were caught and hanged from the gallows' ('in conspectus omnium capti sunt aliqui operarii iniquietatis et suspense sunt in palibulis') (CAI, I.71).

73 For a wider discussion of this text see Alfonso, 'Judicial rhetoric', pp. 74–76.

74 On the recent philological studies about this text, see a detailed summary from a historiographical perspective in Alfonso, 'Vengeance, justice et lutte politique' [Editors' note: For an English translation, see chapter 5 of this volume]. However, for the reasons mentioned there, it is still necessary to use the version published as Menéndez Pidal, ed., *Primera Crónica General*. On the textual development of this work see Gómez Redondo, *Historia de la prosa medieval 1*, pp. 646–86.

75 PCG, ch. 980. This chapter is part of a section covering from Alfonso VII to Fernando III, which has only been preserved in a composite manuscript compiled between 1340 and 1345, using sources that may have been much earlier (Gómez Redondo, *Historia de la prosa medieval 1*, p. 664).

76 'e tan grande fue ell espanto que todos los omnes de la tierra ouieron por este fecho, que non fue ninguno osado en toda la tierra de fazer tuerto a otro. Et esta justicia et otras tales como estas auie fechas ell emperador, por que era ell muy temido de las yentes, et uiuien cada uno en los suyo en paç.' (PCG, ch. 980, p. 660).

The emphasis of the narrative is on the need for toughness on crime to maintain social order, but above all, on the need for the higher authority of the emperor and his justice in the face of the violence of the powerful. Fear, dread and terror were the key drives for that emotional domination, which was justified by the ensuing peace. It should be noted that in these two narratives from different periods (one from the mid-twelfth century and one from the second half of the fourteenth century), similar elements were used to construct a particular political authority linked to the same conception of justice, despite the fact that only the second one followed Roman principles, according to conventional interpretations.

Bodies Defeated in War

In the second part of the *Chronica Adefonsi Imperatoris*, which is dedicated to the fight against the Muslims, the chronicler describes in great detail the treatment that certain Christian captives received. One case was that of Munio Alfonso, a Christian knight whose story deserves to be mentioned here because it brings together many of the elements from which the stories of the fights between Moors and Christians are woven: imprisonments, rescues, killings, beheadings of corpses, dismemberments, exhibitions of a body, burials, humiliations and honours, deserved punishments, or divine vengeance.

The story of this knight occupies almost a quarter of the second book, an unusual length in the chronicle. He appears as the main character in both the defence of the Toledo territory against attacks by Muslims and the harassing raids launched from Toledo to plunder Muslim territories. However, in his first appearance in the chronicle he was defeated, taken prisoner, and sent to Cordoba, where an enormous sum was set for his liberation.[77] Mentioning such a high ransom may well have been the chronicler's way of underlining Munio's status, but it certainly indicates that release after a payment was an option for those captured in war. The knight's second appearance is hardly glorious either, as he was blamed for the loss of the castle of which he was the *alcaide* ('mayor'), which due to his 'negligence' passed into the hands of the king of Sevilla.[78] But the shame of that defeat is presented as the impetus that led Munio to continually fight the Muslims[79] until his valour was recognised by the emperor, who appointed him deputy *alcalde* of Toledo and 'on account of his honesty and military expertise' put him in command of the whole Transierra and Extremadura.[80] His brave actions in the fields of Córdoba (a great deal of plunder, many prisoners and killings)[81] triggered retaliation from the kings of Córdoba and Sevilla. Tactics more symbolic than material were used by him to face them. Success was entrusted to Christ, the Virgin and Santiago and he enthusiastically harangued his troops to fight without fear, by invoking the memory of similar circumstances

---

77 CAI, II.17.
78 CAI, II.46.
79 CAI, II.48.
80 CAI, II.49.
81 CAI, II.67.

when they had been victorious because God had been on their side.[82] Encouraged in this way, and despite their fewer numbers, they defeated the king of Sevilla and cut off his head.[83] Munio Alfonso himself used his spear to kill the fleeing king of Córdoba, who was later beheaded along with many other prisoners. Rich plunder was also obtained. The heads of the two kings and other leaders were placed on the tips of the spears of the royal standards, but the royal bodies were wrapped in silk cloths and returned to the Muslims on the orders of Munio Alfonso.[84] A triumphal entry into Toledo ensued, with the heads of the kings displayed on standards and spears, followed by a procession of chained noble knights and other Muslims with their hands tied. The entourage was completed by Christian troops who carried the rich plunder.[85] The emperor, who had been advised to go and witness such an extraordinary victory,[86] was received outside of the town by Munio Alfonso and his men, who again displayed the heads of the two kings and the warlords and Muslim military commanders, accompanied by the rest of the entourage mentioned above. The emperor expressed his joy and gratitude to God.[87] Then the entry into the royal palaces and the distribution of the booty is described: a large part was offered to the Toledo cathedral; another part was sent to the Cathedral of Santiago de Compostela; a fifth was taken by the emperor and the rest was distributed among the fighters who had accompanied Munio Alfonso.[88] The emperor then ordered that the heads of the Muslim kings and leaders be hung from the top of the citadel, as a testimony to divine help. They remained there until a few days later, the empress took pity and ordered them to be lowered and embalmed and sent to Córdoba to the queens, their wives,

---

82 CAI, II.69, 70.

83 CAI, II.71.

84 'They hung the heads of the kings from the top of the spears upon which were royal standards, and on each of the lances they hung the heads of the commanders and princes. Muño Alfonso ordered the kings' bodies to be wrapped in fine silk materials, he placed them in a green field, and left the Sarracens with them, who were to guard over them until they were taken away from there' ('Capita uero regum suspenderunt in summitate hastarum, in quibus errant uexilla regalia, et capita ducum et principum suspense sunt singulis hastis. Corpora regum iussit Munio Adefonsi inuolui in pannis sericis optimis et posuit ea in quodam campo uiridi et reliquit cum eis Sarracenos, qui ea custodierent usque inde tollerentur') (CAI, II.72, 73).

85 CAI, II.74.

86 CAI, II.76.

87 'After the emperor had seen all these things and the heads of the kings hanging from the tops of the lances upon which were the royal standards, he was astonished and, giving great thanks to the Lord God, he said: "Blessed be *Lord God, Creator of all things, who art fearful and strong, and righteous, and merciful, and the only and gracious King, the only giver of all things, the only just, almighty and everlasting*, who delivered you from the sword of these kings, and from the clutches of the Saracens, and who always delivers me and his followers *from all trouble*"') ('Sed postquam imperator uidit omnia hec et capita regum suspensa in summitate hastarum, in quibus erant uexilla regalia, stupefactus est et magnas gratias agens Domino Deo dixit: "Benedictus sit Dominus Deo omnium creator, terribilis et fortis, iustus et misericordis, qui solus est rex bonus solus prestans, solus iustus omnipotens et eternus, qui uos liberauit de gladio istororum regum et de manibus Sarracenorum et qui me semper liberat de omni malo et suos fideles"') (CAI, II.77).

88 CAI, II.78.

wrapped in rich cloth and tucked into chests of gold and silver.[89] The chronicle then presents the Muslim reaction to this Christian victory, announced by the Almoravid King Taxufin when he heard that the kings of Córdoba and Sevilla had been killed, in terms of revenge against Christians, and specifically, against Munio Alfonso.[90]

Thus, the treatment given by victorious Christians to their defeated Muslim enemies consisted of: the killings in battle; the decapitation of the kings once they were dead (the same may be presumed for the beheaded warlords);[91] the display of these heads at different times and places (on the battlefield, in the triumphal entry into the city, at the king's arrival, and finally, in the centre of the city of Toledo); the heads were displayed as evidence of divine help (as God only helps the good, those who deserve it, those who defend just causes, etc., and victory is in fact described as a miracle); the bodies of the beheaded kings were treated with respect, according to their royal status, as were their heads later on (the political nature of this treatment is evident, but it is necessary to interrogate the symbolic meaning of such acts); women served as intermediaries of the delivery and reception of the bodies of the defeated.

Of the later chapters that recount the subsequent Christian defeat,[92] I will only discuss here those that refer to Munio Alfonso's death.[93] The treatment of his defeated body introduced extraordinary forms of dismemberment. He was not only beheaded, but his right arm was cut off (including the shoulder and hand) as well as his right leg and foot. Each of these parts of the mutilated body functioned as an emissary of the death of the Christian hero in various Muslim areas. The head was sent to the palace of King Azuel's wife in Córdoba, later to the palace of King Avenceta in Sevilla, and then on across waters to King Taxufin's palace, so that what had happened would be known throughout the Muslim territory. The arm and foot along with the heads of the other Christian knights were hung on a high tower in Calatrava, the place of the defeat.[94] The Muslims wrapped in clean linen his dismembered body,

---

89 CAI, II.79.

90 'Take abundant gold and silver from my treasury and go to the land of the Christians and take revenge for our brothers the kings who have been killed' ('Accipe aurum et argentum abundanter de thesauris meis et uade in terra Christianorum et accipe uindictam regum fratrum nostrorum qui occisi sunt') (CAI, II.80).

91 The Toledan Annals record these events without specifying whether the decapitation took place after death: 'Munio Alfonso fought with the Moors and killed two of their kings, the one named Azover, the other Abenzeta, and he brought their heads to Toledo. This battle occurred on the river called Adoro, on the first day of March' ('Lidió Munio Alfonso con moros, è mató a dos Reyes de ellos, è el uno ovo nome Azover, è el otro Abenzeta, è aduxo sus cabezas a Toledo. Esta batalla fue en el Río que dicen Adoro, el primer día de Marcio') Flórez, España Sagrada, 23, p. 389 s. a. 1142.

92 CAI, II.81–86.

93 CAI, II.87–91.

94 'The adalid Farax arrived and cut off his head, his right arm, shoulder and hand, and his right foot and leg, and the stripped off his armour and warpped his mutilated body in clean linen. They cut off many of the Christian knights' heads and sent Muño Alfonso's head to Córdoba, to the palace of the wife of Azuel, and [then] to Seville, to the palace of King Avenceta, and afterwards across the sea to the palace of King Tāshufin, to publish it throughout all the land of the Moabites and Hagarenes. They fastened Muño Alfonso's arm and foot and the heads of the other knights to a high tower which stands in Calatrava' ('Venit autem Farax adali et amputauit caput eius et brachium dextrum cum humero et manum et pedem eius dextrum cum tibia et expoliauit eum armis et truncum corpus eius inuoluit

498   ISABEL ALFONSO

stripped of its weapons, and the people of Toledo collected it, along with those of his companions, and buried it in Toledo Cathedral, where the widows of the victims and their friends came to express their grief for many days after. The chronicler, echoing the Old Testament, compared the love of the people in the city to that of a loving wife for her only husband.[95] As a result, this grief became a great lament for the whole community of Toledo.

In an unexpected argumentative twist, Munio Alfonso's death is explained later in the chronicle as a divine punishment for his impiety. It was a way of atoning for the great sin he committed against God by killing his daughter for having an affair with a young man, and for not following the Lord's teachings to be merciful.[96] This chapter shatters the image heretofore constructed of the knight. The uniqueness of his heroism and courage was contradicted when other nobles sought to comfort the emperor's sorrow at his death by arguing that there were many others like Munio Alfonso and even better throughout the kingdom. This could be a later insertion written by another author for other purposes, which is not relevant to the subject matter here.

Conclusion

I do not intend to make a closed conclusion here, as that would require extending the analysis to a larger number of texts, including chronicles, and legal and hagiographic texts. I will merely highlight some aspects arising from what has been discussed above, pointing to certain lines of study that are worth pursuing.

- The pedagogical and therapeutic conception of violence as an element of the educational process that instils proper ways of behaving: this is a fairly common metaphor for political violence, which involves the intersection of very different social fields (husband/wife, parents/children,[97] teachers/

---

in linteaminibus mundis. Et multa capita Christanorum militum preciderunt et miserunt caput Munionis Adefonsi in Cordubam in domum uxoris Azuuel et in Sibiliam in domun regis Auencete, deinde trans mare in domum regis Texufini, ut annuntiaretur in omnem terram Moabitarum et Agarenorum. Brachium et pedem Munionis Adefonsi et capita aliorum militum suspenderunt super excelsam turrem, que est super Calatraua') (CAI, II.88).

95 'For many days Muño Alfonso's wife with her friends and the othe rwidows would go to the tomb of Muño Alfonso and would lament *with this lamentation* and say: "O Muño Alfonso we are *distressed for thee*. Just as a woman loves her only husband, so the city of Toledo loved you"' ('Sed per multos dies mulier Munius Adefonsis cum amicis suis et cetere uidue ueniebant super sepulcrum Munionis Adefonsi et plangebant planctum huiuscemodi et dicebant: "O Munio Adefonsi, nos dolemus super te. Sicut mulier unicum amat maritum, ita Toletana ciuitas te diligebat"') (CAI, II.89). According to the translator [of the Spanish edition], the passage is inspired in King David's lament for the death of Saul and Jonathan (Pérez González, ed., *Crónica del Emperador Alfonso VII*, p. 122, n. 141). On other famous funerary mournings, see Alfonso, 'Vengeance, justice et lutte politique' [Editors' note: For an English translation, see chapter 5 of this volume].

96 CAI, II.90, 91.

97 In some *fueros* marital and parental violence against women and children is authorised, even with

students,[98] lords/peasants,[99] king/subjects,[100] judges/the judged). The exemplary nature of punishment closely connects with this conception.[101]

- The body as a fundamental site of this violence: abuse/respect are two faces of the same conception of social order. Attention must be drawn to the symbolic meaning of the different types of capital punishment and the various processes of dismemberment and body dispersion that were described in these texts, as well as the recovery of body parts that had been amputated and the joint burial described in some cases. The political ritual of grief clearly shows the high value given to the physical return of 'defeated bodies', and to the fact that 'enemies' deserved the same honour. Punishments for those who dug up corpses or scattered bones illustrate this.[102] Attention needs to be given to those instances in chronicles and legal texts where the total breakup of the body, the complete disappearance of the 'defeated' and/or 'condemned' as a measure of political and moral hygiene was advocated as a kind of medicinal remedy for the health of the social body. Medical metaphors, invoking notions of infections and diseases that need tackling, were used to justify this attitude.[103]

---

impunity if death occurred, as in the *fuero* granted by Alfonso IX to Milmanda in 1199 (González, *Alfonso IX*, Vol. 2, p. 1126). Partidas VII.8.9, however, sets some limits on cruel and unconscionable punishments meted out by parents to their children.

98 The relationships between teachers and students were regulated in Partidas II.21. See Cacho Blecua, 'La crueldad del castigo'; Rodríguez Mediano, 'L'amour, la justice et la crainte'.

99 On metaphors that justified lordly violence, see Algazi, 'Pruning peasants'; Alfonso, 'La rhétorique de légitimation seigneuriale' [Editors' note: For an English translation, see chapter 11 of this volume].

100 Paul Freedman reviewed some reports of executions of people accused of revolting against king and lords: Freedman, 'Atrocities and the Executions'.

101 N. Pancer showed the therapeutic focus of the monastic penal system, the means of repression and how the old rules used the body and shame to effect punishment: Pancer, 'Crimes et châtiments monastiques'. On the punitive functions in the formation of morality and social control, see the arguments in Harding and Ireland, *Punishment*.

102 Partidas VII.9.12: 'What penalty should be accorded to those who destroy tombs and disinter the dead [...] or dishonour the corpse by removing the bones and casting them away or scattering them' ('Pena que merecen los que quebrantan los sepulcros y desentierran a los Muertos [...] o por deshonrrar los cuerpos, sacando los huesos, echandolos, o arrastrandolos'). See Madero Eguía, *Manos violentas*; and Gonthier, *Le châtiment*, pp. 131–33.

103 This is explicitly stated in the measures advocated in Partidas II.23.2 against 'malefactors in the kingdom, [who] resemble poison in the body of a man, who cannot be well as long as it is there' ('los mal fechores en el Reyno, como ponçoña en el cuerpo del ome, que mientra que y esta, non puede ser sano'). These are the internal enemies against whom it was said 'no pestilence has greater power to injure man than a domestic enemy, because he is familiar with all his acts, and can more easily place obstacles in his way' ('ninguna pestilencia non es mas fuerte para empecer al ome, que el enemigo de casa, porque sabe todo su fecho, e puedele estoruar mas de ligero') (Partidas II.19.1); and, in general, against all those who could be deemed to be traitors, based on a conception of betrayal as contagious disease: 'Treason is one of the most serious and odious crimes which a person can commit, and the wise men of the ancients, who had a just knowledge of all things, considered it so wicked that they compared it to leprosy; for just as leprosy is a disease which attacks the entire body, and after it has once been contracted cannot be removed or treated by medicines in such a way that the party who has it can be cured; and which also causes man, after he becomes a leper, to be separated and

500 ISABEL ALFONSO

- The operation of forms of social control through conscious manipulation of some emotions. Fear, dread and shame appear in the texts as positive elements that led to better behaviour. These negative emotions were transformed into the main drive for better justice. Was this not a 'turn of the screw' that justified the violence used to generate them? The study of emotions and their role in terms of social control has become a line of study of great interest.[104] I think, however, that this aspect of the debate on the 'positive' role of 'negative' emotions in promoting justice, in which some medieval scholars seem to agree with the studies on present-day justice, deserves further research and discussion.[105]

- Finally, the ways in which the otherness of the 'enemies' was constructed needs to be especially addressed. The texts commented on show that some 'enemies' were punished or destroyed in a manner that, according to the parameters of the texts themselves (we also have to think about their audience) was more violent than that accorded to prisoners. This might lead to questioning the conceptual opposition between 'captive' and 'prisoner' and to studying 'enmities' in a more complex context.

---

shut off from all others; and, in addition, to this, the disease is so serious that it not only affects the person who has it, but also his descendants in the direct line as well as those who live with him; thus, in the same way, treason affects the reputation of man, for the former injures and corrupts the latter so that it never can be restored, and brings about the separation and estrangement of all those who acknowledge justice and truth; and blackens and tarnishes the reputation of those descended from that family, although they may not be guilty, so that they always remain infamous on account of it' ('Traycion es vno de los mayores yerros, e denuestos, en que los omes pueden caer: e tanto lo touieron por mala los Sabios antiguos, que conocieron las cosas derechamente, que la compararon a la gafedad; ca bien assi, como la gafedad es mal que prende por todo el cuerpo, e después que es presa, non se puede tirar, nin amelecinar, de manera que pueda guarescer el que la ha. E otrosi, que faze a ome, después que es gafo, ser apartado, e alongado de todos los otros. E sin todo esto, es tan fuerte maletia, que non faze mal al que la ha en si tan solamente, mas aun al linaje que por la liña derecha del deciden, a los que con el moran. Otrosi en aquella manera mesma face la traycion en la fama del ome, ca ella la daña e la corrompe, de guisa, que nunca la puede enderezar; e aduze a gran alongança, e a estrañamiento de aquellos que conocen derecho, e verdad; e denegrece, e mancilla la fama de los que de aquel linaje decienden, maguer non ayan en ella culpa; de guisa, que fincan todavía enfamados por ella' (Partidas VII.2, Preamble). In Partidas II.28.2, the treacherous accomplices of the enemy would be exhumed and their bones broken, as they had done with the kingdom.

104 The bibliography is vast. Of interest, among others, are Miller, *Bloodtaking*; Miller, *Humiliation*; Miller, *The Mystery of Courage*; Rosenwein, ed., *Anger's Past*, especially the contributions by G. Althoff, P. Freedman, P. Hyams and S. White; see a critical commentary of the latter book in Alfonso, 'Los nombres de la violencia' [Editors' note: For an English translation, see chapter 16 of this volume]. I have also studied the use of emotions as instruments in Castilian epics and chronicles about revenge in Alfonso, 'Venganza y justicia' [Editors' note: For an English translation, see chapter 5 of this volume]. See also Rosenwein, *Emotional communities*. A study that provides relevant perspectives is Rodriguez Mediano, 'L'amour, la justice et la crainte'.

105 On these current debates, see Solomon, *A Passion for Justice*; McLaughlin and others, eds, *Restorative Justice*; Rivera Beiras, ed., *Mitologías y discursos sobre el castigo*. Perhaps the most interesting aspect of the last reference is to see how the principles underlying some of the currents trends in criminal law and their proposals such as the one referred to as 'Retribucionismo, pena simbólica y *just desert*', seem to implicitly recover some of the ideas supporting the arguments about punishment in the Partidas (Zysman Quirós, 'El castigo penal en Estados Unidos', pp. 253–58).

Bibliography

Alfonso, Isabel, 'Los nombres de la violencia y el control de su legitimación', *Hispania*, 61–208 (2001), 691–706

Alfonso, Isabel, 'Venganza y justicia en el Cantar de Mío Cid', in *El Cid: de la materia épica a las crónicas caballerescas*, ed. by Carlos Alvar Ezquerra, Fernando Gómez Redondo, and Georges Martin (Alcalá de Henares: Universidad de Alcalá, 2002), pp. 41–69

Alfonso, Isabel, 'Judicial Rhetoric and Political Legitimation in Medieval León-Castile', in *Building Legitimacy: Political Discourses and Forms of Legitimacy in Medieval Societies*, ed. by Julio Escalona, Isabel Alfonso, and Hugh Kennedy (Leiden: Brill, 2004), pp. 51–88

Alfonso, Isabel, 'Lenguaje y prácticas de negociar en la resolución de conflictos en la sociedad castellano-leonesa medieval', in *Negociar en la Edad Media/Négocier au Moyen Âge*, ed. by María Teresa Ferrer and others (Barcelona: CSIC, 2005), pp. 45–65

Alfonso, Isabel, 'Vengeance, justice et lutte politique dans l'historiographie castillane du Moyen Âge', in *La vengeance, 400–1200*, ed. by Dominique Barthélemy, François Bougard, and Régine Le Jan (Rome: École française de Rome, 2006), pp. 383–419

Alfonso, Isabel, 'La rhétorique de légitimation seigneuriale dans les fueros de León (XIe–XIIIe siècles)', in *Pour une anthropologie du prélèvement seigneurial dans les campagnes de l'Occident médiéval (XIe–XIVe siècles). Les mots, les temps, les lieux*, ed. by Monique Bourin and Pascual Martínez Sopena (Paris: Publications de la Sorbonne, 2007), pp. 229–52

Alfonso, Isabel, Julio Escalona, and Georges Martin, eds, *Lucha política: condena y legitimación en la España medieval*, Annexes des Cahiers de Civilisation Hispanique Médiévale, 16 (Lyon: ENS Éditions, 2004)

Algazi, Gadi, 'Pruning Peasants: Private War and Maintaining the Lords' Peace in Late Medieval Gsermany', in *Medieval Transformations: Texts, Power and Gifts in Context*, ed. by Esther Cohen and Mayke De Jong (Leiden: Brill, 2001), pp. 245–74

Baloup, Daniel, 'Reconquête et croisade dans la *Chronica Adefonsi imperatoris* (ca. 1150)', *Cahiers de Linguistique et de Civilisation Hispaniques Médiévales*, 25 (2002), 453–80

Baraz, Daniel, *Medieval Cruelty: Changing Perceptions, Late Antiquity to the Early Modern Period* (Ithaca: Cornell University Press, 2003)

Cacho Blecua, José Manuel, 'La crueldad del castigo: el ajusticiamiento del traidor y la "pértiga" educadora en el Libro del Cavallero Zifar', in *Aragón en la Edad Media: sesiones de trabajo. IV Seminario de Historia Medieval* (Zaragoza: Universidad de Zaragoza, 1995), pp. 59–89

Dunbabin, Jean, *Captivity and Imprisonment in Medieval Europe, 1000–1300*, Medieval Culture and Society (New York: Palgrave Macmillan, 2002)

Flórez, Enrique, *España Sagrada. Teatro geográfico-histórico de la Iglesia de España* (Madrid: Antonio Marin, 1767)

Foucault, Michel, *Surveiller et punir. Naissance de la prison* (Paris: Gallimard, 1975)

Freedman, Paul, 'Atrocities and the Executions of Peasant Rebel Leaders in Late Medieval and Early Modern Europe', *Medievalia et Humanistica, New Series*, 31 (2005), 101–13

Gauvard, Claude, *De grace especial: crime, état et société en France à la fin du Moyen Âge*, 2 vols (Paris: Publications de la Sorbonne, 1991)

Gómez Redondo, Fernando, *Historia de la prosa medieval castellana. Vol. 1. La creación del discurso prosístico: el entramado cortesano* (Madrid: Cátedra, 1998)

Gonthier, Nicole, *Le châtiment du crime au Moyen Âge (XIIe–XVIe siècles)* (Rennes: Presses universitaires de Rennes, 1998)

González, Julio, *Alfonso IX*, 2 vols (Madrid: CSIC, 1944)

Guerreau, Alain, *L'avenir d'un passé incertain: quelle histoire du Moyen Age au XXIe siècle?* (Paris: Seuil, 2001)

Harding, Christopher, and Richard W. Ireland, *Punishment: Rhetoric, Rule, and Practice* (New York: Routledge, 1989)

Jacob, Robert, *Images de la justice: essai sur l'iconographie judiciaire du Moyen Âge à l'âge classique* (Paris: Le Léopard d'Or, 1994)

López-Amo y Marín, Ángel, 'El Derecho penal español de la Baja Edad Media', *Anuario de Historia del Derecho Español*, 26 (1956), 337–68

Madero Eguía, Marta, *Manos violentas, palabras vedadas. La injuria en Castilla y León (siglos XIII–XV)* (Madrid: Taurus, 1992)

McLaughlin, Eugene, and others, eds, *Restorative Justice: Critical Issues* (London: Sage – The Open University, 2003)

Menéndez Pidal, Ramón, ed., *Primera Crónica General*, 2 vols (Madrid: Gredos, 1977)

Miller, William I., 'Choosing the Avenger: Some Aspects of the Bloodfeud in Medieval Iceland and England', *Law and History Review*, 1–2 (1983), 159–204

Miller, William I., *Bloodtaking and Peacemaking: Feud, Law, and Society in Saga Iceland* (Chicago: The University of Chicago Press, 1990)

Miller, William I., *Humilation, and other Essays on Honor, Social Discomfort, and Violence* (New York: Cornell University Press, 1993)

Miller, William I., *The Mystery of Courage* (Cambridge, MA: Harvard University Press, 2000)

Orlandis Rovira, José, 'Las consecuencias del delito en el derecho de la alta Edad Media', *Anuario de Historia del Derecho Español*, 18 (1947), 61–165

Pancer, Nira, 'Crimes et châtiments monastiques: aspects du systeme pénal cénobitique occidental (Ve et VIe siècles)', *Le Moyen Âge*, 2 (2003), 261–75

Pérez González, Maurilio, ed., *Crónica del Emperador Alfonso VII. Introducción, traducción, notas e índices* (León: Universidad de León, 1997)

Rivera Beiras, Iñaki, ed., *Mitologías y discursos sobre el castigo: historia del presente y posibles escenarios* (Barcelona: Rubí – Anthropos – Observatori del sistema penal i els drets humans, 2004)

Rodriguez Mediano, Fernando, 'L'amour, la justice et la crainte dans les récits hagiographiques marocains', *Studia Islamica*, 90 (2000), 85–104

Rosenwein, Barbara H., *Emotional Communities in the Early Middle Ages* (Ithaca: Cornell University Press, 2006)

Rosenwein, Barbara H., ed., *Anger's Past* (Ithaca: Cornell University Press, 1998)

Sánchez, Galo, *Fueros castellanos de Soria y Alcalá de Henares* (Madrid: Centro de Estudios Históricos, 1919)

Serna, Justo, 'Los límites de la reclusión carcelaria en la Valencia bajomedieval', *Revista d'Historia Medieval*, 1 (1990), 39–57

Solomon, Robert C., *A Passion for Justice: Emotions and the Origins of the Social Contract* (Reading, MA: Addison-Wesley, 1990)

Tomás y Valiente, Francisco, *El derecho penal de la monarquía absoluta (siglos XVI–XVII–XVIII)* (Madrid: Tecnos, 1969)

Torallas Tovar, Sofía and Inmaculada Pérez Martín, eds, *Castigo y reclusión en el mundo antiguo*, Manuales y anejos de Emérita, 45 (Madrid: CSIC, 2003)

Zysman Quirós, Diego, 'El castigo penal en Estados Unidos: teorías, discursos y racionalidades punitivas del presente', en Rivera Beiras, Iñaki, ed., *Mitologías y discursos sobre el castigo: historia del presente y posibles escenarios* (Barcelona: Rubí – Anthropos – Observatori del sistema penal i els drets humans, 2004), pp. 251–86

CHAPTER 13

On Disputes and Wrongdoings

with a commentary by François Bougard

Conflict, Language, and Social Practice in Medieval Societies: Selected Essays of Isabel Alfonso, with Commentaries, ed. by Julio Escalona Monge, Álvaro Carvajal Castro, and Cristina Jular Pérez-Alfaro, TMC 24 (Turnhout: Brepols, 2024), pp. 503–548

BREPOLS ❧ PUBLISHERS   10.1484/M.TMC-EB.5.132467

FRANÇOIS BOUGARD

Written Disputes

Just the Tip of the Iceberg[*]

The 1980s and 90s were a high point in historical and legal anthropology. This article, published in 1997, is a product of the coming-of-age of this historiographical phase as regards the sources for the north of the Iberian Peninsula. These testify, between the eleventh and the thirteenth centuries, to the diversity of the relationships between the lay 'nobility' and the ecclesiastical institutions, especially the monasteries, with respect to the land and its use. How are we to reconcile the acts of donation found in such numbers in collections of charters and cartularies and the accounts of lawsuits or extrajudicial agreements which denounce in the strongest possible terms the exactions and violence of the laity? If we leave aside the — significant — ambiguity of the words *hereditas* and *hereditarius*, which are likely to confuse those not familiar with the region, and also the existence of particular lexical features, such as the designation *infanzones* for the *milites*, the reality described finds many echoes in other areas, as in France and Italy, even though their sources are less rich and detailed.

We need first to remember something too often forgotten, namely that the legal documentation does not stand alone. Its form and its content make it exceptional, certainly, to the point where it is tempting to select it from among the mass of acts which record items of information in chronological series. It should be regarded, nevertheless, as only one type of evidence amongst others, one element in a wealth of documents in which its presence reflects the change of tone and rhythm imposed by a period of frequent conflict, and by its public expression, in the long history of relations between families and kin groups — more than individuals — and religious establishments. Nor should the act of resorting to the law, whether that of the king or not, be seen as the key moment in a relationship between laity and ecclesiastics, the last resort, coming after a stepping up of hostility, which would bring the conflict to an end thanks to the intervention of an outside authority; it is more a matter of one point in a continuum. The decision of the court, or rather the recognition by one party of the legal right of the other, is only a prelude to other actions and other acts, once a relationship compromised by violence or deception has been re-established: financial compensation, the concession of the 'usurped' property in the form of a lease, or a division between the two parties, and so on. A victory on parchment did not necessarily lead to a victory on the ground. By the eighth century, the Italian sources provide numerous similar instances, linked to the disputes of the abbey of

[*] Translated from the French by Jean Birrell.

François Bougard, Institut de recherche et d'histoire des textes (CNRS, Paris)

Farfa with owners one suspects belonged to the same social level as those at issue here: a minor and middling aristocracy, sufficiently powerful to impose themselves from time to time by force, but not enough to impose themselves over the long term vis-à-vis the monastery.[1] That this was so was also — another point correctly emphasised by this article — because the social forces in play were anything but polarised: it was not a matter of 'the laity' on one side and 'the ecclesiastics' on the other, but rather of groups and families whose members were distributed between the two spheres and whose interests were inevitably linked; many clergy were *infanzones* with a different haircut.

It also emerges clearly, and this is perhaps what is most important, that the relationship to the land was never definitive. On the contrary, it was subject to constant negotiations and renegotiations, which were in fact constant challenges to the current situation, and which might almost be called cyclical: some dictated by the biological vagaries of families, others by political life in general. To regard the donation of a piece of land by a relative as no longer applying in the next generation, however definitive the transfer might seem from the wording of the act, was par for the course. It was equally common to seek to renege on one's own donation, like Fronilde Ovéquiz, in the twelfth century, after she had broken her monastic vows. Similarly, changes of king, bishop or abbot acted as triggers or were seized on as opportunities for challenges. The aim of these claims was not primarily to recover a 'possession' which was one no longer, had sometimes not been for a long time, and where it was easy from a strictly juridical point of view to say to whom it belonged; rather, it was to reactivate a personal tie with the land, usually in the form of a life grant. This reactivation could not simply be a consequence of some documents produced in the office of a notary. Rather, it was effected by a process, by the involvement of the group, by public declarations and, at a given moment, by a meeting: a series of stages which were elements in an almost obligatory process, probably all the more obligatory the higher one was in the social scale. All else being equal, the demands for the confirmation of property by kings obeyed a similar logic: however solemn, a diploma gave only limited assurance if it was not renewed every time a new man took over the beneficiary institution or the occupant of the throne changed. It was necessary, too, to reaffirm at regular intervals a legal relationship with the land: land where those who occupied it and worked it in practice scarcely changed. Time and length of possession were here more a source of uncertainty than the opposite; the reopening of a dossier that had never been completely closed helped to bring the clarity that contemporaries demanded, independently of the presence or absence of written acts which were not in themselves sufficient, at a time when writing did not occupy the rank of absolute 'proof' that it would subsequently acquire.

From the anthropological, thus long-term, perspective, these stages provided structure. An examination of their progression makes it easier to understand certain

---

1 See for example Schiaparelli and Brühl, eds, *Codice diplomatico longobardo*, 4, 1, nos 12, 15; Zielinski, ed., *Codice diplomatico longobardo*, 5, nos 16, 31, 38, discussed by Bougard, *La justice*, p. 345; Costambeys, 'Disputes and Courts'.

aspects of the vocabulary and rhetoric of the acts. Chief among them is perhaps that concerning *invasio*, that is, occupation, too often categorised as 'unwarranted' (here: *entrar*). The physical action of entering land and declaring one's right to it was part of the symbolic 'violences' necessary to getting a process under way. Monastic rhetoric, for its part, prioritised the lexicon of unjust force, of arbitrariness, of the devil and sin; it was a way of constructing two worlds with opposite values. This takes us back to the question of the actual writing of the documents, which it has been possible to study for Italy. In the *regnum Italiae*, where the scribes were from the laity, such a vocabulary did not feature. But scarcely over the frontier, the tone changed, as in the case of the judicial acts involving the abbey of Farfa, depending on whether they were drawn up in the kingdom or on Roman territory: the processes of notaries were not the same as those of monks.[2] Nevertheless, it was not all rhetoric, and the violence was very real, as shown, still in Italy, by the *querimoniae* and other 'polyptyques of misdeeds', in which depredation goes hand in hand with fighting and murder. It would be mistaken, nevertheless, to think that this violence was committed by laymen alone, against whom the only weapon was prayer. On the contrary, it was much more evenly distributed than is generally said. In any case, it was not the act of one historical moment more than another: every link with some 'crisis of the state', as is often proposed, should be rejected. The richness of the acts of Castile and Leon invites us, yet again, to pay more attention to the grey areas, a hundred times more interesting than the black or the white.

---

2 Bougard, 'Écrire le procès'.

Bibliography

Bougard, François, *La justice dans le royaume d'Italie: de la fin du VIIIe siècle au début du XIe siècle* (Paris: École française de Rome, 1995)

Bougard, François, 'Écrire le procès: le compte rendu judiciaire entre VIIIe et XIe siècle', *Médiévales*, 56 (2009), 23–40

Costambeys, Marios, 'Disputes and Courts in Lombard and Carolingian Central Italy', *Early Medieval Europe*, 15 (2007), 265–89

Schiaparelli, Luigi, and Carlrichard Brühl, eds, *Codice diplomatico longobardo, 4, 1*, Fonti per la storia d'Italia, 65 (Roma: Istituto Storico Italiano per il Medio Evo, 1981)

Zielinski, Herbert, ed., *Codice diplomatico longobardo. 5: Le chartae dei Ducati di Spoleto e di Benevento*, Fonti per la storia d'Italia, 66 (Roma: Istituto Storico Italiano per il Medio Evo, 1986)

ISABEL ALFONSO

Land Disputes and *malfetrías* among the Medieval Nobility in Castile and León*

The complex relationships between lay and ecclesiastical aristocrats in the Middle Ages are increasingly better understood. We know of the nobility's generosity with religious institutions, with which they built self-serving ties of varied nature, but also that they were violent towards them. From this it would seem that the alliances between these groups run parallel to their antagonisms, as somewhat shown by both donation charters and judicial records. However, given that interpretations most commonly focus on the legal and economic aspects involved, land disputes between lay and ecclesiastical aristocrats are usually rendered as isolated acts of defence of their respective estates separated from the overall relationship between these groups.

As early as the tenth century monasteries were already litigating against laymen who claimed assets that were to some extent related to estates donated by their ancestors. Sometimes disputes were brought by monasteries complaining of the claims and usurpations they faced and ready to display publicly the written documents that proved their injustice. With this they expected to gain assurance that they would have the right to peaceful ownership of those assets and were eager to see promises ratified accordingly. These claims appear to support the view that ecclesiastical estates were constantly threatened by the ambition and plunder of an ever-harassing lay nobility, of whose violence the clergy considered themselves to be victims. The more or less violent claims of the lay nobility to those assets, however, portray another, not substantially different version. They are presented as acting in defence of family estates increasingly affected by hereditary fragmentation and the pious generosity of their members, and ultimately as reacting against the growing power of the church.[1]

These two aspects of what essentially constitutes a single argument are usually linked to the development of a right to private property defended by monasteries, as opposed to a right to protect the family estate, defended by lay nobles; and to the weakness or crisis of the central political authority, of which the nobility took advantage to lay siege to the ecclesiastical estates. This was a European-wide phenomenon, and the explanations so far considered — which are obviously further qualified in the respective regional historiographies — are widely shared.

Recent studies, focused more on the socio-political aspects involved in land grants, rather than on the legal, religious or purely economic aspects, have provided grounds for a more complex understanding of these disputes. Land, as the source of all power and wealth in medieval societies, was also the major connecting link in all

---

* Original publication: Alfonso, Isabel, 'Litigios por la tierra y "malfetrías" entre la nobleza medieval', *Hispania*, 197 (1997), 917–55. Translated by Julian Thomas.

1 For further discussion on these opposing views, see Weinberger, 'Cours judiciaires'.

social strata. Personal and social ties were built around land and its control. Donations and claims were embedded in local social networks and cannot be explained by mere economic factors.[2]

This study focuses on a series of land disputes between religious institutions and noble groups or individuals that took place between the eleventh and the fourteenth centuries in the area of Castile and León.[3] The aim is to analyse what I consider, as a hypothesis, to be a dynamic of negotiation of local political relations formalised around such disputes, and to identify its underlying structure. The verification of this hypothesis should have an impact on the interpretation of contemporary processes of legal change and political institutionalisation, which will be discussed in the final section.

To illustrate this social dynamic, which I argue is more inherent and structural to the system than has been previously assumed, I have used a series of case studies related to certain individuals who can be identified and connected, both between themselves and with the religious institutions with which they engaged in disputes, through the information provided by other studies.[4] This means not only that long-standing relationships preceding and following disputes can be found between both parties, but also that the manner in which the descendants of the lay individuals and groups inherited and negotiated such relationships can also be observed. These cases come mainly from the archives of two ecclesiastical institutions, the Cathedral of León and the Monastery of Sahagún, and have been selected according to the criteria described above.

This selective criterion relies on the following explicit assumptions made in some studies that I consider to be essential in Legal Anthropology and which have already been established and proven operational:

- A legal dispute is only a specific instance of a wider conflict. In order to understand it, the context of relationships preceding and following that dispute needs to be analysed. It must be understood within the overall social processes of which it is part.

2　Several studies have recaptured and developed the concept of gift exchange originally conceived in the classic essay Mauss, 'Essai sur le don'. These include White, *Custom, Kinship, and Gifts to Saints*; Rosenwein, *To Be the Neighbor of Saint Peter*; Miller, *Bloodtaking*. More recently, this social approach to property has been developed in the papers collected in Davies and Fouracre, eds, *Property and Power*.

3　The term 'land' is used in a very broad sense to refer to a whole series of assets that were the subject matter of proceedings. The content will be specified in each case, only indirectly addressing the distinction between ownership and lordship.

4　Some of the studies on the aristocracy that have been used as reference points and foundations for this work are Martínez Sopena, *Tierra de Campos occidental*; Martínez Sopena, 'Parentesco y poder'; Martínez Sopena, 'El conde Rodrigo de León'; Martínez Sopena, 'La nobleza de León y Castilla'; Estepa Díez, *Estructura social de la ciudad de León*; Estepa Díez, 'Poder y propiedad'. For a useful comparison, see Álvarez Borge, *Poder y relaciones sociales*. Other studies will be cited in the footnotes as appropriate. More particularly, on the importance that the control of, or the ties built with monasteries had for the aristocracy, see Loring García, 'Nobleza e iglesias propias'; Loring García, 'Dominios monásticos'; Martínez Sopena, 'Monasterios particulares'.

LAND DISPUTES AND *MALFETRÍAS*   511

- Having recourse to courts is one among the strategies used in a conflict. When analysing the repercussions of using courts to make certain demands public and have them resolved, the legitimacy that may be obtained from a judicial decision should be considered, but so should other means of dispute resolution as well as the existing relationships, rather than just the opposition, between the parties involved.[5]

Three mid-eleventh century dispute records preserved in the archives of the Cathedral of León provide the grounds for discussing some issues related to land ownership and land holding, and to the social relationships embedded within them. They also enable us to investigate the problems that ownership changes, whether due to transfers between title holders or to the death of one of them, caused for the people tied to the lands in question. This is how I believe we should understand the conflicts, and their settlements thereof, between, on the one hand, the family of countess Sancha Muñiz — founder of the Monastery of San Antolín — and the Cathedral of León, and on the other, the people who disputed their properties.[6]

In 1043 countess Sancha, a descendant of count Munio Fernández, received the *hereditates* that a family group had in the village of Cimanes. They claimed to have acquired them through *comparationes* ('purchases') and other *ganantias* ('gains') and to make the donation freely and without undue pressure — 'with pure heart, devote mind and spontaneous will'.[7] The reason for the donation is not specified, and thus it could be thought to be one of the many made by small to larger property owners. However, another charter from the same date records that the donation of that property was part of a forgiveness ritual.[8] As narrated in the document, those people, qualified as 'homines forciosos' ('forceful men'), had violently claimed properties that they had on lease from count Munio Fernández and afterwards from his son Pedro Muñiz, who were respectively the father and brother of Sancha.

The document also reports that the action took place during the minority of the person that had last inherited the domain over the village, who had transferred it to the monastery of San Antolín. This is documented and two circumstances should be highlighted in connection with it, but I will discuss them in more detail later. The outburst of violence was thus posed as a response to a change in the owning lord.

---

5   Lee Epstein, 'The Case Method'; Roberts and Comaroff, *Rules and Processes*. For some studies on medieval history in which these approaches have been adopted, see White, '*Pactum ... legem vincit*'; White, 'Feuding and Peacemaking'; Davies and Fouracre, eds, *The Settlement of Disputes*; Miller, *Bloodtaking*. See also Alfonso, 'Resolución de disputas'.

6   For the judicial records, see CatLeón887 (1031 [and 1087–1112]); CatLeon1006 (1043); CatLeon1026 (1045); CatLeon1151 (1067). The other charters cited are CatLeon970 (1038); CatLeon971 (1038); CatLeon992 (1040). On the monastery of San Antolín and the family that founded it, see Ser Quijano, 'Un monasterio benedictino'.

7   'corde puro, mente deuota et spontanea uoluntate'.

8   The editor included these documents together, warning that they were copied separately in the cartulary, known as the *Tumbo*, perhaps because they came from two different parchments. I wonder what we would make of the case had the second of the charters been lost. As we will see, this may be the case in many other instances. Such lack of information may lead us to err on our interpretation of the reasons that motivated such donations.

These changes affected the existing personal and material bonds, and could be used by both parties to improve their situation, that is, their position with respect to these properties and the obligations due, which in any case should have been negotiated. Perhaps the most important issue here may be that the village was transferred to a religious institution, rather than along the same family line.

The narration goes on to describe how countess Sancha, aunt of Pedro Muñiz, brought the dispute before king Fernando I.[9] In that *iuncta* ('meeting') held in Sahagún, to which the king had convened 'totos suos barones' ('all of his men'), the countess showed the charter recording the conveyance of the disputed property by Vermudo II to her father. This was enough for the royal assembly to ratify her claims. The arguments made by the other party are unknown, but the written evidence may indicate that the object of the dispute was the ownership of the land by the minor heir, not that it was held on lease.

It seems more interesting to investigate the nature of this litigation, as it may shed some light on the possible status of the litigants in relation to the countess. Why would the countess bring this dispute before the king? Why was her jurisdiction not sufficient to prevail over the men from Cimanes? This poses questions about the scope and effectiveness of lordly justice, a power we know Sancha could avail since other records show that she had received properties as *iudicatum*. Could lords only exert justice in cases between their dependents? Was the intention in this conflict to subjugate people who were not within the sway of their lordly power? Should higher authorities judge the conflicts in which lords themselves were involved? Was this 'weakness' due to her status as a woman? And how should the social status of the litigants be interpreted? They were presented as owners and holders of their land, referred to as their *hereditates*, whether they had been earned or purchased. Were they local elites who negotiated their relationship with more important lords whenever there was a change of ownership, first violently and later judicially?

Other charters provide additional context for this dispute. The endowment of the church of San Antolín in 1038 is certainly relevant, as it became the new owner of all the land and villages of Sancha Muñiz's family. Local power relations must have also been affected when two years later the countess donated San Antolín to the Cathedral of León, together with the monastery of San Salvador, in Baradones, and the village of Cimanes.[10]

---

9 The charter attributes this to Munio Fernández, I believe mistakenly.

10 The reasons why the countess was able to dispose of her nephew's property in favour of the Cathedral are unknown. This has been interpreted as an attempt to protect the minor's rights, which were threatened by the conflict (Ser Quijano, 'Un monasterio benedictino', p. 184). However, it could be thought that the donation that her nephew made shortly afterwards to the monastery — rather than to the cathedral —, which was seemingly confirmed by some of the members of the Orvida family — who had previously litigated against doña Sancha —, could have resulted from attempts by the monastery to maintain its autonomy from the cathedral. If this were the case, could there have been some intra-family tensions whereby some sectors of the Cimanes community may have supported the minor in the conflict with his aunt?

Conflicts emerged again when Havive Donniniz, a successor of the abovementioned family group,[11] representing his own family, raised a *calumpnia* ('charge') against the bishop of León claiming rights to *cortes* and land in Cimanes and Matilla. He argued that his father had bought that property from Pedro Muñiz, doña Sancha's brother. The bishop brought the dispute before Alfonso VI, arguing that that property had been donated to San Antolín. Again, they were opposing arguments as to whether or not the lands had been sold or assigned to one party or the other. Havive made a public demand invoking rights based on both inheritance and purchase. This type of claim was widely acknowledged, but still, it had to be proven.

The bishop, through the holder of the property claimed by Havive, appeared 'ad diem placiti in concilio' ('on the agreed day at court') before the king in Villaquejida, on the banks of river Esla. He brought the charter recording the royal grant made on behalf of Munio Fernández, and all the information related to the transfer that was already in his possession.[12] What matters here was the legitimation of the claim by reference to previous litigation and favourable outcomes. The bishop used the *agnitio* ('recognition') of the cathedral's ownership rights, and the commitment not to disturb them, to render Havive's claim to the king invalid. The information provided should have been enough to prove the bishop's claim, and indeed it is said that king Alfonso and his men saw a *scriptura ueritatis* ('truthful charter') presented by the bishop. However, the bishop was ordered to provide ten witnesses, just as Havive, and the latter was instructed to choose three from those ten to ratify the statement made by the bishop. He also had to swear that his ancestors had never been *hereditarii* in those towns, but rather had the land on lease — and were thus lease holders — of countess Sancha. It was then that Havive acknowledged the *indecentia* ('indecency') of his arguments and relinquished the right to subsequent lawsuits. Interestingly, the ten supporting witnesses provided by the bishop, whose names are listed at the end of the document, included some of the *infanzones* that later appear as his adversaries, as Pelayo and Cipriano Vellitiz, Citi Donelliz, or Diego Ovequiz.

In view of this information, why was the dispute brought before the king? One of the reasons is clearly that the bishop could not impose his power over these local elites, or had limits to do so. Another was that the king's court was a privileged jurisdiction for the bishop to publicise his authority and alliances in order to increase his prestige. The bishop's victory, however, was not as clear as this charter would seemingly indicate, as the process continued. On the same date of his defeat, Havive signed an agreement with the bishop whereby he received the village of Colinas on

---

11 Some form of family relationship can be thought to have existed between them, given the background to the case.

12 First to his son and later to his grandson who, contrary to the argument made by Havive, supposedly transferred it to San Antolín, where he was said to have been buried, and where his aunt, countess Sancha, was 'cultor et domina' ('dweller and lord'). It was described that before Fernando I she had already claimed the properties of the current litigator's 'heredes antecesores' ('preceding inheritors'). The latter would have purportedly received the price that they had paid for the those *hereditates*. This price coincided with that received by the litigants in 1043, which leads to the conclusion that Havive belonged to the same group, given also the parallelisms and similarities of the formulas used.

514   ISABEL ALFONSO

lease, thus becoming the bishop's vassal. This would further seem to show that at times of political change groups of co-heirs like Havive's may have laid claims to lands arguing prior possession, and thus seemingly contesting the rights of current owners, as part of their political strategies.

To recap some information about these cases:

- They were brought before the royal courts of Fernando I and Alfonso VI.

- In both cases the arguments relied on the status of rights, loans, or property, and were discussed and legitimised on the basis of how the latter had been assigned and transferred. The memory recalled covers various transfers made by the initial owners among themselves and to religious institutions; by the beneficiaries among themselves and by purchase from them. It was also discussed whether the land had been assigned or sold, as in the latter case the rights were not merely landholding rights.[13]

- In both cases the proof provided was the charter recording the original royal grant, which passed from one beneficiary to the next along with the lands. In the first case, Fernando I and his men seemed to have made a decision based on this document in favour of those who submitted it, and following the law they ordered that double or triple the value of the disputed property was to be paid, and that a payment had to be made to the king as well. However, Alfonso VI and his men demanded that witnesses had to testify under oath, and this was presented as a reason for the opponent to relinquish his claim.

- In the first case the judgment was not executed, because the losing party begged for forgiveness and donated their lands in the disputed location, while receiving the price that they had supposedly paid for them. In the second case, the losing party recognised that his demand had been wrong and acknowledged the bishop's ownership, but did not deliver anything, and received another village on lease in a separate document, which he would obtain 'in quantum fuero uestro uasallo' ('as long as I am your vassal').

These cases show the difficulties that lay and ecclesiastical aristocracy had in exercising their power locally, both in terms of ownership and jurisdiction. The relationship dynamic between them and the local elites, who did not seem to be of noble status, is clearly shown in these disputes. They were tied to the former through land holding and lease arrangements, and this dynamic may not have been too different from that occurring among those in the higher echelons of society. Claims to *hereditates* and leases were consecutive events already in the eleventh century. Could they be regarded as a usual method to negotiate landholdings and relationships at certain social levels? Were they the means to clarify transfers within the group that expected to receive the inheritance and the social status associated with it? The bishop succeeded in gaining

---

13   With regards to the problems and disputes involving these transactions, and the need to redefine them constantly as they were used to define and establish status and social relationships, see the comments made in Miller, *Bloodtaking*, p. 80.

LAND DISPUTES AND *MALFETRÍAS*   515

total control of the village of Cimanes, but the people who fought over it against him at the same time managed to remain in the bishop's network and enjoy the political, social and economic advantages that arose from this.

Another group of cases over Villaesper[14] also provides a good example of claims to *hereditates* laid against a monastery by descendants of the original or previous donors. It involved a family group whose mother belonged to the higher nobility, the Alfonso kinship group, and whose father was one of the local aristocrats, the Velázquez kinship group.[15] The dispute must have arisen upon the death of María Núñez, who survived the father, Munio Velázquez, by a few years. The litigants were their three children and a niece, who sought to retain ownership of the village for which their father had exchanged charters with the monks from Sahagún, or so they claimed. However, the monks reminded king Alfonso and the magnates in his palace, to whom they brought the case, that what they had transferred to their parents was the holding of the village for life, and therefore that it should be returned to the monastery upon their death. The monks added that Munio Velázquez and his wife had donated their portion of the monastery of San Felices in exchange for the *beneficium* received.

Consequently, whereas one party argued that there had been a *testamentum conmutacionis* ('exchange charter'), the other party alleged that it was a temporary transfer that had taken place. There was no argument about the facts, that is, the transfer of the village by the monastery. This was not challenged. What was rather called into question were the terms of the transfer, that is, the rights of each party.[16] No evidence was submitted or demanded, although both parties seemed to be in a position to furnish documents supporting their claims. The king's decision was that each party should recover its own *hereditas*. What better way could there be to restart the exchange ritual again? This is what they in fact did, as the heirs ratified the donation of their mother's share in the monastery of San Felices — to which they refer as their *hereditate* or 'portio nostra' ('our share') —, which to a certain extent they had recovered as a result of the king's decision. They also restored the relationship with the monastery's saints, whom they made their patron saints. The monks gave them another monastery in exchange, that of San Andres de Pozadurama. The fact that this transaction was formulated as an exchange seemingly implies that those assets had been fully and permanently transferred, and that both parties agreed to honour this arrangement.

---

14 The documents discussed are: SFPSahagun993 (1096); SFPSahagun1247 (1131).

15 The main details about this family can be found in Martínez Sopena, 'Parentesco y poder', p. 65. On the basis of the state of affairs at the end of the eleventh century, Martínez Sopena related these claims to others by members of the same Alfonso family, and interpreted them as a reflection of the protection of that kinship group's estate.

16 Another type of exchange charters carried out by the same institution could serve as a reference to confirm the broad range of forms these businesses could adopt. In 1102 the exchange between Sahagún and Pedro Ansúrez was to remain forever firm 'sicut lex gotica docet' ('as prescribed in Visigothic law') (SFPSahagun1085, 1102). Interestingly, these regulatory arguments may have provided Velasco Muñoz, who was present at the time, with legal support for his own claim. On the contrary, two years later, in 1104, an exchange made between Sahagún and another lay person was formulated as *prestimonial*, since the beneficiaries of the concession, who thereby became vassals to the monastery, were required to return what they acquired in the exchange upon their death (SFPSahagun1104, 1104).

The interest of the charter lies in the information it provides about a transfer made as a *beneficium*, even from a formal point of view, already in the mid-eleventh century. The monastery had granted Munio Velázquez *pro beneficio* a *villa* that was distant from the monastery and which he could *vindicare* ('claim') and *tenere* ('hold') while he was alive, that is, that he could enjoy and defend as his own during his lifetime. In exchange, he and his wife had donated their portion of the family monastery of San Felices. The tie between the two transfers and its nature are evident. Their children seemed to be willing to reassert this connection and declared themselves to be heirs to that relationship in order to ensure that they remained tied to the powerful Sahagún network. Their strategy is well-known: they claimed their rights to the properties that had previously served to establish the bond. Relying on this claim, they were in a stronger position to donate their part in the monastery of San Felices, even if already donated by their parents. By doing so, they proclaimed their blood links to the owners of the monastery, the powerful Banu Mirel kinship group,[17] in the privileged jurisdiction that the royal assembly was. If we acknowledge that the social level of this family line was lower, we should not underestimate the importance of these rituals of public affirmation. They constituted their immaterial inheritance, which was closely related to their material inheritance. These actions also served to argue their position and status within their group of relatives. The rationale behind it, therefore, was not only that of some nobles who were anxious to reconstruct their scattered family estates. We should also contemplate the symbolic capital provided by inherited social ties.[18]

The solution sanctioned by the king seemed to be fully accepted. Sahagún recovered Villaesper and had the share that granted full ownership over the old family monastery of San Felices ratified; the children of Munio Velázquez and María Núñez took the monastery's patron saints as their own and returned what had been their parents' property, and received another monastery in exchange which, despite not being itemised in the document, enabled them to recover an old donation made by their grandmother and their father.[19] We cannot know the reasons for preferring each of the different properties involved in the dispute, or the strategies that underlay the dispute process. However, it is significant that it was precisely at this moment, when a widespread movement of ecclesiastical reform was leading smaller religious institutions to be absorbed by bigger ones, that Sahagún granted these laymen full control over a monastery it had already received from the latter's ancestors back in 1055. In fact, the issue was much more complex. Some prior documents belonging to this family could lead to a hypothetical interpretation that supports the argument

---

17 On this family and the monastery of San Felices, see Martínez Sopena, *Tierra de Campos occidental*, pp. 347–52.

18 On transactions and symbolic capital, see Bourdieu, *Le sens practique*, esp. ch. 7.

19 Evidence for the donation that Tegridia and her son, Munio Velázquez, made to Sahagún for their soul is found in SFPSahagun573 (1055). They referred to Sahagún's saints as their own patron saints and granted them a 'villa propria' ('village of their own') called Becilla, as well as the monastery of San Andrés, in Pozo de Urama, and lands in other locations. The monastery of San Andrés was probably founded by the family or, at least, solely owned by it at that time. In 1090 Munio Velázquez was the lord of Pozo de Urama, the family stronghold.

provided above, namely that the ties created through alms and donations had to be ratified or renegotiated with each generational change. There are no quantitative data available to support this hypothesis, but there is sufficient information to construct it and check its validity. In the case in hand we know that at some unknown date Munio Velázquez had challenged the ownership of some assets that he and his mother had donated in 1055, namely the monastery of San Andrés and two *solares* in *Villa Filal*, and succeeded in obtaining them on lease during his lifetime. In 1091, shortly after his death,[20] his wife and younger children somehow renegotiated those same lands. At this point, they retained possession of the monastery of San Andrés and gave away that of Santa María, together with the two *solares* in *Villa Filal*. His widow and one of their children once again donated Sahagún the *divisa* ('share') they had received among his co-heirs in Castilfalé. These are the children who, upon their mother's death, brought the claim before Alfonso VI. The recovery or ratification of the monastery of San Andrés de Pozo de Urama, which they received as a result of the dispute process, could therefore be also related to the attempt to retain the political power that their father had held in that area.

In any case, the important point here is that thanks to this additional information the court case discussed can be seen as a stage within the long-standing family bond between them and the monastery. This bond was renewed after the process, perhaps under different conditions, and these may not have satisfied the expectations of the parties involved. If the children of Munio Velázquez effectively intended to retain the holding and defence of Villaesper, they failed to do so, although they persisted in their endeavour, as shown in a later version of the same process. In 1131 this *villa* was offered by Sahagún before Alfonso VII to support their claim to it. It was then in the possession of Velasco Muñoz, the only son and main instigator of the dispute held in 1096. He was accused of seizing it, taking advantage of the warlike situation that followed the death of Alfonso VI. *Entramiento* ('seizure') and violence were the arguments adduced by the abbot to delegitimise Velasco Muñoz as a long-term holder of the *villa*. This seizure could be interpreted as yet another episode in the competition between the litigants. However, it could be also seen as a sign of a different political attitude, contrary to that adopted by Sahagún in the violent conflicts surrounding the renewal of the royal political authority that had taken place. No information has been preserved in this case to shed light on the possible connection between the different conflicts, but I would prefer to err on the side of caution when attributing this violence to the unleashed ambition of the nobility.

The resolution of these proceedings before the royal court can be seen as a reconciliation ceremony between the monastery and the noble aggressor, who recognised that his ownership was wrong and unjust, rather than violent: 'recognising my error for I unjustly [...] retained the *hereditas* of Villaesper for my own sake'.[21]

---

20 He appears as *tenente* ('holder') of Pozo de Urama in 1090, following Pedro Ansúrez, count of Saldaña, in the witness list of a charter recording a donation made to Sahagún (SFPSahagun861, 1090). He presided over a dispute between Sahagún and Ildonza Ovéquiz, who was related to Munio through his wife (SFPSahagun863, 1090).

21 'intelligens errorem meum quia iniuste [...] hereditatem de Uilla Asperi michi retinui'.

This is why he returned the charter that his father had been given to establish the terms, and promised not to make any further claims. These arguments were similar to many other renunciations found in charter collections under the names of *manifestum* ('declaration'), *agnitio* ('acknowledgement'), or *deffinitio* ('pronouncement'). In the context of a process of royal restoration, the document discussed was clearly reconstructed by the monastery to show the facts that served their vested interests. The rationale implicit in the narration used such apparently aseptic terms as *autem* ('moreover') or *itaque* ('and so'), which served to emphasise their arguments.[22] Despite this, terms related to violence were also used by the monastery as part of their accusation; as mentioned above, in his recognition of the legal grounds supporting his claims and of his actions the nobleman ultimately invoked his father's former holding. He was not punished or penalised for this violence other than being forced to return the village that he had taken as his own. He took again the monastery's saints as his patron saints and received one hundred silver *solidi* for his renunciation. This case is clearly one instance of a whole process of tensions that characterised the interaction between the large monastery and its lay clients, as both Munio Velázquez and his son Velasco Muñoz regularly subscribed charters recording the monastery's business.

The argument proposed here can be developed further by investigating another set of cases that revolve around Villacorta. For more than a century the locality appears in charters related to the same families, which seemed to have used it in this dynamic of donations, appropriations or claims, denunciations, renunciations and continuity of landholding. This process was related to the ties built with Sahagún and what these represented for these groups and for the relationship between them.

In early 1102, a case was brought before Alfonso VI. This was clearly part of a more extended conflict in which, according to Sahagún, some acts of violence, deemed *barbarus* ('barbarous') by the monastery, had occured. In the hearing, the monastery claimed that its property and share[23] in Villacorta had been donated to it by Pedro Ovéquiz and his wife Ildonza, and that Pedro Sarracínez and his co-heirs 'obsederat more barbarico' ('occupied it barbarously'). In this case, it was the rights rather than the facts that were disputed. Pedro Sarracínez, as implied in his final contrary recognition, seemed to allege that he had a 'divisa por herencia' ('share by inheritance') in that *villa*; in other words, that he had received it 'per directum' ('righteously').[24]

---

22 After narrating how Velasco 'had forcefully seized Villaesper from Sahagún' ('per uim tulerat Uillam Asperi a Sancto Facundo'), the text continues: 'the king then ordered that they should recover the *hereditas* that belonged to them and of which they had been violently deprived' ('iussit, autem, eos rex ut recuperarent hereditatem ad se pertinentem, quam uiolenter perdiderant'). It then adds: 'And so acknowledging the violence he had exerted, Velasco Muñoz returned the charter that his father had granted' ('Cognoscens, itaque Uelasco Monnionis uiolenciam suam, retulit kartam quam dederant patri suo') (SFPSahagun1247, 1131).

23 On this concept and the development of political power based on landed property, see Estepa Díez, 'Proprietà'.

24 Sahagún claimed that Pedro Sarracínez was related to the donors of the disputed village through his sister-in-law, Fronilde Ovéquiz, who I assume was married to his brother, Ordoño Sarracínez. On these two families, see Martínez Sopena, *Tierra de Campos occidental*, pp. 361–62; and Reglero de la Fuente, *Los señoríos de los Montes Torozos*, pp. 91–94.

LAND DISPUTES AND *MALFETRÍAS*   519

In view of the opposing arguments adduced, and despite the written evidence provided by the monks, the king commanded Pedro Ansúrez to perform an inquest not of the violent acts and hereditary claims of the layman, but rather to investigate the truth of the allegations made by the monastery. The outcome of the inquest confirmed the content of the document provided by the monastery — 'what he found was what was recorded in its charter' — as was so often the case, though using a different form of evidence.[25] It operated as a pressure mechanism to force one of the parties to recognise that their claims were wrong and unfair, so it was effective even before its implementation. A full begging and pardon ritual — as aptly studied by Koziol[26] — was then unleashed. This re-established the relationship without even producing any settlement between the parties. In the case in hand, Pedro Sarracínez begged the abbot that he could have the disputed share for life, and the abbot, 'motus misericordia' ('moved by mercy'), granted his wish, subject to the commitment that neither his wife nor his children nor the people of Fontecillas would lay claim to the property against the monks of Sahagún. This illustrates the nature of the problems and differences between the parties.

Another peaceful episode of this conflict took place two years later, when Pedro Sarracínez, together with his daughter, returned the holding of Villacorta to Sahagún. He recalled the claim and the resolution that had previously been issued, yet he declared that now he was delivering his full share over which there had been a dispute before the king.[27] The delivery of his share took place in solemn circumstances, perhaps also before the group of magnates subscribing the charter, and he added to it another share in another location. The reason behind this return/donation was that a property should be received in exchange: the property of Faveces, which is said to have belonged to Diego Osoriz. It was also to be held for life and should therefore be returned upon his death with everything that was found in it. This expression referred to the defence of the monastery's estate, and consequently, to the nature of the link between the parties.

Pedro Sarracínez's social status is known through different sources. This provides more information about the forms of political action taken by this stratum of *infanzones* with whom he belonged. It is worth analysing this in some detail, first, because his children were included among the local notables and property owners that confronted the bishop of León over the ownership of a monastery in 1117. And second, due to his link with the Ovequiz family through the marriage of his brother, Ordoño Sarracínez. Some disputes that involved the latter and his wife's descendants will be dealt with later.

The cases featuring the so-called '*infanzones* of Bernesga' date to 1093, 1115 and 1117. They are well known and have been thoroughly studied, particularly the earliest one.[28] However, a comparative analysis will further their understanding. Given the

---

25 'inuenit sicut in suo testamento habebant'.
26 Koziol, *Begging Pardon*.
27 SFPSahagun1103 (1104).
28 Estepa Díez, 'Formación y consolidación del feudalismo', pp. 212–14; Estepa Díez, *Estructura social de la ciudad de León*, p. 256; Pastor, *Resistencias y luchas campesinas*, p. 82. The charters are CatLeon1279 (1093); CatLeon1350 (1115); CatLeon1358, (1117).

520 ISABEL ALFONSO

inherent interest of these charters, particularly regarding how they were recorded and their narrative structure, an approximate translation of these will be provided.

The first of these, dated 1093, is a formidable text to explore the dynamics analysed here. It is certainly a colourful narration that seems to be the work of a chronicler rather than an account made merely by a scribe at the king's or the bishop's service. It expresses a certain degree of admiration for the *infanzones*. Its narrative structure is also unusual. It starts by announcing the final resolution, the *agnitio*, reached under the triune God's authority, on the *intentiones* ('conflicts') that had arisen between Bishop Pedro de León and those 'knights, who were not born of parents of the lower ranks but are of the kind of nobles and political authorities, who in the common speech are called *infanzones*'.[29] This sentence has become widely used to refer to those social groups whose noble status was clearly defined by their family origin. The conflict is reported to have specifically entailed *hereditates, villae* and men in a broad delimited area of river Bernesga. The narration includes the names of ten people and the relatives accompanying them, all of whom should abide by this *conventio* ('agreement').

The account goes on to explain the events occurred to that point between the reign of Ordoño, donor of those properties, and that of the powerful king Alfonso, son of emperor Fernando. This reference is intended to highlight the continuation of the royal line. In this interval, the grandparents and parents of these *milites* ('knights') seized the *hereditates, villae* and men belonging to the church, which were the ones being divided.

The narration of the dispute at this point includes sentences pretending to reconstruct the discussion that supposedly occurred before the royal court. The bishop lay claim to the *hereditates* unjustly owned by the knights and requested that they should leave it, for *nefarius erat* ('it was nefarious'). Direct speech is used to condemn, as 'scandalous [...] and exceedingly dishonourable' that 'the *hereditates* donated by the king to the church, free from the jurisdiction of political authorities should be separated from the rights of the church'.[30] If this reading is correct, the *infanzones* were thus recognised as holders of the ecclesiastical estate. Hence this would be the same type of dispute as seen above. I will come back to this. Let us now continue with the counter-argument made by the knights, who 'most firmly and as firm as the opposing bishop spoke together in one voice'.[31] Direct speech is also used to narrate that they reminded the bishop of how their parents and grandparents had obtained the possession of the *hereditates* and *villae* under successive kings and bishops. They also argued that this was the reason why they were not willing to return them 'nisi iuditio et imperio regis' ('except by the judgement and command of the king').

---

29 'milites, non infimis parentibus ortos, sed nobiles genere necnon et potestate, qui uulgari lingua infanzones dicuntur'.

30 'turpe [...] et ualde inhoneste [...] ut hereditas que a parte regis Dei Ecclesie fuit dicata, aforastitis potestatibus sit de iuri nostro separata'.

31 'milites firmisissime et tam firmissimo adversus episcopus omnes una uoce dixerunt'.

A vivid summary is therefore provided of the opening defiant ritual of opposition between the parties in front of a large audience. The text moves on to explain the emotional reaction of the bishop to the ferocious and firm statements he had heard. He brought his *querimoniae* ('complains') for their *inquietudines* ('disturbances') before the king, in the knowledge that the monarch was fully aware that the *infanzones* held the *hereditates* unfairly. It is interesting to see how this is in fact part of a previous, direct fight between them, which had taken place before resorting to the 'arbitrio regis et iuditio' ('decision and judgement of the king') for him to judge. The description of the bishop's stern disapproval implies his condemnation of the other party. The narration brings the bishop's argument together with the king's decision made after an inquest — 'inquisiuit ueritatem' ('he investigated the truth') — whereby the porter of the bishop's palace would receive everything that God's church 'lacked due to the negligence and violence of the knights',[32] as it was done.

The text then summarises what followed next. Those who recognised themselves as *milites regis* ('royal knights') did not accept the royal resolution. When they saw the royal order and the bishop receiving all the properties, they met the latter before the king and once again *dimicarent* ('they litigated'). This was a judicial hearing in which the bishop showed his willingness that they should receive *iudicum* ('judgement') on this account. The arguments seem to be repeated, as the king, hearing all parties, provided that three clerics from the cathedral should take an oath regarding the bishop's rights to the *hereditates* he demanded. Direct speech is again used at this point when the knights wondered what they would obtain from this and decided to ask the bishop for mercy instead. It is to be noted how pragmatic the strategies used by the laymen were.

After the knights had acknowledged their false statements, the parties made a 'scripturam firmamenti et agnitionem testamenti' ('charter of confirmation and scripture of agreement') recording the properties to be owned by the bishop and those which, out of his mercy, the knights were allowed to retain. The church then provided details about the names of the *villae* they owned, except for one or two *cortes* — with *hereditas* and without share, or on their own — that belonged to one or another of the knights involved in the dispute. Only some of the *infanzones* named at this point had been mentioned at the beginning, and we can also note that there was also a royal *corte* without share in one of the *villae*. It was also added that they should populate these lands on behalf of the church as much as they could, although it was not made clear whether this referred to some of the places previously mentioned or to all of them.

After listing all the properties, it was then stated that all the *hereditates*, plots of land, vineyards, meadows, fountains, waters and mills that from former times until the present 'they had bought or acquired by force from the [cathedral's] men'[33] should be returned to the bishop. For this they should receive the price they had paid, and had to swear that they would not purchase them again, even in the case

---

32 'negligenter et uiolentia militum amiserat'.
33 'emerunt aut uim rapuerunt ab homibus'.

of debt. Also, no vassal of the Church was to be allowed into the *hereditates* of these knights, 'except the young, the children and the virgins';[34] and that the latter should return home upon their parents' death. Should they refuse, they would be expelled from the *hereditates* of the knights and the bishop should then receive those of their parents. A strict agreement was then made, subject to both spiritual and material penalties to be imposed on any infringers.

The wealth of information provided in this document is certainly important, and I do not seek to make a more thorough analysis at this point. My comments and reflections will focus on several points, but before that it is necessary to present two other cases, given the relationship between them. They can be regarded as discrete acts of that broader conflict, as they refer to that same space.

The 1115 charter outlines an *intentio* between bishop Diego and a group of *infanzones*, one of whom is named, together with his two sons and daughter: 'Miguel Rodríguez and his sons [...] and other *infanzones*'. The object of the dispute was the monastery of San Tirso, on the banks of river Bernesga, in Valdecastro. The charter narrates how each party alleged that the monastery was their *hereditas*. In this situation, the knights, induced by the devil, violently and maliciously appropriated the *hereditas* and its *villae*, and destroyed the monastery's altars and buildings. The bishop excommunicated them — 'misit eos sub gladio anahematis' ('placed them under the sword of anathema') — for all the *sceleris* ('crimes') they had committed. Their excommunication caused them to repent and ask for mercy, although there is a reference to an actual trial and testimony that took place — 'when they found themselves convicted by a strict and righteous judgement, and prompted by a most truthful charter, they begged the bishop for mercy'.[35] Following the usual ritual, they humbly asked the bishop for forgiveness and he pardoned them, with the proviso that they undertook not to lay claim to any part of that monastery or its *villae* ever again.

In this way, Miguel Rodríguez — no other *infanzones* were mentioned at this point —, fearing for the day of his death and seeking to obtain the grace of the Virgin Mary, agreed with his children that they would return their current or future share in the monastery they had destroyed, for it belonged to the cathedral. In so doing, they confirmed their *rationes* ('shares') and affirmed that no one, whether a relative or not, would have the power to claim that *hereditas*, under penalty of excommunication and a higher sanction than in the previous trial. This brought the litigation to a close, with a seemingly clear victory for the bishop.

The 1117 text recorded another phase in this conflict between the same bishop, Diego, and those who claimed to be co-heirs to San Tirso. It seems to me that the way they were named was indicative of the complexity of the parties in dispute. These were not merely the bishop, on the one hand, and the *infanzones*, on the other. Rather, some of the *infanzones* allied with the bishop and engaged in a dispute with the others. It is said that the *intentio* over the monastery of San Tirso was, first, between, on the one hand, don Diego and Pelayo Froilaz and their brothers, and

---

34 'iuuenibus, pueris et uiginibus excussis'.

35 'quando uiderunt se stricti et recte iuditio conuicti, per uerissima testamenta etiam subiecti, pecierunt misericordiam pontifici'.

on the other the sons of Martinus Díaz; second, between Pedro Vermúdez and his sons and on the other the sons of Miguel Rodríguez; and third, between the sons of Rodrigo Cipríaniz and the sons of Pedro Sarracínez.

The arguments adduced were that the latter claimed to be the owners of the *hereditates* of the monastery, whereas the bishop claimed title to them; in other words, the arguments were similar to those used in 1115. It was ultimately found, without specifying how, that bishop don Diego should have half of the monastery, together with Rodrigo Cipríaniz's and Pedro Sarracínez's sons, and that the other half should be owned by the knights mentioned above. This is why 'they agreed at the assembly' and made 'a pact and such an agreement, namely a covenant'[36] specifying that the co-heirs should return the *hereditates* they retained and that the bishop should build and populate the monastery and remove the abbot from office; and that the co-heirs should be their defenders, which entailed a number of advantages for them. These documents are more illustrative than the previous ones regarding the content of the pacts and the nature of the relationship between the parties, over which they fought and negotiated.

These disputes are presented as episodes of a collective struggle for land by some *infanzones*. These have been usually considered as lesser nobility, seemingly under the superior power of the bishop. However, investigating the identity, social status and composition of the parties involved in the dispute, their internal relations and the relations with the powers they confronted, and the nature of their relationship with the peasants, reveals a social fabric that was more complex and less clear-cut than has been usually assumed. This provides information to understand the dynamic of that interaction, which is ultimately the main point of interest here. It is difficult to challenge the interpretation of these fights as a reflection and symptom of a supposed late-eleventh and early-twelfth century crisis marked by a confrontation between the growing power and patrimony of ecclesiastical lords. However, by analysing the better documented disputes, we may begin to better understand the inner links between different forms of antagonism, and also how the political struggle was perceived and represented.

It is not always possible to identify those involved in these disputes on behalf of the church, and what their interests and strategies were. The importance of this knowledge cannot be ignored and needs to be factored in. The two bishops, Pedro y Diego, were uncle and nephew, respectively. The conventional narration is as follows: these two figures played a key role in a highly conflictive political period in the kingdom, which also affected the see of León. They are presented as victims who fought to defend their patrimony from the various threats it faced. There was no direct line of succession between them, as in 1111 Pedro was deposed and expelled by king Alfonso I of Aragón together with other bishops. The seat of León was then usurped by archbishop Mauricio of Braga until Diego became bishop around 1113. To a certain extent, Bishop Diego is presented as restoring and reorganising the bishopric's patrimony, as proven by the texts already discussed, as well as by

---

36 'convenerunt in concilio [...] pactum simul et placitum tali uidelicet pactione'.

two other essential ones: one dated 1116, whereby he solemnly donated numerous properties and churches that had been recovered to the cathedral; and another one dated 1120, which seems to be the first instance of separation between the chapter's and the bishop's benefits, and established stipends payable to the clergy to avoid the difficulties previously caused by poor management. Consequently, Bishop Diego has come to be known as a keen supporter of ecclesiastical reform in León. It is true that both bishops were regarded as followers of queen Urraca in the warlike conflict that was taking place at the time, and some references were also made to the problems caused by the hegemonic aspirations of the archbishop of Toledo, but this information only illustrated the crisis surrounding the episcopate in those years.[37]

Fernández Catón made some insightful comments to his edition of the cathedral's archival documents[38] which lead to question this positivist view. He raised some issues that, in my opinion, show the need — already noted elsewhere[39] — to investigate the internal and external network of relationships involving, or generated by, the members of a given institution. A document dated 1122 contains a wealth of information in this regard. It is a 'charter of pronouncement' ('karta deffinicionis') made on behalf of bishop Diego, and not to the church, but to his family — 'your brothers and sisters' ('fratribus et sororis uestris') by Urraca, 'by God's grace queen of Spain' (Urraca gracia Dei regina Hyspanie'), a title granted by the royal scribe who drafted it.[40] At the end of the text the charter is described as an 'agreement and pronouncement of peace regarding all the evils that had until now arisen between us'.[41] This shows that the alliances between the queen and bishop Diego were as contingent and changing as those involving bishop Pedro.[42] Between the conveyance of immunity over a royal *hereditas* granted to him by the queen in 1113 'as a reward for the good and faithful service that he had performed and performs every day [on the queen's behalf]'[43] and the royal charter dated 1122 some events must have taken place, but this are not illuminated by the narration in the charter. The queen manifests that Diego and his siblings had been accused by their enemies of having kept most of the alms that her father, king Alfonso, had donated to his uncle, bishop Pedro, to be distributed

---

37 Villacorta Rodríguez, *El cabildo catedral de León*, pp. 36–38; Fletcher, *The Episcopate in the Kingdom of León*, pp. 68–69. The charters cited are CatLeon1351 (1116); CatLeon1367 (1120).

38 For these comments, see mainly the comments of the editor, most notably in CatLeon1333 (1110); CatLeon1343 (1113); and CatLeon1370 (1122); and other charters throughout that volume.

39 Alfonso, 'La comunidad campesina', p. 317.

40 'charter of pronouncement [to] your brothers and sisters [by] Urraca gracia Dei regina Hyspanie'.

41 'concordiam pacis et deffinicionem de omnibus que malis que usque nunc inter nos fuerunt'.

42 Bishop Pedro brought a 'substantial accusation' (described both as 'grandem calupniam' and 'grandem querellam') against Urraca while she was still an infant, because she had seized the villages and *hereditas* of the cathedral of León. To solve the case and dispel the 'great trouble and disorder in his kingdom' ('grandem confusionem et grandem baraliam de regno suo'), Alfonso VI forbade the transfers between known lordships (CatLeon1244, 1089). The date should be noted, since it seems that the period of crisis, thought to have lasted from the end of the eleventh century to the beginning of the twelfth century, may have been longer, as further information intimates. For a detailed and qualified comment of this document, see Estepa Díez, 'Formación y consolidación del feudalismo', pp. 206–07.

43 'pro bono et fideli servicio que michi fecistis et quotidie facitis'.

LAND DISPUTES AND *MALFETRÍAS*   525

among churches, the poor and clerics 'both in Spain and ultraports'.[44] This justified
the decision made by the queen to order bishop Diego's sister, María Euláliz, and her
husband, Aznar Cipríaniz, to be detained, and to impose an obligation on them to
pay six thousand *solidi* not to be ever claimed back in the future. This was followed
by the customary ritual of generosity and mercy whereby the queen forgave them
for their 'mala voluntas' ('bad will'), received them in León, and returned them their
houses. In addition, together with the clerics, who appear in the account for the first
time, she authorised the bishop to deliver 'to the altar of the most glorious queen
a silver table and golden box'[45] instead of the 'defined rent' owed on account of his
arcedianos ('archdeacon') and siblings. As a result, the queen ceded two *villae* and
the arrangement was thus completed.

This text clearly reflects that the tensions that affected the seat in León were more
complex than has been traditionally argued. They related to the misuse of royal alms
which, albeit important, was merely a strategy of legitimation to articulate deeper
conflicts. It must be noted that the queen repeated the accusations made by those she
defined as enemies of the accused, and in so doing she took sides with them in a trial
where she seemed to be both a judge and a party. The fact that the enemies included
the clergy was not surprising, considering that the more profound problem at stake
was the distribution and allocation of the ecclesiastic resources of the cathedral. This
was not merely an internal problem, as indicated by the bishop's relatives involved.
In this way, the generous and broad donation made by bishop Diego to the church
of León in 1116 to remedy its chaotic situation — as it was rhetorically stated — and
the 1120 provisions which granted and established financial autonomy for the canons
cannot be interpreted as mere administrative reorganising measures adopted by a
reforming bishop; instead, they need to be understood in the context of a fight for
the land and the power this entails, and thus beyond the purely institutional scope.
In fact, a closer look shows that the 1116 donation, in which the bishop claims to be so
by 'diuina disposicione' ('divine will') was made to the canons, not to the cathedral,
and that it was not his own property that was donated, but the property belonging to
an archdeaconry. This was clearly a new episode of the same conflict-ridden process.
The relationships involved in it are aptly explained in the preamble of the text that
bishop Diego drafted to keep the clergy satisfied. He based his decision on the attempt
to avoid the 'injustice and controversy' ('iniustitiam et controuersiam') that arose
due to the fact that the stipend they received was subject to the prelate's will and
to 'friendship, service, love for his kin, wrath or hate' ('prout amicicia, seruicium,
amor sui generis, uel ira, et odium'), instead of being allocated 'according to the Holy
Canons' ('sicuti santi canones').[46]

These issues would require detailed analysis, but some background information
will suffice for the moment. In those years, bishop Diego Euláliz was actively engaged

---

44 'tam de Ispania quam ultra portos'.
45 'ab altare gloriosisime regine una tabulam argenteam et unam kalsam auream'. This point is not totally
    clear in this document, but I believe the reading of the following charter (CatLeon1370, 1122), where
    this transaction appears again, allows such interpretation.
46 'iniustitiam et controuersiam [...] prout amicicia, seruicium, amor sui generis, uel ira, et odium [...]
    sicuti santi canones'.

in creating a private/family patrimony in Valdoncina, where he must have come from. He obtained a number of royal immunity privileges from queen Urraca in 1113 and from Alfonso VII in 1129 for that patrimony, which he turned into an important seigneurial estate.[47] The emperor claimed that he had made the concession at the request of some friends of bishop Diego Euláliz (including counts Suero Vermúdez and Rodrigo Martínez and other outstanding noblemen). This revealed the extensive and dense network of social relations that underlay all these actions.[48] A scenario fraught with tension and conflict was therefore established, a latent conflictual structure, to use Geary's expression.[49] This affected the internal fabric of the relationships of the church as an institution, as it tended to develop rules to govern their connections as a way of preventing, channelling and solving these disputes.[50] However, it must be clear that this structure of relationships cannot be understood unless other external networks are taken into account. The cathedral as an institution was not only a resource used by its members, but also by other social groups, including the royalty, who in varying degrees and in different ways had expectations and wanted to benefit from both its tangible and intangible assets.

In order to understand these networks and relationships, and the social status of the actors involved in the various disputes, it is interesting to note that some of the *infanzones* that were referred to in 1093 — or their children — reappeared in 1115 or 1117. Rodrigo Cipríaniz was involved in a dispute in 1093, together with three men that could be assumed to be his brothers — Álvaro, Domingo and Aznar — as they had the same surname and their names were copied immediately after his in the document.[51] His children took part in another dispute in 1117 against the same bishop together with the offspring of Pedro Sarracínez, and the latter were granted half of the monastery of San Tirso. In 1093 two men called Martín Cítiz were a party to another dispute. One of them stated he was from Villa Albura and the other from Villaseca. The children of one of them were also involved in the dispute over San Tirso in 1117 together with Pelayo Froilaz and his brothers.[52] Miguel Rodríguez's sons were

---

47 The *realengo* ('royal domain') he received from queen Urraca in 1113 in Santovenia de Valdoncina was delimited by the boundaries of other villages into which he expanded his land further. It was also 'exempted from all royal jurisdiction', and anybody who 'dared to enter [that village] without your command' was to be sanctioned ('eximido de omnem regalem calumniam [...] sine uestra iussione intrauerit audaciter'). In 1129 Alfonso VII granted immunity to Villa de Antimio, which the bishop had included in his private patrimony through purchases and exchange charters in those years (CatLeon1343, 1113; CatLeon1353, 1116; CatLeon1357, 1117; CatLeon1379, 1123; CatLeon1387, 1129; CatLeon1389, 1129).
48 Alfonso VII says: 'this I do for your love, and thanks to the mediation of your friends, the counts' ('hoc autem facio uestro amore, et interuentu uestrorum amicorum, comitum') (CatLeon1389, 1129).
49 Geary, 'Vivre en conflit', p. 1116.
50 CatLeon1367 (1120).
51 Alvar and Rodrigo Cipríaniz also appeared jointly subscribing a charter from the Cathedral of León (CatLeon1300, 1097).
52 I believe that one of these, called Martín Citiz, confirmed a sale made by Fáfila Petríz in 1060 (Carrizo2, 1060), together with Trasmiro Fortes, another litigant. Perhaps he was the same person who made a substantial donation to Sahagún in 1106. His identity can be inferred from the group of people with who he ratified the donations — Pedro and Ordoño Sarracínez, Pelayo Vellitiz, and the Nebzaniz, among others —, rather than from the locations involved.

LAND DISPUTES AND *MALFETRÍAS*   527

reported to have participated in a dispute with their father in 1115, and then in 1117 they re-appeared without their father but together with Pedro Vermúdez and his brothers.

What is more interesting, however, is to identify the importance of this *infanzon* status that they were acknowledged to have. The identity of two of them can be traced from documents that date back to 1093. Cipriano Vellitez was then a litigant together with his nephews and other relatives. He was important due to the fact that he was one of the brothers of Pelayo Vellitiz, an important figure in Alfonso VI's court. Cipriano Vellitez himself was also identified in 1067 as one of the witnesses supporting the previous bishop, don Pelayo, against Havive Donniniz's claims over the vill of Cimanes.[53] The other litigant was Aznar Cipríaniz, who was one of the main actors involved in the events that took place in 1093. His marriage to María Euláliz, niece of bishop Pedro (the other litigant), meant that the dispute took a different turn (even though the marriage took place after the facts described). This couple was reported to have been the unlawful owners of some of the cathedral's assets with the complicity of bishop Diego, who was in office when the other conflicts had taken place. This can account for the fact that in 1117 Aznar's nephews were on the side of the bishop (brother-in-law of their uncle) when half of the monastery in dispute was distributed. This information therefore outlines some points of connection between different conflicts.

From 1117 some additional details are known about the identity of three other *hereditarii*, as they were known at the time. One of them is Pedro Sarracínez, who was awarded some monastic assets after the dispute against Sahagún for Villacorta. His offspring intervened in 1117 together with Rodrigo Cipríaniz's offspring. The second is Pelayo Froilaz, who appeared among the co-heirs that obtained the other half of San Tirso, together with his brothers. Based on the information contained in the cartulary of Carrizo, he can be identified as one of the most powerful noblemen in this area of river Bernesga, in the territory of Luna, where he built a considerable patrimony. I believe he was one of the brothers of the magnate Ramiro Froilaz, with whom he appeared in 1105, and therefore a son of count Froila Díez. They can be identified as siblings based on the fact that their 'archive' was passed on to the monastery of Carrizo, founded by his niece Estefanía Ramírez in the second half of the twelfth century. So was the case with the 'archive' of their relatives, the Flaínez, held in their monastery of Otero de Dueñas. This is not the place to further investigate this noble, who was part of the entourage of the mighty Asturian count Suero Vermúdez. However, it is interesting to note that bishop Diego of León was only mentioned as an authority in two of the documents in which he appeared between 1112 and 1123. This is probably a reflection of the hostilities and problems that occurred in those years.[54]

---

53 See pp. 513–14. I think their family ties can be confirmed, among other evidence, by a donation to Sahagún of the goods he had acquired from Pelayo Vellitiz in Valderaduey — except for Cipriano Vellítiz's plot. Reglero regarded Pelayo and Isidoro Vellitiz as local knights in the area of Torozos (Reglero de la Fuente, *Los señoríos de los Montes Torozos*, pp. 99–100). However, I believe that in this case, as in many others discussed here, one should err on the side of caution about 'how local this local nobility was', as raised in our collective study Pastor and others, 'Baja nobleza'.

54 His patrimony in the area considerably and steadily increased at the beginning of the twelfth century.

The third nobleman recorded in 1117 is Pedro Vermúdez, who participated in the dispute together with his brothers and Miguel Rodríguez's sons, and may have been among those unnamed in 1115. His rare appearances among the court members led Estepa to classify him as a local nobleman.[55] I think he was the same who was expelled from the kingdom on account of his *malfetrias* ('wrong doings') by Alfonso VI, who seized his assets and gave them to the Cathedral of León in 1097. This would make him a son of Vermudo Eriz, and grandson of Ero Salitez, a nobleman whose status would have been similar to that of the previous Froilaz. The term 'local' applied to them is certainly too restrictive.[56]

It would be interesting to understand the types of groups established in this text, and the criteria that divided them into those who sided with the bishop and those who acted separately. These groups may have resulted from the very process by which they became *hereditarii*, and this may be a sign of the various bonds they had created. What seems clear is that the *infanzones* who opposed the bishops of León were people of middle noble status who had family or client links to the lay magnates and who were close to the kings, and had independent economic resources. They may have instigated these actions that gathered the lower-status *infanzones* and the most notable members of the peasant communities. The scarce evidence available points to similarities between their relationships and those established between the ecclesiastical institutions and their lay vassals.

The information available to further investigate the relationship between the lay and the ecclesiastical aristocracy is extremely limited, but it is sufficient to raise some questions that I believe should form an active part of the reflection proposed here.[57] In these disputes there were groups of *infanzones* who harassed and violated the patrimony of the Cathedral of León, that is, the usual ingredients that would seemingly provide evidence for Church vs Nobility conflicts. Some of the evidence so far considered, however, questions this simplistic interpretation. The information about family ties that linked one of the *infanzones* and the prelates, even if exceptional — though perhaps not as difficult to find as it may seem — the mixed private and institutional interests, and the nephew that succeeded his uncle in office, should prevent us from reifying institutions, regardless of their type. It should

---

See Carrizo4, Carrizo5, Carrizo6, Carrizo7, Carrizo8, Carrizo11, Carrizo12, Carrizo13, Carrizo14, Carrizo15, Carrizo16, Carrizo17, Carrizo18, Carrizo19, Carrizo20, Carrizo21, Carrizo22, Carrizo23, Carrizo24, Carrizo25, Carrizo26, Carrizo27. S. Barton discussed and mapped out the patrimony of this nobleman in Barton, *The Aristocracy*, pp. 73–79. Even though he did not consider him quite a magnate, he did place him in a very influential circle, with clientship ties to count Suero Vermúdez, holder of *tenencias* in this area at the time. Barton, however, does not consider the possibility that he was a descendant of count Froila Diez.

55 Estepa Díez, *Estructura social de la ciudad de León*, p. 286.
56 On Pedro Vermúdez, see CatLeon1293 (1097); CatLeon1346 (1114); CatLeon1357 (1117); CatLeon1389 (1129); CatLeon1405 (1133); CatLeon1406 (1133); CatLeon1407 (1133). On the Eriz kinship group, see Reglero de la Fuente, *Los señoríos de los Montes Torozos*, pp. 87–91. See also n. 53 regarding the problems entailed in delimiting the scope of local status.
57 I explicitly use the term 'active' to question a common practice whereby even if very complex aspects of such relationships are identified, its actual implications within such relationships are neglected when drawing conclusions, thus leading towards interpretations that are often mystifying.

encourage research along the lines proposed here, looking at both the internal and external network of personal relationships that they generated or in which they were immersed. The difficulty in studying the social origin of the clergy should be extended to the connections they maintained with their lay family and social networks. In this case, some tentative suggestions could be made about the interwoven bonds and interests that undoubtedly existed between clerics and *infanzones*. Moreover, clientship ties can be observed between these noblemen and the Cathedral in a relationship that Reuter aptly described as symbiotic, based on terms that had to be periodically re-negotiated.[58] The 1117 pact whereby these noblemen remained as defenders of the monastic patrimony, which they committed to enlarge and whose profits they would share in, was very explicit, and its terms repeat themselves in the documents from these centuries. It was specified that 'this *hereditarii* will always defend their possessions [...] and use their power to defend them and increase the *hereditates* of that monastery'.[59] This defence from other powerful parties and also in the relationships with the producing peasants was ultimately what allowed the church to exercise its power. Additionally, some of the functions performed by religious institutions for their lay patrons or proprietors were explicitly established. If any of these *infanzones* 'passed through the monastery and wished to be lodged there, he should receive this as an *hereditarius*, and if he became needy and wished to live in the monastery and serve God, he should be allowed to and honourably enjoy it by the force of the abbot who was at the monastery at that time'.[60]

In the first case analysed, the fact that the conflict was related to *hereditates, villae* and men does not mean that lay powerful parties only prevailed by using force and violence, as their church opponents usually alleged, and that they ruled out avenues to legitimise their true or attempted domination, which could be either proprietary or purely seigniorial. There were various kinds of relationships and dependencies regarding the use of land, the control of which — proprietary or seigniorial — was ultimately in dispute.

A number of terms used in the ecclesiastic discourse in the 1093 document are particularly striking, including *introierunt* ('they invaded'), 'uiolentia militum amiserunt' ('they deployed the violence of knights') or 'uim rapuerunt' ('they seized it by force'). These were employed by the monks to construct the image of their enemies, just as some historians have derived from them a whole model of lordly domination.

However, other more peaceful types of relationships between lay noblemen and peasants could be identified in this text. These were less violent avenues to gain possession of the land, and they were rendered unlawful or prohibited by those who

---

58 On conflicts around the episcopal networks, see Reuter, '*Filii matris nostrae*'; as well as Pascua Echegaray, 'Redes personales', one of the best analyses of this kind. On the interrelationship between lay and church nobility, some useful ideas can be found in Bouchard, *Sword, Miter, and Cloister*.

59 'ipsi hereditarii semper auxilientur suis rebus [...] et defendant pro posse suo, et amplificent illud monasterium suis hereditatibus'.

60 'pertransiens in monasterio hospitari uoluerit, recipiatur sicut hereditarius o si ad inopiam deuenerit, atque in monasaterio morari et ibidem Deo deseruire uoluerit, recipiatur et honeste tenatur pro posse abbatis qui eo tempore monasterio prefuerit'. On the functions of monasteries for their lay patrons or proprietaries, see the studies quoted in n. 4.

claimed to be the lawful owners. It is said that the *infanzones* and their ancestors had purchased many of the assets owned by the people who lived in the villages by the side of River Bernesga, the price of which was paid back to them so that they would abandon those properties and promise not to acquire them again. But these knights had received the bishop's men in their estates, and were later required not to do it ever again except with young people, children and maids who were exempted, and they were obliged to return to their homes upon their parents' death if they did not want to lose their *hereditates*. Years later, both the bishop and the nuns from the monastery of San Pedro de Dueñas seemed to be aware of the danger that alliances between knights and peasants in towns over which they shared some control posed for the effective and legitimate exercise of their power. Hence their attempt to dominate them by controlling land transactions.[61]

Let us now turn to the proceedings of judicial resolution in these disputes as recorded in the charters we are analysing. The arguments adduced by the parties in all three cases referred to opposed proprietary rights and the legitimised ways of acquiring them. In 1093 the bishop accused the *infanzones* and their ancestors of appropriating assets that kings had donated to the church; and of being unlawful owners of those assets. For their part, the *infanzones* defended themselves by alleging that their parents and grandparents had gained those properties. The use of ambiguous terms such as *tenere, possessio* or *aforastitis* makes it difficult to ascertain whether the object of dispute was the holding or the ownership of those assets. To a certain extent, given the allegations made by the bishop and the final resolution, it seems that the *infanzones*, who can be assumed to have owned properties and enjoyed holdings in those towns from ancient times, seemed to have increased the former by purchasing them from some vassals of the cathedral and to have denied that they enjoyed the latter on lease, as the bishop have argued. It may also be the case, as is known from other disputes, that both parties claimed to have lordly power over the people in those towns. In any event, the fragmented nature of land ownership and of the power it entailed, which dated back to former times and did not solve the dispute, was the central component of these antagonisms. In 1115 and 1117 the claims made to the monastery of San Tirso — over its *hereditates* and *villae* and, by implication, over the people who inhabited them — were articulated using similar arguments. The solutions ultimately enshrined the fragmentation of the rights involved.

The first case was brought before King Alfonso VI as demanded by the *infanzones*, who stated that they would only abide by the monarch's resolution in the trial. An inquest was ordered to find the truth about the matter. The form and means used to perform it are unknown, and so is its content; however, it can be inferred from the king's resolution that everything that the church — through negligence or on account of the knights' violence — had lost should be returned to the bishop through the porter of his palace. However, despite the use of the inquest — supposedly the most rational method —, the losing side, now qualified as *milites regis*, refused to

---

61 On these problems and for a commentary of this document, see Alfonso, 'Campesinado y derecho'. [Editors' note: For an English translation, see chapter 9 of this volume].

accept the royal judgment and managed to reopen and continue the procedure. The strategies used by the *infanzones* seemed to have been thwarted by the king's proposal that three clerics from the cathedral should ratify the commitments sworn after the enquiry. This is why they decided to change their tactics and request the bishop's compassion by acknowledging their responsibility. No punishment or penalty was imposed. The outcome was the long *convenientia* ('agreement)' mentioned above. One could wonder to what extent it was effective, since the *infanzones* were in charge of its continued enforcement. All the assurances in the process suggest that there must have been difficulties in this respect.

The procedures used to solve the disputes differed in the two cases that followed. In the 1115 case, explicit reference was made to a previous instance in which the disagreement regarding the ownership of the monastery, which both parties claimed as their own, had resulted in the violent appropriation by the knights and their excommunication by the bishop. It is unknown whether the entire process took place at the meeting where the judicial record was heard and confirmed, and what the nature of the assembly was. In any event, the bishop must have made the excommunication public and the violent acts they had committed must have been the talk of the town. Again, rituals involved submission, return of properties and pardon and compassion. At this point the dispute appeared to be more local, and each party used their weapons: the knights resorted to violence, whereas the bishop used excommunication. Their renouncement stated that they were *hereditarii*, as they had a share in the disputed monastery. At this stage, the *infanzones* seemed to have been totally defeated, and the spiritual *gladio anathematis* proved to be as effective as their actual ones.

Nevertheless, when the dispute was reopened in 1117, the apparently unambiguous victory was somewhat qualified by the actual facts. In practice, the *infanzones* seemingly continued to hold their monastic estates, and agreed to return them in exchange for being recognised as *hereditarii*. In this way, although the bishop's hegemony was established, they also obtained some privileges — as the bishop did — over other *infanzones*, as opposed to, or together with, some peasants. Both parties were bound to provide assurances that they would comply with the pact in this case, which differed from the usual practice in the period — payment of 500 *solidi* —, and no spiritual penalties were imposed. This was the most efficient method to ensure the observance of the long-sought agreement.

The king did not reappear and the political community managed their own affairs in their assemblies under pressure from both sides. There was no more peace or violence than before. Local power relations seemed to prevail, even in opposition to the king, as seen in 1093. The dynamics were changing and provisional, and the different parties were aware of this. There were no complete victories or losses, but disputes, negotiations and agreements to distribute and manage the assets that were part of shared interests. This manipulation of available resources was what politics was made of, and it was the management and reproduction of such resources that was at stake.

The relationships resumed as a result of these agreements were inherited and negotiated by these parties' descendants. This was the case of Pedro Sarracínez, who was one of Sahagún's appointed holders, as previously explained. Following various property claims, his children were in a similar situation with respect to the Cathedral of León. Other members of their family were also involved. At the beginning of the twelfth century, his brother, Ordoño Sarracínez, and the latter's wife, Fronilde Ovéquiz, established a closer link with major monasteries in León, he with Sahagún, she with San Pedro de Dueñas. The negotiations they engaged in regarding the distribution of assets, both between themselves and also with her children from previous marriages, expose issues that, in my view, were closely related to those discussed here, even though they are rarely evident in the record. These conflicts and disputes can be labelled as 'intra-family' — or rather 'intra-kin', in order to circumvent the complexity of 'family' as a concept.

The conflicts that Fronilde was involved in will be briefly discussed here.[62] It is known that she initiated a claim early on against her own father, as she felt that she had been disadvantaged when a third of the family assets were inherited by her mother. She submitted her claim to her relatives and many other *boni homines*, who gathered to settle the case at the family monastery of San Salvador de Villacete, where they ruled against her. Around 1103 she agreed with her husband that she would become a nun and deliver the assets that she had bargained for with her husband and children. This was explicitly intended to prevent any further claims. Many years later she was subject to trial and excommunicated by an ecclesiastic court because she had breached her religious vows and benefited from the patronage of a lay nobleman to whom she had submitted all her *hereditates*.[63]

I have outlined these problems because they show an additional area of tension usually ignored by the historiography, as a natural solidarity is assumed to have existed among family units or kinship groups. More attention needs to be paid to the tensions clearly involved in the allocation and distribution of available resources and to their timeline within family groups. The fact that some of these resources were donated to religious institutions was part of the same process of material and social reproduction by the groups involved. Therefore, land claims and disputes often legitimised by laymen as claims to *hereditates* may be regarded not only as mere attempts to reconstruct previously fragmented patrimonies caused by the grants of prior family members, but also as a means to explicitly assert their rights to a given estate. They may have been perceived as a strategy to have a share in the benefits involved in this relationship, or as a way to question and renegotiate it, as it is here argued.[64]

This dynamic involving donations, harassment and violent occupation, and relinquishing and defending monastic property held as *hereditas* at a given point in the past also underlies some of the known actions of Fronilde Ovéquiz's descendants.

---

62 My discussion builds upon P. Martínez Sopena's analysis of the local knight Pedro Peláez de Arnales, one of her descendants, in Martínez Sopena, *Tierra de Campos occidental*, pp. 405–10.

63 See SFPSahagun424 (1059); SFPSahagun1091 (1103); SFPSahagun1092 (1103); SFPSahagun1093 (1103); SFPSahagun1094 (1103); SFPSahagun1192 (1115).

64 White, *Custom, Kinship, and Gifts to Saints*, pp. 167–90.

Her grandchildren, Bermudo and Pelayo Pérez, made a donation to the Bishop of Astorga in 1135 as reparation for the violent acts committed in the monasteries of his diocese, to which they were attached.[65] In 1129 Fernando Díaz, one of her great-nephews, engaged in disputes with the monastery of Vega but ultimately had to relinquish 'all rights and all the lawsuits that [he was] bringing'[66] in Valdespino, which he received as a holding for life. In that town the grandfather, Pedro Ovéquiz, had donated his share to the monastery of Sahagún in 1048, and he had also given half of his *hereditas* to the monastery of Vega in 1113.[67]

The detailed information that has been preserved about her great-grandson, Pedro Peláez de Arnales, allowed Martínez Sopena to track down the family history and the estate of this local knight. I have taken this information from his work and used it for contextual purposes. He was the holder of Villafrechós, a *villa* in which some of the assets that her great-grandmother had donated to Sahagún were located. His grandfather had also owned some properties there, which he had donated to the cathedral of Astorga, and he continued to be a major landowner both in the locality and in other nearby areas of Tierra de Campos. He was a member of Fernando II's entourage and was closely linked to Sahagún, especially through San Salvador de Villacete, once a family monastery now under his patronage. In practice, this monastery remained as an institutional resource for his lineage, as it became the family vault and an institution that provided support and financial resources. He is entitled *señor* ('lord') in a charter dated to 1197, in which he, together with the prior and three monks, granted his grandson, Pelayo Núñez, the monastery's *hereditas* in Coreses. This was done under customary terms for life leaseholds, which involved the return of any additional gains upon his death, and the obligation of welcoming the prior and the monks of Sahagún when they visited the village.[68]

Although Pedro Peláez did not seem to engage in any court disputes, the documents preserved portray him as an active negotiator regarding his patrimony within the family and in connection with the monasteries that he had links with. The terminology used in these charters also reveals that there must have been certain, more or less open tensions. The 'carta unitatis [et] bona amore' ('charter of unity [and] good love') that he issued in 1185 together with his wife, as well as the various *convenientiae* between 1189 and 1194 with his daughters and sons-in-law, his son — who was the abbot of San Pedro de Montes — and his grandson include detailed and changing disposals of property. They also show the difficulties involved in the distribution of the estate and the negotiations required to reach an agreement. The fact that all of those charters were made before local councils of different villages indicates not only the scope of his patrimony, but also the importance accorded to publicising these

---

65 Quoted in Martínez Sopena, *Tierra de Campos occidental*, p. 407.
66 'omne ius et omnem querelam quam petebam'.
67 MVega19 (1075); MVega28 (1113); MVega34 (1129); MVega36 (1130).
68 See SFPSahagun1388 (1176); SFPSahagun1416 (1185); SFPSahagun1420 (1185); SFPSahagun1428 (1186); SFPSahagun1466 (1192); SFPSahagun1465 (1192); SFPSahagun1484 (1194); SFPSahagun1485 (1194); SFPSahagun1511 (1197); SFPSahagun1512 (1197); SFPSahagun1513 (1197); SFPSahagun1516 (1197).

acts. Likewise, the *conventiones* signed with Sahagún in 1176, which ratified his broad control over the monastery of Villacete despite, or precisely because he had assigned the portion that he still retained — including mutually beneficial provisions that bound him to the monastery —, could have ended one of the conflicts discussed here. There must have been others, as revealed by a donation that he made in 1192. In addition to delivering all of his *hereditas* and share in Cañizo, he confirmed he owned a portion in Villacete and returned two churches that belonged to this monastery. He confessed that he had 'illegally and violently appropriated and taken ownership'[69] of one of them. Until then he had received the tithes, first-fruits and oblations due by the vassals of the prior and monks in the monastery through a cleric he had appointed. Both the donation and the confession may be the outcome of a court process, but they may also have resulted from a direct or mediated agreement that put an end to previous disputes. It is remarkable that in all of these actions there was a wide range of possible transactions involving the same assets. This has led many authors to question its authenticity.

Some additional agreements from the late twelfth and early thirteenth centuries have been documented between people who were close to those listed above and the monastery of Villacete. They provide more thorough information about the processes that led to the settlements. In 1199 Fernando Petri made a *convenientia* with the prior of that monastery before the *boni homines* of Villardiga and Cañizo over an *hereditas* in Villardiga.[70] He confessed that '[he] wanted to appropriate by force and with his relatives what was owned by the house of San Salvador'.[71] The arguments were repeated, albeit justifying the force used by providing rational grounds, claiming 'that it was [his] share' and that the *hereditas* 'had been owned by his parents', and that it had been obtained from the monastery 'under the following agreement: so that he remained a friend and a member of the family of the house of San Salvador forever', and that he would be buried there, as effectively occurred; that he would be given the *hereditas* on lease for life; that he would be entitled to transfer it to his son; and that if the monastery breached the terms agreed, it would be required to transfer another *hereditas* to him.[72] All of this '[was neglected by] the prior, and by no means what he said was true, rather, it was false'.[73] But then Fernando Petri, 'once falsehood had been removed and peace with the other party restored', promised to withdraw his claim and promised not to make any further demands for the sake of his soul 'and for the cleansing of his sinful deeds' and to ensure that the monks would pray for him in life and death.[74] People from the two villages involved were present in this act, perhaps the *boni homines* who might have mediated in reaching this settlement, even

---

69 'per uiolenciam inuasimus e iniuste possedimus'.

70 SFPSahagun1530 (1191).

71 'ego per forciam et per meos parentes uolebam extorquere ut nequa quam eam haberet domus de San Salvador'.

72 'talis erat mea ratio […] fuerat patris meis […] tali convenientia: ut esset amicus et familiaris domus Sancti Saluadoris semper […]'.

73 'et dominus prior dextruebat et nequaquam dicebant esse uerum, set falsum'.

74 'remota perfidia et pace ex utraque parte reformata' […] et pro abluendis peccatorum meorum facinoribus'.

LAND DISPUTES AND *MALFETRÍAS*   535

if their intervention was not acknowledged. More explicit mediation took place in the dispute over a *villa* in Mansilla between the monastery of Villacete and Rodrigo Martínez, a knight from Tiedra.[75] The prior claimed ownership of the vineyard and accused the knight and his father because they 'held it through force' ('tenebat per forciam'). The knight refuted this accusation and said that this was not the case, 'but rather that it was his own *hereditas* as a successor of his father's right'.[76] No evidence was seemingly provided to support their respective claims; however, 'a settlement was reached [by the parties], with the mediation of the *boni homines*.[77] The agreement they reached was as follows: Rodrigo, upon consultation with his brothers, offered a small plot of land located on the monastery's land, which he had on lease for life, and undertook not to make any further claims to the disputed vineyard. The documents explain that the agreement was reached thanks to the mediation of the *boni homines* and that it was witnessed and heard by the whole council of Tiedra and many other people from Villacete. One year later, a similar agreement brought closure to another dispute between this knight and San Isidoro de León. After the knight acknowledged that he had unlawfully held the *hereditates* donated by his parents in Pozuelo, he received others on lease near Tordehumos, and decided to be buried in the collegiate church with which he had settled.

These are good examples of the types of pacts that took place when concessions were formalised, of the expectations they arose, and of the measures for enforcement in the event of a breach. They were private covenants but were concluded publicly, in the presence of their equals, the *boni homines* from these villages, probably in consultation with their council, even though they were not formally institutionalised; the breach of the terms implicitly or explicitly agreed by the grantors resulted in violent methods and strategies to re-establish the rights and relationships involved, and ways of applying pressure to have them restored. Similar *malfetrias* and *facinoras* ('wickedness') presented as sins can also be identified in other acts. Friendship and familiarity continued to be part of these *convenientiae*, which were portrayed, and presumably perceived, as the best resource to re-establish peaceful relationships.

Other documents from this period also show the disputes in which other knights were regularly involved in their relationships with Sahagún. A *carta donationis* ('charter of donation') from 1211 has been preserved whereby half of the church of Valparaíso, together with its *hereditates* was donated. It was issued by Gutierre Díaz de Almadrán, a local descendant of the Alfonso kinship group,[78] together with his wife, nephew and other *coheredibus* ('co-heirs') to appease and pacify the old disputes and controversies once held by his father and brothers on the matter. The text starts by publicising an updated form of *agnitio*,[79] that is, an acknowledgement that he and his father, together with their co-heirs, had 'per iniuriam' ('through wrongdoing')

---

75 SFPSahagun1535 (1201). He is regarded as a local knight from Pozuelo de la Orden in Martínez Sopena, *Tierra de Campos occidental*, p. 412.

76 'set propria esse hereditas et ex paterno iure sibi successisse'.

77 'reconciliacione facta per bonos homines'.

78 SFPSahagun1583 (1211). On his family, see Martínez Sopena, *Tierra de Campos occidental*, pp. 379–80.

79 'I have heard and know that it is true' ('audivi et scio in veritate').

owned and held that church and *hereditas* until then. It is unknown whether this acknowledgement results from a court hearing or not.[80] In this case, the fact that he relinquished the assets does not mean that he had obtained them on lease, but other 'pactum et conuenientia' ('pact and covenant') show that this renewed their bond. The knight became the defender of the monastic property that would be granted to him some years later on lease.[81] Sahagún received assets in Villavicencio from this knight in exchange, which suggests that this could have been an attempt to oust him from the village. However, he was entrusted with the holdings that his father had previously enjoyed, together with other goods. Also, a similar agreement was reached with the monastery of Gradefes, to which he sold a *quiñón* ('share') in a land in Villavicencio. Furthermore, he later appears among the *hereditarii*, share-holders and lords of this *villa*. This, I believe, are all signs of the political power of knights like him. This political power was largely maintained and reproduced through a complex use of the land, whereby alliances enabled them to be part of various power networks, in addition to receiving rents from the institutions of which they were concessionaires.

A number of agreements from the second half of the thirteenth century reflecting similar types of negotiations have also been preserved in the archive of Sahagún. Under these pacts, the monastery received numerous assets from noblemen in exchange for the transfer of other assets to them for life.[82] No reference is made in those documents to any tension between the parties, but the fact that they were recorded as *pacta* ('pacts') and *advenientiae* ('agreements') could indicate that behind these dealings discrepancies similar to those described above may have existed. These were solved through private agreements which bore both the monastery's seal and that of a public institution, such as the local council, for the further assurance of the parties involved.[83]

In the 1270s, Sahagún again brought its claims before the king — first before Alfonso X, and then before his son, the *infante* Sancho. These were disputes on the grounds of forced *entramientos* and holdings in the same vill, Melgar de Abajo. How did this process take place? What differences can be identified with the cases previously documented? What assessment can be made about these conflicts now?

A detailed examination would allow us to discern whether there were any changes in judicial proceedings. The first thing to note is that there were changes in how court

---

80 The fact that this charter was made in Villapando before the authorities and mayors of the town may indicate that this donation was the result of a court hearing, but the means for resolution may have been fully extrajudicial.

81 SFPSahagun1603 (1216).

82 There was a clear relationship between these and the families discussed here. However, this would require further analysis, which will not be conducted here for reasons of space.

83 SFPSahagun1718 (1253); SFPSahagun1719 (1253); SFPSahagun1720 (1253). These agreements had similar provisions to those established after disputes. For example, the defensive and protective role demanded from the grantor is described in detail in one of these agreements. In particular, Sahagún wanted to recover one of the *hereditas* from its then current holder, and in exchange it offered '[our] help and [provided] reassurance that [he would] be able to acquire it' ('nostro adiutorio et dando uobis uocem nostram adquirire poteritis'). This undoubtedly caused conflicts among the monastery's clients.

LAND DISPUTES AND *MALFETRÍAS* 537

procedures were recorded. Several documents have been preserved, and others are likely to have existed.[84] The first two contain the mandate from the *infante* Juan, acting by order of his father Alfonso X, that Pedro Pérez of Sahagún, who is said to be a man serving the king, should go 'to Melgar de Yuso to find out the truth about that *hereditas* that Ferrán Pérez had seized from them.'[85] The other contains a letter to the council, the mayors and the *merinos* of the place where those *hereditates* were located, so that they told the truth in the inquest and enforced it. A third document tells that the king's man gave instructions to the effect that the *hereditates* seized should be delivered after the inquest, including a procedure to verify the assets involved.

The testimony sworn to by the listed '*boni homines* appointed by the council of Melgar'[86] showed the long-standing relationship regarding property issues between the ascendants of the parties, both monastic and lay, in that town. According to those testimonies, Sahagún had owned 'two old plots for such a long time that they did not even remember for how long they had owned them.'[87] These plots were located 'in the half of the *villa* that [Fernando Pérez Ponce and his brothers] had inherited', together with many other *hereditates* including vineyards, land and allotments that 'they had also owned for a long time.'[88] Other assets were also mentioned, as well as the circumstances and transactions related to them. The last of these, a donation made by doña Aldonza, mother of the accused knight, put half of the disputed *villae* in the hands of the monastery, together with the *sexmo* and all their *hereditates* and mills. The witnesses in the inquest stated that 'they had seen the monastery inherit these and its men holding it for six or more years', although we now know that the donation had taken place in 1254 and involved a close, permanent bond between the monastery and its benefactor.[89] The informants ultimately declared that they had always been aware that the monastery had owned these *hereditates* 'until four years ago, when don Ferrán Pérez Ponce sent [his officers] to seize them by force'.[90] Those officers were among the *boni homines* that provided the information. 'Sabida la uerdat' ('when the truth was known'), the king's delegate used these testimonies as a basis to publicly deliver these *hereditates* to Sahagún.

According to traditional interpretations, this case could be used as an example of the more rational, objective and efficient justice that prevailed as royal power become stronger and Roman legal procedures were adopted. It could also be used to illustrate the 'random violence' exerted by the 'rebellious nobility', which to a certain extent were opposed to these developments. However, the inquest was a court method used more frequently than is commonly acknowledged. The arguments used by the lay nobleman, if any, are unknown to us, but the history of long-standing family

---

84 SFPSahagun1813 (1277); SFPSahagun1814 (1278); SFPSahagun1815 (1278).

85 'a Melgar de Yuso e que sepades la uerdad de aquel heredamiento que les tenia Ferran Perez forzado'.

86 'hombres buenos que da el concejo de Melgar'.

87 'dos suelos antigos de tan grant tiempo que se non acordauan quanto tiempo los auien'.

88 'la media uilla que heredauan [...] auian de tienpo antigo'.

89 'esto que lo uieron heredar al monesterio e tenerlo a los sus omnes bien seys annos o mas' (SFPSahagun1815, 1278).

90 'saluo de quatro annos aca, que gelos mando entrar don Fferran Perez Ponz por fuerça'.

relationships with Sahagún suggests that the situation would have been legitimised on fairly similar terms as those discussed above. The enforcement of the resolution was no more lasting and stable than in previous periods. One year later, the mayors of Mayorga had to go back to Melgar in order to investigate and return what had been given to the monks the previous year (on this occasion, it was by order of the *infante* Sancho). The reason was that another knight — whose relationship with the *infante* has not been ascertained — 'had seized it by force', this time 'without justification or right'.[91] This may implicitly indicate that previously there had been rightful reasons to do so, despite the use of force.[92]

The context for these events has been described as more confrontational, as a sign of the renewed and harsher violence of the *malfetrías* perpetrated by noblemen against the large ecclesiastical owners.[93] However, what I am here questioning is the novelty of these wrongdoings and seizures. I argue that they should be considered to be inherent to the competitive practices involving wealth and power, in other words, economic and political benefits, among the dominant groups in the society of the period.

The complexity of the social fabric and the status of property ownership, and the overlapping of rights revealed in the inquest in the *villa* of Melgar discussed above, in which several lords distributed land and people among themselves and competed for power, was the result of complex political developments. Count Ponce de Cabrera, great-grandfather of the previous monastic adversary, had managed to turn the holding of Melgar, from which he had dismissed the Alfonso kinship group, into a seigneurial *villa* that several branches of the family shared in the first third of the thirteenth century.[94] This expansive process had resulted in a conflict between the count and the monastery of Sahagún over a nearby *hereditas*. The count and his family argued that it should be theirs, whereas the abbot and the monks, on the contrary, claimed that it should be *sub iure* ('under the control') of their church 'as reflected in the charters and by the right that they had enjoyed over it since time immemorial'.[95] This language is highly legalistic and rarely found in the documents from the period. There was a direct settlement, maybe due to the high status of this nobleman, whereby the count, having been persuaded by the 'reasons and truths of their charters and authorities' alleged by the monks, delivered the *hereditas*.[96] He did so with not with the intention of being consistent with secular or divine law, but to reach a 'saluber consensus' ('beneficial consensus') between the two. The charter

---

91 'gello entro por ffuerça [...] sin rrazon e sin derecho'.

92 SFPSahagun1820 (1279); SFPSahagun1822 (1280).

93 The classic work on this issues is Moreta, *Malhechores-feudales*. However, most studies quoted in n. 4, share a similar interpretation of these *malfetrias* — particularly of those that took place during a critical period at the end of the thirteenth century — as attacks on ecclesiastical property, of which the monasteries would have defended themselves by resorting to royal courts for support, and also first through land leases and later through assignment.

94 For a good explanation of these developments, see Martínez Sopena, *Tierra de Campos occidental*, pp. 390–92.

95 'secundum scripta testatorum et secundum ius ab antiquis temporibus habitum'.

96 'racionibus et ueris eorum scriptis et auctoritatabus intellectis'.

LAND DISPUTES AND *MALFETRÍAS*   539

also contained threats directed at those who went against this 'just and sound and most truthful and reasonable' settlement reached through 'the most certain and soundest knowledge'.[97] It is worth mentioning that this controversy had taken place a few months before Sahagún received a substantial donation from Ponce de Cabrera for the salvation of his soul and that of his parents 'tota mentis deuotione' ('with the whole mind [committed to] devotion').[98]

Disputes and donations, violence and agreements, were all part of the socio-political fabric in which laymen and clergymen interacted, lived and formed alliances as friends, but also fought and harmed the other party as enemies. Sometimes this close interaction was symbiotic and was affected by breaches in power balance and relationships, but it seems to have been continuously repaired. These practices were varied and resulted from a broad range of situations, but the fact that they were recurrent throughout the period leads to question the interpretations that have linked them to the earlier stages of church institutions, their crises and the persistent ambition of the nobility. Wrongdoers and benefactors should therefore be seen as two possible poles of the same relationship.

* * *

The context considered in this study helps us to understand and assess the effect that the developments in legal and political centralisation had on court practices and forms of political action. The cases discussed above have been analysed in great detail regarding the various jurisdictions that heard them; how the claims were submitted and argued; what procedures were used to make a decision; the role played by legal rules throughout the process; and how resolutions were issued. But my main purpose has been to clarify the role that litigation, the method of opposition and the resolution sought, had for the various parties involved, and the structural factors that caused all of the above. These issues will be recapitulated below.

As seen above, the arguments used by the opposing parties to articulate their demands revolved around two conflicting notions of ownership and landholding. This opposition was made apparent particularly in the different degree of control involved in each of them. Ownership was inherited, not subject to any transfer restrictions, and linked to supposedly *iure hereditario* ('full ownership'). Landholding was a right limited in time and subject to transfer restrictions; it was on held on lease, as a form of assignment. Laymen argued that the disputed assets were their own, based on family inheritance, purchases, exchange charters or donations. That is, their patrimony included inherited assets and others gained through any of the above methods. The sons of Munio Velázquez invoked a 'testamento commutacionis' ('a charter of exchange') before Alfonso VI as a basis for reclaiming against Sahagún the town received by their father. They did so in opposition to the argument provided by the monastery that no exchange charter had been made, but that it had been assigned to them so that 'they would hold it for life'.[99] Another knight also alleged

---

97   'justam et sanam atque verissimam et racionabilem [...] certissiman salubremque cognitionem'.
98   SFPSahagun1329 (1135); and SFPSahagun1327 (1135).
99   'teneret in uita sua'.

540   ISABEL ALFONSO

before queen Urraca that there had been a *cambiatio* ('exchange'), in contrast with the claims made by the bishop that the disputed *villa* was the cathedral's property 'ex dato regum' ('by royal grant'). Much later, at the beginning of the thirteenth century, a knight defended himself from the accusations made by a monastery that he 'held [some land] by force' by arguing 'but rather that it was his own *hereditas* as a successor of his father's right'.[100]

The allegations made by the church were shaped into a self-evident discourse, rather than an actuality: the assets owned by the church resulted from donations of hereditary property, their concessions were for life. However, this does not seem to be a church-like discourse, but rather a lordly discourse. Already in the mid-eleventh century countess Sancha had explained to the royal assembly that the disputed *villa* had been inherited and passed on by her family, whereas her opponents argued that it was part of their own *hereditates*, even though the countess stated that they had them as 'prestamo de suo patre' ('a lease from her father').

This is one of those issues that is key to many of the historiographic discussions about 'legal change', particularly to those that have attempted to ascertain the origins of the right of ownership. This right, according to the more legalistic arguments, only appeared when Roman law was adopted from the twelfth century; when specific rules were invoked both in claims and challenges and in the grounds used for rulings; and when the enforcement of those rulings became assured by a centralised political apparatus. Before then there had been no space for regulatory arguments, as there was no substantive law as such and no distinction between fact and law. In effect, it has often been assumed that conflicts originated due to the lack of clear rules. A large part of the critique on which the so-called 'anthropological model' is built is a criticism of this paradoxically normativist, but at the same time a-juridical conception[101] of early medieval societies.[102]

In the disputes discussed here it can be seen that, albeit no rules were explicitly invoked, an ability to think in legal terms existed and was used; that when there were discussions about certain facts — *tenencias* and *entramientos*, for example — these referred to rules, sometimes implicit and other times explicit, that provided whether or not such facts were legitimate. A regulatory principle, alluded to and operated indirectly, attempted to define and establish lordly patrimony, thus rendering unauthorised transfers unlawful. This principle was developed as a statute and applied as a ruling by Alfonso VI in a famous court assembly in 1089, in which the bishop of León had brought his great lawsuit against queen Urraca. The king ordered that each '*hereditas* should remain fully under the right and power of its lord without the interference of any other *hereditarius*'[103] and defined the four types of known lordships between which such transfers were prohibited.[104] This rule was systematically breached in

---

100   'tenebat per forcia […] set propria esse hereditas et ex paterno iure sibi successisse'.

101   White, among others, has aptly criticised the theses of British law historians Milsom y Palmer in White, 'Inheritances and Legal Arguments'.

102   On this paradox, see the prologue to Bossy, ed., *Disputes and Settlements*.

103   'hereditas integra remaneret in iure et potestate domini sui sine alio herede'.

104   CatLeon1244 (1089). On this decision as an expression of the development of *propiedad dominical*

LAND DISPUTES AND *MALFETRÍAS*   541

practice despite being ratified in later assemblies such as the one held in Nájera at the end of the twelfth century, and compiled in legal systems as Romanised as that of Alcalá in 1348.[105]

However, based on the assemblies that heard these claims, it could be concluded that the major church institutions like Sahagún or the cathedral of León, or even counts, did not succeed in developing sufficient lordly authority to prevail over the nobility bound to them, at least in those cases related to the use of the land. During the eleventh century and part of the twelfth century, the cases discussed here were predominantly brought before the royal court and local assemblies of *boni homines*; during the twelfth century and a large part of the thirteenth century they were subject to direct bilateral negotiations; and at the end of the thirteenth century they were brought before the king again. At first sight, this would seems to confirm that there was a supposedly general process of privatisation of public justice, which was later recovered by the monarchic institutions.[106] However, this perception needs to be qualified, since other data show that different jurisdictions overlapped, rather than followed each other over time; hence some *boni homines* would have appeared in these procedures, at the same time as the kings, and the composition of these assemblies may have been different depending on the parties in dispute or other circumstances unknown to us.[107] In addition, even those cases that were brought before the king's court had been resolved locally before and after the twelfth century, and their outcomes were not substantially different from those in the cases resolved through other extrajudicial means.[108] Further research is needed to reach a firmer conclusion about the relationships between the cases in dispute, the identity of the litigants, the jurisdictions before which they were brought, the procedures conducted and the resolutions issued.

The preferred means of proof used in these processes seems to have been the inquest, the investigation of the truthfulness of the facts alleged or the written evidence provided ordered by the authority that judged the case to decide after hearing the parties' arguments and the testimonies of the witnesses. The fact that this type of

---

('lordly property'), see Estepa Díez, 'Formación y consolidación del feudalismo', pp. 206–07. On the Curia de Nájera as an expression of the consolidation of the *dominio señorial* 'lordly dominion' and literature on this issue, see Álvarez Borge, *Poder y relaciones sociales*, pp. 270–72. One of the approaches I am interested in is analysing these issues as an expression of relationships and alliances established by peasants outside the recognised lordly structures. This involved being subject to various patronages. Their 'mobility' caused some control problems that underlay many of the disputes dealt with here. The continued inquests and the constant prohibitions from transferring their *hereditates* to a different lordship prove how recurrent these practices were.

105 On these regulations, see Pérez-Prendes, *Curso de Historia del Derecho Español 1*. On some problems regarding the production of law, see Iglesia Ferreiros, 'Derecho municipal'.

106 S. D. White, resorting to new analytical approaches, deconstructed such an impression for the case of north-western Francia (White, '*Pactum ... legem vincit*', pp. 285 and ff). If true, this would contrast with the informal methods documented by Cheyette for Provence.

107 For example, bishop Diego disputed and negotiated similar matters during this period, using analogous arguments and resolutions, once before a council — perhaps the one based in León — the nature and composition of which is unknown, and another time before queen Urraca (CatLeon1347, 1114).

108 For greater detail on this matter, see Alfonso, 'Resolución de disputas'.

542   ISABEL ALFONSO

evidence prevailed throughout the period studied here may also serve to question the legal division associated with the adoption of a judicial system inspired by Roman Law, considered to be more rational and impartial than the previous system. However, it is more important to understand the logic involved in its use in a society where the various dominant groups needed to make their domination public in order to be able to exert it. The public nature of social relations, the rights to the land and control over people in a society where power was highly fragmented was achieved mainly by regularly questioning those rights, so that they could be either ratified or reclaimed. These situations, which did not necessarily arise in court hearings, were more common than is usually thought, as they were explicitly promoted in numerous land grants. It should be remembered that in 1055 Munio Velázquez had received the vill from Sahagún *en beneficio* for his service, which would be repeatedly disputed later by his heirs, in order to *inquirire* ('to investigate') and *vindicare* ('to claim') it. But the concessions of specific assets, which were often accompanied by a vague 'et toto quanto puedas invenire' ('and everything that you may find'), could have triggered these types of investigations, as suggested by the expression 'the time of judging came and everyone inquired over his/her *hereditas*', alleged by countess Sancha in 1045 to justify her claims.[109] This allusion seems to refer to periods of lordly justice being imparted, during which the community had to account for their landholdings and obligations, and demarcate the boundaries, uses, transfers of *hereditates* and various other transactions. This time may have taken place with each change of holder, heir and concessionaire, all of which would have mobilised the memory of the community and the rituality of power and submission.[110] The habit of responding to various inquests, of asking the oldest people what they had seen or heard, that is, the appeal to public knowledge, to public fame, that way of building a truth that was tantamount to right, had to do with a specific kind of legal culture. Daniel L. Smail has analysed this in depth, providing further information and studying whether this could be extended to later periods.[111]

This information is also interesting because these inquests exposed an undercurrent of transactions, with their corresponding alliances and client relationships, which seemed to have been beyond the lords' control. This hindered the stability of ownership as provided by the laws, which made local reality more complex than is usually evidenced in the charter record.[112] Taking into account this dense fabric of

---

109 'venit tempus iudicandi que inquiriret unusquisque proximo sua hereditate' (CatLeon1026, 1045).

110 Changes of kings seem to have given rise to similar claims and inquests. These fed a whole rhetoric of restoration that was repeated with every change of king. The inquests ordered by Fernando I in this period aimed at recovering *hereditates* appropriated from or denied to the cathedral of Astorga are interesting because they are connected to the issues discussed here. See FernandoI-29, 1046; and FernandoI-31, 1046. So are the ones ordered by queen Urraca recorded in CatLeon1328 (1109); and CatLeon1329 (1109).

111 Lord Smail, 'Archivos de conocimiento'.

112 An inquest of assets belonging to the cathedral of León in several villages, carried out by one of its archdeacons in the times of Alfonso VII, is a good illustration of these arguments. It details how in one of the villages 'they found three houses that belonged to Santa María held by wrongfully by *infanzones*', and similarly in another they found 'lands that had been wrongfully seized […] from

LAND DISPUTES AND *MALFETRÍAS* 543

interests and social relationships, a better understanding can be gained of how these conflicts originated and evolved, and also of how the resolutions adopted to put an end to litigation — even if momentarily — were the result of negotiations.[113] These were agreements whereby the nobility had their local power recognised, maybe even above church power, while at the same time they became defendants of the institution to which they were linked and of its power. This harassment/protection dialectic provides a context to understand the *malfetrías* and violence perpetrated by the nobility.[114]

The violence constantly attributed in monastic discourse to their opponents was used by monks to build an image of their enemies that still prevails in a large part of Spanish historiography. The litigants in the cases discussed here — the *milites, infanzones* or *hereditarii* — were portrayed, and even recognised themselves, as being *homines forciosos* ('forceful men') whose actions were moved by *forcia* ('force'), *malitia* ('maliciousness') and *uiolenciam* ('violence') and induced by *zelo diabolico* ('diabolic zeal'); as people who *entran* ('seized') and *possidebant iniuste* ('unjustly appropriated') or *false retinuissent* ('unrightfully retained') *hereditates* owned by monasteries, and who did wrong and deprived their vassals of their rights. They were accused of committing all kinds of *rapinae* ('pillages'), *injurium* ('wrongdoings'), *maleficia* ('offences') and *facionora* ('evil deeds'), which were increasingly depicted as sins. The language they used to designate their aggressors also enabled them to build an image of themselves as victims but also — and perhaps more importantly — as compassionate people, who were graceful and forgiving of wrongdoers and willing to negotiate with them,

---

the *infantazgo* by another *infanzon*' ('inuenerunt tres kasas quas tenebant infanzones cum torto, que sunt de Santa Maria' [...] 'terras que prendidit [...] de infantadigo cum torto') (CatLeon1431, [1140–1157]). One of these inquest, performed at the beginning of the thirteenth century, notes that in some villages the bishop of León 'was sent out by our knights, *hereditarii*, and their armed followers' ('iniuiatur nobis milites heredes y armigeri eiusdem'), but also by clerics and by the episcopal vassals themselves (CatLeon1815, [1210–1232]).

113 On the dense lay networks formed around monasteries as the main framework for effective local political action, see White, 'Feuding and peacemaking', pp. 256 and ff. In my study of Galician communities, I showed how this network was used by the monastic group as the most effective means of domination. See Alfonso, 'Poder local y diferenciación interna', pp. 203–24 [Editors' note: For an English translation, see chapter 6 of this volume]; Alfonso, 'La comunidad campesina', pp. 305–72. A broader investigation on monastic networks in Galicia is being currently directed by R. Pastor. [Editors' note: Later published as Pastor and others, *Beyond the Market*].

114 An additional example referring to the *conuenientia* between bishop Manrique of León and the *malhechor* ('wrongdoer') Gonzalo Fernández illustrates this dialectic (CatLeon1734, 1197). The knight returned to the bishop the *hereditates* 'that [the latter] requested from [him] and which [the bishop] said [he] was unlawfully holding', and recognised the injustice that he had committed due to his temerity ('que requirebatis a me, quia dicebatis me tenere eas iniuste [...] propria temeritatem intraueram'). He also promised to compensate the cathedral or reimburse it for all the 'wrongdoings that you know I did, and the ones I ordained to be made or instigated' ('malefactoriis quas uos cognoueretis quas ego eas feci, uel alicuis fecit mandato meo uel instinctu'). He also undertook to repay or compensate the cathedral for all 'the evil that my men did' and which the latter could 'find out about through inquest' ('mala uero que homines mei fecerint [...] inquisitionem inueneritis'). As usual, the bishop, 'attending to [Gonzalo Fernández's] good will' ('attendens uoluntatem uestram bonam') granted him other assets on lease.

544   ISABEL ALFONSO

and therefore interested in building peaceful, amicable relationships with them. This discourse is first and foremost a rhetorical device, a means to legitimise their own demands and delegitimise those made by their enemies. This rhetoric was not the sole remit of the church, although it is this type of ecclesiastical discourse that has been best preserved.

However, as has been proven and documented, violence was not merely a rhetorical instrument, it was a tactic and a strategy used by laymen, albeit not exclusively, in different disputes, those *contiendae* ('contentions') or *intentiones* ('disputes') being the most frequent. It was used to initiate and continue hostilities, but also as a means to assert rights or put pressure to gain them.[115] *Entramientos* ('occupations'), for example, did not have a negative meaning in themselves, and were not necessarily violent. *Entrar* (lit. to enter or to occupy) was the legal term used to receive and take hold of a property.[116] Its unlawfulness was therefore arguable and was disputed on the basis of opposing rights.[117] Even if those rights were not explicitly invoked, there was a regulatory framework where accusations and claims made sense. Thus, violence cannot be merely regarded as an arbitrary, predatory way of prevailing over the peasants, resulting from an 'unpolitical' lordship, as Bisson claimed,[118] but rather as a political action within the process of inter-seigneurial competition for dominion. As I have sought to show in these pages, this competition was enacted both violently and legally. This was not necessarily based on the opposition between the parties, as they were often closely interlinked.

Some of the most important changes in court proceedings identified in the charters of other monasteries from the thirteenth century included: a greater development

---

115   The difficulty in distinguishing between these land disputes and other types of fights, enmities, wars or vengeances has been noted by several authors. See Geary, 'Vivre en conflit'; and, among several of his studies, White, 'Feuding and peacemaking'. White argued that feuding ideology and practice may have facilitated the process whereby some lords consolidated their authority over their clients and extended their power over peasants. He has criticised the purely functionalist interpretations that had been made of these conflicts, according to which these were merely social transactions. An extensive study of the logic of these hostilities is made in Miller, *Bloodtaking*, p. 183. The author notes the moral, legal and always political nature of these feuds.

116   In 1188 an abbot said 'he had got this *hereditas* and received it' from the hands of the royal porter. See AlfonsoVIII-508 (1188); see also AlfonsoVIII-408 (1183).

117   The most obvious and best known cases are those related to *behetrías*. When noblemen were faced with the monasteries' accusations of seizure, they justified their position by turning the accusation against the monks, arguing that the *hereditates* in question had been unlawfully purchased or acquired by the monks in their *behetría* lordship, which was a 'fact' prohibited by 'law'. This type of regulatory allegations was used for any of the known lordships. I dealt with the former in Alfonso, 'Resolución de disputas'. Additional cases are also discussed in Álvarez Borge, *Poder y relaciones sociales*, pp. 298–300. The author sees them as a result of the complicated relationship between ownership and lordship.

118   T. Bisson, the most recent originator of these unconventional arguments, qualified this type of lordship in this way because in his view it was 'an unpolitical mode of affective patrimonial power rooted in will instead of consensus'. See Bisson, 'The "Feudal Revolution"', p. 19. S. White made an important critical contribution based on this article in White, 'The "Feudal Revolution"'. Bisson reiterated his arguments in his reply to White in Bisson, 'The "Feudal Revolution"'; Bisson, 'The Politicising of West European Societies'.

of the royal institutional apparatus; the intervention of people who held specific offices; procedures more consistent with the 'law'; and the ability to appeal due to the lack of 'legal formalities'.[119] They undoubtedly deserve greater analysis than they have received in this study. However, this must not conceal all the other factors that determined the forms and outcomes of disputes, and articulated significant aspects of medieval political life among the dominant groups.

The fact that agreed resolutions and settlements were prevalent, including those in royal courts, which sometimes seem to have been reached through radical forms of adjudication, show that there was an interest in negotiating pre-existing relationships through these clearly political processes. Testimonies that these forms of feuding and negotiating persisted, both in and out of court, have been documented throughout the entire period under study, before and after the twelfth century. These question the impact attributed to the legal and institutional developments that took place, and encourage greater study of the relationships that clearly existed between institutionalised resources and political practices.

---

119 References regarding Moreruela can be found in Alfonso, 'Conflictos'. On Carrizo, see Carrizo506 (1281). On Oña see, Alfonso, 'Resolución de disputas'. On other monasteries in Castile, like Silos or Las Huelgas, see Álvarez Borge, *Poder y relaciones sociales*. In the church realm there was greater legal awareness and rhetoric, and a more elaborated formulation of the expected outcomes. These involved both the greater institutionalisation of settlement procedures and the regulation of the norms to be applied, which were established to objectify and depersonalise the forms of assigning and distributing resources that were not only guided by economic criteria (CatLeon1367, 1120). See *supra*, p. 525.

Bibliography

Alfonso, Isabel, 'Conflictos en el proceso de expansión de un señorío monástico', *Moneda y Crédito*, 129 (1977), 19–33

Alfonso, Isabel, 'La comunidad campesina', in *Poder monástico y grupos domésticos en la Galicia foral (siglos XIII–XV)*, ed. by Reyna Pastor and others (Madrid: CSIC, 1990), pp. 302–72

Alfonso, Isabel, 'Poder local y diferenciación interna en las comunidades rurales gallegas', in *Relaciones de poder, de producción y de parentesco en la Edad Media y Moderna: aproximación a su estudio*, ed. by Reyna Pastor (Madrid: CSIC, 1990), pp. 203–24

Alfonso, Isabel, 'Resolución de disputas y prácticas judiciales en el Burgos medieval', in *Burgos en la Plena Edad Media. III Jornadas Burgalesas de Historia* (Burgos: Asociación Provincial de Libreros de Burgos, 1994), pp. 211–43

Alfonso, Isabel, 'Campesinado y derecho: la vía legal de su lucha (Castilla y León, siglos X–XIII)', *Noticiario de Historia Agraria*, 13 (1997), 15–31

Álvarez Borge, Ignacio, *Poder y relaciones sociales en Castilla en la Edad Media. Los territorios entre el Arlanzón y el Duero en los siglos X al XIV* (Salamanca: Junta de Castilla y León, 1996)

Barton, Simon, *The Aristocracy in Twelfth-Century Leon and Castille* (Cambridge: Cambridge University Press, 1997)

Bisson, Thomas N., 'The "Feudal Revolution"', *Past & Present*, 142 (1994), 6–42

Bisson, Thomas N., 'The Politicising of West European Societies (c. 1175–c. 1225)', in *Georges Duby, l'écriture de l'Histoire*, ed. by Claude Duhamel-Amado and Guy Lobrichon (Bruxelles: DeBoeck Université, 1996), pp. 245–55

Bisson, Thomas N., 'The "Feudal Revolution": Reply', *Past & Present*, 155 (1997), 208–25

Bossy, John, ed., *Disputes and Settlements: Law and Human Relations in the West* (Cambridge: Cambridge University Press, 1983)

Bouchard, Constance Brittain, *Sword, Miter, and Cloister: Nobility and the Church in Burgundy (980–1198)* (Ithaca: Cornell University Press, 1987)

Bourdieu, Pierre, *Le sens practique* (Paris: Éditions de Minuit, 1980)

Davies, Wendy, and Paul Fouracre, eds, *Property and Power in the Early Middle Ages* (Cambridge: Cambridge University Press, 1995)

Davies, Wendy, and Paul Fouracre, eds, *The Settlement of Disputes in Early Medieval Europe* (Cambridge: Cambridge University Press, 1986)

Estepa Díez, Carlos, *Estructura social de la ciudad de León (siglos XI–XIII)* (León: Centro de Estudios e Investigación San Isidoro de León, 1977)

Estepa Díez, Carlos, 'Formación y consolidación del feudalismo en Castilla y León', in *En torno al feudalismo hispánico. I Congreso de Estudios Medievales* (Ávila: Fundación Sánchez-Albornoz, 1989), pp. 157–256

Estepa Díez, Carlos, 'Poder y propiedad feudales en el período astur: las mandaciones de los Flaínez en la Montaña Leonesa', in *Miscel.lània en homenatge al P. Agustí Altisent* (Tarragona: Diputació de Tarragona, 1991), pp. 285–327

Estepa Díez, Carlos, 'Proprietà, evoluzione delle strutture agrarie e trasformazioni sociali in Castiglia (secoli XI–XII)', in *Strutture e trasformazioni della signoria rurale nei secoli X–XIII*, ed. by Gerhard Dilcher and Cinzio Violante (Bologna: Il Mulino, 1996), pp. 411–43

Fletcher, Richard A., *The Episcopate in the Kingdom of León in the Twelfth Century* (Oxford: Oxford University Press, 1978)

Geary, Patrick, 'Vivre en conflit dans une France sans État: typologie des mécanismes de règlement des conflits (1050–1200)', *Annales ESC*, 41–5 (1986), 1107–33

Iglesia Ferreiros, Aquilino, 'Derecho municipal, derecho señorial, derecho regio', *Historia, Instituciones, Documentos*, 4 (1977), 115–97

Koziol, Geoffrey, *Begging Pardon and Favor: Ritual and Political Order in Early Medieval France* (Ithaca: Cornell University Press, 1992)

Lee Epstein, Andrew, 'The Case Method in the Field of Law', in *The Craft of Social Anthropology*, ed. by Andrew Lee Epstein (London: Tavistock, 1969), pp. 205–30

Lord Smail, Daniel, 'Archivos de conocimiento y la cultura legal de la publicidad en la Marsella medieval', *Hispania*, 197 (1997), 1049–77

Loring García, María Isabel, 'Nobleza e iglesias propias en la Cantabria altomedieval', *Studia Historica. Historia Medieval*, 5 (1987), 89–120

Loring García, María Isabel, 'Dominios monásticos y parentelas en la Castilla altomedieval: el origen del derecho de retorno y su evolución', in *Relaciones de poder, de producción y de parentesco en la Edad Media y Moderna: aproximación a su estudio*, ed. by Reyna Pastor (Madrid: CSIC, 1990), pp. 13–50

Martínez Sopena, Pascual, *La Tierra de Campos occidental: poblamiento, poder y comunidad del siglo X al XIII* (Valladolid: Institución Cultural Simancas, 1985)

Martínez Sopena, Pascual, 'Parentesco y poder en León durante el siglo XI. La "casata" de Alfonso Díaz', *Studia Historica. Historia Medieval*, 5 (1987), 33–87

Martínez Sopena, Pascual, 'El conde Rodrigo de León y los suyos. Herencia y expectativa del poder entre los siglos XI y XII', in *Relaciones de poder, de producción y de parentesco en la Edad Media y Moderna: aproximación a su estudio*, ed. by Reyna Pastor (Madrid: CSIC, 1990), pp. 51–84

Martínez Sopena, Pascual, 'Monasterios particulares, nobleza y reforma eclesiástica en León entre los siglos XI y XII', in *Estudios de Historia Medieval. Homenaje a Luis Suárez*, ed. by Miguel Ángel Ladero Quesada, Vicente Álvarez Palenzuela, and Julio Valdeón Baruque (Valladolid: Universidad de Valladolid, 1991), pp. 323–31

Martínez Sopena, Pascual, 'La nobleza de León y Castilla en los siglos XI y XII. Un estado de la cuestión', *Hispania*, 185 (1993), 801–22

Mauss, Marcel, 'Essai sur le don. Forme et raison de l'échange dans les sociétés primitives', *L'Année sociologique*, 1 (1923–1924), 30–180

Miller, William I., *Bloodtaking and Peacemaking: Feud, Law, and Society in Saga Iceland* (Chicago: The University of Chicago Press, 1990)

Moreta, Salustiano, *Malhechores-feudales: violencia, antagonismos y alianzas de clases en Castilla, siglos XIII–XIV* (Madrid: Cátedra, 1978)

Pascua Echegaray, Esther, 'Redes personales y conflicto social: Santiago de Compostela en tiempos de Diego Gelmírez', *Hispania*, 185 (1993), 1069–89

Pastor, Reyna, *Resistencias y luchas campesinas en la época del crecimiento y consolidación de la formación feudal: Castilla y León, siglos X–XIII* (Madrid: Siglo XXI, 1980)

Pastor, Reyna, and others, 'Baja nobleza: aproximación a la historiografía europea y propuestas para una investigación', *Historia Social*, 20 (1994), 23–45

Pastor, Reyna, and others, *Beyond the Market: Transactions, Property and Social Networks in Monastic Galicia, 1200–1300* (Leiden: Brill, 2002)

Pérez-Prendes, José Manuel, *Curso de Historia del Derecho Español. Volumen I. Introducción, fuentes y materiales institucionales* (Madrid: Universidad Complutense de Madrid, 1989)

Reglero de la Fuente, Carlos, *Los señoríos de los Montes Torozos. De la repoblación al Becerro de las 'Behetrías'* (Valladolid: Universidad de Valladolid, 1993)

Reuter, Timothy, '*Filii matris nostrae pugnant adversum nos*: Bonds and Tensions between Prelates and their *milites* in the German High Middle Ages', in *Chiesa e mondo feudale nei secoli X–XII. Atti della dodicesima Settimana internazionale di studio. Mendola 24–28 agosto 1992* (Milan: Università Cattolica del Sacro Cuore, 1995), pp. 241–76

Roberts, Simon, and John Comaroff, L., *Rules and Processes: The Cultural Logic of Dispute in an African Context* (Chicago: The University of Chicago Press, 1981)

Rosenwein, Barbara H., *To Be the Neighbor of Saint Peter: The Social Meaning of Cluny's Property, 909–1049* (Ithaca: Cornell University Press, 1989)

Ser Quijano, Gregorio del, 'Un monasterio benedictino leonés olvidado: San Antolín', in *Semana del historia del monacato cántabro-astur-leonés* (Gijón: Monasterio de San Pelayo, 1982), pp. 175–94

Villacorta Rodríguez, Tomás, *El cabildo catedral de León: estudio histórico-jurídico, siglo XII–XIX* (León: Centro de Estudios e Investigación San Isidoro, 1974)

Weinberger, Stephen, 'Cours judiciaires, justice et responsabilité sociale dans la Provence médiévale: IXe–XIe siècle', *Revue Historique*, 542 (1982), 273–89

White, Stephen D., '*Pactum … legem vincit et amor judicium*: The Settlement of Disputes by Compromise in Eleventh-Century Western France', *The American Journal of Legal History*, 22-4 (1978), 281–308

White, Stephen D., 'Feuding and Peacemaking in Touraine around the Year 1100', *Traditio*, 42 (1986), 196–263

White, Stephen D., 'Inheritances and Legal Arguments in Western France, 1050–1150', *Traditio*, 3 (1987), 55–103

White, Stephen D., *Custom, Kinship, and Gifts to Saints: The Laudatio Parentum in Western France, 1050–1150* (Chapel Hill: University of North Carolina Press, 1988)

White, Stephen D., 'The "Feudal Revolution"', *Past & Present*, 152 (1996), 205–23

CHAPTER 14

On Revolting Noblemen

with a commentary by François Foronda

Conflict, Language, and Social Practice in Medieval Societies: Selected Essays of Isabel Alfonso, with Commentaries, ed. by Julio Escalona Monge, Álvaro Carvajal Castro, and Cristina Jular Pérez-Alfaro, TMC 24 (Turnhout: Brepols, 2024), pp. 549–586

BREPOLS ❧ PUBLISHERS · 10.1484/M.TMC-EB.5.132468

FRANÇOIS FORONDA

Questioning the Evidence

Political History and Social Mentality*

'Desheredamiento and Desafuero' arose at the crossroads of various scholarly dynamics, both collective and personal, and to a certain extent marks the beginning of Isabel Alfonso's greatest contributions to the study of political history.[1] To understand it, we must look back at a context extending roughly from 1996 to 2006 — a decade in the author's career as a researcher. The first dynamic, as suggested by the journal that published the article in 2002 (*Cahiers de linguistique et de civilisation hispaniques médiévales*),[2] is a federated interdisciplinary project led by Georges Martin, who in 2001 created the CNRS-funded *Groupement de Recherches* (GDR) 2378, better known as SIREM (*Séminaire interdisciplinaire de recherches sur l'Espagne médiévale*). The project had already begun to take shape in 1996 through a series of gatherings that, beyond the topics discussed, served to cement a collaboration between various researchers whose respective concentrations provided fertile ground for a dialog between scholars of literature (most of them French) and historians (most of them Spanish). Isabel Alfonso entered this dynamic already in 1996, delivering papers on almost a yearly basis.[3] However, she saw only two of these talks through to publication, first with the article 'Venganza y justicia en el *Cantar de Mio Cid*' (Vengeance and justice in the *Poem of the Cid*), based on her 1999 lecture marking the 900th anniversary of El Cid's death,[4] and then with the present article. '*Desheredamiento y Desafuero*' developed from a conference presentation in 2000, in which she revisited her examination of political conceptions at an earlier seminar, in 1997, but now shifting the focus from the monarchy to the nobility.[5]

---

* Translated from the French by Jean Birrell.
1 Unlike the article in chapter 1, I did not choose this one myself, but was invited to write about it by Julio Escalona.
2 The project affected the form and content of this journal, as can be seen in the successive changes to its title: *Cahiers de linguistique hispanique médiévale*, until issue 23 (2000), *Cahiers de linguistique et de civilisation hispaniques médiévales*, issues 24 to 27 (2001 to 2004), and finally *Cahiers d'études hispaniques médiévales*, as of issue 28 (2005).
3 At the symposium *Alphonse X de Castille ou la Science Politique (1252–1284)*, in November 1996, with the lecture, 'Naturaleza y legitimación del poder regio antes de Alfonso el Sabio'. She delivered the lecture 'Rituales judiciales e ideología política en el siglo XIII' at the seminar *Histoire des idées politiques dans l'Espagne médiévale. Conception et représentations de la royauté-XIIᵉ-XIVᵉ siècles*, in November 1997.
4 Published as 'Venganza y justicia' [Editors' note: For an English translation, see chapter 5 of this volume].
5 As per the symposium's title, *Conceptions politiques de la noblesse dans l'Espagne médiévale*.

François Foronda, Université Paris 1 – Panthéon-Sorbonne

These two articles were Isabel Alfonso's way of accepting the invitation to this dialogue between literary scholars and historians, as the sources she analyses are both 'literary': in the first case the fictional trial of the *Infantes* de Carrión in the *Poem of the Cid*, and in the second the 'letters' — whose documentary nature she disputes — between Alfonso X and the rebels of 1272–1273, found in the Wise King's *Chronicle*.

However, this exploration of 'the literary' is also influenced by another research dynamic that emerged in the first of the two articles we have just mentioned. In her notes, Isabel Alfonso cites a whole array of English-language publications, with which she had become well acquainted during her stays in the UK between 1984 and 1991, at the universities of Edinburgh, Birmingham and London. This wealth of knowledge led her to promote this historiography from the English-speaking world in Spain, as demonstrated by the seminar and special issue of *Hispania* (1997, 197) that she coordinated, titled 'Desarrollo legal, prácticas judiciales y acción política en la Europa medieval', with papers by John Hudson, Stephen D. White, Chris Wickham and Daniel Lord Smail. These papers pointed to two lines of research that had already guided some of Alfonso's own work: economic history and historical anthropology, the core nexus being conflict and its resolution, both judicial and extrajudicial, which also ties in with 'the political'. In the 1997 seminar and special issue, Stephen D. White, whom Alfonso cites several times in 'Vengeance and justice', shifted his focus precisely toward 'the literary' as a useful source for delving into some of the questions that had motivated medievalists to appropriate historical anthropology.[6] In choosing the fictional trial of the *Infantes* de Carrión as a source to develop her ideas in 'Vengeance and justice', Isabel Alfonso was therefore continuing down the methodological path opened up by the 1997 seminar, the same one that would lead to '*Desheredamiento y desafuero*', which weaves together both of these dynamics.

As mentioned earlier, this link, or crossroads, marked the beginning of Alfonso's most important contributions to the field of political history, built upon her independence as director of various funded research projects.[7] The first was *Lucha y legitimación política en León y Castilla, siglos X–XV* (1998–2002), which would yield two collective volumes, one of which came about in collaboration with the University of Saint Andrews,[8] and the other in collaboration with SIREM.[9] The next project, a continuation of the former, was *Cultura, lenguaje y prácticas políticas en las sociedades medievales. Un estudio comparado sobre la construcción de valores compartidos y las formas de su contestación* (2002–2006), which led to a 2007 seminar (the last to be held at the Instituto de Historia's historic building on calle Medinaceli) whose papers were

---

Chronologie, formes, contenus (XIIe–XVe siècles). See Alfonso, 'Desheredamiento y desafuero'.

6 White, 'La traición'.

7 Up until this time she had always taken the role of collaborator in projects led by Reyna Pastor first, and then by Carlos Estepa.

8 A joint collaboration led alongside John Hudson, 'Discursos políticos. Un estudio comparado de formas y ámbitos de legitimación en la Edad Media' (1999–2001): Alfonso, Kennedy, and Escalona, eds, *Building Legitimacy*.

9 This second one was the result of a symposium held in 2001: Alfonso, Escalona, and Martin, eds, *Lucha política*.

published in the journal *e-Spania*,[10] founded by SIREM. I had the opportunity to work with these publications on two occasions.[11] Isabel Alfonso's independence as the director of funded research projects was reinforced in this period when Julio Escalona and Cristina Jular joined the Instituto de Historia. In 2005 the close collaboration of these three researchers gave rise to the Instituto de Historia's research group *Quaestio*. Proof of this newly found harmony is the publication, in the same volume as 'Disinheritance and loss of privilege', immediately after Isabel Alfonso's paper, of an article by Julio Escalona that also examines the same uprising against Alfonso X.[12]

Before highlighting some elements of Alfonso's — as in Isabel Alfonso, not Alfonso the Wise — understanding of this revolt, I would like to point out one last aspect that I find crucial in her approach to 'literary' sources, based on my own personal interactions with her. I can recall my enthusiasm, even elation, shortly after I began my 2000–2002 stay at Casa de Velázquez in Madrid, as I read the first two volumes of *Historia de la prosa medieval castellana* [A History of Castilian Medieval Prose], which Fernando Gómez Redondo began to publish in 1998.[13] I was enthralled by its generosity and exhaustiveness, as it taught what I saw to be a sound methodological lesson through its analysis of the contexts in which the works were produced, in order to establish their influences and intentionality. In so doing, it greatly contributed to granting historians access to 'literature' as a source in its own right. In discussing my perception of Fernando Gómez Redondo's great feat with Isabel Alfonso, I learned that she held the same opinion. This memory, along with Isabel Alfonso's references to the book in '*Desheredamiento y Desafuero*', lead me to believe that, beyond the timeliness of the new 1998 edition of the Wise King's *Chronicle*,[14] she chose this text, and specifically the part containing the dossier of 'correspondence' on the revolt of 1272–1273, in light of Gómez Redondo's prior work on the subject.

Having examined these historiographic and methodological pathways, we can now turn to some of the lines of analysis that Isabel Alfonso follows in the article at hand. All of them tend to question the evidence, in two main ways: either by questioning the facts about the documents, or by questioning the facts about their argumentation. To refer to the dossier analysed by the author, I have used quotation marks in two instances: 'letters' and 'correspondence'. This is because Isabel Alfonso directly questions this documentary addendum to Alfonso X's *Chronicle*, arguing that they are not really 'letters', but rather messages relayed by messengers, sent and received within the framework of a public debate. The content of the messages is therefore influenced by a communications strategy whose final aim is not so much to restore the nobles' obedience as to convince, and thereby to teach a sort of political lesson. Having laid bare the true nature of the dossier, exhuming the communicative framework in which it was produced and wherein it would have proved effective,

---

10 I. Alfonso (dir.), 'Cultura, lenguaje y prácticas políticas en las sociedades medievales', special dossier of the journal e-Spania, 4, 2007.

11 Foronda, 'La *privanza*'; Foronda, 'El miedo al rey'.

12 Escalona, 'Los nobles contra su rey'.

13 Gómez Redondo, *Historia de la prosa medieval 1*; Gómez Redondo, *Historia de la prosa medieval 2*.

14 González Jiménez, ed., *Crónica de Alfonso X*.

Isabel Alfonso can then question the facts as to the messages' own argumentation. As indicated by the article's title, such facts are basically articulated around two arguments, *desheredamiento* ('disinheritance') and *desafuero* ('withdrawal of privileges'), which constitute the cornerstones of the aforementioned lesson. However, both of them are 'negative notions' according to the author, who delves into their semantic content. She thereby underscores the 'positive' aspect of the message: inheritance and privileges, i.e. the common code, shared both personally and collectively, that defined the relationship between the king/lord and nobles/vassals. This makes evident the relational norms and parameters of legitimacy that ought to govern this relationship which had been broken by the revolt. As the author points out, by displacing the discussion towards these norms — with their deep-seated moral, legal, political and cultural aspects — they actually came out reinforced. More than debating facts that are ultimately beyond discussion, the messages manage to delegitimize the position of the rebels, and to situate the rules of the game, whether relational or political, within the realm of 'natural' obligation. With this demonstration, questioning the obvious, Isabel Alfonso points the way toward a method for deconstructing and reconstructing a system of values — a 'social mentality', one might say — which constitutes the hallmark of her contribution to the field of political history.

Bibliography

Alfonso, Isabel, 'Desheredamiento y desafuero, o la pretendida justificación de una revuelta nobiliaria', *Cahiers de linguistique et de civilisation hispaniques médiévales*, 25 (2002), 99–129

Alfonso, Isabel, 'Venganza y justicia en el Cantar de Mío Cid', in *El Cid: de la materia épica a las crónicas caballerescas*, ed. by Carlos Alvar Ezquerra, Fernando Gómez Redondo, and Georges Martin (Alcalá de Henares: Universidad de Alcalá, 2002), pp. 41–69

Alfonso, Isabel, Julio Escalona, and Georges Martin, eds, *Lucha política: condena y legitimación en la España medieval*, Annexes des Cahiers de Civilisation Hispanique Médiévale, 16 (Lyon: ENS Éditions, 2004)

Alfonso, Isabel, Hugh Kennedy, and Julio Escalona, eds, *Building Legitimacy. Political Discourses and Forms of Legitimation in Medieval Societies* (Leiden: Brill, 2004)

Escalona, Julio, 'Los nobles contra su rey. Argumentos y motivacionesde la insubordinación nobiliaria de 1272–1273', *Cahiers d'Études Hispaniques Médiévales*, 25 (2002), 131–62

Foronda, François, 'La *privanza* dans la Castille du bas Moyen Âge. Cadres conceptuels et stratégies de légitimation d'un lien de proximité', in *Lucha política: condena y legitimación en la España medieval*, ed. by Isabel Alfonso Antón, Julio Escalona and Georges Martin (Lyon: ENS Éditions, 2004), pp. 153–97

Foronda, François, 'El miedo al rey. Fuentes y primeras reflexiones acerca de una emoción aristocrática en la Castilla del siglo XIV', *e-Spania*, 4 (2007)

Gómez Redondo, Fernando, *Historia de la prosa medieval castellana. Vol. 1. La creación del discurso prosístico: el entramado cortesano* (Madrid: Cátedra, 1998)

Gómez Redondo, Fernando, *Historia de la prosa medieval castellana. Vol. 2. El desarrollo de los géneros. La ficción caballeresca y el orden religioso* (Madrid: Cátedra, 1999)

González Jiménez, Manuel, ed., *Crónica de Alfonso X* (Murcia: Real Academia Alfonso X el Sabio, 1998)

White, Stephen D., 'La traición en la ficción literaria. Derecho, hecho y ordalías en la narrativa y la épica en francés antiguo', *Hispania*, 57–197 (1997), 957–80

ISABEL ALFONSO

Desheredamiento and *Desafuero*, or the Alleged Justification of a Revolt of the Nobility[*]

It is not often that rebellions staged by the great against royal power are well documented. The *Chronicle of Alfonso X*, however, contains one of the most extensive and detailed accounts of the revolt that the monarch had to face in the early 1270s. This account describes how at the beginning of 1272 the *infante* don Felipe, brother of the king, and the heads of the three main noble lineages, Lara, Haro y Castro, together with other *ricoshombres* ('noblemen'), rose against Alfonso X, to whom they presented a list of important requests. Despite these requests being granted and ratified in the *Cortes*, this did not prevent them from going into exile to Granada, under the king of this kingdom. Only after lengthy negotiations was the dispute resolved by a compromise that reinstated the nobles into the royal service.

This revolt is still historiographically regarded as 'the first manifestation of a struggle between the monarchy, which codified the law and intended to increase its authority, and the nobility, which aimed to preserve or expand its share of power', says González Jiménez, the most recent editor of the *Chronicle*, following Suárez.[1] It therefore seems commonplace to interpret this conflict within the framework of the traditional nobility/monarchy opposition, as a reaction of the nobility to the centralising attempts of the monarch, and to the theoretical formulations of a corporate system that subordinated it to the superiority of a king and his legal code. In this interpretation the royal figure of Alfonso X, his thought, his legal work, his royalist policy, become isolated, in a continuous confrontation with the traditional powers in which he was defeated. It is true that this interpretation has been formulated in various ways. It is also the case that the moral connotations attributed to a fairer legal development proposed by the king against the feudal forces — very obvious in the argument of Ballesteros, who qualified the former as 'scientific' and the latter as 'antediluvian and centennially outdated'[2] — do not appear or are somewhat qualified in later works.[3] There is, however, a broad consensus that this pressure by the nobles, in a particularly favourable situation for them, would derail the legislative plans of the monarch. These plans continue to be endowed with a moral quality derived from the attempt to subdue the 'evil nobles'.[4]

---

[*] Original publication: Alfonso, Isabel, 'Desheredamiento y desafuero, o la pretendida justificación de una revuelta nobiliaria', *Cahiers de linguistique et de civilisation hispaniques médiévales*, 25 (2002), pp. 99–129. Translated by Julian Thomas.

[1] CAX, pp. 60–170. For the quote, see pp. 66, n. 107. The author summarizes the interpretation of this revolt that he had already presented more extensively in González Jiménez, *Alfonso X el Sabio*, pp. 95–107.

[2] Ballesteros Beretta, *Alfonso X el Sabio*, pp. 615, 619 and 622.

[3] O'Callaghan, *El rey Sabio*; Gómez Redondo, *Historia de la prosa medieval 1*; Gómez Redondo, *Historia de la prosa medieval 2*; Pérez-Prendes, 'Las leyes de Alfonso el Sabio'.

[4] So qualified in Pérez-Prendes, 'Las leyes de Alfonso el Sabio', p. 81.

From another perspective, it could certainly be argued that this rebellion, which brought together members of the high nobility who had been traditionally divided, was the first known opposition by nobles in which a set of demands being presented to the king with the aim of limiting the growing power he wanted to arrogate to himself is documented.[5] However, partly as a result of the version transmitted by the chronicle, and partly due to the assumptions of historians regarding what would constitute the best government, there is little sign of such an interpretation.[6]

Nevertheless, the pitfalls and problems involved in these dichotomous arguments justify avoiding this type of discussions. They are also conducive to different approaches to the study of this chronicle material, which certainly deserves careful study as, among other things, it allows to analyse the regulatory standards that informed the political practice of the dominant groups; to explore the various resources provided by the legal culture — or political culture — to social agents to legitimise or justify their behaviour; and to address the more general problem of the relationship between regulations and the social processes in which they were invoked, negotiated, ratified and transformed.[7] The following pages will be dedicated to this analysis.

Texts and Communication

It is well-known that the *Chronicle of Alfonso X* was drafted as a continuation of the *Estoria de España* (*History of Spain*) during the reign of Alfonso XI, probably by his chancellor, Fernán Sánchez de Valladolid, with a purpose and some constraints that cannot be ignored.[8] Chronicling the figure of Alfonso X in the mid-fourteenth century involved facing the contradictory, and therefore difficult task to reconcile the legitimation of a strong king who was able to contain the ambitions of the nobility — a burning question in the times of Alfonso XI, but also continually present in the time of the 'Wise King' — with the recognition of the need for their support to strengthen royal power; and to further justify the ruling dynastic line that had emerged from the confrontation with the king about whom the chronicler had to write. This is the reason why the first of three royal chronicles that this chancellor drafted as ideological support for the fourth one, dedicated to Alfonso XI, is fairly heterogeneous, rather than the nature of the material available, which the chronicler was in fact adopting by reproducing it.

It is true, however, that within the heterogeneous content of the chronicle, the section dedicated to the rebellion stands out for its consistency in delegitimising the demands of the highest nobles of the kingdom, in contrast with data from previous

---

5 This is, for example, how the rebellion by the barons in 1215 in England is interpreted. For a recent summary of this rebellion in the context of other rebellions from which it differs, see Bartlett, *England*, pp. 51–67.

6 A very recent exception is Doubleday, *The Lara Family*, esp. p. 62.

7 Roberts and Comaroff, *Rules and Processes*.

8 Gómez Redondo, 'De la crónica general a la real'; summarized in Gómez Redondo, *Historia de la prosa medieval 1*, pp. 965–68 and 971–76. See also Calderón Calderón, 'La imagen del rey'.

chapters that introduced elements to justify the nobles' opposition.[9] In line with the above, the image of a lavishly generous king, more interested in his personal fame than in the good of his kingdom, as described in the first part, is opposed in this narrative with the image of a king whose problems were due to the insatiable ambitions of high nobility. It is worth examining what means the chronicler used to achieve these effects, and what rhetorical devices were employed, because one of the most striking aspects of the narrative is the way in which the nobles' demands were invalidated, even if they had been granted.

Certainly the question of the nature of the material that could have served as a basis for the writing of the Chronicle is of great importance. In my opinion, the two most recent analyses that seek to reconstruct the process of the chronicle's writing and decipher its textual components differ in substantial aspects despite their apparent similarities. Fernando Gómez Redondo emphasised the ideological nature of the chronicler's work and tried to understand it in relation to the context in which it was written, considering that these factors accounted for the chronological and factual errors found in the chronicle.[10] Manuel González Jiménez, for his part, was more concerned with exploring to what extent the chronicle's narrative matched the diplomatic information available, attributing mismatches to ignorance of the facts. Only in the last part did he argue for the chronicle's partisan nature.[11] Both authors, however, seem to agree on the documentary nature of much of the material included in the chronicle, especially in its second section, which is the focus of the analysis that follows.

The unique information on the rebellion provided in this section, which occupies nearly half of the chronicle — a block of thirty-eight out (from XX to LVIII) of its seventy-eight chapters — has been noted by González Jiménez, highlighting the thorough descriptions of the process and the numerous documents that supposedly compose it.[12] González Jiménez considers this section to be the oldest and the most coherent, and that it resulted from the chronicler's use of a text supposedly written in the court of Alfonso X, in the context of the rebellion orchestrated by his son, the *infante* don Sancho, in order to provide an account of the previous rebellion in which many of those who now supported the *infante* had participated. The work of Sánchez de Valladolid on this part was limited to adapting the account to chronicle form, and

---

9   Undoubtedly, the most important is that of the tribute to Portugal (ch. XIX). Here the chronicler resorts to a fictive episode of clear epic resonances, as it carriers the echoes of the *Poem of Fernán González*, whose popularity was then booming. This gives him an ideal precedent to introduce the account of the rebellion, supplying him with the legitimizing trigger that he lacked, namely, that the king does not accept the nobles' advice to preserve the crown's patrimony, putting his own interests before those of the kingdom. This passage is essential for the argument of the chronicle. It provides a certain legitimacy to the nobles' discontent, thus balancing the discredit the latter suffers in the chapter following those narrating the revolt, in which the image of the king as good doer is opposed to the nobles' wrong doing.

10 On chronological errors due to the specific aims being pursued, rather than to ignorance, see Gómez Redondo, *Historia de la prosa medieval 2*, p. 1280.

11 González Jiménez, *Crónica de Alfonso X*, pp. ix–lxiii.

12 González Jiménez, *Crónica de Alfonso X*, pp. xvii–xx, and especially xxxi–xxxvi.

breaking into chapters a narrative that was supposedly continuous, as well as including formulas that served to indicate the content of the following chapter at the end of the previous one. In González Jiménez's view, this section 'reproduces almost verbatim a story of the nobles' rebellion of 1272–1273 dating from the Alphonsine period'. He also thinks we should be grateful to the fourteenth-century chronicler for not trying to summarise it, because 'due to this, a series of no less than 57 documents have come down to us, some of them complete' that otherwise would have disappeared. González Jiménez included a list of those which, in his opinion, were literally transcribed or were an extract.[13] Meanwhile, Gómez Redondo seems more inclined to believe that it was the fourteenth-century chronicler who, due to his status as royal chancellor, used extensive data from the royal chamber to write this 'purely documentary' account of the disorders affecting the kingdom when Alfonso X failed to subdue the rebellious nobility, in his attempt to contrast the model of a weak monarch such as this, with its counterpart, the Avenger.[14]

Although my intention is not to carry out a textual analysis such as that undertaken by these two philologists, their interpretations of the nature of the material used here are fundamental to understand what political discourse was transmitted and how it was built. Moreover, since it seems to be assumed that one of the features of this chronicle is the large number of documents included, and given the significance or the value — that is, the authority — given to this fact, these arguments merit the discussion in the pages that follow.

The narrative structure of the section that contains the story of the revolt is the following:

1. It begins with a description of the covert pacts that the nobles made between themselves to oppose the king, and the strategies they planned and implemented to conceal their purposes in order to gain time to build support inside and outside of the kingdom (ch. XX–XXI).

2. The king's reaction is then described, first to the rumours about the plot, and later to the discovery of their veracity (ch. XXI–XXIII).

3. The noblemen presented the king with their demands, which were granted in Lerma and then ratified in the Cortes of Burgos (ch. XXIII–XXVII).

4. The king's reaction to the unexpected estrangement with the nobles and their ensuing exile after the concessions were granted (ch. XXVIII–XXXVIII).

5. Exile in Granada. Growing intervention by mediators, due to strategies that relied on force and reconciliation by the parties involved in the negotiation process for the return of the exiled nobles to royal service (ch. XXXIX–LIV).

6. Agreed resolution, final settlement in a context conditioned by the opposing objectives of the parties involved (ch. LV–LVIII)

---

13 González Jiménez, *Crónica de Alfonso X*, pp. xxxiii–xxxvi.
14 Gómez Redondo, *Historia de la prosa medieval 1*, pp. 972 and 975.

DESHEREDAMIENTO AND DESAFUERO 561

My analysis will focus on point 4 of the above, which contains the list of the demands received by the king from the noblemen and the description of the monarch's reaction to their departure from the kingdom, despite the positive response he had given to their demands. It was at this point when, using a supposedly 'epistolary' style, the king reduced the conflict to a verbal discussion on what *desheredamiento* and *desafuero* were. For a better understanding, it is necessary to briefly refer to the previous process.

It is a long process, described in great detail, in which the noble rebels,[15] from the outset and throughout the negotiations, are presented negatively, as they held meetings behind the king's back after he had departed for Murcia, and plotted against him:

> [they all] got together in Lerma and made a pact and agreement: to assist each other in opposing King Alfonso, harming him however they could if he did not grant and fulfil to them the things they would go and demand.[16]

At the same time, they concealed their true intentions by pretending that they were his loyal servants, and at the same time seeking support for their cause. This way of contrasting the opposing attitudes and behaviours of the parties to the conflict had an obvious normative dimension, as this is the means through which the writer ensures that the characters' assessment is presented as objective, according to implicit shared values.

The importance accorded to political rumour in this situation needs to be highlighted, as it was one of the key elements in the narrated action.[17] The king took notice of the rumours that reached him, of the things that he was widely hearing about the conspiracy by the nobility, and sent his *mandaderos* ('messengers') to try to find out indirectly what was happening. He also ordered them to convey to the ringleaders of these noblemen his disbelief about what he had heard, and the seriousness of the situation if the rumours proved to be true. Given the intense exchange of oral and written messages, the importance of the messengers in this process cannot be overstated, as they clearly played a negotiating role in many cases.[18] Thus, the information the reader-listener received through these narrative forms made them a part of the climate of tension being conveyed, in preparation for them to share in

---

15 This group of wealthy men, led by the *infante* don Felipe, the king's brother, and don Nuño de Lara and don Lope Díaz de Haro, was also made up of the heads of other great families: don Esteban Fernández, don Fernando Ruiz de Castro, don Simón Ruiz de los Cameros, don Juan Nuñez and don Alvar Díaz. These are the ones that are mentioned in the different passages of the chronicle. On their identity and for explanatory notes regarding the events narrated, see the neat notes accompanying M. González Jiménez's edition of the chronicle.

16 'juntáronse todos en Lerma e fizieron pleyto e postura de se ayudar todos e ser contra el rey don Alfonso, destruyéndol en lo que pudiesen sy les non otorgase et cumpliese las cosas quel querían demandar' (CAX, p. 60 [76]).

17 'from so many regions [they] sent to warn him, telling him that the meeting was for his great harm and great disservice, that the king immediately sent his letters and his messenger' ('de tantas partes le enbiauan aperçebir diziendo que aquel ayuntamiento eran grand su danno e grand su deseruiçio que enbió luego sus cartas e su mandadero') (CAX, p. 62 [77]).

18 The king ordered that they 'speak with them on his behalf and to do whatever they could to make them desist from that uprising' ('fablasen con ellos de su parte e fiziesen quanto pudiesen por los quitar de aquel alboroço') (CAX, p. 85 [99]).

the emotional reactions of the characters in the story being narrated. The editor of the chronicle had good reason to note the journalistic character of the narrative.[19] However, it would be worth considering that the chronicle also echoes literary genres closer to the public, by using this type of resources to capture the awareness and understanding of the audience. Particularly telling was the message sent to don Nuño, in which the disbelief attributed to the king was related to the expectations of appropriate behaviour. In this regard, it is worth considering the normative nature of these expressions:

> And that because he thought that no other man should do more to protect the king's affairs that don Nuño, that he was so surprised about what they told him, and that it seemed to him so unreasonable he could not believe.[20]

The responses that the king gave, based on each of the reasons that he suspected were behind this *alboroço* ('restlessness') were normative in nature. If it was an attempt 'to frighten the king, he should know that one must not fear proudness and evil, but step up and prepare to confront them'.[21] If it was 'in order to have more goods than he already had, by serving the king he could quickly gain more'.[22] If it was done 'to please some others from the kingdom, he should know well that he would not receive from anyone as much good and as much assistance as from the king'.[23] A moral, and certainly political character, can also be seen when he concluded that 'and that for none of these reasons, nor any other, should he do such wrong against the king'.[24] And therefore, that 'he begged him as a friend and ordered him as a vassal to soften his heart and serve him as he had done before'.[25]

The chronicler does not always resort to this indirect means to discredit the nobles' claims and consequently to construct the figure of the monarch in a positive light. In some cases, he intervenes directly, such as when he reveals the true intentions of Don Nuño concealed behind his advice to the king that he should order the collection of yet another service both in Castile and the Extremaduras to appease some of the councils that 'andauan despagados' ('were unhappy'). The chronicler explains that:

> This [don Nuño] said for two reasons: one, in order to be able to sow enmity among those of the land, and the other, so that they could have money to be able to do what they had agreed to do.[26]

---

19 González Jiménez, *Crónica de Alfonso X*, p. xxxi.

20 'Et porque tenía que ningund omne non deuía fazer más por guardar el fecho del rey que aquel don Nunno, que era marauillado desto que le dezían, et tanto semejaua syn razón, que lo non podía creer' (CAX, pp. 63–64 [78]).

21 'poner miedo al rey, que sopiese que a grand tuerto e gran soberuia non deue onbre auer miedo, ante se deue esforçar e pararse a ello' (CAX, p. 65 [79]).

22 'aver dél más bien de quanto auía, que siruiéndolo podríe ganar más ayna' (CAX, p. 65 [79]).

23 'por fazer plazer a alguno otro del regno, que bien sabía él que de omne del mundo non resçebería tanto bien nin tanta ayuda commo del rey' (CAX, p. 65 [79]).

24 'por ninguna destas razones nin por otra non deuiera fazer tal yerro contra el rey'(CAX, p. 65 [79]).

25 'le rogaua como amigo e le mandaua commo a vasallo que sosegase el coraçón en lo seruir, asy como era tenudo de lo fazer' (CAX, p. 65 [79]).

26 'Et esto dezía él por dos cosas: lo vno por lo poner en enemistad con los de la tierra e lo otro porque

DESHEREDAMIENTO AND DESAFUERO   563

The narrative continues in this climate of constant double-dealing by the rebels, who on the one hand, sent a message to the king that he should believe 'that at no time had they served him in better fashion than then', and on the other, were engaged in causing 'great damage in the land'.[27] It shows how the king, despite warnings to the contrary, agreed to collect those monies, relying on the service that he had been promised. He expected to use them to go to the Empire, and also to maintain the defence of the border against the Moors of Granada. Alfonso X received the refusal of the rebels to provide this service, along with the demand that they had made for him to go to Castile to hear 'algunas cosas quel tenían que decir' ('some things they had to tell him').[28] This occurred at the same time as he had confirmation of the plot through some Arabic letters that were taken from don Nuño's squire, who was carrying them. In these letters, the king of Granada offered to each of these noblemen all the help that they might need in their fight.[29] That was when don Nuño's son informed him about the covenants they wanted to make with the king of Navarre. Alfonso X used this information to advise them, through his messengers, of the implications of such a covenant, invoking what undoubtedly should be seen as a shared political morality:

> on his behalf to tell [Prince Felipe and those noblemen] how the King of Navarre was his enemy and the enemy of the whole kingdom, and that with such a man they should not make a pact of agreement against their natural lord — they being his vassals and having from him the rents of his land — and because he gave them their sums, besides having with them a good friendship as they knew well. He begged that they would not refuse to do it.[30]

But the message this time, as happened later, was also aimed at the rebels' vassals:

> Also, he had the knights, his vassals, and all others who were with them instructed to consider what they were doing in that matter, for they knew well that it was against the loyalty to which they were bound and that they should preserve it.[31]

The answer sent by the noblemen again denied that these *posturas* ('agreements') were real, and also implicitly appealed to a common code that governed their relationships, referring to the usual forms of breaking the vassalage bonds:

---

ouiesen ellos dinero con que pudiesen fazer lo que tenían acordado' (CAX, p. 65 [79]).

27 'que en ningún tiempo nunca le siruier[an] de mejor mente que estonçe [...] muy gran danno a la tierra' (CAX, pp. 68–69 [82–83]).

28 CAX, p. 71 [85].

29 CAX, pp. 72–75 [86–88]. Of the eight letters that are said to have been intercepted, only four are presented as transcribed. Of the rest there is also a reference to a summary of them. Perhaps this is what González Jiménez means, even though he includes all of them in his list of documents.

30 'Que dixiesen de su parte [...] cómmo el rey de Nauarra era su enemigo e de todo el reyno e con tal omne non deuían poner pleyto nin postura contra su sennor natural seyendo ellos sus vasallos e teniendo dél las rentas de su tierra e dándoles él sus dineros, demás auiendo él con ellos buenos debdos asy como ellos saben, et que les rogaua que lo non quisyesen fazer' (CAX, p. 75 [89]).

31 'Otrosy enbió dezir e afrontar a los caualleros sus vasallos e a todos los otros que eran con ellos que catasen lo que fazían en aquel fecho, que bien entendían que era contra la lealtad a que eran tenudos e los deuían guardar' (CAX, p. 75 [89]).

He told [the king] that he knew well how don Nuño had agreements with him, and that he never made a pact with Christians nor Moors without letting him know it, and that until that time he had observed this.[32]

It should be noted how, by repeatedly denying the actions attributed to them, the nobles reaffirm the behaviour that they also deemed to be due and appropriate.[33] Don Nuño clearly emerged as the undisputed leader of the plot against the king, whom he continued to attract to Castile, by sending him the message that 'if he should do so, he would realise that no vassal ever gave better service or advice to his lord';[34] and in that way 'all the uproar and evil that were throughout the land would be removed'.[35] The promise made to the king that they would meet him to 'welcome him as their king and natural lord'[36] was part of a preamble that preceded the meeting where they presented the king with their demands. It was aimed at emphasising their violent behaviour, and again served to highlight the contrast with the way in which they received him, since the king was portrayed as finding that the nobles arrived:

> with a large number of mounted men [...] They all came armed and with a great crowd [...] they were not coming as men who go to their lord but like those who come to face their enemies [even if they kept] promising him many services.[37]

These rhetorical devices, therefore, showed how the noble demands, despite having initially been granted, would eventually be overturned.

In the negotiation process that began at that point, when the parties were already present in the same Castilian region, in Burgos, attention needs to be paid to both place and manners, as these were the elements used but the chronicler to discredit the claims of these magnates. Their demands about the meeting place, and their refusal to enter the city walls due to their suspicion of a potential hostile and repressive action by the king — which we are told was unfounded and seemed to be a projection of their own violence — thwarted the attempt by the king to reach an agreement, and therefore the rebels' strong position prevailed. Eventually the rebels managed to have their demands responded to in the *glera* ('gravelled area') of Burgos, a space outside

---

32   'E dixo al rey que bien sabía cómmo don Nunno auía posturas con él, que don Nunno nunca pusiese postura con christianos nin con moros que ante non gelo fiziese saber, et fasta entonçe que lo guardara' (CAX, p. 75 [89]).

33   By denying what they did by stating what they did not do, one of the ways in which the nobles sought to reassure the king of their loyalty was by fundamentally appealing to his judgment to resolve disputes (CAX, p. 61). This shows that they were fully aware of the meaning of this action because, even though it was a mere strategy, it involved accepting his authority and recognising his power.

34   'sy lo fiziese, que vería que nunca vasallo mejor seruiçio nin consejo dio a su sennor' (CAX, p. 75 [89]).

35   'se tirarían todos los bollyçios e males que andauan en la tierra' (CAX, p. 75 [89]).

36   'acogelle commo a su rey e su sennor natural' (CAX, p. 76 [91]).

37   'con muy grandes gentes de cauallo, e uenían todos armados e con gran asonada [...] no commo omnes que van a su sennor mas commo aquéllos que van a buscar sus enemigos, [aunque] continúen prometiéndol muchos seruiçios' (CAX, p. 77 [92]).

the city that was portrayed as being outside royal control. That was where the king replied to each of the petitions point by point:[38]

- that *hidalgos* be exempted from the *fueros* granted by the king to some towns;

- that Castilian mayors be appointed in his court to judge them;

- understanding of the problems that might result from *prohijamientos* or *profiliaciones* in favour of the royal family; inability to prohibit them as they were lawful (*de fuero*) and customary;

- acceptance of the amounts and ways to collect the rents that they demanded;

- that the *hidalgos* of Burgos be exempted from paying the *alcabala*;

- promise to monitor compliance with the obligations of royal *merinos* and tax collectors and to amend the damage they may have committed;

- referral of the decision about the problem of newly-founded royal *villae* to knights and clerics, as they also claimed to feel aggrieved on that account.

There were no more items on the list presented, but the king added another crucial concession:

- that the accusations made by the king against them would be judged by their peers, who were not linked to the parties at that time, according to the ancient *fuero* used by the preceding kings with their *hidalgos*.

Each of the king's responses was accompanied by comments justifying the issues that they had asked to be rectified, such as for example, when he explained in relation to royal *villae*: 'he would not order a town built on someone else's property and that if [he did so] on his own lands he would not encroach on anyone'.[39]

And when, even though he had agreed to appoint mayors from Castile, he noted that 'él traya buenos alcaldes' ('he had appointed capable [mayors]').[40] To some extent these expressions were intended to show that he agreed to meet their demands, but was not satisfied with the reasons behind them. This justification was most clear in the last royal reason introduced by the narrator at the end of the specific answers for the demands. In this, the narrator refers the claims made against the king and his reputation for being lavish, which were based on two aspects of his policy — namely that 'the king was impoverishing the land by giving wealth to men of other kingdoms and also for the matter concerning the empire'[41] — which he links to some prior episodes of the rebellion already mentioned. The king counters the argument explaining that if he made donations to men from other lands:

---

38 CAX, pp. 78–82 [95–97]. Some of these petitions were analysed in detail in Escalona, 'Los nobles contra su rey'.

39 'que él non mandara fazer puebla en heredat agena, e que faziéndolo él en lo suyo non desaforaua a ninguno' (CAX, p. 81 [96]).

40 CAX, p. 80 [95].

41 'que el rey enpobrescié la tierra dando algos a las gentes de otros reinos et otrosí por lo del Inperio' (CAX, p. 83 [96]).

it was to bring honour to the people of his kingdoms, and that because of it, those of his realm were the most loved and valued men of his realm that ever lived in the whole world, and concerning the empire, the king informed them that [...] he would pursue this for the honour of his realm.[42]

The purpose of this self-representation as a good king was explicit: to invoke the help of this magnates in the imperial election, from which they would also benefit. It constitutes, therefore, a political legitimation of his claim to the Empire based on the appeal to the general good, and particularly to that of the nobles. Even more importantly, the chronicler has the king say that the good he wanted to achieve could not take place without the support of the high nobility. This could certainly be understood as a rhetorical strategy for rallying their support, and therefore as the realisation of a noble political ideal: 'he begged them not to allow such a good king to have such ill fortune, for he wished to do good, but he did not have [anyone] with whom to accomplish it'.[43]

This is followed by the expression of a political reciprocity that articulates a significant proportion of the contents of the chronicle, at least in this part:

For they knew well that there never had been a king in this land who had done so much good and so much favour to them as he had, and that they never were as wealthy or as well supplied, nor possessed as many horses or as many weapons as they did during his time.[44]

On behalf of all involved, don Nuño communicated the overall satisfaction with the king's words and the agreement to accept his answer and place themselves in his service: 'they were very pleased with what he said. They said that because of this, they were obliged to serve the king wherever he ordered them',[45] although they asked for mercy 'that he assembled Cortes and told them those things in Cortes.[46] Thus, it seemed that an assembly of this type, to be held in the city of Burgos some months later to publicly and ritually ratify the solution, would bring these tough political negotiations to a close peacefully and surprisingly easily. However, the circumstances to be described below break with the logic that presides over the previous narrative, in an exaggerated effort to delegitimise the nobles' behaviour. The chronicler presented such behaviour as being excessive and irrational, as they demanded that a truce be signed which would allow them to attend those Cortes,

---

42 'que lo fazía por la honra de las gentes de sus regnos, e por esto que más amados e más presçiados eran los del su regno en todo el mundo que nunca fueran; y en lo relativo al fecho del Inperio, que por la honra de los sus regnos lo siguiera' (CAX, p. 83 [96]).

43 'les rogaua que non quisiesen que seyendo él buen rey fuese de mala ventura que quería fazer bien e non tenía con quien' (CAX, p. 83 [96]).

44 'ca bien sabían que nunca ouiera rey en esta [tierra] que tanto bien e tanta merçet les fiziese commo les él auia fecho, nin fueron nunca tan ricos nin tan abondados nin ouieron tantos cauallos nin tantas armas [commo] en su tiempo' (CAX, p. 83 [96]).

45 'que eran muy pagados con lo que les dizié e que por aquello sennaladamente eran tenudos de le seruir doquier que les él mandase' (CAX, p. 84 [97]).

46 'mandase ayuntar Cortes e que aquellas cosas que gelas dixese por Cortes' (CAX, p. 84 [97]).

alleging that they were fearful of the *infantes* and of the noblemen who came with the king.[47] Further demands were added, to which the king responded in the same conciliatory tone as before. The motivations of the rebels became unintelligible, especially their final reaction to not compromise and to leave the Cortes, and their subsequent exile. In this way, we are informed that 'all of those who were assembled there understood that [the king] was just and lawful and that don Felipe and those noblemen were causing the uprising unjustly'.[48] It has been interpreted that the king's reply is an attempt to negotiate rather than just to give in to everything they asked for. He is depicted as trying to appease them, hence the continuous messages of mediation that he sent them, but he insisted on the obligation to acknowledge political reciprocity: 'he begged they should preserve their service and the [king's] right in all things'.[49] In the narrative, the moral image of the king, but not his power, emerges stronger from the *Cortes*, in which he also had to face the, according to the chronicle, opportunist demands of the bishops, as he is presented fighting against the members of the assembly for 'he thought was of benefit for his kingdom'.[50]

Desheredamiento and *Desafuero*

The block of ten chapters that follows, which narrates the reaction of the king to the break-up promoted by the nobles, is without doubt one of the most interesting part of the *Chronicle*. This is due to the fact that the messages which open and close this set, which were sent to each of the noblemen involved, starting with his brother the *infante* don Felipe and two groups of their vassals, appear to have been transcribed in their entirety. The content and style of this block presents the royal policies in a personalised manner, conveying and furthering the image of the good king in contrast with an evildoing high nobility. If it were true that this part was written still within the reign of Alfonso X, it would seem to be the assessment of a king complaining about the negative response to his good political work, although this content could also apply to other similar situations. The analysis below will be focused on this highly interesting material.

Those who left the kingdom were presented as following the chivalric 'farewell' ritual, but not the chivalric behaviour, since they did not respect the truce granted and when they left they inflected many wrongs in the land. They were quickly sent emissaries from the king to give them his message. The alleged official character that has been attributed to these documents, of being *cartas regias* ('royal charters') that were copied and integrated into the story, seems to have given them a status of

---

47 This statement alone should serve to avoid the temptation to see the conflict as one between nobility and monarchy, fought between two completely separate entities.

48 'todos los que estauan y entendieron que él [rey] tenía razón e derecho, e que don Felipe e aquellos ricos omnes fazían aquel alboroço con muy gran synrazón' (CAX, p. 89 [101]).

49 'les rogaua, pues él quería guardar sus fueros e derechos, que guardasen ellos a él su sennorío e su derecho en todas las cosas' (CAX, p. 90 [101]).

50 'lo que entendió que era pro de su regno' (CAX, p. 92 [104]).

being unquestionably true, a different authority than that given to other information. However, and despite the arguable distinction regarding the credibility of each of the materials, what is presented in these chapters of the chronicle as being transcriptions, are not royal letters, as has been claimed, but the messages transmitted by the king through his messengers.[51] These messengers had letters of credence authorising them to speak on his behalf, and to deliver the message that they had been entrusted with.[52] There was no difference from the messages exchanged before, which structured both the narrative and, to some extent, the negotiations between the rebels and the king. Nevertheless, in this section of the chronicle, the messages are particularly important largely due to the nature of documentary records that has been attributed to them in the historiography.[53]

In my opinion, referring to them as 'letters' has prevented further analysis of the oral structures of these texts, and the communication schemas contained within them. Therefore, more important than discussing whether these messages reproduced existing charters in the royal chamber that the chronicler simply reproduced, is to address the various forms and content of political communication that is presented here as being feasible, and hence, credible. It does not much matter if they are regarded as being mere stylistic resources, simple strategies to give an aura of authenticity to the narrative. It is true that the king is never present, but reading the text of a letter from him is not the same as orally transmitting his message. The communication conveyed in this case was susceptible of being redesigned and reinterpreted, as well and verbally qualified by those charged with delivering it, even if we assume that they were most literal in the reproduction of the content as prescribed by the king.[54] But above all, it was an oral communication style, with the full meaning this has in terms of its rhetorical effects, that is, the very process of receiving it.

It is important, therefore, to consider the way in which these messages from the king were received. Except for two of them, they were personally targeted to each of the noblemen leading the protest, including particular details of the relationship each had

---

51 This is made clear from the titles of each chapter: 'Of the explanations that King Alfonso's knights told' ('De las razones que los mensajeros del rey dixeron'); 'at his bidding' ('de parte del rey'); 'King Alfonso's' ('de don Alfonso').

52 In my opinion, the confusion to which I am referring is due to the fact that the 'letters of credence' with which the messengers are provided so that their message is believed are taken for the message that it is ordered for them to transmit. The credence that such letters confers those who bear them is not always enough, as the example of the Jewish envoy sent by don Nuño shows: 'But the king refused to believe it, since it was being said by that Jew. A day later, a cleric from the Church of Burgos named Pedro Jaime came and brought another letter of credence from don Nuño and told him the very same thing' ('Et el rey non gelo quiso creer por quanto gelo dezía aquel judío. E luego otro día legó y vn clérigo de la iglesia de Burgos que dezían Pero Jaymes et traxo otra carta de creencia de don Nunno e díxol aquella mesma razón') (CAX, p. 71 [86]).

53 A. Ballesteros Beretta refers to them as judicial letters in Ballesteros Beretta, *Alfonso X el Sabio*. F. Gómez Redondo qualifies this as 'a very rich letters collection' in Gómez Redondo, 'De la crónica general a la real', p. 112. Pérez-Prendes speaks of them as a 'collection of political letters' and M. González Jiménez includes them in his aforementioned list of charters.

54 The prominent role played in political negotiation by these messengers, generally eminent nobles, has been mentioned earlier.

DESHEREDAMIENTO AND DESAFUERO 569

with the king. Consequently, one might think that that they were individually received, as what the emissaries conveyed to each magnate seemed to include considerations that were only intended to be communicated privately and individually. Some data, however, suggests the messages were received collectively, as reference is made to summaries of the content delivered to others: 'we say that it is you […] according to what we have already told each one of the others', and to what the king said 'to all of us together'.[55] This is beyond doubt in the first message that was addressed to the group, and the reproach that affected everyone was heard by all. Since the messages were formalised as a royal, highly-personalised reply to the nobles' claims, recognising the public nature of the communication and the political debate that the reader is a witness to, is of great importance in understanding the rhetorical strategies and normative standards used by each party to 'formalise' their own demands.[56] The large space given by the anonymous chronicler to the king's arguments is a clear sign of the effect intended, as in this way it is the monarch's version of the situation which prevails. In addition, to also understand the importance of distinguishing between different forms of communication, it will suffice to observe how it is assumed throughout the chronicle that the practical implications of what is said publicly in council are different from those arising from what is spoken in secret. These two areas are clearly differentiated, despite the possible connection between them. A very explicit example of what a public hearing demanded is in the case of don Juan Nuñez, son of the lord of Lara, who only privately declared that the king was in the right. He apologised to the king for having followed his father, although in the message he received what the narrator/ envoy/king highlighted/reproached the most was his 'treacherous' behaviour, as the king had confided secrets to him during the negotiations of this matter:

> and for this reason he is surprised that this was the motive for which you parted from him; particularly because in this matter of the noblemen, he confided in you, for you were a messenger between them and him. He also thought that you would serve him in this and that you would not disservice him with them.[57]

In the same vein, it should be remembered how the noblemen had asked the king to confirm their demands in the *Cortes*, with its two-fold meaning, institutional and public. Also of note is the awareness that honour and reputation, each person's

---

55 'dezimos que vos […] segunt que auemos dicho a cada vno de los otros […] a todos en uno e a cada uno por sy'. This expression can certainly be confusing, but I interpret it as referring to the content of the messages, either in general or in particular. The collective reception of these can also be deduced from the fact that all of them withdrew together to deliberate after having heard them: 'After Prince Felipe, the noblemen, and the knights had heard what the king's messengers told them, they withdrew in order to reach an agreement' ('Después quel infante don Felipe e los ricos omnes e los caualleros ouieron aydo lo que les dixieron mandaderos del rey, apartáronse auer su acuerdo') (CAX, p. 112 [128]).

56 On formalising practices, see Bourdieu, *El sentido práctico*, pp. 184–85; Roberts and Comaroff, *Rules and Processes*, pp. 70–106. S. White's use of these approaches is particularly interesting, for which see White, 'Strategie rhétorique'.

57 'Et por esto se maravilla qué fue esto que vos enbiastes partir dél, sennaladamente porque en este fecho de los ricos omnes vos metié en su poridat e érades mandadero entre él e ellos, e de uos ternié quel vernié seruiçio en esto e que non le faríedes deseruiçio con ellos' (CAX, p. 109 [124]). It has to be remembered that the son of don Nuño featured as royal envoy in the initial negotiations.

fame, was built through what was said collectively. Looking, then, at these ways and means of communication, and the flow of information,[58] which were also avenues for dispute and negotiation in times of political struggle, is essential to evaluate the material used, because it was well known that communicative intent influenced the narrative then, as it does now: 'say words in such a manner that a man can make those who listen to him believe in what he is saying'.[59] Alfonso X seemly aimed to convince his audience.[60] This audience is reproduced as his message also does in both time and space, because it even appears to reach to the present time, if we observe the involvement of some historians in the debate. It is true that the monarch's immediate objective was to attract these nobles back to his court so as to carry out his imperial project. But beyond this first level, which needed to be surpassed, these messages had a wider political significance. They possessed the quality of direct speech, as if they were addressed to a meeting at which he was present, which was to issue a judgment on the facts that were presented on the dispute being debated. The arguments appealed and referred to some normative standards and moral values that those present understood and shared. And this way of acting and arguing was a feature of the *modus operandi* of medieval justice, one of the most common ways of resolving conflicts. Hence, perhaps, the similarity to the stories found in many *fazañas* ('judicial rulings'), or to the type of exemplary stories that were inserted in chronicles. Further research along these lines would be required to confirm or rectify this working hypothesis, but this is beyond the scope of this charter.

This Alphonsine claim that his reasons are convincing is not trivial, taking into account the way in which his policies were being challenged. Hence the interest in analysing the type of problems that are discussed in this material and the arguments used to do so, especially considering that the most formalised demands made by the noblemen, did not merit such large argumentative development and, as we have seen, were granted as formulated with only minor comments. This narrative style cannot be incidental and was certainly aimed to affect those who read it or heard it in specific ways. But this does not imply that there were not variations in the royal means of communication depending on the forum where they were to be delivered.[61] It would be worth making a contrasted analysis of how the dispute was submitted in each of the different contexts, as a way of understanding the meaning of the different representations of the same events in different situations and circumstances, though this is not our goal here.[62]

---

58 I have addressed these problems on the flow of information and building reputation in Alfonso, 'Venganza y justicia' [Editors' note: For an English translation, see chapter 5 of this volume].

59 'dezir palabras en tal manera que onbre faga creer sus dichos a aquellos que los oyen'. This is a quote by Bruneto Latini contained in Gómez Redondo, *Historia de la prosa medieval 2*, p. 1326. We owe F. Gómez Redondo a splendid analysis of the work of this author and of the meaning of its reception in the Castilian court, for which see Gómez Redondo, *Historia de la prosa medieval 1*, pp. 863–90.

60 The whole structure of the chronicle is aimed to this end, according to Gómez Redondo, *Historia de la prosa medieval 2*, p. 1267.

61 Bloch, *Political Language*.

62 For such a contrast, see Alfonso and Jular Pérez-Alfaro, 'Oña contra Frías'.

DESHEREDAMIENTO AND *DESAFUERO*   571

These messages are truly exceptional pieces, possibly from more points of view than have been pointed out. Through them, Alfonso X, as the wise, literate king that he was, not only accused the group of barons (whose demands he had agreed to shortly before when the *Cortes* were convened) of bad behaviour, but he did so by appealing to a moral and legal code that they seemed to share. They all have the same narrative structure. The king began by reflecting the reasons given by the noblemen for leaving his service before going into exile, and denied them with references to the story of the special relationship he had had with each of them. At the same time, he offered his version of how the conflict had progressed so far, and the facts that had been known in the previous chapters, although not in the same way. In this manner, two of the reasons adduced by the nobles for abandoning the king's service became known, as they were repeated at the beginning of each message, so the king's plea was given unusual prominence: *desheredamiento* and *desafuero*.[63] These two negative notions seemed to concentrate much of the nobles' political thinking about the good and fair government claimed. One referred to personal situations: their patrimonies in the broadest sense: '*desheredamiento* you have received from him' ('deseredamiento que vos fazía'), claimed don Felipe; '[the king] had you *deseredado* and was not granting you the land that your father and your grandfather used to hold',[64] had been don Lope's justification. The other referred to a general situation: the kingdom and the law: 'And this is why you say that the king encroached upon the rights of Castile and León and why you were leaving him',[65] or similar phrases. Since the king, through his messengers, discussed the content of the claims against him on an individual basis, and given that these speeches show how both of the above claims intersected, some of the issues that arose in this dialogue in relation to the existence or not of political conceptions of nobility and monarchy held by each of the parties can be explored.

What did the noblemen understand by *desheredamiento*, or rather, when and why did they consider themselves to be *desheredados*? What kind of assets were affected by this royal measure? The term *desheredar* here seems to refer to inherited assets that they would have been dispossessed of, or that would have been expropriated without cause. Therefore, this term states that the king had failed to comply with one of his duties towards such great vassals. Thus, the *infante* don Felipe argued that 'that [the king] *deseredaua* you, particularly of the *infantadgo* in the land of Léon',[66] a reason also used by don Fernando Ruiz de Castro — 'that you were abandoning him because [the king] had him *deseredado* of the *infantazgo* of the territory of León'.[67] Both magnates received the same response from the king. As he let them know that this estate had been entered, that is, appropriated, without his knowledge, at the command of his son don Fernando, due to the *profiliación* that Queen doña Mencía

---

63   On the effects of this narrative style see White, 'Strategie rhétorique', p. 148.
64   'que porque vos tenía deseredado e non vos daua aquella tierra que solía tener vuestro padre e vuestro avuelo' (CAX, p. 102 [116]).
65   'e porque dezíades que el rey desaforó Castilla e León que vos partides dél' (CAX, p. 102 [116]).
66   'quel rey uos deseredaua, sennaladamente del infantadgo de tierra de León' (CAX, p. 97 [110]).
67   'que porque él vos teníe deseredado del infantazgo de tierra de León, que uos partiedes dél' (CAX, p. 106 [120]).

of Portugal had made on his behalf at the time of her death. In this case, the problem seems that the hereditary expectations they both had as political relatives of the Haro family — to which doña Mencía belonged — had been thwarted. This was due to the legal mechanism that entitled them to *prohijar* and therefore bequeath property to whomever they wished. The removal of this right, it should be remembered, was one of the nobles' demands, although they presented it as a general grievance: 'The other reason for which they perceived themselves to be wronged was due to the *prohijamientos* that the king and his sons received from the noblemen, because they remained *deseredados*.[68] And the king had answered them 'it was law and custom for men to *prohijar* whoever they wished and that in this he could not remove the right his sons had',[69] although he had personally waived his right to it. This issue shows the old recurring problems and tensions that surrounded the distribution and transmission of patrimony within these social groups.

The argument given by don Nuño for abandoning the king's service was that the land granted by the king to him had been taken away from him when he was still in royal service, that is, without cause: 'because while you were serving at Málaga, he took away the land you held from him'.[70] The king's response, after enumerating the countless favours he had granted to don Nuño, was that 'he never took it from you, but instead he increased it so much that there never was a wealthier man in Spain who held so much land from his king or lord'.[71] In this case it should be noted that there was no mention of *deheredar* but rather of *toller* ('to take away'), which seemed to refer to concessions, that is, not *heredades*, but *tenencias*. But the result was to place the king's good behaviour in opposition to that of the bad noble.

Don Lope Díaz justified his abandoning the king's service by saying:

> [that the king] had him *deseredado* and was not granting you the land that your father and your grandfather used to hold, you considered yourself even more [dishonoured], although not [deprived of] the land that your father had left you.[72]

Clearly, the response transmitted in the royal message may lead to the assumption that his arguments were likely to be more detailed, as Orduña y Balmaseda were mentioned as the specific *heredades* referred to in the *desheredamiento* claim. This time the king did not deny the fact, but placed the responsibility on the shoulders of don Lope, since 'it is the law in Castile that if anyone wages war against the king and harms the land

---

68 'E la otra razón por que se tenían por agrauiados era de los porfijamientos que el rey e sus fijos reçebían de los ricos omnes e de los fijosdalgo, por que fincauan deseredados' (CAX, p. 78 [95]).

69 'fuero era et costumbre de porfijar los omnes a quien quisiesen, et que en esto non podía él toller el derecho que sus fijos auían' (CAX, p. 78 [95]).

70 'porque vos, seyendo en su seruiçio en Málaga, que tolliera la tierra que dél teníedes' (CAX, p. 99 [112]).

71 'nunca vos lo tollió ante vos lo cresçió todavía tanto que nunca fue rico omne en Espanna que tanta tierra ouiese del rey o de sennor' (CAX, p. 101 [114]).

72 'que le tenía deseredado e non vos daua aquella tierra que solía tener vuestro padre e vuestro avuelo, que vos teníades por más desonrado avn que non de la heredad que vos dexara vuestro padre' (CAX, p. 102 [117]).

DESHEREDAMIENTO AND DESAFUERO   573

on account of a gift he has granted, then the king is lawfully allowed to seize it'.[73] The king denounced in great detail the actions committed by this member of the Haro family in this land, and therefore ordered that the following message be delivered to him: 'but you *deseredastes* yourself and those who hold you under their authority and protection, for the king could not avoid doing what was lawful and just'.[74]

In this case there seems to be an implicit distinction between *heredades propias* and royal donation. The fact that they were not called *tenencias* like those of don Nuño may indicate that there were different types of concessions. It could be related to the fact that they were donated *iure hereditario* ('with hereditary rights'), and yet they seemed to have a different character from those of family inheritance. However, they could also be a kind of royal concession which, while retaining such status, was assumed to pass from parents to their children, provided that no problems arose. Don Esteban Fernández did not speak of *desheredamiento* either, but he equally alleged personal reasons that affected both his economic situation and his political capital: 'it had been a long time since he gave you your monies, and because he kept you away from your wife, Aldonza Rodríguez',[75] facts that the king denied by stating that many favours had been granted to him. As with don Nuño, don Alvar Díaz's reason for leaving the king's service had been that the land granted to him had been taken away for no reason. The response sent by Alfonso X was along the same lines, it is the breach of the pact of service involved in royal favours — 'you go to disservice him in a very bad mode and in a very wrong manner'[76] – that he reproached, and the reason why he had lost his land. Again, the king's argument invoked a clear political reciprocity that had not been fulfilled, because in this case:

> and [the king] had pleasure in favouring you when [you loved him] with service as you should. Before, you promised him that you would serve him because you had his love and grace.[77]

There was, then, a repeated appeal to a moral and legal order, an exchange of political love and favours for love and services that were also of a political nature.[78]

Certainly the obligations expected and demanded by the king, which his discourse assumes to be intrinsic to his power and prestige, included inheriting from his vassals, raising them, marrying them off, granting them money from the royal revenues,[79] mediating their conflicts, judging and punishing their *malfetrías*

---

73 'fuero es de Castilla que si de la donaçión que el rey da, le fazen guerra e mal en la tierra, que la pueda tomar con fuero e con derecho' (CAX, p. 104 [117]).
74 'uos mesmo vos deseredastes et aquéllos que vos tenían en poder et en guarda, ca el rey non pudo escusar de fazer lo que era fuero e derecho' (CAX, p. 104 [117–18].
75 'que porque auía grant tiempo que uos non diera vuestros dineros e porque vos tenía a Aldonça Rodríguez vuestra esposa por fuerça' (CAX, p. 107 [122]).
76 'ese deseruir en muy mal son e en muy mala manera' (CAX, p. 110 [125]).
77 'él auié sabor de uos fazer bien quando vos lo amásedes con seruiçio así commo deuédes, ante le prometiestes quel seruiríedes porque oviésedes su amor e su merçed' (CAX, p. 110 [125]).
78 On 'political love' see the very interesting contribution Martin, 'Amour'.
79 The king thus states when he is blamed of *desaforar* Castile and León that 'he does not do it, nor is it his will to do it, for he favours and has favoured in his court many men of noble descent, and he

('evil-doings'), etc. The monarch's messages are excellent sources of information, because in describing his relationships with each of the noblemen that they were directed to, they emphasised the personal ties and the specific favours and honours that each had received. Thus special focus was placed on the *debdos* ('obligations') that each of them had contracted, making their behaviour even more reprehensible and unjustifiable, which aggravated the acts that they had committed.

It is in the messages to don Nuño de Lara and to don Lope Díaz de Haro, the heads of the two main noble factions — traditionally in confrontation but now acting together — where the emphasis on the uniqueness of the favours received was mostly placed, not only in terms of quantity, but also in terms of their context and how they were granted. The king's relationship with don Nuño was presented as having been very close since childhood, as they grew up together and when he was still *infante* he had protected him, even against the wishes of his father, and also helped his allies, preventing the repression that their uprising and the *deservicio* ('disservice') would have deserved. The king also granted him favours against his father's will. He had don Nuño accepted into the royal circle, knighted him and arranged his marriage.[80] Not only that, when Alfonso X was still *infante* he had supported don Nuño, both in

---

arranged marriages for them, made them knights, granted them lands and did many good things for them, more than any other king who was in Spain until his time' ('non lo faze nin es su voluntat de lo fazer, mas crió e cría en su casa muchos fijosdalgo e dióles casamientos e fízolos caualleros e heredólos e fízoles mucho bien, más que otro rey en Espanna fuese fasta en el su tiempo') (CAX, p. 104 [118]).

80 'You know that you received from him much honour and favour, more than any man of your station ever received from any other king. For being a child, you grew up with him, and being Prince, when he began to rule, because of the love he felt for you, he placed Gonzalo Nuño, your brother, under his protection and favour. When king Fernando refused to make you a knight or give you land and had no wish to do you good but instead wanted to harm you and all your lineage, Count Fernando and Count Álvaro, your uncles, and Count Gonzalo, your father, who lived when he began to rule, rebelled and waged a great war against him. But King Alfonso, as a prince, gave you Écija contrary to his father's will, which you held through him, and it was the first thing King Fernando gave his son in Andalusia, being a prince. The first time that King Alfonso went to the kingdom of Murcia, being a prince, he granted you land and later on pleaded and asked King Fernando, his father, to give other holdings, to make you a knight, and to give you in marriage doña Teresa Alfonso, his first cousin and granddaughter of the King of León. And King Fernando, because of his son's plea, granted against his will these favours to you' ('Et vos sabedes que del rey resçebistes mucha honra e mucha merçet, más que nunca reçibió en Espanna omne de la vuestra guisa de otro rey, ca, seyendo él ninno, criástesvos con él, e seyendo él infante, quando començó a tener casa, por lo vuestro tomó en su casa e en la su merçet a Gonçalo Núnnez, vuestro hermano. E el rey don Fernando non vos quería fazer cauallero nin daruos tierra nin auía voluntad de fazer[vos] bien, ante quería mal a vos e a todo vuestro linaje por quel conde don Fernando e el conde don Aluaro, vuestros tíos, et el conde don Gonçalo, vuestro padre, que era quando él començó a regnar, se le alçaron e le desiruieron mucho faziéndole grant guerra. Et el rey don Alfonso seyendo infante, contra voluntad de su padre, dio a vos don Nunno a Éçija que la touiésedes por él, que fue la primera cosa quel rey don Fernando le dio en el Andaluzía seyendo infante. Et la primera vez que el rey don Alfonso fue al regno de Murçia, seyendo infante, dióvos heredat. E después rogó e pidió al rey don Ferrando, su padre, que vos diese tierra et vos fiziese cauallero et vos diese en casamiento a donna Teresa Alfonso, su cormana, nieta del rey de León. Et el rey don Ferrando, por ruego del rey don Alfonso su fijo, fízouos estas merçedes muy contra su voluntat') (CAX, p. 99 [112]).

the dispute over an *heredamiento* with the father of don Lope, his current ally, even though he knew that the claim was illegal, as in the revolts he led in Castile.[81] These benefits granted to don Nuño — he reminded him — increased when he became king to such an extent that the leader of the Haros asked many times 'not to do it, for everything he did for you was to his disadvantage'.[82] So many favours were granted to him in income, land and services that don Diego de Haro left the kingdom because this was 'an honour to you and a very great loss for [don Diego]', and he could never have him in his service, and moreover 'he did him disservice [...] with all of those he understood wished to harm the king'.[83] Reference is clearly made here to favourable treatment and political exclusion as being inherent to the dynamics of power, which the king in his message insisted on bringing to don Nuño's attention: 'you should understand how much the King did for you in losing someone like don Diego in order to make you the best in his kingdom'.[84]

This dynamic that should not be forgotten when explaining the processes of internal political competition in which these magnates were involved, which was derived from their limited political resources and their forms of access and allocation. The accuracy of the data contained in the messages is less interesting than the certainty or likelihood of the processes involved.

In the same way, in his message to don Lope, the king also reminded him of important aspects of the personal relationship between them: how after the death of his father he was welcomed into his home despite his father's disservice; he knighted him with great honour and gave him a lot of money on the wedding day of his son,

---

81 'Afterward, you started a dispute with don Diego concerning the estate of La Montaña. And notwithstanding that King Alfonso knew that you were wrongly demanding it, he behaved with you in such a fashion that the estate remained yours, worrying his father, because King Alfonso favoured you more than anything else. After this, you, don Nuño, brought your conniving to Castile, and King Alfonso, being a prince, gave you so many friends in that time that you preserved your honour' ('Et después tomastes contienda con don Diego sobre eredamiento de la Montanna, et commo quier que sabía el rey don Alfonso que vos lo demandáuades con tuerto, pero tóuose conbusco de manera que la heredat fincó vuestra, pesando al rey su padre. En que tobo que vos fizo merçet más que en ninguna otra cosa. Et después desto, vos don Nunno ouiestes vuestras asonadas en Castiella et tantos amigos vos dio el rey don Alfonso en aquel tiempo, seyendo infante, que vos fincastes en vuestra honra').

82 'merçed que lo non fiziese, ca todo lo que en vos fazía era desfallesçimiento dél' (CAX, p. 99 [113]).

83 'muy grant honra para vos e muy grant quebranto para él [...] le deseruio [...] con todos aquellos quél entendió que querían mal al rey' (CAX, pp. 99–100 [113]).

84 'deuiedes entender quánto fizo el rey por vos en perder tal omne como don Diego por fazer a uos el mejor de su regno' (CAX, pp. 100 [113]). Other favours are also listed, including some that had called into question the king's prestige such as granting land to sons in the lifetime of their father: 'In your time, the king gave land to your sons don Juan Núñez and Nuño González, and to grant holdings to the sons while the father still lived was something that was never done during the time of any other king, and many from the kingdom had much to say about this' ('Et en el vuestro tiempo dio el rey tierra a vuestros fijos don Juan Núnnez e Nunno Gonçález, lo cual ante nunca fue fecho en tiempo de ningunt rey que en vida del padre diese tierra a los fijos. E desto ouieron los del regno mucho que dezir') (CAX, p. 100 [113]). Ultimately, the honour and the favours were so many that 'you were the most powerful and honourable man that any lord had in all of Spain' ('vos erades el más poderoso omne que sennor ouiesse e mas honrado de Espanna') (CAX, p. 101 [114]).

the *infante* don Fernando.[85] But he highlighted, above all, how he had supported him in the dispute against don Nuño over Durango and Vizcaya, to the point of offending don Nuño; therefore, his greatest favour was to make enemies in order to help him.[86] It is shown how the help given in this case by the king to don Lope worked in the opposite way to the support provided to don Nuño with his father, although in both cases the claim of don Nuño was said to have been unlawful. This data shows how these different actions seemed to be strategies of convenience accorded to various specific situations rather than to follow abstract ethical or legal principles. They spoke of experiences of hostilities and reconciliations between kings and noble families, of how inherited enmities could be maintained or forgiven as appropriate. This is where, in my opinion, the chronicler may have made good use of his great political experience and knowledge.

Desafuero, the other major reason given by the noblemen as justification for their break with the king and exile was not raised as a personal issue, but as an action that affected the kingdom. What were the acts that nobles considered to be *desafuero*? What was the *fuero* that they invoked to define them as such? Did the monarch allude to a different *fuero*? The term *fuero* in the texts of the period was certainly, even in strictly legal terms, one of the most flexibly used and with the most varied semantic content. Hence the interest in exploring its meaning within specific contexts, and analysing its ability to articulate opposing arguments that enabled its strategic manipulation. What follows is to be understood as an approach along these lines, which should be contrasted with many other texts.

Alfonso X's brother, don Felipe, had sent a message to the king to inform him that he was abandoning his service due to the *desafueros* that the king did in the land. Alfonso X in his defence, alluded and admitted to the possible *desaguisados*

---

85 'Don Lope Díaz, you know how many favours he did you, for when your father, don Diego, died — notwithstanding that he was doing disservice to the king — you came to him later on and he welcomed you in his home; and he honoured you much and commanded that on his wedding day his son Prince Fernando make you a knight; and he gave you much honour and money, which he ordered given to you each year' ('Don Lope Díaz, vos sabedes quantas merçedes vos fizo ca quando murió don Diego vuestro padre, commo quier que él andaua en deseruiçio del rey, luego vos venistes a él et tomóvos en la su casa et tráxovos mucho honradamiente et fizo al infante don Fernando su fijo que vos fiziese cauallero en el día de sus bodas e dióvos mucha honra et muchos dineros que vos puso para de cada anno') (CAX, pp. 102–03 [116]).

86 'So many favours and so much help the king did for you in this that it is one of the major complaints don Nuño holds against the king' ('E tanta merçet e tanta ayuda vos fizo el rey en esto, que vna de las mayores querellas que don Nunno ha del rey es ésta') (CAX, p. 103 [116]). The king justifies this help as a defence of the rights of a minor under his protection before a forceful action against the latter. He further presents himself as fostering peaceful rather than violent means to settle disputes, as he adds that he had told don Nuño 'to demand the land from you, as he should, and said he would make just payment to don Nuño on your behalf. The king would not allow that he use force against you, being young and in his power. On this account you received Vizcaya, because if he had not protected it for you, you would have lost hereditary right to it. In this and in other things the king did much good and honour' ('que vos demandase commo deuía et que faría de uos conplimiento de derecho, mas que non consentié que vos fiziese fuerça seyendo vos pequenno e estando en su poder. Et por esto ouiestes vos a Viscaya, ca si él non vos la guardara, deseredado fuérades della. Et en esto e en otras cosas vos fizo él mucho bien e mucha honra') (CAX, p. 103 [116–17]).

(‘wrongdoings’) of his officers, which he had already had amended. Are these the acts that the *infante* thought were *desafueros*? For the king, *desafueros* were those committed by the *infante*, and he proceeded to list them: he had stolen and taken everything he could from the *hidalgos* and townsmen, as well as from monasteries and religious orders; he had also refused to give him the service due resulting from the favours and monies conceded; he had made a pact with the king's worst enemy; and ultimately all the actions that he had been involved in,[87] because 'in all of these things you *desaforades* the land and you *deseredades* yourself, and he did not *desafura* you nor *desereda* you'.[88] Don Nuño had also given orders for the king to be told that he would be leaving his service 'because he [*desaforaua*] Castile and León'.[89] The royal response, which sought to turn the accusation back on don Nuño, provided a more specific description of the term *desafuero* than his previous message to don Felipe. This description was expressed very forcefully by the envoy, who referred to the illegal

---

87 'Regarding what you told the king, that he breached the customs of [desaforaba] Castile and León, he never did it nor was it his will to do it; and even if any of his officers committed any wrong, he always regretted it and exiled that officer for it. But you, sir Prince Felipe, illegally deprived the kingdoms of Castile and León, stealing and seizing from those of noble descent and from townsmen and monasteries of the Orders all you could seize. And besides the king's doing these favours and these honours, and giving you sums from his rents so that you could serve him wherever he ordered you to do it, and having sent word to you that he was in need of your service in the war against the Moors and that you should go to be with Prince Fernando, his son, you refused to do it. Now he orders you to return the sums that you took from him and the land that you hold from him, that you send him guarantors for the crimes you committed in the land; and if not, he considers that you were disobedient; and because of what you have said, he cannot avoid what is the law in Castile. Moreover, he sends words that they told him you were going to the kingdom of Granada to be on its side, knowing that the King of Granada is the enemy of God and of the Faith, and of the king and his kingdoms, and the enemy of all of noble descent who there are in Castile and León, and of all of those from these other kingdoms. And you, being the son of King Fernando and of Queen Beatriz, and brother of King Alfonso, he considers that you ought to protect better the lineage from which you come and the duty you have toward him' ('Et lo que enbiastes dezir quel rey desaforaua Castilla e León, nunca lo él fizo nin fue su voluntad de lo fazer. Et avn sy alguno de sus ofiçiales fizieron algunt desaguisado, pesól dende e estrannó gelo. Mas vos, sennor infante don Felipe, desaforastes los regnos de Castilla e de León robando e tomando a los fijosdalgo e a los de las villas e a los de los monesterios e de las Órdenes todo lo que vos podistes tomar, et demás faziéndouos el rey estas merçedes et estas honras e dándovos los dineros de las sus rentas e seyendo su vasallo, e tomándouos dél otra quantía grand de dineros de las sus rentas para le yr seruir do él mandase. Et enbiándovos dezir que avía menester vuestro seruiçio en la guerra de los moros e que fuésedes estar con el infante don Ferrando su fijo, non lo quesistes fazer. Llámavos agora quel vayades seruir los dineros que dél tomastes et la tierra que dél tenedes, e que enbiedes darle fiadores por las malfetrías que fezistes en la tierra. Si non sabet quel rey tiene quel fuestes desmandado et por lo que avedes dicho non puede escusar de fazer contra vos lo que es fuero de Castilla e León. Et más vos enbía dezir quel dixieron que vos yuades al regno de Granada a ser en su ayuda, veyendo uos quel rey de Granada es enemigo de Dios e de la fe e del rey e de los sus regnos e enemigo de quantos fijosdalgo ha en Castilla e en León e de todos los otros de sus regnos. E seyendo uos fijo del rey don Fernando et de la reyna donna Beatriz et hermano del rey don Alfonso, fazer esto tiene que deuiedes mejor guardar el linaje donde venides e el debdo que con él avedes') (CAX, p. 98 [110–11]).

88 'en todas estas cosas vos desforades la tierra e vos deseredades, e el rey no vos desafuera nin vos desereda' (CAX, p. 98 [111]).

89 'porque desaforaua a Castilla e León' (CAX, p. 110 [112]).

demands that don Nuño had made on the land that the king had entrusted him with, and in connection with other people and places, as well as the unauthorised tax raised by him (*conduchos* and *martiniegas*). The text was expressed in direct speech, and was very expressive and certainly worthy of reproduction:

> As to what you say, don Nuño, that the king *desaforaua* Castile and León, it was you who *desaforastes* the king, his nobles, and the vassals of king and Church, by imposing taxes in all of the land in which the king left you in charge while he was at the frontier. Don Nuño, you know that the king asked you whether the taxes you imposed in his land were legal, and you said no but that others imposed them before you and that for this reason you had done it. And the king told you that because this was not the law, it was force and robbery; and the king forbade you from ever again committing such outrage that you had done, and you promised him that you would put an end to it. Afterward, and disregarding his prohibition, while the king was in Seville, you dispatched another requirement on all nobles, knights and squires, and ladies and damsels in his royal holdings, and in his Orders, and you [collected the *conducho* and] the taxes payable to him on Saint Martin's Day without his authority and ordinances. You had it collected in a very disorderly fashion, and thusly, you *desaforaste* the land.[90]

It is evident that the normative standards invoked, both by the king and by the noble rebels were the same, for the discrepancies, as noted before, seem to have more to do with specific political situations that brought together various forces than with opposing theoretical views with respect to a different legal code.

In his answer to this member of the Haro family, the king used similar arguments and attributed the *desafuero* to him. He redirected his reply to be based on honour, and the ways in which '[the king has favoured] many men of noble descent [...] more than any other king who was in Spain until this time'[91] and on the dishonour caused by don Lope, '[because you have] done many unlawful things in the land, dishonouring those of noble descent and their wives, [sons] and many other relatives [and many other royal estates]'.[92]

---

90 'Et a lo que vos dezides que desaforaua el rey a Castilla e a León, don Nunno, vos desaforastes al rey e desaforastes los sus fijosdalgo et los realengos e todos los abadengos echando uos pedido en toda la tierra en quanto la dexó en vuestra encomienda, estando él en la frontera. Et don Nunno, vos sabedes quel rey vos preguntó los pedidos que fezistes en su tierra si era fuero e vos dixiestes que non, mas que lo fizieran ante otros que vos e que por esto lo fiziérades vos. Et dixouos el rey que pues non era fuero, que era fuerça e robo, et defendióuos que de allí adelante non fiziésedes aquellos desafueros et aquellas fuerças que auíades fecho. Et vos otorgastes gelo así que lo guardaríades. Et después sobre su defendimiento, estando el rey en Seuilla, echastes otro pedido en todos los fijosdalgo, caualleros et escuderos e duennas e donzellas en sus realengos et en sus ordenes, et tomaste conducho e cogistes sus martiniegas syn su mandado e sin sus cartas e fezísteslo coger muy desaguisadamente. E asi vos desaforastes la tierra' (CAX, p. 101 [114]).

91 'el rey ha honrado a muchos fijos dalgo [...] mas que otro rey que en Espanna fuese fasta en el su tiempo' (CAX, p. 104 [118]).

92 'porque feziste muchas cosas syn fuero, deshonrando los fijosdalgo e sus mugeres e sus fijos e sus parientes e otros muchos realengos' (CAX, p. 104 [118]).

This dishonour and *desafuero* had also been previously associated by the king with the effects of imposed taxes attributed to don Nuño; *desafuero* also included not going to war when summoned by the king, having been paid to do so, committing *malfetrías* and 'el gran alboroço' ('the great uproar') of armed people who had risen against him.[93]

In all these things we have said, don Lope Díaz, you have *desaforado* the king and all of those of noble descent in Castile and León, and all [the royal and the abbatial estates], and what you do is against the law and against justice. You cannot say that the king *desafuera* you, for you *desaforades* the king: you took away horses and weapons that you purchased with the money he gave you with which you should serve him. And you are going to do him a disservice in it.[94]

---

93 'Besides, you know that the king, being in Murcia, sent to tell you about how the Moors were waging war and that because you had accepted his monies, he ordered and begged you go to be with his son Prince Fernando in that war, but you refused to do it. Although in this fashion you disobeyed him, he now sends to beg you to go to the frontier with Prince Fernando and serve your king with the land and monies that you received from him. If you refuse to do this, he sends to tell you to go to give him securities in exchange for the evil acts that you committed so that you could pay for them as the law demands it, and if not, the king will order that they be paid from your wealth, according to the law of Castile. Also, you know that when the king, your lord, came to Burgos in order to lull you back into his service, you came forth at him supported by many armed men on foot and on horses as no one from your lineage ever came to their king and sovereign lord. And you and the other noblemen demanded from him whatever you wished, and the king granted it to you. About this, he assembled the *cortes* at your request so that he could grant, before all, what he had promised you. And the king being at the palace and before his court, you made him other demands and left the palace where he was without speaking to him and with a great uproar of armed men, and you pillaged the land. Now he is told that while you were his vassal and while you were holding his land and monies, you made a treaty against him with the King of Granada. You know that the King of Granada is an enemy of the Faith, of the king, of you, and of all of those of noble descent in Castile and León, and that you do disservice to the king by making an alliance with such a man as this, who has lied to him and broken whatever treaties he made with him, and who has broken truces' ('E demás, uos sabesdes que el rey estando en Murçia que vos enbió dezir de cómmo los moros fazían guerra, e que pues auíades tomado sus dineros, que vos mandaua e rogaua que fuésedes estar en aquella guerra con el infante don Ferrando, su fijo, e vos non lo quisiste fazer. Et commo quier que en esto le fuestes desmandado, enbíavos rogar agora e dezir que vayades estar en la frontera con el infante don Ferrando et que le siruades con la tierra e dineros que uos dél tomastes. E si esto non quisierades fazer, enbíauos el rey dezir que le vayades dar fiadores por las malfetrías que feziestes, para las entregar así commo es fuero. E si non, quel rey mandará entregar de los vuestros bienes segunt que es fuero de Castiella. Et otrosí uos sabedes que el rey vuestro sennor, veniendo a Burgos por uos sosegar en el su seruiçio, salistes a él ason[n]ando con muchas gentes de pie e de a cauallo armados commo nunca vinieron aquéllos onde vos venides a su rey e a su sennor natural. E uos e otros ricos omnes demandástele las cosas que quesistes et el rey otorgóuoslas. Et sobre esto, a vuestro pedimiento, fizo ayuntar Cortes para uos otorgar ante todos lo que uos auía dicho. Et estando el rey en palaçio ante toda su corte, fezístele otras demandas e saliéstesle del palaçio do estaua e fuestes con grant alboroço de gentes armados sin le dezir ninguna cosa e robastes la tierra. Et agora fiziéronle entender que seyendo uos su vasallo e teniendo dél su tierra et sus dineros, que posistes pleito con el rey de Granada contra él. Et uos sabedes que el rey de Granada es enemigo de la fe e del rey e vuestro e de todos los fijosdalgo de Castilla e de León, e querédesle deseruir con tal omne commo éste que le ha mentido e falsado quantos pleitos puso con él e que quebrantadas las treguas') (CAX, pp. 104–05 [118–19]).

94 'Por todas estas cosas que avemos dicho, vos don Lope Díaz auedes desaforado al rey e a todos los

Desafuero had therefore become a common argument used by these magnates to legitimise and muster support for their cause. This is why they all received a similar answer from the king, although using different words, as can be clearly seen in the message to don Fernando Ruiz de Castro. It referred to the arguments previously used with the other noblemen: 'dezimos que vos la desaforades, según que auemos dicho a cada vno de los otros',[95] summing up the same kind of charges that justified the royal action in this regard: 'if the king had done to you what is law in Castile, you should understand that the blame is on you'.[96] This can also be seen in the king's message to don Alvar Díaz, which said that 'the *desafuero* and the wrong came from you, and from you it comes to the king and the kingdom, and you cannot say it is just'.[97]

In this discourse the *desheredamiento* alleged by the rebels ultimately becomes a consequence — a legal penalty for their actions — of the *desafuero* that they themselves, not the king, had committed. In short, the king's messages to the rebels made it very clear what he meant by *fuero* and what *desafuero* was. To do so, he did not invent or invoke a new code or new rules, but alluded and referred to an ancient *fuero*, that of Castile, which they also allegedly invoked. Here, however, rather than discussing what could be the *fuero* they referred to,[98] among those preserved, I want to draw attention here to the appeal made to a legal system that was well known to all. It was precisely its breach, and the lack of respect for it, that pointed towards the betrayal of this noblemen, without using that term or directly calling them traitors. Again in this narrative the king is represented as being incredulous that those vassals whom he had indulged the most were the ones who had betrayed him, hence the rhetorical effects of the detailed list of favours and repeated breaches by the nobles. This disbelief, as noted earlier, implicitly referred to a shared code of values and standards. The notion of the *fuero* in this context alludes not only to a legal framework but also to a moral and political one. Within it, the two poles of the

---

fijos dalgo de Castilla e de León e a todos los realengos e abadengos, e lo que fazedes es contra fuero e contra derecho, e non podedes dezir que el rey vos desafuera, mas vos lo desaforades, que leuades los cauallos et las armas que conprastes de los sus dineros que vos él dio con que le siruiésedes et vos ysle deseruir con ello' (CAX, p. 105 [118–19]).

95 CAX, p. 106 [121].

96 'Et si por todas estas cosas fiziera contra vos lo que es fuero de Castilla, entenderedes que es vuestra culpa' (CAX, p. 106 [121]).

97 'el desafuero et el tuerto de vos vino e de vos viene al rey e al regno, et ál non podedes dezir que de derecho sea' (CAX, p. 110 [125]).

98 Pérez-Prendes considers that the legal principles underlying these allegations made by Alfonso X are also the backbone of the *Espéculo*, a legislative work that he sees as being the 'main organic nerve of the political constitution' used by the king to try to modify 'the abusive custom-based lordly statute'. In his view, around 1272 two different alternatives existed: that offered by the monarch and that of the nobility (Pérez-Prendes, 'Las leyes de Alfonso el Sabio', pp. 76–82). Interestingly, González Jiménez, who claimed to follow Pérez-Prendes's interpretation and also believed that the reasons for the rebellion were based on the opposition to the new law that Alfonso X sought to impose, also says that the laws in the *Espéculo* did not result in any changes to the requests that king could make under traditional law (CAX, p. 67, n. 107). The contradiction and error of this reference are not without interest because they show the interpretative problems that the texts discussed give rise to. But mostly they are a warning of the difficulties in capturing the historical context within which they had meaning, something I do not intend to solve here.

DESHEREDAMIENTO AND DESAFUERO   581

exchange relationship and of the political reciprocity that characterised relationships between lord and vassal were defined: love and favours in exchange for love and service, as indicated above.[99] *Desafuero* therefore becomes a form of negative reciprocity, derived from the breach of loyalty oaths and of the mutual obligations that they entailed. Both in this case and in general terms, the rebellion consisted of that 'disservice [...] in a very bad mode and in a very wrong manner' that the king reproached them.[100] It could be thought that this was Alfonso X's attempt to break the group of nobles who opposed him, but it rather seems to be an act of political propaganda that appealed to some shared parameters of legitimacy to dispel the reasoning underlying the rebel discourse.

It is perhaps when the collective message again detailed the events 'to all you of noble descent and knights who are here and to those who are not here'[101] where the delegitimation of the *desaforado* behaviour of the nobles appeared most clearly. Very subtle rhetorical strategies were deployed here. There were two important aspects here that enhanced the authority of the monarch: on the one hand, the demands that the nobles had made to the king in Burgos (which he had agreed to as they were 'for the benefit of the land') became pieces of advice; this was a way to reframe an action that could be understood as a full concession as something good and reasonable.[102] On the other hand, the duties owed to the king by these nobles were presented as having been breached in such a way that their own vassals in turn were authorised to breach their vassalage agreed with them. So, he sent word to these vassals of the rebels, appealing to their supposed knowledge of the facts, but also to the complicity of their implications, as to how:

---

99 The formulas vary: 'had pleasure in favouring you when [you loved him] with service as you should' ('auié sabor de uos fazer bien quando vos lo amásedes con seruiçio así como deuedes') (CAX, p. 110 [125]); '[loving and serving him] he would pardon and do favour [to them]' ('ellos amándol e seruiéndol [...] que les faría gran merçet') (CAX, p. 131 [149]).

100 'ese deseruir en muy mal son e en muy mala manera' (CAX, 110 p. [125]). In the political vocabulary used in these texts there are no terms or expressions to refer to what we would currently call 'revolt', 'rebellion', or 'uprising'. The expressions used in the chronicle speak of disservice (*deservicio*), uproar (*alboroço*), 'wrong and bedlam' ('tuerto e desaguisado'), misconduct (*yerro*), 'scheme against the king' ('ayuntamiento contra el rey'), enmity (*enemistad*), unrest (*desasosiego*), conflict (*desavenencia*), damages (*dannos*), 'tumults and evil doings' ('bolliçios e males'), war (*guerra*), *desafuero*, deprivation of public fama (*desfamar*), uprising (*alçar*), and their explicit opposites.

101 'A todos los infançones et caualleros fijosdalgo que sodes aquí et a los que non sodes aquí' (CAX, p. 111 [126]).

102 'For if they demanded rights, he have them and granted them through his word in the courts and through his privilege. Other things they told him that they advised him to do, which were for the land's benefit, and he tried to do them just as the noblemen of Castile and León advised' ('Ca, si fuero demandaron, dieron gelo e otorgaron gelo por su palabra en corte e por preuillejio. Et otras cosas quel dixieron quel consejauan que era pro de la tierra quísolas él fazer así commo ellos et los ricos omnes de Castilla e de León gelo consejaron') (CAX, p. 111 [126]). This is a similar strategy to the one he would use later with the municipality of Almagro, when he changed the character of the rebels' demands and turned them into general royal concessions for the good of the kingdom. In this way he attributed to himself the success of the negotiations, in other words, of having achieved a compromise (ch. XLVII).

the king gave them good and large territories and many *maravedís* so that they could serve him with them; and now, with that which he gave them for you, in this fashion they take it to the enemies of God, of the Faith, and of the king,[103]

referring to the alliances that they had made with the king of Granada. In this way, the royal envoy continued, 'and with the very same wealth, which the king ordered them to give you so that you could serve him, with that [money] they take you to where you can disservice him, without God nor reason',[104] and appealing to the memory of their parents' loyalties, who 'always considered loyalty and justice [...] in the *fueros* and other things that they requested from him',[105] he clarified that they were not obliged to follow those lords. In this way the king not only exempted them from responsibility, but also appealed to their duty towards their natural lord, from whom the money they had received had come:

> we say that you should not go with them against your [natural] lord. As for what they gave you because you are their vassals, the king gave it to them, it did not come from their possessions; if they did not give you something, you would not be his vassals, nor would you be with them for reasons of kinship nor because of the debts you owed them. And since the vassalage you owe them is because of the moneys they gave you, which they got from the king, it is to me that you must render service, as your natural lord.[106]

This way in which the king delegitimised the high nobility's rebellion precisely in front of those who promoted it reiterated the enforcement of reciprocal obligations. These were not solely limited, as it might seem at first glance, to the exchange of money for services, and vice versa, but affected the behaviour that was seen as desirable within these social groups, according to a set of normative regulations and cultural values that were — crucially — both moral and political at the same time. Reputation, prestige, virtue, and personal honour were intangible and contingent assets which depended on compliance with the referred values and regulations. These, as the king warned in his message to these knights, were granted by the community, both divine and human, 'therefore, we tell you to consider loyalty and justice and the law and to do so in order that neither God nor man may have anything to question

---

103 'el rey les dio grandes tierras e buenas e muchos marauedís que diesen a vos para le servir con ellos, pero que en vez de este servicio lléuanlos a enemigos de Dios e de la fe e del rey' (CAX, p. 111 [126]).

104 'con aquel aver mesmo que el rey uos mandó dar con quel seruiésedes, con aquello vos lieuan a do lo desiruades syn Dios et syn razon' (CAX, p. 111 [126]).

105 'que siempre cataron lealtad e derecho [...] en fueros et en otras cosas quel pidieron' (CAX, p. 111 [126]).

106 'dezimos que non deuedes de yr con ellos contra vuestro sennor natural, ca aquello que ellos vos dieron porque sodes sus vasallos, el rey gelo dio de lo suyo e non vos lo dieron ellos de sus heredades. Et si algo non vos diesen, non seríades sus vasallos nin yríades con ellos por parentesco nin por debdo que con ellos ayades. Et pues la razón del vasallaje que an de vos es por los dineros que vos dieron de los quel rey les dio a ellos, et por estos dineros avedes a fazer serviçio e a mí avedes de seruir donde viene el auer que vos fue dado, mayormente a vuestro sennor natural' (CAX, p. 111 [127]).

you about'.[107] Given the clear hegemony of the reciprocity principle, which was the standard against which behaviour was measured and judged — not only in courts of justice but also in the sphere of public fame, extended into the divine realm[108]—, this invoked moral/normative order appeared as a 'natural order' rather than an ideological one.[109]

It is noteworthy that in this political debate — as it is presented in this process of struggle and negotiation — the chivalric *fuero* used to articulate the opposing demands of the two conflicted parties was strengthened. The king did not dispute that the nobles' actions could have been justified, if he had really committed the acts alleged against him — taking their land or *desheredarles* for no reason, without deserving it, and so on. But he did not engage in such acts. And this contrast between the two types of behaviour — which articulated the royal messages discussed here — was used again to reveal to his son Fernando the hidden reasons that were behind the noble's shifting actions:

> These noblemen did not go against me for reason of *fuero* nor for the wrong that I did to them. For I never took away any *fuero*, but even if I had taken it away, they should be pleased and happy that I granted it back to them. Also, I never did them any wrong; but even if I had done the greatest in the world, I wanted to right it for them well within their sight so that they had no cause to demand more. Also, they do not do it for the benefit of the land, for there was no other who wanted to do more than I, to whom the inheritance belongs, and they have little benefit in it but the good that we do them. But the reason why they did it was this: in order to have kings always under pressure and to take from them what is theirs, looking for ways to disinherit and dishonour them like those from where they come have tried before. For though the kings nurtured them, they made an effort to destroy and take away the kingdoms even while some of them were young; and just as soon as the kings bestowed inheritance upon them, they made an effort to *desheredar* them, first taking counsel with their enemies, then by plundering the land, taking away what was the king's little by little and denying it to him. And just as kings made them powerful and honoured them, they strove to make the kings less powerful and to dishonour them in so many ways, which would be long and very shameful to relate.[110]

---

107 'Porque vos dezimos que catedes lealtad e derecho e fuero e lo que deuedes de fazer porque Dios nin los ommes non ayan qué dezir' (CAX, p. 111 [127]).

108 The social control exercised through public reputation and fame appeared in various contexts. The term *malandantes* ('bad knight errant') applied to don Nuño's lineage to allude to his 'mad' behaviour towards kings (CAX, p. 148 [169]), and to the knights returning to the royal service because they knew they were *malandantes* (CAX, p. 148 [169]), were clearly the opposite good knight errant. Moreover, the prestige of the king was also constructed in that way, that is, it could be affected by what was said about his actions.

109 On this process of ideological 'naturalization', and together with the classic work Bourdieu, *El sentido práctico*; see the valuable reformulation in Comaroff and Comaroff, *Ethnography*, pp. 27–29.

110 'Estos ricos omes non se mouieron contra mi por razón de fuero nin por tuerto que les yo touiese, ca fuero nunca gelo yo tollí, Más, que gelo touiese tollido, pues que gelo otorgaua, mas pagados deuieran

584 ISABEL ALFONSO

These warnings full of bitter irony were used by the king to make his son understand that 'this is the *fuero* and the benefit for the land that they always wanted.'[111] It is therefore not the law that is being questioned, but the facts, by reference to *fueros* which Alfonso X had supposedly abolished. And the same is true of the rebels, or better of the *desavenidos* ('discordant') nobles as they called themselves, who in the collective response explicitly assumed the terms of the exchange invoked by the king, which could be described as obligations by *fuero*, but strategically manipulating their contents:

> As to what you say, that the king gave us his land and his *maravedís* so that we ought to serve him, you speak rightly; and we are sending to tell him that if he wants our service, we shall serve him. But asking it of us now is at a time in which we are not able to do so.[112]

They contradict, or scoff at, these terms at the end of their response: 'because since we do not live with him nor have his favour, we cannot avoid searching for a place where we may live.'[113] Although it is not my intention to extend the analysis to the full material of the chronicle, it is worth remembering this strategic use of common resources, of a common legal culture which is also seen in all of the royal discourse. This is particularly evident in the last message addressed to all the knights referred to earlier. It gave them reasons to break with their lords, eliminate the intermediation of the nobility, and assert the primacy of the natural tie upon which he aimed to base

---

ser et quedar deuieran contentos. Otrosi tuerto nunca gelo fiz. Mas que gelo ouiese fecho el mayor del mundo, pues que gelo quería emendar a su bien vista dellos, non auién por qué más demandar. Otrosí por pro de la tierra non lo fazen, ca esto non lo querían tanto ninguno commo yo, cuya es la heredat, e muy poca pro han ellos ende sy non el bien que les nos fazemos. Mas la razón porque lo fezieron fue ésta: porque querían tener syempre los reyes apremiados e leuar dellos lo suyo pesándoles e buscando carreras por do los deseredasen e los desonrasen, commo lo buscaron aquéllos donde ellos vienen. Et asy commo los reyes criaron a ellos, punaron ellos de los descriar e de tollerles los reynos, algunos dellos seyendo ninnos. E asy commo los reyes los heredaron, punaron ellos de los desheredar lo vno consejeramente con sus enemigos, lo ál a furto en la tierra, leuándoles lo suyo, poco a poco anagenándogelo. Et asy commo los reyes les apoderaron e los onraron, ellos punaron en los desapoderar e los desonrar en tantas maneras que serían muchas de contar e muy vergonnosas' (CAX, pp. 145–46 [166]).

111 'esto es el fuero e pro de la tierra que ellos syempre quisieron' (CAX, p. 146 [166]). This text, so rich in information as well as literary beauty, has also been considered a literal transcription made by the chronicler of a royal charter. However, I disagree with this interpretation, or at least question it due to lack of evidence, because I think we should not rule out the possibility that it was yet another of the sophisticated rhetorical devices from the quill of Alfonso XI's chancellor. Does this 'letter' not condense the whole of a tradition which was very much alive at the time of writing, in accounts with the same didactic/counselling character? Although Fernando Gómez Redondo holds to the first view, his book — masterly on many points — contains the data to support my arguments. On the letter, see Gómez Redondo, *Historia de la prosa medieval 1*, p. 972, n. 205.

112 'A lo que dezides que pues el rey nos dio su tierra e sus marauedís que le deuemos seruir, dezides derecho e nos le enbiamos dezir que sy quiere nuestro seruiçio, que le seruiremos. Mas agora demándanoslo en tiempo que lo non podemos fazer' (CAX, p. [128]).

113 'pues con él non beuimos nin su merçet non avemos, non podemos escusar que non vayamos buscar do biuamos' (CAX, p. 112 [128]).

his authority — a tie where obligation and nature are closely linked).[114] The *fuero* and the law served as a metaphor of the political reciprocity that they demanded from each other. This notion encompassed the rights of both parties, maintaining their hierarchy, as shown in the final compromise when the king (at the behest of the queen and his son) by granting them 'the *fueros*, uses, and customs they had during the time of the kings of Castile and León,'[115] assumed the same commitment as they did, 'keeping for the king his lordship, *fueros* and rights'.[116]

Are we therefore faced here with a manifestation of an aristocratic royalist model, in which the nobility shared the government of the kingdom with the king, which Alfonso X was forced to specify further in his second *Partida*?[117] Admittedly, it is true that the greatest strength of the king's image in this chronicle, and of the political discourse contained in his messages, lies in the accusations and recriminations that he made against the rebel noblemen for having violated the chivalric code and their own rules of coexistence. These were the rules of the political game — using modern parlance — which, as we are told, the nobles attempted to defend against more royalist projects than that of Alfonso the Wise.

---

114 Undoubtedly, this is not the place to address the many problems raised by this notion. This topic has been insufficiently studied, and I think it is necessary to return to it. I will merely include two quotes from the fourth *Partida* that I believe relate to this: 'Natural relationship means an obligation which men are under to others to love and cherish them for some just reason. The following distinction exists between it and nature, namely; nature is a force which causes everything to remain in the condition directed by the bond of God; natural relationship is something which resembles nature and assists everything derived from it to exist and be preserved' ('Naturaleza tanto quiere dezir como debdo que han los omes unos con otros, por alguna derecha razón en se amar e en se querer bien. E el departimiento que ha entre natura e naturaleza es éste. Ca natura es una virtud que faze ser todas las cosas en aquel estado que Dios las ordenó. Naturaleza es cosa que semeja a la natura e que ayuda a ser e mantener en todo lo que desciende d'ella') (Partidas IV.24.1); 'To denaturalize himself according to the Spanish language, is for a man to abandon the relation which he holds to his lord, or to the country in which he lives. And because this is, as it were, a debt of nature, this relation cannot be dissolved except for some just reason' ('Desnaturar segund lenguaje de España tanto quiere dezir como salir ome de la naturaleza que ha con su señor, o con la tierra en que bive. E porque esto es como debda de natura, non se puede desatar, si non por alguna derecha razón') (Partidas IV.25.5).

115 'los fueros e vsos e costumbres que ouieron en tiempo de los reyes de Castilla e de León' (CAX, p. 159 [181]).

116 'guardando ellos al rey su sennorío e sus fueros e sus derechos' (CAX, p. 159 [181]).

117 Fernando Gómez Redondo seems to interpret it in this way, as he sees the chivalric ideal imposed on the nobility by the king — following the uprising reported by the chronicle — reflected in that *Partida* (Gómez Redondo, *Historia de la prosa medieval* 1, pp. 536–69). An opinion recently disputed by Georges Martin for whom, on the contrary, that *Partida* represented the royal model to subdue the nobility (Martin, 'Control regio de la violencia nobiliaria'). This discussion dovetails with that presented in n. 99. For an analysis of the ideal of kingship advanced in the *Especulo* compared with that presented in the second *Partida*, see Gómez Redondo, *Historia de la prosa medieval* 1, pp. 354–57, 516–19 and 547–70.

Bibliography

Alfonso, Isabel, 'Venganza y justicia en el Cantar de Mío Cid', in *El Cid: de la materia épica a las crónicas caballerescas*, ed. by Carlos Alvar Ezquerra, Fernando Gómez Redondo, and Georges Martin (Alcalá de Henares: Universidad de Alcalá, 2002), pp. 41–69

Alfonso, Isabel, and Cristina Jular Pérez-Alfaro, 'Oña contra Frías o el pleito de los cien testigos: una pesquisa en la Castilla del siglo XIII', *Edad Media: Revista de Historia*, 3 (2000), 61–88

Ballesteros Beretta, Antonio, *Alfonso X el Sabio*, 2 edn (Barcelona: El Albir, 1984 [1963)])

Bartlett, Robert J., *England under the Norman and Angevin Kings, 1075–1225* (Oxford: Oxford University Press, 2000)

Bloch, Maurice, *Political Language and Oratory in Traditional Society* (London: Academic Press, 1975)

Bourdieu, Pierre, *El sentido práctico* (Madrid: Taurus, 1991)

Calderón Calderón, Manuel, 'La imagen del rey en la Crónica de Alfonso X', *Boletín de la Real Academia de la Historia*, 2 (2000), 255–66

Comaroff, John, L., and Jean Comaroff, *Ethnography and the Historical Imagination* (Oxford: Westview, 1992)

Doubleday, Simon, *The Lara Family. Crown and Nobility in Medieval Spain* (Cambridge, MA: Harvard University Press, 2001)

Escalona, Julio, 'Los nobles contra su rey. Argumentos y motivacionesde la insubordinación nobiliaria de 1272–1273', *Cahiers d'Études Hispaniques Médiévales*, 25 (2002), 131–62

Gómez Redondo, Fernando, *Historia de la prosa medieval castellana. Vol. 1. La creación del discurso prosístico: el entramado cortesano* (Madrid: Cátedra, 1998)

Gómez Redondo, Fernando, *Historia de la prosa medieval castellana. Vol. 2. El desarrollo de los géneros. La ficción caballeresca y el orden religioso* (Madrid: Cátedra, 1999)

Gómez Redondo, Fernando, 'De la crónica general a la real: transformaciones ideológicas en Crónica de tres reyes', in *La historia alfonsí: el modelo y sus destinos* (siglos XIII–XV), ed. by Georges Martin (Madrid: Casa de Velázquez, 2000), pp. 95–123

González Jiménez, Manuel, *Crónica de Alfonso X* (Murcia: Real Academia Alfonso X el Sabio, 1999)

González Jiménez, Manuel, *Alfonso X el Sabio* (Palencia: Diputación Provincial de Palencia, 1993)

Martin, Georges, 'Amour (Une notion politique)', *Cahiers d'Études Hispaniques Médiévales*, 11 (1997), 169–206

Martin, Georges, 'Control regio de la violencia nobiliaria: la caballería según Alfonso X de Castilla (comentario al título XXI de la "Segunda partida")', in *Lucha política: condena y legitimación en las sociedades medievales*, ed. by Isabel Alfonso Antón, Julio Escalona, and Georges Martin (Lyon: ENS Éditions, 2004)

O'Callaghan, Joseph F., *El rey Sabio. El reinado de Alfonso X de Castilla, 1252–1284* (Sevilla: Universidad de Sevilla, 1996)

Pérez-Prendes, José Manuel, 'Las leyes de Alfonso el Sabio', *Revista de Occidente*, 43 (1984), 67–84

Roberts, Simon, and John Comaroff, L., *Rules and Processes: The Cultural Logic of Dispute in an African Context* (Chicago: The University of Chicago Press, 1981)

White, Stephen D., 'Strategie rhétorique dans la Conventio de Hugues de Lusignan', in *Histoire et Société. Mélanges offerts à Georges Duby* (Aix-en-Provence: Presses de L'Université de Provence, 1992), pp. 147–57

Part IV

Historians' Minds

Concepts, Language, and Debates

CHAPTER 15

On Cistercians and Feudalism

with a commentary by Peter Coss

Conflict, Language, and Social Practice in Medieval Societies: Selected Essays of Isabel Alfonso, with Commentaries, ed. by Julio Escalona Monge, Álvaro Carvajal Castro, and Cristina Jular Pérez-Alfaro, TMC 24 (Turnhout: Brepols, 2024), pp. 589–624

BREPOLS ❦ PUBLISHERS   10.1484/M.TMC-EB.5.132469

PETER COSS

Commentary

Isabel Alfonso's important intervention in the evolution of Cistercian studies came at a particular juncture. Studies published across the preceding decade had questioned some of the assumptions of the traditional historiography. Archival work had opened up regional perspectives that dented the Cistercian reputation as reclaimers of waste lands *par excellence*, showing that their settlements were very often located in areas that were already inhabited and that their reputation as technical innovators had shallow foundations. Moreover, the much-lauded grange economy was not practised exclusively, even in the twelfth century, and existed alongside more traditional forms of landlord-tenant relations and/or was predicated upon their prior existence.[1] Alfonso contended that much of the recent reinterpretation had retained in essence the traditional tendency to extol Cistercian economic practice, especially before the mid-thirteenth century. In place of their role in reclamation, scholars now tended to stress their managerial efficiency and their predilection for rational practices, while continuing to see the retreat from directly cultivated demesnes in favour of rent and the decline of the lay brother system as a movement away from Cistercian ideals. Evidence for seigneurial exploitation tended to be explained away in one way or another. She pointed to the tendency to stress 'technical and economic factors relating to efficiency and productivity' over social structure, and the danger of distortion if the seigneurial aspects of Cistercian enterprises continued to be neglected or played down in favour of voluntary and contractual relations. She called for further study of the relations between the monastic communities and the peasant world, including the links between monastic granges and village communities, and greater attention to the lay brothers or *conversi* and their milieu. In short, the 'complexities of social articulation will show us much about the structures of domination in which the Cistercians were involved'. Although elements of the traditional interpretation remain strong, subsequent work has underlined the force of her insights and advanced scholarly awareness of the features she emphasized.

Scholarly interpretation of the numerous dimensions to Cistercian history have been synthesised recently by Janet Burton and Julie Kerr, by Emilia Jamroziak, and in the new *Cambridge Companion to the Cistercian Order*, all published between 2011 and 2014.[2] Many of the historiographical trends apparent in 1991 have been developed in subsequent studies. The regional emphasis has been maintained, with

---

1 For the definition of grange and the content of the grange economy see in particular Berman, *Medieval Agriculture*, especially ch. IV, 'The profits of grange agriculture'.

2 Burton and Kerr, *The Cistercians*; Jamroziak, *The Cistercian Order*; Bruun, ed., *Cambridge Companion*.

Peter Coss, Cardiff University

important work on Scandinavian and Polish monasteries for example.[3] Careful study has revealed considerable variation in economic practices so that the belief in a single Cistercian model regulated by the order's normative texts is no longer viable. Estates were conditioned by property acquired from benefactors, so much so that 'the reorganisation of land that has already been under cultivation was the hallmark of Cistercian activities to a much greater degree than taking virgin land into cultivation and other pioneering activities, which for a long time was believed to be the "Cistercian speciality"'.[4] In Eastern Europe the Cistercians were not as much in the van in founding new settlements as had been thought. In Bohemia only one of the Cistercian abbeys, Zlatá Koruna, seems to have been involved in large-scale colonisation.[5] Nor has a particular Cistercian propensity for technological innovation been sustained, although they did participate in the diffusion of a variety of agricultural techniques. By contrast the quality of their administration and the economies of scale involved in the formation of granges have continued to be emphasized. The sheer variety of economic activities practised, depending on the terrain and on ecological factors, has become increasingly apparent, from the pastoral emphasis in Spain, Northern England and Scotland, through horse breeding in Denmark to fisheries in Saxony, Silesia and elsewhere. Water mills and their monopolisation was one speciality. Salt production was another.[6] And so on. Cistercian involvement in commercialisation and in credit has also been stressed, as has the role of this supposedly most rural of orders in towns.[7] Regions where there were concentrations of urban property include the Rhineland, the Moselle Valley, Champagne and the territory of the Hanseatic League.[8] The location of nunneries in urban centres has been specifically noted, as has their location near the fairs of Champagne.[9] All of these phenomena can be seen as aspects of the regionalisation of the order.

What, then, of the specific issue raised by Alfonso? First of all, we need to look at the relationship between the monks and aristocratic society. They were themselves, of course, drawn from aristocratic families, deliberately and self-consciously so. In their economic activities the Cistercians reveal themselves as very much a part of the aristocratic world. In a work published in the same year as Isabel's essay, Constance Bouchard subjected their economic activities in their Burgundian heartland to close

---

3 For the former see France, *The Cistercians in Scandinavia*. The Polish studies are drawn on in Jamroziak, *The Cistercian Order*, ch. 6, 'Economy: Not Just Sheep and Grain'.

4 Jamroziak, *The Cistercian Order*, p. 185.

5 Charátová, 'Mindful of Reality', pp. 179 and 181. In Gascony by contrast, research shows that the Cistercians were involved in the foundation of around 40 fortified towns or *bastides*: Berman, 'From Cistercian Granges to Cistercian Bastides', p. 205. For the economic functions of the *bastides* see Hilton, *English and French Towns*, pp. 35–37.

6 Bond, 'Cistercian Mills', pp. 368–73; Jamroziak, *The Cistercian Order*, p. 193; Berman, 'Agriculture and Economics', p. 119.

7 By 1195 Cistercian *conversi* were involved in banking: Waddell, ed., *Twelfth-Century Statutes*, year 1195, no. 29. See also Madden, 'Business Monks', pp. 347–48, 355. She sees the Cistercian houses in England as agricultural banks' and as 'credit establishments for the wool trade'.

8 Jamroziak, *The Cistercian Order*, p. 198.

9 Lester, *Creating Cistercian Nuns*.

analysis.[10] Over half of those men and women who were involved in transactions with them belonged to the social elite, many of them castellans or knights. As she says, 'it is not surprising that someone who came to the abbey to make a gift or engage in another transaction should have come accompanied by his friends, relatives, lords and vassals. But, in addition, the monks themselves seem actively to have sought the presence and support of their networks of secular friends'.[11] These were, of course, men and women who often enjoyed seigneurial rights and powers over the peasants. The types of property conveyed to the monks from early in their history, and increasingly as the twelfth century progressed, included not only both uncultivated and cultivated land but also a whole gamut of additional interests. Prominent among these were rents from peasant tenants and jurisdiction over them. Also included were churches and tithes. Notwithstanding the Cistercian legislation as to which forms of property were suitable and which were not — whose dating and transmission is in any case problematic — the diversity of interests was undoubtedly there from the beginning.[12] The antithesis between ideal and reality, and with it the search for a date from which the order became compromised, is not therefore a very useful one. The first Cistercians simply 'did not define themselves in terms of what sorts of economic activities they did or did not undertake'.[13] It was not just a matter of the gifts they were given. The Cistercians were involved in purchases, sales and exchanges, all of which were useful as 'consolidation tools'. As Constance Bouchard has said, leasing and the holding of land in mortgage also 'helped create bonds of friendship and mutual dependence between monks and secular neighbours'.[14] As with other transactions, the patching up of quarrels and compromises with their aristocratic neighbours often involved the granting of spiritual benefits and counter-gifts. The survey by Burton and Kerr of recent work on the spread of the Cistercian order is revealing in itself in terms of the breadth of the monks' involvement in the interests of the secular world. In Wales, for example, their benefactors were rewarded in myriad ways: 'by recording their deeds and writing their history; by preserving Welsh culture through the copying of manuscripts; by providing them with hospitality; and by safeguarding their muniments', quite apart from the 'spiritual support for their regimes and practical expertise and assistance in the formation of their political power'.[15] The higher reaches of the secular church also played a major part in the expansion of the order. The role of bishops and archbishops was crucial in Scandinavia for example.[16] Wherever we look we see the ambitions of the socially and politically powerful.

---

10 Bouchard, *Holy Entrepreneurs*.

11 Bouchard, *Holy Entrepreneurs*, p. 173.

12 Bouchard cites Auberger, *L'unanimité cistercienne primitive*, as well as her own Bouchard, 'Cistercian Ideals'.

13 Bouchard, *Holy Entrepreneurs*, p. 188.

14 Bouchard, *Holy Entrepreneurs*, p. 33.

15 Burton and Kerr, *The Cistercians*, p. 46. See also Pryce, 'Patrons and Patronage'.

16 See McGuire, *Conflict and Continuity*, pp. 9–19, who examines the activities of Archbishop Eskil of Lund, Bishop Absalon of Rockilde, his successor, and Bishop Valdemar of Sleswig. See also France, 'Cistercian Foundation Narratives'.

594   PETER COSS

It is against this background of aristocratic interaction that we can most usefully approach the Cistercian enterprises. We need to pay close attention to the *conversi*. The phenomenon has to be understood not only in terms of the needs of the specific enterprise of the grange but also in terms of the seigneurial world that the Cistercians inhabited. Of great significance are the steps that were taken to ensure the distinction between the lay brothers and the choir monks. The customary which was drawn up to regulate the role of the lay brothers, the *Usus Conversorum*, not only separated them in terms of function — to shelter the monks from involvement in worldly affairs — but forbade them to be literate.[17] The lay brothers effectively 'formed a separate community which ran in tandem but parallel to the choir monks'.[18] They inhabited a different part of the precinct and had their own stalls in the nave of the church. They wore work clothes not monastic habits and were not tonsured but displayed fringes and beards. Furthermore, they had different career trajectories: according to Cistercian legislation the *conversi* were not to become monks. As so often with medieval quests for social separation, when contacts actually took place barriers might come down and friendships develop; some of these are evidenced. These were more likely when obedientiaries, as opposed to simple choir monks, worked and travelled on business alongside *conversi*. Although some of the lay brothers seem to have been drawn from knightly ranks, this was commoner early on when they may have been allocated pastoral duties; it was forbidden by the General Chapter in 1188.[19] The great majority were undoubtedly of peasant stock, and drawn from the locality of the granges on which they worked. This takes us directly into the relationship between the monks and peasant communities. Constance Berman had already shown in her studies of the Cistercians in southern France how the formation of granges involved the displacement of peasant communities.[20] The same has been shown in England and Wales: at Fountains, Byland, Holm Cultram and Furness, at Neath and Margam.[21] In many cases the peasants were absorbed into the new system.[22] As Julie Kerr points out, the Cistercians often invited the local peasantry to become lay brothers or hired workers; 'they might be allowed to remain on the land for the rest of their lives or be moved to a new tenancy by their former lord'.[23] Some relinquished their tenancies and joined the order as lay brothers.[24] Often existing landlord/peasant relations were left in place.[25] Moreover, cartularies reveal not only the gift but also

---

17   Or if they were literate they should refrain from reading, presumably to avoid lapsing into error (Waddell, ed., *Cistercian Lay Brothers*, p. 182).

18   Burton and Kerr, *The Cistercians*, p. 152.

19   For lay brothers of knightly extraction see Berman, 'Distinguishing Between the Humble Cistercian', and Kinder, *Cistercian Europe*, p. 308.

20   Berman, *Medieval Agriculture*, pp. 59–60.

21   See, for example, Coppack, *Fountains Abbey*; Williams, *The Cistercians*, p. 278; Burton, *The Monastic Orders in Yorkshire*, p. 255.

22   See, for example, Wright, 'Casting down the altars'. See also Berman, *Medieval Agriculture*, pp. 47–59 and Burton, *The Monastic Orders in Yorkshire*, pp. 255–56.

23   Burton and Kerr, *The Cistercians*, p. 170.

24   Berman, *Medieval Agriculture*, pp. 79–82.

25   Williams, *The Cistercians*, pp. 288–89; Toepfer, *Die Konversen der Zisterzienster*, pp. 106–09, 116–21.

the purchase of peasant cultivators.[26] In eastern Europe, in particular, much use was made of unfree labour. Alternatively, a monastery might forge a relationship with a peasant community and engage in social transactions with it, as has been shown in Galicia.[27] Whatever glosses one puts on the Cistercian economy, the plain fact is that what we are witnessing here is the exercise of seigneurial power, as Alfonso indicated. It is little wonder that John of Forde Abbey, who wrote a life of the saintly recluse Wulfric of Haselbury during the 1180s, should have his subject criticise the Cistercians for being 'insufficiently mindful of their duty to those committed to their lordship'.[28]

It is not surprising that there were many incidents of *conversi* violence against the order. The order's statutes record no less than 103 incidents of revolt between 1190 and 1308, although 27 of them involved monks as well as *conversi*. Most of these were in England, France and Italy.[29] The leasing of demesne land in the thirteenth century, which threatened the *conversi* with redundancy, served to exacerbate matters.[30] Traditionally, Cistercian scholars have seen *conversi* discontent either in terms of their moral laxity[31] or as a direct reaction to oppression.[32] In an important essay of 2006 Brian Noell broke with both of these and argued that the problems were caused by rising expectations on the one hand and a thwarted desire for parity on the other.[33] To understand this, as he argues, it is necessary to look more closely at the actual position of the *conversi*. The *Usus Conversorum* envisaged them in a subordinate but necessary role within the context of monastic self-sufficiency. They were to engage in a whole range of practical activities, like animal husbandry, stable keeping, milling, baking, weaving, leather working and shoemaking.[34] When the granges come into view we see that the lay brothers themselves were actually assisted in their work by a variety of other groups including servants, hired labourers and *familiares* or 'familiars'. These last mentioned helped to sustain Cistercian houses but lacked the religious profession and obligations of the *conversi*. Noell sees them as intermediate in status between the lay brothers on the one hand and the hired workers on the other. By the early thirteenth century these groups appear more frequently in the sources, suggesting to Noell that their proportion to the lay brothers may have tended to increase over the course of time.[35] Consequently, '*conversi* appear more frequently as managers

---

26 See Platt, *The Monastic Grange*, ch. 4, 'The staffing of the grange', esp. p. 83.

27 Pascua Echegaray, 'Vassals and Allies in Conflict', and Pastor, 'Social Mobility'.

28 Burton and Kerr, *The Cistercians*, p. 186, citing Forde, 'Life of Wulfric', pp. 253–54.

29 See also Donnelly, *The Decline of the Medieval Cistercian Laybrotherhood*; Newman, *The Boundaries of Charity*.

30 Noell, 'Expectations and Unrest', pp. 273–74.

31 See Donnelly, *The Decline of the Medieval Cistercian Laybrotherhood*; Lekai, *The Cistercians*.

32 Sayers, 'Violence in the Medieval Cloister', pp. 535, 539–40; Newman, *The Boundaries of Charity*, pp. 241–46; Cassidy-Welch, *Monastic Spaces*, pp. 167–93.

33 Noell, 'Expectations and Unrest', pp. 270–74.

34 Waddell, ed., *Cistercian Lay Brothers*, ch. XIV, p. 72.

35 Noell, 'Expectations and Unrest', p. 265, citing Chauvin, 'Réalités et évolution de l'économie cistercienne', p. 28; Barrière, 'Les patrimoines cisterciens', p. 50; and Toepfer, *Die Konversen der Zisterzienster*, p. 36. It seems that the *familiares* tended to cause disciplinary problems in the late

and administrators in Cistercian enterprises'.[36] Thus they played an important role in the economic development of their communities. Michael Toepfer has revealed the breadth of their activities in Germany. At Altenberg in the thirteenth century, for example, they oversaw not only granges but also *stadthof* (urban distribution centres), managed donated property and handled marketing. At Salem they functioned as 'craftsmen, guest masters, work bosses, overseers of the abbey's salt mines, *stadthof* masters, agents in property transactions, document carriers, purchasing managers, and grange masters'.[37] And so on. Similarly, at Beaulieu in Hampshire, judging from its account book of 1270, the *conversi* appear to have worked essentially as supervisors, given that the labourers outnumbered them.[38] For some, then, *conversi* status could bring opportunities and Noell is able to point to some who wielded considerable influence and some who were quite exceptional characters. It is in this context that he examines the various disturbances. An early example of unrest took place at Schönau near Heidelberg in 1168 when an abbot withheld from the *conversi* the annual issue of new boots which they shared with the choir monks. In retaliation the lay brothers planned to destroy the monks' boots on Christmas eve while they were attending services.[39] In England and Wales, curbing the consumption of alcohol was a particular issue and could lead to strife. At Cwmhir the *conversi* retaliated by denying the abbot his horses.[40] Various other acts of sabotage are reported, such as denying hospitality at granges for monks in transit. There were occasionally risings of a wholly different order, one of the most spectacular being in early fourteenth-century Flanders where the *conversus* William of Saeftingen led a rising at Ter Doest in 1308 which led to his wounding the abbot and killing the cellarer.[41] What is striking, though, is that however variable the roles performed by the *conversi* may have been, for the most part the incidents and acts of sabotage highlighted, often over what might seem to us to be relatively trivial matters, appear to parallel those frequently found among peasant communities resisting their lords.

As Alfonso's own work indicated, however, there were many others of peasant stock working for the order. If the *conversi* were by no means monolithic in terms of their role they were also variable in number. In East-Central Europe *conversi* numbers seem to have been generally smaller than in the west. In such circumstances it is hardly surprising that they should have functioned more as managers and specialists with the manual work being undertaken very largely by hired workers and by the unfree peasantry. But it was not just a matter of numbers. In Bohemia, Hungary and Poland

---

thirteenth century. Though abolished as an institution by the general chapter in 1293 they continued to exist in other guises (Kinder, *Cistercian Europe*, p. 308).

36 Noell, 'Expectations and Unrest', p. 265.

37 Toepfer, *Die Konversen der Zisterzienster*, pp. 71–94; Noell, 'Expectations and Unrest', pp. 268–69.

38 Noell, 'Expectations and Unrest', p. 269, citing Hockey, ed., *The Account Book of Beaulieu Abbey*, pp. 9–23.

39 Noell, 'Expectations and Unrest', p. 271, citing *Exordium magnum* V, p. 10.

40 Waddell, ed., *Twelfth-Century Statutes*, year 1195, no. 62.

41 Noell, 'Expectations and Unrest', p. 274, citing Schneider, *Vom Klosterhaushalt zum Stadt- und Staathaushalt*, pp. 67–70.

serfdom was a regular component of Cistercian estates.[42] In Iberia, too, manual work was undertaken by tenants. These were often heavily indebted and hardly in a position to exercise choice. Here again we find *mercenarios* as well as *familiares* attached to the estates. In recent decades, considerable advances have been made in our understanding of the effects of commercialization on the economy and society of the central middle ages. The extent of rational decision-making has been explored and the rise of accounting and accountability has been stressed.[43] This has had two effects which are especially pertinent here. One is that the peculiarity of the Cistercians as landlords — as lying somehow outside of the norms of the 'feudal' world or as harbingers of capitalism — becomes even less tenable. The other is the tendency of some scholars when identifying the prevalence of contractual relationships to downplay the potential weight of seigneurial exploitation.[44] In reality, of course, these phenomena are by no means incompatible, let alone mutually exclusive. We should never lose sight of the severely unequal power relations that characterised the world of lords and peasants. In this context in particular Isabel Alfonso's landmark essay remains, and will remain in the future, an important focus of study.

---

42 See Jamroziak, *The Cistercian Order*, p. 188, works cited there.
43 See for example Stone, *Decision-Making in Medieval Agriculture*, and Sabapathy, *Officers and Accountability*.
44 See, for example, Bailey, *The Decline of Serfdom*, ch. 14: 'From Bondage to Freedom: Towards a Reassessment'.

Bibliography

Auberger, Jean-Baptiste, *L'unanimité cistercienne primitive: mythe ou réalité?* (Achel: Editions Sine Parvulos, 1986)

Bailey, Mark, *The Decline of Serfdom in Late Medieval England* (Woodbridge: Boydell, 2014)

Barrière, Bernadette, 'Les patrimoines cisterciens en France: Du faire valoir direct au fermage et à la sous-traitance', in *L'espace cistercien*, ed. by Léon Pressouyre (Paris: Comité des travaux historiques et scientifiques, 1994), pp. 45–69

Berman, Constance Hoffman, *Medieval Agriculture, the Southern French Countryside, and the Early Cistercians: A Study of Forty-three Monasteries* (Philadelphia: The American Philosophical Society, 1986)

Berman, Constance Hoffman, 'From Cistercian Granges to Cistercian Bastides: Using the Order's Records to Date Landscape Transformation', in *L'espace cistercien*, ed. by Léon Pressouyre (Paris: Comité des travaux historiques et scientifiques, 1994), pp. 204–15

Berman, Constance Hoffman, 'Distinguishing Between the Humble Cistercian Lay Brother and Sister, and the Converted Knight in Southern France', in *Religious and Laity in Western Europe, 1000–1400: Interaction, Negotiation and Power*, ed. by Emilia Jamroziak and Janet Burton (Turnhout: Brepols, 2006), pp. 263–83

Berman, Constance Hoffman, 'Agriculture and Economics', in *Cambridge Companion to the Cistercian Order*, ed. by Mette Bruun (Cambridge: Cambridge University Press, 2012), pp. 112–24

Bond, C. James, 'Cistercian Mills in England and Wales: A Preliminary Survey', in *L'espace cistercien*, ed. by Léon Pressouyre (Paris: Comité des travaux historiques et scientifiques, 1994), pp. 364–77

Bouchard, Constance Brittain, 'Cistercian Ideals versus Reality: 1134 Reconsidered', *Citeaux*, 39 (1988), 217–31

Bouchard, Constance Brittain, *Holy Entrepreneurs: Cistercians, Knights, and Economic Exchange in Twelfth-Century Burgundy* (Ithaca: Cornell University Press, 1991)

Bruun, Mette, ed., *Cambridge Companion to the Cistercian Order* (Cambridge: Cambridge University Press, 2012)

Burton, Janet, *The Monastic Orders in Yorkshire, 1069–1215* (Cambridge: Cambridge University Press, 1999)

Burton, Janet, and Julie Kerr, *The Cistercians in the Middle Ages* (Woodbridge: Boydell Press, 2011)

Cassidy-Welch, Megan, *Monastic Spaces and their Meanings: Thirteenth-century English Cistercian Monasteries* (Turnhout: Brepols, 2001)

Charátová, Kateřina, 'Mindful of Reality, Faithful to Traditions: Development of Bohemian Possessions of the Cistercian Order, from the 12th to the 13th Centuries', in *L'espace cistercien*, ed. by Léon Pressouyre (Paris: Comité des travaux historiques et scientifiques, 1994), pp. 177–84

Chauvin, Benoît, 'Réalités et évolution de l'économie cistercienne dans les duché et comté de Bourgogne au Moyen Âge. Essai de synthèse', in *L'économie cistercienne: geographie, mutations, du Moyen Âge aux temps modernes: troisiemes journées internationales d'histoire, 16–18 septembre 1981* (Auch: Centre Culturel Départemental de l'Abbaye de Flaran, 1983), pp. 13–52

Coppack, Glyn, *Fountains Abbey: the Cistercians in Northern England* (Stroud: Tempus, 2003)

Donnelly, James S., *The Decline of the Medieval Cistercian Laybrotherhood* (New York: Fordham University Press, 1949)

Forde, John of, 'Life of Wulfric of Haselbury', in *The Cistercian World: Monastic Writings of the Twelfth Century*, ed. by Pauline Matarasso (London: Penguin, 1993)

France, James, 'Cistercian Foundation Narratives in Scandinavia in their Wider Context', *Citeaux*, 43 (1992), 119–60

France, James, *The Cistercians in Scandinavia* (Kalamazoo, MI: Cistercian Publications, 1992)

Hilton, Rodney H., *English and French Towns in Feudal Society* (Cambridge: Cambridge University Press, 1992)

Hockey, Stanley F., ed., *The Account Book of Beaulieu Abbey* (London: Royal Historical Society, 1975)

Jamroziak, Emilia, *The Cistercian Order in Medieval Europe, 1090–1500* (Abingdon: Routledge, 2013)

Kinder, Terryl N., *Cistercian Europe: Architecture of Contemplation* (Grand Rapids, MI: Eerdmans, 2000)

Lekai, Louis Julius, *The Cistercians: Ideals and Reality* (Ohio: Kent State University Press, 1977)

Lester, Anne E., *Creating Cistercian Nuns: The Women's Religious Movement and its Reform in Thirteenth-Century Champagne* (Ithaca: Cornell University Press, 2011)

Madden, Sister James Eugene, 'Business Monks, Banker Monks, Bankrupt Monks: The English Cistercians in the Thirteenth Century', *The Catholic Historical Review*, 49–3 (1963), 341–64

McGuire, Brian Patrick, *Conflict and Continuity at Øm Abbey: A Cistercian Experience in Medieval Denmark* (Copenhagen: Museum Tusculanum, 1976)

Newman, Martha, *The Boundaries of Charity: Cistercian Culture and Ecclesiastical Reform 1098–1180* (Stanford, CA: Stanford University Press, 1996)

Noell, Brian, 'Expectations and Unrest among Cistercian Lay Brothers in the Twelfth and Thirteenth Centuries', *Journal of Medieval History*, 32 (2006), 253–74

Pascua Echegaray, Esther, 'Vassals and Allies in Conflict: Relations between Santa Maria de Montederramo and Local Galician Society in the Thirteenth Century', in *Beyond the Market: Transactions, Property and Social Networks in Monastic Galicia, 1200–1300*, ed. by Reyna Pastor and others (Leiden: Brill, 2002), pp. 23–106

Pastor, Reyna, 'Social Mobility and the Personal Networks of "Low-intermediate Social Groups": Relations Between Communities of Peasants and *Foreros* and the Monastery of Oseira in the Thirteenth Century', in *Beyond the Market: Transactions, Property and Social Networks in Monastic Galicia, 1200–1300*, ed. by Reyna Pastor and others (Leiden: Brill, 2002), pp. 235–324

Platt, Colin, *The Monastic Grange in Medieval England: A Reassessment* (London: MacMillan, 1969)

Pryce, Huw, 'Patrons and Patronage among the Cistercians in Wales', *Archaeologia Cambrensis*, 154 (2007), 81–95

Sabapathy, John, *Officers and Accountability in Medieval England 1170–1300* (Oxford: Oxford University Press, 2014)

Sayers, Jane, 'Violence in the Medieval Cloister', *Journal of Ecclesiastical History*, 41–4 (1990), 533–42

Schneider, Reinhard, *Vom Klosterhaushalt zum Stadt- und Staathaushalt der zisterziensische Beitrag* (Stuttgart: Hiersemann, 1994)

Stone, David, *Decision-Making in Medieval Agriculture* (Oxford: Oxford University Press, 2005)

Toepfer, Michael, *Die Konversen der Zisterzienster* (Berlin: Duncker & Humblot, 1983)

Waddell, Chrysogonus, ed., *Cistercian Lay Brothers: Twelfth-century Usages with Related Texts* (Brecht: Citeaux, 2000)

Waddell, Chrysogonus, ed., *Twelfth-Century Statutes from the Cistercian General Chapter* (Brecht: Cîteaux, 2002)

Williams, David H., *The Cistercians in the Early Middle Ages* (Leominster: Gracewing, 1998)

Wright, Robert, 'Casting down the altars and levelling everything before the Ploughshare? The Expansion and Evolution of the Grange Estates of Kirkstall Abbey', in *Thirteenth Century England IX. Proceedings of the Durham Conference 2001*, ed. by Michael Prestwich, Richard Britnell, and Robin Frame (Woodbridge: Boydell, 2003), pp. 187–200

ISABEL ALFONSO

Cistercians and Feudalism*

This article is concerned with the conventional assumption that the Cistercians, in their early period, lived outside the manorial system. My interest focuses on the way in which this assumption — not always explicit — has been argued. The Cistercian order has been seen as a movement of religious reform which emerged at the end of the eleventh century as a reaction to contemporary practice in monastic life, and which aimed to restore the letter and spirit of true Benedictine monasticism. In order to pursue the monastic vocation according to St Benedict's ideal, the early Cistercians as they themselves recount, and as was enshrined in their statutes[1] — renounced the revenues from churches, altars, oblations, burials, tithes, ovens, mills, villages and dependent peasants.[2] They were to live by the fruits of their own labour, frugally and austerely, in sites remote from human habitation. With the assistance of lay brothers (*conversi*), or even hired labour, and by organizing their estates into granges (directly managed units), they would be in a position to fulfil this ideal.[3]

The Cistercian interpretation of the Rule of St Benedict has generally been accepted as 'an economic program that implied a departure from the economic practices of contemporary monastic and secular estates', an attempt 'to base monastic existence on an altogether different socio-economic system', and 'to divorce Cistercian land cultivation from manorialism'.[4] Put another way, 'the basic unorthodoxy introduced by the settlers at Citeaux was the rejection of the manorial system both as a way of life and as a source of income'.[5]

As a result of the emphasis placed on the economic side of monastic life by the founders of Citeaux, historians have tended to refer to their religious-economic precepts in order to assess the actual development of Cistercian abbeys. They have

---

* Original publication: Alfonso, Isabel, 'Cistercians and Feudalism', *Past & Present*, 49–133 (1991), 3–30. An earlier version of this article was published as an epilogue to my book Alfonso, *La colonización cisterciense*. This version, which pays greater attention to the English bibliography, has benefited from the comments of colleagues in the School of History of the University of Birmingham, in particular Christopher Dyer. I am especially grateful to Rodney Hilton, whose warm interest and encouragement have been instrumental in the completion of this version, and to Jean Birrell, for her crucial assistance with the English translation.

1 The *Exordium parvum sacri ordinis Cisterciensis* was composed by Stephen Harding, third abbot of Citeaux. There are many editions. I use here Berga Rosell, ed., *Exordio parvo*, based on the Latin version by Rixheim. The *Exordium* was reaffirmed by the statutes of the General Chapter of the order: Canivez, ed., *Statuta capitulorum generalium ordinis Cisterciensis (1933–1941)*. On the dating of these documents, see Knowles, 'The Primitive Cistercian Documents'. The standard institutional study is Mahn, *L'ordre cistercien*.

2 *Exordium*, ch. 16. p. 38; *Statuta* I (1134), p. 14.

3 *Exordium*, p. 40; *Statuta* I (1134), pp. 12–16.

4 Roehl, 'Plan and Reality', pp. 84–85; Berman, *Medieval Agriculture*, p. 1.

5 Graves, 'The Economic Activities of the Cistercians', p. 5.

602   ISABEL ALFONSO

also judged whether the abbeys conformed or not to these ideals and, according to this, have identified stages of prosperity or decadence.

The outcome of this close association between religious *ideal* and *reality* was a model, today regarded as 'traditional', which describes how the Cistercians, in seeking places 'far from human habitation' — and given that the better lands were occupied — settled in unpopulated and unclaimed areas, resorting to large-scale land clearance and reclamation. The direct exploitation of monastic lands consolidated in compact granges practised by the monks and *conversi* made their estates more productive. Savings derived from this rational organization and from their ascetic life could be used to extend and improve their patrimony. That is to say, these monks, by putting into practice the letter and the spirit of the Rule unintentionally obtained a certain amount of surplus production. Trade developed as a necessary way of dealing with this surplus produce, and this in turn provided further opportunity for territorial expansion.[6] However, one consequence of this involuntary economic prosperity was a growing deviation from their original principles, which led to a transformation in the religious quality of the monks' life. Eventually they became landlords in receipt of rent like other seigneurial groups and, at the same time, declined economically.[7]

Spiritual ideals have thus long been used to account both for the paradoxical success of the Cistercian monks, who were 'the voluntary poor', but became 'the involuntary rich', and for their rapid expansion throughout Europe.

This interpretation, which has generally portrayed the Cistercians as *pioneers, labouring monks* and *reclaimers of waste*, has been influenced by the 'frontier thesis',

---

6   For David Knowles, this meant that 'the wheel had come full circle' (Knowles, *The Monastic Order*, p. 349). This is the circle that some liberal economists in our day would label as the 'virtuous circle of wealth' in contrast to the 'vicious circle of poverty'. The notion of a circle to explain the logic of the Cistercian growth has been adopted by many recent historians. Knowles wrote about 'the superior agricultural methods of the Cistercians, whose demesne organisation gave to their enterprises many of the advantages possessed in the modern world by the multiple-branch concern or vertically controlled group-industry over the small manufacturer and trader' (Knowles, *The Monastic Order*, p. 352). He thought that the disappearance of the *conversi* left the 'Cistercian monks as capitalist in the full sense' (Knowles, *The Monastic Order*, p. 349).

7   For an example of the standard account which has had widespread influence, see Knowles, *The Monastic Order*, pp. 346 ff., 632 ff. We can consider Lekai, *The White Monks* — which brings together and disseminates what I believe to be the key elements of this traditional discourse — the point of contact between the old and the new literature on the subject. Lekai, himself a Cistercian monk, asserts that his predecessors 'turned their back to the staggering system of feudal administration of monastic property [...] The manorial system divided the large feudal estates into isolated and virtually independent units, where the peasantry, handicapped by servility of status and tenure, was left alone to its own primitive devices without any large scale planning or unifying organisation, for the lord's interest usually was strictly limited to the collection of revenues'. In contrast, for the Cistercians, 'who rejected the traditional manorial system together with all sorts of incomes of feudal origin, there was certainly no other choice but to organise a group of lay religious for agricultural work' (Lekai, *The White Monks*, pp. 209–10 and 230). There is another version of this book (Lekai, *The Cistercians*), which Lekai himself labels as a 'new history of the Cistercian order'. He has certainly used a 'large number of recent studies' which, in his opinion, have 'revolutionized our traditional views on Cistercian beginnings' (Lekai, *The Cistercians*, p. ix). However, in my view he persists with the traditional global interpretation.

which compares Cistercian monks to the prairie settlers of the New World who derived unexpectedly large yields from rich soils which had never previously been cultivated.[8] According to this view, in seeking a life of asceticism and apostolic poverty the Cistercian monks were twelfth-century predecessors of Weber's Puritans, and, like those later Protestants, ironically reaped a rich reward for their efforts.

I believe this idealized picture to be important as an expression of the outlook and attitudes of a historiography originating in the nineteenth century. Such historiography seems, in this as in other fields, to have sought justifications and antecedents for its own political models in the Middle Ages. The past is interpreted according to certain nineteenth-century values — large and concentrated estates (although not directly managed); productive labour forces and productive investment — in contrast to what were seen as manorial ways of production.[9] We must not forget that the central decades of the last century were considered the 'Golden Age' of European agriculture, with British and French 'high farming' as the most significant examples.[10]

This traditional model has had a widespread influence over a long period, since it has generally been accepted by economic and social historians when assessing the contribution of the white monks to medieval economic growth.[11] It is worth noting that Lester Little, in his *Religious Poverty and the Profit Economy in Medieval Europe* (1978), still repeats this same argument, his secondary sources being B. H. Slicher van Bath, Georges Duby and David Knowles.[12]

Recent monographs on the monasteries, granges and economic activities of the Cistercians, based on archival evidence from the medieval houses of the order in different parts of Europe, however, have questioned some of the elements composing this traditional model. A preoccupation with a regional perspective is the most relevant feature of this new historical literature. The conference held at Flaran in 1981 on the Cistercian economy exemplifies this regional approach, as Charles Higounet points out in his introduction to the conference papers. He stresses both the attempt to avoid generalizations on the basis of data observed in a particular area or estate, and the tendency to moderate and play down the exceptional role which has been attributed to the monks' economic activities.[13] The papers presented at this conference carefully examine the characteristics, patterns of settlement and the socio-economic

---

8 Berman, *Medieval Agriculture*, p. 8, ch. 1.
9 See, for example, Winter, *Die Cistercienser des nordöstlichen Deutschlands*; Schulze, *Die Kolonisierung*; Uhlhorn, 'Die Kulturthätigkeit der Cisterzienser'; Inama-Sternegg, 'Sallandstudien'; Caffi, *Dell'abbazia di Chiaravalle*; Gabotto, *L'agricoltura nella regione Saluzzese*; Donna, *Lo sviluppo storico delle bonifiche*; Marie-Henri, *Études sur l'état intérieur des abbayes cisterciennes*; Parker Mason, 'The Beginnings of the Cistercian Order'; Mullin, *A History of the Work of the Cistercians*. Many of these works are referred to in the more recent regional studies listed in n. 14 and 16.
10 For that period see Abel, *Crises agraires*; Thompson, 'Free Trade and the Land'.
11 See, for example, Slicher van Bath, *The Agrarian History of Western Europe*, pp. 153 ff.; Duby, *The Early Growth of the European Economy*, pp. 219 ff.; Genicot, *Countours of the Middle Ages*; Postan, *The Medieval Economy*, p. 92; Pounds, *An Economic History*, pp. 171–73. Note that not all these studies accept the outstanding role of Cistercians in reclaiming waste land.
12 Little, *Religious Poverty*, pp. 90–96.
13 Higounet, 'Avant-propos', p. 8.

organization of the regions in which the Cistercians established their houses. They provide excellent syntheses of regional research in Burgundy, north-west Europe, south-west France, Portugal, north-west Italy and western Germany.[14] A further paper on Cistercian granges contrasts the norms of the order with the evidence of practice.[15] Similar studies exist for monasteries in eastern Germany, England and Wales, the Iberian peninsula and Bohemia.[16] Together, they constitute a useful summary of the debate on the Cistercian economy in the period of expansion, and I will draw on them extensively in what follows.

The most questionable part of the traditional thesis holds that the Cistercians were *reclaimers of waste, pioneers* who created new arable land out of the wilderness. Many local studies have revealed that their settlements were almost entirely located in previously inhabited areas, where much clearance and reclamation had already taken place. Constance Berman has shown how much the traditional model has been influenced by the 'frontier thesis'; she is highly critical of this interpretation, the origins of which she locates in the twelfth century, when the early Cistercians had to legitimize their settlements in terms of the statutes of the order. Showing that the Cistercians of southern France acquired property not through the clearance and reclamation of unoccupied land, but rather by careful purchase and the reorganization of holdings which often had a long history of cultivation, she argues that the Cistercians in this region were *entrepreneurs* and *managers*, not *frontiersmen* or *pioneers*.[17] Robert Fossier also stresses that the conservation of forests was a prime concern of the white monks in north-west Europe, while Coburn Graves considers that, in the case of the English

---

14 For Burgundy, see Chauvin, 'Réalités et évolution de l'économie cistercienne'; for north-west Europe, see Fossier, 'L'économie cistercienne'; for south-west France, see Barrière, 'L'économie cistercienne'; for southern France, see also Berman, *Medieval Agriculture*; for Portugal, see Durand, 'L'économie cistercienne'; for north-west Italy, see Comba, 'Aspects économiques'; Comba, 'I cistercensi', reprinted in Comba, *Contadini, signori e mercanti*; for other Italian Cistercians, see Chiappa Mauri, 'La costruzione del paesaggio agrario padano'; for western Germany, see Rösener, 'L'économie cistercienne'.

15 Higounet, 'Essai sur les granges cisterciennes'.

16 For eastern Germany, see Roehl, 'Plan and Reality'; for England and Wales, see Graves, 'The Economic Activities of the Cistercians'; Platt, *The Monastic Grange*; Donkin, *The Cistercians*; Williams, *The Welsh Cistercians*. Research on Cistercian houses in the Iberian Peninsula is still very scarce, though it has developed greatly in recent years. The spread of the order into the peninsula is well described by Cocheril, *Études sur le monachisme*. There is also a synthesis of work on the Galician Cistercians: Portela, *La colonización cisterciense*. The general works by Álvarez Palenzuela, *Monasterios cistercienses*; and Pérez-Embid Wamba, *El Cister en Castilla y León*, are not effective synthesis, being very superficial. For this region, refer to Alfonso, *La colonización cisterciense*; Castán Lanaspa, 'La formación y la explotación'. For Catalonia, see Santacana Tort, *El monasterio de Poblet*; Altisent, *Historia de Poblet*; McCrank, 'The Cistercians of Poblet'. For Bhemia, see Charvatova, 'Le modèle économique cistercien'.

17 Berman, *Medieval Agriculture*, pp. 5–10. However, Berman refers only to a very narrow concept of 'frontier', and does not take account of the new developments of this thesis as presented by L. J. McCrank, writing on monastic and ecclesiastical movements on the frontier of New Catalonia. McCrank has questioned the rigid application of the frontier thesis by F. J. Turner and most American historians after him, who came from a Protestant background (McCrank, 'The Cistercians of Poblet', pp. 355–59).

Cistercians, 'the work of *défrichement* was not outstanding'.[18] This is not to deny that the Cistercians, in some areas, made a considerable contribution to the expansion of arable land. We know from the studies under discussion that both activities could be combined within the monastic estate as a whole with its varied geographical areas, in order to make best use of resources.[19]

Innovations in agriculture and rural industry have also been associated with the Cistercian estates. In fact it has not been demonstrated that the Cistercians were responsible for the introduction of any such innovations, as opposed to being important agents in their diffusion and improvement.[20] Skill in the use of water, and in the mining of coal, iron and salt, seems to have been highly developed in certain abbeys,[21] but this always seems to reflect the socio-economic and cultural context of the surrounding region.[22] Though the importance of the Cistercians as good arable farmers has not been questioned, emphasis has been put rather on their specialization in other activities, namely sheep-farming,[23] and industry and trade.[24]

These remarks are not meant to provide a comprehensive survey of all the dominant trends in current historical writing on the Cistercians. I have tried, rather, to draw attention to some criticisms of the old model, as well as to the most relevant

---

18 Fossier, 'L'économie cistercienne'; Graves, 'The Economic Activities of the Cistercians'. See also Chauvin, 'Réalités et évolution de l'économie cistercienne', pp. 20–21, which argues that '"forest" monks (*moines forestarii*) are referred to in many abbeys, at Cîteaux, La Ferté and Fontenay, among others, during the second half of the twelfth century'.

19 'Cistercian assarting took different forms depending on the place and abbey; here, scarcely at all, there, sporadic, elsewhere again, large-scale and systematic. It is high time that we stopped arguing in terms simply of assarters or non-assarters' (Higounet, 'Avant-propos', p. 8).

20 For example, Comba says that 'we have no grounds for believing that the Cistercians introduced any technological innovations' (Comba, 'I cistercensi', p. 256). Roehl argues that 'in fact, there seems to be virtually no firm evidence that the Cistercians employed any technology which was not available to and practiced by their contemporaries' (Roehl, 'Plan and Reality', p. 94). Barrière believes that 'as far as technical equipment is concerned, the Cistercians seem not so much to have innovated as to have improved existing techniques' (Barrière, 'L'économie cistercienne', p. 82). However, Portela found evidence that a very advanced plough (*vassadoiro*) was used on the granges of the Galician monastery of Sobrado, as well as new schemes for crop rotation (Portela, *La colonización cisterciense*, pp. 108–13).

21 Chauvin, 'Réalités et évolution de l'économie cistercienne', p. 21; Barrière, 'L'économie cistercienne', p. 82. On mining and iron production, see Verna-Navarre, 'La sidérurgie cistercienne', pp. 207–18; Graves, 'The Economic Activities of the Cistercians', pp. 17–18.

22 Higounet, 'Avant-propos', p, 8; Comba, 'I cistercensi', pp. 239 and 252. See also Durand, 'L'économie cistercienne', p. 109; Alfonso, *La colonización cisterciense*, pp. 178–79 and SMMoreruela104, 1242.

23 For England, see Graves, 'The Economic Activities of the Cistercians', pp. 19–32; for Italy, see Comba, 'I cistercensi', pp. 252–54; for France, see Fossier, 'L'économie cistercienne', p. 71; Chauvin, 'Réalités et évolution de l'économie cistercienne', pp. 25–26; Berman, *Medieval Agriculture*, pp. 94–117. On 'pastoral granges', see Higounet, 'Essai sur les granges cisterciennes', pp. 174–75; Alfonso, 'Las granjas de Moreruela'.

24 See, for example, Comba, 'I cistercensi', pp. 255–60; Alfonso, *La colonización cisterciense*, pp. 179–84; Chauvin, 'Réalités et évolution de l'économie cistercienne', p. 30. For the wool trade and woollen cloth manufacture in England, see Graves, 'The Economic Activities of the Cistercians', pp. 19–33. Rösener, 'L'économie cistercienne', analyses the specialization of Cistercian production consequent on its growing orientation towards the market economy. See also Berman, *Medieval Agriculture*, p. 121; Durand, 'L'économie cistercienne', p. 109.

new contributions to our understanding of the economy of the white monks. These studies undoubtedly improve our knowledge of the rural history of the various regions in which the Cistercians settled. Nevertheless, in my opinion, this historiography retains the underlying traditional global interpretation, though this is not always readily apparent. Thus these historians — who do not make full use of the evidence on which their studies are based — assert the non-manorial character of the primitive Cistercians, and/or see the Cistercian economy as foreshadowing the early capitalist economy.

To illustrate this point, I would like to discuss — without distorting or decontextualizing them — those descriptions and assessments of the granges which have generally been accepted. These reveal, clearly and eloquently, the persistence, in different ways, of the traditional picture. At the same time, I would like to suggest, first, that the relationships of domination and subordination within the granges should not be overlooked, even though the labour of the *conversi* or hired labourers might appear to be 'voluntary' and 'free' when compared with the services of tenants; and secondly, that the study of the nature of Cistercian land accumulation and the role of tenancies — that is, land indirectly managed — in the functioning of the estates, both of which should be considered in relation to the granges, reveals that the Cistercian monks held and exercised seigneurial power from an early period in their existence.

We know from the recent studies that, though with many regional variations, all Cistercian abbeys, in aiming at self-sufficiency, planned and controlled their economy through a complementary network of granges, which were well adapted to the agricultural conditions of the areas in which they were located. On these granges, a large, unpaid, voluntary and highly motivated work-force, composed mainly of lay brothers, but assisted by hired workers, cultivated the soil, tended the cattle, worked the iron or salt mines, and manufactured their products, not only for their own consumption, but to produce surpluses. These brought financial benefits which were, in turn, used to improve and expand the patrimony.[25]

In the century before 1250, a period of general economic expansion, the Cistercian granges reached a high peak of development, which varied in intensity with monastery and region.[26] During this period, however, they departed considerably from the ideals of the founding fathers. These deviations were gradually accepted and, as they became common practice, were eventually incorporated by the annual assembly of abbots of all monasteries in the General Chapter into the rules of the order.[27] From then on the leasing-out of land in various forms made the monks the recipients of income from

---

25 Higounet, 'Essai sur les granges cisterciennes', pp. 157–80, sums up the debate on granges, examining both theory and 'the testimony of the facts' concerning this institution and its evolution. It is interesting to note how, in spite of the wide variety of types of granges documented by historians, this standard view prevails in the end.

26 On the question of overall chronology, Higounet argues that '[i]n general, the grange system remained in full vigour up to the mid-thirteenth century' (Higounet, 'Essai sur les granges cisterciennes', pp, 164–65). See also Chauvin, 'Réalités et évolution de l'économie cistercienne', pp. 20–39.

27 Higounet examines the statutes created between 1208 and 1305, which show how the 'mutation of the system [...] was progressively accepted and made possible' (Higounet, 'Essai sur les granges

rent, and disrupted the original Cistercian economy.[28] A decline in the recruitment of *conversi* is assumed to be the main reason for the disintegration of the demesnes.[29]

The introduction of a grange system, variously described as 'a monument to Cistercian organizational skills', 'the key to Cistercian economy', 'fundamental to abbatial prosperity' and 'the basis for the high quality of organisation', has won all kinds of praise — for its efficiency, its profitability, its rationality and its superiority.[30] It resulted in 'a new scientific agriculture', 'an ideal system, perfectly balanced', which in the less-developed areas became a model for others to follow.[31] Scholars continue to employ such terms to describe the consolidation and organization of land in granges, the work-force used to exploit them, the planning of complementary activities, and the management of these centres which reflected 'the spirit of the order', and which were, indeed, 'founded to carry it out'.[32] Thus the old story is repeated, although historians now tend to stress Cistercian organizational and managerial skills rather than their ability to reclaim wasteland.[33]

It is not my intention to question the existence of such granges, or the exceptional efficiency of such demesnes, although, from the beginning, as we shall see, there were other forms of estate organization and other types of labour. What I wish to draw attention to are certain inferences which are being drawn. According to these accounts, the most distinctive feature of the Cistercian economy before 1250 was the direct farming of large and compact demesnes by, instead of tenants, a work-force which did not pay rents. Hence it is described as a programme, model or system

---

cisterciennes', p. 176, cf. pp. 160–61. See also Barrière, 'L'économie cistercienne', p. 94; Roehl, 'Plan and Reality', p. 106.

28 According to Chauvin 'before 1250, the Cistercian economy shows evidence of a rapid emergence, then continuous progress coupled with a permanent concern to adapt [...] Once past the watershed of the 1250s, what had by then become *the economy of the Cistercians* was to experience internal decline as a result of the passage of time' (Chauvin, 'Réalités et évolution de l'économie cistercienne', p. 44 – emphasis added). See also Higounet, 'Essai sur les granges cisterciennes', pp. 177 ff.

29 Higounet says that '[w]hen the crisis of manpower became acute, the dissolution of the granges, or of part of the granges, and their conversion into rent-paying tenements, from having been exceptional emerged as a common means of survival' (Higounet, 'Essai sur les granges cisterciennes', p. 177). In his introduction to the volume in which this essay appears, however, he recognizes that other causes have been suggested (Higounet, 'Avant-propos', p. 9). See also Graves's comments on the classic studies Donnelly, *The Decline of the Medieval Cistercian Laybrotherhood*; Donnelly, 'Changes in the Grange Economy'; cf. Graves, 'The Economic Activities of the Cistercians', pp. 4–5 and 19. See also Roehl, 'Plan and Reality', pp. 112–13.

30 Berman, *Medieval Agriculture*, p. 61; Platt, *The Monastic Grange*, p. 13; Higounet, 'Essai sur les granges cisterciennes', p. 157; Barrière, 'L'économie cistercienne', p. 84.

31 Platt, *The Monastic Grange*, p. 13; Berman, *Medieval Agriculture*, pp. 61 and 93; Barrière, 'L'économie cistercienne', p. 88; Williams, *The Welsh Cistercians*, p. 242.

32 Platt, *The Monastic Grange*, p. 13; Barrière, 'L'économie cistercienne', pp. 84, 89. See also Fossier, 'L'économie cistercienne', pp. 66–67.

33 Durand, for example, observes that 'All in all, whatever has been said, in Portugal one finds few "assarting monks", and even fewer "monastic agronomists", but instead top-rank managers' (Durand, 'L'économie cistercienne', p. 117). See also Berman, *Medieval Agriculture*, p. 93. Roehl, 'Plan and Reality', p. 94 redefines the liberal economic theory embodied in the Cistercian programme of religious reform which seems to him to be a model of economic rationality. In this essay he clearly applies Keynesian theory, as in Roehl, 'Patterns and Structure of Demand', pp. 107–42.

608   ISABEL ALFONSO

which did not resemble the manorial economy, but was rather 'an island of advanced organisation in a sea of peasant tenements and feudal demesnes'.[34]

Is it possible to argue that the primitive Cistercians were independent of the manorial structures which they claimed to have rejected? A casual glance at the titles of studies of the Cistercians or of medieval rural history, for example, would be enough to show that the seigneurial character of the Cistercians is commonly accepted. Nevertheless it is also customary to contrast *manorial* monasticism as represented by Cluny with the new labouring orders, and — more specifically — with the Cistercians, whose members 'chose not to live by the labor of other men and so took a stance outside the seigniorial mode of production'.[35]

While this interpretation is not always explicit in these studies, its presence is frequently betrayed in other expressions. It seems to me that, as long as historians (and I acknowledge certain exceptions) write about the first Cistercian century as a century of purity, of the renunciation of all standard feudal revenues, and of the exclusively self-sufficient cultivation of land, the white monks will only be characterized as seigneurial lords in the century during which they leased out their demesnes. Thus Higounet, for example, describes a process by which, at the end of the thirteenth century, these granges 'travel ever further towards a seigneurial type of organization', so that 'Cistercians were henceforth no more than rentiers like other lay and ecclesiastical landlords'.[36] Similarly, Werner Rösener shows how, 'from the thirteenth century, the tendency to rent out newly acquired property strengthened at Salem, and there gradually emerged an unequivocally domanial system', though he concedes that 'in the economy of Salem, there was already, in the twelfth century, in addition to the granges cultivated by the monks, an important group of farmed-out lands, which the monks had primarily acquired through donations in very scattered locations'.[37] D. H. Williams also describes 'the transition of a grange economy to a manorial structure' on the part of the Welsh Cistercians and 'the transformation of the monastic communities from directly-involved farmers to financially-interested landlords', although he also recognizes that at Strata Florida in central Wales, 'many of its vast "granges" [...] were based upon a semi-manorial Celtic pattern, with attendant dues and customs'.[38]

There is, in fact, an almost imperceptible tendency to associate the manorial system with a form of estate management in which the landlord received rents — in kind, cash and/or labour — from his tenants: that is to say, in which the lord lived *by*

---

34   Donkin, *The Cistercians*, p. 173. See the works listed in n. 4 and n. 5 for similar assumptions.

35   Duby, *The Three Orders*, p. 222. See also Duby, *The Early Growth of the European Economy*, p. 219, though noting that on p. 220 he refers to the granges as seigneurial centres.

36   Higounet, 'Essai sur les granges cisterciennes', p. 162; Higounet, 'Avant-propos', p. 9.

37   Rösener, 'L'économie cistercienne', p. 152. Rösener attempts to differentiate German monasteries according to their degree of self-sufficiency; however, he is forced to conclude that 'it was only during the initial phase and in some abbeys that a wholly self-sufficient economy was found. The majority of monasteries in the twelfth and thirteenth centuries had a mixed economic system; as well as the lands which the monks cultivated themselves, a great deal of land was rented out and cultivated by dependent peasants'.

38   Williams, *The Welsh Cistercians*, pp. 243 and 267.

the sweat of others. This conjures up, both from an economic and a social standpoint, all kinds of negative associations, such as idleness, luxury and avarice, in contrast to the hard work, austerity and poverty attributed to the Cistercians.

We need to question the implicit meaning of the type of associations which are to be found in the analysis contained in this historiographical discourse. Most relevant, in my opinion, is the one which associates seigneurial exploitation with rent collection, of whatever type, from a tenant peasantry. Even though rent — as the appropriation of part of peasant production — was a key element in shaping class structure in a feudal society, this connection tends to obscure our understanding of social relationships and their characteristics on the Cistercian estates which, we are told, consisted wholly of directly cultivated demesne. We will see that evidence from an early date — quoted in the studies already referred to — of other monastic land held by tenants, has generally been regarded as exceptional, and has not been taken into account in the analysis of the Cistercian economy of that period.

All the same, even if we are to accept that all monastic land was organized in granges and cultivated mainly by *conversi*, and that, though unpaid, these lay brothers were not totally disinterested,[39] we need to remember that the character of the relationship between monks and labourers should not be assumed, but must be analysed. It is often suggested that it was through the efforts of the *conversi*, assisted by hired workers, that the granges made the Cistercians rich[40] — though the lack of quantitative evidence for this is also generally admitted.[41] The higher degree of commitment, the strong

---

39 Here I am referring both to material subsistence and the symbolic capital (the prestige and spiritual advantages of being a monk) that they expected to share with the monks as a part of the religious community.

40 For example, to Lekai, it was the 'heroic labour' of these *conversi* which was 'the key to the phenomenal economic success of the early Cistercian establishments' (Lekai, *The White Monks*, p. 232). Donkin also says that 'without lay brothers, the typical Cistercian grange [...] would hardly have been possible' (Donkin, *The Cistercians*, p. 173). See also Fossier, 'L'économie cistercienne', p. 67; Berman, *Medieval Agriculture*, p. 56.

41 For example, Chauvin, after saying that 'the world of the lay brethren remains almost totally unknown', claims that 'in Burgundy as elsewhere, [they] made [...] a large contribution to the fortunes and renown of Citeaux [...] and as the meagre sources confirm up to the middle of the thirteenth century, nothing indicates the crisis of recruitment found in other regions at this period' (Chauvin, 'Réalités et évolution de l'économie cistercienne', p. 28, cf. p. 40). Barriere also says that 'despite its abundance, the documentation provides only scanty evidence as to the quantitative importance of the lay brothers, and barely enables us to add to our modest knowledge of this monastic population' (Barrière, 'L'économie cistercienne', p. 85, cf. p. 92). As 'the number of lay brothers is always difficult to establish', Comba calls for the use of other historical sources, such as chronicles, since 'the lay brother was a category of person who, in principle, escaped the documentation collected in the cartularies'. He seems, nevertheless, to accept that there was an initial period in which Cistercian granges in the north of Italy were worked by *conversi* (Comba, 'Aspects économiques', p. 128, n. 50). Higounet, despite admitting that 'the number of *conversi* working on the grange generally eludes us', concludes that '[i]n sum, charged initially with work on the land, the lay brethren became a small body of experienced and specialized foremen, all the more competent in that regional recruitment favoured knowledge of local agricultural practices', which implies that their number had previously been larger (Higounet, 'Essai sur les granges cisterciennes', p. 172 — emphasis added). See also Berman, *Medieval Agriculture*, pp. 78, 125 and 126. I have criticized elsewhere similar internal inconsistencies in Spanish studies (Alfonso, *La colonización cisterciense*, pp. 202–03). This

motivation and the pious devotion of the lay brothers, together with the austerity of their lives, have long been adduced to explain the exceptional level of productivity typical of Cistercian granges in comparison with earlier or contemporary agrarian units worked by villein tenants.[42] In addition there have recently been attempts to assess the major advantages that the *conversi* offered the Cistercian economy in terms of *cost functions*. Most important on the theoretical level, according to Richard Roehl, was that the use of *conversi* reduced dependency costs for labour, because 'they were not feeding wives, children or the elderly, but (in terms of labour cost) had only to feed and clothe themselves'. In other words, 'the unit cost of subsistence per labourer was significantly lower on Cistercian granges than it had been on the peasant farms which had preceded those granges. The immediate effect was decreasing cost and thereby increasing the order's net yields'.[43] It is interesting to note that Roehl, in his assessment of 'the ratio of economically productive to economically non-productive individuals supported by the estate', includes among the latter those members of peasant families that he considers to be 'economic parasites (children, women, and the ailing, infirm and aged)', but not the monks, since they 'intended to be active participants in the work of production'.[44]

Berman devotes a whole chapter to 'The Profits of Grange Agriculture', in which she uses a 'hypothetical example' to demonstrate the saving on dependants derived from *conversi* labour which, she argues, must be 'recognised as one of the reasons why direct cultivation by lay brothers and hired laborers was so attractive'. She also tackles the problem of the reproduction of the *conversi* work-force, since 'it did not replace itself from generation to generation as had the peasant farm family'.[45] It is striking

---

inconsistency in part results from supposing, on insufficient evidence, the existence and importance of the *conversi* from the beginning. The use of other types of manpower on the granges — such as serfs, hired workers and dependent peasants — has been demonstrated, but the importance of these labourers is passed over when the leasing out of granges is attributed to the reduction in the number of *conversi*.

42 For example, Roehl writes about the implications of their 'austere, even puritanical consumption regime' (Roehl, 'Plan and Reality', p. 92). For Berman, '*conversi* must have been highly motivated, seeing their work in the fields as a form of prayer' (Berman, *Medieval Agriculture*, p. 82); further, 'Cistercian asceticism and stress on simplicity in religious practice promoted the saving which allowed capital accumulation' (Berman, *Medieval Agriculture*, p. 83).

43 I have used Berman's quotations from Roehl to demonstrate that she accepts this analysis (Berman, *Medieval Agriculture*, p. 79).

44 Roehl, 'Plan and Reality', pp. 92–94.

45 Berman, *Medieval Agriculture*, pp. 81 and 79. I believe that, among other considerations, she contradicts herself in the last chapter of her book, where she claims that monastic houses, by providing a secure and respectable place of retirement for parents, favoured earlier marriage and, indirectly, population expansion. See Berman, *Medieval Agriculture*, p. 119. If this were true, I think the result would have been a higher level of dependency, not perhaps on the *conversi* as individuals, but on the whole religious community. What is more, in her 'hypothetical' estimation, Berman compares granges to peasant holdings rather than to other types of demesne; when comparing demesnes, she finds it necessary to observe that the calculation is only possible 'if the monks are treated as landlords living on rent just as Cluniac ones would have been' (Berman, *Medieval Agriculture*, p. 81, n. 80). She nevertheless explicitly denies the manorial character of the Cistercian estates (Berman, *Medieval Agriculture*, pp. 20–21).

that in assessing the work performed by *conversi* both she and Roehl use the classic arguments employed to evaluate the advantages and disadvantages of slave labour.

The inferior status of the lay brothers with respect to the choir monks is a commonplace throughout this historical literature. They were 'enlarged *famuli*', 'half monks', 'villeins in monastic dress', 'bound by the same vows as were the monks', 'theoretically reckoned equal members of the community, but their role was to be first and foremost that of workers'. However, these explicit acknowledgements of the existence of unequal relationships within the monastic communities seem to be forgotten when — while it is stated that choir monks hardly worked at all — we are told that the Cistercians re-established immediate, direct and physical manual labour for all their members.[46]

Indeed, it is the assumption that all the members of the community worked which ultimately conceals and legitimizes the relationship of domination within the monastic community of monks over labourers — whether unpaid and subject to monastic discipline, or paid wages.[47] Fossier, for example, says that the Cistercians did not oppress their men, as the latter either earned wages or did not exist.[48] He seems here to refuse to acknowledge the exploitation of lay brothers and hired workers which, it seems to me, he implicitly assumes elsewhere, as when he attributes the high yields of Cistercian granges to the unpaid or badly paid work-force which the order had at its disposal until 1250–1275.[49] I have already noted the view that the white monks did not live by the labour of others until they began to lease out their demesnes, evidence — we are told — of the complete transformation of the Cistercian spirit and the decadence of their original economy.[50]

The real nature of relations within the monastic community similarly seems to me to have been commonly ignored — perhaps it might even be said, misrepresented — when the granges have been lauded as being efficient, profitable, modern, rational and so on, on the basis of their size and homogeneity, and the considerable managerial ability of the monks in purely technical terms. In these

---

46 Duby, *The Three Orders*, p. 222; Duby, *The Early Growth of the European Economy*, p. 219. There are internal inconsistencies on this subject in the considerable body of work produced by Duby, because, in spite of the statement already quoted (see above, p. 608), he also clearly asserts that the Cistercian community was divided into two classes, choir monks and lay brothers, reflecting the social origins of those who were drawn into the monasteries (Duby, *The Three Orders*, p. 225; Duby, *Saint Bernard*, p. 80). See also Berman, *Medieval Agriculture*, pp. 41 and 54.

47 On the concealment of domination and economic exploitation within kinship relations, see Vernier, 'Putting Kin and Kinship to Good Use'.

48 Fossier, *Peasant Life*, p. 133.

49 For example, when he argues that 'up to 1250–1275, it is reasonable to say that, in the successive habits of the devoted lay brother, then the consenting oblate, and finally the full-time wage-labourer, the order always had a work-force at its disposal which was unpaid or underpaid, and it was this which lay at the root of its overproduction, its progress and its entry into the market' (Fossier, 'L'économie cistercienne', p. 72). See above, n. 40.

50 For example, for Chauvin, 'The dominant influence, which was fully prevalent from the mid-thirteenth century until around 1330, was the disruption and then gradual disappearance of the chief foundations of the triumphant Cistercian economy' (Chauvin, 'Réalités et évolution de l'économie cistercienne', p. 40).

cases, the inequality and mechanisms of social exploitation are relegated to a subsidiary role. It is in this context that we can understand the emphasis placed in this historiography on the concern of the monks for the *rational use of their estates*, on their *economic sensibility* and their *organizational skills*. They are considered active, experienced, even *Schumpeterian managers*, with whom the era of great entrepreneurs begins to take shape.[51] From this perspective, the Cistercian demesne represents a different model, clearly superior to its underdeveloped environment,[52] one in which the monks' managerial efficiency does not appear to be related to the monastic power which they employed, and in which, therefore, oppression and coercion of the *conversi* — unpaid labour — or of hired workers — underpaid labour — was not a factor.[53]

This same line of thought inspires Gonzalo Anes, a Spanish historian specializing in the *ancien régime*, to argue that the demesnes of a Castilian Cistercian monastery in the eighteenth century 'were not seigneurial because the monks paid their labourers high wages and, above all, because they were managed according to the criteria of profitability, that is to say, capitalist criteria'. He neglects, however, the civil and criminal jurisdiction which the monks still possessed at that date.[54]

I have argued above that, though the Cistercian estates were supposedly wholly directly managed, there was nevertheless a socio-economic hierarchy internal to the monastic community which differentiated choir monks from lay brothers and other labourers, and also that the integration of Cistercian granges into an aristocratically dominated society in which the monks had much in common with other landlords needs to be stressed. The Cistercian granges have to be understood in the context of the social and economic system of which they formed a part. I believe that a consideration of two other topics that illustrate this, the nature of Cistercian land accumulation and the issue of indirectly managed monastic land, will make it possible to pursue further this reconstruction of the ideological framework of the historiography under discussion.

Throughout the literature, the study of the formation of monastic estates is closely related to the analysis of the granges. The gradual accumulation of these compact,

---

51 The quotation comes from Moulin, *La vie quotidienne des religieux*, p. 250. It is obviously something of an exaggerated version of current thinking.

52 Barrière, 'L'économie cistercienne', p. 91. See also the works cited in n. 32.

53 For Fossier, 'the essential contribution of Citeaux to the economy of medieval Europe [...] lay [...] in the development of wage-labour; the labour paid for by these men of the church gained a dignity in which I am tempted to see one of the reasons for its later development' (Fossier, 'L'économie cistercienne', p. 72). One should remember here the inconsistencies already mentioned (see above, n. 48 and 49). Should we believe that the number of wage-earning labourers increased because their work became more dignified, as Fossier seems to imply? It must be emphasized that neither *conversi* nor hired workers in this period can be considered as workers selling their labour. Hence, the notion of a labour-market used, for instance, by Comba can also be misleading (Comba, 'Aspects économiques', p. 128). I wish to thank Rodney Hilton for his comment on this point.

54 Remarks made at the Economic History Congress held in Alcalá de Henares (Spain) in December 1981 in response to J. M. Lopez's paper, 'Una aportación al estudio de las reservas señoriales en Castilla: la explotación de la abadía cisterciense de la Santa Espina', now published in López García, 'Una aportación al estudio de las "reservas señoriales"', pp. 215, 323–26.

homogeneous units, through a sometimes laborious and lengthy process of land acquisition, is seen as the result of economic planning on the part of the monks. This policy, we are told, allowed more efficient organization, since the monks had greater freedom to organize production and labour unimpeded by common rights.

Fossier argues that in Normandy through pursuing this policy the Cistercians disrupted the harmony of the open-field system and the agro-pastoral balance characteristic of the traditional medieval 'eco-system'. However, he thinks that in compensation the monks favoured 'virtually capitalist development' by leasing out their granges to the wealthiest peasants.[55]

The greatest contribution of the Cistercian monks to the transformation of the landscape in the north of Italy, according to Rinaldo Comba, was a concentration and reorganization of the land, which involved a reimposition of 'absolute ownership' ('proprietà assoluta') over what had previously been tenancies. In the course of this process, conflicts originated, above all as a result of the contradiction between this form of agricultural organization and the *irrationality* of the other forms of possession ('irrazionalità della repartizione dei diritti di possesso') and the collective use of land. He stresses that the effects of monastic expansion in mountainous areas started a *process of capitalistic expropriation* of land previously under collective control.[56]

Berman argues that by adopting careful procedures for the acquisition and *rationalization of land*, in southern France — where there was an absence of wasteland — the white monks could similarly amass 'large, compacted holdings which were transformed into granges of which they were *the only owners*'. Thus simply by consolidating holdings and reassembling fragmented units of land, the Cistercians could ensure that granges in that region would have 'produced larger net yields than the estates and farms which preceded them, even with the same nominal acreage'.[57] According to R. Donkin, the general aim of Cistercian houses in England and Wales was similarly to assemble fairly compact demesnes that were *independent of communal agriculture*, in order to produce a *more rational* and *efficient arrangement*.[58] To Rösener, it seems that in Germany the 'revolutionary requirements' of Cistercian economic precepts obliged monks and lay brothers to extend and organize their lands in 'units large enough to be profitable'.[59] In Galicia (north-west Spain), where there was a rapid accumulation of land in Cistercian hands, Ermelindo Portela states that for this reason alone the construction and widespread expansion of many granges and the abbeys themselves — especially in their aspect as agrarian units — can be considered

---

55 Fossier, 'L'économie cistercienne', pp. 65–66 — emphasis added.

56 Comba, 'I cistercensi', pp. 250–53. However, he elsewhere points out that the white monks were not alone in this (Comba, 'Aspects économiques', p. 126).

57 Berman, *Medieval Agriculture*, pp. 43 and 76 — emphasis added.

58 Donkin, *The Cistercians*, pp. 61–62 — my emphasis.

59 For Rösener, 'the ideal form' is 'the isolated farm [...] economically, such granges constituted extremely productive agricultural units, since they had no need to take account of the division of land in the community between villagers, or of pasture rights, with the result that the management of the unit could easily be adapted' (Rösener, 'L'économie cistercienne', pp. 140–41). However, he gives examples of other types of granges with their lands 'scattered and intermingled with those of village communities' (see above, n. 37).

a 'real change' (*revulsivo*) in the rural economy of that region in the second half of the twelfth century. The granges were active centres in the renovation of Galician agriculture as a result of their size, specialization, the farming tools used and, most important of all, their rationality.[60]

We must bear in mind the ideological content of the terms italicized above, which refer to a particular type of large-scale, concentrated, homogeneous and undivided landed property, as opposed to the irrationality of other types of fragmented landownership, presumed to be less efficient and profitable. That is to say, the growth of absolute property rights seems to be regarded as a step towards a more productive economy.[61]

However, the white monks' accumulation of land, and its subsequent or simultaneous organization into granges, is a process which, in my opinion, should be considered as a result of the acquisition and application of what we refer to as 'seigneurial' or 'feudal' power, since it implied personal domination. This power was asserted in different ways and conditions, ranging from the usurpation and eviction of peasants in order to transform their settlements into granges, to the maintenance and control of the peasant population in their villages. The formation of the monastic patrimony represented the exercise of seigneurial power, whether or not it took a jurisdictional form, through which relationships of dependence became institutionalized.

The exercise of seigneurial power, frequently documented, is generally presented as something exceptional, for which a variety of explanations are put forward. The attempt to explain an inherent element of the social system thus acquires a justificatory aspect. There are a number of curious and sometimes contradictory examples of this in the historiography we are considering, which reflect some of the ways in which historians have presented monastic power. Let us look at some of them. Robert Durand, in a valuable synthesis concerning Portuguese Cistercian estates, points out as the most *remarkable peculiarity* of the Cistercian economy in this area the fact it was not only based upon landed property and its cultivation, but also upon possession of seigneurial power. Portuguese Cistercian monasteries, he says, obtained from their very foundation privileges which made the monks landlords with prerogatives of coercion and granted them the subsequent profits. He goes on

---

60 Portela, *La colonización cisterciense*, pp. 108–09 and 112 — my emphasis.

61 I cannot refrain from including Moulin's exaltation of the rationality of those monks whom he considers 'the enlightened teachers of the rural masses [...] With respect to the peasants who remained profoundly attached to their ardent animist beliefs, the action of the monks was a vital factor in their rationalization' (Moulin, *La vie quotidienne des religieux*, p. 250). 'To the routine of the peasant', he goes on, 'to his deep-seated irrationality, the monk opposed the spirit of innovation and the desire to make reasoning, if not always reason, intervene' (Moulin, *La vie quotidienne des religieux*, p. 251). Berman also remarks that 'it is often mentioned that *conversi* labourers were free from the constraint of peasant mentality' (Berman, *Medieval Agriculture*, p. 78). On property as a historical concept, see the highly interesting work Peset, *Dos ensayos*; articles by P. Grossi collected in Grossi, *Historia del derecho de propiedad*. On property myths and misunderstandings, see Ellerman, 'Property Theory'. To understand the historical and class origins of rationality as a concept, and its relation to certain forms of *property*, it is useful to refer to MacPherson, *The Political Theory of Possessive Individualism*. Of great interest on this subject is Hollis, *Rational Economic Man*. I have discussed this problem in Alfonso, 'Sobre la organización del terrazgo'.

to explain that these prerogatives were undoubtedly necessary for them to carry out the task of repopulation in this *sparsely populated region*.[62] While his assertions are correct, the studies discussed here provide evidence of such privileges throughout the Cistercian order, which make it impossible to describe them as specific to the Portuguese or Spanish monasteries as has been assumed. Rösener, for example, when synthesizing research on the Cistercians in Germany, says that in some areas of grange settlement the monks could not achieve productive exploitation unless they acquired seigneurial and feudal powers and evicted the peasantry. He explains that this was due to the *high density of population*.[63]

Berman has made a very interesting study of the careful acquisition procedures adopted by the Cistercians in southern France, which had a long history of settlement. She claims that there was a close relationship between land acquisition and the recruitment of *conversi*. In view of 'the general economic dependency of most peasants on their lords', she argues that, for them, 'the opportunity to become *conversi* only existed if the Cistercians became their landlords [...] Once Cistercians had lordship over dependent tenants, they could encourage them to become lay brothers [...] The charters generally imply that the men and women living in the village or on the farms conveyed to the Cistercians were treated as appurtenances to the lordship of those holdings; authority over such tenants was automatically conveyed to the monks along with ownership or *dominium* of land. Once *dominium* was acquired, the Cistercians either transformed those tenants into *conversi* or removed them from their tenancies, usually by a simple purchase of their tenurial claims'. Occasionally, this removal 'was made only under pressure'.[64] Nevertheless Berman concludes that 'the monks rarely sought or obtained *bannal* or seigneurial rights so often associated with rural lordship or manorialism [...] When they obtained already-existing villages, or churches or tithes, or other manorial properties, such acquisitions were a step towards transforming those manorial resources into new non-manorial holdings — Cistercian granges — rather than the beginnings of seigneurialism'. She contends that 'practices verging on seigneurialism must all be viewed as reflecting *needs* of the order, in its introduction of grange agriculture into settled areas, or of capital investment, rather than as lapses from the order's ideals which forbade ownership of such tithes or profiting from seigneurialism'.[65] Berman's account speaks for itself; further comment is superfluous.

---

62 Durand, 'L'économie cistercienne', pp. 105–08 — my emphasis.

63 Rösener, 'L'économie cistercienne', p. 141 — my emphasis.

64 Berman describes some examples of such removals and organized, but unsuccessful, resistance to the monks' expansion. However, according to her, 'the success of the order in Southern France denotes a generally positive reception by the neighbouring communities' (Berman, *Medieval Agriculture*, pp. 53–60).

65 Berman, *Medieval Agriculture*, pp. 90, 128 and 91 – emphasis added. Berman does not achieve her aim — made explicit in the preface — of breaking with the schemes that contrast the realm of the 'ideal' with 'reality', or legislation with local practice. References to religious precepts are numerous throughout the book, but especially in the last chapter. She also believes that 'indirectly, of course, the eventual loss of religious idealism may have been a result of rural economic success (Berman, *Medieval Agriculture*, p. 129).

We have already seen how Williams writes of the 'transition of a grange economy to a manorial structure' and of the transformation of the Cistercians from *farmers* into *landlords*, although he documents 'much more evidence of the continued enjoyment of jurisdictional rights by the Welsh Cistercians'.[66] In northern Italy, though from a different perspective, Comba also describes a carefully planned policy of the acquisition of land with jurisdictional rights. He maintains that the monks' power was not always used to collect rents, but rather to counter the eventual exercise of power by other lords with the objective of guaranteeing their territorial boundaries — and control of the population living inside them[67] – within which boundaries they had unrestricted freedom of action.[68] Similarly, Luisa Chiappa argues that in the valley of the Po in Italy, 'the monks had acquired seigneurial rights in order to eliminate external interference rather than to exercise them'. Yet, she recognizes, in my opinion correctly, that 'to hold even nominally the *dominicatus* entailed the possibility of enjoying further rights'.[69] This is something which should, I think, be accepted as general rather than exceptional, since the first grants of land to the white monks, often by kings or nobles, were generally made with jurisdictional rights.[70]

On the basis of these historians' own descriptions, I would argue that this process of land accumulation should not be equated, as some seem to imply, with capitalistic land accumulation.[71] Further, analysis and evaluation of the functioning of the granges should not be divorced from consideration of the power that white monks held and used in order to construct compact estates, recruit the work-force and manage their agrarian economy.

The organization of Cistercian properties that were not granges should also be understood in relation to this monastic power as well as seigneurial interests. The detailed research that we have already examined shows that many Cistercian monasteries possessed land farmed by tenants from the beginning. Rösener, for instance, has stressed that from the twelfth century many monasteries in western

---

66 Williams, *The Welsh Cistercians*, pp. 243 and 250.

67 I refer here to the monks' interest in controlling labour resources in the areas where the granges were established. For example, Platt quotes disputes and agreements between the monks and other landlords regarding the recruitment of labourers (Platt, *The Monastic Grange*, pp. 84–86).

68 Comba, 'I cistercensi', p. 248.

69 Chiappa Mauri, 'La costruzione del paesaggio agrario padano', pp. 294–95.

70 For example, in Bohemia, see Charvatova, 'Le modèle économique cistercien'.

71 As usual, Moulin exaggerates. This is what he says about land accumulation: 'In the nature of things, the regime of life imposed by faith created the optimum conditions for *primitive capitalist accumulation*' (Moulin, *La vie quotidienne des religieux*, p. 252 — emphasis added), from a chapter entitled 'The Spiritual Engenders the Economic'. It is significant that Roehl refers to 'their unique economic programme, which was a prerequisite to the realisation of their programme of religious reform' (Roehl, 'Plan and Reality', p. 92, n. 27). A good counterpoint on the process of land accumulation in the feudal system can be found in Bois, *The Crisis of Feudalism*. He identifies two main features of feudal accumulation — 'its discontinuity and its contradictory character' — in contrast to those of capitalism (Bois, *The Crisis of Feudalism*, pp. 386–89. See also Nell, *Growth, Profits and Property*, esp. introduction, and ch. 1, 2, 15.

Germany were profitable thanks to rents collected from the tenants who farmed their holdings.[72] Therefore, he has to accept that a 'mixed economic system' existed in most abbeys.[73] However, like many others, he only seems to take into account 'the relationship between the grange economy and leasing out after the crisis of the Cistercian economy in the late Middle Ages'.[74]

Roehl, with reference to eastern German monasteries, finds that 'the Cistercians did begin to retain lands on which peasant cultivators resided, and on which they remained'. But he feels that 'the most serious difficulty in making a defence of the purity of the monks' intentions is that they acquired rent-returning lands not only as passive agents, but also in substantial measure by their own voluntary acts of purchase […] it does indicate that the economies of Cistercian monasteries could quite often become characterised by a very strong element of rentier landlordship'. He nevertheless also tries to explain what he considers 'a growing dichotomization between plan and reality in the Cistercian economy' of the abbeys he studied.[75] On this question, Fossier says that 'at the beginning […] it was only a matter of being given rent-paying tenements, even of buying them and evicting the worker; the difficulties encountered in implementing this "final solution" led them to retain the tenant'. Yet he also states that 'the Cistercians were rarely the owners of lands which were rented out'.[76] Williams argues that 'serfs on the lands early granted to the monks, if not displaced, would have become villeins of the abbot', and that 'the servile tenants were simply inherited by the monks'. He documents the grant of manors to the Welsh Cistercian abbeys at their foundation, but continues to argue for the 'transition of a grange economy to a manorial structure'.[77]

Higounet, in his general essay on Cistercian granges, provides extensive evidence of how very early on the monks had to employ hired workers, serfs or tenants, because the *conversi* were above all a small team of experienced supervisors.[78] He nevertheless interprets this as a 'degradation' of the ideal of direct exploitation of all monastic lands in granges, as a 'mutation of the system', which, from 1208, was accepted and sanctioned by the General Chapter in its statutes.[79] Thus we see that this account of 'degradation' is almost as widespread as the evidence for existence of peasants with holdings on the early Cistercian estates, and even of these peasants' contribution to the cultivation of the granges.

---

72 'From the twelfth century, many monasteries in west Germany benefited, thanks to rent, from land which was cultivated outside the granges and leased to the peasantry' (Rösener, 'L'économie cistercienne', p. 151).

73 See above, n. 82.

74 Rösener, 'L'économie cistercienne', p. 137.

75 Roehl, 'Plan and Reality', pp. 104–05. We must bear in mind that to Roehl, 'the "successful" functioning of the Cistercian economy' was 'the operation consistent with the plan' (Roehl, 'Plan and Reality', p. 96).

76 Fossier, 'L'économie cistercienne', p. 64.

77 Williams, *The Welsh Cistercians*, p. 243.

78 'It was therefore necessary at a very early date to resort to the labour of paid agricultural workers and small rent-paying peasant tenants' (Higounet, 'Essai sur les granges cisterciennes', p. 173).

79 Higounet, 'Essai sur les granges cisterciennes', pp. 176–77.

618   ISABEL ALFONSO

In this context, Spanish and Portuguese monasteries, which exhibited such tendencies from their foundation, should in my opinion be considered less unusual than is generally thought. On the basis of data contained in the studies discussed here, we should also question the marginal and exceptional character which has been attributed to such tendencies in other Cistercian estates prior to the generalization of the leasing-out of demesnes from the mid-thirteenth century onwards. As the role of tenant-holdings has been overlooked in the global analysis of the early Cistercian economy, I would like to emphasize the complementary relationship which existed, in a variety of ways, between these holdings and the granges within the estate as a whole.

Certainly, the links between demesne and tenancies on Cistercian estates were closer and more complex than has generally been recognized. In the early period, since the monks assumed the direction of production, the retention of tenants on their holdings seems above all to have facilitated control of the peasantry as a work-force. We can quote cases in which tenants were obliged to work on the granges; in which they were associated with the tasks of clearing and reclaiming land; where the rents from their holdings were used to pay hired labourers to work on the granges; or when the cultivation of the peasants' vineyards was organized from specialized granges.

For Colin Platt, 'the high price of temporary assistance, as well as its uncertain availability, no doubt explains the precautions that the Cistercians took to acquire land outside their granges, almost as much as within them'. He considers that because lay brethren were never intended to yield a squad of inexpensive labourers, tied or hired labour on the grange would seem a necessary condition of its functioning. He questions the widespread view of the Cistercians as genuine depopulators. 'As a programme of resettlement rather than depopulation, the Cistercian agricultural system assumes a somewhat different role. Needing the labour of a dependent peasantry to maintain their estates, the Cistercians competed with their contemporaries to recruit it'. By the use of archaeological evidence, Platt has shown the close association with many of the known Yorkshire granges of remains of former peasant settlements, unremarked in the records and sometimes attributed to early depopulation. He argues that 'the grange, perhaps even from its very beginnings, was a mixed community in which lay brothers, supervisors, servants and tied peasantry equally played their parts'. His account of this association seems not to have received the attention it deserves. However, given these statements, it is difficult to understand why this same author claims that the Cistercians did not form part of the manorial system.[80]

In north-west Spain I myself have found similar links between granges and peasant communities. Many of the granges of the abbey of Moreruela were in their origins small villages which were received, together with their inhabitants (*collazos*) through royal benefactions. Thus the peasants passed under monastic authority. This dependent peasantry was employed by the white monks to cultivate their lands or in other directly managed work, such as mining or stock-raising.[81] The role of the rural community as a reserve labour force is clearly apparent from other monastic evidence, which suggests the complexity of the socio-economic relationship between

---

80   Platt, *The Monastic Grange*, pp. 76–93.
81   Alfonso, *La colonización cisterciense*, pp. 190–204.

the monks and the peasants of the villages. The Cistercian monks of Sobrado, the most powerful Galician monastery, could demand labour from the *homines* of their *cotos* (areas under monastic jurisdiction) to perform a variety of tasks.[82] Granges and peasant communities were similarly connected on the estates of the Cistercian abbey of Poblet right from its foundation, as is well documented in the records of donations of lands together with their *homines*.[83]

The related organization of granges and a tied peasantry in Portuguese Cistercian estates has been described in detail by Durand, who claims that 'the Portuguese Cistercians [were] simultaneously, in the same place and at the same time, both masters of agricultural enterprises, if not cultivators, and also rentiers'.[84] In Valera the Italian Cistercians of Chiaravalle managed to concentrate land in a large and homogeneous grange. This, according to Chiappa, was established on the boundaries of the village of Valera, which the monks wished to keep as a community of labourers. For Chiappa, the Cistercians' most innovative contribution to the Lombard countryside was the direct control they exerted over this peasant work-force through short-term leases which allowed them to direct production as well as dispose easily of available land.[85] In the second half of the thirteenth century, through collective agreements with peasants, the monks 'sanctioned the creation of a new organization for the rural community' which they continued to control.[86] New settlements on monastic estates, quite common in the phase of economic expansion, are now beginning to be interpreted as the most effective way of exploiting peasant labour, rather than a solution to an adverse financial situation. The case of the abbey of Grandselve, in Aquitaine, and its *bastide* of Beaumont illustrates this; by settling peasants in the new village, with the obligation to plant vineyards, the monks could respond to the growing demand for wine, the sale of which they continued to control.[87]

Obviously, much research still needs to be done in the field of the social relations of production on Cistercian estates. I would argue here for a widening of the problem of linkages between monastic granges and village communities; that the study of the *conversi* should also be related to that of the peasant household and family structures, since it is, I think, a mistake to ignore or neglect the ties of *conversi* both with their families and with the peasant communities from which they were drawn.[88] Further the various relationships established between monks and peasants as donors, sellers, creditors and hired and tenant labourers need to be investigated in more depth. The complexities of social articulation will show us much about the structures of domination in which the Cistercians were involved.

---

82 Alfonso, *La colonización cisterciense*, pp. 204–12.
83 Santacana Tort, *El monasterio de Poblet*, pp. 354–56.
84 Durand, 'L'économie cistercienne', p. 110.
85 Chiappa Mauri, 'La costruzione del paesaggio agrario padano', p. 305.
86 Chiappa Mauri, 'La costruzione del paesaggio agrario padano', pp. 305 ff.
87 Barrière, 'L'économie cistercienne', pp. 97–98. See also Comba, 'Aspects économiques', pp. 128–29, where he discusses the different conditions in which the direct management of the demesnes was possible.
88 On the issue of the social strata from which the *conversi* came, see Comba, 'I cistercensi', pp. 246–47 and 260–61.

In this article, I have criticized the historical 'discourse' on the Cistercian economy, in which technical and economic factors relating to efficiency and productivity have been stressed, and the importance of social structures has been neglected. I have tried to demonstrate that relations of domination and subjection were present in the organization of production on Cistercian estates, and should not be associated solely with more traditional forms of manorial organization. If we do not recognize this — if we fail to see that the Cistercian economy involved seigneurial coercion and domination — we will fundamentally misunderstand how it functioned. There is also a danger that if we ignore the importance of these structures on the Cistercian estates, we will incorrectly portray socio-economic relations on the granges as purely voluntary and contractual, and imply the absence of such forms of domination from capitalistic enterprises of the kind with which the Cistercian granges have often been associated. Our understanding of both feudal and capitalistic social formations would be seriously skewed if we were to associate feudalism with social organization involving exploitation and domination, and capitalism with contractual, free and voluntary relations. After all, this would mean accepting the very ideology which legitimizes exploitation in our own society.

Bibliography

Abel, Wilhelm, *Crises agraires en Europe (XIIIe–XXe siècle)* (Paris: Flammarion, 1973)

Alfonso, Isabel, 'Las granjas de Moreruela. Notas para el estudio de la colonización cisterciense en la Meseta del Duero', in *Semana de Historia del Monacato Cantabro-Astur-Leonés* (Oviedo: Monasterio de San Pelayo, 1982), pp. 361–76

Alfonso, Isabel, 'Sobre la organización del terrazgo en Tierra de Campos', *Agricultura y sociedad*, 23 (1982), 217–32

Alfonso, Isabel, *La colonización cisterciense en la Meseta del Duero. El dominio de Moreruela (siglos XII–XIV)* (Zamora: Instituto de Estudios Zamoranos Florián de Ocampo, 1986)

Altisent, Agustí, *Historia de Poblet* (Poblet: Abadía de Poblet, 1974)

Álvarez Palenzuela, Vicente, *Monasterios cistercienses en Castilla (siglos XII–XIII)* (Valladolid: Universidad de Valladolid, 1978)

Barrière, Bernadette, 'L'économie cistercienne du sud-ouest de la France', in *L'économie cistercienne: geographie, mutations, du Moyen Âge aux temps modernes: troisièmes journées internationales d'histoire, 16–18 septembre 1981* (Auch: Centre Culturel Départemental de l'Abbaye de Flaran, 1983), pp. 75–99

Berga Rosell, Ramón, ed., *Exordio parvo y carta de caridad de la sagrada orden cisterciense: versión latina según la edición de Rixheim y traducción ilustrada con notas por D. Ramón Berga Rossell* (Poblet: Monasterio de Santa María de Poblet, 1953)

Berman, Constance Hoffman, *Medieval Agriculture, the Southern French Countryside, and the Early Cistercians: A Study of Forty-Three Monasteries* (Philadelphia: The American Philosophical Society, 1986)

Bois, Guy, *The Crisis of Feudalism: Economy and Society in Eastern Normandy c. 1300–1550* (Cambridge: Cambridge University Press, 1984)

Caffi, Michele, *Dell'abbazia di Chiaravalle in Lombardia* (Milan: G. Gnocchi, 1842)

Canivez, Joseph M, ed., *Statuta capitulorum generalium ordinis Cisterciensis ab anno 1116 ad 1786*, 8 vols (Louvain: Bureaux de la Revue d'histoire ecclésiastique, 1933–1941)

Castán Lanaspa, Guillermo, 'La formación y la explotación del dominio del monasterio de Villaverde de Sandoval (siglos XII–XIII)', in *León y su historia. Miscelánea histórica IV* (León: Centro de Estudios e Investigación San Isidoro, 1977), pp. 215–317

Charvatova, Katefina, 'Le modèle économique cistercien et son application pratique en Bohême', *Cahiers de civilisation médiévale*, 30–117 (1987), 65–70

Chauvin, Benoît, 'Réalités et évolution de l'économie cistercienne dans les duché et comté de Bourgogne au Moyen Âge. Essai de synthèse', in *L'économie cistercienne: geographie, mutations, du Moyen Âge aux temps modernes: troisièmes journées internationales d'histoire, 16–18 septembre 1981* (Auch: Centre Culturel Départemental de l'Abbaye de Flaran, 1983), pp. 13–52

Chiappa Mauri, Luisa, 'La costruzione del paesaggio agrario padano: I cistercensi e la grangia di Valera', *Studi Storici*, 26–2 (1985), 263–313

Cocheril, Maur, *Études sur le monachisme en Espagne et au Portugal* (Paris: Les Belles Lettres, 1966)

Comba, Rinaldo, 'Aspects économiques de la vie des abbayes cisterciennes de l'Italie du Nord-Ovvest (XIIe–XIVe siècles)', in *L'économie cistercienne: geographie, mutations, du Moyen Âge aux temps modernes: troisièmes journées internationales d'histoire, 16–18 septembre 1981* (Auch: Centre Culturel Départemental de l'Abbaye de Flaran, 1983), pp. 119–33

Comba, Rinaldo, 'I cistercensi fra città e campagne nei secoli XII e XIII. Una sintesi mutevole di orientamenti economici e culturali nell'italia nord-occidentale', *Studi Storici*, 26–2 (1985), 237–61

Comba, Rinaldo, *Contadini, signori e mercanti nel Piemonte medievale* (Roma: Lampi di Stampa, 1999)

Donkin, Robert Arthur, *The Cistercians: Studies in the Geography of Medieval England and Wales* (Toronto: Pontifical Institute of Mediaeval Studies, 1978)

Donna, Giovanni, *Lo sviluppo storico delle bonifiche e dell'irrigazione in Piemonte* (Turin: L'Impronta, 1939)

Donnelly, James S., *The Decline of the Medieval Cistercian Laybrotherhood* (New York: Fordham University Press, 1949)

Donnelly, James S., 'Changes in the Grange Economy of English and Welsh Cistercian Abbeys, 1300–1540', *Traditio*, 10 (1954), 399–458

Duby, Georges, *The Early Growth of the European Economy: Warriors and Peasants from the Seventh to the Twelfth Century* (London: Weidenfeld & Nicolson, 1974)

Duby, Georges, *Saint Bernard: l'art cistercien* (Paris: Arts et Métiers Graphiques, 1976)

Duby, Georges, *The Three Orders: Feudal Society Imagined* (Chicago: University of Chicago Press, 1980)

Durand, Robert, 'L'économie cistercienne au Portugal', in *L'économie cistercienne: geographie, mutations, du Moyen Âge aux temps modernes: troisièmes journées internationales d'histoire, 16–18 septembre 1981* (Auch: Centre Culturel Départemental de l'Abbaye de Flaran, 1983), pp. 101–17

Ellerman, David, 'Property Theory and Orthodox Economics', in *Growth, Profits and Property: Essays in the Revival of Political Economy*, ed. by Edward J. Nell (Cambridge: Cambridge University Press, 1980), pp. 250–63

Fossier, Robert, 'L'économie cistercienne dans les plaines du nord-ouest de l'Europe', in *L'économie cistercienne: geographie, mutations, du Moyen Âge aux temps modernes: troisièmes journées internationales d'histoire, 16–18 septembre 1981* (Auch: Centre Culturel Départemental de l'Abbaye de Flaran, 1983), pp. 53–74

Fossier, Robert, *Peasant Life in the Medieval West* (Oxford: Basil Blackwell, 1988)

Gabotto, Ferdinando, *L'agricoltura nella regione Saluzzese dal secolo XI al XV* (Turin: Tip. Chiantore-Mascarelli, 1901)

Genicot, Léopold, *Countours of the Middle Ages* (London: Routledge & Kegan Paul, 1967)

Graves, Coburn V., 'The Economic Activities of the Cistercians in Medieval England', *Analecta Sacri Ordinis Cisterciensis*, 13 (1957), 3–62

Grossi, Paolo, *Historia del derecho de propiedad: la irrupción del colectivismo en la conciencia europea* (Barcelona: Ariel, 1986)

Higounet, Charles, 'Avant-propos', in *L'économie cistercienne: geographie, mutations, du Moyen Âge aux temps modernes: troisièmes journées internationales d'histoire, 16–18 septembre 1981* (Auch: Centre Culturel Départemental de l'Abbaye de Flaran, 1983)

Higounet, Charles, 'Essai sur les granges cisterciennes', in *L'économie cistercienne: geographie, mutations, du Moyen Âge aux temps modernes: troisièmes journées internationales d'histoire, 16–18 septembre 1981* (Auch: Centre Culturel Départemental de l'Abbaye de Flaran, 1983), pp. 157–80

Hollis, Martin, *Rational Economic Man: A Philosophical Critique* (London: Cambridge University Press, 1975)

Inama-Sternegg, Karl Theodor, 'Sallandstudien', in *Festgabe für Georg Hanssen* (Tübingen: Verlag der H. Laupp'schen Buchhandlung, 1889), pp. 73–118

Knowles, David, *The Monastic Order in England: A History of Its Development from the Times of St Dunstan to the Fourth Lateran Council, 943–1216* (London: Cambridge University Press, 1940)

Knowles, David, 'The Primitive Cistercian Documents', in *Great Historical Enterprises: Problems in Monastic History*, ed. by David Knowles (Edinburgh: Thomas Nelson and Sons, 1963)

Lekai, Louis Julius, *The White Monks: A History of the Cistercian Order* (Okauchee, WI: Cistercian Fathers – Our Lady of Spring Bank, 1953)

Lekai, Louis Julius, *The Cistercians: Ideals and Reality* (Ohio: Kent State University Press, 1977)

Little, Lester K., *Religious Poverty and the Profit Economy in Medieval Europe* (Ithaca: Cornell University Press, 1978)

López García, José Miguel, 'Una aportación al estudio de las "reservas señoriales" en Castilla: la explotación de la Abadía cisterciense de la Santa Espina', *Revista de Historia Económica – Journal of Iberian and Latin American Economic History*, 2–3 (1984), 215–31

MacPherson, Crawford B., *The Political Theory of Possessive Individualism: Hobbes to Locke* (Oxford: Oxford University Press, 1964)

Mahn, Jean-Berthold, *L'ordre cistercien et son gouvernement des origines au milieu du XIIIᵉ siècle (1098–1265)* (Paris: E. de Boccard, 1945)

Marie-Henri, d'Arbois de Jubainville., *Études sur l'état intérieur des abbayes cisterciennes, et principalement de Clairvaux, aux XIIᵉ et XIIIᵉ siècles* (Paris: Auguste Durand, 1858)

McCrank, Lawrence, 'The Cistercians of Poblet as Medieval Frontiersmen: An Historiographic Essay and Case Study', in *Estudios en homenaje a Don Claudio Sánchez Albornoz en sus 90 años* ed. by Mª. del Carmen Carlé, Hilda Grassotti, and Germán Orduna (Buenos Aires: Instituto de Historia de España, 1983), pp. 313–60

Moulin, Léo, *La vie quotidienne des religieux au Moyen Âge (Xᵉ–XVᵉ siècles)* (Paris: Hachette, 1978)

Mullin, Francis Anthony, *A History of the Work of the Cistercians in Yorkshire* (Washington: Catholic University of America, 1932)

Nell, Edward J., *Growth, Profits and Property: Essays in the Revival of Political Economy* (Cambridge: Cambridge University Press, 1980)

Parker Mason, W. A., 'The Beginnings of the Cistercian Order', *Transactions of the Royal Historical Society*, 19 (1905), 169–207

Pérez-Embid Wamba, Javier, *El Cister en Castilla y León: monacato y dominios rurales (siglos XII–XV)* (Salamanca: Junta de Castilla y León, 1986)

Peset, Mariano, *Dos ensayos sobre la historia de la propiedad de la tierra* (Madrid: Editoriales del Derecho Reunidas, 1982)

Platt, Colin, *The Monastic Grange in Medieval England: A Reassessment* (London: MacMillan, 1969)

Portela, Ermelindo, *La colonización cisterciense en Galicia (1142–1250)* (Santiago de Compostela: Universidad de Santiago de Compostela, 1981)

Postan, Michael M., *The Medieval Economy and Society: An Economic History of Britain in the Middle Ages* (London: Weidenfeld & Nicolson, 1972)

Pounds, Norman J. G., *An Economic History of Medieval Europe* (London: Longman, 1974)

Roehl, Richard, 'Plan and Reality in a Medieval Monastic Economy: The Cistercians', *The Journal of Economic History*, 29–1 (1969), 180–82

Roehl, Richard, 'Patterns and Structure of Demand, 1000–1500', in *The Fontana Economic History of Europe: The Middle Ages*, ed. by Carlo M. Cipolla (London: Collins, 1976), pp. 107–42

Rösener, Werner, 'L'économie cistercienne de l'Allemagne occidentale (XIIe–XVe siècles)', in *L'économie cistercienne: geographie, mutations, du Moyen Âge aux temps modernes: troisièmes journées internationales d'histoire, 16–18 septembre 1981* (Auch: Centre Culturel Départemental de l'Abbaye de Flaran, 1983), pp. 135–56

Santacana Tort, Jaime *El monasterio de Poblet (1151–1181)* (Barcelona: CSIC, 1974)

Schulze, Eduard O., *Die Kolonisierung und Germanisierung der Gebiete zwischen Saale und Elbe* (Leipzig: Hirzel Verlag, 1896)

Slicher van Bath, Bernard H., *The Agrarian History of Western Europe, A.D. 500–1850* (London: Edward Arnold, 1963)

Thompson, Francis, M. L., 'Free Trade and the Land', in *The Victorian Countryside*, ed. by Gordon E. Mingay (London: Routledge & Kegan Paul, 1981), pp. 103–17

Uhlhorn, Gerhard, 'Die Kulturthätigkeit der Cisterzienser in Niedersachsen', *Zeitschrift des historischen Vereins für Niedersachsen*, 52 (1890), 84–110

Verna-Navarre, Catherine, 'La sidérurgie cistercienne en Champagne méridionale et en Bourgogne du Nord (XIIe–XVe siècles)', in *L'économie cistercienne: geographie, mutations, du Moyen Âge aux temps modernes: troisièmes journées internationales d'histoire, 16–18 septembre 1981* (Auch: Centre Culturel Départemental de l'Abbaye de Flaran, 1983), pp. 207–12

Vernier, Bernard, 'Putting Kin and Kinship to Good Use: The Circulation of Goods, Labour, and Names on Karpathos (Greece)', in *Interest and Emotion: Essays on the Study of Family and Kinship*, ed. by Hans Medick and David W. Sabean (Cambridge: Cambridge University Press, 1984), pp. 28–76

Williams, David H., *The Welsh Cistercians*, 2 vols (Pontypool: Griffin Press, 1969)

Winter, Franz, *Die Cistercienser des nordöstlichen Deutschlands: ein Beitrag zur Kirchen- und Culturgeschichte des deutschen Mittelalters* (Gotha: Perthes, 1868)

CHAPTER 16

Three Review Articles

with a commentary by Jesús Rodríguez Velasco

Conflict, Language, and Social Practice in Medieval Societies: Selected Essays of Isabel Alfonso, with Commentaries, ed. by Julio Escalona Monge, Álvaro Carvajal Castro, and Cristina Jular Pérez-Alfaro, TMC 24 (Turnhout: Brepols, 2024), pp. 625–677

BREPOLS PUBLISHERS   10.1484/M.TMC-EB.5.132470

JESÚS RODRÍGUEZ VELASCO

How to Read

The moment I take an academic book in my hands, I feel enormous trepidation. Will I be able to read it well? Will I be able to understand it? Wil I be able to delve into its pages opening wide my eyes to listen to what the book says and what the book does not say? Will I be up to the challenge of capturing the intricate web of sources, ideas, and traditions? Will I understand fully the many layers, diachronic and synchronic, of the debates that are taking place in the pages of books that, at their turn, have been the result of years, decades, lifetimes devoted to those books by their authors? Will I be able to see the insights they convey? Will I be a generous thinker, rather than a grumpy armchair reader? Will I be able to think with the book, instead of against it? And yet, will I be able to see, while the arguments, theses and sources unfold before my eyes, that there are questions that have not been asked, ideas than have been taken for granted, assumptions that need to be submitted to a second exam — or a third one? Will I be able to be, not just a good reader, but, mostly, a good critic? What kind of teachings will I get from my reading? Will they become part of my ongoing training? Will I be able to accept that such training has not ended, even though I am a gainfully employed scholar, and that this very book I now hold in my hands is going to be an important piece in my process of thinking and doing research? Will I ... This book ... All that just by having the book in my hands, maybe with my notebook and a few pencils around me. All that trepidation ...

Sounds difficult. But Maribel Alfonso's way of reading makes it monumentally simple, while choosing the most complex books to write her 'critical notes' published in *Hispania* throughout the years. Dominique Barthélemy's study on the Vendôme from the Ancient world to the Middle Ages and up to the fourteenth and fifteenth century, in which the French historian sees radical changes while denying that there is a mutation between the ancient and the medieval world, but rather a continuity, is an almost 1200-page long book in which the accumulation of data and sources seems overwhelming to the same reviewer who cuts across its theses, methodologies, theoretical contributions, and qualms with the precision of a neurosurgeon. When Maribel Alfonso opens up this book and decides to delve into each of its chapters, she understands the challenge of finding her way in the immense forest of data that the author has compiled, selected, and criticized in order to form his argument. Maribel Alfonso sees through those sources underscoring the right arguments. Those that focus on vocabulary, like the appearance or disappearance of the word allodium and what this means for the feudal organization, and that allow Maribel Alfonso to make certain that changes, even radical, and the denial of early medieval mutationism are theoretically non-exclusive. Those that focus on methodologies, like the limitations of the prosopographical methodology, which tends to transmit

| **Jesús Rodríguez Velasco**, Yale University

stability in kinship and power — Maribel Alfonso understands how Barthélemy uses and criticizes the method at the same time, because she is also aware of those methodological limitations. And, finally, those that focus on what, to me, seems among the most important concerns for her: what is this that I do to the sources when, as a historian, I order them, read them, and make a series of arguments and narratives about them? And Barthélemy's, for Maribel Alfonso, is a good argument, because it allows her to focus on the question of political and juridical organization of stateless societies versus state (or even modern state) societies. And Maribel Alfonso would have liked the author to engage with his own way of making history, and then posits the right question, the question, perhaps, that should have dominated Barthélemy's impeccable analysis: We know that the debates regarding the State are taking an extraordinary complexity, but the centrality of the State, isn't it the result of a historical revelation — the fruit of current interests that we would need to determine further — rather than the result of a historical reality?[1] Isn't it, indeed, one of the obsessions of the liberal state organization, and the opposition of what is stateless, not just of what constitutes the State? But notice that Maribel Alfonso does not retroactively criticize the book: she moves forward, because the question she is asking is the theme for a future, necessary, and mostly difficult research.

Georges Martin's book, *Les Juges de Castille*, which results from his thèse d'état, is a 675-page long brick, written by a relentless scholar who is able to fit three major ideas within each of his sentences (I am talking here with the admiration a student owes to his master), and Maribel Alfonso gets it all, writes about everything this project enlightens, understands and promotes its theoretical contribution and still finds time to think beyond it to propose a vision of the theory of history: 'to draw attention to the difficulties in grasping the social context is to stand at the horizon of today's 'historical knowledge,' and to acknowledge its limitations',[2] and therefore devote oneself to the fabric of language that is also history. Maribel Alfonso, again, pursues in detail every single element in Martin's argument: from the emergence of the two judges and their authority expressed in baldness capital, to the many transformations of the myth to become part not of the Castilian historiography, but rather of the Navarran one; Maribel Alfonso reads and comments on every single one of Martin's theses (which abound) and thinks with him along the sources, and, with him, thinks that if history is discourse it is because discourse is history. In other words, that the reason to operate the way Martin is operating is not to fulfil the theoretical desire of a 'linguistic turn' or a post-modern challenge, but rather the importance of the semiological, conceptual, and linguistic maps deployed in the process of history writing. And not just because they were operative in the past — but because they will dictate, if we do not submit them to criticism, the ways in which we ourselves will deal with our own history. And history weights like a nightmare on the minds of all the living generations — Marx said, *irgendwo* … That is why, Maribel Alfonso concludes it is essential to understand that the most important contribution of the

---

1 See below, pp. 641–42.
2 See below, p. 657.

book is the need to investigate 'into the process behind the construction of this historical knowledge, of this discourse of the past that is created out of the needs and interests of the social groups of each present time'.[3] The past is the succession of those discourses of the present. Not focusing on how they are written, how they express themselves, how they speak to the future from the past, is like renouncing to any historical knowledge.

Why one book, when Maribel Alfonso could be reading three books, engaging with the work of dozens of authors and their editors? In one of her critical notes, she indeed delves into the question of violence, reading at the same time, and establishing connections among them, and between them and the other many books that are not part of this review — from Paul Freedman to Jacques Derrida or Emmanuel Levinas — the works of Bisson (*Tormented Voices*), Barbara Rosenwein (editor, *Anger's Past*), and Guy Halsall (editor, *Violence and Society in the Early Medieval West*). In this critical note, Maribel Alfonso deals with every single one of the proposals in those books, and even helps the editors (and readers) to, retroactively, reorder the book: Halsall's introduction would have been more useful at the end of the book, or, I don't know, the articles devoted to Celtic and Muslim sources, that seem an appendage the way they have been put in the book, should have been collected in other, different sections of the book. But in the end, what really matters is the insight that she provides, the lesson that she learns for us about the very concept of violence. Because she was not reading those books just to read those books, but to reflect about this concept that crosses disciplines (cuts across them, really) and that rejects being defined at all. Here, Maribel Alfonso does not go into the difficult, but frequently used resource of thinking about violence with Walter Benjamin (and she is writing at a time in which Žižek has not yet published his book on this subject); she tries to engage with the question of what do we do with the concept of violence given that it is constantly present, but it cannot be properly defined to mean one thing? And she concludes with a theoretical consideration that provokes the need to continue thinking with her:

> control over legitimacy has much to do with the names given to violence, with the definition imposed on a conflict. However, there is more at play that mere word choice: the fact of describing an act or process as violent cannot be regarded as separate from the power relations and process of political domination that produced it. Naming, describing, legitimating and condemning violence are in and of themselves forms of political struggle. In this sense, historians' lack of agreement as to how to describe, name and define the types of violence they observe in political competition, and the extent of their debates, says little about the ambiguity and flexibility of these names. Rather, it speaks to the very fact that naming and other discursive strategies are elements of this same struggle, and that legitimacy depends to a large extent on the name that prevails once a conflict has ceased. For this reason the terms we encounter in our sources should

---

3 See below, p. 657.

largely be regarded as the result of these struggles, as the product of a recognized power or authority.[4]

Now, this is not just the result of a review, or a critical note about one (or three) books. This is one of the venues in which Maribel Alfonso finds her path to theory. Reading, for her, is not just learning. It is a theoretical revelation. But, see? This is yet another instance in which what she wants to mention is that no matter how interested we are in the past, the fact of the matter is that the past is at its turn the moment of revelation of a discourse that has been shaped with specific political interests, and that the best we can do is to focus on how those discourses have been shaped as well the way we talk about the past and, therefore, about our own struggles in the political and social fields.

It is a common trope in academic-administrative life that reviews do not count in one's CV. And maybe this is right for most people or for most reviews in which the reviewer simply describes perfunctorily the content of the book and makes a passing remark about the size of the font or the typographical errors in the final index. Maybe it is right for those other reviews-of-combat in which rivals engage in ad hominem remarks that are good for occasional gossiping, but useless for everything else. Maribel Alfonso's reviews and critical notes do count because they are an incredible occasion of generous thinking that finally produces something rarely seen: a theoretical revelation, a question for the future, an indictment to historians to reflect on how we do what we do.

---

4 See below, p. 671.

ISABEL ALFONSO

Continuity and Documentary Revelation, or Mutation and Feudal Revolution?*

It is stimulating to see the intensity surrounding the discussion, debate, and therefore historiographical reflection on historical processes rendered ever more comprehensible by studies such as the one I will be discussing here. The title of this brief article refers to the main debate in which this study takes part, namely the transition from antiquity to feudalism. This debate, one of the most fruitful in recent decades, has seen regular periods of renewal, and to this day remains open. The author, questioning what he considers to be the dominant interpretive paradigm, and one which he himself had previously adopted — i.e. that of a sudden and radical shift — now offers a 'counter model' which explains the transitions through 'successive adjustments' to and the 'reorganization' of institutional and social structures, rather than a 'violent mutation'.[1]

This is without a doubt yet another great 'regional' thesis from one of France's leading historians,[2] which is in itself cause to celebrate. It constitutes a vast volume that is exceptionally rich given its rigor and erudition, and especially because for each topic of the many covered the author conducts a survey of the existing debates in the field, validating or criticizing the most recent arguments and theses. Let me say from the outset that I find this to be one of Barthélemy's greatest contributions, because it enables him, without straying from a classical structure and a tradition built around Marc Bloch, Duby and Toubert, to incorporate truly novel approaches to the majority of the areas he covers. I will attempt to provide a general account of this aspect of the text.

The book is divided into three parts, along with an extensive introduction. The first part analyses in great detail the sources upon which the study is based, as well as the socioeconomic evolution and historical formation of the Vendôme area in western France. The second part (970–1150), which is perhaps the most interesting and constitutes the book's core, sets out to demonstrate that there was no political, economic or social rift after the year 1000. It attempts to gauge the extent of this continuity and, given that it is not synonymous with immutability, to determine the

---

* Original publication: Alfonso, Isabel, '¿Continuidad y revelación documental o mutación y revolución feudal?', *Hispania*, 189 (1995), 301–13. Translated by Nicholas Callaway. Barthélemy, *La société dans le comté de Vendôme* (pp. 1118, includes 'cartes, planches et généalogies').

1 Following the new edition of Poly and Bournazel, *La mutation féodale*, Barthélemy questioned whether such a mutation really took place, summarizing what he had been presenting as a *contre-modèle* to 'mutationism'. See Barthélemy, 'La mutation féodale a-t-elle eu lieu?'; and Barthélemy, 'Dominations châtelaines'. The continued relevance of this debate is reflected in recent publications such as: Violante and Fried, eds, *Il secolo XI*; and Bisson, 'The "Feudal Revolution"'.

2 By way of example, let us recall Duby, *La société aux XIe et XIIe siècles*; Fossier, *La Terre et les hommes*; Toubert, *Les structures du Latium médiéval*; Bonnassie, *La Catalogne*; Poly, *La Provence*; and many others cited in the book under review.

632   ISABEL ALFONSO

characteristics of the changes that did occur. The third part of the book (1150–1359) sets out to demonstrate that the true turning point in the history of feudalism was the twelfth century, and puts forth various types of transformations that, it argues, took place from the mid-twelfth to fourteenth century. Each of these parts is accompanied by several annexes expanding upon the information and particularities of the various chapters, to which I will now turn. Because, as mentioned, the book is quite dense, I believe that each chapter deserves to be commented on separately.

The fact that the main element of his argument is what he terms *documentary mutations* forces him to conduct an exhaustive analysis of the extant sources, to which he dedicates chapter 1. This is no small task, as it is an area that is often overlooked, but, above all, this sort of analysis is not usually approached from the perspective of inquiring as to the function and changes in the very production of the source material, in relation to cultural transformations and the interests of the groups from which they originate.[3] In any case, the author is keenly aware of the limitations of this documentation, and of the significance of gaps in the collections employed, and takes measures against the construction of models that, while acknowledging these difficulties, easily lose sight of them in their overall discourse. For the area under study, the greatest abundance of source material dates from 1040–1150, and comes from Marmoutier and La Trinité, the county's two most important monasteries. As the thirteenth century represents a great void without municipal charters or major inventories, he uses retrospectively the *Livre de Feuds* and the *Comptes*, both from the fourteenth century.

From his close examination he verifies the legacy of the Roman-Frankish legal experience in the continuity of Carolingian written instruments into the eleventh century (donations, sales, manumissions, census grants or *manufirma* and notices of lawsuits). In his opinion, the novelty resides in the forms of narration and recording, passing from an ancient style that is more laconic and conventional, to a new, more narrative style that takes hold in the mid-eleventh century and is dominant until the thirteenth, when another more cultivated and stereotyped style takes root. His hypothesis is that the changes and conflicts of the last third of the eleventh century, considered a key period, are not in themselves novel, and that their presence in earlier periods can and should be brought to light, as they are indicative of a social pressure on the law, which other authors have shown to have begun already in antiquity. He considers the most important historical phenomenon to be the development of monastic organization and culture. It is in the first third of the thirteenth century when, according to Barthélemy, a true documentary mutation occurred, in parallel to an increasing social complexity. This is especially reflected in the new instrumental character acquired by written agreements, and the resulting reorganization of archives, with a growing importance placed upon jurisdictional seals. In any case, this cultivated style that eventually came to predominate is only a formal break; the

---

3   One contribution along these lines to the debate around the year 1000 'mutation' is Patrick Geary's recent book, which asserts that the period's greatest shift was the transformation in the nature of the written document as regards changes in the perception of the individual and the group. See Geary, *Phantoms of Remembrance.*

CONTINUITY AND DOCUMENTARY REVELATION   633

author insists that ultimately it is just a matter of evolution. An evolution, however, that will imply a greater definition of social relations, status, powers, rights, etc.; in short, a systematic record of *féodalité* itself.

One could say that in this lengthy documentary analysis the author, concerned as he is with the relationship between *changements documentaires* and *changements réels*, gets ahead of himself, covering content he will go on to develop in later chapters. Such is the case, for example, when he examines the practice of manumissions more than their rhetoric of freedom; of the information found in lawsuits, whose interpretation demonstrates how crucial it is to take into consideration anthropology's most recent contributions to this field. These are aspects that he will deal with *in extenso* when addressing servitude or justice, two topics that, as we shall see, are of vital importance to the study of medieval societies, about which debates never remain closed for long. The annexes to this chapter go into detail about documents from Marmoutier and La Trinité, and pieces which justify his arguments.

Chapter 2 contains a reflection on the rhythms and modalities of rural and urban growth in the County of Vendôme, an entity which does not constitute a natural region, and whose 'regional identity' is therefore the result of complex sociopolitical processes. The main interest of this chapter is precisely this attempt to record the fate of the different geographical areas bound together through history. In the evolution of their settlement patterns and economies we once again find no great fractures. The annex on new place names as an instrument of analysis is indispensable.

In chronological terms, the second part of the book hinges around the period before and after the year 1000. In social terms, it is structured around the black monks: what they are ceded (land and men) and who cedes it to them (noble knights and other powerful figures), as well as their various forms of domination. In the first chapter Barthélemy analyses the political development of the county from *c.* 1075, showing that despite the use of public service terminology, the counts' relationship to the king is one of vassalage. Moreover, their regional power is based not only on a military and judicial organization, but also a fiscal one. Lastly, he argues that around the year 1000 there are indications that Vendôme is a relatively autonomous and functional unit. However, during the eleventh century, the violent disputes over the power of the count — 'the counts' wars' — seem to back up, for Vendôme too, the arguments about social disorder in early feudalism among those who see this period as marking a catastrophic shift. However, drawing inspiration from anthropology and making use of the prosopographical method, Barthélemy takes on the documentary evidence from a different perspective and offers alternative 'continuist' interpretations to three of the main elements of the 'mutationist' model: political conflict, 'bad' customs, and the disappearance of the allodium.

The counts' political power struggles are considered part of the conflictive structures of 'kinship'. As such, what emerges is the conflict's constructive role in social reproduction (a point to which we will return). The *consuetudines* are considered 'bad' not so much because of their actual novelty, but due to the ideology of the monks during their process of political affirmation. The monks of the eleventh century had a marked tendency to term as *violentia* any legality concurrent with their own, but there is not an unprecedented proliferation of consuetudinary levying in the eleventh century, nor is there a dislocation of the *pagus*, although the nobility did reaffirm its position through the creation of new castles.

To demonstrate this, the author examines an inventory of the 'customs' due to the count prior to the year 1000, which he subjects to a rigorous analysis. This study will enable him to determine a great deal about the sociopolitical structure of the county, and of the aristocratic group itself, allowing him to conclude that there is a continuity between the *vassalli* of the tenth century and the castle lords of the eleventh, with the *viri illustri* at the top and a small, almost invisible aristocracy at the bottom. For the reader it is fascinating to find 'the simultaneous mixing and distinction between similar ranks,' the verifiable ties between them. Likewise, another important takeaway from this section is the varied nature of the 'holdings' in the hands of these groups, which reflects complexity more than the fabled simplicity that had been ascribed to the 'origins' of the feudal system. Barthélemy pays special attention to the group of noblemen who take turns with the count to each month guard the castle of Vendôme, the military and judicial centre of the *pagus*, considering that in terms of control there is a model of parity between them, in a spirit that he finds very 'Carolingian.' This entails recognizing that these noblemen had a power of their own, a point which will lead him to raise the issue of noble *allodiality*.

It is the document cited above that makes it possible to discern the image of a *pagus* divided among areas subject to the consuetudinary taxation of the count and the two or three noble lineages. These areas are neither homogeneous nor continuous, and in them the prominent men enjoy the same type of rights and taxes. They are 'domains,' 'lands,' 'fiefs' — spaces of taxation, really — that live on as such, in both geographic and fiscal terms, into the Low Middle Ages, according to another document from 1355, the *Livre*, which he uses for comparison. Of course there are many difficulties in interpreting the very nature of these taxes, as the 'custom' is listed as a unit, wherein *vicaria* (justice) and *commandisia* (protection) are the dominant binary. However, the very use of the term 'taxes' indicates that the author takes issue with historians' usual opposition between 'public' and 'private,' asserting that the new castles of the eleventh century are neither more 'private' nor less 'public' than those of previous centuries. On the contrary, Barthélemy confirms that there is indeed an equivalence, in the identical principals of taxation, between the castle of Vendôme and other peripheral castles. The temporary changes in the greater or lesser strength of the count or the vassals, or the new forms of levying taxes, are not indications of a crisis of structures in the eleventh century. The struggles against the 'bad' customs, as we have said, are part of the process of the establishment of monastic privileges.

Against that *tournant* of 'mutationism' that is the disappearance of the allodia and of the independent peasantry that owned them, the author levels a far-reaching critique, showing that before 1060 the allodium of the Vendôme is in fact a local manor, whose organization can be partially discerned based on donations to monasteries. The series of donations between 1030–1060 does not signal the demise of an entire class, but rather the establishment of the normal ties between the local nobility and the monasteries, whether new or restored, as can be found throughout the High Middle Ages. The decline of the allodium, then, comes down to a vocabulary shift: it is replaced by the term 'fief' as the patrimonial land unit par excellence.

It will take Barthélemy four more chapters to deal separately and in extreme detail with some of the topics mentioned. This involves a certain degree of redundancy and an excess of information, which at times threatens to overshadow some of what I consider to be the most interesting achievements of his research.

The primary objective is to explain the black monks' success by attempting to reconstruct the chains of solidarity through which they exerted their influence, and the cultural model that lent meaning to the benefits they received. He therefore examines their links with the local society, the networks of relationships that they established, and their dynamics — not all of them peaceful. In so doing, he highlights the socio-religious nature of the donations, and the limited but violent character of the conflicts, which in most cases involving laying claim to and usurping the donated lands. It is the study of the common framework of *familiarity*, in which the transactions between the area's monks and knights take place, that makes it possible to play down the influence of the Gregorian reform on the movement to restore churches. This movement, which had already begun earlier, does not entail a weakening, as has been argued in the case of the knights' estates, since they reserve for themselves the tithes and devise formulas of joint lordship. This is also the framework through which he proposes we understand the land 'market.' He talks of 'para-feudality' in the pacts between knights and monks, full of peace and friendship rituals, which defy the rigid pattern traditionally proposed for the feudal-vassalage ritual.

The monks' success can be explained by the function they satisfied in a society run by knights, to whom they offered the traditional role attributed to 'religion' as opposed to the nobility: that of ensuring the rights of passage through the appropriate signs of distinction, and of moulding the people's anger, addressing conflicts by casting them in sacred terms, mediating in their resolution, and acting as redistributors of wealth, in a role that is difficult to assess if one accepts that their demands were also directed against the nobility. The conclusion of the chapter on the *morbidité* with which the monks infused feudal society, their moral pressure, seems at the very least unnecessary and somewhat forced, even misguided, as it maintains and reproduces the tired dichotomy between secular and ecclesiastical nobility. Many of his arguments on the dialectical relationship between the two groups are therefore rendered unusable by their ineffectiveness, as the foregoing considerations to a certain extent override them.

A much more interesting chapter is the one about the local manor's control over lands and men, and the forms of domination. He distinguishes between various forms of local manor that were not confined to the demesne, but also included certain jurisdictional powers. He highlights three aspects of the 'Vendômois model' and proposes checking for them throughout the entire Loire region. They are as follows: 1) The allodium does not pose an obstacle in the chains of subordination, as is sometimes claimed. It neither prolongs an 'antifeudal' society, nor is the distinguishing characteristic of an independent peasantry doomed to disappear in the year 1000, but rather tends to describe a land holding of the nobility. 2) The local manor (allodium, *tetra* or *villa*) is a fundamental unit of power, income and social life. In the castles, the 'manor' is no more than the second floor of the building, a type of superstructure for supporting and articulating the 'allodial' infrastructure. 3) The 'dependence' or servitude of the eleventh century does not differ from that of the Carolingian system, since it is with traditional instruments of social control that the manorial order of the eleventh and twelfth centuries is reconstructed, prolonged and extended.

Another chapter in this second part returns to donors and sellers — essentially noble knights — to study the double system of solidarity/antagonism structuring this class: kinship and vassalage. As in other sections of the book, Barthélemy exhibits a broad command of the most recent literature in both history and anthropology. As such, he expresses interest in Bourdieu's notion of *practical kinship*.[4] Likewise, following White's conclusions about the *laudatio*,[5] he uses the transactions with the monasteries, and relatives' consent to these transactions — or subsequent complaints — in order to study the empirical composition of the authorizing groups. They do not identify with a theoretical notion of family, as had previously been assumed; rather, their makeup could be related to the origins of the goods ceded, or to interests that were specific but also changed each time. Such interests were related to an overarching desire to associate themselves with the spiritual and material benefits of the relationship with the receiving monastery, and the reinforcement of kinship ties. The latter was particularly necessary in moments of great change in the donor's life, which was, indeed, when donations were usually made. The part which deserves the most attention is his thoughts on the structural nature of intra-family conflicts, which call into question the all-too-common interpretations about the solidarity of family behaviour. In this sense, the medieval European nobility's frequent disputes with the monasteries, claiming items once donated by their ancestors, may be situated within a more complex context than the mere 'united' defence of a family estate diminished by erstwhile extravagance. Instead, he relates these quarrels to problems of hierarchical transformation emerging in the very heart of the aristocratic family.

It would take up far too much space to address all the rich content of this chapter. It is, however, worth mentioning the second part, which studies the clientship structures among the knighthood. It likewise highlights the ambivalence of the vocabulary surrounding knighthood and vassalage, and therefore the typology of knights and vassals. This is explored through a number of case studies that help to better explain the hard-to-define hierarchical differences that are detected between these two categories. Another contribution, then, is the reconstruction of lineages and maps of estates, describing, as much as he can, the functions, means of upward mobility, and varyious ties to the castles, as well as the existence of multiple vassalages, a fact which did not have the eroding effect on the system that the traditional historiography had supposed. Once again his conclusion is that, while there were conflictive, structural factors at the heart of the dominant class, there was not widespread disorder, as the class's regulatory mechanisms were highly effective at reestablishing peace, as he will seek to demonstrate in the last chapter of this second part.

It is worth pointing out the usefulness of the prosopographical study offered here for comparative purposes. Equally important is the annex on personal names and their mutation, a very thorough dossier establishing the state of the art in studies

---

4 In Bourdieu, *Le sens practique*, p. 282.
5 White, *Custom, Kinship, and Gifts to Saints*.

on this topic. He warns — as K. F. Werner once did — that an uncritical use of the prosopographical method can lead us to overestimate the degree of social stability, as by its very nature it brings to light only continuities.

Underlying Barthélemy's basic argument — and at times explicit in it — is the society/state dichotomy, and an aim: to show that the latter is not synonymous with order, and that its absence cannot be equated with anarchy. In this way, he devotes special attention to explaining the workings of what he calls *puissance sociale* in terms of its two most important aspects: justice, and its place in the chain of reciprocity or 'gift exchange.'

In his analysis of justice, the author insists on questioning the catastrophist theses, heirs to a whole school of traditional history of law, which detect in the eleventh century a degraded and inefficient system of justice, associating the castles with the advent of a 'class justice.' Instead, he offers a positive assessment of its workings at the concrete scale. As we have already indicated, he places himself within a relatively recent body of studies in this field aimed at renewal, and which feeds off of very interesting contributions from anthropology. It is from this perspective that he analyses the resolution procedures both in Vendôme and in other castles, with keen observations as to intervening parties other than the litigants themselves, exploring the possible relationships between them, the places hearings are held, whether or not they are public, etc. His conclusion is that feudal society possessed suitable means with which to handle its conflicts. As it was more interested in building and reaching agreements than in repression, it managed to pacify the various parties, set compensations and affect the relationships of force. Thus, it represents the success of a *justice* that tends toward peace and the reestablishment of relations between the members of the dominant class.

It is in this same line of analysis, which tries to cover 'tout ce qui est marqueur social,' that he also addresses the complex field of transactions of goods. The display of erudition in this section is, if possible, even more overwhelming than in the others. Once again armed with ideas from anthropology, he examines the various documented forms and objects of exchange, trying to demonstrate that their social and economic aspects should not be differentiated or separated. Business deals are always about more than economics, and are literally inserted (*enchâssé*) within a given social context. These considerations apply equally to donations and sales, to loans with an estate as collateral, or to the land 'market' in general. The social nature of the relationship between parties is, in short, what imbues a transaction with diverse components.

As we have seen, there is an attempt to get to the bottom of a social logic in a period that has often been placed between the parentheses of the crisis of Carolingian public power and the reconstruction of monarchic power starting in the mid-twelfth century. It is true that in this book Barthélemy traces continuities before and after these dates, but the reference models he uses, and which he only partially critiques, no doubt condition the model of 'manorial order' that he puts forth.

As with Coucy,[6] although with minor differences, Barthélemy holds that it is in the mid-twelfth century that we can find a major change, albeit gradual, within feudal structures, ushering in yet another period in the system's development. The nature

---

6 Barthélemy, *Les deux âges de la seigneurie banale.*

of these transformations, then, constitutes the subject of the third part of the book, which, although shorter than the second, is no less dense, making it equally difficult to recount all of the rich information it contains. In this period the institutions of the countship are better documented, a fact undoubtedly related to the reinforcement of 'central' power taking place at the regional level. And it is for this reason that the author has organized this part of the study around the history of the counts. He writes at great length about the principal families, as well as the contrasting evolution of the knights and the bourgeoisie in Vendôme. It is worth mentioning in the first place the main points of this process of 'unprecedented social change,' which Barthélemy confesses he would term 'radical,' if it were not so redolent of the rejected notion of 'mutation.' The points are as follows:

- The knights gradually dissociate themselves from the castles and move out into the countryside. This evolution is related to the decline in conflicts between neighbours and the resulting obsolescence of the knights' basic function.

- The strengthening of the power of the count in relation to the concentration of castles under his control and to the development of the tax and judicial systems. There is also a strengthening of a hierarchical centre — Vendôme — in parallel to the increased dynamism of its patriciate.

- The institutionalization of Vendôme's 'autonomy' within the broader framework of the kingdom or, rather, the monarchic state.

I will go over what I find to be the most relevant points of this part, which sheds light on phenomena in the previous period, clarifying the author's arguments. Such is the case with the nature of the 'wars,' those 'private' wars 'between neighbours,' which Barthélemy presents as the very *raison d'être* of the knighthood, and which tended to reproduce and justify the social order, spawning homologous and rival units, i.e. the groups of knights at each castle. It is, he tells us, the means of reproduction of the 'first age.' This violent, endemic, repetitive, regulated conflict is internal to the dominant class, whose ultimate goal is to engender the need for protection that legitimizes their taxation of the productive class. In this period it will change valence, gradually ceasing to be functional as another repressive ideological apparatus is institutionalized into a system of law and taxation. The scale of the wars changes, pitting larger political units against one another, and with combatants who are neither strictly local nor limited to the knighthood. One can start to make out — he says, taking the argument a step further — the traits of what will one day be national or state-level wars, as in the conflict between the Capetians and the House of Plantagenet, which took place in the county of Vendôme.

I think that Barthélemy is right in drawing a connection between the strengthening process of the monarchy, that of the countship, and the changes in manorial organization. However, I believe that the application of the term 'modernization' to describe political power in this period is debatable. The barony belongs to the count of Vendôme, the only lord *châtelain* of both these areas and of numerous castle estates. His 'house' rises above the principal local families, and customary law is rewritten in favour of lineages like his own. There is a development of taxation and the legal system in a 'modern sense,' in relation to which a concept of territory emerges that materializes in carefully crafted feudal borders that precisely define the space of 'feudal assistance,' by now a tax, and that of control over the high spheres of justice. However, local families have not yet disappeared, and their power continues to keep that of the local barony in check. The relative unalterability of the powerful — says Barthélemy — is the perennial backdrop upon which we can describe the modernization of the county's administration. The new posts, new staff and regular accounts pointing to feudal sovereignty's solid legal system, are some of its important triumphs.

The knights, as they leave the castle courts and take up residence on their rural properties, which they fortify,[7] cease to be the expression of 'social power' that they were in the eleventh century, but do not disappear either. It cannot even be said that there is a breakup of the armed retinue of the castles, which in fact never existed as such, since the knights had always constituted a heterogeneous class with diverse ties among themselves. At this point Barthélemy demonstrates the importance of having a deep grasp on the preceding period in order to offer a sound comparative reference that, moreover, allows him to detect the continuity in the top and mid-ranking families up until the fourteenth century.

The city (*villa*), instead of the castle, will now become the centre of the manorial estate. The title of lord spreads, and the number of places with lords increases, without this process signifying an unprecedented fragmentation of local power. On the contrary, it is within the very process of strengthening the castle-related institutions that the local manor is also reinforced. Barthélemy actually explains in detail how this manor is accompanied by new forms of agrarian exploitation: the *métayages*, the new legal form of servitude. The types of tenancies comprised under this term vary, but this exploitation of the 'reserves' through new forms of letting based on equally new legal guarantees will strengthen manorial structures that maintain continuity with other prior forms of leasing. Thus, he warns, we are not to interpret this reorganization simplistically as the 'return to the land' of a nobility with an 'eye for profit.' Despite the constant pressure of the Church, which intensifies starting in the thirteenth century and which they continue to resist, the local lords hold onto tithed income and use it in this period as an important source of credit granted to them by the Church itself.

There is no indication of a crisis of manorial income, although it can be deduced indirectly from the crisis of the knights' lineage. Indeed, the author refers to an 'obsolescence of the knighthood' after 1250, and labels the society of the first half of the fourteenth century as 'post-knight,' as the very title seems to lose weight. He makes an interesting and, as always, detailed analysis of the terms *miles* and *armiger*, differentiating between their statutory and relational meanings, in order to conclude that the increased proportion of squires signals an important break in the history of the nobility. Likewise, it is indicative of the difficulties in being knighted, even if

---

7 To understand this process he proposes excavations and includes an annex with elements for a reflection on this type of secondary fortresses (Barthélemy, *La société dans le comté de Vendôme*, Annex III, pp. 811–13).

the noble title lives on. The development of the *armigérat* (the squireship) therefore takes place alongside the impoverishment of noble families. Barthélemy is right to emphasize, however, that this does not amount to a 'crisis of the aristocracy' as is normally argued whenever a renovation of the elites is observed. Rather, there are documented cases of those who not only survive but prosper and acquire new fiefs. On the other hand, among the newly rich, the process is longer and more difficult, though not impossible, for urban fortunes than rural ones. This may simply indicate greater prejudice towards merchants, bourgeoisie and jurists than towards well-off farmers.

It could therefore be said, then, that in parallel to the strengthening of the manor there is a shift in what the author refers to as *puissance sociale*, from the knights to the bourgeoisie. The progress of the bourgeois fortunes is in fact presented as incontestable. The rise of the urban notables starting in the mid-thirteenth century entails the formation of an urban patriciate that inserts itself within the feudal *nomenklatura*. Not only did they emerge in relation to lay and ecclesiastical manors, but also, after 1230, will boast manors of their own. The dynamism of this 'patriciate,' which is surprising in this area of France and undeterred by the lack of written urban charters, is what I find noteworthy here. This absence of autonomy and communal power in Vendôme, and the presence of a significant bourgeoisie, can be explained, in Barthélemy's opinion, by the fact that it lives and grows wealthy at the service of the count, and secures freedoms individually, as in Reims, Paris or Chartres. The author does not find it far-fetched to assume that urban notables were among those who inspired and benefited from some of the count's initiatives. Moreover, it serves to remind us the extent to which the *commune* really could contribute to the longevity of the manorial order, blocking *de jure* the *de facto* progression toward greater freedoms. This is why it is important to study the makeup of this bourgeoisie, the material foundations supporting its power, its connections, and its means of upward social mobility. In this way, in some of the case studies we can see how access to feudal property was gained through multiple simultaneous dependencies.

What Barthélemy seeks to demonstrate in the book's last chapter is that the origin and social mobility of the urban notables does not follow the simple pathways of ministerialism and marriage alliances with the old nobility. Rather, the classical renewal of the old elite is contemporaneous with the emergence of the new elite. He applies what he terms the 'theory of elite renewal,' whereby a dominant class persists *despite* and *because of* certain families entering and exiting the fold. In other words, there are cycles or sequences of social ascent and decline.

The author's conclusions clearly express the two concerns or threads that have structured the book, namely: 1) criticizing one periodization while advocating for another; and 2) proposing a positive analysis of feudal society. At the risk of being overly repetitive, it is worth commenting on these final pages because, having shed the overwhelming quantity of information that accompanies the rest of the text, they bring to the fore ideas which in the foregoing explanations were only implicit. Without a doubt, the most important of them has to do with the classical opposition — so dear to the social sciences — of society and state. Indeed, for Barthélemy, the social (principle of vassalage; relationships of dependency) will prevail over the culture of the state (monarchic principle) already in the ninth and tenth centuries, although it will not be *revealed* as such until the eleventh century. And it is this *society without a state* (or 'modern state,' as he sometimes says) that he has tried, in the way of an anthropologist, to analyse in terms of its forms of maintaining order. Here, he synthesizes them as follows: 1) The Church, especially its monastic sphere, with its double function of mediating and redistributing wealth, is an immanent force, i.e. one that is not external to feudal society. As such, it should not always be viewed as a pacifying force, but one that generates tensions of its own. 2) The feudal institutions and their regulating principles, among which he includes those of kinship. 3) Warfare itself; controlled, limited violence that, together with social disparities, he considers to be a powerful societal factor.

While it would be unfair to deny the author's pursuit of originality, it is only honest to acknowledge his debts, first of all to anthropology, as we have seen. This is especially true in his analysis of the particular formalization of violence and the negotiated resolution of conflicts in the society of the eleventh and twelfth century, which he describes as 'wars between neighbours' and 'pledged justice.' He is even indebted to some 'mutationists' (such as Duby, Poly and Bournazel), accepting, as they have, that the manorial 'disorder,' which was a reality, should not be attributed so much to the feudal institutions themselves as to their 'imperfections,' and that it is when they are eventually reinforced that the state emerges.

In this line of argumentation it should come as no surprise that Barthélemy connects his shift — which he prefers to call 'deep' instead of 'radical' — to the eleventh-century genesis of the state, or that he describes a 'passage from knighthood to statehood.'

In my opinion, this argument brings with it important contributions, such as his reflection on the relationships between the central and local powers (although he does not phrase it in these terms), and his view that the transformations affect all units of power. It is for this reason that it is hard to accept his opposition between the 'modernization of justice' or 'domestication of the nobility' and 'pledge justice' or 'wars between neighbours' as essentially different phenomena from concurrent relationships at the heart of the dominant class, both lay and ecclesiastical. It is as if conflicts and their resolutions depended closely on a political power, and not on the nature of the social relations under consideration.

Ultimately, in Barthélemy's discourse one encounters a clearly state-centred outlook, which I think is indebted to a liberal political theory insufficiently subjected to criticism. He therefore tends to postulate the autonomy of the political power in parallel to its 'modern' centralization. In this way, for example, social-level factors highlighted in order to elucidate the workings of medieval society in this 'stateless' period are overlooked in his explanation of the later period. There, it is implicitly assumed by contrast that the so-called 'private' wars or the judicial pledges — to use examples we have already seen — disappear in favour of state-based law and justice, generating 'peace' and 'conflicts' of a different order.[8] The increasing complexity of the debate surrounding the state is well known to all. However, its centrality throughout

---

8 In my opinion, some of the legal anthropology studies that Barthélemy uses invite a similar critique, which I intend to develop elsewhere, in particular Geary, 'Vivre en conflit'; Cheyette, 'Suum Cuique Tribuere'; Cheyette, 'The invention of the state'.

the book leads me to wonder whether it is not more of a historiographical *revelation* stemming from current concerns, than an actual historical reality.

These last observations are intended to underscore, once again, the study's richness and interest, which stretch far beyond their contribution to our historical understanding of Vendômois feudal society. Indeed, they elicit and enable broader theoretical questions that are necessary for history's development as a social science. Along these lines, it is also worth drawing attention to the index, which further develops the most important notions used in the book, and which are the product of a dialogue with sociology and anthropology that has by now become indispensable.

Bibliography

Barthélemy, Dominique, *Les deux âges de la seigneurie banale: Pouvoir et société dans la terre des sîres de Coucy (milieu XIe–milieu XIIIe siècles)* (Paris: Publications de la Sorbonne, 1984)

Barthélemy, Dominique, 'Dominations châtelaines de l'an Mil (Le modèle vendômois pour la Francia/Nord de la Loire)', in *La France de l'an Mil*, ed. by Robert Delort (Paris: Éditions du Seuil, 1990), pp. 101–13

Barthélemy, Dominique, 'La mutation féodale a-t-elle eu lieu? (note critique)', *Annales. Économies, Sociétés, Civilisations*, 47–3 (1992), 767–77

Barthélemy, Dominique, *La société dans le comté de Vendôme de l'an mil au XIVe siècle* (Paris: Librairie Artheme Fayard, 1993)

Bisson, Thomas N., 'The "Feudal Revolution"', *Past & Present*, 142 (1994), 6–42

Bonnassie, Pierre, *La Catalogne du milieu du Xe à la fin du XIe siècle: croissance et mutations d'une société* (Toulouse: Association des Publications de l'Université de Toulouse-Le Marail, 1976)

Bourdieu, Pierre, *Le sens practique* (Paris: Éditions de Minuit, 1980)

Cheyette, Fredric L., 'Suum Cuique Tribuere', *French Historical Studies*, 6–3 (1976), 287–99

Cheyette, Fredric L., 'The Invention of the State', in *Essays in Medieval Civilization: The Walter Prescott Webb Memorial Lectures*, ed. by Bede Karl Lackner and Kenneth Roy Philip (Austin: University of Texas Press, 1978), pp. 143–78

Duby, Georges, *La société aux XIe et XIIe siècles dans la région mâconnaise* (Paris: Armand Colin, 1953)

Fossier, Robert, *La Terre et les hommes en Picardie jusqu'à la fin du XIIIe siècle* (Paris–The Hague: Béatrice-Nauwelaerts, 1968)

Geary, Patrick, 'Vivre en conflit dans une France sans État: typologie des mécanismes de règlement des conflits (1050–1200)', *Annales ESC*, 41–5 (1986), 1107–33

Geary, Patrick, *Phantoms of Remembrance: Memory and Oblivion at the End of the First Millennium* (Princeton: Princeton University Press, 1994)

Poly, Jean-Pierre, *La Provence et la société féodale* (Paris: Bordas, 1976)

Poly, Jean-Pierre, and Eric Bournazel, *La mutation féodale, X^e–XIIe siècles* (Paris: Presses Universitaires de France, 1991 [1980])

Toubert, Pierre, *Les structures du Latium médiéval: le Latium méridional et la Sabine du IXe siècle à la fin du XIIe siècle* (Rome: École français de Rome, 1973)

Violante, Cinzio, and Johannes Fried, eds, *Il secolo XI. Una svolta? Atti della XXXII settimana di studio, 10–14 settembre 1990* (Bologna: Il Mulino, 1993)

White, Stephen D., *Custom, Kinship, and Gifts to Saints: The Laudatio Parentum in Western France, 1050–1150* (Chapel Hill: University of North Carolina Press, 1988)

ISABEL ALFONSO

Historical Discourse as History*

The first words of Georges Martin's book,[1] which state that *history is discourse*, could be seen as part of the language-based 'post-structuralist challenge' that, for the past several years, many historians have regarded as a threat to their discipline.[2] However, the study under review here, by a linguist, will show that such fears are based only on the most simplistic and radical claims of the so-called 'linguistic turn.' In fact, the author's stated aim is to 'make the historian understand that *discourse is history*'. These two statements sum up the two fields into which his research falls, and his methodological approach, which leads him to criticize both the traditional philological perspective, as well the conventional history of historiography. The study of a fictional account at the heart of the Castilian imagination, namely the legend of the Castilian Judges, is undertaken through a semiotics of history which attempts to understand texts as facts. As the author explicitly acknowledges, this aim conditions his own semiological options, paying more attention to concepts than to linguistics, more to the grammar of values than to that of signs, more to the signified than to the signifier. Therefore, the study we will be commenting on can be assessed within the framework of this broad, complex debate on the relationships between history and language,[3] although today, of course, restricting oneself to this framework is, as we shall see, reductionist. By shying from abstract discussions without omitting them completely, Georges Martin makes a highly important practical contribution to an approach that, in my opinion, should be more widespread in the study of the written material of the past.

Martin's theoretical perspective is actually more akin to the new approaches in history and social science that reflect on ways of perceiving and remembering the past in different periods and contexts; on how 'social memory' works and what its function is, to use one of the most recent and relevant expressions.[4] However Martin

---

* Original publication: Alfonso, Isabel, 'El discurso histórico como historia', *Hispania*, 192 (1996), 349–63. Translated by Nicholas Callaway.

1 Martin, *Les juges de Castille*.

2 Stone, 'History and Post-Modernism'.

3 On this debate, see the different articles included in the section Controvèrsies about 'Historia y Postmodernismo', in *Taller d'Historia*, 1 (1993), a Spanish translation of the responses elicited by the aforementioned article by L. Stone, first published in *Past & Present* (1991–1992). Two works by G. M. Spiegel, a medievalist who also has taken part in this debate, are interesting: Spiegel, 'History, Historicism'; and her book, Spiegel, *Romancing the Past*. A worthwhile discussion of these problems can be found in Fouracre, 'Merovingian History'. In Spain, see Moradiellos, 'Últimas corrientes en historia'. I. Burdiel and M. C. Romeo have written a highly interesting article in which the authors reflect on the usefulness of this 'challenge' for historians, in Burdiel and Cruz Romeo, 'Historia y lenguaje'.

4 Fentress and Wickham, *Social Memory*. Although these are not the first authors to use the expression 'social memory', they are the first to give it a meaning of its own that sets it apart from other similar

goes one step further than the rest. The interest of his contribution resides in his examination of the nature, construction and function of historical discourse — in this case a fictional one — by studying its own history, i.e. its successive reinterpretations. Indeed, the process of transmission and dissemination is in itself clearly historical. It is a historical discourse that for the author means knowledge formalized with its own specific themes, function and means of expression. This understanding allows him to point out the false dichotomy that is normally drawn between historiography as scientific literature, and literature and epic as literary or 'poetic' history. The story he studies, and its variations, shows that there is but one discourse, and that the legendary and the historical are closely intertwined.

The legend narrates how the people of Castile elected two judges — Nuño Rasura and Laín Calvo — to govern them, and discusses their lines of descent, tracing Rasura's down to the monarchs of Castile, and Calvo's to El Cid. The causes behind their election, and the chronology, procedure and workings of this judicial diarchy, are the basic elements of this foundational fiction, which in turn covers three broad topics: the history of the Peninsular monarchies, the foundations of royal power, and the relations between the Crown and the aristocracy. It is this basic core that will be modified in the successive versions. Martin identifies semiotically, between 1277 and 1312, three states of the legend that make up a unit he considers to be the basis of all of the major systems that the contemporary and subsequent historical discourse will reproduce and recover. The book centres on: 1) the *Liber Regum*, written in Navarre in the late twelfth century, which contains the first version of the legend; 2) the versions contained in the thirteenth-century Castilian-Leonese historiographic series (*Chronicon Mundi, De Rebus Hispaniae* and *Estoria de España*); and 3) those from the late thirteenth and early fourteenth century found in *La Crónica de Castilla* and in the *Poema de las Mocedades de Rodrigo*. I will now summarize the main threads of the complex analysis that the author undertakes in order to explain the major semantic themes of this variation. He follows neither the traditional approach of the Menéndez Pidal school with regard to supposed lost sources, nor a formalist and textual logic concerning its development, but rather reconstructs the sociopolitical and cultural context that endow them with meaning.

In order to establish the *primordial corpus*, he carries out a philological and historical examination of the source material in order to date it and situate its genealogy. Of the four internally connected works containing traces of the legend (the *Liber Regum Villarensis*; the *Linaje de Rodrigo Díaz*; the *Chronica Naierensis* and the *Historia Roderici*), this examination allows him to demonstrate that it is the *Liber Regum* — a political and genealogical narration of the royal dynasty founded by García Ramírez, and

---

notions. Of equal interest along these lines is Geary, *Phantoms of Remembrance*, and the articles collected in Magdalino, ed., *The Perception of the Past*. On the writing of history and its functions, see Stock, *Listening for the Text*. On Spanish historiography, one must cite the vast work of Linehan, *History and the Historians*, a very particular interpretation of Spanish medievalism during and after the Franco regime, and of the concerns that have articulated the history of Spain as far back as the medieval period itself. Special attention should be paid to his remarks on the sociopolitical contexts in which the medieval chronicles were written.

HISTORICAL DISCOURSE AS HISTORY   647

written in the area of Navarre in the second half of the twelfth century — where we find the first version of the legendary system under study. However, it is the semantic analysis of the text and its historical contextualization that allow Martin to understand the reasons behind the formation of this anonymous historical representation, for which there is no supporting historical evidence.

I believe that the semantic study of this first version constitutes a model of analysis that historians have every interest in understanding. It involves comprehending the text within a cultural universe made up of a body of knowledge (historical, legal, sociological, political), an imaginary and a general semiotics. This enables him to identify the points where the legend breaks with the dominant historiography, and to inquire as to their meaning. The legend, in effect, in this first version, is inserted within the succession of post-Visigothic kings; in other words, within an ancient body of historical knowledge perpetuated by the chronicles without any noteworthy variation, both adapting to and altering it. The first novelty is the extinction of the royal line founded by Pelayo upon the death of Alfonso II. While the rest of the historiography extols the spiritual virtues of the latter's chastity, the *Liber* is only interested in its consequences for the dynasty and the power vacuum that it creates. The election of the judges is described as an effect of this state of affairs. Moreover, the use of the term *Castile* by the authors of the *Liber* also marks a change in the geopolitical history of this territory, a spatial shift whose aim is to confuse the history of Castile with the post-Visigothic monarchy of León from its very foundation.

This twofold break with the facts and with the contemporary body of knowledge, which characterizes what Martin refers to as the initial narrative unity of the legend, makes sense in relation to the information in the central unit: agreement upon and election of two judges to fill the vacuum created by the accidental interruption in the continuity of royal power. A king is thus replaced by two judges, a solution that breaks with homologous responses to similar situations. The analysis of this central unit sheds much light on the aims of the *Liber*'s authors. There are two fundamental notions that characterize the judges in the legend: *primordiality* or genetic independence, in that their names make no reference to their fathers' names, such that the judges constitute starting points whose value is based not on their ancestors but on their own nature; *parity* or nominal identicality based on the analogous meaning of their last names, Rasura ('shave') and Calvo ('bald'). The semantic domain of baldness exhibits the ambivalence and functional duplicity of the term, which combines a degrading quality with the fact of overcoming it, symbolizing the two poles of decline/sublimation. In this way, the naming system, in addition to identifying each of the judges, also connects them with a whole series of myths where the hero emerges by making up for a natural defect or by breaking with his or her line. It is, thus, a classic origin tale, a foundational myth, that encompasses this symbology, and thus the notion of primordiality shows up as well in the symbolism of the judges' names. It is worth highlighting the richness of Georges Martin's highly nuanced inquest into the symbolic meaning of baldness in the medieval imaginary.

The legend mentions just one descendant of each judge (from Nuño Rasura, Alfonso VII the Emperor, and from Laín Calvo, El Cid), inserting the legend into prior genealogies, which is precisely one of the *Liber*'s aims. As is now well known,[5] this narrative genre has its own specific imaginary and a semiotics with its own set of rules that the author highlights with extreme clarity regarding the known social processes behind the aristocracy's hereditary transmission and structural hierarchy. We could say that the 'family history' constituted by the genealogies was a legitimizing representation of the practices of dividing up and transmitting goods and power. Martin employs the implicit rules of this linguistic system as a guide to unravel the meaning of the narration, taking the descendants as signs in the genealogical text, pointing out their place within the circulation of goods, and identifying and tracking their path down to the last recipient. This is how he examines the legacy of the two judges.

Nuño Rasura's genealogy supports a double political legacy: that of the counts of Castile and of the monarchs of Navarre. The *Liber* version, as we have mentioned, breaks with the dominant representation of the royalty (*Crónica de don Pelayo, Historia Silensis, Genealogías de Roda*). There, the dynasty of the Counts of Castile was largely overlooked, and the first king, Fernando I, did not accede to the throne until after the death of his son-in-law, King Vermudo III of León, in the battle of Tamarón. In this understanding, Castile only came into its own as a derivative of the Kingdom of León. In the *Liber* the aforementioned alterations constitute a *reinterpretation* of the Castilian royalty, as Fernando receives the throne from the monarchy of Navarre naturally through paternal inheritance. This is achieved by referring to the authority of Sancho the Great to the west of Navarre as that of a 'lord' rather than a 'king,' thereby avoiding all mention of León and its monarchs. Fernando's Leonese marriage is thus erased, along with the entire traditional interpretation of his accession to the throne. Fernando is referred to as king after naming his mother, Infanta Elvira of Castile, and his father, Sancho of Navarre. Therefore it is implicitly through the Navarran monarchy that Fernando inherits his *potestas regalis*, as well as the *territorium*, inherited from his mother, over which he exercises it, and which had been under the authority of Nuño Rasura. In this way, through the encounter between the judge's legacy and the Navarran royal line, the rights of Fernando I of León transfer over to Navarre. This political legacy is what the *Liber* attempts to construct. The last descendant mentioned in this genealogy is Alfonso VII, and the authors appear to be interested only in his network of alliances, known to be significant. Indeed, this king stands at the centre of a kinship system extending to all of the monarchs in the peninsula, as well as those of France, England and the Emperor, all of whom are included in the kinship web of the *Liber*.

The genealogy of the first judge, however, would not make sense without that of the second, as the two lineages together form a system structured around a common heritage. The lineage of Laín Calvo culminates with El Cid. The latter's ancestors came from a more humble background, but demonstrated the importance of marriage alliances and battlefield exploits for social mobility. El Cid's military experience reproduces his genealogy, insofar as both represent a progression up to the threshold of royalty. What the legend does is provide a historical perspective to the Cid myth by

---

5   The relationship between this literary genre and its content is studied by Spiegel, 'Genealogy'.

relating it to the ancestral parity of the judges. In this way, parity with the monarchs represents not just a *conquest*, but, more importantly, an *inheritance*. However, the one who benefits from this inheritance is not El Cid himself. Rather, following the female side of the line, the last figure is Sancho of Navarre, who was king at the time the *Liber* was written. Martin demonstrates that the actual intended point of arrival of the Cid line is the royal dynasty of Navarre, making it heir to the accumulated worth of El Cid, in other words of a symbolic capital that is also an immaterial inheritance, to use the concepts of P. Bourdieu and G. Levi, respectively. In a way, this establishes an equivalence between the Castilian and Navarran dynasties, equating Fernando I of Castile with García Ramírez of Navarre, and placing the latter at the centre of a kinship network similar to, though not as vast as, that of Alfonso VII.

Historical contextualization — another of the text's genetic or determining factors — therefore allows Martin to argue that the fiction falls within the dynastic problem upsetting the political life of the Kingdom of Navarre in the twelfth century, largely due to the aftermath of King Sancho Garcés IV of Navarre's murder at Peñalén in 1076. On top of the breakup of the kingdom and the alienation of the Aragonese monarchy were the problems of succession following Alfonso I the Battler's death without issue and the suspicions surrounding his will, which Navarre would attempt to turn to its advantage in order to restore its monarchy. It would manage to achieve this restoration only amidst serious political troubles, and with the support of Castile, which was interested in securing its position in La Rioja. According to Martin, it is against the backdrop of this uncertain restoration that we are to understand not only the first version of the legend, but also more generally the fine architecture of Spanish historiography's first chronicle in Romance vernacular, the *Liber Regum*. Inserting the legend within the royal genealogies is thus aimed at constructing similar origins for the rulers of Castile and Navarre through a shared heroic ancestor. García Ramírez and his descendants found in their Castilian ancestor Laín Calvo, companion and peer of Nuño Rasura, a historical foundation for the parity between the Emperor's descendants. In this way, through a system of institutional and historical equivalences, the authors of the *Liber* set out to legitimize the Navarran restoration.

However, Georges Martin is not content to merely examine and help us understand the context giving rise to the legend and its workings. Rather, out of an interest in the fate of a text that broke with the Spanish historiographical tradition, he seeks to understand the causes behind its perpetuation, and the features and processes of its variation through space and time. How — he asks — did the book become so successful and widespread? How are we to understand the fact that historians who were heirs to the great Asturian-Leonese tradition would adopt a legend that stood at odds with the interests of the very Crowns they were serving?

Through an examination of the works of Lucas de Tuy, Jiménez de Rada and Alfonso X, he attempts to determine why and how the episode was integrated into a system against which it was originally created. Thus, in the second part of the book he proposes to track the rewritings of the legend in three works written in the first half of the thirteenth century in the Kingdom of Castile and León by royal commission. As time goes by, the episode continues to evolve, transforming into a political ideology where, Martin argues, upon the structure of the original tale, subsequent authors place the elements of a new social and political discourse. Given their dates (the first half of the thirteenth century), place of composition (Kingdom of Castile and León), royal patronage (Queen Berenguela, King Fernando III and King Alfonso X), and writing style (each author is familiar with and rewrites the preceding version), they form a homogeneous body and a closed textual system. Contextualization is a much easier task here, as it is possible to learn the historian's perspective, interpret it and reveal each one's writing strategies.

The person Queen Berenguela commissioned to write the *Chronicon mundi* was Lucas, deacon of the Basilica of San Isidoro in León and later bishop of Tuy. The queen asked him to collect the writings of the historians of Spain, and to continue them down to her son Fernando III, once he was consolidated as king. According to Martin, this astute queen was aware of the importance of history for the idea of the monarchy, and her initiative set in motion the greatest historiographical movement in medieval Iberia. The work produced by the Leonese monk, which Martin argues is of critical importance, is a sociopolitical interpretation of the history of Spain, conceived as an *ars regendi*, and a *speculum principis* that the queen would give to her son in order to instruct him in the art of governing himself and his subjects. It contains the image of the good prince as conceived by the Church, and the role that the latter attributes itself within such a government. The core of the *Chronicon*, however, is the relationship between the royalty and the lay aristocracy. The royalty is represented as being constantly pushed to the limits of the law by an aristocracy avid for power, quick to rebel, and eager to have its say over royal succession. To this social group Lucas attributes all responsibility for the kingdom's many periods of unrest, distorting and falsifying the reasons behind the monarchy's interventions in such conflicts. The work's underlying message, then, is clearly anti-nobility, although it is the Castilian nobility in particular that receives the most negative portrayal, as the embodiment of the unruly spirit the author attributes to the knighthood.

It is within this sociopolitical context that Martin argues we should understand Lucas's version of the legend, which transforms its content and radically inverts its meaning. Lucas uses fiction to proclaim a specific political ideology, which consists of affirming the providential nature of the monarchy's power and its hereditary nature; the need for the political order imposed by this power, as opposed to the turbulent and tyrannical behaviour of an aristocracy cast as the sole culprit behind Castile's dissidence; and, on a territorial level, a defence of León's sovereignty over Tierra de Campos. Martin shows, through a long and detailed analysis, how the changes Lucas makes to the legend are pieces in a semantic device that matches up with the chronicler's stated aim. By moving the election of the judges back to the reign of Fruela, these alterations transform into rebellion what in the *Liber Regum* was, in a sense, a public health measure taken in the face of a power vacuum. This enables Lucas to condemn the actions of the Castilians and minimize this event's influence on the Peninsular monarchies. Moreover, the sociological characterization of the actors, identifying two separate hierarchical levels at their very core, allows him to implicate just the aristocracy in Castile's dissidence. It is worth highlighting Martin's depiction of the sociological categories used in these three thirteenth-century works to refer to the characters in the legendary episode, and the semantic analysis that he carries out. Indeed, the differing characterization of the social actors in the works under study is one of the linguistic tools most extensively employed to endow a single story with multiple meanings. Several years later in a different political situation, when the kingdom's territory was rapidly expanding, thereby enabling the consolidation and reinforcement of royal authority and an increase in the estates of the grandees, Fernando III commissioned Archbishop of Toledo Rodrigo Jiménez de Rada to write the history *De rebus Hispaniae.*

According to Martin, the analysis of the personality and thought of this important lord and archbishop indicates that he was personally involved in the contradiction deriving from the aforementioned development of royal power and noble power at odds with one another. The political model outlined in *De rebus* is based on a substantially different conception of the relationship between monarchy and nobility than that of the *Chronicon* of Lucas de Tuy, insofar as it illustrates the need for a harmonious union between these two social poles by respecting and fulfilling their mutual obligations. Jiménez de Rada relies on a notion of *faith* whose semantic valence is broader than that of mere *fealty*, encompassing the full range of political relations by making it the source of all forms of obligation. This core role assigned to the *pledge of faith*, its origin in homage and other personal-type contracts, the frequent mention of fiefs and the rituals by which they are granted, held and alienated, leads Martin to wonder whether the general political representation promoted by Jiménez de Rada is governed by the model of the 'feudal monarchy' that was prevailing in France at the time. However, according to Martin — and here we see, as I will discuss further along, how the historical knowledge adopted by the contemporary scholar (i.e. Martin himself) interferes in the construction of the context of the past in which his own object of study is situated — *De rebus* cannot be read as a feudal proclamation for Castile, because it does not understand its political organization as a pyramid of feudal vassalage dependencies. He sees Jiménez de Rada as 'deeply rooted in the imaginary and institutional universe of feudalism,' which in turn leads him to laud *fides* and *fidelitas* as values giving structure and cohesion to the world, and to situate the political edifice upon personal commitment and reciprocal obligation and dependence, as opposed to the providential and absolute monarchy put forward by Lucas de Tuy.

In this context, the modifications that Archbishop Rodrigo introduces into the legend as passed down in the *Chronicon* are meticulous and radical. His revision affects not only its meaning but also the field of representation in which it unfolds. This thereby creates a new horizon of meaning by offering a different origin for the political history of Castile. Martin's semantic and historical analysis of this revision strikes me as exemplary, truly illuminating the construction of foundation myths in the Castilian political system. The election of the judges is presented as having been carried out by the Castilian nobles to escape their mistreatment at the hands of the monarchs of León, but without the element of political rebellion in Lucas de Tuy's version. Instead, he accentuates the legal nature of the causes and purposes of the institution founded in Castile, which thereby takes on the appearance of a local reorganization of judicial power. Moreover, the features of political rupture are now attributed to Count Fernán González, and the legend woven around him serves to downplay the gravity of the founders' actions. Thus, in Jiménez de Rada's version, the election of the judges ceases to be a marginal incident within the history of Asturias and León, and instead becomes an endogenous process of independence — and not mere restoration, as in the *Liber* — of Castilian power. This inaugural history — says Martin — is more than just a revision of the origins and evolution of the spaces of power. By shifting the meaning of the legend of the judges and its continuation via the history of the counts of Castile, it leaves behind the sphere of dynastic deviations that were central to the *Liber* version, as well as that of a fundamental ideology of royal order in the *Chronicon*, instead composing a foundation myth of Castilian law and order.

What is crucial in the construction of this order is the quality accorded to the nature of the relations between a community — essentially the Castilian aristocracy — and its leader. Jiménez de Rada's retouches to the legend are revealing as to his own agenda. He reevaluates the role of the social actors who brought the judges to power, turning the rebellious noblemen of the *Chronicon* into the innocent victims of royal injustice and, more importantly, into defenders of the community. However, he also reclassifies the categories of the aristocratic group through a lexical-notional reorganization that entails a new approach to the narrative roles as a whole. On the one hand, he identifies, within the nobility, the group closest to the monarch — the *magnates* — whose members carry out the most important political functions and hold the top government posts. On the other, taking advantage of the functional meaning of *miles*, he merges *knighthood* and *nobility*, which allows him to portray aristocratic society as uniform, and to impose a political representation of consensus among the secular aristocracy and the sovereign authority. And yet, there is more. In his version of the legend, Jiménez de Rada attributes a distinct function to each judge: the ancestor of the monarchs enacts justice, while that of the grandees focuses on the military. He then has these two functions — justice and the military — reunite further down the line in the figure of Fernán González, to whom he attributes Castile's highest political authority. The novelty in this representation — Martin points out — is that the instigator of this twofold institution is the aristocracy. The aristocracy is the origin of the supreme authority thanks to its historical claim to the military. In this way, unlike the representation proposed by Lucas de Tuy in the *Chronicon* of a royalty providentially quashing the tyrannical aspirations of the nobility, in *De rebus* it is the aristocracy that, in accordance with Providence, founds and sustains the power of the Crown.

However, it is possible to read even further into the legend, as Martin does so well, and highlight the judicial nature of the title given since its origin to the elected Castilians, in an attempt to understand how Jiménez de Rada brings this latent meaning of the legend up to date. Unlike the *Liber* or the *Chronicon*, Archbishop Rodrigo is the first to base his assessment of the judge on the definition of his practice and — in Martin's reading — advocates for the benefits of 'amicable settlements' over the injustice of the 'rulings' that had characterized justice as practiced by the royal court of León. He pits two legal spaces against each other: the bad sort practiced by the royal court of Asturias and León, and the good sort initiated in Castile by the aristocracy. Martin points out that the text comes against the backdrop of an increasing Romanization of the legal code, and an increasing centralization of the justice system. Thus, he believes that the reference to the 'amicable resolution of disputes', more than a symptom of the nobility's preventive measures against the coercive application of the law, constitutes a defence of royal arbitration between the grandees. Archbishop Rodrigo transforms Lucas de Tuy's telling of the legend in three major ways. First, he restores the importance of the judges' election within the process of Castile's independence from León. Second, he constructs the first myth of the legendary Fernán González. Lastly, he turns Lucas's sociopolitical thesis on its head by postulating the necessity of a political order based on the harmonious relationship between monarchy and aristocracy.

For the version of the legend from the time of Alfonso X, Martin uses two copies that he believes belong to the corpus of the *Estoria de España*, placing special emphasis on studying the workings of this historiographic enterprise promoted by the king himself. He examines how the task of compilation was carried out so as to formalize historical knowledge and endow it with a new status, what new procedures were used in recovering this past and adapting it to the needs of its time, and, ultimately, what overall aims are reflected in this act of recovery.

What Martin traces throughout this section is Alfonso X's political ideology in relation to his body of work. His territorial conception of history, which implies a 'natural' definition, due to the kingdom where it arose, is that of a history of mankind written out of a notion of 'nature' regarded as the basis of political relations. The timing of the text likewise reflects the king's interest in defining, gathering together and organizing his political legacy in line with his imperial designs. But it is in the very telling of the events where Martin observes the modelling of a power structure in accordance with Alfonso's ideal. In this sense, the most relevant are the passages referring to relations with the nobility, illustrated for the most part with heroic tales that introduce innovations into the historical knowledge of prior generations. Thus, in the legends of both Bernardo del Carpio and the Infantes de Lara,[6] the modifications generally aim to demonstrate the need for a code to regulate the various systems of obligations, and to hierarchically order the systems of the 'natural', i.e. dependence — a critical topic in the Alfonsine legal corpus. In Martin's view, the centralist, codifying project likewise governs the tales of aristocratic disputes, by substituting the old forms of resolution with new ones regulated through written law. Especially illuminating is Martin's analysis of the transformation of the *faith/fealty* of Jiménez de Rada's model, into the *law/loyalty* of Alfonso X's, as a pillar of political relations. Thus, there is a shift from a system of dependence based on personal commitment, to a system based on the new *natural* conception of law.

Alfonso's version of the legend responds to this same centralizing political aim, such that Martin discerns the desire to ascribe a 'totality' (and then a unity, a centralism) to the justice exercised by Nuño Rasura. Accentuating the territorial character of

---

6 A very interesting interpretation of this legend has been proposed by Julio Escalona, who focuses on the transformations in the spatial context of Lara in which the legend plays out; see Escalona, 'Transformaciones sociales'. [Editor's note: The relevant section was later published as Escalona, 'Épica, crónicas y genealogías'].

the judges serves to confer a foundational character upon the legal centralization of Castile. Of particular interest are the pages dedicated to the Alfonsine compilers' task of reconstruction, crafting a meaningful relationship between a representation of authority and a representation of the aristocracy. They show how the most vigorous revision is to be found, once again, in the sociological characterization of the episode's protagonists. Here Martin makes a crucial contribution by studying the sociological vocabulary employed and exploited by the compilers of the *Historia*. Indeed, Martin demonstrates the function that the work's varied social lexicon plays within the text's aims. Although this lexicon is not new, its meaning and distribution are, and this is not because of a shift in the nature of the social facts the terms refer to, but rather due to the compilers' aims. The translation from Latin into Romance goes hand in hand with a semantic revision that therefore responds to the work's objectives.

It is particularly interesting to see the semantic reworking of the term *hombres buenos*. Its latent meaning (i.e. 'good men') is exploited so that the moral meaning prevails over its use as a term of social status, attributing to the phrase all the roles that contribute to reinforcing sovereign authority. Likewise, the lexical differentiation of different statuses within the nobility makes it possible to distinguish a separate, powerful segment, and attribute to it all the monarchy's ills.

Martin also identifies three major changes introduced by the Alfonsine compilers that make their version of the legend distinct. While Lucas brought out the fissures within the aristocracy in order to better denounce the threat that a powerful nobility posed for the monarchy, and Rodrigo cast the nobility in a positive light by integrating it into a single, uniform aristocracy by and large devoted to the crown, the *Historia* neither condemns nor praises the nobility. Rather, its objective is to point out the right path for it to take, through a dynamic, 'benevolent' assessment inviting the nobility to join the only worthwhile elite: the public elite of the 'good men' (of which they are but one part), which are the cornerstone of sovereign political authority and a pillar of the royal enterprise.

Georges Martin takes on a third major version of the legend arising in Castile between the late thirteenth and early fourteenth centuries in the context of an expansion of the figure of El Cid at the heart of a chanson de geste. There are two works with a significant impact on the subsequent historiography that make up the corpus of this version: the *Crónica de Castilla* and the *Poema de las Mocedades de Rodrigo*. In both texts the legend of the judges opens the tale of Rodrigo's youth, distancing itself from the history of the monarchy and instead veering toward heroic fiction. Martin examines the similarities and differences between these two works, their dates, as well as the variations and continuities with respect to the versions we have already seen. He does so with his characteristic thorough and careful understanding of the meanings behind the legend's renewal. It is this approach which allows him to question the arguments of traditional philology and historiography as to the poetic origin of the heroes' tales in the chronicles. He likewise challenges the ideological criteria used to date texts such as the *Poema de las Mocedades*, where, because the hero does not match the common representations found in the Castilian heroic tradition, scholars have argued it belongs to a subsequent period when epic poetry was already in decline.

These texts, like the *Liber regum* containing the first version of the legend, are undated, and contain no information as to their patrons, authors or explicit aims. However, the complexity of Martin's analysis makes it possible not only to propose a new chronology, but also to better understand its meaning. In the *Crónica de Castilla* the core theme is Rodrigo's ascent in the shadow of the Crown, his upward social mobility in the service of the king, whose power is never called into question. In the *Poema* it is vassalage, the establishment of a personal dependence through homage, that is a prerequisite for effective lordship. However, the focus is on the merits, deeds and competence of the vassal, more than on the authority of his lord. It is the hero, a knight, who establishes prerequisites to his recognition of the king's lordship over him. Both works' political ideology reflects the social aspirations of the knighthood. Indeed, the knighthood encompassed second-born and illegitimate offspring — marginalized by a hereditary system that increasingly privileged first-born sons and estate confiscation — as well as groups belonging to the emerging urban oligarchy.

The telling of the legend included in these texts works off of the *Liber Regum* and the version of Jiménez de Rada. Its function is to affirm, more than ever before, through an insistence on the original twofold power of the ancestor of the monarchs and the ancestor of the knights, that Castilian political relations are based on a foundational balance between royal and aristocratic power. Moreover, the legend provides a radically new definition of the aristocracy, as beneath the political parity of the judges there emerges a social disparity between nobility and knighthood: Nuño Rasura is given the title of count, while the children of Laín Calvo are made knights. And out of this disparity emerges the heroic core of the *Mocedades*, the social bloc mentioned above.

The sociopolitical purpose that Martin reads into the text are the specific historical circumstances surrounding Fernando IV and Alfonso XI's accession to the throne as children. The high nobility took advantage of these moments of royal weakness, but at the same time the idea of vassalage to the king, which the *Poema* puts forth as a solution to the problem of noble dominance, underwent enormous development.

Martin's historical contextualization of the works (despite a lack of studies that he himself points out) therefore enables him to confirm his semiotic analysis by showing the traits and ambitions of the rising social groups, that secular social group united especially around the urban knighthood, which the monarchy turned to for support in the second half of the thirteenth century and beginning of the fourteenth century. Martin argues that this social group had by this point learned an alternative version of history transmitting a systematic interpretation of the nobility's political behaviour as the main threat to the kingdom's well-being. What is more, despite these groups' apparent desire to assimilate into the aristocracy, Martin considers that this last version of the legend is an 'independent manifesto,' an 'autonomous proclamation' of a 'true, non-derivative ideology of the knighthood' that expresses the specific interests of the knights, who, to the detriment of the nobility, assert the superiority of their capacity to reinforce the monarchy. In this way, one can see the importance for this social group of controlling and expressing its own past, its historical memory, as an element of its social identity and a fundamental factor in the formalization of its political aspirations.

The study of this legendary tale, and the reconstruction of its process of transmission, clearly show that the historical factuality of the narration is less important than its correspondence with contemporary circumstances, in other words, with the context within which the tale was written, recovered and rewritten. This perspective avoids the decontextualization inherent both in textual analyses aimed only restoring the internal meaning of the narration, as well as in positivist historical analyses interested more in extracting 'the truth' from a story, in separating 'the historical' from 'the literary,' than in understanding the relationship between empirical reality and its representation. By contrast, Martin shows that it is the contextualization of this *text object* and its successive variations, all of them pure historical discourse, that makes it a historical source, insomuch as the process of reinterpretation enables us to understand real processes of social and cultural change. In this case, he says, it reflects 'the mental profiles and thought processes of the elites, the antagonisms and transformations of a society, the construction of royal power.'

And it is along the lines of the issues surrounding the very notion of context that I think it is worth making a few closing observations. As he has clearly demonstrated throughout the book, Martin conceives of *context* as the set of genetic factors behind the text. This implies, as we have seen, inquiring into the personal, cultural and social circumstances that limit and condition the discourse, in this case of each textual version of the legend. As such, social reality emerges as the ultimate point of reference for the interpretation of the text, one which is never rhetorical. Martin, by contrast, does not only rely on historical studies on the society in which the legend emerges and is successively rewritten; one of his merits is to identify the gaps in the research and to attempt to bridge them.

And yet, reconstructing the context remains an enormously difficult task. Martin says so explicitly in his introduction. I will mention a few such difficulties that, in my opinion, he has not always managed to overcome. They stem not so much from a lack of historical studies as from the type of studies employed. I have already referred to this problem above when mentioning that the author's institutional conception of feudalism seems to have influenced the conception he attributes to Jiménez de Rada. I believe that the dynamic of noble/royal relations he describes is ultimately undermined by an overly linear argumentation (contradicting the more complex and precise reasoning of his textual analysis). This can likewise be attributed to the studies he uses as a reference, wherein the common assumption is that the monarchy is strong when it dominates the nobility, and vice versa. This process, which tends to form the core of more traditional, established interpretations of Spanish political history, is rightly questioned through more complex theoretical approaches. Such approaches show that the strengthening and centralization of the monarchy in the late Middle Ages was not undertaken at the expense of the political capacities of the nobility. Rather, the power of the nobility as a group was also reinforced, in opposition to, but also in alliance with, rising social groups, whose identity we have seen commemorated in *Las Mocedades*, in their pursuit of control over the apparatuses or policies of the state.[7]

---

7 For theoretical considerations, see Monsalvo Antón, 'Poder político y aparatos de Estado'. The

Another aspect that I believe could be read differently is Martin's assessment of judicial practice in the work of Jiménez de Rada. The archbishop seems to juxtapose amicable resolutions and rulings not so much to argue which of the two conflict-resolution methods is most beneficial for society, as to differentiate between judicial jurisdictions and spaces using specific decision-making procedures. To accept the latter argument about differentiation is to implicitly accept that the traditional legal discourse's dichotomy between allocation and settlement is a false one. Moreover, the fact that the Alfonsine version of the legend is assessed in similar terms also calls into question another age-old assumption (or another aspect of the same one): that the strengthening and centralization of royal power, and the resulting development of the royal tribunals, displaced the use of informal methods of conflict resolution.[8]

My point is that to draw attention to the difficulties in grasping the social context is to stand at the horizon of today's 'historical knowledge,' and to acknowledge its limitations. I do so precisely to highlight what I consider to be the main contribution of Martin's book, which is his investigation into the process behind the construction of this historical knowledge, of this discourse of the past that is created out of the needs and interests of the social groups of each present time. This kind of creating takes place through an active process of recuperation that suppresses alternative discourses, and transforms and manipulates materials inherited from the past, using 'all the resources of language' to do so. As we have seen, this 'social use of language' to give meaning to the past takes the form of models of political reflection that are in competition, insofar as they formalize, in the framework of power relations, the different and often opposing aspirations of these groups. In this sense the medieval historical discourse, as Martin concludes, was one of the major pillars of the political discourse.

The most important aspect of this book therefore resides in the reflection it arouses regarding how history is practiced today, contributing to a debate in the field of history that is more alive than we would often like to admit. Questioning the dominant social discourses from different angles, this debate fosters research that takes an in-depth look at the nature of the relationship between social reality and the language used to explain it.

---

process of constructing Castile's feudal monarchy and the development of the nobility's power from such a perspective has recently been studied by Rodríguez López, *La consolidación territorial*; Jular Pérez-Alfaro, *Los adelantados y merinos mayores*; Álvarez Borge, *Monarquía feudal y organización territorial*. Pastor and others, 'Baja nobleza'. Also, Martínez Sopena, 'La nobleza de León y Castilla'.

8   For more on these topics and a critical review thereof, see Alfonso, 'Resolución de disputas'.

Bibliography

Alfonso, Isabel, 'Resolución de disputas y prácticas judiciales en el Burgos medieval', in *Burgos en la Plena Edad Media. III Jornadas Burgalesas de Historia* (Burgos: Asociación Provincial de Libreros de Burgos, 1994), pp. 211–43

Álvarez Borge, Ignacio, *Monarquía feudal y organización territorial. Alfoces y merindades en Castilla (siglos X–XIV)* (Madrid: CSIC, 1993)

Burdiel, Isabel, and María Cruz Romeo, 'Historia y lenguaje: la vuelta al relato dos décadas después', *Hispania*, 56–192 (1996), 333–46

Escalona, Julio, 'Transformaciones sociales y organización del espacio en el alfoz de Lara en la Alta Edad Media' (unpublished PhD, Universidad Complutense de Madrid, 1996)

Escalona, Julio, 'Épica, crónicas y genealogías. En torno a la historicidad de la Leyenda de los Infantes de Lara', *Cahiers de Linguistique Hispanique Médiévale*, 23 (2000), 113–73

Fentress, James, and Chris Wickham, *Social Memory* (Oxford: Blackwell, 1992)

Fouracre, Paul, 'Merovingian History and Merovingian Hagiography', *Past & Present*, 127 (1990), 3–38

Geary, Patrick, *Phantoms of Remembrance: Memory and Oblivion at the End of the First Millennium* (Princeton: Princeton University Press, 1994)

Jular Pérez-Alfaro, Cristina, *Los adelantados y merinos mayores de León (siglos XIII–XV)* (León: Universidad de León, 1990)

Linehan, Peter, *History and the Historians of Medieval Spain* (Oxford: Clarendon Press, 1993)

Magdalino, Paul, ed., *The Perception of the Past in Twelfth-Century Europe* (Rio Grande, OH: Hambledon Press, 1992)

Martin, Georges, *Les juges de Castille. Mentalités et discours historique dans l'Espagne médiévale*, Annexes des Cahiers de linguistique hispanique médiévale. 6 (Paris: Klincksieck, 1992)

Martínez Sopena, Pascual, 'La nobleza de León y Castilla en los siglos XI y XII. Un estado de la cuestión', *Hispania*, 53–185 (1993), 801–22

Monsalvo Antón, José María, 'Poder político y aparatos de Estado en la Castilla bajomedieval. Consideraciones sobre su problemática', *Studia Historica, Historia Medieval*, 4 (1986), 101–67

Moradiellos, Enrique, 'Últimas corrientes en historia', *Historia Social*, 16 (1993), 97–113

Pastor, Reyna and others, 'Baja nobleza: aproximación a la historiografía europea y propuestas para una investigación', *Historia Social*, 20 (1994), 23–45

Rodríguez López, Ana, *La consolidación territorial de la monarquía feudal castellana. Expansión y fronteras durante el reinado de Fernando III* (Madrid: CSIC, 1994)

Spiegel, Gabrielle, 'Genealogy: Form and Function in Medieval Historical Narrative', *History and Theory*, 22–1 (1983), 43–53

Spiegel, Gabrielle, 'History, Historicism, and the Social Logic of the Text in the Middle Ages', *Speculum*, 65–1 (1990), 59–86

Spiegel, Gabrielle, *Romancing the Past: The Rise of Vernacular Prose Historiography in Thirteenth-Century France* (London: University of California Press, 1993)

Stock, Brian, *Listening for the Text: On the Uses of the Past* (Baltimore, MD: Johns Hopkins University Press, 1990)

Stone, Lawrence, 'History and Post-Modernism', *Past & Present*, 131 (1991), 217–18

ISABEL ALFONSO

Naming Violence and Controlling its Legitimation*

Prompted by the bloody conflict in the Balkans, a well-known author recently wrote in one of Spain's most widely read newspapers about the 'unfathomable mystery of human cruelty', stating that one had to 'humbly accept [it] as something natural, the effect of a mineral imbalance in some recess of the brain'. He was less disconcerted by the violence itself as by the spectacle of its justification via terms such as 'legitimate self-defence', 'just war' or 'humanitarian war' imposed by those waging it.[1]

Those of us who study society are well aware of the force of language in imposing authority, whether it is held or disputed. As historians, the tenacity of such discourses of legitimization through time never ceases to surprise us. The immediacy of a conflict like the Yugoslav Wars seems to have reawakened old questions and debates as to whether violence is a matter of nature or nurture, as to the persistence and multiplicity of its forms, as to the causes that give rise to it, and as to how it might be eradicated or restricted. Although these questions have traditionally been linked to issues of social order and peace-keeping, of control and legitimacy, more and more academic disciplines have taken a keen interest in the social processes through which we perceive, assess and represent violence as such.

These problems are the subject of the books I will review here,[2] since although the word 'violence' only appears in the title of one of them, in all of them it is the central topic. To write these notes, the wide range of sources used and perspectives offered is at once one of the greatest incentives and greatest difficulties, and as such my aim is not to write a full overview of their contents, but rather to point out the debates in which the authors either explicitly situate themselves, or which constitute their implicit point of reference. I hope to reflect on the role of historians and their position in a chain, as observers of violence, perceiving and interpreting the information on violence that they find in the materials they use, and also as architects constructing a narration with its own set of conventions and rhetorical strategies.[3] Indeed, the most important debates found in these books have to do with our own

---

* Original publication: Alfonso, Isabel, 'Los nombres de la violencia y el control de su legitimación', *Hispania*, 208 (2001), pp. 691–706. Translated by Nicholas Callaway. The reflections contained in the following pages are part of a broader study within the framework of the research project *Lucha y legitimación política en León y Castilla (siglos X–XV)* [PB98–0655]. I would like to thank Julio Escalona for all of his useful feedback on this article.

1 Vicent, 'La crueldad'.

2 Halsall, ed., *Violence and Society*; Rosenwein, ed., *Anger's Past*; Bisson, *Tormented Voices*.

3 The role of the observer in this triad of actors who take part in assessing violence has been marvellously highlighted by Miller, *Humiliation*.

660   ISABEL ALFONSO

perceptions, which are also constructed, altered, ratified or called into question through the writing of history.

Thomas Bisson's book seems to have been written to ratify, with some qualifications, the old, deeply rooted image of the violent anarchy of feudalism, adopting the role of spokesperson for its victims in what he refers to as a 'compassionate history'.[4] By contrast, the other two books, both by multiple authors, seem to share the common aim, highlighted by the coordinators of each volume, of questioning historians' widespread depiction of the Middle Ages as dark and violent. They thus embark on a serious attempt to identify this violence's various forms, to explore the contexts in which these arose, and to understand the roles they played — ultimately in order to get at the logic behind the workings of the societies under study. The volume coordinated by Guy Halsall, which contains eleven chapters by so many authors, takes on aspects of violence in different areas of early medieval Europe. The volume coordinated by Barbara Rosenwein contains ten articles, also by multiple authors, which, as indicated by the subtitle, explore the social use of one of its most emotional expressions. To a certain extent the two books complement one another, since whereas the former pays more attention to issues of political vocabulary and social legitimization, the latter focuses on the emotional aspects of violent reactions, and on their representation and perception. Bisson's work participates in both spheres, centring on the period from 1140–1200, when, in his opinion, there was a crisis of the old political order in the Catalan countryside, giving way to 'disorder' and lords' 'arbitrary violence'.

Halsall's lengthy introduction to *Violence and Society* (pp. 1–45), which appears aimed at lending it overall coherence and revealing the interests that motivated his work as editor, should have been included at the end as an epilogue or conclusion, since more than presenting the studies, it dialogues with them, relating the problems they raise, and reflecting on the principal debates. I feel that it is a more useful read after the other chapters, and so I will save my discussion of it for the end. The articles in this book can be grouped around two core themes: violence and sociopolitical order for the first eight articles, and violence by and against women for the last three. Luis García Moreno ('Legitimate and illegitimate violence in Visigothic law,' pp. 46–59) describes the violence of what he refers to as the proto-feudalization of Visigothic society, starting with its condemnation in royal law. Waged by the powerful, this violence, he says, threatened the stability of the rule of law that the Gothic kingdom purported to ensure. This author's assessment of aristocratic violence in Visigothic society differs from Paul Fouracre's view on the coeval Merovingian society ('Attitudes towards violence in seventh and eighth century Francia,' pp. 60–75) He is especially critical of positivist readings of the materials used by historians, and is less interested in quantifying violence than in understanding how it is constructed socially. He does

---

4   While it is true that Bisson does not actually use this term, he himself pointed out in his response to the criticism prompted by his article 'The "Feudal Revolution"', that he does find the concept of 'anarchy' to be well documented (p. 211, n. 37). See the contributions to this debate by Barthélemy, 'The "Feudal Revolution": I'; White, 'The "Feudal Revolution": II'; Reuter, 'Debate: The "Feudal Revolution": III'; Wickham, 'Debate: The "Feudal Revolution": IV', as well as Bisson's 'The "Feudal Revolution": Reply'.

not, however, deny that it existed, but rather sees it as an element of Merovingian political organization, which depended to a large extent on the rivalry between different noble factions capable of exerting their power militarily. Rarely used on a large scale, this violence was a means of redistributing power within the royal court, and therefore saw the participation of the monarchs themselves. Thus, in Fouracre's opinion, it never put social stability in jeopardy, since it reinforced more than eroded the power structure and social hierarchy. Despite the moralization of politics through an increasingly Christianized lexicon, he observes the development of a pragmatic attitude toward violence, judged as good or bad on a case-by-case basis. Thus, the more widespread violence that seems to characterize late Merovingian society can largely be explained, says the author, by how it is construed later on within the framework of the Carolingian legitimation, and by a change in the orientation of the extant sources, which shifted from hagiographies centred on internal conflicts to histories centred on external ones. In this same vein, Janet Nelson ('Violence in the Carolingian world and the ritualization of ninth-century warfare,' pp. 90–107) insists on the importance of ecclesiastic influence on the new ideological and liturgical resources that justified violence — whether directed outwards, or into the heart of the Carolingian Empire — in defence of the Christian *res publica*. The names for the conflicts change: private rivalries and disputes, she points out, become 'civil war' when the Carolingians face off against one another. As a means of legitimizing these wars, ecclesiastic ritualization likewise helped make possible the formation of the new political structures of the medieval kingdoms that arose once the empire was divided up, as well as making them more acceptable. The process, invoking divine will, also entailed the validation of the violence committed by the knightly military elite. The article thus deals with an essential topic: legitimized state violence, institutionalized as a necessary element for both the construction and reproduction of authority, in a perspective that goes beyond the legal recognition of specific forms of violence.

The problem of the relationship between violence and the creation of a new sociopolitical order is also taken up by S. J. Speight ('Violence and the creation of socio-political order in post-conquest Yorkshire,' pp. 157–74), in this case focusing on Yorkshire in the wake of the Norman conquest. Although the conquest was particularly violent in this area, Speight argues that it was no different from the violence employed by the English and Scottish kings in their prior *attempts* to control this same region. The author rightly points out that the way in which the intervention was carried out had to do with the type of relations the conquerors were, or were not, able to establish with various local powers, and the way in which subsequent chroniclers described this violence is part of the process of legitimation or condemnation of the new power, in contrast with the assessment of these same actions by those who opposed its establishment. She also points out problems stemming from land distribution as inherent to the vicious competition over land found among Normans and Saxons alike, and draws attention to the use of psychological intimidation and humiliation as weapons on par with physical violence, in the process of *imposing* the new order and *subjugating* the native population. To a certain extent, although it is not an imported form of domination, Guy Morris ('Violence and late Viking Age Scandinavian social order,' pp. 141–56) researches a similar problem when dealing with the use of violence among the Vikings as they asserted social and political order within Scandinavian society. Royal-sponsored violence here was justified, as it was almost everywhere else as well, by decrying the treachery of those against whom it was directed. This had to do with the monarchy's self-portrayal as the supreme authority over an aristocracy that had strict internal hierarchies, and with the formation of territorial borders against other kingdoms.

A specific form of violence — ritual regicide apparently aimed at masking power struggles in both intra-dynastic succession and in wars between different kingdoms — is the subject of Nick B. Aitchison's chapter on Ireland ('Regicide in early medieval Ireland,' pp. 108–25). The rituals in which the monarchs are put to death are presented as acts carried out for the health of the kingdom, which the victims had put into danger by infringing their sacred royal duties. The legitimizing function of these rituals remained in force in the ninth century, such that, as the author points out, they cannot be attributed to tribal practices of the Irish monarchy.

This same concern with questioning widespread assumptions and criticizing positivist readings of the sources is shared by Tom S. Brown ('Urban violence in early medieval Italy: The cases of Rome and Ravenna,' pp. 76–89), on conflicts in early medieval Italian cities. He demonstrates that the city as a pacifying sphere or an expression of civilized order is a myth, or rather is a rhetorical element of those in power. He likewise shows that the existence of factional strife is not a phenomenon exclusive to the Late Middle Ages, but in fact arose much earlier. In the context of the Papal 'wars of succession' in Rome, he points to the legitimizing character of the appeals to popular intervention within the context of factional strife. As for Ravenna, his reading of the source material also reveals a narrative in which violence attributed to others served as a rhetorical element to highlight the unifying and pacifying role of the Bishop. He therefore calls into question the perspective put forth by the urban clergy of an integrating violence asserting the community's identity in the face of Byzantine influence. This study implies a redefinition of the traditional characterization — or concealment — of these struggles.

However, it is in the article by Matthew Bennet ('Violence in eleventh-century Normandy: Feud, warfare and politics,' pp. 126–40) where the nature of violence is most explicitly discussed regarding the terminology used, both then and now, to describe conflict. Focusing on the conflicts in eleventh-century Normandy, he argues against characterizing them as 'feuds,' thereby challenging historians' traditional characterization of the period as one of anarchy. In his opinion, we should instead regard them as expressions of 'politics' and 'warfare,' i.e. as forms of resolving power struggles between political rivals equipped with the means to face off militarily. While I find valuable this author's attempts to discern and identify different types of conflict, and to uncover their causes and the ways they were resolved, I nevertheless question his vision of the term 'feud,' restricted to its modern sense as personal or family-based vengeance in cases of mortal enmity. The authors he cites (White, Barlett, Hyams, Miller) have painted a more complex picture of the power struggles and political competition designated by such terms.[5] And unlike Bennet, their recognition of the

---

5 White, 'Feuding and Peace-Making'; Bartlett, '"Mortal Enmities"'; Hyams, 'Feud in Medieval England'; Miller, *Bloodtaking*.

political nature of these conflicts is at the same time their argument against the idea that the violence they generated amounted to anarchy. However, his own distinction between 'political' and 'non-political' conflicts — indicative of a very narrow notion of the political sphere — in my opinion implies an acceptance of the old dichotomy between 'public' and 'private' that he seems to criticize (pp. 130–31).[6] Ultimately, the problem is displaced to whatever notion one adopts of politics, which is just as problematic as violence. If reduced to a mere naming convention, the argument can easily become circular. In the type of society that he describes, in which the groups represent and articulate themselves through ties of kinship, friendship and fealty, the conflicts must necessarily be more interwoven than this author would make them seem. It would be more interesting to research how some conflicts get mixed up with others, at times even deliberately, and how personal matters end up expanding into broader spheres.[7] Indeed, some of his examples would readily allow for such an approach (e.g. p. 130). There are therefore two important problems that Bennet's article raises but, in my opinion, does not resolve: what determines whether the conflicts under study are granted or denied a political nature, and the relationship between political structures and forms of violence. We will return to them later on, as they take up the bulk of the editor's introduction and underlie the rest of the articles, not only in this book, but also in the other two that we will be discussing.

The last three chapters of *Violence and Society* deal with important aspects of what is known as 'gender-based violence,' although we should find a better term, insofar as women, like all other actors, can be victims or observers of violence, but can also wage or incite it. It is true that in the sources they show up mainly as victims, only rarely are recognized as aggressors, and are underrepresented as witnesses to violence.[8] Nevertheless, Nancy Wicker's article ('Selective female infanticide as partial explanation for the dearth of women in Viking Age Scandinavia,' pp. 204–21) shows how obscured and hidden their visibility can be even as victims, and proposes a new reading of the archaeological record, whose importance she defends, in order to tackle the difficult subject of domestic violence (which I find more suitable than 'private violence,' the term used by the author), in particular violence against newborn girls. The practice of different types of selective infanticide is what, in her opinion, would explain the scarcity of female archaeological remains, as well as their relatively smaller presence in documents. Julie Coleman ('Rape in Anglo-Saxon England,' pp. 193–204) also centres on a type of violence directed specifically at women: rape, although this crime also produced a collateral group of victims beyond those directly affected, representing an affront to the women's families and entailing a breach of the royal peace. Wicker shows the diverse attitudes and perceptions that such violence elicited regarding the family and social status of raped women in Anglo-Saxon England. Ross Balzaretti's article ("'These are things that men do, not women": The Social Regulation of Female Violence in Longobard Italy,' pp. 175–92)

---

6 For example, when he contrasts 'private' and 'political' murder (p. 132).

7 Work in this direction is the aim of our current research project, cited in note 1.

8 Incitement seems to be the role that corresponds to them culturally. Interesting pages in this sense are those of Miller, *Bloodtaking*, pp. 212–14.

looks into women as the subjects of violence, and the ways in which such violence was represented in the legal sources of Longobard Italy. He argues that the negation and legal punishment of female violence that he has observed is corollary not only to their political exclusion and relegation to the domestic sphere, but also to the dominant construction of heroic masculinity. These chapters bring up a number of points that certainly deserve a more in-depth discussion than is possible here. Among them are the rhetorical elements that we find in the representation of violence suffered by women, constructed as a criterion of disorder in relation to a masculine rhetoric of protection and patronage. There is also the character, whether political or otherwise, of female violence, or the reproduction of gender inequality resulting from persistent positivist readings of the sources.

The studies in *Anger's Past* seem to be concerned with addressing issues and difficulties with our sources that can give us insight into emotional processes and, through them, enhance our understanding of how society works. Anger is, indeed, the emotion that best expresses the violent sentiments in medieval European societies. Representations and perceptions of anger, and attitudes toward it, are the subject of the ten articles that make up the book, which is divided into four parts. Part I, 'Monks and Saints,' includes an article by Lester Little ('Anger in Monastic Curses,' pp. 9–35) on monastic anger and its liturgical expression, which he sees as a ritual that inhibits violent emotional outbursts and has bearing on the civilizing process.[9] We also find Catherine Peyroux's contribution ('Gertrude's *furor*: Reading Anger in an Early Medieval Saint's *Life*,' pp. 36–58) on the angry reaction of a girl and future saint against an offer of secular marriage, as she was already betrothed to Christ. The author provides a convincing explanation for this reaction based on the socio-cultural and political context of both the players and the narration's intended audience, as well as in relation to how marriage alliances were negotiated in that society.

Part II, 'Kings and Emperors,' covers royal and imperial ire. Gerd Althoff ('*Ira Regis*: Prolegomena to a History of Royal Anger,' pp. 59–74) offers us a preview of the history of royal anger that he is currently writing. He interprets this anger as one of the fundamental instruments of a personal-type political system whose legitimacy had to overcome a long tradition favouring mildness and patience dating back to Carolingian times. Geneviève Bührer-Thierry ('"Just Anger" or "Vengeful Anger"? The Punishment of Blinding in the Early Medieval West,' pp. 75–91) also deals with the process by which anger went from being condemned as an abuse of power — a tradition that she traces back to classical antiquity — to becoming a manifestation of legitimate authority under the Visigoths and Carolingians. These new systems transformed the punishment of blinding political opponents from a cruel act into a pious one, through the influence of the clergy on the court in defining the emperor's function as that of illuminating the Christian community. In the last article in this section ('What Did Henry III of England Think in Bed and in French about Kingship and Anger,' pp. 92–126), Paul Hyams offers a rather sophisticated rumination on the

---

9 In a recent article, Alain Boureau has discussed the ineffectiveness of this liturgical policy and the use of a different one starting in the thirteenth century. However, like Little, he regards the monastery as a 'fabrique de la civilité' (Boureau, 'Les moines anglais', p. 640).

processes by which a thirteenth-century English king internalized 'civilized' ideas, based on, among other influences, the iconography decorating the royal chamber, which included depictions of the virtue of clemency triumphing over the sin of wrath.

Part III deals with the anger of 'Lords and Peasants.' Stephen D. White ('The Politics of Anger,' pp. 127–52) investigates the nature and political function of the lords' anger and its implications, in an argument that explicitly questions widespread assumptions that view it as a sign of animal emotion and, therefore, as political irrationality (further on we will return to this interesting notion of 'politics'). Instead, he argues that it was in fact employed as a strategic element in the course of disputes. Likewise, Richard Barton ('"Zealous Anger" and the Renegotiation of Aristocratic Relationships in Eleventh- and Twelfth-Century France,' pp. 153–70) deals with anger as an essential component of the lords' power. As a sign and effect of legitimate authority, it allowed this authority to be reproduced through processes of negotiation when under threat. In this sense, he makes clear the positive social force of expressions of anger as a means to 'peacefully' resolve disputes. However, Barton seems to reserve the feeling of anger for the aristocrats alone, or at least limits his research to the emotional motivations behind this particular group's behaviour. But we might wonder: is it the sole property of the nobles to feel irate? Is anger an emotion specific to the lords or the aristocracy? What happens when peasants become enraged? These are the questions that Paul Freedman's article ('Peasant Anger in the Late Middle Ages,' pp. 171–90) attempts to answer, to a certain extent complementing Barton's study. Thus, he shows that the nobility's prerogative seems to be specifically 'just' anger, whereas that of peasants is generally represented in negative terms. It is either ridiculous and comical, or terrifying and murderous, depending on whether its protagonists are individuals or collectives, and is in all cases cast as irrational and instinctive. Freedman essentially argues that the 'weapons of the weak,' borrowing James Scott's well-known phrase, were not bravery and open confrontation, but cunning and astuteness, as they did not have any officially recognized honour or dignity to defend. The image of the peasantry constructed and passed down by the medieval sources on the one hand ascribes to them savage violence, while on the other denying them the emotional bonds of love, honour and anger reserved for the knights. But just as the discourse is not univocal in the case of the aristocracy, peasant anger too, as we shall see, can be recognized as just in some contexts, when their oppressors are represented negatively as tyrants. Thus, positive portrayals of peasant violence tend to go hand in hand with a rhetoric of restoration celebrating a good ruler in the face of another ruler condemned as unjust.[10]

The fourth and final part of the book, 'Celts and Muslims,' consists of two articles that are, in my opinion, a bit forced, insofar as they approach their subject through insufficiently justified geographic and religious criteria. One of them, by Wendy Davies ('Anger and the Celtic Saint,' pp. 191–202), could have been included in Part I, as it covers the destructive function of saints' curses in Celtic areas, which are not associated with anger but rather with prayer. In the hagiographical material dealing with anger, the

---

10 For more on portrayals of the peasantry, see Freedman, *Images of the Medieval Peasant*.

666   ISABEL ALFONSO

emotion is more closely associated with bad monarchs and aristocrats than with saints, as would befit a punishable sin. However, within the framework of military ethics it is construed as a suitable condition for the domination of a bellicose aristocracy in early medieval peasant cultures. Davies expressly connects anger's function as a defence of honour and status to the highly limited or largely non-formalized apparatuses of the state. The other article ('From Anger on Behalf of God to "Forbearance" in Islamic Medieval Literature,' pp. 203–32) could have been included in Part II, which more specifically deals with the institutional control of anger. The author, Zouhair Ghazzal, analyses this process extending from 'divine anger' to 'tolerance' in Islamic literature, offering useful comparative data. Her study contains a very interesting analysis of the notion of tolerance or self-control (*hilm* in ninth-century *adab* literature) and the difficulty of conceptualizing it, whether as ethically determined uprightness, or as a Machiavellian *virtù* based on pure political strategizing.

The material and arguments offered in these chapters take on greater significance and coherence in light of the texts by the editor, Rosenwein, whose introductory pages (pp. 1–6), and especially her conclusion ('Controlling Paradigms,' pp. 233–47) do not merely present the articles' content, but arrange it within a theoretical framework, signalling the points that are open to debate and the disagreements between the authors, as well as weighing in on the debates herself. It is worthwhile for us, too, in this review, to follow her lead and add our own perspective to these debates. First, however, there is one more book to present.

The eponymous *Tormented Voices* of Thomas Bisson, the well-known and highly regarded historian of medieval Catalonia, are a good counterpoint to the 'wild' and 'irrational' image of peasant anger that Freedman has shown to be an aristocratic construct. Bisson presents us with Catalan peasants who were justifiably angry about the new forms of domination spreading across the region in the mid-1100s, a violence that, he tells us, these people experienced as a terrible, arbitrary break with an age-old order. The issue of violence, and of the shift in mentality regarding its social function (which elsewhere was central to this author's thesis on the feudal revolution),[11] this break and appropriation of legitimate authority at the hands of local powers, is reexamined in this book with what strikes me as deliberate provocation. In a more impressionistic manner than in his previous work, he insists on highlighting the violence produced through the imposition of new methods of oppression by a lordship that was doing away with the 'normative public order' that had survived in Catalonia through the crisis of the eleventh century, and was legitimizing its own arbitrariness. This long survival makes the process of change appear slower than Bisson had proposed in his famous thesis, and to a certain extent is closer to Freedman's proposal as to the origins of servitude in Catalonia.[12] What is up for debate here is neither the

---

11   Bisson, 'The "Feudal Revolution"'. Of particular interest within the debate sparked by this article — one of the journal's most interesting and furthest reaching — were the discussions as to the role of violence in the construction of a new political order, or perhaps of a new legitimacy. See note 4 above. The debate is discussed in Halsall's introduction (pp. 5–6).

12   Freedman's part in the debate on the 'feudal revolution' can be found in Freedman, 'La servidumbre catalana'.

pace nor the timeline of this shift, although Bisson stands by those already proposed (n. 12, p. 148), but rather the reality of this arbitrary violence brought about by poor lordship, which is the book's true leitmotiv. This reality, the author argues, is denied, or at least undervalued, by those who contextualize said violence within processes of conflict, and/or hold that it was the way disputes were resolved in stateless societies. For Bisson, these 'dispute resolutionists',[13] as he refers to what he considers to be a 'new school' of historians, construe the existence of violence in stateless societies as normal. His provocation stems from the positivist reading, based on 'compassionate common sense,' that he proposes in order to grasp the 'historical truth' of his sources (pp. 144–46).[14] This discussion touches on the central problem of historians' role in constructing the realities about which they write or attempt to explain — in short, the reading that they make of the information before them — a problem mentioned by each and every one of the authors we have discussed.

Bisson regards the 'records of grievance,' as he refers to the documents from which he draws his information, as forgotten remnants containing the voices of peasants protesting and complaining about the violence inflicted upon them by their new lords as they imposed a new form of domination to replace the lordship of the counts or monarchs, which they regarded as having been more benign. It is this appeal to a normative order, to an idea of supposedly broken justice, that he finds important. The information provided by this material seems to essentially have arisen from disputes brought before the authority of the count/monarch, or surveys and investigations ordered by said authority within its domains.[15] However, Bisson, who pays attention only to the 'pain' of the plaintiffs, turns a blind eye to the framework in which such legal documents arose, i.e. a power struggle, even if taken in the broad sense. He likewise fails to pay attention to the few cases in which violence, as he himself points out, appears to be the result of wars between lords (pp. 26, 96). The underlying and sometimes explicit (p. 144) question is whether we are to understand these references to violence as a rhetorical strategy against a backdrop of conflict, or as the reflection of a reality. The phrasing of this question is somewhat faulty, as it should be a given that any sort of strategy forms part of the reality we are studying and its internal processes, in which it carries out one or more functions. To interrogate the function carried out by the representation of a situation, in this case that of the violence being reported, does not entail denying the situation, but does imply trying to understand it in a more complex way, without moralistic dichotomies that distort the social processes we are analysing. Thus, verifying the framework of conflict in which the documents used by Bisson were written should serve not only to echo the tormented voices of the victims, but also, perhaps, to understand how these

---

13 This phrase seems to mock his opponents' arguments instead of discussing them rationally, respectfully and without 'violence'.

14 These expressions are found on pp. 147 and VI, respectively. Pierre Bourdieu warns against the traps of 'common sense' in *The Logic of Practice*, esp. Book I, c. 2.

15 The analysis of the seventeen documents used, which Bisson presents in chapter 1 (pp. 1–27), is extremely thorough. He reflects on the diversity and nature of these records in chapter three (pp. 72–80).

complaints might have been used as an instrument in order to construct or regain power in the face of those singled out as aggressors. This also means asking whether the victims suffered not just from the arbitrary violence of a group of aristocrats, but also from these broader power struggles. This is not to downplay the pain or violence they suffered, but just to understand — as demonstrated by many of the articles we have seen here — that struggles to impose a new power structure, or to restore or maintain an old one, are in and of themselves violent. But Bisson, despite recognizing the biased and problematic nature of his evidence, is invested in demonstrating that the violence reported by *his* peasants was derived from the coercion of the lords, and was not the product of personal wars or feuds in a stateless society.[16]

The discussion therefore affects the relationship established between forms of violence and the presence or absence of organized political structures. Some pages ago I mentioned that this issue merited further attention, as it either explicitly articulates or implicitly informs a large portion of the articles contained in these three books. It constitutes the bulk of Halsall's introductory remarks, is crucial in Bisson's argument, and is inseparable from Rosenwein's thesis about the civilizing process. The most commonly held opinion seems to be that certain forms of violence and political competition only took place in societies where power was either not institutionalized politically or else was very weak. In other words, they are associated with a lack of 'state' and, by extension, a lack of 'politics.' Nevertheless, behind what would appear to be a common assumption there are numerous conceptions, not in the least because the modern-day terms used to refer to violence and power do not all share the same referent. Illustrative, then, is the debate sparked by how we are to translate and understand conflicts that in the sources appear as *inimicitia, guerra, bellum, vindicatio, quaerimonia,* or *intentio,* to name those that are commonly found across medieval European sources.

To a large extent the studies examined here have been motivated by the socially structuring function that some anthropologists have attributed to conflicts in societies lacking a formalized political organization (or at least formalized to the extent of our own cultural frame of reference). This is coupled with a very strict, modern-day understanding of one type of violence, used as a self-defence mechanism across endless exchanges of vindictive strife (as in the English term 'feud' or the Spanish *venganza de sangre*). However, this does not match up with the majority of the information we have about these conflicts from the Middle Ages. Evidence has emerged demonstrating that some of these conflicts may have ended via compensation rather than bloodshed. Violence in some cases was just a strategic threat, which was a frequent and legally regulated practice, and at times conflicts were resolved through judicial intervention. This has pushed scholars to attempt to distinguish between these different sorts of practices, and to find better names for them. This is why Halsall proposes 'customary vengeance' as more appropriate than 'feud' to describe the local power struggles in early medieval societies, in an epigraph that he

---

16 I have used the possessive pronoun to indicate that this is his interpretation, as some of the information he puts forward calls into doubt whether they were, in fact, peasants. For example, in one case they claim to have had their horses confiscated (pp. 49, 131).

NAMING VIOLENCE AND CONTROLLING ITS LEGITIMATION   669

expressively titles 'Feud, vengeance and "civil" war' (pp. 19–29). Instead of accepting, as other authors have,[17] the variety of names used for these struggles in the sources, and rejecting the limited valence of the modern-day sense of 'feud,' he makes the effort to find a term specific to this medieval violence. He ultimately decides that the only *true* feuds are those that respond to the term's dictionary definition, thus linking it to stateless societies or moments of political weakness.[18] Although interesting, his remarks on the notion of war are also problematic and debatable, insofar as he seems to reserve a political element for war that he does not assign to feuds. He illustrates well the difficulties in tracing out a typology of violence, or of establishing criteria for how different types of violence should be named. He is therefore correct to say that assessments of the period under study are marked by the nature attributed to these conflicts in arguments that, in my opinion, often become circular, as the debate also affects, as we have seen, the meaning that the historian ascribes to the notion of the 'state.' When this notion is of the ideal, Weberian sort, violence and aristocratic political action are always seen as rooted in the personal. However, it might be wiser and more useful to research the extent and nature of the political apparatus's control over these local-scale conflicts, as Halsall himself proposes, delving into the changes in how violence is expressed and controlled, represented and legitimized, in relation to changes in the power structure. This should not, in any case, pit state development against the disappearance of 'feuds.' In other words, justice and revenge should not be cast as logical opposites.[19]

These problems are closely related to the debate surrounding the civilizing process, in turn linked to a notion of the state and to a linear evolutionary development toward phases that are increasingly civilized and, as such, less violent, and at times with greater cognitive development,[20] and, in any case, where emotions are more inhibited. As Rosenwein states, the texts in her volume are essentially differentiated based either on their more or less explicit acceptance of the 'civilizing process'

---

17 White, 'Feuding and Peace-Making'; Miller, *Bloodtaking*; Alfonso, 'Litigios por la tierra' [Editors' note: For an English translation, see chapter 13 of this volume].

18 Once again, the problem is which term to use, which seems to be the factor that has forced Halsall to distinguish between 'feuds' in the absence of the state, and 'customary vengeance' controlled by the state, a distinction that to a certain extent allows for the opposition he had set out to avoid. He develops these arguments at greater length, but with no more clarity, in Halsall, 'Reflections on Early Medieval Violence'.

19 Robert Barlett questions the axiom, and the implications thereof, that 'the strength of legal enmity and that of the state vary inversely' (Bartlett, '"Mortal Enmities"', p. 13). Paul Hyams, in pointing out that these forms of struggle must have been seen as an integral part of the culture of the medieval nobility throughout Europe, even in areas with a well-defined central authority, calls for a 'softening of conventional contrasts between [England's] precociously centralized regimes and some in continental Europe' (Hyams, 'Feud in Medieval England', p. 21). For a critique of the opposition between justice and revenge, see Alfonso, 'Venganza y justicia' [Editors' note: For an English translation, see chapter 5 of this volume]. Of great interest for this debate are some of the ideas in Dean, 'Marriage and Mutilation' and Smail, 'Common Violence'.

20 Very significant in this respect are the arguments of Little, who takes up the well-known thesis of Ch. Radding (see Radding, *A World Made by Men*) on the different levels of cognitive development ranging from lower to higher rationality.

paradigm (in particular as understood as one of emotional control), or on proposing alternative models of interpretation. She herself seems to fall into the latter group, which understands historical change not as the civilizing restriction of uncontrolled emotions and violence, but rather as the transformation of one set of conventions and repressions into another. Thus, considering it a mistake to seek out clear 'turning points' in the development of civilization, she lends a different meaning to those articles that, taking on the thesis of Elias, had merely pushed them further back in time or situated them in other spaces of socialization, e.g. Little regarding monastic liturgy, or Hyams on the use of liturgy in judicial practice. What is more, she says that the 'violent' eleventh century was perhaps just as civilized as the sixteenth, if by civilized we mean having and following social codes that limit conduct (p. 233).

It is interesting to note that unlike in the other two books, the notion of politics discussed in this context, and therefore of political action or politicization, does not refer solely to formalized structures of government or a specific level of administrative development, but rather to the degree of development detected in the emotional structures. As such, they inquire, for example, into whether the irate displays of the kings are expressions of impulsive, spontaneous emotion, or political resources at their disposal. Some texts may leave us wondering whether the English kings became civilized by taming their anger and practicing tolerance through the influence of the clergy, as Hyams would have it,[21] or if they used and repressed the emotion for political ends, as White argues. The implications of one response or the other are quite different. Whereas the first interpretation falls within the idea of the civilizing process, the second denies the very existence of such a process. Moreover, the latter proposes that we understand expressions of anger as a political practice extending far beyond individual experience, along the same lines as Ghazzal's findings, drawn from a different cultural context. White is right to point out the serious implications of associating anger with emotionality, violence with political irrationality. His Foucaultian response, to which I subscribe, is that the forms of royal or lordly anger (both lay and ecclesiastical), whether open or symbolic, were elements in a 'technology of power,' and/or referenced a specific ethics. Rosenwein warns against broad generalizations about the political institutions available to medieval rulers, and suggests that we be alert to moments in which anger is justified or condemned.

These considerations ultimately lead us to the final point: that of narrative construction as a discourse for legitimating or condemning this or that sort of violence; that of control and the criteria for exerting it. These are the issues I brought up at the outset of this paper — in which I have preferentially referred to the forms of violence resulting from competition and political struggle in the broad sense — and which are present in the studies under review here. Based on these studies one gathers, as Miller states, that violence as a notion lacks a precise, fixed meaning. It is an inherently problematic category of analysis, and, as a social process, we should

---

21 This author's interpretation is undoubtedly more complex, as on the one hand he seems to regard education as a process of internalizing emotional control, and on the other points to royal justice and its rights as the instruments that do away with the anger of the lords.

understand its perception, description and representation to be culturally, historically and normatively conditioned.[22]

As we have seen, control over legitimacy has much to do with the names given to violence, with the definition imposed on a conflict. However, there is more at play that mere word choice: the fact of describing an act or process as violent cannot be regarded as separate from the power relations and process of political domination that produced it. Naming, describing, legitimating and condemning violence are in and of themselves forms of political struggle. In this sense, historians' lack of agreement as to how to describe, name and define the types of violence they observe in political competition, and the extent of their debates, says little about the ambiguity and flexibility of these names. Rather, it speaks to the very fact that naming and other discursive strategies are elements of this same struggle, and that legitimacy depends to a large extent on the name that prevails once a conflict has ceased. For this reason the terms we encounter in our sources should largely be regarded as the result of these struggles, as the product of a recognized power or authority.

It is well known that violent acts bolster legitimacy when cast as being carried out in the name of general interests (whose scope is taken to encompass the members of the target audience) that are frequently characterized as public. This construction of a notion of the 'public' as the reference *par excellence* for all forms of legitimacy is a crucial rhetorical resource that, in my opinion, deserves to be studied in greater depth. However, beyond this, it would make sense to inquire into the historical construction of other concepts that legitimize power, and the violence that they entail. We would do well to determine how they contribute to the naturalization of the established order, and to seek out alternatives that have questioned and opposed such violence. It is in this sense that we must accept that the deconstruction of these concepts, of the conventions that they involve, contains, in and of itself, the power of change.[23] The varied contribution to this task of the books discussed here is worth highlighting.

---

22 Miller, *Humiliation*, ch. 2, contains reflections that are highly useful for making us aware of our own perception of violence.

23 On deconstruction as an ethical project, see Critchley, *The Ethics of Deconstruction*.

Bibliography

Alfonso, Isabel, 'Litigios por la tierra y "malfetrías" entre la nobleza medieval', *Hispania*, 57–197 (1997), 917–55

Alfonso, Isabel, 'Venganza y justicia en el Cantar de Mío Cid', in *El Cid: de la materia épica a las crónicas caballerescas*, ed. by Carlos Alvar Ezquerra, Fernando Gómez Redondo, and Georges Martin (Alcalá de Henares: Universidad de Alcalá, 2002), pp. 41–70

Barthélemy, Dominique, 'The "Feudal Revolution": I', *Past and Present*, 152 (1996), 197–205

Bartlett, Robert J., '"Mortal Enmities": The Legal Aspect of Hostility in the Middle Ages', in *Feud, Violence and Practice: Essays in Medieval Studies in Honor of Stephen D. White*, ed. by Belle Stoddard Tuten and Tracey Lynn Billado (Farnham: Ashgate, 2010), pp. 197–212

Bisson, Thomas N., 'The "Feudal Revolution"', *Past & Present*, 142 (1994), 6–42

Bisson, Thomas N., 'The "Feudal Revolution": Reply', *Past & Present*, 155 (1997), 208–25

Bisson, Thomas N., *Tormented Voices: Power, Crisis and Humanity in Rural Catalonia, 1140–1200* (Cambridge, MA: Harvard University Press, 1998)

Bourdieu, Pierre, *The Logic of Practice* (Stanford: Stanford University Press, 1990)

Boureau, Alain, 'Les moines anglais et la construction du politique (début du 13e siècle)', *Annales. Histoire, Sciences Sociales*, 54–3 (1999), 637–66

Critchley, Simon, *The Ethics of Deconstruction: Derrida and Levinas* (Oxford: Blackwell 1992)

Dean, Trevor, 'Marriage and Mutilation: Vendetta in Late Medieval Italy', *Past & Present*, 157 (1997), 3–36

Freedman, Paul H., 'La servidumbre catalana y el problema de la revolución feudal', *Hispania*, 193 (1996), 425–46

Freedman, Paul H., *Images of the Medieval Peasant* (Stanford: Stanford University Press, 1999)

Halsall, Guy, 'Reflections on Early Medieval Violence: The Example of the "Blood Feud"', *Memoria y Civilización. Anuario de Historia*, 2 (1999), 7–29

Halsall, Guy, ed., *Violence and Society in the Early Medieval West* (Woodbridge: Boydell & Brewer, 2002)

Hyams, Paul, 'Feud in Medieval England', *The Haskins Society Journal*, 3 (1991), 1–21

Miller, William I., *Bloodtaking and Peacemaking: Feud, Law, and Society in Saga Iceland* (Chicago: The University of Chicago Press, 1990)

Miller, William I., *Humiliation, and other Essays on Honor, Social Discomfort, and Violence* (New York: Cornell University Press, 1993)

Radding, Charles M., *A World Made by Men: Cognition and Society, 400–1200* (Chapel Hill: University of North Carolina Press, 1985)

Reuter, Timothy, 'Debate: The "Feudal Revolution": III', *Past & Present*, 155 (1997), 177–95

Rosenwein, Barbara, ed., *Anger's Past* (Ithaca: Cornell University Press, 1998)

Smail, Daniel L., 'Common Violence and Inquisition in Fourteenth-Century Marseille', *Past & Present*, 151 (1996), 28–59

Vicent, Manuel, 'La crueldad', *El País*, 2/04/1999

White, Stephen D., 'Feuding and Peace-Making in Touraine around the Year 1100', *Traditio*, 42 (1986), 196–263

White, Stephen D., 'The "Feudal Revolution": II', *Past & Present*, 152 (1996), 205–23

Wickham, Chris, 'Debate: The "Feudal Revolution": IV', *Past & Present*, 155 (1997), 196–208

Full List of Publications by Isabel Alfonso

PhD Thesis

1980. 'La colonización cisterciense en la Meseta del Duero: el ejemplo de Moreruela'. Universidad Complutense de Madrid.

Monographs

1983. *La colonización cisterciense en la Meseta del Duero. El ejemplo de Moreruela (siglos XII–XIV)*. Madrid. Universidad Complutense. 2 vols

1986. *La colonización cisterciense en la Meseta del Duero. El dominio de Moreruela (siglos XII–XIV)*. Zamora: Instituto de Estudios Zamoranos 'Florián de Ocampo' — CSIC.

1983. (with Luis García de Valdeavellano and others). *El Fuero de León. Comentarios*. León: Hullera Vasco-Leonesa.

1990. (with Reyna Pastor, Ana Rodríguez and Pablo Sánchez León). *Poder monástico y grupos domésticos en la Galicia foral, siglos XIII–XV*. Biblioteca de Historia 4. Madrid: CSIC.

Editions

Costa, Joaquín, *Introducción a un Tratado de Política, sacado textualmente de los refraneros, romanceros y gestas de la Península (Reedición de la primera: Madrid, Imprenta de la Revista de legislación, 1881)*, ed. by Isabel Alfonso. Zaragoza: Institución 'Fernando el Católico' (CSIC) – Diputación de Zaragoza, 2012.

Editions of Collected Volumes

2004. (with Julio Escalona and Georges Martin). *Lucha política: condena y legitimación en la España medieval*. Annexes des Cahiers de Civilisation Hispanique Médiévale 16. Lyon: ENS Éditions.

2004. (with Hugh Kennedy and Julio Escalona). *Building Legitimacy: Political Discourses and Forms of Legitimation in Medieval Societies*. The Medieval Mediterranean 53. Leiden: Brill.

2007. *The Rural History of Medieval European Societies: Trends and Perspectives*. The Medieval Countryside 1. Turnhout: Brepols. (Spanish transl.: 2008. *La historia rural de las sociedades medievales europeas. Tendencias y perspectivas*. Valencia: Publicacions de la Universitat de València).

2010. (with José Antonio Jara Fuente and Georges Martin) 2010. *Construir la identidad en la Edad Media. Poder y memoria en la Castilla de los siglos VII a XV*. Cuenca: Universidad de Castilla-La Mancha.

forthcoming. (with José M. Andrade Cernadas and André Evangelista Marques). *Records and Processes of Dispute Settlement in Early Medieval Societies: Iberia and Beyond*. Leiden: Brill.

674 FULL LIST OF PUBLICATIONS BY ISABEL ALFONSO

Editions of Journal Special Issues

1997. 'Desarrollo legal, prácticas judiciales y acción política en la Europa medieval.' *Hispania* 197.

2003. 'La historia rural de las sociedades medievales europeas: trayectorias y perspectivas, 1.' *Historia Agraria* 31.

2004. 'La historia rural de las sociedades medievales europeas: trayectorias y perspectivas, 2.' *Historia Agraria* 33. The whole collection later reprinted in Spanish (2008. *La historia rural ...*) and in English (2007. *The Rural History ...*).

2007. 'Cultura, lenguaje y prácticas políticas en las sociedades medievales'. *e-Spania* 4: http://e-Spania.revues.org/document3853.html

Journal Articles

1973. 'Sobre la *amicitia* en la España medieval. Un documento de interés para su estudio.' *Boletín de la Real Academia de la Historia* 170: 379–86.

1974. 'Las sernas en León y Castilla. Contribución al estudio de las relaciones socio-económicas en el marco del señorío medieval.' *Moneda y Crédito* 129: 153–210.

1977. 'Conflictos en el proceso de expansión de un señorío monástico.' *Moneda y Crédito* 129: 19–33.

1981. 'La penetración del Císter en la Península. Polémica en torno a Moreruela.' *Revista Española de Teología* 41–1: 147–61.

1982. 'Sobre la organización del terrazgo en Tierra de Campos durante la Edad Media.' *Agricultura y sociedad* 23: 217–32.

1991. 'Cistercians and Feudalism.' *Past & Present* 49–133: 3–30.

1994. (with Reyna Pastor, Carlos Estepa, Julio Escalona, Cristina Jular Pérez-Alfaro, Esther Pascua Echegaray and Pablo Sánchez León). 'Baja nobleza: aproximación a la historiografía europea y propuestas para una investigación.' *Historia Social* 20: 23–45.

1995. '¿Continuidad y revelación documental o mutación y revolución feudal?' *Hispania* 189: 301–13.

1996. 'El discurso histórico como historia.' *Hispania* 192: 349–63.

1997. 'Campesinado y derecho: la vía legal de su lucha (Castilla y León, siglos X–XIII).' *Noticiario de Historia Agraria* 13: 15–31.

1997. 'Introducción: desarrollo legal, prácticas judiciales y acción política en la Europa medieval.' *Hispania* 47 (197): 879–83.

1997. 'Litigios por la tierra y "malfetrías" entre la nobleza medieval.' *Hispania* 197: 917–55.

2000. (with Cristina Jular Pérez-Alfaro). 'Oña contra Frías o el pleito de los cien testigos: una pesquisa en la Castilla del siglo XIII.' *Edad Media: Revista de Historia* 3: 61–88.

2000. (with Pascual Martínez Sopena). 'Formas y funciones de la renta: un estudio comparado de la fiscalidad señorial en la Edad Media Europea (1050–1350).' *Historia Agraria* 22: 231–347.

2000. 'La organización del trabajo en el mundo rural y sus evoluciones históricas. Época medieval.' *Historia Agraria* 20: 15–23.

2001. 'Los nombres de la violencia y el control de su legitimación.' *Hispania* 208: 691–706.

2002. 'Desheredamiento y desafuero, o la pretendida justificación de una revuelta nobiliaria.' *Cahiers de linguistique et de civilisation hispaniques médiévales* 25: 99–129.

2007. 'Cultura, lenguaje y prácticas políticas en las sociedades medievales. Propuestas para su estudio.' *e-Spania* 4: http://e-spania.revues.org/document3853.html

Book Chapters

1982. 'Renta señorial en la Edad Media de León y Castilla.' In *Historia de la Hacienda española (épocas antigua y medieval). Homenaje al profesor García de Valdeavellano*, 57–65. Madrid: Instituto de Estudios Fiscales.

1982. 'Las granjas de Moreruela. Notas para el estudio de la colonización cisterciense en la Meseta del Duero.' In *Semana de Historia del Monacato Cantabro-Astur-Leonés*, 361–76. Oviedo: Monasterio de San Pelayo.

1988. 'El monacato. Zamora en la Edad Media.' In *Catálogo de Exposición I Congreso de historia de Zamora*, 20–25. Zamora: Caja de Zamora.

1989. 'Feudalismo. Instituciones feudales en la Península Ibérica.' In *En torno al Feudalismo Hispánico. I Congreso de Estudios Medievales*, 57–67. León: Fundación Sánchez Albornoz.

1990. 'Poder local y diferenciación interna en las comunidades rurales gallegas.' In *Relaciones de poder, de producción y de parentesco en la Edad Media y Moderna: aproximación a su estudio*, ed. by Reyna Pastor. Biblioteca de Historia 1, 203–23. Madrid: CSIC.

1990. 'La comunidad campesina.' In *Poder monástico y grupos domésticos en la Galicia foral (siglos XIII–XV)*, ed. by Reyna Pastor, Isabel Alfonso, Ana Rodríguez and Pablo Sánchez León. Biblioteca de Historia 4, 302–72. Madrid: CSIC.

1991. 'Comunidades campesinas en Zamora.' In *I Congreso de Historia de Zamora. Tomo III: Historia Medieval y Moderna*, 137–46. Zamora: Instituto de Estudios Zamoranos 'Florián de Ocampo' – Diputación de Zamora.

1993. 'Cistercienses y feudalismo. Notas para un debate historiográfico.' In *Señorío y feudalismo en la Península Ibérica (ss. XII–XIX)*, ed. by Esteban Sarasa Sánchez and Elíseo Serrano Núñez. 11–40. Zaragoza: Diputación de Zaragoza – Institución 'Fernando el Católico' (CSIC).

1993. 'Clases sociales en Zamora.' In *Civitas. MC Aniversario de la ciudad de Zamora*, 34–43. Zamora: Junta de Castilla y León.

1994. 'Resolución de disputas y prácticas judiciales en el Burgos medieval.' In *Burgos en la Plena Edad Media. III Jornadas Burgalesas de Historia*, 211–43. Burgos: Asociación Provincial de Libreros de Burgos.

2001. 'Conflictos en las behetrías.' In *Los señoríos de behetría*, ed. by Carlos Estepa Díez and Cristina Jular Pérez-Alfaro. Biblioteca de Historia 47, 227–60. Madrid: CSIC.

2002. 'Venganza y justicia en el Cantar de Mío Cid.' In *El Cid: de la materia épica a las crónicas caballerescas*, ed. by Carlos Alvar Ezquerra, Fernando Gómez Redondo and Georges Martin. 41–69. Alcalá de Henares: Universidad de Alcalá.

2004. 'Judicial Rhetoric and Political Legitimation in Medieval León-Castile.' In *Building Legitimacy: Political Discourses and Forms of Legitimacy in Medieval Societies*, ed. by Julio Escalona, Isabel Alfonso and Hugh Kennedy. 51–88. Leiden: Brill.

2004. (with Julio Escalona) 'Introduction.' In *Building Legitimacy: Political Discourses and Forms of Legitimacy in Medieval Societies*, ed. by Isabel Alfonso, Hugh Kennedy, and Julio Escalona. ix–xxiii. Leiden: Brill.

2004. 'La contestation paysanne face aux exigences de travail seigneuriales en Castille et Léon: Les formes et leur signification symbolique.' In *Pour une anthropologie du prélèvement seigneurial dans les campagnes médiévales (XIe–XIVe siècles): réalités et représentations paysannes. Colloque tenu à Medina del Campo du 31 mai au 3 juin 2000*, ed. by Monique Bourin and Pascual Martínez Sopena. 291–320. Paris: Publications de la Sorbonne.

676 FULL LIST OF PUBLICATIONS BY ISABEL ALFONSO

2005. 'Lenguaje y prácticas de negociar en la resolución de conflictos en la sociedad castellano-leonesa medieval.' In *Negociar en la Edad Media/Négocier au Moyen Âge*, ed. by María Teresa Ferrer, Jean-Marie Moeglin, Stéphane Péquignot and Manuel Sánchez. Anejos del Anuario de Estudios Medievales 61, 45–65. Barcelona: CSIC.

2006. 'Vengeance, justice et lutte politique dans l'historiographie castillane du Moyen Âge.' In *La vengeance, 400–1200*, ed. by Dominique Barthélemy, François Bougard and Régine Le Jan. 383–419. Rome: École française de Rome.

2007. 'Exploring Difference within Rural Communities in the Northern Iberian Kingdoms, 1000–1300.' In *Rodney Hilton's Middle Ages: An Exploration of Historical Themes*, ed. by Christopher Dyer, Peter Coss, and Chris Wickham. Past and Present, Supplement 2, 87–100. Oxford: Oxford University Press.

2007. '¿Muertes sin venganza? La regulación de la violencia en ámbitos locales (Castilla y León, siglo XIII).' In *El lugar del campesino. En torno a la obra de Reyna Pastor*, ed. by Ana Rodríguez. 261–87. Valencia: Publicaciones de la Universidad de Valencia.

2007. 'Comparing National Historiographies of the Medieval Countryside: An Introduction.' In *The Rural History of Medieval European Societies: Trends and Perspectives*, ed. by Isabel Alfonso. 1–20. Turnhout: Brepols.

2007. 'La rhétorique de légitimation seigneuriale dans les *fueros* de León (XIe–XIIIe siècles).' In *Pour une anthropologie du prélèvement seigneurial dans les campagnes de l'Occident médiéval (XIe–XIVe siècles). Les mots, les temps, les lieux*, ed. by Monique Bourin and Pascual Martínez Sopena. 229–52. Paris: Publications de la Sorbonne.

2008. 'El cuerpo del delito y la violencia ejemplar.' In *El cuerpo derrotado: Cómo trataban musulmanes y cristianos a los enemigos vencidos (Península Ibérica, ss. VIII–XIII)*, ed. by Maribel Fierro and Francisco García Fitz. 397–431. Madrid: CSIC.

2008. 'Moreruela revisitada: viejos documentos, nuevos interrogantes.' In *Moreruela. Un monasterio en la historia del Císter*, ed. by Hortensia Larrén Izquierdo. 57–78. Valladolid: Junta de Castilla y León.

2008. 'Moreruela en época cisterciense.' In *Moreruela. Un monasterio en la historia del Císter*, ed. by Hortensia Larrén Izquierdo. 119–42. Valladolid: Junta de Castilla y León.

2008. (with Julio Escalona and Francisco Reyes). 'Arqueología e historia de los paisajes medievales. Apuntes para una agenda de investigación.' In *El paisaje en perspectiva histórica. Formación y transformación del paisaje en el mundo mediterráneo*, ed. by Ramón Garrabou and José Manuel Naredo. Monografías de Historia Rural 6. 91–116. Zaragoza: Prensas Universitarias de Zaragoza.

2008. 'La contestación campesina a las exigencias de trabajo señoriales en Castilla y León. Las formas y su significación simbólica.' In *Habitar, producir, pensar el espacio rural. De la Antigüedad al Mundo Moderno*, ed. by Paola Miceli and Julián Gallego. 257–89. Buenos Aires: Miño y Dávila.

2008. 'Las historiografías nacionales sobre el mundo rural medieval: una aproximación comparativa.' In *La historia rural de las sociedades medievales europeas. Tendencias y perspectivas*, ed. by Isabel Alfonso. 11–30. Valencia: Publicacions de la Universitat de València.

2009. 'Conflict in the Behetrías.' In *Land, Power, and Society in Medieval Castile: A Study of Behetría Lordship*, ed. by Cristina Jular Pérez-Alfaro and Carlos Estepa Díez. The Medieval Countryside 3, 275–316. Turnhout: Brepols.

FULL LIST OF PUBLICATIONS BY ISABEL ALFONSO   677

2010. 'Iglesias rurales en el norte de Castilla: una dimensión religiosa de las luchas campesinas en la Edad Media.' In *Sombras del Progreso. Las huellas de la historia agraria. Estudios en homenaje a Ramón Garrabou*, ed. by Ricardo Robledo. 27–65. Barcelona: Crítica.

2010. 'The Language and Practice of Negotiation in Medieval Conflict Resolution (Castile-León, Eleventh-Thirteenth Centuries).' In *Feud, Violence and Practice: Essays in Medieval Studies in Honor of Stephen D. White*, ed. by Belle S. Tuten and Tracey L. Billado. 157–74. Farnham: Asghate.

2010. 'Memoria e identidad en las pesquisas judiciales en el área castellano-leonesa medieval.' In *Construir la identidad en la Edad Media. Poder y memoria en la Castilla de los siglos VII a XV*, ed. by José Antonio Jara Fuentes, Georges Martin and Isabel Alfonso. 248–79. Cuenca: Universidad de Castilla-La Mancha.

2012. 'Presentación.' In *Joaquín Costa, Introducción a un Tratado de Política, sacado textualmente de los refraneros, romanceros y gestas de la Península*, ed. by Isabel Alfonso. vi–xlvi. Zaragoza: Institución 'Fernando el Católico' (CSIC) – Diputación de Zaragoza.

2013. 'El formato de la información judicial en la Alta Edad Media peninsular.' In *Chartes et cartulaires comme instruments de pouvoir: Espagne et Occident chrétien (VIIIe–XIIe siècles)*, ed. by Julio Escalona and Hélène Sirantoine. 191–218. Toulouse: Méridiennes-Université de Toulouse-Le Mirail – CSIC.

2016 (with Julio Escalona and Cristina Jular Pérez-Alfaro) 'El medievalismo, lo medieval y el CSIC en el primer franquismo.' In *El franquismo y la apropiación del pasado. El uso de la historia, de la arqueología y de la historia del arte para la legitimación de la dictadura*, ed. by Francisco José Moreno Martín. 159–88. Madrid: Editorial Pablo Iglesias.

2017 'La retórica de legitimación sensorial en las concesiones forales leonesas (siglos XI–XIII).' In *Instituciones políticas, comportamientos sociales y atraso económico en España (1580–2000). Homenaje a Ángel García Sanz*, ed. by Francisco Comín, Ricardo Hernández and Javier Moreno. Salamanca: Universidad de Salamanca.

forthcoming. 'León: Documentation from the Ninth–Eleventh Centuries'; 'Navarre-Aragon: Documentary Evidence between the Ninth and Eleventh Centuries'; 'Documentary Production and Dispute Records in Castile before the Year 1100', chapters 3, 4 and 5 of *Records and Processes of Dispute Settlement in Early Medieval Societies: Iberia and Beyond* ed. by Isabel Alfonso, José M. Andrade Cernadas, and André Evangelista Marques. Leiden: Brill.